Mobil Travel Guide

Mid-Atlantic

2005

Delaware

Maryland

New Jersey

Pennsylvania

Virginia

District of Columbia

West Virginia

ExxonMobil
Travel Publications

Acknowledgements

We gratefully acknowledge the help of our representatives for their efficient and perceptive inspections of the lodging and dining establishments listed; the establishments' proprietors for their cooperation in showing their facilities and providing information about them; and the many users of previous editions who have taken the time to share their experiences. Mobil Travel Guide is also grateful to all the talented writers who contributed entries to this book.

Printing Acknowledgement: North American Corporation of Illinois

www.mobiltravelguide.com

Front cover photo: Meade Statue and Cannon on Cemetery Ridge, Gettysburg

ISBN: 0-7627-3582-1

ISSN: 1090-6975

Manufactured in the United States of America.

10 9 8 7 6 5 4 3 2 1

Contents

Maps

Mid-Atlantic

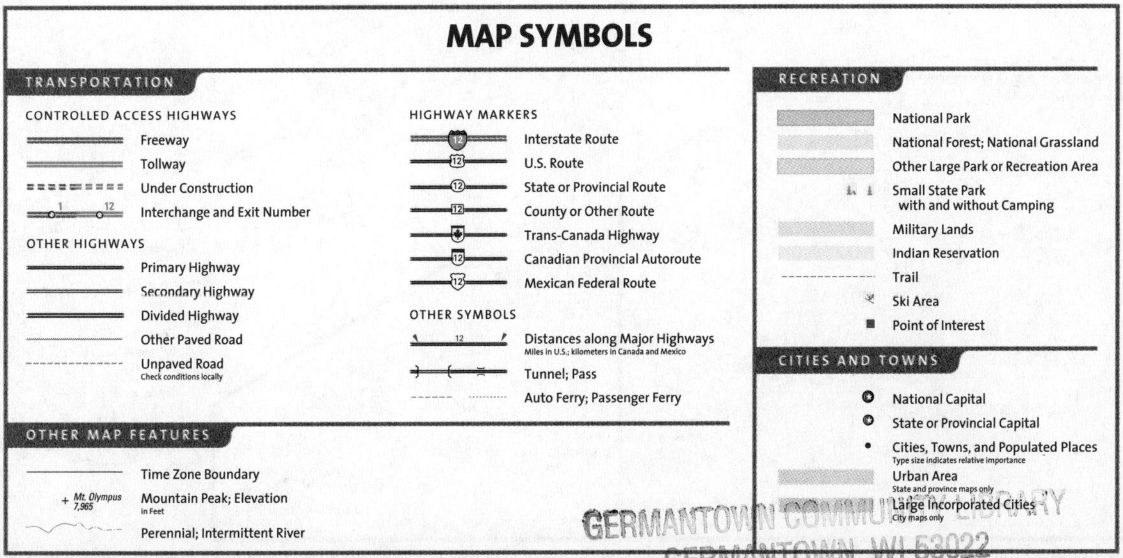
MAP SYMBOLS
TRANSPORTATION
CONTROLLED ACCESS HIGHWAYS
Freeway
Tollway
Under Construction
Interchange and Exit Number
OTHER HIGHWAYS
Primary Highway
Secondary Highway
Divided Highway
Other Paved Road
Unpaved Road
Check conditions locally
HIGHWAY MARKERS
Interstate Route
U.S. Route
State or Provincial Route
County or Other Route
Trans-Canada Highway
Canadian Provincial Autoroute
Mexican Federal Route
OTHER SYMBOLS
Distances along Major Highways
Miles in U.S.; kilometers in Canada and Mexico
Tunnel; Pass
Auto Ferry; Passenger Ferry
OTHER MAP FEATURES
Time Zone Boundary
Mt. Olympus 7,965
Mountain Peak; Elevation
in Feet
Perennial; Intermittent River
RECREATION
National Park
National Forest; National Grassland
Other Large Park or Recreation Area
Small State Park
with and without Camping
Military Lands
Indian Reservation
Trail
Ski Area
Point of Interest
CITIES AND TOWNS
National Capital
State or Provincial Capital
Cities, Towns, and Populated Places
Type size indicates relative importance
Urban Area
State and province maps only
Large Incorporated Cities
City maps only

BRITISH COLUMBIA
ALBERTA
SASKATCHEWAN
MANITOBA
Vancouver
Calgary
Regina
Winnipeg
WASHINGTON
OREGON
IDAHO
MONTANA
NORTH DAKOTA
SOUTH DAKOTA
WYOMING
NEVADA
UTAH
COLORADO
CALIFORNIA
ARIZONA
NEW MEXICO
NEBRASKA
KANSAS
OKLAHOMA
TEXAS
MEXICO
CHIHUAHUA
SONORA
COAHUILA
NUEVO LEÓN
TAMAULIPAS
GREAT BASIN
ROCKY MOUNTAINS
COLORADO PLATEAU
GREAT PLAINS
COLUMBIA PLATEAU
LLANO ESTACADO
EDWARDS PLATEAU
COAST RANGES
SIERRA NEVADA
CASCADE RANGE
PACIFIC OCEAN
Seattle
Spokane
Portland
Boise
Salt Lake City
Reno
Sacramento
San Francisco
San Jose
Fresno
Bakersfield
Los Angeles
Long Beach
San Diego
Tijuana
Mexicali
Las Vegas
Phoenix
Tucson
Albuquerque
Santa Fe
Denver
Colorado Springs
Cheyenne
Billings
Great Falls
Helena
Rapid City
Pierre
Bismarck
Lincoln
Wichita
Oklahoma City
Amarillo
Lubbock
El Paso
Ciudad Juárez
Fort Worth
Dallas
Austin
San Antonio
Monterrey
Saltillo
Corpus Christi
Brownsville
Matamoros
ALASKA
ARCTIC OCEAN
BROOKS RANGE
ALASKA RANGE
Fairbanks
Anchorage
Juneau
NORTHWEST TERRITORIES
YUKON TERRITORY
CANADA
BRITISH COLA.
RUSSIA
Gulf of Alaska
PACIFIC OCEAN
HAWAII
Kaua'i
O'ahu
Honolulu
Moloka'i
Maui
Hawai'i
Hilo
PACIFIC OCEAN
© MQST

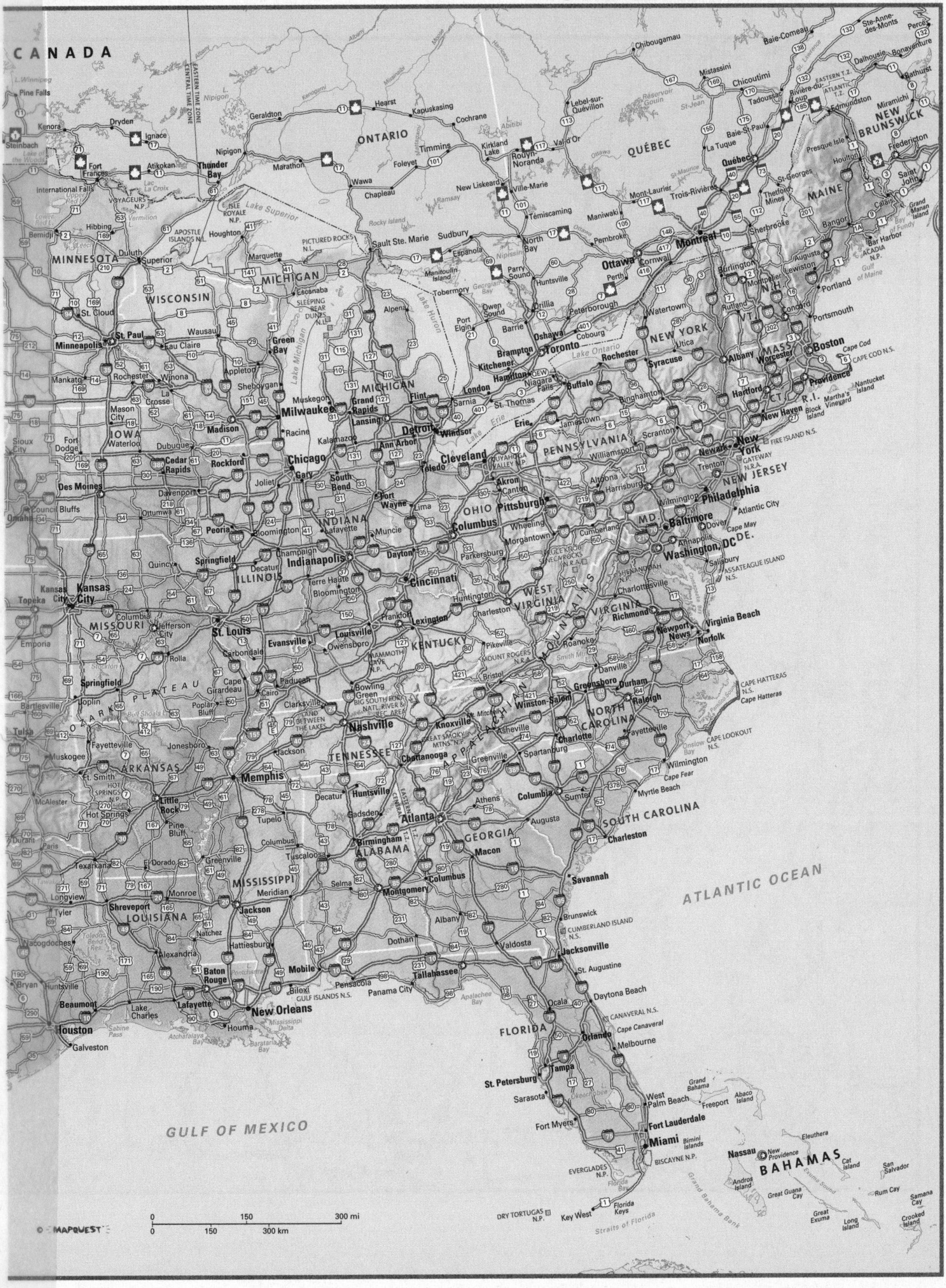
CANADA
ONTARIO
QUÉBEC
NEW BRUNSWICK
MAINE
N.H.
VT.
MASS.
R.I.
CT.
NEW YORK
NEW JERSEY
PENNSYLVANIA
DE.
MD.
Washington, DC
WEST VIRGINIA
VIRGINIA
NORTH CAROLINA
SOUTH CAROLINA
GEORGIA
FLORIDA
ALABAMA
MISSISSIPPI
LOUISIANA
ARKANSAS
TENNESSEE
KENTUCKY
OHIO
INDIANA
ILLINOIS
MICHIGAN
WISCONSIN
MINNESOTA
IOWA
MISSOURI
OZARK PLATEAU
APPALACHIAN MOUNTAINS
Lake Superior
Lake Michigan
Lake Huron
Lake Erie
Lake Ontario
ATLANTIC OCEAN
GULF OF MEXICO
BAHAMAS
Nassau
Chicago
Detroit
Cleveland
Pittsburgh
Philadelphia
New York
Boston
Montreal
Toronto
Ottawa
Baltimore
Richmond
Atlanta
Nashville
Memphis
St. Louis
Indianapolis
Columbus
Cincinnati
Louisville
Milwaukee
Minneapolis
St. Paul
Kansas City
Des Moines
Houston
New Orleans
Jacksonville
Tampa
Orlando
Miami
Charlotte
Raleigh
Birmingham
Jackson
Little Rock
Shreveport
0 150 300 mi
0 150 300 km
© MAPQUEST

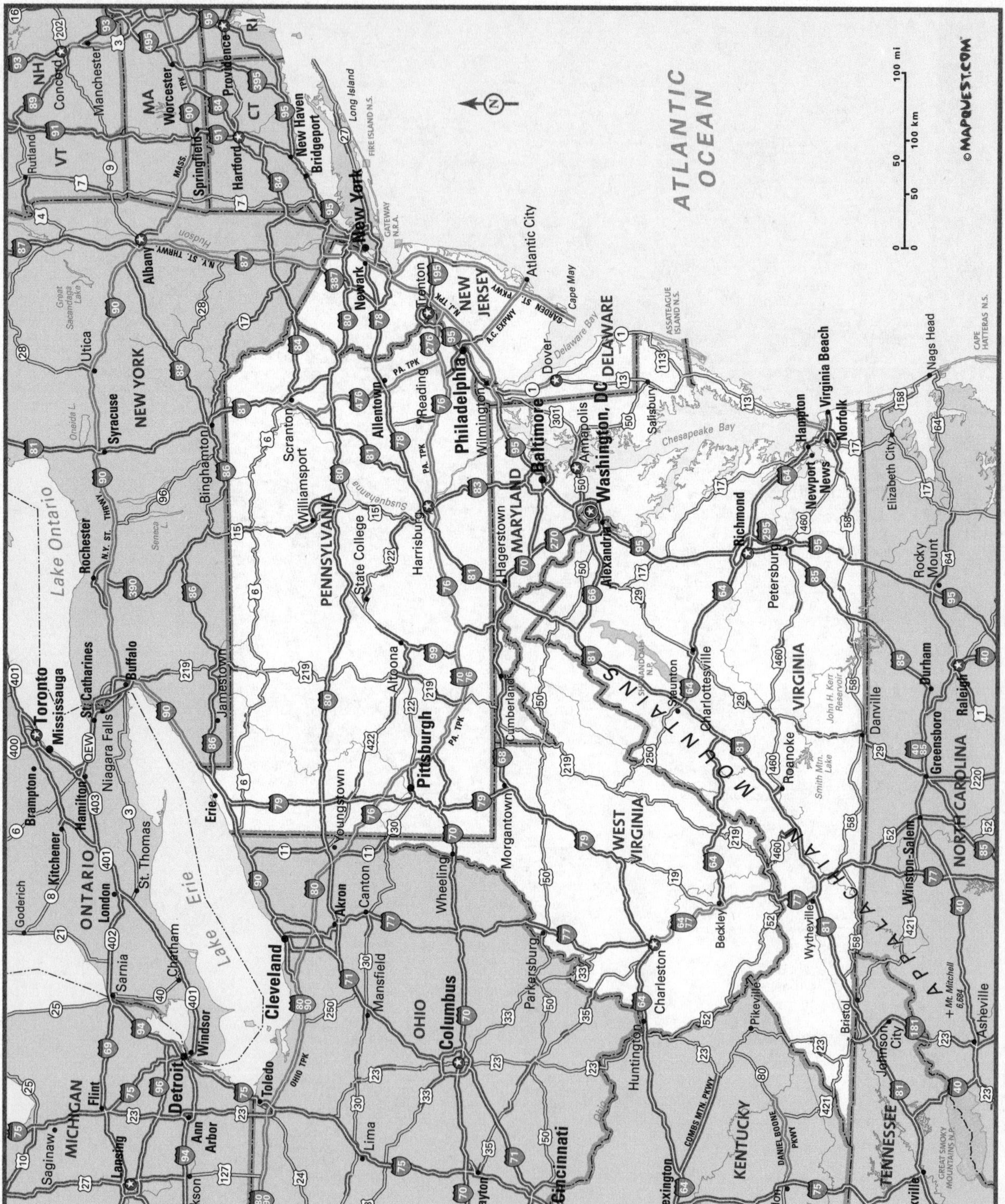

ATLANTIC OCEAN
Lake Ontario
Lake Erie
NEW YORK
PENNSYLVANIA
NEW JERSEY
DELAWARE
MARYLAND
WEST VIRGINIA
VIRGINIA
NORTH CAROLINA
KENTUCKY
TENNESSEE
OHIO
MICHIGAN
ONTARIO
VT
NH
MA
CT
RI
APPALACHIAN MOUNTAINS
New York
Newark
Trenton
Philadelphia
Baltimore
Washington, DC
Alexandria
Annapolis
Dover
Wilmington
Atlantic City
Cape May
Albany
Syracuse
Rochester
Buffalo
Utica
Binghamton
Jamestown
Erie
Scranton
Williamsport
Allentown
Reading
Harrisburg
State College
Altoona
Pittsburgh
Youngstown
Hagerstown
Cumberland
Morgantown
Wheeling
Parkersburg
Charleston
Huntington
Beckley
Staunton
Charlottesville
Richmond
Petersburg
Newport News
Hampton
Norfolk
Virginia Beach
Salisbury
Roanoke
Wytheville
Bristol
Danville
Rocky Mount
Elizabeth City
Nags Head
Durham
Raleigh
Greensboro
Winston-Salem
Asheville
Johnson City
Knoxville
Lexington
London
Pikeville
Cincinnati
Dayton
Columbus
Lima
Mansfield
Canton
Akron
Cleveland
Toledo
Detroit
Windsor
Ann Arbor
Lansing
Jackson
Flint
Saginaw
Sarnia
Chatham
London
St. Thomas
Kitchener
Goderich
Hamilton
Brampton
Toronto
Mississauga
St. Catharines
Niagara Falls
Concord
Manchester
Rutland
Worcester
Springfield
Hartford
Providence
New Haven
Bridgeport
Long Island
FIRE ISLAND N.S.
GATEWAY N.R.A.
ASSATEAGUE ISLAND N.S.
CAPE HATTERAS N.S.
GREAT SMOKY MOUNTAINS N.P.
Mt. Mitchell 6,684
Chesapeake Bay
Delaware Bay
Smith Mtn. Lake
John H. Kerr Reservoir
PA. TPK
N.J. TPK
N.Y. ST. THRWY
OHIO TPK
COMBS MTN. PKWY
DANIEL BOONE PKWY
GARDEN ST. PKWY
A.C. EXPWY
0 50 100 mi
0 50 100 km
© MAPQUEST.COM

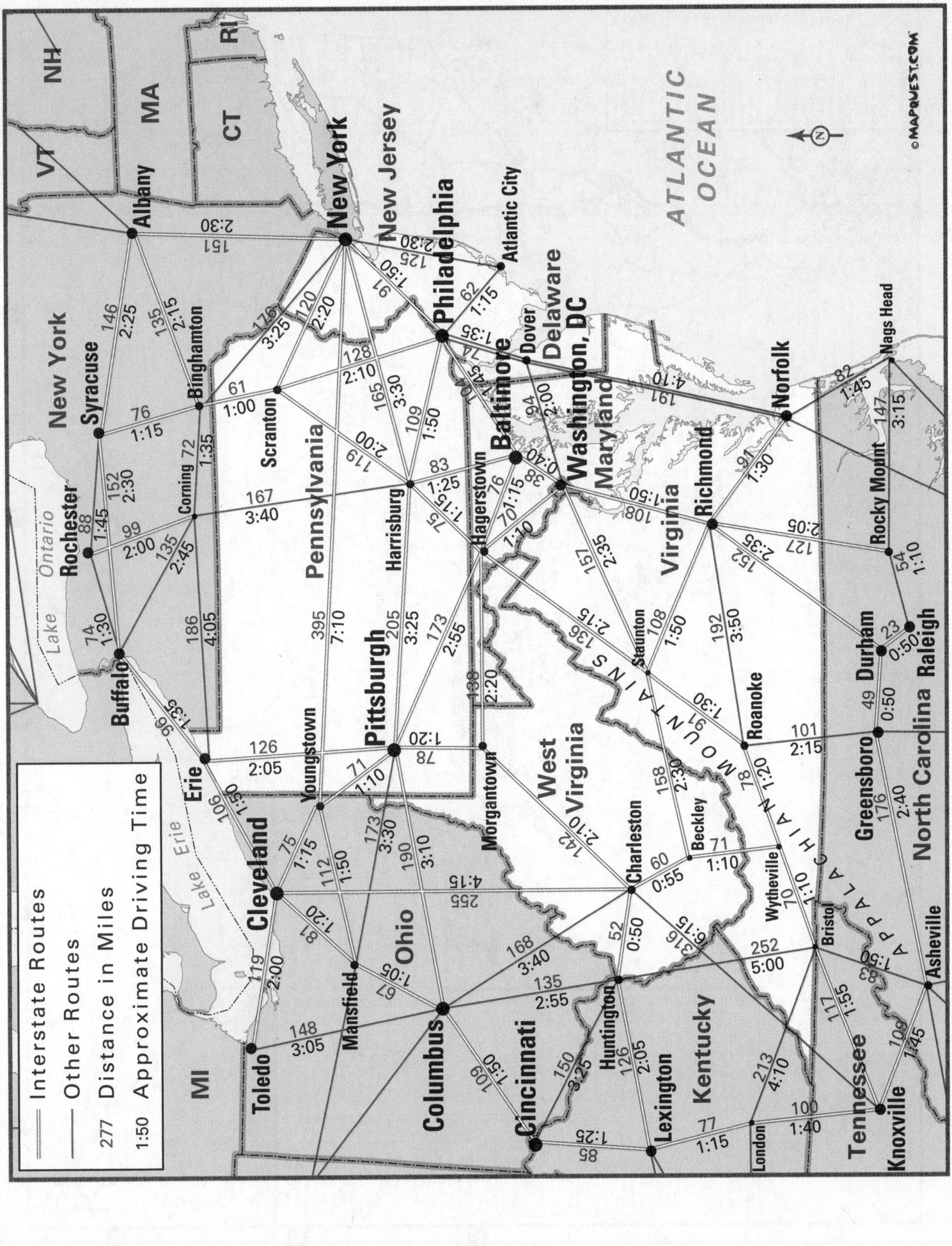
Interstate Routes
Other Routes
277 Distance in Miles
1:50 Approximate Driving Time
ATLANTIC OCEAN
© MAPQUEST.COM
NH
VT
MA
CT
RI
New York
New Jersey
Delaware
Maryland
Pennsylvania
Virginia
West Virginia
North Carolina
Ohio
Kentucky
Tennessee
MI
Lake Ontario
Lake Erie
APPALACHIAN MOUNTAINS
Albany
Syracuse
Rochester
Buffalo
Binghamton
Corning
Scranton
New York
Philadelphia
Atlantic City
Dover
Baltimore
Washington, DC
Harrisburg
Hagerstown
Pittsburgh
Erie
Youngstown
Cleveland
Toledo
Mansfield
Columbus
Cincinnati
Morgantown
Charleston
Huntington
Beckley
Staunton
Richmond
Norfolk
Roanoke
Wytheville
Bristol
Lexington
London
Knoxville
Asheville
Greensboro
Durham
Raleigh
Rocky Mount
Nags Head

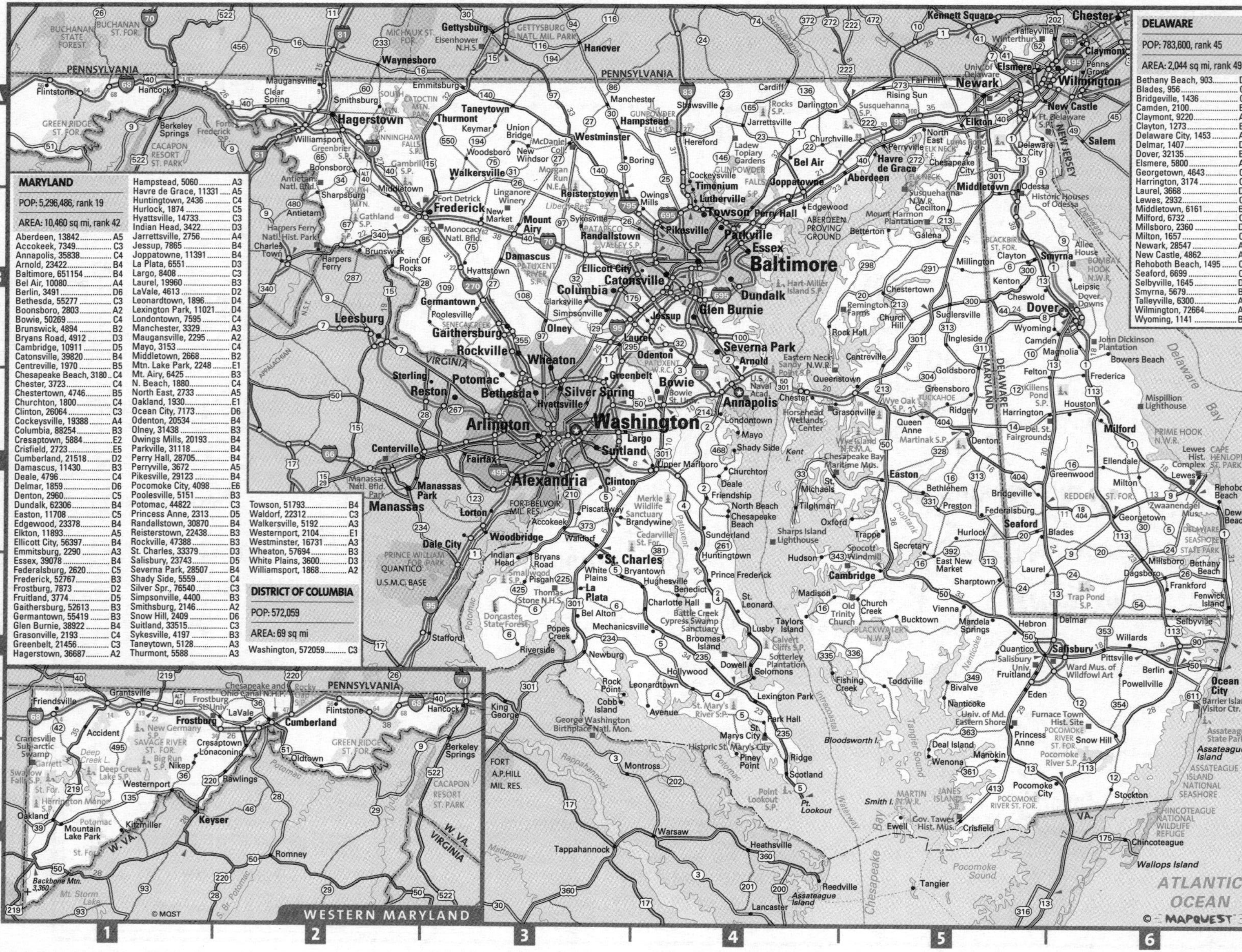

MARYLAND

POP: 5,296,486, rank 19

AREA: 10,460 sq mi, rank 42

Aberdeen, 13842	A5
Accokeek, 7349	C3
Annapolis, 35838	C4
Arnold, 23422	B4
Baltimore, 651154	B4
Bel Air, 10080	A4
Berlin, 3491	D6
Bethesda, 55277	C3
Boonsboro, 2803	A2
Bowie, 50269	C4
Brunswick, 4894	B2
Bryans Road, 4912	D3
Cambridge, 10911	D5
Catonsville, 39820	B4
Centreville, 1970	B5
Chesapeake Beach, 3180	C4
Chester, 3723	C4
Chestertown, 4746	B5
Churchton, 1800	C4
Clinton, 26064	C3
Cockeysville, 19388	A4
Columbia, 88254	B3
Cresaptown, 5884	E2
Crisfield, 2723	E5
Cumberland, 21518	D2
Damascus, 11430	B3
Deale, 4796	C4
Delmar, 1859	D6
Denton, 2960	C5
Dundalk, 62306	B4
Easton, 11708	C5
Edgewood, 23378	B4
Elkton, 11893	A5
Ellicott City, 56397	B4
Emmitsburg, 2290	A3
Essex, 39078	B4
Federalsburg, 2620	C5
Frederick, 52767	B3
Frostburg, 7873	D2
Fruitland, 3774	D5
Gaithersburg, 52613	B3
Germantown, 55419	B3
Glen Burnie, 38922	B4
Grasonville, 2193	C4
Greenbelt, 21456	C3
Hagerstown, 36687	A2
Hampstead, 5060	A3
Havre de Grace, 11331	A5
Huntingtown, 2436	C4
Hurlock, 1874	C5
Hyattsville, 14733	C3
Indian Head, 3422	D3
Jarrettsville, 2756	A4
Jessup, 7865	B4
Joppatowne, 11391	B4
La Plata, 6551	D3
Largo, 8408	C3
Laurel, 19960	B3
LaVale, 4613	D2
Leonardtown, 1896	D4
Lexington Park, 11021	D4
Londontown, 7595	C4
Manchester, 3329	A3
Maugansville, 2295	A2
Mayo, 3153	C4
Middletown, 2668	B2
Mtn. Lake Park, 2248	E1
Mt. Airy, 6425	B3
N. Beach, 1880	C4
North East, 2733	A5
Oakland, 1930	E1
Ocean City, 7173	D6
Odenton, 20534	B4
Olney, 31438	B3
Owings Mills, 20193	B4
Parkville, 31118	B4
Perry Hall, 28705	B4
Perryville, 3672	A5
Pikesville, 29123	B4
Pocomoke City, 4098	E6
Poolesville, 5151	B3
Potomac, 44822	C3
Princess Anne, 2313	D5
Randallstown, 30870	B4
Reisterstown, 22438	B3
Rockville, 47388	B3
St. Charles, 33379	D3
Salisbury, 23743	D5
Severna Park, 28507	B4
Shady Side, 5559	C4
Silver Spr., 76540	C3
Simpsonville, 4400	B3
Smithsburg, 2146	A2
Snow Hill, 2409	D6
Suitland, 33515	C3
Sykesville, 4197	B3
Taneytown, 5128	A3
Thurmont, 5588	A3
Towson, 51793	B4
Waldorf, 22312	C3
Walkersville, 5192	A3
Westernport, 2104	E1
Westminster, 16731	A3
Wheaton, 57694	B3
White Plains, 3600	D3
Williamsport, 1868	A2

DISTRICT OF COLUMBIA

POP: 572,059

AREA: 69 sq mi

Washington, 572059	C3

DELAWARE

POP: 783,600, rank 45

AREA: 2,044 sq mi, rank 49

Bethany Beach, 903	D6
Blades, 956	C5
Bridgeville, 1436	C5
Camden, 2100	B6
Claymont, 9220	A6
Clayton, 1273	B5
Delaware City, 1453	A5
Delmar, 1407	D6
Dover, 32135	B6
Elsmere, 5800	A5
Georgetown, 4643	C6
Harrington, 3174	C6
Laurel, 3668	D6
Lewes, 2932	C6
Middletown, 6161	B5
Milford, 6732	C6
Millsboro, 2360	D6
Milton, 1657	C6
Newark, 28547	A5
New Castle, 4862	A5
Rehoboth Beach, 1495	C6
Seaford, 6699	C5
Selbyville, 1645	D6
Smyrna, 5679	B5
Talleyville, 6300	A6
Wilmington, 72664	A6
Wyoming, 1141	B6

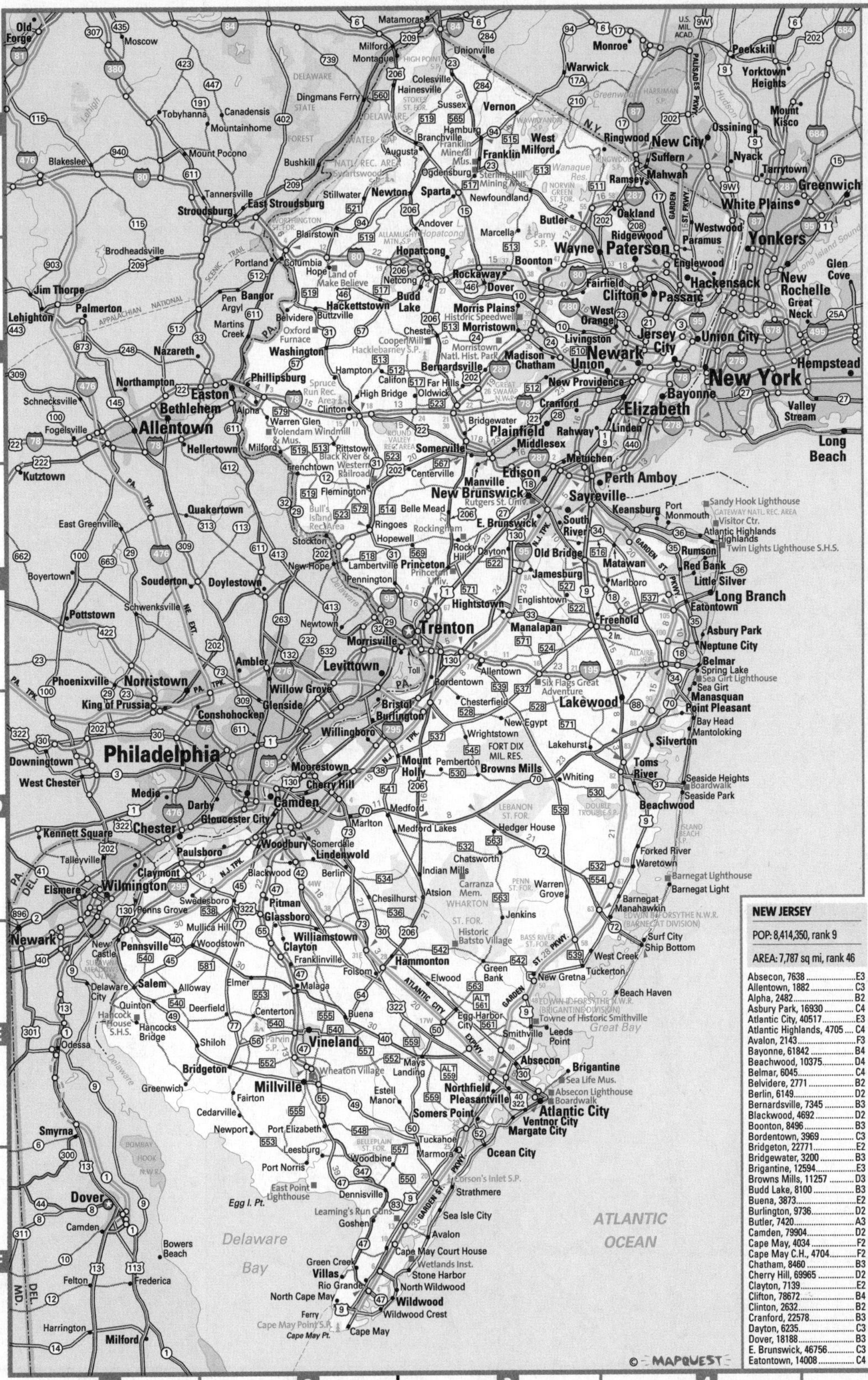

NEW JERSEY

POP: 8,414,350, rank 9

AREA: 7,787 sq mi, rank 46

Absecon, 7638	E3
Allentown, 1882	C3
Alpha, 2482	B2
Asbury Park, 16930	C4
Atlantic City, 40517	E3
Atlantic Highlands, 4705	C4
Avalon, 2143	F3
Bayonne, 61842	B4
Beachwood, 10375	D4
Belmar, 6045	C4
Belvidere, 2771	B2
Berlin, 6149	D2
Bernardsville, 7345	B3
Blackwood, 4692	D2
Boonton, 8496	B3
Bordentown, 3969	C3
Bridgeton, 22771	E2
Bridgewater, 3200	B3
Brigantine, 12594	E3
Browns Mills, 11257	D3
Budd Lake, 8100	B3
Buena, 3873	E2
Burlington, 9736	D2
Butler, 7420	A3
Camden, 79904	D2
Cape May, 4034	F2
Cape May C.H., 4704	F2
Chatham, 8460	B3
Cherry Hill, 69965	D2
Clayton, 7139	E2
Clifton, 78672	B4
Clinton, 2632	B2
Cranford, 22578	B3
Dayton, 6235	C3
Dover, 18188	B3
E. Brunswick, 46756	C3
Eatontown, 14008	C4
Edison, 97687	C3
Egg Harbor City, 4545	E3
Elizabeth, 120568	B4
Englewood, 26203	B4
Englishtown, 1764	C3
Fairfield, 7063	B3
Fairton, 2253	E2
Flemington, 4200	C2
Folsom, 1972	E2
Forked River, 4914	D4
Franklin, 5160	A3
Freehold, 10976	C3
Glassboro, 19068	E2
Gloucester City, 11484	D2
Hackensack, 42677	B4
Hackettstown, 10403	B2
Hamburg, 3105	A3
Hammonton, 12604	E2
High Bridge, 3776	B2
Highlands, 5097	C4
Hightstown, 5216	C3
Hopatcong, 15888	B3
Hopewell, 2035	C3
Jamesburg, 6025	C3
Jersey City, 240055	B4
Keansburg, 10732	C4
Lakehurst, 2522	D3
Lakewood, 36065	D4
Lambertville, 3868	C2
Linden, 39394	B4
Lindenwold, 17414	D2
Little Silver, 6170	C4
Livingston, 27391	B3
Long Branch, 31340	C4
Madison, 16530	B3
Mahwah, 5200	A4
Manahawkin, 2004	D4
Manasquan, 6310	C4
Manville, 10343	B3
Margate City, 8193	E3
Marlboro, 3300	C4
Marlton, 10260	D2
Matawan, 8910	C4
Mays Landing, 2321	E3
Medford, 3500	D2
Medford Lakes, 4173	D2
Metuchen, 12840	B3
Middlesex, 13717	B3
Millville, 26847	E2
Moorestown, 13860	D2
Morris Plains, 5236	B3
Morristown, 18544	B3
Mt. Holly, 10600	D2
Neptune City, 5218	C4
Netcong, 2580	B3
Newark, 273546	B4
New Brunswick, 48573	C3
New Egypt, 2519	D3
New Providence, 11907	B3
Newton, 8244	A3
N. Cape May, 3618	F2
Northfield, 7725	E3
N. Wildwood, 4935	F2
Oakland, 12466	A4
Ocean City, 15378	E3
Ogdensburg, 2638	A3
Old Bridge, 22833	C3
Paramus, 25737	B4
Passaic, 67861	B4
Paterson, 149222	B4
Paulsboro, 6160	D2
Pennington, 2696	C2
Penns Grove, 4886	D1
Pennsville, 11657	E1
Perth Amboy, 47303	C3
Phillipsburg, 15166	B2
Pitman, 9331	D2
Plainfield, 47829	B3
Pleasantville, 19012	E3
Pt. Pleasant, 19306	D4
Port Monmouth, 3742	C4
Princeton, 14203	C3
Rahway, 26500	B3
Ramsey, 14351	A4
Red Bank, 11844	C4
Ridgewood, 24936	A4
Ringwood, 12396	A4
Rio Grande, 2444	F2
Rockaway, 6473	B3
Rumson, 7137	C4
Salem, 5857	E1
Sayreville, 40377	C3
Sea Girt, 2148	C4
Sea Isle City, 2835	F3
Seaside Hts., 3155	D4
Seaside Park, 2263	D4
Silverton, 9200	D4
Smithville, 3100	E3
Somerdale, 5192	D2
Somers Pt., 11614	E3
Somerville, 12423	B3
S. River, 15322	C3
Sparta, 9755	A3
Spring Lake, 3567	C4
Sussex, 2145	A3
Swedesboro, 2055	D1
Toms River, 86327	D4
Trenton, 85403	C3
Tuckerton, 3517	E3
Union, 54405	B4
Union City, 67088	B4
Ventnor City, 12910	E3
Villas, 9064	F2
Vineland, 56271	E2
Washington, 6712	B2
Wayne, 54069	B3
W. Milford, 26410	A3
W. Orange, 44943	B4
Westwood, 10999	A4
Whiting, 1800	D3
Wildwood, 5436	F2
Wildwood Crest, 3980	F2
Williamstown, 11812	E2
Willingboro, 36300	D2
Woodbine, 2716	F2
Woodbury, 10307	D2
Woodstown, 3136	E1

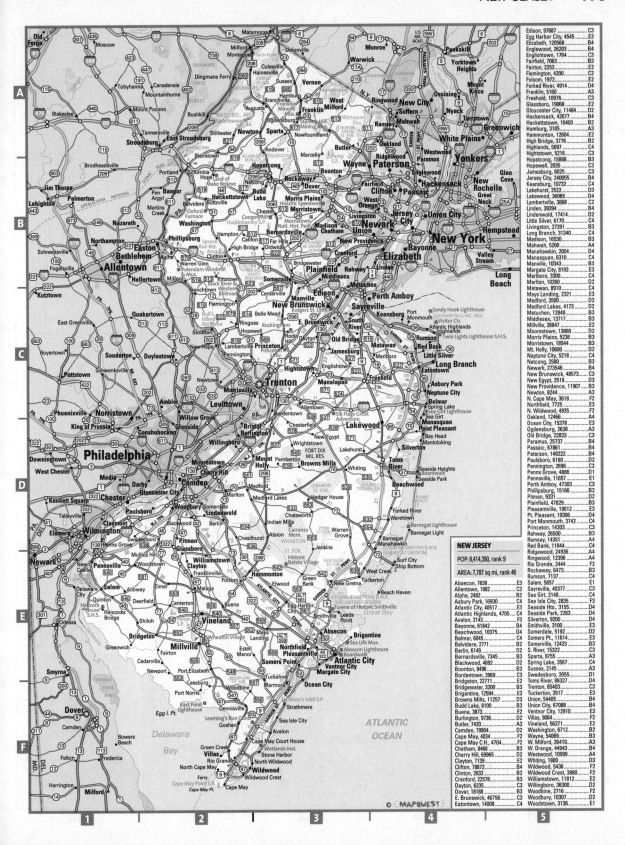

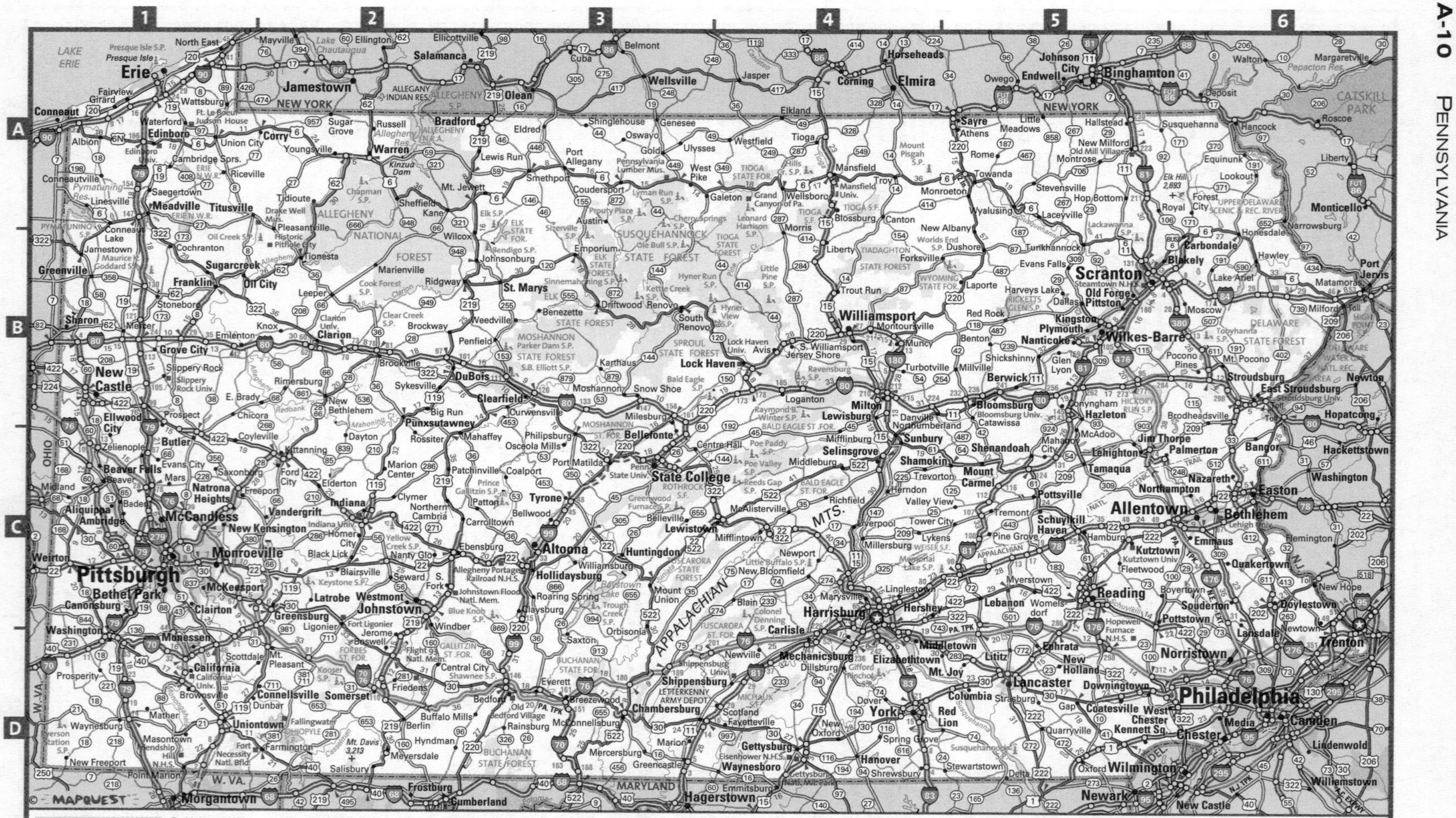

PENNSYLVANIA

POP: 12,281,054, rank 6

AREA: 45,308 sq mi, rank 33

Aliquippa, 11734 .... C1
Allentown, 106632 .... C6
Altoona, 49523 .... C3
Ambridge, 7769 .... C1
Athens, 3415 .... A5
Baden, 4377 .... C1
Bangor, 5319 .... C6
Beaver, 4775 .... C1
Beaver Falls, 9920 .... C1
Bedford, 3141 .... D3
Bellefonte, 6395 .... C3
Berlin, 2192 .... D2
Berwick, 10774 .... B5
Bethel Park, 33556 .... C1
Bethlehem, 71329 .... C6
Blairsville, 3607 .... C2
Blakely, 7027 .... B5
Bloomsburg, 12375 .... B5
Boyertown, 3940 .... C5
Bradford, 9175 .... A2
Brookville, 4230 .... B2
Brownsville, 2804 .... D1
Butler, 15121 .... C1
California, 5274 .... D1
Cambridge Sprs., 2363 .... A1
Canonsburg, 8607 .... C1
Carbondale, 9804 .... B6
Carlisle, 17970 .... D4
Chambersburg, 17862 .... D3
Chester, 36854 .... D6
Clairton, 8491 .... C1
Clarion, 6185 .... B2
Clearfield, 6631 .... B3
Coatesville, 10838 .... D5
Columbia, 10311 .... D5
Connellsville, 9146 .... D2
Corry, 6834 .... A2
Coudersport, 2650 .... A3
Curwensville, 2650 .... B3
Dallas, 2557 .... B5
Danville, 4897 .... B5
Downingtown, 7589 .... D5
Doylestown, 8227 .... C6
DuBois, 8123 .... B2
Easton, 26263 .... C6
E. Stroudsburg, 9888 .... B6
Ebensburg, 3091 .... C2
Edinboro, 6950 .... A1
Elizabethtown, 11887 .... D5
Ellwood City, 8688 .... C1
Emmaus, 11313 .... C6
Emporium, 2526 .... B3
Ephrata, 13213 .... D5
Erie, 103717 .... A1
Fayetteville, 2774 .... D4
Fleetwood, 4018 .... C5
Ford City, 3451 .... C2
Franklin, 7212 .... B1
Gettysburg, 7490 .... D4
Girard, 3164 .... A1
Greencastle, 3722 .... D3
Greensburg, 15889 .... C2
Greenville, 6380 .... B1
Grove City, 8024 .... B1
Hamburg, 4114 .... C5
Hanover, 14535 .... D4
Harrisburg, 48950 .... C4
Harveys Lake, 2888 .... B5
Hazleton, 23329 .... B5
Hershey, 12771 .... C4
Hollidaysburg, 5368 .... C3
Honesdale, 4874 .... B6
Huntingdon, 6918 .... C3
Indiana, 14895 .... C2
Jersey Shore, 4482 .... B4
Jim Thorpe, 4804 .... C5
Johnsonburg, 3003 .... B2
Johnstown, 23906 .... C2
Kane, 4126 .... A2
Kennett Square, 5273 .... D5
Kingston, 13855 .... B5
Kittanning, 4787 .... C2
Kutztown, 5067 .... C5
Lancaster, 56348 .... D5
Lansdale, 16071 .... C6
Latrobe, 8994 .... C2
Lebanon, 24461 .... C5
Lehighton, 5537 .... C5
Lewisburg, 5620 .... B4
Lewistown, 8998 .... C4
Liberty, 2670 .... B4
Linglestown, 6414 .... C4
Lititz, 9029 .... D5
Lock Haven, 9149 .... B4
Mahanoy City, 4647 .... C5
Mansfield, 3411 .... A4
Marysville, 2306 .... C4
Masontown, 3611 .... D1
Matamoras, 2312 .... B6
McAdoo, 2274 .... C5
McCandless, 29022 .... C1
McKeesport, 24040 .... C1
Meadville, 13685 .... A1
Mechanicsburg, 9042 .... D4
Media, 5533 .... D6
Mercer, 2391 .... B1
Meyersdale, 2473 .... D2
Middletown, 9242 .... D4
Midland, 3137 .... C1
Mifflinburg, 3594 .... C4
Millersburg, 2562 .... C4
Milton, 6650 .... B4
Monessen, 8669 .... D1
Monroeville, 29349 .... C1
Montoursville, 4777 .... B4
Mt. Carmel, 6390 .... C5
Mt. Joy, 6765 .... D5
Mt. Pleasant, 4728 .... D2
Mt. Pocono, 2742 .... B6
Mt. Union, 2504 .... C3
Muncy, 2663 .... B4
Myerstown, 3171 .... C5
Nanticoke, 10955 .... B5
Nanty Glo, 3054 .... C2
Natrona Hts., 10934 .... C1
Nazareth, 6023 .... C6
New Castle, 26309 .... B1
New Holland, 5092 .... D5
New Hope, 2252 .... C6
New Kensington, 14701 .... C1
Newtown, 2312 .... C6
Norristown, 31282 .... D6
Northampton, 9405 .... C6
N. East, 4601 .... A1
Northern Cambria, 4199 .... C2
Northumberland, 3714 .... C4
Oil City, 11504 .... B1
Old Forge, 8798 .... B5
Oxford, 4315 .... D5
Palmerton, 5248 .... C6
Philadelphia, 1517550 .... D6
Philipsburg, 3056 .... C3
Pittsburgh, 334563 .... C1
Pittston, 8104 .... B5
Plymouth, 6507 .... B5
Port Allegany, 2355 .... A3
Pottstown, 21859 .... C5
Pottsville, 15549 .... C5
Punxsutawney, 6271 .... B2
Quakertown, 8931 .... C6
Reading, 81207 .... C5
Red Lion, 6149 .... D5
Ridgway, 4591 .... B2
Roaring Spr., 2418 .... C3
St. Marys, 14502 .... B3
Sayre, 5813 .... A5
Schuylkill Haven, 5548 .... C5
Scottdale, 4772 .... D2
Scranton, 76415 .... B5
Selinsgrove, 5383 .... C4
Shamokin, 8009 .... C5
Sharon, 16328 .... B1
Shenandoah, 5624 .... C5
Shippensburg, 5586 .... D4
Shrewsbury, 3378 .... D4
Slippery Rock, 3068 .... B1
Somerset, 6762 .... D2
Souderton, 6730 .... C6
S. Williamsport, 6412 .... B4
State College, 38420 .... C3
Strasburg, 2800 .... D5
Stroudsburg, 5756 .... B6
Sugarcreek, 5331 .... B1
Sunbury, 10610 .... C4
Tamaqua, 7174 .... C5
Titusville, 6146 .... A1
Towanda, 3024 .... A5
Tyrone, 5528 .... C3
Union City, 3463 .... A1
Uniontown, 12422 .... D1
Vandergrift, 5455 .... C2
Warren, 10259 .... A2
Washington, 15268 .... D1
Waynesboro, 9614 .... D4
Waynesburg, 4184 .... D1
Wellsboro, 3328 .... A4
W. Chester, 17861 .... D6
Westmont, 5523 .... C2
Wilkes-Barre, 43123 .... B5
Williamsport, 30706 .... B4
Windber, 4395 .... D2
Womelsdorf, 2599 .... C5
York, 40862 .... D4
Zelienople, 4123 .... C1

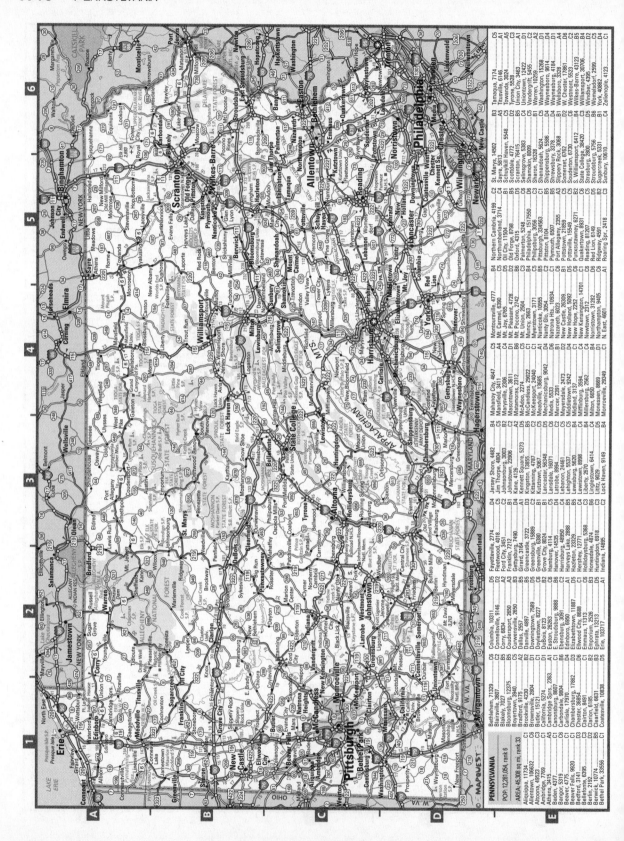

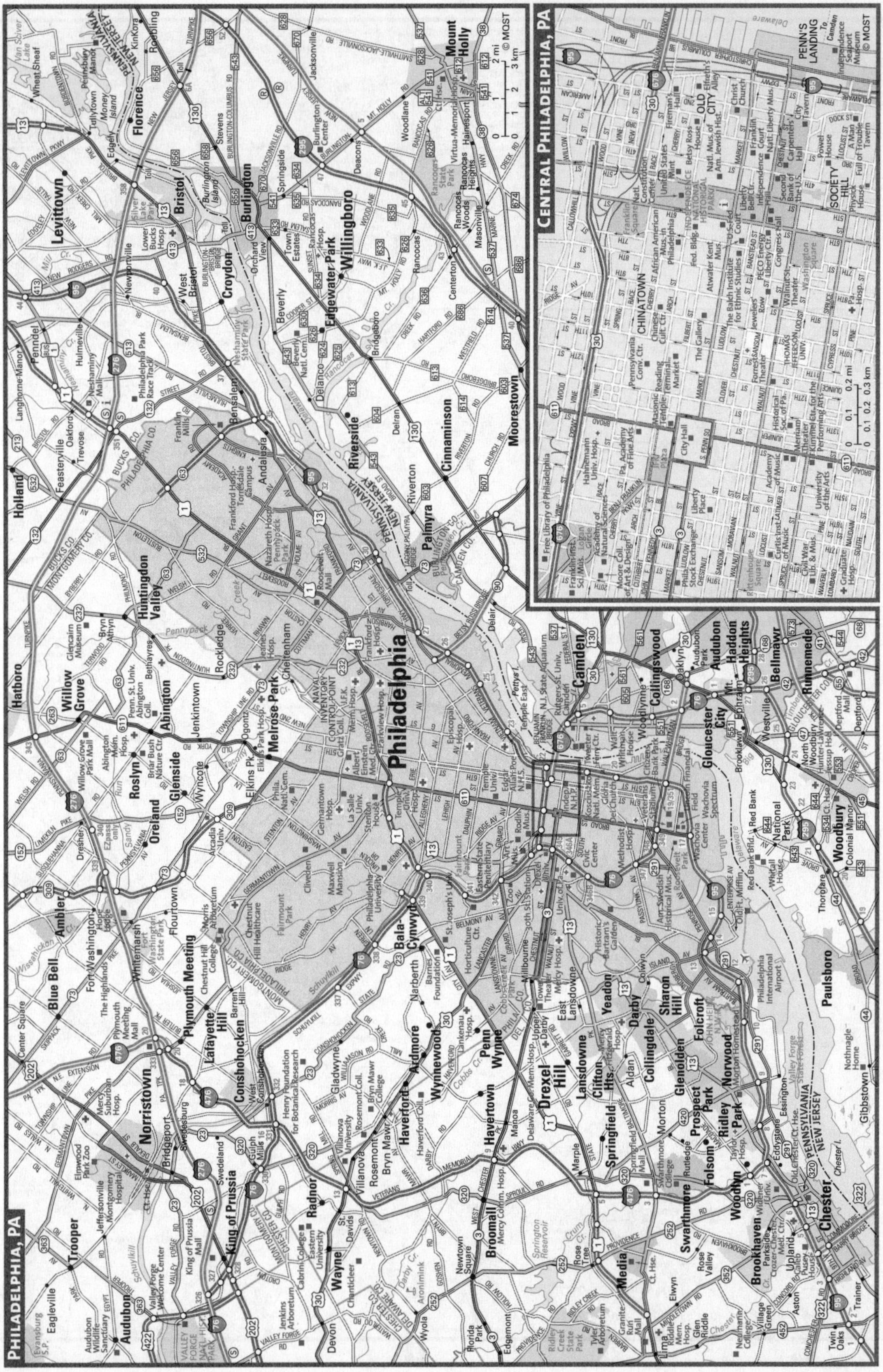
PHILADELPHIA, PA
CENTRAL PHILADELPHIA, PA
© MOST

WEST VIRGINIA

POP: 1,808,344, rank 37

AREA: 24,231 sq mi, rank 41

Alderson, 1091	D4
Amherstdale, 1785	D3
Ansted, 1576	D4
Athens, 1102	E4
Barboursville, 3183	D2
Beckley, 17254	D3
Belington, 1788	C5
Belmont, 1036	B3
Bluefield, 11451	E3
Bradley, 2371	D3
Bridgeport, 7306	B4
Buckhannon, 5725	C4
Buffalo, 1171	C3
Cameron, 1212	B4
Chapmanville, 1211	D2
Charleston, 53421	D3
Charles Town, 2907	B7
Chester, 2592	A4
Clarksburg, 16743	B4
Clendenin, 1116	C3
Craigsville, 2204	D4
Dunbar, 8154	D3
Eleanor, 1345	C3
Elizabeth, 994	C3
Elkins, 7032	C5
Elkview, 1182	D3
Fairmont, 19097	B5
Fayetteville, 2754	D4
Ft. Ashby, 1354	B6
Glenville, 1544	C4
Grafton, 5489	B5
Hamlin, 1119	D2
Harrisville, 1842	C4
Harts, 2361	D2
Hinton, 2880	E4
Huntington, 51475	D2
Hurricane, 5222	D2
Inwood, 2084	B7
Keyser, 5303	B6
Kingwood, 2944	B5
Lewisburg, 3624	D4
Logan, 1630	D3
Madison, 2677	D3
Mannington, 2124	B4
Marlinton, 1204	D5
Marmet, 1693	D3
Martinsburg, 14972	B7
Milton, 2206	D2
Mineral Wells, 1860	C3
Moorefield, 2375	C6
Morgantown, 26809	B5
Moundsville, 9998	B4
Mt. Gay, 2623	D2
Mt. Hope, 1487	D3
Mullens, 1769	E3
New Cumberland, 1099	A4
New Haven, 1559	C3
New Martinsville, 5984	B4
Nitro, 6824	D3
Oak Hill, 7589	D3
Oceana, 1550	E3
Paden City, 2860	B4
Parkersburg, 33099	B3
Parsons, 1463	C5
Pennsboro, 1199	B4
Petersburg, 2423	C6
Philippi, 2870	C5
Pt. Pleasant, 4637	C2
Princeton, 6347	E3
Rainelle, 1545	D4
Rand, 2300	D3
Ravenswood, 4031	C3
Richwood, 2477	D4
Ripley, 3263	C3
Romney, 1940	B6
Ronceverte, 1557	D4
Rupert, 940	D4
St. Albans, 11567	D3
St. Marys, 2017	B3
Salem, 2006	B4
Shady Spr., 2078	E3
Shinnston, 2295	B4
Sissonville, 4399	C3
Sistersville, 1588	B4
Sophia, 1301	E3
S. Charleston, 13390	D3
Spencer, 2352	C3
Summersville, 3294	D4
Sutton, 1011	C4
Switzer, 1138	D2
Terra Alta, 1456	B5
Vienna, 10861	B3
Wayne, 1105	D2
Weirton, 20411	A4
Welch, 2683	E3
Wellsburg, 2891	A4
Weston, 4317	C4
Wheeling, 31419	A4
White Sulphur Sprs., 2315	D4
Williamson, 3414	E2
Williamstown, 2996	B3
Winfield, 1858	C3

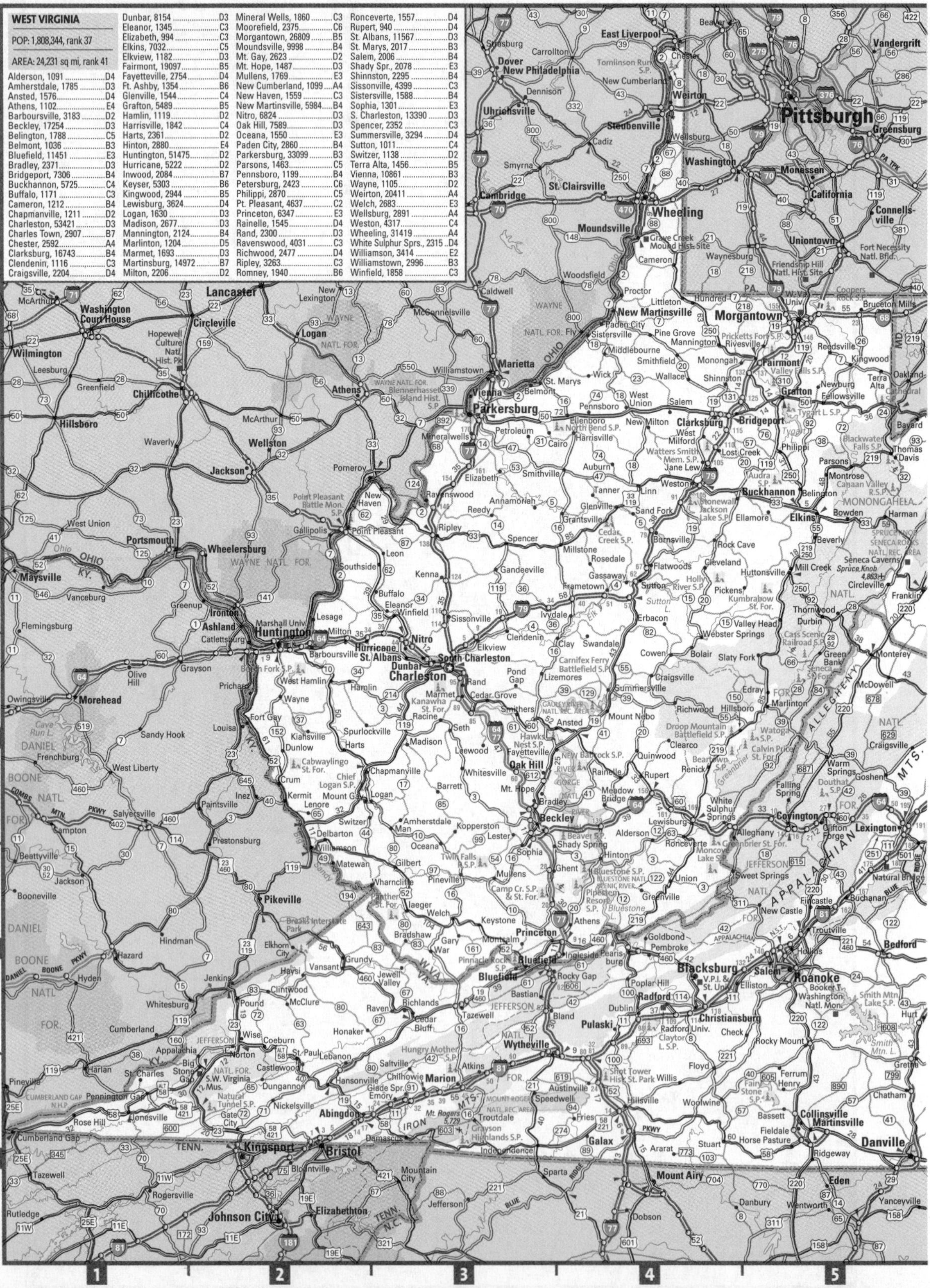

VIRGINIA

POP: 7,078,515, rank 12

AREA: 40,767 sq mi, rank 36

Abingdon, 7780 .... F2
Alexandria, 128283 .... C8
Altavista, 3425 .... E6
Amherst, 2251 .... E6
Appalachia, 1839 .... F2
Appomattox, 1761 .... E6
Arlington, 189453 .... C8
Ashland, 6619 .... D8
Bassett, 1338 .... F5
Bealeton, 2100 .... C7
Bedford, 6299 .... E5
Berryville, 2963 .... C7
Big Stone Gap, 4856 .... F2
Blacksburg, 39573 .... E4
Blackstone, 3675 .... E7
Bluefield, 5078 .... E3
Bridgewater, 5203 .... D6
Bristol, 17367 .... F2
Broadway, 2192 .... C6
Buena Vista, 6349 .... E6
Castlewood, 2036 .... F2
Centreville, 48661 .... C8
Charlottesville, 45049 .... D6
Chase City, 2457 .... F6
Chatham, 1338 .... F5
Chesapeake, 199184 .... F9
Chester, 17890 .... E8
Chesterfield, 3558 .... E8
Chilhowie, 1827 .... F3
Chincoteague, 4317 .... D10
Christiansburg, 16947 .... E4
Clarksville, 1329 .... F6
Clifton Forge, 4289 .... D5
Clintwood, 1549 .... E2
Coeburn, 1996 .... E2
Collinsville, 7777 .... F5
Colonial Beach, 3228 .... D8
Colonial Hts., 16897 .... E8
Courtland, 1270 .... F8
Covington, 6303 .... D5
Crewe, 2378 .... E7
Crimora, 1796 .... D6
Culpeper, 9664 .... D7
Dale City, 55971 .... C8
Danville, 48411 .... F5
Dublin, 2288 .... E4
Dumfries, 4937 .... C8
Elkton, 2042 .... D6
Emory, 2266 .... F3
Emporia, 5665 .... F8
Fairfax, 21498 .... C8
Farmville, 6845 .... E7
Ferrum, 1313 .... F5
Fishersville, 4998 .... D6
Forest, 8006 .... E6
Franklin, 8346 .... F8
Fredericksburg, 19279 .... D8
Front Royal, 13589 .... C7
Galax, 6837 .... F4
Gate City, 2159 .... F2
Glade Spr., 1374 .... F3
Gloucester, 2269 .... E9
Gloucester Pt., 9429 .... E9
Gordonsville, 1498 .... D7
Grottoes, 2114 .... D6
Halifax, 1389 .... F6
Hampden Sydney, 1264 .... E6
Hampton, 146437 .... E9
Harrisonburg, 40468 .... D6
Hillsville, 2607 .... F4
Hollins, 14309 .... E5
Hopewell, 22354 .... E8
Horse Pasture, 2255 .... F5
Hurt, 1276 .... E5
Lawrenceville, 1275 .... F7
Lebanon, 3273 .... F2
Leesburg, 28311 .... C7
Lexington, 6867 .... D5
Louisa, 1401 .... D7
Luray, 4871 .... C6
Lynchburg, 65269 .... E6
Manassas, 35135 .... C8
Marion, 6349 .... F3
Martinsville, 15416 .... F5
Mt. Jackson, 1664 .... C6
New Market, 1637 .... C6
Newport News, 180150 .... E9
Norfolk, 234403 .... F9
Norton, 3904 .... E2
Onancock, 1525 .... D9
Orange, 4123 .... D7
Pearisburg, 2729 .... E4
Pennington Gap, 1781 .... F1
Petersburg, 33740 .... E8
Poquoson, 11566 .... E9
Portsmouth, 100565 .... F9
Pulaski, 9473 .... E4
Purcellville, 3584 .... C7
Radford, 15859 .... E4
Raven, 2593 .... E3
Reston, 56407 .... C8
Richlands, 4144 .... E3
Richmond, 197790 .... E8
Roanoke, 94911 .... E5
Rocky Mount, 4066 .... E5
Rustburg, 1271 .... E6
Salem, 24747 .... E5
Saltville, 2204 .... F3
Shenandoah, 1878 .... C6
Smithfield, 6324 .... E9
S. Boston, 8491 .... F6
S. Hill, 4403 .... F7
Spotsylvania, 3833 .... D7
Stafford, 3000 .... D8
Stanley, 1326 .... C6
Staunton, 23853 .... D6
Strasburg, 4017 .... C7
Stuarts Draft, 8367 .... D6
Suffolk, 63677 .... F9
Tappahannock, 2068 .... D8
Tazewell, 4206 .... E3
Timberville, 1739 .... C6
Toano, 1400 .... E8
Triangle, 5500 .... C8
Verona, 3638 .... D6
Victoria, 1821 .... E7
Virginia Beach, 425257 .... F9
Warrenton, 6670 .... C7
Warsaw, 1375 .... D8
Waverly, 2309 .... E8
Waynesboro, 19520 .... D6
W. Point, 2866 .... E8
Williamsburg, 11998 .... E8
Winchester, 23585 .... C7
Wise, 3255 .... E2
Woodbridge, 31941 .... C8
Woodstock, 3952 .... C6
Wytheville, 7804 .... F3

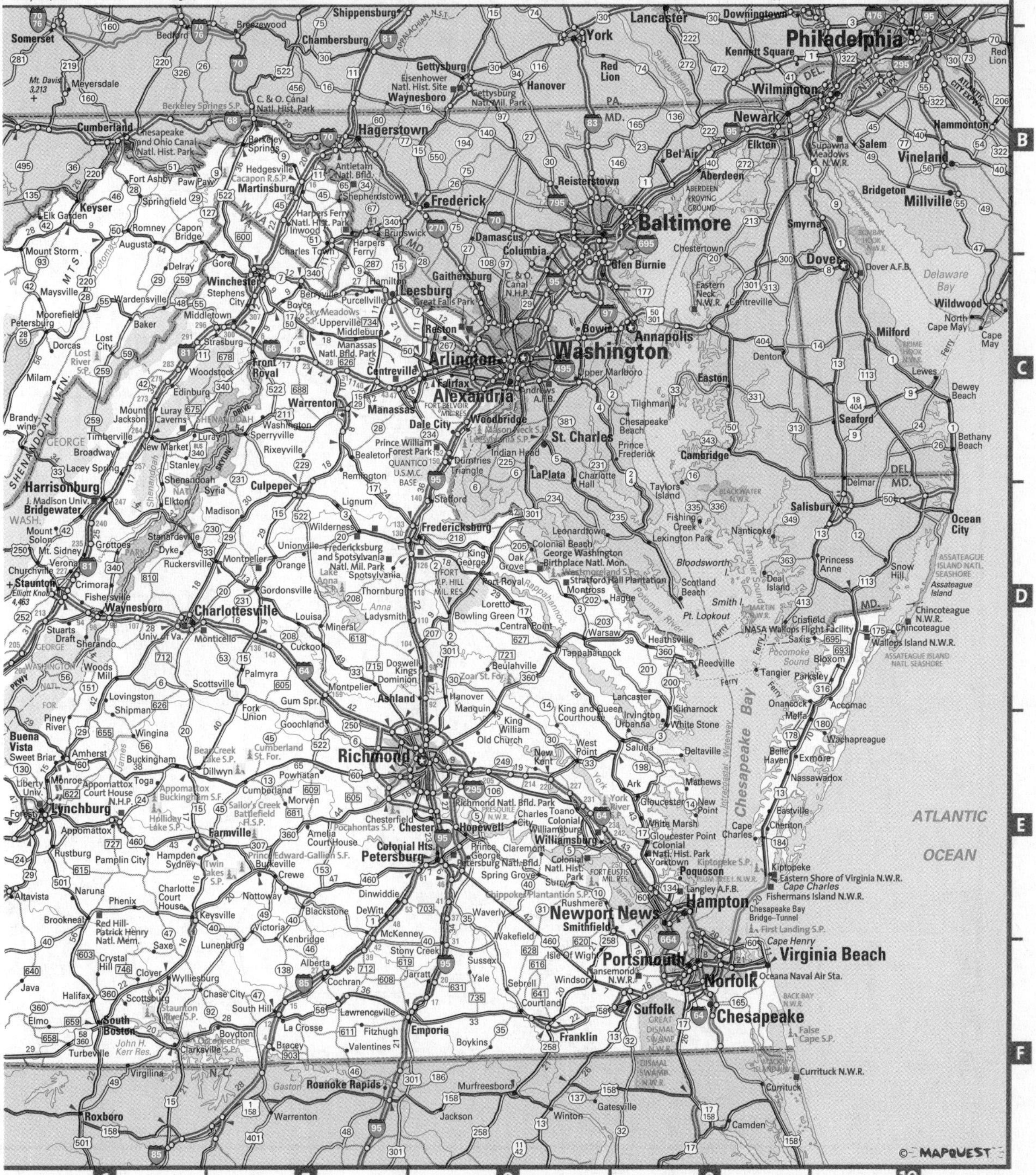

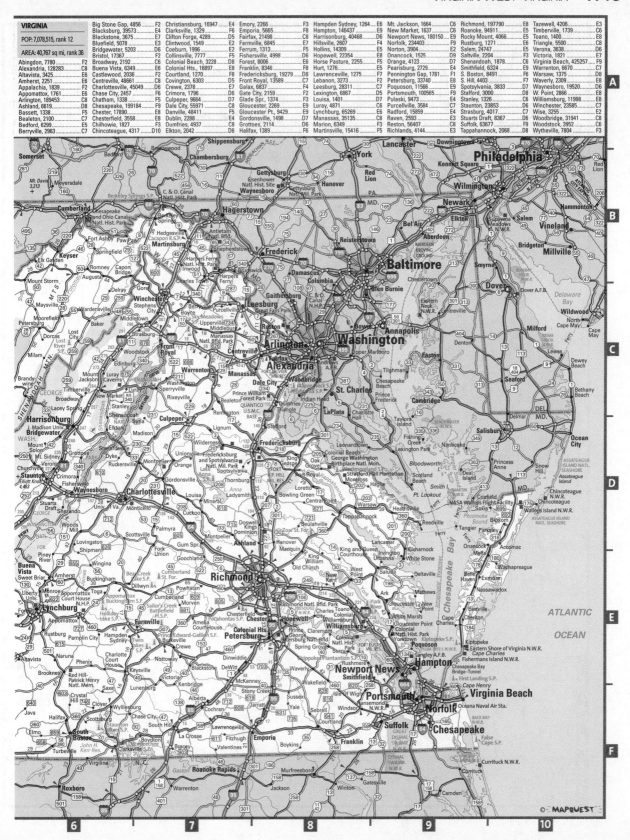

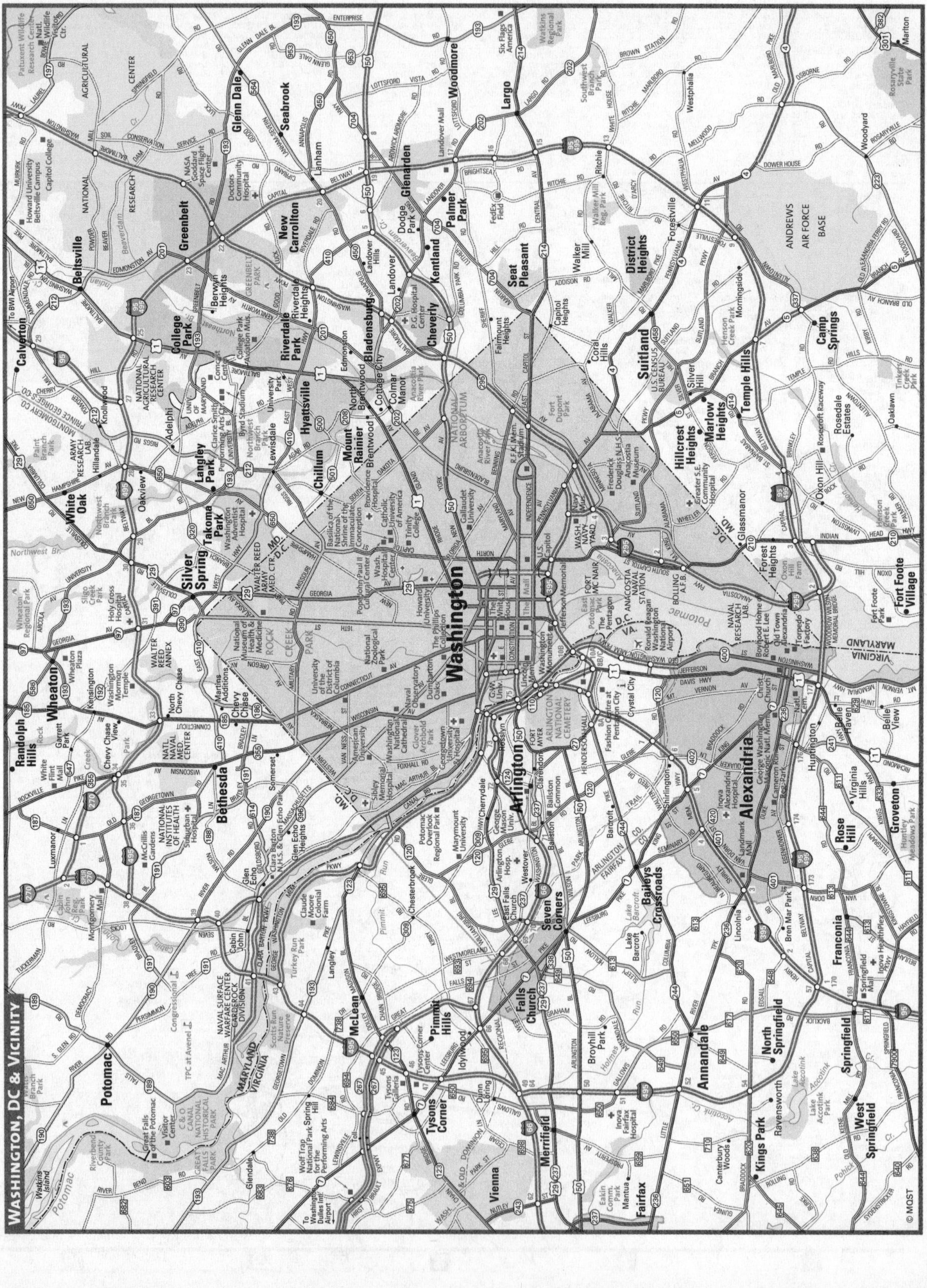
WASHINGTON, DC & VICINITY
Washington
Arlington
Alexandria
Silver Spring
Bethesda
Takoma Park
Wheaton
College Park
Greenbelt
Beltsville
Calverton
White Oak
Langley Park
Hyattsville
Chillum
Mount Rainier
Brentwood
Bladensburg
Cheverly
Riverdale Park
New Carrollton
Lanham
Seabrook
Glenn Dale
Glenarden
Woodmore
Largo
Landover
Kentland
Palmer Park
Seat Pleasant
District Heights
Forestville
Suitland
Camp Springs
Temple Hills
Marlow Heights
Hillcrest Heights
Glassmanor
Oxon Hill
Forest Heights
Fort Foote Village
Randolph Hills
Chevy Chase
Potomac
McLean
Pimmit Hills
Tysons Corner
Vienna
Merrifield
Falls Church
Seven Corners
Baileys Crossroads
Annandale
North Springfield
Springfield
West Springfield
Franconia
Kings Park
Fairfax
Huntington
Rose Hill
Groveton
ANDREWS AIR FORCE BASE
ARLINGTON NATIONAL CEMETERY
NATIONAL ARBORETUM
ROCK CREEK PARK
VIRGINIA
MARYLAND
MD.
D.C.
VA.
Potomac
© MQST

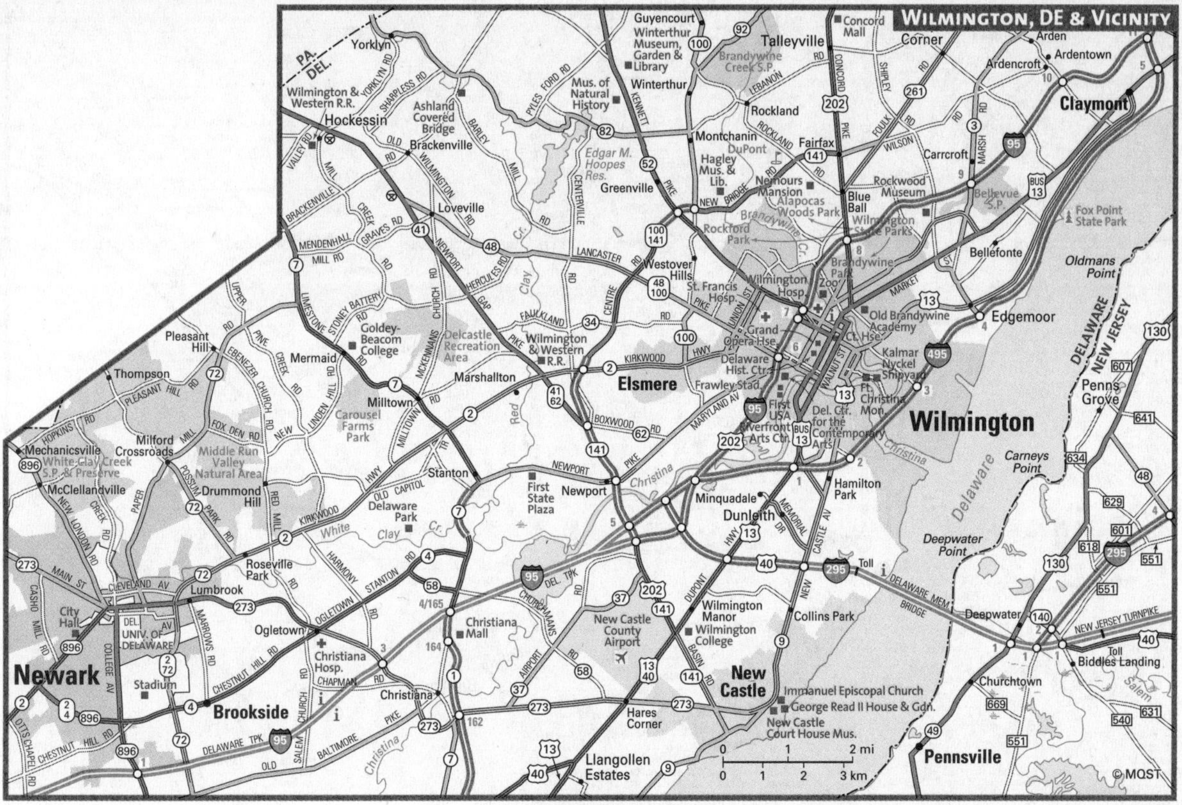
WILMINGTON, DE & VICINITY
Guyencourt
Winterthur Museum, Garden & Library
Winterthur
Talleyville
Concord Mall
Corner
Arden
Ardentown
Ardencroft
Claymont
Yorklyn
PA. DEL.
Wilmington & Western R.R.
Hockessin
Ashland Covered Bridge
Brackenville
Mus. of Natural History
Brandywine Creek S.P.
Rockland
Montchanin
DuPont
Fairfax
Carrcroft
Edgar M. Hoopes Res.
Hagley Mus. & Lib.
Greenville
Nemours Mansion
Alapocas Woods Park
Blue Ball
Rockwood Museum
Bellevue S.P.
Fox Point State Park
Loveville
Rockford Park
Wilmington State Parks
Bellefonte
Oldmans Point
Westover Hills
St. Francis Hosp.
Wilmington Hosp.
Brandywine Park
Zoo
Old Brandywine Academy
Edgemoor
Pleasant Hill
Goldey-Beacom College
Mermaid
Delcastle Recreation Area
Wilmington & Western R.R.
Grand Opera Hse.
Ct. Hse.
Kalmar Nyckel Shipyard
Thompson
Marshallton
Elsmere
Delaware Hist. Ctr.
Frawley Stad.
Ft. Christina Mon.
Penns Grove
Milltown
Carousel Farms Park
First USA Riverfront Arts Ctr.
Del. Ctr. for the Contemporary Arts
Wilmington
Mechanicsville
White Clay Creek S.P. & Preserve
Milford Crossroads
Middle Run Valley Natural Area
Stanton
Newport
First State Plaza
Christina
Carneys Point
McClellandville
Drummond Hill
Delaware Park
Minquadale
Dunleith
Hamilton Park
Delaware
Deepwater Point
Roseville Park
Lumbrook
DELAWARE NEW JERSEY
City Hall
Del. Univ. of Delaware
Ogletown
Christiana Hosp.
Christiana Mall
New Castle County Airport
Wilmington Manor
Wilmington College
Collins Park
Deepwater
Newark
Stadium
Brookside
Christiana
Hares Corner
New Castle
Immanuel Episcopal Church
George Read II House & Gdn.
New Castle Court House Mus.
Churchtown
Biddles Landing
Toll
Salem
Llangollen Estates
Pennsville
0 1 2 mi
0 1 2 3 km
© MQST

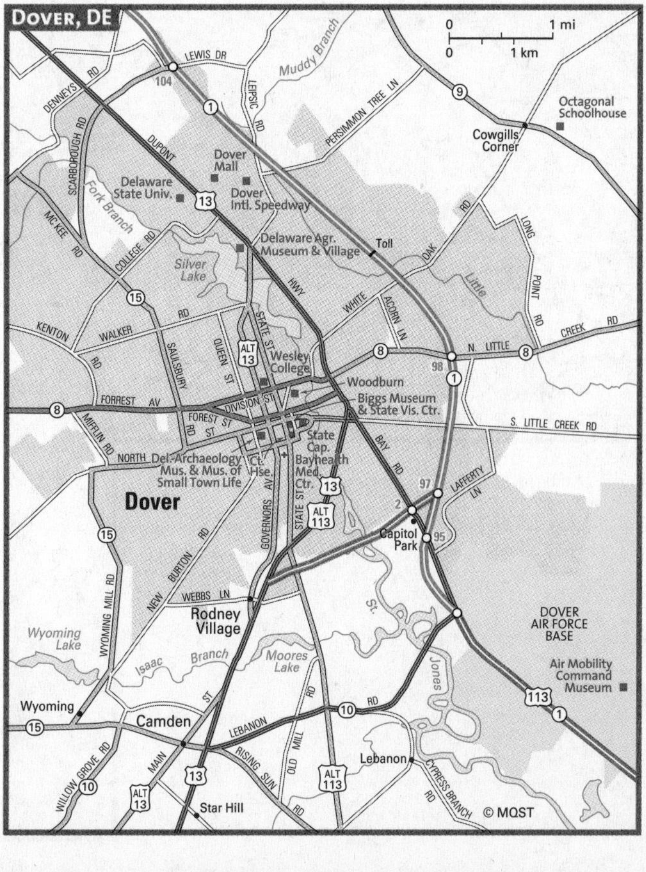
DOVER, DE
0 1 mi
0 1 km
Lewis Dr
Muddy Branch
Octagonal Schoolhouse
Cowgills Corner
Dover Mall
Delaware State Univ.
Dover Intl. Speedway
Fork Branch
Delaware Agr. Museum & Village
Toll
Silver Lake
Little
Wesley College
Woodburn
Biggs Museum & State Vis. Ctr.
State Cap.
Bayhealth Med. Ctr.
Del. Archaeology Mus. & Mus. of Small Town Life
Ct. Hse.
Dover
Capitol Park
Rodney Village
St.
DOVER AIR FORCE BASE
Air Mobility Command Museum
Wyoming Lake
Isaac Branch
Moores Lake
Jones
Wyoming
Camden
Lebanon
Star Hill
© MQST

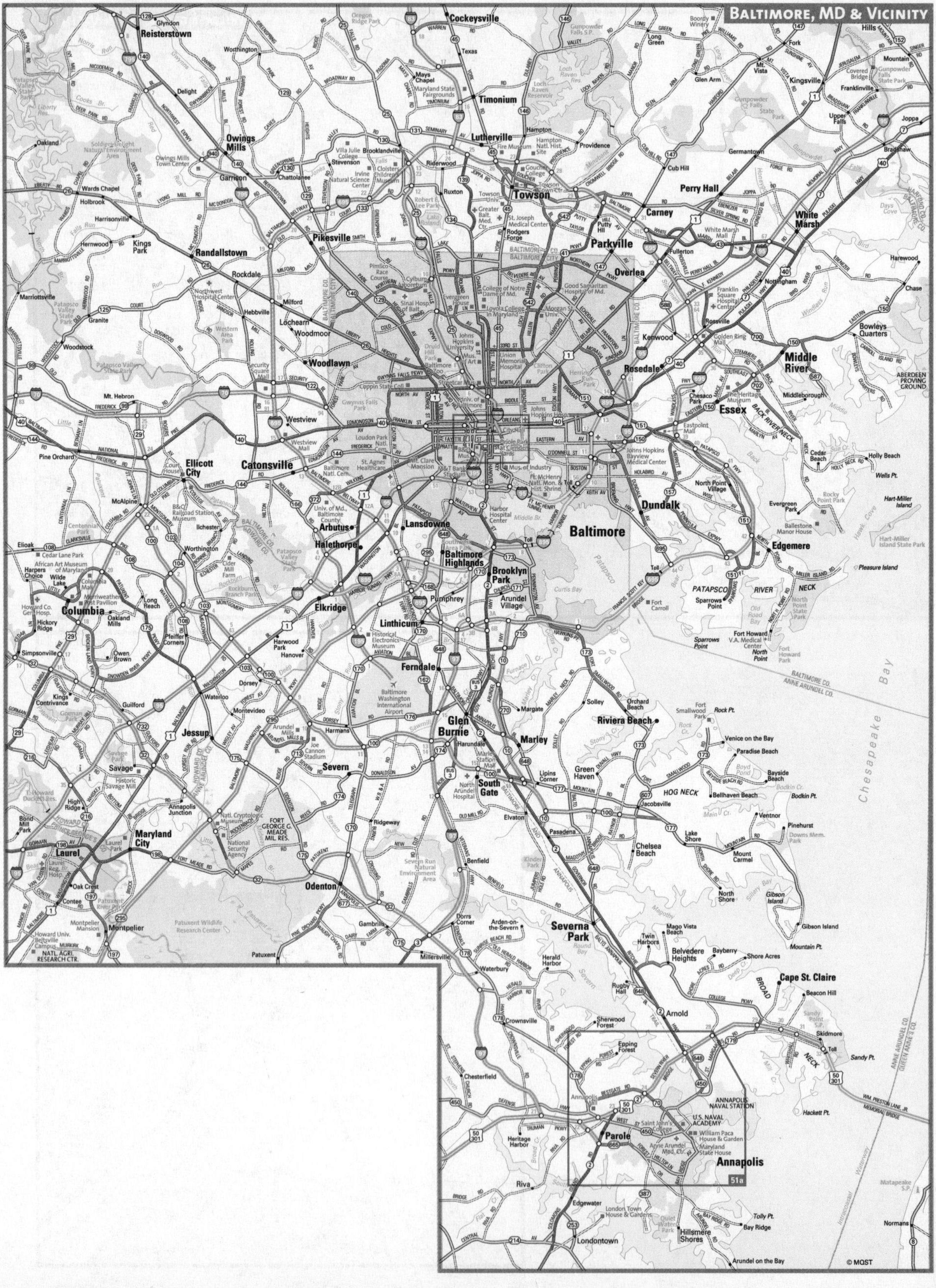
BALTIMORE, MD & VICINITY
Cockeysville
Reisterstown
Glyndon
Worthington
Texas
Timonium
Lutherville
Owings Mills
Towson
Pikesville
Randallstown
Parkville
Carney
Perry Hall
White Marsh
Overlea
Rosedale
Middle River
Essex
Dundalk
Edgemere
Baltimore
Catonsville
Ellicott City
Woodlawn
Westview
Arbutus
Halethorpe
Lansdowne
Baltimore Highlands
Brooklyn Park
Elkridge
Columbia
Linthicum
Ferndale
Glen Burnie
Riviera Beach
Marley
Jessup
Savage
Severn
South Gate
Laurel
Maryland City
Odenton
Severna Park
Arnold
Cape St. Claire
Parole
Annapolis
Londontown
Baltimore Washington International Airport
Patapsco Valley State Park
Gunpowder Falls State Park
Loch Raven Reservoir
Curtis Bay
Patapsco River
Chesapeake Bay
BALTIMORE CO.
ANNE ARUNDEL CO.
51a
© MQST

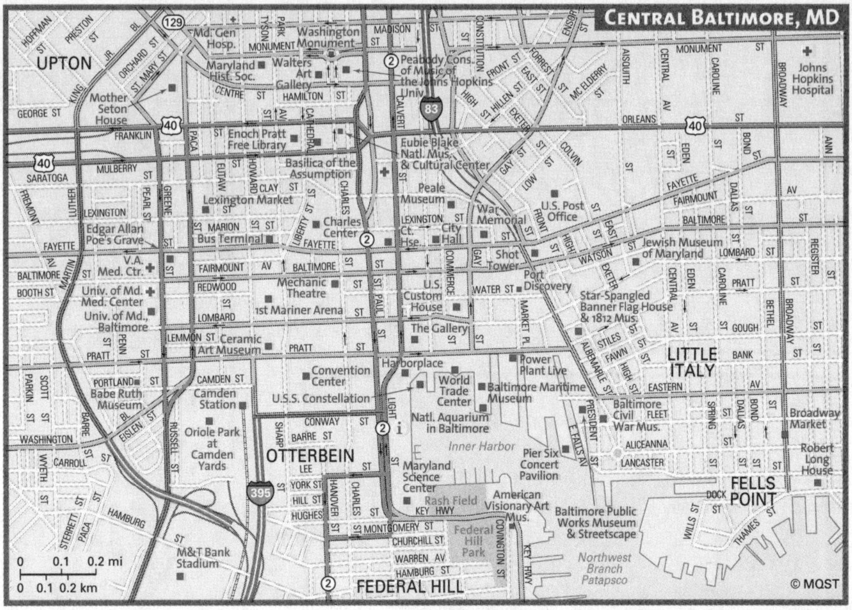
CENTRAL BALTIMORE, MD
UPTON
Md. Gen. Hosp.
Washington Monument
Peabody Cons. of Music of the Johns Hopkins Univ.
Maryland Hist. Soc.
Walters Art Gallery
Mother Seton House
Enoch Pratt Free Library
Eubie Blake Natl. Mus. & Cultural Center
Basilica of the Assumption
Johns Hopkins Hospital
Lexington Market
Peale Museum
Edgar Allan Poe's Grave
Bus Terminal
Charles Center
City Hall
War Memorial
U.S. Post Office
V.A. Med. Ctr.
Shot Tower
Jewish Museum of Maryland
Mechanic Theatre
Univ. of Md. Med. Center
U.S. Custom House
Port Discovery
Univ. of Md. Baltimore
1st Mariner Arena
Star-Spangled Banner Flag House & 1812 Mus.
The Gallery
Ceramic Art Museum
LITTLE ITALY
Power Plant Live
Harborplace
Convention Center
Babe Ruth Museum
World Trade Center
Baltimore Maritime Museum
Camden Station
U.S.S. Constellation
Baltimore Civil War Mus.
Broadway Market
Oriole Park at Camden Yards
Natl. Aquarium in Baltimore
OTTERBEIN
Inner Harbor
Pier Six Concert Pavilion
Robert Long House
Maryland Science Center
FELLS POINT
Rash Field
American Visionary Art Mus.
Baltimore Public Works Museum & Streetscape
Federal Hill Park
M&T Bank Stadium
Northwest Branch Patapsco
FEDERAL HILL
0 0.1 0.2 mi
0 0.1 0.2 km
© MQST

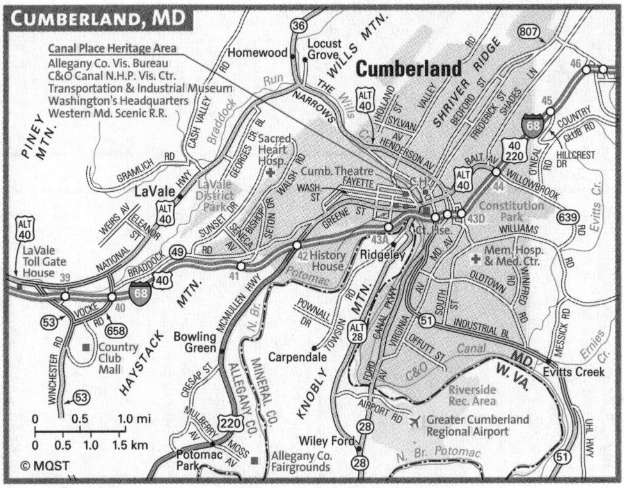
CUMBERLAND, MD
Canal Place Heritage Area
Allegany Co. Vis. Bureau
C&O Canal N.H.P. Vis. Ctr.
Transportation & Industrial Museum
Washington's Headquarters
Western Md. Scenic R.R.
Homewood
Locust Grove
Cumberland
WILLS MTN.
SHRIVER RIDGE
PINEY MTN.
Sacred Heart Hosp.
Cumb. Theatre
LaVale
LaVale District Park
Constitution Park
Mem. Hosp. & Med. Ctr.
Ct. Hse.
LaVale Toll Gate House
History House
Ridgeley
HAYSTACK MTN.
Country Club Mall
Bowling Green
Carpendale
KNOBLY MTN.
Evitts Creek
C&O Canal
MD. W. VA.
Riverside Rec. Area
Greater Cumberland Regional Airport
Wiley Ford
Potomac Park
Allegany Co. Fairgrounds
N. Br. Potomac
0 0.5 1.0 mi
0 0.5 1.0 1.5 km
© MQST

HAGERSTOWN, MD
0 1 2 mi
0 1 2 3 km
Maugansville
To Hagerstown Reg. Airport
Orchard Hills
Paramount
Fountain Head
Huyett
Cedar Lawn
Fiddlersburg
Security
County Frgnds.
Hager House
Hagerstown
City Park
Bridgeport
Washington Co. Health System
Washington Co. Mus. of Fine Arts
Greenberry Hills
Colonial Park
Valley Mall
Miller House
Halfway
Bright-wood Acres
Tammany Manor
Funkstown
© MQST

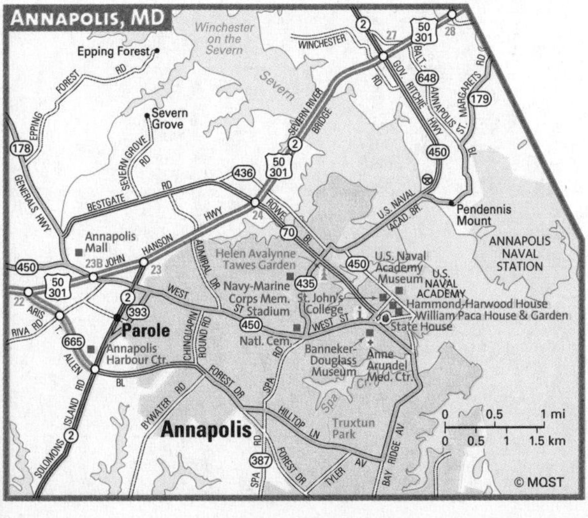
ANNAPOLIS, MD
Winchester on the Severn
Epping Forest
Severn
Severn Grove
Pendennis Mount
ANNAPOLIS NAVAL STATION
Annapolis Mall
Helen Avalynne Tawes Garden
U.S. Naval Academy Museum
U.S. NAVAL ACADEMY
Navy-Marine Corps Mem. Stadium
St. John's College
Hammond-Harwood House
William Paca House & Garden
State House
Parole
Annapolis Harbour Ctr.
Natl. Cem.
Banneker-Douglass Museum
Anne Arundel Med. Ctr.
Spa Cr.
Truxtun Park
Annapolis
0 0.5 1 mi
0 0.5 1 1.5 km
© MQST

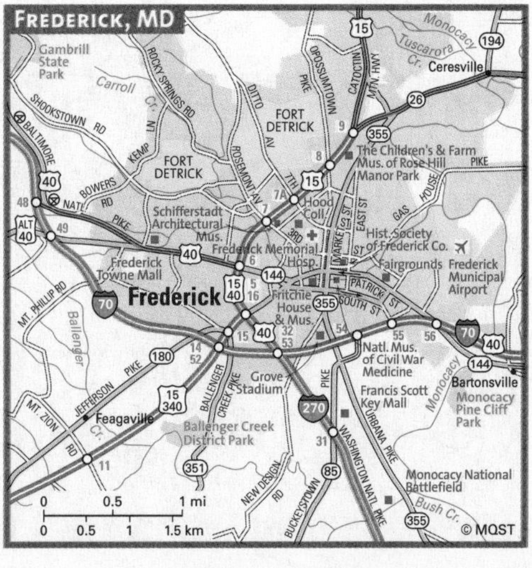
FREDERICK, MD
Gambrill State Park
Monocacy
Tuscarora Cr.
Ceresville
Carroll Cr.
FORT DETRICK
The Children's & Farm Mus. of Rose Hill Manor Park
Hood Coll.
Schifferstadt Architectural Mus.
Hist. Society of Frederick Co.
Frederick Memorial Hosp.
Frederick Towne Mall
Fairgrounds
Frederick Municipal Airport
Frederick
Fritchie House & Mus.
Natl. Mus. of Civil War Medicine
Bartonsville
Grove Stadium
Francis Scott Key Mall
Monocacy Pine Cliff Park
Feagaville
Ballenger Creek District Park
Monocacy National Battlefield
Bush Cr.
0 0.5 1 mi
0 0.5 1 1.5 km
© MQST

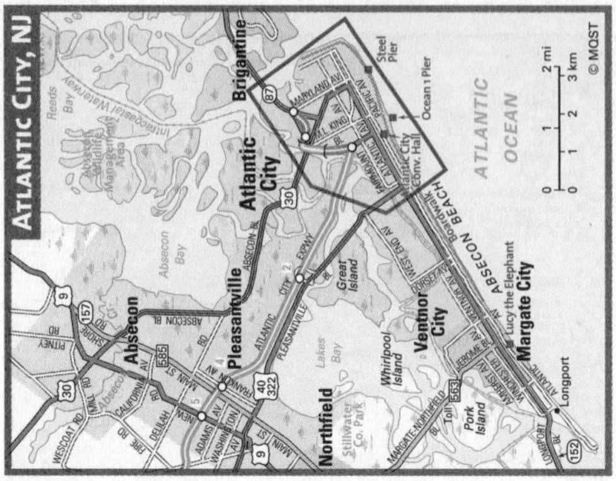
ATLANTIC CITY, NJ
ATLANTIC OCEAN
© MQST

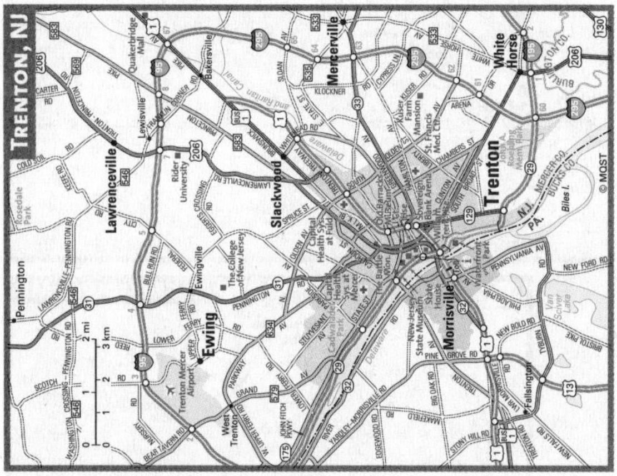
TRENTON, NJ
© MQST

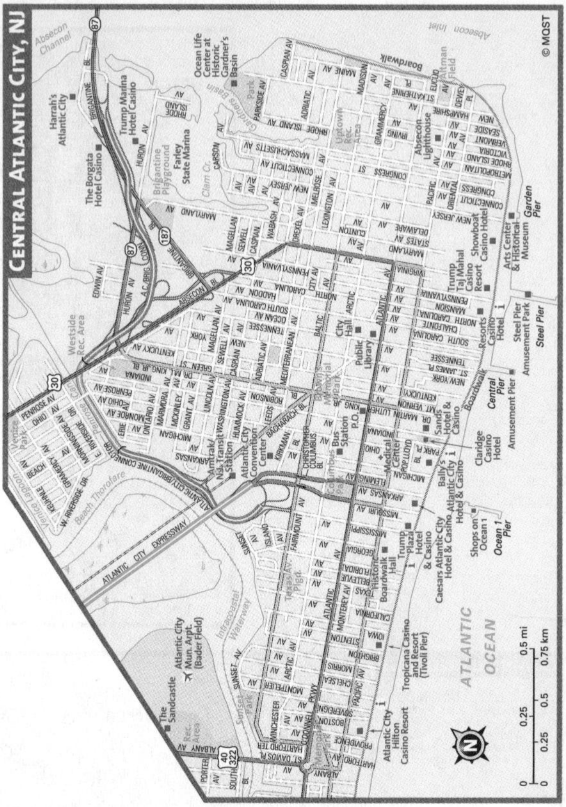
CENTRAL ATLANTIC CITY, NJ
ATLANTIC OCEAN
© MQST

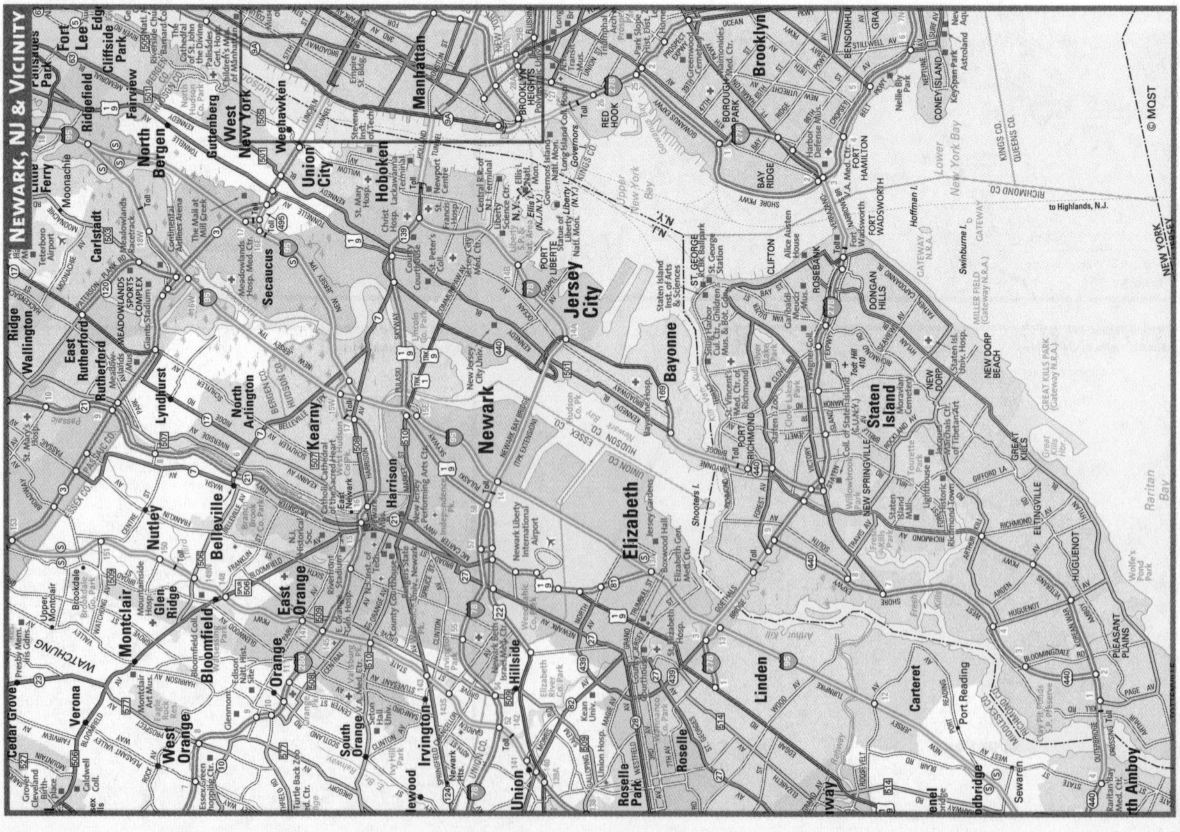
NEWARK, NJ & VICINITY
© MQST

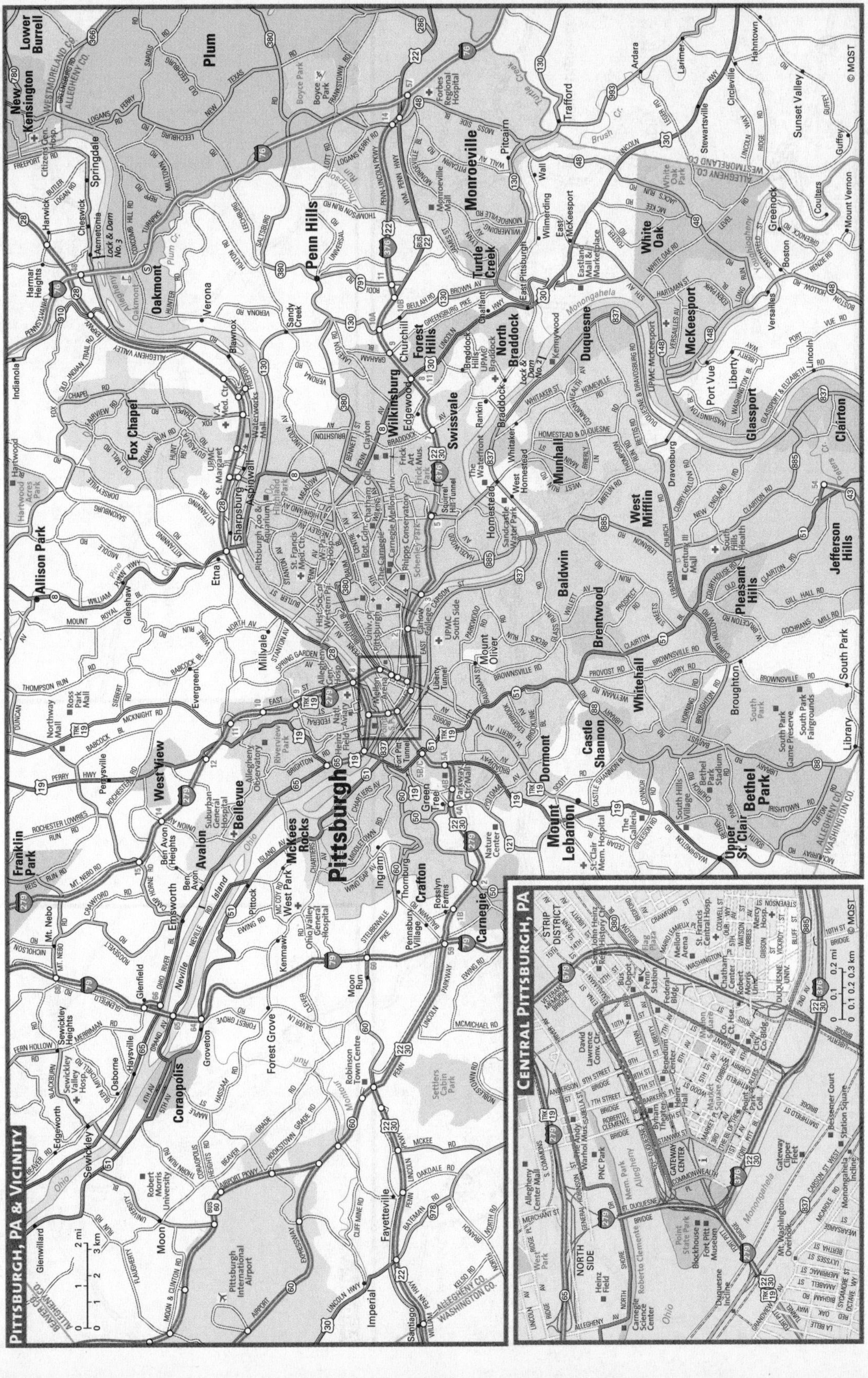
PITTSBURGH, PA & VICINITY
0 1 2 mi
0 1 2 3 km
CENTRAL PITTSBURGH, PA
0 0.1 0.2 mi
0 0.1 0.2 0.3 km
© MQST
Pittsburgh
Penn Hills
Monroeville
Plum
Oakmont
Fox Chapel
Wilkinsburg
Swissvale
Braddock
Homestead
West Mifflin
Munhall
Duquesne
McKeesport
White Oak
Clairton
Jefferson Hills
Pleasant Hills
Baldwin
Brentwood
Whitehall
Castle Shannon
Dormont
Mount Lebanon
Upper St. Clair
Bethel Park
Crafton
Carnegie
McKees Rocks
Bellevue
Avalon
West View
Allison Park
Franklin Park
Coraopolis
Moon
Imperial
Fayetteville
Pittsburgh International Airport
Robert Morris University
Sewickley
Glenwillard
Monongahela
Allegheny
Ohio

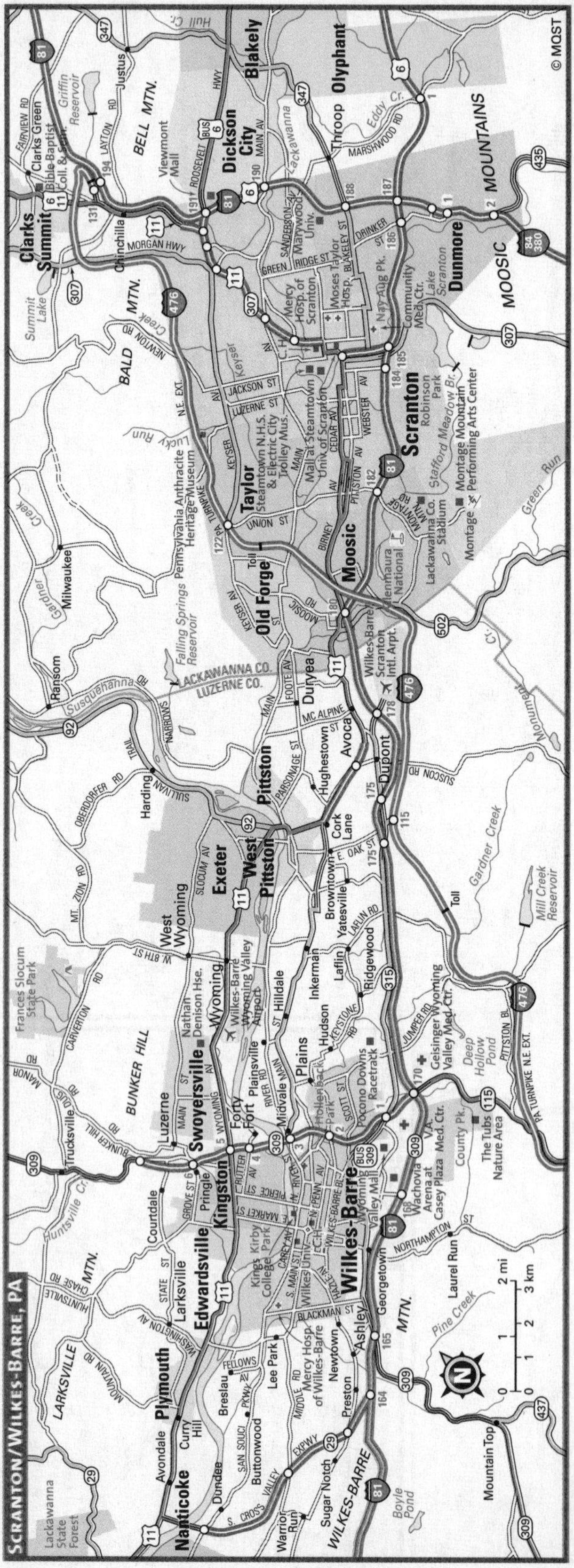
SCRANTON/WILKES-BARRE, PA

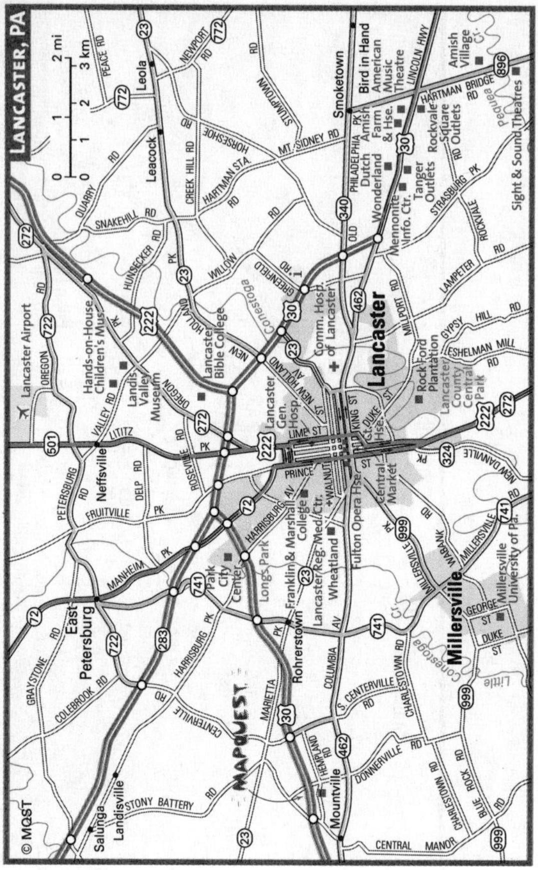
LANCASTER, PA

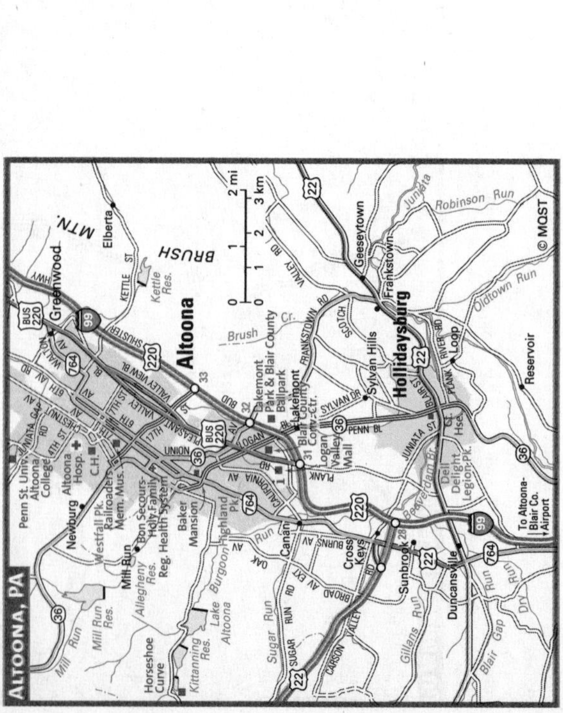
ALTOONA, PA

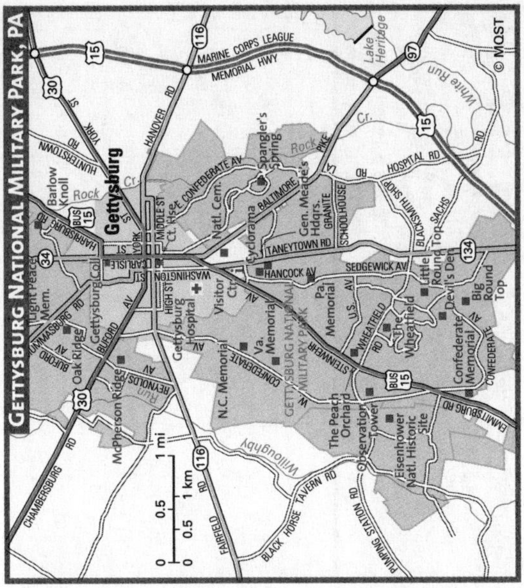
GETTYSBURG NATIONAL MILITARY PARK, PA
Gettysburg
© MQST

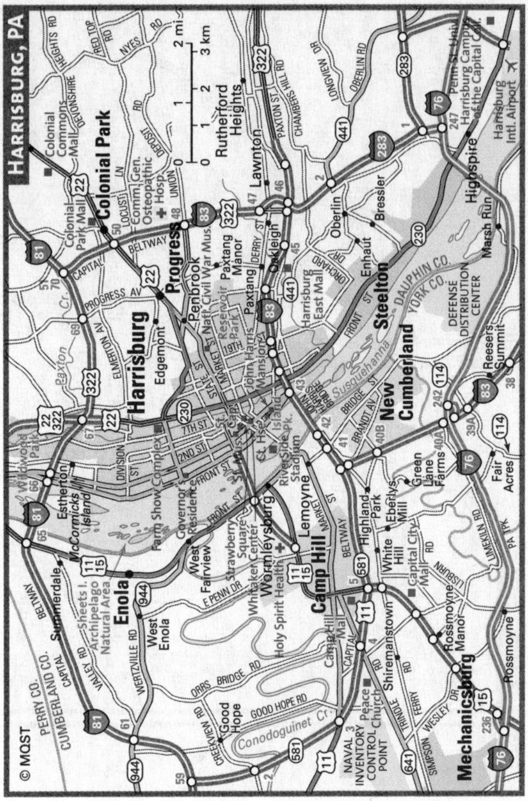
HARRISBURG, PA
Harrisburg
© MQST

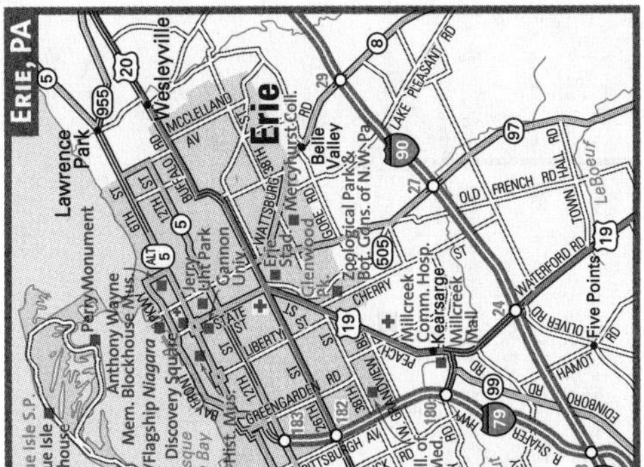
ERIE, PA
Erie
LAKE ERIE
© MQST

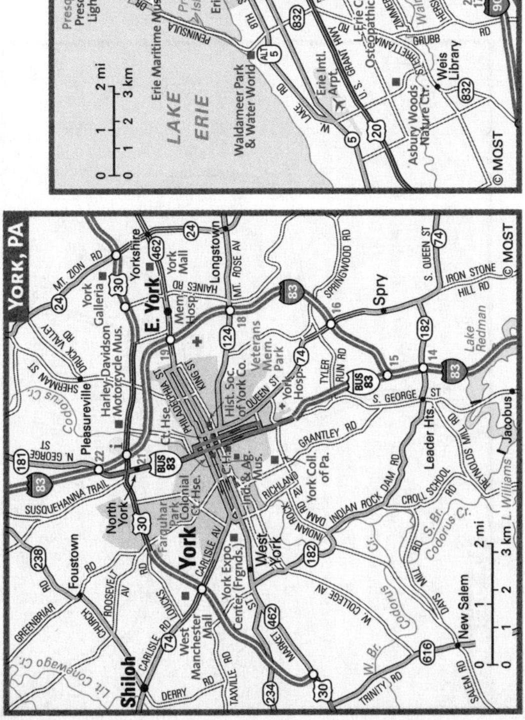
YORK, PA
York
© MQST

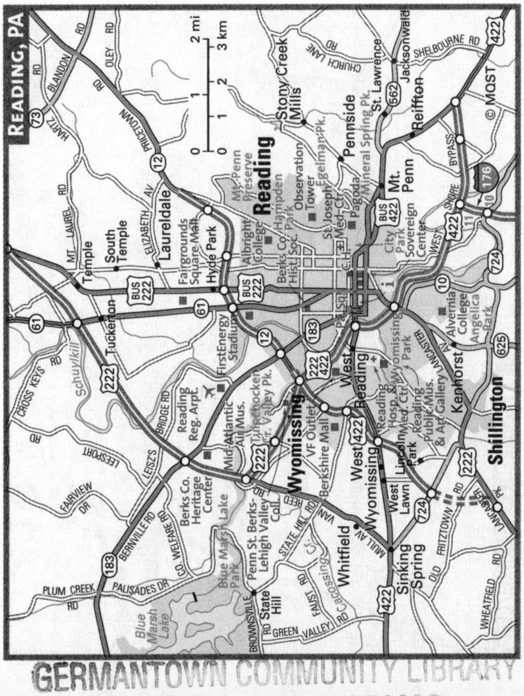
READING, PA
Reading
© MQST

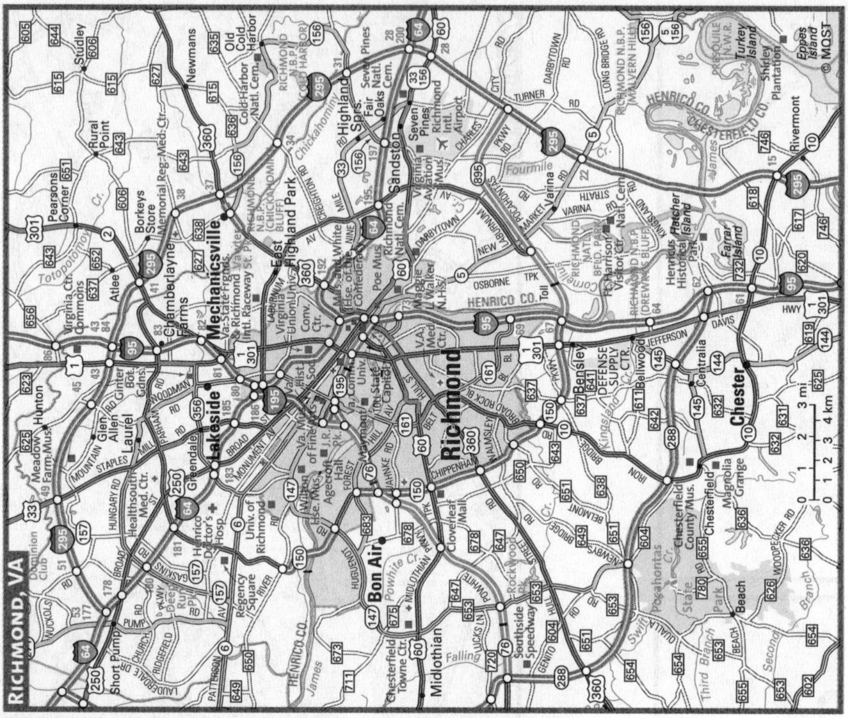
RICHMOND, VA
Richmond
Mechanicsville
Lakeside
Bon Air
Chester
Highland Park
Sandston
Midlothian
© MOST

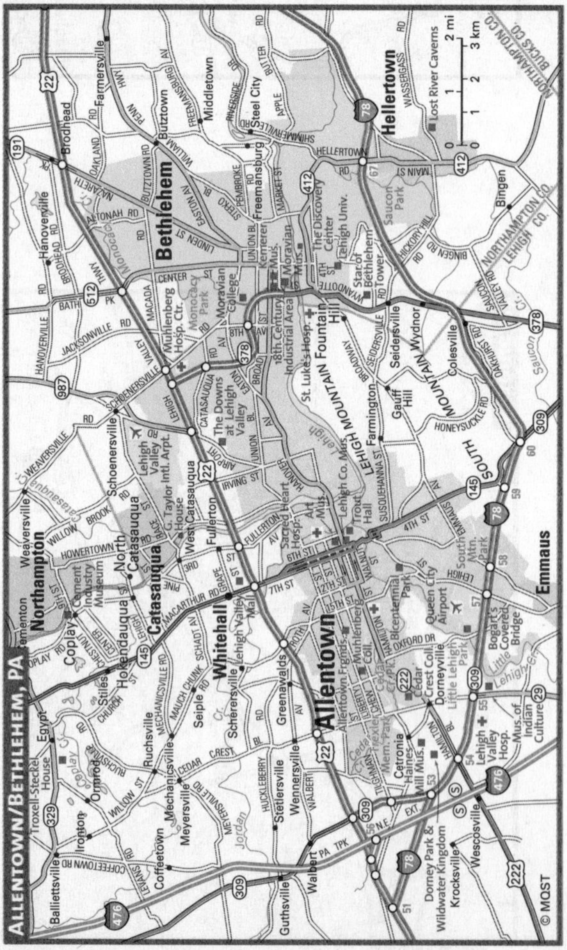
ALLENTOWN/BETHLEHEM, PA
Allentown
Bethlehem
Hellertown
Whitehall
Catasauqua
Northampton
Emmaus
© MOST

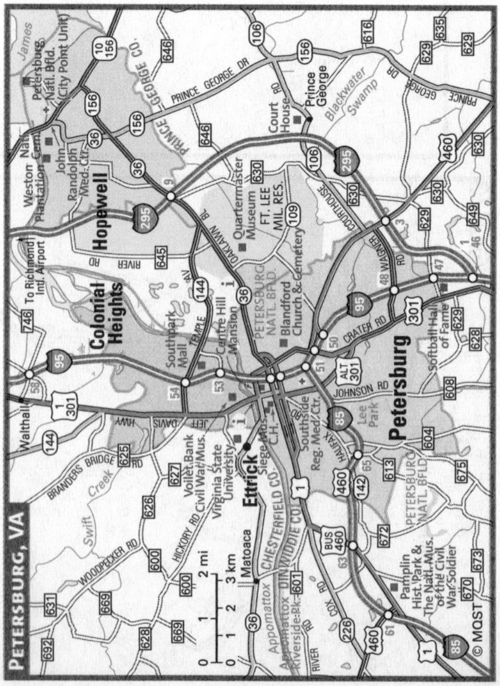
PETERSBURG, VA
Petersburg
Colonial Heights
Hopewell
Ettrick
© MOST

NORFOLK/VIRGINIA BEACH, VA
© MQST
ATLANTIC OCEAN
Chesapeake Bay
Norfolk
Virginia Beach
Hampton
Newport News
Portsmouth
Chesapeake
Suffolk
Poquoson
Smithfield
Cape Charles
Kiptopeke
Fishermans Island
Cape Henry
CHESAPEAKE BAY BRIDGE-TUNNEL
HAMPTON ROADS BRIDGE-TUNNEL
MONITOR-MERRIMAC MEM. BRIDGE TUNNEL
JAMES RIVER BRIDGE
LITTLE CREEK NAVAL AMPHIBIOUS BASE
NORFOLK NAVAL STATION
OCEANA N.A.S.
FORT MONROE
LANGLEY A.F.B.
NASA RESEARCH CENTER
FORT EUSTIS MIL. RES.
GREAT DISMAL SWAMP N.W.R.
BACK BAY N.W.R.
NANSEMOND N.W.R.
Norfolk Intl. Airport
Newport News/Williamsburg Intl. Airport
Cape Henry Memorial
Old Cape Henry Lighthouse
Old Coast Guard Station
Royal London Wax Museum
First Landing State Park
Virginia Zoological Park
Chrysler Museum
Mariners Museum
Virginia Air & Space Center
Fort Wool
Willoughby Spit
Craney Island
James
Elizabeth
Nansemond
0 2 4 mi
0 2 4 6 km

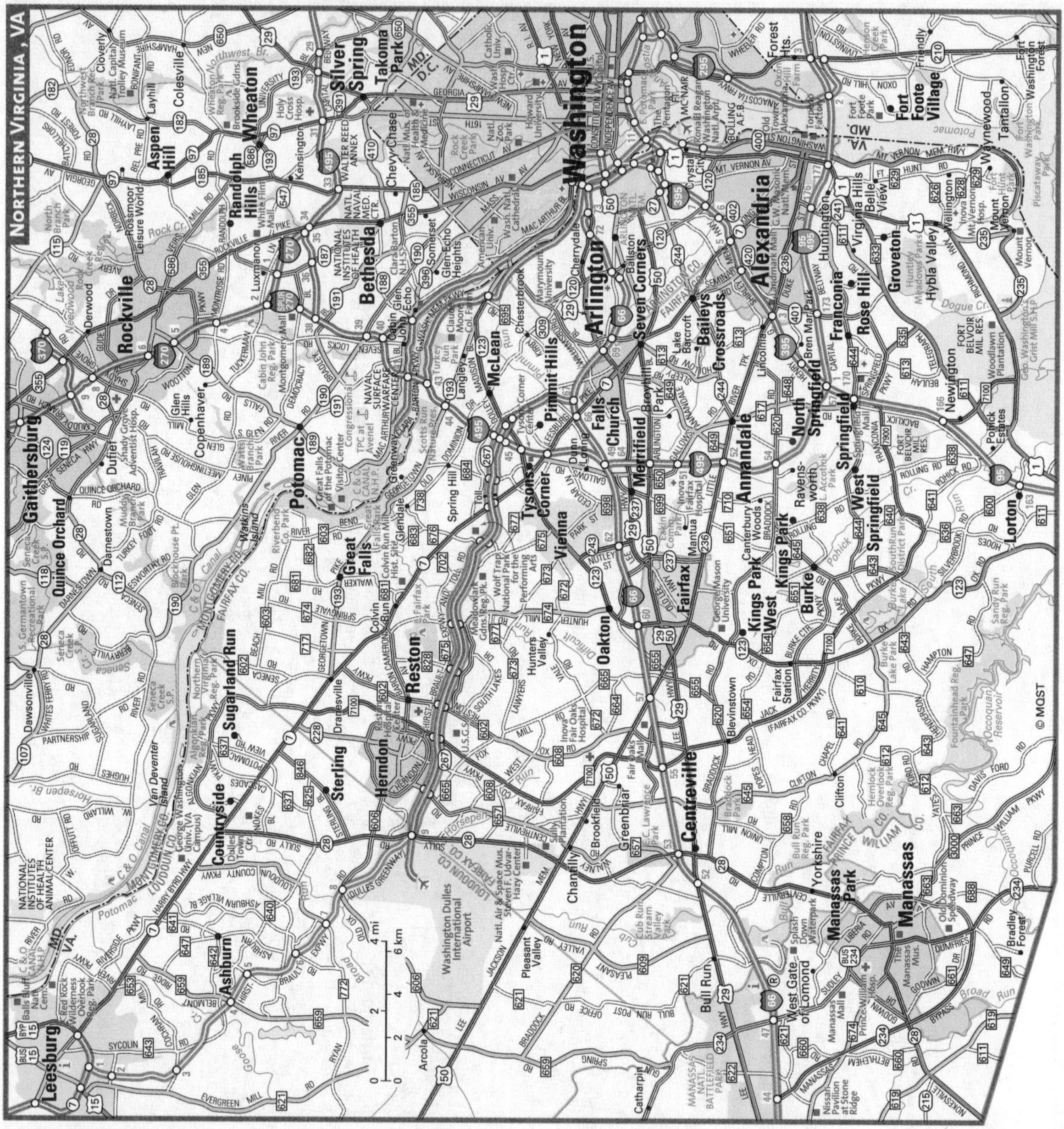
NORTHERN VIRGINIA, VA
© MQST

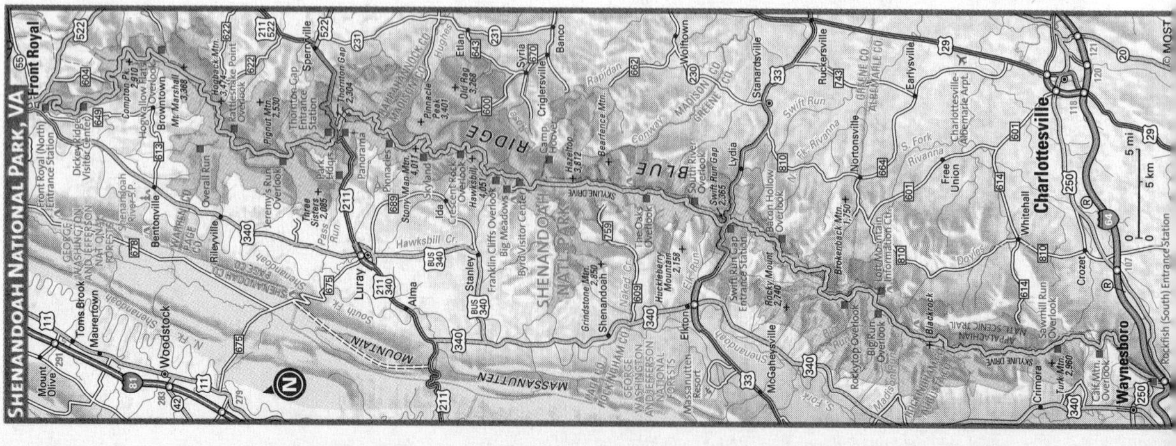
SHENANDOAH NATIONAL PARK, VA
© MQST

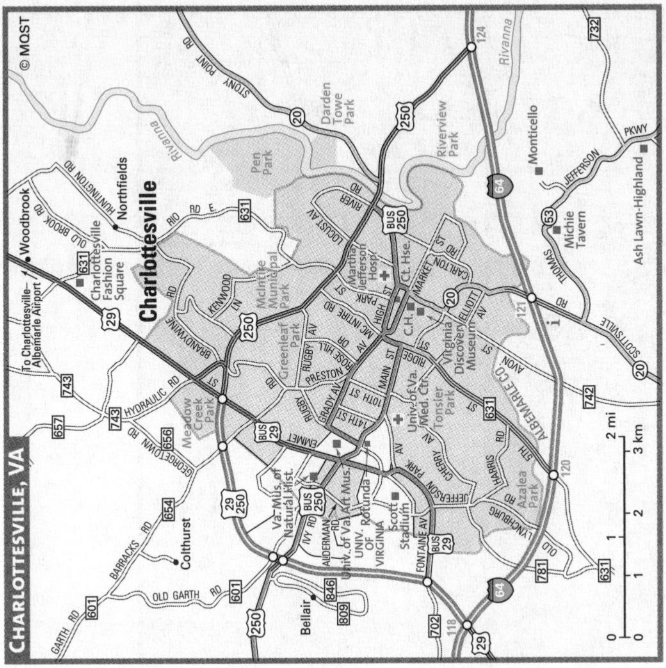
CHARLOTTESVILLE, VA
© MQST
Charlottesville
0 1 2 mi
0 1 2 3 km

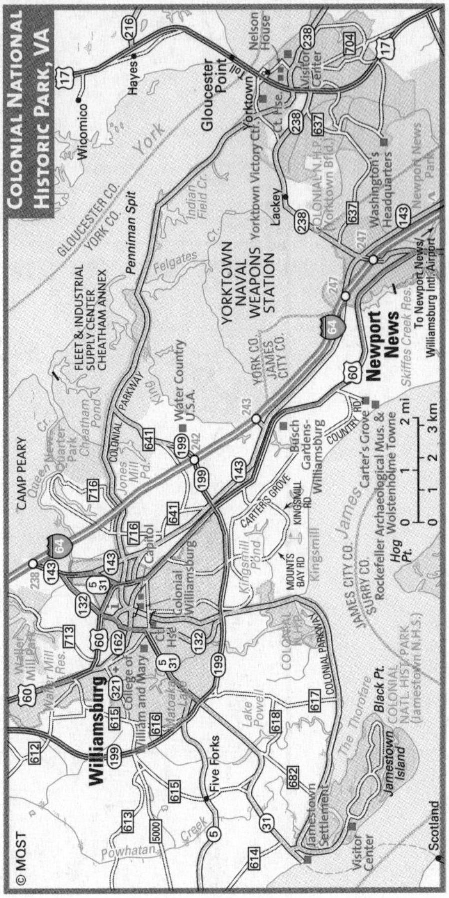
COLONIAL NATIONAL HISTORIC PARK, VA
© MQST
Williamsburg
Newport News
YORKTOWN NAVAL WEAPONS STATION
0 1 2 mi
0 1 2 3 km

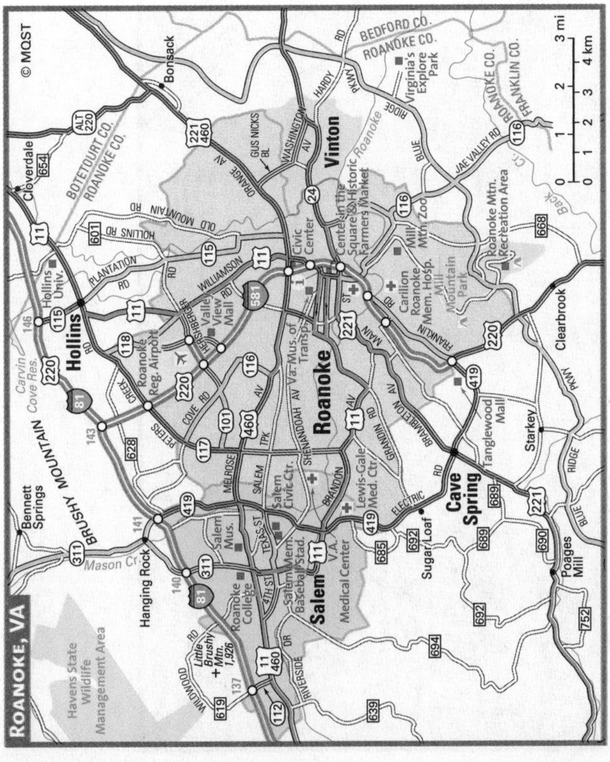
ROANOKE, VA
© MQST
Roanoke
Salem
Vinton
Hollins
Cave Spring
0 1 2 3 mi
0 1 2 3 4 km

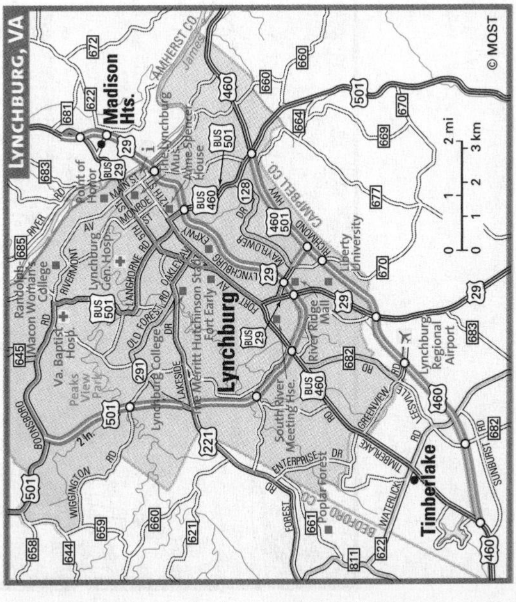
LYNCHBURG, VA
© MQST
Lynchburg
Madison Hts.
Timberlake
0 1 2 mi
0 1 2 3 km

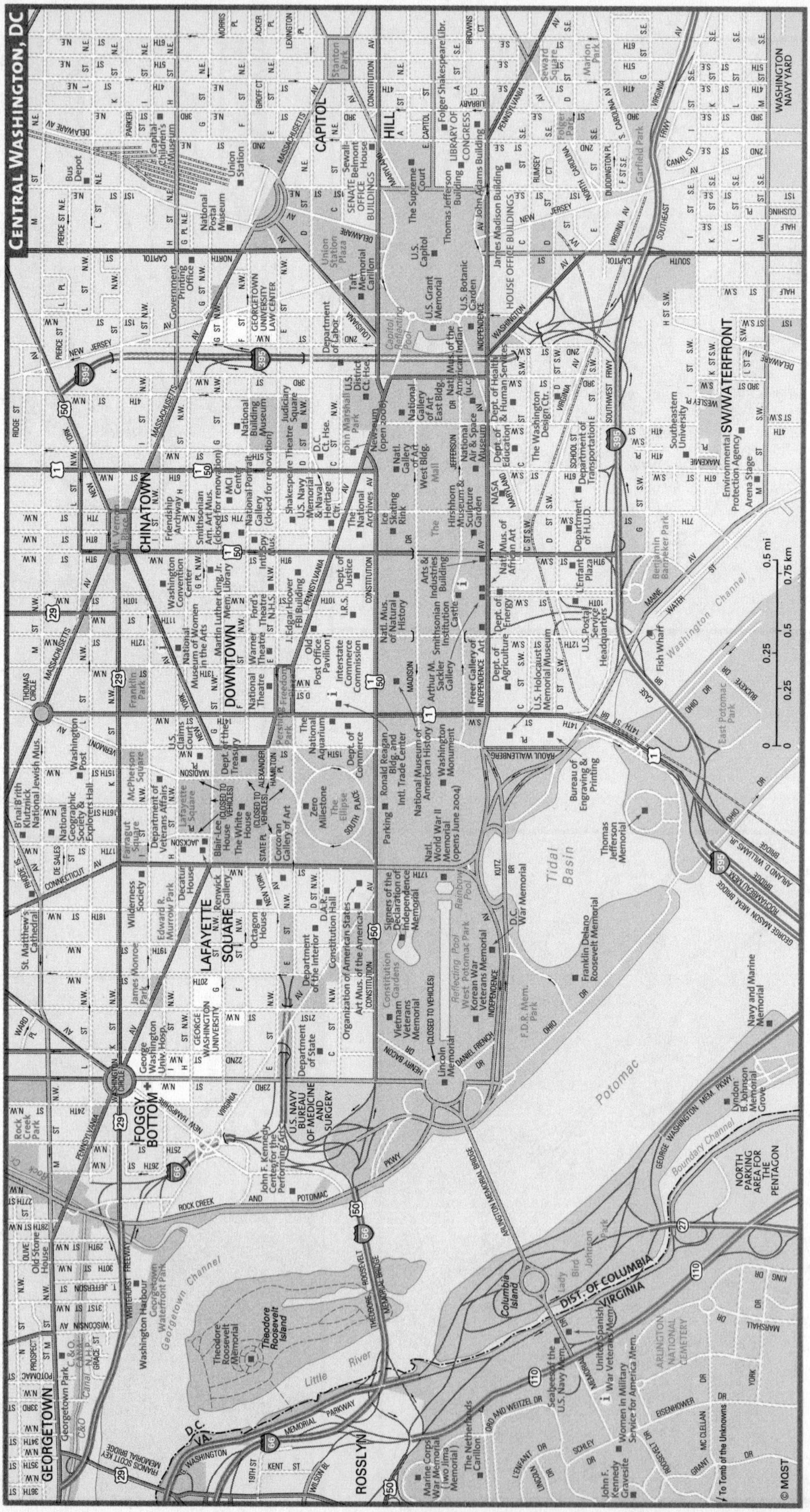
CENTRAL WASHINGTON, DC
CAPITOL HILL
CHINATOWN
DOWNTOWN
LAFAYETTE SQUARE
FOGGY BOTTOM
GEORGETOWN
ROSSLYN
SW WATERFRONT
U.S. Capitol
The Supreme Court
Union Station
National Postal Museum
Library of Congress
Folger Shakespeare Libr.
Stanton Park
Government Printing Office
Georgetown University Law Center
Taft Memorial Carillon
U.S. Grant Memorial
U.S. Botanic Garden
House Office Buildings
Senate Office Buildings
Department of Labor
National Building Museum
Judiciary Square
National Archives
National Gallery of Art East Bldg.
Natl. Gallery of Art West Bldg.
Natl. Air & Space Museum
Natl. Mus. of the American Indian
Hirshhorn Museum & Sculpture Garden
Smithsonian Institution Castle
Arts & Industries Building
Freer Gallery of Art
Arthur M. Sackler Gallery
Natl. Mus. of African Art
Natl. Mus. of Natural History
National Museum of American History
Washington Monument
Natl. World War II Memorial (opens June 2004)
U.S. Holocaust Memorial Museum
Bureau of Engraving & Printing
Thomas Jefferson Memorial
Tidal Basin
Franklin Delano Roosevelt Memorial
Korean War Veterans Memorial
Vietnam Veterans Memorial
Lincoln Memorial
Reflecting Pool
Constitution Gardens
The Ellipse
Zero Milestone
The White House
Lafayette Square
Dept. of the Treasury
Corcoran Gallery of Art
Renwick Gallery
Department of the Interior
Department of State
Organization of American States
John F. Kennedy Center for the Performing Arts
George Washington University
Washington Convention Center
Ford's Theatre
J. Edgar Hoover FBI Building
Old Post Office Pavilion
National Aquarium
Dept. of Commerce
Dept. of Justice
Pershing Park
Freedom Plaza
National Theatre
Warner Theatre
MCI Center
National Portrait Gallery
Smithsonian Am. Art Mus.
Friendship Archway
National Museum of Women in the Arts
Franklin Park
McPherson Square
Farragut Square
Thomas Circle
Washington Circle
Dupont Circle
National Geographic Society
Washington Post
St. Matthew's Cathedral
Theodore Roosevelt Island
Theodore Roosevelt Memorial
Little River
Georgetown Channel
Washington Harbour
Georgetown Waterfront Park
Old Stone House
Rock Creek Park
Potomac
Columbia Island
Lady Bird Johnson Park
Lyndon B. Johnson Memorial Grove
Navy and Marine Memorial
East Potomac Park
Washington Channel
Fish Wharf
Benjamin Banneker Park
Southeastern University
Environmental Protection Agency
Arena Stage
Washington Navy Yard
Arlington National Cemetery
Marine Corps War Memorial (Iwo Jima Memorial)
The Netherlands Carillon
John F. Kennedy Gravesite
Women in Military Service for America Mem.
Seabees of the U.S. Navy Mem.
To Tomb of the Unknowns
DIST. OF COLUMBIA
VIRGINIA
NORTH PARKING AREA FOR THE PENTAGON
0 0.25 0.5 mi
0 0.25 0.5 0.75 km
© MOST

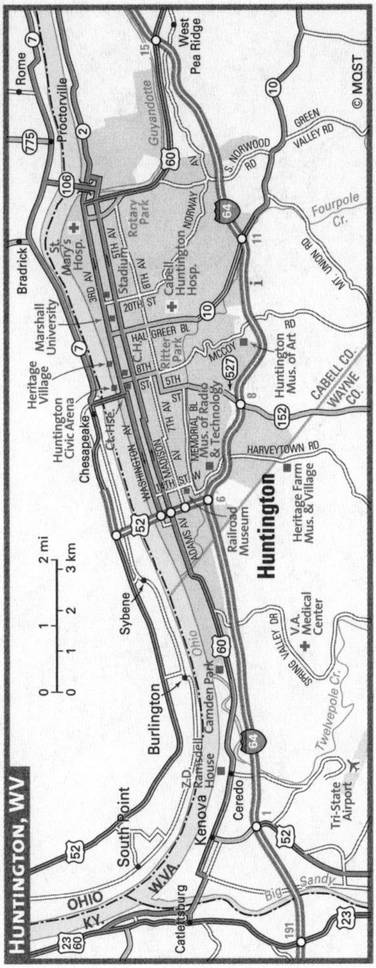
HUNTINGTON, WV

MORGANTOWN, WV

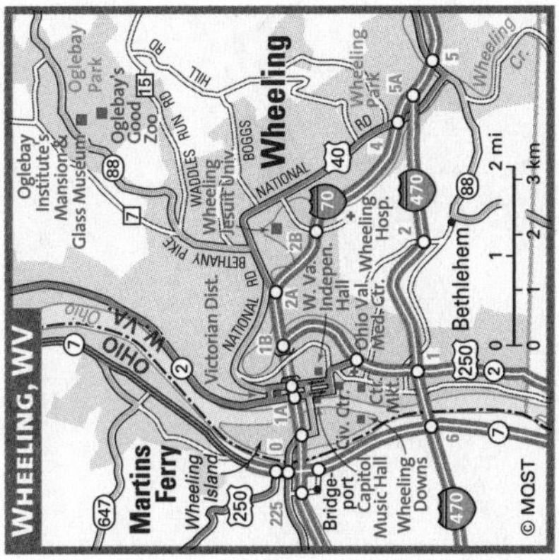
WHEELING, WV

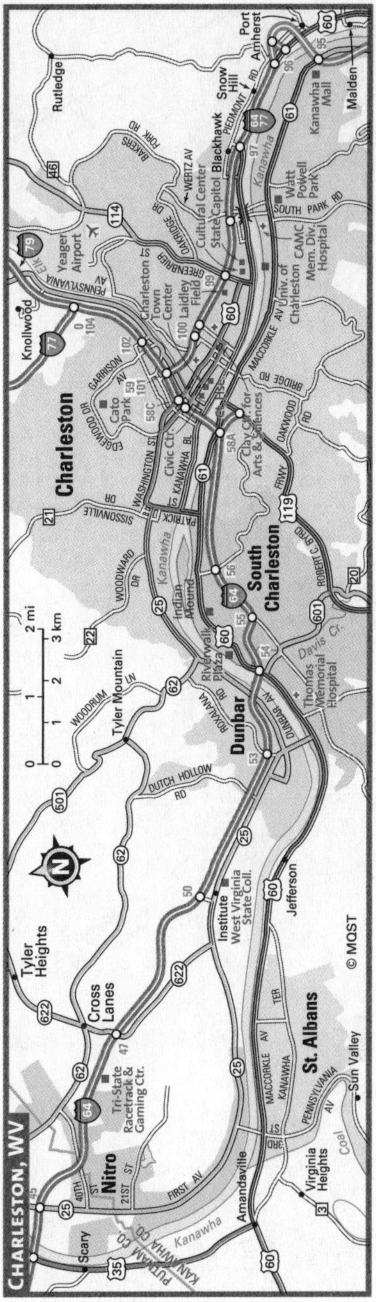
CHARLESTON, WV

Central New York City, NY
Queens
West New York
Union City
Weehawken
NEW YORK
NEW JERSEY
Hudson
UPPER EAST SIDE
UPPER WEST SIDE
LINCOLN CENTER
THEATER DISTRICT
MIDTOWN
ROCKEFELLER CENTER
TURTLE BAY
MURRAY HILL
FASHION CENTER
CLINTON
CHELSEA
Central Park
Roosevelt Island
UNITED NATIONS
Times Square
Herald Square
Bryant Park
Riverside Park
Chelsea Park
Dewitt Clinton Park
Gantry Plaza State Park
Belmont I.
LINCOLN TUNNEL
QUEENS-MIDTOWN TUNNEL
Jacob Javits Convention Center
Intrepid Sea-Air-Space Museum
Passenger Ship Terminal
CHELSEA PIERS SPORTS & ENTERTAINMENT COMPLEX
Empire State Building
Grand Central Terminal
The New York Public Library
Metropolitan Museum of Art
American Museum of Natural History
Solomon R. Guggenheim Museum
Whitney Museum of American Art
Carnegie Hall
Radio City Music Hall
Madison Square Garden
Pennsylvania Station
General Post Office
Port Authority Bus Terminal
to LaGuardia Arpt.
to Lincoln Harbor
to Battery Park

Manhattan
Brooklyn
LONG ISLAND CITY
GREENPOINT
WILLIAMSBURG
STUYVESANT TOWN
GRAMERCY PARK
EAST VILLAGE
LOWER EAST SIDE
GREENWICH VILLAGE
WEST VILLAGE
SOHO
LITTLE ITALY
CHINATOWN
TRIBECA
FINANCIAL DISTRICT
BATTERY PARK CITY
BROOKLYN NAVY YARD
FORT GREENE
BROOKLYN HEIGHTS
East
WILLIAMSBURG BRIDGE
MANHATTAN BRIDGE
BROOKLYN BRIDGE
HOLLAND TUNNEL
BROOKLYN-BATTERY TUNNEL
BROOKLYN-QUEENS EXPWY
Wallabout Bay
Bushwick Inlet
Newtown Cr.
East River Park
Tompkins Square
Washington Square
Union Sq.
Seward Park
Foley Sq.
Columbus Park
Hudson Square
Cadman Plaza
Barry Park
Battery Park
Bellevue Hosp. Ctr.
V.A. Med. Ctr.
Beth Israel Medical Center
Police Academy Museum
Theodore Roosevelt Birthplace N.H.S.
Forbes Galleries
Salmagundi Club
Washington Arch
Grace Church
Public Theater
THE COOPER UNION
Ukrainian Museum
Old Merchant's House
Lower East Side Tenement N.H.S.
New Mus. of Contemporary Art
Alternative Museum
Mus. of the Chinese in the Americas
Criminal Courts Bldg.
U.S. Court House
Municipal Bldg.
City Hall
Pace Univ. N.Y.C. Campus
St. Paul's Chapel
Woolworth Bldg.
WORLD TRADE CENTER SITE
WORLD FINANCIAL CENTER
Winter Garden
N.Y. Mercantile Exchange
Fed. Res. Bank
Federal Hall Natl. Mem.
New York Stock Exchange
Trinity Church
Cunard Bldg.
Natl. Mus. of the American Indian
Fraunces Tavern
Shrine of Elizabeth Ann Seton
Castle Clinton Natl. Mon.
Mus. of Jewish Heritage
Downtown Athletic Club
Fulton Fish Market
Pier 17 Pavilion
SOUTH ST. SEAPORT
Seaport Mus.
Plymouth Church of the Pilgrims
Brooklyn Historical Society
N.Y.C. TECH. COLL. (C.U.N.Y.)
Empire-Fulton Ferry S.P.
Fire Museum
St. Vincent's Hosp. & Medical Ctr.
to Hoboken, N.J.
to Highlands, N.J.
to Staten Island
to Liberty I.
to Ellis I.
to Port Liberte, N.J.
to Staten I.
0 0.25 0.5 mi
0 0.25 0.5 0.75 km
© MQST

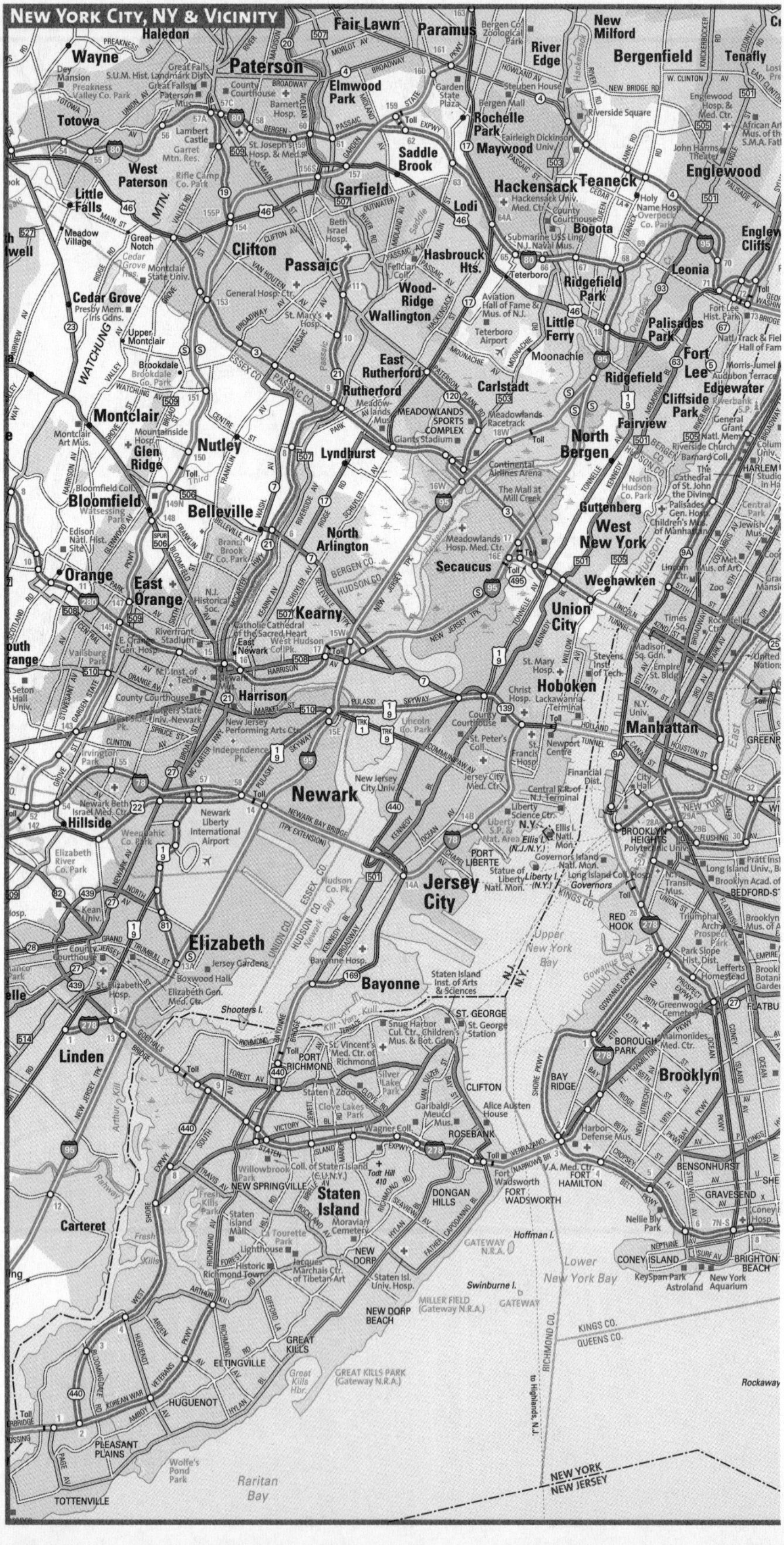
NEW YORK CITY, NY & VICINITY
Fair Lawn
Paramus
Haledon
Wayne
Paterson
Bergenfield
Tenafly
Elmwood Park
Totowa
Rochelle Park
Maywood
Saddle Brook
West Paterson
Englewood
Garfield
Hackensack
Teaneck
Little Falls
Lodi
Bogota
Clifton
Passaic
Hasbrouck Hts.
Leonia
Wood-Ridge
Wallington
Ridgefield Park
Cedar Grove
Little Ferry
Palisades Park
Moonachie
East Rutherford
Fort Lee
Rutherford
Carlstadt
Ridgefield
Edgewater
Montclair
Cliffside Park
Fairview
Nutley
Lyndhurst
North Bergen
Glen Ridge
Bloomfield
Belleville
North Arlington
Guttenberg
West New York
Secaucus
Weehawken
Orange
East Orange
Kearny
Union City
Harrison
Hoboken
Manhattan
Newark
Hillside
Jersey City
Elizabeth
Bayonne
Linden
Brooklyn
Staten Island
Carteret
Upper New York Bay
Lower New York Bay
Raritan Bay
NEW YORK
NEW JERSEY

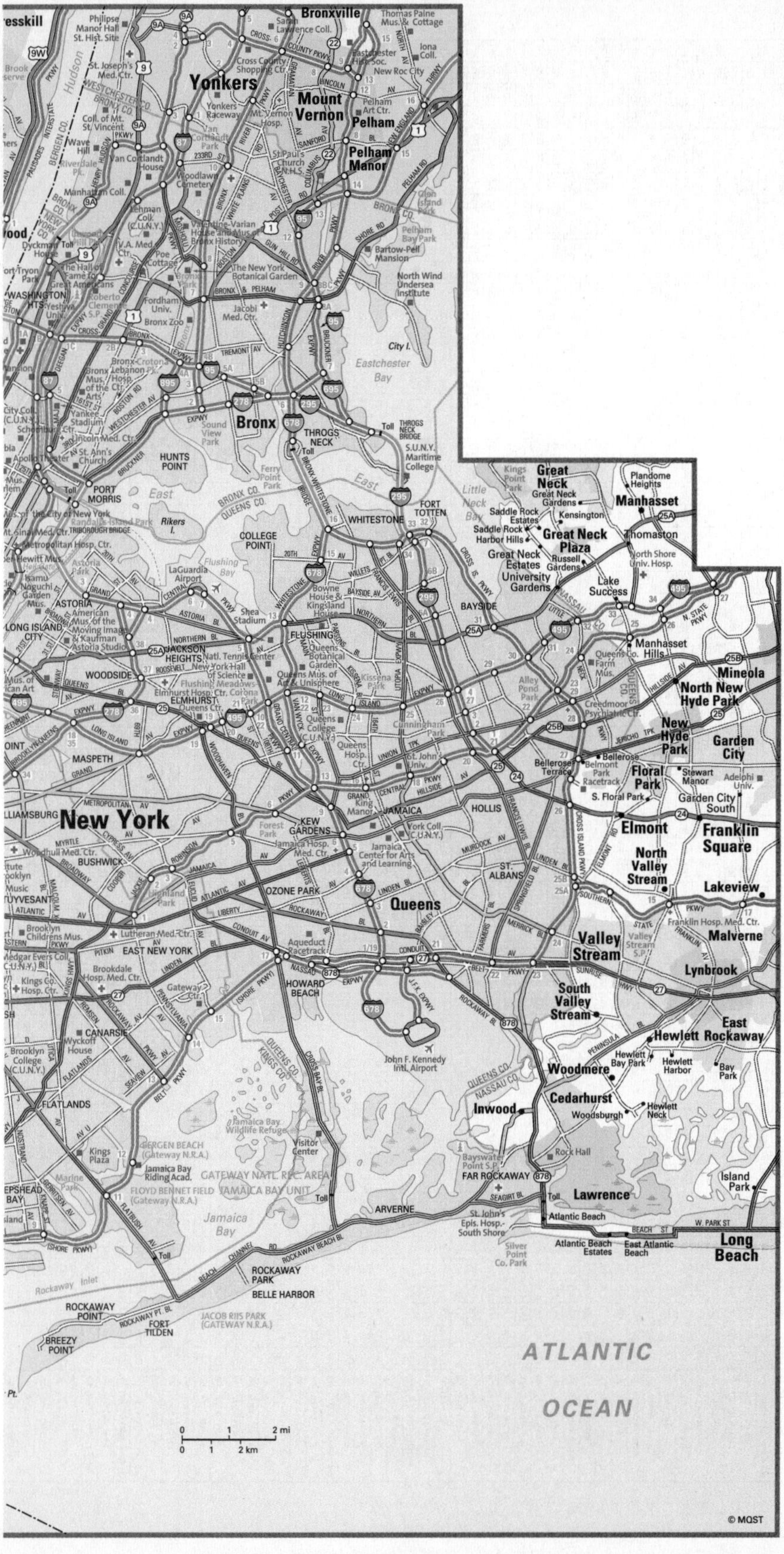
Bronxville
Sarah Lawrence Coll.
Thomas Paine Mus. & Cottage
Philipse Manor Hall St. Hist. Site
Iona Coll.
Eastchester Hist. Soc.
New Roc City
St. Joseph's Med. Ctr.
Cross County Shopping Ctr.
Yonkers
Mount Vernon
Pelham
Pelham Art Ctr.
Yonkers Raceway
Mt. Vernon Hosp.
Coll. of Mt. St. Vincent
Wave Hill
Van Cortlandt House
Van Cortlandt Park
St. Paul's Church N.H.S.
Pelham Manor
Woodlawn Cemetery
Manhattan Coll.
Lehman Coll. (C.U.N.Y.)
Valentine-Varian House and Mus. of Bronx History
Pelham Bay Park
Bartow-Pell Mansion
V.A. Med. Ctr.
Poe Cottage
Dyckman House
The New York Botanical Garden
North Wind Undersea Institute
Fordham Univ.
Bronx Zoo
Jacobi Med. Ctr.
Yeshiva Univ.
WASHINGTON HTS.
City I.
Eastchester Bay
Bronx Mus. of the Arts
Yankee Stadium
Bronx-Lebanon Hosp. Ctr.
City Coll. (C.U.N.Y.)
Lincoln Med. Ctr.
St. Ann's Church
Bronx
Sound View Park
THROGS NECK
Toll
S.U.N.Y. Maritime College
HUNTS POINT
PORT MORRIS
Ferry Point Park
East
Rikers I.
Randalls Island Park
Mus. of the City of New York
Mt. Sinai Med. Ctr.
Metropolitan Hosp. Ctr.
TRIBOROUGH BRIDGE
BRONX CO.
QUEENS CO.
COLLEGE POINT
WHITESTONE
FORT TOTTEN
Little Neck Bay
Kings Point Park
Great Neck
Great Neck Gardens
Saddle Rock Estates
Saddle Rock
Harbor Hills
Kensington
Great Neck Plaza
Great Neck Estates
Russell Gardens
University Gardens
Plandome Heights
Manhasset
Thomaston
North Shore Univ. Hosp.
Lake Success
LaGuardia Airport
Flushing Bay
Astoria Park
Isamu Noguchi Garden Mus.
ASTORIA
American Mus. of the Moving Image & Kaufman Astoria Studio
LONG ISLAND CITY
Shea Stadium
Bowne House & Kingsland House
FLUSHING
BAYSIDE
JACKSON HEIGHTS
Natl. Tennis Center
New York Hall of Science
Queens Botanical Garden
Flushing Meadows Corona Park
Queens Mus. of Art
Unisphere
Kissena Park
WOODSIDE
Elmhurst Hosp. Ctr.
ELMHURST
Queens Ctr.
Queens College (C.U.N.Y.)
Alley Pond Park
Queens Co. Farm Mus.
Manhasset Hills
Mineola
North New Hyde Park
Creedmoor Psychiatric Ctr.
Cunningham Park
New Hyde Park
Garden City
MASPETH
Queens Hosp. Ctr.
St. John's Univ.
Bellerose Terrace
Bellerose
Belmont Park Racetrack
Floral Park
Stewart Manor
Adelphi Univ.
S. Floral Park
Garden City South
New York
King Manor
JAMAICA
HOLLIS
KEW GARDENS
Forest Park
Jamaica Hosp. Med. Ctr.
York Coll. (C.U.N.Y.)
Jamaica Center for Arts and Learning
Elmont
Franklin Square
North Valley Stream
Woodhull Med. Ctr.
BUSHWICK
ST. ALBANS
Lakeview
Highland Park
OZONE PARK
Queens
Franklin Hosp. Med. Ctr.
Malverne
Brooklyn Childrens Mus.
Lutheran Med. Ctr.
EAST NEW YORK
Aqueduct Racetrack
Valley Stream
Valley Stream S.P.
Lynbrook
Medgar Evers Coll. (C.U.N.Y.)
Kings Co. Hosp. Ctr.
Brookdale Hosp. Med. Ctr.
Gateway Ctr.
HOWARD BEACH
South Valley Stream
East Rockaway
Hewlett
Hewlett Bay Park
Hewlett Harbor
Bay Park
CANARSIE
Wyckoff House
Brooklyn College (C.U.N.Y.)
John F. Kennedy Intl. Airport
Woodmere
Cedarhurst
Hewlett Neck
Woodsburgh
Inwood
FLATLANDS
Jamaica Bay Wildlife Refuge
Visitor Center
Kings Plaza
BERGEN BEACH (Gateway N.R.A.)
Jamaica Bay Riding Acad.
GATEWAY NATL. REC. AREA JAMAICA BAY UNIT
FLOYD BENNET FIELD (Gateway N.R.A.)
Bayswater Point S.P.
FAR ROCKAWAY
Rock Hall
Island Park
Lawrence
Jamaica Bay
ARVERNE
St. John's Epis. Hosp.-South Shore
Atlantic Beach
Long Beach
Silver Point Co. Park
Atlantic Beach Estates
East Atlantic Beach
ROCKAWAY PARK
BELLE HARBOR
Rockaway Inlet
ROCKAWAY POINT
FORT TILDEN
JACOB RIIS PARK (GATEWAY N.R.A.)
BREEZY POINT
ATLANTIC
OCEAN
0 1 2 mi
0 1 2 km
© MQST

Distances in chart are in miles. To convert miles to kilometers, multiply the distance in miles by 1.609

Example:
New York, NY to Boston, MA
= 215 miles or 346 kilometers
(215 x 1.609)

	ALBUQUERQUE, NM	ATLANTA, GA	BALTIMORE, MD	BILLINGS, MT	BIRMINGHAM, AL	BISMARCK, ND	BOISE, ID	BOSTON, MA	BUFFALO, NY	BURLINGTON, VT	CHARLESTON, SC	CHARLESTON, WV	CHARLOTTE, NC	CHEYENNE, WY	CHICAGO, IL	CINCINNATI, OH	CLEVELAND, OH	DALLAS, TX	DENVER, CO	DES MOINES, IA	DETROIT, MI	EL PASO, TX	HOUSTON, TX	INDIANAPOLIS, IN	JACKSON, MS	KANSAS CITY, MO	LAS VEGAS, NV	LITTLE ROCK, AR	LOS ANGELES, CA	LOUISVILLE, KY	MEMPHIS, TN	MIAMI, FL	MILWAUKEE, WI	MINNEAPOLIS, MN	MONTRÉAL, QC	NASHVILLE, TN	NEW ORLEANS, LA	NEW YORK, NY	OKLAHOMA CITY, OK	OMAHA, NE	ORLANDO, FL	PHILADELPHIA, PA	PHOENIX, AZ	PITTSBURGH, PA	PORTLAND, ME	PORTLAND, OR	RAPID CITY, SD	RENO, NV	RICHMOND, VA	ST. LOUIS, MO	SALT LAKE CITY, UT	SAN ANTONIO, TX	SAN DIEGO, CA	SAN FRANCISCO, CA	SEATTLE, WA	TAMPA, FL	TORONTO, ON	VANCOUVER, BC	WASHINGTON,DC	WICHITA, KS
ALBUQUERQUE, NM		1490	1902	991	1274	1333	966	2240	1808	2178	1793	1568	1649	538	1352	1409	1619	754	438	1091	1608	263	994	1298	1157	894	578	900	806	1320	1033	2155	1426	1339	2172	1248	1276	2015	546	973	1934	1954	466	1670	2338	1395	841	1020	1876	1051	624	818	825	1111	1463	1949	1841	1597	1896	707
ATLANTA, GA	1490		679	1889	150	1559	2218	1100	910	1158	317	503	238	1482	717	476	726	792	1403	967	735	1437	800	531	386	801	2067	528	2237	419	389	661	813	1129	1241	242	473	869	944	989	440	782	1868	676	1197	2647	1511	2440	527	549	1916	1000	2166	2618	2705	455	958	2838	636	989
BALTIMORE, MD	1902	679		1959	795	1551	2401	422	370	481	583	352	441	1665	708	521	377	1399	1690	1031	532	2045	1470	600	1032	1087	2445	1072	2705	602	933	1109	805	1121	564	716	1142	192	1354	1168	904	104	2366	246	520	2830	1626	2623	152	841	2100	1671	2724	2840	2775	960	565	2908	38	1276
BILLINGS, MT	991	1889	1959		1839	413	626	2254	1796	2181	2157	1755	2012	455	1246	1552	1597	1433	554	1007	1534	1255	1673	1432	1836	1088	965	1530	1239	1547	1625	2554	1175	839	2093	1648	1955	2049	1227	904	2333	2019	1199	1719	2352	889	379	960	2053	1341	548	1500	1302	1176	816	2348	1762	949	1953	1067
BIRMINGHAM, AL	1274	150	795	1839		1509	2170	1215	909	1241	466	578	389	1434	667	475	725	647	1356	919	734	1292	678	481	241	753	1852	381	2092	369	241	812	763	1079	1289	194	351	985	729	941	591	897	1723	763	1313	2599	1463	2392	678	501	1868	878	2021	2472	2657	606	958	2791	758	838
BISMARCK, ND	1333	1559	1551	413	1509		1039	1846	1388	1773	1749	1347	1604	594	838	1144	1189	1342	693	675	1126	1597	1582	1024	1548	801	1378	1183	1702	1139	1337	2224	767	431	1685	1315	1734	1641	1136	616	2003	1611	1662	1311	1944	1301	320	1372	1645	1053	960	1599	1765	1749	1229	2018	1354	1362	1545	934
BOISE, ID	966	2218	2401	626	2170	1039		2697	2239	2624	2520	2182	2375	737	1708	1969	2040	1711	833	1369	1977	1206	1952	1852	2115	1376	760	1808	1033	1933	1954	2883	1748	1465	2535	1976	2234	2491	1506	1234	2662	2462	993	2161	2795	432	930	430	2496	1628	342	1761	1096	646	500	2677	2204	633	2395	1346
BOSTON, MA	2240	1100	422	2254	1215	1846	2697		462	214	1003	741	861	1961	1003	862	654	1819	2004	1326	741	2465	1890	940	1453	1427	2757	1493	3046	964	1353	1529	1100	1417	313	1136	1563	215	1694	1463	1324	321	2706	592	107	3126	1921	2919	572	1181	2395	2092	3065	3135	3070	1380	570	3204	458	1616
BUFFALO, NY	1808	910	370	1796	909	1388	2239	462		375	899	431	695	1502	545	442	197	1393	1546	868	277	2039	1513	508	1134	995	2299	1066	2572	545	927	1425	642	958	397	716	1254	400	1262	1005	1221	414	2274	217	560	2667	1463	2460	485	749	1936	1665	2632	2677	2612	1276	106	2745	384	1184
BURLINGTON, VT	2178	1158	481	2181	1241	1773	2624	214	375		1061	782	919	1887	930	817	567	1763	1931	1253	652	2409	1916	878	1479	1366	2684	1437	2957	915	1297	1587	1027	1343	92	1086	1588	299	1632	1390	1383	371	2644	587	233	3052	1848	2845	630	1119	2322	2036	3020	3062	2997	1438	419	3130	517	1554
CHARLESTON, SC	1793	317	583	2157	466	1749	2520	1003	899	1061		468	204	1783	907	622	724	1109	1705	1204	879	1754	1110	721	703	1102	2371	900	2554	610	760	583	1003	1319	1145	543	783	773	1248	1290	379	685	2184	642	1101	2948	1824	2741	428	850	2218	1310	2483	2934	2973	434	1006	3106	539	1291
CHARLESTON, WV	1568	503	352	1755	578	1347	2182	741	431	782	468		265	1445	506	209	255	1072	1367	802	410	1718	1192	320	816	764	2122	745	2374	251	606	994	601	918	822	395	926	515	1022	952	790	454	2035	217	839	2610	1422	2403	322	512	1880	1344	2393	2620	2571	845	537	2705	346	953
CHARLOTTE, NC	1649	238	441	2012	389	1604	2375	861	695	919	204	265		1637	761	476	520	1031	1559	1057	675	1677	1041	575	625	956	2225	754	2453	464	614	730	857	1173	1003	397	713	631	1102	1144	525	543	2107	438	959	2802	1678	2595	289	704	2072	1241	2405	2759	2827	581	802	2960	397	1145
CHEYENNE, WY	538	1482	1665	455	1434	594	737	1961	1502	1887	1783	1445	1637		972	1233	1304	979	100	633	1241	801	1220	1115	1382	640	843	1076	1116	1197	1217	2147	1012	881	1799	1240	1502	1755	773	497	1926	1725	1004	1425	2059	1166	305	959	1760	892	436	1046	1179	1176	1234	1941	1468	1368	1659	613
CHICAGO, IL	1352	717	708	1246	667	838	1708	1003	545	930	907	506	761	972		302	346	936	1015	337	283	1543	1108	184	750	532	1768	662	2042	299	539	1382	89	409	841	474	935	797	807	474	1161	768	1819	467	1101	2137	913	1930	802	294	1406	1270	2105	2146	2062	1176	510	2196	701	728
CINCINNATI, OH	1409	476	521	1552	475	1144	1969	862	442	817	622	209	476	1233	302		253	958	1200	599	261	1605	1079	116	700	597	1955	632	2215	106	493	1141	398	714	815	281	820	636	863	736	920	576	1876	292	960	2398	1219	2191	530	350	1667	1231	2234	2407	2368	935	484	2501	517	785
CLEVELAND, OH	1619	726	377	1597	725	1189	2040	654	197	567	724	255	520	1304	346	253		1208	1347	669	171	1854	1328	319	950	806	2100	882	2374	356	742	1250	443	760	588	531	1070	466	1073	806	1045	437	2085	136	751	2469	1264	2262	471	560	1738	1481	2437	2478	2413	1101	303	2547	370	995
DALLAS, TX	754	792	1399	1433	647	1342	1711	1819	1393	1763	1109	1072	1031	979	936	958	1208		887	752	1218	647	241	913	406	554	1331	327	1446	852	466	1367	1010	999	1772	681	525	1589	209	669	1146	1501	1077	1246	1917	2140	1077	1933	1309	635	1410	271	1375	1827	2208	1161	1441	2342	1362	367
DENVER, CO	438	1403	1690	554	1356	693	833	2004	1546	1931	1705	1367	1559	100	1015	1200	1347	887		676	1284	701	1127	1088	1290	603	756	984	1029	1118	1116	2069	1055	924	1843	1162	1409	1799	681	541	1847	1744	904	1460	2102	1261	404	1054	1688	855	531	946	1092	1271	1329	1862	1512	1463	1686	521
DES MOINES, IA	1091	967	1031	1007	919	675	1369	1326	868	1253	1204	802	1057	633	337	599	669	752	676		606	1283	992	481	931	194	1429	567	1703	595	720	1632	378	246	1165	725	1117	1121	546	136	1411	1091	1558	791	1424	1798	629	1591	1126	436	1067	1009	1766	1807	1822	1426	834	1956	1025	390
DETROIT, MI	1608	735	532	1534	734	1126	1977	741	277	652	879	410	675	1241	283	261	171	1218	1284	606		1799	1338	318	960	795	2037	891	2310	366	752	1401	380	697	564	541	1079	622	1062	743	1180	592	2074	292	838	2405	1201	2198	627	549	1675	1490	2373	2415	2350	1194	233	2483	526	984
EL PASO, TX	263	1437	2045	1255	1292	1597	1206	2465	2039	2409	1754	1718	1677	801	1543	1605	1854	647	701	1283	1799		758	1489	1051	1085	717	974	801	1499	1112	1959	1617	1530	2363	1328	1118	2235	737	1236	1738	2147	432	1893	2563	1767	1105	1315	1955	1242	864	556	730	1181	1944	1753	2032	2087	2008	898
HOUSTON, TX	994	800	1470	1673	678	1582	1952	1890	1513	1916	1110	1192	1041	1220	1108	1079	1328	241	1127	992	1338	758		1033	445	795	1474	447	1558	972	586	1201	1193	1240	1892	801	360	1660	449	910	980	1572	1188	1366	1988	2381	1318	2072	1330	863	1650	200	1487	1938	2449	995	1561	2583	1433	608
INDIANAPOLIS, IN	1298	531	600	1432	481	1024	1852	940	508	878	721	320	575	1115	184	116	319	913	1088	481	318	1489	1033		675	485	1843	587	2104	112	464	1196	279	596	872	287	826	715	752	618	975	655	1764	370	1038	2280	1101	2073	641	239	1549	1186	2122	2290	2249	990	541	2383	596	674
JACKSON, MS	1157	386	1032	1836	241	1548	2115	1453	1134	1479	703	816	625	1382	750	700	950	406	1290	931	960	1051	445	675		747	1735	269	1851	594	211	915	835	1151	1514	423	185	1223	612	935	694	1135	1482	988	1550	2544	1458	2337	914	505	1813	644	1780	2232	2612	709	1183	2746	996	771
KANSAS CITY, MO	894	801	1087	1088	753	801	1376	1427	995	1366	1102	764	956	640	532	597	806	554	603	194	795	1085	795	485	747		1358	382	1632	516	536	1466	573	441	1359	559	932	1202	348	188	1245	1141	1360	857	1525	1805	710	1598	1085	252	1074	812	1695	1814	1872	1259	1028	2007	1083	192
LAS VEGAS, NV	578	2067	2445	965	1852	1378	760	2757	2299	2684	2371	2122	2225	843	1768	1955	2100	1331	756	1429	2037	717	1474	1843	1735	1358		1478	274	1874	1611	2733	1808	1677	2596	1826	1854	2552	1124	1294	2512	2500	285	2215	2855	1188	1035	442	2444	1610	417	1272	337	575	1256	2526	2265	1390	2441	1276
LITTLE ROCK, AR	900	528	1072	1530	381	1183	1808	1493	1066	1437	900	745	754	1076	662	632	882	327	984	567	891	974	447	587	269	382	1478		1706	526	140	1190	747	814	1446	355	455	1262	355	570	969	1175	1367	920	1590	2237	1093	2030	983	416	1507	600	1703	2012	2305	984	1115	2439	1036	464
LOS ANGELES, CA	806	2237	2705	1239	2092	1702	1033	3046	2572	2957	2554	2374	2453	1116	2042	2215	2374	1446	1029	1703	2310	801	1558	2104	1851	1632	274	1706		2126	1839	2759	2082	1951	2869	2054	1917	2820	1352	1567	2538	2760	369	2476	3144	971	1309	519	2682	1856	691	1356	124	385	1148	2553	2538	1291	2702	1513
LOUISVILLE, KY	1320	419	602	1547	369	1139	1933	964	545	915	610	251	464	1197	299	106	356	852	1118	595	366	1499	972	112	594	516	1874	526	2126		386	1084	394	711	920	175	714	739	774	704	863	678	1786	394	1062	2362	1215	2155	572	264	1631	1125	2144	2372	2364	878	589	2497	596	705
MEMPHIS, TN	1033	389	933	1625	241	1337	1954	1353	927	1297	760	606	614	1217	539	493	742	466	1116	720	752	1112	586	464	211	536	1611	140	1839	386		1051	624	940	1306	215	396	1123	487	724	830	1035	1500	780	1451	2382	1247	2175	843	294	1652	739	1841	2144	2440	845	975	2574	896	597
MIAMI, FL	2155	661	1109	2554	812	2224	2883	1529	1425	1587	583	994	730	2147	1382	1141	1250	1367	2069	1632	1401	1959	1201	1196	915	1466	2733	1190	2759	1084	1051		1478	1794	1671	907	874	1299	1609	1654	232	1211	2390	1167	1627	3312	2176	3105	954	1214	2581	1401	2688	3140	3370	274	1532	3504	1065	1655
MILWAUKEE, WI	1426	813	805	1175	763	767	1748	1100	642	1027	1003	601	857	1012	89	398	443	1010	1055	378	380	1617	1193	279	835	573	1808	747	2082	394	624	1478		337	939	569	1020	894	880	514	1257	865	1892	564	1198	2063	842	1970	899	367	1446	1343	2145	2186	1991	1272	607	2124	799	769
MINNEAPOLIS, MN	1339	1129	1121	839	1079	431	1465	1417	958	1343	1319	918	1173	881	409	714	760	999	924	246	697	1530	1240	596	1151	441	1677	814	1951	711	940	1794	337		1255	886	1337	1211	793	383	1573	1181	1805	881	1515	1727	606	1839	1216	621	1315	1257	2014	2055	1654	1588	924	1788	1115	637
MONTRÉAL, QC	2172	1241	564	2093	1289	1685	2535	313	397	92	1145	822	1003	1799	841	815	588	1772	1843	1165	564	2363	1892	872	1514	1359	2596	1446	2869	920	1306	1671	939	1255		1094	1632	383	1625	1300	1466	454	2637	607	282	2963	1758	2756	714	1112	2232	2043	2931	2972	2907	1522	330	3041	600	1547
NASHVILLE, TN	1248	242	716	1648	194	1315	1976	1136	716	1086	543	395	397	1240	474	281	531	681	1162	725	541	1328	801	287	423	559	1826	355	2054	175	215	907	569	886	1094		539	906	703	747	686	818	1715	569	1234	2405	1269	2198	626	307	1675	954	2056	2360	2463	701	764	2597	679	748
NEW ORLEANS, LA	1276	473	1142	1955	351	1734	2234	1563	1254	1588	783	926	713	1502	935	820	1070	525	1409	1117	1079	1118	360	826	185	932	1854	455	1917	714	396	874	1020	1337	1632	539		1332	731	1121	653	1245	1548	1108	1660	2663	1643	2431	1002	690	1932	560	1846	2298	2731	668	1302	2865	1106	890
NEW YORK, NY	2015	869	192	2049	985	1641	2491	215	400	299	773	515	631	1755	797	636	466	1589	1799	1121	622	2235	1660	715	1223	1202	2552	1262	2820	739	1123	1299	894	1211	383	906	1332		1469	1258	1094	91	2481	367	313	2920	1716	2713	342	956	2189	1861	2839	2929	2864	1150	507	2998	228	1391
OKLAHOMA CITY, OK	546	944	1354	1227	729	1136	1506	1694	1262	1632	1248	1022	1102	773	807	863	1073	209	681	546	1062	737	449	752	612	348	1124	355	1352	774	487	1609	880	793	1625	703	731	1469		463	1388	1408	1012	1124	1792	1934	871	1727	1331	505	1204	466	1370	1657	2002	1403	1295	2136	1350	161
OMAHA, NE	973	989	1168	904	941	616	1234	1463	1005	1390	1290	952	1144	497	474	736	806	669	541	136	743	1236	910	618	935	188	1294	570	1567	704	724	1654	514	383	1300	747	1121	1258	463		1433	1228	1440	928	1561	1662	525	1455	1263	440	932	927	1630	1672	1719	1448	971	1853	1162	307
ORLANDO, FL	1934	440	904	2333	591	2003	2662	1324	1221	1383	379	790	525	1926	1161	920	1045	1146	1847	1411	1180	1738	980	975	694	1245	2512	969	2538	863	830	232	1257	1573	1466	686	653	1094	1388	1433		1006	2169	963	1422	3091	1955	2884	750	993	2360	1180	2467	2918	3149	82	1327	3283	860	1434
PHILADELPHIA, PA	1954	782	104	2019	897	1611	2462	321	414	371	685	454	543	1725	768	576	437	1501	1744	1091	592	2147	1572	655	1135	1141	2500	1175	2760	678	1035	1211	865	1181	454	818	1245	91	1408	1228	1006		2420	306	419	2890	1686	2683	254	895	2160	1774	2779	2900	2835	1062	522	2968	140	1330
PHOENIX, AZ	466	1868	2366	1199	1723	1662	993	2706	2274	2644	2184	2035	2107	1004	1819	1876	2085	1077	904	1558	2074	432	1188	1764	1482	1360	285	1367	369	1786	1500	2390	1892	1805	2637	1715	1548	2481	1012	1440	2169	2420		2136	2804	1335	1308	883	2343	1517	651	987	358	750	1513	2184	2307	1655	2362	1173
PITTSBURGH, PA	1670	676	246	1719	763	1311	2161	592	217	587	642	217	438	1425	467	292	136	1246	1460	791	292	1893	1366	370	988	857	2215	920	2476	394	780	1167	564	881	607	569	1108	367	1124	928	963	306	2136		690	2590	1386	2383	341	611	1859	1519	2494	2599	2534	1019	321	2668	240	1046
PORTLAND, ME	2338	1197	520	2352	1313	1944	2795	107	560	233	1101	839	959	2059	1101	960	751	1917	2102	1424	838	2563	1988	1038	1550	1525	2855	1590	3144	1062	1451	1627	1198	1515	282	1234	1660	313	1792	1561	1422	419	2804	690		3223	2019	3016	670	1279	2493	2189	3162	3233	3168	1478	668	3301	556	1714
PORTLAND, OR	1395	2647	2830	889	2599	1301	432	3126	2667	3052	2948	2610	2802	1166	2137	2398	2469	2140	1261	1798	2405	1767	2381	2280	2544	1805	1188	2237	971	2362	2382	3312	2063	1727	2963	2405	2663	2920	1934	1662	3091	2890	1335	2590	3223		1268	578	2925	2057	771	2322	1093	638	170	3106	2633	313	2824	1775
RAPID CITY, SD	841	1511	1626	379	1463	320	930	1921	1463	1848	1824	1422	1678	305	913	1219	1264	1077	404	629	1201	1105	1318	1101	1458	710	1035	1093	1309	1215	1247	2176	842	606	1758	1269	1643	1716	871	525	1955	1686	1308	1386	2019	1268		1151	1720	963	628	1335	1372	1368	1195	1970	1429	1328	1620	712
RENO, NV	1020	2440	2623	960	2392	1372	430	2919	2460	2845	2741	2403	2595	959	1930	2191	2262	1933	1054	1591	2198	1315	2072	2073	2337	1598	442	2030	519	2155	2175	3105	1970	1839	2756	2198	2431	2713	1727	1455	2884	2683	883	2383	3016	578	1151		2718	1850	524	1870	642	217	755	2899	2426	898	2617	1568
RICHMOND, VA	1876	527	152	2053	678	1645	2496	572	485	630	428	322	289	1760	802	530	471	1309	1688	1126	627	1955	1330	641	914	1085	2444	983	2682	572	843	954	899	1216	714	626	1002	342	1331	1263	750	254	2343	341	670	2925	1720	2718		834	2194	1530	2684	2934	2869	805	660	3003	108	1274
ST. LOUIS, MO	1051	549	841	1341	501	1053	1628	1181	749	1119	850	512	704	892	294	350	560	635	855	436	549	1242	863	239	505	252	1610	416	1856	264	294	1214	367	621	1112	307	690	956	505	440	993	895	1517	611	1279	2057	963	1850	834		1326	968	1875	2066	2125	1008	782	2259	837	441
SALT LAKE CITY, UT	624	1916	2100	548	1868	960	342	2395	1936	2322	2218	1880	2072	436	1406	1667	1738	1410	531	1067	1675	864	1650	1549	1813	1074	417	1507	691	1631	1652	2581	1446	1315	2232	1675	1932	2189	1204	932	2360	2160	651	1859	2493	771	628	524	2194	1326		1419	754	740	839	2375	1902	973	2094	1044
SAN ANTONIO, TX	818	1000	1671	1500	878	1599	1761	2092	1665	2036	1310	1344	1241	1046	1270	1231	1481	271	946	1009	1490	556	200	1186	644	812	1272	600	1356	1125	739	1401	1343	1257	2043	954	560	1861	466	927	1180	1774	987	1519	2189	2322	1335	1870	1530	968	1419		1285	1737	2275	1195	1714	2410	1635	624
SAN DIEGO, CA	825	2166	2724	1302	2021	1765	1096	3065	2632	3020	2483	2393	2405	1179	2105	2234	2437	1375	1092	1766	2373	730	1487	2122	1780	1695	337	1703	124	2144	1841	2688	2145	2014	2931	2056	1846	2839	1370	1630	2467	2779	358	2494	3162	1093	1372	642	2684	1875	754	1285		508	1271	2481	2601	1414	2720	1531
SAN FRANCISCO, CA	1111	2618	2840	1176	2472	1749	646	3135	2677	3062	2934	2620	2759	1176	2146	2407	2478	1827	1271	1807	2415	1181	1938	2290	2232	1814	575	2012	385	2372	2144	3140	2186	2055	2972	2360	2298	2929	1657	1672	2918	2900	750	2599	3233	638	1368	217	2934	2066	740	1737	508		816	2933	2643	958	2834	1784
SEATTLE, WA	1463	2705	2775	816	2657	1229	500	3070	2612	2997	2973	2571	2827	1234	2062	2368	2413	2208	1329	1822	2350	1944	2449	2249	2612	1872	1256	2305	1148	2364	2440	3370	1991	1654	2907	2463	2731	2864	2002	1719	3149	2835	1513	2534	3168	170	1195	755	2869	2125	839	2275	1271	816		3164	2577	140	2769	1843
TAMPA, FL	1949	455	960	2348	606	2018	2677	1380	1276	1438	434	845	581	1941	1176	935	1101	1161	1862	1426	1194	1753	995	990	709	1259	2526	984	2553	878	845	274	1272	1588	1522	701	668	1150	1403	1448	82	1062	2184	1019	1478	3106	1970	2899	805	1008	2375	1195	2481	2933	3164		1383	3297	916	1448
TORONTO, ON	1841	958	565	1762	958	1354	2204	570	106	419	1006	537	802	1468	510	484	303	1441	1512	834	233	2032	1561	541	1183	1028	2265	1115	2538	589	975	1532	607	924	330	764	1302	507	1295	971	1327	522	2307	321	668	2633	1429	2426	660	782	1902	1714	2601	2643	2577	1383		2711	563	1217
VANCOUVER, BC	1597	2838	2908	949	2791	1362	633	3204	2745	3130	3106	2705	2960	1368	2196	2501	2547	2342	1463	1956	2483	2087	2583	2383	2746	2007	1390	2439	1291	2497	2574	3504	2124	1788	3041	2597	2865	2998	2136	1853	3283	2968	1655	2668	3301	313	1328	898	3003	2259	973	2410	1414	958	140	3297	2711		2902	1977
WASHINGTON, DC	1896	636	38	1953	758	1545	2395	458	384	517	539	346	397	1659	701	517	370	1362	1686	1025	526	2008	1433	596	996	1083	2441	1036	2702	596	896	1065	799	1115	600	679	1106	228	1350	1162	860	140	2362	240	556	2824	1620	2617	108	837	2094	1635	2720	2834	2769	916	563	2902		1272
WICHITA, KS	707	989	1276	1067	838	934	1346	1616	1184	1554	1291	953	1145	613	728	785	995	367	521	390	984	898	608	674	771	192	1276	464	1513	705	597	1655	769	637	1547	748	890	1391	161	307	1434	1330	1173	1046	1714	1775	712	1568	1274	441	1044	624	1531	1784	1843	1448	1217	1977	1272	

Speedpass

Welcome

Dear Traveler,

Since its inception in 1958, Mobil Travel Guide has served as a trusted advisor to auto travelers in search of value in lodging, dining, and destinations. Now in its 47th year, the Mobil Travel Guide is the hallmark of our ExxonMobil family of travel publications, and we're proud to offer an array of products and services from our Mobil, Exxon, and Esso brands in North America to facilitate life on the road.

Whether you're looking for business or pleasure venues, our nationwide network of independent, professional evaluators offers their expertise on thousands of travel options, allowing you to plan a quick family getaway, a full-service business meeting, or an unforgettable Mobil Five-Star celebration.

Your feedback is important to us as we strive to improve our product offerings and better meet today's travel needs. Whether you travel once a week or once a year, please take the time to contact us at www.mobiltravelguide.com. We hope to hear from you soon.

Best wishes for safe and enjoyable travels.

Lee R Raymond

Lee R. Raymond
Chairman and CEO
Exxon Mobil Corporation

A Word to Our Readers

Travelers are on the roads in great numbers these days. They're exploring the country on day trips, weekend getaways, business trips, and extended family vacations, visiting major cities and small towns along the way. Because time is precious and the travel industry is ever-changing, having accurate, reliable travel information at your fingertips is critical. Mobil Travel Guide has been providing invaluable insight to travelers for more than 45 years, and we are committed to continuing this service well into the future.

The Mobil Corporation (known as Exxon Mobil Corporation since a 1999 merger) began producing the Mobil Travel Guide books in 1958, following the introduction of the US interstate highway system in 1956. The first edition covered only five Southwestern states. Since then, our books have become the premier travel guides in North America, covering all 50 states and Canada.

Since its founding, Mobil Travel Guide has served as an advocate for travelers seeking knowledge about hotels, restaurants, and places to visit. Based on an objective process, we make recommendations to our customers that we believe will enhance the quality and value of their travel experiences. Our trusted Mobil One- to Five-Star rating system is the oldest and most respected lodging and restaurant inspection and rating program in North America. Most hoteliers, restaurateurs, and industry observers favorably regard the rigor of our inspection program and understand the prestige and benefits that come with receiving a Mobil Star rating.

The Mobil Travel Guide process of rating each establishment includes:

- Unannounced facility inspections
- Incognito service evaluations for Mobil Four-Star and Mobil Five-Star properties
- A review of unsolicited comments from the general public
- Senior management oversight

For each property, more than 450 attributes, including cleanliness, physical facilities, and employee attitude and courtesy, are measured and evaluated to produce a mathematically derived score, which is then blended with the other elements to form an overall score. These quantifiable scores allow comparative analysis among properties and form the basis that we use to assign our Mobil One- to Five-Star ratings.

This process focuses largely on guest expectations, guest experience, and consistency of service, not just physical facilities and amenities. It is fundamentally a relative rating system that rewards those properties that continually strive for and achieve excellence each year. Indeed, the very best properties are consistently raising the bar for those that wish to compete with them. These properties proactively respond to consumers' needs even in today's uncertain times.

Only facilities that meet Mobil Travel Guide's standards earn the privilege of being listed in the guide. Deteriorating, poorly managed establishments are deleted. A Mobil Travel Guide listing constitutes a positive quality recommendation; every listing is an accolade, a recognition of achievement. Our Mobil One- to Five-Star rating system highlights its level of service. Extensive in-house research is constantly underway to determine new additions to our lists.

- The Mobil Five-Star Award indicates that a property is one of the very best in the country and consistently provides gracious and courteous service, superlative quality in its facility, and a unique ambience. The lodgings and restaurants at the Mobil Five-Star level consistently and proactively respond to consumers' needs and continue their commitment to excellence, doing so with grace and perseverance.
- Also highly regarded is the Mobil Four-Star Award, which honors properties for outstanding achievement in overall facility and for providing very strong service levels in all areas. These

award winners provide a distinctive experience for the ever-demanding and sophisticated consumer.

- The Mobil Three-Star Award recognizes an excellent property that provides full services and amenities. This category ranges from exceptional hotels with limited services to elegant restaurants with a less-formal atmosphere.
- A Mobil Two-Star property is a clean and comfortable establishment that has expanded amenities or a distinctive environment. A Mobil Two-Star property is an excellent place to stay or dine.
- A Mobil One-Star property is limited in its amenities and services but focuses on providing a value experience while meeting travelers' expectations. The property can be expected to be clean, comfortable, and convenient.

Allow us to emphasize that we do not charge establishments for inclusion in our guides. We have no relationship with any of the businesses and attractions we list and act only as a consumer advocate. In essence, we do the investigative legwork so that you won't have to.

Keep in mind, too, that the hospitality business is ever-changing. Restaurants and lodgings—particularly small chains and stand-alone establishments—change management or even go out of business with surprising quickness. Although we make every effort to double-check information during our annual updates, we nevertheless recommend that you call ahead to make sure the place you've selected is still open and offers all the amenities you're looking for. We've provided phone numbers; when available, we also list fax numbers and Web site addresses.

We hope that your travels are enjoyable and relaxing and that our books help you get the most out of every trip you take. If any aspect of your accommodation, dining, or sightseeing experience motivates you to comment, please drop us a line. We depend a great deal on our readers' remarks, so you can be assured that we will read your comments and assimilate them into our research. General comments about our books are also welcome. You can write to us at Mobil Travel Guide, 1460 Renaissance Drive, Suite 401, Park Ridge, IL 60068, or send an e-mail to info@mobiltravelguide.com.

Take your Mobil Travel Guide books along on every trip you take. We're confident that you'll be pleased with their convenience, ease of use, and breadth of dependable coverage.

Happy travels!

How to Use This Book

The Mobil Travel Guide Regional Travel Planners are designed for ease of use. Each state has its own chapter, beginning with a general introduction that provides a geographical and historical orientation to the state and gives basic statewide tourist information, from climate to calendar highlights to seatbelt laws. The remainder of each chapter is devoted to travel destinations within the state—mainly cities and towns, but also national parks and tourist areas—which, like the states, are arranged in alphabetical order.

The following sections explain the wealth of information you'll find about those travel destinations: information about the area, things to see and do there, and where to stay and eat.

Maps and Map Coordinates

At the front of this book in the full-color section, we have provided state maps as well as maps of selected larger cities to help you find your way around once you leave the highway. You'll find a key to the map symbols on the Contents page at the beginning of the map section.

Next to most cities and towns throughout the book, you'll find a set of map coordinates, such as C-2. These coordinates reference the maps at the front of this book and help you find the location you're looking for quickly and easily.

Destination Information

Because many travel destinations are close to other cities and towns where travelers might find additional attractions, accommodations, and restaurants, we've included cross-references to those cities and towns when it makes sense to do so. We also list addresses, phone numbers, and Web sites for travel information resources—usually the local chamber of commerce or office of tourism—as well as pertinent statistics and, in many cases, a brief introduction to the area.

Information about airports, ground transportation, and suburbs is included for large cities.

Driving Tours and Walking Tours

The driving tours that we include for many states are usually day trips that make for interesting side excursions, although they can be longer. They offer you a way to get off the beaten path and visit an area that travelers often overlook. These trips frequently cover areas of natural beauty or historical significance.

Each walking tour focuses on a particularly interesting area of a city or town. Again, these tours can provide a break from everyday tourist attractions. The tours often include places to stop for meals or snacks.

What to See and Do

Mobil Travel Guide offers information about nearly 20,000 museums, art galleries, amusement parks, historic sites, national and state parks, ski areas, and many other types of attractions. A white star on a black background ★ signals that the attraction is a must-see—one of the best in the area. Because municipal parks, public tennis courts, swimming pools, and small educational institutions are common to most towns, they generally are not mentioned.

Following an attraction's description, you'll find the months, days, and, in some cases, hours of operation; the address/directions, telephone number, and Web site (if there is one); and the admission price category. The following are the ranges we use for admission fees, based on one adult:

- **FREE**
- **$** = Up to $5
- **$$** = $5.01-$10
- **$$$** = $10.01-$15
- **$$$$** = Over $15

Special Events

Special events are either annual events that last only a short time, such as festivals and fairs, or longer, seasonal events such as horse racing, theater, and summer concerts. Our Special Events listings also include infrequently occurring occasions that mark certain dates or events, such as a centennial or other commemorative celebration.

Listings

Lodgings, spas, and restaurants are usually listed under the city or town in which they're located. Make sure to check the related cities and towns that appear right beneath a city's heading for additional options, especially if you're traveling to a major metropolitan area that includes many suburbs. If a property is located in a town that doesn't have its own heading, the listing appears under the town nearest it, with the address and town given immediately after the establishment's name. In large cities, lodgings located within 5 miles of major commercial airports may be listed under a separate "Airport Area" heading that follows the city section.

LODGINGS

Travelers have different wants and needs when it comes to accommodations. To help you pinpoint properties that meet your particular needs, Mobil Travel Guide classifies each lodging by type according to the following characteristics.

Mobil Rated Lodgings

- **Limited-Service Hotel.** A limited-service hotel is traditionally a Mobil One-Star or Mobil Two-Star property. At a Mobil One-Star hotel, guests can expect to find a clean, comfortable property that commonly serves a complimentary continental breakfast. A Mobil Two-Star hotel is also clean and comfortable but has expanded amenities, such as a full-service restaurant, business center, and fitness center. These services may have limited staffing and/or restricted hours of use.
- **Full-Service Hotel.** A full-service hotel traditionally enjoys a Mobil Three-Star, Mobil Four-Star, or Mobil Five-Star rating. Guests can expect these hotels to offer at least one full-service restaurant in addition to amenities such as valet parking, luggage assistance, 24-hour room service, concierge service, laundry and/or dry-cleaning services, and turndown service.
- **Full-Service Resort.** A resort is traditionally a full-service hotel that is geared toward recreation and represents a vacation and holiday destination. A resort's guest rooms are typically furnished to accommodate longer stays. The property may offer a full-service spa, golf, tennis, and fitness facilities or other leisure activities. Resorts are expected to offer a full-service restaurant and expanded amenities, such as luggage assistance, room service, meal plans, concierge service, and turndown service.
- **Full-Service Inn.** An inn is traditionally a Mobil Three-Star, Mobil Four-Star, or Mobil Five-Star property. Inns are similar to bed-and-breakfasts (see below) but offer a wider range of services, most significantly a full-service restaurant that serves at least breakfast and dinner.

Specialty Lodgings

Mobil Travel Guide recognizes the unique and individualized nature of many different types of lodging establishments, including bed-and-breakfasts, limited-service inns, and guest ranches. For that reason, we have chosen to place our stamp of approval on the properties that fall into these two categories in lieu of applying our traditional Mobil Star ratings.

- **B&B/Limited-Service Inn.** A bed-and-breakfast (B&B) or limited-service inn is traditionally an owner-occupied home or residence found in a residential area or vacation destination. It may be a structure of historic significance. Rooms are often individually decorated, but telephones, televisions, and private bathrooms may not be available in every room. A B&B typically serves only breakfast to its overnight guests, which is included in the room rate. Cocktails and refreshments may be served in the late afternoon or evening.
- **Guest Ranch.** A guest ranch is traditionally a rustic, Western-themed property that specializes in stays of three or more days. Horseback riding is often a feature, with stables and trails found on the property. Facilities can range from clean, comfortable establishments to more luxurious facilities.

Mobil Star Rating Definitions for Lodgings

- ★★★★★ : A Mobil Five-Star lodging provides consistently superlative service in an exceptionally distinctive luxury environment, with expanded services. Attention to detail is evident throughout the hotel, resort, or inn, from bed linens to staff uniforms.
- ★★★★ : A Mobil Four-Star lodging provides a luxury experience with expanded amenities in a distinctive environment. Services may include, but are not limited to, automatic turndown service, 24-hour room service, and valet parking.
- ★★★ : A Mobil Three-Star lodging is well appointed, with a full-service restaurant and expanded amenities, such as a fitness center, golf course, tennis courts, 24-hour room service, and optional turndown service.
- ★★ : A Mobil Two-Star lodging is considered a clean, comfortable, and reliable establishment that has expanded amenities, such as a full-service restaurant on the premises.
- ★ : A Mobil One-Star lodging is a limited-service hotel, motel, or inn that is considered a clean, comfortable, and reliable establishment.

Information Found in the Lodging Listings

Each lodging listing gives the name, address/location (when no street address is available), neighborhood and/or directions from downtown (in major cities), phone number(s), fax number, total number of guest rooms, and seasons open (if not year-round). Also included are details on business, luxury, recreational, and dining facilities at the property or nearby. A key to the symbols at the end of each listing can be found on the page following the "A Word to Our Readers" section.

For every property, we also provide pricing information. Because lodging rates change frequently, we list a pricing category rather than specific prices. The pricing categories break down as follows:

- **$** = Up to $150
- **$$** = $151-$250
- **$$$** = $251-$350
- **$$$$** = $351 and up

All prices quoted are in effect at the time of publication; however, prices cannot be guaranteed. In some locations, short-term price variations may exist because of special events, holidays, or seasonality. Certain resorts have complicated rate structures that vary with the time of year; always confirm rates when making your plans.

Because most lodgings offer the following features and services, information about them does not appear in the listings:

- Year-round operation
- Bathroom with tub and/or shower in each room
- Cable television in each room
- In-room telephones
- Cots and cribs available
- Daily maid service
- Elevators
- Major credit cards accepted

Although we recommend every lodging we list in this book, a few stand out—they offer noteworthy amenities or stand above the others in their category in terms of quality, value, or historical significance. To draw your attention to these special spots, we've included the magnifying glass icon to the left of the listing, as you see here.

SPAS

Mobil Travel Guide is pleased to announce its newest category: hotel and resort spas. Until now, hotel and resort spas have not been formally rated or inspected by any organization. Every spa selected for inclusion in this book underwent a rigorous inspection process similar to the one Mobil Travel Guide has been applying to lodgings and restaurants for more than four decades. After spending a year and a half researching more than 300 spas and performing exhaustive incognito inspections of more than 200 properties, we narrowed our list to the 48 best spas in the United States and Canada.

Mobil Travel Guide's spa ratings are based on objective evaluations of more than 450 attributes. Approximately half of these criteria assess basic expectations, such as staff courtesy, the technical proficiency and skill of the employees, and whether the facility is maintained properly and hygienically.

Several standards address issues that impact a guest's physical comfort and convenience, as well as the staff's ability to impart a sense of personalized service and anticipate clients' needs. Additional criteria measure the spa's ability to create a completely calming ambience.

The Mobil Star ratings focus on much more than the facilities available at a spa and the treatments it offers. Each Mobil Star rating is a cumulative score achieved from multiple inspections that reflects the spa management's attention to detail and commitment to consumers' needs.

Mobil Star Rating Definitions for Spas

- ★★★★★ : A Mobil Five-Star spa provides consistently superlative service in an exceptionally distinctive luxury environment with extensive amenities. The staff at a Mobil Five-Star spa provides extraordinary service above and beyond the traditional spa experience, allowing guests to achieve the highest level of relaxation and pampering. A Mobil Five-Star spa offers an extensive array of treatments, often incorporating international themes and products. Attention to detail is evident throughout the spa, from arrival to departure.
- ★★★★ : A Mobil Four-Star spa provides a luxurious experience with expanded amenities in an elegant and serene environment. Throughout the spa facility, guests experience personalized service. Amenities might include, but are not limited to, single-sex relaxation rooms where guests wait for their treatments, plunge pools and whirlpools in both men's and women's locker rooms, and an array of treatments, including at a minimum a selection of massages, body therapies, facials, and a variety of salon services.
- ★★★ : A Mobil Three-Star spa is physically well appointed and has a full complement of staff to ensure that guests' needs are met. It has some expanded amenities, such as, but not limited to, a well-equipped fitness center, separate men's and women's locker rooms, a sauna or steam room, and a designated relaxation area. It also offers a menu of services that at a minimum includes massages, facial treatments, and at least one other type of body treatment, such as scrubs or wraps.

RESTAURANTS

All Mobil Star rated dining establishments listed in this book have a full kitchen and offer seating at tables; most offer table service.

Mobil Star Rating Definitions for Restaurants

- ★★★★★ : A Mobil Five-Star restaurant offers one of few flawless dining experiences in the country. These establishments consistently provide their guests with exceptional food, superlative service, elegant décor, and exquisite presentations of each detail surrounding a meal.
- ★★★★ : A Mobil Four-Star restaurant provides professional service, distinctive presentations, and wonderful food.
- ★★★ : A Mobil Three-Star restaurant has good food, warm and skillful service, and enjoyable décor.
- ★★ : A Mobil Two-Star restaurant serves fresh food in a clean setting with efficient service. Value is considered in this category, as is family friendliness.
- ★ : A Mobil One-Star restaurant provides a distinctive experience through culinary specialty, local flair, or individual atmosphere.

Information Found in the Restaurant Listings

Each restaurant listing gives the cuisine type, street address (or directions if no address is available), phone and fax numbers, Web site (if available), meals served, days of operation (if not open daily year-round), and pricing category. Information about appropriate attire is provided, although it's always a good idea to call ahead and ask if you're unsure; the meaning of "casual" or "business casual" varies widely in different parts of the country. We also indicate whether the restaurant has a bar, whether a children's menu is offered, and whether outdoor seating is available. If reservations are recommended, we note that fact in the listing. When valet parking is available, it is noted in the description. In many cases, self-parking is available at the restaurant or nearby.

Because menu prices can fluctuate, we list a pricing category rather than specific prices. The pricing categories are defined as follows, per diner, and assume that you order an appetizer or dessert, an entrée, and one drink:

- **$** = $15 and under
- **$$** = $16-$35
- **$$$** = $36-$85
- **$$$$** = $86 and up

Again, all prices quoted are in effect at the time of publication, but prices cannot be guaranteed.

Although we recommend every restaurant we list in this book, a few stand out—they offer noteworthy local specialties or stand above the others in their category in terms of quality, value, or experience. To draw your attention to these special spots, we've included the magnifying glass icon to the left of the listing, as you see here.

SPECIAL INFORMATION FOR TRAVELERS WITH DISABILITIES

The Mobil Travel Guide D symbol indicates that an establishment is not at least partially accessible to people with mobility problems. When the D symbol follows a listing, the establishment is not equipped with facilities to accommodate people using wheelchairs or crutches or otherwise needing easy access to doorways and rest rooms. Travelers with severe mobility problems or with hearing or visual impairments may or may not find the facilities they need. Always phone ahead to make sure that an establishment can meet your needs.

AMERICA'S BYWAYS™

Mobil Travel Guide is pleased to announce a new partnership with the National Scenic Byways Program. Under this program, the US Secretary of Transportation recognizes certain roads as National Scenic Byways or All-American Roads based on their archaeological, cultural, historic, natural, recreational, and scenic qualities. To be designated a National Scenic Byway, a road must possess at least one of these six intrinsic qualities. To receive an All-American Road designation, a road must possess multiple intrinsic qualities that are nationally significant and contain one-of-a-kind features that do not exist elsewhere. The road or highway also must be considered a destination unto itself.

America's Byways are a great way to explore the country. From the mighty Mississippi to the towering Rockies to the Historic National Road, these routes take you past America's most treasured scenery and enable you to get in touch with America's past, present, and future. Bringing together all the nationally designated Byways in the Mid-Atlantic, this bonus section of the book is a handy reference whether you're planning to hop in the car tomorrow or you're simply looking for inspiration for future trips. Look for it at the end of the front section, before page 1.

Understanding the Symbols

What to See and Do

★	=	One of the top attractions in the area
$	=	Up to $5
$$	=	$5.01 to $10
$$$	=	$10.01 to $15
$$$$	=	Over $15

Lodgings

$	=	Up to $150
$$	=	$151 to $250
$$$	=	$251 to $350
$$$$	=	Over $350

Restaurants

$	=	Up to $15
$$	=	$16 to $35
$$$	=	$36 to $85
$$$$	=	Over $85

Lodging Star Definitions

★★★★★ A Mobil Five-Star lodging establishment provides consistently superlative service in an exceptionally distinctive luxury environment with expanded services. Attention to detail is evident throughout the hotel/resort/inn from the bed linens to the staff uniforms.

★★★★ A Mobil Four-Star lodging establishment is a hotel/resort/inn that provides a luxury experience with expanded amenities in a distinctive environment. Services may include, but are not limited to, automatic turndown service, 24-hour room service, and valet parking.

★★★ A Mobil Three-Star lodging establishment is a hotel/resort/inn that is well appointed, with a full-service restaurant and expanded amenities, such as, but not limited to, a fitness center, golf course, tennis courts, 24-hour room service, and optional turndown service.

★★ A Mobil Two-Star lodging establishment is a hotel/resort/inn that is considered a clean, comfortable, and reliable establishment, but also has expanded amenities, such as a full-service restaurant on the premises.

★ A Mobil One-Star lodging establishment is a limited-service hotel or inn that is considered a clean, comfortable, and reliable establishment.

Restaurant Star Definitions

★★★★★ A Mobil Five-Star restaurant is one of few flawless dining experiences in the country. These restaurants consistently provide their guests with exceptional food, superlative service, elegant décor, and exquisite presentations of each detail surrounding the meal.

★★★★ A Mobil Four-Star restaurant provides professional service, distinctive presentations, and wonderful food.

★★★ A Mobil Three-Star restaurant has good food, warm and skillful service, and enjoyable décor.

★★ A Mobil Two-Star restaurant serves fresh food in a clean setting with efficient service. Value is considered in this category, as is family friendliness.

★ A Mobil One-Star restaurant provides a distinctive experience through culinary specialty, local flair, or individual atmosphere.

Symbols at End of Listings

- Facilities for people with disabilities not available
- Pets allowed
- Ski in/ski out access
- Golf on premises
- Tennis court(s) on premises
- Indoor or outdoor pool
- Fitness room
- Major commercial airport within 5 miles
- Business center

Making the Most of Your Trip

A few hardy souls might look back with fondness on a trip during which the car broke down, leaving them stranded for three days, or a vacation that cost twice what it was supposed to. For most travelers, though, the best trips are those that are safe, smooth, and within budget. To help you make your trip the best it can be, we've assembled a few tips and resources.

Saving Money

ON LODGING

Many hotels and motels offer discounts—for senior citizens, business travelers, families, you name it. It never hurts to ask—politely, that is. Sometimes, especially in the late afternoon, desk clerks are instructed to fill beds, and you might be offered a lower rate or a nicer room to entice you to stay. Simply ask the reservation agent for the best rate available. Also, make sure to try both the toll-free number and the local number. You may be able to get a lower rate from one than from the other.

Timing your trip right can cut your lodging costs as well. Look for bargains on stays over multiple nights, in the off-season, and on weekdays or weekends, depending on the location. Many hotels in major metropolitan areas, for example, have special weekend packages that offer leisure travelers considerable savings on rooms; they may include breakfast, cocktails, and/or dinner discounts.

Another way to save money is to choose accommodations that give you more than just a standard room. Rooms with kitchen facilities enable you to cook some meals yourself, reducing your restaurant costs. A suite might save money for two couples traveling together. Even hotel luxury levels can provide good value, as many include breakfast or cocktails in the price of a room.

State and city taxes, as well as special room taxes, can increase your room rate by as much as 25 percent per day. We are unable to include information about taxes in our listings, but we strongly urge you to ask about taxes when making reservations so that you understand the total cost of your lodgings before you book them.

Watch out for telephone-usage charges that hotels frequently impose on long-distance, credit-card, and other calls. Before phoning from your room, read the information given to you at check-in, and then be sure to review your bill carefully when checking out. You won't be expected to pay for charges that the hotel didn't spell out. Consider using your cell phone if you have one; or, if public telephones are available in the hotel lobby, your cost savings may outweigh the inconvenience of using them.

Here are some additional ways to save on lodgings:

- Stay in B&B accommodations. They're generally less expensive than standard hotel rooms, and the complimentary breakfast cuts down on food costs.
- If you're traveling with children, find lodgings at which kids stay free.
- When visiting a major city, stay just outside the city limits; these rooms are usually less expensive than those in downtown locations.
- Consider visiting national parks during the low season, when prices of lodgings near the parks drop by 25 percent or more.
- When calling a hotel, ask whether it is running any special promotions or if any discounts are available; many times reservationists are told not to volunteer these deals unless they're specifically asked about them.
- Check for hotel packages; some offer nightly rates that include a rental car or discounts on major attractions.
- Search the Internet for travel bargains. Web sites that allow for online booking of hotel rooms and travel planning, such as *www.mobiltravelguide.com,* often deliver lower rates than are available through telephone reservations.

ON DINING

There are several ways to get a less expensive meal at an expensive restaurant. Early-bird dinners are popular in many parts of the country and offer considerable savings. If you're interested in visiting a Mobil Four- or Five-Star establishment, consider going at lunchtime. Although the prices are probably still relatively high at midday, they may be half of those at dinner, and you'll experience the same ambience, service, and cuisine.

ON ENTERTAINMENT

Although many national parks, monuments, seashores, historic sites, and recreation areas may be visited free of charge, others charge an entrance fee and/or a usage fee for special services and facilities. If you plan to make several visits to national recreation areas, consider one of the following money-saving programs offered by the National Park Service:

- **National Parks Pass.** This annual pass is good for entrance to any national park that charges an entrance fee. If the park charges a per-vehicle fee, the pass holder and any accompanying passengers in a private noncommercial vehicle may enter. If the park charges a per-person fee, the pass applies to the holder's spouse, children, and parents as well as the holder. It is valid for entrance fees only; it does not cover parking, camping, or other fees. You can purchase a National Parks Pass in person at any national park where an entrance fee is charged; by mail from the National Park Foundation, PO Box 34108, Washington, DC 20043-4108; by calling toll-free 888/467-2757; or at www.nationalparks.org. The cost is $50.
- **Golden Eagle Sticker.** When affixed to a National Parks Pass, this hologram sticker, available to people who are between 17 and 61 years of age, extends coverage to sites managed by the US Fish and Wildlife Service, the US Forest Service, and the Bureau of Land Management. It is good until the National Parks Pass to which it is affixed expires and does not cover usage fees. You can purchase one at the National Park Service, the Fish and Wildlife Service, or the Bureau of Land Management fee stations. The cost is $15.
- **Golden Age Passport.** Available to citizens and permanent US residents 62 and older, this passport is a lifetime entrance permit to fee-charging national recreation areas. The fee exemption extends to those accompanying the permit holder in a private noncommercial vehicle or, in the case of walk-in facilities, to the holder's spouse and children. The passport also entitles the holder to a 50 percent discount on federal usage fees charged in park areas, but not on concessions. Golden Age Passports must be obtained in person and are available at most National Park Service units that charge an entrance fee. The applicant must show proof of age, such as a driver's license or birth certificate (Medicare cards are not acceptable proof). The cost is $10.
- **Golden Access Passport.** Issued to citizens and permanent US residents who are physically disabled or visually impaired, this passport is a free lifetime entrance permit to fee-charging national recreation areas. The fee exemption extends to those accompanying the permit holder in a private noncommercial vehicle or, in the case of walk-in facilities, to the holder's spouse and children. The passport also entitles the holder to a 50 percent discount on usage fees charged in park areas, but not on concessions. Golden Access Passports must be obtained in person and are available at most National Park Service units that charge an entrance fee. Proof of eligibility to receive federal benefits (under programs such as Disability Retirement, Compensation for Military Service-Connected Disability, and the Coal Mine Safety and Health Act) is required, or an affidavit must be signed attesting to eligibility.

A money-saving move in several large cities is to purchase a **CityPass.** If you plan to visit several museums and other major attractions, CityPass is a terrific option because it gets you into several sites for one substantially reduced price. Currently, CityPass is available in Boston, Chicago, Hollywood, New York, Philadelphia, San Francisco, Seattle, southern California (which includes Disneyland, SeaWorld, and the San Diego Zoo), and Toronto. For more information or to buy one, call toll-free 888/330-5008 or visit www.citypass.net. You can also buy a CityPass from any participating CityPass attraction.

Here are some additional ways to save on entertainment and shopping:

- Check with your hotel's concierge for various coupons and special offers; they often have two-for-one tickets for area attractions and coupons for discounts at area stores and restaurants.

- Purchase same-day concert or theater tickets for half-price through the local cheap-tickets outlet, such as TKTS in New York or Hot Tix in Chicago.
- Visit museums on their free or "by donation" days, when you can pay what you wish rather than a specific admission fee.

ON TRANSPORTATION

Transportation is a big part of any vacation budget. Here are some ways to reduce your costs:

- If you're renting a car, shop early over the Internet; you can book a car during the low season for less, even if you'll be using it in the high season.
- Rental car discounts are often available if you rent for one week or longer and reserve in advance.
- Get the best gas mileage out of your vehicle by making sure that it's properly tuned up and keeping your tires properly inflated.
- Travel at moderate speeds on the open road; higher speeds require more gasoline.
- Fill the tank before you return your rental car; rental companies charge to refill the tank and do so at prices of up to 50 percent more than at local gas stations.
- Make a checklist of travel essentials and purchase them before you leave; don't get stuck buying expensive sunscreen at your hotel or overpriced film at the airport.

FOR SENIOR CITIZENS

Always call ahead to ask if a discount is being offered, and be sure to carry proof of age. Additional information for mature travelers is available from the American Association of Retired Persons (AARP), 601 E St NW, Washington, DC 20049; phone 202/434-2277; www.aarp.org.

Tipping

Tips are expressions of appreciation for good service. However, you are never obligated to tip if you receive poor service.

IN HOTELS

- Door attendants usually get $1 for hailing a cab.
- Bell staff expect $2 per bag.
- Concierges are tipped according to the service they perform. Tipping is not mandatory when you've asked for suggestions on sightseeing or restaurants or for help in making dining reservations. However, a tip of $5 is appropriate when a concierge books you a table at a restaurant known to be difficult to get into. For obtaining theater or sporting event tickets, $5 to $10 is expected.
- Maids should be tipped $1 to $2 per day. Hand your tip directly to the maid, or leave it with a note saying that the money has been left expressly for the maid.

IN RESTAURANTS

Before tipping, carefully review your check for any gratuity or service charge that is already included in your bill. If you're in doubt, ask your server.

- Coffee shop and counter service waitstaff usually receive 15 percent of the bill, before sales tax.
- In full-service restaurants, tip 18 percent of the bill, before sales tax.
- In fine restaurants, where gratuities are shared among a larger staff, 18 to 20 percent is appropriate.
- In most cases, the maitre d' is tipped only if the service has been extraordinary, and only on the way out. At upscale properties in major metropolitan areas, $20 is the minimum.
- If there is a wine steward, tip $20 for exemplary service and beyond, or more if the wine was decanted or the bottle was very expensive.
- Tip $1 to $2 per coat at the coat check.

AT AIRPORTS

Curbside luggage handlers expect $1 per bag. Car-rental shuttle drivers who help with your luggage appreciate a $1 or $2 tip.

Staying Safe

The best way to deal with emergencies is to avoid them in the first place. However, unforeseen situations do happen, so you should be prepared for them.

IN YOUR CAR

Before you head out on a road trip, make sure that your car has been serviced and is in good working order. Change the oil, check the battery and belts, make sure that your windshield washer fluid is full and your tires are properly inflated (which can also improve your gas mileage). Other inspections recommended by the vehicle's manufacturer should also be made.

Next, be sure you have the tools and equipment needed to deal with a routine breakdown:

- Jack
- Spare tire
- Lug wrench
- Repair kit
- Emergency tools
- Jumper cables
- Spare fan belt
- Fuses
- Flares and/or reflectors
- Flashlight
- First-aid kit
- In winter, a windshield scraper and snow shovel

Many emergency supplies are sold in special packages that include the essentials you need to stay safe in the event of a breakdown.

Also bring all appropriate and up-to-date documentation—licenses, registration, and insurance cards—and know what your insurance covers. Bring an extra set of keys, too, just in case.

En route, always buckle up! In most states, wearing a seatbelt is required by law.

If your car does break down, do the following:

- Get out of traffic as soon as possible—pull well off the road.
- Raise the hood and turn on your emergency flashers or tie a white cloth to the roadside door handle or antenna.
- Stay in your car.
- Use flares or reflectors to keep your vehicle from being hit.

IN YOUR HOTEL

Chances are slim that you will encounter a hotel or motel fire, but you can protect yourself by doing the following:

- Once you've checked in, make sure that the smoke detector in your room is working properly.
- Find the property's fire safety instructions, usually posted on the inside of the room door.
- Locate the fire extinguishers and at least two fire exits.
- Never use an elevator in a fire.

For personal security, use the peephole in your room door and make sure that anyone claiming to be a hotel employee can show proper identification. Call the front desk if you feel threatened at any time.

PROTECTING AGAINST THEFT

To guard against theft wherever you go:

- Don't bring anything of more value than you need.
- If you do bring valuables, leave them at your hotel rather than in your car.
- If you bring something very expensive, lock it in a safe. Many hotels put one in each room; others will store your valuables in the hotel's safe.
- Don't carry more money than you need. Use traveler's checks and credit cards or visit cash machines to withdraw more cash when you run out.

For Travelers with Disabilities

To get the kind of service you need and have a right to expect, don't hesitate when making a reservation to question the management about the availability of accessible rooms, parking, entrances, restaurants, lounges, or any other facilities that are important to you, and confirm what is meant by "accessible."

The Mobil Travel Guide [D] symbol indicates establishments that are not at least partially accessible to people with special mobility needs (people using wheelchairs or crutches or otherwise needing easy access to buildings and rooms). Further information about these criteria can be found in the earlier section "How to Use This Book."

A thorough listing of published material for travelers with disabilities is available from the Disability Bookshop, Twin Peaks Press, Box 129, Vancouver, WA 98666; phone 360/694-2462; disabilitybookshop.virtualave.net. Another reliable organization is the Society for Accessible Travel & Hospitality (SATH), 347 Fifth Ave, Suite 610, New York, NY 10016; phone 212/447-7284; www.sath.org.

Important Toll-Free Numbers and Online Information

Hotels

Adams Mark 800/444-2326
www.adamsmark.com
AmericInn 800/634-3444
www.americinn.com
AmeriHost Inn 800/434-5800
www.amerihostinn.com
Amerisuites 800/833-1516
www.amerisuites.com
Baymont Inns 877/BAYMONT
www.baymontinns.com
Best Inns & Suites 800/237-8466
www.bestinn.com
Best Value Inn 888/315-BEST
www.bestvalueinn.com
Best Western 800/780-7234
www.bestwestern.com
Budget Host Inn 800/BUDHOST
www.budgethost.com
Candlewood Suites 888/CANDLEWOOD
www.candlewoodsuites.com
Clarion Hotels 800/252-7466
www.choicehotels.com
Comfort Inns and Suites 800/252-7466
www.choicehotels.com
Country Hearth Inns 800/848-5767
www.countryhearth.com
Country Inns & Suites 800/456-4000
www.countryinns.com
Courtyard by Marriott 800/321-2211
www.courtyard.com
Cross Country Inns (KY and OH) 800/621-1429
www.crosscountryinns.com
Crowne Plaza Hotels and Resorts 800/227-6963
www.crowneplaza.com
Days Inn 800/544-8313
www.daysinn.com
Delta Hotels 800/268-1133
www.deltahotels.com
Destination Hotels & Resorts 800/434-7347
www.destinationhotels.com
Doubletree Hotels 800/222-8733
www.doubletree.com
Drury Inn 800/378-7946
www.druryinn.com
Econolodge 800/553-2666
www.econolodge.com
Embassy Suites 800/362-2779
www.embassysuites.com
ExelInns of America 800/FOREXEL
www.exelinns.com
Extended StayAmerica 800/EXTSTAY
www.extstay.com
Fairfield Inn by Marriott 800/228-2800
www.fairfieldinn.com
Fairmont Hotels 800/441-1414
www.fairmont.com
Four Points by Sheraton 888/625-5144
www.starwood.com/fourpoints
Four Seasons 800/545-4000
www.fourseasons.com
Hampton Inn 800/426-7866
www.hamptoninn.com
Hard Rock Hotels, Resorts, and Casinos 800/HRDROCK
www.hardrock.com
Harrah's Entertainment 800/HARRAHS
www.harrahs.com
Hawthorn Suites 800/527-1133
www.hawthorn.com
Hilton Hotels and Resorts (US) 800/774-1500
www.hilton.com
Holiday Inn Express 800/465-4329
www.hiexpress.com
Holiday Inn Hotels and Resorts 800/465-4329
www.holiday-inn.com
Homestead Studio Suites 888/782-9473
www.homesteadhotels.com
Homewood Suites 800/225-5466
www.homewoodsuites.com
Howard Johnson 800/406-1411
www.hojo.com
Hyatt 800/633-7313
www.hyatt.com
Ian Schrager .... Contact individual hotel
www.ianschragerhotels.com
Inns of America 800/826-0778
www.innsofamerica.com
InterContinental 888/567-8725
www.intercontinental.com
Joie de Vivre 800/738-7477
www.jdvhospitality.com
Kimpton Hotels 888/546-7866
www.kimptongroup.com
Knights Inn 800/843-5644
www.knightsinn.com

La Quinta 800/531-5900
www.laquinta.com
Le Meridien 800/543-4300
www.lemeridien.com
Leading Hotels of the World 800/223-6800
www.lhw.com
Loews Hotels 800/235-6397
www.loewshotels.com
MainStay Suites 800/660-6246
www.choicehotels.com
Mandarin Oriental 800/526-6566
www.mandarin-oriental.com
Marriott Hotels, Resorts, and Suites 800/228-9290
www.marriott.com
Microtel Inns & Suites 800/771-7171
www.microtelinn.com
Millennium & Copthorne Hotels 866/866-8086
www.mill-cop.com
Motel 6 . . . . 800/4MOTEL6
www.motel6.com
Omni Hotels 800/843-6664
www.omnihotels.com
Pan Pacific Hotels and Resorts 800/327-8585
www.panpac.com
Park Inn & Park Plaza 888/201-1801
www.parkhtls.com
The Peninsula Group . . . . Contact individual hotel
www.peninsula.com
Preferred Hotels & Resorts Worldwide 800/323-7500
www.preferredhotels.com
Quality Inn 800/228-5151
www.qualityinn.com
Radisson Hotels 800/333-3333
www.radisson.com
Raffles International Hotels and Resorts . . . 800/637-9477
www.raffles.com
Ramada Plazas, Limiteds, and Inns 800/2RAMADA
www.ramada.com
Red Lion Inns 800/733-5466
www.redlion.com
Red Roof Inns 800/733-7663
www.redroof.com
Regal Hotels 800/222-8888
www.regal-hotels.com
Regent International 800/545-4000
www.regenthotels.com
Relais & Chateaux 800/735-2478
www.relaischateaux.com
Renaissance Hotels 888/236-2427
www.renaissancehotels.com
Residence Inn 800/331-3131
www.residenceinn.com
Ritz-Carlton 800/241-3333
www.ritzcarlton.com
Rockresorts 888/FORROCKS
www.rockresorts.com
Rodeway Inn 800/228-2000
www.rodeway.com
Rosewood Hotels & Resorts 888/767-3966
www.rosewood-hotels.com
Select Inn 800/641-1000
www.selectinn.com
Sheraton 888/625-5144
www.sheraton.com
Shilo Inns 800/222-2244
www.shiloinns.com
Shoney's Inn 800/552-4667
www.shoneysinn.com
Signature/Jameson Inns 800/822-5252
www.jamesoninns.com
Sleep Inn 800/453-3746
www.sleepinn.com
Small Luxury Hotels of the World 800/525-4800
www.slh.com
Sofitel 800/763-4835
www.sofitel.com
SpringHill Suites 888/236-2427
www.springhillsuites.com
SRS Worldhotels 800/223-5652
www.srs-worldhotels.com
St. Regis Luxury Collection 888/625-5144
www.stregis.com
Staybridge Suites 800/238-8000
www.staybridge.com
Summerfield Suites by Wyndham 800/833-4353
www.summerfieldsuites.com
Summit International 800/457-4000
www.summithotels.com
Super 8 Motels 800/800-8000
www.super8.com
The Sutton Place Hotels 866/378-8866
www.suttonplace.com
Swissôtel 800/637-9477
www.swissotel.com
TownePlace Suites 888/236-2427
www.towneplace.com
Travelodge 800/578-7878
www.travelodge.com
Vagabond Inns 800/522-1555
www.vagabondinns.com
W Hotels 888/625-5144
www.whotels.com
Wellesley Inn and Suites 800/444-8888
www.wellesleyinnandsuites.com
WestCoast Hotels 800/325-4000
www.westcoasthotels.com
Westin Hotels & Resorts 800/937-8461
www.westin.com

Wingate Inns 800/228-1000
www.wingateinns.com
Woodfin Suite Hotels 800/966-3346
www.woodfinsuitehotels.com
Wyndham Hotels & Resorts 800/996-3426
www.wyndham.com

Airlines

Air Canada 888/247-2262
www.aircanada.ca
AirTran 800/247-8726
www.airtran.com
Alaska Airlines 800/252-7522
www.alaskaair.com
American Airlines 800/433-7300
www.aa.com
America West 800/235-9292
www.americawest.com
ATA 800/435-9282
www.ata.com
Continental Airlines 800/523-3273
www.flycontinental.com
Delta Air Lines 800/221-1212
www.delta.com
Frontier Airlines 800/432-1FLY
www.frontierairlines.com
Jet Blue Airways 800/JET-BLUE
www.jetblue.com
Midwest Express 800/452-2022
www.midwestexpress.com
Northwest Airlines 800/225-2525
www.nwa.com
Southwest Airlines 800/435-9792
www.iflyswa.com
Spirit Airlines 800/772-7117
www.spiritair.com
United Airlines 800/241-6522
www.ual.com
US Airways 800/428-4322
www.usairways.com
Vanguard Airlines 800/VANGUARD
www.flyvanguard.com

Car Rentals

Advantage 800/777-5500
www.arac.com
Alamo 800/327-9633
www.goalamo.com
Avis 800/831-2847
www.avis.com
Budget 800/527-0700
www.budgetrentacar.com
Dollar 800/800-4000
www.dollarcar.com
Enterprise 800/325-8007
www.pickenterprise.com
Hertz 800/654-3131
www.hertz.com
National 800/227-7368
www.nationalcar.com
Payless 800/729-5377
www.800-payless.com
Rent-A-Wreck.com 800/535-1391
www.rent-a-wreck.com
Thrifty 800/847-4389
www.thrifty.com

Meet the Stars

Mobil Travel Guide 2005 **Five-Star** *Award Winners*

CALIFORNIA

Lodgings

The Beverly Hills Hotel, *Beverly Hills*
Chateau du Sureau, *Oakhurst*
Four Seasons Hotel San Francisco, *San Francisco*
Hotel Bel-Air, *Los Angeles*
The Peninsula Beverly Hills, *Beverly Hills*
Raffles L'Ermitage Beverly Hills, *Beverly Hills*
The Ritz-Carlton, San Francisco, *San Francisco*

Restaurants

The Dining Room, *San Francisco*
The French Laundry, *Yountville*
Gary Danko, *San Francisco*

COLORADO

Lodgings

The Broadmoor, *Colorado Springs*
The Little Nell, *Aspen*

CONNECTICUT

Lodging

The Mayflower Inn, *Washington*

FLORIDA

Lodgings

Four Seasons Resort Palm Beach, *Palm Beach*
The Ritz-Carlton, Naples, *Naples*
The Ritz-Carlton, Palm Beach, *Manalapan*

GEORGIA

Lodgings

Four Seasons Hotel Atlanta, *Atlanta*
The Lodge at Sea Island Golf Club, *St. Simons Island*

Restaurants

The Dining Room, *Atlanta*
Seeger's, *Atlanta*

HAWAII

Lodging

Four Seasons Resort Maui at Wailea, *Wailea, Maui*

ILLINOIS

Lodgings

Four Seasons Hotel Chicago, *Chicago*
The Peninsula Chicago, *Chicago*
The Ritz-Carlton, A Four Seasons Hotel, *Chicago*

Restaurants

Charlie Trotter's, *Chicago*
Trio, *Evanston*

MASSACHUSETTS

Lodgings

Blantyre, *Lenox*
Four Seasons Hotel Boston, *Boston*

NEW YORK

Lodgings

Four Seasons Hotel New York, *New York*
The Point, *Saranac Lake*
The Ritz-Carlton New York, Central Park, *New York*
The St. Regis, *New York*

Restaurants

Alain Ducasse, *New York*
Jean Georges, *New York*
Masa, *New York*

NORTH CAROLINA

Lodging

The Fearrington House Country Inn, *Pittsboro*

OHIO

Restaurant

Maisonette, *Cincinnati*

PENNSYLVANIA

Restaurant

Le Bec-Fin, *Philadelphia*

SOUTH CAROLINA

Lodging

Woodlands Resort & Inn, *Summerville*

Restaurant

Dining Room at the Woodlands, *Summerville*

TEXAS

Lodging

The Mansion on Turtle Creek, *Dallas*

VERMONT

Lodging

Twin Farms, *Barnard*

VIRGINIA

Lodgings

The Inn at Little Washington, *Washington*
The Jefferson Hotel, *Richmond*

Restaurant

The Inn at Little Washington, *Washington*

Mobil Travel Guide has been rating establishments with its Mobil One- to Five-Star system since 1958. Each establishment awarded the Mobil Five-Star rating is one of the best in the country. Detailed information on each award winner can be found in the corresponding regional edition listed on the back cover of this book.

Four- and Five-Star Establishments in Mid-Atlantic

Pennsylvania

★★★★ Lodgings
Four Seasons Hotel Philadelphia, *Philadelphia*
The Hotel Hershey, *Hershey*
Nemacolin Woodlands Resort & Spa, *Farmington*

★★★★★ Restaurant
Le Bec-Fin, *Philadelphia*

★★★★ Restaurants
Brasserie Perrier, *Philadelphia*
Lacroix at the Rittenhouse, *Philadelphia*

Virginia

★★★★★ Lodgings
The Inn at Little Washington, *Washington*
The Jefferson Hotel, *Richmond*

★★★★ Lodgings
The Ritz-Carlton, Pentagon City, *Arlington*
The Ritz-Carlton, Tyson's Corner, *McLean*
Williamsburg Inn, *Williamsburg*

★★★★★ Restaurant
The Inn at Little Washington, *Washington*

★★★★ Restaurant
Maestro, *McLean*

District of Columbia

★★★★ Lodgings
Four Seasons Hotel Washington, DC, *Washington*
The Hay-Adams, *Washington*
The Ritz-Carlton, Georgetown, *Washington*
The Ritz-Carlton, Washington, DC, *Washington*
The St. Regis Washington, DC, *Washington*

★★★★ Restaurants
Gerard's Place, *Washington*
Michel Richard Citronelle, *Washington*

West Virginia

★★★★ Lodging
The Greenbrier, *White Sulphur Springs*

★★★★ Restaurant
The Tavern Room, *White Sulphur Springs*

America's Byways™ are a distinctive collection of American roads, their stories, and treasured places. They are roads to the heart and soul of America. In this section, you'll find the nationally designated Byways in Maryland, Pennsylvania, and West Virginia.

The Historic National Road

MARYLAND

Part of a multistate Byway; see also PA, WV.

As the first federally funded road, the Historic National Road provided a gateway to the West for thousands of settlers who followed it from Baltimore through the Appalachians to Vandalia, Illinois. The road's history traces the evolution of transportation and commemorates the movement that ultimately stretched the nation's boundaries from the Atlantic to the Pacific.

It all began in 1806, when Congress authorized a road running west from Cumberland, Maryland. The proposed Historic National Road was the impetus for Maryland's General Assembly to create a turnpike, run by private interests, connecting Baltimore and Cumberland. Maryland's Baltimore to Cumberland section of the road was designated the Historic National Pike.

QUICK FACTS

Length: 170 miles.

Time to Allow: 4.5 hours.

Best Time to Drive: April through October. Many migratory birds return in the spring, and autumn paints the area in vibrant reds and oranges. The busiest season is from June to August, while November to March is considered Maryland's off-season. Despite the bare trees and chill in the air, you will still enjoy traveling the Byway during the less-crowded times.

Byway Travel Information: Byway local Web site: www.marylandroads.com/exploremd/scenicbyways/scenicbyways.asp; Byway travel and tourism Web site: www.mdisfun.org.

Special Considerations: You may want to plan stops for gas and food, because this is a long Byway. You'll also find numerous historic sites and museums to visit, so you may wish to plan additional time to drive the Byway.

Bicycle/Pedestrian Facilities: The roadways on this Byway vary in width and traffic. However, a majority of the Byway roads have paved shoulders that allow plenty of room for bikers.

Many layers of urbanization have modified this historic route, but the diligent traveler still may follow the old Historic National Pike through the streets of Baltimore westward into the historic Maryland countryside. Today, with the construction of new roads, many historic towns and sites originally connected to the Historic National Pike lure modern travelers with rugged charm, including a host of antique shops, specialty shops, and unique restaurants. These elements make the National Historic Road a treat for everyone.

The Byway Story

The Historic National Road tells cultural, historical, natural, recreational, and scenic stories that make it a unique and treasured Byway.

CULTURAL

The culture along the Historic National Road is one of pioneering spirit. As the first federally funded road, this Byway originally blazed a trail for the emerging nation to follow. Maryland's Baltimore to Cumberland section of the Historic National Road was designated the Historic National Pike. Soon, hardy travelers began seeking faster routes west, leading to a system of canals and railroads. Towns and cities along the pike began to spring up to provide comforts for weary travelers heading west. Even in modern times, travelers along the Historic National Pike can find a ready smile and a warm handshake.

Modern travelers of the Historic National Pike will find communities proud of their vibrant historical heritage. With Interstate 70 bypassing many of the original Historic National Pike cities, they have developed into artistic communities with a passion for diversity. Coffeehouses, small restaurants, antique shops, and cafés welcome modern travelers of the Historic National Pike to share in central Maryland's pioneering spirit.

HISTORICAL

In the late 18th century, as the population of the United States began to grow, President Thomas Jefferson convinced the US Congress to undertake a massive investment in new territory to the west. In 1803, the Louisiana Purchase more than doubled the size of the United States. Almost immediately, Jefferson dispatched Lewis and Clark on their mission to explore the new territory. At the same time, closer to home, Jefferson encouraged the development of a transportation infrastructure that would connect the eastern seaboard with points farther inland.

The construction of the National Road westward from Cumberland was the first such investment by the federal government. The construction of an "eastern connection" from Baltimore to Cumberland started before construction on the National Road had begun. This early start had a practical purpose: connecting the burgeoning population of Baltimore with new markets to the west. Without a road, the region's prosperity would not be assured. In the 1830s, the federal government gave the road back to the state of Maryland.

NATURAL

From the shores of the Chesapeake Bay to the majestic Negro Mountain, the Historic National Road offers many natural wonders. Many state parks along the Byway offer quiet breaks in the long drive. As the Byway continues into western Maryland, it passes through many mountain peaks, which constantly hindered early travel west. Before the Byway continues into Pennsylvania, it journeys through the city of Cumberland, which is nestled in a small mountain valley. Here, mountains tower 1,000 feet around the city.

The most magnificent feature to note in the Byway is the Narrows, located northwest of Cumberland. The Narrows is an unusual geologic formation near Cumberland that provides a pass through the Allegheny Mountains. Wills Creek runs north and south through the Narrows, creating the narrow gorge through Wills Mountain. The National Road was rerouted through the Narrows in 1834 because the original grade that traversed Wills Mountain was too steep. It was easier to take the water-level route up Mechanic Street through the Narrows and beyond. A good six-horse hitch could make this grade relatively easily with a few stops to let the team rest. Today, however, it accommodates automobiles quite well.

RECREATIONAL

Without question, the Historic National Road has a stellar array of recreational activities. Many people come here expecting to spend a day relaxing but change their plans to stay longer because of the large number of outstanding activities. This Byway is known not only for its historical highlights but also for its recreational qualities.

Perhaps the most popular destination in all of Maryland is Baltimore's Inner Harbor, where you'll find outdoor performances, numerous eateries, the Baltimore National Aquarium and Marine Mammal Pavilion, the Maryland Science Center and Davis Planetarium, the Pier 6 Concert Pavilion, historic ships, Harborplace shops, and much more.

If you love outdoor activity, this Byway features fantastic biking, boating, hiking, and rock climbing. If you're a sportsman, you won't get bored on the Historic National Road. You can find numerous places to fish as well as hunt deer, turkey, grouse, squirrel, rabbits, quail, and waterfowl. Furthermore, this area features one of the only special hunting spots in the nation dedicated to disabled persons. If you like to view animals but not necessarily hunt them, you can also find excellent bird-watching areas.

SCENIC

From the picturesque shores of the Chesapeake Bay to the towering mountains surrounding Cumberland, the Historic National Road delivers breathtaking

scenery every step of the way. You will see early stone bridges, Pennsylvania-German back barns with limestone-faced gable ends, and the last toll-booth left on the Maryland part of the Historic National Road.

The Blue Ridge is a mountain chain with two ridges in Maryland (South Mountain to the west and Catoctin Mountain to the east). Views are quite beautiful approaching South Mountain, from the top of the mountain (Washington Monument State Park), and around Middletown. Washington Monument State Park on South Mountain contains a spectacular overlook located approximately 1 mile from the Byway, from which the surrounding Middletown Valley can be admired. The Appalachian Trail crosses by this landmark.

Leaving South Mountain, the Byway passes through historic and scenic Turner's Gap on its way into Middletown. You can stop off at an overlook here to admire the view into town.

The Historic National Road

PENNSYLVANIA

Part of a multistate Byway; see also MD, WV.

As America entered the 19th century, the young nation faced one of its first challenges: how to link the people and cities along the Eastern seaboard to those on the frontiers west of the Allegheny Mountains. Settlers moving west faced perils aggravated by the lack of a well-defined roadway. And easterners were unable to take advantage of the abundant produce and goods from the western frontier without a road to transport them over the Alleghenies. The solution was the National Road, America's first interstate highway, and the only one constructed entirely with federal funds.

Construction began in 1811, and by 1818, the road stretched from Cumberland, Maryland, to what is now Wheeling, West Virginia. In time, the National Road ran the whole way to Vandalia, Illinois, a distance of 600 miles. The story of the National Road is a human tale of how Native American pathways became the settlers' lifeline and eventually a major artery, allowing the east-to-west interchange of the nation's commerce. It is the story of visionaries, mercenaries, common people, and most uncommon acts. The history of the National Road is high drama that deserves to be told, relived, and imparted to future generations.

QUICK FACTS

Length: 90 miles.

Time to Allow: 2 hours to 1 day.

Best Time to Drive: The colors of fall make it a great time to travel the National Road.

Byway Travel Information: Byway local Web sites: www.nationalroadpa.org and www.dcnr.state.pa.us/recreation/heritage/nationalroad.htm.

Bicycle/Pedestrian Facilities: Transportation along the National Road is predominantly automobile or tour bus. No pedestrian facilities exist along the road itself; however, numerous areas just off the road are friendly to bike and pedestrian travel.

For three decades, the history, influence, and heritage of the National Road has been celebrated at the annual National Road Festival, held on the third weekend each May. The festival features memorable festivities and a wagon train that comes into town—quite a sight to see.

The Byway Story

The National Historic Road tells cultural, historical, natural, and scenic stories that make it a unique and treasured Byway.

CULTURAL

The National Road was developed from existing Native American pathways and, by the 1840s, was the busiest transportation route in America. Over its miles lumbered stagecoaches, Conestoga wagons with hopeful settlers, and freight wagons pulled by braces of mules, along with peddlers, caravans, carriages, foot travelers, and mounted riders. In response to demand, inns, hostels, taverns, and retail trade sprang up to serve the many who traveled the road. Today, reminders of National Road history are still visible along this corridor, designed as one of Pennsylvania's heritage parks to preserve and interpret history throughout the region.

HISTORICAL

The first cries for a "national road" were heard before there was even a nation. Such a road would facilitate settlement and help the budding nation expand in order to survive and flourish. Economic considerations weighed heavily in favor of a national road, which would be a two-way street, allowing farmers and traders in the west to send their production east in exchange for manufactured goods and other essentials of life. By the end of the 18th century, there was a growing consensus that a national road was needed. In May 1820, Congress appropriated funds to lay out the road from Wheeling to the Mississippi. Construction in Ohio did not commence until 1825. Indiana's route was surveyed in 1827, with construction beginning in 1829. By 1834, the road extended across the entire state, albeit in various stages of completeness. The road began to inch across Illinois in the early 1830s, but shortages of funds and national will, plus local squabbles about its destination, caused it to end in Vandalia rather than on the shore of the Mississippi River.

The major engineering marvels associated with the National Road may have been the bridges that carried it across rivers and streams. The bridges came in a wide variety of styles and types and were made of stone, wood, iron, and, later, steel. They were the wonder of their day, and bridge-building did much to advance engineering knowledge in America before the Civil War. One bridge style often associated with the road was the S-type. Contrary to the popular, misguided opinion of the day, the bridges were not the product of the fevered, whiskey-inspired imagination of an engineer, but were built that way because it was easier to construct them in that configuration than as a straight span at that time. As the bridges indicate, an amazing variety of skills were needed to build the road: surveyors laid out the path; engineers oversaw construction; carpenters framed bridges; and masons cut and worked stones for bridges and milestones.

Initial cost estimates for the National Road were $6,000 per mile, but, like many other government projects, this estimate proved optimistic. Portions of the road through the hilly sections of Pennsylvania cost $9,000 to $13,000 per mile. Expenditures were sometimes lower as the road stretched across the flatlands of western Indiana and eastern Illinois.

NATURAL

One hundred eighty years ago, the National Road was a lifeline, bringing people and prosperity to the regions of the country removed from the eastern coast. First a Native American trail cutting through the mountains and valleys, and then a primitive wagon trail to the first federal highway, the National Road is surrounded by the views of history. You'll see pristine hardwood forests blanketing rolling hills, vintage homes and barns, historic farmlands, orchards, and hunting grounds. The view laid out along your route is a blended cacophony of sights and sounds that cannot be described, only experienced.

SCENIC

The scenic qualities of the Historic National Road can be described as a rich tapestry that changes with the seasons. Obvious reference can be made to the beauty of the budding leaves in the vast mountain woodlands, and the lush green look of the trees and fields in summer, or the vibrant colors of autumn. Some of the real beauty, however, arrives with winter, with the starkness of the woods and barren trees. It is then

that the whole landscape reveals itself to the visitor, seeing further into the viewshed to the ruts of the original trails, the traces of the Historic National Road and buildings nestled therein.

One of the most amazing sights along the road occurs just after you climb the Summit Mountain traveling west from Farmington and Chalk Hill at the Historic Summit Inn. Just over the crest of that "hill," your eyes fall onto a vast, endless valley, with rolling hills and a lushness that makes you believe you have found the promised land. This breathtaking view beckons you to imagine the sense of jubilation that pioneers must have felt after struggling to cross the Appalachians, realizing that the mountains were behind them as they began their final, steep descent down the western side.

The Historic National Road

WEST VIRGINIA

Part of a multistate Byway; see also MD, PA.

West Virginia's National Historic Road takes you on a trip through history. In 1863, West Virginia developed into a new state—the only state to successfully break off from another. The building where the Restored Government of Virginia was established is located along the Byway—many important decisions and debates regarding the Civil War took place in this building. You can tour this historic site that has been painstakingly preserved and beautifully restored.

The Historic National Road boasts many impressive museums and art galleries. One of the most popular museums along the Byway is the Kruger Street Toy and Train Museum, where the annual Marx Toy Convention is held. The Byway also features restored mansions, such as the Oglebay Institute Mansion Museum. This 16-mile attraction offers a high level of historic aesthetics and cleanliness. On almost every spot along this Byway, you see historic buildings and bridges, not to mention beautiful scenery. To make this route even more accommodating, you find bike paths and paved trails through most of the Byway's highlights.

The Byway Story

The Historic National Road tells cultural, historical, recreational, and scenic stories that make it a unique and treasured Byway.

CULTURAL

The cultural qualities of the Historic National Road are many in number and offer diverse experiences. Two of perhaps the most meaningful include music (particularly Jamboree USA) and religion.

The Capitol Music Hall, located next to the famous Wheeling Suspension Bridge, is home to both Jamboree USA and the Wheeling Symphony Orchestra. The Jamboree is the longest-running live radio program in America's history. Since 1933, famous artists from all over the nation have come to perform to an eager audience and have their show aired live over the radio each Saturday night. It was founded with the idea of promoting the regional country music that is dear to the South. When the Jamboree first began, fans drove hundreds of miles for this weekly event. This tradition continues today, as many still drive great distances to participate in the yeehawin' fun.

Religion has played a powerful role in shaping the communities along the Byway. Places of worship dot this area, some with beautiful aesthetics and architecture. Churches along the route tell the story of the great diversity of those who traveled the road and settled along the nation's first interstate. You can view beautiful cemeteries near the churches with many unique monuments and headstones indicative of the artistry of earlier eras.

QUICK FACTS

Length: 16 miles.

Time to Allow: Less than 1 hour.

Best Time to Drive: The Byway is open all year, but many feel it is best to drive during the summer, the high season, when more cultural activities are taking place.

Byway Travel Information: Wheeling Convention and Visitors Bureau: phone toll-free 800/828-3097.

Bicycle/Pedestrian Facilities: A paved trail is available for bikers and pedestrians along most of the Byway.

HISTORICAL

Without question, the historic qualities here are the richest attribute this Byway has to offer. With two national historic landmarks, numerous designated historic districts, and National Register structures, the Historic National Road had a great impact on not only West Virginia's past, but on America's, too. From Monument Place, the oldest home standing in Wheeling, to the Elm Grove Stone Arch Bridge, the oldest stone bridge in the state, the Byway is steeped in history.

The National Road Corridor Historic District consists of a variety of homes built by Wheeling's wealthy industrial class. It also includes Wheeling Park, Greenwood Cemetery, and Mount Calvary Cemetery. In 1888, farms outside the city began to be developed as "suburbia." The Woodsdale-Edgewood Neighborhood Historic District is a result of this type of development. The district contains many high-style houses, such as Queen Anne, Colonial Revival, and Shingle styles. As the route descends Wheeling Hill into the city of Wheeling, you enter the North Wheeling Historic District. Ebenezer Zane, the founder of Wheeling, laid out the Victorian district in 1792. The houses include a variety of simple Federal townhouses offset with the high styles of Italianate, Queen Anne, Second Empire, and Classical Revival architecture.

The Wheeling Suspension Bridge crosses the Ohio River to Wheeling Island. The engineering marvel spans 1,010 feet and was the first bridge to cross the Ohio River. Designed by Charles Ellet Jr, it was the longest single span in the United States at the time of its completion in 1849. You cross the bridge to get to Wheeling Island, one of the largest inhabited river islands in the country. The Wheeling Island Historic District includes a diverse collection of lavish 19th-century residential homes.

RECREATIONAL

Why do over a million people come each year to the city of Wheeling to watch dogs? Simple. They come to view and bet on some of the world's fastest canines in the races. This popular event is usually open every day all year long.

Visitors go to Wheeling Downs to watch the races in person. These sleek thoroughbreds give quite a show as they thunder along the tracks at speeds of up to 40 miles per hour. Here at the Downs, people can enjoy the luxury of attending the races while eating at a fine diner that overlooks the track. Each of the tables also has tabletop televisions that relay the race and broadcast any replays and results. Many have found the restaurant's service, coupled with the excitement of the live races, an invigorating experience not easily forgotten.

SCENIC

Time almost stands still while looking down on the city of Wheeling from Mount Wood Overlook. Looking carefully, you can spot old, restored Victorian homes, as well as other important buildings in the nation's history. This vantage point, resting on top of Wheeling Hill, also overlooks the mighty Ohio River. It's at these heights that the observer starts to appreciate the accomplishment of the early Americans who constructed the single-spanned Wheeling Bridge across this wide river. At the time of its completion in the early 1800s, this was the longest single-spanned bridge in the world. As you continue to gaze in the area around Wheeling, more sights become visible. Ancient deciduous forests surround the city and small streams make their way to the grand Ohio. Maple trees thrive here, and some of the locals harvest the syrup. The area is a saturated green during the warm months and a calm white during the winter ones.

Delaware

Delaware "… is like a diamond, diminutive, but having within it inherent value," wrote John Lofland, the eccentric "Bard of Milford," in 1847. The state is 96 miles long and from 9 to 35 miles wide. With more than half of its 1,982 square miles (excluding marshes) used for farming, Delaware produces a flood of agricultural products. Poultry makes up approximately half of the state's total farm income; soybeans, corn, tomatoes, strawberries, asparagus, fruit, and other crops bring in about $170 million each year. Booming industry in northern and central Delaware balances the agricultural sector of the economy. Consistent state corporate policies have persuaded more than 183,000 corporations to make their headquarters in the "corporate capital of the world." Forty major US banks alone have established lending and credit operations in the state.

Population: 783,600
Area: 1,982 square miles
Elevation: 0-447 feet
Peak: Ebright Road (New Castle County)
Entered Union: First state to ratify Constitution (December 7, 1787)
Capital: Dover
Motto: Liberty and independence
Nickname: First State, Small Wonder, The Diamond State, Blue Hen State
Flower: Peach Blossom
Bird: Blue Hen
Tree: American Holly
Fair: July in Harrington (see Dover)
Time Zone: Eastern
Web site: www.state.de.us
Fun Facts:

- Delaware was the first state to ratify the United States constitution. It did so on December 7, 1787.
- Horseshoe crabs may be viewed in large numbers up and down the Delaware shore in May. The crabs endure extremes of temperature and salinity. They can also go for a year without eating and have remained basically the same since the days of the dinosaur.

Compact but diverse, Delaware has rolling, forested hills in the north, stretches of bare sand dunes in the south, and mile upon mile of lonely marsh along the coast. Visitors can tour a modern agricultural or chemical research center in the morning and search for buried pirate treasures in the afternoon. The *deBraak,* which foundered off Lewes in 1798, was raised in 1986 because of the belief that it may have had a fortune in captured Spanish coin or bullion aboard. The coins, which frequently come ashore at Coin Beach below Rehoboth, are believed to come from the *Faithful Steward,* a passenger vessel lost in 1785.

Delaware's history started on a grim note. The first colonists, 28 men under Dutch auspices, landed in the spring of 1631 near what is now Lewes. A year later, after an argument with a Lenni-Lenape chief, the bones of all 28 were found mingled with those of their cattle and strewn over their burned fields. In 1638, a group of Swedes established the first permanent settlement, Fort Christina, at a spot now in Wilmington. This was also the first permanent settlement of Swedes in North America. Dutch, English, Scottish, and Irish colonists soon followed, with German, Italian, and Polish groups coming in the late 19th century.

Henry Hudson, in Dutch service, discovered Delaware Bay in 1609. A year later, Thomas Argall reported it to English navigators, naming it for his superior, Lord de la Warr, Governor of Virginia. Ownership changed rapidly from Swedish to Dutch to English hands. Later the area was claimed by both Lord Baltimore and the Penn family. The Maryland-Delaware boundary was set by British court order in 1750 and surveyed as part of the Mason-Dixon Line in 1763-1767. The boundary

Calendar Highlights

May

Wilmington Garden Day *(Wilmington).* Tour of famous houses and gardens.

June

Zwaanendael Heritage Garden Tour *(Lewes). Phone 302/645-8073.* Tour of the hidden gardens of Lewes. Vendors.

July

Delaware State Fair *(Harrington). Phone 302/398-3269.* Arts and crafts, home and trade show, carnival rides, and entertainment; homemaking, agricultural, and livestock exhibits.

October

Sea Witch Halloween and Fiddlers' Festival *(Rehoboth Beach). Phone 800/441-1329, ext 11.*

with New Jersey, also long disputed, was confirmed by the Supreme Court in 1935.

The "First State" (first to adopt the Constitution—December 7, 1787) is proud of its history of sturdy independence, both military and political. During the Revolution, the "Delaware line" was a crack regiment of the Continental Army. After heavy casualties in 1780, the unit was reorganized. The men would "fight all day and dance all night," according to a dispatch by General Greene. How well they danced is open to question, but they fought with such gallantry that they were mentioned in nearly all of the General's dispatches.

Delaware statesman John Dickinson, "penman of the Revolution" and one of the state's five delegates to the Constitutional Convention, was instrumental in the decision to write a new document rather than simply patch up the Articles of Confederation. Later he effected the compromise on representation, a problem that had threatened to break up the convention completely.

In addition to Lofland and Dickinson, Delaware has produced many literary figures, including the 19th-century playwright and novelist Robert Montgomery Bird, writer and illustrator Howard Pyle, Henry Seidel Canby (founder of the Saturday Review), and novelist John P. Marquand.

A fine highway network tempts motorists to drive through diminutive Delaware without really seeing it. Those who take time to leave the major highways and explore the countryside will find much that is rewarding.

When to Go/Climate

Delaware's climate is generally mild; long Indian summers are not unusual and there's seldom frost until late autumn. Temperatures at the shore can be 10° F higher in winter or lower in summer than inland temperatures.

AVERAGE HIGH/LOW TEMPERATURES (° F)

Wilmington

Jan 39/22	**May** 73/52	**Sept** 78/58
Feb 42/25	**June** 81/62	**Oct** 67/46
Mar 52/33	**July** 86/67	**Nov** 56/37
Apr 63/42	**Aug** 84/66	**Dec** 44/28

Parks and Recreation

Water-related activities, hiking, riding, various other sports, picnicking, and visitor centers are available in many state parks. Delaware state parks are open all year, 8 am-sunset, except Fort Delaware (late Apr-late Sept). Most areas have fishing, boat ramps, and picnicking. There is a vehicle entrance fee from Memorial Day-Labor Day, daily; May and Sept-Oct, weekends and holidays. Camping is available from mid-Mar-mid-Nov at Delaware Seashore; Apr-Oct at Lums Pond, Trap Pond, and Cape Henlopen; year-round at Killens Pond. There is a two-week maximum stay at campgrounds; reservations encouraged; campsites run from $12-$26/night/site. For further information contact Department of Natural Resources and Environmental Control, Division of Parks and Recreation, 89 Kings Highway, Dover 19901; 302/739-4702.

FISHING AND HUNTING

Both fresh and saltwater fishing are excellent. The state owns, leases, or licenses 33,000 acres of game lands and fishing waters. More than 50 well-stocked state and privately owned ponds are scattered throughout the state. Many miles of ocean shoreline between Rehoboth Beach and Indian River Inlet are ideal for surf fishing. Common saltwater fish include trout, bluefish, porgie, sea bass, flounder, and croaker; freshwater fish include bass, bluegill, pickerel, crappie, perch, and trout.

An annual nonresident hunting license is $86; nonresident 3-day small game license $35; nonresident trapping license $25; additional single deer permit $10. An annual resident freshwater fishing license is $8.50; nonresident license $15; 7-day nonresident license $5.20. A license is not required for tidal saltwater fishing. For further information on fishing or hunting, contact the Department of Natural Resources and Environmental Control, Division of Fish and Wildlife, 89 Kings Highway, Dover 19901; phone 302/739-4431 or toll-free 800/523-3336.

Driving Information

Safety belts are mandatory for all persons in front seat of vehicle. Children under 4 years and 40 pounds in weight must be in approved safety seats anywhere in vehicle; children ages 4-15 must use regulation seat belts anywhere in vehicle. Phone 302/739-5938.

INTERSTATE HIGHWAY SYSTEM

The following alphabetical listing of Delaware towns in this book shows that these cities are within 10 miles of the indicated interstate highway. Check a highway map for the nearest exit.

Highway Number	Cities/Towns within 10 Miles
Interstate 95	Newark, New Castle, Wilmington.

Additional Visitor Information

Delaware Tourism Office, 99 Kings Highway, Dover 19901, will provide tourist information; phone 800/441-8846.

Visitor centers also provide information and brochures on points of interest in the state. Their locations are as follows: Delaware Memorial Bridge Plaza, junction I-295 and the bridge at New Castle; I-95 rest area, Greater Wilmington Convention and Visitors Bureau, Wilmington; Delaware State Information Center, Duke of York & Federal sts, Dover; Smyrna, 1 mile N on Hwy 13; Bethany-Fenwick Area Chamber of Commerce, Hwy 1, N of Fenwick Island.

ATLANTIC BEACHES

Graced with a beautiful 25-mile stretch of Atlantic beach, Delaware has done more than many Eastern states to preserve much of the land from excessive development. From north to south, three impressive state parks maintain the coast's natural look, and between these parks, several small resort towns retain an old-fashioned, early-20th-century flavor. The charm quotient is high and honky-tonk lures are minimal. Though most people think of the beach as a summer destination, you will find this one-day, 25-mile drive rewarding any time of the year. Indeed, many visitors, especially bird watchers and shell collectors, enjoy hiking the beaches in spring and fall when the summer sunbathers are absent. Begin in Lewes, a community that dates its founding to a Dutch whaling colony in 1631. Stroll tree-shaded 2nd Street, the main street, to browse the town's shops and view its rich architectural heritage, then drive east about a mile on Savannah Road, following the signs to 3,785-acre Cape Henlopen State Park. On your left, you will pass the dock for the Cape May-Lewes Ferry, which shuttles across Delaware Bay between Delaware and New Jersey, a 70-minute crossing. The park juts between the bay and the ocean, offering hiking and bicycling trails that meander among pine forests, salt marshes, and grass-topped dunes. Just inside the park, the Seaside Nature Center features a small aquarium displaying examples of local sea life, including the region's famed blue crabs. In mid-May, the park is a resting stop for shore birds migrating north from South America to their summer breeding grounds in the Arctic. The park enjoys a long beach of golden sand. From the parking lot, a high boardwalk crosses the dunes, leaving the cars hidden behind. Only a bath house invades the otherwise unblemished seascape. From Lewes, take Highway 9 west briefly to State Route 1 south, which parallels the coast for the length of this drive. You will detour from it only once—at Rehoboth Beach, the next stop. One of the Mid-Atlantic's most popular beach resorts, Rehoboth hasn't lost its small-town appeal. The beach is long and inviting, and at sunset, many people promenade on the boardwalk that links one end of the community to the other. In recent years, Rehoboth has blossomed into a sophisticated destination, evidenced by its numerous fine bed-and-breakfast inns; upscale restaurants; and quality shops selling designer beach attire, expensive antiques, and excellent contemporary crafts and home furnishings. But you can also find more typical beach wear and fare, such as burgers and hot dogs, on the boardwalk. There's even a small amusement arcade called Funland. South of Rehoboth on Route 1 is Dewey Beach, a much smaller resort town with a cluster of lively pubs that have a reputation of attracting a young singles crowd. To the south is 2,656-acre Delaware Seashore State Park, another natural preserve offering such traditional beach activities as swimming, surfing, fishing, picnicking, hiking, and boating on Indian River Bay. Further south is the little resort town of Bethany Beach, favored by families renting a vacation home or condominium, and beyond that is 442-acre Fenwick Island State Park, another natural area. End the tour just across the state line in sprawling Ocean City, Maryland, a bustling beach town that is the antithesis of Delaware's quieter beach experience. **(Approximately 25 miles)**

BRANDYWINE VALLEY

Cut by slender Brandywine Creek, the Brandywine Valley, just north of Wilmington, is a serene canvas of rolling hills, broad fields of corn and yellow sunflowers, rambling split-rail fences, horse pastures, ancient stone barns, and narrow country roads lined by towering old trees. Scattered within this scenic realm, one of the Mid-Atlantic's loveliest, is a wonderfully diverse collection of fine arts, history, and house museums, most of which were bequeathed by the du Pont family, the wealthy industrialists whose forebear, Pierre Samuel du Pont, arrived from France in 1800. Pierre's son, Eleuthere Irenee (E. I.) du Pont, established a black powder factory, harnessing the Brandywine for power and creating the du Pont fortune. Brandywine Creek flows southeast from Pennsylvania's Chester County through prosperous Wilmington suburbs to the Delaware River. The wealth here has earned the valley the nickname of "Chateau Country" because of its many grand homes, typically set far back from the road. For more than 30 years, an environmental organization called the Brandywine Conservancy has worked to protect the valley's open pastoral look from the threatening sprawl of both Philadelphia and Wilmington. Begin this one day, 50-mile tour into the scenic and artistic riches of the region in Wilmington. Your first stop is the Delaware Art Museum at 2301 Kentmere Parkway, which features a strong collection of American sculpture and painting, including works by Brandywine resident Andrew Wyeth. To reach the museum from downtown Wilmington, take 12th Street north to State Route 52 north. Take a right on North Bancroft to Kentmere. Founded in 1912, the museum also houses a premier collection of the works of Howard Pyle, a famous Wilmington illustrator of that era. Many of his illustrations depict pirates, witches, and other fanciful characters drawn to accompany adventure stories in magazines and books. More realistic is Pyle's 1911 portrait of General Robert E. Lee surrendering his Confederate army at Appomattox, commissioned to illustrate a piece in *Harper's Monthly Magazine*. From the museum, return to Route 52 north. Turn right at Route 141 to the Hagley Museum, which sits on the site of the first du Pont powder works, amid 230 acres of gardens and exhibits. The museum recalls industrial life in mid-19th-century America. A bit further upstream along Brandywine Creek is Eleutherian Mills, the lovely Georgian-style house E. I. du Pont built in 1803. Double back on Route 141 to Route 100 north (Montchanin Road) to the village of Montchanin. Here, 11 varied structures that served as homes for workers at the du Pont mills have been converted into a luxury retreat, the 37-room Inn at Montchanin Village. Even if you aren't a guest, stroll the block-long cobblestone main street, which is named Privy Lane for the comical row of gray concrete privies standing behind the dwellings in military precision. Today the privies, a reminder of an earlier era, store garden equipment. Consider lunch at the inn's whimsically named restaurant, Krazy Kat's, one of Brandywine's best. Continue north on Route 100 to Brandywine State Park for a chance to hike along Brandywine Creek. Stay on Route 100 north to Smiths Bridge Road, where you make a left turn. Continue west via Centerville Road to Route 52, and turn south (left). At the sign, turn left into Winterthur, a nine-story museum of American decorative arts set in the midst of 985 acres of gardens. This was the estate of Henry Francis du Pont, who collected antique furniture, porcelain, silver, rugs, and draperies crafted from 1640 to 1860. These items are organized in period rooms, including a 17th-century Lancaster, Pennsylvania, bedroom and an 18th-century Tidewater, Virginia plantation sitting room. The gardens reflect du Pont's goal of creating a masterpiece of 20th-century American naturalism. Return to Wilmington on Route 52 south. **(Approximately 50 miles)**

Bethany Beach (D-6)

See also Fenwick Island, Lewes, Rehoboth Beach

Founded 1901
Population 903
Elevation 8 ft
Area Code 302
Zip 19930
Information Bethany-Fenwick Area Chamber of Commerce, Coastal Hwy/DE 1, PO Box 1450; phone 302/539-2100 or toll-free 800/962-7873
Web site www.bethany-fenwick.org

A quiet beach town on the Atlantic Ocean, Bethany Beach was founded as a site for revival camp meetings; hence the biblical name. Surf fishing and swimming are excellent here.

What to See and Do

Holts Landing State Park. *8 miles NW via Hwy 26 and Hwy 346, N of Millville. Phone 302/539-9060. www.destateparks.com/holts/hlsp.htm.* A 203-acre park located along the Indian River Bay. Fishing, crabbing, clamming, sailing, boating (launch ramp providing access to bay); picnicking, playground, ball fields.

Special Event

Boardwalk Arts Festival. *The Boardwalk, Garfield Pkwy, Bethany Beach. Phone 302/539-2100.* Juried, original handmade works; woodcarving, photography, jewelry, batik, watercolor paintings. Early Sept.

Limited-Service Hotel

★ HOLIDAY INN EXPRESS BETHANY BEACH. *710 S Coastal Hwy, Bethany Beach (19930). Phone 302/541-9200; fax 302/541-4057. www.holiday-inn.com.* 100 rooms. Check-in 3 pm, check-out 11 am. Outdoor pool, whirlpool. **$**

Restaurants

★★ THE BIG EASY SEAFOOD AND STEAKHOUSE. *116 Market Pl, Bethany Beach (19930). Phone 302/539-7482.* Cajun/Creole menu. Lunch, dinner. Bar. Children's menu. Casual attire. Outdoor seating. **$$**

★ MANGO'S. *97 Garfield Pkwy, Bethany Beach (19930). Phone 302/537-6621. www.mangomikes.com.* Caribbean menu. Lunch, dinner. Closed Dec-Feb except Dec 31; also Mon-Thurs late Mar-May and late Sept-Nov. Bar. Children's menu. Casual attire. Outdoor seating. **$$**

Dover (B-6)

See also Odessa, Smyrna

Founded 1717
Population 32,135
Elevation 36 ft
Area Code 302
Zip 19901
Information Central Delaware Chamber of Commerce, 9 E Loockerman St, Suite 2-A, PO Box 576, 19903; phone 302/734-7513
Web site www.cdcc.net

The capital of Delaware since 1777, Dover was laid out by William Penn around the city's lovely green. For almost 200 years there were coach houses and inns on King's Road between Philadelphia and Lewes. Circling the green north and south on State Street are fine 18th- and 19th-century houses.

Today, because of Delaware's favorable corporation laws, more than 60,000 US firms pay taxes in Dover. At Dover Air Force Base, south off Rte 113, the Military Airlift Command operates one of the biggest air cargo terminals in the world, utilizing the giant C5-A Galaxy aircraft. Dover is also the home of Delaware State College, Wesley College, and the Terry campus of Delaware Technical and Community College.

What to See and Do

Delaware Agricultural Museum and Village. *866 N DuPont Hwy, Dover (Rte 13) (19901). Phone 302/734-1618. www.agriculturalmuseum.org.* Museum of farm life from early settlement to 1960. Main exhibition hall and historic structures representing a late-19th-century farming community; includes gristmill, blacksmith-wheelwright shop, farmhouse, outbuildings, one-room schoolhouse, store, and train station. Gift shop. (Tues-Sat 10 am-4 pm; Sun 1-4 pm; closed Sun in winter) **$**

Delaware Public Archives. *121 Duke Of York St, Dover (19901). Phone 302/744-5000. www.state.de.us/sos/dpa/*

collections/hours.shtml. Delaware's historical public records.(Mon-Tues, Fri-Sat 8 am-4:30 pm; Wed-Thurs 8 am-8 pm; closed Sun, holidays) **FREE**

Delaware State Museums. *316 S Governors Ave, Dover (19901). www.destatemuseums.org.* Complex of three buildings:

Delaware Archeology Museum. *Phone 302/739-3260.* (1790) Housed in an old church, exhibits devoted to archaeology. (Tues-Sat 10 am-3:30 pm; closed holidays) **FREE**

Johnson Victrola Museum. *Phone 302/739-4266.* Tribute to Eldridge Reeves Johnson, founder of the Victor Talking Machine Company. Collection of talking machines, Victrolas, early recordings, and equipment. (Tues-Sat 10 am-3:30 pm; closed holidays) **FREE**

Museum of Small Town Life. *Phone 302/739-3261.* Turn-of-the-century drugstore, printing press, pharmacy, carpenter shop, general store, post office, shoemaker's shop, and printer's shop; Johnson building. (Tues-Sat 10 am-3:30 pm; closed holidays) **FREE**

Delaware State Visitor Center. *The Green, 406 Federal St, Dover (19901). Phone 302/739-4266. www.destatemuseums.org/vc/.* Administered by the Delaware State Museums, the center offers information on attractions throughout the state. Exhibit galleries. (Mon-Sat 8:30 am-4:30 pm, Sun 1:30-4:30 pm; closed holidays) **FREE**

Dover Heritage Trail. *1071 S Governors Ave, Dover (19901). Departs from State Visitor Center. Phone 302/739-4266.* Guided walking tour of historic areas, buildings, and other attractions. (By appointment only) **$$**

John Dickinson Plantation. *340 Kitts Hummrock Rd, Dover (19901). 6 miles SE, near junction Rte 113 and Hwy 9. Phone 302/739-3277. www.destatemuseums.org/jdp.* (1740) Restored boyhood residence of Dickinson, the "penman of the Revolution." Reconstructed farm complex. (Tues-Sat; also Sun afternoons Mar-Dec) **FREE**

Killens Pond State Park. *5025 Killens Pond Rd, Felton (19901). 13 miles S via Rte 13. Phone 302/284-4526. www.destateparks.com/kpsp/kpsp.htm.* A 1,083-acre park with a 66-acre pond. Swimming pool, fishing, boating (rentals); hiking, fitness trails, game fields, picnicking, camping (hookups, dump station).

The Old State House. *The Green, 406 Federal St, Dover (19901). Phone 302/739-4266. www.destatemuseums.org/sh.* (1792) Delaware's seat of government since 1777, the State House, restored in 1976, contains a courtroom, ceremonial governor's office, legislative chambers, and county offices, including Levy Courtroom. A portrait of George Washington in the Senate Chamber was commissioned in 1802 by the legislature as a memorial to the nation's first president. Although Delaware's General Assembly moved to nearby Legislative Hall in 1934, the State House remains the state's symbolic capitol. (Tues-Sat 10 am-4:30 pm, Sun 1:30-4:30 pm; closed holidays) **FREE**

Trap Pond State Park. *Rte 24 and Trap Pond Rd, Laurel (19956). Phone 302/875-5153. www.destateparks.com/tpsp/tpsp.htm.* Boating, canoeing, fishing; hiking, biking, camping.

Special Events

Delaware State Fair. *Rtes 316 and 13, Harrington (19952). 17 miles S on Rte 13. Phone 302/398-3269. www.delawarestatefair.com.* Arts and crafts, home and trade show, carnival rides, shows; homemaking, agricultural, and livestock exhibits. Mid-July. **$**

Dover Downs. *1131 N DuPont Hwy, Dover (19901). Phone 302/674-4600; toll-free 800/711-5882. www.doverdowns.com.* Racing events include NASCAR Winston Cup auto racing (June, Sept); harness racing (mid-Nov-Apr). Call for fees and schedule.

Harrington Raceway. *Fairgrounds, 15 W Rider Rd, Harrington (19952). 17 miles S on Rte 13. Phone 302/398-RACE. www.harringtonraceway.com.* Harness racing. Betting most nights. Sept-Apr.

Old Dover Days. *Phone toll-free 800/233-5368.* Tours of historic houses and gardens not usually open to the public. Crafts exhibits, many other activities. Contact Kent County Tourism. First weekend in May.

Limited-Service Hotel

★ COMFORT INN. *222 S DuPont Hwy, Dover (19901). Phone 302/674-3300; toll-free 800/228-5150; fax 302/674-5439. www.choicehotels.com.* 94 rooms,

2 story; all suites. Complimentary continental breakfast. Check-in 2 pm, check-out noon. High-speed Internet access. Outdoor pool. **$**

Full-Service Hotel

★★★ **SHERATON DOVER HOTEL.** *1570 N Du Pont Hwy, Dover (19901). Phone 302/678-8500; toll-free 800/544-5064; fax 302/678-9073. www.sheratondover.com.* This hotel is conveniently located just minutes from shopping and local attractions in historic Dover. 152 rooms, 7 story. Check-in 3 pm, check-out noon. Restaurant, bar. Fitness room. Indoor pool, whirlpool. **$**

Restaurants

★★ **BLUE COAT INN.** *800 N State St, Dover (19901). Phone 302/674-1776; fax 302/674-1807.* Lake setting. Seafood, steak menu. Lunch, dinner. Closed Dec 25. Bar. Children's menu. Casual attire. **$$$**

★★ **VILLAGE INN.** *DE 9, Little Creek (19901). Phone 302/734-3245; fax 302/734-3238.* Lunch, dinner. Closed Dec 25. Bar. **$$**

Fenwick Island (D-6)

See also Bethany Beach, Lewes, Rehoboth Beach; also see Ocean City, MD

Population 342
Elevation 4 ft
Area Code 302
Zip 19944
Information Bethany-Fenwick Area Chamber of Commerce, Coastal Hwy/DE 1, PO Box 1450, Bethany Beach 19930; phone 302/539-2100 or toll-free 800/962-7873
Web site www.bethany-fenwick.org

Fenwick Island, at the southeast corner of Delaware, was named for Thomas Fenwick, a wealthy Virginia landowner who purchased the land in 1686. For a time, a dispute raged over whether Fenwick Island was part of Maryland or Pennsylvania. It ended in 1751 when the Transpeninsular Line placed Fenwick Island in Delaware. In 1775, James and Jacob Brasure, residents of the island, began extracting salt from the ocean and until 1825, "salt making" was big business. In the latter part of the 19th century, Fenwick Island grew as a religious-oriented summer campground. After World War I, Fenwick Island became fashionable as a summer resort.

What to See and Do

DiscoverSea Shipwreck Museum. *708 Ocean Hwy, Fenwick Island (19944). Phone 302/539-9366; toll-free 888/743-5524. www.discoversea.com.* Contains changing exhibits of shipwreck artifacts recovered on the Delmarva Peninsula. (June-Aug: daily 10 am-9 pm; Sept-May: Sat-Sun 11 am-4 pm) **FREE**

Fenwick Island Lighthouse. *142nd St and Lighthouse Ln, Fenwick Island (19970). W of town via Hwy 54. Phone 302/539-4115.* Historic 87-foot-tall lighthouse; light was first turned on Aug 1, 1859. (June-Aug, two Wed afternoons per month; also by appointment)

Fenwick Island State Park. *3 1/2 miles S of Bethany Beach on Hwy 1. Phone 302/539-9060. www.destateparks.com/fenwick/fisp.asp.* This 208-acre seashore park is located between the Atlantic Ocean and Little Assawoman Bay. Surfing, swimming, bathhouse, surf fishing, sailing (rentals).

Special Event

Surf Fishing Tournaments. *Hwy 1, North, Fenwick Island (19970). Phone 302/539-2100.* Second Sat in May and Columbus Day weekend.

Limited-Service Hotel

★ **ATLANTIC COAST INN.** *Ocean Hwy and Hwy 54, Fenwick Island (19944). Phone 302/539-7673; toll-free 800/432-8038; fax 302/539-7673. www.atlanticcoastinn.com.* 48 rooms, 2 story. Closed Nov-mid-Apr. Check-out 11 am. Outdoor pool. **$**

Restaurant

★★ **TOM & TERRY'S.** *Hwy 54 at the Bay, Fenwick Island (19944). Phone 302/436-4161; fax 302/227-7980.* Lunch, dinner. Closed Dec 25. Bar. **$$**

Fort Delaware State Park (A-5)

See also New Castle, Newark, Odessa, Wilmington

(On Pea Patch Island, opposite Delaware City)

This grim gray fort was built as a coastal defense in 1860. The fort was used as a prisoner of war depot for three years, housing up to 12,500 Confederate prisoners at a time. The damp, low-lying terrain and the poor conditions encouraged epidemics, leading to some 2,400 deaths. The fort was modernized in 1896 and remained in commission until 1943.

Restoration of the site is a continuing process. Available are overlook of heronry, picnicking, and living history programs. Museum has a scale model of the fort, model Civil War relics, and an orientation video. There are special events throughout summer and a boat trip to the island from Delaware City (mid-June-Labor Day: Wed-Sun; last weekend Apr-mid-June and Sept: Sat, Sun, and holidays). No pets. Contact the Park Superintendent, 45 Clinton St, PO Box 170, Delaware City 19706; phone 302/834-7941. Round trip **$$$**

Lewes (C-6)

See also Bethany Beach, Fenwick Island, Rehoboth Beach

Settled 1631
Population 2,932
Elevation 10 ft
Area Code 302
Zip 19958
Information Chamber of Commerce, Fisher-Martin House, 120 Kings Hwy, PO Box 1; phone 302/645-8073
Web site www.leweschamber.com

Lewes (LOO-is) has been home base to Delaware Bay pilots for 300 years. Weather-beaten, cypress-shingled houses still line the streets where pirates plundered and Captain Kidd bargained away his loot. The treacherous sandbars outside the harbor have claimed their share of ships, and stories of sunken treasures have circulated for centuries. Some buildings show scars from cannonballs that hit their mark when the British bombarded Lewes in the War of 1812. Traces of the original stockade were discovered in 1964.

What to See and Do

Cape Henlopen State Park. *42 Cape Henlopen Dr, Lewes (19958). 1 mile E of ferry terminal. Phone 302/645-8983. www.destateparks.com/chsp/chsp.htm.* More than 3,000 acres at the confluence of Delaware Bay and the Atlantic Ocean; site of decommissioned Fort Miles, part of the US coastal defense system during World War II. Supervised swimming, fishing; nature center, programs, trails, picnicking, concession, camping (water hookups, dump station).

Lewes-Cape May, NJ, Ferry. *43 Henlopen Dr, Lewes (19958). Phone 302/644-6030; toll-free 800/643-3779 (reservations). www.capemaylewesferry.com.* Sole connection between Hwy 13 (Ocean Hwy) on the Delmarva Peninsula and southern terminus of Garden State Parkway (NJ). Trip across Delaware Bay (16 miles) takes 70 minutes. (Daily; 22 crossings in summer, 10 in winter, 14-18 in spring and fall) **$$$$**

Lewes Historical Society Complex. *110 Shipcarpenter St, Lewes (19958). Shipcarpenter and Third sts. Phone 302/564-7670. www.historiclewes.org.* The restored buildings located here were moved here to create a feel for Lewes' early days. (June-Labor Day, Tues-Sat) Tickets at Rabbit's Ferry House. Walking tours and varied events take place during summer season. **$$** Buildings include

Burton-Ingram House. *Secon St, Lewes (19958). www.historiclewes.org/complex/bih.html.* (Circa 1800) Log home made from hand-hewn timbers with cypress shingles. Houses beautiful antiques.

Cannonball House & Marine Museum. *118 Front St, Lewes (19958). www.historiclewes.org/complex/cbh.html.* Built in late 18th century. Originally called the David Rowland Home, it was hit by a cannonball during the War of 1812 and was renamed.

Early Plank House. *www.historiclewes.org/complex/eph.html.* Swedish log cabin restored to reflect the home of an early settler.

Hiram R. Burton House. *Second and Shipcarpenter sts, Lewes (19958). www.historiclewes.org/complex/hrbh.html.* (Circa 1740) Houses antique furnish-

Dutch Heritage in Lewes

As an Atlantic beach destination, historic Lewes (pronounced Loo-is) is an offbeat choice, a place that recommends itself to vacationers for whom sand and sea (about a mile away) are only part of the pleasure. Dating its origins to a Dutch attempt at establishing a whaling station in 1631, it is Delaware's oldest community and enjoys a rich architectural heritage. The neighborhood adjacent to the pleasure boat harbor on the Lewes & Rehoboth Canal is dotted with beautifully restored cottages and mansions from the 18th and 19th centuries, which once housed ship's pilots working Delaware Bay. A 1-mile, one-hour stroll through the Historic District is an engaging journey into the past. Begin at the Zwaanendael Museum, a red-brick curiosity with a delightful stair-stepping gable decorated with carved stonework. Built in 1931, it was adapted from the 17th-century town hall of Hoorn in the Netherlands, from which Lewes' first colonists arrived. As the museum, which details the town's history, explains, all 28 (some sources say 32) were killed in a dispute with local Native Americans. In 1682, the area became part of an English grant to William Penn, the founder of Pennsylvania. Behind the museum, the gambrel-roofed Fisher-Martin House (1730) houses the Visitor Information Center. From the museum, head up 2nd Street, Lewes' "main street," in the shade of a canopy of giant, old trees. Take time out to nibble on an ice cream cone while resting on a park bench. At 218 2nd Street, Lewes' oldest home, the little red and yellow shingled Ryves Holt House, is believed to have been built in about 1665. Once a colonial inn, it also housed the Officer of the Port. A few steps to the right at 118 Front Street, which parallels the canal, a cannonball fired by a British vessel in the War of 1812 still juts from the brick foundation of the Cannonball House Marine Museum (1797). Inside are nautical exhibits. Many of the town's Victorian homes are richly adorned with gingerbread trim, and several are brightly painted. One of the prettiest, just off 2nd Street (double back to get here), is the Ann Eliza Baker House, a dazzler in yellow, gold, purple, and orange. This house is a fine example of Lewes' "folk Victorian" style: note the lovely flower gardens and small fountains in this neighborhood. Head north up 3rd Street to Shipcarpenter Street, where the Lewes Historical Society maintains an outdoor museum of early Delaware architecture. Several are "scooter" houses; that is, they are relocated from elsewhere—a local custom. Conclude this tour just up Shipcarpenter to the west at Shipcarpenter Square, an attractive development of restored 18th- and 19th-century scooter homes, all private residences, set around a nicely landscaped mall.

ings and an 18th-century kitchen. Also includes a reading room with materials dedicated to Delaware history.

Old Doctor's Office. *Third St, Lewes (19958). www.historiclewes.org/complex/odo.html.* (Circa 1836) Medical and Dental museum.

Rabbit's Ferry House. *Third St, Lewes (19958). www.historiclewes.org/complex/rfh.html.* (Circa 1789) An 18th-century farmhouse with original paneling and period pieces.

Thompson Country Store. *Third St, Lewes (19958). www.historiclewes.org/tcs/store.html.* (1800) Moved from original location in Tompsonville. The Thompson family ran it as a store until 1962.

Zwaanendael Museum. *102 Kings Hwy, Lewes (19958). Savannah Rd and Kings Hwy. Phone 302/645-1148. www.destatemuseums.org/zwa/zwahistory.html.* This adaptation of the Hoorn, Holland, town hall was built in 1931 as a memorial to the original Dutch founders of Lewes (1631). It highlights the town's maritime heritage with colonial, Native American, and Dutch exhibits. (Tues-Sat 10 am-4:30 pm, Sun 1:30-4:30 pm; closed holidays) **FREE**

Special Events

Coast Day. *University of Delaware Marine Studies Complex, 700 Pilottown Rd, Lewes (19958). Phone 302/831-8083. www.ocean.udel.edu/coastday/.* Facilities and research vessel open to the public; marine exhibits, research demonstrations, nautical films. First Sun in Oct.

Great Delaware Kite Festival. *Cape Henlopen State Park, 42 Henlopen Dr, Lewes (19958). Phone 302/645-8983. www.destateparks.com/chsp/chsp.htm.* Festival heralds the beginning of spring on the Fri before Easter.

Lewes Garden Tour. *Zwaanendael Park, 120 Kings Hwy, Lewes (19958). Phone 302/645-8073.* Visit the hidden gardens of Lewes. Vendors. Third Sat in June.

Full-Service Inns

★★★ INN AT CANAL SQUARE. *122 Market St, Lewes (19958). Phone 302/644-3377; toll-free 888/644-1911; fax 302/644-3565. www.theinnatcanalsquare.com.* Adjacent to the beautiful historic district, this charming bed-and-breakfast is the only waterfront inn in Lewes. 26 rooms, 4 story. Pets accepted, some restrictions. Complimentary continental breakfast. Check-in 3 pm, check-out 11 am. Restaurant. **$$**

★★★ ZWAANENDAEL INN. *142 2nd St, Lewes (19958). Phone 302/645-6466; toll-free 800/824-8754; fax 302/645-7196.* Listed in the National Historic Register, this antique-filled inn pleases guests with its charm and elegance. Guests can enjoy nearby antique shopping and beaches. 26 rooms, 4 story. Check-out 11 am. Restaurant. **$**

Restaurants

★ ASHBY'S OYSTER HOUSE. *24 Peddlers Village, Lewes (19958). Phone 302/945-4070; fax 302/945-4057.* Seafood menu. Breakfast, lunch, dinner. Closed Thanksgiving, Dec 25. Bar. Children's menu. Casual attire. **$$**

★★★ THE BUTTERY. *102 2nd St, Lewes (19958). Phone 302/645-7755; fax 302/644-4909. www.butteryrestaurant.com.* This charming restaurant, located in the restored Trader Mansion, will tempt every appetite. Guests can choose from a variety of tasty salads or entrées and will not be disappointed. Try the English bangers at Sunday brunch. French menu. Lunch, dinner, brunch. **$$$**

★ LIGHTHOUSE. *Savannah Rd at Anglers Rd, Lewes (19958). Phone 302/645-6271; fax 302/645-1608. www.lighthouselewes.com.* Seafood menu. Breakfast, lunch, dinner. Closed Thanksgiving, Dec 24-25. Bar. Children's menu. Outdoor seating. **$$**

Little Creek

(See Dover)

New Castle (A-5)

See also Fort Delaware State Park, Newark, Wilmington

Settled 1651
Population 4,862
Elevation 19 ft
Area Code 302
Zip 19720
Information Mayor and Council of New Castle, 220 Delaware St; phone 302/322-9801
Web site www.newcastlecity.net

New Castle—meeting place of the Colonial assemblies, first capital of the state, and an early center of culture and communication—was one of Delaware's first settlements. Its fine harbor made it a busy port in the 18th century until its commerce was taken over by Wilmington, which is closer to Philadelphia. Today, New Castle is a historian's and architect's delight—charming, mellow, and relaxed. Three signers of the Declaration of Independence made their homes here: George Read, Thomas McKean, and George Ross, Jr. (considered a Pennsylvanian by some). New Castle lies at the foot of the Delaware Memorial Bridge, which connects with the southern end of the New Jersey Turnpike.

What to See and Do

Amstel House Museum. *2 E 4th St, New Castle (19720). 4th St at Delaware St. Phone 302/322-2794. www.newcastlehistory.org.* (1730) Restored brick mansion of seventh governor of Delaware; an earlier structure was incorporated into the service wing. Houses colonial furnishings and arts; complete colonial kitchen. (Tues-Sat 11 am-4 pm, Sun 1-4 pm; closed holidays) Combination ticket available with Old Dutch House. **$**

George Read II House. *42 The Strand, New Castle (19720). Phone 302/322-8411.* (1804) A Federal-style house with elegant interiors: gilded fanlights, silver door hardware, carved woodwork, and relief plasterwork. It's furnished with period antiques, and the garden design dates from 1847. (Mar-Dec: Tues-Sat 10 am-4 pm, Sun noon-4 pm; Jan-Feb: Sat 10 am-4 pm, Sun noon-4 pm, weekdays by appointment) **$**

The Green. *Delaware and 3rd sts (19720).* Laid out by direction of Peter Stuyvesant, this public square of the old town is surrounded by dozens of historically important buildings. Located here

Old New Castle Court House Museum. *211 Delaware St, New Castle (19720). Phone 302/323-4453. www.destatemuseums.org/ncch/museum.html.* (1732) Original colonial capitol and oldest surviving courthouse in the state; furnishings and exhibits on display; cupola is the center of a 12-mile circle that delineates the Delaware-Pennsylvania border. (Tues-Sat 10 am-3:30 pm, Sun 1:30-4:30 pm; closed holidays) **FREE**

Old Dutch House. *32 E 3rd St, New Castle (19720). Phone 302/322-2794. www.newcastlehistory.org.* (late 17th century) Thought to be Delaware's oldest dwelling in its original form; Dutch colonial furnishings; decorative arts. (Mar-Dec, Tues-Sat 11 am-4 pm, Sun 1-4 pm; rest of year by appointment; closed holidays) Combination ticket available with Amstel House Museum. **$**

Old Library Museum. *40 E 3rd St, New Castle (19720). Phone 302/322-2794. www.newcastlehistory.org.* (1892) Unusual semioctagonal Victorian building houses temporary exhibits relating to area. (Mar-late Dec, Sat-Sun 1-4 pm) **FREE**

Special Events

Band concerts. *Battery Park, New Castle. Phone 302/328-4188.* Wed evenings, June-early Aug.

Separation Day. *Battery Park, New Castle. Phone 302/322-9802.* Observance of Delaware's declaration of independence from Great Britain. Regatta, shows, bands, concerts, fireworks. June.

Limited-Service Hotel

★ RAMADA INN NEW CASTLE - WILMINGTON. *1612 N DuPont Hwy, New Castle (19720). Phone 302/658-8511; fax 302/658-3071. www.ramada.com.* 120 rooms, 2 story. Complimentary continental breakfast. Check-in 2 pm, check-out noon. Outdoor pool. **$**

Restaurants

★★ AIR TRANSPORT COMMAND. *143 N DuPont Hwy, New Castle (19720). Phone 302/328-3527; fax 302/328-3832.* Lunch, dinner, Sun brunch. Bar. Children's menu. Reservations recommended. Outdoor seating. Replica of World War II-era Scottish farmhouse; war memorabilia. **$$**

★★ ARSENAL AT NEW CASTLE. *30 Market St, New Castle (19720). Phone 302/328-1290; fax 302/328-3106. www.arsenal1812.com.* Lunch, dinner. Closed Mon. Building constructed in 1809 by the Federal government; originally used as arsenal. **$$$**

★ SALTY SAM'S PIER 13. *130 S DuPont Hwy, New Castle (19720). Phone 302/323-1408; fax 302/323-1232.* Seafood menu. Lunch, dinner. Closed holidays. Bar. Children's menu. Casual attire. Outdoor seating. **$$**

Newark (A-5)

See also Fort Delaware State Park, Newark, Wilmington

Settled 1685
Population 28,547
Elevation 124 ft
Area Code 302
Information Greater Wilmington Convention & Visitors Bureau-Visitors Center, 100 W 10th St, Wilmington 19801; phone 302/737-4059

Newark grew up at the crossroads of two well-traveled Native American trails. The site of the only Revolutionary War battle on Delaware soil is at nearby

Cooch's Bridge, southeast of Newark. According to tradition, Betsy Ross's flag was first raised in battle at Cooch's Bridge on September 3, 1777.

What to See and Do

University of Delaware. *196 S College Ave, Newark (19716). Phone 302/831-2791. www.udel.edu.* (1743) (18,000 students) Founded as a small private academy; stately elm trees, fine lawns, and Georgian-style brick buildings adorn the central campus. Tours from Visitors Center (Mon-Fri, Sat). On campus is

> **University of Delaware Mineral Collection.** *Mineralogical Museum in Penny Hall, Academy St, Newark (19716). Phone 302/831-8242. www.udel.edu/geology/min/.* Also fossil exhibit. (Tues-Wed, Thurs noon-4 pm; Sat-Sun 1-4 pm; closed holidays) **FREE**

White Clay Creek State Park. *425 Wedgewood Rd, Newark (19711). 3 miles NW via Hwy 896. Phone 302/368-6900. www.destateparks.com/wccsp/index.asp.* A 1,483-acre day park with farmlands, forest, and streams. Fishing; nature and fitness trails, picnicking.

Limited-Service Hotels

★★ BEST WESTERN DELAWARE INN & CONFERENCE CENTER. *260 Chapman Rd, Newark (19702). Phone 302/738-3400; toll-free 800/633-3203; fax 302/738-3414. www.bestwestern.com.* 99 rooms, 2 story. Complimentary continental breakfast. Check-out noon. Restaurant, bar. Outdoor pool. **$**

★★ HOLIDAY INN. *1203 Christiana Rd, Newark (19713). Phone 302/737-2700; toll-free 800/465-4329; fax 302/737-3214. www.holiday-inn.com.* 144 rooms, 2 story. Check-in 3 pm, check-out noon. Restaurant, bar. Outdoor pool. **$**

Full-Service Hotel

★★★ HILTON WILMINGTON/CHRISTIANA. *100 Continental Dr, Newark (19713). Phone 302/454-1500; fax 302/366-0448. www.hilton.com.* 266 rooms, 4 story. Check-out 11:30 am. Restaurant, bar. Fitness room. Outdoor pool, whirlpool. Business center. **$**

Restaurant

★ KLONDIKE KATE'S. *158 E Main St, Newark (19711). Phone 302/737-6100; fax 302/737-6199. www.klondikekates.com.* American, Southwestern menu. Lunch, dinner. Closed Thanksgiving, Dec 25. Bar. Children's menu. Outdoor seating. In former courthouse/jail. **$$**

Odessa (B-5)

See also Dover, Fort Delaware State Park, New Castle, Smyrna, Wilmington

Settled 1721
Population 286
Elevation 50 ft
Area Code 302
Zip 19730

Once a prosperous grain shipping center, Odessa tried to protect its shipping trade by haughtily telling the Delaware Railroad, in 1855, to lay its tracks elsewhere. To glorify itself that same year, the town changed its name from Cantwell's Bridge to that of the Russian grain port on the Black Sea. But the sloops and schooners that transported grain eventually found less shortsighted ports of call. Odessa was an important station on the Underground Railroad for many years before the Civil War. Now it is a crossroads town at the junction of Highways 13 and 299. The town exhibits numerous fine examples of 18th- and 19th-century domestic architecture.

What to See and Do

Lums Pond State Park. *1068 Howell School Rd, Bear (19701). Approximately 3 miles W on Hwy 299 to Middletown, then 8 miles N on Hwys 301 and 71. Phone 302/368-6989. www.destateparks.com/lpsp/lpsp.asp.* More than 1,800-acre park centered around 200-acre pond. Fishing, boating (rentals); hiking and fitness trails, game courts, picnicking, camping (showers, dump station; Apr-Oct). **$$**

Rehoboth Beach (C-6)

See also Bethany Beach, Fenwick Island, Lewes

Settled 1872
Population 1,495
Elevation 16 ft
Area Code 302
Zip 19971
Information Rehoboth Beach-Dewey Beach Chamber of Commerce, 501 Rehoboth Ave, PO Box 216; phone 302/227-2233 or toll-free 800/441-1329
Web site www.beach-fun.com

The "nation's summer capital" got its nickname by being a favorite with Washington diplomats and legislators. A 2 1/2-hour drive from Washington, DC, the largest summer resort in Delaware began as a spot for camp meetings amid sweet-smelling pine groves. In the 1920s, real estate boomed, triggering Rehoboth Beach's rebirth as a resort town with a variety of accommodations, shopping areas, and eateries. Deep sea and freshwater fishing, sailing, swimming, and biking and strolling along cherry tree-lined Rehoboth Avenue have kept it a favorite retreat from Washington's summer heat.

What to See and Do

Delaware Seashore State Park. *850 Inlet Rd, Rehoboth Beach (19971). 6 miles S on Hwy 1. Phone 302/227-2800. www.destateparks.com/dssp/dssp.asp.* This 7-mile strip of land separates Rehoboth and Indian River bays from the Atlantic. Bay and ocean swimming, fishing, surfing, boating (marina, launch, rentals); picnicking, concession, primitive and improved campsites (hookups).

Special Events

Bandstand concerts. *501 Rehoboth Ave, Rehoboth Beach (19971). Phone 302/227-6181.* Open-air concerts. Sat and Sun evenings, Memorial Day-Labor Day. **FREE**

Sea Witch Halloween and Fiddlers' Festival. *501 Rehoboth Ave, Rehoboth Beach (19971). Phone 302/227-2233; toll-free 800/441-1329.* This annual festival features contests, a parade, music and food. Late Oct.

Limited-Service Hotels

★ BEST WESTERN GOLD LEAF. *1400 Hwy 1, Dewey Beach (19971). Phone 302/226-1100; toll-free 800/422-8566; fax 302/226-9785. www.bestwesterngoldleaf.com.* 75 rooms, 4 story. Complimentary continental breakfast. Check-in 3 pm, check-out 11 am. Ocean 1/2 block; swimming beach. Outdoor pool. **$$**

★ BRIGHTON SUITES HOTEL. *34 Wilmington Ave, Rehoboth Beach (19971). Phone 302/227-5780; toll-free 800/227-5788; fax 302/227-6815. www.brightonsuites.com.* 66 rooms, 4 story, all suites. Check-in 3 pm, check-out 11 am. Fitness room. Indoor pool. **$**

★ COMFORT INN. *4439 Hwy 1, Rehoboth Beach (19971). Phone 302/226-1515; fax 302/226-1550. www.comfortinnrb.com.* 97 rooms. Complimentary continental breakfast. Check-in 4 pm, check-out noon. Outdoor pool. **$**

Full-Service Hotel

★ ★ ★ BOARDWALK PLAZA HOTEL. *Olive Ave and the Boardwalk, Rehoboth Beach (19971). Phone 302/227-7169; toll-free 800/332-3224; fax 302/227-0561. www.boardwalkplaza.com.* The charm and comfort of this Victorian-style hotel on Rehoboth Beach will delight guests. Enjoy the scenic ocean views at Victoria's restaurant. 84 rooms, 4 story. Check-in 3 pm, check-out 11 am. Restaurant, bar. Fitness room. On beach; ocean swimming. Indoor pool. **$$$**

Specialty Lodgings

The following lodging establishments are approved by Mobil Travel Guide, but due to their unique and individualized nature have not been given a traditional Mobil Star rating. Included in this listing you may find bed-and-breakfasts, limited-service inns, guest ranches, and other unique hotel properties.

THE BELLMOOR INN. *6 Christian St, Rehoboth Beach (19971). Phone 302/227-5800; toll-free 800 425-2355; fax 302/227-0323. www.thebellmoor.com.* 78 rooms, 2 story. Complimentary full breakfast. Check-in 3 pm, check-out 11 am. Fitness room, spa. Two outdoor pools, whirlpool. **$$$**

CHESAPEAKE LANDING. *101 Chesapeake St, Rehoboth Beach (19971). Phone 302/227-2973; fax 302/227-2973. www.chesapeakelanding.com.* Guests will feel like they are in their own home at this cozy bed and breakfast. Enjoy lakeside paddleboating or the nearby beaches and outlet shopping. 4 rooms, 3 story. Children over 16 years only. Complimentary full breakfast. Check-in 2 pm, check-out noon. Outdoor pool. **$$**

Restaurants

★ ★ **BLUE MOON.** *35 Baltimore Ave, Rehoboth Beach (19971). Phone 302/227-6515; fax 302/227-3702. www.bluemoonrehoboth.com.* American menu. Dinner, Sun brunch. Closed three weeks in Jan. Bar. **$$$**

★ ★ ★ **CHEZ LA MER.** *210 2nd St, Rehoboth Beach (19971). Phone 302/227-6494; fax 302/227-6797. www.chezlamer.com.* Decorated French-country style, this restaurant offers a number of different settings with their own charm. French menu. Dinner. Closed Nov-Mar. Bar. Restored house with French Provinçal décor. Outdoor seating. Sun porch. **$$$**

★ **IGUANA GRILL.** *52 Baltimore Ave, Rehoboth Beach (19971). Phone 302/227-0948; fax 302/227-5967. www.iguanagrill.com.* Southwestern, American menu. Lunch, dinner. Closed Nov-first weekend of Mar. Bar. Casual attire. Outdoor seating. **$**

★ ★ **LA LA LAND.** *22 Wilmington Ave, Rehoboth Beach (19971). Phone 302/227-3887; fax 302/227-4877. www.lalalandrestaurant.com.* American menu. Dinner. Closed Dec 31-Easter; also Mon-Wed from Easter-Memorial Day and Oct-Dec 31. Bar. Casual attire. Reservations recommended. Outdoor seating. **$$**

★ ★ **LAMP POST SEAFOOD RESTAURANT.** *4534 Hwy 1, Rehoboth Beach (19971). Phone 302/645-9132; fax 302/645-9026.* Seafood, steak menu. Lunch, dinner. Closed Dec 25. Bar. Children's menu. Casual attire. **$$**

★ **RUSTY RUDDER.** *113 Dickinson St, Dewey Beach (19971). Phone 302/227-3888; fax 302/226-2402.* Seafood menu. Lunch, dinner, late-night, Sun brunch. Bar. Children's menu. Casual attire. Outdoor seating. **$$**

★ ★ **SYDNEY'S BLUES AND JAZZ RESTAURANT.** *25 Christian St, Rehoboth Beach (19971). Phone 302/227-1339; toll-free 800/808-1924; fax 302/227-1332.* Creole menu. Dinner. Closed Thanksgiving, Dec 25. Restored old schoolhouse. Bar. Reservations recommended. Outdoor seating. **$$**

★ **TIJUANA TAXI.** *207 Rehoboth Ave, Rehoboth Beach (19971). Phone 302/227-1986; fax 302/645-9427.* Mexican menu. Dinner. Closed Dec 25. Bar. Children's menu. Casual attire. **$$**

Seaford (C-5)

Restaurant

★ ★ **GEORGIA HOUSE.** *119 Main St, Millsboro (19966). Phone 302/934-6737.* American menu with Southern influences. Lunch, dinner. Closed Sun, Mon; holidays. Children's menu. Casual attire. **$$**

Smyrna (B-5)

See also Dover, Odessa

Founded 1768
Population 5,679
Elevation 36 ft
Area Code 302
Zip 19977
Information Chamber of Commerce, PO Box 576, Dover 19903; phone 302/653-9291; or visit the Smyrna Visitors Center, 5500 DuPont Hwy; phone 302/653-8910

Named in 1806 for the chief seaport of Turkish Asia Minor, Smyrna in the 1850s was an active shipping center for produce grown in central Delaware.

What to See and Do

Bombay Hook National Wildlife Refuge. *2591 Whitehall Neck Rd, Smyrna (19977). 5 miles E on Hwy 6, then 3 miles S on Hwy 9. Phone 302/653-6872. bombayhook.fws.gov.* Annual fall and spring resting and feeding spot for migratory waterfowl, including a variety of ducks and tens of thousands of snow geese and Canada geese; also home for bald eagles, shorebirds, deer, fox, and muskrat. Auto tour route (12 miles), wildlife foot trails, observation towers; visitor center offering interpretive and environmental education programs. (Spring and fall, daily, summer and winter, Mon-Fri) Golden Eagle, Golden Age, and Golden Access passports accepted (see MAKING THE MOST OF YOUR TRIP). **$$**

Smyrna Museum. *11 S Main St, Smyrna (19977). Phone 302/653-1320.* Furnishings and memorabilia from early Federal to late Victorian periods; changing exhibits. (Sat 1-4 pm) **FREE**

Restaurants

★ ★ THOMAS ENGLAND HOUSE. *1165 S DuPont Blvd (Hwy 13), Smyrna (19977). Phone 302/653-1420; fax 302/653-1352.* American menu. Dinner. Bar. Children's menu. Reservations recommended. Colonial building; housed troops during Revolutionary War; was stop on Underground Railroad. **$$$**

★ WAYSIDE INN. *103 N DuPont Hwy, Smyrna (19977). Phone 302/653-8047.* Seafood, steak menu. Lunch, dinner. Children's menu. **$$**

Wilmington (A-6)

See also Fort Delaware State Park, New Castle, Newark, Odessa; In PA, see also Chester, Kennett Square, Philadelphia

Settled 1638
Population 72,664
Elevation 120 ft
Area Code 302
Information Greater Wilmington Convention & Visitors Bureau, 100 W 10th St, 19801; phone 302/652-4088
Web site www.wilmcvb.org

Wilmington, the "chemical capital of the world," international hub of industry and shipping, is the largest city in Delaware. The Swedish, Dutch, and British have all left their marks on the city. The first settlement was made by Swedes seeking their fortunes; they founded the colony of New Sweden. In 1655, the little colony was taken without bloodshed by Dutch soldiers under Peter Stuyvesant, governor of New Amsterdam. Nine years later, the English became entrenched in the town, which grew—under the influence of wealthy Quakers—as a market and shipping center. Abundant water power in creeks of the Brandywine River Valley plus accessibility to other eastern ports stimulated early industrial growth. When Eleuthére du Pont built his powder mill on Brandywine Creek in 1802, the valley had already known a century of industry. From here come vulcanized fiber, glazed leathers, dyed cotton, rubber hose, autos, and many other products.

What to See and Do

Amtrak Station. *Martin Luther King Blvd and French St, Wilmington (19801). Phone 302/429-6530.* Restored Victorian railroad station, which continues to function as such, designed by master architect Frank Furness. (Daily)

Banning Park. *22 S Heald St, Wilmington (19801). 2 miles S on Hwy 4. Middleboro Rd and Maryland Ave. Phone 302/323-6422.* Fishing; tennis, playing fields, picnicking, and pavilions. (Daily) **FREE**

Bellevue State Park. *800 Carr Rd, Wilmington (19809). 4 miles NE via I-95, Marsh Rd exit. Phone 302/761-6963 (voice). www.destateparks.com/bvsp/bvsp.htm.* Fishing; nature, fitness, and horseback riding trails; bicycling, tennis, game courts, picnicking (pavilions).

Brandywine Creek State Park. *Rtes 92 and 100, Wilmington (19807). 4 miles N on Hwy 100. Phone 302/577-3534. www.destateparks.com/bcsp/bcsp.asp.* A 1,000-acre day-use park. Fishing; nature and fitness trails; cross-country skiing. Picnicking. Nature center. **$$**

Brandywine Springs Park. *3300 Faulkland Rd, Wilmington (19805). 4 miles W on Hwy 41. Phone 302/395-5652.* Site of a once-famous resort hotel (1827-1845) for Southern planters and politicos. Here, Lafayette met Washington under the Council Oak before the Battle of Brandywine in 1777. Picnicking, fireplaces, pavilions, baseball fields. Pets on leash only. (Daily) **FREE**

Brandywine Zoo and Park. *1001 N Park Dr, Wilmington (19802). On both sides of Brandywine River, from Augustine to Market St bridges. Phone 302/571-7788. www.brandywinezoo.org.* Designed by Frederick Law Olmsted, the park includes Josephine Garden with a fountain and roses; stands of Japanese cherry trees. The zoo, along North Park Drive, features animals from North and South America. Picnicking, playgrounds. (Daily 10 am-4 pm) **$**

Delaware Art Museum. *800 S Madison St, Wilmington (19806). Phone 302/571-9590. www.delart.org.* Expanded facility features Howard Pyle Collection of American Illustrations with works by Pyle, N. C. Wyeth, and Maxfield Parrish; American painting collection, with works by West, Homer, Church, Glackens, and Hopper; Bancroft Collection of English Pre-Raphaelite art, with works by Rossetti and Burne-Jones; and Phelps Collection of Andrew Wyeth works; also changing exhibits, children's participatory gallery; store. (Tues-Fri 10 am-4 pm, Sat 10 am-5 pm, Sun 1-5 pm; closed holidays) Guided tours by appointment. **$$**

Delaware History Museum. *504 Market St, Wilmington (19801). Phone 302/656-0637. www.hsd.org/dhm.htm.* Changing exhibits on history and decorative arts. (Mon-Fri noon-4 pm, Sat 10 am-4 pm; closed holidays) **$**

Delaware Museum of Natural History. *4840 Kennett Pike, Greenville (19807). 5 miles NW on Hwy 52. Phone 302/658-9111. www.delmnh.org.* Exhibits of shells, birds, mammals; also the largest bird egg and a 500-pound clam. (Mon-Sat 9:30 am-4:30 pm, Sun noon-4:30 pm; closed holidays) **$**

Fort Christina Monument. *Foot of E 7th St, Wilmington (19801).* Monument marks the location where Swedes settled in 1638. The monument was presented in 1938 to Wilmington by the people of Sweden. It consists of black granite plinth surmounted by pioneers' flagship, the Kalmar Nyckel, sculpted by Carl Milles. Complex includes nearby log cabin, moved to this location as a reminder of Finnish and Swedish contributions to our nation.

Grand Opera House. *818 Market St Mall, Wilmington (19801). Phone 302/658-7898. www.grandopera.org.* (1871) Historic landmark built by Masons, this restored Victorian theater now serves as Delaware's Center for the Performing Arts, home of Opera Delaware (Nov-May) and the Delaware Symphony (Sept-May). The facade is fine example of the style of the Second Empire interpreted in cast iron. **$$$$**

Hagley Museum and Library. *298 Buck Rd, Wilmington (19807). 3 miles NW off Hwy 141. Phone 302/658-2400. www.hagley.lib.de.us/museum.html.* Old riverside stone mill buildings, a one-room schoolhouse, and a millwright shop highlight 19th-century explosive manufacturing and community life; 240-acre historic site of E. I. du Pont's original black powder mills includes an exhibit building with working models and dioramas, an operating waterwheel, a stationary steam engine, and a fully operable 1875

Wilmington's Public Art

The Brandywine Valley, just outside Wilmington, is noted for its magnificent museums and gardens. What is often overlooked is the wealth of outdoor statuary in public squares and office courtyards in the historic heart of the old city. Much of it is representational, but there are abstract pieces and a whimsical work or two. Indeed, a picture book describing the collection has been published for several years. On a one-hour, 1-mile walk through the city's commercial center, you can almost imagine you are in a sculpture garden. Begin at Rodney Square outside the elegant Hotel du Pont at 11th and Market streets. Dominating the view is the famous 1923 statue of Caesar Rodney, which shows him astride his horse galloping toward Philadelphia, about 30 miles north, to cast the deciding vote for the Declaration of Independence in 1776. A city hallmark, the Rodney statue is one of the world's rare equestrian sculptures of a horse in full gallop, its two front legs in the air and the weight of the statue resting on the two rear hooves. The challenge of balancing the statue was solved in part by weighting the horse's tail. Head north on Market Street to 13th Street and two blocks west (left) to Orange Street to the Brandywine Gateway, where you'll see the intriguing kinetic fountain at the foot of the Hercules Building (facing 13th Street) in Hercules Plaza. Three solid granite balls rest on three marble pillars in the middle of a large pool. The spheres are arranged so that water flowing over them suggests they are rotating. Retrace your path to 8th and Market and then turn east (left) to Spencer and Freedom plazas between French and Market streets. In Spencer Plaza, *Father and Son*, a larger-then-life bronze statue, touchingly depicts a black man with a child in his arms. It is the work of Charles Park, a local artist. A plaque notes that this was the one-time site of the Mother African Union Methodist Protestant Church, the first black church in America wholly controlled by descendants of Africans. Just across French Street in Freedom Plaza, in the shadow of a cluster of modern municipal buildings, is an arresting statue, *The Holocaust*. Both abstract and realistic, it shows the tortured bodies of the victims pressed against three unyielding pillars, a symbol of the force of destruction. End your tour on a more positive note at the plaque honoring abolitionists Harriet Tubman and Thomas Garrett and the Underground Railroad, the road north to freedom for Southern slaves before the Civil War.

machine shop. Admission includes a bus ride along the river for a tour of 1803 Eleutherian Mills, a residence with antiques reflecting five generations of du Ponts, a 19th-century garden, and a barn with a collection of antique wagons. Museum store. (Mid-Mar-Dec: daily; rest of year: Sat-Sun, limited hours Mon-Fri; closed holidays) **$$$**

Holy Trinity (Old Swedes) Church and Hendrickson House. *606 Church St, Wilmington (19801). Phone 302/652-5629. www.oldswedes.org.* Founded by Swedish settlers in 1698, the church stands as originally built and still holds regular services. The house, a Swedish farmhouse built in 1690, is now a museum containing 17th- and 18th-century artifacts. (Mon-Sat; closed holidays) **DONATION**

Nemours Mansion and Gardens. *1600 Rockland Rd, Wilmington (19899). Rockland Rd between Hwys 141 and 202. Phone 302/651-6912; toll-free 800/651-6912. www.nemours.org/no/mansion.* Country estate (300 acres) of Alfred I. du Pont. Mansion (1910) is modified Louis XVI, by Carrère and Hastings, with 102 rooms of rare antique furniture, Asian rugs, tapestries, and paintings dating from the 12th century. Formal French gardens extend 1/3 of a mile along the main vista from the house with terraces, statuary, and pools. Tours (May-Oct: Tues-Sat 9 am, 11 am, 1 pm, 3 pm; Sun 11 am, 1 pm, 3 pm; Nov-Dec: limited basis; reservations required). Over 12 years only. **$$**

Rockwood Museum. *610 Shipley Rd, Wilmington (19809). Phone 302/761-4340.* A 19th-century Gothic Revival estate with gardens in English Romantic style. On grounds are manor house, conservatory, porter's lodge, and other outbuildings. Museum furnished with English, European, and American decorative arts of the 17th to 19th centuries. Guided tours (Mar-Dec: Tues-Sun; Jan and Feb: Tues-Sat). (See SPECIAL EVENTS) **$$**

Willingtown Square. *505 N Market St Mall, Wilmington (19801). Phone 302/655-7161.* Historic square surrounded by four 18th-century houses moved to this location between 1973 and 1976. Serves as office and conference space.

Wilmington & Western Railroad. *Greenbank Station, 2201 Newport Gap Pike, Wilmington (19808). 4 miles SW, near junction Hwys 2 and 41. Phone 302/998-1930. www.wwrr.com.* Round-trip steam-train ride (9 miles) to and from Mount Cuba picnic grove. (May-Oct, Sun; rest of year, schedule varies) **$$$**

Winterthur Museum, Garden, and Library. *Hwy 52 (Kennett Pike), Winterthur (19735). 6 miles NW on Hwy 52. Phone 302/888-4907; toll-free 800/448-3883. www.winterthur.org.* Henry Francis du Pont established this world-class antiques museum, naturalistic garden, and Americana library on a 979-acre grand country estate in the early 1950s. Inspiring period rooms showcase thousands of objects made or used in America between 1640 and 1860, ranging from historic clothing and craftsmen's tools to metalworks, ceramics, and paintings. On the grounds are rolling hills, streams, meadows, and forests and a garden that blooms from late January to November. Cooks will enjoy demonstrations of open-hearth cooking and kitchen gardening. Little ones can ride a garden tram or gently finger growing things in a fairy-tale garden or the Enchanted Woods. Walkers can stroll on gentle paths, and history buffs will enjoy African-American history presentations as well as the thousands of exquisite collectibles. (Museum and Garden Tues-Sun 10 am-5 pm; closed holidays; Library Mon-Fri 8:30 am-4:30 pm). **$$$**

Special Events

Harvest Moon Festival. *Coverdale Farm, Ashland Nature Center, 543 Way Rd, Greenville (19707). 3 miles NW via Hwy 41, at Ashland Nature Center. Phone 302/239-2334. www.delawarenaturesociety.org.* Cider-pressing demonstrations, hay rides, nature walks, farm animals, arts and crafts, musical entertainment, pony rides, and games. First weekend in Oct. **$$**

Horse racing. Delaware Park. *777 Delaware Park Blvd, Wilmington (19804). 7 miles S on I-95 exit 4B. Phone 302/994-2521. www.delpark.com.* Thoroughbred racing. Slots facility. Restaurants. Late Apr-mid-Nov.

Victorian Ice Cream Festival. *Rockwood Museum, 610 Shipley Rd, Wilmington (19809). Phone 302/761-4340.* Victorian festival featuring high-wheeled bicycles, hot-air balloons, marionettes, old-fashioned medicine show, baby parade, and crafts; homemade ice cream. Mid-July.

Wilmington Garden Day. *Phone 302/428-6172. www.gardenday.org.* Tour of famous gardens and houses. First Sat in May. **$$$$**

Winterthur Point-to-Point Races. *Hwy 52, Wilmington (19801). Phone 302/888-4600; toll-free 888/448-3883. www.thebrandywine.com/special.* An old-fashioned country horse race that features five races. The gates open at 9 am. May. **$$$$**

Limited-Service Hotels

★ BEST WESTERN BRANDYWINE VALLEY INN. *1807 Concord Pike, Wilmington (19803). Phone 302/656-9436; toll-free 800/537-7772; fax 302/656-8564. www.bestwestern.com.* 95 rooms, 2 story. Complimentary continental breakfast. Pets accepted. Check-out noon. Fitness room. Outdoor pool, children's pool, whirlpool. **$**

★★ BRANDYWINE SUITES HOTEL. *707 N King St, Wilmington (19801). Phone 302/656-9300; toll-free 800/756-0070; fax 302/656-2459.* Located in the heart of Wilmington, this small, luxurious European-style hotel offers intimate attention to visitors, and comfortable and spacious suites. 49 rooms, 4 story, all suites. Complimentary continental breakfast. Check-in 3 pm, check-out noon. Restaurant, bar. Airport transportation available. **$**

★★ COURTYARD BY MARRIOTT. *1102 West St, Wilmington (19801). Phone 302/429-7600; fax 302/429-9167. www.courtyard.com.* 126 rooms, 10 story. Check-in 3 pm, check-out noon. High-speed Internet access. Fitness room. Airport transportation available. **$$**

★★ **DOUBLETREE HOTEL.** *4727 Concord Pike, Wilmington (19803). Phone 302/478-6000; toll-free 888/478-2923; fax 302/477-1492. www.doubletree.com.* 244 rooms, 7 story. Check-in 3 pm, check-out noon. Restaurant, bar. Fitness room. Indoor pool, whirlpool. **$$**

★★ **HOLIDAY INN.** *630 Naamans Rd, Claymont (19703). Phone 302/792-2700; fax 302/798-6182. www.holiday-inn.com.* 193 rooms, 7 story. Pets accepted; fee. Check-in 3 pm, check-out noon. Restaurant, bar. Fitness room. Pool. Airport transportation available. **$**

Full-Service Hotels

★★★ **HOTEL DU PONT.** *11th and Market sts, Wilmington (19801). Phone 302/594-3100; toll-free 800/441-9019; fax 302/594-3108. www.hoteldupont.com.* The Hotel du Pont has been a Delaware institution since its opening in 1913. Constructed to rival the grand hotels of Europe, this palatial hotel carries a distinguished air. Located in downtown Wilmington, the hotel enjoys proximity to the city's attractions while remaining in the heart of the scenic Brandywine Valley, where championship golf and estate tours are *de rigueur*. Luxury is in the details here, from the ornate plasterwork to the gleaming brass. The guest rooms are classically decorated with mahogany furnishings, cream tones, and imported linens. Patrons dine on sublime French cuisine while listening to the gentle strains of a harp at the Green Room. From its coffered ceiling to its oak-paneled walls, its turn-of-the-century décor is the height of elegance. The Brandywine Room (see) offers a delightful change of pace with its inviting ambience resembling a private club and its contemporary American fare. 217 rooms, 10 story. Pets accepted, some restrictions; fee. Check-in 3 pm, check-out noon. Restaurant, bar. Fitness room. Airport transportation available. Business center. **$$**

★★★ **SHERATON SUITES WILMINGTON.** *422 Delaware Ave, Wilmington (19801). Phone 302/654-8300; fax 302/654-6036. www.sheraton.com.* 228 rooms, 16 story, all suites. Check-in 3 pm, check-out noon. High-speed Internet access. Restaurant, bar. Fitness room. Indoor pool. Airport transportation available. Business center. **$**

★★★ **WYNDHAM WILMINGTON HOTEL.** *700 King St, Wilmington (33140). Phone 302/655-0400; fax 302/655-0430. www.wyndham.com.* 219 rooms, 9 story. Check-in 3 pm, check-out noon. High-speed Internet access. Restaurant, bar. Fitness room. Indoor pool, whirlpool. Business center. **$**

Full-Service Inn

★★★ **INN AT MONTCHANIN VILLAGE.** *Rte 100 and Kirk Rd, Montchanin (19710). Phone 302/888-2133; toll-free 800/269-2473; fax 302/888-0389. www.montchanin.com.* Experience the charm of a 19th-century hamlet while staying at The Inn at Montchanin Village in Delaware's historic Brandywine Valley. Once part of the Winterthur Estate and located on the National Register of Historic Places, the inn endears itself to visitors with its white picket fence, winding walkways, and country sensibilities. This winsome inn is a perfect base for travelers perusing nearby antique stores, enjoying scenic country drives, or admiring the glorious blooms at Longwood Gardens (see Kennett Square, PA). The warm innkeepers pay meticulous attention to detail, incorporating luxurious amenities while maintaining the integrity of this quaint village. Four-poster and canopy beds set a romantic tone, while marble bathrooms add a sophisticated element to the lovely guest rooms. Gourmets cross state lines just for a meal at Krazy Kat's (see), where refined nouvelle cuisine takes on the tranquil countryside. 28 rooms, 3 story. Check-in 3 pm, check-out 11 am. Restaurant. Fitness room. **$$**

Specialty Lodgings

The following lodging establishments are approved by Mobil Travel Guide, but due to their unique and individualized nature have not been given a traditional Mobil Star rating. Included in this listing you may find bed-and-breakfasts, limited-service inns, guest ranches, and other unique hotel properties.

THE BOULEVARD BED AND BREAKFAST. *1909 Baynard Blvd, Wilmington (19802). Phone 302/656-9700; fax 302/656-9701.* This red brick bed-and-breakfast, built in 1913, provides relaxation and comfort. Wake up to a delicious breakfast that might include lemon pancakes with raspberry syrup, or enjoy mulled apple cider in the afternoon. 6 rooms, 3 story. Complimentary full breakfast. Check-in 2 pm, check-out 11 am. **$**

DARLEY MANOR INN. *3701 Philadelphia Pike, Claymont (19703). Phone 302/792-2127; toll-free 800/824-4703; fax 302/798-6143. www.darinn.com.* Visitors will appreciate this intimate bed-and-breakfast set in the quiet countryside. 6 rooms, 3 story. Children over 6 years only. Complimentary full breakfast. Check-in 4 pm, check-out noon. Fitness room. Whirlpool. **$**

Restaurants

★ ★ BACK BURNER. *425 Hockessin Corner, Hockessin (19707). Phone 302/239-2314; fax 302/234-3212. www.backburner.com.* Enjoy intimate conversation at this darkly lit restaurant converted from an old barn. Lunch, dinner. Closed Sun; Jan 1, Dec 25. Bar. Eleegant dining in a country atmosphere; renovated barn with arched walls and a display kitchen. Reservations recommended. **$$**

★ ★ ★ COLUMBUS INN. *2216 Pennsylvania Ave, Wilmington (19806). Phone 302/571-1492; fax 302/571-1111. www.columbusinn.com.* This charming restaurant attracts an eclectic crowd with cuisine that has a flavorful twist. American menu. Lunch, dinner. Closed Memorial Day, Labor Day, Dec 25. Bar. Children's menu. Casual attire. Valet parking. Outdoor seating. **$$$**

★ ★ ★ GREEN ROOM. *11th and Market sts, Wilmington (19801). Phone 302/594-3154; toll-free 800/441-9019; fax 302/594-3070. www.hoteldupont.com.* The menu offers a variety of selections with a continental flair. French menu. Breakfast, lunch, dinner, Sun brunch. Bar. Children's menu. Jacket required (dinner). Valet parking. **$$$**

★ ★ ★ HARRY'S SAVOY GRILL. *2020 Naaman's Rd, Wilmington (19810). Phone 302/475-3000; fax 302/475-9990. www.harrys-savoy.com.* American, seafood, steak menu. Lunch, dinner, late-night, Sun brunch. Closed Dec 25. Bar. Children's menu. Outdoor seating. **$$**

★ KID SHELLEENS. *1801 W 14th St, Wilmington (19806). Phone 302/658-4600; fax 302/658-7910. www.kidshelleens.com.* American menu. Lunch, dinner. Closed Thanksgiving, Dec 25. Bar. Children's menu. Casual attire. Outdoor seating. **$$**

★ ★ ★ KRAZY KAT'S. *Rte 100 and Kirk Rd, Montchanin (19710). Phone 302/888-2133; toll-free 800/269-2473; fax 302/888-0389. www.montchanin.com.* Serving bold yet refined French-Asian cuisine, Krazy Kat's is set in a romantic 19th-century blacksmith's shop neighboring the charming and historic Inn at Montchanin Village (see). With its wild, whimsical animal-themed décor (the seats are covered in plush zebra and leopard prints), you may not know what to expect. The kitchen's inventive menu includes signatures like grilled wild boar tenderloin satay with ginger jus, sesame-roasted fingerling potatoes, and red cabbage daikon slaw—a robust warmer for a cold winter's night. The wine list is extensive and spans the globe, from America's Northwest to Italy, France, Australia, and New Zealand. Breakfast, lunch, dinner. Jacket required. Outdoor seating. **$$$**

★ ★ ★ RESTAURANT 821. *821 Market St, Wilmington (19801). Phone 302/652-8821; fax 302/652-4481. www.restaurant821.com.* Located directly across from Wilmington's historic opera house, this is the perfect spot for taking in dinner before or after a show. The atmosphere is sophisticated, and the American menu with international accents includes many excellent choices. American menu. Lunch, dinner. Closed Sun. **$$$**

★ ★ TOSCANA KITCHEN AND BAR. *1412 N DuPont St, Wilmington (19806). Phone 302/654-8001; fax 302/655-8090. www.toscanakitchen.com.* This restaurant is a favorite for private and intimate parties. Italian menu. Dinner. Closed holidays. Bar. Casual attire. Reservations recommended. **$$**

★★★ **VINCENTE'S.** *1601 Concord Pike, Wilmington (19803). Phone 302/652-5142; fax 302/652-0514.* With a variety of creative menu items, this upscale but casual restaurant is always superb, and diners will leave with a happy palate. French, Italian menu. Lunch, dinner. Closed Sun; holidays. Bar. Children's menu. Casual attire. Reservations recommended. **$$$**

★★★ **ZANZIBAR BLUE.** *1000 West St, Wilmington (19801). Phone 302/472-7000; fax 302/472-7002. www.zanzibarblue.com.* Eclectic menu. Lunch, dinner, Sun brunch. Bar. **$$$**

Maryland

Maryland prides itself on its varied terrain and diverse economy. Metropolitan life around the great cities of Baltimore and Washington, DC (the land was ceded from Maryland in 1791) is balanced by the rural atmosphere in central and southern Maryland and on the Eastern Shore, across the Chesapeake Bay. Green mountains in the western counties contrast with white Atlantic beaches. A flourishing travel industry, agricultural and dairy wealth in central Maryland, the seafood industry of the Bay and its tidal rivers, manufacturing and commerce in the cities, plus federal government and defense contracts combine to make the state prosperous.

Population: 5,296,486
Area: 9,838 square miles
Elevation: 0-3,360 feet
Peak: Backbone Mountain (Garrett County)
Entered Union: Seventh of original 13 states (April 28, 1788)
Capital: Annapolis
Motto: Manly Deeds, Womanly Words
Nickname: Old Line State, Free State
Flower: Black-Eyed Susan
Bird: Baltimore Oriole
Tree: White Oak
Fair: Late August-early September in Timonium (see Towson)
Time Zone: Eastern
Web site: www.mdisfun.org

Maryland's three-and-one-half centuries of history began in March 1634 when Lord Baltimore's brother, Leonard Calvert, solemnly knelt on tiny St. Clements Island, near the wide mouth of the Potomac, and named his new province in honor of Henrietta Maria, wife of Charles I, King of England. Calvert's awkward little ships, the *Ark* and the *Dove*, then carried the 222 passengers, including religious refugees, to a Native American village a few miles away. They purchased the village and named it "Saint Maries Citty" (now St. Mary's City). Religious tolerance was practiced from the colony's founding and was assured by law in 1649. The land was cleared, tobacco was planted, and over the years, profits built elegant mansions, many of which still stand.

Maryland was one of the 13 original colonies. Its first capital was St. Mary's City. In 1694, the capital was transferred to Annapolis, where it remains today.

Every war waged on US soil has seen major action by Marylanders. In 1755, British General Edward Braddock, assisted by Lieutenant Colonel George Washington, trained his army at Cumberland for the fight against the French and Indians. In the Revolution, General William Howe invaded Maryland at the head of Chesapeake Bay, and a battle was joined at Brandywine Creek in Pennsylvania before the British moved on to capture Philadelphia. Maryland troops in the Battle of Long Island made a heroic bayonet coverage of the retreat. The courageous action of the "Old Line" gave the state one of its nicknames. The War of 1812 saw Fort McHenry at Baltimore withstand attack by land and sea, with the action immortalized in the national anthem by Francis Scott Key, a Frederick lawyer. In the Civil War, Maryland was a major battleground at Antietam; troops moved back and forth through the state for the four bloody years of destruction.

A border state with commercial characteristics of both North and South, Maryland found its original dependence on tobacco relieved by the emerging Industrial Revolution. Modern factories, mills, and ironworks around Baltimore became important to the state's economy. Educational institutions were established and the port of Baltimore, at the mouth of the Patapsco River, flourished. In the mid-19th

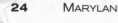

Calendar Highlights

February

National Outdoor Show *(Cambridge). Phone 800/522-TOUR.* Goose and duck calling, log sawing, crab picking, and trap setting contests; entertainment.

April

Point-to-Point Steeplechase *(Cockeysville). Phone 410/557-9466.* Three well-known meets on consecutive weekends—My Lady's Manor, Grand National, and Maryland Hunt Cup.

May

Maryland Preakness Celebration *(Baltimore). Phone 410/837-3030.* Statewide festival; events include a hot-air balloon festival, parade, steeplechase, celebrity golf tournament, block parties, and schooner race.

Mid-Atlantic Maritime Festival *(St. Michaels). Chesapeake Bay Maritime Museum. Phone 410/745-2916.* Nautical celebration with fly-fishing demonstration, skipjack races, boat building contest, boat parade, seafood festival, and cooking contest.

August

Montgomery County Agricultural Fair *(Gaithersburg). Phone 301/926-3100.* One of the East Coast's leading county fairs; emphasis on agriculture, 4-H activities; animal exhibits, home arts; antique farm equipment; tractor pull, horse pull, demolition derby; rodeo; entertainment.

State Fair *(Towson). Timonium Fairgrounds. Phone 410/252-0200.* Ten-day festival of home arts; entertainment, midway; agricultural demonstrations, thoroughbred horse racing, livestock presentations.

September

New Market Days *(Frederick). In New Market. Phone 301/831-6755.* Nostalgic revival of the atmosphere of a 19th-century village; costumed guides, period crafts, and events held in the "Antiques Capital of Maryland."

October

Autumn Glory Festival *(Oakland). Phone 301/387-4386.* Celebrates fall foliage. Features arts and crafts, five-string banjo contest, state fiddle contest, western Maryland tournament of bands, parades, and antique show.

St. Mary's County Oyster Festival *(Leonardtown). County Fairgrounds. Phone 301/863-5015.* National oyster shucking contests; oyster cook-off, seafood and crafts.

November

Annapolis by Candlelight *(Annapolis). For information, contact Historic Annapolis Foundation, phone 800/603-4020.*

century, with the Baltimore & Ohio Railroad and the Chesapeake & Ohio Canal carrying freight to the fast-developing western states, Maryland thrived.

Sports enthusiasts have always thought well of Maryland. The state's thousands of miles of tidal shoreline allow plenty of elbow room for aquatic diversion. Maryland's race tracks include Pimlico (see BALTIMORE), featuring the nationally known Preakness Stakes, and Laurel. The "Maryland Million" is held alternately at Laurel and Pimlico. Deer hunting is allowed in most counties and goose hunting on the Eastern Shore. Historical sites cover the landscape, and more are constantly being opened up to the public by the state and National Park Service. Highways are good; reaching places in the Baltimore-Washington, DC, area is simplified by direct, high-speed, four-lane highways constructed around, between, and radiating from these cities.

When to Go/Climate

Spring and autumn are popular times to visit Maryland. Winter weather is unpredictable and summers can be hot and humid.

AVERAGE HIGH/LOW TEMPERATURES (° F)

Baltimore

Jan 40/23	**May** 74/53	**Sept** 79/58
Feb 44/26	**June** 83/62	**Oct** 67/46
Mar 54/34	**July** 87/67	**Nov** 57/37
Apr 64/43	**Aug** 85/66	**Dec** 42/28

Parks and Recreation

Water-related activities, hiking, riding, various other sports, picnicking and visitor centers, as well as camping, are available in many of Maryland's parks. Most state-maintained areas have small charges for parking and special services. Camping: $2-$22/site/night; stays limited to two weeks; most areas are open late March-early December, but the season varies from one park to the next; check-out is 3 pm; reservations for a stay of one week are available at Assateague—they may be obtained by writing directly to the park. Pets are allowed at the following parks (some special restrictions may apply; phone ahead): Green Ridge Forest, Elk Neck, Patapsco (Hollofield), Point Lookout, Rocky Gap, Savage River Forest, Susquehanna, Swallow Falls, Garrett Forest, Potomac Forest, and Pocomoke River (Milburn Landing). Day use: 8 am-sunset; closed Dec 25; fee Mar-Oct. For complete information, including information on cabins, contact the Maryland Department of Natural Resources, State Forest and Park Service, Tawes State Office Building E-3, 580 Taylor Ave, Annapolis 21401; phone toll-free 888/432-2267 or 800/830-3974. It is advisable to call parks before visiting, as some may be closed during the off-season.

FISHING AND HUNTING

Nontidal, nonresident fishing license, $20; five-day, $7; trout stamp, $5. Chesapeake Bay nonresident fishing license, $12; five-day, $4.

Nonresident hunting licenses: consolidated, $86-$135, depending on state of residence; three-day, $35; waterfowl stamp $6; regular deer stamp, $9.50; bow hunting deer stamp, $3.50; black powder deer stamp, $3.50; second deer stamp, $10. For the latest information, including Maryland Sportfishing Guide or the Guide to Hunting, Trapping in Maryland, contact Maryland Department of Natural Resources, Licensing & Registration Service, 580 Taylor Ave B-1, Annapolis 21404-1869; phone 410/260-8200.

Driving Information

Safety belts are mandatory for the driver and passengers in the front seat of a vehicle. Any child 10 years and under must be in approved passenger restraints anywhere in a vehicle. Any child under 4 years or weighing 40 pounds or less must be in an approved safety seat. For more information, phone 410/486-3101.

INTERSTATE HIGHWAY SYSTEM

The following alphabetical listing of Maryland towns shows that these cities are within 10 miles of the indicated interstate highways. Check a highway map for the nearest exit.

Highway Number	Cities/Towns within 10 Miles
Interstate 68	Cumberland.
Interstate 70	Baltimore, Columbia, Ellicott City, Frederick, Hagerstown.
Interstate 81	Hagerstown.
Interstate 83	Baltimore, Cockeysville, Towson.
Interstate 95	Aberdeen, Baltimore, College Park, Elkton, Havre de Grace, Laurel, Silver Springs, Towson.

Additional Visitor Information

The Maryland guide to travel, *Destination Maryland*, and a calendar of events can be obtained from the Maryland Office of Tourism Development, 217 E Redwood St, Baltimore 21202; phone 800/543-1036.

There are several visitor information centers in Maryland; visitors who stop by will find information and brochures helpful in planning stops at points of interest. Their locations are as follows: on I-95 (N and S) near Laurel; on I-70 (E and W) between Hagerstown and Frederick; on Hwy 15 S at Emmitsburg; on I-95 S near North East; on Hwy 48 E near Friendsville; on Hwy 13 N near Maryland-Virginia line; in the State House, Annapolis; Crain memorial, on Hwy 301 N, Newburg; and in Bay Country, on Hwy 301 N/S, Centreville. (Daily; closed holidays)

DEEP CREEK LAKE, MARYLAND'S WESTERN PLAYGROUND

Out in western Maryland's Garrett County, the local folks like to call massive Deep Creek Lake the state's "hidden secret." But the secret is getting out, and the massive lake has become the centerpiece for a wealth of vigorous outdoor adventures: water skiing, whitewater rafting, hiking, back-road bicycling, kayaking, fly-fishing, canoeing, sailing, and swimming. On a drive around the lake, you can partake in as many activities as you choose—outfitters are on hand to rent all the necessary equipment—or simply enjoy the sublime mountain views. Maryland's largest freshwater lake, Deep Creek, is 12 miles long, but so etched with fingerlike coves that the shoreline stretches for 65 miles. Surrounded by the forested ridges and splashing streams of mountain wilderness, the lake, at an altitude of 2,300 feet, treats summer visitors to a cooling respite from the city. Begin this two-day, 400-mile drive in Baltimore and head west on I-70 and I-68 to exit 14 at Keysers Ridge. Take Highway 219 south to the Visitor Center, which is on the right just outside the village of McHenry. Plan to spend the night in one of McHenry's inns, hotels, or motels. The trip from Baltimore to McHenry is about 180 miles, a scenic ride that carries you across a series of green mountain ridges. To break up the trip, pull off I-68 at Cumberland, immediately recognizable by the castle-like spires and turrets of its courthouse and churches. George Washington is said to have assumed his first military command at Fort Cumberland, and his one-room log cabin and remnants of the fort can still be seen here. Cumberland is the terminus of the Chesapeake and Ohio Canal, which originates in Washington, DC, and you can rent a bicycle and ride along the tow path for miles. At Deep Creek Lake, follow the signs to Deep Creek Lake State Park, which maintains a nice 700-foot-long sandy swimming beach, a lovely place to relax after the trip from the city. The Discovery Center, an attractive structure of stone, wood, and soaring windows, features displays about the region's natural history and mining heritage. Ranger talks, walks, and canoe trips are offered. On the second day of your trip, take Highway 219 south from McHenry to the turn-off to Swallow Falls State Park. For an easy hike, follow the 1 1/2-mile path that scrambles in a loop past four waterfalls. At the trail head, the park has preserved a 37-acre stand of virgin hemlock and white pine estimated to be 300 years old. After 1/4 mile, Muddy Creek Falls—the state's highest at 52 feet—cascades down a staircase of rocks into a large pool. You are welcome to splash in the many pools along this trail. Next, follow signs south to the town of Oakland and then begin your scenic return to Baltimore via Route 135 northeast to Highway 220 north to I-68 east. Just beyond Bloomington on Route 135, make a detour left on Savage River Road. For about 5 1/2 miles along this road, the Savage River splashes. So narrow, mean, and harrowing is the course, say local tourism officials, that it was picked as the site of the 1989 Whitewater World Championships and the 1992 US Canoe & Kayak Team Olympic Trails. A couple of suspension bridges built for the events still leap the river. While here, imagine yourself trying to negotiate a kayak through the frenzied chaos of water and rocks. Retrace your path to Route 135 northeast. About 10 miles east of Cumberland, take a break at Rocky Gap State Park, two minutes off the interstate, which tempts with a couple of fine sandy beaches in a forested mountain setting. **(Approximately 400 miles)**

EASTERN SHORE OF THE CHESAPEAKE BAY

North America's largest estuary, the Chesapeake Bay commands more than 4,500 miles of shoreline, much of it in Maryland. A vast sea known for its rich history and savory shellfish, it is one of the Mid-Atlantic's most popular destinations. Inviting inns, other lodgings, and fine seafood restaurants are plentiful on Maryland's Eastern Shore. A two-day driving tour covering about 250 miles makes a fine introduction to the bay and to the watermen and their families who harvest the seafood that appears on every menu. Begin your drive in Annapolis, Maryland's beautiful old capital, which doubles as the bay's sailing headquarters. In summer, catch the regular Wednesday evening races, when as many as 100 boats may compete. The finish is easily visible from City Dock at the foot of the city's colonial-era streets. From Annapolis, take Highway 50 east across the soaring Chesapeake Bay Bridge. Just before you reach the bridge, a five-minute detour leads to Sandy Point State Park, the only stop on this drive where you can take a dip in the bay. At the eastern end of the bridge, turn north onto Highway 301 to Route 213 north to Chestertown. Founded in 1706, Chestertown is a pretty village with a collection of 18th- and 19th-century homes, several of them situated along the scenic Chester River. After browsing in the shops of High and Cross streets, take Route 20 west to Rock Hall, a sailing and charter fishing port. Retrace your path to Chestertown, and take Route 213 south to Highway 50 south. In Easton, take Route 33 west to the historic sailing port of St. Michaels, an inviting place to spend the night. One of the Mid-Atlantic's prettiest little towns, its lovely inns, fine restaurants, offbeat shops on Talbot Street, and expansive bay views are irresistible. So, too, are the charming little back streets, lined with lovely homes dating back to the 18th and 19th centuries. Your first stop should be the Chesapeake Bay Maritime Museum, which focuses on the Chesapeake. The museum's 18-acre harbor site features more than a dozen historic structures, including a fully restored 1879 lighthouse complete with flashing light. Stop by Waterman's Wharf, where you can try your skill at crab fishing. The Waterfowling Building displays beautifully carved duck decoys. Boat builders are often at work restoring historic bay work boats for the museum's large collection. The *Patriot*, a cruise ship departing from the museum's dock, takes visitors on a 60-minute tour up the Miles River, a bay tributary. From St. Michaels, follow Route 33 to its end at Tilghman Island, a charter fishing port. Plan on having lunch at one of its waterside seafood houses. On the return trip to St. Michaels, stop about 3 miles east of the city and take the road south (right) to Bellevue. There you can catch the little Bellevue-Oxford Ferry for a ten-minute ride across the Tred Avon River to Oxford, a sleepy pleasure boat port dating back to 1694. To stretch your legs, take a walk along the Strand, a lovely river promenade, or rent a bicycle and pedal among the quiet streets. From Oxford, return to Annapolis via Route 333 and Highway 50, stopping briefly in Easton to admire its attractive, colonial-looking town center and to investigate its engaging shops and galleries. **(Approximately 250 miles)**

Aberdeen (A-5)

Population 13,842
Elevation 83 ft
Area Code 410
Zip 21001

This is the home of the 75,000-acre Aberdeen Proving Grounds, a federal reservation along Chesapeake Bay. Various types of army materiel, ranging from gunsights to tanks, are tested under simulated combat conditions.

What to See and Do

PECO Energy Company. *4948 Conowingo Rd, Aberdeen (21034). 7 miles NE on Hwy 40 or I-95, then 11 miles NW on Hwy 222 to Conowingo. Phone 410/457-5011.* Hydroelectric plant on the Susquehanna River. Limited area of plant is open for guided tours (Apr-Sept: Sat; rest of year: by appointment; closed holidays). Contact the Conowingo Information Center. **FREE** Nearby is

Recreation area. *Phone 410/457-5011.* Fourteen-mile-long man-made lake; swimming pool (fee), boating (ramps, marinas), fishing; fishermen's gallery (over 12 years only); picnicking, hiking. **FREE**

US Army Ordnance Museum. *2601 Maryland Blvd, Aberdeen (21005). At Aberdeen Proving Ground, off I-95, exit 85, 3 miles E on Hwy 22, follow signs. Phone 410/278-3602. www.goordnance.apg.army.mil/odmuseum.htm.* Tanks, artillery, self-propelled artillery, extensive small arms, and an ammunition collection. Obtain a day pass at the Maryland Boulevard gate. (Daily 9 am-4:45 pm; closed holidays) **FREE**

Limited-Service Hotel

★ ★ HOLIDAY INN. *1007 Beards Hill Rd, Aberdeen (21001). Phone 410/272-8100; toll-free 800/465-4329; fax 410/272-1714. www.holiday-inn.com/aberdeenmd.* 122 rooms, 5 story. Pets accepted. Check-in 2 pm, check-out noon. Restaurant, bar. Fitness room. Indoor pool, whirlpool. **$**

Annapolis (C-4)

See also Baltimore, Baltimore/Washington International Airport Area

Founded 1649
Population 35,838
Elevation 57 ft
Area Code 410 and 443
Information Annapolis and Anne Arundel County Conference and Visitors Bureau, 26 West St, 21401; phone 410/268-TOUR. Information is also available at the Visitor Information Booth located at the city dock.
Web site www.visit-annapolis.org

The capital of Maryland, gracious and dignified in the colonial tradition, Annapolis has had a rich history for more than 300 years. Planned and laid out as the provincial capital in 1695, it was the first peacetime capital of the United States (Congress met here November 26, 1783 to August 13, 1784). In 1845, the US Naval Academy was established here at the Army's Fort Severn. Town life centers on sport and commercial water-oriented activities, state government, and the academy. Every May, at commencement time, thousands of visitors throng the narrow brick streets.

Annapolis Fun Fact

The United States Naval Academy was founded on October 10, 1845, at Annapolis.

What to See and Do

Boat Trips. *980 Awald Rd, #202, Annapolis (21403). From city dock at foot of Main St. Phone 410/268-7600 (Baltimore).* Forty-minute narrated tours of city harbor, USNA, and Severn River aboard *Harbor Queen* (Memorial Day-Labor Day, daily); 90-minute cruises to locations aboard *Annapolitan II* and *Rebecca*, cruises to St. Michael's aboard the *Annapolitan II* (Memorial Day-Labor Day); 40-minute cruises up Spa Creek, residential areas, city harbor, and USNA aboard the *Miss Anne* and *Miss Anne II* (Memorial Day-Labor Day). Some cruises early spring and late fall, weather permitting. Fees vary.

Chesapeake Bay Bridge. *357 Pier 1 Rd, Annapolis (21666).* The 7 1/4-mile link of Hwy 50 across the Bay. Toll (charged eastbound only) **$$**

History and Government in Annapolis

In the years just prior to the American Revolution, the colonial elite flocked to the bustling seaport of Annapolis, Maryland's capital on the Chesapeake Bay. This was the city's "golden age," and many, George Washington among them, were drawn by its spirited social life and elegant mansions built by wealthy tobacco planters. You can see some of the same sights Washington might have enjoyed on a one-hour, one-mile stroll through the city's well-preserved Historic District. Begin at the Visitor Center, 26 West Street, where tourist parking is available. From the center head east (left) on West Street; detour around St. Anne's Church (1859), noting its Tiffany windows; pause on School Street to view Government House, the Georgian-style Maryland Governor's residence (remodeled 1936); and then climb the stairs, as Washington surely did, to the Maryland State House on State Circle (1772), the oldest state capitol in continuous legislative use. Perched atop the city's highest hill, the State House provides a panoramic view of the bay. Inside, the Old Senate Chamber appears as it did on December 23, 1783, when Washington resigned his commission as the victorious commander of the Continental Army. At 21 State Circle, the John Shaw House (1720s) was the home of the city's premier cabinet maker, whose furniture is displayed in the State House. Continue east from State Circle on Maryland Avenue, lined with antique shops, to the Hammond-Harwood Home (1774) at No. 19. A house museum, this Georgian structure features what is considered by many to be the most beautiful doorway in America. Double back one block on Maryland Avenue, pausing briefly at the Chase-Lloyd House (1769), another elegant Georgian mansion where Francis Scott Key, author of "The Star-Spangled Banner," was married in 1802. Turn toward the harbor (left) onto Prince George Street. The William Paca House (1765) at No. 186 and its 2-acre colonial garden, carefully restored for authenticity, are national treasures. Now a house museum, the Paca house was the home of Maryland's Revolutionary War governor and a signer of the Declaration of Independence. Built in the symmetrical five-part structure of the city's finest colonial homes, it is considered one of the best examples of a Georgian home in America. Neighboring Brice House (1767) at 42 East Street is another magnificent Georgian mansion built by a wealthy merchant. To conclude this tour, continue downhill on Prince George Street, and turn west (right) one block onto Randall Street to City Dark for refreshments at Middleton Tavern. Once an "Inn for Seafaring Men," it has been serving Annapolis visitors since 1754.

Chesapeake Sailing School. *7074 Bembe Beach Rd, Annapolis (21403). Phone 410/269-1594; toll-free 800/966-0032. www.sailingclasses.com.* There's nothing like sun, water, and a stiff breeze for shaking off doldrums. This school offers everything from weekend sailing classes for beginners (no experience necessary) to live-aboard five-day cruises on gorgeous Chesapeake Bay, with basic and advanced instruction for individuals, families, and corporate groups. Depending on the class, you might cast off in a zippy 22-foot Tanzer or a state-of-the-art catamaran. You can also rent sailboats and go out on your own. (Apr-Oct) **$$$$**

Government House. *Between State and Church cirs. Phone 410/974-3531. www.mdarchives.state.md.us/msa/homepage/html/govhouse.html.* (1868) This Victorian structure was remodeled in 1935 into a Georgian country house; furnishings reflect Maryland's history and culture. Tours by appointment (Mon, Wed, Fri 10:30 am-2:30 pm). **FREE**

Hammond-Harwood House. *19 Maryland Ave, Annapolis (21401). At King George St, one block W of US Naval Academy. Phone 410/269-1714. www.hammondharwoodhouse.org.* (1774) Georgian house designed by William Buckland; antique furnishings; garden. Matthias Hammond, a Revolutionary patriot, was its first owner. Guided tours. (Daily; closed Jan 1, Thanksgiving, Dec 25) **$$**

Historic Annapolis Foundation. *18 Pinkney St, Annapolis (21401). Tours leave from museum store. Phone 410/267-7619; toll-free 800/603-4020; fax 410/267-6189. www.annapolis.org.* Self-guided audiocassette walking tours. Includes Historic District, State House, Old Treasury, US Naval Academy, and William Paca House. (Mar-Nov, daily) **$$**

William Paca House. *186 Prince George St, Annapolis (21401). Phone 410/263-5553.* Paca built this five-part Georgian mansion in 1765. (Mon-Sat, also Sun afternoons; closed Thanksgiving, Dec 25) **$$**

William Paca Garden. Restored 2-acre pleasure garden originally developed in 1765 by William Paca, a signer of the Declaration of Independence and governor of Maryland during the Revolutionary War. Includes waterways, formal parterres, and a garden wilderness. (Mon-Sat, also Sun afternoons; closed Thanksgiving, Dec 25) **$$** Also here is

Historic Annapolis Foundation Welcome Center and Museum Store. *77 Main St, Annapolis (21401). Phone 410/268-5576; toll-free 800/639-9153. www.hafmuseumstore.com.* This 1815 building stands on the site of a storehouse for Revolutionary War troops that burned in 1790. Audiocassette walking tours. Products reflecting Annapolis history. (Mon-Thurs 10 am-6 pm, Fri-Sat 10 am-9 pm, Sun 10 am-6 pm; closed Thanksgiving, Dec 25)

London Town. *839 Londontown Rd, Edgewater (21037). 8 miles SE via MD 2 S (Mayo Rd). Phone 410/222-1919. www.historiclondontown.com.* (Circa 1760) Once considered a site for Maryland's capital; the only surviving structure of the Lost Town is the William Brown House, a Georgian mansion on the banks of South River. Has 8 acres of woodland gardens. Museum and garden shop; boat docking. Special events. Guided tours. (Tues-Sat 10 am-3 pm, Sun noon-3 pm; William Brown House closed Jan-Mar) **$$**

Sailing Tours. *80 Compromise St, Annapolis (21401). Phone 410/263-8619. www.schooner-woodwind.com.* Two-hour narrated trips through Chesapeake Bay aboard 74-foot sailing yacht *Woodwind.* (May-Sept: Tues-Sun four trips daily, Mon Sunset Sail only; Apr, Oct, Nov: schedule varies) Departs from Pusser's Landing Restaurant at the Annapolis Marriott Waterfront Hotel. **$$$$**

Sandy Point State Park. *1100 E College Pkwy, Annapolis (21401). 7 miles E on Hwy 50, at W end of Chesapeake Bay Bridge. Phone 410/974-2149; toll-free 888/432-2267. www.dnr.state.md.us/publiclands/southern/sandypoint.html.* On 786 acres. The park's location on the Atlantic Flyway makes it a fine area for bird-watching; view of Bay Bridge and oceangoing vessels. Swimming in the bay at two guarded beaches, two bathhouses, surf fishing, crabbing, boating (rentals, launches); concession. (See SPECIAL EVENTS) (Daily hours vary; call for schedule)

St. John's College. *60 College Ave, Annapolis (21401). Phone 410/263-2371; toll-free 800/727-9238. www.sjca.edu/main.html.* (1784) (475 students) Nonsectarian liberal arts college. This 36-acre campus, one of the oldest in the country, is a National Historic Landmark. The college succeeded King William's School, founded in 1696. George Washington's two nephews and step-grandson studied here; Francis Scott Key was an alumnus. On campus are

Charles Carroll, Barrister House. *107 Duke of Gloucester St, Annapolis (21401). Phone 410/269-1737. www.sjca.edu/college/tour/carrbarr.phtml.* (1722) Birthplace of the author of the Maryland Bill of Rights; moved in 1955 to the campus and restored; now an administration building. Not open to the public.

Elizabeth Myers Mitchell Art Gallery. *Mellon Hall, 60 College Ave, Annapolis (21401). Phone 410/626-2556. www.sjca.edu/college/tour/mitchell.phtml.* Displays museum-quality traveling exhibitions. (Academic year, Tues-Sun noon-5 pm, Fri 7-8 pm) **FREE**

McDowell Hall. *60 College Ave, Annapolis (21401). www.sjca.edu/college/tour/mcdowell.phtml.* (begun 1742, finished 1789) Named for St. John's first president; originally built as the Governor's Mansion. Lafayette was feted here in 1824. Not open to the public.

State House. *350 Rowe Blvd, State Circle (21401). Center of town. Phone 410/974-3400; toll-free 800/235-4045.* (1772-1779) Oldest state house in continuous legislative use in US, this was the first peacetime capitol of the US. Here in 1784, a few weeks after receiving George Washington's resignation as commander-in-chief, Congress ratified the Treaty of Paris, which officially ended the Revolutionary War. Visitors Information Center. Guide service (closed Jan 1, Thanksgiving). (Daily; closed Dec 25) **FREE**

Three Centuries Tours of Annapolis. *26 West St, Annapolis (21401). Morning tour leaves from Visitor Center at 26 West St; afternoon tour leaves from Visitor Information Booth on City Dock. Phone 410/263-5401*

(departure points and schedule). www.annapolis-tours.com. Walking tours of US Naval Academy and Historic District conducted by guides in colonial attire. Tour includes historic Maryland State House, St. John's College, Naval Academy Chapel, crypt of John Paul Jones, Bancroft Hall dormitory, and Armel-Leftwich Visitor Center. (Apr-Oct, daily) **$$$**

United States Naval Academy. *121 Blake Rd, Annapolis (21402). From Baltimore, take I-97 S or Rte 2 S for 26 miles and get off on Rowe Blvd (exit 24). Take Rowe Blvd 1.6 miles to where it dead-ends at College Ave and turn left. At the first stoplight, which is King George St, turn right. Follow King George St for two blocks. Enter Gate 1; visitor parking is on your right. Phone 410/263-6933. www.usna.edu.* Opened in 1845, the Naval Academy is located in Maryland's picturesque capital, Annapolis, a 30-minute drive from Baltimore. The beautiful campus sits at the edge of the Chesapeake Bay and Severn River, occupying 338 acres. Tours of the campus are available through the academy's Armel-Leftwich Visitor Center, where you can immerse yourself in naval history and life. You will see the tomb of John Paul Jones, the chapel, the midshipmen's living quarters, and the naval museum. The center also shows the orientation film *To Lead and to Serve*, exhibits the original wooden figurehead of the Tecumseh, and displays the *Freedom 7* space capsule. If you time your visit right, you can witness the Noon Formation. During this impressive daily event, all present midshipmen gather, line up, and march in for the noon meal with military precision. Note: Access to the Academy grounds is limited. Please check the current security restrictions before planning a visit. All visitors over the age of 16 must have a valid picture ID. **$$**

Special Events

Annapolis by Candlelight. *18 Pinkney St, Annapolis (21401). Phone 410/267-7619. www.annapolis.org.* For information and reservations contact Historic Annapolis Foundation. Early Nov. **$$$$**

Chesapeake Appreciation Days. *Sandy Point State Park, 1100 E College Pkwy, Annapolis (21401). Phone 410/974-2149.* Skipjack sailing festival honors state's oystermen. Last weekend in Oct.

Christmas in Annapolis. *Annapolis. Phone 410/268-8687.* Features decorated 18th-century mansions, parade of yachts, private home tours, pub crawls, concerts, holiday meals, First Night celebration, caroling by candlelight at the State House and other events. Call Visitors Bureau for free events calendar. Thanksgiving-Jan 1.

Maryland Renaissance Festival. *1821 Crownsville Rd, Annapolis (21401). Phone 410/266-7304; toll-free 800/296-7304. www.rennfest.com/mrf/.* Food, crafters, minstrels, dramatic productions. Usually last week in Aug-third weekend in Oct. **$$$$**

Maryland Seafood Festival. *Sandy Point State Park, 1100 E College Pkwy, Annapolis (21401). Phone 410/268-7682. www.mdseafoodfestival.com.* This family-friendly event offers up hearty portions of Maryland's favorite seafood dishes, including crab cakes, flounder, oysters, clams, trout, and shrimp salad. Held at Sandy Point State Park near historic Annapolis, visitors will enjoy the beauty of the Chesapeake Bay, more than 50 quality arts and crafts exhibitors, and live musical entertainment. The nearby National Aquarium and US Naval Academy make nice side trips. Weekend after Labor Day. **$$**

US Powerboat Show. *100 Severn Ave, Annapolis (21401). City dock and harbor. Phone 410/268-8828. www.usboat.com.* Extensive in-water display of powerboats; exhibits of related marine products. Mid-Oct. **$$$$**

US Sailboat Show. *100 Severn Ave, Annapolis (21401). City dock and harbor. Phone 410/267-6711. www.usboat.com.* Features world's largest in-water display of sailboats; exhibits of related marine products. Early-mid-Oct. **$$$$**

Limited-Service Hotels

★ BEST WESTERN ANNAPOLIS. *2520 Riva Rd, Annapolis (21401). Phone 410/224-2800; toll-free 800/780-7234; fax 410/266-5539. www.bestwesternannapolis.com.* 151 rooms, 2 story. Complimentary continental breakfast. Check-in 3 pm, check-out 11 am. High-speed Internet access. Fitness room. Outdoor pool. **$**

★ GIBSON'S LODGINGS. *110 Prince George St, Annapolis (21401). Phone 410/268-5555; toll-free 877/330-0057; fax 410/268-2775. www.gibsonlodgings.com.* 20 rooms, 3 story. Children over 10 years only. Complimentary continental breakfast. Check-in 2 pm, check-out 11 am. **$$**

★ ★ RADISSON HOTEL ANNAPOLIS. *210 Holiday Ct, Annapolis (21401). Phone 410/224-3150; toll-free 800/266-7631; fax 410/224-3413. www.radisson.com/annapolismd.* 219 rooms, 6 story. Pets accepted; fee. Check-in 4 pm, check-out noon. High-speed Internet access. Restaurant, bar. Fitness room. Outdoor pool. **$**

Full-Service Hotels

★ ★ ★ LOEWS ANNAPOLIS HOTEL. *126 West St, Annapolis (21401). Phone 410/263-7777; toll-free 800/235-6397; fax 410/263-0084. www.loewshotels.com.* Located in the heart of downtown Annapolis, this hotel is within walking distance to many of the city's historical sites. It also has 17,000 square feet of flexible meeting space that business travelers will find convenient and comfortable. 217 rooms, 6 story. Pets accepted. Check-in 3 pm, check-out noon. Wireless Internet access. Two restaurants, bar. Fitness room, fitness classes available. Airport transportation available. Business center. **$$**

★ ★ ★ MARRIOTT ANNAPOLIS WATERFRONT. *80 Compromise St, Annapolis (21401). Phone 410/268-7555; toll-free 800/336-0072; fax 410/269-5864. www.annapolismarriott.com.* With guest rooms overlooking Chesapeake Bay, this hotel is conveniently located to nearby shops and restaurants in colonial Annapolis. 150 rooms, 6 story. Check-in 4 pm, check-out 11 am. Wireless Internet access. Restaurant, bar. Fitness room. On the waterfront. **$$$**

★ ★ ★ THE O'CALLAGHAN HOTEL. *174 West St, Annapolis (21401). Phone 410/263-7700; fax 410/990-1400. www.ocallaghanhotels.com.* 120 rooms. Check-in 3 pm, check-out noon. Restaurant, bar. Business center. **$$**

★ ★ ★ SHERATON BARCELO ANNAPOLIS. *173 Jennifer Rd, Annapolis (21401). Phone 410/266-3131; toll-free 800/325-3535; fax 410/266-6247. www.sheraton.com/annapolis.* 196 rooms, 6 story. Pets accepted, some restrictions; fee. Check-in 3 pm, check-out noon. High-speed Internet access. Restaurant, bar. Fitness room. Indoor pool, whirlpool. Business center. **$$**

Specialty Lodgings

The following lodging establishments are approved by Mobil Travel Guide, but due to their unique and individualized nature have not been given a traditional Mobil Star rating. Included in this listing you may find bed-and-breakfasts, limited-service inns, guest ranches, and other unique hotel properties..

GOVERNOR CALVERT HOUSE. *58 State Cir, Annapolis (21401). Phone 410/263-2641; toll-free 800/847-8882; fax 410/268-3613. www.annapolisinns.com/calverthouse.html.* Formerly inhabited by two Maryland governors named Calvert, this tastefully restored colonial and Victorian residence also has a contemporary conference center. 51 rooms, 4 story. Check-in 3 pm, check-out noon. **$$**

ROBERT JOHNSON HOUSE. *23 State Cir, Annapolis (21401). Phone 410/263-2641; toll-free 800/847-8882; fax 410/268-3613. www.annapolisinns.com.* 29 rooms, 4 story. Check-in 3 pm, check-out noon. Consists of 18th-century mansion plus two connecting townhouses of the same period. **$$**

WILLIAM PAGE INN. *8 Martin St, Annapolis (21401). Phone 410/626-1506; toll-free 800/364-4160; fax 410/263-4841. www.1908-williampageinn.com.* 5 rooms, 3 story. Closed Jan. Children over 12 years only. Complimentary full breakfast. Check-in 4-6 pm, check-out noon. Wireless Internet access. Former clubhouse (1908). **$$**

Restaurants

★ ★ ★ BREEZE. *126 West St, Annapolis (21401). Phone 410/263-1299; fax 410/263-0084. www.loewsannapolis.com.* Located in the Loews Annapolis Hotel (see), this restaurant has a creative menu with tempting flavors. Seafood, steak menu. Breakfast, lunch, dinner, Sun brunch. Bar. Children's menu. Valet parking. **$$$**

★★★ **CAFÉ BRETTON.** *849 Baltimore-Annapolis Blvd, Severna Park (21146). Phone 410/647-8222.* French menu. Dinner. Closed Sun-Mon; holidays. Bar. Reservations recommended. **$$$**

★★ **CAFE NORMANDIE.** *185 Main St, Annapolis (21401). Phone 410/263-3382; fax 410/263-6470.* French menu. Breakfast, lunch, dinner. Bar. Children's menu. **$$$**

★ **CANTLER'S RIVERSIDE INN.** *458 Forest Beach Rd, Annapolis (21401). Phone 410/757-1311.* Seafood menu. Lunch, dinner. Bar. Children's menu. Casual attire. Outdoor seating. **$$**

★ **CHICK & RUTH'S DELLY.** *165 Main St, Annapolis (21401). Phone 410/269-6737; fax 410/269-6738. www.chickandruths.com.* Deli menu. Breakfast, lunch, dinner. Children's menu. Casual attire. No credit cards accepted. **$**

★★ **GRIFFIN'S.** *22 Market Space, Annapolis (21401). Phone 410/268-2576; fax 410/280-0195. www.griffins-citydock.com.* Seafood, steak menu. Lunch, dinner, Sun brunch. Closed Dec 25. Bar. Children's menu. **$$**

★★ **HARRY BROWNE'S.** *66 State Cir, Annapolis (21401). Phone 410/263-4332; fax 410/263-8049. www.harrybrownes.com.* Known as one of the best upscale restaurants in town, Harry Browne's looks up at the Maryland State House in downtown Annapolis. The fare is consistently good, the ambience inviting, and the service pleasurable. American menu. Lunch, dinner. Closed Jan 1, Dec 25. Bar. Valet parking. **$$**

★★ **LEWNES' STEAKHOUSE.** *401 4th St, Annapolis (21403). Phone 410/263-1617.* Seafood, steak menu. Dinner. Closed Thanksgiving, Dec 25. Bar. Reservations recommended. **$$$**

★★ **MIDDLETON TAVERN.** *2 Market Space, Annapolis (21401). Phone 410/263-3323; fax 410/263-3807. www.middletontavern.com.* Seafood menu. Lunch, dinner. Bar. Restored building (1750), traditional tavern décor. Outdoor seating. **$$$**

★ **MR. WANG'S HUNAN.** *1957 West St, Annapolis (21401). Phone 410/224-0552; fax 410/224-4543.* Chinese, Japanese, Thai menu. Lunch, dinner. Closed Thanksgiving. Bar. Casual attire. **$**

★★★ **NORTHWOODS.** *609 Melvin Ave, Annapolis (21401). Phone 410/268-2609; fax 410/268-0930.* This rustic, upscale seafood restaurant has a warm and romantic feel. With a good wine selection and a variety of fresh local seafood, it is a favorite for both business meals and intimate dinners. American menu. Dinner. Closed holidays. Outdoor seating. **$$**

★★ **O'LEARY'S SEAFOOD.** *310 3rd St, Annapolis (21403). Phone 410/263-0884; fax 410/263-5869.* Seafood menu. Dinner. Closed Thanksgiving, Dec 24-25. Bar. Children's menu. **$$$**

★★ **TREATY OF PARIS.** *58 State Cir, Annapolis (21401). Phone 410/263-2641; fax 410/268-3813.* This landmark is praised for its game and seafood selections. With menu items such as warm duck breast salad, beef Wellington, or rack of lamb, guests will bask in both the presentation and flavors of the masterful fares. French, American menu. Lunch, dinner, Sun brunch. Closed Jan 1. Bar. Reservations recommended. Valet parking. **$$**

Antietam National Battlefield (A-2)

(11 miles S on Hwy 65)

On September 17, 1862, the bloodiest day in Civil War annals, more than 23,000 men were killed or wounded as Union forces blocked the first Confederate invasion of the North. A Union advantage was gained beforehand when a soldier accidentally found Lee's orders wrapped around some cigars. In spite of knowing Lee's tactical game plan, McClellan moved cautiously. The battle, critical because British aid to the Confederacy depended on the outcome, was a tactical draw but a strategic victory for the North. This victory allowed Lincoln to issue the Emancipation Proclamation, which expanded the war from simply reuniting the country to a crusade to end slavery. The rebels withdrew across the Potomac on the night of September 18, but for some reason McClellan, with twice the manpower, delayed his pursuit. Lincoln relieved him of command of the Army of the Potomac seven weeks later. Clara Barton, who was to found the Red Cross 19 years later, tended the wounded at a field hospital on the battlefield.

Approximately 350 iron tablets, monuments, and battlefield maps, located on 8 miles of paved avenues, describe the events of the battle. The Visitor Center houses a museum and offers information, literature, and a 26-minute orientation movie (shown on the hour). Visitor Center (daily; closed January 1, Thanksgiving, December 25); battlefield (daily); ranger-conducted walks, talks, and demonstrations (Memorial Day-Labor Day, daily). Golden Age Passport (see MAKING THE MOST OF YOUR TRIP). For information phone 301/432-5124. Entrance fee per person. **$**

Baltimore (B-4)

See also Annapolis

Settled 1661
Population 654,154
Elevation 32 ft
Area Code 410 and 443
Information Baltimore Area Convention & Visitors Association, 100 Light St, 12th floor, 21202; phone 410/659-7300 or toll-free 800/343-3468
Web site www.baltimore.org
Suburbs Aberdeen, Cockeysville, Columbia, Ellicott City, Pikesville, Towson.

Metropolis of Maryland and one of America's great cities, Baltimore is a city of neighborhoods built on strong ethnic foundations, a city of historic events that helped shape the nation, and a city that has achieved an incredible downtown renaissance in the past 20 years. It is a major East Coast manufacturing center and, almost from its beginning, a world seaport. Several colleges and universities, foremost of which is Johns Hopkins, make their home here.

Lying midway between north and south and enjoying a rich cultural mixture of both, Baltimore is one of the nation's oldest cities. When British troops threatened Philadelphia during the Revolutionary War, the Continental Congress fled to Baltimore, which served as the nation's capital for a little more than two months.

In October 1814, a British fleet attacked the city by land and sea. The defenders of Fort McHenry withstood the naval bombardment for 25 hours until the British gave up. Francis Scott Key saw the huge American flag still flying above the fort and was inspired to pen "The Star-Spangled Banner."

Rapid growth in the early 19th century resulted from the opening of the National Road and then the nation's first railroad, the Baltimore & Ohio.

Politics was a preoccupation in those days, and the city hosted many national party conventions. At least seven presidents and three losing candidates were nominated here. Edgar Allan Poe's mysterious death in the city may have been at the hands of shady electioneers.

Untouched physically by the Civil War, effects came later when Southerners flooded in to rebuild their fortunes and commerce was disrupted by the loss of Southern markets. A disastrous fire in 1904 destroyed 140 acres of the business district but the city recovered rapidly and, during the two World Wars, was a major shipbuilding and naval repair center.

In the 1950s and early 1960s, Baltimore was the victim of the apathy and general decay that struck the industrial Northeast. But the city fought back, replacing hundreds of acres of slums, rotting wharves, and warehouses with gleaming new office plazas, parks, and public buildings. The Inner Harbor was transformed into a huge public area with shops, museums, restaurants, and frequent concerts and festivals. Millions of tourists and proud Baltimoreans flock downtown to enjoy the sights and activities.

Famous residents and native sons and daughters include Babe Ruth; Edgar Allan Poe; H. L. Mencken; Mother Elizabeth Ann Seton; Eubie Blake; Ogden Nash; Thurgood Marshall; Wallis Warfield Simpson, who became the Duchess of Windsor; and more recent sports legends Brooks Robinson, Johnny Unitas, Jim Palmer, and Cal Ripken.

Additional Visitor Information

For additional accommodations and airport information, see BALTIMORE/WASHINGTON INTERNATIONAL AIRPORT AREA, which follows BALTIMORE.

Maps, brochures, and calendars of events are available at the Baltimore Area Visitors Center, 301 E Pratt St, Constellation Pier, 21202; phone 410/837-INFO or toll-free 800/282-6632.

Public Transportation

Bus and subway (Mass Transit Administration), phone 410/539-5000.

What to See and Do

American Visionary Art Museum. *800 Key Hwy, Baltimore (21230). Phone 410/244-1900. www.avam.org.* Visitors with a penchant for the offbeat or the just plain bizarre should not miss this singular museum. The Whirligig—a 55-foot-tall, wind-powered, pinwheel-like sculpture made from bicycle wheels, car parts, and cables—stands in Sculpture Plaza as a towering symbol of the museum's mission. The museum defines visionary art as works produced by individuals without formal training whose art stems from an inner vision. Opened in 1995, the museum has more than 4,000 pieces in its collection. The main building holds seven indoor galleries. Separate from this building are the wildflower garden, a wedding chapel and altar built out of tree limbs and flowers, and the tall sculpture barn, which once showcased psychic Uri Geller's art, including a car he covered with 5,000 psychically bent forks and spoons. The museum also plans to add a "Thou Art Creative Center," an interactive area for visitors. (Tues-Sun 10 am-6 pm; closed Mon, Thanksgiving, Dec 25) **$$**

Antique Row. *N Howard and W Read sts, Baltimore (21201).* Antique Row, which has existed in Baltimore for over 100 years, is an antique lover's paradise. With more than 20 dealers and shops that also include restoration services, the area offers enough displayed and hidden treasures to satisfy diehard shoppers and casual browsers alike. The different shops specialize in items such as European furniture, Tiffany lamps, china, and rare books.

The Avenue in Hampden. *36th St, Baltimore (21211). www.hampdenmainstreet.org.* Although the four blocks that make up the Avenue total only a half mile, visitors will be amazed at all there is to see in this eclectic North Baltimore neighborhood. Novelty shops, vintage clothing stores, casual restaurants, and art galleries line Hampden's main drag, and the treasures that guests can find in these shops range from kitschy to sublime. If you're looking for a down-home meal, drop in at Mamie's Café or Café Hon.

B & O Railroad Museum. *901 W Pratt St, Baltimore (21223). Phone 410/752-2490. www.borail.org.* This museum, affiliated with the Smithsonian, celebrates the birthplace of railroading in America and depicts the industry's economic and cultural influences. Encompassing 40 acres, the museum's collection of locomotives is the oldest and most comprehensive in the country. Its exhibits are divided among three main buildings. In the Roundhouse, visitors can board and explore more than a dozen of the "iron horses," which include a rail post office car and the Tom Thumb train. The second floor of the Annex building has an impressive display of working miniature-scale trains. The Mount Clair Station, exhibiting the story of the B & O Railroad, was built in 1851 to replace the 1829 original, which was the first rail depot in the country. Outside, the museum features more trains, such as the *Chessie*, the largest steam locomotive. On certain weekends, visitors can take a train ride. In 2003, the museum marked its 175th anniversary. It also marked a tragic event. In February of 2003, the museum suffered severe damage during a snowstorm. Since that time, it has been undergoing restoration, with visitor access by appointment only. As of mid-November, 2004, the museum's renovation will be complete, and will resume regular hours, as well as offer new exhibits, programs, and activities. (Apr-Oct: Mon-Sun 10 am-5 pm; to 7 pm on all Orioles home games; Nov-Mar: Mon-Sun 10 am-4 pm; closed Jan 1, Thanksgiving, Dec 25) **$$**

Babe Ruth Birthplace and Museum. *216 Emory St, Baltimore (21230). Phone 410/727-1539. www.baberuthmuseum.com.* Although Babe Ruth played for the New York Yankees, Baltimore calls him one of its native sons. The house where this legend was born has been transformed into a museum that showcases his life and career. Visitors can see rare family photographs as well as a complete record of his home runs. The museum also features exhibits about the Baltimore Colts and Orioles. Every February 6, the museum commemorates Babe Ruth's birthday by offering free admission to all visitors. (Apr-Oct:

Baltimore crab

A visit to Charm City wouldn't be complete without a sampling of the local delicacy. Crab is a staple of Maryland's economy and diet. It comes prepared in a variety of forms: deep-fried, soft-shelled, or flaked and served as crab cakes. However, the classic version is steamed hard crabs. Restaurants serve steamed crab without adornment. Don't be put off when your waiter covers the table with plain brown paper and then hands you a wooden mallet, paper napkins, and a plastic bib. When the crabs come to the table, they will be hot, red from the steam, and covered in Old Bay Seasoning. Once you crack open the shell and taste the sweet, white meat, you'll be hooked. Crab is in season from March to October, but peak season is July through September.

Mon-Sun 10 am-5 pm; to 7 pm on all Orioles home games; Nov-Mar: Mon-Sun 10 am-4 pm; closed Jan 1, Thanksgiving, Dec 25) **$$**

Baltimore Maritime Museum. *802 S Caroline St, Baltimore (21231). Inner Harbor area. Phone 410/396-3453. www.baltomaritimemuseum.org.* This museum's featured ships include the USS *Torsk*, a World War II submarine; the Coast Guard cutter *Taney*; and the lightship *Chesapeake*. All the ships have been designated National Historic Landmarks. (Spring, summer, and fall, Sun-Thurs 10 am-5:30 pm, Fri-Sat until 6:30 pm; winter, Fri-Sun 10:30 am-5 pm) **$$**

Baltimore Museum of Art. *10 Art Museum Dr, Baltimore (21218). Near N Charles and 31st sts. Phone 410/396-7100. www.artbma.org.* Located near Johns Hopkins University, this museum opened in 1923 and was designed by John Russell Pope, the architect of the National Gallery in Washington, DC. The museum has eight permanent exhibits featuring works from the periods of Impressionism to modern art. It boasts the second largest collection of works by Andy Warhol. However, its jewel is the Cone collection, which includes more than 3,000 pieces by artists such as Picasso, Van Gogh, Renoir, Cézanne, and Matisse. The Matisse collection is the largest in the Western Hemisphere. Visitors will also want to see the 3-acre sculpture garden, which contains art by Alexander Calder and Henry Moore. (Wed-Fri 11 am-5 pm, Sat-Sun 11 am-6 pm; closed holidays) Free admission the first Thurs of each month. **$$**

Baltimore Museum of Industry. *1415 Key Hwy, Baltimore (21230). Inner Harbor South. Phone 410/727-4808. www.thebmi.org.* This museum educates visitors about the vital role that industry and manufacturing played in Baltimore's economic and cultural development. Located in a renovated oyster cannery on the west side of the Inner Harbor, the museum opened in 1977. Its exhibits showcase such trades as printing, garment making, canning, and metalworking. Guests will learn about the invention of Noxema, the disposable bottle cap, and even the first umbrella. Or they can explore the SS *Baltimore*, the only operating coal-fired tugboat on the East Coast that is now a National Historic Landmark. Visitors can also see the Mini-Mariner, a restored 1937 working prototype of the World War II boat bomber. The museum also has "Theatre on the Harbor," which presents touring and in-house productions. Past shows have included "Gizmo's Invention Show" and "Right Place, Right Time, Wright Brothers." (Mon-Sat 10 am-4 pm, Sun 11 am-4 pm; closed Thanksgiving, Dec 24-25) **$$**

Baltimore Streetcar Museum. *1901 Falls Rd, Baltimore (21211). Under North Ave Bridge. Phone 410/547-0264. www.baltimoremd.com/streetcar/.* Eleven electric streetcars and two horsecars used in the city between 1859 and 1963; 1 1/4-mile rides (fee). (June-Oct, Sat noon-5 pm; rest of year, Sun noon-5 pm; also open Memorial Day, July 4, Labor Day) **$$**

Baltimore Orioles (MLB). *Oriole Park at Camden Yards, 333 W Camden St, Baltimore (21201). Phone 410/685-9800. www.orioles.mlb.com.* The ballpark is one of the top five in the nation in which to see a game, combining new technology with a throwback sense found in parks like Wrigley Field and Fenway Park.

Baltimore Ravens (NFL). *Ravens Stadium, 1101 Russell St, Baltimore (21230). Phone 410/261-7283. www.baltimoreravens.com.* Winners of Super Bowl XXXV in 2001, the Ravens, formerly the Cleveland Browns, are

Baltimore's beloved NFL team. The team's home base is Ravens Stadium, a state-of-the art facility located across from Camden Yards baseball park. So that fans don't miss a minute of the action, a 100-foot-long and 25-foot-high Smartvision video board sits in each end zone. The stadium seats more than 69,000 people, and the upper deck seating has a unique split architecture design that allows fans to catch a breathtaking view of the city skyline in addition to an exciting game of football.

Baltimore Zoo. *1 Druid Hill Park Lake Dr, Baltimore (21217). Phone 410/366-5466. www.baltimorezoo.org.* Located in Druid Hill Park, this third-oldest zoo in the United States covers 180 acres and features more than 2,250 animals. Children will be intrigued by the scaly inhabitants of the reptile house. They can also travel to another continent by visiting the giraffes and elephants in the African Safari exhibit, as well as ride the carousel or try out the climbing wall. The zoo also hosts special events during Halloween and Christmas. (Daily 10 am-4 pm; closed Thanksgiving, Dec 25) **$$$**

Basilica of the National Shrine of the Assumption. *408 N Charles St, Baltimore (21201). Cathedral and Mulberry sts, downtown. Phone 410/727-3565. www.baltimorebasilica.org.* Now a co-cathedral, this was the first Roman Catholic cathedral in the US. Bishop John Carroll, head of the diocese of Baltimore from its establishment in 1789, blessed the cornerstone in 1806. The church was dedicated in 1821. Architectural design by B. H. Latrobe. Tours Sun after 10:45 am mass or by appointment. (Masses said Daily)

Battle Monument. *Calvert and Fayette sts, Baltimore (21222).* (1815) Memorial to those who fell defending the city in the War of 1812. Climb the 228 steps to the top of the monument for a breathtaking view. (Wed-Sun 10 am-4 pm, first Thurs of every month until 8 pm) **$**

Boordy Vineyards. *12820 Long Green Pike, Hydes (21082). Phone 410/592-5015. www.boordy.com.* Guests who live by the maxim *In Vino Veritas* should visit Maryland's oldest family-run winery. Only a 15-minute drive from Baltimore, Boordy sits in the serene countryside. With its rows and rows of delicate plants and 19th-century farm buildings, this winery will surely charm visitors. Daily tours are available, and Boordy hosts special events, such as wine tastings and live musical performances. (Mon-Sat 10 am-5pm, Sun from 1pm) **FREE**

Charles Center. *36 S Charles St, Baltimore (21201). Bounded by Charles, Liberty, Saratoga, and Lombard sts, downtown.* Business area with European-style plazas, part of an overhead walkway system, shops, restaurants, and outdoor activities. Prize-winning office building by Mies van der Rohe borders center plaza. Also here is

The Morris A. Mechanic Theatre. *25 Hopkins Plz, Baltimore (21201). Phone 410/481-7328. www.themechanic.org.* Hosts Broadway productions.

Church Home and Hospital. *Broadway and Fairmount aves, East Baltimore (21231).* Edgar Allan Poe died here in 1849.

City Court House. *100 N Calvert St, Baltimore (21202). St. Paul and Fayette sts, downtown.* (1900) On the steps is a statue of Cecil Calvert, brother of Leonard and founder of Maryland as the second Lord Baltimore.

City Hall. *100 N Holiday St, Baltimore (21202). Downtown. Phone 410/396-3100.* Post-Civil War architecture, restored to original detail. Tours by appointment. **FREE**

City of Baltimore Conservatory. *Druid Hill Park, 2600 Madison Ave, Baltimore (21217). Phone 410/396-0180. www.ci.baltimore.md.us/government/recnparks/conservatory.html.* This graceful building (circa 1885) houses a large variety of tropical plants. Special shows during Easter, November, and the Christmas season. (Thurs-Sun 10 am-3 pm) **FREE**

Clyburn Arboretum. *4915 Greenspring Ave, Baltimore (21209). Phone 410/367-2217. www.cylburnassociation.org.* Marked nature trails. Nature museum, ornithological room, horticultural library in a restored mansion; shade and formal gardens, All-American Selection Garden, Garden of the Senses. (Grounds are open from dawn to dusk; Mansion Mon-Fri 7:30 am-3:30 pm; Museums Tues, Thurs 1-3 pm) **FREE**

Edgar Allan Poe Grave. *Westminster Hall and Burial Grounds. 509 W Fayette St, Baltimore (21201). Downtown. Phone 410/706-2072.* Baltimore's oldest cemeteries also contain the graves of many prominent early Marylanders. Westminster Burying Ground and Catacomb tours by appointment (Apr-Nov, first and third Fri and Sat). **$$**

Edgar Allan Poe House and Museum. *203 N Amity St, Baltimore (21223). Phone 410/396-7932. www.ci.baltimore.md.us/government/historic/poehouse.html.* The famed author and father of the macabre lived in this house from 1832 to 1835. The faint of heart should beware, as several psychics have reported ghostly presences here. Haunted or not, the house and museum scare up many Poe artifacts, such as period furniture, a desk and telescope owned by Poe, and Gustave Dore's illustrations of "The Raven." Around January 19, the museum hosts a birthday celebration that includes readings and theatrical performances of Poe's work. (Apr-July: Wed-Sat noon-3:45 pm; Aug-Sept: Sat noon-3:45 pm; Oct-Dec, Wed-Sat noon-3:45 pm) **$**

Enoch Pratt Free Library. *400 Cathedral St, Baltimore (21201). At Franklin St, downtown. Phone 410/396-5430. www.pratt.lib.md.us.* City's public library. Includes H. L. Mencken and Edgar Allan Poe collections. (Mon-Wed 10 am-8 pm, Thurs to 5:30 pm, Fri-Sat to 5 pm; Also Sun 1-5 pm from Sept-May; closed holidays)

Federal Hill. *Charles and Cross sts, Baltimore (21227). Bordered by Hughes St, Key Hwy, Hanover St, and Cross St. Inner Harbor area.* View of the city harbor and skyline. Named after a celebration that occurred here in 1788 to mark Maryland's ratification of the Constitution.

Fell's Point. *812 S Ann St, Baltimore (21231). Broadway, S of Fleet St to the harbor. www.fellspoint.us.* Shipbuilding and maritime center, this neighborhood dates back to 1730; approximately 350 original residential structures. Working tugboats and tankers can be observed from the docks.

First Unitarian Church. *Charles and Franklin sts, Baltimore (21201). Phone 410/685-2330.* (1817) William Ellery Channing preached a sermon here that hastened the establishment of the Unitarian denomination. Example of Classic Revival architecture.

★ The Flag House & Star-Spangled Banner Museum. *844 E Pratt St, Baltimore (21202). Phone 410/837-1793. www.flaghouse.org.* Open to the public for over 75 years, this museum was the home of Mary Pickersgill, sewer of the flag that Francis Scott Key eternalized in America's national anthem. Although the flag now hangs in the Smithsonian's National Museum of American History, visitors can tour the house to learn about its origins and Pickersgill's life. The house has an adjoining War of 1812 museum, which exhibits military and domestic artifacts and presents an award-winning video. (Tues-Sat 10 am-4 pm, Sun noon-5 pm) **$**

Fort McHenry National Monument and Historic Shrine. *End of E Fort Ave, Baltimore (21230). Phone 410/962-4290 (visitor center). www.nps.gov/fomc.* Fort McHenry boasts a stunning view of the harbor, authentic re-created structures, and a wealth of living history that will fascinate both history buffs and casual visitors. In addition to being the site of the battle that inspired Francis Scott Key to pen "The Star-Spangled Banner" in 1814, the fort was a defensive position during the Revolutionary War, a POW camp for Confederate prisoners during the Civil War, and an army hospital during World War I. The fort's exhibits showcase these events. Park rangers are knowledgeable and helpful, and they encourage visitors to participate in the twice-daily flag changes. Summer weekends feature precision drill and music performed by volunteers in Revolutionary War uniforms. (Labor Day-Memorial Day: daily 8 am-4:45 pm; Memorial Day-Labor Day: daily 8 am-7:45 pm; closed Jan 1, Dec 25) **$**

Narrated cruises. *Baltimore. Phone 410/962-4299.* The *Baltimore Patriot* departs from Inner Harbor Finger Pier to Fort McHenry and Fell's Point (Memorial Day-Labor Day). Also departures from Fort McHenry and Fell's Point. For other tours, contact Maryland Tours, Inc. **$$$**

Gunpowder Falls State Park. *2813 Jerusalem Rd, Kingsville (21087). Phone 410/592-2897; toll-free 888/432-2267. www.dnr.state.md.us/publiclands/central/gunpowder.html.* Approximately 16,000 acres, located in the Gunpowder River Valley.

Harbor cruises. *301 Light St, Baltimore (21202). Depart from Inner Harbor.* **$$$**

Baltimore Patriot. *Pier 1, Inner Harbor's Constellation dock, 301 E Pratt St (21202). Phone 410/685-4288.* Ninety-minute tours around Baltimore's Inner Harbor. Three daily departures. (Apr-Oct, daily)

***Minnie V* Harbor Tours.** *Docks near Pier 1, Pratt St, Inner Harbor area. Phone 410/685-9062.* A 45-foot Chesapeake Bay skipjack sloop built in 1906.

Ninety-minute harbor tours give 24 passengers the opportunity to help crew the boat (open summer weekends).

MV *Lady Baltimore*. *301 Light St, Baltimore (21202). West Bulkhead. Phone 410/727-3113; toll-free 800/695-5239.* Round-trip cruises to Annapolis (June-Aug, Wed); also cruises to the Chesapeake & Delaware Canal (three selected Sun in Oct). *Bay Lady* has lunch and dinner cruises (Apr-Oct, daily; limited schedule rest of year).

Harborplace. *200 E Pratt St, Baltimore (21202). Phone 410/332-4191. www.harborplace.com.* This shopping center is the most recognizable symbol of Baltimore's downtown and harbor renaissance. With its architecture of glass and exposed pipes and beams, Harborplace serves as a model for other cities' revitalization plans. Developed by James W. Rouse, the shopping mecca opened in 1980 and boasts more than 130 stores and restaurants. Visitors who want to take a break can go outside and walk on the brick-paved promenade that runs along the water's edge. Harborplace also has a small outdoor amphitheater, where, in good weather, guests are treated to free performances by jugglers, musicians, singers, and military and concert bands. (Daily)

Holocaust Memorial. *Water, Gay, and Lombard sts, Baltimore (21202). Downtown. Phone 410/752-2630.* A simple marble slab memorial to the victims of the Holocaust.

The Jewish Museum of Maryland. *15 Lloyd St, Baltimore (21202). Downtown. Phone 410/732-6400. www.jhsm.org.* Buildings include Lloyd St Synagogue (1845), the oldest in Maryland; B'nai Israel Synagogue (1876); and the Jewish Museum of Maryland. (Tues-Thurs, Sun noon-4 pm or by appointment; closed Jewish holidays) Research archives (Mon-Fri, by appointment). **$**

Johns Hopkins University. *3400 N Charles St, Baltimore (21218). Charles and 34th sts, 2 miles N. Phone 410/516-8000. www.jhu.edu.* Founded in 1876 and located in northern Baltimore, Johns Hopkins is an impressive institution of scholarship and research. It enrolls 18,000 students and is renowned for the Bloomberg School of Public Health, the Peabody Institute (a music conservatory) and its Applied Physics Laboratory, located 30 minutes outside of Baltimore. *US News & World Report* continuously ranks its affiliated hospital, which has its own separate campus in eastern Baltimore, as one of the top medical facilities in the country. Guests to the campus should visit the Homewood mansion. This elegant, Federal red-bricked building was once owned by Charles Carroll, one of the signers of the Declaration of Independence. It was deeded to the university in 1902 and now serves as a historic home. Guided tours are available. On grounds are

Bufano Sculpture Garden. *Dunning Park, behind Mudd Hall. www.jhu.edu/tour/bufano.html.* A wooded retreat with animals sculpted by artist Beniamino Bufano. **FREE**

Evergreen House. *4545 N Charles St, Baltimore (21218). Approximately 2 miles N of Homewood campus. Phone 410/516-0341. www.jhu.edu/evrgreen/evergreen.html.* On 26 wooded acres; features Classical Revival architecture and a formal garden. Library (35,000 volumes). Post-impressionist paintings, Japanese and Chinese collections, and Tiffany glass. Tours (daily). **$$**

Homewood House Museum. *3400 N Charles St, Baltimore. Near 34th St. Phone 410/516-5589. www.jhu.edu/hwdhouse/.* (1801) Former country home of Charles Carroll, Jr., whose father was a signer of the Declaration of Independence; period furnishings. (Tues-Sat 11 am-4 pm, Sun noon-4 pm; closed holidays) Guided tours every half hour. **$$**

Johns Hopkins Medical Institutions. *550 N Broadway, Baltimore (21205). Broadway and Monument sts. Phone 410/955-7894. www.hopkinsmedicine.org.* (1889) Widely known as a leading medical school, research center, and teaching hospital. Victorian buildings.

Peabody Institute of the Johns Hopkins University. *609 N Charles St, Baltimore (21202). In Mount Vernon Place area. Phone 410/659-8124 (box office). www.peabody.jhu.edu.* (1857) (550 students) Music conservatory founded by philanthropist George Peabody; now affiliated with Johns Hopkins. Research and reference collection in library accessible to the public (Mon-Fri; closed holidays). The Miriam A. Friedberg Concert Hall seats 800. Orchestral, recital, and opera performances.

Joseph Meyerhoff Symphony Hall. *1212 Cathedral St, Baltimore (21201). Phone 410/783-8000. www.baltimoresymphony.org.* Permanent residence of the Baltimore Symphony Orchestra.

Lacrosse Hall of Fame Museum. *113 W University Pkwy, Baltimore (21210). Phone 410/235-6882. www.lacrosse.org/museum/.* Team trophies, display of lacrosse artifacts and memorabilia, including rare photographs and art, vintage equipment and uniforms. Also historical video documentary. (Feb-May: Tues-Sat 10 am-3 pm; June-Jan: Mon-Fri 10 am-3 pm; closed holidays) **$**

Lexington Market. *400 W Lexington St, Baltimore (21201). Between Eutaw and Paca sts, downtown. Phone 410/685-6169. www.lexingtonmarket.com.* This under-roof market is more than two centuries old. Covering two blocks, it has more than 130 stalls offering fresh vegetables, seafood, meats, baked goods, and prepared foods that will whet any appetite. Vendors outside the market sell clothing, jewelry, T-shirts, and other miscellaneous items. Throughout the year, the market hosts several events, such as the Chocolate Festival in October, which boasts free samples and a chocolate-eating contest. But the most anticipated event at the market is Lunch with the Elephants. Every March, Ringling Brothers and Barnum & Bailey Circus elephants parade up Eutaw Street accompanied by fanfare, live music, and clowns. When they finally reach the market, they are served "lunch," which consists of 1,100 oranges, 1,000 apples, 500 heads of lettuce, 700 bananas, 400 pears, and 500 carrots. (Mon-Sat 8:30 am-6 pm; closed holidays) **FREE**

Lovely Lane Museum. *The Lovely Lane United Methodist Church, 2200 St. Paul St, Baltimore (21218). Phone 410/889-4458.* Permanent and changing exhibits of items of Methodist church history since 1760. Guided tours (Mon-Fri; also Sun after services and by appointment; closed holidays). **FREE**

Maryland Historical Society. *201 W Monument St, Baltimore (21201). Phone 410/685-3750. www.mdhs.org.* The state's oldest cultural institution includes a library, a museum, and even a small press that promotes scholarship about Maryland's history and material culture. The library has more than 5.4 million works and is a valuable resource for genealogists. The society's collection of historical artifacts includes the original draft of "The Star Spangled Banner" and the world's largest collection of 19th-century American silver. It also sponsors educational programs, such as lectures and living history presentations. (Museum: Wed-Fri 10 am-5 pm; to 8 pm the first Thurs of every month; Sat 9 am-5 pm, Sun 11 am-5 pm. History and Geneaology Reading Room: Wed-Sat 10 am-4:30 pm. Special Collections Reading Room: Wed-Fri 10 am-4:30 pm; also open to the public on the third Sat of every month) **$**

Maryland Institute, College of Art. *1300 Mount Royal Ave, Baltimore (21217). Main building, at Lanvale St. Phone 410/669-9200. www.mica.edu.* (1826) (880 students) Institute hosts frequent contemporary art exhibitions. Campus distinguished by recycled buildings and white marble Italianate main building. (Daily)

Maryland Science Center & Davis Planetarium. *601 Light St, Baltimore (21230). Phone 410/685-5225 (recording). www.mdsci.org.* This interactive center proves that science is anything but boring. Located in the Inner Harbor, the three-story building contains hundreds of exhibits guaranteed to spark young (and older) minds. In the Chesapeake Bay exhibit, you can learn about the delicate ecosystem that exists beneath the water. Or you can explore the mysteries of the human body in BodyLink. The Kids Room, for guests eight and younger, gives children the chance to operate a fish camera or dress up like turtles. Don't miss the Hubble Space Telescope National Visitor Center, a 4,000-square-foot interactive space gallery, which has more than 20 hands-on activities and 120 high-resolution images that allow guests to see space through the Hubble's eye. Those who can't get enough of outer space should also visit the Davis Planetarium and the Crosby-Ramsey Memorial Observatory, both on site. The center's IMAX theater will thrill guests with its five-stories-tall movie screen and 3-D capability. (Tues-Fri 10 am-5 pm, Sat 10 am-6 pm, Sun noon-5 pm. IMAX theater is open later) **$$$**

Morgan State University. *1700 E Cold Spring Ln, Baltimore (21251). At Hillen Rd. Phone 443/885-3333. www.morgan.edu.* (1867) (5,100 students) The James E. Lewis Museum of Art has changing exhibits (Mon-Fri; weekends by appointment; closed holidays).

Mother Seton House. *600 N Paca St, Baltimore (21201). Downtown. Phone 410/523-3443. www.baltimoretourism.com/mothersetonhouse.* Home of St. Elizabeth Ann Bayley Seton from 1808 to 1809. Here she established the forerunner of the parochial school system, as well as an order of nuns that eventually became the Daughters & Sisters of Charity in the US and Canada. (Sat-Sun 1-3 pm, also by appointment; closed Jan 1, Easter, Dec 25) **FREE**

Mount Clare Museum House. *1500 Washington Blvd, Baltimore (21230). In Carroll Park. Phone 410/837-3262. www.cr.nps.gov/nr/travel/baltimore/b2.htm.* (1760) Oldest mansion in Baltimore, former home of Charles Carroll, barrister. Eighteenth- and 19th-century furnishings. Guided tours on the hour. (Tues-Fri 11 am-3 pm; Sat-Sun 1-3 pm; closed Jan, holidays) **$$**

Mount Vernon Place United Methodist Church. *10 E Mount Vernon Pl, Baltimore (21202). Phone 410/685-5290.* (Circa 1850) Brownstone with balcony and grillwork extending the entire width of the house; spiral staircase suspended from three floors; library with century-old painting on the ceiling; drawing room. (Mon-Fri 9 am-3 pm, Sat by appointment; closed holidays and the Mon after Easter) **FREE**

MPT (Maryland Public Television). *11767 Owings Mills Blvd, Baltimore (21117). Phone 410/356-5600; toll-free 800/223-3678 (surrounding states). www.mpt.org.* Tours of the state's television network studios. (By appointment) **FREE**

★ **National Aquarium.** *501 E Pratt St, Baltimore (21202). Inner Harbor area. Phone 410/576-3800. www.aqua.org.* This aquarium's glass-and-steel pyramid shape is as unusual and stunning as the more than 15,000 sea creatures it houses. Located in the Inner Harbor, the National Aquarium introduces guests to stingrays, sharks, puffins, seals, and even a giant Pacific octopus. Visitors can explore the danger and mystery of a living South American tropical rain forest complete with poisonous frogs, exotic birds, piranha, and swinging tamirin monkeys, or delight in the underwater beauty of the replicated Atlantic coral reef. The Children's Cove, a touch pool, provides an interactive experience for kids. In the Marine Mammal Pavilion, a high-tech dolphin show entertains and teaches guests about these intelligent creatures. Visitors particularly enjoy watching trainers feed the animals. Daily feeding schedules are posted in the lobby. (Daily 9 am-7 pm, Fri until 10 pm; closed Thanksgiving, Dec 25) **$$$$** Visitors cross an enclosed skywalk to reach the adjacent wing, which houses

Marine Mammal Pavilion. *www.aqua.org.* This unique structure features a 1,300-seat amphitheater surrounding a 1.2-million-gallon pool, which houses Atlantic bottlenose dolphins; underwater viewing areas enable visitors to observe the mammals from below the surface. A life-size replica of a humpback whale spans two levels of the atrium. The Discovery Room houses a collection of marine artifacts; the Resource Center is an aquatic learning center for school visitors; and the library boasts an extensive collection of marine science material. An educational arcade with computerized video screens and other participatory exhibits is found around the pavilion's upper deck. (Daily)

Old Otterbein United Methodist Church. *112 W Conway St, Baltimore (21201). At Sharp st, Inner Harbor area. Phone 410/685-4703. www.oldotterbein.com.* (1785-1786) Fine Georgian architecture; mother church of United Brethren. Tours of historic building (Apr-Oct, Sat).

Old Town Mall. *414 N Gay St, Baltimore (21202). 400 and 500 blocks of N Gay St. Phone 410/239-6930.* This 150-year-old, brick-lined commercial area has been beautifully refurbished; it's closed to vehicular traffic. Nearby is

Stirling Street. *1000 block of Monument St, 1 block W of mall.* First community urban "homesteading" venture in the US. Renovated homes date to the 1830s. Original facades have been maintained; interior rehabilitation ranges in style from the antique to the avant garde.

Oriole Park at Camden Yards. *333 W Camden St, Baltimore (21201). Phone 410/685-9800. www.baltimore.orioles.mlb.com.* The crack of the bat and the roar of the crowd signal that the Orioles are home. Opened in 1992 and located just blocks from the Inner Harbor, Camden Yards is considered by many to be the best baseball stadium in the US. With its steel trusses, arched brick façade, and natural turf, the stadium's design is reminiscent of the great ballparks built in the early 1900s. It holds 48,876 fans and memorializes local legends Brooks Robinson, Earl Weaver, and Cal Ripken, Jr. The old B&O Warehouse sits behind right field and has long been a target for batters aiming for a home run. Guests can sit anywhere in the stadium and enjoy an unobstructed view of the game. Tours of the stadium are also available and allow visitors to sit in the dugout, see the press box, and explore the clubhouse. (Season Mar-Sept; tours held mid-Feb-late Dec, daily except on days of afternoon home games)

Duckpin Bowling

Despite its name, no ducks play a part in this game, which originated in Baltimore in 1900. The object of the game is similar to that of bowling except that the pins and balls are smaller. However, first-time players should not be fooled by the diminutive pieces. They'll soon discover that the smaller they are, the pins are, in fact, even harder to knock down! Alleys are open throughout Baltimore, including at Taylor's Stoneleigh Duckpin Bowling Center, 6703 York Rd, phone 410/377-8115.

Otterbein "Homesteading". *Area around S Sharp St, Inner Harbor area.* The original neighborhood dates back to 1785. Houses have been restored.

Patterson Park. *200 S Linwood Ave, Baltimore (21231). Baltimore St, Eastern, Linwood, and Patterson Park aves. Phone 410/396-7931. www.pattersonpark.com.* Defenses here helped stop the British attack in 1814. Breastworks and artillery pieces are displayed.

Port Discovery. *35 Market Pl, Baltimore (21202). Phone 410/727-8120. www.portdiscovery.org.* Port Discovery is three floors and 80,000 square feet of pure imagination. Ranked the fourth best children's museum in the country by *Child* magazine, the museum opened in 1998 in collaboration with Walt Disney Imagineering. Its exhibits are interactive, innovative, and educational. Kids will have a blast exploring the three-story urban tree house. In MPT Studioworks, they can become producers of their own television broadcasts. Sensation Station will overload their senses of sight, sound, and touch. Kids can even travel back to ancient Egypt and uncover the mystery of the pyramids and Pharaoh's tomb. The museum also operates the HiFlyer, a giant helium balloon that's anchored 450 feet above the Inner Harbor. The enclosed gondola holds 20 to 25 passengers and offers a spectacular view of the city. (Oct-May: Tues-Fri 9:30 am-4:30 pm, Sat 10 am-5 pm, Sun noon-5 pm; Memorial Day-Labor Day: Mon-Sat 10 am-5 pm, Sun noon-5 pm; closed Thanksgiving, Dec 25) **$$$**

The Power Plant. *601 E Pratt St, Baltimore (21202). Phone 410/752-5444.* As its name implies, this commercial complex was once a power plant owned by Baltimore Gas & Electric. Located in the Inner Harbor next to the National Aquarium (see), the renovated plant now houses a two-story Barnes & Noble bookstore; a Hard Rock Café; and the original ESPN Zone, a 35,000-square-foot sports-themed restaurant and arcade. **FREE**

Pride of Baltimore II. *Inner Harbor (21202). Phone 410/539-1151; toll-free 888/55-PRIDE. www.intandem.com/newpridesite.* This replicated 1812-style Baltimore Clipper is Maryland's goodwill ambassador. The ship has sailed to more than 40 countries in North and South America, Europe, and Asia to promote the state's tourism and economical interests. In 1986, the original *Pride of Baltimore* sank in a storm near Puerto Rico, killing the entire crew. When the *Pride of Baltimore II* is docked in the Inner Harbor, visitors can board for a tour. Day sails and overnight passages between ports are also available.(Daily 10 am-5 pm; (tour hours vary, so call or see the Web site for port schedule) **$$$$**

Public Works Museum & Streetscape. *Pier 7, 751 Eastern Ave, Baltimore (21202). At Inner Harbor East. Phone 410/396-5565.* Museum exhibits the history and artifacts of public works. Located in a historic sewage pumping station. Streetscape sculpture outside depicts the various utility lines and ducts under a typical city street, in a walk-through model. (Tues-Sun 10 am-4 pm) **$**

Sail Baltimore. *1809 Thames St, Baltimore (21231). Phone 410/522-7300. www.sailbaltimore.org.* Because boats are to Baltimore as cows are to farms, Sail Baltimore, a nonprofit organization, informs the public about a variety of citywide boating events that take place throughout the year. Its Web site provides an updated schedule of the different boats and ships that will be visiting the Inner Harbor. It also hosts the Great Chesapeake Bay Schooner Race in October, among other seasonal events.

Senator Theatre. *5904 York Rd, North Baltimore (21212). Phone 410/435-8338. www.senator.com.* Movie buffs will appreciate the charm and history of the Senator, which *USA Today* rated one of the top theaters in the country. Showing first-run, independent, and classic films, the theater seats 900 and has a 40-foot-wide screen. Listed on the National Register of Historic Places, its architecture is elegant Art Deco. The theater has also premiered several films by directors John Waters and Barry Levinson, who are Baltimore natives. The theater recently added its own mini "Walk of Fame" outside its entrance. **$$$**

Sherwood Gardens. *Stratford Rd and Greenway, Baltimore (21218). In the residential community of Guilford in northern Baltimore. Phone 410/323-7982.* More than 6 acres in size, the gardens reach their peak of splendor in late April and early May, when thousands of tulips, azaleas, and flowering shrubs bloom. (Daily dawn-dusk) **FREE**

Six Flags America. *13710 Central Ave, Mitchellville (20721). From Baltimore, take I-695 to I-97 S, Rte 3/301 S to Rte 214 W, and go 3 miles (follow signs). From Washington, take I-495/I-95 to exit 15A and go 5 miles (follow signs). Phone 301/249-1500. www.sixflags.com/parks/america/home.asp.* This colorful theme park offers thrills both gentle and extreme, with everything from an old-fashioned carousel to classic 50-mph wooden roller coasters and the high-tech Batwing, which gives riders the feeling of free-flight. Smaller kids will love Looney Tunes MovieTown, where Bugs Bunny and his cartoon pals roam free. Too hot to ride? Cool down with Paradise Island Water Park's splash-happy water slides, wave pool, inner-tube ride, and interactive water tree house. (June-Aug, daily; limited schedule in Apr, May, Sept, and Oct) **$$$$**

Top of the World. *401 E Pratt St, Baltimore (21202). World Trade Center, Inner Harbor area. Phone 410/837-8439.* Observation deck and museum on the 27th floor of the World Trade Center, which was designed by I. M. Pei. Exhibits describe the city's history, famous residents, and the activities of the port. (Sept-Memorial Day: Wed-Sun 10 am-6 pm; Memorial Day-Labor Day: daily 10 am-9 pm) **$**

University of Maryland at Baltimore. *520 W Lombard St, Baltimore (21201). Lombard, Greene, and Redwood sts, downtown. Phone 410/706-7820. www.umaryland.edu.* 5,476 students. The 32-acre downtown campus includes six professional schools; the University of Maryland Medical System, and the Graduate School. Davidge Hall (1812) is the oldest medical teaching building in continuous use in the western hemisphere.

USS *Constellation*. *301 E Pratt St, Pier 1, Baltimore (21202). Phone 410/539-1797. www.constellation.org.* This retired sloop, anchored at Pier 1 in the Inner Harbor, has a proud naval history that spans from the Civil War to World War II. Visitors can board the ship for a self-guided audio tour. Kids can participate in the Powder Monkey program, in which they learn what it was like to serve in President Lincoln's navy. In 1999, a restoration project returned the ship to its original Civil War appearance. (May-mid-Oct: daily 10 am-6 pm; mid-Oct-Apr: daily 10 am-4 pm. Extended hours may be available June-Aug) **$$**

Vagabond Players. *806 S Broadway, Baltimore (21231). Phone 410/563-9135. www.vagabondplayers.com.* Oldest continuously operating "little theater" in the US. Recent Broadway shows, revivals, and original scripts are performed. (Fri-Sun) **$$**

Walters Art Museum. *600 N Charles St, Baltimore (21201). Phone 410/547-9000. www.thewalters.org.* This museum's collection is so comprehensive that it spans 55 centuries and traces the history of the world from ancient times to the present day. Father and son William and Henry Walters gifted the museum and its numerous holdings to Baltimore, although the New York Metropolitan Museum of Art also coveted it. Located in the historic neighborhood of Mount Vernon and containing more than 30,000 pieces of art, the collection, which is housed in three buildings, is renowned for its French paintings and Renaissance and Asian art. The museum also exhibits Fabergé eggs; paintings by the Old Masters, such as Raphael and El Greco; and an impressive assortment of ivories and Art Deco jewelry. Visitors will also want to check out the unique Roman sarcophagus. (Tues-Sun 10 am-5 pm; closed holidays) **$$**

Washington Monument. *600 Charles St, Baltimore (21202). In Mount Vernon Pl area. Phone 410/396-1049.* (1815-1842) The first major monument to honor George Washington. There's a museum in the base; view the city from the top. Other monuments nearby honor Lafayette, Chief Justice Roger Brooke Taney, philanthropist George Peabody, lawyer Severn Teackle Wallis, and Revolutionary War hero John Eager Howard.

Special Events

American Craft Council Baltimore-Winter Show. *Convention Center, 1 W Pratt St, Baltimore (21201). Phone 410/649-7000. www.craftcouncil.org.* Craft festival features the works of nearly 800 artisans, with crafts ranging from clay and glass to furniture and toys. Three-day weekend in late Feb. **$$$**

Artscape. *1200 block of Mount Royal Ave, Baltimore (21217). Phone toll-free 877/225-8466. www.artscape.org.* This festival celebrates the area's abundance of visual, literary, and performing arts. The three-day event, which occurs in late July, takes place in the "cultural corridor" of the city's Bolton Hill neighborhood. It features live music performances, poetry and fiction readings by regional writers, and even a one-act opera. Past festival performers and guests have included John Waters, Buckwheat Zydeco, Kool & the Gang, and India.Arie. The Artists' Market exhibits and sells the work of more than 140 artists. The festival includes a wide variety of activities for children, which in the past have included a youth Shakespearean performance and an interactive art tent. The event also presents a charity wine-tasting hosted by a regional vineyard. Mid-July. (Fri 6-10 pm, Sat-Sun noon-10 pm) **FREE** (Small fee for some indoor events)

Cockpit in Court Summer Theatre. *Essex Community College, 7201 Rossville Blvd, Baltimore (21237). Phone 410/780-6369 (box office).* Theater in residence at Essex Community College. Four separate theaters offer a diverse collection of plays, including Broadway productions, contemporary drama, revues, and Shakespeare. Mid-June-mid-Aug.

Harbor Expo. *3001 Boston St, Baltimore (21224). Middle Branch and Canton waterfront. Phone 410/396-7931.* Boat parades, seafood festival; entertainment; events. Mid-June.

Maryland Film Festival. *107 E Read St, Baltimore (21202). Phone 410/752-8083. www.mdfilmfest.com.* Initiated in 1999, this four-day festival has become a premiere cinema event for Baltimore, presenting more than 120 foreign, domestic, and short films throughout the city's movie houses, including the famous Senator Theatre (see). Most screenings are followed by a discussion with the film's director or producer; past directors in attendance have included Barry Levinson and John Waters. In addition to featuring cutting-edge contemporary movies, its Guest Host Program invites members from the film community to screen and discuss films that have influenced their own work. The festival has also hosted films for children, such as a silent movie version of *Peter Pan* accompanied by an orchestra. The festival's committee holds film-related events in Baltimore throughout the year. Late Apr or early May. **$$$$**

Maryland House and Garden Pilgrimage. *1105-A Providence Rd, Towson (21286). Phone 410/821-6933. www.mhgp.org.* More than 100 homes and gardens throughout the state are open. Late Apr-early May. **$$$$**

New Year's Eve Extravaganza. *Convention Center and Inner Harbor, 1 W Pratt St, Baltimore (21201). Phone 410/649-7144.* Parties, entertainment, big bands, and fireworks. (Fee for some activities)

Pier 6 Concert Pavilion. *731 Eastern Ave, Pier 6, Baltimore (21202). Inner Harbor area. Phone 410/625-3100 (for schedule). www.piersixpavilion.com.* Summertime outdoor concerts and plays at the water's edge. Some covered seating. June-Sept. (Evenings) **$$$$**

Pimlico Race Course. *5201 Park Heights Ave, Baltimore (21215). Phone 410/542-9400. www.marylandracing.com.* Home to the world-famous Preakness Stakes (see), this track is well steeped in thoroughbred horseracing tradition. Pimlico features a 70-foot-wide and 1-mile-long track. It can easily meet the needs of horseracing fans with more than 750 betting windows and a clubhouse and two grandstands that can accommodate more than 13,000 people. In the lounge, visitors can view broadcasts of races at other tracks. (Wed-Sun, Apr-June) **$**

Preakness Stakes and Celebration Week. *Pimlico Race Course, 5201 Park Heights Ave, Baltimore (21215). Also Statewide festival. Phone 410/837-3030.* The Preakness Stakes, the second jewel in horse racing's Triple Crown, is a time-honored tradition in Baltimore. Every year, on the third Saturday in May, nearly 100,000 people from Maryland and around the world gather at the Pimilico Race Course. Celebration festivities begin one week before the race. The week is packed with activities that include a parade, a hot-air balloon festival, outdoor concerts, boat races, and 5K and 10K runs. On race day, the track's gates open at 8:30 am, with the first races beginning at 11 am. The

Preakness itself is the second-to-last race of the day and begins at around 5:30 pm. Visitors looking for a good value and an eye-level view of the horses should reserve seats in the infield. Those willing to spend more money—and dress more formally—should choose seats in the clubhouse or grandstand.

Showcase of Nations Ethnic Festivals. *200 W Lombard St, Baltimore (21201). Various downtown locations. Phone 410/752-8632.* Presenting the food, music, and crafts of a different culture each weekend. June-Sept. **$**

Taste of Baltimore. *Oriole Park at Camden Yards, 333 W Camden St, Baltimore (21201). Phone 410/494-1066. www.tasteofbaltimore.com.* Dozens of restaurants descend upon the ballpark to offer hungry attendees samples of their finest dishes. From Polish sausage and cheese steak to pizza and Italian ice, you're sure to find something to tempt your taste buds. Part of the proceeds from the event go to the Children's Cancer Foundation, so you can indulge without guilt (or with a little less guilt, at least). Live music and family activities provide entertainment between bites. Mid-Sept. **$**

Limited-Service Hotels

★ ★ BROOKSHIRE INNER HARBOR SUITE HOTEL. *120 E Lombard St, Baltimore (21202). Phone 410/625-1300; toll-free 800/647-0013; fax 410/649-2635. www.harbormagic.com.* This hotel welcomes guests with the quiet elegance and sophisticated grace of a luxury retreat. 95 rooms, 11 story. Pets accepted. Complimentary full breakfast. Check-in 3 pm, check-out noon. High-speed Internet access. Fitness room. Business center. **$$**

★ ★ CLARION HOTEL PEABODY COURT. *612 Cathedral St, Baltimore (21201). Phone 410/727-7101; toll-free 800/292-5500; fax 410/789-3312. www.peabodycourt.snbhotels.com.* Listed with the Historic Hotels of America and the National Historic Register, this intimate hotel prides itself on providing guests with personal attention. Located in Mt. Vernon, it is in the heart of Baltimore's cultural corridor, just steps away from the theater, opera, art museums, and several historic churches. Most of the guest rooms look out at the stunning George Washington Monument, which stands in the center of the neighborhood's square. 104 rooms, 14 story. Pets accepted. Check-in 3 pm, check-out 11 am. Restaurant. Fitness room. Restored hotel built in 1927. **$$**

★ ★ DAYS INN INNER HARBOR HOTEL. *100 Hopkins Pl, Baltimore (21201). Phone 410/576-1000; toll-free 800/329-7466; fax 410/576-9437. www.daysinnerharbor.com.* This chain hotel puts you close to the exciting Inner Harbor without breaking your pocketbook. The Inner Harbor, Baltimore's premier waterfront area, features some of the city's best shopping and dining. You'll also be within walking distance to many major attractions, such as the National Aquarium and Oriole Park at Camden Yards. 250 rooms, 9 story. Check-in 3 pm, check-out 11 am. High-speed Internet access. Restaurant, bar. Fitness room. Outdoor pool. Business center. **$**

★ ★ INN AT THE COLONNADE. *4 W University Pkwy, Baltimore (21218). Phone 410/235-5400; fax 410/235-5572. www.colonnadebaltimore.com.* Here you'll find elegance at an affordable price. The European decorated lobby with its hardwood floors and elaborately painted mural ceilings preview the guest rooms' comfort and beauty. The hotel is located across from Johns Hopkins University, is close to Baltimore's Museum of Art, and only 4 miles from the Inner Harbor. Guests will also want to try the hotel's Polo Grill, a brasserie-type restaurant. 125 rooms, 3 story. Check-in 3 pm, check-out noon. Restaurant. Fitness room. Indoor pool, whirlpool. Business center. **$$**

★ ★ TREMONT PARK HOTEL. *8 E Pleasant St, Baltimore (21202). Phone 410/576-1200; toll-free 800/873-6668; fax 410/685-4216. www.tremontsuitehotel.com.* 58 rooms, 13 story, all-suites. Complimentary continental breakfast. Check-out noon. Restaurant, bar. **$$**

Full-Service Hotels

★ ★ ★ HARBOR COURT HOTEL. *550 Light St, Baltimore (21202). Phone 410/234-0550; toll-free 800/824-0076; fax 410/659-5925. www.harborcourt.com.* The Harbor Court Hotel is a distinguished residence for travelers while visiting Baltimore's Inner Harbor. This hotel recreates the spirit of a grand English manor home, and its magnificent sweeping staircase is the first indication of dignified things to come. The professional staff attends to every need, even offering hot, buttery popcorn for guests enjoying in-room movies. Guest services are plentiful, from dry cleaning and child care to spa treatments, and the hotel has a fitness center and yoga studio for athletic-minded guests. Dining is top-notch here, with the American-inspired Hampton's (see), the relaxed elegance of Café Brightons, and the clubby feel of the Explorers Lounge, where live jazz entertains nightly. 200 rooms, 8 story. Check-out noon. High-speed Internet access. Two restaurants, bar. Fitness room, fitness classes available, spa. Indoor pool, whirlpool. Tennis. Airport transportation available. Business center. **$$$**

★ ★ ★ HYATT REGENCY BALTIMORE ON THE INNER HARBOR. *300 Light St, Baltimore (21202). Phone 410/528-1234; toll-free 800/233-1234; fax 410/685-3362. www.baltimore.hyatt.com.* If you want convenience, luxury, and sophistication, this hotel is for you. With a skywalk that connects you to Harborplace, the Inner Harbor's shopping and dining attractions are literally just across the street. Take advantage of the hotel's numerous amenities, such as two outdoor tennis courts, a jogging track, half court basketball, or fitness center with aerobic classes. The staff will also arrange for you to play golf at one of two nearby golf courses. 486 rooms, 15 story. Check-in 3 pm, check-out noon. Two restaurants, two bars. Fitness room, fitness classes available. Outdoor pool. Tennis. Business center. **$$**

★ ★ ★ MARRIOTT BALTIMORE WATERFRONT. *700 Aliceanna St, Baltimore (21202). Phone 410/385-3000; toll-free 800/228-9290; fax 410/895-1900. www.marriotthotels.com.* This beautiful and modern hotel knows how to pamper its guests. From large rooms that offer stunning views of the harbor to luxurious amenities, such as feather pillows and plush duvet-covered beds, this hotel does not skimp on its service. Its location puts you in the center of Baltimore's Inner Harbor and downtown area. You can walk (or even take a water taxi) to some of the city's premier tourist destinations—Little Italy, Pier 6 Concert Pavilion, or Harborplace. 751 rooms, 32 story. Check-in 3 pm, check-out noon. High-speed Internet access. Two restaurants, two bars. Fitness room. Indoor pool. Airport transportation available. Business center. **$$**

★ ★ ★ RENAISSANCE HARBORPLACE HOTEL. *202 E Pratt St, Baltimore (21202). Phone 410/547-1200; toll-free 800/535-1200; fax 410/539-5780. www.renaissancehotels.com.* Located on the waterfront at Baltimore's scenic Inner Harbor and amidst all of downtown's delights, this hotel offers friendly service and elegantly appointed guest rooms. Nearby attractions include the Gallery, Convention Center, and World Trade Center. 657 rooms, 12 story. Check-out noon. Restaurant, bar. Fitness room. Indoor pool, whirlpool. Business center. **$$$**

Full-Service Inn

★ ★ ★ ABACROMBIE BADGER BED AND BREAKFAST. *58 W Biddle St, Baltimore (21201). Phone 410/244-7227; toll-free 888/9-BADGER; fax 410/244-8415. www.badger-inn.com.* Originally an 1880s townhouse, this delightful inn welcomes both business and leisure travelers, enveloping guests with gracious tranquility and a serene atmosphere. Nearby attractions include the Meyerhoff Symphony Hall, Lyric Opera House, and the start to the fashionable Antique Row. 12 rooms, 4 story. Children over 10 years only. Complimentary continental breakfast. Check-in 4-6 pm, check-out noon. Restaurant, bar. **$**

Specialty Lodgings

The following lodging establishments are approved by Mobil Travel Guide, but due to their unique and individualized nature have not been given a traditional Mobil Star rating. Included in this listing you may find bed-and-breakfasts, limited-service inns, guest ranches, and other unique hotel properties.

ADMIRAL FELL INN. *888 S Broadway, Historic Fell's Point, Baltimore (21231). Phone 410/522-7377; toll-free 800/292-4667; fax 410/522-0707. www.admiralfell.com.* This renovated urban inn is conveniently located downtown in the scenic historic waterfront area. From the custom-designed Federal-style furnishings and meeting rooms, which offers guests an empowering view of the skyline and harbor, to the warm and attentive service, this hotel is a delight. Enjoy a stroll along the quaint brick sidewalks to the numerous antique shops, gourmet restaurants, galleries, and friendly pubs. 83 rooms, 5 story. Pets accepted. Complimentary continental breakfast. Check-in 4 pm, check-out noon. Bar. **$$**

BRIDGESTREET HENDERSONS WHARF. *1000 Fell St, Baltimore (21231). Phone 410/522-7777; fax 410/522-7087.* This quiet and well-maintained inn, located in Fells Point, is steeped in history and charm. The building, a converted tobacco warehouse, is listed on the National Historic Register and sits on a marina. Boats are available for rent by the inn's owner. You will be close to a variety of eclectic shops and restaurants, as well as the Inner Harbor. The inn serves a deluxe continental breakfast, and the rooms offer either a harbor or garden view. 38 rooms. Pets accepted; fee. Complimentary continental breakfast. Check-in 3 pm, check-out noon. Fitness room. 19th-century tobacco warehouse. On the waterfront; dockage available. **$$**

CELIE'S WATERFRONT INN. *1714 Thames St, Baltimore (21231). Phone 410/522-2323; toll-free 800/432-0184; fax 410/522-2324. www.celieswaterfront.com.* Located in the heart of the Fell's Point waterfront district, this inn beckons to travelers with its atmospheric seafaring past. Rooms are airy and graced with skylights, offering scenic views of the harbor and well-maintained gardens. 9 rooms, 3 story. Children over 10 years only. Complimentary continental breakfast. Check-in 3 pm, check-out 11 am. **$**

INN AT GOVERNMENT HOUSE. *1125 N Calvert St, Baltimore (21202). Phone 410/539-0566; fax 410/539-0567. www.baltimorecity.gov.* Located in the scenic Mount Vernon historic district, this elegant inn is known to welcome Baltimore's visiting dignitaries. Comprised of three townhouses and charmingly appointed with an elegant Victorian décor, this inn guarantees a welcoming respite as well as warm and friendly service. 18 rooms, 4 story. Pets accepted. Complimentary continental breakfast. Check-in after 11 am, check-out 11 am. **$**

MR. MOLE BED AND BREAKFAST. *1601 Bolton St, Baltimore (21217). Phone 410/728-1179; fax 410/728-3379. www.mrmolebb.com.* This charming 19th-century bed-and-breakfast, decorated with many beautiful antiques, offers you an elegant residential atmosphere without neglecting personal attention. The first floor's 14-foot ceilings, bay windows, and marble fireplace give you a taste of historic sophistication. The inn also serves a full breakfast that features homemade cakes and biscuits. You can choose among five different rooms, each with its own private bath. The inn's Bolton Hill location puts you close to numerous city attractions, including Antique Row. Public transportation is also easily accessible. 5 rooms, 5 story. Children over 10 years only. Complimentary full breakfast. Check-in 4-6 pm, check-out 11 am. **$**

Restaurants

★★ **ANGELINA'S.** *7135 Harford Rd, Baltimore (21234). Phone 410/444-5545; toll-free 800/272-2225. www.crabcake.com.* Italian, American menu. Lunch, dinner. Closed Mon; Thanksgiving, Dec 25. Bar. Children's menu. Casual attire. **$$**

★★ **THE BAYOU CAFE.** *8133A Honeygo Blvd, Baltimore (21236). Phone 410/931-2583. www.thebayoucafe.com.* American, Cajun menu. Lunch, dinner. Bar. Children's menu. Casual attire. Outdoor seating. **$$**

★ **BERTHA'S.** *734 S Broadway, Baltimore (21231). Phone 410/327-5795; fax 410/732-1548.* Seafood menu. Lunch, dinner, Sun brunch. Closed holidays. Bar. Reservations recommended. Historic 19th-century building. **$$**

★★★ **BOCCACCIO.** *925 Eastern Ave, Baltimore (21231). Phone 410/234-1322; fax 410/727-6318.* Italian menu. Lunch, dinner. Closed holidays. Bar. Casual attire. **$$$**

★ **CAFE HON.** *1002 W 36th St, Baltimore (21211). Phone 410/243-1230; fax 410/243-6461. www.cafehon.com.* Breakfast, lunch, dinner, Sun brunch. Closed holidays. Bar. Children's menu. **$$**

★★★ **CHARLESTON.** *1000 Lancaster St, Baltimore (21202). Phone 410/332-7373; fax 410/332-8425. www.charlestonrestaurant.com.* Chef/owner Cindy Wolf's stunning regional American restaurant is one of the most exciting and luxurious dining experiences to be had in Baltimore. This upscale restaurant is warmed by an amber glow that makes you feel ten years younger, and the food is even better. Sautéed heads-on gulf shrimp with andouille sausage and Tasso ham with creamy stone-milled grits, a signature dish, is a perfect example of the robust, home-style low-country cooking served here. The restaurant also has an impressive wine program that includes several dozen sparkling wines and a selection of about 600 well-chosen whites and reds from the New World (Australia, South Africa, New Zealand, and Chile) and the Old World (France, Italy, and Spain). If wine doesn't appeal to you, Charleston offers more than a dozen microbrews and imported beers and a splashy cocktail list that contains some inventive sippers as well as a great variety of classics. American menu. Dinner. Closed Sun, holidays. Bar. Outdoor seating. **$$$**

★★ **CHIAPPARELLI'S OF LITTLE ITALY.** *237 S High St, Baltimore (21202). Phone 410/837-0309; fax 410/783-7985. www.chiapparellis.com.* Italian menu. Lunch, dinner. Closed Thanksgiving, Dec 25. Bar. Children's menu. Casual attire. Valet parking. Built in 1870; original brick walls, oak paneling. Seven dining rooms on two levels. **$$$**

★★ **CITY LIGHTS.** *301 Light St, Baltimore (21202). Phone 410/244-8811; fax 410/244-8815. www.citylightsseafood.com.* Seafood menu. Lunch, dinner. Closed Thanksgiving, Dec 24-25. Bar. Children's menu. Outdoor seating. **$$**

★★★ **DALESIO'S OF LITTLE ITALY.** *829 Eastern Ave, Baltimore (21202). Phone 410/539-1965; fax 410/576-8749. www.dalesios.com.* Italian menu. Lunch, dinner. Closed Thanksgiving. Bar. Casual attire. Valet parking. Outdoor seating. **$$**

★★★ **DELLA NOTTE.** *801 Eastern Ave, Baltimore (21202). Phone 410/837-5500; fax 410/837-2600.* Italian menu. Lunch, dinner. Closed Dec 25. Bar. Children's menu. Casual attire. **$$**

★★ **GERMANO'S TRATTORIA.** *300 S High St, Baltimore (21202). Phone 410/752-4515; fax 410/625-6472. www.germanostrattoria.com.* Tuscan, regional Italian menu. Lunch, dinner. Closed Thanksgiving, Dec 25. Bar. Children's menu. Casual attire. **$$**

★★★ **HAMPTON'S.** *550 Light St, Baltimore (21202). Phone 410/234-0550; fax 410/659-5925. www.harborcourt.com.* Located in the Harbor Court Hotel (see), Hampton's is a luxurious restaurant that serves marvelous seasonal American fare matched by serene and romantic views of Baltimore's Inner Harbor. The kitchen stays true to classic technique, using pristine regional ingredients and clever modern tweaks to add a savvy edge to the plate. Specialties include lobster bisque flecked with chives and mushrooms, seared dry-aged beef tenderloin, and a kickin' horseradish Caesar salad. The wine list is exceptional as well, focusing on small, independent producers and rare vintages that pair up seamlessly with the inspired menu. Nightly live piano and a jazz quartet on the weekends fill the room with an old-world elegance and charm. American menu. Dinner, Sun brunch. Closed Mon. Jacket required. Reservations recommended. Valet parking. **$$$**

★★ **THE HELMAND.** *806 N Charles St, Baltimore (21201). Phone 410/752-0311.* Afghan menu. Dinner. Closed Mon. Bar. Casual attire. **$**

★★ **HENNINGER'S TAVERN.** *1812 Bank St, Baltimore (21231). Phone 410/342-2172. www.henningerstavern.com.* American menu. Dinner. Closed Sun, Mon; Jan 1, Dec 25. Bar. Casual attire. **$$**

★★ **IKAROS.** *4805 Eastern Ave, Baltimore (21224). Phone 410/633-3750.* Greek, American menu. Lunch, dinner. Closed Tues; Thanksgiving, Dec 25. **$$**

★★ **IXIA.** *518 N Charles St, Baltimore (21201). Phone 410/727-1800; fax 410/727-1887. www.ixia-online.com.* Mediterranean menu. Dinner, late-night. Closed Sun-Mon. **$$$**

★★ **JEANNIER'S.** *105 W 39th St, Baltimore (21211). Phone 410/889-3303; fax 410/889-6813.* French menu. Lunch, dinner. Closed Sun; holidays. Bar. **$$**

★★ **JOHN STEVEN, LTD.** *1800 Thames St, Baltimore (21231). Phone 410/327-5561; toll-free 877/732-3460; fax 410/327-0513. www.johnstevenltd.com.* American, eclectic, seafood menu. Lunch, dinner. Bar. Casual attire. Outdoor seating. Building built in 1838. **$$**

★★ **JOY AMERICA CAFE.** *800 Key Hwy, Baltimore (21230). Phone 410/244-6500; fax 410/244-6363. www.avam.org/joyamerica/.* "Nothing Without Joy" is the fitting motto at this whimsical restaurant housed on the top floor of Baltimore's unique Visionary Arts Museum. The food is as creative as the décor, and many dishes have a Latin flair. American menu. Lunch, dinner, Sun brunch. Closed Mon; Labor Day, Thanksgiving, Dec 25. Bar. Children's menu. Outdoor seating. **$$$**

★★ **KAWASAKI.** *413 N Charles St, Baltimore (21201). Phone 410/659-7600; fax 410/625-0607. www.kawasaki-restaurant.com.* Japanese menu. Lunch, dinner. Closed Sun; holidays. Bar. Casual attire. **$$**

★★★ **LA SCALA.** *1012 Eastern Ave, Baltimore (21202). Phone 410/783-9209; fax 410/783-5949. www.lascaladining.com.* Italian menu. Dinner. Closed Jan 1, Thanksgiving, Dec 25. Bar. Casual attire. **$$$**

★★ **MT. WASHINGTON TAVERN.** *5700 Newbury St, Baltimore (21209). Phone 410/367-6903; fax 410/542-9023. www.mtwashingtontavern.com.* American menu. Lunch, dinner, Sun brunch. Closed Dec 25. Bar. **$$$**

★★ **OBRYCKI'S CRAB HOUSE.** *1727 E Pratt St, Baltimore (21231). Phone 410/732-6399; fax 410/522-4637. www.obryckis.com.* Lunch, dinner. Closed mid-Dec-Mar. Bar. Children's menu. **$$$**

★★ **PIERPOINT.** *1822 Aliceanna St, Baltimore (21231). Phone 410/675-2080; fax 410/563-2855. www.pierpointrestaurant.com.* American menu. Lunch, dinner. Closed Mon; Jan 1, Dec 25. Bar. Casual attire. **$$**

★★★ **THE PRIME RIB.** *1101 N Calvert St, Baltimore (21202). Phone 410/539-1804; fax 410/837-0244. www.theprimerib.com.* It's no surprise that The Prime Rib has been voted the best steakhouse in town—it has been serving consistently good steaks, chops, and seafood for three decades. With an upscale atmosphere, it is known as "the civilized steakhouse." Steak, seafood menu. Dinner. Closed Thanksgiving. Bar. Jacket required. Black lacquered walls. **$$$**

★★ **ROCCO'S CAPRICCIO.** *846 Fawn St, Baltimore (21202). Phone 410/685-2710; toll-free 888/685-2710; fax 410/539-4261.* Italian, Mediterranean menu. Lunch, dinner. Closed Thanksgiving, Dec 25. Bar. Children's menu. Casual attire. **$$$**

★★★ **RUBY LOUNGE.** *802 N Charles St, Baltimore (21201). Phone 410/539-8051.* This is a sophisticated spot to spend an evening. The elegantly apportioned restaurant and bar are upscale. The menu presents appetizers and entrées that are a cut above, and the skilled and efficient bar staff whip up fanciful concoctions that are sure to please. American menu. Dinner. Closed Sun-Mon; also holidays. Bar. Casual attire. Valet parking. **$$**

★★★ **RUTH'S CHRIS STEAK HOUSE.** *600 Water St, Baltimore (21202). Phone 410/783-0033; toll-free 800/544-0808; fax 410/783-0049. www.ruthschris.com.* Sizzling hot, custom-aged steaks are the specialty at this branch of the famed national chain. Portions are big enough to share, and there's a courtesy shuttle to all major Inner Harbor hotels. Dinner. Closed Jan 1, Thanksgiving, Dec 25; also Super Bowl Sun. Bar. **$$$**

★★ **SOTTO SOPRA.** *405 N Charles St, Baltimore (21201). Phone 410/625-0534; fax 410/625-2642. www.sottosoprainc.com.* Italian menu. Lunch, dinner. Casual attire. **$$$**

★★★ **SPIKE AND CHARLIE'S.** *1225 Cathedral St, Baltimore (21201). Phone 410/752-8144. www.spikeandcharlies.com.* Here, food is art. Eclectic culinary creations are served in an ultrachic dinner salon. American menu. Dinner. Closed Mon; holidays. Bar. Reservations recommended. **$$**

★★ **TIO PEPE.** *10 E Franklin St, Baltimore (21202). Phone 410/539-4675; fax 410/837-7288.* Spanish menu. Lunch, dinner. Closed holidays. Bar. Jacket required. Reservations recommended. **$$$**

★★ **VELLEGGIA'S.** *829 E Pratt St, Baltimore (21202). Phone 410/685-2620; fax 410/837-5176.* Italian menu. Lunch, dinner. Closed Dec 24-25. Bar. Children's menu. Casual attire. **$$**

Baltimore/ Washington International Airport Area

See also Annapolis, Baltimore; also see District of Columbia

Airport Information

Airport Baltimore/Washington International Airport

Information Phone 410/859-7111 (in Baltimore area), phone 301/201-1000 (in DC area), or 800/IFLY-BWI

Lost and Found Phone 410/859-7387

Airlines Aer Lingus, Air Canada Jazz, Air Jamaica, Air Tran Airways, American Airlines, America West, British Airways, Continental Airlines, Delta Air Lines, Frontier Airlines, Ghana Airways, Hooters Air, Icelandair, Midwest Airlines, Northwest Airlines, Pan Am, Southwest Airlines, United Airlines, US Airways, USA 3000 Airlines

Limited-Service Hotels

★★ EMBASSY SUITES. *1300 Concourse Dr, Linthicum (21090). Phone 410/584-1400; toll-free 800/EMBASSY; fax 410/859-0816. www.embassy-suites.com.* 251 rooms, 8 story, all suites. Complimentary full breakfast. Check-in 3 pm, check-out noon. High-speed Internet access. Restaurant, bar. Fitness room. Indoor pool, whirlpool. Airport transportation available. Business center. **$$**

★ HAMPTON INN. *829 Elkridge Landing Rd, Linthicum (21090). Phone 410/850-0600; toll-free 800/426-7866; fax 410/691-2119. www.hamptoninn.com.* 182 rooms, 5 story. Pets accepted. Complimentary continental breakfast. Check-in 3 pm, check-out noon. High-speed Internet access. Fitness room. Airport transportation available. **$**

Full-Service Hotels

★★★ MARRIOTT BALTIMORE WASHINGTON INTERNATIONAL AIRPORT. *1743 W Nursery Rd, Linthicum (21240). Phone 410/859-8300; toll-free 800/228-9290; fax 410/691-4555. www.marriott.com.* 310 rooms, 10 story. Check-in 3 pm, check-out noon. Restaurant, two bars. Fitness room. Indoor pool, whirlpool. Airport transportation available. Business center. **$$**

★★★ SHERATON INTERNATIONAL HOTEL ON BWI AIRPORT. *7032 Elm Rd, Baltimore (21240). Phone 410/859-3300; toll-free 800/638-5858; fax 410/859-0565. www.sheraton.com.* Whether you are homeward bound or heading out for business or pleasure, this hotel situated on the site of Baltimore's major airport, can be your "stepping stone" to your final destination. It includes all the thoughtful amenities you would expect—Internet access, fitness center, and an onsite restaurant. And don't worry, you can see more than just planes taking off. City attractions, such as the Inner Harbor, Camden Yards, and Laurel Racecourse, are less than 20 minutes away. 201 rooms, 2 story. Pets accepted. Check-in 3 pm, check-out 11 am. Restaurant, bar. Fitness room. Outdoor pool. Airport transportation available. **$$**

Bethesda (C-3)

Also see District of Columbia

Population 55,277
Elevation 305 ft
Area Code 301
Information The Greater Bethesda-Chevy Chase Chamber of Commerce, Landow Building, 7910 Woodmont Ave, Suite 1204, 20814; phone 301/652-4900
Web site www.bccchamber.org

A suburb of Washington, DC, Bethesda is the home of both the National Institutes of Health, research arm of the Public Health Service, and Bethesda Naval Hospital.

What to See and Do

Cabin John Regional Park. *7700 Tuckerman Ln, Rockville (20854). Approximately 3 miles N on Hwy 355*

then W on Tuckerman Ln. Phone 301/299-0024. This 551-acre park has playgrounds, miniature train ride; nature center; concerts (summer evenings; free); tennis courts, game fields, ice rink, nature trails, and picnicking. Fee for some activities. (Daily)

Clara Barton National Historic Site. *5801 Oxford Rd, Glen Echo (20812). 3 miles W via Hwy 191, Goldsboro Rd. Phone 301/492-6245. www.nps.gov/clba.* (See DISTRICT OF COLUMBIA)

National Library of Medicine. *8600 Rockville Pike, Bethesda (20894). Phone 301/496-6308; toll-free 888/346-3656. www.nlm.nih.gov.* World's largest biomedical library; rare books, manuscripts, prints; medical art displays. (Mon-Sat; closed holidays and Sat before Mon holidays) Visitors center and guided tour (Mon-Fri, one departure each day). **FREE**

Limited-Service Hotels

★ ★ HOLIDAY INN. *5520 Wisconsin Ave, Chevy Chase (20815). Phone 301/656-1500; toll-free 800/465-4329; fax 301/656-5045. www.holiday-inn.com.* 215 rooms, 12 story. Pets accepted, some restrictions; fee. Check-in 3 pm, check-out 11 am. Restaurant, bar. Fitness room. Outdoor pool. Business center. **$**

★ ★ MARRIOTT SUITES BETHESDA. *6711 Democracy Blvd, Bethesda (20817). Phone 301/897-5600; toll-free 800/228-9290; fax 301/530-1427. www.marriotthotels.com.* Whether traveling for business or pleasure, this hotel welcomes guests with spacious and well-appointed guest rooms, some with extravagant marbled baths. Nearby attractions include the Kennedy Center, Mormon Temple, and National Zoo. 274 rooms, 11 story, all suites. Check-in 4 pm, check-out 11 am. High-speed Internet access. Restaurant. Fitness room. Indoor, outdoor pools; whirlpool. Business center. **$$**

Full-Service Hotel

★ ★ ★ HYATT REGENCY BETHESDA. *1 Bethesda Metro Ctr, Bethesda (20814). Phone 301/657-1234; fax 301/657-6453. www.bethesda.hyatt.com.* Guests will delight in all the amenities this hotel has to offer. Located at Metro Center and within steps to restaurants, theaters, and some of the best shopping, this hotel is perfect for both the business and leisure traveler. 390 rooms, 12 story. Check-in 3 pm, check-out noon. Restaurant, bar. Children's activity center. Fitness room. Indoor pool. Business center. **$$**

Restaurants

★ ★ AUSTIN GRILL. *7278 Woodmont Ave, Bethesda (20814). Phone 301/656-1366; fax 301/656-1398. www.austingrill.com.* Tex-Mex menu. Lunch, dinner, late-night, brunch. Closed Thanksgiving, Dec 24-25. Bar. Children's menu. Casual attire. Outdoor seating. **$$**

★ ★ BACCHUS BETHESDA. *7945 Norfolk Ave, Bethesda (20814). Phone 301/657-1722; fax 301/657-4406. www.bacchusrestaurant.com.* Middle Eastern menu. Lunch, dinner. Closed Jan 1, Thanksgiving, Dec 25. Casual attire. Valet parking. Outdoor seating. **$$**

★ BETHESDA CRAB HOUSE. *4958 Bethesda Ave, Bethesda (20814). Phone 301/652-3382; fax 301/652-4669. www.bethesdacrabhouse.com.* Seafood menu. Lunch, dinner, late-night. Closed Dec 25. Casual attire. Outdoor seating. Rustic décor; established 1961. **$$**

★ ★ BUON GIORNO. *8003 Norfolk Ave, Bethesda (20814). Phone 301/652-1400; fax 301/654-5508.* Italian menu. Dinner. Closed Mon; holidays; also mid-Aug-mid-Sept. Bar. Valet parking (dinner). **$$**

★ ★ CAFE BETHESDA. *5027 Wilson Ln, Bethesda (20814). Phone 301/657-3383.* French bistro menu. Lunch, dinner. Closed Mon; holidays; also Super Bowl Sun. Casual attire. Valet parking. Outdoor seating. **$$**

★ ★ ★ CESCO TRATTORIA. *4871 Cordell Ave, Bethesda (20814). Phone 301/654-8333; fax 301/654-8874.* Reminiscent of a Tuscan villa, Cesco Trattoria features breads that are baked fresh daily in a wood-burning oven that is visible to diners. Entrées are light, yet hearty, and desserts are simply delicious. Italian menu. Lunch, dinner. Closed holidays. Bar. Casual attire. Valet parking (dinner). Outdoor seating. **$$$**

★★ **FOONG LIN.** *7710 Norfolk Ave, Bethesda (20814). Phone 301/656-3427; fax 301/215-7985. www.foonglin.com.* Chinese menu. Lunch, dinner. Closed Thanksgiving. Bar. Casual attire. **$$**

★★ **FRASCATI.** *4806 Rugby Ave, Bethesda (20814). Phone 301/652-9514; fax 301/656-5538. www.ilfrascati.com.* Italian menu. Lunch, dinner. Closed Mon; Jan 1, Easter, Dec 25. Reservations recommended. Outdoor seating. **$$**

★★ **JEAN-MICHEL.** *10223 Old Georgetown Rd, Bethesda (20814). Phone 301/564-4910; fax 301/569-4912.* French menu. Lunch, dinner. Closed holidays; also Sun in July-Aug. Casual attire. **$$$**

★★★ **LA FERME.** *7101 Brookville Rd, Chevy Chase (20815). Phone 301/986-5255; fax 301/951-4450. www.lafermerestaurant.com.* A pretty country house setting is the draw at this comfortable French restaurant. French menu. Lunch, dinner. Closed Mon; Dec 25. Reservations recommended. Outdoor seating. **$$**

★★★ **LE VIEUX LOGIS.** *7925 Old Georgetown Rd, Bethesda (20814). Phone 301/652-6816; fax 301/652-8221.* American and Scandinavian cooking adds to the dining experience. French menu. Dinner. Closed Sun; Jan 1, Dec 25. Casual attire. Free valet parking. Outdoor seating. **$$$**

★★ **MONTGOMERY'S GRILLE.** *7200 Wisconsin Ave, Bethesda (20814). Phone 301/654-3595; fax 301/654-3596.* American menu. Lunch, dinner, Sun brunch. Closed Thanksgiving, Dec 25. Bar. Children's menu. Casual attire. Outdoor seating. **$$**

★ **NAPA THAI.** *4924 St. Elmo, Bethesda (20814). Phone 301/986-8590; fax 301/986-8490.* Thai menu. Lunch, dinner. Closed July 4, Thanksgiving. Casual attire. Outdoor seating. **$$**

★ **RAKU.** *7240 Woodmont Ave, Bethesda (20814). Phone 301/718-8680; fax 301/718-8683.* Pan-Asian menu. Lunch, dinner. Closed Thanksgiving, Dec 25. Children's menu. Outdoor seating. **$$**

★★★ **RUTH'S CHRIS STEAK HOUSE.** *7315 Wisconsin Ave, Bethesda (20814). Phone 301/652-7877; fax 301/718-8463. www.ruthschris.com.* Steak menu. Dinner. Closed Thanksgiving, Dec 25. Bar. Casual attire. Valet parking. Lobster tank; cigar lounge. **$$$**

★★ **THYME SQUARE.** *4735 Bethesda Ave, Bethesda (20814). Phone 301/657-9077; fax 301/657-4505.* American menu. Lunch, dinner. Closed Dec 25. Bar. Children's menu. Casual attire. Outdoor seating. **$$**

★★★ **TRAGARA.** *4935 Cordell Ave, Bethesda (20814). Phone 301/951-4935; fax 301/951-0401. www.tragara.com.* Tragara is one of Bethesda's most elegant and romantic restaurants, offering satisfying Italian cuisine and impeccable service. Bathed in soft light, with fresh roses on every linen-topped table, Tragara is serene and relaxing—a lovely place to dine and then linger. Tables fill up quickly at lunch and dinner with smartly dressed business executives and stylish quartets of 30-something couples. The impressive Italian kitchen draws them all in with a tempting menu of pastas, fish, meat, and antipasti, but be sure to save room to indulge in the house-made gelato before saying, "Ciao." Italian menu. Lunch, dinner. Closed holidays. Casual attire. Valet parking. **$$$**

Boonsboro (A-2)

See also Frederick, Hagerstown

Settled 1787
Population 2,803
Elevation 591 ft
Area Code 301
Zip 21713
Information Hagerstown/Washington County Chamber of Commerce, 111 W Washington St; phone 301/739-2015
Web site www.hagerstown.org

What to See and Do

Crystal Grottoes Caverns. *19821 Shepherdstown Pike, Boonsboro (Washington County) (21713). 1 mile SW on Hwy 34. Phone 301/432-6336. www.goodearthgraphics.com/showcave/md/crystal.html.* Limestone caverns may be viewed from walkways. Picnicking. Guided tours (Apr-Oct, daily 9 am-6 pm; Nov-Mar, Sat-Sun 11 am-4 pm). **$$$**

Gathland State Park. *In Washington and Frederick Counties, 1 mile W of Burkittsville, off Rte 17. Phone 301/791-4767. www.dnr.state.md.us/publiclands/western/gathland.html.* On 140 acres. A site once owned by George Townsend, Civil War reporter. A monument was built in 1896 to honor Civil War correspondents. The visitor center contains original papers. Picnicking, walking tour, winter sports.

Washington Monument State Park. *21843 National Pike Rd (21713). 3 miles SE off Hwy 40A. Phone 301/791-4767. www.dnr.state.md.us/publiclands/western/washington.html.* On 147 acres. A 34-foot tower of native stone (1827) was the first completed monument to honor George Washington. Views of nearby battlefields, two states (Pennsylvania and West Virginia). History Center displays firearms and Civil War mementos (by appointment). The Appalachian Trail leads through the park; hiking and picnicking. **FREE**

Restaurant

★ ★ OLD SOUTH MOUNTAIN INN. *6132 Old National Pike (Alt Hwy 40), Boonsboro (21713). Phone 301/371-5400; fax 301/432-2211. www.oldsouthmountaininn.com.* American menu. Lunch, dinner, Sun brunch. Closed Mon; Dec 25. Bar. Children's menu. Reservations recommended. Outdoor seating. Founded in 1732; was once a stagecoach stop. **$$$**

Bowie (C-4)

See also College Park, Silver Spring; also see District of Columbia

Population 50,269
Elevation 150 ft
Area Code 301 and 204
Information Greater Bowie Chamber of Commerce, 6770 Race Track Rd, Hilltop Plaza, 20715; phone 301/262-0920. Information is also available from Prince George's Conference & Visitors Bureau, 9475 Lottsford Rd, #130, Landover 20785; phone 301/925-8300

What to See and Do

Belair Mansion. *12207 Tulip Grove Dr, Bowie (20715). Phone 301/809-3089. www.cityofbowie.org/comserv/museums.htm.* Georgian-style home (circa 1745) was home of Governor Samuel Ogle in the 1700s; later owned by the Woodward family, prominent racehorse breeders in the first half of the 20th century. Tours. (Wed-Sun noon-4 pm, groups by appointment) **DONATION**

Belair Stable Museum. *2835 Belair Dr, Bowie (20715). Phone 301/809-3089. www.cityofbowie.org/comserv/museums.htm.* Part of famed Belair Stud, one of the premier Thoroughbred racing stables of the '30s, '40s, and '50s. Was home to two Triple Crown winners—Gallant Fox and Omaha—and the 1955 Horse of the Year, Nashua. (Wed-Sun noon-4 pm, groups by appointment) **FREE**

Marietta House Museum. *5626 Bell Station Rd, Glenn Dale (20769). 3 miles W. Phone 301/464-5291.* A modest Federal-style plantation house built by Gabriel Duvall, an associate justice of the US Supreme Court (1811-1835). Tours. (Mar-Dec: Fri 11 am-3 pm; Sun noon-4 pm. Groups by appointment. Library open Sat noon-4 pm) **$**

Special Event

Heritage Day. *Belair Mansion and Stable. 2835 Belair Dr, Bowie (20715). Phone 301/809-3089.* Performance by Congress' Own Regiment; tour of stables and grounds; battle reenactments; demonstrations of colonial crafts. Third Sun in May.

Limited-Service Hotel

★ HAMPTON INN BOWIE. *15202 Major Lansdale Blvd, Bowie (20716). Phone 301/809-1800; fax 301/809-2515. www.hamptoninn.com.* 301 rooms. Check-in 3 pm, check-out noon. Fitness room. Outdoor pool, whirlpool. **$**

Cambridge (D-5)

See also Easton, Salisbury

Founded 1684
Population 10,911
Elevation 14 ft
Area Code 410
Zip 21613
Information Dorchester County Visitors Center, 2 Rose Hill Pl; phone 410/228-1000 or toll-free 800/522-TOUR
Web site www.tourdorchester.org

On the Eastern Shore, Cambridge is Maryland's second-largest deep-water port. Boating and fishing opportunities are found in the Choptank and Honga rivers and Chesapeake, Tar, and Fishing bays.

What to See and Do

Blackwater National Wildlife Refuge. *2145 Key Wallace Dr (21613). 12 miles S via Hwy 16, 335. Phone 410/228-2677. blackwater.fws.gov.* Over 20,000 acres of rich tidal marsh, freshwater ponds, and woodlands. One of the chief wintering areas for Canada geese and ducks using the Atlantic Flyway; in fall, as many as 33,000 geese and 17,000 ducks swell the bird population. Also a haven for the bald eagle, the Delmarva fox squirrel, and the peregrine falcon. Scenic drive, woodland trails, photo blind. Visitor center (Daily; closed Thanksgiving, Dec 25). Golden Age, Golden Eagle, and Golden Access passports (see MAKING THE MOST OF YOUR TRIP). **$**

Old Trinity Church, Dorchester Parish. *8 miles SW on Hwy 16 in Church Creek. Phone 410/228-2940.* (Circa 1675) One of the oldest churches in US still holding regular services; faithful restoration of interior. (By appointment) **FREE**

Special Events

Antique Aircraft Fly-In. *Dorchester Heritage Museum, 1904 Horn Point Rd, Cambridge (21613). 5 miles W on Hwy 343. Phone 410/228-5530; toll-free 800/522-8687.* Old and new planes on display. Third weekend in May.

National Outdoor Show. *Phone toll-free 800/522-8687.* Goose and duck calling, log sawing, crab picking, trap setting contests; entertainment. Last weekend in Feb.

Chesapeake and Ohio Canal National Historical Park (D-2)

As early as 1754 the enterprising George Washington, only in his twenties, proposed a system of navigation along the Potomac River valley. His Potowmack Canal Company, organized in 1785, cleared obstructions and built skirting canals to facilitate the transportation of goods from settlements beyond the Allegheny Mountains to the lower Potomac River towns.

The eventual inadequacy of these improvements and the renowned success of the Erie Canal spurred the formation in 1828 of the Chesapeake and Ohio Canal Company, whose purpose was to connect Georgetown with the Ohio Valley by river and canal. On July 4, 1828, President John Quincy Adams led the traditional groundbreaking ceremony declaring, "To subdue the earth is preeminently the purpose of this undertaking." Unfortunately, the earth was not easily subdued. President Adams bent his shovel after several attempts before breaking into an energetic frenzy and successfully getting a shovelful of dirt.

The difficulty of the groundbreaking ceremony foreshadowed the canal's short-lived future as a major transportation artery. Completed in 1850 as far as Cumberland, Maryland (184 1/2 miles from Georgetown), the waterway was used extensively for the transportation of coal, flour, grain, and lumber. Financial and legal difficulties, the decline of commerce after the Civil War, the Baltimore & Ohio Railroad, and the advent of improved roads cut deeply into the commerce of the waterway, and it gradually faded into obsolescence. The canal still had limited commercial use as late as 1924, when a flood destroyed many of the canal locks and nothing was restored.

The unfortunate demise of the C & O Canal is now a blessing for hikers, canoeists, and bikers, who can find access to the towpath along the banks of the waterway. Remaining as one of the least altered of old American canals, the Chesapeake and Ohio is flanked by ample foliage throughout most of its 20,239 acres.

Many points of interest can be seen along the waterway. Exhibits are offered in Cumberland, Georgetown, Hancock, and Williamsport and at a museum near the Great Falls of the Potomac. At the Great Falls there are interpretive programs, including self-guiding trails, picnic facilities, and a working lock. Mule-drawn canal boat rides are offered April-October at Georgetown and Great Falls (fee). Camping for hikers and bikers is available throughout the park.

For information about the canal contact the Chief of Visitor Services, C & O Canal National Historical Park, PO Box 4, Sharpsburg, MD 21782; phone 301/739-4200. Visitor centers are located in Cumberland, Georgetown, Great Falls, Hancock, and Williamsport.

Chesapeake Bay Bridge Area (B-5)

The majestic twin spans of the Chesapeake Bay Bridge carry visitors to the Eastern Shore, a patchwork of small picturesque towns, lighthouses, and fishing villages tucked away from the city. Scenic rivers and bays, wildlife, gardens, and wildflowers fill the countryside. The main attractions of any visit, however, are the many fine inns and the restaurants specializing in local seafood.

What to See and Do

Wye Oak State Park. *Hwy 662, Wye Mills (21657). On the Eastern Shore in Talbot County, approximately 1 mile from the junction of Rtes 50 and 404. Phone 410/820-1668. www.dnr.state.md.us/publiclands/eastern/wyeoak.html.* The official state tree of Maryland is in this 29-acre park; it is the largest white oak in the US (108 feet high, 28 feet around) and is believed to be over 460 years old; a new tree has been started from an acorn. A restored 18th-century one-room schoolhouse and the Old Wye Mill (late 1600s) are nearby.

Limited-Service Hotel

★ COMFORT INN. *160 Scheeler Rd, Chestertown (21666). Phone 410/810-0555; toll-free 800/424-6423; fax 410/810-0286. www.chestertown.com/comfortsuites.* 53 rooms, 3 story, all suites. Complimentary continental breakfast. Check-in 3 pm, check-out 11 am. Indoor pool. **$**

Full-Service Inn

★ ★ ★ KENT MANOR INN. *500 Kent Manor Dr, Stevensville (21666). Phone 410/643-7716; toll-free 800/820-4511; fax 410/643-8315. www.kentmanor.com.* 24 rooms, 3 story. Complimentary continental breakfast. Check-in 3 pm, check-out 11 am. Wireless Internet access. Restaurant, bar. Outdoor pool. Built in 1820. On Thompson Creek. **$$**

Specialty Lodgings

The following lodging establishments are approved by Mobil Travel Guide, but due to their unique and individualized nature have not been given a traditional Mobil Star rating. Included in this listing you may find bed-and-breakfasts, limited-service inns, guest ranches, and other unique hotel properties.

HUNTINGFIELD MANOR. *4928 Eastern Neck Rd, Rock Hall (21661). Phone 410/639-7779; toll-free 800/720-8788; fax 410/639-2924. www.huntingfield.com.* 6 rooms, 2 story. Pets accepted, some restrictions. Complimentary continental breakfast. Check-in 2 pm, check-out noon. Outdoor pool. Telescope-type house on a working farm that dates to the middle 1600s. **$**

INN AT MITCHELL HOUSE. *8796 Maryland Pkwy, Chestertown (21620). Phone 410/778-6500; fax 410/778-2861. www.chestertown.com/mitchell.* Built in 1743, this elegant and historic manor house welcomes guests with friendly service and a serene atmosphere, set amidst lush woods and 10 beautiful acres. Guests will delight in views of the Stoneybrook Pond and the tranquility of this charming inn. 5 rooms, 2 story. Complimentary full breakfast. Check-in 3 pm, check-out noon. **$$**

WHITE SWAN TAVERN. *231 High St, Chestertown (21620). Phone 410/778-2300; fax 410/778-4543. www.chestertown.com/whiteswan/.* 6 rooms, 2 story. Complimentary continental breakfast. Check-in

3-10 pm, check-out noon. Former house and tavern built in 1733 and 1793, respectively; restored with antique furnishings; museum. **$**

Restaurants

★ ★ FISHERMAN'S INN AND CRAB DECK. *316 Main St, Kent Narrows (21638). Phone 410/827-8807; fax 410/827-5705. www.fishermansinn.com.* Seafood menu. Lunch, dinner. Closed Dec 24-25. Bar. **$$**

★ HARRIS CRAB HOUSE. *433 Kent Narrows Way N, Grasonville (21638). Phone 410/827-9500; fax 410/827-9057. www.harriscrabhouse.com.* Seafood menu. Lunch, dinner. Closed Thanksgiving, Dec 25. Bar. Outdoor seating. Gazebo. **$**

★ ★ ★ NARROWS. *3023 Kent Narrows Way S, Grasonville (21638). Phone 410/827-8113; fax 410/827-8436.* This restaurant offers waterfront dining with a spectacular view of the narrows. Regional Eastern Shore menu. Lunch, dinner, brunch. Closed Dec 24-25. Bar. Children's menu. **$$**

★ ★ OLD WHARF INN. *Cannon St, Chestertown (21620). Phone 410/778-3566; fax 410/778-2989.* American menu. Lunch, dinner, Sun brunch. Closed Dec 25. Bar. Children's menu. Outdoor seating. **$**

★ WATERMAN'S CRAB HOUSE. *21055 Sharp St, Rock Hall (21661). Phone 410/639-2261; fax 410/639-2819.* Seafood menu. Lunch, dinner. Closed Thanksgiving; also Jan-Feb. Bar. Children's menu. Outdoor seating. On Rock Hall Harbor. **$**

Cheverly

Restaurant

★ FRATELLI. *5820 Landover Rd, Cheverly (20784). Phone 301/209-9006; fax 301/209-9012.* Italian menu. Lunch, dinner. Bar. **$$**

Chevy Chase

(See Bethesda)

Cockeysville (A-4)

See also Baltimore, Towson

Population 19,388
Elevation 260 ft
Area Code 410
Zip 21030
Information Baltimore County Chamber of Commerce, 102 W Pennsylvania Ave, Suite 402, Towson 21204; phone 410/825-6200

What to See and Do

Ladew Topiary Gardens. *3535 Jarrettsville Pike, Monkton (21111). Phone 410/557-9466. www.ladewgardens.com.* The Garden Club of America once described these gardens as the best in the country. Created by Harvey S. Ladew in the 1930s, the property contains 15 thematic gardens that total 22 acres. In addition to seeing the gardens, visitors can walk a 1.5-mile nature trail that runs through the property or tour the Ladew Manor House, furnished with Ladew's own antique English furniture and fox-hunting memorabilia. (Mid-Apr-Oct: Mon-Fri 10 am-4 pm, Sat-Sun 10:30 am-5 pm; last house tour 3 pm weekdays, 4 pm weekends) **$$$**

Special Event

Point-to-Point Steeplechase. *Phone 410/825-6200.* Three well-known meets on consecutive wkends: **My Lady's Manor.** In Monkton. Mid-Apr. **Grand National.** In Butler; phone 410/666-7777. Mid-Apr. **Maryland Hunt Cup.** In Glyndon; Phone 410/666-7777. Late Apr.

Full-Service Hotel

★ ★ ★ MARRIOTT HUNT VALLEY INN. *245 Shawan Rd, Hunt Valley (21031). Phone 410/785-7000; fax 410/785-0341. www.marriott.com.* Located 20 minutes north of Baltimore's Inner Harbor and on 18 acres of land, this hotel offers comfortable guest rooms with the amenities that business and leisure travelers expect. Workout in the health club facilities that include a whirlpool; sauna; indoor/outdoor pools; and tennis courts; or play a round of golf at one of the six nearby golf courses. Your dining needs will be met at any of the three on-site restaurants. For your business needs, take advantage of Marriott's

Wired for Business program that offers high-speed Internet access and unlimited local and long distance calls for a low daily fee. You'll also have access to WiFi in the hotel's meeting and public areas. 390 rooms, 4 story. Check-in 4 pm, check-out noon. High-speed Internet access. Restaurant, bar. Fitness room. Indoor pool, outdoor pool, whirlpool. Tennis. Business center. **$$**

Restaurants

★★★ **THE MILTON INN.** *14833 York Rd, Sparks (21152). Phone 410/771-4366; fax 410/771-4184. www.miltoninn.com.* This old stone house has been restored for use as a country inn that serves exceptional food in an authentic colonial atmosphere. Seafood menu. Dinner. Closed holidays. Bar. Children's menu. Outdoor seating. **$**

★★★ **THE OREGON GRILLE.** *1201 Shawan Rd, Hunt Valley (21030). Phone 410/771-0505; fax 410/771-9837. www.theoregongrille.com.* Steakhouses tend to blur together after a while. You find meat, creamed spinach, mashed potatoes, some sort of hash browns, and overpriced cabernets, and that's pretty much the standard formula. It takes a special place to break the cookie-cutter mold. The Oregon Grille succeeds in differentiating itself from the fray by offering not only a terrific selection of impeccably prepared steaks (all beef is dry-aged USDA Prime), but also a creative selection of classic American cuisine, including free-range poultry, fresh seafood, and vibrant first courses that stay true to regional ingredients. But it's not just the food that sets it apart. The attentive, tuxedoed waitstaff succeeds in making every diner in the room feel special, and the décor takes a step back from the typical boys' club. The restaurant, set in a renovated 19th-century stone farmhouse, has four fireplaces and is filled with deep, luxurious banquettes. Its long, rich, mahogany bar is the perfect spot for lingering pre- or post-steak. American menu. Lunch, dinner, Sun brunch. Closed Dec 25. Bar. Jacket required after 5 pm. Outdoor seating. **$$$**

★★ **YORK INN.** *10010 York Rd, Cockeysville (21030). Phone 410/666-0006; fax 410/666-7612.* Continental menu. Lunch, dinner, Sun brunch. Closed Dec 25. Bar. Children's menu. Casual attire. Reservations recommended. **$$$**

College Park

See also Bowie, Silver Spring; also see District of Columbia

Population 24,657
Elevation 190 ft
Area Code 301
Zip 20740
Information Prince George's County Conference & Visitors Bureau, 9200 Basil Ct, #101, Largo 20774; phone 301/925-8300 or toll-free 888/925-8300
Web site www.goprincegeorgescounty.com

What to See and Do

College Park Aviation Museum. *1985 Corporal Frank Scott Dr, College Park (20740). Phone 301/864-6029 (recording). www.collegeparkaviationmuseum.com.* World's oldest operating airport, started by Wilbur Wright in 1909 to train two military officers in the operation of aircraft. First airplane machine gun and radio-navigational aids tested here; first air mail and controlled helicopter flights. Museum (daily 10 am-5 pm; closed holidays). **$**

Greenbelt Park. *6565 Greenbelt Rd, College Park (20770). E off Kenilworth Ave, Hwy 201, exit 23. Phone 301/344-3948.* A 1,100-acre wooded park operated by the National Park Service that includes 174 sites. Nature trails, picnicking, camping (dump station, showers; seven-day limit Memorial Day-Labor Day; 14-day limit rest of year). Self-registration; first-come, first-served.

NASA/Goddard Visitor Center. *SE on I-95 to Baltimore-Washington Pkwy, exit 22 A Greenbelt, then follow signs. Phone 301/286-8981. www.gsfc.nasa.gov/vc/.* Satellites, rockets, capsules, and exhibits in all phases of space research. (Mon-Fri 9 am-4 pm) **FREE**

University of Maryland. *Hwy 1, College Park (20742). Phone 301/405-1000. www.umd.edu.* (1865) (35,000 students) Tawes Fine Arts Theater has plays, musicals, concerts, dance, opera, and music festivals. Tours.

Limited-Service Hotels

★★ **COURTYARD BY MARRIOTT.** *6301 Golden Triangle Dr, Greenbelt (20770). Phone 301/441-3311;*

toll-free 800/321-2211; fax 301/441-4978. www.courtyard.com. 152 rooms, 4 story. Check-in 3 pm, check-out noon. High-speed Internet access. Restaurant, bar. Fitness room. Indoor pool, whirlpool. **$**

★★ HOLIDAY INN. *10000 Baltimore Ave, College Park (20740). Phone 301/345-6700; toll-free 800/465-4329; fax 301/441-4923. www.holiday-inn.com.* 222 rooms, 4 story. Check-in 3 pm, check-out noon. Restaurant, bar. Fitness room. Indoor pool, whirlpool. Business center. **$**

Full-Service Hotels

★★★ MARRIOTT GREENBELT. *6400 Ivy Ln, Greenbelt (20770). Phone 301/441-3700; toll-free 800/228-9290; fax 301/441-3995. www.marriott.com.* 287 rooms, 18 story. Check-in 4 pm, check-out noon. High-speed Internet access. Two restaurants, bar. Children's activity center. Fitness room. Indoor pool, outdoor pool, whirlpool. Tennis. Business center. **$$**

★★★ SHERATON COLLEGE PARK. *4095 Powder Mill Rd, Beltsville (20705). Phone 301/937-4422; toll-free 800/325-3535; fax 301/730-1290. www.sheraton.com.* 205 rooms, 9 story. Pets accepted, fee. Check-in 3 pm, check-out noon. High-speed Internet access. Restaurant, bar. Fitness room. Outdoor pool. Business center. **$**

Restaurants

★★ CHEF'S SECRET. *5810 Greenbelt Rd, Greenbelt (20770). Phone 301/345-6101; fax 301/345-6102.* Superb Thai seafood courses are served in a most elegant setting. Don't let the small warehouselike exterior fool you. Thai menu. Lunch, dinner. Closed Labor Day, Dec 25. **$$**

★ SANTA FE CAFE. *4410 Knox Rd, College Park (20740). Phone 301/779-1345; fax 301/779-4522. www.santafecafe.com.* Southwestern, American menu. Lunch, dinner. Closed Sun; Thanksgiving, Dec 25. Bar. Outdoor seating. Casual Southwestern décor; murals, buffalo heads, Native American rugs. **$**

Columbia (B-3)

See also Baltimore

Population 88,254
Elevation 402 ft
Area Code 410 & 443
Information Howard County Tourism Council, 8267 Main St, PO Box 9, Ellicott City 21041; phone 410/313-1900 or toll-free 800/288-TRIP
Web site www.visithowardcounty.com

A planned city built on a tract of land larger than Manhattan Island, Columbia comprises 11 villages surrounding a central downtown service area. Construction of the city began in 1966.

What to See and Do

African Art Museum of Maryland. *5430 Vantage Point Rd, Columbia (21044). In Historic Oakland at Town Center. Phone 410/730-7106. www.africanartmuseum.org.* Masks, sculptured figures, textiles, basketry, household items, and musical instruments displayed in a 19th-century manor. (Tues-Fri 10 am-4 pm, Sun noon-4 pm; closed holidays) **$**

Howard County Center of African-American Culture. *5434 Vantage Point Rd, Columbia (21045). Phone 410/715-1921.* Contains artifacts and memorabilia depicting images of African-Americans over the last 200 years. Extensive collection of spiritual, jazz, and rap music; more than 2,000 books and periodicals; hands-on exhibit for children. (Tues-Fri noon-5 pm, Sat noon-4 pm, Sun by appointment; closed holidays) **$$**

Special Events

Columbia Festival of Arts. *10221 Wincopin Cir, Columbia (21044). Phone 410/715-3089. www.columbiafestival.com.* Music, dance, theater, lakeside entertainment. Ten days in mid-June. **$$$$**

Symphony of Lights. *Phone 410/313-1900.* Animated lighting displays along a 1 1/2-mile park route. Late Nov-early Jan.

Wine in the Woods. *Symphony Woods, 10475 Little Patuxent Pkwy, Columbia (21044). Phone 410/313-7275. www.wineinthewoods.com.* Symphony Woods at Merriweather Post Pavilion. Two-day celebration featuring Maryland wines, gourmet food, entertainment, arts and crafts. Third weekend in May. **$$$$**

Full-Service Hotels

★★★ HILTON COLUMBIA. *5485 Twin Knolls Rd, Columbia (21045). Phone 410/997-1060; toll-free 800/235-0653; fax 410/997-0160. www.hilton.com.* Located in the heart of Columbia and set amidst a parklike setting, this hotel offers a very relaxing stay. From the exquisitely glassed atrium to the elegantly appointed guest rooms, this hotel is a delight. 152 rooms, 4 story. Check-in 3 pm, check-out 11 am. High-speed Internet access. Restaurant, bar. Fitness room. Indoor pool, whirlpool. Business center. **$$**

★★★ SHERATON COLUMBIA HOTEL. *10207 Wincopin Cir, Columbia (21044). Phone 410/730-3900; toll-free 800/638-2817; fax 410/730-1319. www.sheraton.com.* Recognized for its gracious accommodations, superb service and handsomely appointed guestrooms, this hotel is a welcome retreat for both business and leisure travelers. 288 rooms, 10 story. Pets accepted, some restrictions. Check-in 3 pm, check-out noon. High-speed Internet access. Restaurant, bar. Fitness room. Pool. **$$**

Restaurants

★★ CLYDE'S. *10221 Wincopin Cir, Columbia (21044). Phone 410/730-2829; fax 410/596-4052. www.clydes.com.* American menu. Lunch, dinner, Sun brunch. Closed Dec 25. Bar. Children's menu. Outdoor seating. **$$**

★★★ KING'S CONTRIVANCE. *10150 Shaker Dr, Columbia (21046). Phone 410/995-0500; fax 410/730-8063.* A mansion built in 1900 is the casual setting for this regional seafood restaurant with excellent crab cakes. Landlubbers can feast on rack of lamb, and all can enjoy the house baked goods. American menu. Lunch, dinner. Bar. Reservations recommended. Enclosed porch dining. **$$**

Crisfield (E-5)

See also Pocomoke City

Population 2,723
Elevation 4 ft
Area Code 410
Zip 21817
Information Crisfield Area Chamber of Commerce, 906 W Main St, PO Box 292; phone 410/968-2500
Web site www.crisfield.org

What to See and Do

Janes Island State Park. *26280 Alfred Lawson Dr, Crisfield (21817). Approximately 2 miles NE via Hwy 413, then 1 1/2 miles N on Hwy 358. Phone 410/968-1565; toll-free 888/432-2267 (reservations). www.dnr.state.md.us/publiclands/eastern/janesisland.html.* These 3,147 acres are nearly surrounded by Chesapeake Bay and its inlets. Swimming, fishing, boat ramp (rentals); cabins, camping.

Tangier Island Cruises. *1001 W Main St, Crisfield (21817). Phone 410/968-2338.* Trips to the fishing village of Tangier Island, VA. (Mid-May-Oct) **$$$$**

Tyler's Cruises. *Somers Cove Marina, 7th St, Crisfield. Phone 410/425-2771. www.smithislandcruises.com/daycruise.html.* The *Chelsea's Lane Tyler* and the *Captain Tyler* make approximately one-hour cruises to Smith Island. Bus tour of the two villages that compose the island, with spare time to visit the rest of the island; lunch available (fee). Tour length approximately 4 1/2 hours. (Memorial Day weekend-mid-Oct) **$$$$**

Special Event

National Hard Crab Derby & Fair. *Somers Cove Marina, 7th St, Crisfield (21817). Phone 410/968-2500; toll-free 800/782-3913. www.crisfield.org/crabderby.cfm.* Cooking, crab picking, boat docking contests; crab racing; fireworks and parade. Fri-Sun, Labor Day weekend. **$**

Limited-Service Hotel

★ PINES MOTEL. *127 N Somerset Ave, Crisfield (21817). Phone 410/968-0900; fax 410/968-0900.* 40 rooms. Check-out 11 am. Outdoor pool. In scenic, wooded section. **$**

Cumberland (D-2)

Settled 1750
Population 21,518
Elevation 688 ft
Area Code 301 and 240
Zip 21502
Information Allegany County Convention & Visitors Bureau, 13 Canal St; phone 301/777-5132 or toll-free 800/425-2067
Web site www.mdmountainside.com

Far to the west in the state, Cumberland is nestled between Pennsylvania and West Virginia. The Potomac River and its tributary, Wills Creek, flow peaceably by this onetime western outpost of the colonies.

British General Edward Braddock was sent here to conquer the French and Native Americans in 1755; unprepared for the wilderness, he met with defeat and death. George Washington, who defended the town in that period, felt the main east-west route would pass through Cumberland eventually. In 1833, the National Road (Hwy 40 Alternate) made the town a supply terminus for overland commerce. The road was extended farther west, the B & O Railroad reached here in 1842, and eight years later came the Chesapeake and Ohio Canal (see CHESAPEAKE AND OHIO CANAL NATIONAL HISTORICAL PARK), bringing prosperous business. Today's economy no longer depends on industry alone but includes services and recreational facilities.

What to See and Do

Dans Mountain State Park. *Water Station Run, Lonaconing (21539). 10 miles W on I-68, then 8 miles S on Hwy 36, 2 miles SE of Lonaconing. Phone 301/463-5564; toll-free 888/432-2267 (reservations). www.dnr.state.md.us/publiclands/western/dansmountain.html.* On 481 acres. Nearby Dans Rock affords a panoramic view of surrounding region from a height of 2,898 feet. Swimming pool (fee), fishing; picnicking, playground, hiking, sledding.

Fort Cumberland Trail. Walking trail covers several city blocks downtown around the site of Fort Cumberland. Includes boundary markers, narrative plaques.

George Washington's Headquarters. *Greene St, Cumberland (21502). In Riverside Park, downtown. Phone 310/777-8214.* (Circa 1755) His first military headquarters. Taped narration. **FREE**

Gordon-Roberts House. *218 Washington St, Cumberland (21502). In Victorian Historic District. Phone 301/777-8678. www.historyhouse.allconet.org/house.* (Circa 1867) Restored 18-room Victorian house with nine period rooms; costumes; research room. (Tues-Sat 10 am-5 pm) **$$$**

Green Ridge State Forest. *28700 Headquarters Dr NE, Flintstone (21530). 21 miles E off I-68 at exit 64. Phone 301/478-3124. www.dnr.state.md.us/publiclands/western/greenridge.html.* These 44,000 acres of forest land stretch across mountains of western Maryland and occupy portions of Town Hill, Polish Mountain, and Green Ridge Mountain. Abundant wildlife. Fishing, boat launch, canoeing; hiking trails, camping, winter sports. C & O Canal runs through here into 3,118-foot Paw-Paw Tunnel.

The Narrows. Picturesque 1,000-foot gap through Alleghenies (Hwy 40A) used by pioneers on their way to the West.

Rocky Gap State Park. *12500 Pleasant Valley Rd NE, Cumberland (21530). 6 miles E on I-68, exit 50. Phone 301/777-2139; toll-free 888/432-2267 (reservations). www.dnr.state.md.us/publiclands/western/rockygap.html.* Mountain scenery around 243-acre lake with three swimming beaches. Swimming, fishing, boating (electric motors only; rentals); nature and hiking trails, picnicking, cafe, improved camping (reservations accepted one year in advance), winter activities. Resort; 18-hole golf course. (See SPECIAL EVENTS) **$**

Toll Gate House. *Hwy 40, LaVale (21502). Approximately 6 miles W on Hwy 40A, in La Vale. Phone 301/729-3047.* (1836) Built to collect tolls from users of Cumberland Rd (National Rd); only remaining toll house in state; restored. (Late May-late Oct, Sat-Sun 1:30-4:30 pm) **$**

Western Maryland Station Center. *13 Canal St, Cumberland (21502). Phone 301/724-3655. www.cr.nps.gov/nr/travel/cumberland/wmd.htm.* This 1913 railroad station houses Canal Place Authority, Industrial and Transportation Museum; C & O Canal

National Historical Park Visitors Center and Allegany County Visitors Center. (Daily; closed holidays) **FREE** This is also the departure point for

Western Maryland Scenic Railroad. *Phone 301/759-4400; toll-free 800/872-4650. www.wmsr.com/newindex.html.* Excursion train makes scenic trip 17 miles to Frostburg and back. (May-Oct: Tues-Sun; Nov-mid-Dec: weekends) **$$$$**

Special Events

Agricultural Expo and Fair. *Allegany County Fairgrounds, 11490 Moss Ave Ext, Cumberland (21501). Phone 301/729-1200. www.alleganycofair.org.* Poultry, livestock, carnival, entertainment. Late July. **$$**

Drumfest. *Greenway Ave Stadium, Greenway Ave, Cumberland. Phone 301/777-8325.* Drum and bugle corps championship. Last Sat in July.

Rocky Gap Music Festival. *Allegany College, 12401 Willow Brook Rd SE, Cumberland (21502). Phone toll-free 888/762-5942.* Features bluegrass and country music; children's activities, crafts, workshops. Fri-Sun, First weekend Aug.

Street Rod Roundup. *6 miles S on Hwy 220, at fairgrounds. Phone 301/729-5555.* Hundreds of pre-1950 hot rods on display and in competitions. Labor Day weekend.

Limited-Service Hotels

★★ BEST WESTERN BRADDOCK MOTOR INN. *1268 National Hwy, La Vale (21502). Phone 301/729-3300; toll-free 800/528-1234; fax 301/729-3300. www.bestwestern.com.* 105 rooms, 3 story. Complimentary continental breakfast. Check-in 2 pm, check-out 11 am. Restaurant, bar. Fitness room. Indoor pool, whirlpool. Airport transportation available. **$**

★★ HOLIDAY INN. *100 S George St, Cumberland (21502). Phone 301/724-8800; toll-free 877/426-4672; fax 301/724-4001. www.holiday-inn.com.* 130 rooms, 5 story. Pets accepted; fee. Check-in 3 pm, check-out noon. Restaurant, bar. Fitness room. Outdoor pool. Airport transportation available. Business center. **$**

★★ ROCKY GAP LODGE & GOLF RESORT. *16701 Lakeview Rd NE, Flintstone (21530). Phone 301/784-8400; toll-free 800/724-0828; fax 301/784-8408.* This hotel offers you a peaceful and relaxed stay in a beautiful rustic setting just two hours outside of Baltimore. You can spend time on the 243-acres of Lake Habeeb or explore some of the 3,000 acres of Rocky Gap State Park. Pass a leisurely day fishing, kayaking, or hiking, or hit the greens—this hotel has the only Jack Nicklaus Signature Golf Course in Maryland. The guest rooms are spacious and warm and feature all the expected amenities, as well as custom-made Shaker furniture. Some suites include a gas fireplace, two bathrooms, and whirlpool bathtub. Deluxe rooms offer a stunning view of the lake, while superior rooms overlook the golf course. 217 rooms, 6 story. Pets accepted, fee. Check-in 3 pm, check-out 11 am. Restaurant, bar. Children's activity center. Fitness room, spa. Outdoor/indoor pool, whirlpool. Golf, 18 holes. Tennis. Airport transportation available. Business center. **$$**

★ SUPER 8. *1301 National Hwy, La Vale (21502). Phone 301/729-6265; toll-free 800/800-8000; fax 301/729-6265. www.super8.com.* 63 rooms, 3 story. Complimentary continental breakfast. Pets accepted. Check-in 2 pm, check-out 11 am. **$**

Specialty Lodging

The following lodging establishment is approved by Mobil Travel Guide, but due to its unique and individualized nature has not been given a traditional Mobil Star rating. Included in this listing you may find bed-and-breakfasts, limited-service inns, guest ranches, and other unique hotel properties.

INN AT WALNUT BOTTOM. *120 Greene St, Cumberland (21502). Phone 301/777-0003; toll-free 800/286-9718; fax 301/777-8288. www.iwbinfo.com.* At this elegant retreat, guests are offered their choice of two equally charming accommodations. The Georgian-style architecture of the Cowden House welcomes guests with a formal doorway and chimneys at each end, while the Queen Anne-style Dent House delights guests with the distinctly round turret on the corner. Either place is guaranteed to enchant guests with the history behind it, with their charmingly appointed guest rooms and wonderful antiques. 12 rooms, 3 story. Complimentary full breakfast. Check-in 3 pm, check-out 11 am. **$**

Restaurant

★ ★ WARNER'S GERMAN RESTAURANT. *Hwy 220 S McMullen Hwy, Cresaptown (21505). Phone 301/729-2361.* German menu. Lunch, dinner. Closed Mon; Jan 1, July 4, Dec 25. Bar. Children's menu. Casual attire. Outdoor seating. **$$**

Easton (C-5)

See also Cambridge, St. Michael's

Settled 1682
Population 11,708
Elevation 28 ft
Area Code 410
Zip 21601
Information Talbot County Chamber of Commerce, PO Box 1366, Easton Plaza Suite 53; phone 410/822-4653
Web site www.talbotchamber.org

What to See and Do

Academy Art Museum. *106 South St, Easton (21601). Phone 410/822-2787. www.eastonarts.com/academy .html.* Housed in renovated 1820s schoolhouse, the Academy exhibits works of local and national artists in its permanent collection. Also hosts over 250 visual and performing arts programs annually. (Mon-Sat 10 am-4 pm, Wed 10 am-9 pm) **$**

Historical Society of Talbot County. *25 S Washington, Easton St (21601). Phone 410/822-0773. www.hstc.org.* A three-gallery museum in a renovated early commercial building; changing exhibits, museum shop. Historic houses: 1810 Federal town house, 1700s Quaker cabinetmaker's cottage, period gardens; tours. (Mon-Sat 10 am-4 pm, by advance appointment) **FREE**

Third Haven Friends Meeting House. *405 S Washington St, Easton (21601). Phone 410/822-0293.* (1682-1684) One of the oldest frame-construction houses of worship in US. (Daily) **FREE**

Tuckahoe State Park. *13070 Crouse Mill Rd, Queen Anne (21657). 5 miles N of Queen Anne, off Hwy 404. Phone 410/820-1668; toll-free 888/432-2267 (reservations). www.dnr.state.md.us/publiclands/eastern/tuckahoe.html.* A 60-acre lake and Tuckahoe Creek provide a secluded atmosphere in this 3,800-acre park. The Adkins Arboretum (500 acres) propagates trees, plants, and shrubs indigenous to Maryland. Fishing, boating; hunting, hiking, picnicking, camping (electric hook-ups, dump station).

Special Events

Eastern Shore Chamber Music Festival. *21 S Harrison St, Easton (21601). Various locations. Phone 410/819-0380. www.musicontheshore.org.* World-class chamber music; young people's concert. Two weeks in June.

Tuckahoe Steam and Gas Show and Reunion. *210 Marlboro Ave, Easton (21601). 5 miles N via Hwy 50, opposite Woodlawn Memorial Park. Phone 410/643-6123 or 410/820-9868 (during event).* Old steam and gas engines; antique tractors and cars. Demonstrations in soap and broom making; flour milling. Gas and steam wheat threshing; sawmill working; flea market, crafts, parade, entertainment. Usually weekend after July 4.

Waterfowl Festival. *40 S Harrison St, Easton (21601). Downtown and various locations in and around town. Phone 410/822-4606. www.waterfowlfestival.org.* Exhibits on waterfowl; pictures, carvings; food. First or second weekend in Nov. **$$$**

Limited-Service Hotel

★ HOLIDAY INN EXPRESS. *8561 Ocean Gateway, Easton (21601). Phone 410/819-6500; toll-free 877/327-8661; fax 410/819-6505. www.hiexpresseaston .com.* 73 rooms, 4 story. Complimentary continental breakfast. Check-in 3 pm, check-out 11 am. Wireless Internet access. Indoor pool, whirlpool. Business center. **$**

Full-Service Inn

★ ★ ★ ROBERT MORRIS INN. *314 N Morris St, Oxford (21654). Phone 410/226-5111; toll-free 866/642-4363; fax 410/226-5744. www. robertmorrisinn.com.* This is a family inn that provides quiet, comfortable lodging, great food, and a location that is perfect for exploring the local area. Guests can relax on the beach, visit the marine museum, go biking or antiquing, or play a game of golf or tennis. 35 rooms, 3 story. Closed Dec-Mar. Children over 10 years only. Check-in 3 pm, check-out noon. Restaurant. **$$**

Specialty Lodging

The following lodging establishment is approved by Mobil Travel Guide, but due to its unique and individualized nature has not been given a traditional Mobil Star rating. Included in this listing you may find bed-and-breakfasts, limited-service inns, guest ranches, and other unique hotel properties.

BISHOP'S HOUSE. *214 Goldsborough St, Easton (21601). Phone 410/820-7290; toll-free 800/223-7290. www.bishopshouse.com.* 5 rooms, 3 story. Closed Jan-Feb. Children over 12 years only. Complimentary full breakfast. Check-in 4-5 pm, check-out 11 am. Wireless Internet access. Built in 1880; antiques, toys, porcelains. **$**

Restaurant

★★★ **HUNTER'S TAVERN.** *101 E Dover St, Easton (21601). Phone 410/822-1300; fax 410/820-8847. www.tidewaterinn.com.* A hunting theme predominates at this casual tavern-style restaurant, which serves regional specialties, including wild game. American menu. Breakfast, lunch, dinner, Sun brunch. Bar. Valet parking. Outdoor seating. **$$**

Elkton (A-5)

See also Havre de Grace

Population 11,893
Elevation 30 ft
Area Code 410
Zip 21921
Information Elkton Chamber of Commerce, 101 E Main St; phone 410/398-1640

What to See and Do

Elk Neck State Forest. *4395 Turkey Point Rd, North East (21901). 4 miles W off Hwy 7, near North East. Phone 410/287-5333; toll-free 888/432-2267 (reservations). www.dnr.state.md.us/publiclands/central/elkneck.html.* Has 3,165 acres. Forest wildlife, particularly whitetail deer, can be seen; food plots have been established. Hunting, hiking, bridle trail, picnicking, primitive camping, shooting range, winter sports. Pets allowed. **$**

Elk Neck State Park. *4395 Turkey Point Rd, North East (21901). 14 miles SW via Hwys 40, 272, near North East. Phone 410/287-5333; toll-free 888/432-2267 (reservations). www.dnr.state.md.us/publiclands/central/elkneck.html.* This park has 2,188 acres of sandy beaches, marshlands and heavily wooded bluffs. Swimming, fishing, boating (launch, rentals); miniature golf (fee), hiking and nature trails, picnicking, concession, winter sports, camping, cabins.

Specialty Lodging

The following lodging establishment is approved by Mobil Travel Guide, but due to its unique and individualized nature has not been given a traditional Mobil Star rating. Included in this listing you may find bed-and-breakfasts, limited-service inns, guest ranches, and other unique hotel properties.

INN AT THE CANAL. *104 Bohemia Ave, Chesapeake City (21915). Phone 410/885-5995; fax 410/885-3585. www.innatthecanal.com.* 7 rooms, 3 story. Children over 10 years only. Complimentary full breakfast. Check-in 2-6 pm, check-out 11 am. Mansion built in 1870; antiques. Overlooks Chesapeake and Delaware Canal. **$**

Restaurant

★★ **SCHAEFER'S CANAL HOUSE.** *208 Bank St, Chesapeake City (21915). Phone 410/885-2200; fax 410/885-2206. www.schaeferscanalhouse.com.* Seafood menu. Breakfast, lunch, dinner, Sun brunch. Closed Dec 25. Bar. Children's menu. Outdoor seating. **$$**

Ellicott City (B-4)

See also Baltimore

Settled 1772
Population 56,397
Elevation 233 ft
Area Code 410
Information Howard County Tourism Council, 8267 Main St, PO Box 9, 21041; phone 410/313-1900 or toll-free 800/288-TRIP
Web site www.visithowardcounty.com

The town was originally named Ellicott Mills for the three Quaker brothers who founded it as the site of their gristmill. Charles Carroll of Carrollton, whose

Doughoregan Manor can still be seen nearby, lent financial help to the Ellicotts and the town eventually became the site of ironworks, rolling mills, and the first railroad terminus in the United States. The famous Tom Thumb locomotive race with a horse took place near here. Many of the town's original stone houses and log cabins, on hills above the Patapsco River, have been preserved.

What to See and Do

Ellicott City B & O Railroad Station Museum. *2711 Maryland Ave, Ellicott City (21043). At Main St. Phone 410/461-1944 (recording). www.ecbo.org.* Two restored buildings (circa 1830 and 1885) house historic rooms, railroad displays and memorabilia, operating HO model railroad of the first 13 miles of the B & O track, photographs, dioramas. Full-size B & O caboose and museum store. Civil War reenactments of military and civilian life, June-Sept. (Fri-Sat 11 am-4 pm, Sun noon-5 pm; last admission is one half-hour before closing) **$**

Patapsco Valley State Park. *8020 Baltimore National Pike, Ellicott City (21043). NE and SE of town; 5 miles from I-695 exits 12 and 15, 50 yards from I-195 exit 1. Phone 410/461-5005; toll-free 888/432-2267. www.dnr.state.md.us/publiclands/central/patapscovalley.html.* Spread across three counties, this great nature and recreational area runs along a 32-mile stretch of the scenic Patapsco River, spans 14,000 acres, and contains five sites. Guests can hike, bike, ride horses, fish, camp, canoe, tube, or picnic. The park also includes the world's largest multiple arched stone railroad bridge, a 300-foot suspension bridge, and a paved hiking trail for the disabled. (Park: daily dawn-dusk. Information desk: daily 8 am-4:30 pm) **$**

Special Events

Howard County Fair. *2210 Fairgrounds Rd, West Friendship (21794). Phone 410/442-1022. www.howardcountyfair.com.* Rides, entertainment, concessions, 4-H exhibits, horse-pulling contests, and other events. Early-Aug. **$$**

Maryland Sheep and Wool Festival. *2210 Fairgrounds Rd, West Friendship (21794). Phone 410/442-1022. www.sheepandwoolfestival.org.* Sheep breeds and other wool-bearing animals; sheepdog demonstration. Crafters sell products related to sheep and wool; spinning, weaving, and sheep-shearing contests; wool dyeing; entertainment. First weekend in May. **FREE**

Full-Service Resort

★ ★ ★ TURF VALLEY RESORT AND CONFERENCE CENTER. *2700 Turf Valley Rd, Ellicott City (21042). Phone 410/465-1500; toll-free 888/833-8873; fax 410/465-8280. www.turfvalley.com.* 223 rooms, 7 story. Check-in 4 pm, check-out noon. High-speed Internet access. Two restaurants, three bars. Fitness room, spa. Indoor/outdoor pool, whirlpool. Golf, 36 holes. Tennis. Business center. **$$**

Restaurants

★ ★ CRAB SHANTY. *3410 Plumtree Dr, Ellicott City (21042). Phone 410/465-9660; fax 410/750-0154. www.crabshanty.com.* Seafood menu. Lunch, dinner. Bar. Children's menu. **$$**

★ SIDESTREETS. *8069 Tiber Alley, Ellicott City (21043). Phone 410/461-5577; fax 410/750-8096.* Seafood menu. Lunch, dinner, Sun brunch. Closed Thanksgiving, Dec 25. Bar. **$$**

★ ★ ★ TERSIGUEL'S. *8293 Main St, Ellicott City (21043). Phone 410/465-4004; fax 410/461-1421. www.tersiguels.com.* Guests will find fine dining in a 19th-century home with six individual dining rooms serving a combination of authentic French-style cooking and rustic country fare. Seasonal cuisine is prepared with fresh vegetables and herbs from their garden, and chevre cheese is made daily. French menu. Lunch, dinner. Closed Dec 25. Bar. Historic building; mementos from Brittany, France. **$$$**

Emmitsburg (A-3)

See also Frederick, Hagerstown, Thurmont

Settled 1785
Population 2,290
Elevation 449 ft
Area Code 301
Zip 21727
Information Tourism Council of Frederick County, 19 E Church St, Frederick 21701; phone 301/228-2888
Web site www.visitfrederick.org

Civil War Sites of Frederick

A well-preserved city of elegant 18th- and 19th-century structures, Frederick should be placed on anyone's tour of important Civil War landmarks. It is an especially appropriate sequel to a visit to nearby Antietam National Battlefield, which has entered the history books as the site on September 17, 1862 of the single bloodiest day of the Civil War. At the end of the battle, thousands of Union wounded were transported to the small city, where 29 buildings were turned into makeshift hospitals. President Lincoln later praised townsfolk for their humanity. This heritage proved an important factor when Frederick was chosen from among 15 communities vying to be the site of the National Museum of Civil War Medicine. Begin an hour-long, 1-mile walking tour of the city's Historic District at the museum at 48 East Patrick Street. The museum tells the story of radical improvements in medical treatment during the four years of the war, as the divided nation coped with the flood of ill or wounded soldiers on both sides of the Mason-Dixon line. As the museum points out, the use of ambulances and the technique of embalming both emerged during the war. From the museum, walk three blocks west (left) to the reconstructed Barbara Frietchie House & Museum at 154 West Patrick. Fritchie was immortalized in John Greenleaf Whittier's Civil War poem, *Barbara Frietchie*: "Shoot if you must, this old gray head, But spare your country's flag." According to legend, she waved a Union flag defiantly at "Stonewall" Jackson, who was leading a Confederate army through the city. In truth, she may have waved a flag, but to honor Union troops passing by later. Double back on Patrick Street to Court Street and walk north (left) one block to tour Courthouse Square. On Court Street, opposite City Hall, is the small office where Francis Scott Key, author of "The Star-Spangled Banner," practiced law. Revolutionary War General Lafayette was a guest at 103 Council Street during his ceremonial US tour in 1824. At 119 Record Street, Lincoln visited a wounded general and addressed a crowd from its steps after the Antietam battle. Head east (left) on West Church Street. At No. 108, you'll see a cast-iron model of the pet dog of John Tyler, a pioneer ophthalmologist. The statue was stolen by Confederates seeking to melt it into bullets, but later it was found near an Antietam battlefield. Conclude your tour two blocks east at the Historical Society of Fredericksburg at 24 East Church. A large 1820 home, it is maintained as a house museum furnished with local antiques—appropriately so, because nearby East Patrick Street has been dubbed "Antique Row" for its many antique shops.

What to See and Do

Mount St. Mary's College and Seminary. *16300 Old Emmitsburg Rd, Emmitsburg (21727). 3 miles S on Hwy 15. Phone 301/447-6122. www.msmary.edu.* (1808) (1,800 students) Oldest independent Catholic college in the US. Liberal arts and sciences. Near the campus is the

National Shrine Grotto of Lourdes. *Mount St. Mary's College and Seminary, 16300 Old Emmitsburg Rd, Emmitsburg. Phone 301/447-5318. www.msmary.edu/grotto.* This replica of the French shrine is 1/3 the size of the original; oldest replica in the Western Hemisphere. Pangborn Memorial Campanile, constructed of native stone and located at the entrance, is 120 feet tall and is surmounted by a 25-foot bronze gold-leaf statue of the Blessed Virgin Mary. (Apr-Oct: daily; rest of year: Tues-Sun) **FREE**

★ **Seton Shrine Center.** *333 S Seton Ave, Emmitsburg (21727). Phone 301/447-6606. www.screensaves.com/seton.htm.* National Shrine of St. Elizabeth Ann Seton, first US female saint, canonized 1975. Includes Stone House (1750), White House (1810), home in which Mother Seton died; video presentation, basilica, museum, and cemetery. (Tues-Sun, or by appointment; closed holidays; also last two weeks in Jan) **FREE**

Frederick (B-3)

See also Boonsboro, Emmitsburg, Hagerstown, Thurmont

Settled 1745
Population 52,767
Elevation 290 ft
Area Code 301 and 240
Zip 21701
Information Tourism Council of Frederick County, 19 E Church St; phone 301/663-8687 or toll-free 800/999-3613
Web site www.visitfrederick.org

Home of dauntless Barbara Frietchie, who reportedly spoke her mind to Stonewall Jackson and his "rebel hordes," Frederick is a town filled with history. Named for Frederick Calvert, sixth Lord Baltimore, it is the seat of one of America's richest agricultural counties. Francis Scott Key and Chief Justice Roger Brooke Taney made their homes here. Court House Square was the scene of several important events during the Revolutionary War, including the famed protest against the Stamp Act, in which an effigy of the stamp distributor was burned.

During the Civil War, Frederick was a focal point for strategic operations by both sides. In the campaign of 1862, the Confederacy's first invasions of the North were made at nearby South Mountain and Sharpsburg, at Antietam Creek. Wounded men by the thousands were cared for here. Troop movements continued for the duration of the war; cavalry skirmishes took place in the streets. In July 1864, the town was forced to pay a $200,000 ransom to Confederate General Jubal Early before he fought the Battle of Monocacy a few miles south. Frederick today is an educational center, tourist attraction, location of Fort Detrick army installation, and home of diversified small industry. A 33-block area has been designated a Historic District.

What to See and Do

Barbara Fritchie House and Museum. *154 W Patrick St, Frederick (21701). Phone 301/698-0630.* Exhibits include quilts, clothing made by Fritchie, her rocker and Bible, the bed in which she died, and other items; ten-minute film; also garden. (Apr-Sept: Mon, Thurs-Sun; Oct-Nov: Sat-Sun) **$$**

Brunswick Railroad Museum. *40 W Potomac St, Brunswick (21716). Phone 301/834-7100. www.brrm.net.* Furnishings and clothing interpret life in a turn-of-the-century railroad town; large model train exhibit. Special events are held on selected weekends. (Fri 10 am-2 pm, Sat 10 am-4 pm, Sun 1-4 pm) **$**

Children's Museum of Rose Hill Manor. *1611 N Market St, Frederick (21701). Phone 301/694-1648; toll-free 800/999-3613.* Hands-on exhibits of 19th-century family life; carriage museum; colonial herb and fragrant gardens; farm museum; blacksmith shop; log cabin. (Apr-Oct: daily; Nov: Sat-Sun) **$$**

Gambrill State Park. *8602 Gambrill Park Rd, Frederick (21702). Phone 301/271-7574; toll-free 888/432-2267 (reservations). www.dnr.state.md.us/publiclands/western/gambrill.html.* Park has 1,136 acres with two developed areas. Fishing; nature and hiking trails, picnicking, tent and trailer sites (standard fees). Tea room. Two overlooks.

Historical Society of Frederick County Museum. *24 E Church St, Frederick (21701). Phone 301/663-1188.* House, built in early 1800s, shows both Georgian and Federal details; leaded side and fan-lights, Doric columns inside, double porches in rear, and boxwood gardens. Portraits of early Frederick residents. Genealogy library (Tues-Sat). (Mon-Sat; also Sun afternoons) **$**

Horse-drawn carriage tours. *The Frederick Carriage Company, 811 Trail Ave (21701). Phone 301/694-7433.* (Daily, by appointment)

Monocacy National Battlefield. *4801 Urbana Pike, Frederick (21704). 3 miles S on Hwy 355. Phone 301/662-3515. www.nps.gov/mono/home.htm.* On July 9, 1864, Union General Lew Wallace with 5,000 men delayed General Jubal Early and his 23,000 Confederate soldiers for 24 hours, during which Grant was able to reinforce, and save, Washington, DC, New Jersey, Vermont, and Pennsylvania. Confederate monuments mark the area. (Labor Day-Memorial Day: 8 am-4:30 pm, Memorial Day-Labor Day: 8:30 am-5 pm; closed Jan 1, Thanksgiving, Dec 25) **FREE**

Mount Olivet Cemetery. *515 S Market St, Frederick (21701). S end of Market St. Phone 301/662-1164.* (1852) Monuments mark graves of Francis Scott Key and Barbara Fritchie. Flag flies over Key's grave.

Roger Brooke Taney Home and Francis Scott Key Museum. *121 S Bentz St, Frederick (21701). Phone 301/663-8687.* Chief Justice of the US from 1835-1864, Taney was chosen by Andrew Jackson to succeed John Marshall. He swore in seven presidents, including Abraham Lincoln, and issued the famous Dred Scott Decision. He is buried in the cemetery of St. John's Catholic Church at E 3rd and East sts. (Apr-Oct, weekends) **$$**

Schifferstadt Architectural Museum. *1110 Rosemont Ave, Frederick (21701). Phone 301/663-3885. www.smallmuseum.org/schifferstadt.htm.* (1756) Fine example of German Colonial farmhouse architecture. Tours of architectural museum. Gift shop. (Apr-mid Dec: Wed-Fri 10 am-4 pm; Sat-Sun noon-4 pm; closed Thanksgiving) **DONATION**

Trinity Chapel. *W Church St, Frederick (21701). Phone 301/694-2489.* (1763) Graceful colonial church; Francis Scott Key was baptized here. Steeple houses town clock and ten-bell chimes; chimes play every Saturday evening. **$$$** The chapel is now used as Sunday School for

Evangelical Reformed Church. *15 W Church St, Frederick (21701). Phone 301/662-2762.* United Church of Christ (1848). *Opposite Trinity Chapel.* A Grecian-style building modeled after the Erechtheum, with two towers resembling Lanterns of Demosthenes. Here Stonewall Jackson slept through a pro-Union sermon before the Battle of Antietam; Barbara Fritchie was a member.

Special Events

Beyond the Garden Gates Tour. *19 E Church St, Frederick (21701). Downtown. Phone 301/663-8687.* Tour historic and contemporary gardens. Early May. **FREE**

Fall Festival. *Rose Hill Manor, 1611 N Market St, Frederick (21701). Phone 301/694-1650. www.co.frederick.md.us/Parks/rosehill.html.* Apple butter making, music, crafts demonstrations, tractor pull, hay rides, country cooking. Early Oct. **$**

Great Frederick Fair. *797 E Patrick St, Frederick (21705). Phone 301/663-5895. www.thegreatfrederickfair.com.* Frederick county fair. Mid-late Sept. **$**

Lotus Blossom Festival. *Lilypons Water Garden, 6800 Lilypons Rd, Frederick (21717). 10 miles S via Hwy 85. Phone 301/874-5133; toll-free 800/999-5459.* Endless blooms of water lilies and lotus, water garden; arts and crafts, food, entertainment, lectures. First double-digit weekend in July.

New Market Days. *2 W Main St, New Market (21774). 8 miles E. Phone 301/831-6755.* Nostalgic revival of the atmosphere of a 19th-century village; costumed guides, period crafts and events; held in New Market, the town dedicated to being the "Antiques Capital of Maryland." Last full weekend in Sept.

Limited-Service Hotels

★ FAIRFIELD INN. *5220 Westview Dr, Frederick (21703). Phone 301/631-2000; fax 301/631-2100. www.fairfieldinn.com.* 105 rooms, 3 story. Complimentary continental breakfast. Check-in 3 pm, check-out noon. High-speed Internet access. Fitness room. Indoor pool, whirlpool. **$**

★ ★ HAMPTON INN. *5311 Buckeystown Pike, Frederick (21704). Phone 301/698-2500; toll-free 800/426-7866; fax 301/695-8735. www.hamptoninn.com.* 161 rooms, 6 story. Pets accepted, some restrictions; fee. Complimentary continental breakfast. Check-in 3 pm, check-out noon. Restaurant, bar. Fitness room. Outdoor pool. **$**

Specialty Lodgings

The following lodging establishments are approved by Mobil Travel Guide, but due to their unique and individualized nature have not been given a traditional Mobil Star rating. Included in this listing you may find bed-and-breakfasts, limited-service inns, guest ranches, and other unique hotel properties.

CATOCTIN INN. *3619 Buckeystown Pike, Buckeystown (21717). Phone 301/874-5555; fax 301/831-8102. www.catoctininn.com.* 23 rooms, 3 story. Complimentary full breakfast. Check-in 4 pm, check-out noon. Built in the 1780s; parlor with antique sofas. **$**

INN AT BUCKEYSTOWN. *3521 Buckeystown Pike, Buckeystown (21717). Phone 301/874-5755; toll-free 800/272-1190; fax 301/831-1355. www.innatbuckeystown.com.* This stately and elegant mansion opened its doors in 1981, and today continues to enchant guests with touches of luxury and the charm of another era. Located in a National Registered Historic Village, this mansion delights with its warm hospitality, Victorian-style décor, and wonderful appointment of collectibles and period pieces. 5 rooms, 3 story. Children over 12 years only. Check-in 4 pm, check-out 11 am. Restaurant. (public by reservation). Near river. **$$$**

Restaurants

★★ BROWN PELICAN. *5 E Church St, Frederick (21701). Phone 301/695-5833; fax 301/695-5876.* American menu. Lunch, dinner. Closed Jan 1, Thanksgiving, Dec 25; also Super Bowl Sun. Bar. Reservations recommended. In basement of antebellum bank. **$$**

★★ GABRIEL'S. *4730 Ijamsville Rd, Ijamsville (21754). Phone 301/865-5500; fax 301/698-9880.* French menu. Dinner. Closed Mon-Wed; Jan 1. Bar. French Provinçal inn atmosphere; building constructed in 1862. Reservations recommended. **$$**

★★ TAURASO'S. *6 East St, Frederick (21701). Phone 301/663-6600; fax 301/663-6677. www.tauraso.com.* Italian, American menu. Lunch, dinner. Closed Dec 25. Bar to midnight. Outdoor seating. In restored factory building (late 1800s). **$$**

Frostburg (D-2)

Restaurant

★★★ AU PETIT PARIS. *86 E Main St, Frostburg (21532). Phone 301/689-8946; fax 301/689-0268. www.aupetitparis.com.* The atmosphere at Au Petit Paris is intimate, not rushed. The a la carte menu will satisfy the most discriminating gourmet. The wine cellar boasts the most extensive collection in western Maryland. French menu. Dinner. Closed Sun-Mon; holidays. Bar. Children's menu. **$$$**

Gaithersburg (B-3)

See also Rockville

Population 52,613
Elevation 508 ft
Area Code 301
Information Chamber of Commerce, 9 Park Ave, 20877; phone 301/840-1400

What to See and Do

Seneca Creek State Park. *11950 Clopper Rd, Gaithersburg (20878). 2 1/2 miles W of I-270 on Hwy 117. Phone 301/924-2127; toll-free 888/432-2267 (reservations). www.dnr.state.md.us/publiclands/central/seneca.html.* Stream valley park of 6,109 acres with 90-acre lake. Historic sites with old mills, an old schoolhouse, stone quarries. Fishing, boating (rentals); picnicking, disk golf, hiking, bicycle and bridle trails, winter sports. **$**

Special Event

Montgomery County Agricultural Fair. *16 Chestnut St, Gaithersburg (20877). Phone 301/926-3100. www.mcagfair.com.* One of the East Coast's leading county fairs; emphasis on agriculture, 4-H activities; animal exhibits, home arts; antique farm equipment; tractor pull, horse pull, demolition derby; rodeo; entertainment. Mid-late Aug. **$$**

Limited-Service Hotels

★ COMFORT INN. *16216 Frederick Rd, Gaithersburg (20877). Phone 301/330-0023; toll-free 888/605-9100; fax 301/258-1950. www.choicehotels.com.* 126 rooms, 7 story. Pets accepted. Complimentary full breakfast. Check-in 3 pm, check-out 11 am. High-speed Internet access. Fitness room. Outdoor pool. Business center. **$**

★★ COURTYARD BY MARRIOTT. *805 Russell Ave, Gaithersburg (20879). Phone 301/670-0008; toll-free 800/336-6880; fax 301/948-4538. www.courtyard.com.* 203 rooms, 7 story. Check-in 3pm, check-out noon. High-speed Internet access. Restaurant, bar. Fitness room. Outdoor pool, whirlpool. Tennis. **$**

★ HAMPTON INN. *20260 Goldenrod Ln, Germantown (20876). Phone 301/428-1300; fax 301/428-9034. www.hamptoninn.com.* 178 rooms, 6 story. Complimentary continental breakfast. Check-in 3 pm, check-out noon. High-speed Internet access. Restaurant. Fitness room. Outdoor pool. **$**

★ ★ HOLIDAY INN. *2 Montgomery Village Ave, Gaithersburg (20879). Phone 301/948-8900; toll-free 800/465-4329; fax 301/258-1940. www.holiday-inn.com.* 300 rooms, 8 story. Pets accepted, some restrictions; fee. Check-in 3 pm, check-out noon. High-speed Internet access. Restaurant, bar. Fitness room. Indoor pool, whirlpool. Business center. **$**

Full-Service Hotels

★ ★ ★ HILTON GAITHERSBURG. *620 Perry Pkwy, Gaithersburg (20877). Phone 301/977-8900; toll-free 800/599-5111; fax 301/977-3450. www.hilton.com.* 301 rooms, 12 story. Restaurant, bar. Fitness room. Indoor pool, outdoor pool. **$**

★ ★ ★ MARRIOTT GAITHERSBURG WASHINGTONIAN CENTER. *9751 Washingtonian Blvd, Gaithersburg (20878). Phone 301/590-0044; fax 301/212-6155. www.marriott.com.* This hotel is conveniently connected to restaurants, retail stores, and a multiplex theater. 284 rooms, 11 story. Check-in 4 pm, check-out noon. High-speed Internet access. Restaurant, bar. Fitness room. Indoor pool, whirlpool. Business center. **$$**

Restaurants

★ CHRIS' STEAK HOUSE. *201 E Diamond Ave, Gaithersburg (20877). Phone 301/869-6116.* American menu. Lunch, dinner. Closed Sun; holidays. Bar. Children's menu. Football memorabilia. **$**

★ ★ FLAMING PIT. *18701 N Frederick Ave, Gaithersburg (20879). Phone 301/977-0700; fax 301/840-9633.* American menu. Lunch, dinner. Closed holidays. Bar. Children's menu. Reservations recommended. Skylight; hanging baskets. **$$$**

★ ★ GOLDEN BULL GRAND CAFE. *7 Dalamar St, Gaithersburg (20877). Phone 301/948-3666; fax 301/948-4542.* American menu. Lunch, dinner. Closed Dec 25. Bar. Children's menu. **$$$**

★ IL FORNO PIZZERIA. *8941 Westland Dr, Gaithersburg (20877). Phone 301/977-5900; fax 301/977-5902.* Italian menu. Lunch, dinner. Closed holidays. Outdoor seating. **$$**

★ ★ OLD SIAM. *108 E Diamond Ave, Gaithersburg (20877). Phone 301/926-9199; fax 301/926-9132.* Thai menu. Lunch, dinner. Casual attire. **$**

★ ★ PEKING CHEERS. *519 Quince Orchard Rd, Gaithersburg (20878). Phone 301/216-2090; fax 301/216-1473.* Chinese menu. Lunch, dinner. Casual décor; large murals. **$$**

★ PEKING SUPREME. *19204 Montgomery Village Ave, Montgomery Village (20886). Phone 301/963-8088; fax 301/963-8318.* Chinese menu. Lunch, dinner. Closed Thanksgiving. Bar. **$**

★ ROY'S PLACE. *2 E Diamond Ave, Gaithersburg (20877). Phone 301/948-5548; fax 301/948-4840. www.roysplacerestaurant.com.* Lunch, dinner. Closed Thanksgiving, Dec 24-25. Bar. **$**

★ ★ SIR WALTER RALEIGH. *19100 Montgomery Village Ave, Gaithersburg (20886). Phone 301/258-0576; fax 301/590-9357. www.sirwalterraleigh.com.* American menu. Lunch, dinner. Closed Dec 25. Bar. Children's menu. **$$**

Grantsville (D-1)

See also Cumberland, Oakland

Population 619
Elevation 2,300 ft
Area Code 301
Zip 21536
Information Garrett County Chamber of Commerce, 15 Visitors Center Dr, McHenry 21541; phone 301/387-4386
Web site www.garrettchamber.com

What to See and Do

Casselman River Bridge State Park. *E of Grantsville on Rte 40. Phone 301/895-5453. www.dnr.state.md.us/publiclands/western/casselman.html.* This single-span stone arch bridge over the Casselman River was built in 1813.

New Germany State Park. *349 Headquarters Ln, Grantsville (21536). 5 miles SE of Grantsville, in Savage River State Forest. Phone 301/895-5453; toll-free 888/432-2267 (reservations). www.dnr.state.md.us/publiclands/western/newgermany.html.* A 13-acre lake built on site of a once prosperous milling center. Swimming, fishing, boating; nature, hiking trails, winter sports, picnicking, playground, concession, improved campsites, cabins (fee). Pets not permitted. **$**

Savage River State Forest. *349 Headquarters Ln (21536). W and S via Rte 40 and I-68. Phone 301/895-5759. www.dnr.state.md.us/publiclands/western/savageriver.html.* Largest of Maryland's state forests comprises about 52,800 acres of near wilderness. A strategic watershed area, the northern hardwood forest surrounds the Savage River Dam. Fishing; hunting, hiking trails, winter sports, primitive camping (permit required).

Springs Museum. *Rte 669, Springs (15562). 2 miles N via Hwy 669, in Springs, PA. Phone 814/662-2625. www.pennalps.com/Museum.html.* Depicts life of settlers of Casselman Valley; 18th-century farming tools, fossil collection, other exhibits. (Memorial Day-early Oct: Wed-Fri 1-5 pm, Sat 9 am-2 pm)

Spruce Forest Artisan Village. *177 Casselman Rd, Grantsville (21536). 1 mile E on Rte 40, near Penn Alps. Phone 301/895-3332. www.spruceforest.org.* Original log cabins plus other historic buildings serve as studios for a potter, internationally recognized bird carver, weaver, spinner, stained-glass maker, and other artisans. Village (Mon-Sat 10 am-5 pm). Special events (summer; fee). Restaurant. (See SPECIAL EVENTS) **FREE**

Special Events

Springs Folk Festival. *Springs Museum, Hwy 669, Springs (15562). Phone 814/662-2625. www.pennalps.com/festival.html.* On grounds of Springs Museum (see). Pennsylvania Dutch food, music. First Fri and Sat in Oct. **$**

Spruce Forest Summerfest and Quilt Show. *Spruce Forest Artisan Village, 177 Casselman Rd, Grantsville (21536). Phone 301/895-3332. www.spruceforest.org.* More than 200 quilts on display; more than 70 craftspeople demonstrate their various skills. Second full Thurs, Fri, and Sat weekend in July.

Restaurant

★★ PENN ALPS. *125 Casselman Rd, Gaithersburg (21536). Phone 301/895-5985; fax 301/895-9542. www.pennalps.com.* Dutch menu. Breakfast, lunch, dinner, Sun brunch. Closed Dec 24-25. Children's menu. **$$**

Hagerstown (A-2)

See also Antietam National Battlefield, Boonsboro, Emmitsburg, Frederick, Thurmont

Settled 1762
Population 36,687
Elevation 552 ft
Area Code 301
Zip 21740
Information Hagerstown/Washington County Tourism Office, 16 Public Sq; phone 301/791-3246 or toll-free 800/228-7829
Web site www.marylandmemories.org

Within the city of Hagerstown there is a walking tour with points of interest marked on downtown sidewalks and walking paths in city parks. South Prospect Street is one of the city's oldest neighborhoods, listed on the National Register of Historic Places. The tree-lined street is graced by homes dating back to the early 1800s.

What to See and Do

Fort Frederick State Park. *11100 Fort Frederick Rd, Big Pool (21711). 18 miles W of junction I-81 and I-70 to Big Pool, then 1 mile SE via Rte 56, unnumbered road. Phone 301/842-2155; toll-free 888/432-2267 (reservations). www.dnr.state.md.us/publiclands/western/fortfrederick.html.* Erected in 1756 during the French and Indian War, the fort is considered a fine example of a pre-Revolutionary stone fort. It overlooks Chesapeake and Ohio Canal National Historical Park (see). The barracks, interior, and wall of the fort have been restored; military reenactments are staged throughout year. Fishing, boating (rentals); nature and hiking trails, picnicking (shelter), playground, unimproved camping. Museum, orientation film, and historical programs. Winter hours may vary.

Greenbrier State Park. *21843 National Pike, Boonsboro (21713). 6 miles E via Rte 40. Phone 301/791-4767; toll-free 888/432-2267 (reservations). www.dnr.state.md.us/publiclands/western/greenbrier.html.* The Appalachian Trail passes near this 1,275-acre park and its 42-acre man-made lake. Swimming (Memorial Day-Labor Day, daily), fishing, boating (rentals; no gas motors); nature and hiking trails, picnicking.

Hagerstown Roundhouse Museum. *300 S Burhans Blvd, Hagerstown (21741). Across the tracks from City Park. Phone 301/739-4665. www.roundhouse.org.* Museum houses photographic exhibits of the seven railroads of Hagerstown; historic railroad memorabilia, tools, and equipment; archives of maps, books, papers, and related items. Gift shop. (Fri-Sun 1-5 pm) (See SPECIAL EVENTS) **$**

Jonathan Hager House and Museum. *110 Key St, Hagerstown (21740). In City Park. Phone 301/739-8393. www.fortedwards.org/cwffa/hager.htm.* (1739) Stone house in park setting; authentic 18th-century furnishings. (Apr-Dec: Tues-Sat 10 am-4 pm, Sun 2-5 pm) **$$**

Miller House. *135 W Washington St, Hagerstown (21740). Phone 301/797-8782.* Washington County Historical Society Headquarters. Federal townhouse (circa 1820); three-story spiral staircase; period furnishings; garden; clock, doll, and Bell pottery collections; Chesapeake and Ohio Canal and Civil War exhibits; 19th-century country store display. (Apr-Dec: Wed-Sat 1-4 pm, Sun afternoons; closed holidays; also first two weeks in Dec) **$**

Washington County Museum of Fine Arts. *91 Key St, Hagerstown (21741). In City Park, S on Hwy 11 (Virginia Ave). Phone 301/739-5727. www.washcomuseum.org.* Paintings, sculpture, changing exhibits; concerts, lectures. (Tues-Fri 9 am-5 pm, Sat 9 am-4 pm, Sun 1-5 pm; closed holidays) **FREE**

Special Events

Alsatia Mummers Halloween Parade Festival. *Phone 301/739-2044.* Sat, weekend closest to Halloween.

Hagerstown Railroad Heritage Days. *Hagerstown Roundhouse Museum, 300 S Burhans Blvd, Hagerstown (21741). Phone 301/739-4665. www.roundhouse.org.* Special events centered on the Roundhouse Museum. Mid-June. **$**

Jonathan Hager Frontier Craft Day. *Jonathan Hager House and Museum, 110 Key St, Hagerstown (21740). Phone 301/739-8393. www.fortedwards.org/cwffa/hager.htm.* Colonial crafts demonstrated and exhibited. Bluegrass music; food. First weekend in Aug. **FREE**

Leitersburg Peach Festival. *21378 Leiters Mill Rd, Hagerstown (21742).* Peach-related edibles, farmers market, bluegrass music. Second weekend in Aug.

Williamsport C & O Canal Days. *30 W Potomac St, Hagerstown (21740).* Arts and crafts, Indian Village, National Park Service activities; food. Late Aug.

Limited-Service Hotels

★ ★ CLARION HOTEL & CONFERENCE CENTER ANTIETAM CREEK. *901 Dual Hwy, Hagerstown (21740). Phone 301/733-5100, fax 301/733-9192. www.clarion.com.* 210 rooms, 5 story. Check-out 11 am. Restaurant, bar. Fitness room. Indoor pool. Airport transportation available. **$**

★ ★ PLAZA HOTEL. *1718 Underpass Way, Hagerstown (21740). Phone 301/797-2500; toll-free 800/826-4534; fax 301/797-6209. www.plazahotelhagerstown.com.* 163 rooms, 6 story. Check-in 3 pm, check-out noon. High-speed Internet access. Restaurant, bar. Fitness room. Indoor pool, whirlpool. Airport transportation available. **$**

Restaurants

★ JUNCTION 808. *808 Noland Dr, Hagerstown (21740). Phone 301/791-3639; fax 301/791-3639.* American menu. Breakfast, lunch, dinner. Closed Sun; July 4, Dec 24-26. Children's menu. **$**

★ ★ RED HORSE STEAK HOUSE. *1800 Dual Hwy, Hagerstown (21740). Phone 301/733-3788.* Steak, seafood menu. Dinner. Closed holidays. Bar. Children's menu. **$**

★ RICHARDSON'S. *710 Dual Hwy, Hagerstown (21740). Phone 301/733-3660; fax 301/733-3662. www.richardsonsrestaurant.com.* Seafood menu. Breakfast, lunch, dinner. Closed Dec 24 evening, Dec 25. Bar. Children's menu. **$**

Havre de Grace (A-5)

See also Aberdeen, Elkton

Settled 1658
Population 11,331
Elevation 52 ft
Area Code 410 and 443
Zip 21078
Information Chamber of Commerce, 224 N Washington St, PO Box 339; phone 410/939-3303 or toll-free 800/851-7756
Web site www.hdgchamber.com

What to See and Do

Concord Point Lighthouse. *At foot of Lafayette St.* (1827) Built of granite, considered the oldest continuously used lighthouse on the East Coast. It was automated in 1928. (May-Oct, weekends and holidays only) **FREE**

Decoy Museum. *215 Giles St, Havre de Grace (21078). At the bay. Phone 410/939-3739. www.decoymuseum.com.* Adjacent to the blue waters of Chesapeake Bay is a museum dedicated to a sport the locals lovingly call waterfowling. The museum houses a large collection of working and decorative decoys used in the Chesapeake Bay area. The museum offers workshops on creating effective decoys, honors some of the great decoy makers and hunters of the area, and even hosts talks from those currently in the practice of decoy making. Approximately 2,700 decoys line the walls of the building, which sits on historic Susquehanna Flats, making it an intriguing find for hunters, historians, and bird lovers alike. (Daily 11 am-4 pm; closed holidays) **$**

Susquehanna State Park. *3 miles NW of Havre de Grace off Rte 155 in Harford County. Phone 410/557-7994; toll-free 888/432-2267 (reservations). www.dnr.state.md.us/publiclands/central/susquehanna.html.* A 2,639-acre park. Fishing, boat launch; nature, riding, and hiking trails; cross-country skiing, picnicking, camping (May-Sept; fee). In the park is

Steppingstone Museum. *461 Quaker Bottom Rd, Havre de Grace (21078). Phone 410/939-2299. www.steppingstonemuseum.org.* Self-guided tour of museum grounds includes sites of a once working Harford County farm; farmhouse is furnished as a turn-of-the-century country home; nearby shops and barn hold many displays and exhibits of the 1880-1920 period; demonstrations of rural arts and crafts of the period. Also here are blacksmith, woodworking, cooper, and dairy shops. (May-first Sun in Oct, Sat-Sun 1-5 pm) Special events held throughout the year (see SPECIAL EVENTS). **$**

Special Events

Decoy & Wildlife Art Festival. *Decoy Museum, 215 Giles St, Havre de Grace (21078). Phone 410/939-3739. www.decoymuseum.com.* Decoys on display, auction. Carving, gunning, and calling contests. Refreshments. Early May.

Fall Harvest Festival and Craft Show. *Steppingstone Museum, 461 Quaker Bottom Rd, Havre de Grace (21078). Phone 410/939-2299. www.steppingstonemuseum.org.* Features activities related to the harvest and preparation for winter: apple pressing, scarecrow stuffing, and other events. Entertainment. Last full weekend in Sept. **$**

Specialty Lodging

The following lodging establishment is approved by Mobil Travel Guide, but due to its unique and individualized nature has not been given a traditional Mobil Star rating. Included in this listing you may find bed-and-breakfasts, limited-service inns, guest ranches, and other unique hotel properties.

VANDIVER INN. *301 S Union Ave, Havre de Grace (21078). Phone 410/939-5200; toll-free 800/245-1655; fax 410/939-5202. www.vandiverinn.com.* This elegant Victorian mansion was built in 1886 and is listed on the National Historic Register. Located just blocks from the Chesapeake Bay, charming antique stores, and numerous water activities, this delightful inn offers a welcome respite from the daily hustle and bustle of life. Guests will delight in everything from the relaxing veranda to the elegantly appointed guest rooms. 17 rooms, 3 story. Complimentary full breakfast. Check-in 3-9 pm, check-out 11 am. **$**

Restaurants

★★ **BAYOU.** *927 Pulaski Hwy (Rte 40), Havre de Grace (21078). Phone 410/939-3565; fax 410/939-5396.* American, seafood menu. Lunch, dinner. Closed Mon; Dec 24-26. Children's menu. Reservations recommended. **$$**

★★ **CRAZY SWEDE.** *400 N Union Ave, Havre de Grace (21078). Phone 410/939-5440; fax 410/939-8020. www.crazyswederestaurant.com.* Eclectic/International menu. Lunch, dinner, Sun brunch. Closed Thanksgiving, Dec 25. Bar. Children's menu. Reservations recommended. **$$**

La Plata (D-3)

See also Waldorf; also see District of Columbia

Population 6,551
Elevation 193 ft
Area Code 301
Zip 20646
Information Charles County Chamber of Commerce, 6360 Crain Hwy, phone 301/932-6500; or the Department of Tourism, phone 301/645-0558
Web site www.ccc-md.org

What to See and Do

Doncaster Demonstration Forest. *Rte 1, Box 425, Indian Head (20640). 13 miles W on Hwy 6, near Doncaster. Phone 301/934-2282.* Heavily forested with yellow poplar, sweet gum, red and white oaks, and pine throughout its 1,477 acres. Hunting, 13 miles of hiking trails, bridle trails, picnic area, cross-country skiing.

Port Tobacco. *Chapel Point Rd, Port Tobacco. 3 miles SW on Hwy 6. Phone 301/934-4313.* Infrared aerial photography and archaeological excavation revealed the site of one of the oldest continuously inhabited English settlements in North America. Appearing as a Native American village on Captain John Smith's map of the area (1608), the area was colonized by the English as early as 1638. The town was chartered in 1727, and the first courthouse was erected in 1729. Among the remaining buildings are the Chimney House (1765) and Stagg Hall (1732), an original colonial home still a private residence, Burch (Catslide) House (1700), the reconstructed Quenzel Store, and a Federal period courthouse, with the Port Tobacco Museum on the second floor; archeological items on display, replicas of Colonial houses; Civil War and John Wilkes Booth exhibits, 30-minute audiovisual film, *The Story of Port Tobacco.* (Apr-Dec, Sat-Sun afternoons) **$**

Smallwood State Park. *2750 Sweden Point Rd, Marbury (20658). 16 miles W via Hwys 225, 224, near Rison. Phone 301/743-7613; toll-free 888/432-2267 (reservations). www.dnr.state.md.us/publiclands/southern/smallwood.html.* Restored home of Revolutionary General William Smallwood. Guided tour and historical program during summer. Marina. Boating (launch, rentals), fishing; hiking, picnicking. Retreat house. Park (April-Oct: daily 5 am-sunset; Nov-Mar: daily 8 am-sunset). **$**

Limited-Service Hotel

★ **BEST WESTERN LA PLATA INN.** *6900 Crain Hwy; Rte 301, La Plata (20646). Phone 301/934-4900; toll-free 800/780-7234; fax 301/934-5389. www.bestwestern.com.* 73 rooms, 2 story. Complimentary continental breakfast. Check-in 3 pm, check-out noon. Fitness room. Outdoor pool. **$**

Laurel (B-3)

See also Bowie, College Park, Silver Spring; also see District of Columbia

Population 19,960
Elevation 160 ft
Area Code 240 and 301
Information Baltimore/Washington Corridor Chamber of Commerce, 312 Marshall Ave, Suite 104; phone 301/725-4000
Web site www.laurel.md.us

What to See and Do

Montpelier Mansion. *9401 Montpelier Dr, Laurel (20708). 3 miles SE on Hwy 197 at Muirkirk. Phone 301/953-1376. www.pgparks.com/places/historic/montpelier.html.* (Circa 1780) Built and owned for generations by Maryland's Snowden family; Georgian architecture. George Washington and Abigail Adams were among its early visitors. On the grounds are boxwood gardens, an 18th-century herb garden, and a small summer house. Tours; purchase ticket in gift shop. (Mar-Nov: Sun-Thurs noon-3 pm (on the hour), Dec-Feb: Sun 1 pm, 2 pm; weekday groups by appointment; closed holidays) Candlelight tours held in early Dec. **$**

National Wildlife Visitor Center. *10901 Scarlet Tanager Loop, Laurel (20708). Phone 301/497-5760. patuxent.fws.gov/vcdefault.html.* A 12,750-acre national wildlife refuge and research area. Interactive exhibits focus on global environmental issues, migratory birds, wildlife habitats, and endangered species. Tram tours available of surrounding forests and lakes (weather permitting; fee). Trails. Gift shop. (Daily 10 am-5:30 pm; closed Dec 25) **FREE**

Special Event

Thoroughbred racing. *Laurel Race Course, Racetrack Rd and Rte 198, Laurel (20725). Phone 301/725-0400; toll-free 800/638-1859. www.marylandracing.com/laurel.html.* Entrances accessible from northbound or southbound on Hwy 1, I-95, or from Baltimore-Washington Pkwy, Hwy 198 exit. **$**

Limited-Service Hotel

★★ HOLIDAY INN. *3400 Fort Meade Rd, Laurel (20724). Phone 301/498-0900; toll-free 800/477-7410; fax 301/498-3203. www.holiday-inn.com.* 166 rooms, 2 story. Check-in 1 pm, check-out 11 am. Restaurant, bar. Fitness room. Outdoor pool. **$**

Leonardtown (D-4)

See also St. Mary's City

Population 1,896
Elevation 87 ft
Area Code 301
Zip 20650
Information St. Mary's County Division of Tourism, 23115 Leonard Hall Dr, PO Box 653; phone 301/475-4411 or toll-free 800/327-9023
Web site www.co.saint-marys.md.us

What to See and Do

Calvert Marine Museum. *14150 Solomons Island Rd, Leonardtown (20688). 1 mile SE on Hwy 5, then 11 miles NE on Hwy 4, cross bridge and turn right on Solomons Island Rd; follow signs. Phone 410/326-2042. www.calvertmarinemuseum.com.* Museum complex with exhibits relating to the culture and marine environment of Chesapeake Bay and Patuxent River estuary; fossils of marine life; estuarine biology displays, aquariums, touch-tank; maritime history exhibits, includes boat-building gallery. Also here is the restored Drum Point Lighthouse, built in 1883; 1/2 mile S is the JC Lore Oyster House, with exhibits on the area's seafood industry. Gift shop. (Daily 10 am-5 pm; closed Jan 1, Thanksgiving, Dec 25) **$**

Old Jail Museum. *11 Court House Dr, Leonardtown (20650). Phone 301/475-2467.* Local historical exhibits housed in an old jail; also a genealogy library for researchers. A cannon from Leonard Calvert's ship, the *Ark*, is mounted in front. (Tues-Sat 10 am-4 pm; closed holidays; also last week in Dec) **FREE**

Sotterley Plantation. *44300 Sotterley Rd, Hollywood (20636). 9 miles E on Hwy 245. Phone 301/373-2280; toll-free 800/681-0850. www.sotterley.com.* (Circa 1715) Overlooks Patuxent River. Working plantation; house in original condition. Chinese Chippendale staircase, antiques, original pine paneling in three rooms. Farming exhibit. (Grounds open May-Oct, Tues-Sat 10 am-4 pm (the last tour is at 3 pm), Sun noon-4 pm; individual tours of manor house on weekends; group tours by appointment only) **$$**

St. Clements Island-Potomac River Museum. *38370 Point Breeze Rd, Colton's Point (20626). 5 miles W via Hwy 234 to Clements, then 9 miles S on Hwy 242. Phone 301/769-2222.* Maryland colonists first landed on the island in 1634. Exhibits trace 12,000 years of local history and pre-history. Museum includes Little Red School House (circa 1821) and country store. Picnic area; fishing and crabbing. (Late Mar-Sept: Mon-Fri 9 am-5 pm, Sat-Sun noon-5 pm; Oct-late Mar: Wed-Sun noon-4 pm; closed holidays) **$**

Special Events

Blessing of the Fleet and Historical Pageant. *St. Clements Island-Potomac River Museum, 38370 Point Breeze Rd, Colton's Point (20626). Phone 301/769-2222.* Celebration commemorates first Roman Catholic Mass held on Maryland soil and Governor Leonard Calvert's proclamation of religious freedom. Blessing of oyster and clam fishing fleets. Folk dances, historical exhibits, concerts. Boat rides to the island. First weekend in Oct.

St. Mary's County Fair. *County Fairgrounds, Rte 5, Leonardtown (20650). Phone 301/475-2256.* Midway, seafood, horse shows. Late Sept.

St. Mary's County Oyster Festival. *County Fairgrounds, Rte 5, Leonardtown (20650). Phone 301/863-5015. www.usoysterfest.com.* National oyster shucking contest; oyster cook-off, seafood and crafts. Third weekend in Oct.

Oakland (E-1)

See also Grantsville

Settled 1851
Population 1,930
Elevation 2,384 ft
Area Code 301
Zip 21550
Information Garrett County Chamber of Commerce, 200 S Third St; phone 301/387-4386
Web site www.garrettchamber.com

What to See and Do

Backbone Mountain. *8 miles S on Hwy 219, then W on Hwy 50.* Highest point in the state (3,360 feet).

Deep Creek Lake State Park. *898 State Park Rd, Swanton (Garrett Co) (21561). From I-68, 10 miles SE off Hwy 219. Phone 301/387-4111; toll-free 888/432-2267 (reservations). www.dnr.state.md.us/publiclands/western/deepcreeklake.html.* Approximately 1,800 acres with 3,900-acre man-made lake. Swimming, bathhouse, fishing, boating (rowboat rentals); nature and hiking trails, picnicking (shelters), playground, concession, improved campsites (fee). **$**

Garrett State Forest. *222 Herrington Ln, Oakland (Garrett Co) (21550). 5 miles NW on County 20. Phone 301/334-2038. www.dnr.state.md.us/publiclands/western/garrett.html.* Approximately 6,800 acres. The forest contains much wildlife. Fishing; hunting, hiking and riding trails, winter activities, primitive camping. Forestry demonstration area. Within the forest are

Herrington Manor State Park. *Phone 301/334-9180; toll-free 888/432-2267 (reservations). www.dnr.state.md.us/publiclands/western/herringtonmanor.html.* Well-developed 365-acre park with housekeeping cabins, 53-acre lake. Swimming, fishing, boating (launch, rentals); hiking trails, concession, picnicking, cross-country skiing (rentals). Interpretive programs (summer). No pets.

Swallow Falls State Park. *Phone 301/387-6938; toll-free 888/432-2267 (reservations). www.dnr.state.md.us/publiclands/western/swallowfalls.html.* Surrounding 257 acres, the Youghiogheny River tumbles along the park's boundaries, passing through shaded rocky gorges and over sunny rapids. Muddy Creek produces a 52-foot waterfall. Here the last remaining stand of virgin hemlock dwarfs visitors. Fishing; nature trails, hiking, picnicking, improved campsites. Pets at registered campsites only.

Potomac State Forest. *1431 Potomac Camp Rd, Oakland (Garrett Co) (21550). 9 miles SE off Hwy 560, along Potomac River. Phone 301/334-2038. www.dnr.state.md.us/publiclands/western/potomacforest.html.* More than 10,685 acres for hiking, riding, and hunting. Primitive camping. Timber is harvested regularly here and the area is important in the management of watershed and wildlife programs.

Special Events

Autumn Glory Festival. *Countywide. Phone 301/387-4386. www.garrettchamber.com.* Celebrates fall foliage. Features arts and crafts, five-string banjo contest, state fiddle contest, western Maryland tournament of bands, parades, antique show. Mid-Oct.

Garrett County Fair. *Garrett County Fairgrounds, Rte 219, McHenry (21541). Phone 301/334-1948.* Early Aug.

McHenry Highland Festival. *Rte 219, McHenry (21541). Deep Creek Lake in McHenry.* Traditional Scottish and Celtic festival. First Sat in June. **$$**

Winterfest. *15 Visitors Center Dr, Oakland (Garrett Co) (21541). Deep Creek Lake in McHenry.* Ski races, parade, fireworks. Late Feb or early Mar.

Specialty Lodgings

The following lodging establishments are approved by Mobil Travel Guide, but due to their unique and individualized nature have not been given a traditional Mobil Star rating. Included in this listing you may find bed-and-breakfasts, limited-service inns, guest ranches, and other unique hotel properties.

CARMEL COVE BED AND BREAKFAST. *105 Monastery Way, Swanton (21550). Phone 301/387-0067; fax 301/387-2394. www.carmelcoveinn.com.* This bed-and-breakfast was once a monastery and now offers fine accommodations surrounded by beautiful mountains and the clear lake. 10 rooms, 2 story. Children over 12 years only. Complimentary full breakfast. Check-in 4 pm, check-out 11 am. Whirlpool. Tennis. Built in 1945. **$$**

HALEY FARM BED AND BREAKFAST. *16766 Garrett Hwy, Oakland (21550). Phone 301/387-9050; toll-free 888/231-3276; fax 301/387-9050. www.haleyfarm.com.* Built in 1923; formerly a working farm; near Deep Creek Lake, Swallow Falls, and five state parks. 10 rooms, 2 story. Children over 12 years only. Complimentary full breakfast. Check-in 3 pm, check-out noon. **$**

Restaurant

★★ POINT VIEW INN. *609 Deep Creek Dr, Mc Henry (21541). Phone 301/387-5555. www.pointviewinn.com.* African, American, seafood menu. Breakfast, lunch, dinner. Closed Easter, Dec 25. Bar. Children's menu. Casual attire. Outdoor seating. **$$**

Ocean City (D-6)

See also Fenwick Island

Founded 1869
Population 7,173
Elevation 7 ft
Area Code 410
Zip 21842
Information Chamber of Commerce, 12320 Ocean Gateway; phone 410/213-0552
Web site www.oceancity.org

Deep-sea fishing is highly regarded in Maryland's only Atlantic Ocean resort. The white sand beach, 3-mile boardwalk, amusements, golf courses, and boating draw thousands of visitors every summer.

What to See and Do

★ Assateague Island National Seashore. *7206 National Seashore Ln, Berlin (21811). There are two entrances to Assateague Island National Seashore. The N entrance is at the end of Rte 611, 8 miles S of Ocean City, MD. The S entrance is at the end of Rte 175, 2 miles from Chincoteague, VA. There is no vehicle access between the two entrances. Vehicles must return to the mainland to access the N or S entrance. Phone 410/641-1441 (information); toll-free 800/365-2267 (camping). www.assateagueisland.com.* Visitors interested in sandy beaches and wildlife should visit Assateague Island, which is about a four-hour drive from Baltimore. Straddling Maryland and Virginia, it contains a state park and a wildlife refuge. Visitors have their choice of activities: swimming, 7677676hiking, canoeing, sea kayaking, biking, camping on the beach, and some of the best surf-fishing on the Atlantic Coast. In addition to the seashore's beauty, guests also come to see the wild horses. According to legend, the horses, which are only the size of ponies, swam to the island from a shipwrecked Spanish galleon. On every last Wednesday and Thursday in July, the world-famous "Pony Penning" event occurs. During this event, the horses swim from the Maryland side of the island to the Virginia side with a crowd of spectators cheering them on. The visitor center offers more information about the horses as well as the seashore's many activities. (Daily; closed Thanksgiving, Dec 25) **$$** Also on the island is

Assateague State Park. *7307 Stephen Decatur Hwy, Berlin. Phone 410/641-2120; toll-free 888/432-2267 (reservations). www.dnr.state.md.us/publiclands/eastern/assateague.html.* Has 755 acres with 2 miles of ocean frontage and gentle, sloping beaches. Swimming, fishing, boat launch; picnicking, concession (summer), bicycle and hiking trails, camping (Apr-Oct). **$**

Special Events

Fishing contests and tournaments. *Phone 410/213-0552.* Many held throughout the year. For exact dates contact the Chamber of Commerce.

Harness racing. Ocean Downs. *10218 Racetrack Rd, Berlin (21811). 4 miles W on Hwy 50. Phone 410/641-0600. www.oceandowns.com.* Nightly Tues-Sun. Children with adult only. Late July-Labor Day.

Limited-Service Hotels

★ BEST WESTERN FLAGSHIP OCEANFRONT. *2600 Baltimore Ave, Ocean City (21842). Phone 410/289-3384; toll-free 800/837-3585; fax 410/289-1743. www.bestwestern.com.* 93 rooms, 3 story. Closed two weeks in Dec and weekdays Dec 26-Feb 14. Check-in 3 pm, check-out 11 am. Fitness room. Indoor pool, outdoor pool, children's pool, whirlpool. Tennis. **$$**

★ ★ CLARION HOTEL. *10100 Coastal Hwy, Ocean City (21842). Phone 410/524-3535; fax 410/524-3834. www.clarioninn.com.* Visitors can enjoy the sunrise and sunset from their rooms. The hotel offers a wide range of shops, restaurants, lounges and services, as well as recreational facilities such as a health spa. 250 rooms, 16 story. Pets accepted, some restrictions; fee. Check-in 4 pm, check-out 11 am. High-speed Internet access. Restaurant, bar. Fitness room. Indoor pool, whirlpool. Airport transportation available. Business center. **$$**

★ COMFORT INN. *507 Atlantic Ave, Ocean City (21842). Phone 410/289-5155; toll-free 800/228-5150; fax 410/289-6547. www.comfortinnboardwalk.com.* 84 rooms, 5 story. Closed Dec-Feb. Complimentary continental breakfast. Check-out 11 am. On ocean. Indoor pool, outdoor pool. **$$**

★ ★ HOLIDAY INN. *6600 Coastal Hwy, Ocean City (21842). Phone 410/524-1600; toll-free 800/638-2106; fax 410/524-1135. www.holiday-inn.com.* 216 rooms, 8 story. Check-in 3 pm, check-out 11 am. Restaurant, bar. Children's activity center. Fitness room. Beach. Indoor pool, outdoor pool, children's pool, whirlpool. Tennis. **$$**

★ ★ QUALITY INN. *5400 Coastal Hwy, Ocean City (21842). Phone 410/524-7200; toll-free 800/837-3586; fax 410/723-0018. www.qualityinn.com.* 126 rooms, 5 story. Check-in 3 pm, check-out 11 am. Restaurant, bar. Fitness room. On ocean, swimming beach. Indoor pool, outdoor pool, children's pool, whirlpool. Tennis. **$**

★ RAMADA. *Oceanfront and 32nd St, Ocean City (21842). Phone 410/289-6444; toll-free 800/837-3589; fax 410/289-0108. www.ramada.com.* 76 rooms, 3 story. Complimentary continental breakfast. Check-in 3 pm, check-out 11 am. Balconies overlook beach. Outdoor pool. **$$**

Full-Service Inn

★ ★ ★ BERLIN ATLANTIC. *2 N Main St, Berlin (21811). Phone 410/641-0189; toll-free 800/814-7672; fax 410/641-4928. www.atlantichotel.com.* Centrally located in Berlin's historic district, this elegant inn is perfect for a relaxing stay and quiet getaway. 17 rooms, 3 story. Complimentary full breakfast. Check-in 3 pm, check-out 11 am. Restaurant, bar. **$**

Full-Service Resort

★ ★ PRINCESS ROYALE OCEANFRONT RESORT. *9100 Coastal Hwy, Ocean City (21842). Phone 410/524-7777; toll-free 800/476-9253; fax 410/524-1623. www.princessroyale.com.* This hotel is located on the white sandy beaches of Ocean City. It offers two-room suites and two- or three-room condominiums. An Olympic-sized pool is found in a glass atrium overlooking the ocean. Golfers will enjoy the 11 nearby courses. 310 rooms, 5 story. Check-out 11 am. Restaurant, bar. Fitness room. Swimming beach, ocean deck, private boardwalk. Indoor pool, whirlpool. Tennis. Business center. **$**

Specialty Lodgings

The following lodging establishments are approved by Mobil Travel Guide, but due to their unique and individualized nature have not been given a traditional Mobil Star rating. Included in this listing you may find bed-and-breakfasts, limited-service inns, guest ranches, and other unique hotel properties.

THE LIGHTHOUSE CLUB HOTEL. *56th St in the Bay, Ocean City (21842). Phone 410/524-5400; toll-free 888/371-5400; fax 410/524-3928. www.fagers.com.* Located directly on the Isle of Wight Bay at Fager's Island, this three-story octagonal hotel affords spectacular views of waterfowl in flight and sunsets over the natural wetlands. The elegant, beachy accommodations are decorated with lush greenery, taupe and cream-colored fabrics, blond wood, and marble baths, and all 23 one-bedroom suites include continental breakfast. 23 rooms, 3 story. Complimentary continental breakfast. Check-in 4 pm, check-out noon. **$$**

MERRY SHERWOOD PLANTATION. *8909 Worcester Hwy, Berlin (21811). Phone 410/641-2112; toll-free 800/660-0358; fax 410/641-9528. www.merrysherwood.com.* 8 rooms. Children over 8 years only. Complimentary full breakfast. Check-in 2 pm, check-out 11 am. Built in 1859; on grounds of former plantation. **$$**

Restaurants

★★ **BONFIRE.** *71st St, Ocean City (21842). Phone 410/524-7171; fax 410/524-4228.* American menu. Dinner. Closed Mon-Thurs in winter. Bar. Children's menu. **$$**

★★ **EMBERS.** *2305 Philadelphia Ave, Ocean City (21842). Phone 410/289-3322; fax 410/289-0609. www.embers.com.* American menu. Dinner. Closed Dec-Feb. Bar. Children's menu. **$$**

★★★ **FAGER'S ISLAND.** *201 60th St, Ocean City (21842). Phone 410/524-5500; fax 410/723-2055. www.fagers.com.* The outdoor deck overlooking the bay is the perfect spot to take in a glorious summer sunset. The menu does well with standard and creative seafood preparations as well as other classics like prime rib. Choose a wine from a list that features over 500 bottles to accompany your meal. Pacific-Rim/Pan-Asian, seafood menu. Lunch, dinner, brunch. Bar. **$$**

★★ **HARRISON'S HARBOR WATCH.** *806 S Boardwalk, Ocean City (21842). Phone 410/289-5121.* Breathtaking ocean views, a bountiful raw bar, and fresh seafood keep this enormous restaurant packed on summer weekends. Seafood menu. Dinner. Closed Mon-Thurs Dec-Mar. Bar. Children's menu. **$$**

★★★ **HOBBIT.** *81st St and Bay, Ocean City (21842). Phone 410/524-8100; fax 410/524-5290.* This restaurant serves many of your old favorites, as well as creative new items from time to time. After dinner, browse through the unique gift shop for your Hobbit memorabilia. American, seafood menu. Lunch, dinner. Closed Dec 24-25. Bar. Children's menu. **$$**

★ **MARINA DECK RESTAURANT.** *306 Dorchester St, Ocean City (21842). Phone 410/289-4411. www.marinadeckrestaurant.com.* Seafood, steak menu. Breakfast, lunch, dinner. Closed mid-Nov-mid-Mar. Bar. Children's menu. Casual attire. Outdoor seating. **$**

★★ **OCEAN CLUB.** *49th St, Ocean City (21842). Phone 410/524-7500; fax 410/524-5086.* Seafood menu. Breakfast, lunch, dinner. Closed Dec 25; Mon-Tues off-season; mid Jan-Feb. Bar. Children's menu. **$$**

★★ **PHILLIPS CRAB HOUSE.** *2004 Philadelphia Ave, Ocean City (21842). Phone 410/289-6821; fax 410/289-2053. www.phillipsoc.com.* Seafood menu. Lunch, dinner. Closed Nov-Mar. Bar. Children's menu. **$$**

★★ **PHILLIPS SEAFOOD HOUSE.** *14101 Coastal Hwy, Ocean City (21842). Phone 410/250-1200. www.phillipsseafoodhouse.com.* Seafood menu. Lunch, dinner. Closed late Nov-late Feb. Bar. Children's menu. **$$**

Owings Mills (B-4)

Restaurants

★★ **DUE.** *25 Crossroads Dr, Owings Mills (21117). Phone 410/356-4147; fax 410/581-7836. www.linwoods.com.* Italian menu. Dinner. Closed holidays. Bar. **$$**

★★★ **LINWOOD'S CAFE.** *25 Crossroads Dr, Owings Mills (21117). Phone 410/356-3030; fax 410/581-7836. www.linwoods.com.* American menu. Lunch, dinner. Closed holidays. Bar. Reservations recommended. Outdoor seating. **$$**

Pikesville (B-4)

See also Baltimore

Population 29,123
Area Code 410
Zip 21208

Full-Service Hotel

★★★ **HILTON PIKESVILLE.** *1726 Reisterstown Rd, Pikesville (21208). Phone 410/653-1100; toll-free 800/283-0333; fax 410/415-6231. www.pikesville.hilton.com.*

This property is located 8 miles from the Baltimore/Washington International Airport, and is a short drive from local attractions like the Inner Harbor. Six indoor tennis courts, and a restaurant and lounge are on site. 171 rooms, 5 story. Check-in 3 pm, check-out noon. High-speed Internet access. Restaurant, bar. Fitness room (fee), fitness classes available. Outdoor pool. Business center. **$$**

Specialty Lodging

The following lodging establishment is approved by Mobil Travel Guide, but due to its unique and individualized nature has not been given a traditional Mobil Star rating. Included in this listing you may find bed-and-breakfasts, limited-service inns, guest ranches, and other unique hotel properties.

GRAMERCY BED AND BREAKFAST. *1400 Greenspring Valley Rd, Stevenson (21153). Phone 410/486-2405; toll-free 800/553-3404; fax 410/486-1765. www.gramercymansion.com.* This Tudor-style mansion provides elegant accomodations, and is minutes away from downtown Baltimore's shopping, museums, and fine restaurants. 11 rooms, 3 story. Complimentary full breakfast. Check-in 3-6 pm, check-out 11 am. Outdoor pool. **$$**

Pocomoke City (E-6)

See also Crisfield

Founded 1670
Population 4,098
Elevation 22 ft
Area Code 410 and 443
Zip 21851
Information Pocomoke Chamber of Commerce, 144 Market St; phone 410/957-1919
Web site www.pocomoke.com

Specialty Lodging

The following lodging establishment is approved by Mobil Travel Guide, but due to its unique and individualized nature has not been given a traditional Mobil Star rating. Included in this listing you may find bed-and-breakfasts, limited-service inns, guest ranches, and other unique hotel properties.

RIVER HOUSE INN. *201 E Market St, Snow Hill (21863). Phone 410/632-2722; fax 410/632-2866. www.riverhouseinn.com.* 8 rooms, 3 story. Pets accepted; fee. Built in 1860. On river. **$**

Potomac (C-3)

Restaurants

★★★ NORMANDIE FARM. *10710 Falls Rd, Potomac (20854). Phone 301/983-8838. www.popovers.com.* The relaxed feeling of being in a country home is part of what makes Normandie Farm a favorite among locals. The French fare is appetizing, and there is no lack of attention to detail. French, seafood menu. Lunch, dinner, brunch. Closed Mon. Bar. **$$**

★★★ OLD ANGLER'S INN. *10801 MacArthur Blvd, Potomac (20854). Phone 301/299-9097; fax 301/983-0630. www.oldanglersinn.com.* Located in a Tudor-style house built in 1860, the rustic dining room is a perfect spot for a cozy evening. In winter get a table near the fireplace, but in summer the terrace provides a lovely setting. Seafood menu. Lunch, dinner. Closed Mon. Bar. Outdoor seating. **$$**

Riverdale

Restaurants

★★ ALAMO. *5508 Kenilworth Ave, Riverdale (20737). Phone 301/927-8787; fax 301/927-3400.* Mexican menu. Lunch, dinner. Bar. Children's menu. **$$**

★★ CALVERT HOUSE INN. *6211 Baltimore Ave, Riverdale (20737). Phone 301/864-5220; fax 301/927-6612. www.calverthouseinn.com.* Seafood, steak menu. Lunch, dinner. Closed Dec 25. Bar. Children's menu. Reservations recommended. **$**

Rockville (B-3)

See also Gaithersburg

Population 47,388
Elevation 451 ft
Area Code 240 and 301
Information Chamber of Commerce, 250 Hungerford Dr, Suite L10, 20850; phone 301/424-9300
Web site www.rockvillechamber.org

The second-largest city in the state of Maryland, Rockville is the seat of Montgomery County, located at the north edge of the District of Columbia. The Great Falls of the Potomac are 9 miles south off Highway 189. This series of small falls was pretty but unnavigable, so the Chesapeake and Ohio Canal (see CHESAPEAKE AND OHIO CANAL NATIONAL HISTORICAL PARK) was built from Washington, DC, to Cumberland to simplify travel. Stone locks and levels are still visible. The graves of F. Scott and Zelda Fitzgerald are in St. Mary's Cemetery.

What to See and Do

Beall-Dawson House. *103 W Montgomery Ave, Rockville (20850). Phone 301/762-1492.* (1815) Federal architecture; period furnishings; library; museum shop; 19th-century doctor's office. Tours guided by docents. (Tues-Sat noon-4 pm; closed holidays) **$**

Special Event

Hometown Holidays. *Phone 301/424-9300.* Family entertainment; carnival rides and games ($), arts and crafts, music, food, skate park. Memorial Day weekend.

Limited-Service Hotels

★ ★ COURTYARD BY MARRIOTT. *2500 Research Blvd, Rockville (20850). Phone 301/670-6700; fax 301/670-9023. www.courtyard.com.* 147 rooms, 2 story. Check-in 3 pm, check-out noon. High-speed Internet access. Restaurant, bar. Indoor pool, whirlpool. **$**

★ ★ DOUBLETREE HOTEL. *1750 Rockville Pike, Rockville (20852). Phone 301/468-1100; fax 301/468-0163. www.doubletree.com.* This hotel is only minutes from many attractions of the nation's capital, including great shopping at the White Flint Mall. 315 rooms, 8 story. Check-out noon. Restaurant, bar. Fitness room. Indoor, outdoor pool, whirlpool. Business center. **$$**

★ QUALITY INN. *3 Research Ct, Rockville (20850). Phone 301/840-0200; fax 301/869-3080. www.qualityinn.com.* 124 rooms, 3 story. Complimentary full breakfast. Check-in 3 pm, check-out noon. Fitness room. Outdoor pool. Business center. **$**

Restaurants

★ A AND J. *1319-C Rockville Pike, Rockville (20852). Phone 301/251-7878.* Chinese menu. Lunch, dinner. Casual attire. **$**

★ ★ ADDIE'S. *11120 Rockville Pike, Rockville (20852). Phone 301/881-0081; fax 301/881-0082.* American menu. Lunch, dinner, brunch. Closed Sun; Jan 1, Thanksgiving, Dec 25. Bar. Children's menu. Outdoor seating. Eclectic décor; collection of whimsical clocks; wood-burning grill. **$$**

★ ★ ANDALUCIA. *12300 Wilkens Ave, Rockville (20852). Phone 301/770-1880. www.tasteandalucia.com.* Spanish menu. Lunch, dinner. Closed Mon; Jan 1. Bar. Reservations recommended. **$$**

★ ★ BOMBAY BISTRO. *98 W Montgomery Ave, Rockville (20850). Phone 301/762-8798; fax 301/762-8799. www.bombaybistro.com.* Indian, vegetarian menu. Lunch, dinner. Closed Labor Day, Thanksgiving. **$$**

★ ★ COPELAND'S OF NEW ORLEANS. *1584 Rockville Pike, Rockville (20852). Phone 301/230-0968; fax 301/230-0949. www.copelands.net.* Cajun/Creole, seafood menu. Lunch, dinner. Closed Dec 25. Bar. Children's menu. **$**

★ HARD TIMES CAFE. *1117 Nelson St, Rockville (20850). Phone 301/294-9720; fax 301/424-7116. www.hardtimes.com.* American menu. Lunch, dinner. Closed Thanksgiving, Dec 25. Bar. Children's menu. **$**

★★ **IL PIZZICO.** *15209 Frederick Rd, Rockville (20850). Phone 301/309-0610; fax 301/340-1227.* Italian menu. Lunch, dinner. Closed Sun; holidays. Bar. **$**

★★ **KUZINE.** *302 King Farm Blvd, Rockville (20850). Phone 301/963-3400; fax 301/963-9505.* Eastern European menu. Lunch, dinner. Children's menu. Casual attire. Outdoor seating. **$$**

★ **RED HOT & BLUE.** *16811 Crabbs Branch Way, Rockville (20855). Phone 301/948-7333; fax 301/926-7090. www.redhotandblue.com.* Barbecue menu. Lunch, dinner. Closed Thanksgiving, Dec 25. Bar. Children's menu. Outdoor seating. Blues memorabilia. **$$**

★ **RICCIUTI'S.** *3308 Olney-Sandy Spring Rd, Olney (20832). Phone 301/570-3388; fax 301/570-5351. www.ricciutis.com.* Italian menu. Lunch, dinner. Closed holidays. Children's menu. Outdoor seating. **$**

★ **SEVEN SEAS.** *1776 E Jefferson St, Rockville (20852). Phone 301/770-5020; fax 301/770-5083.* Chinese, Japanese menu. Lunch, dinner. Closed Thanksgiving. Bar. **$$**

★ **SILVER DINER.** *11806 Rockville Pike, Rockville (20852). Phone 301/770-1444; fax 301/770-1940. www.silverdiner.com.* American menu. Breakfast, lunch, dinner. Closed Dec 25. Children's menu. 1950s-style diner; jukeboxes. Servers dressed in period clothing. **$**

★★ **TARA ASIA.** *199D E Montgomery Ave, Rockville (20850). Phone 301/315-8008; fax 301/315-9082.* Pan-Asian menu. Lunch, dinner. Bar. Casual attire. Outdoor seating. **$$**

★★ **TASTE OF SAIGON.** *410 Hungerford Dr, Rockville (20850). Phone 301/424-7222.* Vietnamese menu. Lunch, dinner. Closed Thanksgiving, Dec 25. Bar. Outdoor seating. **$$**

★★ **THAT'S AMORE.** *15201 Shady Grove Rd, Rockville (20850). Phone 301/670-9666; fax 301/670-0810. www.thatsamore.com.* Italian menu. Lunch, dinner. Closed Labor Day, Thanksgiving, Dec 25. Bar. Early 20th-century mens' club atmosphere. Stained-glass windows. **$$**

St. Mary's City (D-4)

See also Leonardtown, Waldorf; also see District of Columbia

Settled 1634
Population 1,300
Elevation 36 ft
Area Code 240 and 301
Zip 20686
Information St. Mary's County Division of Tourism, 23115 Leonard Hall Dr, PO Box 653, Leonardtown 20650; phone 301/475-4411 or toll-free 800/327-9023
Web site www.co.saint-marys.md.us

Maryland's first colonists bought a Native American village on this site upon their arrival in the New World under Leonard Calvert. The settlement was the capital and hub of the area until 1694, when the colonial capital was moved to Annapolis. The town gradually disappeared. The city and county are still rich in historical attractions.

What to See and Do

Historic St. Mary's City. *Rte 5 and Rosecroft Rd, St. Mary's City (20686). Phone 301/475-4411; toll-free 800/327-9023. www.stmaryscity.org.* Outdoor museum at site of Maryland's first capital (1634) includes reconstructed State House (1676), replica of the original capitol building; other exhibits include the *Maryland Dove*, replica of a 17th-century ship, and archaeological exhibits. Also seasonal living history programs, a 17th-century tobacco plantation, reconstructed 17th-century inn; visitor center, outdoor cafe. Call or visit the Web site for hours. **$$** Also here is

> **Margaret Brent Memorial.** Gazebo overlooking the river; memorial to the woman who, being a wealthy landowner, requested the right to vote in the Maryland Assembly in 1648, in order to settle Leonard Calvert's affairs after his death.

Leonard Calvert Monument. *Trinity Churchyard, 18751 Hogaboom Ln (20686).* Monument to Maryland's first colonial governor.

Point Lookout State Park. *13 miles S on Rte 5 at the junction of the Potomac River and Chesapeake Bay. Phone 301/872-5688; toll-free 888/432-2267* *(reservations). www.dnr.state.md.us/publiclands/southern/pointlookout.html.* Site of Confederate Monument, the only memorial erected by US government to honor POWs who died in Point Lookout Prison Camp during Civil War (3,384 died here). Swimming, fishing, boating; hiking, picnicking, improved camping (Apr-Oct; self-contained camping units year-round). Nature center. Civil War museum. (May-Sept, weekends) **$**

Special Events

Crab Festival. *41348 Medley's Neck Rd, St. Mary's City (20686).* Steamed crabs, other seafood and nonseafood dishes. Arts and crafts, antique and classic car show. First Sun in June.

Maryland Days. *38370 Point Breeze Rd, St. Mary's City (20686).* Boat rides, seafood, 17th-century militia musters. Third weekend in Mar.

Restaurants

★ ALOHA. *2025 MD 235, California (20619). Phone 301/862-4838; fax 301/862-4158.* Chinese, Japanese menu. Lunch, dinner. Closed Thanksgiving, Dec 25. Bar. Children's menu. **$$**

★ EVANS SEAFOOD. *16680 Piney Point Rd, St. Mary's City (20674). Phone 301/994-2299; fax 301/994-2848. www.evansseafood.com.* American menu. Lunch, dinner. Closed Mon. Bar. Children's menu. **$$**

St. Michaels (C-4)

See also Easton

Population 1,193
Elevation 7 ft
Area Code 410
Information Talbot County Chamber of Commerce, PO Box 1366, Easton Plaza Suite 53, Easton 21601; phone 410/822-4653
Web site www.talbottschamber.org

Chartered in 1804, St. Michaels has become a boating and tourist center with its abundance of shops, marinas, restaurants, bed-and-breakfasts, and country inns. It is a town with many Federal- and Victorian-period buildings.

What to See and Do

Chesapeake Bay Maritime Museum. *Mill St and Navy Point, St. Michaels (21663). Phone 410/745-2916. www.cbmm.org.* This waterside museum consists of nine buildings and includes a historic lighthouse, floating exhibits, boat-building shop with working exhibit, ship models, small boats; paintings; waterfowl exhibits; workboats and mechanical propulsion. Special events are held throughout the year (see SPECIAL EVENT). (Daily 9 am-5 pm; summer to 6 pm; winter to 4 pm; closed Jan 1, Thanksgiving, Dec 25) **$$**

The Footbridge. *109 S Talbot St, St. Michaels (21663). Joins Navy Point to Cherry St.* Only remaining bridge of three that once connected the town with areas across the harbor.

The *Patriot*. *Chesapeake Bay Museum Dock, St. Michaels (21663). Phone 410/745-3100. www.patriotcruises.com.* A one-hour narrated cruise on Miles River. Four trips daily at 11 am, 12:30 pm, 2:30 pm, 4 pm. (Apr-Oct) **$$$**

St. Mary's Square. This public square was laid out in 1770 by Englishman James Braddock. Several buildings date to the early 1800s, including the Cannonball House and Dr. Miller's Farmhouse. The Ship's Carpenter Bell was cast in 1842; across from the bell stand two cannons, one dating from the Revolution, the other from the War of 1812. Also here is

> **St. Mary's Square Museum.** *409 St. Mary's Square, St. Michaels. Phone 410/745-9561. www.stmichaelsmd.org/lodging/smba903.htm.* Mid-19th-century home of "half-timber" construction; one of the earliest buildings in St. Michael's. Exhibits of historical and local interest. (Early May-late Oct: Sat-Sun 10 am-4 pm; also by appointment) Inquire about the town walking tour brochures. Contact the Town Office. **DONATION**

Special Event

Mid-Atlantic Maritime Festival. *Chesapeake Bay Maritime Museum, Mill St at Navy Point, St. Michaels (21663). Phone 410/745-2916. www.midatlanticmaritime.com.* Nautical celebration with fly-fishing demonstration, skipjack races, boat building contest, boat parade, seafood festival cooking contest. Three days in mid-May.

Full-Service Resorts

★ ★ HARBOURTOWNE GOLF RESORT. *Rte 33 and Martingham Dr, St. Michaels (21663). Phone 410/745-9066; toll-free 800/446-9066; fax 410/745-9124. www.harbourtowne.com.* 111 rooms, 2 story. Complimentary full breakfast. Check-in 3 pm, check-out 11 am. Restaurant, bar. Fitness room. Outdoor pool. Golf. Tennis. Business center. **$$**

★ ★ ★ THE INN AT PERRY CABIN. *308 Watkins Ln, St. Michaels (21663). Phone 410/745-2200; toll-free 800/722-2949; fax 410/745-3348. www.perrycabin.com.* The Inn at Perry Cabin marries the charm of a country inn and the intimacy of a private home with the service of a world-class resort. Nestled on the shores of eastern Maryland in the quaint Victorian town of St. Michaels, the inn is a well-heeled country getaway. Built just after the War of 1812, it looks and feels like a gracious manor house. English and early American styles blend in the lovely guest rooms, where mahogany sleigh beds, antiques, and enchanting views of the Miles River warm visitors' hearts. Cycling, golfing, and sailing are popular pastimes. A definitive British influence is evident throughout the inn, from the high tea and scones with Devonshire cream to the shortbread served at evening turndown. The bounty of the Chesapeake is celebrated on the menu at the exquisite Sherwood Landing restaurant (see also). 81 rooms, 3 story. Pets accepted, some restrictions. Children over 10 years only. Check-in 3 pm, check-out noon. Restaurant, bar. Fitness room. Outdoor pool. Business center. **$$$**

Full-Service Inn

★ ★ ★ ST. MICHAELS HARBOR INN. *101 N Harbor Rd, St. Michaels (21663). Phone 410/745-9001; toll-free 800/955-9001; fax 410/745-9150. www.harbourinn.com.* From this waterfront resort, visitors can take a short stroll down the main road to shops, museums and historical sites. 46 rooms, 3 story. Check-in 4 pm, check-out noon. Restaurant, bar. Fitness room. Outdoor pool, whirlpool. **$$$**

Specialty Lodgings

The following lodging establishments are approved by Mobil Travel Guide, but due to their unique and individualized nature have not been given a traditional Mobil Star rating. Included in this listing you may find bed-and-breakfasts, limited-service inns, guest ranches, and other unique hotel properties.

CHESAPEAKE WOOD DUCK INN. *21490 Gibsontown Rd at Dogwood Harbor, Tilghman Island (21671). Phone 410/886-2070; toll-free 800/956-2070; fax 413/677-7256. www.woodduckinn.com.* This waterfront Victorian-style bed-and-breakfast was first used as a boarding house, but has since been remodeled to provide comfortable and intimate lodging for visitors to the area. 7 rooms, 3 story. Complimentary full breakfast. Check-in 4-6 pm, check-out 11 am. **$$**

LAZYJACK INN. *PO Box 248, Tilghman Island (21671). Phone 410/886-2215; toll-free 800/690-5080; fax 410/886-2635. www.lazyjackinn.com.* This waterfront home was built in 1855 and is located within walking distance of fine dining and antique shops. It offers spacious rooms, many with views of the water. 4 rooms, 2 story. Children over 12 years only. Complimentary full breakfast. Check-in 4-7 pm, check-out 11 am. **$$**

PARSONAGE INN. *210 N Talbot, St. Michaels (21663). Phone 410/745-5519; toll-free 800/394-5519. www.bestinns.net.* This inn is in the National Historic District and colonial seaport of St. Michaels near the Maritime Museum, fine restaurants, and shops. Rooms are furnished with period reproductions, and some feature fireplaces. 8 rooms, 2 story. Pets accepted, some restrictions. Complimentary full breakfast. Check-in 2 pm, check-out 11 am. **$$**

WADE'S POINT INN. *Wades Point Rd, St. Michaels (21663). Phone 410/745-2500; toll-free 888/923-3466; fax 410/745-3443. www.wadespoint.com.* This bed-and-breakfast is located just outside historic St. Michaels. It is situated on 120 acres of fields, woodlands, and 1/2 mile of coastline that overlooks Chesapeake Bay. The inn is perfect for relaxation or recreation. 24 rooms, 3 story. Closed mid-Dec-mid-Mar. Complimentary continental breakfast. Check-in 2-8 pm, check-out 11 am. **$$**

Restaurants

★★★ **208 TALBOT.** *208 N Talbot St, St. Michaels (21663). Phone 410/745-3838; fax 410/745-6507. www.208talbot.com.* One of the top dining destinations in quaint St. Michaels, 208 Talbot is full every night with those who appreciate the creative, seasonal approach to seafood and other regional specialties. The townhouse setting is comfortable and romantic, and furnished with many antiques. American menu. Dinner, Sun brunch. Closed Mon-Tues; Dec 24-25; also mid-Feb-mid-Mar. Bar. Casual attire. **$$$**

★★ **BAY HUNDRED RESTAURANT.** *6178 Tilghman Island Rd, Tilghman (21671). Phone 410/886-2126; fax 410/886-2455.* Seafood menu. Lunch, dinner, brunch. Children's menu. Outdoor seating. **$**

★★ **BISTRO ST. MICHAELS.** *403 S Talbot St, St. Michaels (21663). Phone 410/745-9111; fax 410/745-3447. www.bistrostmichaels.com.* French bistro menu. Dinner. Closed Tues-Wed; Feb. Bar. Casual attire. Outdoor seating. Over 100 years old. **$$$**

★★ **THE BRIDGE.** *6316 Tilghmand Island Dr, Tilghman (21671). Phone 410/886-2330. www.bridgerestaurant.com.* American menu. Lunch, dinner. Closed Thanksgiving, Dec 25. Bar. Children's menu. Casual attire. Reservations recommended. Outdoor seating. **$$**

★★ **CHESAPEAKE LANDING SEAFOOD.** *23713 St. Michael's Rd, St. Michaels (21663). Phone 410/745-9600; fax 410/745-5165.* Seafood menu. Lunch, dinner. Closed Dec 25. Children's menu. Casual attire. **$$**

★★★ **HARBOUR LIGHTS.** *101 N Harbor Rd, St. Michaels (21663). Phone 410/745-5102; toll-free 800/955-9001; fax 410/745-9150. www.harbourinn.com.* This intimate dining room offers professional service and one of the finest water views on the Eastern Shore. Seafood menu. Dinner. Bar. Casual attire. **$$$**

★★★ **SHERWOOD'S LANDING.** *308 Watkin Ln, St. Michaels (21663). Phone 410/745-2200; toll-free 800/722-2949; fax 410/745-3348. www.perrycabin.com.* Located in the magnificent, manor-style Inn at Perry Cabin (see also THE INN AT PERRY CABIN) in the Victorian resort town of St. Michaels, Sherwood Landing features eclectic continental cuisine, an international wine list, and thoughtful, knowledgeable service. The restaurant is formal and elegant, swathed in soothing sandy tones, filled with gorgeous flower arrangements, and lined with luxurious tables cloaked in creamy linens and topped with crystal glasses and fine china. The menu takes classic French technique and marries it with regional Chesapeake Bay flair and the best local produce, fish, poultry, and meats. Crispy maple leaf duck leg on celery, chayote, and raisin slaw with carrot-orange vinaigrette; honey-glazed lamb shank with a casserole of Welsh leeks, potatoes, and thyme; and jumbo lump crab with saffron sauce are a few of the signature dishes on the menu. American menu. Breakfast, lunch, dinner. Bar. Children's menu. Valet parking. Outdoor seating. **$$$**

★ **ST. MICHAELS CRAB HOUSE.** *305 Mulberry St, St. Michaels (21663). Phone 410/745-3737; fax 410/745-2471. www.stmichaelscrabhouse.com.* Seafood menu. Lunch, dinner. Closed Wed; mid-Dec-Mar. Bar. Children's menu. Casual attire. Outdoor seating. **$$**

Salisbury (D-5)

See also Cambridge, Ocean City

Founded 1732
Population 20,592
Elevation 33 ft
Area Code 410 and 443
Zip 21801
Information Wicomico County Convention & Visitors Bureau, 8480 Ocean Hwy, Delmar 21875; phone 410/548-4914 or toll-free 800/332-TOUR. Information is also available from the Chamber of Commerce, 300 E Main St, PO Box 510, 21803; phone 410/749-0144
Web site www.salisburyarea.com

"Central City of the Eastern Shore" and of the Delmarva Peninsula, Salisbury has a marina on the Wicomico River providing access to Chesapeake Bay.

It lies within 30 miles of duck hunting and deep-sea fishing. Gasoline pumps, hydraulic lifts, canned and frozen foods, seafood, and poultry come from this area.

What to See and Do

Mason-Dixon Line Marker. *5 miles N on Hwy 13, 13A, then 7 miles W on Rte 467.* The Mason-Dixon Line was the boundary between the free states and the slave states during the American Civil War. The marker bears the coats of arms of Lord Baltimore and William Penn.

Nassawango Iron Furnace. *Pocomoke Forest, 3816 Old Furnace Rd, Snow Hill (21863). 16 miles S via Rte 12 to Old Furnace Rd. Phone 410/632-2032.* One of the oldest industrial sites in Maryland and one of the earliest hot blast mechanisms still intact. The stack was restored in 1966; archaeological excavations were made and a canal, a dike, and a portion of the old waterwheel used in the manufacturing process were found. The remains of the area are undergoing restoration. (Apr-Oct: daily 11 am-5 pm) **$** Surrounding the iron furnace is

> **Furnace Town.** *Phone 410/632-2032.* This 1840s industrial village occupies 22 acres around the iron furnace and also includes six historic structures; a working 19th-century blacksmith shop and broom making shop has demonstrations on selected days; a museum and company store; archaeological excavations; a nature trail and picnic area. Special events take place throughout the season. (Same hours and fees as Nassawango Iron Furnace)

Poplar Hill Mansion. *117 Elizabeth St, Salisbury (21801). Phone 410/749-1776. www.ci.salisbury.md.us/PoplarHillMansion/poplar_hill.html.* (Circa 1805) Example of Georgian- and Federal-style architecture; Palladian and bull's-eye windows; large brass box locks on doors, woodwork, mantels, and fireplaces. Period furniture; country garden. (Sun 1-4 pm; Tues-Sat by appointment; closed Mon, holidays) Admission is free on Sun. **$**

Princess Anne. *13 miles SW on Hwy 13.* This town was the home of Samuel Chase, signer of the Declaration of Independence. Buildings of the Colonial and Federal periods are of architectural interest.

Salisbury Zoological Park. *755 S Park Dr, Salisbury (21802). Phone 410/548-3188. www.salisburyzoo.org.* Natural habitats for almost 400 mammals, birds, and reptiles. Major exhibits include bears, monkeys, jaguars, bison, waterfowl. Also exotic plants. (Memorial Day-Labor Day: daily 8 am-7:30 pm; rest of year: daily 8 am-4:30 pm) **FREE**

Ward Museum of Wildfowl Art. *909 S Schumaker Dr, Salisbury (21804). At Beaglin Park Dr. Phone 410/742-4988. www.wardmuseum.org.* Displays include the history of decoy and wildfowl carving in North America; wildfowl habitats; contemporary wildfowl art. Changing exhibits. Gift shop. (Mon-Sat 10 am-5 pm, Sun noon-5 pm; closed Easter, Thanksgiving, Dec 25) **$$**

Limited-Service Hotels

★ COMFORT INN. *2701 N Salisbury Blvd, Salisbury (21801). Phone 410/543-4666; toll-free 800/638-7949; fax 410/749-2639. www.choicehotels.com.* 96 rooms, 2 story. Pets accepted, some restrictions. Complimentary continental breakfast. Check-in 3 pm, check-out 11 am. **$**

★ ★ RAMADA INN. *300 S Salisbury Blvd, Salisbury (21801). Phone 410/546-4400; fax 410/546-2528. www.ramada.com.* 156 rooms, 5 story. Pets accepted, some restrictions; fee. Check-in 3 pm, check-out noon. Restaurant, bar. Indoor pool. Airport transportation available. On river. **$**

Specialty Lodging

The following lodging establishment is approved by Mobil Travel Guide, but due to its unique and individualized nature has not been given a traditional Mobil Star rating. Included in this listing you may find bed-and-breakfasts, limited-service inns, guest ranches, and other unique hotel properties.

WATERLOO COUNTRY INN. *28822 Mt. Vernon Rd, Princess Anne (21853). Phone 410/651-0883; fax 410/651-5592. www.waterloocountryinn.com.* Built in the 1750s, this waterfront estate offers canoes and bikes to explore the area, and gardens and forests to walk through and relax. 6 rooms, 3 story. Closed Jan-Feb.

Children over 9 years only. Complimentary full breakfast. Check-out 11 am. Outdoor pool, whirlpool. **$**

Silver Spring (C-3)

See also Bowie, College Park, Laurel, Rockville; also see District of Columbia

Population 76,540
Elevation 350 ft
Area Code 240 and 301
Information Chamber of Commerce, 8601 Georgia Ave, Suite 203, 20910; phone 301/565-3777
Web site www.gsscc.org

What to See and Do

Brookside Gardens. *1800 Glenallan Ave, Wheaton (20902). N on Rte 97, right on Randolph Rd, right on Glenallan Ave. Phone 301/949-8230.* A 50-acre display garden with two conservatories, flowering displays; variety of flowering plants in eight gardens; educational programs. Grounds (daily sunrise to sunset; closed Dec 25). Conservatories (daily 10 am-5 pm). **FREE**

National Capital Trolley Museum. *1313 Bonifant Rd, Colesville (20905). Northwest Branch Park, about 7 miles N on Bonifant Rd, just off Hwy 650. Phone 301/384-6088. www.dctrolley.org.* Rides on old-time American and European trolleys; exhibits depict history of streetcars. Special events during year. (Jan-Nov: Sat-Sun noon-5 pm; mid-Mar-mid-May, Oct-mid-Nov: Sat-Sun, Thurs-Fri 10 am-2 pm; mid-June-mid-Aug: Sat-Sun, Thurs-Fri 11 am-3 pm; also open Memorial Day, July 4, Labor Day noon-5 pm) **$$**

Restaurants

★ ★ **BLAIR MANSION INN.** *7711 Eastern Ave, Silver Spring (20912). Phone 301/588-6646. www.blairmansion.com.* American menu. Lunch, dinner. Closed Mon. Bar. 1890s Victorian mansion; gaslight chandelier, 7 fireplaces. Murder mystery dinners Thurs-Sun. **$$**

★ ★ **CRISFIELD.** *8606 Colesville Rd, Silver Spring (20910). Phone 301/588-1572; fax 301/588-1574.* Seafood menu. Lunch, dinner. Closed Thanksgiving, Dec 25. Bar. Children's menu. Reservations recommended. **$$**

★ ★ **MRS. K'S TOLL HOUSE.** *9201 Colesville Rd, Silver Spring (20910). Phone 301/589-3500; fax 301/589-0768. www.mrsks.com.* American menu. Lunch, dinner, Sun brunch. Closed Mon; Dec 25. Century-old tollhouse; antique china, glass. **$$$**

★ **VICINO.** *959 Sligo Ave, Silver Spring (20910). Phone 301/588-3372; fax 301/585-8151.* Italian menu. Lunch, dinner. Closed holidays. Children's menu. Outdoor seating. **$$**

Taneytown (A-3)

Specialty Lodging

The following lodging establishment is approved by Mobil Travel Guide, but due to its unique and individualized nature has not been given a traditional Mobil Star rating. Included in this listing you may find bed-and-breakfasts, limited-service inns, guest ranches, and other unique hotel properties.

ANTRIM 1844. *30 Trevanion Rd, Taneytown (21787). Phone 410/756-6812; toll-free 800/858-1844; fax 410/756-2744. www.antrim1844.com.* This country inn is located on 23 acres of property in the Catoctin Mountains. Guest rooms and suites are decorated with antiques. 27 rooms, 3 story. Complimentary full breakfast. Check-in 3 pm, check-out 11 am. High-speed Internet access. Restaurant, bar. Spa. Outdoor pool. Tennis. **$$**

Restaurant

★ ★ ★ **ANTRIM 1844.** *30 Trevanion Rd, Taneytown (21787). Phone 410/756-6812; fax 410/756-2744. www.antrim1844.com.* This restaurant is known for its superb cuisine. When weather permits dinner may be served on the veranda overlooking the formal gardens or in the "Smokehouse," with a brick floor and large fireplaces. American, French menu. Dinner. Closed Jan 1, Dec 25. Reservations recommended. Outdoor seating. **$$$**

Thurmont (A-3)

See also Emmitsburg, Frederick, Hagerstown

Settled 1751
Population 5,588
Elevation 523 ft
Area Code 301
Zip 21788
Information Tourism Council of Frederick County, 19 E Church St, Frederick 21701; phone 301/228-2888 or toll-free 800/999-3613
Web site www.visitfrrederick.org

What to See and Do

Catoctin Mountain National Park. *Park Central Rd, Thurmont (21788). From Rte 15 N, exit onto Rte 77 W. Go approximately 3 miles and then turn right onto Park Central Rd; the visitor center is on the right. Phone 301/663-9388. www.nps.gov/cato/.* Located one hour outside Baltimore, this 5,810-acre forest is an easily accessible nature retreat. The park is adjacent to two state parks and Camp David, the weekend mountain home of the US president. If you go, you probably won't see the President, but you will be treated to beautiful overlook views and wildlife as well as scenic hiking trails. The park also offers camping, picnicking areas, fishing, and playgrounds. (Park: Open year-round during daylight hours. Visitor Center: Mon-Thurs 10 am-4:30 pm, Fri 10 am-5 pm, Sat-Sun 8:30 am-5 pm; closed holidays) **FREE**

Cunningham Falls State Park. *14039 Catoctin Hollow Rd, Thurmont (21788). Phone 301/271-7574; toll-free 888/432-2267 (reservations). www.dnr.state.md.us/publiclands/western/cunninghamfalls.html.* This state park encompasses 4,950 acres in the Catoctin Mountains. Two recreation areas: Houck, 5 miles west of town, has swimming, fishing, boating (rentals); picnicking, camping, hiking trails that lead to 78-foot falls and scenic overlooks. Manor Area, 3 miles south of town on Rte 15, has picnicking, camping, playground. Trout fishing in Big Hunting Creek. Ruins of Iron Masters Mansion and the industrial village that surrounded it are also here. (See SPECIAL EVENTS)

Special Events

Catoctin Colorfest. *6602 Foxville Rd, Thurmont (21788). Phone 301/271-4432. www.colorfest.org.* Fall foliage; arts and crafts show. Second weekend in Oct. **FREE**

Maple Syrup Demonstration. *Cunningham Falls State Park, 14039 Catoctin Hollow Rd, Thurmont (21788). Phone 301/271-7574. www.dnr.state.md.us/publiclands/western/cunninghamfalls.html.* Tree tapping, sap boiling; carriage rides; food; children's storytelling corner. Usually second and third weekends in Mar.

Limited-Service Hotel

★★ COZY COUNTRY INN THURMONT. *103 Frederick Rd, Thurmont (21788). Phone 301/271-4301; fax 301/271-4301. www.cozyvillage.com.* This is a small property located near Camp David, many historic sites, and numerous antique shops. Many visiting dignitaries have stayed here. 21 rooms, 2 story. Check-in 3 pm, check-out noon. Complimentary continental breakfast. Restaurant, bar. **$**

Restaurant

★★ COZY. *103 Frederick Rd (Hwy 806), Thurmont (21788). Phone 301/271-7373; fax 301/271-4301. www.cozyvillage.com.* Breakfast, lunch, dinner. Closed Dec 24, 25. Bar. Children's menu. Outdoor seating. **$$**

Towson (B-4)

See also Baltimore, Cockeysville

Population 51,793
Elevation 465 ft
Area Code 410 and 443
Zip 21204
Information Baltimore County Chamber of Commerce, 102 W Pennsylvania Ave, Suite 402; phone 410/825-6200
Web site www.baltcountycc.com

What to See and Do

Fire Museum of Maryland. *1301 York Rd, Lutherville (21093). 1 block N of I-695 exit 26B. Phone 410/321-7500. www.firemuseummd.org.* More than 60 pieces of antique firefighting equipment; includes motorized and hand/horse-drawn units from 1822 to 1957. (May-Dec: Sat 11 am-4 pm; June-Aug: Tues-Sat 11 am-4 pm) **$$**

Hampton National Historic Site. *535 Hampton Ln, Towson (21286). 1/2 mile off Dulaney Valley Rd; I-695 exit 27 B. Phone 410/823-1309 (visitor information). www.nps.gov/hamp.* Includes ornate Georgian mansion (circa 1790) (tours), formal gardens, and plantation outbuildings. Gift shop. (Grounds: daily 9 am-5 pm; closed Jan 1, Thanksgiving, Dec 25; Mansion tours: daily on the hour, 9 am-4 pm) Tea room open for luncheon (Daily; closed six weeks mid-Jan-early Mar). **$$**

Soldiers Delight Natural Environment Area. *5100 Deer Park Rd, Ownings Mills (21117). 7 miles W on I-695, then W on Rte 26, then 5 miles N on Deerpark Rd to overlook. Phone 410/922-3044. www.dnr.state.md.us/publiclands/central/soldiers.html.* This 1,725-acre park has 19th-century chrome mines; restored log cabin; scenic overlook; hiking and nature trails, picnicking (at visitor center only). It is the only undisturbed serpentine barren in the state. Pets must be on leash. (Visitor center: Wed-Sun 9 am-4 pm)

Towson State University. *8000 York Rd, Towson (21252). Phone 410/830-2787 (information on entertainment and events). www.towson.edu.* (1866) (15,000 students) On campus are three art galleries, including Holtzman Art Gallery, with an extensive collection of art media (Sept-May, Tues-Sat). Concerts and sporting events are held in the Towson Center.

Special Event

State Fair. *Timonium Fairgrounds, 2100 York Rd, Timonium (21094). 3 miles N on York Rd. Phone 410/252-0200. www.marylandstatefair.com.* Ten-day festival of home arts; entertainment, midway; agricultural demonstrations, Thoroughbred horse racing, livestock presentations. Late Aug-early Sept. **$**

Full-Service Hotel

★ ★ ★ SHERATON BALTIMORE NORTH. *903 Dulaney Valley Rd, Towson (21204). Phone 410/321-7400; toll-free 800/433-7619; fax 410/296-9534. www.sheraton.com.* 284 rooms, 12 story. Pets accepted, some restrictions; fee. Check-in 3 pm, check-out noon. High-speed Internet access. Restaurant, bar. Fitness room. Indoor pool, whirlpool. Business center. **$**

Restaurants

★ ★ CAFE TROIA. *28 W Allegheny Ave, Towson (21204). Phone 410/337-0133. www.cafetroia.com.* Italian menu. Lunch, dinner. Bar. Outdoor seating. **$$**

★ ★ LIBERATORE'S. *9515 Derreco Rd, Timonium (21093). Phone 410/561-3300; fax 410/561-2404. www.liberatores.com.* With an elegant Mediterranean ambiance, this restaurant serves authentic Italian specialties. Italian menu. Lunch, dinner. Closed holidays. Bar. **$$**

★ ★ PEERCE'S PLANTATION. *12460 Dulaney Valley Rd, Phoenix (21131). Phone 410/252-3100; fax 410/560-0718. www.peerces.com.* American menu. Lunch, dinner, brunch. Closed Dec 25. Bar. Children's menu. Jacket required. Valet parking. Outdoor seating. **$$$**

★ ★ ROTHWELL'S GRILLE. *106 W Padonia Rd, Timonium (21093). Phone 410/252-0600; fax 410/252-0946.* American menu. Lunch, dinner. Closed holidays. Bar. Outdoor seating. **$$**

Upper Marlboro (C-4)

What to See and Do

Marlton Golf Club. *9413 Midland Turn, Upper Marlboro (20772). Phone 301/856-7566. www.marltongolf.com.* Marlton is a very narrow course that, like many others in the area, requires the ability to play a number of different types of shots. Some holes require arrow-straight drives, some fly over large expanses of water to medium-sized greens, and some make approaching the green impossible from one side of the fairway. However, for the challenge, the price is cheap: just $24 for 18 holes on weekdays. A good course for the money within a short drive of the capital. **$$$$**

Waldorf (C-3)

See also La Plata, St. Mary's City

Population 22,312
Elevation 215 ft
Area Code 301
Information Tourism Director, PO Box 2150, La Plata 20646; phone 301/645-0558 or toll-free 800/766-3386
Web site www.explorecharlescomd.com

What to See and Do

Cedarville State Forest. *10201 Bee Oak Rd, Brandywine (20613). 4 miles E off Hwy 301 on Cedarville Rd. Phone 301/888-1410; toll-free 888/432-2267 (reservations). www.dnr.state.md.us/publiclands/southern/cedarville.html.* Includes 3,697 acres of woodland, once home of the Piscataway, who settled around the Zekiah Swamp. Fishing; hunting, nature and hiking trails, picnicking.

Farmer's Market and Auction. *29890 Three Notch Rd, Waldorf (20622). 13 miles SE on Hwy 5. Phone 301/884-3108.* Nearby Amish farms offer fresh baked goods and produce (auction Wed) for sale; more than 90 shops. Antique dealers. (Wed and Sat)

★ **John Wilkes Booth Escape Route.** *www.nps.gov/foth/escapjwb.htm.* After shooting Abraham Lincoln on April 14, 1865, John Wilkes Booth fled south into Maryland to rendezvous with his accomplice, David Herold, at

Surratt House and Tavern. *9118 Brandywine Rd, Clinton (20735). (then Surrattsville). Phone 301/868-1121. www.surratt.org/su_part.html.* (1852) Where they recovered arms they had hidden there. Though she may have been innocent, Mary Surratt was hanged for conspiracy. Eight period rooms, museum; guides in period costumes; Dec candlelight tours; special events and exhibits throughout the year. (Jan-mid-Dec, Thurs-Fri 11 am-3 pm, Sat-Sun noon-4 pm; closed Easter, July 4) **$**

Dr. Samuel A. Mudd House Museum. *3725 Dr. Samuel Mudd Rd, Waldorf (20601). From Hwy 301, take Hwy 5, then left on Hwy 205, turn right on Poplar Hill Rd approximately 4 miles, right on Dr. Samuel Mudd Rd, continue to house; sign at entrance. Phone 301/645-6870. www.somd.lib.md.us/MUSEUMS/Mudd.htm.* (Circa 1830) Where Dr. Mudd set Booth's broken leg, unaware that Booth had just shot the president. Mudd was convicted and imprisoned for life, but pardoned four years later by President Andrew Johnson. Tours conducted by costumed docents, some of whom are Dr. Mudd's descendants. (Apr-Nov, Sat-Sun, Wed 11 am-4 pm; last tour at 3:30 pm; closed Easter, Thanksgiving) **$**

Maryland Indian Cultural Center. *16816 Country Ln, Waldorf (20601). Phone 301/372-1932. www.somd.com/Detailed/1482.php.* Exhibits reflect diverse tribal structures, art, lodging construction, and cultures of Native Americans. (Tues, Thurs, Sun afternoons) **FREE**

Special Event

John Wilkes Booth Escape Route Tour. *Surrat House and Tavern, 9118 Brandywine Rd, Waldorf (20735). Phone 301/868-1121. www.surratt.org/su_bert.html.* Day-long bus tour of Booth's route from Ford's Theatre, Washington, through southern Maryland to site of Garrett's farm, Virginia, with expert commentary. Select dates in Apr, May, Sept, and Oct. **$$$$**

Limited-Service Hotel

★★ **HOLIDAY INN.** *45 St. Patrick's Dr, Waldorf (20603). Phone 301/645-8200; toll-free 800/465-4329; fax 301/843-7945. www.holiday-inn.com.* 191 rooms, 3 story. Check-in 3 pm, check-out 11 am. Wireless Internet access. Restaurant, bar. Fitness room. Outdoor pool. **$**

Westminster (A-3)

See also Baltimore, Frederick

Founded 1764
Population 16,731
Elevation 717 ft
Area Code 410 and 443

Westminster, a Union supply depot at the Battle of Gettysburg, saw scattered action before the battle. It is the county seat of Carroll County, first in the United States to offer complete rural free delivery mail service (started in 1899 with four two-horse wagons).

Limited-Service Hotel

★ **BEST WESTERN WESTMINSTER CATERING & CONFERENCE CENTER.** *451 WMC Dr, Westminster (21158). Phone 410/857-1900; fax 410/857-9584. www.bestwesternwestminster.com.* 102 rooms, 2 story. Complimentary continental breakfast. Check-in 3 pm, check-out 11 am. Outdoor pool, whirlpool. **$**

Restaurants

★★ **JOHANSSON'S.** *4 W Main St, Westminster (21157). Phone 410/876-0101; fax 410/848-1707.* Seafood menu. Lunch, dinner. Closed Thanksgiving, Dec 25. Bar. Children's menu. English pub atmosphere, originally a nickel-and-dime store; colored glass artwork. Outdoor seating. **$**

★★ **RUDY'S 2900.** *2900 Baltimore Blvd, Finksburg (21048). Phone 410/833-5777. www.rudys2900.com.* American menu. Lunch, dinner. Closed Mon; holidays. Reservations recommended. Vocalist Wed. **$$**

New Jersey

Tree-shaded 18th-century towns and history-hallowed grounds, on which Revolutionary battles were fought, make this state one of dignified beauty and democratic tradition. More than 800 lakes and ponds, 100 rivers and streams, and 1,400 miles of freshly stocked trout streams are scattered throughout its wooded, scenic northwest corner. The swampy meadows west of the New Jersey Turnpike have been reclaimed and transformed into commercial and industrial areas. The Meadowlands, a multimillion-dollar sports complex, offers horse racing, the New York Giants and the New York Jets NFL football teams, the New Jersey Devils NHL hockey team, and the New Jersey Nets NBA basketball team. The coastline, stretching 127 miles from Sandy Hook to Cape May, offers excellent swimming and ocean fishing.

Population: 7,730,188
Area: 7,504 square miles
Elevation: 0-1,803 feet
Peak: High Point Mountain (Sussex County)
Entered Union: Third of original 13 states (December 18, 1787)
Capital: Trenton
Motto: Liberty And Prosperity
Nickname: Garden State
Flower: Purple Violet
Bird: Eastern Goldfinch
Tree: Red Oak
Time Zone: Eastern
Web site: www.state.nj.us/travel

George Washington spent a quarter of his time here as commander-in-chief of the Revolutionary Army. On Christmas night in 1776, he crossed the Delaware and surprised the Hessians at Trenton. A few days later, he marched to Princeton and defeated three British regiments. He then spent the winter in Morristown, where the memories of his campaign are preserved in a national historical park.

New Jersey often is associated only with its factories, oil refineries, research laboratories, and industrial towns. But history buffs, hunters, anglers, scenery lovers, and amateur beachcombers need only to wander a short distance from its industrial areas to find whatever they like best.

When to Go/Climate

Moderate temperatures in spring and fall make these the best times to visit New Jersey. Summers can be hot and humid; winters can be bitterly cold, particularly in the inland mountain areas. Beaches are lovely, and coastal temperatures are often 5° F lower in summer and higher in winter than inland areas.

AVERAGE HIGH/LOW TEMPERATURES (° F)

Atlantic City

Jan 40/27	**May** 66/54	**Sept** 74/62
Feb 42/29	**June** 74/62	**Oct** 64/51
Mar 49/36	**July** 80/68	**Nov** 55/42
Apr 57/44	**Aug** 80/68	**Dec** 46/33

Newark

Jan 38/23	**May** 72/53	**Sept** 78/60
Feb 41/25	**June** 82/63	**Oct** 67/48
Mar 51/33	**July** 87/69	**Nov** 55/39
Apr 62/43	**Aug** 85/67	**Dec** 43/29

Parks and Recreation

Bathing at inland beaches, Memorial Day-Labor Day; at ocean beaches from mid-June; cabins ($20-$100); campsites ($10-$12), lean-tos ($15); reservations accepted ($7, nonrefundable).
Most areas are wildlife sanctuaries. In addition, 1,700 acres of Palisades Interstate Parks (see) on the Hudson are in New Jersey. There are also more than 20 state-owned historic sites (clearly marked); some with museums and guides. For detailed information contact Division of Parks and Forestry, PO Box 404, Trenton 08625; phone 609/984-0370 or toll-free 800/843-6420.

Calendar Highlights

APRIL

Tulip Festival *(Cape May). Phone 609/884-5508.* Celebrate Dutch heritage with ethnic foods and dancing, a craft show, street fair, and garden and house tours.

JUNE

IBM/USET Festival of Champions *(Somerville). Hamilton Farm. Phone 908/234-0555.* Competition of three Olympic equestrian disciplines.

JULY

Night in Venice *(Ocean City). Phone 800/ BEACH-NJ.* Decorated boat parade.

OCTOBER

Atlantic City Marathon *(Atlantic City). Phone 609/601-1RUN.*

DECEMBER

Reenactment of Crossing of the Delaware *Washington Crossing State Park. (Trenton).* Departs PA side on the afternoon of Dec 25.

Water-related activities, hiking, riding, various sports, picnicking, camping, and visitor centers are available in many state parks. There is a $1 per person (12-62 years) walk-in/bicycle fee in some areas; there is a parking fee ($2-$7) in many areas. In most areas, fees are collected Memorial Day weekend-Labor Day weekend; fees collected year-round at Island Beach (see SEASIDE PARK). No pets in bathing, camping areas or buildings; in other day-use areas, pets must be attended and kept on a 6-foot leash.

FISHING AND HUNTING

Fishing opportunities abound in New Jersey's fresh and salt waters. No license is required for deep-sea or surf fishing along the 127-mile coastline; however, a license is required for taking shellfish. Nonresident clam license: $20; under age 16, $2. A license is required for freshwater fishing for everyone over 16 years of age. Nonresident fishing license: $34; nonresident trout stamp: $20; 7-day nonresident vacation fishing license: $19.50.

Hunting licenses are required for everyone over 10 years of age. Firearm or bow and arrow: nonresident, $135.50 each; small game only: nonresident, two-day, $36.50; pheasant and quail stamp: $40 (for wildlife management areas only). Hunter Education Course or resident license from previous year required to purchase license. For information contact Department of Environmental Protection, Division of Fish, Game, and Wildlife, PO Box 400, Trenton 08625-0400; 609/292-2965.

Driving Information

Safety belts are mandatory for all persons in front seat of vehicle. Children under 5 years must be in approved passenger restraints anywhere in a vehicle: ages 18 months-5 years may use regulation safety belts in back seat; however, in front seat, children must use approved safety seats; children under 18 months must use approved safety seats anywhere in a vehicle. For further information phone 609/633-9300.

INTERSTATE HIGHWAY SYSTEM

The following alphabetical listing of New Jersey towns in this book shows that these cities are within 10 miles of the indicated Interstate highways. Check a highway map for the nearest exit.

Highway Number	Cities/Towns within 10 Miles
Interstate 78	Clinton, Plainfield, Scotch Plains, Somerville, Union.
Interstate 80	Fort Lee, Hackensack, Hackettstown, Paramus, Parsippany, Rockaway, Saddle Brook, Wayne.
Interstate 95	Elizabeth, Fort Lee, Newark, Trenton, Woodbridge.

Additional Visitor Information

The State Division of Travel and Tourism, PO Box 820, Trenton 08625-0820, phone 609/292-2470 or 800/JERSEY-7, publishes a variety of materials for travelers. There are also two periodicals: *New Jersey Monthly* (write Subscription Department, Box 936, Farmingdale, NY 11737; phone 888/419-0419); *New Jersey Outdoors* (write Department of Environmental Protection & Energy, CN-402, Trenton 08625).

There are eight tourist welcome centers and numerous information centers in New Jersey. At these centers visitors will find information racks with brochures to help plan trips to points of interest. For a publication with the locations of the centers contact the State Division of Travel and Tourism.

THE AMUSEMENTS OF THE JERSEY SHORE

Pennsylvania Route 40 leads to the Jersey Shore, where you'll find some of the best-known New Jersey resort towns: Atlantic City, Ocean City, and historic Cape May. People of all ages are sure to find something fun to do in Atlantic City. Children are delighted by Lucy the Margate Elephant, a six-story elephant-shaped building. If you climb Lucy's legs to the observation area on her back, your children can add "riding an elephant," to the things they've done on their summer vacation–and they'll have a great story to share with their classmates when vacation is over! Storybook Land, which includes more than 50 storybook buildings, rides, animals, and a playground, is also a hit with the little ones. A trip to the fantastic world of the Ripley's Believe It or Not Museum may be of more interest to older children. Adults will enjoy the guided tour of Renault Winery, a visit to the Noyes Museum, and the specialty shops and restaurants of historic Smithville. Still at a loss for entertainment? A visit to one of the recreation areas along the coast is a surefire way to please any family member, young or old. Or spend some time at one of the amusement piers, where shopping and food provide distractions for even the hardest to please. Other noteworthy attractions include the Marine Mammal Stranding Center & Museum, which also offers dolphin- and whale-watching tours, and Edwin B. Forsythe National Wildlife Refuge. Looking for the wilder side of Atlantic City? Test your luck at one of a dozen casinos, where the action never stops and fortunes are won and lost in an instant. It might be safest to stick to the slot machines.

Head south from Atlantic City to Ocean City, a popular family resort where you can enjoy swimming, fishing, and boating on 8 miles of beaches. A walk on the boardwalk bordering the Jersey Shore is a must. Take a ride to the top of the 140-foot-tall Ferris wheel for breathtaking views that stretch for miles. Video arcades, roller coasters, and water slides will keep the kids entertained. In fact, at Li'l Buc's Bay, adults are admitted only if they're accompanied by children–your kids are bound to get a kick out of that! Stop for a snack at one of the outdoor cafés or fill up on sweet goodies like cotton candy and ice cream. After all, you're on vacation!

Cape May, the nation's oldest seashore resort, is at the southernmost tip of New Jersey. History enthusiasts will enjoy exploring historic Cold Spring Village, a restored 1870 South Jersey farm village with craft shops and demonstrations. Take the ferry across Delaware Bay or explore on foot with a guided walking tour of the Historic District or a one-hour Ocean Walk tour of area beaches and marine life. As in Atlantic City and Ocean City, there are plenty of opportunities for swimming, boating, and fishing in the Atlantic or in Delaware Bay. **(Approximately 125 miles)**

A NORTHERN NEW JERSEY LOOP

Begin in Fort Lee, just south of the George Washington Bridge at Fort Lee Historic Park, part of Palisades Interstate Park, off of County Route 505 (Hudson Terrace/Main Street). The park's Visitor Center and Museum focuses on the role of Fort Lee in the American Revolution. See a reconstructed 18th-century soldier hut and campsite, reconstructed gun batteries, and beautiful Manhattan views. Turn left, leaving the Historic Park. Go one block and turn left at the stop sign (Main Street). In about 50 yards, an unmarked parking lot appears on the left. Turn into it and follow the narrow roadway, Henry Hudson Drive, down toward the river. Follow this tree-covered, 25-mph lane to its end (about 25 minutes), admiring the river views. Stops can be made at one of the two marinas along the way where walking trails can be accessed. Henry Hudson Drive ends at exit 2 of the Palisades Parkway. Take the parkway north. At exit 3, State Line Lookout is set on the highest point on the Palisades Cliffs, commanding views of the Hudson River, Westchester County, and beyond. There's hiking, a snack bar, information center, and gift shop.

Follow the Parkway into New York State and turn onto I-87/287 (NY Thruway) North. At Suffern, follow I-287 South back into New Jersey. At exit 57 (Oakland), follow Skyline Drive, which travels over Ramapo Mountain and offers some fun-to-drive, twisting mountain roads. At the end, turn right onto Country Road 511 North. Expansive, picturesque Wanaque Reservoir is on the left. County 511 leads to Ringwood State Park, site of the historic homes Ringwood Manor and Skylands Manor, and the NJ State Botanical Garden. Leaving the park, return to 511 and follow it into Greenwood Lake. Continue straight onto Warwick Turnpike, through Upper Greenwood Lake, skirting Waywayanda State Park (a good place for hiking, mountain biking, or swimming), and up into New York State again. At Route 94, turn south (left), driving back into New Jersey and through the town of Vernon. You'll pass Mountain Creek Resort, a major ski center in winter and water/adventure sports park in summer, a great place to stop with the kids. Continue on Route 94 to Route 23, turn right (north) and go into the town of Sussex. In summertime, Sussex is the site of the annual Sussex Air Show, one of the best small-airport shows of its kind, and the Sussex Horse & Farm Show/NJ State Fair.

If kids are along for the ride, detour to Space Farms Zoo & Museum by following County Route 628 West out of Sussex, turning left onto County Route 519. A private attraction, Space Farms offers a fascinating collection of animals, as well as antique cars and farm equipment. Return to (or continue north from Sussex on) Route 23 into High Point State Park, site of the state's highest elevation. Stop here for a picnic, climb the obelisk that marks the state zenith, swim, or camp. Continue on Route 23 North into Port Jervis, NY, and take US 209 South, which follows the upper Delaware River on the Pennsylvania side. In Milford, PA, take US 206 South. At Tuttles Corner, turn right onto County Route 580, then left onto County Route 615 to Peters Valley, an arts and crafts center where artists can be watched as they work. The annual crafts fair here is one of the state's finest and biggest. Return to US 206 at Tuttles Corner; this is the heart of Stokes State Forest, which holds a variety of hiking opportunities. Follow US 206 south into Augusta. In the summer, the New Jersey Cardinals minor league baseball team plays here. At Ross Corner, leave US 206 for Route 15 South, traveling into Lafayette, known for its large number of antique emporia.

Out of Lafayette, follow Route 94 South back to US 206 South, into Stanhope. Here, Waterloo Village offers a living-history look at an iron works and Morris Canal town (circa 1831), a re-created Lenape Indian Village (circa 1625), and a summer-long series of music concerts. Follow County Route 602 into Hopatcong State Park. Lake Hopatcong is the state's largest lake and offers excellent boating and swimming. Follow the local roads around the lake into the village of Hopatcong for some good lakeside dining. From here, take I-80 East back to Fort Lee/New York City. **(Approximately 110 miles)**

A Southern New Jersey Loop

From Philadelphia, follow Route 70 East through the suburbs to the junction of Route 72, and turn right onto 72 East. In a few miles, you'll see the entrance to Lebanon State Forest on the left. Stop at the Visitors Center and pick up a park map, and drive north through the park to Whitesbog Village. This is the heart of the famous Jersey Pinelands, and the village, almost a ghost-town, was once a thriving cranberry/blueberry producing community, the place where the blueberry was first commercially grown and processed. Stroll among the old buildings and talk to the folks who are trying to preserve the place–their office is at the main crossroad. Also in Lebanon State Forest is access to the Batona Trail, south Jersey's longest hiking trail, and a variety of places to hike and swim. Return to Route 72, turn right, and then quickly left onto County 563, a local, two-lane, tree-lined road that meanders south past forest and meadows into Wharton State Forest. Passing through the tiny hamlets of Jenkins and Maxwell, turn right onto County Route 542 westbound at Green Bank. Route 542 parallels the picturesque Mullica River. Follow it to Batsto, and stop for a visit to Historic Batsto Village.

Batsto was an ironworks (supplying munitions for the Revolutionary War and the War of 1812) and a glassmaking center. The restored village includes a mansion and several workers' houses, some of which are occupied today by artisans who are happy to show their work. There's a small nature center, as well as picnic grounds, a nature trail, and plenty of hiking, mountain biking (on some 500 miles of unpaved roads), and canoeing. Canoeing can also be done on the Mullica River from the nearby towns of Sweetwater or Pleasant Mills.

Leave Batsto, heading south on County 623, then turn left onto County 643, following the other side of the Mullica River through Sweetwater. At County 612 (Elwood Weekstown Road), turn right on County 563. Turn right at Alternate 511 (Mill Road), and visit the Renault Winery. Renault is a bit "touristy," but their glass collection and very good restaurant (especially for Sunday brunch) make this stop worthwhile. Return to County 563 and turn left. In Egg Harbor City County 563 will become Route 50. Continue south to Tuckahoe, then turn right onto Route 49 West into Millville, home to Wheaton Village. Wheaton Village pays homage to Millville's storied glassmaking heritage with the Museum of American Glass, one of the world's finest collections. The Village also holds the T. J. Wheaton Glass Factory and Crafts & Traders' Row, where glass- and craft-making demonstrations are staged, the Down Jersey Folklife Center, many stores, a miniature train ride, and a long list of special events. A nice motel is on-site.

After Millville, consider a detour to Bivalve. (If not, continue on Route 49 West to Bridgeton.) The local roads pass through bucolic fields producing fruits, vegetables, and ornamentals, as well as dairy, poultry, and swine farms. Follow County 555 South out of Millville to County 553 East (left turn) at the tiny hamlet of Dividing Creek. In slightly less than 4 miles, turn right onto Shell Road, which becomes Lighthouse Road into Bivalve. This tiny spot was once the capital of the oyster industry, and it displays a series of industrial buildings (some half-ruined, some fully functioning) that create a compelling atmosphere. Return to County 553, turn right into Port Norris, and visit the restored A. J. Meerwald, New Jersey's official "tall ship" and an archetype for the heyday of oystering. This is a great chance to explore this little-known facet of New Jersey's heritage.

Follow County 553 back to the west until it reunites with Route 49. Turn left. Three miles before entering Bridgeton is Berry's Farm Market (739 Shiloh Pike/Rte 49), one of several terrific farm markets in the area. In town, follow the signs to the Bridgeton Historical District on East Broad Street. This is New Jersey's largest historical district, holding some 2,200 Colonial, Victorian, and Federalist buildings. Downtown has paved-brick walkways, and a scenic promenade fronts the river. A 1,100-acre city park has four museums, a zoo, canoe rentals, swimming, and picnicking. A handful of small restaurants and nice shops can be found here, too. Leave Bridgeton on Route 49, passing through Salem to Fort Mott State Park, a small park that is noteworthy because of its fortifications (built in 1896), good walking trails, and picnic grounds. Return to Route 49, accessing I-295 back to Philadelphia. **(Approximately 180 miles)**

PHILADELPHIA AND WESTERN NEW JERSEY

This drive meanders up New Jersey's western border, following the scenic Delaware River from the greater Philadelphia area through the timberlands of Delaware Water Gap National Recreation Area.

From Philadelphia, follow Route 130 to Route 73 North. Turn left, and make a right onto County Route 543. From here, the drive becomes leisurely, following local roads for quite a distance. The scenic Delaware River is on your left, and the road passes through the small towns of Palmyra, Riverton, and Riverside. It merges with Route 130, a major thoroughfare just south of Burlington. In Burlington, go left onto High Street, the main intersection, and into the Historic District, which dates back to 1677. (Ben Franklin learned the printing trade here.) Walking tours are offered by the Burlington Center (phone 609/387-8300), and the Burlington County Historical Society is at 457 High Street. Tours are also offered of the James Fenimore Cooper house. Several fine restaurants are found here, including the Café Gallery, which overlooks the river at 219 High Street.

Leave Burlington northbound on County Route 656, which loops alongside the river and comes back to Route 130. Take 130 North into Trenton, the state capital. Among the worthwhile stops in Trenton are the Old Barracks Museum, an original French and Indian War Barracks; the State House, seat of NJ government; the Contemporary Victorian Museum; the War Memorial Theater; and the New Jersey State Museum and Planetarium. For a good meal and jazz, try Joe's Mill Hill Saloon. Leave Trenton on Route 29 North. Near the junction of I-95 stands the New Jersey State Police Museum and, soon after in Titusville, Washington Crossing State Park. Here, each Christmas Day, Washington's crossing of the Delaware is re-enacted. The park also contains nice walking paths, river views, picnic areas, and historical information. Also in Titusville is the Howell Living History Farm, (101 Hunter Road, just off Rte 29), a circa 1900 horse-powered farm where visitors join in field, barn, and craft programs on weekends.

Continue on Route 29 northbound into Lambertville. An exceptionally well-maintained historic town with many Federal-style and Victorian buildings, Lambertville is a treasure trove of antiques shopping, fine dining, bed-and-breakfast lodging, and access to the Delaware & Raritan Canal State Park, where walking, boating, canoeing, biking, fishing, cross-country skiing, and picnicking are possible. Route 29 continues north along the river. In Stockton, the Stockton Inn on Main Street offers pleasant accommodations. The Prallsville Mills at Delaware & Raritan Canal State Park consist of nine structures dating from 1796 and historical exhibits. The Bull's Island Recreation Area offers 30 miles of hiking trails and superb birdwatching. In Frenchtown, Hunterdon House and The Guesthouse at Frenchtown Brown's Old Homestead are two excellent bed-and-breakfast inns, and Poor Richard's Winery offers tours and tastings.

In Frenchtown, jog left on Ridge Street, then right on Harrison Street, which becomes Milford-Frenchtown Road and eventually Frenchtown Road, leading into Milford, site of The Ship Inn, New Jersey's first brew pub and an excellent spot to stop and dine. Follow County Route 627 out of Milford. In Holland Township, the Vollendam Windmill Museum shows its operational gristmill and replica windmills on summer weekends. In Mount Joy, Route 627 veers inland. Follow it to a merge with Route 173, bearing right, then to the junction of I-78 (exit 6). Take I-78 westbound to exit 4, and follow County Route 687 towards Lower Harmony, switching to County Route 519 northbound in Harmony. Follow Route 519 to Belvidere and visit Four Sisters Winery at Matarazzo Farms, which not only produces some surprisingly nice wines, but has an excellent bakery and stages many special events. Also in town is the Pequest River Book Company, which stocks historic local books, and has an art gallery and café.

Continue on Route 519 north until it meets Route 46/I-80 at Columbia. Follow I-80 westbound to exit 1, exiting for a visit to the Delaware Water Gap National Recreation Area, a magnificent outdoor wonderland with swimming, fishing, canoeing, tubing, hiking, camping, biking, cross-country skiing, and all manner of other outdoor activities. The Kittatiny Ranger Station offers information, an audio-visual program, and displays, and rangers present impromptu "Terrace Talks" on weekends. Make the trip to Millbrook Village, located about 12 miles north of I-80 along Old Mine Road (the park's main north-south route), a 19th-century settlement in an ongoing process of restoration. **(Approximately 115 miles)**

NORTHERN SHORE TO ATLANTIC CITY

New Jersey has some 130 miles of coastline. This tour covers the shore from Atlantic Highlands to Atlantic City. While many local roads are noted, the main north-south route is the Garden State Parkway (a toll road). At any given time, the local roads can be abandoned for a quick run down the Parkway to the next desired shore point.

Coming out of the New York metro area, access the Parkway south. Leave the Parkway at exit 117, and follow Route 36 into Atlantic Highlands. Just as the highway crosses the bridge into Highlands, you'll see Gateway National Recreation Area on the left. There's a swimming beach here, but the highlights are Sandy Hook Lighthouse, Fort Hancock (including World War II fortifications remnants), and the Visitor Center, which sponsors nature and maritime history programs.

Route 36 continues south through the beach towns of Sea Bright, Monmouth Beach, and Long Branch, then turns inland. Turn right on Route 35. In about 7 1/2 miles, turn right onto Route 33 and head to Ocean Grove. First founded as a religious retreat, Ocean Grove holds a great collection of Victorian architecture. It's also home to the Ocean Grove Auditorium, an extraordinary all-wood structure with one of the world's great organs. Stop in for a bite to eat–or stay the night–at the Manchester Inn & Secret Garden Restaurant. Follow Route 35 south to County 71 and turn right on Jersey Avenue to get to the heart of Spring Lake, which can also be accessed from the Garden State Parkway via exit 98, once known as the Irish Riviera, now known for its extensive collection of fine bed-and-breakfast inns. This is a great place to spend the night.

The next stop is Point Pleasant Beach, a must for those traveling with small children. It's reached by returning to Route 35 South. Turn right on Route 88, then left on Ocean Avenue. Here Jenkinson's Pavilion Boardwalk & Amusement Park is a shore-side heaven for little ones. It has a terrific small aquarium, and its beach, boardwalk, rides, fun house, arcades, restaurants, shops, and miniature golf are all family-oriented.

Moving south, Ocean Avenue becomes Route 35, and travels through a number of shore towns, most of which attract second-home owners or summer-home renters. In about 7 miles, the highway becomes Central Avenue, the main street in Seaside Heights/Seaside Park, a mecca for teens and young adults, filled with amusements, a long boardwalk, and much noise and action. (MTV set up its summer beach house here a few years back.) To the south, Central Avenue becomes the entryway to Island Beach State Park, one of the state's most pristine environments, ideal for those who want the beach without the amusements. The park also has nature trails and hosts excellent nature programs.

Returning north out of the park and into Seaside Heights, turn left onto Route 37, and enter the Garden State Parkway at exit 82. At exit 63, leave the Parkway onto Route 72 East, which leads to Long Beach Island, a collection of small towns that are very popular with vacationers. Turn right onto Route 9 southbound and in about 5 miles, after passing through several towns, enter Tuckerton, site of the Barnegat Bay Decoy and Baymen's Museum, an excellent small museum that preserves maritime history, heritage, and the lifestyle of the Jersey shore and its baymen. Drive south on Route 9 for 10 miles or so into Oceanville. Following the signs, turn left on East Great Creek Road and right onto Lily Lake Road to reach The Noyes Museum of Art, a surprisingly fine facility set almost literally in the middle of nowhere. From the museum, return to East Great Creek Road, turn right, and follow the signs to the Forsythe Wildlife Refuge, a 42,000-acre tract with a beautiful 8-mile wildlife auto trail that reveals magnificent wetlands and ocean views, and has terrific bird-watching.

Return to Route 9 South. At the junction of Route 30 turn left (east) to go into Atlantic City. Famous for its casinos, "AC" is not everyone's cup of tea, but it does offer an excellent race track, a good (albeit small) historical museum, minor league baseball, the Ocean Life Center for Marine Education, the world's most famous boardwalk, and two of the region's best golf courses–Blue Heron Pines Golf Club and the Seaview Marriott Resort. **(Approximately 160 miles)**

Allaire State Park (C-4)

See also Asbury Park, Freehold

Web site www.state.nj.us/dep/parksandforests/parks/allaire.html

Allaire State Park has more than 3,000 acres and offers a fishing pond for children under 14; multi-use trails, picnic facilities, playground, camping (dump station, summer), and the opportunity to visit a historic 19th-century village (see below). Park (daily). For more information, contact PO Box 220, Farmingdale 07727.

What to See and Do

Historic Allaire Village. *524 Allaire Rd, Farmingdale (07727). Phone 732/938-2253. www.allairevillage.org.* In 1822, James Allaire bought this site as a source of bog ore for his ironworks. The furnace also produced cast-iron items such as hollow-ware pots and kettles, stoves, sadirons, and pipes for New York City's waterworks. Today, visitors can explore the bakery, general store, blacksmith and carpentry shops, worker's houses, the community church, and other buildings still much as they were in 1836. Village grounds and center (daily 10 am-4 pm); village buildings (Memorial Day-Labor Day: Wed-Sun 11 am-5 pm; Labor Day-Nov: Sat-Sun 10 am-4 pm); special events (Feb-Dec). **FREE**

Train Rides. *Historic Allaire Village, Allaire State Rd, Farmingdale (07727). Phone 732/938-5524.* Narrow-gauge steam and diesel locomotive rides (Apr-mid-Oct, daily). **$$**

Asbury Park (C-4)

See also Allaire State Park

Settled 1871
Population 16,930
Elevation 21 ft
Area Code 732
Zip 07712
Information Greater Asbury Park Chamber of Commerce, 308 Main St, PO Box 649; phone 732/775-7676
Web site www.asburyparkchamber.com

This popular shore resort was bought in 1871 by New York brush manufacturer James A. Bradley and named for Francis Asbury, first American Bishop of the Methodist Episcopal Church. Bradley established a town for temperance advocates and good neighbors. The beach and the three lakes proved so attractive that, by 1874, Asbury Park had grown into a borough, and by 1897, a city. It is the home of the famous boardwalk, Convention Hall, and the Paramount Theatre. In September 1934, the SS *Morro Castle* was grounded off this beach and burned with a loss of 122 lives. Asbury Park became the birthplace of a favorite sweet when a local confectioner introduced "saltwater taffy" and watched the sales curve rise with the tide. Today, this is a popular resort area for swimming and fishing.

What to See and Do

Stephen Crane House. *508 4th Ave, Asbury Park (07712). Phone 732/775-5682.* Early home of the author of *The Red Badge of Courage* contains photos, drawings, and other artifacts. Tours (by appointment). **FREE**

The Stone Pony. *913 Ocean Ave, Asbury Park (07712). Phone 732/502-0600. www.stoneponyonline.com.* This legendary nightclub is known for unexpected visits from rock musician Bruce Springsteen and others. Includes the Asbury Park Gallery, with a collection of photographs and other memorabilia from the resort town's glory days. (Daily)

Special Events

Concerts at the Great Auditorium. *54 Pitman Ave, Ocean Grove (07756). Phone 732/774-1391; toll-free 800/388-4768. www.oceangrovenj.com/auditorium.htm.* Pipe organ recitals. June-Sept: Wed evenings, Sat afternoons.

Horse racing. Monmouth Park. *175 Oceanport Ave, Oceanport (07757). Via Hwy 35 N to Hwy 36; or via Garden State Pkwy exit 105, then E on Hwy 36. Phone 732/222-5100. www.monmouthpark.com.* Thoroughbred racing. Memorial Day-Labor Day: Wed-Sun. **$**

Jazz Fest. *1 Municipal Plz, Asbury Park (07712). Phone 732/775-7676.* Late June.

Metro Lyric Opera Series. *Paramount Theatre, Asbury Park.* At the Paramount Theatre on the Boardwalk. Sat evenings, July-Aug.

Ocean Grove House Tour. *50 Pitman Ave, Ocean Grove (07756). Phone 732/774-1869. www.oceangrove.org.* Tour of Victorian cottages. July.

Restaurant

★ ★ MOONSTRUCK. *517 Lake Ave, Asbury Park (07712). Phone 732/988-0123; fax 732/775-4493.* Italian, Mediterranean menu. Dinner. Closed Mon-Tues; Dec 25; also Jan-mid-Feb. Outdoor seating. **$$**

Atlantic City (E-3)

See also Ocean City

Settled 1854
Population 40,517
Elevation 8 ft
Area Code 609
Information Atlantic City Convention & Visitors Authority, 2314 Pacific Ave, 08401; phone 609/449-7147, toll-free 888/ACVISIT, or 800/BOARDWALK
Web site www.atlanticcitynj.com

Honeymooners, conventioneers, Miss America, and some 37 million annual visitors have made Atlantic City the best-known New Jersey beach resort. Built on Absecon Island, the curve of the coast shields it from battering northeastern storms while the nearby Gulf Stream warms its waters, helping to make it a year-round resort. A 60-foot-wide boardwalk extends along 5 miles of beaches. Hand-pushed wicker rolling chairs take visitors up and down the Boardwalk. Absecon Lighthouse ("Old Ab"), a well-known landmark, was first lit in 1857 and now stands in an uptown city park.

Atlantic City Fun Fact

- Atlantic City is where the street names came from for the game Monopoly.

What to See and Do

Absecon Lighthouse. *31 S Rhode Island Ave, Atlantic City (08401). Phone 609/449-1360 (voice). www.abseconlighthouse.org.* Climb the 228 steps to the top of this 1857 lighthouse, designed by Civil War general George Gordon Meade. Tallest lighthouse in New Jersey, third-tallest in US. (July-Aug: daily 10 am-5 pm; Sept-June: Thurs-Mon 11 am-4 pm; closed holidays) **$**

Atlantic City Boardwalk Hall. *2301 Boardwalk, Atlantic City (08401). Phone 609/348-7000. www.boardwalkhall.com.* Seats 13,800; special events, concerts, boxing, ice shows, sports events; site of the annual Miss America Pageant.

Edwin B. Forsythe National Wildlife Refuge, Brigantine Division. *Box 72, Great Creek Rd, Oceanville (08231). 9 miles N on Hwy 9. Phone 609/652-1665. forsythe.fws.gov.* Wildlife drive; interpretive nature trails (daily). Over the years, more than 200 species of birds have been observed at this 45,000-acre refuge. Public-use area has an 8-mile wildlife drive through diversified wetlands and uplands habitat; most popular in the spring and fall, during the course of the waterbird migration, and at sunset, when the birds roost for the evening. Refuge headquarters (Mon-Fri 8 am-4 pm). **$$**

Fishing. Surf and deep-sea fishing. License may be required, check locally. Charter boats (Mar-Nov). Many tournaments are scheduled. Contact Atlantic City Party and Charter Boat Association.

Garden Pier. *Boardwalk at New Jersey Ave, Atlantic City (08401). Phone 609/347-5837.* The Atlantic City Art Center and Atlantic City Historical Museum are located here. (Daily 10 am-4 pm) **FREE**

Historic Gardner's Basin. *800 New Hampshire Ave, Atlantic City (08401). At N end of city. Phone 609/348-2880.* An 8-acre, sea-oriented park featuring the working lobstermen; Ocean Life Center, eight tanks totalling 29,800 gallons of aquariums, exhibiting more than 100 varieties of fish and marine animals, 10 exhibits featuring themes on the marine and maritime environment. Picnicking. (Daily; closed Jan 1, Thanksgiving, Dec 25)

Historic Town of Smithville and the Village Greene at Smithville. *1 N New York Rd, Smithville (08205). 7 miles W on Hwy 30 to Absecon, then 6 miles N on Hwy 9, at Moss Mill Rd. Phone 609/652-4040 (Village Greene). www.online96.com/smithville.* (1787) Restored 18th-century village with specialty shops and restaurants. Also carousel, train ride, and paddle boats. Village. Special events throughout the year (daily).

Lucy, the Margate Elephant. *9200 Atlantic Ave, Margate City (08402). Phone 609/823-6473. www.lucytheelephant.org.* The only elephant in the world you can walk through and come out alive. Guided tour and exhibit inside this six-story elephant-shaped building. Built in 1881; spiral stairs in Lucy's legs lead to main hall and observation area on her back. Gift shop. (Mid-June-Labor Day: daily; Sept-Dec: Sat-Sun 10 am-5 pm) **$**

Marine Mammal Stranding Center & Museum. *3625 Atlantic Brigantine Blvd, Brigantine (08203). Over bridge and 2 miles N. Phone 609/266-0538. www.mmsc.org.* This is one of the few marine mammal rescue and rehabilitation centers in the US. Injured dolphins, turtles, and other marine animals are brought to the center for treatment and then released back into the wild. The museum offers exhibits on mammal species; recuperating animals can be viewed at the center. Dolphin and whale-watch trips are available (fee; reservations required). (Visiting hours change seasonally or according to daily activities and operations, call for schedule) **DONATION**

Noyes Museum. *Lily Lake Rd, Oceanville (08231). 12 miles NW via Hwy 9. Phone 609/652-8848. www.noyesmuseum.org.* Rotating and permanent exhibits of American art; collection of working bird decoys. (Tues-Sat 10 am-4:30 pm, Sun noon-5 pm; closed Jan 1, Dec 25). **$**

Recreation areas. Beach (Memorial Day-mid-Sept; free), surfing at special areas (daily), boating; bicycling and rolling chairs on Boardwalk (daily), golf, tennis.

Renault Winery. *72 N Bremen Ave, Egg Harbor City (08215). 16 miles W on Hwy 30. Phone 609/965-2111. www.renaultwinery.com.* Guided tour (approximately 45 minutes) includes wine-aging cellars; press room; antique wine-making equipment; free wine tasting. Restaurants. (Guided tours and wine tasting: Mon-Fri 11 am-4 pm, Sat 11 am-8 pm, Sun noon-4 pm) **$** Free tour with dinner on Saturday night.

The Shops on Ocean One. *1 Atlantic Ocean, Atlantic City (08401). Boardwalk at Arkansas Ave. Phone 609/347-8082.* A 900-foot, three-deck shopping pier houses shops, food court, and restaurants. (Jan-May: daily 10 am-7 pm; June-Aug: daily 10 am-9 pm; Sept-Dec: daily 10 am-8 pm) **FREE**

Storybook Land. *6415 Black Horse Pike, Egg Harbor Township (08234). 10 miles W via Hwy 40, 322. Phone 609/641-7847 (recording). www.storybookland.com.* More than 50 storybook buildings and displays depicting children's stories; live animals; rides; picnic area, concession. Christmas Fantasy with Lights and visiting with Mr. and Mrs. Santa (Thanksgiving-Dec 30, nightly). Admission includes attractions and unlimited rides. (Schedule varies, call for hours.) **$$$**

Special Events

Atlantic City Marathon. *PO Box 2181, Boardwalk Runners Club, Atlantic City (08406). Phone 609/601-1786. www.visitac.com/marathon.* Mid-Oct.

Miss America Pageant. *Atlantic City Boardwalk Hall, 2301 Boardwalk, Atlantic City (08401). Phone 609/449-2064. www.missamerica.com.* Usually first or second weekend after Labor Day. **$$$$**

ShopRite LPGA Atlantic City Classic. *Seaview Marriott Resort & Spa, 401 S New York Rd, Galloway Township (08205). Phone 609/927-7888. www.seaviewmarriott.com.* Late June.

Limited-Service Hotels

★★ CLARION HOTEL. *8029 Black Horse Pike, West Atlantic City (08232). Phone 609/641-3546; toll-free 800/999-9466; fax 609/641-9740. www.clarionhotel.com.* 110 rooms, 2 story. Check-in 3 pm, check-out 11 am. Restaurant. Children's activity center. Fitness room. Outdoor pool, children's pool. Tennis. Airport transportation available. **$**

★ DAYS INN. *6708 Tilton Rd, Egg Harbor City (08234). Phone 609/641-4500; toll-free 800/329-7466; fax 609/645-8295. www.daysinn.com.* 117 rooms, 5 story. Complimentary continental breakfast. Check-in 3 pm, check-out 11 am. **$**

★ HAMPTON INN. *7079 Black Horse Pike, West Atlantic City (08232). Phone 609/484-1900; toll-free 800/426-7866; fax 609/383-0731. www.hamptoninn.com.* 143 rooms, 6 story. Complimentary continental breakfast. Check-in 3 pm, check-out 11 am. **$**

★ ★ HOLIDAY INN. *111 S Chelsea Ave, Atlantic City (08401). Phone 609/348-2200; toll-free 800/548-3037; fax 609/348-0168. www.atlanticcity.holiday-inn.com.* 220 rooms, 21 story. Check-in 4 pm, check-out 11 am. High-speed Internet access. Restaurant. Outdoor pool. **$$**

Full-Service Hotels

★ ★ ★ BALLY'S PARK PLACE CASINO RESORT. *Park Place and Boardwalk, Atlantic City (08401). Phone 609/340-2000; toll-free 800/225-5977; fax 609/340-4713. www.ballysac.com.* A geometric glass chandelier twinkles overhead at the entrance to this large, classic casino. There are several dining options to choose from, including some that fit into the Wild West theme of the hotel's annex casino. 1,246 rooms, 49 story. Check-in 3 pm, check-out 11 am. Restaurant, bar. Fitness room, spa. On beach. Indoor pool, outdoor pool, whirlpool. Casino. **$$**

★ ★ ★ BORGATA CASINO HOTEL & SPA. *One Borgata Way, Atlantic City (08401). Phone 609/317-1000; toll-free 888/950-4575. www.atlantic-city-casinos.net.* 2,002 rooms, all suites. Check-in 3 pm, check-out noon. Five restaurants, five bars. Casino. **$$$**

★ ★ ★ CAESARS ATLANTIC CITY HOTEL CASINO. *2100 Pacific and Arkansas aves, Atlantic City (08401). Phone 609/348-4411; toll-free 800/524-2867; fax 609/441-2261. www.caesars.com.* Touted as "Rome on the Jersey shore" this opulent oceanfront hotel and 120,231-square-foot casino houses 26,000 square feet of meeting space. There are Chinese, Japanese, and American restaurants, Roman-themed eateries, as well as many other casual restaurants and lounges. 1,144 rooms, 20 story. Check-in 4 pm, check-out noon. Nine restaurants, five bars. Fitness room, spa. Beach. Outdoor pool, whirlpool. Tennis. Airport transportation available. Casino. **$$**

★ ★ ★ HILTON CASINO RESORT. *Boston and the Boardwalk, Atlantic City (08401). Phone 609/347-7111; toll-free 877/432-7139; fax 609/340-4858. www.hiltonac.com.* 804 rooms, 22 story. Check-in 4 pm, check-out noon. Eight restaurants, bar. Fitness room, spa. Indoor pool, whirlpool. On beach. Casino. **$$**

★ ★ ★ RESORTS ATLANTIC CITY. *1133 Boardwalk, Absecon (08401). Phone 609/344-6000; toll-free 800/336-6378; fax 609/340-7684. www.resortsac.com.* The rooms in this oceanfront casino property have a summery décor with bright plaid comforters and white wood furniture. Fine dining options are numerous highlighting Asian, Italian, and French cuisines, and the Le Palais' Sunday champagne brunch is worth a visit. First casino in Atlantic City. 412 rooms, 15 story. Check-in 3 pm, check-out noon. Six restaurants, bar. Fitness room. Indoor pool, outdoor pool, whirlpool. Airport transportation available. Casino. **$$**

★ ★ ★ SHERATON ATLANTIC CITY CONVENTION CENTER HOTEL. *2 Miss America Way, Atlantic City (08401). Phone 609/344-3535; fax 609/441-2999. www.sheraton.com.* 502 rooms, 12 story. Check-out noon. Restaurant, bar. Fitness room. Indoor pool, whirlpool. Business center. Casino. **$$**

★ ★ ★ TRUMP PLAZA HOTEL & CASINO. *The Boardwalk and Mississippi Ave, Atlantic City (08401). Phone 609/441-6000; toll-free 800/677-7378; fax 609/441-7881. www.trumpplaza.com.* 904 rooms, 38 story. Check-out noon. Eight restaurants, three bars. Fitness room. Indoor pool, whirlpool. Tennis. Casino. **$$**

★ ★ ★ TRUMP TAJ MAHAL CASINO RESORT. *1000 Boardwalk, Atlantic City (08401). Phone 609/449-1000; toll-free 800/825-8888; fax 609/449-6818. www.trumptaj.com.* 1,250 rooms, 52 story. Check-in 4 pm, check-out 11 am. Nine restaurants, bar. Fitness room, spa. Indoor pool. Business center. Casino. **$$**

Full-Service Resort

★ ★ ★ MARRIOTT SEAVIEW RESORT AND SPA. *401 S New York Rd, Absecon (08201). Phone 609/652-1800; toll-free 800/932-8000; fax 609/652-2307. www.marriott.com.* A golfer's dream, this hotel is located on 650 acres near Reeds Bay and offers two 18-hole championship golf courses. 297 rooms, 3 story. Check-in 4 pm, check-out 12:30 pm. High-speed Internet access. Restaurant, bar. Fitness room. Indoor pool, outdoor pool, whirlpool. Golf. Tennis. Business center. **$$**

Restaurants

★★★ **BRIGHTON STEAKHOUSE.** *Indiana Ave at Brighton Park, Atlantic City (08401). Phone 609/441-4300. www.acsands.com.* In addition to thick cuts of steak, veal, and lamb as well as the usual seafood, this surf 'n turf spot in the Sands casino also serves up live piano music. Steak menu. Dinner. Closed Tues, Wed. Bar. Casual attire. Reservations recommended. **$$$**

★★ **CHEF VOLA'S.** *111 S Albion Pl, Atlantic City (08401). Phone 609/345-2022; fax 609/266-2649.* Italian, American menu. Dinner. Closed Mon; Thanksgiving, Dec 24-25. Casual attire. Reservations recommended. Photographs of celebrities. **$$$**

★★ **DOCK'S OYSTER HOUSE.** *2405 Atlantic Ave, Atlantic City (08401). Phone 609/345-0092; fax 609/345-7893. www.docksoysterhouse.com.* Seafood, steak menu. Dinner. Bar. Children's menu. Casual attire. **$$$**

★ **IRISH PUB AND INN.** *St. James Pl and Boardwalk, Atlantic City (08401). Phone 609/344-9063; fax 606/344-7225. www.theirishpub.com.* American, Irish menu. Breakfast, lunch, dinner, late-night. Bar. Casual attire. Outdoor seating. **$**

★★ **OLD WATERWAY INN.** *1660 W Riverside Dr, Atlantic City (08401). Phone 609/347-1793; fax 609/347-0075. www.oldwaterwayinn.com.* American menu. Dinner. Closed Mon; also three weeks in Jan. Bar. Children's menu. Casual attire. Outdoor seating. **$$**

★★ **RAM'S HEAD INN.** *9 W White Horse Pike, Galloway City (08205). Phone 609/652-1700; fax 609/652-1572.* This continental restaurant is also a busy banquet facility that can accommodate up to 350 people. Dine in a glass-enclosed veranda, ballroom, or brick courtyard. American menu. Lunch, dinner. Closed Mon; Labor Day, Dec 24. Bar. Children's menu. Jacket required. Valet parking. Outdoor seating. **$$**

★★★ **RENAULT WINERY.** *72 N Bremen Ave, Egg Harbor City (08215). Phone 609/965-2111; fax 609/965-1847. www.renaultwinery.com.* This gourmet restaurant offers three different dining experiences: guests may enjoy a six-course dinner with two wine samplings (reservations are required), relax at the garden cafe for an afternoon meal, or try the Sunday country brunch. Dinner, Sun brunch. Closed Mon-Thurs; Dec 25. Reservations recommended. **$$$**

★ **SCANNICCHIO'S.** *119 S California Ave, Atlantic City (08401). Phone 609/348-6378; fax 609/345-5711.* Italian menu. Dinner. Closed holidays. Bar. Children's menu. Casual attire. **$$**

★★ **STEVE AND COOKIE'S BY THE BAY.** *9700 Amherst Ave, Margate (08402). Phone 609/823-1163; fax 609/823-9571. www.steveandcookies.com.* American menu. Dinner, brunch. Closed Dec 24-25. Bar. Children's menu. Casual attire. **$$**

Avalon (F-3)

Restaurant

★★ **MIRAGE.** *7888 Dune Dr, Avalon (08202). Phone 609/368-1919; fax 609/368-1849.* American menu. Breakfast, dinner. Closed Nov-Mar. Bar. Children's menu. **$$**

Batsto (E-3)

See also Atlantic City

Area Code 609
Zip 08037

The Batsto Iron Works, established in 1766, made munitions for the Revolutionary Army from the bog iron ore found nearby. Its furnaces shut down for the last time in 1848. Eighteen years later, Joseph Wharton, whose immense estate totaled nearly 100,000 acres, bought the land. In 1954, the state of New Jersey bought nearly 150 square miles of land in this area, including the entire Wharton tract, for a state forest.

What to See and Do

Batsto State Historic Site. *4110 Nesco Rd (main office), Hammonton (08037). Phone 609/561-3262.* Restored early 19th-century iron and glassmaking community. General store, gristmill, blacksmith shop, wheelwright shop, sawmill, workers' houses, and visitor center are open seasonally to the public. Parking fee (Memorial Day-Labor Day, weekends and holidays). **$$$**

Wharton State Forest. *4110 Nesco Rd, Hammonton (08037). Along Hwy 206 near Atsion. Crossed by Hwys 542, 563. Phone 609/561-0024. www.state.nj.us/dep/parksandforests/parks/wharton.html.* Streams wind through 110,000 acres of wilderness. Swimming, fishing, canoeing; limited picnicking, tent and trailer sites, cabins. Also here is

Atsion Recreation Area. *744 Hwy 206, Batsto (08037). Phone 609/268-0444.* Swimming, canoeing; picnicking, camping.

Bernardsville (B-3)

See also Basking Ridge, Morristown

Population 7,345
Elevation 400 ft
Area Code 908
Zip 07924

What to See and Do

Great Swamp National Wildlife Refuge. *152 Pleasant Plains Rd, Basking Ridge (07920). 1 mile N on Hwy 202, W on N Maple Ave, 2 miles E on Madisonville Rd, 1 1/2 miles NE on Lee's Hill Rd, then right on Long Hill Rd. Phone 973/425-1222. northeast.fws.gov/nj/grs.htm.* Nature trails, boardwalk. Observation blind; wilderness area. More than 200 species of birds, fish, reptiles, frogs, ducks, geese, and fox may be seen in this 7,300-acre refuge. Headquarters (Mon-Fri 8 am-4:30 pm; closed holidays). Trails and information booth (daily, dawn-dusk). **FREE**

Full-Service Hotel

★★★ SOMERSET HILLS HOTEL. *200 Liberty Corner Rd, Warren (07059). Phone 908/647-6700; toll-free 800/688-0700; fax 908/647-8053. www.shh.com.* Visitors will find that this hotel, located in the Watchung Mountains, combines the service of a country inn with the facilities, entertainment, and accommodations expected from a full-service hotel. 111 rooms, 4 story. Pets accepted, some restrictions; fee. Check-in 3 pm, check-out noon. High-speed Internet access. Two restaurants, bar. Fitness room. Outdoor pool. Business center. **$$**

Full-Service Inn

★★★ BERNARDS INN. *27 Mine Brook Rd, Bernardsville (07924). Phone 908/766-0002; toll-free 888/766-0002; fax 908/766-4604. www.bernardsinn.com.* This historic property, located in quaint Bernardsville, is a favored retreat for locals looking for a night out. Guest rooms are individually decorated with antiques and reproductions, and are quite roomy. The restaurant serves sophisticated American food in an upscale, clubby setting. 20 rooms, 5 story. Complimentary continental breakfast. Check-in 4 pm, check-out 11 am. Restaurant, bar. **$$**

Restaurant

★★★ THE BERNARDS INN. *27 Mine Brook Rd, Bernardsville (07924). Phone 908/766-0002; fax 908/766-4604. www.bernardsinn.com.* This traditional dining room features chef Edward Stone's creative contemporary American menu in a rustic, intimate setting that's just a short drive from New York City. Few others can match the graceful, elegant service (or the 8,000-bottle wine cellar). Lunch, dinner. Closed Sun; holidays. Bar. Jacket required (Sat). Reservations recommended. Outdoor seating. **$$$**

Bordentown (C-3)

See also Trenton

Settled 1682
Population 3,969
Elevation 72 ft
Area Code 609
Zip 8505
Information Historical Society Visitors Center, Old City Hall, 13 Crosswicks St, PO Box 182; phone 609/298-1740

A long and honorable history has left an indelible stamp on this town. Bordentown was once a busy shipping center and a key stop on the Delaware and Raritan Canal. In January 1778, Bordentown citizens filled numerous kegs with gunpowder and sent them down the Delaware River to Philadelphia hoping to blow up the British fleet stationed there. But the plan was discovered, and British troops intercepted the kegs and discharged them. In 1816, Joseph Bonaparte, exiled king of Spain and brother of Napoleon, bought 1,500 acres and settled here.

What to See and Do

Clara Barton Schoolhouse. *142 Crosswicks St, Bordentown (08505). Phone 609/298-0676.* This building was in use as a school in Revolutionary days. In 1851, Clara Barton, founder of the American Red Cross, established one of the first free public schools in the country in this building. (By appointment) **FREE**

Limited-Service Hotel

★ DAYS INN. *1073 Hwy 206, Bordentown (08505). Phone 609/298-6100; fax 609/298-7509. www.daysinn .com.* 131 rooms, 2 story. Check-in 2 pm, check-out 11 am. Bar. Outdoor pool. **$**

Branchville (A-3)

See also Vernon

Population 845
Elevation 529 ft
Area Code 201
Zip 07826
Information Sussex County Chamber of Commerce, 120 Hampton House Rd, Newton 07860; phone 201/579-1811
Web site www.sussexcountychamber.org

This town in Sussex County is near many attractions in New Jersey's scenic northwest corner.

What to See and Do

Peters Valley. *19 Kuhn Rd, Layton (07851). 8 miles NW via Hwy 206, County 560, then S on County 615. Phone 973/948-5200. www.pvcrafts.org.* Historic buildings in the Delaware Water Gap National Recreation Area (see DELAWARE WATER GAP, PA) serve as residences and studios for professional craftspeople and summer crafts workshops in blacksmithing, ceramics, fine metals, photography, fibers, and woodworking. Studios. Contemporary craft store and gallery (Fri-Wed 11 am-5 pm). **FREE**

Space Farms Zoo & Museum. *Rte 519, Sussex (07461). 6 miles N on County 519. Phone 973/875-5800. www. spacefarms.com.* Collection of more than 500 wild animals; early American museum in main building, additional museums on grounds; picnic area, concession; gift shop. Zoo and museum (May-Oct: daily 9 am-5 pm). **$$$**

Stokes State Forest. *Hwy 206, Branchville (07826). 4 miles N on Hwy 206. Phone 973/948-3820. www.state .nj.us/dep/parksandforests/parks/stokes.html.* Located on the Kittatinny Ridge, this 15,482-acre forest includes some of the finest mountain country in New Jersey. Swimming, fishing; hunting, picnicking, camping. Scenic views from Sunrise Mountain; Tillman Ravine, a natural gorge, is in the southern corner of the park.

Swartswood State Park. *1091 County Rd 619, Swartswood (07877). 2 miles S on County 519, then continue 2 miles on County 627, left 3 miles on County 521 to Swartswood, left 1 mile on County 622, right on County 619, 1/2 mile to park entrance. Phone 973/ 383-5230. www.state.nj.us/dep/parksandforests/parks/ swartswood.html.* A 1,470-acre park on Swartswood Lake. Swimming (Memorial Day-Labor Day), bathhouse, fishing, boating (rentals, Memorial Day-Labor Day); hunting, picnicking, concession, camping.

Special Event

Peters Valley Craft Fair. *Sussex County Fairgrounds, 37 Plains Rd, Augusta (07822). 10 miles from Peters Valley campus. Phone 973/948-5200. www.pvcrafts.org.* More than 150 juried exhibitors; demonstrations, music, food. Last weekend in Sept. **$$**

Bridgeton (E-2)

See also Millville

Settled 1686
Population 22,771
Elevation 40 ft
Area Code 856
Zip 08302
Information Bridgeton-Cumberland Tourist Association, 50 E Broad St; phone 856/451-4802 or toll-free 800/319-3379

The city of Bridgeton has been recognized as New Jersey's largest historic district, with more than 2,200 registered historical landmarks. There are many styles of architecture here, some of which date back nearly 300 years.

What to See and Do

City Park. *Mayor Aitken Dr, Bridgeton (08302). Off Hwy 49. Phone 856/455-3230.* A 1,100-acre wooded area with swimming (protected beaches, Memorial Day-Labor Day), fishing, boating (floating dock), canoeing. Picnic grounds, recreation center; zoo. (Daily) Also here is

New Sweden Farmstead Museum. Reconstruction of first permanent European settlement in Delaware Valley. Seven log buildings including smokehouse/sauna; horse barn, cow and goat barn, threshing barn; storage house; blacksmith shop; family residence with period furnishings. Costumed guides. (May-Labor Day: Sat 11 am-5 pm, Sun noon-5 pm; rest of year: by appointment) **$**

George J. Woodruff Museum of Indian Artifacts. *Bridgeton Public Library, 150 E Commerce St, Bridgeton (08302). Phone 856/451-2620.* Approximately 20,000 local Native American artifacts, some up to 10,000 years old; clay pots, pipes, implements. (Sept-May: Mon-Sat 1-4 pm; June-Aug: Sat 10 am-1 pm; rest of year: by appointment; closed holidays) **DONATION**

Gibbon House. *960 Ye Greate St, Greenwich (08323). 7 miles SW. Phone 856/455-4055.* (1730) Site of New Jersey's only 18th-century tea burning party; genealogical research library. Events scheduled throughout year. Gibbon House (early Apr-late Nov, Tues-Sat; closed Sun in July-Aug); tours (weekdays). **DONATION**

Old Broad Street Church. *W Broad St and West Ave, Bridgeton (08302).* (1792) Outstanding example of Georgian architecture, with Palladian window, high-backed wooden pews, wine glass pulpit, brick-paved aisles, and brass lamps that once held whale oil.

Parvin State Park. *701 Almond Rd, Pittsgrove (08318). From Rte 55 north or south, take exit 35 and follow signs to the park. The Park is located between Centerton and Vineland on Rte 540. Phone 856/358-8616. www.state.nj.us/dep/parksandforests/parks/parvin.html.* This 1,125-acre park offers swimming, bathhouse, fishing, boating, canoeing (rentals); picnicking, concessions, playgrounds, camping (dump station), cabins.

Special Event

Concerts. *Riverfront. Phone 856/451-9208.* Performances by ragtime, military, country and western bands, and others. Sun nights. Nine weeks in July-Aug.

Bridgewater (B-3)

(See Somerville)

Burlington (D-2)

See also Bordentown, Mount Holly; also see Philadelphia, PA

Settled 1677
Population 9,736
Elevation 13 ft
Area Code 609, 856
Zip 08016
Information Burlington County Chamber of Commerce, 900 Briggs Rd, Mount Laurel, 08054; phone 856/439-2520

In 1774, Burlington, along with New York, Philadelphia, and Boston, was a thriving port. A Quaker settlement, it was one of the first to provide public education. A 1682 Act of Assembly gave Matinicunk (now Burlington) Island in the Delaware River to the town with the stipulation that the revenue it generated would be used for public schools; that act is still upheld. Burlington was the capital of West Jersey; the legislature met here, and in the East Jersey capital of Perth Amboy, from 1681 until after the Revolution. In 1776, the Provincial Congress adopted the state constitution here.

What to See and Do

Burlington County Historical Society. *451 High St, Burlington (08016). Phone 609/386-4773.* The society maintains **D. B. Pugh Library**, in the Corson-Poley Center, genealogical and historical holdings;

Revolutionary War exhibit; **James Fenimore Cooper House** (circa 1780), birthplace of the famous author; **Bard-How House** (circa 1740) with period furnishings; **Captain James Lawrence House**, birthplace of the commander of the Chesapeake during the War of 1812 and speaker of the immortal words "Don't give up the ship," contains 1812 objects and costume display. Tour of historic houses (Tues-Sat 1-5 pm; tours leave every 50 minutes). **$**

Friends Meeting House. *340 High St, Burlington (08016). Phone 609/387-3875.* (1784) The house is now a regional conference center for Southeastern Pennsylvania/New Jersey Quakers. It is operated by the Philadelphia Yearly Meeting. (By appointment) **$$**

Historic tours. *Foot of High St. Phone 609/386-3993.* Guided walking tours of 33 historic sites (1685-1829), eight of which are open to the public. (Daily; no tours Easter, Dec 25) **$$**

Old St. Mary's Church. *145 W Broad St, Burlington (08016). W Broad and Wood sts. Phone 609/386-0902.* (1703) The oldest Episcopal Church building in the state. (By appointment)

Thomas Revell House. *213 Wood St, Burlington (08016). Phone 609/386-3993.* (1685) The oldest building in Burlington County. Included in Burlington County Historical Society home tour (see). (By appointment and during Wood Street Fair; see SPECIAL EVENT) **FREE**

Special Event

Wood Street Fair. Re-creation of colonial fair; crafts, antique exhibits; food; entertainment. First Sat after Labor Day.

Restaurant

★★★ CAFE GALLERY. *219 High St, Burlington (08016). Phone 609/386-6150. www.cafegalleryburlington.com.* French menu. Lunch, dinner, Sun brunch. Closed holidays. Bar. Children's menu. Outdoor seating. **$$**

Caldwell

See also Newark, Newark International Airport Area

Population 7,584
Elevation 411 ft
Area Code 973
Zip 07006

What to See and Do

Grover Cleveland Birthplace State Historic Site. *207 Bloomfield Ave, Caldwell (07006). Phone 973/226-0001. westessexguide.com/gcb.* Built in 1832, this building served as the parsonage of the First Presbyterian Church. It is the birthplace of President Grover Cleveland, the only president born in New Jersey. He lived here from 1837 to 1841. The house is listed on the New Jersey and National Registers of Historic Places. Self-guided and guided tours are available, and reservations are recommended. (Wed-Sun afternoons, call for hours; closed holidays) **FREE**

Camden (D-2)

See also Cherry Hill; also see Philadelphia, PA

Settled 1681
Population 79,904
Elevation 23 ft
Area Code 856

Camden's growth as the leading industrial, marketing, and transportation center of southern New Jersey dates from post-Civil War days. Its location across the Delaware River from Philadelphia prompted large companies such as Campbell Soup (national headquarters) to establish plants here. Walt Whitman spent the last 20 years of his life in Camden.

What to See and Do

Battleship *New Jersey*. *Camden Waterfront, Docked on the Camden waterfront, across the Delaware River from Penn's Landing, Philadelphia, and adjacent to the Tweeter Entertainment Center, S of the NJ State Aquarium. Phone 856/966-1652 (office); toll-free 866/877-6262. www.battleshipnewjersey.org.* The United States Navy permanently berthed the USS *New Jersey* (or "Big J"), one of the nation's largest and most decorated battleships, at the Camden Waterfront in 2000 and has transformed it into a floating museum. First launched in 1942, the ship was commissioned for operations during World War II at Iwo Jima and Okinawa. The ship conducted its last mission, to provide fire support to Marines in embattled Beirut, Lebanon, in 1983. Military history buffs will be awed by the guided two-hour tour through this 887-foot, 11-story, 212,000-horsepower, Iowa-class ship. "Big J" is available for special events, retreats, and overnight encampments. (Apr-Sept: daily 9 am-5 pm; Oct-Mar: daily 9 am-3 pm) **$$$**

Camden County Historical Society-Pomona Hall. *1900 Park Blvd, Camden (08103). Phone 856/964-3333. www.cchsnj.com.* (1726/1788) Brick Georgian house that belonged to descendants of William Cooper, an early Camden settler; period furnishings. Museum exhibits focus on regional history and include antique glass, lamps, toys, and early hand tools; fire-fighting equipment; Victor Talking Machines. Library (fee) has more than 20,000 books, as well as maps (17th century-present), newspapers (18th-20th century), oral history tapes, photographs, and genealogical material. (Tues-Thurs, Sun; closed holidays, also Aug) **$**

New Jersey State Aquarium. *1 Riverside Dr, Camden (08103). I-676 exit Mickle Blvd. Phone 856/365-3300. www.njaquarium.org.* This home to more than 4,000 fish of some 500 species is just minutes across the Ben Franklin Bridge in Camden, New Jersey, on the Delaware River waterfront. (You can also get there via the Delaware River Aerial Tram, coming soon.) At the aquarium, curious kids can find out how fish sleep and which fish can change from male to female and back again. You will also find exhibits of seals, penguins, sharks, turtles, and tropical fish, as well as elaborate rain forest, water filtration, and conservation awareness displays. (Mid-Sept-mid-Apr: Mon-Fri 9:30 am-4:30 pm, Sat-Sun 10 am-5 pm; mid-Apr-mid-Sept: daily 9:30 am-5:30 pm; closed Jan 1, Thanksgiving, Dec 25) **$$$**

Tomb of Walt Whitman. *Harleigh Cemetery, 1640 Haddon Ave, Camden (08103). Phone 856/963-0122.* The vault of the "good gray poet," designed by the poet himself, is of rough-cut stone with a grillwork door.

Walt Whitman Arts Center. *2nd and Cooper sts, Camden (08102). Phone 856/964-8300. www.waltwhitmancenter.org.* Poetry readings, concerts, and gallery exhibits (Oct-May). Children's theater (late June-Aug, Fri). Art gallery; statuary. Center (Mon-Fri).

★ **Walt Whitman House State Historic Site.** *328 Mickle Blvd, Camden (08103). Phone 856/964-5383. www.ci.camden.nj.us/htdocs/walt.html.* The last residence of the poet and the only house he ever owned; he lived here from 1884 until his death on March 26, 1892. Contains original furnishings, books, and mementos. (Wed-Sat, also Sun afternoons) **FREE**

Restaurant

★ **BROOKLAWN DINER.** *Hwy 130, Gloucester City (08030). Phone 856/742-0035; fax 856/742-0130.* Greek, American menu. Breakfast, lunch, dinner. Closed Dec 25. Bar. Children's menu. **$$**

Cape May (F-2)

See also Wildwood and Wildwood Crest

Settled 1631
Population 4,034
Elevation 14 ft
Area Code 609
Zip 08204
Information Chamber of Commerce, PO Box 556; phone 609/884-5508. Welcome Center, 405 Lafayette St; phone 609/884-9562
Web site www.capemaychamber.com

Cape May, the nation's oldest seashore resort, is located on the southernmost tip of the state surrounded by the Atlantic Ocean and Delaware Bay. Popular with Philadelphia and New York society since 1766, Cape May has been host to Presidents Lincoln, Grant, Pierce, Buchanan, and Harrison, as well as notables such as John Wanamaker and Horace Greeley. The entire town has been proclaimed a National Historic Landmark because it has more than 600 Victorian homes and buildings, many of which have been restored. The downtown Washington Street Victorian Mall features three blocks of shops and restaurants. Four miles of beaches and a 1 1/4-mile paved promenade offer vacationers varied entertainment. "Cape May diamonds," often found on the shores of Delaware Bay by visitors, are actually pure quartz, rounded by the waves.

Cape May: An Architectural Bounty

The Center for the Arts, located at the historic Emlen Physic Estate at 1048 Washington Street (phone 609/884-5404), is a good place to begin a walking tour that explores some of the more than 600 Victorian-era buildings in Cape May. Enjoy the 45-minute house tour, which imparts an excellent, concise history of Cape May. Leaving the estate, turn left, go right onto Madison, and, having arrived at the corner of Virginia Street, turn left and walk amid the grid created by Madison, Philadelphia, and Reading streets as they intersect Virginia, Ohio, Cape May Idaho, Maryland, New York, and New Jersey streets. The entire neighborhood is rich in antique homes.

Having completed as much neighborhood viewing as you want, return to Madison. Turn left onto Sewell, then right onto Franklin. At the corner of Columbia Avenue, note the Clivedon Inn (709 Columbia) on the right. Turn left on Columbia. Here stand the Henry Sawyer Inn (722 Columbia) with its magnificent garden; the Dormer House (800 Columbia), a Colonial Revivalist home; The Inn at Journey's End (710 Columbia); and the Mainstay Inn (635 Columbia), once a gentlemen's gambling house.

Walk toward the ocean on Howard Street. At Beach Drive stands the Hotel Macomber (727 Beach Dr), built in the Shingle style. Turn right, walk three blocks to Ocean Street, turn right, and look for the Queen Anne-style Columbia House (26 Ocean St) and Twin Gables (731 Ocean St), with its pair of Gothic gables. Go left on Hughes to Decatur, turn right, and in three short blocks enter the downtown shopping district. Here, along the Washington Street Mall, Lyle Lane, Jackson Street, and Perry Street are dozens of shops, restaurants, and inns. Stop at the corner of the Washington Street Mall and Perry to look at Congress Hall, a gargantuan hotel. At 9 Perry, near Beach Drive, stands the King's Cottage, built in the Mansard style with Stick-style detailing. Another excellent Queen Anne-style building, The Inn at 22 Jackson, is found on Jackson Street parallel to Perry. Nearby, the Virginia Hotel (25 Jackson) serves elegant meals in its upscale dining room. You could also take a meal at the Mad Batter (19 Jackson), a Victorian bed-and-breakfast inn, where breakfast on the veranda is a long-standing Cape May tradition.

For a classic Jersey shore finish, return to the beach (at Jackson and Beach Dr) and stroll along the water's edge, or shop and snack along the Promenade. On a summer's eve, another option is to take in a play performed by the professional Cape May Stage. To reach them, stroll back up Jackson (away from the ocean), past the Washington Street Mall to Lafayette Street. Turn right-the theater is in the Visitor Center.

What to See and Do

Cape May-Lewes (DE) Ferry. *Sandman Blvd and Lincoln Dr, North Cape May (08204). Phone 609/889-7200; toll-free 800/643-3779. www.capemaylewesferry.com.* Sole connection between southern terminus of Garden State Pkwy and Hwy 13 (Ocean Hwy) on the Delmarva Peninsula. 17-mile, 80-minute trip across Delaware Bay. (Daily) **$$$$**

Emlen Physick Estate. *1048 Washington St, Cape May (08204). Phone 609/884-5404.* (1879) Authentically restored 18-room Victorian mansion designed by Frank Furness. Mansion is also headquarters for the Mid-Atlantic Center for the Arts. (Daily) **$$**

Historic Cold Spring Village. *720 Rte 9, Cape May (08204). 3 miles N via Rte 109. Phone 609/898-2300. www.hcsv.org.* Restored early 1800s South Jersey farm village; 25 restored historic buildings on 22 acres. Craft shops; spinning, blacksmithing, weaving, pottery, broom making, ship modeling demonstrations; folk art; bakery and food shops; restaurant. (Late May-mid-June: Sat-Sun 10 am-4:30 pm; mid-June-early Sept: Tues-Sun 10 am-4:30 pm; early Sept-mid-Sept: Sat-Sun 10 am-4:30 pm) **$$**

Swimming, fishing, boating. Beaches with lifeguards (fee). Fishing is very good at the confluence of the Atlantic and Delaware Bay. A large harbor holds boats of all sizes; excellent for sailboating and other small-boat activity.

Tours. *1048 Washington St, Cape May (08204). Phone 609/884-5404. www.capemayac.org.* The Mid-Atlantic Center for the Arts offers the following tours. Contact PO Box 340; Cape May, 08204.

Cape May INNteriors Tour & Tea. *202 Ocean St, Cape May (08204).* Features a different group of houses each week, visiting five or more bed-and-breakfast inns and guesthouses. Innkeepers greet guests and describe experiences. (Summer: Mon; rest of year: Sat; no tours Dec-Jan) **$$$$**

Combination Tours. *Begin at Emlen Physick Estate.* Approximately two hours; includes trolley tour and guided tour of Physick Estate. (June-Oct: daily; rest of year: Sat and Sun) **$$$**

Mansions by Gaslight. Three-hour tour begins at Emlen Physick Estate. Visits four Victorian landmarks: Emlen Physick House (see), the Abbey (1869), Mainstay Inn (1872), and Humphrey Hughes House (1903); shuttle bus between houses. (Mid-June-Sept: Wed evenings; rest of year: holiday and special tours) **$$$$**

Ocean Walk Tours. *Promenade and Beach drs, Cape May.* A 1 1/2-hour guided tour of Cape May's beaches. Guide discusses marine life and history of the beaches, including legends of buried treasure. (May-Sept: Tues-Sat) **$$**

Trolleys. Half-hour tours on enclosed trolley bus or open-air carriage; three routes beginning at Ocean St opposite the Washington St Mall. (June-Oct, daily; reduced schedule rest of year; no tours Thanksgiving) **$$**

Walking Tours of the Historic District. Begin at Information Booth on Washington St Mall at Ocean St. Three 90-minute guided tours give historical insight into the customs and traditions of the Victorians and their ornate architecture. (June-Sept, daily; reduced schedule rest of year) **$$**

Special Events

Promenade Art Show. *Cape May.* Early July.

Tulip Festival. *513 Washington, Cape May (08204). Phone 609/884-5508.* Celebrate Dutch heritage with ethnic foods and dancing, craft show, street fair, garden and house tours. Apr.

Victorian Week. Tours, antiques, crafts, period fashion shows. Mid-Oct.

Limited-Service Hotels

★ AVONDALE BY THE SEA. *Beach and Gurney aves, Cape May (08204). Phone 609/884-2332; toll-free 800/676-7030; fax 609/884-2073. www.avondalebythesea.com.* 46 rooms, 3 story. Complimentary continental breakfast. Check-out 11 am. Outdoor pool. **$$**

★ ★ MONTREAL INN. *1019 Beach Dr, Cape May (08204). Phone 609/884-7011; toll-free 800/525-7011; fax 609/884-4559. www.montreal-inn.com.* 70 rooms, 4 story. Closed Jan-Feb. Check-out 11 am. Restaurant, bar. Fitness room. Outdoor pool, children's pool, whirlpool. Airport transportation available. **$**

★ QUEEN'S HOTEL. *601 Columbia Ave, Cape May (08204). Phone 609/884-1613. www.queenshotel.com.* 11 rooms, 3 story. Check-in 3 pm, check-out 11 am. **$**

Full-Service Hotel

★ ★ ★ VIRGINIA HOTEL. *25 Jackson St, Cape May (08204). Phone 609/884-5700; toll-free 800/732-4236; fax 609/884-1236. www.virginiahotel.com.* This hotel, built in 1879, has been recently remodeled. No detail was overlooked in creating a warm and welcoming environment for guests to relax in and enjoy. 24 rooms, 3 story. Complimentary continental breakfast. Check-in 3 pm, check-out noon. Restaurant, bar. **$**

Full-Service Inn

★ ★ ★ CARROLL VILLA HOTEL. *19 Jackson St, Cape May (08204). Phone 609/884-9619; fax 609/884-0264. www.madbatter.com.* 22 rooms, 3 story. Complimentary full breakfast. Check-in 2 pm, check-out 11 am. Restaurant. **$**

Specialty Lodgings

The following lodging establishments are approved by Mobil Travel Guide, but due to their unique and individualized nature have not been given a traditional Mobil Star rating. Included in this listing you may find bed-and-breakfasts, limited-service inns, guest ranches, and other unique hotel properties.

ANGEL OF THE SEA. *5 Trenton Ave, Cape May (08204). Phone 609/884-3369; toll-free 800/848-3369; fax 609/884-3331. www.angelofthesea.com.* Guests will be pleased with their stay at this quiet Victorian inn. Room sizes range from standard up to the Angel Suite. All rooms are decorated with antiques, have a private bath, and color TVs. The inn is across the street from a great beach. 27 rooms, 3 story. Children over 8 years only. Complimentary full breakfast. Check-in 2 pm, check-out 11 am. **$$**

COLVMNS BY THE SEA BED & BREAKFAST. *1513 Beach Dr, Cape May (08204). Phone 609/884-2228; fax 609/884-4789. www.colvmnscapemay.com.* 11 rooms, 3 story. Children over 7 years only. Complimentary full breakfast. Check-in 2 pm, check-out 11:30 am. Beach. **$$**

MAINSTAY INN. *635 Columbia Ave, Cape May (08204). Phone 609/884-8690. www.mainstayinn.com.* Guests will enjoy their stay in this elegant inn, decorated in Victorian style and located by the sea. Each morning a continental breakfast will be served to guests to enjoy by the fireplace or on the private porch. 9 rooms, 3 story. Complimentary full breakfast. Check-in 2 pm, check-out 11 am. **$**

THE QUEEN VICTORIA B & B INN. *102 Ocean St, Cape May (08204). Phone 609/884-8702. www.queenvictoria.com.* The property is located near the ocean and blocks from shops and fine dining. Walk through the historic town or take one of the available bicycles from the inn. 17 rooms, 3 story. Complimentary full breakfast. Check-in 3 pm, check-out 11 am. **$$**

THE SOUTHERN MANSION. *720 Washington St, Cape May (08204). Phone 609/884-7171; toll-free 800/381-3888; fax 609/898-0492. www.thesouthern-mansion.com.* Originally built as a country estate in 1863 by Philadelphia industrialist George Allen, the Victorian décor of this painstakingly restored home has graced the covers of several magazines. This is true transplanted southern hospitality. 24 rooms, 3 story. Children over 8 years only. Complimentary full breakfast. Check-in 3 pm, check-out 11 am. **$$**

VICTORIAN LACE INN. *901 Stockton Ave, Cape May (08204). Phone 609/884-1772; fax 609/884-0983. www.victorianlaceinn.com.* 5 rooms, 3 story. Closed early Jan-mid-Feb. Complimentary full breakfast. Check-in 2 pm, check-out 10 am. Built in 1869. **$$**

Restaurants

★★ 410 BANK STREET. *410 Bank St, Cape May (08204). Phone 609/884-2127; fax 609/884-7796. www.410bankstreet.com.* Louisiana French menu. Dinner. Closed Nov-Apr. Children's menu. Outdoor seating. Restored 1840 Cape May residence. **$$$**

★★ ALEATHEA'S. *7 Ocean Dr, Cape May (08204). Phone 609/884-5555. www.aleatheas.com.* Breakfast, dinner. Closed holidays; also Sept-mid-May. Bar. Children's menu. Property built in 1894; view of ocean. **$$$**

★★ ALEXANDER'S INN. *653 Washington St, Cape May (08204). Phone 609/884-2555; fax 609/884-8883. www.alexandersinn.com.* French menu. Dinner, Sun brunch. Closed Mon, Tues; Jan 1, Thanksgiving, Dec 25. Victorian décor; antiques. **$$$**

★★★ EBBITT ROOM. *25 Jackson St, Cape May (08204). Phone 609/884-5700; fax 609/884-1236. www.virginiahotel.com.* This intimate dining room inside Cape May's Virginia Hotel, named after the inn's original founders, has been offering a seasonally changing menu for over ten years. American cuisine with Asian influences. Dinner. Bar. Valet Parking. Intimate Victorian dining room. **$$**

★★ MAD BATTER. *19 Jackson St, Cape May (08204). Phone 609/884-9619. www.madbatter.com.* American menu. Dinner. Closed Sun; holidays; Jan. Children's menu. Outdoor seating. Victorian inn (1882). **$$**

★★ MERION INN. *106 Decatur St, Cape May (08204). Phone 609/884-8363. www.merioninn.com.* Seafood, steak menu. Lunch, dinner. Closed Jan-Mar; also Mon-Thurs Apr-May and mid-Oct-Dec. Bar.

Children's menu. Outdoor seating. Turn-of-the-century Victorian décor. Built in 1885. **$$$**

★★ PELICAN CLUB. *501 Beach Ave, Cape May (08204). Phone 609/884-3500; fax 609/884-7036. www.pelicanclubcapemay.com.* Dinner. Closed Dec 24-25. Bar. Children's menu. Valet parking in season. Victorian setting with view of Atlantic Ocean. **$$$**

★ RUSTY NAIL. *205 Beach Dr, Cape May (08204). Phone 609/884-0220. www.coachmansmotorinn.com.* Breakfast, lunch, dinner. Closed Nov-mid-Apr. Bar. Children's menu. **$$**

★★★ WASHINGTON INN. *801 Washington St, Cape May (08204). Phone 609/884-5697; fax 609/884-1620. www.washingtoninn.com.* Insiders know that the intimate cellar is the place for a romantic meal at this historic Victorian inn. American menu. Dinner. Closed Thanksgiving, Dec 24-25. Bar. Children's menu. Reservations recommended. Outdoor seating. Fireside seating. Former plantation house (1848). **$$**

★★ WATER'S EDGE. *Beach and Pittsburgh aves, Cape May (08204). Phone 609/884-1717; fax 609/884-1885. www.watersedgerestaurant.com.* Seafood, steak menu. Dinner. Closed Thanksgiving, Dec 25. Bar. Children's menu. Outdoor seating. **$$$**

Cape May Court House (F-2)

See also Cape May, Stone Harbor, Wildwood and Wildwood Crest

Population 4,704
Elevation 18 ft
Area Code 609
Zip 08210
Information Cape May County Chamber of Commerce, PO Box 74; phone 609/465-7181
Web site www.cmccofc.com

To be accurately named, this county seat would have to be called Cape May Court Houses, for there are two of them—one is a white, 19th-century building now used as a meeting hall.

What to See and Do

Cape May County Historical Museum. *504 N Hwy 9, Cape May Court House (08210). Shore Rd, 1 mile N on Hwy 9. Phone 609/465-3535.* Period dining room (predating 1820), 18th-century kitchen, doctor's room, military room with Merrimac flag, Cape May diamonds. Barn exhibits; whaling implements; Indian artifacts; pioneer tools; lens from Cape May Point Lighthouse. Genealogical library. (Mid-Apr-Nov: Tues-Sat; rest of year: Sat only) **$**

Cape May County Park. *707 N Hwy 9, Cape May Court House (08210). On Hwy 9 at Crest Haven Rd. Phone 609/465-5271.* Zoo has over 100 types of animals. Jogging path, bike trail, tennis courts, picnicking, playground. (Daily) **DONATION**

Leaming's Run Gardens. *Cape May Court House, 1845 N Hwy 9, Swainton (08210). Approximately 4 miles N on Hwy 9, between Pkwy exits 13 and 17. Phone 609/465-5871.* Amid 20 acres of lawns, ponds, and ferneries are 25 gardens, each with a separate theme. Eighteenth-century colonial farm grows tobacco and cotton; farm animals. (Mid-May-mid-Oct, daily) **$$$**

Victorian houses. Over 600 fine examples of 19th-century architecture located in the area. Information can be obtained at the Chamber of Commerce Information Center, Crest Haven Rd and Garden State Pkwy, milepost 11 (Easter-mid-Oct: daily; rest of year: Mon-Fri; closed holidays).

Specialty Lodging

The following lodging establishment is approved by Mobil Travel Guide, but due to its unique and individualized nature has not been given a traditional Mobil Star rating. Included in this listing you may find bed-and-breakfasts, limited-service inns, guest ranches, and other unique hotel properties.

THE DOCTORS INN. *2 N Main St, Cape May Court House (08210). Phone 609/463-9330; fax 609/463-9194. www.doctorsinn.com.* This romantic bed-and-breakfast, housed in a renovated 19th-century home, is a good location for a Jersey shore vacation. Walk the winding brick drive up to the wicker-filled porch before settling into one of the antique-filled rooms. 7 rooms, 3 story. Complimentary full breakfast. Check-in 2 pm, check-out 11 am. **$$**

Chatham (B-3)

Population 10,686
Elevation 244 ft
Area Code 973
Zip 07928
Information Township of Chatham, 58 Meyersville Rd; phone 973/635-4600
Web site www.chathamtownship.org

What to See and Do

Great Swamp National Wildlife Refuge. *152 Pleasant Plains Rd, Basking Ridge (07920). Phone 973/425-1222.* SW of city (see BERNARDSVILLE).

Restaurant

★ ★ ★ **RESTAURANT SERENADE.** *6 Roosevelt Ave, Chatham (07928). Phone 973/701-0303; fax 973/701-0613. www.restaurantserenade.com.* Owned by husband and wife James and Nancy Sheridan Laird, Restaurant Serenade is a product of love on a number of levels. The couple met at the Ryland Inn, where James was a sous chef and Nancy was an intern. They fell in love and decided to merge their collective passion for fine dining and each other, marrying in 1996 and opening Restaurant Serenade six months later. Restaurant Serenade is a sophisticated and intimate gastronomic temple, with soft-toned walls, dark-wood moldings, and gorgeous flower arrangements that add warmth and serenity to the elegant space. The kitchen shows a deep respect for seasonal, local ingredients, serving innovative, contemporary French cuisine cleverly and deftly tinged with Asian flair. While James consistently dazzles the palate, Nancy welcomes guests with grace. Dining in their care is a delight from start to finish. Lunch, dinner. Closed Sun; holidays. Bar. Jacket required. Reservations recommended. **$$$**

Cherry Hill (D-2)

See also Camden, Haddonfield

Population 69,965
Elevation 30 ft
Area Code 856
Information Chamber of Commerce, 1060 Kings Hwy N, Suite 200, 08034; phone 609/667-1600
Web site www.cherryhillnj.com

What to See and Do

Barclay Farmstead. *209 Barclay Ln, Cherry Hill (08034). Phone 856/795-6225.* One of the earliest properties settled in what is now Cherry Hill; origins traced to 1684. The township-owned site consists of 32 acres of open space; restored Federal-style farmhouse; operating forge barn; corn crib; Victorian spring house. Grounds (all year); house tours (Tues-Fri, first Sun each month; and by appointment). **$**

Limited-Service Hotels

★ ★ **CLARION HOTEL.** *1450 Rte 70 E, Cherry Hill (08034). Phone 856/428-2300; fax 856/354-7662. www.choicehotels.com.* 213 rooms, 4 story. Check-in 3 pm, check-out noon. Restaurant, bar. Fitness room. Outdoor pool. Tennis. Airport transportation available. Business center. **$**

★ **HAMPTON INN.** *121 Laurel Oak Rd, Voorhees (08043). Phone 856/346-4500; fax 856/346-2402. www.hamptoninn.com.* 122 rooms, 4 story. Complimentary continental breakfast. Check-in 3 pm, check-out noon. Outdoor pool. **$**

★ ★ **HOLIDAY INN.** *Rte 70 and Sayer Ave, Cherry Hill (08034). Phone 856/663-5300; fax 856/662-2913. www.holiday-inn.com.* 186 rooms, 6 story. Pets accepted, some restrictions. Check-in 3 pm, check-out noon. Restaurant, bar. Fitness room. Indoor pool, outdoor pool, children's pool. Business center. **$**

★ ★ **RADISSON HOTEL MOUNT LAUREL.** *915 Rte 73, Mount Laurel (08054). Phone 856/234-7300; fax 856/802-3912. www.radisson.com.* This hotel offers a continental breakfast, evening cocktails and hors d'oeuvres, movies, and a 24 hour copy and fax service. 283 rooms, 10 story. Check-out noon. Restaurant, bar. Fitness room. Outdoor pool. Tennis. **$**

★ **TOWNEPLACE SUITES BY MARRIOTT MOUNT LAUREL.** *450 Century Pkwy, Mount Laurel (08054). Phone 856/778-8221; fax 856/778-8226. www.towneplacesuites.com.* Guests planning on a longer stay will find comfort in the spacious studios and one- and two-bedroom suites complete with fully equipped kitchens and large work spaces. 95 rooms, 3 story, all suites. Check-in 4 pm, check-out noon. Outdoor pool. **$**

Full-Service Hotel

★ ★ ★ **HILTON.** *2349 W Marlton Pike, Cherry Hill (08002). Phone 856/665-6666; fax 856/662-3676. www.hilton.com.* This suburban hotel is located only ten minutes from Philadelphia's historic and business districts and just a few miles from the Aquarium and the Cherry Hill Mall. 408 rooms, 14 story. Check-in 3 pm, check-out noon. Restaurant, bar. Fitness room. Outdoor pool, children's pool. Business center. **$**

Restaurants

★ ★ **CAFFE LA BELLA.** *61 E Main St, Morristown (08057). Phone 856/234-7755.* Italian menu. Lunch, dinner, Sun brunch. Closed holidays. Children's menu. Reservations recommended. **$$**

★ ★ ★ **LA CAMPAGNE.** *312 Kresson Rd, Cherry Hill (08034). Phone 856/429-7647; fax 856/429-0037. www.lacampagne.com.* This 150-year-old restaurant and farmhouse serves country French cuisine with an emphasis on the Provençal region of Southeast France. French menu. Lunch, dinner, Sun brunch. Closed Mon. Children's menu. Outdoor seating. **$$$**

★ ★ **LOS AMIGOS MEXICAN RESTAURANT.** *461 Rte 73, West Berlin (08091). Phone 856/767-5247; fax 856/767-5566. www.losamigosrest.com.* Southwestern menu. Dinner. Closed Mon; some holidays. Bar. Children's menu. Outdoor seating. **$$**

★ ★ **MELANGE CAFE.** *1601 Chapel Ave, Cherry Hill (08002). Phone 856/663-7339. www.melangecafe.com.* Italian, Louisianian menu. Lunch, dinner. Closed Mon; also July 4, Thanksgiving, Dec 25. Children's menu. Upscale casual dining. Outdoor seating. **$$**

★ **RED HOT & BLUE.** *Rte 70 and Sayer Ave, Cherry Hill (08034). Phone 856/665-7427; fax 856/665-8204. www.redhotandblue.com.* Barbecue menu. Lunch, dinner. Closed Easter, Thanksgiving, Dec 25. Bar. Children's menu. Casual attire. Blues Fri, Sat. **$$**

★ ★ **SIRI'S THAI FRENCH CUISINE.** *2117 Rte 70W, Cherry Hill (08002). Phone 856/663-6781; fax 856/663-6128.* Thai, French menu. Lunch, dinner. Closed holidays. **$$**

Clifton (B-4)

See also Flemington

Population 78,682
Elevation 70 ft
Area Code 973
Information North Jersey Regional Chamber of Commerce, 1033 Rte 46 E, PO Box 110, 07011; phone 973/470-9300
Web site www.njrcc.org

What to See and Do

Hamilton House Museum. *971 Valley Rd, Clifton (07013). Phone 973/744-5707.* Early 19th-century sandstone farmhouse with period furniture; country store; exhibits. Open-hearth cooking demonstrations by costumed guides. (Mar-Dec, First Sun each month, Tues-Thurs afternoons; closed holiday weekends) **FREE**

Limited-Service Hotel

★ **WELLESLEY INN.** *265 Rte 3 E, Clifton (07014). Phone 973/778-6500; toll-free 800/444-8888; fax 973/778-8724. www.wellesleyinnonline.com.* 225 rooms, 4 story. Complimentary continental breakfast. Pets accepted, some restrictions. Check-in 3 pm, check-out noon. Fitness room. Indoor pool. **$**

Clinton (B-2)

Population 2,632
Elevation 195 ft
Area Code 908
Zip 08809

What to See and Do

Red Mill Museum Village. *56 Main St, Clinton (08809). Off I-78. Phone 908/735-4101.* Four-story gristmill (circa 1810). Ten-acre park houses education center, quarry and lime kilns, blacksmith shop, general store, one-room schoolhouse, log cabin, machinery sheds, herb garden. Also home of Clinton's landmark red mill. Gift shop. (Apr-Oct, Tues-Sun) Outdoor concerts some Sat evenings in summer (fee). **$$**

Round Valley State Park. *1220 Lebanon Stanton Rd, Clinton (08833). Off Hwy 22, E of jct I-78; follow signs. Phone 908/236-6355.* A 4,003-acre park. Swimming, fishing, boating; picnicking, concession (Memorial Day-Labor Day), wilderness camping (access to campsites via hiking or boating only).

Spruce Run State Recreation Area. *1 Van Syckles Rd, Clinton (08809). 3 miles NW off Hwy 31. Phone 908/638-8572.* 1,290 acres of water, 600 of acres park. Swimming, fishing, boating (launch, rentals); picnicking, concession, camping (dump station) (Apr-Oct).

Limited-Service Hotel

★★ HOLIDAY INN. *111 Rte 173, Clinton (08809). Phone 908/735-5111; toll-free 888/452-5770; fax 908/730-9768. www.holiday-inn.com.* 142 rooms, 5 story. Check-in 3 pm, check-out noon. Restaurant, bar. Fitness room. Indoor pool. Business center. **$**

Specialty Lodging

The following lodging establishment is approved by Mobil Travel Guide, but due to its unique and individualized nature has not been given a traditional Mobil Star rating. Included in this listing you may find bed-and-breakfasts, limited-service inns, guest ranches, and other unique hotel properties.

STEWART INN. *708 S Main St, Stewartsville (08886). Phone 908/479-6060; fax 908/479-4211. www.bbianj.com/stewartinn.* 7 rooms, 2 story. Children over 12 years only. Complimentary full breakfast. Check-in 3 pm, check-out 11 am. Outdoor pool. Stone manor house built in 1770s, set amidst 16 acres of lawns, gardens, woods, stream, and pasture. Trout stream, barns and outbuildings with farm animals. **$**

Restaurants

★★ CLINTON HOUSE. *2 W Main St, Clinton (08809). Phone 908/730-9300; fax 908/735-5490. www.theclintonhouse.com.* Lunch, dinner. Closed Dec 25. Bar. Children's menu. Built in 1743; former stagecoach stop. **$$**

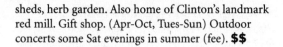

★★★ SONOMA GRILL. *64 Hoboken Rd, East Rutherford (07073). Phone 201/507-8989; fax 201/507-5191. www.sonomagrill.net.* American menu. Lunch, dinner. Closed Sun; holidays. Bar. Casual attire. **$$**

Eatontown (C-4)

See also Red Bank

Population 14,008
Elevation 46 ft
Area Code 732
Zip 07724

Full-Service Hotel

★★★ SHERATON EATONTOWN HOTEL. *Rte 35, at Industrial Way E, Eatontown (07724). Phone 732/542-6500; toll-free 800/544-5064; fax 732/542-6607. www.sheraton.com.* 208 rooms, 6 story. Check-in 4 pm, check-out noon. Restaurant, bar. Fitness room. Indoor, outdoor pool, whirlpool. Business center. **$$**

Edison (C-3)

See also Woodbridge

Population 97,687
Elevation 95 ft
Area Code 732
Information Chamber of Commerce, 100 Menlo Park, 3rd Fl, PO Box 2103, 08818-2103; phone 732/494-0300
Web site www.edisonchamber.com

Although Thomas A. Edison's house here has been destroyed, Menlo Park and the Edison Memorial Tower stand in tribute to the great American inventor. Here, on December 6, 1877, the 30-year-old Edison invented the phonograph. Two years later, he perfected the first practical incandescent light, designing and constructing various kinds of electrical equipment we now take for granted. His workshop has been moved to the Ford Museum in Dearborn, Michigan. Edison also built the first electric railway locomotive here in 1880; it ran 1 1/2 miles over the fields of Pumptown.

What to See and Do

Edison Memorial Tower and Menlo Park Museum. *37 Christie St, Edison (08820). 1/2 mile SW of Garden*

State Pkwy exit 131 off Rte 27 in Menlo Park. Phone 732/549-3299. A 131-foot tower topped by a 13 1/2-foot-high electric light bulb stands at the birthplace of recorded sound. Museum contains some of Edison's inventions, including phonographs and lightbulbs (Tues-Sat 10 am-4 pm). **FREE**

Limited-Service Hotel

★ ★ CLARION HOTEL. *2055 Lincoln Hwy, Edison (08817). Phone 732/287-3500; toll-free 800/424-6423; fax 732/287-8190. www.choicehotels.com.* 169 rooms, 5 story. Complimentary continental breakfast. Check-in 3 pm, check-out noon. High-speed Internet access. Restaurant, bar. Fitness room. Airport transportation available. Business center. **$**

Full-Service Hotel

★ ★ ★ SHERATON EDISON HOTEL RARITAN CENTER. *125 Raritan Center Pkwy, Edison (08837). Phone 732/225-8300; fax 732/225-0037. www.sheraton.com.* 275 rooms, 12 story. Pets accepted, restrictions, fee. Check-in 3 pm, check-out noon. Restaurant, bar. Fitness room. Indoor pool, whirlpool. **$$**

Restaurants

★ ★ CHARLIE BROWN'S. *222 Plainfield Rd, Edison (08820). Phone 732/494-6135; fax 732/494-7257. www.charliebrowns.com.* Lunch, dinner. Closed Dec 25. Bar. Children's menu. Outdoor seating. **$$**

★ ★ MOGHUL. *1665-195 Oaktree Center, Edison (08820). Phone 732/549-5050; fax 732/540-5052. www.moghul.com.* Indian menu. Lunch, dinner, brunch. Closed Mon. **$$**

Elizabeth (B-4)

See also Jersey City, Newark, Newark International Airport Area

Settled 1664
Population 120,568
Elevation 36 ft
Area Code 908
Information Union County Chamber of Commerce, 135 Jefferson Ave, 07207; phone 908/352-0900

More than 1,200 manufacturing industries are located in Elizabeth and Union County. Long before the Revolution, Elizabeth was not only the capital of New Jersey, but also a thriving industrial town. The first Colonial Assembly met here from 1669-1692. Princeton University began in Elizabeth in 1746 as the College of New Jersey. More than 20 pre-Revolutionary buildings still stand. Many noteworthy people were citizens of Elizabeth: William Livingston, first governor of New Jersey; Elias Boudinot, first president of the Continental Congress; Alexander Hamilton; Aaron Burr; General Winfield Scott; John Philip Holland, builder of the first successful submarine; and Admiral William J. Halsey. The Elizabeth-Port Authority Marine Terminal is the largest container port in the United States.

What to See and Do

Boxwood Hall State Historic Site. *1073 E Jersey St, Elizabeth (07201). 1 1/2 blocks W of Hwy 1. Phone 973/648-4540.* Home of Elias Boudinot, lawyer, diplomat, president of the Continental Congress (1783), and director of the US Mint. Boudinot entertained George Washington here on Apr 23, 1789, when Washington was on his way to his inauguration. (Mon-Sat; closed Jan 1, Thanksgiving, Dec 25)

First Presbyterian Church and Graveyard. *42 Broad St, Elizabeth (07201). Broad St and Caldwell Pl. Phone 908/353-1518.* The first General Assembly of New Jersey convened in an earlier building in 1668. The burned-out church was rebuilt in 1785-1787, and again in 1949. The Reverend James Caldwell was an early pastor. Alexander Hamilton and Aaron Burr attended an academy where the parish house now stands.

Warinanco Park. *Elizabethtown Town Plaza. St. George's Ave, border of Elizabeth and Roselle. Phone 908/527-4900.* One of the largest Union County parks. Fishing, boating (rentals June-Sept, daily); running track, parcourse fitness circuit, tennis (late Apr-early Oct), handball, horseshoes, indoor ice skating (early Oct-early Apr, daily). Henry S. Chatfield Memorial Garden features tulip blooms each spring; azaleas and Japanese cherry trees; summer and fall flower displays. Some fees. **FREE**

Flemington (C-2)

See also Clinton, Somerville

Settled 1738
Population 4,200
Elevation 160 ft
Area Code 908
Zip 08822
Information Hunterdon County Chamber of Commerce, 2200 Rte 31, Suite 15, Lebanon 08833; phone 908/735-5955
Web site www.hunterdon-chamber.org

Originally a farming community, Flemington became a center for the production of pottery and cut glass at the turn of the century.

What to See and Do

Black River & Western Railroad. *Rte 12, Flemington (08822). Phone 908/782-9600.* Excursion ride on old steam train, 11-mile round trip to Ringoes. Picnic area; museum. (July-Aug: Thurs-Sun; Apr-June and Sept-Dec: Sat-Sun and holidays) **$$**

County Courthouse. *Main St, Flemington.* (1828) For 46 days in 1935, world attention was focused on this Greek Revival building where Bruno Hauptmann was tried for the kidnapping and murder of the Lindbergh baby.

Fleming Castle. *5 Bonnell St, Flemington (08822). Phone 908/782-8840.* (1756) Typical two-story colonial house built as a residence and inn by Samuel Fleming, for whom the town is named. DAR headquarters. (By appointment) **DONATION**

Kase Cemetery. *Bonnell St, W of Fleming Castle, Flemington (08822).* John Philip Kase, Flemington's first settler, purchased a tract from William Penn. His family's crumbling gravestones date from 1774 to 1856. Kase's Native American friend, Chief Tuccamirgan, is also memorialized here.

Special Events

Hunterdon County 4-H Agricultural Fair. *Rte 179, Ringoes (08822). Phone 908/782-2413.* Late Aug.

Restaurants

★★★ **HARVEST MOON INN.** *1039 Old York Rd, Ringoes (08551). Phone 908/806-6020; fax 908/806-7111. www.harvestmooninn.com.* Lunch, dinner. Closed Mon; holidays. Bar. **$$**

★★ **UNION HOTEL.** *76 Main St, Flemington (08822). Phone 908/788-7474; fax 908/788-0135.* Lunch, dinner. Closed holidays. Bar. Children's menu. In ornate Victorian hotel (1878) opposite historical county courthouse. **$$**

Folsom (E-2)

Restaurant

★ **HARLEY DAWN DINER.** *1402 Black Horse Pike, Folsom (08037). Phone 609/567-6084.* Breakfast, lunch, dinner. Closed Dec 25. Children's menu. **$$**

Forked River (D-4)

See also Toms River

Population 4,914
Elevation 19 ft
Area Code 609
Zip 08731

Restaurant

★★ **CAPTAIN'S INN.** *E Lacey Rd, Forked River (08731). Phone 609/693-3351; fax 609/242-1302.* American menu. Breakfast, lunch, dinner. Closed Dec 25. Bar. Children's menu. Built in 1831. Docking. **$$**

Fort Lee (B-4)

See also Hackensack

Population 35,461
Elevation 314 ft
Area Code 201
Zip 07024
Information Greater Fort Lee Chamber of Commerce, 2357 Lemoine Ave; phone 201/944-7575

North and south of the George Washington Bridge, Fort Lee is named for General Charles Lee, who served in the Revolutionary Army under George Washington. Its rocky bluff achieved fame as the cliff from which Pearl White hung in the early movie serial *The Adventures of Pearl White*. From 1907-1916, 21 companies and seven studios produced motion pictures in Fort Lee. Stars such as Mary Pickford, Mabel Normand, Theda Bara, and Clara Kimball Young made movies here.

What to See and Do

Fort Lee Historic Park. *Hudson Terr and Palisades Interstate, Fort Lee (07024). Phone 201/461-3956.*

Palisades Interstate Parks. *Palisades Interstate Parks Commission, Administration Building, Bear Mountain (10911). Phone 914/786-2701.* This 81,008-acre system of conservation and recreation areas extends along the west side of the Hudson River from the George Washington Bridge at Fort Lee, NJ, to Saugerties, NY. The main unit is the 51,680-acre tract of Bear Mountain and Harriman state parks. Included in the system are 17 parks and six historic sites. Parks include

Bear Mountain (5,067 acres) extends westward from the Hudson River opposite Peekskill. Only 45 miles from New York City via the Palisades Interstate Parkway, this is a popular recreation area, with all-year facilities, mainly for one-day visits. Bear Mountain has picnic areas, hiking trails, a swimming pool with bathhouse, boating on Hessian Lake, fishing, and an artificial ice rink. Perkins Memorial Drive goes to the top of Bear Mountain, where there is a picnic area and a sightseeing tower. Near the site of Fort Clinton, just west of Bear Mountain Bridge, is Trailside Museums and Wildlife Center, with native animals and exhibit buildings (daily; phone 914/786-2701). **$**

Harriman (46,613 acres), southwest of Bear Mountain, consists of wilder country. Fishing, boating, scenic drives, lakes, bathing beaches at Lakes Tiorati, Welch and Sebago; tent camping at Lake Welch and cabins (primarily for family groups) at Lake Sebago. The Silver Mine Area, 4 miles west of Bear Mountain, has fishing, boating, and picnicking. (All year) Charges for parking and for most activities vary. **$$**

Limited-Service Hotels

★ ★ HOLIDAY INN. *2339 Rte 4 E, Fort Lee (07024). Phone 201/944-5000; toll-free 800/836-8533; fax 201/944-0623. www.holiday-inn.com.* 184 rooms, 6 story. Check-in 3 pm, check-out noon. Restaurant, bar. Fitness room. Outdoor pool. **$**

★ ★ RADISSON HOTEL ENGLEWOOD. *401 S Van Brunt St, Englewood (07631). Phone 201/871-2020; toll-free 800/333-3333; fax 201/871-7116. www.radisson.com.* 194 rooms, 9 story. Pets accepted, some restrictions; fee. Check-in 3 pm, check-out noon. High-speed Internet access. Restaurant, bar. Fitness room. Indoor pool. Business center. **$$**

Full-Service Hotel

★ ★ ★ HILTON FORT LEE GEORGE WASHINGTON BRIDGE. *2117 Rte 4, Fort Lee (07024). Phone 201/461-9000; toll-free 800/445-8667; fax 201/585-9807. www.hilton.com.* This hotel is located at the gateway to the "Big Apple" and offers its guests two restaurants, a lounge, a karaoke night club, an indoor pool, and a modern fitness center. 236 rooms, 15 story. Check-in 3 pm, check-out noon. High-speed Internet access. Two restaurants, two bars. Fitness room. Indoor pool, whirlpool. Business center. **$$**

Freehold (C-3)

See also Allaire State Park, Eatontown, Hightstown, Lakewood

Founded 1715
Population 10,976
Elevation 154 ft
Area Code 732
Zip 07728
Information Western Monmouth Chamber of Commerce, 17 Broad St; phone 732/462-3030
Web site www.wmchamber.com

George Washington and the Revolutionary Army defeated the British under General Sir Henry Clinton at the Battle of Monmouth near here on June 28, 1778. Molly Hays carried water to artillerymen in a pitcher and from that day on she has been known as "Molly Pitcher." Formerly known as Monmouth Courthouse, Freehold is the seat of Monmouth County.

What to See and Do

Covenhoven House. *150 W Main St, Freehold (07728). Phone 732/462-1466.* (1756) House with period furnishings; once occupied by General Sir Henry Clinton prior to the Battle of Monmouth in 1778. (May-Sept, Tues, Thurs, Sat, and Sun afternoons) **$**

Monmouth County Historical Museum and Library. *70 Court St, Freehold (07728). Phone 732/462-1466.* Headquarters of the Monmouth County Historical Association. Changing exhibits center on aspects of life in Monmouth county and include collections of silver, ceramics, and paintings, the exhibits on Battle of Monmouth. Museum (Tues-Sat, also Sun afternoons); library (Wed-Sat; both closed holidays). **$**

Turkey Swamp Park. *200 Georgia Rd, Freehold (07728). 2 miles SW off I-195, exit 22, County 524 to Georgia Rd. Phone 732/462-7286.* An 1,004-acre park with fishing, boating (rentals); hiking trails, ice skating, picnicking (shelter), playfields, camping (Mar-Nov; fee; electric and water hookups). Special events. **FREE**

Special Event

Harness racing. *Freehold Raceway, Rtes 9 and 33, Freehold (07728). Junction Rtes 9, 33. Phone 732/462-3800.* Tues-Sat, mid-Aug-May.

Limited-Service Hotel

★★ FREEHOLD GARDENS HOTEL & CONFERENCE CENTER. *50 Gibson Pl, Freehold (07728). Phone 732/780-3870; toll-free 800/448-8355; fax 732/780-8725. www.freeholdgardens.com.* 114 rooms, 5 story. Pets accepted, some restrictions. Complimentary continental breakfast. Check-out noon. Restaurant. Outdoor pool. **$**

Restaurant

★ GOLDEN BELL DINER. *3320 Rte 9, Freehold (07728). Phone 732/462-7259; fax 732/462-7194.* Italian, American menu. Lunch, dinner. Children's menu. Greenhouse atrium. **$$**

Gateway National Recreation Area (Sandy Hook Unit) (C-4)

See also Red Bank

(5 miles E of Atlantic Highlands on Rte 36).

Sandy Hook is a barrier peninsula that was first sighted by the crew of Henry Hudson's Half Moon (1609). It once was owned (1692) by Richard Hartshorne, an English Quaker, but has been government property since the 18th century. Fort Hancock (1895) was an important harbor defense from the Spanish-American War through the Cold War era. Among Sandy Hook's most significant features are the Sandy Hook Lighthouse (1764), the oldest operating lighthouse in the United States, and the US Army Proving Ground (1874-1919), the army's first new-weapons testing site.

The park offers swimming (lifeguards in summer), fishing; guided and self-guided walks, picnicking, and a concession. Visitors are advised to obtain literature at the Visitor Center (daily). There is no charge for entrance and activities scheduled by the National Park Service. Parking fee, Memorial Day weekend-Labor Day. (Daily, sunrise-sunset; some facilities closed in winter) Contact Superintendant, PO Box 530, Fort Hancock 07732; 732/872-5970.

What to See and Do

Twin Lights State Historic Site. *Rte 36 and Light House Rd, Highlands (07732). Phone 732/872-1814.* (1862) A lighthouse built to guide ships into New York harbor; now a marine museum operated by the State Park Service. (May-Oct: daily 10am-5 pm; rest of year: Wed-Sun daily 10 am-5 pm) **DONATION**

Restaurants

★★ BAHR'S RESTAURANT & MARINA. *2 Bay Ave, Highlands (07732). Phone 732/872-1245; fax 732/872-0495. www.bahrs.com.* Seafood menu. Lunch, dinner, Sun brunch. Closed Dec 25. Bar. Children's menu. **$$**

★★ **DORIS & ED'S.** *348 Shore Dr, Highlands (07732). Phone 732/872-1565; fax 732/872-2299. www.doris-and-eds.com.* Dinner. Closed Mon-Tues; also Jan-Feb. Children's menu. **$$$**

Gibbstown

Population 3,758
Elevation 15 ft
Area Code 856
Zip 08027
Information Township of Greenwich, 420 Washington St; phone 856/423-1038 or 856/423-4913

What to See and Do

Hunter-Lawrence-Jessup House. *58 N Broad St, Woodbury (08096). Approximately 7 miles NW via Rte 45, County 534. Phone 856/848-8531.* (1765) Headquarters of Gloucester County Historical Society. Museum contains 16 rooms of furnishings and memorabilia from 17th- to 19th-century New Jersey. (Mon, Wed, Fri, last Sat-Sun of each month; closed holidays) **$**

Nothnagle Home. *406 Swedesboro Rd, Gibbstown (08027). Phone 856/423-0916.* (1638-1643) America's oldest log house. (By appointment) **FREE**

Limited-Service Hotel

★★ **HOLIDAY INN.** *1 Pureland Dr, Swedesboro (08085). Phone 856/467-3322; fax 856/467-3031. www.holiday-inn.com.* 149 rooms, 4 story. Check-out noon. Restaurant, bar. Fitness room. Indoor pool, whirlpool. **$**

Hackensack (B-4)

See also Fort Lee, Paterson

Settled 1647
Population 42,677
Elevation 20 ft
Area Code 201
Information Chamber of Commerce, 190 Main St, 07601; phone 201/489-3700

Hackensack was officially known as New Barbados until 1921 when it received its charter under its present name, thought to be derived from the Native American word *Hacquinsacq.* The influence of the original Dutch settlers who established a trading post here remained strong even after British conquest. A strategic point during the Revolutionary War, the city contains a number of historical sites from that era. Hackensack is the hub for industry, business, and government in Bergen County. Edward Williams College is located here.

What to See and Do

The Church on the Green. *42 Court St, Hackensack (07601). NE corner of the Green, S end of Main St, opposite County Court House. Phone 201/845-0957.* Organized in 1686, the original building was built in 1696 (13 monogrammed stones preserved in east wall), and rebuilt in 1791 in Stone Dutch architectural style. It is the oldest church building in Bergen County. Museum contains pictures, books, and colonial items. Enoch Poor, a Revolutionary War general, is buried in the cemetery. Tours (weekdays on request). **FREE**

Steuben House State Historic Site. *1209 Main St, River Edge (07661). Approximately 1/4 mile N of Rte 4, overlooking river. Phone 201/487-1739.* (1713) Museum of the Bergen County Historical Society. Enlarged in 1752 as home of Jan and Annetie Zabriskie. The house was confiscated during the Revolutionary War because the Zabriskies were Loyalists; it was given to Baron von Steuben, by the state of New Jersey, as a reward for his military services. The baron later sold it back to the original owners. Colonial furniture, glassware, china; Native American artifacts. (Wed-Sat and Sun afternoons; closed Jan 1, Thanksgiving, Dec 25)

USS *Ling* Submarine. *Court and River sts, Hackensack (07601). Phone 201/342-3268.* Restored World War II fleet submarine; New Jersey Naval Museum. (Sat-Sun afternoons; closed holidays)

Full-Service Hotels

★★★ **HILTON HASBROUCK HOUSE.** *650 Terrace Ave, Hasbrouck Heights (07604). Phone 201/288-6100; fax 201/288-4717. www.hilton.com.* 355 rooms, 12 story. Check-in 3 pm, check-out 11 am. Pets accepted, fee. Restaurant, bar. Fitness room.

High-speed Internet access. Outdoor pool. Business center. Airport transportation available. **$$**

★★★ **MARRIOTT GLENPOINTE.** *100 Frank W Burr Blvd, Teaneck (07666). Phone 201/836-0600; toll-free 800/228-9290; fax 201/836-0638. www.marriott.com.* 347 rooms, 15 story. Check-in 4 pm, check-out noon. High-speed Internet access. Restaurant, bar. Fitness room, fitness classes available, spa. Indoor pool, whirlpool. Business center. Near Meadowlands. **$$**

Restaurant

★★★ **STONY HILL INN.** *231 Polifly Rd, Hackensack (07601). Phone 201/342-4085; fax 201/342-1046.* American menu. Lunch, dinner. Closed Dec 25. Bar. Jacket required. Landmark Dutch colonial house (1818); period furnishings. **$$$**

Hackettstown (B-2)

Settled circa 1760
Population 10,403
Elevation 571 ft
Area Code 908
Zip 07840
Information Town Hall, 215 Stiger St; phone 908/852-3130

First called Helm's Mills and then Musconetcong, citizens renamed the town for Samuel Hackett, the largest local landowner. His popularity increased when he provided unlimited free drinks at the christening of a new hotel. Hackettstown is located in the Musconetcong Valley between the Schooleys and Upper Pohatcong mountains.

What to See and Do

Allamuchy Mountain State Park, Stephens Section. *800 Willow Grove St, Hackettstown (07840). 1 1/2 miles N of Rte 46. Phone 908/852-3790 (Stephens).* Allamuchy Mountain State Park (7,263 acres) is divided into three sections. The Stephens Section (482 acres) is developed; the rest (Allamuchy) is natural. Fishing in Musconetcong River; hunting, hiking, picnicking, playground, camping.

Land of Make Believe. *354 Great Meadows Rd, Hope. I-80 exit 12, on County 611. Phone 908/459-9000.* Amusement park at foot of Jenny Jump Mountain includes the Tornado; Old McDonald's Farm; the Red Baron airplane; Santa Claus at the North Pole; a Civil War train; a maze; water park; hayrides; picnic grove; fudge factory. (Mid-June-Labor Day: daily; Memorial Day weekend-mid-June: weekends; Sept: weekend after Labor Day) **$$$$**

Full-Service Inn

★★★ **THE INN AT MILLRACE POND.** *313 Johnsonberg Rd, Rte 519 N, Hope (07844). Phone 908/459-4884; toll-free 800/746-6467; fax 908/459-5276. www.innatmillracepond.com.* 18 rooms, 2 story. Complimentary full breakfast. Check-in 3 pm, check-out noon. Restaurant. Tennis. Airport transportation available. Rooms individually decorated with colonial-style furniture and period reproductions. **$**

Haddonfield

See also Camden, Cherry Hill

Settled circa 1713
Population 11,659
Elevation 95 ft
Area Code 856
Zip 08033
Information Visitor/Information Center, 114 Kings Hwy E; phone 856/216-7253

Named for Elizabeth Haddon, a Quaker girl of 20 whose father sent her here from England in 1701 to develop 400 acres of land. This assertive young woman built a house, started a colony, and proposed to a Quaker missionary who promptly married her. The "Theologian's Tale" in Longfellow's *Tales of a Wayside Inn* celebrates Elizabeth Haddon's romance with the missionary.

What to See and Do

Greenfield Hall. *343 King's Hwy E (Rte 41), Haddonfield (08033). Phone 856/429-7375.* Haddonfield's Historical Society headquarters in old Gill House (1747-1841) contains personal items of Elizabeth Haddon; furniture; costumes; doll collection. Boxwood garden; library on local history.

On grounds is a house (circa 1735) once owned by Elizabeth Haddon. (Library: Tues, Thurs mornings; Museum: Wed-Fri afternoons, other days by appointment; closed Aug) **$**

Indian King Tavern Museum State Historic Site. *233 King's Hwy E, Haddonfield (08033). Phone 856/429-6792.* Built as an inn; state legislatures met here frequently, passing a bill (1777) substituting "State" for "Colony" in all state papers. Colonial furnishings. Guided tours. (Wed-Sun; closed Jan 1, Thanksgiving, Dec 25; also Wed if following a Mon or Tues holiday) **DONATION**

The Site of the Elizabeth Haddon House. *Wood Ln and Merion Ave, Haddonfield.* Isaac Wood built this house in 1842, on the foundation of Elizabeth Haddon's 1713 brick mansion, immediately after it was destroyed by fire. The original brew house Elizabeth built (1713) and the English yew trees she brought over in 1712 are in the yard. Private residence; not open to the public.

High Point State Park (A-3)

(7 miles NW of Sussex on Rte 23).

High Point's elevation (1,803 feet), the highest point in New Jersey, gave this 15,000-acre park its name. The spot is marked by a 220-foot stone war memorial. The view is magnificent, overlooking Tri-State—the point where New Jersey, New York, and Pennsylvania meet—with the Catskill Mountains to the north, the Pocono Mountains to the west, and hills, valleys, and lakes all around. Elsewhere in the forests of this Kittatinny Mountain park are facilities for swimming, fishing, boating; nature center, picnicking, tent camping (no trailers). Phone 973/875-4800.

Hightstown (C-3)

See also Freehold

Population 5,216
Elevation 84 ft
Area Code 609
Zip 08520

Limited-Service Hotel

★ RAMADA. *399 Monmouth St, East Windsor (08520). Phone 609/448-7000; toll-free 888/298-2054; fax 609/443-6227. www.ramada.com.* 200 rooms, 4 story. Check-in 2 pm, check-out noon. Bar. Fitness room. Outdoor pool. **$**

Ho-Ho-Kus

See also Paramus

Population 4,060
Elevation 111 ft
Area Code 201
Zip 07423
Information Borough of Ho-Ho-Kus, 333 Warren Ave; phone 201/652-4400

In colonial times, Ho-Ho-Kus was known as Hoppertown. Its present name is derived from the Chihohokies, who also had a settlement on this spot.

What to See and Do

The Hermitage. *335 N Franklin Tpke, Ho-Ho-Kus (07423). Phone 201/445-8311.* Stone Victorian house of Gothic Revival architecture superimposed on original 18th-century house. Its span of history includes ownership by the Rosencrantz family for more than 150 years. Grounds consist of 5 wooded acres, including a second stone Victorian house. Docents conduct tours of site and the Hermitage. Changing exhibits. Special events held throughout the year. Tours. **$$**

Hoboken

See also Jersey City, Secaucus

Settled 1640
Population 38,577
Elevation 5 ft
Area Code 201
Zip 07030
Information Hoboken Community Development, 94 Washington St; phone 201/420-2013

In the early 19th century, beer gardens and other amusement centers dotted the Hoboken shore, enticing New Yorkers across the Hudson. John Jacob

Astor, Washington Irving, William Cullen Bryant, and Martin Van Buren were among the fashionable visitors. By the second half of the century, industries and shipping began to encroach on the fun. From 1928-1929, Christopher Morley and Cleon Throckmorton presented revivals of *After Dark* and *The Black Crook* to enchanted New Yorkers. Hoboken is connected to Manhattan by the PATH rapid-transit system.

What to See and Do

Stevens Institute of Technology. *Castle Point, E of Hudson St between 5th and 9th sts. Phone 201/216-5105. www.stevens.edu.* (1870) (3,600 students) A leading college of engineering, science, computer science management, and the humanities; also a center for research. Campus tours. On campus are

Davidson Laboratory. *Hudson and 7th sts, Hoboken. W end of the campus. Phone 201/216-5290.* One of the largest privately owned hydrodynamic labs of its kind in the world. Testing site for models of ships, hydrofoils, the America's Cup participants, and the *Apollo* command capsule. (Limited public access)

Samuel C. Williams Library. *Phone 201/216-5198.* (1969) Special collections include a set of facsimiles of every drawing by Leonardo da Vinci; library of 3,000 volumes by and about da Vinci; Alexander Calder mobile; the Frederick Winslow Taylor Collection of Scientific Management. (Academic year)

Stevens Center. (1962) The 14-story hub of campus. Excellent view of Manhattan from George Washington Bridge to the Verrazano Bridge.

Restaurants

★★ **BAJA MEXICAN CUISINE.** *104 14th St, Hoboken (07030). Phone 201/653-0610; fax 201/239-9034.* Mexican menu. Dinner. Closed Jan 1, Thanksgiving, Dec 25. Bar. Casual attire. **$$$**

★ **CAFE MICHELINA.** *423 Bloomfield St, Hoboken (07030). Phone 201/659-3663.* Italian menu. Lunch, dinner. Closed Mon; holidays. Casual attire. **$$**

★ **GRIMALDI'S.** *133 Clinton St, Hoboken (07030). Phone 201/792-0800. www.grimaldis.com.* Italian menu. Lunch, dinner. Closed Mon; Easter, Thanksgiving, Dec 25. Outdoor seating. **$$**

★ **MARGHERITAS'.** *740 Washington St, Hoboken (07030). Phone 201/222-2400; fax 201/222-3440.* Italian menu. Lunch, dinner. Closed Mon; Easter, Thanksgiving, Dec 25. **$$**

★ **ODD FELLOWS.** *80 River St, Hoboken (07030). Phone 201/656-9009; fax 201/656-0484. www.oddfellowsrest.com.* Creole/Cajun menu. Lunch, dinner. Closed Thanksgiving, Dec 25. Bar. Casual attire. Outdoor seating. Blues Thurs, Sun. **$$**

Jackson

See also Lakewood, Toms River

Population 42,816
Elevation 138 ft
Area Code 732
Zip 08527
Information Chamber of Commerce, 1080 N County Line Rd, PO Box A-C; phone 732/363-1080

What to See and Do

Six Flags Great Adventure Theme Park/Six Flags Wild Safari Animal Park. *299 Cherry Hill Rd, Parsippany (07054). On Rte 537, 1 mile S of I-195. Phone 732/928-1821.* This family entertainment center includes a 350-acre drive-through safari park with more than 1,200 free-roaming animals from six continents; 125-acre theme park featuring more than 100 rides, shows and attractions. (Late Mar-late Oct; schedule varies). **$$$$**

Jersey City (B-4)

See also Elizabeth, Hoboken, Newark, Newark International Airport Area

Settled 1629
Population 240,055
Elevation 11 ft
Area Code 201
Information Jersey City Cultural Affairs, 1 Chapel Ave, 07305; phone 201/547-5522

Jersey City's location on the Hudson River, due west of the southern end of Manhattan Island, has aided its growth to such a degree that it is now the second-largest city in New Jersey. New Yorkers across the bay tell time by the Colgate-Palmolive Clock at 105 Hudson Street; the dial is 50 feet across, and the minute hand, weighing 2,200 pounds, moves 23 inches each minute. Jersey City's major links with New York are the 8,557-foot Holland Tunnel, which is 72 feet below water level; the Port Authority Trans-Hudson (PATH) rapid-transit system; and New York Waterways Ferries, which run between Exchange Place, the city's Financial District, and the World Financial Center in lower Manhattan.

What to See and Do

Liberty State Park. *Morris Pesin Dr, Jersey City (07305). Off NJ Tpke, exit 14B; on the New York Harbor, less than 2,000 feet from the Statue of Liberty. Phone 201/915-3400. www.libertystatepark.com.* Offers breathtaking view of New York City skyline; flag display includes state, historic, and US flags; boat launch; fitness course, picnic area. Historic railroad terminal has been partially restored. The Interpretive Center houses an exhibit area; adjacent to the Center is a 60-acre natural area consisting mostly of salt marsh. Nature trails and observation points complement this wildlife habitat. Boat tours and ferry service to Ellis Island and Statue of Liberty are available. (Daily) Also in park is

> ★ **Liberty Science Center.** *251 Phillip St, Jersey City (07305). Phone 201/200-1000. www.lsc.org.* Four-story structure encompasses Environment, Health, and Invention exhibit areas that feature more than 250 hands-on exhibits. Geodesic dome houses IMAX Theater with a six-story screen. (Daily; closed Thanksgiving, Dec 25) **$$$$**

Lake Hopatcong (B-3)

(Approximately 15 miles N and W of Dover via Rte 15 and an unnumbered road)

The largest lake in New Jersey, Hopatcong's popularity as a resort is second only to the seacoast spots. It covers 2,443 acres and has a hilly shoreline of approximately 40 miles. The area offers swimming, stocked fishing, and boating.

What to See and Do

Hopatcong State Park. *Lakeside Blvd, Landing. SW shore of lake. Phone 973/398-7010.* A 113-acre park with swimming, bathhouse, fishing; picnicking, playground, concession. Historic museum (Sun afternoons).

Limited-Service Hotel

★ ★ COURTYARD BY MARRIOTT. *15 Howard Blvd, Mount Arlington (07856). Phone 973/770-2000; toll-free 800/321-3211; fax 973/770-1287. www.marriot.com/ewrma.* 125 rooms, 5 story. Check-in 3 pm, check-out noon. Wireless Internet access. Restaurant, bar. Fitness room. Indoor pool, whirlpool. **$**

Lakewood (D-4)

See also Freehold, Jackson, Toms River

Settled 1800
Population 36,065
Elevation 67 ft
Area Code 732
Zip 08701
Information Chamber of Commerce, 395 Rte 70 W, Suite 125; phone 732/363-0012

A well-known winter resort in the 1890s, many socially prominent New Yorkers such as the Astors, the Goulds, the Rhinelanders, the Rockefellers, and the Vanderbilts maintained large homes on the shores of Lake Carasaljo.

What to See and Do

Ocean County Park #1. *659 Ocean Ave, Lakewood. 1 mile E on Rte 88. Phone 732/370-7380.* The 325-acre former Rockefeller estate. Lake swimming, children's fishing lake; tennis, platform tennis, picnicking (grills), playground, athletic fields. (Daily) Entrance fee (July-Aug, weekends). **$**

Limited-Service Hotel

★ ★ BEST WESTERN LEISURE INN. *1600 Rte 70, Lakewood (08701). Phone 732/367-0900; fax 732/370-4928. www.bestwestern.com.* 105 rooms, 2 story. Check-out 11 am. Restaurant, bar. Outdoor pool. **$**

Lambertville (C-2)

See also Trenton

Settled 1705
Population 3,868
Elevation 76 ft
Area Code 609
Zip 08530
Information Lambertville Area Chamber of Commerce, 239 N Union St; phone 609/397-0055
Web site www.lambertville.org

What to See and Do

John Holcombe House. *260 N Main St, Lambertville (08530).* Washington stayed here just before crossing the Delaware. Privately owned residence.

Marshall House. *62 Bridge St, Lambertville (08530). Phone 609/397-0770.* (1816) James Marshall, who first discovered gold at Sutter's Mill in California in 1848, lived here until 1834. Period furnishings; memorabilia of Lambertville; small museum collection. (May-mid-Oct, weekends or by appointment) **FREE**

Full-Service Inn

★★★ INN AT LAMBERTVILLE STATION. *11 Bridge St, Lambertville (08530). Phone 609/397-4400; toll-free 800/524-1091; fax 609/397-9744. www.lambertvillestation.com.* 45 rooms, 3 story. Complimentary continental breakfast. Check-out noon. Restaurant. Victorian antiques. View of Delaware River. **$**

Specialty Lodgings

The following lodging establishments are approved by Mobil Travel Guide, but due to their unique and individualized nature have not been given a traditional Mobil Star rating. Included in this listing you may find bed-and-breakfasts, limited-service inns, guest ranches, and other unique hotel properties.

CHIMNEY HILL FARM ESTATE. *207 Goat Hill Rd, Lambertville (08530). Phone 609/397-1516; toll-free 800/211-4667; fax 609/397-9353. www.chimneyhill.com.* 12 rooms, 3 story. Children over 12 years only. Complimentary full breakfast. Check-in 3 pm, check-out 11 am. Elegant stone and frame manor house built in 1820; furnishings are antiques and period reproductions. **$$**

WOOLVERTON INN. *6 Woolverton Rd, Stockton (08559). Phone 609/397-0802; toll-free 888/264-6648; fax 609/397-0987. www.woolvertoninn.com.* 10 rooms, 2 story. Complimentary full breakfast. Check-in 3-8 pm, check-out 11 am. **$**

Restaurants

★★ ANTON'S AT THE SWAN. *43 S Main St, Lambertville (08530). Phone 609/397-1960. www.antons-at-the-swan.com.* American menu. Dinner. Closed Mon; also Jan 1, Dec 25. Bar. **$$$**

★★ LAMBERTVILLE STATION. *11 Bridge St, Lambertville (08530). Phone 609/397-8300; fax 609/397-4262. www.lambertvillestation.com.* Lunch, dinner, Sun brunch. Bar. Children's menu. Renovated train station with three dining areas; one dining room is an old station platform. Victorian-style décor. **$$**

Livingston (B-3)

Population 27,391
Elevation 307 ft
Area Code 973
Zip 07039

This suburban community in southwestern Essex County is named for William Livingston, the first governor of New Jersey.

Restaurant

★★ AFTON. *2 Hanover Rd, Florham Park (07932). Phone 973/377-1871; fax 973/377-6362. www.theafton.com.* Lunch, dinner, Sun brunch. Closed Mon; Dec 25. Bar. **$$**

Long Beach Island (B-5)

Web site www.nealcomm.com/lbi/index.htm

Six miles out to sea, this island is separated from the New Jersey mainland by Barnegat and Little Egg Harbor bays. Route 72, going east from Manahawkin

Lambertville's Unique Shopping

This tour can cover anywhere from about 1 1/2 miles to many miles, depending on whether you stay within the town proper or extend the walk along the Delaware & Raritan Canal, or even cross the Delaware River into New Hope, Pennsylvania. Lambertville is rich in history, antique shops, fine restaurants, and historic homes. The town has long been the state's shad fishing center, and still celebrates the annual Shad Festival. It was also the country's hairpin-making capital during the early 20th century. Today, Lambertville is a fine antiques and art center. The streets are set out in a grid, with Union and Main Streets running north and south, parallel to the river, and a series of short cross-streets passing between them. A variety of historic homes in the Federalist and Victorian styles can be found here.

Start at the historic Marshall House at 62 Bridge Street. A classic Federalist building, this is the home of the Lambertville Historical Society, which leads one-hour guided walking tours from late June through September, presents a 30-minute film on Lambertville's history, and can supply you with a guide to the town's historic buildings. After visiting the Marshall House, proceed west to Union Street, and head north into the heart of the shopping district. Along this street you'll encounter Phoenix Books (49 North Union), a treasure trove of rare and out-of-print volumes; the Five and Dime (40 North Union), which houses an equally fascinating collection of antique toys; and, all along the street, a number of high-quality antique shops and galleries, from The People's Store at the corner of Union and Church streets and Broadmoor Antiques at 6 North Union to the Best of France at 204 North Union, with many others between. At the north end of Union (ten blocks north), turn right onto Cherry Street. Follow Cherry to North Main, turn right, and begin weaving among the cross streets between North Union and North Main back to Bridge Street. Along North Main, A Mano Gallery specializes in American crafts, jewelry, and glass, while Almirah focuses on colonial-era Indian antique furniture and gifts. Shopping, window shopping, or gallery hopping are best done on Perry, York, Coryell, Church Bridge, and Ferry streets. More shops can be found on Kline's Court (one block on the left from Bridge Street) and Lambert Lane (just across the canal on the right). From Lambert Lane, cross the footbridge onto Lewis Island, home of Fred Lewis, the state's only commercially licensed freshwater shad fisherman.

Back on Bridge Street, take a break at Lambertville Station, which serves New American cuisine, or return to town for other dining options, including The Fish House (2 Canal Street) for local catches of the day, Anton's at the Swan (43 South Main Street) for upscale dining in an historical building, or the Church Street Bistro (11 Church Street) for intimate dining.

For those with stamina, add one of the two extended walk options. To get in touch with nature, follow the walking/biking path along the Delaware & Raritan Canal, which travels south for many miles, presenting a bucolic view of the canal and the Delaware River. Another option is to cross the Delaware on the Bridge Street bridge and enter New Hope, Pennsylvania, a treasure trove of antique shops and restaurants.

on the mainland, enters the island at Ship Bottom. The island is no more than three blocks wide in some places, and extends 18 miles from historic Barnegat Lighthouse to the north. It includes towns such as Loveladies, Harvey Cedars, Surf City, Ship Bottom, Brant Beach, and the Beach Havens at the southern tip. The island is a popular family resort with excellent fishing, boating, and other water sports. For swimming, the bay is calm, while the ocean offers a vigorous surf.

Tales are told of pirate coins buried on the island, and, over the years, silver and gold pieces occasionally have turned up. Whether they are part of pirate treasure or the refuse of shipwrecks remains a mystery.

What to See and Do

Barnegat Lighthouse State Park. *At N end of island. Phone 609/494-2016.* Barnegat Lighthouse, a 167-foot red and white tower, was engineered by General George G. Meade and completed in 1858; a 217-step spiral staircase leading to the lookout offers a spectacular view. Fishing; picnicking. Park (daily); lighthouse (Memorial Day-Labor Day: daily; May and Labor Day-Oct: weekends only).

Fantasy Island Amusement Park. *320 W 7th St, Beach Haven (08008). Phone 609/492-4000.* Family-oriented amusement park featuring rides and games; family casino arcade. (June-Aug: daily; May and Sept: weekends; schedule varies)

Special Event

Surflight Theatre. *Beach and Engleside aves, Beach Haven. Phone 609/492-9477. www.surflight.org.* Engleside and Beach aves, Beach Haven. Broadway musicals nightly. Children's theater, Wed-Sat. May-mid-Oct.

Limited-Service Hotel

★★ THE ENGLESIDE INN. *30 E Engleside Ave, Beach Haven (08008). Phone 609/492-1251; toll-free 800/762-2214; fax 609/492-9175. www.engleside.com.* 72 rooms, 3 story. Check-out 11 am. Restaurant, bar. Fitness room. Outdoor pool. On beach. **$$**

Specialty Lodging

The following lodging establishment is approved by Mobil Travel Guide, but due to its unique and individualized nature has not been given a traditional Mobil Star rating. Included in this listing you may find bed-and-breakfasts, limited-service inns, guest ranches, and other unique hotel properties.

AMBER STREET INN BED & BREAKFAST. *118 Amber St, Beach Haven (08008). Phone 609/492-1611; fax 609/492-9165. www.amberstreetinn.com.* 6 rooms, 3 story. Children over 10 years only. Complimentary full breakfast. Check-in 3 pm, check-out 11 am. Restaurant. Built in 1885; antiques. **$$**

Restaurants

★★ BUCKALEW'S. *101 N Bay Ave, Beach Haven (08008). Phone 609/492-1065; fax 609/492-2975.* American menu. Breakfast, lunch, dinner. Closed Dec 25. Bar. Children's menu. **$$**

★★ LEEWARD ROOM. *30 Engleside Ave, Beach Haven (08008). Phone 609/492-5116. www.engleside.com.* Japanese, American menu. Breakfast, lunch, dinner, Sun brunch. Closed Dec 25. Bar. Children's menu. **$$$**

★ ROBERTO'S DOLCE VITA. *12907 Long Beach Blvd, Beach Haven Terrace (08008). Phone 609/492-1001.* Italian menu. Dinner. Casual attire. Reservations recommended. Outdoor seating. **$**

★★ TUCKER'S. *Engleside Ave and West St, Long Beach Island (08008). Phone 609/492-2300; fax 609/492-8160.* Lunch, dinner. Closed Dec 25. Bar. Children's menu. Outdoor seating. **$$**

Madison (B-3)

See also Chatham, Morristown

Settled circa 1685
Population 16,530
Elevation 261 ft
Area Code 973
Zip 07940
Information Chamber of Commerce, 155 Main St, PO Box 152; phone 973/377-7830

For many years, the quiet suburban town of Madison was called the "Rose City" because of the thousands of bouquets produced in its many greenhouses.

What to See and Do

Drew University. *36 Madison Ave, Madison (07940). Phone 973/408-3000.* (1867) (2,100 students) A 186-acre wooded campus west of town. College of Liberal Arts, Theological School, and Graduate School. On campus are a Neoclassical administration building (1833), the United Methodist Archives and History Center, and the Rose Memorial Library containing Nestorian Cross collection, government and UN documents and manuscripts, and memorabilia of early Methodism. Tours.

Fairleigh Dickinson University-Florham-Madison Campus. *285 Madison Ave, Madison (07940). Rte 124. Phone 973/443-8661.* (1958) (3,889 students) (One of three campuses) On site of Twombly Estate (1895); many original buildings still in use. Friendship Library houses numerous special collections including Harry A. Chesler collection of comic art, and collections devoted to printing and the graphic arts. (Academic year, Mon-Fri; closed school holidays) Tours of campus by appointment.

Museum of Early Trades and Crafts. *9 Main St, Madison (07940). Main St (Rte 124) at Green Village Rd. Phone 973/377-2982.* Hands-on look at 18th- and 19th-century artisans. Special events include Bottle Hill Craft Festival (Oct). Tours. (Tues-Sat, also Sun afternoons; closed holidays) **$$**

Special Event

New Jersey Shakespeare Festival. *36 Madison Ave, Madison (07940). Phone 973/408-5600 or 973/408-3278.* In residence at Drew University. Professional theater company. Includes Shakespearean, classic, and modern plays; special guest attractions and classic films.(Mid-May-Dec).

Maple Shade

Restaurant

★ **GOLDEN EAGLE DINER.** *Rte 73 S at I-295, Maple Shade (08052). Phone 856/235-8550; fax 856/222-4767.* Breakfast, lunch, dinner. Bar. Children's menu. **$$**

Matawan (C-4)

See also Freehold

Population 8,910
Elevation 55 ft
Area Code 732
Zip 07747
Information Matawan-Aberdeen Chamber of Commerce, PO Box 522; phone 732/290-1125

What to See and Do

Cheesequake State Park. *300 Gordon Rd, Matawan (07747). Garden State Pkwy, exit 120, right at first traffic light and right at next traffic light onto Gordon Rd, 1/4 mile to entrance. Phone 732/566-2161.* This 1,300-acre park offers swimming, bathhouse, fishing; nature tours, picnicking, playground, concession, camping (fee; dump station).

Special Event

Concerts. *PNC Bank Arts Center, Telegraph Hill Park on the Garden State Pkwy, exit 116, Holmdel (07095). Phone 732/442-9200. artscenter.com.* A 5,302-seat amphitheater; lawn area seats 4,500-5,500. Contemporary, classical, pop, and rock concerts. Mid-June-Sept.

Limited-Service Hotel

★ **WELLESLEY INN.** *3215 Rte 35, Hazlet (07730). Phone 732/888-2800; fax 732/888-2902. www.wellesleyinnandsuites.com.* 89 rooms, 3 story. Pets accepted, some restrictions; fee. Complimentary continental breakfast. Check-out 11 am. **$**

Restaurant

★★ **BUTTONWOOD MANOR.** *845 Rte 34, Matawan (07747). Phone 732/566-6220; fax 732/566-3801. www.buttonwoodmanor.com.* Seafood, steak menu. Lunch, dinner. Bar. Children's menu. Lakeside dining. **$$**

Millburn

See also Newark, Newark International Airport Area

Settled 1720s
Population 19,765
Elevation 140 ft
Area Code 973
Zip 07041
Information Chamber of Commerce, 343 Millburn Ave, PO Box 651; phone 973/379-1198
Web site www.millburn.com

Once bristling with paper mills and hat factories, Millburn today boasts a thriving downtown with a regional theater, a quiet residential area, and direct access to New York City.

What to See and Do

Cora Hartshorn Arboretum and Bird Sanctuary. *324 Forest Dr S, Short Hills (07078). 2 miles W on Forest Dr. Phone 973/376-3587.* A 17-acre sanctuary with nature trails; guided walks. Stone House Museum with nature exhibits (late Sept-mid-June, Tues, Thurs, and Sat). Grounds (Daily). **FREE**

Paper Mill Playhouse. *Brookside Dr and Old Shore Hills Rd, Millburn (07041). Phone 973/376-4343 (box office).* State Theater of New Jersey. A variety of plays, musicals, and children's theater (Wed-Sun); matinees (Thurs, Sat, and Sun).

Full-Service Hotel

★★★ **HILTON SHORT HILLS.** *41 John F. Kennedy Pkwy, Short Hills (07078). Phone 973/379-0100; toll-free 800/445-8667; fax 973/379-6870. www.hilton.com.* The Hilton Short Hills appeals to both business and leisure visitors with its tasteful style, central location, and abundant amenities. Executives visiting the New York metropolitan area appreciate its proximity to Manhattan, New Jersey's businesses, and Newark airport, yet this hotel is not just a destination for corporate travelers. Located across from the fabulous Short Hills Mall, well known for its selection of exclusive stores, this hotel is also a favorite stomping ground of shopaholics. A beauty salon keeps guests properly primped, while a fitness center and pool are a boon for fitness enthusiasts. The hotel enjoys a parklike setting on beautifully landscaped grounds, and its rooms and suites are the perfect match for its sophisticated clientele. 308 rooms, 7 story. Pets accepted, some restrictions; fee. Check-in 3 pm, check-out noon. High-speed Internet access. Two restaurants, bar. Fitness room, spa. Indoor pool, outdoor pool, whirlpool. Tennis. Airport transportation available. Business center. **$$**

Restaurant

★★★ **THE DINING ROOM.** *41 John F Kennedy Pkwy, Short Hills (07078). Phone 973/379-0100; fax 973/379-6870. www.hilton.com.* American, French menu. Dinner. Closed Sun. Bar. Jacket required. Valet parking. **$$$**

Millville (E-2)

See also Bridgeton

Population 26,847
Elevation 37 ft
Area Code 856
Zip 08332
Information Chamber of Commerce, 4 City Park Dr; phone 856/825-2600
Web site www.millville-nj.com

What to See and Do

Wheaton Village. *1501 Glasstown Rd, Millville (08332). 2 miles NE via County 552. Phone 856/825-6800.* Buildings include the Museum of American Glass, which houses an extensive glass collection; working factory where demonstrations of glassmaking are given; general store; restored train station; 1876 one-room schoolhouse. Crafts demonstrations, arcade, shops. Restaurant, hotel. Self-guided tours. (Jan-Feb: Fri-Sun; Mar: Wed-Sun; Apr-Dec: daily; closed holidays) **$$$**

Limited-Service Hotel

★★ **COUNTRY INNS & SUITES.** *1125 Village Dr, Millville (08332). Phone 856/825-3100; fax 856/825-1317. www.countryinns.com.* 100 rooms, 2 story. Restaurant, bar. Outdoor pool. **$**

Montclair

See also Newark, Newark International Airport Area

Settled 1666
Population 38,977
Elevation 337 ft
Area Code 973
Information Chamber of Commerce, 26 Park St, Suite 2025, 07042; phone 973/226-5500
Web site www.montclairchamber.org

Originally a part of Newark, the area that includes Montclair was purchased from Native Americans in 1678 for "two guns, three coats, and thirteen cans of rum." The first settlers were English farmers from Connecticut who came here to form a Puritan church of their own. Shortly after, Dutch from Hackensack arrived, and two communities were created: Cranetown and Speertown. The two communities later were absorbed into West Bloomfield.

During the Revolutionary War, First Mountain served as a lookout point and as a barrier, preventing the British from crossing into the Upper Passaic valley. In the early 1800s, manufacturing began, new roads opened and the area grew. In 1856-57, a rail controversy arose: West Bloomfield citizens wanted a rail connection with New York City; Bloomfield residents saw no need for it. In 1868, the two towns separated and West Bloomfield became Montclair. This railroad helped to make Montclair the suburban, residential town it is today. One of the town's schools is named for painter George Inness, who once lived here.

What to See and Do

Eagle Rock Reservation. *West Orange. 1/2 mile W on Bloomfield Ave, then S on Prospect Ave to Eagle Rock Ave.* (see).

Israel Crane House. *110 Orange Rd, Montclair (07042). Phone 973/744-1796.* (1796) Federal mansion with period rooms; working 18th-century kitchen; school room; special exhibits during the year. Country Store and Post Office have authentic items; old-time crafts demonstrations. Research library. (June-Aug: Thurs-Sat; Sept-May: Sun afternoons; other times by appointment) **$$**

The Montclair Art Museum. *3 S Mountain Ave, Montclair (07042). At Bloomfield Ave. Phone 973/746-5555.* American art; Native American gallery; changing exhibits. (Tues-Sun; closed holidays Gallery lectures (Sun). Concerts; jazz; film series. **$$**

Presby Iris Gardens. *Mountainside Park, 474 Upper Mountain Ave, Montclair (07043). Phone 973/783-5974.* Height of bloom in mid-May or early June.

Morristown (B-3)

See also Bernardsville, Madison

Settled circa 1710
Population 18,554
Elevation 327 ft
Area Code 973
Information Historic Morris Visitors Center, 6 Court St, 07960; phone 973/631-5151
Web site www.morristourism.org

Today, Morristown is primarily residential, but the iron industry, so desperately needed during the Revolutionary War, was responsible for the development of the town and the surrounding county. George Washington and his army spent two winters here, operating throughout the area until the fall of 1781. The first successful experiments with the telegraph were made in Morristown by Samuel F. B. Morse and Stephen Vail. Cartoonist Thomas Nast, writers Bret Harte and Frank Stockton, and millionaire Otto Kahn all lived here. Morristown rises to a 597-foot peak at Fort Nonsense; the Whippany River runs through the town.

What to See and Do

Acorn Hall. *68 Morris Ave, Morristown (07960). Phone 973/267-3465.* (1853) Victorian Italianate house; original furnishings; reference library; restored garden. (Mon, Thurs, Sun; group tours by appointment; closed holidays) **$$**

Fosterfields Living Historical Farm. *73 Kahdena Rd, Morristown (07960). Off County Rte 510. Phone 973/326-7645.* Turn-of-the-century living history farm (200 acres). Self-guided trail; displays; audiovisual presentations; workshops, farming demonstrations; restored Gothic Revival house. Visitor Center. (Apr-Oct, Wed-Sun) **$$**

Frelinghuysen Arboretum. *53 E Hanover Ave, Morristown (07962). 1 1/2 miles NE via Morris Ave, Whippany Rd; entrance from E Hanover Ave. Phone 973/326-7600.* Features 127 acres of forest and open fields; natural and formal gardens; spring and fall bulb displays; labeled collections of trees and shrubs; Braille trail; gift shop. Grounds (daily). **FREE**

Historic Speedwell. *333 Speedwell Ave, Morristown (07960). Phone 973/540-0211.* Home and factory of Stephen Vail, iron master, who in 1818 manufactured the engine for the SS *Savannah*, the first steamship to cross the Atlantic. In 1838, Alfred Vail (Stephen's son) and Samuel F. B. Morse perfected the telegraph and first publicly demonstrated it here in the factory. Displays include period furnishings in the mansion, exhibit on Speedwell Iron Works, exhibits on history of the telegraph; water wheel, carriage house, and granary. Gift shop. Picnic area. (May-Sept, Sun, Thurs; closed July 4) **$$**

Macculloch Hall Historical Museum. *45 Macculloch Ave, Morristown (07960). Phone 973/538-2404.* Restored 1810 house and garden; home of George P. Macculloch, initiator of the Morris Canal, and his descendants for more than 140 years. American, European decorative arts from the 18th and 19th centuries. Illustrations by Thomas Nast. Garden. (Wed, Thurs, and Sun afternoons; closed holidays) **$$**

Morris Museum. *6 Normandy Heights Rd, Morristown (07960). Phone 973/971-3700.* Art, science, and history exhibits; permanent and changing. Musical, theatrical events; lectures and films. (Tues-Sun; closed holidays) Free admission Thurs afternoons. **$$$**

Schuyler-Hamilton House. *5 Olyphant Pl, Morristown (07960). Phone 973/267-4039.* (1760) Former home of Dr. Jabez Campfield. Alexander Hamilton courted Betsy Schuyler here. Period furniture; colonial garden. (Sun afternoons; other times by appointment; closed Easter, Dec 25) **$$**

Full-Service Hotels

★ ★ ★ THE MADISON HOTEL. *1 Convent Rd, Morristown (07960). Phone 973/285-1800; toll-free 800/526-0729; fax 973/540-8566. www.themadisonhotel.com.* 200 rooms, 4 story. Complimentary continental breakfast. Check-in 3 pm, check-out noon. High-speed Internet access. Restaurant, bar. Fitness room. Indoor pool, whirlpool. Business center. **$$**

★ ★ ★ THE WESTIN GOVERNOR MORRIS. *2 Whippany Rd, Morristown (07960). Phone 973/539-7300; toll-free 800/937-8461; fax 973/984-1036. www.westin.com/morristown.* 230 rooms, 6 story. Pets accepted, some restrictions. Check-in 3 pm, check-out noon. High-speed Internet access. Restaurant, two bars. Fitness room. Outdoor pool. Business center. **$$$**

Restaurant

★ ★ ROD'S STEAK AND SEAFOOD GRILLE. *Hwy 124, Convent Station (07961). Phone 973/539-6666; fax 973/285-0586. www.rodssteak-seafoodgrill.com.* Seafood, steak menu. Lunch, dinner. Closed Dec 25. Bar. Children's menu. Casual attire. Valet parking. Display of authentic Victorian antiques. **$$$**

Morristown National Historical Park (B-3)

See also Bernardsville, Morristown

(Approximately 3 miles S of Morristown on Rte 202)

This national historical park, the first to be established and maintained by the federal government, was created by an Act of Congress in 1933. Its three units cover more than 1,600 acres, all but Jockey Hollow and the New Jersey Brigade Area being within Morristown's limits. The main body of the Continental Army stayed here in the winter of 1779-1780.

Headquarters and museum (daily 9 am-5 pm); Jockey Hollow buildings (summer, daily; rest of year schedule varies, phone ahead; closed Jan 1, Thanksgiving, Dec 25). Contact Chief of Interpretation, Washington Pl, Morristown 07960.

What to See and Do

Ford Mansion. *10 Washington Pl, Morristown (07960). Phone 973/539-2085.* One of the finest early houses in Morristown was built in 1772-74 by Colonel Jacob Ford, Jr., who produced gunpowder for American troops during the Revolutionary War. His widow rented the house to the army for General and Mrs. Washington when the Continental Army spent the winter of 1779-1780 here.

Fort Nonsense. *Ann St.* Its name came long after residents had forgotten the real reason for earthworks constructed here in 1777. Overlook commemorates fortifications which were built at Washington's order to defend military supplies stored in the village.

Jockey Hollow. *10 Washington Pl, Morristown (07960). 5 miles SW of Morristown. Phone 973/539-2085.* The site of the Continental Army's winter quarters in 1779-80 and the 1781 mutiny of the Pennsylvania Line. Signs indicate locations of various brigades. There are typical log huts and an officer's hut, among other landmarks. Demonstrations of military and colonial farm life (summer). Visitor center has exhibits and audiovisual programs.

Wick House. *30 Washington St, Morristown (07960). Jockey Hollow.* Farmer Henry Wick lived here with his wife and daughter. Used as quarters by Major General Arthur St. Clair in 1779-1780. Restored with period furnishings.

Mount Holly (D-2)

See also Burlington

Settled 1676
Population 10,728
Elevation 52 ft
Area Code 609
Zip 08060

The mountain that gives this old Quaker town its name is only 183 feet high. For two months in 1779, Mount Holly was the capital of the state; today, it is the seat of Burlington County.

What to See and Do

John Woolman Memorial. *99 Branch St, Mount Holly (08060). Phone 609/267-3226.* (1783) John Woolman, the noted Quaker abolitionist whose Journal is still appreciated today, owned the property on which this small, three-story red brick house was built; garden. Picnicking. (Wed-Fri; also by appointment) **DONATION**

Mansion at Smithville. *801 Smithville Rd, Mount Holly (08060). Phone 609/265-5068.* (1840) Victorian mansion and village of inventor/entrepreneur Hezekiah B. Smith; home of the "Star" hi-wheel bicycle. Guided tours (May-Oct, Wed and Sun). Victorian Christmas tours (Dec; fee). **$$**

Mount Holly Library. *307 High St, Mount Holly (08060). Phone 609/267-7111.* Chartered in 1765 by King George III, the library is currently housed in Georgian mansion built in 1830. Historic Lyceum contains original crystal chandeliers, blue marble fireplaces, boxwood gardens; archives date to original 1765 collection. (July-Aug: Tues-Thurs; rest of year: Mon-Sat, limited hours) **FREE**

Limited-Service Hotel

★ QUALITY INN. *21 Wrightstown/Cookstown Rd, Cookstown (08511). Phone 609/723-6500; fax 609/723-7895. www.qualityinn.com.* 100 rooms, 2 story. Complimentary full breakfast. Check-in 3 pm, check-out 11 am. High-speed Internet access. Outdoor pool. **$**

Specialty Lodging

The following lodging establishment is approved by Mobil Travel Guide, but due to its unique and individualized nature has not been given a traditional Mobil Star rating. Included in this listing you may find bed-and-breakfasts, limited-service inns, guest ranches, and other unique hotel properties.

ISSAC HILLARD HOUSE B&B. *31 Hanover St, Pemberton (08068). Phone 609/894-0756; toll-free 800/371-0756; fax 609/894-7899.* 4 rooms, 2 story. Complimentary full breakfast. Check-in 3 pm, check-out 11 am. Pool. Victorian house built in mid-18th century. **$**

Restaurants

★★★ BEAU RIVAGE. *128 Taunton Blvd, Medford (08055). Phone 856/983-1999; fax 856/988-1136.* The well-trained staff provides guests with attentive tableside service that includes boning fish and offering helpful suggestions for wine selection. French menu. Lunch, dinner. Closed Mon; holidays; also 2 weeks before Labor Day. Jacket required. Two dining areas, one upstairs. **$$**

★★ BRADDOCK'S TAVERN. *39 S Main St, Medford Village (08055). Phone 609/654-1604; fax 609/654-8180. www.braddocks.com.* This casual restaurant features traditional American cuisine with European influences. Don't miss the cooking classes held throughout the year. Lunch, dinner, Sun brunch. Closed Jan 1, Dec 25. Bar. Children's menu. **$$$**

★ CHARLEY'S OTHER BROTHER. *1383 Monmouth Rd, Mount Holly (08060). Phone 609/261-1555; fax 609/261-7577. www.charleysotherbrother.com.* Lunch, dinner. Closed Dec 25. Bar. Children's menu. Country setting; Tiffany lamps. **$$**

New Brunswick (C-3)

Settled 1681
Population 48,573
Elevation 42 ft
Area Code 732
Information Middlesex County Regional Chamber of Commerce, One Distribution Way, Suite 101, Monmouth Junction 08852; phone 732/821-1700

New Brunswick, the seat of Middlesex County, is on the south bank of the Raritan River. It is both a college town and a diversified commercial and retail city. Rutgers University, the eighth-oldest institution of higher learning in the country and the only state university with a colonial charter, was founded in 1766 as Queens College, and opened in 1771 with a faculty of one—aged 18. Livingston College, Cook College, and Douglass College (for women), all part of the university, are also located here. One of New Brunswick's most important industries is Johnson and Johnson; its company headquarters are located downtown. Joyce Kilmer, the poet, was born in New Brunswick; his house, at 17 Joyce Kilmer Avenue, is open to visitors.

What to See and Do

Buccleuch Mansion. *George St and Easton Ave, New Brunswick (08901). In 78-acre Buccleuch Park. Phone 732/745-5094.* Built in 1739 by Anthony White, son-in-law of Lewis Morris, a colonial governor of New Jersey. Period rooms. (June-Oct, Sun afternoons; closed holidays) Under 10 only with adult. **FREE**

Crossroads Theatre. *7 Livingston Ave, New Brunswick (08901). Phone 732/729-9559.* Professional African-American theater company offering plays, musicals, touring programs, and workshops. (Oct-May, Wed-Sun)

George Street Playhouse. *9 Livingston Ave, New Brunswick (08901). Phone 732/246-7717 (box office, daily except Mon).* Regional theater; six-show season of plays and musicals; touring Outreach program for students. A 379-seat house. Stage II Theater; cafe; cabaret. (Tues-Sun)

Hungarian Heritage Center. *300 Somerset St, New Brunswick (08901). Phone 732/846-5777.* Museum of changing exhibits that focus on Hungarian folk life, fine and folk art; library, archives. (Tues-Sun; closed holidays) **DONATION**

New Jersey Museum of Agriculture. *103 College Farm Rd, New Brunswick (08901). Phone 732/249-2077.* Large collection of farm implements; covers three centuries of farming history. Interactive science and history exhibits. (Tues-Sun) **$$**

Rutgers-The State University of New Jersey. *126 College Ave, New Brunswick (08901). Phone 732/932-1766 (general information). www.rutgers.edu.* (1766) (50,000 students) Multiple campuses include 30 colleges serving students at all levels through post-doctoral studies; main campus on College Ave. On campus are

Geology Museum. *George and Somerset sts, New Brunswick. Phone 732/932-7243.* Displays of New Jersey minerals; dinosaur; mammals, including a mastodon; Egyptian exhibit with mummy. (Mon-Fri; call for weekend/summer hours; closed holidays) **FREE**

Jane Voorhees Zimmerli Art Museum. *George and Hamilton sts, New Brunswick. Phone 732/932-7237.* Paintings from early 16th century through the present; changing exhibits. (Tues-Fri, also Sat and Sun afternoons; closed holidays) **$$**

The Rutgers Gardens. *Ryder's Ln (Rte 1). Phone 732/932-8451.* Features extensive display of American holly. (Daily) **FREE**

Special Event

Middlesex County Fair. *East Brunswick. Cranbury-South River Rd. Phone 732/356-7400. Aug.*

Limited-Service Hotel

★ ★ DOUBLETREE HOTEL. *200 Atrium Dr, Somerset (08873). Phone 732/469-2600; toll-free 800/222-8733; fax 732/469-4617. www.somerset.doubletree.com.* This hotel is located in the business district with easy access to shopping, restaurants, and other local attractions. 361 rooms, 6 story. Check-in 3 pm, check-out noon. High-speed Internet access. Two restaurants, bar. Fitness room. Indoor pool, outdoor pool, whirlpool. Tennis. Business center. **$$**

Full-Service Hotels

★ ★ ★ HILTON EAST BRUNSWICK. *3 Tower Center Blvd, East Brunswick (08816). Phone 732/828-2000; toll-free 800/445-8667; fax 732/828-6958. www.hilton.com.* 405 rooms, 15 story. Check-in 4 pm, check-out noon. Pets accepted, some restrictions; fee. Two restaurants, two bars. Fitness room. Indoor pool, whirlpool. Airport transportation available. Business center. **$$**

★ ★ ★ HYATT REGENCY NEW BRUNSWICK. *2 Albany St, New Brunswick (08901). Phone 732/873-1234; toll-free 800/233-1234; fax 732/873-1382. www.hyatt.com.* This property is located downtown on a 6-acre lot, midway between New York and Philadelphia. The central location offers easy access to shopping, restaurants and nearby attractions. 258 rooms, 6 story. Check-in 3 pm, check-out noon. High-speed Internet access. Two restaurants, bar. Fitness room. Indoor pool, whirlpool. Tennis. Business center. **$$**

★ ★ ★ MARRIOTT SOMERSET. *110 Davidson Ave, Somerset (08873). Phone 908/560-0500; fax 908/560-3669. www.marriott.com.* 442 rooms, 10 story. Check-in 3 pm, check-out 11 am. High-speed Internet access. Restaurant, bar. Fitness room. Indoor, outdoor pool, whirlpool. Tennis. Business center. **$**

Restaurants

★ ★ 2 ALBANY. *2 Albany St, New Brunswick (08901). Phone 732/867-2300; toll-free 800/233-1234; fax 732/867-1382. www.hyatt.com.* American menu. Breakfast, lunch, dinner. Children's menu. Casual attire. **$$**

★ ★ ANTONIA'S. *40 Livingston Ave, New Brunswick (08901). Phone 732/828-7080; fax 732/828-7090.* Italian menu. Lunch, dinner. Closed Sat, Sun; also holidays. Bar. Children's menu. Casual attire. Patriotic décor; turn-of-the-century pictures. **$$**

★ ★ DELTA'S. *19 Dennis St, New Brunswick (08901). Phone 732/249-1551; fax 732/249-7922. www.deltasrestaurant.com.* Southern menu. Lunch, dinner. Closed Jan 1, July 4, Dec 25. Bar. **$$**

★ ★ ★ THE FROG AND THE PEACH. *29 Dennis St, New Brunswick (08901). Phone 732/846-3216; fax 732/846-4820. www.frogandpeach.com.* Housed in a converted factory, this New American landmark has been in business since 1983. American menu. Lunch, dinner. Closed holidays. Bar. Children's menu. Casual attire. Reservations recommended. Outdoor seating. Factory motif; painted brick walls, exposed duct work. **$$$**

★ ★ ★ LA FONTANA. *120 Albany St, New Brunswick (08901). Phone 732/249-7500; fax 732/214-1811. www.lafontanaristorante.com.* Executive chef Oscar Romero and partner Jose Akena offer a traditional BYOB Italian experience. Italian menu. Lunch, dinner. Closed Sun. Bar. Children's menu. Casual attire. Valet parking. **$$$**

★ ★ MAKEDA ETHIOPIAN RESTAURANT. *338 George St, New Brunswick (08901). Phone 732/545-5115; fax 732/545-8740. www.makedas.com.* Ethiopian menu. Lunch, dinner. Closed holidays. Bar. Casual attire. **$$**

★ MARITA'S CANTINA. *1 Penn Plz, New Brunswick (08901). Phone 732/247-3840; fax 732/247-7852.* Mexican, Southwestern menu. Lunch, dinner. Closed Easter, Thanksgiving, Dec 25. Bar. Children's menu. Casual attire. Outdoor seating. **$$**

★ ★ THE OLD BAY. *61-63 Church St, New Brunswick (08901). Phone 732/246-3111; fax 732/246-2049. www.oldbay.com.* French Creole menu.

Lunch, dinner. Closed Sun; holidays. Bar. Outdoor seating. **$$**

★ RUSTY NAIL. *Rte 130 S, North Brunswick (08902). Phone 732/821-4141; fax 732/821-7856.* American menu. Lunch, dinner. Bar. Children's menu. **$$**

★ ★ ★ STAGE LEFT: AN AMERICAN CAFE. *5 Livingston Ave, New Brunswick (08901). Phone 732/828-4444; fax 732/828-6228. www.stageleft.com.* American menu. Lunch, dinner. Closed Mon; also Jan 1, Memorial Day, Dec 25. Bar. Valet parking. Outdoor seating. **$$$**

★ ★ SZECHWAN GOURMET. *3 Livingston Ave, New Brunswick (08901). Phone 732/846-7878; fax 732/846-3779.* Chinese menu. Lunch, dinner. Closed Thanksgiving. Casual attire. **$$**

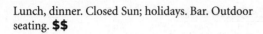

★ ★ TERESA'S. *48 Easton Ave, New Brunswick (08901). Phone 732/545-3737; fax 732/545-9405.* Italian menu. Lunch, dinner. Closed Easter, Thanksgiving, Dec 25. Bar. Children's menu. Outdoor seating. **$$**

Newark (B-4)

See also Caldwell, Elizabeth, Jersey City, Millburn, Montclair

Settled 1666
Population 273,546
Elevation 146 ft
Area Code 973
Web site www.state.nj.us/travel

Once a strict Puritan settlement, Newark has grown to become the largest city in the state and one of the country's leading manufacturing cities. Major insurance firms and banks have large offices in Newark, dominating the city's financial life. Newark was the birthplace of Stephen Crane (1871-1900), author of *The Red Badge of Courage*, and Mary Mapes Dodge (1838-1905), author of the children's book *Hans Brinker, or the Silver Skates*. Newark is also an educational center with Newark College of Rutgers University, College of Medicine and Dentistry of New Jersey, New Jersey Institute of Technology, Seton Hall Law School, and Essex County College.

Public Transportation

Trains, buses (NJ Transit), phone 973/491-9400.

Airport For additional accommodations, see NEWARK INTERNATIONAL AIRPORT AREA, which follows NEWARK.

What to See and Do

Minor Basilica of the Sacred Heart. *89 Ridge St, Newark (07104). At Clifton and 6th aves.* French Gothic in design, it resembles the cathedral at Rheims. Hand-carved reredos. (Daily) **DONATION**

New Jersey Historical Society. *52 Park Pl, Newark (07102). Phone 973/596-8500. www.jerseyhistory.org.* Museum with collections of paintings, prints, furniture, decorative arts; period room; special exhibitions. Reference and research library of state and local history; manuscripts, documents, maps. (Tues-Sat 10 am-5 pm) **FREE**

New Jersey Performing Arts Center. *1 Center St, Newark (07102). Phone toll-free 888/466-5722. www.njpac.org.* Home of the New Jersey Symphony Orchestra and host to many other performances.

The Newark Museum. *49 Washington St, Newark (07102). Phone 973/596-6550. www.newarkmuseum.org.* Museum of art and science, with changing exhibitions. American paintings and sculpture; American and European decorative arts; classical art; the arts of Asia, the Americas, and the Pacific; numismatics and the natural sciences. Also here are the Junior Museum, Mini Zoo, Dreyfuss Planetarium, Garden, with its 1784 schoolhouse, and the Newark Fire Museum. Special programs, lectures, concerts; cafe (lunch). (Wed-Sun noon-5 pm)

Old Plume House. *407 Broad St, Newark (07104). Phone 973/483-8202.* Now the rectory of the adjoining House of Prayer Episcopal Church, it is thought to have been standing as early as 1710, which would make it the oldest building in Newark.

Symphony Hall. *1030 Broad St, Newark (07102). Phone 973/643-4550.* (1925) A 2,811-seat auditorium; home of New Jersey State Opera and the New Jersey Symphony Orchestra; also here is the famous Terrace Ballroom.

The Wars of America. *Military Park, bounded by Broad St, Park Pl, Rector St, Raymond Blvd.* Sculptured bronze group by Gutzon Borglum features 42 human figures representing soldiers in the major conflicts in US history. Other works by Borglum are

Bridge Memorial. *N of Washington Park (Broad St, Washington Pl, and Washington St).* This sculpture of a Native American and a Puritan stands on the site of a colonial marketplace.

Statue of Abraham Lincoln. *Springfield Ave and Market St, Newark. Essex County Courthouse.*

Full-Service Hotel

★★★ HILTON NEWARK GATEWAY. *One Gateway Center - Raymond Blvd, Newark (07102). Phone 973/622-5000; toll-free 800/932-3322; fax 973/824-2188. www.hilton.com.* This hotel is found 3 miles from Newark Airport and in the heart of the business district, making it convenient for all travelers. 263 rooms, 8 story. Check-in 3 pm, check-out noon. Restaurant, bar. Fitness room. Outdoor pool. Airport transportation available. Business center. **$**

Newark International Airport Area (B-4)

See also Caldwell, Elizabeth, Jersey City, Millburn, Montclair, Newark

Airport Information

Airport Newark Liberty International Airport.

Information Phone 201/961-6000

Lost and Found Phone 201/961-6230

Airlines Air Canada, Air Europa, Air France, Air India, Air Jamaica, Air Tran Airways, Alaska Airlines, Alitalia, Allegro, America West, American Airlines, American Eagle ATA, British Airways, Chautauqua, Comair, Continental Airlines, Continental Express, Czech Airlines, Delta Air Lines, Delta Express, EL AL, Ethiopian Airlines, EVA Airways, Hooters Air, Jetsgo, LOT Polish Airlines, Lufthansa, Malaysia, Mexicana, Midwest, Northwest Airlines, Qantas, SAS (Scandinavian Airlines), Singapore Airlines, Song, Southeast Airlines, SWISS, Tap Air Portugal, United Airlines, United Express, USA 3000 Airlines, US Airways, US Airways Express, Virgin Atlantic

Full-Service Hotel

★★★ HILTON NEWARK AIRPORT. *1170 Spring St, Elizabeth (07201). Phone 908/351-3900; toll-free 800/445-8667; fax 908/351-9556. www.newarkairport.hilton.com.* 374 rooms, 12 story. Check-in 3 pm, check-out noon. High-speed Internet access. Restaurant, bar. Fitness room. Indoor pool, whirlpool. Airport transportation available. Business center. **$$**

★★★ MARRIOTT NEWARK LIBERTY INTERNATIONAL AIRPORT. *Newark International Airport, Newark (07114). Phone 973/623-0006; toll-free 800/882-9290; fax 973/623-1419. www.marriott.com.* 591 rooms, 10 story. Check-in 4 pm, check-out noon. High-speed Internet access. Two restaurants, bar. Fitness room. Indoor pool, outdoor pool, whirlpool. Airport transportation available. Business center. **$$**

Ocean City (E-3)

See also Atlantic City

Population 15,378
Elevation 4 ft
Area Code 609
Zip 08226
Information Public Relations Department, City of Ocean City, 9th and Asbury Ave; phone 609/525-9300

Families from all over the country come to this popular resort year after year, as do conventions and religious conferences. In accordance with its founder's instructions, liquor cannot be sold here. Ocean City is an island that lies between the Atlantic Ocean and Great Egg Harbor. It has 8 miles of beaches, more than 2 miles of boardwalk, an enclosed entertainment auditorium on the boardwalk, and excellent swimming, fishing, boating, golf, and tennis.

Ironbound Newark

Newark, once moribund, is in renaissance, and the city offers a combination of fascinating history, modern facilities, and some of the finest Spanish-Portugese dining anywhere. This walk first covers the historic Ironbound section, named for the surrounding railroads, the settling site for immigrant groups since the 1830s, now home to about 40 ethnic groups. It continues into the resurgent Four Corners/Military Park section.

Start at Pennsylvania Station, built in 1933 and beautifully decorated with Art Deco wall reliefs and ceiling sculptures. Walk east on Market Street, passing diminutive Mother Cabrini Park, site of a bust of Jose Marti, liberator of Cuba. Turn right onto Union Street. In one block, at Ferry Street, Our Lady of Mount Carmel Roman Catholic Church stands opposite at McWhorter Street. Originally opened in 1848, this building is now home to the Ironbound Educational and Cultural Center. Turn left onto Ferry Street. This is the commercial heart of the Ironbound, and is filled with shops and restaurants. Among the eateries of note are Fornos of Spain (47 Ferry St) Iberia Peninsula Restaurant (63-69 Ferry St), Iberia Restaurant (82-89 Ferry St), and Brasilia Restaurant (132 Ferry St).

Turn right onto Prospect Street. In 1/2-bock at Number 76 is the Gothic Revival-style Christ Episcopal Church, completed in 1850. Destroyed by vandalism and fire, it was restored in 1978, and now serves as the Chancery Professional Center. At the corner of Lafayette Street stands St. Joseph's Roman Catholic Church, circa 1858, now called Immaculate Heart of Mary. In the basement are hidden catacombs that are replicas of those found in Rome, complete with crypts featuring wax likenesses of Spanish saints. Turn left on Lafayette and walk six blocks to Van Duren. Turn right two blocks to Independence Park. Covering 12 1/2 acres, this was one of the city's first neighborhood parks (circa 1896). Turn left on New York Avenue, go one block, and turn right on Pulaski Street. Pass East Side High School, and come to St. Casimir's Roman Catholic Church, built in 1919 in the Italian Renaissance style. Continue to Chestnut Street and turn right. Five blocks down the road stand the remains of the Murphy Varnish Company, once comprising six major structures; note the carving of a Roman chariot carrying a can of Murphy Varnish on the west side of the building.

Follow Chestnut under the railroad and across McCarter Highway to Broad Street. Turn right and walk through the business district to the Prudential Building at the heart of the Four Corners Historic District. Among the many historic buildings are the National Newark Building, (744 Broad St), a 34-story neoclassical structure completed in 1930; and 1180 Raymond Boulevard, another Depression-era skyscraper. In two more blocks, Military Park appears. Walk on the left side of the park to the New Jersey Historical Society (52 Park Pl), which has an on-site museum and is next door to the historic Robert Treat Hotel. At the end of the park on Center Street stands the architecturally stunning New Jersey Performing Arts Center. Opened in 1997, it has become a world-renowned performance space. Return on Center Street towards Military Park, turn left on Central Street, and go two blocks to the Newark Museum (49 Washington St), site of the largest collection of Tibetan art outside Tibet, the Dreyfus Planetarium, and the historic 1885 Ballantine House.

What to See and Do

Historic House. *1139 Wesley Ave, Ocean City (08226). Phone 609/399-1801.* Furnishings and fashions circa 1920-1930. Tours. (Apr-Dec, Mon-Sat) **DONATION**

Ocean City Historical Museum. *1735 Simpson Ave, Ocean City (08226). At 17th St. Phone 609/399-1801.* Victorian furnishings and fashions; doll exhibit; local shipwreck; historical tours; research library; gift shop. (Mon-Sat) **DONATION**

Special Events

Boardwalk Art Show. *Ocean City Arts Center, 1735 Simpson Ave, Ocean City (08226).* International and regional artists. Aug.

Concerts. *Hwys 152 and 40, Ocean City. Music Pier. Phone 732/316-1095.* Pops orchestra and dance band. Mon-Wed, Sun. Late June-Sept.

Flower Show. *Ocean City. Music Pier.* June.

Hermit Crab Race, Miss Crustacean Contest. *Ocean City. 12th St Beach. Phone 609/525-9300; toll-free 800/232-2465.* Crab beauty pageant, races. Early Aug.

Night in Venice. *Ocean City.* Decorated boat parade. Mid-July.

Limited-Service Hotels

★ ★ BEACH CLUB HOTEL. *1280 Boardwalk, Ocean City (08226). Phone 609/399-8555. www.ochotels.com.* 82 rooms, 3 story. Closed Dec-Apr. Check-out 11 am. Restaurant. Pool, children's pool. Beach. **$$**

★ DAYS INN. *7th St and Boardwalk, Ocean City (08226). Phone 609/398-2200; fax 609/391-2050. www.daysinn.com.* 80 rooms, 4 story. Closed Nov-Mar. Check-in 3 pm, check-out 11 am. Outdoor pool. **$$**

Full-Service Resort

★ ★ PORT-O-CALL HOTEL. *1510 Boardwalk, Ocean City (08226). Phone 609/399-8812; toll-free 800/334-4546; fax 609/399-0387. www.portocallhotel.com.* 99 rooms, 9 story. Check-out 11 am. Restaurant. Children's activity center. Fitness room. Outdoor pool. Airport transportation available. **$**

Specialty Lodging

The following lodging establishment is approved by Mobil Travel Guide, but due to its unique and individualized nature has not been given a traditional Mobil Star rating. Included in this listing you may find bed-and-breakfasts, limited-service inns, guest ranches, and other unique hotel properties.

SERENDIPITY BED & BREAKFAST. *712 E 9th St, Ocean City (08226). Phone 609/399-1554; toll-free 800/842-8544; fax 609/399-1527. www.serendipitynj.com.* 6 rooms, 3 story. Children over 10 years only. Complimentary full breakfast. Check-in 2 pm, check-out 11 am. Renovated inn built in 1912. Ocean City Boardwalk 1/2 block. **$**

Paramus (B-4)

See also Hillsdale, Ho-Ho-Kus

Settled 1660
Population 25,737
Elevation 58 ft
Area Code 201
Zip 07652
Information Chamber of Commerce, 58 E Midland Ave, PO Box 325; phone 201/261-3344
Web site www.paramuschamber.com

This old Dutch farm community was an important hub of transportation as long ago as the Revolutionary War; western Paramus became headquarters for the Continental Army as a result. Paramus has grown as a residential community from 4,000 inhabitants in 1946 to its present size.

What to See and Do

New Jersey Children's Museum. *599 Valley Health Plz, Paramus (07652). Phone 201/262-5151. www.njcm.com.* Interactive displays in 30 rooms. Including displays on aviation, firefighting, TV studio, hospital. Gift shop. (Daily; closed holidays) **$$$**

Schoolhouse Museum. *650 E Glen Ave, Ridgewood (07450). At Rte 17. Phone 201/652-4584.* Exhibits in 1873 schoolhouse depict life from colonial times through 19th century, with emphasis on local history. Native American relics; early maps; Dutch genealogies; farm implements; doll and toy displays; clothing. Tours (by appointment). (May-late Oct, Sun afternoons; closed holidays) **FREE**

Van Saun County Park. *216 Forest Ave, Paramus (07652). 1 1/2 miles N of Rte 4. Phone 201/262-2627.* Fishing lake; bike trail, tennis (fee), horseshoes, shuffleboard, ice skating, sledding, picnicking, concession, playgrounds, ball fields (permit). Zoo; train, pony rides (fees). Garden surrounding historic Washington Spring; farmyard. Park (daily). **FREE**

Limited-Service Hotel

★ ★ **RADISSON INN PARAMUS.** *601 From Rd, Paramus (07652). Phone 201/262-6900; toll-free 800/333-3333; fax 201/262-4955. www.radisson.com.* 120 rooms, 2 story. Check-in 3 pm, check-out noon. High-speed Internet access. Restaurant, bar. **$$**

Park Ridge

Restaurant

★ ★ **VALENTINO'S.** *103 Spring Valley Rd, Park Ridge (07645). Phone 201/391-2230; fax 201/391-3646.* Italian menu. Lunch, dinner. Closed Sun; holidays. Bar. Casual attire. **$$**

Parsippany

Population 50,649
Elevation 282 ft
Area Code 973
Zip 07054

Limited-Service Hotel

★ **HAMPTON INN.** *3535 Rte 46 E, Parsippany (07054). Phone 973/263-0095; fax 973/263-6133. www.hamptoninn.com.* 109 rooms, 4 story. Complimentary continental breakfast. Check-in 3 pm, check-out noon. High-speed Internet access. Fitness room. Business center. **$**

Full-Service Hotel

★ ★ ★ **HILTON PARSIPPANY.** *1 Hilton Ct, Parsippany (07054). Phone 973/267-7373; toll-free 877/671-5744; fax 973/984-6853. www.hilton.com.* The Hilton Parsippany is located 25 minutes from the Newark International Airport, 3 miles from New Jersey, and 27 miles from New York. It offers accommodations for business, leisure, and group travelers. 509 rooms, 6 story. Pets accepted, some restrictions; fee. Check-in 3 pm, check-out noon. High-speed Internet access. Two restaurants, two bars. Fitness room. Indoor pool, outdoor pool, whirlpool. Tennis. Airport transportation available. Business center. **$$**

Paterson (B-4)

See also Clifton, Hackensack, Newfoundland, Wayne

Settled 1711
Population 149,222
Elevation 100 ft
Area Code 973
Information Great Falls Visitor Center, 65 McBride Ave, across from the Great Falls, 07501-1715; phone 973/279-9587. Special Events Office, 72 McBride Ave, 07501; phone 973/523-9201

Named after Governor William Paterson, this city owes its present and historic eminence as an industrial city to Alexander Hamilton. He was the first man to realize the possibility of harnessing the Great Falls of the Passaic River for industrial purposes. As secretary of the Treasury, he helped form the Society for Establishing Useful Manufactures in 1791 and, a year later, was instrumental in choosing Paterson as the site of its initial ventures. Paterson was the country's major silk-producing town in the late 1800s. Today, it is a diversified industrial center. The area surrounding the Great Falls is now being restored and preserved as a historic district. Paterson is the seat of Passaic County.

Paterson Fun Fact

- The first radio station and broadcast was in Paterson.

What to See and Do

American Labor Museum-Botto House National Landmark. *83 Norwood St, Haledon (07508). Phone 973/595-7953.* The history of the working class is presented through restored period rooms, changing exhibits, and ethnic gardens. Tours, seminars, and workshops are offered. (Wed-Sat afternoons; closed holidays) **$**

Garret Mountain Reservation. *Rifle Camp Rd and Mountain Ave, Paterson (07522). Phone 973/881-4994.* A 575-acre woodland park on a 502-foot-high plateau. Fishing pond (stocked with trout), boat dock, rowboats, paddleboats; trails, stables, picnic groves. **FREE**

★ **Great Falls Historic District Cultural Center.** *65 McBride, Paterson (07501). Phone 973/279-9587. www.patersongreatfalls.org.* Includes 77-foot-high falls, park and picnic area, renovated raceway system, restored 19th-century buildings. **DONATION** Also here is

> **Paterson Museum.** *Thomas Rogers Building, 2 Market St, Paterson (07501). Phone 973/881-3874.* Contains shell of original 14-foot submarine invented by John P. Holland in 1878; also his second submarine (31 feet), built in 1881. Paterson-Colt gun collection (1836-1840); mineral display; exhibits on Paterson history, including the silk and locomotive industries; two locomotives; Curtiss-Wright airplane engines; changing art exhibits. (Tues-Sun; closed holidays) **DONATION**

Lambert Castle. *3 Valley Rd, Paterson (07503). Phone 973/247-0085. www.lambertcastle.com.* Built by an immigrant who rose to wealth as a silk manufacturer. The 1893 castle of brownstone and granite houses a local-history museum; restored period rooms; art-history gallery; changing exhibits; library (Wed, Fri, Sun; closed holidays). **$$**

Rifle Camp Park. *Rifle Camp Rd, West Paterson (07424). Phone 973/881-4832.* This 158-acre park is 584 feet above sea level. Includes nature and geology trails, nature center with astronomical observatory; walking paths, fitness course. Picnic areas. **FREE**

Plainfield (B-3)

Settled 1685
Population 47,829
Elevation 118 ft
Area Code 908
Information Central Jersey Chamber of Commerce, 120 W 7th St, #217, 07060; phone 908/754-7250
Web site www.erols.com/cjcc

Plainfield, directly south of the Watchung Mountains, is actually the center of a group of associated towns: Scotch Plains (see), Watchung, North and South Plainfield, Fanwood, Green Brook, Warren Township, Dunellen, Middlesex, and Piscataway, all of which are mainly residential. Plainfield is also home to a number of industries.

What to See and Do

Drake House Museum. *602 W Front St, Plainfield (07060). Phone 908/755-5831.* (1746) General Washington's headquarters in 1777; now the Historical Society of Plainfield headquarters. Period furnishings; diorama depicts Battle of Shorthills. (Sun afternoons) **$$**

Littell-Lord Farmhouse Museum. *31 Horseshoe Rd, Berkeley Heights (07922).* Museum includes a pre-Revolutionary farmstead, 1878 Victorian House, spring house, 1914 pump house, summer kitchen, spring house, corn crib. (Third Sun of each month or by appointment) **DONATION**

Limited-Service Hotel

★★ **HOLIDAY INN.** *4701 Stelton Rd, South Plainfield (07080). Phone 908/753-5500; toll-free 877/214-6161; fax 908/753-5500. www.holiday-inn.com.* 174 rooms, 4 story. Pets accepted. Check-in 3 pm, check-out noon. High-speed Internet access. Restaurant, bar. Fitness room. Indoor pool, whirlpool. **$$**

Point Pleasant Beach (D-4)

Restaurants

★ **FAMILY TREE TAVERN.** *2420 Rte 35, Manasquan (08736). Phone 732/528-5950.* American menu. Lunch, dinner. Bar. Children's menu. **$$**

★★ **HEAT WAVE CAFE.** *530 Main St, Bay Head (08742). Phone 732/714-8881; fax 732/714-7055. www.heatwavecafe.com.* Dinner. Closed Mon; Jan 1, Thanksgiving, Dec 25. Outdoor seating. **$$$**

★★ **MARLINS CAFE.** *1901 Ocean Ave, Point Pleasant Beach (08742). Phone 732/714-8035; fax 732/714-7777.* American menu. Lunch, dinner. Bar. Children's menu. **$$**

★★ **TESAURO'S.** *401 Broadway, Point Pleasant Beach (08742). Phone 732/892-2090; fax 732/892-5694. www.tesaurosrestaurant.com.* Italian, American menu. Dinner. Closed Mon; also Thanksgiving, Dec 25. Bar. Valet parking. **$$**

Princeton (C-3)

See also Trenton

Settled 1685
Population 14,203
Elevation 215 ft
Area Code 609
Information Chamber of Commerce, 216 Rockingham Row, 08540; phone 609/520-1776
Web site www.princetonchamber.org

In 1776, the first State Legislature of New Jersey met in Princeton University's Nassau Hall. Washington and his troops surprised and defeated a superior British Army in the 1777 Battle of Princeton. From June to November 1783, Princeton was the new nation's capital. Around the same time, Washington was staying at Rockingham in nearby Rocky Hill, where he wrote and delivered his famous "Farewell Orders to the Armies."

Princeton's life is greatly influenced by the university, which opened here in 1756; at that time it was known as the College of New Jersey. In 1896, on the 150th anniversary of its charter, the institution became Princeton University. Woodrow Wilson, the first president of the university who was not a clergyman, held the office from 1902-1910. Princeton is also the home of the Institute for Advanced Study, where Albert Einstein spent the last years of his life.

What to See and Do

Bainbridge House. *158 Nassau St, Princeton (08542). Phone 609/921-6748.* (Circa 1766) Birthplace of commander of the USS *Constitution* during War of 1812. Changing exhibits on Princeton history; research library (Tues, Sat; fee), photo archives. Museum shops. Also offers walking tours of historic district (Sun; fee). **FREE**

Kuser Farm Mansion and Park. *Newkirk Ave. 10 miles SE via Rte 206, I-295 to Olden Ave in Hamilton, then 1/2 mile W to Newkirk Ave. Phone 609/890-3630.* Farm and 1890s summer mansion of Fred Kuser; more than 20 rooms open; many original furnishings. Grounds consist of 22 acres with original buildings including coachman's house, chicken house; tennis pavilion; clay tennis court. Park with picnic areas; quoit courts, lawn bowling, walking trails; formal garden, gazebo. Tours (May-Nov: Thurs-Sun; Feb-Apr: Sat and Sun; limited hours, call for schedule and holiday closings); self-guided tour maps of grounds. Special programs, lectures, and video evenings throughout the year. **FREE**

Morven. *55 Stockton St, Princeton (08540). Phone 609/683-4495 (schedule).* (Circa 1750) House of Richard Stockton, signer of the Declaration of Independence. Ransacked during Revolutionary War; was frequently visited by General Washington and other colonial leaders. (Apr-Oct, Wed-Fri, Sun).

Princeton Battle Monument. *On Monument Dr, off Stockton St, near Morven.* The work of Frederick W. MacMonnies, this 50-foot block of Indiana limestone commemorates the famous 1777 battle when George Washington's troops defeated the British.

Princeton Cemetery. *Witherspoon and Wiggens sts, Princeton (08542). Phone 609/924-1369.* Buried in the Presidents' Plot are 11 university presidents, including Aaron Burr, Sr., Jonathan Edwards, and John Witherspoon. Monument to Grover Cleveland and grave of Paul Tulane, in whose honor Tulane University was named.

Princeton University. *1 Nassau Hall, Princeton (08544). Phone 609/258-3603. www.princeton.edu.* (1746) (4,500 undergraduate students, 1,650 graduate students) An Ivy League college that has been coeducational since 1969. A campus guide service shows the visitor points of interest on the main campus. (Daily, closed holidays) On campus are

McCarter Theatre. *91 University Place, Princeton (08540).* Professional repertory company performs classical and modern drama; concerts; ballet; other special programs year-round.

Nassau Hall. *Phone 609/258-3000.* (1756) Provided all college facilities, classrooms, dormitories, library, and prayer hall for about 50 years. New Jersey's first legislature met here in 1776, and the Continental Congress met here in 1783, when Princeton was the capital. During the Revolution, it served as a barracks and hospital for Continental and British troops.

The Putnam Sculptures. One of the largest modern outdoor sculpture showcases in the country, with 19 sculptures on display throughout the campus, including pieces by Picasso, Moore, Noguchi, Calder, and Lipchitz.

Woodrow Wilson School of Public and International Affairs. *Phone 609/258-4831.* Designed by Minoru Yamasaki; reflecting pool and "Fountain of Freedom" by James Fitzgerald.

Rockingham State Historic Site. *108 County Rd, Sight 18, Rocky Hill (08540). 4 miles N on Rte 206, then 2 miles E on County 518. Phone 609/921-8835.* On this 5-acre site are three buildings: a kitchen, a wash house, and the main building. This was Washington's headquarters Aug 23-Nov 10, 1783, where he wrote his "Farewell Orders to the Armies"; ten rooms with period furnishings. (Wed-Sat, also Sun afternoons; closed holidays) **FREE**

Limited-Service Hotels

★ ★ NASSAU INN. *10 Palmer Sq, Princeton (08542). Phone 609/921-7500; toll-free 800/862-7728; fax 609/921-9385. www.nassauinn.com.* Visitors to Princeton University are lucky to have this inn in such a convenient downtown location. Red armchairs, oriental rugs and beamed ceilings create a rustic country charm, and the nightly, fresh-baked chocolate chip cookies are a welcome treat. 216 rooms, 5 story. Pets accepted; fee. Check-out noon. Restaurant, bar. Fitness room. Business center. **$$**

★ ★ RADISSON HOTEL PRINCETON. *4355 Rte 1 S, Princeton (08540). Phone 609/452-2400; fax 609/452-2494. www.radisson.com.* 242 rooms, 6 story. Check-out noon. Restaurant, bar. Fitness room. Indoor pool. **$**

Full-Service Hotels

★ ★ ★ DORAL FORRESTAL. *100 College Rd E, Princeton (08540). Phone 609/452-7800; toll-free 800/222-1131; fax 609/452-7883. www.forrestal.com.* Located on 25 wooded acres, this hotel is decorated with turn-of-the-century arts and crafts. 290 rooms, 4 story. Check-out noon. Restaurant, bar. Fitness room. Indoor pool, whirlpool. Tennis. Airport transportation available. Business center. **$**

★ ★ ★ HYATT REGENCY PRINCETON. *102 Carnegie Center, Princeton (08540). Phone 609/987-1234; fax 609/987-2584. www.hyatt.com.* This hotel is nestled on 16 acres of landscaped property just 1 mile from the city's business center and near the Princeton Junction Train Station. Guests receive a complimentary shuttle to anywhere within a 5-mile radius of the property. 348 rooms, 4 story. Check-out noon. Restaurant, bar. Fitness room. Indoor, outdoor pool, whirlpool. Tennis. Airport transportation available. Business center. **$**

Specialty Lodging

The following lodging establishment is approved by Mobil Travel Guide, but due to its unique and individualized nature has not been given a traditional Mobil Star rating. Included in this listing you may find bed-and-breakfasts, limited-service inns, guest ranches, and other unique hotel properties.

PEACOCK INN. *20 Bayard Ln, Princeton (08540). Phone 609/924-1707; fax 609/924-2229. www.peacockinn.com.* 17 rooms, 3 story. Pets accepted. Complimentary full breakfast. Check-in 2 pm, check-out 11 am. Restaurant. Historic late Georgian Colonial house, built in 1775 and relocated from Nassau St to its present site. Two blocks from Princeton University campus. **$$**

Restaurants

★ ★ ALCHEMIST AND BARRISTER. *28 Witherspoon, Princeton (08540). Phone 609/924-5555; fax 609/921-2634. www.alchemistandbarrister.com.* Lunch, dinner, Sun brunch. Closed Jan 1, July 4, Dec 25. Bar. Outdoor seating. **$$$**

★ ANNEX. *128 1/2 Nassau St, Princeton (08542). Phone 609/921-7555; fax 609/921-7556.* American menu. Lunch, dinner. Closed Sun; holidays. Bar. Children's menu. Casual attire. **$$**

★ ★ GOOD TIME CHARLEY'S. *4591 Rte 27, Kingston (08528). Phone 609/924-7400; fax 609/924-7070. www.gtcharleys.com.* Lunch, dinner. Closed Dec 25; also holidays. Bar. Tiffany lamps; posters. **$$**

★★★ **TRE PIANI.** *120 Rockingham Row, Princeton (08540). Phone 609/452-1515.* Italian, Mediterranean menu. Lunch, dinner. Bar. Casual attire. Outdoor seating. **$$$**

Ramsey (A-4)

Population 14,351
Elevation 373 ft
Area Code 201
Zip 7446

What to See and Do

Campgaw Mountain Ski Area. *200 Campgaw Rd, Mahwah (07430). Rte 17 N, exit Rte 202 Suffern, 1.6 miles S on Rte 202, left on Darlington Ave 1 block, stay to right, 1 mile on Campgaw Rd. Phone 201/327-7800.* Two double chairlifts, T-bar, two rope tows; patrol, school, rentals; snowmaking; cafeteria. Eight runs, longest run 600 feet; vertical drop 275 feet. (Early Dec-mid-Mar, daily) Lighted cross-country trails; half-pipe; cross-country and snowboard rentals; night skiing (Mon-Sat); snow tubing. **$$$$**

James A. McFaul Environmental Center. *Crescent Ave, Wyckoff. 3 miles NW off Rte 208. Phone 201/891-5571.* An 81-acre wildlife sanctuary includes museum with natural history displays, lectures, film programs; woodland trail; waterfowl pond; picnic area. Arboretum and perennial gardens. (Daily; closed morning weekends and holidays)

Full-Service Hotel

★★★ **SHERATON CROSSROADS HOTEL.** *One International Blvd, Rte 17 N, Mahwah (07495). Phone 201/529-1660; toll-free 800/325-3535; fax 201/529-4709. www.sheraton.com/crossroads.* This hotel offers rooms with a garden or a fountain view as well as an indoor heated pool, tennis courts, two restaurants, and two lounges. Golfers will enjoy the nearby courses, and all will enjoy shopping and other attractions close to this hotel. 225 rooms, 22 story. Pets accepted, some restrictions. Check-in 3 pm, check-out noon. High-speed Internet access. Two restaurants, two bars. Fitness room. Indoor pool, whirlpool. Tennis. Business center. **$$**

Restaurant

★★★ **CAFE PANACHE.** *130 E Main St, Ramsey (07446). Phone 201/934-0030.* Located near the center of the town, this restaurant serves upscale French cuisine in an elegant atmosphere. French menu. Lunch, dinner. Closed Sun; holidays. Casual attire. **$$$**

Red Bank (C-4)

See also Eatontown, Gateway National Recreation Area (Sandy Hook Unit)

Population 11,844
Elevation 35 ft
Area Code 732
Zip 07701

Red Bank, an historic community on the shores of the Navesink River, includes a central business area with shops, restaurants, brokerage firms, and an antique center.

What to See and Do

Allen House. *400 Sycamore Ave, Shrewsbury (07702). 2 miles S on Rte 35, at junction Sycamore Ave. Phone 732/462-1466.* (Circa 1750) Lower floor restored as tavern of the Revolutionary period; traveler's bedrooms upstairs. (Days same as Holmes House) **$**

Holmes-Hendrickson House. *62 Longstreet Rd, Holmdel (07733). W on Rte 520. Phone 732/462-1466.* (Circa 1750) A 14-room Dutch Colonial farmhouse with period furnishings. (May-Sept, Tues, Thurs, Sat-Sun; closed holidays) **$**

Monmouth Museum. *761 Newman Springs Rd, Lincroft (07738). 5 miles W on Newman Springs Rd; on campus of Brookdale Community College. Phone 732/747-2266.* Changing exhibits of art, science, nature, and cultural history; children's hands-on wing. (Tues-Sun; closed holidays) **$$$**

Limited-Service Hotel

★★ **COURTYARD BY MARRIOTT.** *245 Half Mile Rd, Red Bank (07701). Phone 732/530-5552; fax 732/530-5756. www.courtyard.com.* 146 rooms, 3 story. Check-out noon. Restaurant, bar. Fitness room. Indoor pool, whirlpool. **$$**

Restaurants

★ ★ **2 SENZA RISTORANTE.** *2 Bridge Ave, Building 5, Red Bank (07701). Phone 732/758-0999; fax 732/758-9399. www.2senza.com.* Italian, Mediterranean menu. Lunch, dinner. Closed Mon. Children's menu. Casual attire. Outdoor seating. **$$**

★ ★ **DOWNTOWN CAFE.** *8 W Front St, Red Bank (07701). Phone 732/741-8844. www.dtcafe.com.* American, sushi menu. Dinner, late-night. Bar. Casual attire. **$$**

★ ★ ★ **FROMAGERIE.** *26 Ridge Rd, Rumson (07760). Phone 732/842-8088; fax 732/842-6625. www.fromagerierestaurant.com.* This romantic French restaurant first opened in 1972. Classical French cuisine is paired with an award winning selection of wines, some of which may be sampled during special gourmet wine dinners. French menu. Lunch, dinner. Closed Dec 25. Bar. Jacket required. Valet parking. **$$$**

★ **GAETANO'S.** *10 Wallace St, Red Bank (07701). Phone 732/741-1321. www.gaetanosrebank.com.* Italian menu. Lunch, dinner. Casual attire. Outdoor seating. **$$**

★ ★ **JOE & MAGGIE'S BISTRO.** *591 Broadway, Long Branch (07740). Phone 732/571-8848; fax 732/728-1885.* American menu. Lunch, dinner. Closed Thanksgiving, Dec 25; also day after Labor Day, Super Bowl Sun. Bar. Casual attire. Reservations recommended. **$$**

★ **LITTLE KRAUT.** *115 Oakland St, Red Bank (07701). Phone 732/842-4830.* German menu. Dinner. Closed Mon. Bar. Children's menu. Casual attire. Outdoor seating. **$$**

★ ★ ★ **MOLLY PITCHER INN.** *88 Riverside Ave, Red Bank (07701). Phone 732/747-2500; toll-free 800/221-1372; fax 732/747-2713. www.mollypitcher-oysterpoint.com.* This restaurant is located in a waterfront hotel on the banks of the Navensink river. Breakfast, lunch, dinner, Sun brunch. Bar. Children's menu. Jacket required. **$$**

★ ★ ★ **THE RAVEN & THE PEACH.** *740 River Rd, Fair Haven (07704). Phone 732/747-4666; fax 732/747-3633.* Guests will enjoy dining at this popular, casual restaurant. French menu. Lunch, dinner. Closed Dec 25. Bar. Children's menu. Valet parking. Outdoor seating. **$$$**

★ ★ ★ **SHADOWBROOK.** *Rte 35, Shrewsbury (07702). Phone 732/747-0200; toll-free 800/634-0078; fax 732/747-1830. www.shadowbrook.com.* Established in 1942, this restaurant is set in an authentic Georgian mansion. Catering for weddings is their specialty, with bridal suites, attended restrooms, and beautiful gardens for cocktail parties or receptions. Dinner. Closed Mon; Dec 24. Bar. Children's menu. Jacket required. Valet parking. Fireplace; in Georgian mansion; Victorian antiques. **$$$**

Rutherford

Population 18,110
Elevation 100 ft
Area Code 201

What to See and Do

Fairleigh Dickinson University-Rutherford Campus. *W Passaic and Montross aves, Rutherford. Phone 201/692-7032.* (1942) (2,300 students) On campus is the Kingsland House (1670), in which George Washington stayed in August 1783; and the Castle, an 1888 copy of Chateau d'Amboise in France.

Meadowlands Racetrack. *50 Hwy 120, East Rutherford (07073). Take NJ Transit Bus from Port Authority to the track. Call 800/772-2222 or 201/762-5100 for bus departures. Phone 201/935-8500. www.meadowlands.com.* The suburban leafy Meadowlands complex offers fine thoroughbred racing from September to mid-December and harness racing for the remainder of the year. An evening at the races can always be fun (especially if you win!), but waiting for a bus at sleazy Port Authority is not the most pleasant experience. You may want to consider renting a car for the day. (Wed-Sun) **$**

MetroStars (MLS). *Giants Stadium, 50 Hwy 120, East Rutherfold (07073). Phone 201/583-7000. www.metrostars.com.* Professional soccer team.

New Jersey Devils (NHL). *Continental Airlines Arena, 50 Hwy 120 N, East Rutherford. Phone toll-free 800/653-3845.*

New Jersey Nets (NBA). *Continental Airlines Arena, 50 Hwy 120, East Rutherford. Phone 201/935-8888.*

Limited-Service Hotels

★ ★ COURTYARD BY MARRIOTT MEADOWLANDS. *1 Polito Ave, Lyndhurst (07071). Phone 201/896-6666; toll-free 800/321-2211; fax 201/896-1309. www.marriott.com.* 227 rooms, 6 story. Check-in 3 pm, check-out noon. High-speed Internet access. Restaurant, bar. Fitness room. Indoor pool. **$$**

★ FAIRFIELD INN. *850 Paterson Plank Rd, East Rutherford (07073). Phone 201/507-5222; toll-free 800/228-2800; fax 201/507-0744. www.fairfieldinn.com.* 141 rooms, 5 story. Complimentary continental breakfast. Check-in 3 pm, check-out noon. High-speed Internet access. Fitness room. **$**

★ ★ HOLIDAY INN HARMON MEADOW SPORTPLEX. *300 Plaza Dr, Secaucus (07094). Phone 201/348-2000; toll-free 800/222-2676; fax 201/348-6035. www.holiday-inn.com/secaucusnj.* 161 rooms, 8 story. Check-in 3 pm, check-out noon. Restaurant, bar. Fitness room. **$**

Full-Service Hotel

★ ★ ★ SHERATON MEADOWLANDS HOTEL AND CONFERENCE CENTER. *2 Meadowlands Plz, East Rutherford (07073). Phone 201/896-0500; toll-free 800/325-3535; fax 201/896-9696. www.sheraton.com.* This hotel is only minutes from Manhattan and is perfect for business or leisure travelers. A restaurant, sports pub and lounge are available, as well as many recreational facilities. 443 rooms, 21 story. Pets accepted; fee. Check-in 3 pm, check-out noon. Two restaurants, two bars. Fitness room. Indoor pool, whirlpool. Airport transportation available. Business center. **$$**

Salem (E-1)

Founded circa 1675
Population 5,857
Elevation 19 ft
Area Code 856
Zip 08079
Information Salem County Chamber of Commerce, 91A S Virginia Ave, Carneys Point, 08069; phone 856/299-6699
Web site www.salemnjchamber.com

Salem is said to be the oldest English settlement on the Delaware River. The town and its surrounding area have more than 60 18th-century houses and buildings, as well as many points of historical interest. In the Friends Burying Ground on Broadway is the 600-year-old Salem Oak, under which John Fenwick, the town's founder, signed a treaty with the Lenni-Lenape tribe.

What to See and Do

Alexander Grant House. *79-83 Market St, Salem (08079). Phone 856/935-5004.* (1721) Headquarters of Salem County Historical Society. Twenty rooms with period furniture; Wistarburg glass; Native American relics; dolls; paintings; genealogy library; stone barn. (Tues-Fri afternoons; also open the second Sat afternoon of each month) **$$**

Fort Mott State Park. *454 Fort Mott Rd, Pennsville (08070). Phone 856/935-3218.* A 104-acre park at Finns Point; established in 1837 as a defense of the port of Philadelphia. North of the park is Finns Point National Cemetery, where more than 2,500 Union and Confederate soldiers are buried. Fishing, ferry ride, picnicking, playground; overlook.

Special Event

Cowtown Rodeo. *780 Rte 40, Pilesgrove (08098). 12 miles NE on Rte 45, then 3 miles W on Rte 40, near Woodstown. Phone 609/769-3200. www.cowtownrodeo.com* PRCA sanctioned. Sat evenings, Memorial Day-late Sept. **$$$**

Skylands at Ringwood State Park

Skylands is the official state garden of New Jersey. The walking here is largely on marked dirt paths, with some paved drives and paths. Skylands Manor House is the park's centerpiece. A circa 1922 Tudor-style manor house, it holds, among other items of note, an outstanding collection of antique stained-glass medallions set in leaded windows. Guided house tours are offered one Sunday a month from March through December (phone 973/962-9534). In all, the botanical garden covers 96 acres.

Start at the Visitors Center/Carriage House and pick up a self-guiding tour brochure. Walk first to the right (in the general direction of Parking Lot A), skirting the manor house counter-clockwise. The Winter Garden contains New Jersey's largest Jeffery pine, a century-old upright beech, and an elegant weeping beech. The Japanese umbrella pine is distinctive for its dark green needles. Also on display here are Atlas cedars and an Algerian fir, a tree that produces 7-inch-tall, purple standing cones.

Walk around the house along the lawn to the Terrace Garden. This garden is comprised of five terraces, each with its own particular ambience. The first centers on an octagonal pool with a swan fountain. Its rock garden is filled with a variety of dwarf plants, including a not-so-dwarf-like 20-foot-tall Dwarf Alberta Spruce. Continue past a pair of Sweet Bay Magnolias, especially beautiful during June, to the third level. Here the centerpiece is a rectangular reflecting pool that, in summer, displays water lilies and tropical fish. Surrounding it are a large collection of azaleas and rhododendrons that bloom in many colors. Next comes the Summer Garden, home to annuals and day lilies, followed by the final terrace level, the Peony Garden.

Walk to the left into the Lilac Garden, which peaks in mid-May. Step onto Maple Avenue, the paved lane, and walk back toward the house. On the right, you'll see the Perennial Garden. A constant flow of color is maintained here from March until November. Just beyond that stands the Annual Garden, a frequently changing formal garden centered on a 16th-century Italian marble well. Move from there to the right, turn around and walk along Crab Apple Vista, a 1,600-foot grassy allee (or corridor) of 166 Carmine crab apple trees that erupts into full bloom in early- to mid-May. At the end of the Vista stands a series of sculptures known as the Four Continents Statues and, to the left, a collection of horsechestnut trees.

Turn left at the horsechestnut trees, and another world appears, revealing woodland paths that travel past Swan Ponds and through a bog. Following the interlaced and meandering dirt paths here, you'll see a wetland in which duck families, as well as the occasional frog, can be spotted. The paths also travel through a cactus collection, a wildflower garden, and a heather garden, and end at a colorful and flashy, yet formal, Rhododendron Display Garden. From here, follow East Cottage Road as it winds its way back to the Carriage House.

Restaurant

★★ **J.G. COOK'S RIVERVIEW INN.** *60 Main St, Pennsville (08070). Phone 856/678-3700; fax 856/678-2087. www.riverviewinn.net.* Lunch, dinner. Closed Mon; Jan 1, Dec 25. Bar. Children's menu. Outdoor seating. **$$$**

Scotch Plains

See also Plainfield

Settled 1684
Population 22,732
Elevation 119 ft
Area Code 908
Zip 07076

What to See and Do

Watchung Reservation. *Between Rtes 22 and 78. 1 mile NE. Phone 908/527-4900.* A 2,000-wooded-acre reservation in the Watchung Mountains includes the 25-acre Surprise Lake. Nature and bridle trails, ice skating, picnic areas, playground. Ten-acre nursery and rhododendron display garden. Also here is

> **Trailside Nature and Science Center.** *452 New Providence Rd, Mountainside (07092). Phone 908/789-3670.* Nature exhibits; special programs; planetarium shows (Sun; fee). Museum (late Mar-mid-Nov: daily; rest of year: weekends only; closed some holidays). Visitor Center with live reptile exhibit (daily, afternoons). Gift shop. Grounds (daily). **FREE**

Restaurant

★ ★ ★ **STAGE HOUSE INN.** *366 Park Ave, Scotch Plains (07076). Phone 908/322-4224; fax 908/322-4225.* A local favorite, this establishment offers lightened versions of classic French dishes, beautifully presented and full of flavor. Guests enjoy the simple, refined atmosphere and the casual patio dining. Lunch, dinner. Closed Mon; Dec 25. Bar. Jacket required. Outdoor seating. **$$$**

Seaside Park (D-4)

Population 2,263
Elevation 6 ft
Area Code 732
Zip 08752

What to See and Do

Island Beach State Park. *S on Central Ave. Phone 732/793-0506.* This strip of land (3,002 acres) is across the water, north of Long Beach Island (see), and faces Barnegat Lighthouse. There are two natural areas (Northern Area and Southern Area) and a recreational zone in the center. Excellent swimming and fishing in Atlantic Ocean (seasonal). Nature tours. Picnicking. (Daily)

Limited-Service Hotel

★ ★ **WINDJAMMER MOTOR INN.** *1st and Central aves, Seaside Park (08752). Phone 732/830-2555.* 39 rooms, 3 story. Check-out 11 am. Restaurant, bar. Beach privileges. Pool. **$**

Somers Point (E-3)

Restaurants

★ ★ **CRAB TRAP.** *2 Broadway, Somers Point (08244). Phone 609/927-7377; fax 609/927-5979.* Lunch, dinner. Closed Dec 24-25. Bar. Children's menu. On the bay. **$$$**

★ **GREGORY'S.** *900 Shore Rd, Somers Point (08244). Phone 609/927-6665; fax 609/927-2681. www.gregorysbar.net.* American menu. Lunch, dinner. Bar. Children's menu. **$$**

★ ★ **MAC'S.** *908 Shore Rd, Somers Point (08244). Phone 609/927-4360; fax 609/927-0033.* Italian, American menu. Dinner. Closed Dec 25. Bar. **$$**

Somerville (B-3)

See also Bridgewater, Flemington, New Brunswick

Population 12,423
Elevation 54 ft
Area Code 908
Zip 08876
Information Somerset County Chamber of Commerce, 64 W End Ave, PO Box 833; phone 908/725-1552
Web site www.somersetcountychamber.org

What to See and Do

Duke Gardens. *Rte 206 S, Somerville. About 1 1/4 miles S of Somerville Cir. Phone 908/722-3700.* Features 11 gardens under glass, including colonial, desert, Italian, Asian, English, and tropical (closed Jan 1, Thanksgiving, Dec 25); 45-minute guided tour (Oct-May, daily). No high heels, no cameras. Reservations required; contact Duke Gardens Foundation (Mon-Fri).

Golf House–USGA Museum and Library. *Rte 512, Liberty Corner Rd, Far Hills. Rte 287 to Rte 512. Phone toll-free 800/223-0041.* Georgian colonial mansion originally designed as private residence by John Russel Pope, now houses exhibits tracing the evolution of golf. Equipment and artifacts donated by golf's greatest champions, including Bobby Jones, Byron Nelson, Jack Nicklaus, and Arnold Palmer. Interactive displays. Library with over 13,000 volumes on golf; USGA Research and Test Center. (Daily; closed holidays)

Old Dutch Parsonage State Historic Site. *38 Washington Pl, Somerville (08876). Phone 908/725-1015.* (1751) Moved from its original location, this brick building was the home of the Reverend Jacob Hardenbergh from 1758 to 1781. He founded Queens College, now Rutgers University, while residing in this building. Some furnishings and memorabilia on display. (Wed-Sun; closed holidays; hours may vary)

Wallace House State Historic Site. *38 Washington Pl, Somerville (08876). Phone 908/725-1015.* General and Mrs. Washington made their headquarters here immediately after the house was built in 1778, while the army was stationed at Camp Middlebrook. Period furnishings. (Wed-Sun; closed holidays; hours may vary)

Special Event

IMB/USET Festival of Champions. *Hamilton Farm, Pottersville Rd, Bedminster (07934). Hamilton Farm, 10 miles N on Rte 206. Phone 908/234-0555.* Competition of three Olympic equestrian disciplines. Mid- or late June.

Limited-Service Hotel

★ **DAYS INN.** *118 Rte 206 S, Hillsborough (08844). Phone 908/685-9000; toll-free 800/329-7466; fax 908/685-0601. www.daysinn.com.* 100 rooms, 2 story. Pets accepted, some restrictions; fee. Complimentary continental breakfast. Check-in 2 pm, check-out 11 am. High-speed Internet access. Fitness room. Outdoor pool. **$**

Restaurant

★★★ **THE RYLAND INN.** *Rte 22 W, Whitehouse (08888). Phone 908/534-4011; fax 908/534-6592. www.therylandinn.com.* Using ingredients culled from his 7 acres of gardens, chef-owner Craig Shelton creates a deceivingly simple seasonal French cuisine at this country-estate restaurant. The decor ranges from homey to hunting lodge, and the wine list is long and varied. French menu. Lunch, dinner. Closed Mon; first week in Jan. Bar. Jacket required. Valet parking. Cigar room. Organic garden. **$$$$**

Spring Lake (C-4)

See also Asbury Park

Population 3,567
Elevation 25 ft
Area Code 732
Zip 07762

Limited-Service Hotel

★★ **BREAKERS HOTEL.** *1507 Ocean Ave, Spring Lake (07762). Phone 732/449-7700; fax 732/449-0161. www.breakershotel.com.* 67 rooms. Check-out noon. Restaurant. Outdoor pool, whirlpool. Restored Victorian oceanfront hotel. **$$**

Full-Service Inns

★★★ **HEWITT WELLINGTON HOTEL.** *200 Monmouth Ave, Spring Lake (07762). Phone 732/974-1212; fax 732/974-2338. www.hewittwellington.com.* Found lakeside, with a view of the ocean, this Victorian-style hotel was renovated in 1988, yet still keeps its old world charm and grace. 29 rooms, 3 story. Children over 12 years only. Check-out 11 am. Restaurant. Outdoor pool. **$$**

★★★ **THE SANDPIPER INN.** *7 Atlantic Ave, Spring Lake (07762). Phone 732/449-6060; toll-free 800/824-2779; fax 732/529-3390. www.sandpiperinn.com.* 15 rooms, 4 story. Children over 16 years only.

Complimentary continental breakfast. Check-in 3 pm, check-out noon. Restaurant. Indoor pool. Victorian inn built in 1888; casual atmosphere in elegant surroundings. Opposite beach. **$$**

Specialty Lodgings

The following lodging establishments are approved by Mobil Travel Guide, but due to their unique and individualized nature have not been given a traditional Mobil Star rating. Included in this listing you may find bed-and-breakfasts, limited-service inns, guest ranches, and other unique hotel properties.

ASHLING COTTAGE. *106 Sussex Ave, Spring Lake (07762). Phone 732/449-3553; toll-free 888/274-5464; fax 732/449-9067. www.ashlingcottage.com.* 11 rooms, 3 story. Closed mid-Dec-mid-Feb. Complimentary full breakfast. Check-in 2 pm, check-out 11 am. Victorian-style frame house (1877). **$$**

BAY HEAD GABLES. *200 Main Ave, Bay Head (08742). Phone 732/892-9844; toll-free 800/984-9536; fax 732/295-2196. www.bayheadgables.com.* This oceanfront bed-and-breakfast sits at the head of Barnegat Beach Island. Its Georgian-style, 150-foot wraparound porch, cedar-shingled façade, and manicured grounds are well regarded in this fashionable area. Point Pleasant Beach is nearby for walking the boardwalk or sunbathing. 11 rooms, 3 story. Closed Jan-Mar. Complimentary full breakfast. Check-in 1 pm, check-out 11 am. **$$**

CHATEAU INN. *500 Warren Ave, Spring Lake (07762). Phone 732/974-2000; toll-free 877/974-5253; fax 732/974-0007. www.chateauinn.com.* 38 rooms, 2 story. Beach. Renovated Victorian hotel (1888). Overlooks parks, lake. **$$**

THE INN AT THE SHORE. *301 4th Ave, Belmar (07719). Phone 732/681-3762; fax 732/280-1914. www.theinnattheshore.com.* 10 rooms. Complimentary full breakfast. Check-in 2 pm, check-out noon. Victorian-style ambience in a house built in 1888; many antiques. **$**

NORMANDY INN. *21 Tuttle Ave, Spring Lake (07762). Phone 732/449-7172; toll-free 800/449-1888; fax 732/449-1070. www.normandyinn.com.* 19 rooms, 3 story. Complimentary full breakfast. Built as a private residence in 1888; 19th-century antiques. **$$**

WHITE LILAC INN. *414 Central Ave, Spring Lake (07762). Phone 732/449-0211; fax 732/974-0568. www.whitelilac.com.* 10 rooms, 2 story. Closed Jan. Children over 14 years only. Complimentary full breakfast. Check-in 2 pm, check-out 11 am. Southern accent; built in 1880. **$**

Restaurants

★★★ **OLD MILL INN.** *101 Old Mill Rd, Spring Lake (07762). Phone 732/449-1800. www.themillatslh.com.* American menu. Lunch, dinner. Closed Mon. Bar. Children's menu. Casual attire. Outdoor seating. **$$**

★★ **THE SANDPIPER.** *7 Atlantic Ave, Spring Lake (07762). Phone 732/449-4700; fax 732/449-9825. www.sandpiperrestaurant.com.* American menu. Lunch, dinner. Children's menu. Candlelit dining in Victorian setting. **$$**

Stanhope

See also Lake Hopatcong, Rockaway

Population 3,584
Elevation 882 ft
Area Code 973
Zip 07874

What to See and Do

Waterloo Village Restoration. *525 Waterloo Rd, Stanhope (07874). I-80 exit 25; follow signs. Phone 973/347-0900.* Known as the Andover Forge during the Revolutionary War, it was once a busy town on the Morris Canal. The 18th-century buildings include Stagecoach Inn, houses, craft barns, gristmill, apothecary shop, general store. Music festival during summer (fee). (Mid-Apr-mid-Nov, Wed-Sun; closed Thanksgiving, Dec 25) **$$$**

Specialty Lodging

The following lodging establishment is approved by Mobil Travel Guide, but due to its unique and individualized nature has not been given a traditional Mobil Star rating. Included in this listing you may find bed-and-breakfasts, limited-service inns, guest ranches, and other unique hotel properties.

THE WOODEN DUCK B & B. *140 Goodale Rd, Newton (07860). Phone 973/300-0395. www.woodenduckinn.com.* A shuttered façade and neat little brick steps are a prelude to the residential, lived-in interior of this small bed-and-breakfast in rural Sussex County. All guest rooms feature elegant country décor, as well as queen-sized beds and modern amenities. 10 rooms, 2 story. Children over 8 years only. Complimentary full breakfast. Check-in 2 pm, check-out 11 am. Outdoor pool. **$$**

Restaurant

★ ★ THE BLACK FOREST INN. *249 Rte 206 N, Stanhope (07874). Phone 973/347-3344; fax 973/347-0176. www.blackforestinn.com.* German menu. Lunch, dinner. Closed Tues; holidays. Bar. Casual attire. **$$**

Stone Harbor (F-3)

See also Cape May Court House

Population 1,128
Elevation 5 ft
Area Code 609
Zip 08247
Information Stone Harbor Chamber of Commerce, 212 96th St, PO Box 422; phone 609/368-6101. Cape May County Chamber of Commerce, PO Box 74, Cape May Court House 08210; phone 609/465-7181

What to See and Do

Wetlands Institute. *1075 Stone Harbor Blvd, Stone Harbor (08247). 3 miles E off Garden State Pkwy exit 10. Phone 609/368-1211.* Environmental center focusing on coastal ecology. Also includes observation tower; marsh trail; aquarium; films and guided walks (July and Aug, daily). Bookstore. (Mid-May-mid-Oct: daily; rest of year: Tues-Sat; closed Easter, July 4, Thanksgiving; also two weeks in late Dec-early Jan) **$$**

Special Events

Sail into Summer Boat Show. *Stone Harbor. Phone 609/368-6101.* Pleasure boating, family entertainment, musicians, food. First weekend in May.

Wings 'n Water Festival. *1075 Stone Harbor Blvd, Stone Harbor (08247). Phone 609/368-1211.* Arts and crafts, decoys; entertainment; seafood. Third full weekend in Sept.

Full-Service Resorts

★ ★ AVALON GOLDEN INN HOTEL & COFERENCE CENTER. *7849 Dune Dr, Avalon (08202). Phone 609/368-5155; fax 609/368-6112. www.goldeninn.com.* This is an oceanfront hotel with a relaxed atmosphere. Guest rooms are tastefully decorated, food is delicately prepared in the dining room, and a wide variety of activities can be found only minutes away. 154 rooms, 3 story. Check-out 11 am. Restaurant, bar. Children's activity center. Outdoor pool, children's pool. Beach. **$**

★ ★ DESERT SAND RESORT COMPLEX. *7888 Dune Dr, Avalon (08202). Phone 609/368-5133; toll-free 800/458-6008; fax 609/368-1849. www.desertsand.com.* 90 rooms, 3 story. Closed Nov-mid-Apr. Check-out 11 am. Restaurant, bar. Fitness room. Indoor pool, outdoor pool, whirlpool. **$**

Strathmore

Restaurant

★ ★ DEAUVILLE INN. *201 Willard Rd, Strathmere (08248). Phone 609/263-2080; fax 609/391-1327. www.deauvilleinn.com.* Lunch, dinner. Closed Dec 25-26. Bar. Children's menu. Valet parking. Outdoor seating. **$$$**

Toms River (D-4)

See also Forked River, Jackson, Lakewood

Population 7,524
Elevation 40 ft
Area Code 732
Information Toms River-Ocean County Chamber of Commerce, 1200 Hooper Ave, 08753; phone 732/349-0220

What to See and Do

Cooper Environmental Center. *1170 Cattus Island Blvd, Toms River (08753). E on Rte 37 to Fischer Blvd, follow signs. Phone 732/270-6960.* A 530-acre facility with 3-mile bay front. Boat tours (summer; free); 7 miles of marked trails, picnicking (grills), playground. Nature center. (Daily) **FREE**

Limited-Service Hotels

★★ HOLIDAY INN. *290 Rte 37 E, Toms River (08753). Phone 732/244-4052; fax 732/244-4000. www.holiday-inn.com.* 122 rooms, 4 story. Check-out noon. Restaurant, bar. Indoor pool, whirlpool. **$**

★★ RAMADA INN. *2373 Rte 9, Toms River (08755). Phone 732/905-2626; fax 732/905-8735. www.ramada.com.* 154 rooms, 3 story. Complimentary continental breakfast. Check-in 3 pm, check-out noon. Restaurant, bar. Fitness room. Outdoor pool, whirlpool. Tennis. **$**

Trenton (C-3)

See also Bordentown, Lambertville, Princeton

Settled 1679
Population 85,403
Elevation 50 ft
Area Code 609
Information Mercer County Chamber of Commerce, 214 W State St, 08608-1002; phone 609/393-4143
Web site www.mercerchamber.org

The capital of New Jersey since 1790, Trenton is one of the fastest growing business and industrial areas in the country and a leading rubber-manufacturing center since colonial times. After crossing the Delaware on December 26, 1776, George Washington attacked the British-held town eight miles to the northwest.

What to See and Do

College of New Jersey. *4 miles N on Rte 31. Phone 609/771-1855. www.trenton.edu.* (1855) (6,150 students) A 250-acre wooded campus with two lakes. Tours of campus. On campus is the

College Art Gallery. *Phone 609/771-2652.* (Feb-May and Sept-Dec: Mon-Fri, Sun; closed holidays) **FREE**

New Jersey State Museum. *205 W State St, Trenton (08608). Adjacent to Capitol. Phone 609/292-6464. www.newjerseystatemuseum.org.* (Tues-Sun; closed holidays). **FREE** Includes

Auditorium. Lectures; films; music; children's theater. Some fees.

Main Building. Fine art, cultural history, archaeology and natural science exhibits. (Tues-Sun; closed state holidays) **FREE**

Planetarium. *Phone 609/292-6303.* One of few Intermediate Space Transit planetaria (duplicates motions of space vehicles) in the world. Programs (weekends; July-Aug, Tues-Sun). Over four years only except children's programs. Tickets 30 minutes in advance. **$$**

The Old Barracks Museum. *Barrack St, Opposite W Front St. Phone 609/396-1776. www.oldbarracks.org.* One of the finest examples of colonial barracks in the US. Built between 1758 and 1759, it housed British, Hessian, and Continental troops during the Revolutionary War. Museum contains restored soldiers' squad room; antique furniture; ceramics; firearms; dioramas. Guides in period costumes. (Daily; closed holidays) **$$$**

Sesame Place. *Rte 1 S to Oxford Valley exit. Phone 215/752-7070.* A family play park featuring characters from Sesame Street. **$$$$**

★ Washington Crossing State Park. *355 Washington Crossing-Pennington Rd, Titusville (08560). 8 miles NW on Rte 29. Phone 609/737-0623. www.state.nj.us/dep/forestry/parks/washcros.* This 996-acre park commemorates the famous crossing on Christmas night, 1776, by the Continental Army, under the command of General George Washington. Continental Lane, at the park, is the road over which Washington's army began its march to Trenton, Dec 25, 1776. Natural trails. Picnicking, playground. Visitor center and nature center (Wed-Sun); open-air summer theater (fee). Also in park is

Ferry House State Historic Site. *Phone 609/737-2515.* This building sheltered Washington and some of his men on Dec 25, 1776, after they had crossed the Delaware from the Pennsylvania side. It is believed that the strategy to be used for the attack on Trenton was discussed here. Restored as a living history colonial farmhouse; special programs throughout the year. (Wed-Sun)

William Trent House. *15 Market St, Trenton (08611). Phone 609/989-3027.* (1719) Trenton's oldest house is an example of Georgian architecture. It was the home of Chief Justice William Trent, for whom the city was named. Colonial garden. (Daily, afternoons; closed holidays) **$$**

Special Events

Heritage Days. *Trenton.* First weekend in June.

Reenactment of Crossing of the Delaware. *Washington Crossing State Park, 355 Washington Crossing Rd, Trenton (08560).* Departs PA side on the afternoon of Dec 25.

Trenton Kennel Club Dog Show. *Trenton. Mercer County Central Park.* Early May.

Full-Service Hotel

★★★ **LAFAYETTE YARD MARRIOTT.** *1 W Lafayette St, Trenton (08608). Phone 609/421-4000; fax 609/421-4002. www.marriott.com.* 197 rooms. Check-in 4 pm, check-out noon. High-speed Internet access. Restaurant, bar. Fitness room. Airport transportation available. Business center. **$$**

Restaurants

★★ **DIAMONDS.** *132 Kent, Trenton (08611). Phone 609/393-1000; fax 609/393-1672. www.diamondsrestaurant.com.* Italian, seafood, steak menu. Lunch, dinner. Closed Thanksgiving, Dec 25. Bar. Valet parking. **$$**

★★ **MARSILIO'S.** *541 Roebling Ave, Trenton (08611). Phone 609/695-2986; fax 609/695-2986.* Italian menu. Lunch, dinner. Closed Sun; holidays. Bar. Children's menu. **$$**

Vernon (A-3)

See also Branchville

Population 1,737
Elevation 564 ft
Area Code 973
Zip 7462
Information Vernon Township Municipal Building, 21 Church St; phone 973/764-4055

What to See and Do

Action Park. *200 Rte 94, Vernon. Phone 973/827-2000.* Theme park includes 75 self-operative rides, shows and attractions. Action Park has more than 40 water rides, including river rides and Tidal Wave Pool; also Grand Prix race cars, bungee jumping, miniature golf, children's park; food, picnic area. Three daily shows, weekend festival series. (Mid-June-Labor Day: daily; late May-mid-June: Thurs-Sun) **$$$$** Also here is

Mountain Creek Ski Resort. *www.mountaincreek.com.* Gondola; four quad, triple, double chairlifts; three surface lifts, rope tow; school, rentals; snowmaking; cafeterias, restaurants, bars, night club; nursery. Forty-three runs; vertical drop 1,040 feet. (Dec-Mar, daily) Night skiing. Spa, country club (daily). **$$$$**

Specialty Lodging

The following lodging establishment is approved by Mobil Travel Guide, but due to its unique and individualized nature has not been given a traditional Mobil Star rating. Included in this listing you may find bed-and-breakfasts, limited-service inns, guest ranches, and other unique hotel properties.

APPLE VALLEY INN. *967 Rte 517, PO Box 302, Glenwood (07418). Phone 973/764-3735; fax 973/764-1050. www.applevalleyinn.com.* 7 rooms, 3 story. Complimentary full breakfast. Check-in before 9 pm, check-out 11 am. Built in 1831; antiques. **$**

Wayne (B-3)

See also Newfoundland, Paterson

Population 54,069
Elevation 200 ft
Area Code 973
Zip 07470
Information Tri-County Chamber of Commerce, 2055 Hamburg Tpke; phone 973/831-7788
Web site www.tricounty.org

Wayne is the home of William Paterson University of New Jersey (1855).

What to See and Do

Dey Mansion. *199 Totowa Rd, Wayne (07470). Phone 973/696-1776.* (circa 1740) Restoration of Washington's headquarters (1780); period furnishings. Guided tours. Picnic tables. (Wed-Sun; closed holidays) **$**

Ringwood State Park. *On the New Jersey, New York border. Phone 973/962-7031.* Ringwood State Park lies in upper Passaic County, near the town of Ringwood, within the heart of the Ramapo Mountains. Consisting of 6,196 acres, the park is reached by routes 23 and 511 from the west and Route 17 and Sloatsburg Road from the east. Standard fees are charged for each section Memorial Day-Labor Day.

Ringwood Manor Section. This section features a 51-room mansion containing a collection of Americana; relics of iron-making days (1740); formal gardens. Interpretive tours. Fishing in Ringwood River. Picnic facilities nearby. Tours (Wed-Sun).

Shepherd Lake Section. A 541-acre wooded area has trap and skeet shooting all year (fee). The 74-acre Shepherd Lake provides a swimming beach and bathhouse, fishing, boating (ramp). Also available is picnicking (tables and grills).

Skylands Section. Located here is a 44-room mansion modeled after an English baronial house (open to the public on select days). The gardens (90 acres) surrounding the manor house comprise the only botanical garden in the state park system (guided tours upon request; phone 973/962-7527). This 1,119-acre section also offers fishing; hunting, hiking, mountain biking.

Terhune Memorial Park (Sunnybank). *Terbune Dr and Lamereux, Wayne (07470). 2 1/2 miles N on Rte 202 N. Phone 973/694-1800.* Estate of the late Albert Payson Terhune, author of *Lad, a Dog* and many other books about his collies. Scenic garden; picnic area. (Daily) **FREE**

Van Riper-Hopper (Wayne) Museum. *533 Berdan Ave, Wayne (07470). Phone 973/694-7192 (for schedule and fees).* (Circa 1786) Dutch Colonial farmhouse with 18th- and 19th-century furnishings; local historical objects; herb garden; bird sanctuary. Also here is

Mead Van Duyne House. *530 Berdan Ave, Wayne (07470) Phone 973/694-7192.* Restored Dutch farmhouse.

Limited-Service Hotels

★★ BEST WESTERN FAIRFIELD EXECUTIVE INN. *216-234 Rte 46 E, Fairfield (07004). Phone 973/575-7700; fax 973/575-4653. www.bwfei.com.* 170 rooms, 4 story. Complimentary full breakfast. Check-in 3 pm, check-out noon. Restaurant, bar. Fitness room. Indoor pool, whirlpool. Business center. **$**

★★ PRIME HOTEL AND SUITES FAIRFIELD. *690 Rte 46 E, Fairfield (07004). Phone 973/227-9200; toll-free 866/937-7746; fax 973/227-4308. www.primehotelsandresorts.com.* 204 rooms, 5 story. Pets accepted, some restrictions. Check-in 3 pm, check-out noon. Restaurant, bar. Fitness room. Indoor pool. Business center. **$$**

★ WELLESLEY INN. *1850 NJ 23 and Ratzer Rd, Wayne (07470). Phone 973/696-8050; toll-free 800/444-8888. www.wellesleyonline.com.* 146 rooms, 2 story. Pets accepted, some restrictions. Complimentary continental breakfast. Check-in 2 pm, check-out noon. High-speed Internet access. Outdoor pool. **$**

West Orange (B-4)

See also Newark, Newark International Airport Area

Population 44,943
Elevation 368 ft
Area Code 973
Zip 07052
Information West Orange Chamber of Commerce, PO Box 83; phone 973/731-0360
Web site www.westorange.com

What to See and Do

Eagle Rock Reservation. *Prospect and Eagle Rock aves, West Orange (07052). NW via Main St and Eagle Rock Ave. Phone 973/268-3500.* A 644-foot elevation in the Orange Mountains; visitors see a heavily populated area that stretches from the Passaic River Valley east to New York City. Hiking trails, picnicking, bridle paths. Restaurant. (Daily)

★ **Edison National Historic Site.** *Main St and Lake Side Ave, West Orange (07052). Phone 973/736-5050.* Here is

> **Edison Laboratory.** Built by Edison in 1887, it was his laboratory for 44 years. During that time, he was granted more than half of his 1,093 patents (an all-time record). Here he perfected the phonograph, motion picture camera, and electric storage battery. One-hour lab tour (no video cameras, strollers) includes the chemistry lab and library; demonstrations of early phonographs. Visitor center has exhibits; films (Daily; closed Jan 1, Thanksgiving, Dec 25). **$**

Turtle Back Zoo. *560 Northfield Ave, West Orange (07052). 3 miles W on I-280, exit 10, in South Mountain Reservation. Phone 973/731-5800.* This 20-acre park features animals in natural surroundings; sea lion pool; miniature train ride (1 mile). Picnicking, concessions. Gift shop (hours vary). (Daily; closed Thanksgiving, Dec 25; limited schedule Dec-Mar) **$$$** Adjacent is

> **South Mountain Arena.** *Phone 973/731-3828.* Indoor ice rink. Hockey games, special events.

Restaurants

★★★ **HIGHLAWN PAVILION.** *Eagle Rock Reservation, West Orange (07052). Phone 973/731-3463; fax 973/731-0034. www.highlawn.com/home.html.* American menu. Lunch, dinner. Closed Dec 24. Bar. Jacket required. Valet parking. Outdoor seating. **$$$**

★★★ **THE MANOR.** *111 Prospect Ave, West Orange (07052). Phone 973/731-2360; fax 973/731-2348. www.themanorrestaurant.com.* One of the most well-known (and most formal) restaurants in New Jersey continues to excel at all items on the menu, especially the seafood. Try the cilantro-sesame-seed-coated halibut filet, the pan-seared veal tournados or the lobster bisque. American menu. Lunch, dinner. Closed Mon. Bar. Jacket required. **$$$**

Wildwood and Wildwood Crest (F-2)

See also Cape May, Cape May Court House

Population 5,463
Elevation 8 ft
Area Code 609
Zip 08260
Information Greater Wildwood Chamber of Commerce, 3306 Pacific Ave, PO Box 823; phone 609/729-4000
Web site www.gwcoc.com

Wildwood's busy boardwalk extends for approximately 2 miles along the 5 miles of protected sandy beach it shares with North Wildwood and Wildwood Crest, two neighboring resorts. The area offers swimming, waterskiing, ocean and bay fishing, boating, sailing; bicycling, golf, tennis, and shuffleboard.

What to See and Do

Boat trips. *6006 Park Blvd, Wildwood Crest (08260). Capt Sinn's Dock. Phone 609/522-3934.* Sightseeing and whale-watching cruises aboard *Big Flamingo.* (July-Nov, daily) Also aboard the *Big Blue Sightseer.* (June-Sept, daily)

Limited-Service Hotels

★ ★ ADVENTURE MOTOR INN. *5401 Ocean Ave, Wildwood Crest (08260). Phone 609/729-1200; fax 609/523-1485.* 104 rooms, 6 story. Closed Nov-mid-Apr. Check-out 11 am. Restaurant. Beach. Outdoor pool, children's pool. **$$**

★ ARMADA BY THE SEA. *6503 Ocean Ave, Wildwood Crest (08260). Phone 609/729-3000; toll-free 800/399-3001; fax 609/729-7472. www.armadamotel.com.* 56 rooms, 5 story. Closed Oct-mid-Apr. Check-out 11 am. Outdoor pool, children's pool. **$$**

★ ★ CRUSADER OCEAN FRONT RESORT. *PO Box 1308, Wildwood Crest (8260). Phone 609/522-6991; toll-free 800/462-3260; fax 609/522-2280. www.crusaderresort.com.* 61 rooms, 3 story. Closed Nov-Mar. Check-out 11 am. Restaurant. Outdoor pool, children's pool. **$$**

★ ★ EL CORONADO MOTOR INN. *8501 Atlantic Ave, Wildwood Crest (08260). Phone 609/729-1000; toll-free 800/227-5302; fax 609/729-6557. www.elcoronado.com.* 113 rooms, 6 story. Closed Nov-Apr. Check-out 11 am. Restaurant. Children's activity center. Outdoor pool, children's pool, whirlpool. **$**

★ FLEUR DE LIS. *6105 Ocean Ave, Wildwood Crest (08260). Phone 609/522-0123; fax 609/523-0893. www.fleurdelismotel.com.* 44 rooms, 3 story. Closed mid-Oct-mid-Apr. Check-out 11 am. Outdoor pool, children's pool. On beach. **$**

★ JOLLY ROGER MOTEL. *6805 Atlantic Ave, Wildwood Crest (08260). Phone 609/522-6915; toll-free 800/337-5232; fax 609/522-3767. www.jollyrogermotel.com.* 74 rooms, 3 story. Closed late Sept-mid-May. Check-out 11 am. Children's activity center. Outdoor pool, children's pool. Tennis. **$**

★ NASSAU INN. *6201 Ocean Ave, Wildwood Crest (08260). Phone 609/729-9077; toll-free 800/336-9077; fax 609/729-2208. www.nassauinnmotel.com.* 56 rooms, 5 story. Closed mid-Oct-Apr. Check-out 11 am. Outdoor pool, children's pool. On beach. **$**

★ ★ PAN AMERICAN HOTEL. *5901 Ocean Ave, Wildwood Crest (08260). Phone 609/522-6936; fax 609/522-6937. www.panamericanhotel.com.* 78 rooms, 4 story. Closed mid-Oct-mid-May. Check-out 11 am. Restaurant. Children's activity center. Outdoor pool, children's pool. **$$**

★ ★ PORT ROYAL HOTEL. *6801 Ocean Ave, Wildwood Crest (08260). Phone 609/729-2000; fax 609/729-2051. www.portroyalhotel.com.* Take a swim in the hourglass-shaped pool, play with the kids in their own kid pool, or relax in the sun pool side on the patio. Guests will find golf, tennis, boating, fine restaurants, theater, and many more activities nearby. 100 rooms, 6 story. Closed mid-Oct-Apr. Check-out 11 am. Restaurant. Children's activity center. Outdoor pool, children's pool. **$$**

Specialty Lodging

The following lodging establishment is approved by Mobil Travel Guide, but due to its unique and individualized nature has not been given a traditional Mobil Star rating. Included in this listing you may find bed-and-breakfasts, limited-service inns, guest ranches, and other unique hotel properties.

CANDLELIGHT INN. *2310 Central Ave, North Wildwood (08260). Phone 609/522-6200; toll-free 800/992-2632; fax 609/522-6125. www.candlelight-inn.com.* 10 rooms, 4 story. No children allowed. Complimentary full breakfast. Check-in 1 pm, check-out 11 am. Queen Anne/Victorian-style house (circa 1905); restored. **$$**

Restaurants

★★ **GARFIELD'S GIARDINO RISTORANTE.** *3800 Pacific Ave, Wildwood (08260). Phone 609/729-0120; fax 609/729-2643. www.garfieldsnj.com.* Italian, seafood menu. Dinner. Bar. Children's menu. 2 dining areas in garden setting. **$$**

★ **MENZ RESTAURANT AND BAR.** *985 Rte 47 S, Rio Grande (08242). Phone 609/886-5691; fax 609/886-4092.* Dinner. Closed winter months. Children's menu. **$$**

Woodbridge

See also Edison

Settled 1664
Population 97,203
Elevation 21 ft
Area Code 732
Zip 07095
Information Chamber of Commerce Visitor Center, 52 Main St; phone 732/636-4040

Here, where the first cloverleaf interchange in the US was constructed in 1929, cross two of the country's busiest roads—the Garden State Parkway and the New Jersey Turnpike. Also in Woodbridge are seaway and river port areas visited by thousands of vessels annually.

What to See and Do

Barron Arts Center. *582 Rahway Ave, Woodbridge (07095). Phone 732/634-0413.* Built in 1877 in Romanesque Revival style. Originally the first free public library in Middlesex County, now an arts and cultural center with art exhibits; workshops; lectures; poetry sessions; concerts; special events. Gallery (Sun-Fri; closed holidays). **FREE**

Pennsylvania

Population: 11,881,643	
Area: 44,892 square miles	
Elevation: 0-3,213 feet	
Peak: Mount Davis (Somerset County)	
Entered Union: Second of original 13 states (December 12, 1787)	
Capital: Harrisburg	
Motto: Virtue, Liberty, And Independence	
Nickname: Keystone State	
Flower: Mountain Laurel	
Bird: Ruffed Grouse	
Tree: Eastern Hemlock	
Fair: (Pennsylvania State Farm Show), January in Harrisburg	
Time Zone: Eastern	
Web site: www.state.pa.us	

From its easternmost tip near Bordentown, New Jersey, to its straight western boundary with Ohio and West Virginia, Pennsylvania's 300-mile giant stride across the country covers a mountain-and-farm, river-and-stream, mine-and-mill topography. Its cities, people, and resources are just as diverse. Philadelphia is a great city in the eastern part of the state, a treasure house of tradition and historical shrines; Pittsburgh is a great city in the western part, a mighty arsenal of industry. In this state are the Pennsylvania Dutch, their barns painted with vivid hex signs; here also are steel mills. Pennsylvania miners dig nearly all the anthracite coal in the United States and still work some of the oldest iron mines in the country. Oil employees work more than 19,000 producing wells, and 55,000 farm families make up 20 percent of the Pennsylvania work force.

Pennsylvania, the keystone of the original 13 states, remains one of the keystones in modern America. A leader in steel and coal production, the state also is a leader in cigar leaf tobacco, apples, grapes, ice cream, chocolate products, mushrooms (nearly half of the United States total), and soft drinks, plus factory and farm machinery, electronics equipment, scientific instruments, watches, textile machines, railroad cars, ships, assorted metal products, and electrical machinery. This fifth most populous state is also a major factor in national politics.

Pennsylvania has been a keystone of culture. The first serious music in the colonies was heard in Bethlehem; today, it resounds throughout the state—Pittsburgh has an acclaimed symphony, as does Philadelphia. There are 140 institutions of higher learning (including the oldest medical school in the United States at the University of Pennsylvania), celebrated art galleries, and hundreds of museums.

Despite its size, all of Pennsylvania is within the motorist's grasp. Its 44,000 miles of state highways, including the 470-mile Pennsylvania Turnpike (pioneer of superhighways), plus 69,363 miles of other roads make up one of the largest road networks in the nation.

Swedes made the first settlement on this fertile land at Tinicum Island in the Delaware River in 1643. The territory became Dutch in 1655 and British in 1664. After Charles II granted William Penn a charter that made him proprietor of "Pennsilvania," this Quaker statesman landed here in 1682 and invested the land with his money, leadership, and fellow Quakers. The Swedes, Finns, and Dutch already in the new land were granted citizenship; soon came Welsh, Germans, Scots, Irish, and French Huguenots. Of these, the Germans left the strongest imprint on the state's personality. Commercial, agricultural, and industrial growth came quickly, and all these resources were contributed to the Revolution. In Pennsylvania, Washington camped at Valley Forge, the Declaration of Independence was signed, and the Constitution drafted.

Calendar Highlights

JANUARY

Pennsylvania State Farm Show *(Harrisburg). Phone 717/787-5373.* State fair.

FEBRUARY

Chocolate Lovers' Extravaganza *(Hershey). Hotel Hershey. For reservations, phone 800/533-3131.* Everything chocolate—tasting and sampling, chef-taught classes, decorating instruction, and more.

MAY

Devon Horse Show *(Philadelphia). Horse Show Grounds in Devon. Phone 610/964-0550.* One of America's leading equestrian events. More than 1,200 horses compete; country fair; antique carriage drive.

JUNE

CoreStates US Pro Cycling Championship *(Philadelphia).* Longest single-day cycling event in the country—156 miles.

Three Rivers Arts Festival *(Pittsburgh). Point State Park. Phone 412/281-8723.*Juried, original works of local and national artists; paintings, photography, sculpture, crafts, and videos; artists' market in outdoor plazas. Ongoing performances include music, dance, and performance art. Special art projects; film festival; food; children's activities.

JULY

Civil War Heritage Days *(Gettysburg). Phone 717/334-6274.* Lectures by historians; Civil War collectors' show; entertainment; Civil War book show; firefighters' festival; fireworks.

Folk Festival *(Kutztown). Festival grounds. Phone 215/679-9610.* Celebration of Pennsylvania Dutch folk culture; quilts, music, dancing, and food of Plain and Fancy Dutch. Craftspeople make baskets, brooms, rugs, toleware, and other handcrafts.

AUGUST

Das Awkscht Festival *(Allentown). Macungle Memorial Park. Phone 610/967-2317.* 2,500 antique, classic and special-interest autos; arts and crafts; antique toy show, entertainment, food, fireworks.

Musikfest *(Bethlehem). Phone 610/861-0678.* Nine sites in downtown historic area. Nine-day festival celebrating Bethlehem's rich musical and ethnic heritage. More than 600 performances of all types of music from folk to rock.

SEPTEMBER

Ligonier Highland Games and Gathering of the Clans of Scotland *(Ligonier). Idlewild Park. Phone 724/238-3666.* Sports; massed pipe bands, Highland dancing competitions, Scottish fiddling; sheep dog, wool spinning, and weaving demonstrations; geneology booth, Scottish fair.

Wine Country Harvest Festival *(North East). Gravel Pit Park and Gibson Park. Phone 814/725-4262.* Arts and crafts, bands, buses to wineries, food.

DECEMBER

Army-Navy Football Game *(Philadelphia). John F. Kennedy Memorial Stadium or Veterans Stadium.*

With Philadelphia the capital of the new nation, tides of pioneers pushed west and north to develop far corners of the state. The Civil War brought fresh industrial development, and for the past century Pennsylvania has continued to develop at an ever-quickening industrial pace. Today, the Keystone State is an empire of industry and a storehouse of historic traditions.

When to Go/Climate

Pennsylvania's lands and hill country enjoy typical East Coast seasonal temperatures—hot, humid summers; relatively mild winters; crisp falls; and wet springs. The mountains, however, experience short summers and cold, snowy winters.

AVERAGE HIGH/LOW TEMPERATURES (° F)

Philadelphia

Jan 38/23	**May** 73/53	**Sept** 78/59
Feb 41/25	**June** 82/62	**Oct** 66/47
Mar 52/33	**July** 86/67	**Nov** 55/38
Apr 63/42	**Aug** 85/66	**Dec** 43/28

Pittsburgh

Jan 34/19	**May** 71/48	**Sept** 74/54
Feb 37/20	**June** 79/57	**Oct** 63/42
Mar 49/30	**July** 83/62	**Nov** 50/34
Apr 60/39	**Aug** 81/60	**Dec** 39/24

Parks and Recreation

Water-related activities, hiking, riding, various other sports, picnicking, and environmental interpretive centers, as well as camping, are available in many state parks. More than 116 state parks and 4 environmental centers are scattered throughout the commonwealth. A total of 57 campgrounds offer camping. Seven are open all year; the rest are open from 2nd Fri Apr-3rd Sun Oct or Dec. Occupancy is limited to 2 consecutive weeks; $9-$14 resident, $11-$16 nonresident/night (primitive areas); $11-$14 resident, $13-$16 nonresident/night (modern areas). Cabins (daily and weekly rentals spring, fall, and winter; 1 week only, Fri after Memorial Day-Fri before Labor Day). Boat launching (annually) $10 resident, $15 nonresident. No pets allowed in overnight areas. Write to Bureau of State Parks, PO Box 8551, Harrisburg 17105-8551, for detailed information. Cabin reservations are made by calling the park directly. For other state park information, phone 888/PA-PARKS.

FISHING AND HUNTING

Pennsylvania is one of the country's leading states in the amount of waters open to public and private fishing. There are nearly 5,000 miles of trout streams stocked annually, and many thousands of miles of warm-water streams, plus thousands of acres of lakes with walleye, panfish, muskellunge, and bass. A nonresident fishing license is $35; a 3-day tourist license is $15; a 7-day tourist license is $30. A $5.50 trout/salmon stamp also is required (for trout fishing only). Write to Pennsylvania Fish and Boat Commission, PO Box 67000, Harrisburg 17106-7000, or phone 717/705-7800, for the annual "Summary of Fishing Regulations and Laws," as well as maps and other useful information.

A license is required to hunt, take, trap, or kill any wild bird or animal in the state. Nonresident hunting license, $101; children 12-16, $41. The license tag must be displayed on the back of outer garment, between the shoulders, at all times. For big-game and tukey hunting and small-game hunting in the fall, 250 square inches of fluorescent orange must be worn on the head, chest, and back combined. For the Official Digest, Pennsylvania Hunting and Trapping Regulations, contact the Pennsylvania Game Commission, 2001 Emerton Ave, Harrisburg 17110-9797, phone 717/787-4250.

Driving Information

Safety belts are mandatory for all persons in the front seat of a vehicle. Children under 4 years must be in an approved passenger restraint anywhere in the vehicle: age 4 and older may use a regulation safety belt; ages 1-3 may use a regulation safety belt in back seat only. Children under 4 years must use an approved safety seat in front seat; under age 1 must use an approved safety seat anywhere in the vehicle. Phone 717/787-6853.

INTERSTATE HIGHWAY SYSTEM

The following alphabetical listing of Pennsylvania towns in Mobil Travel Guide shows that these cities are within 10 miles of the indicated Interstate highways. Check a highway map for the nearest exit.

Highway Number	Cities/Towns within 10 Miles
Interstate 70	Bedford, Breezewood, Donegal, Greensburg, New Stanton, Somerset, Washington.
Interstate 78	Allentown, Bethlehem, Easton, Hamburg, Kutztown, Lebanon, Shartlesville.
Interstate 79	Conneaut Lake, Edinboro, Erie, Harmony, Meadville, Mercer, Pittsburgh, Washington.

Interstate 80	Belefonte, Bloomsburg, Brookville, Clarion, Clearfield, Danville, Du Bois, Hazleton, Lewisburg, Lock Haven, Mercer, Mount Pocono, Sharon, Shawnee on Delaware, Stroudsburg, Tannersville, White Haven.
Interstate 81	Ashland, Carlisle, Chambersburg, Harrisburg, Hazleton, Scranton, Wilkes-Barre.
Interstate 83	Harrisburg, York.
Interstate 84	Milford, Scranton.
Interstate 90	Erie, North East.
Interstate 95	Bristol, Philadelphia.

Additional Visitor Information

A free visitors guide is available by calling 800/VISIT-PA, at the Pennsylvania Office of Travel, Tourism, and Film Promotion, Department of Community & Economic Development, PO Box 61, Warrendale 15086.

There are 14 state-run traveler information centers in Pennsylvania; visitors who stop by will find information and brochures most helpful in planning stops at points of interest. Their locations are as follows: I-79 Edinboro (southbound), 1 mile S of the Edinboro exit; I-81 Greencastle (northbound), 1 mile N of the Pennsylvania/Maryland border; I-95 Linwood (northbound), 1/2 miles N of the Pennsylvania/Delaware border; I-70 Warfordsburg (westbound), 1 mile from the Pennsylvania/Maryland border; I-80 West Middlesex (eastbound), 1/2 miles E of the Pennsylvania/Ohio border; Neshaminy Welcome Center, Mile Marker 351 (westbound) on the Pennsylvania Turnpike, 7 miles W of the Pennsylvania/New Jersey border, located inside the plaza building; I-78 Easton (westbound), 1 mile W of the Pennsylvania/New Jersey border; Sideling Hill Welcome Center, Mile Marker 172 (eastbound and westbound) on the Pennsylvania Turnpike, 10 miles E of the Breezewood exit, located inside the plaza building; I-81 Lenox (southbound), 4 miles S of the Lenox exit 64; I-83 Shrewsbury (northbound), 1/2 miles N of the Pennsylvania/Maryland border; Zelienople Welcome Center, Mile Marker 21 (eastbound), 21 miles E of the Pennsylvania/Ohio border, located inside the plaza building; I-79 northbound, N of the Pennsylvania/West Virginia line; I-70 Washington County, E of the Pennsylvania/West Virginia line.

Ride with Me—Pennsylvania, Interstate 81 is a 90-minute audio cassette tape that provides information on points of interest along I-81, from New York to Maryland. Topics such as the history of the Pennsylvania Dutch, notable battlegrounds and areas related to the Civil War, and anthracite coal miners are discussed. Contact RWM Associates, PO Box 1324, Bethesda, MD 20817; 301/299-7817.

BUCKS COUNTY

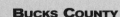

Over the years, literary references to Bucks County, just north of Philadelphia, have been plentiful, and with good reason. This woodland retreat along the Delaware River has been favored by notable Manhattanite literati for decades, including Broadway's Moss Hart and George S. Kaufman, and the acerbic writer Dorothy Parker. Though estate-sized homes are popping up everywhere in the privileged realm, the rumpled landscape still retains the look of a Currier and Ives print. Stately old fieldstone houses stand beneath towering trees, and stalks of ripening corn march across the fields. In fall, pumpkins peek from among patches of vines. Nearby, the wide and peaceful Delaware flows quietly past. A one-day, 75-mile loop drive out of New Hope provides a rewarding glimpse of Bucks County's scenic and cultural appeal. Begin in New Hope, a small town noted as a romantic weekend getaway destination. A colonial-era ferry crossing on the main road between Philadelphia and New York, the town is dotted with old stone structures sandwiched between the river and the Delaware Canal. The shops they house are well worth a look; several feature exquisite handmade crafts of local and national artisans. Many visitors come simply to stroll the old streets and enjoy the cafés, pubs, and ice cream parlors. You can hike or bicycle on the canal tow path. If you're in town on Saturday or Tuesday morning, drop by Rice's Market on Greenhill Road, a ten-minute drive northwest of New Hope. Set in a 30-acre field, the market is the next best thing to an old-fashioned county fair. More than 200 vendors haul in booths selling merchandise of all kinds–produce, plants and flowers, crafts, furniture pieces, clothing, you name it–often at bargain prices. To see more of the county, return to New Hope and take River Road (State Route 32) north. The road winds alongside the Delaware River for about 25 miles to Kintnersville, providing gorgeous river views the entire way. Quaint river towns, mostly a cluster of old homes, dot the route. In places, the road narrows as it skirts a stone wall. The stretch of road between New Hope and Lumberville passes a river setting that, in the early years of the century, drew a number of landscape artists who formed a colony of Pennsylvania Impressionists in the hamlet of Phillips Mill. You can't miss it; River Road makes a sharp turn here. Today, their work can be seen in a permanent exhibit called "Visual Heritage of Bucks County" at the James A. Michener Art Museum in Doylestown, ahead on this drive. In Kintnersville, take Route 611, the Lackawanna Trail, south to Doylestown. Visit the Michener Museum, which also features a diverting exhibit detailing the Broadway and Hollywood legends who have lived in the county. Save plenty of time for the three fantastical castle-like structures that archaeologist and historian Henry Chapman Mercer bequeathed his hometown. Turrets, towers, and parapets adorn the buildings, all built between 1908 and 1916 in a free-form style of reinforced concrete. The Moravian Pottery and Tile Works, which resembles a Spanish-colonial mission, houses Mercer's innovative tile factory. Good-quality artistic tiles are still made here by hand. On the same 70-acre, park-like grounds stands Fonthill, Mercer's 44-room mansion, a fairy-tale creation of strange nooks and crannies adorned with decorative tiles from his factory and around the world. A mile away, the seven-story Mercer Museum houses an important collection of furnishings, folk art, and implements of early America. Conclude this drive by returning to New Hope via Routes 202 and 179. **(Approximately 75 miles)**

LAUREL HIGHLANDS

As the name suggests, the Laurel Highlands–spread across the Allegheny Mountains in southwestern Pennsylvania–is a region of lofty wooded ridges, slender farm valleys, splashing streams, and quiet lakes, many boasting swimming beaches. Here and there you come upon covered bridges. George Washington once trod these hills, acquiring the military skills he would need as the Revolutionary War commander. Early on, the beauty of the setting drew many travelers–and continues to do so. Today, the Highlands serve as a year-round playground, where you can raft, kayak, fish, swim, and bicycle. This two-day, 150-mile drive meanders though this appealing setting while visiting several important historic sites. This is a one-way trip between Bedford in the east and Uniontown in the west. You can drive in either direction; we'll begin at Bedford, just off the Pennsylvania Turnpike. Stop in Bedford at the Old Bedford Village, which preserves more than 40 original farm buildings and other structures from bygone days in a village-like cluster. One that catches the eye is the eight-sided frame schoolhouse built nearby in 1851. Called an Eight Square, the octagon shape had a specific purpose: it gave every student an equal share of window light and proximity to the pot-bellied stove in the center. In summer, craftsmen demonstrate blacksmithing, barrel-making, broom-making, and other pioneer skills. From Bedford, take I-99 North to State Route 56 northwest to Johnstown. Two sites here capture the horror of the Johnstown Flood of 1889, which struck the small steel-manufacturing city with a sudden ferocity that left 2,200 people dead. Just east of the city, the National Park Service operates the Johnstown Flood National Memorial. It overlooks the dry basin of what was once a man-made lake that emptied when heavy rains collapsed an earthen dam. In Johnstown itself, the Johnstown Flood Museum illustrates the damage wrought by the flood and Johnstown's determination to rebuild. Ahead on the drive, two reconstructed 18th-century forts, Fort Ligonier in Ligonier and Fort Necessity National Battlefield near Farmington, recount British colonial efforts to wrest the Ohio River Valley west of the Alleghenies from French control. Both forts played a role in the ultimate defeat of the French at Fort Duquesne, which became the site of Pittsburgh. Ligonier is the most imposing of the two forts, but Fort Necessity may be more memorable. To reach it, take Route 271 West from Johnstown to Ligonier, and plan to spend the night there. To reach Fort Necessity, head 2 miles southeast on US 30 to Route 381 to Farmington, and turn right on US 40. At Fort Necessity, a modest ring of stakes thrusting from the earth marks the site of George Washington's only military surrender, a lesson that surely must have aided him two decades later as commander of the Continental Army. The route from Ligonier to Farmington edges past Fallingwater, architect Frank Lloyd Wright's masterpiece on Bear Run. The structure, stair-stepping down a wooded mountainside, combines architecture and nature in a glorious piece of artwork. A stop here is a must, but allow at least three hours to take an escorted tour and to walk the grounds. Exhibits at the Entrance Pavilion explain the construction of the house, built in 1936 as a mountain retreat for a wealthy Pittsburgh department store owner. Inside the house, you'll learn about Wright's daring use of new construction materials and his fascination with the possibilities of space, as well as his idiosyncracies. Short in stature, Wright designed the house with surprisingly low ceilings. A couple of miles down the road, the village of Ohiopyle is a center for whitewater rafting. Sign up for thrills, or watch helmet-clad rafters arriving or departing on upper and lower stretches of the Youghiogheny River (also called the "Yock"). From Fort Necessity, continue west on US 40 to Uniontown to conclude this tour. **(Approximately 150 miles)**

Allentown (C-6)

See also Bethlehem, Bucks County, Easton, Kutztown, Quakertown (Bucks County)

Founded 1762
Population 106,632
Elevation 364 ft
Area Code 484 and 610
Information Lehigh Valley Convention & Visitors Bureau, PO Box 20785, Lehigh Valley 18002-0785; phone 610/882-9200

Allentown, situated in the heart of Pennsylvania Dutch country, is conveniently accessible via a network of major highways. Allentown was originally incorporated as Northamptontown. The city later took the name of its founder, William Allen, a Chief Justice of Pennsylvania. Allentown was greatly influenced by the Pennsylvania Germans who settled the surrounding countryside and helped the city become the business hub for a rich agricultural community.

What to See and Do

Bear Creek Ski Area. *Macungie. 12 miles SW, 4 1/2 miles off Hwy 100, just N of Hereford. Phone 610/682-7100.* Four chairlifts, one handle tow, T-bar, two rope tows; 15 slopes; patrol, school, rentals, snowmaking; night skiing and snowboarding; tubing park; restaurant, cafeteria, bar; nursery. Longest run 1 1/2 miles; vertical drop 500 feet. (Dec-mid-Mar, daily) **$$$$**

Blue Mountain. *1660 Blue Mountain Dr, Palmerton. 17 miles N via Hwy 145, Treichlers exit, at "Y" turn right to Cherryville, and on to Danielsville, to top of Blue Mountain. Phone 610/826-7700. www.skibluemt .com.* Seven chairlifts, T-bar; school, rentals, snowmaking; cafeteria, bar, lodge. Vertical drop 1,082 feet. Also 27 trails with day and night skiing. (Dec-Apr, daily) **$$$$**

Cedar Crest College. *100 College Dr, Allentown. Phone 610/437-4471.* (1867) (1,700 women) An 84-acre campus that includes nationally registered William F. Curtis Arboretum (tours); chapel with stained-glass windows portraying outstanding women in history; art galleries, sculpture gardens, museum, and theater. Campus tours.

Dorney Park and Wildwater Kingdom. *3830 Dorney Park Rd, Allentown (18104). Phone 610/395-3724. www.dorneypark.com.* This amusement and water park is one of the country's oldest. A former fish hatchery, the 200-acre park is home to nearly 100 rides, 11 water slides, and four roller coasters. It's just an hour from Philadelphia, and there are activities here to engage every member of the family. Little ones can discover frog slides, turtle fountains, and squirt guns. Bigger kids can climb, slide, splash, and play on a submarine and an octopus. Older kids (and grownup ones) may want to torpedo through an enclosed tube or float slowly down a 1,600-foot winding river. In addition to rides, there are song and dance revues and 40 food locations, including two air-conditioned, dine-in restaurants. (Daily; closed Nov-Apr) **$$$$**

Frank Buchman House. *117 N 11th St, Allentown. Phone 610/435-4664.* Constructed in 1892, this three-story row house, typical of Allentown's inner city, is an example of Victorian architecture; period rooms. (Sat and Sun afternoons; also by appointment) **FREE**

George Taylor House and Park. *501 W Hamilton St, Catasauqua. 4 miles N off Hwy 22, at Lehigh and Poplar sts. Phone 610/435-4664.* (1768) House of a signer of the Declaration of Independence; 18th-century restoration period rooms; museum; walled garden. Guided tours. (June-Oct, Sat and Sun afternoons; also by appointment) **$**

Haines Mill Museum. *3600 Dorney Park Rd, Centronia. 3 miles W via Hamilton St. Phone 610/435-4664.* (Circa 1760) Operating gristmill (reconstructed 1909); exhibits portray the development and importance of the gristmill in rural America. (May-Sept, Sat and Sun afternoons; also by appointment; closed holidays) **FREE**

Lehigh County Museum. *501 W Hamilton St, Allentown. Old Courthouse, 5th and Hamilton sts. Phone 610/435-4664.* Exhibits illustrate economic, social, and cultural history of the county. (Mon-Sat, Sun afternoons; closed holidays) **FREE**

Liberty Bell Shrine. *622 Hamilton, Allentown. At Church St. Phone 610/435-4232.* Reconstructed Zion's church has shrine in basement area where Liberty Bell was hidden in 1777; contains a full-size replica of the original bell; a 46-foot mural depicts the journey of the bell; other historical exhibits, art collection. (Mon-Sat afternoons; closed holidays) **FREE**

Lock Ridge Furnace Museum. *525 Franklin St, Allentown. Phone 610/435-4664.* Exhibits on the development of the US iron and steel industry; emphasis on the anthracite-coal-heated iron industry. Located in a reconstructed 19th-century iron furnace. (May-Sept, Sat and Sun afternoons; also by appointment) **FREE**

Muhlenberg College. *2400 W Chew St, Allentown (18104). Phone 484/664-3100.* (1848) (2,000 students) Founded by the Lutheran Church to honor patriarch of Lutheranism in America. On campus is the Gideon F. Egner Memorial Chapel, an example of Gothic architecture. Also here is the Center for the Arts, a dramatic building designed by renowned architect Philip Johnson, which houses the Muhlenberg Theater Association. Campus tours.

Saylor Park Cement Industry Museum. *245 N 2nd, Coplay. Phone 610/435-4664.* Outdoor historic site featuring remains of cement kilns. (Daily, year-round) **FREE**

Trexler-Lehigh County Game Preserve. *5150 Game Preserve Rd, Allentown (18078). 4 miles W on Hwy 22, then 6 miles N on Hwy 309, near Schnecksville. Phone 610/799-4171.* A 1,200-acre zoo, petting farm, and wilderness tour that is home to more than 350 animals. Scenic overlooks; picnic area. (Mid-Apr-Oct, daily) **$$$**

Trexler Memorial Park. *Cedar Crest Blvd and Broadway, Allentown. Phone 610/437-7628.* Spring outdoor bulb display (Apr-May). Gross Memorial Rose Garden (at peak second week June) and Old-Fashioned Garden, Cedar Pkwy (June-Aug). Trout Nursery and Fish-for-Fun stream, Lehigh Pkwy; picnic areas. West Park, 16th and Turner. Band concerts (June-Aug). **FREE**

Trout Hall. *414 Walnut St, Allentown (18102). Phone 610/435-4664.* (1770) Oldest house in city, Georgian Colonial; restored. Period rooms, museum. Guided tours (Apr-May & Sept-Nov, Sat & Sun afternoons; June-Aug, Tues-Sun afternoons; also by appointment; closed holidays) **$**

Troxell-Steckel House and Farm Museum. *4229 Reliance St, Egypt. 6 miles N on Hwy 145, then 1 mile W on Hwy 329. Phone 610/435-4664.* (1756) Stone house is an example of German medieval architecture. Period rooms; museum. Swiss-style bank barn adjacent has exhibits of farm implements, carriages, and sleighs. Guided tours. (June-Oct, Sat and Sun afternoons; also by appointment) **$**

Special Events

Das Awkscht Fescht. *Macungie Memorial Park, Allentown. Phone 610/966-4289.* 2,500 antique, classic, and special-interest autos; arts and crafts; antique toy show, entertainment, food, fireworks. First weekend in Aug.

Drum Corps International-Eastern Regional Championship. *21st and Linden sts, Allentown. J. Birney Crum Stadium. Phone 610/966-5344.* Drum and bugle corps competition. Sept.

Great Allentown Fair. *Fairgrounds, 17th and Chew sts, Allentown. Phone 610/435-SHOW.* Farm and commercial exhibits, rides, games, food, entertainment. Late Aug-early Sept.

Mayfair Festival of the Arts. *Phone 610/437-6900.* Allentown parks. Family arts festival with 150 free musical performances; crafts and food. Mon and Thurs-Sun, Memorial Day weekend.

Limited-Service Hotels

★ COMFORT INN. *3712 Hamilton Blvd, Allentown (18103). Phone 610/437-9100; fax 610/437-0221. www.choicehotels.com.* 122 rooms, 4 story. Complimentary continental breakfast. Check-out noon. Restaurant, bar. Airport transportation available. **$**

★★ CROWNE PLAZA. *904 Hamilton Mall, Allentown (18101). Phone 610/433-2221; fax 610/433-6455.* Located downtown, it is only 6 miles from the ABE International Airport and within walking distance of the Liberty Bell. 224 rooms, 9 story. Check-out 11 am. Restaurant, bar. Fitness room. Outdoor pool. Airport transportation available. **$**

★ ★ **FOUR POINTS BY SHERATON.** *3400 Airport Rd, Allentown (18109). Phone 610/266-1000; toll-free 888/610-2662; fax 610/266-1888.* 147 rooms, 3 story. Pets accepted; fee. Check-out noon. Restaurant, bar. Indoor pool, whirlpool. **$**

★ **HAMPTON INN.** *7471 Keebler Way, Allentown (18106). Phone 610/391-1500; toll-free 800/426-7866; fax 610/391-0386. www.hamptoninn.com.* 124 rooms, 5 story. Complimentary continental breakfast. Check-out noon. Fitness room. Airport transportation available. **$**

Full-Service Inn

★ ★ ★ **THE GLASBERN INN.** *2141 Pack House Rd, Fogelsville (18051). Phone 610/285-4723; fax 610/285-2862. www.glasbern.com.* 37 rooms, 2 story. Complimentary full breakfast. Check-in 4 pm, check-out noon. Restaurant. Outdoor pool. Farmhouse, barn, gate house and carriage house built in late 1800s; antiques. **$**

Restaurants

★ ★ ★ **APPENNINO.** *3079 Willow St, Allentown (18104). Phone 610/799-2727; fax 610/799-2741.* Northern Italian menu. Dinner. Closed Sun; holidays. Bar. Restored hotel (1800s); imported Italian lamps, chandeliers and tapestry on chairs. Jacket required. **$$$**

★ ★ **ARTEPASTA TOO.** *2071 31st Street Sw, Allentown (18103). Phone 610/791-3500; fax 610/791-9448.* Italian menu. Lunch, dinner. Closed Mon. Bar. Children's menu. Casual attire. **$$**

★ ★ **BAY LEAF.** *935 W Hamilton St, Allentown (18101). Phone 610/433-4211; fax 610/433-2652.* Thai menu. Lunch, dinner. Closed Sun; holidays. Bar. **$$**

★ ★ **FEDERAL GRILL.** *536 Hamilton St, Allentown (18101). Phone 610/776-7600; fax 610/776-3660.* Seafood menu. Lunch, dinner, brunch. Closed holidays. Bar. Reservations recommended. Outdoor seating. **$$**

Altoona (C-3)

See also Ebensburg

Founded 1849
Population 49,523
Elevation 1,170 ft
Area Code 814
Information Allegheny Mountains Convention & Visitors Bureau, One Convention Center Dr, 16602; phone 814/943-4183 or toll-free 800/842-5866
Web site www.alleghenymountains.com

The rough, high Alleghenies ring this city, which was founded by the Pennsylvania Railroad. Altoona expanded rapidly after 1852, when the difficult task of spanning the Alleghenies with track, linking Philadelphia and Pittsburgh, was completed. The railroad shops still offer substantial employment for residents of the city and Blair County, but new and diversified industries now provide the economic base.

What to See and Do

Allegheny Portage Railroad National Site. *110 Federal Park Rd, Gallitzin (16641). Phone 814/886-6150.* View authentic Lemon House and original rehabbed Engine House; learn how canal boats were taken over the Allegheny Mountains before the Horseshoe Curve was built. (Daily; closed Dec 25) **$$$**

Baker Mansion Museum. *3500 Oak Ln, Altoona. Phone 814/942-3916.* (1844-1848) Stone Greek Revival house of early ironmaster; now occupied by Blair County Historical Society. Hand-carved Belgian furniture of the period; transportation exhibits, gun collection, clothing, housewares. (Memorial Day-Labor Day: Tues-Sun; mid-Apr-Memorial Day and Labor Day-Oct: Sat-Sun; closed holidays) **$$**

Canoe Creek State Park. *12 miles E via Hwy 22. Phone 814/695-6807.* Approximately 950-acre park features 155-acre lake. Swimming beach, fishing, boating (launches, rentals); hiking, picnicking (reservations for pavilion), cross-country skiing, sledding, ice boating, ice skating, cabins.

Delgrossos Park. *10 miles N on Hwy 220, in Tipton. Phone 814/684-3538.* More than 30 rides and attractions include antique carousel, miniature golf, and pony rides. Also here are arcade games, picnic pavilions, and restaurant. (May-Sept, Tues-Sun) **$$$$**

Fort Roberdeau. *8 miles NE via Hwy 220, Kettle St exit onto Hwy 1013. Phone 814/946-0048.* Reconstructed Revolutionary War fort with horizontal logs; contains lead smelter, blacksmith shop, lead miners' hut, barracks, storehouse, officers' quarters, powder magazine. Costumed guides; weekend reenactments. Visitor center. Picnicking, nature trails. (Mid-May-early Oct, Tues-Sun) **$$**

Horseshoe Curve Visitors Center. *5 miles W via well-marked, unnumbered road. Phone 814/946-0834.* World-famous engineering feat, carrying main-line Conrail and Amtrak trains around western grade of 91 feet per mile. Curve is 2,375 feet long and has a central angle of 220 degrees. Funicular runs between interpretive center and observation area. Gift shop. (Apr-Dec, daily) **$$**

Lakemont Park. *700 Park Ave, Altoona. Frankstown Rd and I-99. Phone 814/949-7275.* An amusement park with more than 30 rides and attractions; home of the nation's oldest wooden roller coaster; water park, miniature golf, entertainment. (May-Sept, daily) **$$$**

Prince Gallitzin State Park. *Hwy 53 and Beaver Valley Rd, Flinton (16640). 8 miles NW on Hwy 36, then 1 1/4 miles NW off Hwy 53, then W on Hwy 1026. Phone 814/674-1000.* Approximately 6,200 acres; 26 miles of shoreline on 1,600-acre lake. Swimming beach, fishing, boating (rentals, mooring, launching, marina); hiking trails, horseback riding, cross-country skiing, snowmobiling, ice skating, ice fishing, picnicking, snack bar, store, laundry facilities, tent and trailer sites, cabins.

Railroader's Memorial Museum. *1300 9th Ave, Altoona. Phone 814/946-0834.* Exhibits feature railroad artifacts, art, and theme displays. Railroad rolling stock, steam and electric locomotive collections. (Daily) **$$$**

Wopsononock Mountain. *6 miles NW on Juniata Gap Rd.* Lookout provides view of six-county area from height of 2,580 feet; offers one of the best views in the state.

Special Events

Blair County Arts Festival. *Penn State Altoona Campus, 3000 Ivyside Park, Altoona (16601).* Arts, crafts, hobbies on display. Mid-May.

Keystone Country Festival. *Lakemont Park, 700 Park Ave, Altoona.* Arts and crafts, continuous music; food. Contact Convention and Visitors Bureau for details. Weekend after Labor Day.

Railfest. *1300 9th Ave, Altoona. Phone 814/946-0834.* A celebration of Altoona's rich rail heritage. Oct.

Limited-Service Hotel

★★ **RAMADA.** *1 Sheraton Dr, Altoona (16601). Phone 814/946-1631; fax 814/946-0785. www.ramada.com.* 215 rooms, 3 story. Pets accepted, some restrictions; fee. Complimentary continental breakfast. Check-out noon. Restaurant, bar. Fitness room. Indoor pool, children's pool, whirlpool. Airport transportation available. Business center. **$**

Restaurant

★★ **ALLEGRO.** *3926 Broad Ave, Altoona (16601). Phone 814/946-5216; fax 814/946-4635. www.allegro-restaurant.com.* Locals favor Allegro Ristorante for special occasions due to the candlelit setting and stately ambience. The Italian food is not innovative, but classic dishes are tried and true. American, Italian menu. Dinner. Closed Sun; holidays. Bar. Children's menu. **$$**

Ambridge (C-1)

See also Beaver Falls, Pittsburgh

Founded 1901
Population 7,769
Elevation 751 ft
Area Code 724
Zip 15003
Information Beaver County Recreation & Tourism Department, Brady's Run Park, RD 1, Box 526, Beaver Falls, PA, 15010; phone 724/891-7030
Web site www.co.beaver.pa.us

Founded by and taking its name from the American Bridge Company, this city rests on part of the site of Old Economy Village. In 1825, under the leadership of George Rapp, the Harmony Society established a communal pietistic colony that, for many decades, was important in the industrial life and development of western Pennsylvania. Despite its spiritual emphasis, Old Economy Village enjoyed a great material prosperity; farms were productive, craft shops were busy, and factories made textiles widely acclaimed for their quality. Surplus funds financed railroads and industrial enterprises throughout the upper Ohio Valley. After celibacy was adopted and unwise investments were made, the community's productivity decreased. Officially dissolved in 1905, the remains of the community were taken over by the Commonwealth of Pennsylvania in 1916.

What to See and Do

★ **Old Economy Village.** *14th and Church sts, Ambridge. Phone 724/266-4500.* Seventeen original Harmony Society buildings located on 6 acres, restored and filled with furnishings of the community. Included are the communal leader's 32-room Great House, the Feast Hall, the Grotto in the Gardens, wine cellars, a five-story granary, shops, dwellings, and community kitchens. Cobblestone streets link the buildings. Special festivals and events. (Tues-Sun; closed holidays)

Raccoon Creek State Park. *3000 Hwy 18, Hookstown (15050). 9 miles W on Hwy 151, then 7 miles S on Hwy 18, near Frankfort Springs. Phone 724/899-2200.* Approximately 7,300 acres. Swimming beach, fishing, boating (rentals, mooring, launching); hunting, hiking, horseback riding, cross-country skiing, sledding, snowmobiling, ice skating, ice fishing, snack bar, tent and trailer sites. Nature and historical centers.

Special Event

Nationality Days. Ethnic cultural displays, foods; native music, dancing. Mid-May.

Ashland

See also Hazleton

Population 3,283
Elevation 1,000 ft
Area Code 717
Zip 17921
Information Schuylkill County Visitors Bureau, 91 S Progress Ave, Pottsville 17901; phone 717/622-7700 or toll-free 800/765-7282
Web site www.schuylkill.org

What to See and Do

Museum of Anthracite Mining. *Pine and 17th sts, Ashland. Phone 570/875-4708.* Museum on geology and technology of mining "hard" coal. (May-Oct: Mon-Sat, also Sun afternoons; rest of year: Tues-Sat, also Sun afternoons; closed holidays) **$$**

Pioneer Tunnel Coal Mine and Steam Lokie Ride. *19th and Oak sts, Ashland. Phone 717/875-3850.* Tour and explanation of mining in original coal mine tunnel; indoor temperature 52° F. Narrow-gauge steam train ride; picnic park. (call for hours) **$$$**

Beaver Falls (C-1)

See also Ambridge, Harmony

Founded 1806
Population 9,920
Elevation 800 ft
Area Code 724
Zip 15010
Information Beaver County Recreation & Tourism Department, Brady's Run Park, RD 1, Box 526, Beaver Falls, PA, 15010; phone 724/891-7030
Web site www.co.beaver.pa.us

Founded as Brighton, the town changed its name for the falls in the Beaver River. The plates from which US currency is printed are made in Beaver Falls. Geneva College (1848) is located here.

Limited-Service Hotels

★ **BEAVER VALLEY MOTEL.** *7257 Big Beaver Blvd, Beaver Falls (15010). Phone 724/843-0630; toll-free 800/400-8312; fax 724/843-1610. www.bvmotel.com.* 27 rooms. Check-out 11 am. **$**

★ ★ **CONLEY INN.** *Big Beaver Blvd, Beaver Falls (15010). Phone 724/843-0630; toll-free 800/345-6819; fax 724/843-9039.* 56 rooms. Check-out 11 am. Restaurant, bar. **$**

★ ★ **HOLIDAY INN.** *7195 Eastwood Rd, Beaver Falls (15010). Phone 724/846-3700; toll-free 800/613-1490; fax 724/846-7008. www.holiday-inn.com.* 156 rooms, 3 story. Pets accepted, some restrictions. Check-out noon. Restaurant, bar. Indoor pool, whirlpool. **$**

Restaurant

★ ★ **WOODEN ANGEL.** *308 Leopard Ln, Beaver (15009). Phone 724/774-7880; fax 724/774-7994. www.wooden-angel.com.* This cozy dining room has old-fashioned elegance with dark-wood paneling and rustic chandeliers reminiscent of soft candlelight. The monthly changing menu is market inspired. Seafood menu. Lunch, dinner. Closed Sun-Mon; holidays. Bar. **$$$**

Bedford (D-3)

Settled 1751
Population 5,417
Elevation 1,106 ft
Area Code 814
Zip 15522
Information Bedford County Conference & Visitors Bureau, 141 S Juliana St; phone 814/623-1771 or toll-free 800/765-3331
Web site www.bedfordcounty.net

Fort Bedford was a major frontier outpost in pre-Revolutionary War days. After the war, it became an important stopover along the route of western migration and has remained so up until the present. Garrett Pendergrass, the second settler here, built Pendergrass's Tavern, which figures in a number of novels by Hervey Allen.

What to See and Do

Bedford County Courthouse. *230 S Juliana St, Building 2, Bedford (15522). Phone 814/623-4807.* Federal-style building constructed in 1828 has unique hanging spiral staircase; oldest courthouse still in operation in Pennsylvania. (Mon-Fri; closed holidays) **FREE**

Blue Knob Ski Area. *RR 1, Claysburg. Phone 814/239-5111; toll-free 800/458-3403 (snow conditions). www.blueknob.com.* Two triple, two double chairlifts; three platter pulls; patrol, school, rentals; snowmaking; bar, cafeteria; nursery. Longest run approximately 2 miles; vertical drop 1,072 feet. (Dec-Mar, daily) Half-day rates available. **$$$$**

Blue Knob State Park. *124 Park Rd, Imler (16655). 10 miles N on Hwy 220, then 8 miles NW on Hwy 869. Phone 814/276-3576.* Approximately 6,000 acres. Swimming pool, fishing; hunting, hiking, cross-country skiing, snowmobiling, sledding, picnicking, playfield, camping (mid-Apr-mid-Oct).

Fort Bedford Park and Museum. *Fort Bedford Dr, Bedford. N end of Juliana St, park along Raystown River. Phone 814/623-8891.* Log blockhouse, erected during Bedford's bicentennial. Contains large-scale replica of original fort, displays of colonial antiques and relics, Native American artifacts. (May-late Oct, daily)

Old Bedford Village. *220 Sawblade Rd, Bedford (15522). Phone 814/623-1156.* More than 40 authentic log and frame structures (1750-1851) house historical exhibits; crafts demonstrations; operating pioneer farm. Many special events throughout the year. (Memorial Day weekend-Labor Day) **$$$**

Shawnee. *132 State Park Rd, Schellsburg (15559). 8 miles W on Hwy 30. Phone 814/733-4218.* Approximately 450-acre lake surrounded by 3,840 acres. Swimming beach, fishing, boating (rentals, mooring, launching); hunting, cross-country skiing, snowmobiling, sledding, ice skating, ice fishing, picnicking, playfield, snack bar, camping; tent and trailer sites.

Special Events

Civil War Reenactment. *Old Bedford Village.* Early Sept.

Fall Foliage Festival Days. *141 S Juliana St, Bedford (15522).* Entertainment, ethnic foods, antique cars, more than 350 craft booths. First two full weekends in Oct.

Limited-Service Hotels

★ ★ **BEST WESTERN BEDFORD INN.** *4517 Business 220, Bedford (15522). Phone 814/623-9006; toll-free 800/752-8592; fax 814/623-7120. www.bestwestern.com.* 105 rooms, 2 story. Pets accepted, some restrictions; fee. Check-out noon. Restaurant, bar. Fitness room. Outdoor pool, whirlpool. **$**

★ ★ **QUALITY INN.** *4407 Business 220, Bedford (15522). Phone 814/623-5188; fax 814/623-0049. www.choicehotels.com.* 66 rooms. Pets accepted, some restrictions; fee. Complimentary continental breakfast. Check-out 11 am. Restaurant, bar. Outdoor pool. **$**

Restaurant

★ ★ **ED'S STEAK HOUSE.** *4476 Business 220, Bedford (15522). Phone 814/623-8894; fax 814/623-2643.*

Seafood, steak menu. Breakfast, lunch, dinner. Closed Thanksgiving, Dec 25. Bar. Children's menu. **$$**

Bellefonte (C-3)

See also State College

Settled 1770
Population 6,395
Elevation 809 ft
Area Code 814
Zip 16823
Information Bellefonte Intervalley Area Chamber of Commerce, Train Station, 320 W High St; phone 814/355-2917
Web site bellefontechamber.org

When the exiled French minister Talleyrand saw the Big Spring here in 1794, his exclamation—"Beautiful fountain"—gave the town its name. Bellefonte is perched on seven hills at the southeast base of Bald Eagle Mountain.

What to See and Do

Black Moshannon State Park. *N via Hwy 144/150, SW via Hwy 220, then approximately 12 miles W on Hwy 504. Phone 814/342-5960.* Approximately 3,450 acres. Swimming beach, fishing, boating (rentals, mooring, launching); hunting, hiking, cross-country skiing, snowmobiling, ice skating, ice fishing, ice boating, picnicking, snack bar, tent and trailer sites, cabins. Interpretive program.

Centre County Library and Historical Museum. *200 N Allegheny St, Bellefonte. Phone 814/355-1516.* Local historical museum includes central Pennsylvania historical and genealogical books, records. (Mon-Sat; closed holidays) **FREE**

Restaurant

★★ **GAMBLE MILL RESTAURANT.** *160 Dunlap St, Bellefonte (16823). Phone 814/355-7764; fax 814/355-1571. www.gamblemill.com.* American menu. Lunch, dinner. Closed Sun; Thanksgiving, Dec 25. Bar. Restored mill (1786); rustic early American décor. **$$**

Bethlehem (C-6)

See also Allentown, Bucks County, Easton, Quakertown (Bucks County)

Founded 1741
Population 71,329
Elevation 340 ft
Area Code 484 and 610
Information Bethlehem Tourism Authority, 52 W Broad St, 18018; phone 610/868-1513 or toll-free 800/360-8687
Web site www.bethtour.org

The city is famous throughout the world for Bethlehem Steel products and is also well known for its Bach Festival, for Lehigh University (1865), Moravian College (1807), Musikfest, its historic district, and as "America's Christmas city."

Moravians, members of a very old Protestant denomination that came here to the banks of the Lehigh River, assembled on Christmas Evening 1741 in the only building, a log house that was part stable. Singing a hymn that praised Bethlehem, they found a name for their village. The musical heritage, too, dates from this moment; string quartets and symphonies were heard here before any other place in the colonies.

The opening of the Lehigh Canal in 1829 started industrialization of the area and development of the borough of South Bethlehem (1865), which was incorporated into the city of Bethlehem in 1917.

What to See and Do

Apothecary Museum. *424 Main St, Bethlehem (18018). In rear; entry gate next to book shop. Phone 610/867-0173.* Original fireplace (1752), where prescriptions were compounded; collection of artifacts includes retorts, grinders, mortars and pestles, scales, blown-glass bottles, labels, and a set of Delft jars (1743); herb and flower garden. (By appointment) **$**

Brethren's House. *Church and Main sts, Bethlehem. Phone 610/861-3916.* (1748) Early residence and shop area for single men of the Moravian Community. Used as a general hospital by the Continental Army during the Revolutionary War. Now serves Moravian College as its Center for Music and Art.

Central Moravian Church. *40 W Church St, Bethlehem (10818).* (1806) Federal-style with hand-carved detail, considered foremost Moravian church in the US. Noted for its music, including a trombone choir in existence since 1754.

God's Acre. *Church and Market sts, Bethlehem (18018).* (1742-1910) Old Moravian cemetery following Moravian tradition that all gravestones are laid flat, indicating that all are equal in the sight of God.

Hill-to-Hill Bridge. *Main St, Hwy 378 over Lehigh River.* Joins old and new parts of the city and provides excellent view of historic area, river, and Bethlehem Steel plant.

Historic Bethlehem Inc's 18th-Century Industrial Quarter. *459 Old York Rd, Bethlehem (18018). Ohio Rd and Main St (pedestrian entrance); Old York Rd and Union Blvd (parking lot entrance). Phone 610/691-0603.* Guided tours (July-Aug: Sat; late Nov-late Dec: weekends). (See SPECIAL EVENTS) **$$** Tour of area includes

Goundie House. *501 Main St, Bethlehem.* (1810) Restored Federal-style brick house has period-furnished rooms and interpretive exhibits.

Luckenbach Mill. (1869) Restored gristmill contains contemporary craft gallery and museum shop; also the offices of Bethlehem Area Chamber of Commerce and Historic Bethlehem Inc. Interpretive display here is included in guided tour.

Springhouse. (1764) Reconstruction on site of original spring that served Moravian community as a water source from the time of settlement in 1741 until 1912.

Tannery. (1761) Exhibits Moravian crafts, trades, and industries. Includes a working model of the original oil mill.

Waterworks. (1762) with reconstructed 18-foot wooden waterwheel and pumping mechanisms.

Kemerer Museum of Decorative Arts. *427 N New St, Bethlehem. Phone 610/691-0603.* Exhibits include art, Bohemian glass, toys, prints, china; regional German folk art from 1750-1900; Federal furniture; period room settings. (Tues-Sun; closed holidays) **$$$**

Lost River Caverns. *726 Durham St, Hellertown. 3 miles SE via Hwy 412. Phone 610/838-8767.* Stalagmites, stalactites, other formations. Picnic area; Gilman Museum with rocks and minerals, ancient and modern armor; also jungle garden (free). 30-minute guided tours. (Daily; closed Jan 1, Thanksgiving, Dec 25) **$$$**

Moravian Museum (Gemein Haus). *66 W Church St, Bethlehem. Phone 610/867-0173.* (1741) This five-story log building is the oldest structure in the city; docents interpret the history and culture of early Bethlehem and the Moravians. 45-minute tour. (Tues-Sun; closed holidays, including Good Friday, Holy Saturday, also Jan)

Old Chapel. *Heckewelder Place, adjacent to Moravian Museum.* (1751) Once called the "Indian chapel" because so many Native Americans attended the services, this stone structure, the second church for the Moravian congregation, is still used frequently. May be toured only in combination with Moravian Museum community walking tour.

Special Events

Bach Festival. *Packer Church, Lehigh University campus. Phone 610/866-4382.* One of the country's outstanding musical events. Famous artists and the Bach Choir of Bethlehem participate. Mid-late May.

Christmas. *52 W Broad St, Bethlehem. Phone 610/868-1513; toll-free 800/360-8687.* Bethlehem continues more than two centuries of Christmas tradition with candlelight, music, and a number of special events. Moravians sing their own Christmas songs intermingled with Mozart and Handel. A huge "Star of Bethlehem" shines from the top of South Mountain and the Hill-to-Hill Bridge has special lighting. The community "Putzes," a Moravian version of nativity scenes, are open to the public daily. Thousands of people post their Christmas cards from Bethlehem. Night Light Tours of city's Christmas displays and historical areas are offered (Dec) by the Bethlehem Tourism Authority. Reservations suggested. Thanksgiving-Jan 1.

Live Bethlehem Christmas Pageant. *Phone 610/867-2893.* Scores of volunteers (garbed in biblical costumes) and live animals (including camels, horses, donkey and sheep) join together to re-create the nativity story; narrated. First weekend in Dec.

Moravian College Alumni Association Antiques Show. *Johnston Hall, Moravian College Campus, 1200 Main St, Bethlehem (18018). Phone 610/861-1366.* Early June.

Musikfest. *25 W 3rd St, Bethlehem (18015). Phone 610/861-0678.* Nine-day festival celebrating Bethlehem's rich musical and ethnic heritage. More than 600 performances (most free) of all types of music including folk, big-band, jazz, country-western, chamber, classical, gospel, rock, swing; held at nine different sites in downtown historic area. Also children's activities. Late Aug.

Shad Festival. *Phone 610/691-0603* . Historic Bethlehem's 18th-century Industrial Quarter. Old-fashioned planked shad bake (reservations required for dinner), exhibits, demonstrations. First Sun in May.

Limited-Service Hotels

★ COMFORT INN. *3191 Highfield Dr, Bethlehem (18020). Phone 610/865-6300; toll-free 800/732-2500; fax 610/865-5074. www.choicehotels.com.* 116 rooms, 2 story. Pets accepted; fee. Complimentary continental breakfast. Check-out noon. Bar. **$**

★ ★ HOLIDAY INN. *3560 Bath Pike; Rtes 512 and 22, Bethlehem (18017). Phone 610/866-5800; toll-free 888/222-8512; fax 610/867-9120. www.holiday-inn.com.* 192 rooms, 2 story. Check-out noon. Restaurant, bar. Fitness room. Outdoor pool, children's pool. Airport transportation available. Business center. **$**

Specialty Lodging

The following lodging establishment is approved by Mobil Travel Guide, but due to its unique and individualized nature has not been given a traditional Mobil Star rating. Included in this listing you may find bed-and-breakfasts, limited-service inns, guest ranches, and other unique hotel properties.

WYDNOR HALL INN. *3612 Old Philadelphia Pike, Bethlehem (18015). Phone 610/867-6851; toll-free 800/839-0020; fax 610/866-2062.* 5 rooms, 3 story. Complimentary continental breakfast. Check-in 2-8 pm, check-out 11 am. Built in 1895. European-style inn. **$**

Restaurants

★ ★ CAFE. *221 W Broad St, Bethlehem (18018). Phone 610/866-1686.* International menu. Lunch, dinner. Closed Sun-Mon. Reservations recommended. **$$**

★ ★ CANDLELIGHT INN. *4431 Easton Ave, Bethlehem (18020). Phone 610/691-7777; fax 610/691-8378.* American menu. Lunch, dinner. Bar. Children's menu. **$$$**

★ EASTERN CHINESE. *3926 Linden St, Bethlehem (18020). Phone 610/868-0299; fax 610/868-1321.* Chinese menu. Lunch, dinner. Closed Thanksgiving. Bar. Reservations recommended. **$$**

★ ★ INN OF THE FALCON. *1740 Seidersville Rd, Bethlehem (18015). Phone 610/868-6505; fax 610/868-6507. www.innofthefalcon.com.* The landmark status of this charming restaurant is evident from the red shutters, flower-filled window boxes, and rustic stone facade of its home. Chef/owner Shirlee Neumeyer turns out creative dishes in the cozy, authentically furnished dining room. American menu. Dinner. Closed Sun; holidays. Bar. Building built in 1800s. Reservations recommended. **$$**

★ ★ ★ MAIN STREET DEPOT. *61 W Lehigh St, Bethlehem (18018). Phone 610/868-7123.* American menu. Lunch, dinner. Closed Sun; holidays. Bar. 1873 Victorian railway station; old train pictures, gas chandeliers. Reservations recommended. **$$$**

★ ★ MINSI TRAIL INN. *626 Stefko Blvd, Bethlehem (18018). Phone 610/691-5613. www.minsitrailinn.com.* American, Greek menu. Lunch, dinner, Sun brunch. Closed holidays. Bar. Children's menu. Reservations recommended. **$$**

Bird-in-Hand

See also Ephrata, Lancaster

Population 700
Elevation 358 ft
Area Code 717
Zip 17505
Information Pennsylvania Dutch Convention and Visitors Bureau, 501 Greenfield Rd, Lancaster 17601; phone 717/299-8901 or toll-free 800/723-8824
Web site www.800padutch.com

This Pennsylvania Dutch farming village got its name from the signboard of an early inn.

What to See and Do

Amish Village. *Hwy 896, Strasburg. 1 mile W on Hwy 340, then 3 miles S on Hwy 896. Phone 717/687-8511.* Reconstructed and original buildings include blacksmith shop, schoolhouse, operating smokehouse; livestock. Guided tours of Amish farmhouse. (Mar-Dec: daily; rest of year: most weekends; closed week of Thanksgiving, also Dec 25) **$$$**

Bird-in-Hand Farmers' Market. *Hwy 340 and Maple Ave, Bird-in-Hand. Phone 717/393-9674.* Indoor market with a wide variety of Pennsylvania Dutch foods and gifts. (July-Oct: Wed-Sat; Apr-June and Nov: Wed, Fri, and Sat; rest of year: Fri and Sat; closed Jan 1, Thanksgiving, Dec 25)

Folk Craft Center & Museum. *441 Mt Sidney Rd, Witmer. 1 1/2 miles W on Hwy 340, then N on Mt. Sidney Rd. Phone 717/397-3609.* Early 18th-century buildings display tools, household implements, stoneware pottery, toys, Stiegel glass, quilts, coverlets, and early Pennsylvania Dutch memorabilia; log cabin loom house (1762); herb and ornamental gardens; turn-of-the-century woodworking and print shops; audiovisual presentation. (Apr-Nov, daily) **DONATION**

The People's Place. *3513 Old Philadelphia Pike, Intercourse. Phone 717/768-7171.* Arts and heritage center features three-screen documentary on the Amish; interpretive museum with hands-on exhibits; Amish quilt museum. Also bookstore, art gallery. 5 miles E on Hwy 340, on Main St in Intercourse. (Mon-Sat; closed Jan 1, Thanksgiving, Dec 25)

Weavertown One-Room Schoolhouse. *2916 Old Philadelphia Pike, Bird-in-Hand (17505). 1 mile E via Hwy 340. Phone 717/768-3976.* Life-size animated re-creation of activities at a one-room schoolhouse. (Early April-Oct: daily; Mar and Nov: weekends) **$$**

Full-Service Inn

★★★ BIRD-IN-HAND FAMILY INN. *2740 Old Philadelphia Pike, Bird-in-Hand (17505). Phone 717/768-8271; toll-free 800/665-8780; fax 717/768-1117. www.bird-in-hand.com.* This quiet inn is found in the small town of Bird-in-Hand, and is within walking of the local attractions including the general store, farmers market, craft shops, and factory outlet stores. 100 rooms, 2 story. Check-out 11 am. Restaurant. Indoor pool, outdoor pool. Tennis. **$**

Specialty Lodgings

The following lodging establishments are approved by Mobil Travel Guide, but due to their unique and individualized nature have not been given a traditional Mobil Star rating. Included in this listing you may find bed-and-breakfasts, limited-service inns, guest ranches, and other unique hotel properties.

GREYSTONE MANOR BED AND BREAKFAST. *2658 Old Philadelphia Pike, Bird-in-Hand (17505). Phone 717/393-4233; fax 717/393-0616. www.800padutch.com/greystone.html.* This inn was built in the mid-1880s and is used today as a heritage lodging site. Situated on 8 acres of landscaped property, the inn offers guests Victorian charm and style for a relaxing stay. 10 rooms, 3 story. Closed Jan. Complimentary full breakfast. Check-in 3 pm, check-out 11 am. Victorian mansion built in 1883; Carriage House once a barn (1880s). **$**

VILLAGE INN. *2695 Old Philadelphia Pike, Bird-in-Hand (17505). Phone 717/293-8369; toll-free 800/914-2473; fax 717/768-1117. www.bird-in-hand.com/villageinn.* 3 story. Closed early Dec-early Feb. Children over 13 years old only. Complimentary continental breakfast. Check-in 3 pm, check-out noon. Built in 1734 as inn on Old Philadelphia Pike. Victorian interior ambience. **$**

Restaurants

★★ AMISH BARN. *3029 Old Philadelphia Pike, Bird-in-Hand (17505). Phone 717/768-8886; fax 717/768-7396. www.amishbarnpa.com.* Pennsylvania Dutch menu. Breakfast, lunch, dinner. Closed Jan 1, Dec 25. Children's menu. Outdoor seating. **$$**

★ PLAIN AND FANCY FARM. *3121 Old Philadelphia Pike, Bird-in-Hand (17505). Phone 717/768-4400; fax 717/768-4444. www.plainandfancyfarm.com.* Pennsylvania Dutch menu. Lunch, dinner. Closed Dec 24-25. Children's menu. **$$**

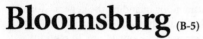

Bloomsburg (B-5)

See also Danville

Settled 1802
Population 12,375
Elevation 530 ft
Area Code 570
Zip 17815
Information Columbia-Montour Visitors Bureau, 121 Papermill Rd; phone 570/784-8279 or toll-free 800/847-4810
Web site www.cmtpa.org

Situated on the north bank of the Susquehanna River, Bloomsburg is the county seat of Columbia County. The town was a center of mining, transportation, and industry during the 19th and early 20th centuries. Although manufacturing continues to be the largest employer here, Bloomsburg retains the relaxed atmosphere of earlier days with its lovely scenery and many covered bridges. In nearby Orangeville, 9 miles west on Highway 487, Fishing Creek offers trout, bass, and pickerel.

The only incorporated town in the state (all the others are boroughs or cities), Bloomsburg has silk and rayon manufacturers; it also produces architectural aluminum, processed foods, and electronic products. During the Civil War, Union troops came here to crush the "Fishing Creek Confederacy," a group of alleged draft dodgers who were reportedly building fortifications; no fort was found, and the men were released. One of the "Molly Maguire" murder trials was held here. (The Molly Maguires was a miners' society seeking improved conditions through force and violence.)

What to See and Do

Bloomsburg University of Pennsylvania. *400 2nd St, Bloomsburg (17815). Phone 570/389-4316.* (1839) 6,600 students. On campus are Carver Hall (1867); the Harvey A. Andruss Library (1966); Haas Center for the Arts (1967) with 2,000-seat auditorium and art gallery; McCormick Center for Human Services (1985); Redman Stadium and Nelson Field House. Tours (academic year, Mon-Fri).

The Children's Museum. *2 W Seventh St, Bloomsburg (17815). Phone 570/389-9206. www.the-childrens-museum.org.* This kid-friendly museum has more than 50 hands-on activities that aim to make learning about our world and the environment fun. The museum has a new theme each year, and most of the exhibits change as well. (June-early Sept: Tues-Fri 10 am-4 pm, Sat 2-5 pm; early Sept-mid-Dec: Tues-Fri 10 am-3 pm, Sat 2-5 pm; Jan-Mar: call for hours; groups by appointment) **$**

Columbia County Historical Society. *410 Main St, Orangeville. 6 miles N on Hwy 487. Phone 570/784-1600.* Museum and Edwin M. Barton Library with local history exhibits, pioneer items. (Apr-Oct, Thurs-Sat; closed holidays) **$**

Historic District. *Bounded by West, 5th, 1st, Lake sts. Phone 570/784-7703.* More than 650 structures spanning architectural styles from Georgian to Art Deco. Center of town.

Twin covered bridges. *10 miles N on Hwy 487.* Believed to be the only twin covered bridges in the US. There are more than 20 other covered bridges in the area.

Special Events

Bloomsburg Fair. *4 Yardly Ave, Fallsington (19054). Fairgrounds, W side of town.* Fair held since 1854. Agricultural and industrial exhibits; harness racing. Eight days in late Sept.

Bloomsburg Theatre Ensemble. *Alvina Krause Theatre, 226 Center St, Bloomsburg (17815). Phone 717/784-8181.* Three to four weeks of performances for each of six plays. Main stage Oct-June (special performances rest of year).

Covered Bridge & Arts Festival. *I-80, exit 35.* Tours of covered bridges; apple butter boil; weaving; old-fashioned arts and crafts. Early Oct.

Limited-Service Hotel

★ BUDGET HOST PATRIOT INN. *6305 Columbia Blvd, Bloomsburg (17815). Phone 570/387-1776; toll-free 800/873-1180; fax 570/387-9611. www.budgethost.com.* 48 rooms. Check-out noon. Bar. **$**

Full-Service Inn

★ ★ ★ INN AT TURKEY HILL. *991 Central Rd, Bloomsburg (17815). Phone 570/387-1500; fax 570/784-3718. www.innatturkeyhill.com.* 18 rooms, 2 story.

Pets accepted, some restrictions; fee. Complimentary continental breakfast. Check-in 2 pm, check-out noon. Restaurant, bar. Airport transportation available. Old homestead (1839); guest rooms overlook landscaped courtyard; gazebo, lily pond. **$**

Specialty Lodging

The following lodging establishment is approved by Mobil Travel Guide, but due to its unique and individualized nature has not been given a traditional Mobil Star rating. Included in this listing you may find bed-and-breakfasts, limited-service inns, guest ranches, and other unique hotel properties.

MAGEE'S MAIN STREET INN. *20 W Main St, Bloomsburg (17815). Phone 570/784-3200; toll-free 800/331-9815; fax 570/784-5517. www.magees.com.* 8 rooms, 3 story. Pets accepted, some restrictions. Complimentary full breakfast. Check-out noon. Restaurant, bar. **$**

Bradford (A-2)

See also Kane, Warren

Settled 1827
Population 9,175
Elevation 1,442 ft
Area Code 814
Zip 16701
Information Bradford Area Chamber of Commerce, 10 Marilyn Horne Way, PO Box 135; phone 814/368-7115
Web site www.bradfordpa.com

When oil was discovered here, the price of land jumped from about six cents to $1,000 an acre; wells appeared on front lawns, in backyards, even in a cemetery. An oil exchange was established in 1877, two years after the first producing well was brought in. Diversified industry now provides the city's economic base. A Ranger District office of the Allegheny National Forest (see WARREN) is located here.

What to See and Do

Bradford Landmark Society. *45 E Corydon St, Bradford (16701). Phone 814/362-3906.* Headquartered in restored bakery; local history exhibits, period rooms. (Mon, Wed, and Fri; closed holidays) **FREE**

Crook Farm. *Seaward Ave Ext. Near the Tuna Crossroad. Phone 814/362-3906.* (1848) Original home of Erastus and Betsy Crook; restored to the 1870s period. (May-Sept, Tues-Fri afternoons, also Sat by appointment; closed holidays) (See SPECIAL EVENT) **$**

Carpenter Shop. (Circa 1870) Reconstruction of original; old hand tools.

Old Barn. (Circa 1870) Identical to the original; moved to Crook Farm in 1981 and rebuilt on the site of the original barn.

Old One-Room Schoolhouse #8. (1880) Authentic structure where classes are still held occasionally.

Special Event

Crook Farm Country Fair. *Crook Farm, Seaward Ave at Tuna Crossroad, Bradford. Phone 914/362-3906.* Arts and crafts, exhibits, entertainment, food. Last weekend in Aug.

Limited-Service Hotel

★★ **BEST WESTERN.** *100 S Davis St, Bradford (16701). Phone 814/362-4501; toll-free 800/344-4656; fax 814/362-2709. www.bestwestern.com.* 120 rooms, 3 story. Check-out noon. Restaurant, bar. Outdoor pool. **$**

Full-Service Inn

★★★ **GLENDORN.** *1000 Glendorn Dr, Bradford (16701). Phone 814/362-6511; toll-free 800/843-8568; fax 814/368-9923. www.glendorn.com.* Luxurious and restful, Glendorn provides the perfect escape for world-weary travelers seeking a blissful change of pace. Set on 1,280 acres, this one-time private estate offers a sophisticated twist on the traditional wooded retreat. A long private drive welcomes visitors to this hideaway, where guests enjoy walks in the woods, canoe and fishing trips, hiking and biking adventures, and a host of other outdoor pursuits. The accommodations in the Big House reflect a warm, country house spirit, while the cabin suites have a rugged charm. Fine dining is a hallmark of this country lodge, and with hearty country breakfasts, delicious lunches, and four-course prix-fixe dinners, palates are surprised and delighted here. 18 rooms,

2 story. Children over 12 years only. Check-in 2 pm, check-out 11 am. Restaurant. Fitness room. Outdoor pool. Tennis. **$$$$**

Breezewood (D-3)

See also Bedford, Chambersburg

Population 180
Elevation 1,356 ft
Area Code 814
Zip 15533

Limited-Service Hotels

★ ★ BEST WESTERN PLAZA MOTOR LODGE. *16407 Lincoln Hwy, Breezewood (15533). Phone 814/735-4352; fax 814/735-3036. www.bestwestern.com.* 89 rooms, 2 story. Check-out 11 am. Restaurant. Outdoor pool. **$**

★ QUALITY INN. *16621 Lincoln Hwy, Breezewood (15533). Phone 814/735-4311; toll-free 800/721-4311; fax 814/735-3433. www.choicehotels.com.* 50 rooms, 2 story. Check-out noon. Outdoor pool, children's pool. **$**

Bristol (Bucks County)

See also Philadelphia

Settled 1697
Population 9,923
Elevation 20 ft
Area Code 215 & 267
Zip 19007
Information Bucks County Conference and Visitors Bureau, Inc, 152 Swamp Rd, Doylestown 18901; phone 215/345-4552 or toll-free 800/836-BUCKS
Web site www.buckscountycvb.org

Bristol, founded in 1681, was the main thoroughfare from Philadelphia to New York. It has been frequented by famous visitors including Joseph Bonaparte, brother of Napoleon, and General Lafayette. There are homes dating from the 1700s; most of these have been restored.

What to See and Do

Grave of Captain John Green. *St. James Protestant Episcopal Church Burial Ground, Cedar and Walnut sts, Bristol (Bucks Co).* Grave of US Navy captain who piloted the *Columbia* around the world in 1787-1789 on first such voyage by vessel flying American flag.

Historic Fallsington. *4 Yardley Ave, Fallsington (19054). 5 miles N of Hwy Tpke, off Hwy 13. Phone 215/295-6567.* Restored 17th-, 18th-, and 19th-century buildings. Guided tours of 17th-century log house, Burges-Lippincott house, tavern. Also museum store. (See SPECIAL EVENT) (Mid-May-Oct, daily; closed holidays) **$$**

Pennsbury Manor. *400 Pennsbury Memorial Rd, Morrisville (19067). 5 miles NE, off Bordentown Rd. Phone 215/946-0400.* Reconstruction of William Penn's 17th-century country manor; formal and kitchen gardens; livestock. Craft demonstrations; hands-on workshops. (Tues-Sun; closed holidays) **$$**

Sesame Place. *100 Sesame Rd, Langhorne (19047). Approximately 7 miles N, near Oxford Valley Mall (Langhorne), just N of Philadelphia off I-95 between Philadelphia and Trenton, NJ. Phone 215/752-7070.* Family theme park combines fun with learning. More than 50 outdoor physical play activities develop skills and coordination with kid-powered units. The indoor interactive and science galleries offer games to challenge the mind. Sesame Food Factory: visible kitchen-in-the-round serves wholesome favorites. Mr. Hooper's Emporium: complete shop for all Sesame Street items. Sesame Island area with Caribbean theme; water activities include Big Bird's Rambling River and Sky Splash. Musical revue with Sesame Street characters. (May-Labor Day: daily; after Labor Day-late Oct: weekends only) **$$$$**

Special Event

Fallsington Day. *In Fallsington.* Outdoor fair; restored buildings open; colonial craft demonstrations; entertainment. Second Sat in Oct.

Brookville (B-2)

See also Clarion

Settled 1830
Population 4,230
Elevation 1,269 ft
Area Code 814
Zip 15825
Information Brookville Area Chamber of Commerce, 70 Pickering St; phone 814/849-8448

What to See and Do

Clear Creek State Park. *8 miles N on Hwy 36, then 4 miles NE on Hwy 949. Contact Park Manager, RD 1, Box 82, Sigel, 15860. Phone 814/752-2368.* Approximately 1,600 acres. Swimming beach, fishing, canoeing; hiking trails, cross-country skiing, picnicking, playing field, camping, cabins (dump station). Nature center; interpretive activities.

Special Event

Western Pennsylvania Laurel Festival. *Brookville. Phone 814/849-2024.* Third week in June.

Limited-Service Hotel

★ HOLIDAY INN EXPRESS. *235 Allegheny Blvd, Brookville (15825). Phone 814/849-8381; fax 814/849-8386. www.holiday-inn.com.* 68 rooms, 3 story. Pets accepted; fee. Complimentary continental breakfast. Check-out noon. **$**

Restaurant

★★ MEETING PLACE. *209 Main St, Brookville (15825). Phone 814/849-2557.* American menu. Breakfast, lunch, dinner. Closed Sun, holidays. Bar. Children's menu. Restored Victorian building (1871); casual dining. **$$**

Bucks County

Web site www.buckscountycvb.org

Bucks County's great natural resources, location, and waterway transportation were known to the Leni-Lenape centuries ago. Dutch explorers, followed by Swedes, English Quakers, and Germans, began to take possession of the area in the 1600s. William Penn established his country estate in this area in the 17th century.

The county's historic importance is highlighted in the central section—it was here that General George Washington crossed the Delaware River with the Continental Army during the Revolutionary War. More recently, artists and writers have settled in and around New Hope, giving rise to the village's fame as an art center. Bucks County's scenic beauty and rich history make it a popular tourist spot.

Following are the places in Bucks County included in this book. For full information on any one of them, see the individual alphabetical listing: Bristol, Doylestown, New Hope, Quakertown, Washington Crossing Historic Park.

Bushkill

See also Milford

Population 900
Elevation 365 ft
Area Code 570
Zip 18324
Information Pocono Mountains Vacation Bureau, 1004 Main St, Stroudsburg 18360; phone 570/424-6050; for free brochures phone toll-free 800/POCONOS
Web site www.poconos.org

What to See and Do

Bushkill Falls. *2 miles N off Hwy 209 on local road. Phone 570/588-6682.* Largest series of falls in Pocono Mountains. Main falls have 100-foot drop. Scenic gorge. Fishing, boating; picnicking. Wildlife exhibit of mounted animals and birds of Pennsylvania. (Apr-mid-Nov, daily) **$$$**

Pocono Indian Museum. *3 miles S on Hwy 209. Phone 570/588-9338.* Traces history of the Delaware through displays of artifacts, weapons, and tools. Gift shop. (Daily; closed Thanksgiving, Dec 25) **$$**

Butler (C-1)

See also Harmony, Pittsburgh

Settled 1793
Population 15,121
Elevation 1,077 ft
Area Code 724
Zip 16003
Information Butler County Chamber of Commerce, PO Box 1082; phone 724/283-2222
Web site www.butlercountychamber.com

This is a manufacturing city nestled amid rolling hills that were owned by Robert Morris of Philadelphia, financier of the Revolutionary War. The city and county are named for General Richard Butler, who died in the St. Clair Indian Expedition. During the 1930s, the Butler-based American Austin Company—later called American Bantam Company—pioneered the development of small, lightweight cars in America and invented the prototype of the jeep.

What to See and Do

Cooper Cabin. *199 Cooper Rd, Cabot (16023). Phone 724/283-8116.* (Circa 1810) A family homestead on 4 acres with heirlooms and memorabilia; spinning house, spring house, tool shed. Self-guided nature trail and herb garden; live history demonstrations and tours. (Call for hours and events) **$**

Jennings Environmental Education Center. *2951 Prospect Rd, Slippery Rock (16057). 12 miles N, at junction Hwys 8, 528, 173. Phone 724/794-6011.* Blazing Star, a relict prairie wildflower, blooms profusely here late July-early Aug. Trails, guided walks, interpretive center; picnicking. (Memorial Day-Labor Day: daily; rest of year: Mon-Fri, some Sun) **FREE**

Moraine State Park. *225 Pleasant Valley Rd, Portersville (16051). 12 miles NW on Hwy 422. Phone 724/368-8811.* A 3,225-acre lake in a 16,180-acre park. Swimming beaches, fishing, boating (rentals, mooring, launching, marina); hunting, hiking, bicycle trails (rentals), horseback riding, cross-country skiing, snowmobiling, sledding, ice skating, ice fishing, ice boating, picnicking, playground, snack bar, restaurant, cabin rentals. Waterfowl observation area; interpretive programs. Pontoon boat tours. **FREE**

Limited-Service Hotel

★ FAIRFIELD INN BY MARRIOTT BUTLER. *200 Fairfield Lane, Butler (16001). Phone 724/283-0009; toll-free 800/228-2800; fax 724/283-1045. www.fairfieldinn.com.* 75 rooms. Check-in 3 pm, check-out noon. Indoor pool, whirlpool. **$**

Full-Service Resort

★ ★ CONLEY RESORT. *740 Pittsburgh Rd, Butler (16002). Phone 724/586-7711; toll-free 800/344-7303; fax 724/586-2944. www.conleyresort.com.* 56 rooms, 3 story. Check-out 1 pm. Restaurant, bar. Indoor pool, whirlpool. Golf. Tennis. 150-foot indoor water park. **$**

Specialty Lodging

The following lodging establishment is approved by Mobil Travel Guide, but due to its unique and individualized nature has not been given a traditional Mobil Star rating. Included in this listing you may find bed-and-breakfasts, limited-service inns, guest ranches, and other unique hotel properties.

APPLEBUTTER INN. *666 Centreville Pike, Slippery Rock (16057). Phone 724/794-1844; toll-free 888/275-3466; fax 724/794-3319. www.pathway.net/applebutterinn.* Built in 1844, this charming inn offers guests a truly delightful stay. Guests are welcomed to relax amongst handsomely appointed guest rooms, including one room boasting an exquisite 1810 four-poster bed complete with a beautiful fish net canopy and antique chest. Make sure to take time to pamper yourself with one of the hot tub, spa, or massage packages. 11 rooms, 2 story. No children allowed. Complimentary full breakfast. Check-in 3-8 pm, check-out 11 am. **$**

Canadensis

Population 1,200
Area Code 570
Zip 18325

What to See and Do

Holley Ross Pottery. *Hwy 191, La Anna. S on Hwy 390, NW on Hwy 447, on Hwy 191 N. Phone 570/676-3248.* Twenty-minute guided tours with demonstration of pottery making (Mon-Fri). Swinging bridge, park, sawdust trails. (May-mid-Dec, daily) **FREE**

Full-Service Resort

★★★ **SKYTOP LODGE.** *1 Skytop, Mt. Pocono (18357). Phone 570/595-7401; toll-free 800/345-7759; fax 570/595-9618. www.skytop.com.* Skytop Lodge is the ultimate mountain getaway for outdoor enthusiasts, with an 18-hole golf course, seven tennis courts, a clay shooting range, indoor and outdoor pools, and even fly fishing in the natural streams found throughout the property. This retreat in the heart of the Poconos is easily accessed from New York or Philadelphia, yet its wilderness setting will calm the soul of any city dweller. Accommodations are found within the historic hotel, four-bedroom cottages, or the intimate golf course inn, and all offer comfortable environments in which to relax and recharge. The continental menu at the Windsor Dining Room (jacket required) draws a crowd, while more casual dining is available at the Lake View Dining Room and the Tap Room. 185 rooms, 4 story. Check-in 4 pm, check-out 1 pm. Three restaurants, bar. Children's activity center. Fitness room. Indoor pool, outdoor pool, children's pool, whirlpool. Golf, 18 holes. Tennis. Beach. **$$$$**

Full-Service Inn

★★★ **CRESCENT LODGE.** *191 Paradise Valley, Mt. Pocono (18326). Phone 570/595-7486; toll-free 800/392-9400; fax 570/595-3452. www.crescentlodge.com.* Nestled in the heart of the Pocono Mountains, guests should be prepared to enter a truly elegant country inn, where the welcomes are warm and the ambience is one of pure serenity. Guests will find delight in the charmingly furnished guest rooms, each with its own distinctive flair, with some rooms offering a sunken Jacuzzi as well as private patios and sundecks overlooking the lush and well-maintained grounds. 31 rooms. Complimentary continental breakfast. Check-in 2 pm, check-out 11 am. Restaurant, bar. Tennis. **$**

Specialty Lodgings

The following lodging establishments are approved by Mobil Travel Guide, but due to their unique and individualized nature have not been given a traditional Mobil Star rating. Included in this listing you may find bed-and-breakfasts, limited-service inns, guest ranches, and other unique hotel properties.

BROOKVIEW MANOR INN. *2960 Hwy 447, Canadensis (18325). Phone 570/595-2451; toll-free 800/585-7974; fax 570/595-5065. www.brookviewmanor.com.* This bed-and-breakfast offers the traveler an ideal retreat from the workday world. Each room offers a panoramic view of the forest, stream, and mountains. The inn is convenient to many popular Pocono activities, a wide selection of outlet stores, and unique country craft and antiques shops. 10 rooms, 3 story. Children over 12 years only. Complimentary full breakfast. Check-in 3 pm, check-out noon. **$$**

PINE KNOB INN. *Hwy 447, Canadensis (18325). Phone 570/595-2532; toll-free 800/426-1460; fax 570/595-6429. www.pineknobinn.com.* 28 rooms. Check-in 2 pm, check-out 11 am. Tennis. **$$**

Restaurant

★★★ **PUMP HOUSE INN.** *Hwy 390 N, Canadensis (18325). Phone 570/595-7501. www.pumphouseinn.com.* Located in a big house in the country—guest rooms are upstairs—the Pump House pleases diners with well prepared American fare and congenial service. There are a variety of specials that change every night. American, French menu. Lunch, dinner. Closed Mon; Dec 25. Bar. Country inn (1842). **$$**

Carbondale (B-6)

See also Hawley, Scranton

Founded 1822
Population 9,804
Elevation 1,070 ft
Area Code 570
Zip 18407
Information Northeast Pennsylvania Convention and Visitors Bureau, 99 Glenmaura National Blvd, Scranton, 18507; phone toll-free 800/229-3526
Web site www.visitnepa.org

Carbondale, located in the heart of the northeast Pocono area, has excellent sports facilities. There are 33 lakes within an 8-mile radius and 201 more lakes within 25 miles. One of the first railroad lines in the country was built to haul coal from Carbondale.

What to See and Do

Elk Mountain Ski Center. *RR2, Union Dale (18470). NW on Hwy 106, E on Hwy 374. Phone 570/679-4400; toll-free 800/233-4131 (snow conditions). www.elkskier.com.* At an elevation of 2,693 feet, this is eastern Pennsylvania's highest mountain. Quad, five double chairlifts; patrol, school, rentals; cafeteria, restaurant, bar. Longest run 2 miles; vertical drop 1,000 feet. (Early Dec-late Mar, daily) Half-day rate. **$$$$**

Merli-Sarnoski Park. *1/2 mile off Hwy 106. Phone 570/876-1714.* Covers 850 acres of woodlands with 40-acre lake. Swimming beach (lifeguards), fishing (seasonal), boating (launch); hiking trails, picnicking. Winter activities include cross-country skiing, ice skating, ice fishing. (Daily)

Mount Tone Ski Resort. *Wallerville Rd, Lake Como. N via Hwy 171, E via Hwy 370 to Lakewood, then S on Hwy 247 to Lake Como, follow signs. Phone 570/798-2707. www.mttone.com.* Triple chairlift, T-bar, rope tow, mighty mite; school, rentals; snowmaking; cafeteria; lodge. Vertical drop 450 feet. (Late Dec-mid-Mar) Two mountains, ten trails; also night skiing, cross-country trails. **$$$$**

Carlisle (D-4)

See also Harrisburg

Settled 1720
Population 17,970
Elevation 478 ft
Area Code 717
Zip 17013
Information Greater Area Chamber of Commerce, 212 N Hanover St, PO Box 572; phone 717/243-4515
Web site www.carlislechamber.org

In the historically strategic Cumberland Valley, Carlisle was a vital point for Native American fighting during the Revolutionary and Civil wars.

Carlisle Barracks is one of the oldest military posts in America. Soldiers mounted guard here as early as 1750 to protect the frontier. From here began British campaigns that drove the French from the Ohio Valley and, in 1763, the march to relieve Fort Pitt. In 1794 President Washington reviewed troops assembled to march against the "Whiskey Rebels." Troops went from the Barracks to the Mexican and Civil wars. The famous Carlisle Indian Industrial School, the first nonreservation school, was here until 1918. The Barracks was reopened in 1920 as the Medical Field Service School. It is now the home of the US Army War College.

George Ross, James Wilson, and James Smith, all signers of the Declaration of Independence, lived in Carlisle, as did Molly Pitcher.

What to See and Do

Carlisle Barracks. *22 Ashburn Dr, Carlisle (17013). 1 mile N on Hwy 11. Phone 717/245-3611.* Army War College, senior school in US Army's educational system. Includes the US Army Military History Institute and Hessian Powder Magazine Museum (1777), built by prisoners captured at the Battle of Trenton. The Carlisle Indian Industrial School (1879-1918) was one of the first institutions of higher learning for Native Americans. Also includes the Omar Bradley Museum, containing a collection of personal and military memorabilia of the five-star general. Jim Thorpe and other famous Native American athletes studied here. Military History Institute and the Omar Bradley Museum (Mon-Fri; closed federal holidays). Post/grounds (Daily; closed federal holidays). **FREE**

Cumberland County Historical Society and Hamilton Library Association. *21 N Pitt St, Carlisle (17013). Phone 717/249-7610. www.historicalsociety.com.* Woodcarvings, furniture, silver, tools, redware, ironware, tall-case clocks, coverlets, paintings by local artisans; mementos of the Carlisle Indian School; special exhibits and programs. Library contains books, tax lists, early photographs, genealogical material. (Tues-Sat, Mon evenings; closed holidays) **FREE**

Dickinson College. *242 W High St, Carlisle. Phone 717/243-5121.* (1773) 1,900 students. Tenth college chartered in US; President James Buchanan was a graduate. On campus is "Old West" (1804), a building registered as a National Historic Landmark that was designed by Benjamin Henry Latrobe, one of the designers of the Capitol in Washington. Tours of campus. Also here is

The Trout Gallery. *West High St, Carlisle. Emil R. Weiss Center for the Arts. Phone 717/245-1711.* Permanent and temporary exhibits. (Sept-mid-June, Tues-Sat) **FREE**

Grave of Molly Pitcher. *South St. In Old Graveyard, E South St.* (Mary Ludwig Hays McCauley) Soldiers in the Battle of Monmouth (June 1778) gave Molly her nickname because of her devotion to her husband and others who were fighting by bringing them pitchers of water. When her husband was wounded, Molly took his place at a cannon and continued fighting for him.

Huntsdale Fish Hatchery. *195 Lebo Rd, Huntsdale (17013). 10 miles SW. Phone 717/486-3419.* Springs and mountain stream fill tanks and ponds of brown, rainbow, and palomino trout, muskellunge and walleye; visitor center. (Daily) **FREE**

Pine Grove Furnace State Park. *1212 Pine Grove Rd, Carlisle (17234). 10 miles SW on I-81, exit 11, then 8 miles S on Hwy 233. Phone 717/486-7575.* Pre-Revolutionary iron, slate, and brick works were in this area. Approximately 696 acres. Swimming beaches, fishing, boating (rentals, mooring, launching); hunting, hiking, bicycling (rentals), cross-country skiing, ice skating, ice fishing, picnicking, snack bar, store, tent and trailer sites. Visitor center. Lodging available.

Special Events

Art Festival and Octoberfest. *Carlisle.* Oct.

Summerfair. *Carlisle. Downtown Carlisle.* Early July.

Limited-Service Hotels

★★ CLARION HOTEL. *1700 Harrisburg Pike, Carlisle (17013). Phone 717/243-1717; toll-free 800/692-7315; fax 717/243-6648. www.clarioncarlisle.com.* 270 rooms. Pets accepted; fee. Check-out 11 am. Restaurant, bar. Indoor pool, whirlpool. Tennis. **$**

★ DAYS INN. *101 Alexander Spring Rd, Carlisle (17013). Phone 717/258-4147; fax 717/258-1207. www.daysinn.com.* 130 rooms, 3 story. Complimentary continental breakfast. Check-out noon. Fitness room. Outdoor pool. Airport transportation available. **$**

★★ HOLIDAY INN. *1450 Harrisburg Pike, Carlisle (17013). Phone 717/245-2400; toll-free 800/465-4329; fax 717/245-9070.* 100 rooms, 2 story. Pets accepted; fee. Check-out noon. Restaurant, bar. Outdoor pool. **$**

★ QUALITY INN. *1255 Harrisburg Pike, Carlisle (17013). Phone 717/243-6000; fax 717/258-4123. www.qualityinn.com.* 96 rooms, 2 story. Pets accepted, some restrictions. Complimentary continental breakfast. Check-out noon. Bar. Outdoor pool, children's pool. **$**

Full-Service Resort

★★ ALLENBERRY RESORT INN. *1559 Boiling Springs Rd, Boiling Springs (17007). Phone 717/258-3211; toll-free 800/430-5468; fax 717/960-5293. www.allenberry.com.* 69 rooms. Check-out noon. Restaurant, bar. Pool, children's pool, whirlpool. Tennis. Airport transportation available. On 57 wooded acres, 200-year-old trees; several remodeled limestone buildings date from 1785, 1812. Professional theater. On Yellow Breeches Creek. **$**

Restaurants

★ ★ **BOILING SPRINGS TAVERN.** *Front and First sts, Boiling Springs (17007). Phone 717/258-3614; fax 717/258-5250.* American menu. Lunch, dinner. Closed Sun-Mon; holidays. Bar. Children's menu. Old stone structure (1832), originally an inn. **$$**

★ ★ **CALIFORNIA CAFE.** *38 W Pomfret St, Carlisle (17013). Phone 717/249-2028; fax 717/249-0330. www.calcaf.com.* California, French menu. Lunch, dinner. Closed Memorial Day weekend, Dec 25. **$$**

Chalfont

Restaurant

★ **LOS SARAPES.** *17 Moyer Rd, Chalfont (18914). Phone 215/822-8858; fax 215/822-6149. www.lossarapes .com.* Mexican menu. Lunch, dinner, brunch. Closed Mon; holidays. Bar. Casual attire. Outdoor seating. **$$**

Chambersburg (D-3)

See also Breezewood

Settled 1730
Population 17,862
Elevation 621 ft
Area Code 717
Zip 17201
Information Chamber of Commerce, 75 S Second St; phone 717/264-7101. Information is also available at the Visitors Station, 1235 Lincoln Way E; phone 717/261-1200
Web site www.chambersburg.org

Named for Colonel Benjamin Chambers, a Scottish-Irish pioneer, this is an industrial county seat amid peach and apple orchards. John Brown had his headquarters here. During the Civil War, Confederate cavalry burned down the town, destroying 537 buildings after the citizens refused to pay an indemnity of $100,000.

What to See and Do

Caledonia State Park. *40 Rocky Mountain Rd, Fayetteville (17222). 10 miles E on Hwy 30. Phone 717/352-2161.* Confederate General Jubal A. Early came through here during the Civil War and destroyed an iron furnace, which had been producing arms for the Union armies. Approximately 1,100 acres. Swimming pool (fee), fishing; nature and hiking trails, bicycling, 18-hole golf course, cross-country skiing, picnicking, playground, snack bar, tent and trailer sites. (See SPECIAL EVENTS)

Capitol Theatre. *159 S Main St, Chambersburg. Phone 717/263-0202.* This 1927 movie house presents performances ranging from classical concerts to big bands; theatrical presentations. Features a 1928 Moller pipe organ. Call for performances and fees.

The Old Jail. *175 E King St, Chambersburg. Phone 717/264-6364.* Jail complex (1818) restored and renovated for use as the Kittochtinny Historical Society's Museum and Library. An 1880 cell block houses community cultural activities, art and historical exhibits; other events. Also on grounds are Colonial, Fragrance, and Japanese gardens; 19th-century barn; agricultural museum. Cultural programs (May-Oct). Tours (May-Nov, Thurs-Sat). **FREE**

Special Events

ChambersFest. *Emil R. Weiss Center for the Performing Arts, Caledonia State Park, 75 S 2nd St, Chambersburg. Phone 717/264-7101.* Civil War festival with crafts, food, reenactments, parade of pets. July.

Franklin County Fair. *Rod and Gun Club Farm, 5995 Warm Springs, Chambersburg. Phone 717/369-4100.* Arts and crafts displays, needlework, home and dairy products, state turkey-calling contest, tractor pull, agricultural and livestock exhibits, entertainment. Third full week in Aug.

Totem Pole Playhouse. *Caledonia State Park, 9555 Golf Course Rd, Chambersburg. Phone 717/352-2164.* Resident professional theater company performs dramas, comedies, and musicals in 453-seat proscenium theater. Tues-Sun evenings; matinees Wed, Sat-Sun. June-Aug.

Limited-Service Hotels

★ **HAMPTON INN.** *955 Lesher Rd, Chambersburg (17201). Phone 717/261-9185; fax 717/261-1984. www.hamptoninn.com.* 124 rooms, 3 story. Complimentary continental breakfast. Check-out noon. Fitness room. **$**

★ ★ **QUALITY INN.** *1095 Wayne Ave, Chambersburg (17201). Phone 717/263-3400; toll-free 800/465-4329; fax 717/263-8386. www.choicehotels.com.* 139 rooms, 2 story. Pets accepted, some restrictions; fee. Check-out noon. Restaurant, bar. Pool. **$**

Full-Service Inn

★ ★ ★ **MERCERSBURG INN.** *405 S Main St, Mercersburg (17236). Phone 717/328-5231; fax 717/328-3403. www.mercersburginn.com.* Located between the civil war battlefield and other historic sites is this 15-room country inn. Golf courses, tennis facilities, skiing, fly fishing, mountain biking and hiking trails are all located within a short distance. 15 rooms, 3 story. Complimentary full breakfast. Check-in 3 pm, check-out 11 am. Restaurant. **$**

Restaurant

★ ★ **COPPER KETTLE.** *1049 Lincoln Way E (Hwy 30), Chambersburg (17201). Phone 717/264-3109.* Seafood, steak menu. Dinner. Closed Sun; holidays. Bar. Children's menu. **$$**

Chester (D-6)

See also Kennett Square, King of Prussia, Media, Philadelphia, West Chester, Wilmington

Settled 1643
Population 41,856
Area Code 484, 610
Information Delaware County Convention & Tourist Bureau, 200 E Estate St, Suite 100, Media 19063; phone 610/565-3679 or toll-free 800/343-3983

The oldest settlement in the state, Chester was established by the Swedish Trading Company as Upland. William Penn came to Upland in 1682 to begin colonization of the land granted to him by King Charles II. He renamed the settlement in honor of Chester, a Quaker center in Cheshire, England. The first Assembly here adopted Penn's Framework of Government, enacted the first laws, and organized the county of Chester—from which Delaware County broke off in 1789. On the Delaware River, 15 miles southwest of Philadelphia, Chester is a busy port and home of shipyards where every type of vessel has been built for the navy and merchant marine.

What to See and Do

Caleb Pusey Home, Landingford Plantation. *15 Race St, Upland (19015). Phone 610/874-5665.* (1683) Built for manager and agent of Penn's mill; only remaining house in state visited by William Penn. Period furniture. Also on 27 acres of original plantation are a log house (1790), stone schoolhouse-museum (1849), and herb garden. (May-Sept, Sat and Sun afternoons; also by appointment; closed holidays) **FREE**

Morton Homestead. *100 Lincoln Ave, Prospect Park. 4 miles NE on Hwy 13, then SW on Hwy 420. Phone 610/583-7221.* (Circa 1655) Two-part log house built by ancestors of John Morton, signer of Declaration of Independence. Contemporary outdoor exhibits on Pennsylvania's Swedish Period, log-house construction, Morton family. (Wed-Sat) **FREE**

Penn Memorial Landing Stone. *Front and Penn sts, Chester.* Marks spot where William Penn first landed Oct 28, 1682.

Swarthmore College. *500 College Ave, Swarthmore (19081). 4 miles N on Hwy 320. Phone 610/328-8000.* (1864) (1,320 students) Coeducational; on wooded 330-acre campus are Friends Historical Library and Peace Collection, an art gallery, concert hall, performing arts center, observatory, terraced grass amphitheater, Friends Meeting House, Scott Arboretum, a collection of trees, shrubs, and herbaceous plants throughout campus. Symposia, exhibits, music, and dance programs are open to the public.

Widener University. *3800 Vartan Rd, Chester (17110). 14th and Walnut sts. Phone 610/499-4000.* (1821) (7,000 students) On campus are Old Main, a national historic landmark, and the University Art Museum, with a permanent collection of 19th- and 20th-century American Impressionist and European academic art as well as contemporary exhibits (Sept-May: Tues-Sat; June and Aug: Mon-Thurs; closed July). Also here is Wolfgram Memorial Library. Campus tours.

Clarion (B-2)

See also Brookville

Founded 1839
Population 8,491
Elevation 1,491 ft
Area Code 814
Zip 16214
Information Clarion Area Chamber of Business and Industry, 41 S Fifth Ave; phone 814/226-9161
Web site www.clarionpa.com

Once the forests were so thick and tall here that, according to tradition, the wind in the treetops sounded like a distant clarion. That's how the town, county, and river got their names. Today many campers and sports and outdoors enthusiasts enjoy the beauty and recreation that the Clarion area offers.

What to See and Do

Clarion County Historical Society. *18 Grant St, Clarion (16214). Phone 814/226-4450.* Museum housed in mid-19th century Sutton-Ditz house. Contains exhibits on county industry and business; Victorian bedroom and parlor; genealogical and historical library (researchers may call ahead for appointment other than regular hours); changing exhibits. (Apr-Dec, Tues, Thurs, and Fri afternoons; closed holidays) **FREE**

Cook Forest State Park. *River Rd, Cooksburg. 11 miles NE on Clarion to Cook Forest Rd, then 3 miles S on Hwy 36. Phone 814/744-8407.* Approximately 6,700 acres. Swimming pool (fee), fishing; hunting, hiking, bicycling, horseback riding, cross-country skiing (rentals), snowmobiling, sledding, ice skating, picnicking, tent and trailer sites, cabins (rentals). Nature and historical center.

Tionesta Reservoir. *5 miles NW on Hwy 322, then 20 miles NW on Hwy 66, in Allegheny National Forest.* (see WARREN)

Special Events

Autumn Leaf Festival. Parade, carnival, autorama, scholarship pageants, concerts, flea market, craft shows. Late Sept-early Oct.

Spring Fling. Concerts, food concessions, games, entertainment. Early May.

Limited-Service Hotels

★★ HOLIDAY INN. *45 Holiday Inn Dr, Clarion (16214). Phone 814/226-8850; toll-free 800/596-1313; fax 814/226-9055. www.holiday-inn.com.* 122 rooms, 2 story. Pets accepted; fee. Check-out noon. Restaurant, bar. Indoor pool. Airport transportation available. **$**

★ SUPER 8. *I-80 and Rte 68, Clarion (16214). Phone 814/226-4550; toll-free 800/800-8000; fax 814/227-2337. www.super8.com.* 99 rooms. Pets accepted. Complimentary continental breakfast. Check-out noon. Outdoor pool. **$**

Clearfield (Clearfield County) (B-3)

Settled 1805
Population 6,631
Elevation 1,109 ft
Area Code 814
Zip 16830
Information Clearfield Chamber of Commerce, 125 E Market St, PO Box 250; phone 814/765-7567

The old and important Native American town of Chinklacamoose occupied this site until it was burned in 1757. Coal and clay mining and more than 20 diversified plants producing school supplies, firebrick, fur products, precision instruments, electronic products, and sportswear now occupy what used to be cleared fields. Easy access to other parts of the state and rich river bottom land led to the establishment of the county seat here.

What to See and Do

Parker Dam. *14 miles NW on Hwy 153, 6 miles off I-80 exit 18, then 2 miles E on unnumbered road. Phone 814/765-0630.* Approximately 950 acres in

Moshannon State Forest. Swimming beach, fishing, boating (launch, rentals); hiking, cross-country skiing, snowmobiling, sledding, ice skating, ice fishing, snack bar, tent and trailer sites (electric hookups), cabins. Nature center.

S. B. Elliott. *9 miles N, off Hwy 153, just N of I-80 exit 18. Phone 814/765-7271.* Approximately 300 acres in the heart of the Moshannon State Forest; entirely wooded; display of mountain laurel in season. Fishing in small mountain streams surrounding the park. Hiking, snowmobile trails, tent and trailer sites, cabins.

Special Events

Central Counties Concerned Sportsmen Annual Show. *Clearfield County Fairgrounds, Mill Rd and Turnpike Ave. Phone 814/765-9495.* Fri-Sun mid-Mar.

Clearfield County Fair. *Clearfield County Fairgrounds, Mill Rd and Turnpike Ave. Phone 814/765-4629.* Late July-early Aug.

High Country Arts & Craft Fair. *S. B. Elliott State Park, Clearfield. Phone 814/765-9804.* Sun after July 4.

Laurel Tour. Late June-early July.

Limited-Service Hotel

★ **DAYS INN.** *Hwy 879 and I-80, Clearfield (16830). Phone 814/765-5381; fax 814/765-7885. www.daysinn.com.* 119 rooms, 2 story. Pets accepted; fee. Complimentary continental breakfast. Check-out noon. Fitness room. Outdoor pool. **$**

Conneaut Lake (A-1)

See also Edinboro, Meadville

Population 708
Elevation 1,100 ft
Area Code 814
Zip 16316
Information Crawford County Convention & Visitors Bureau, 211 Chestnut St, Meadville 16335; phone 814/333-1258 or toll-free 800/332-2338
Web site www.visitcrawford.org

Located on the largest natural lake in Pennsylvania (929 acres), this resort town has swimming, boating, and excellent fishing for perch, muskellunge, walleye, bass, and crappie.

What to See and Do

Conneaut Cellars Winery. *12005 Conneaut Lake Rd, Conneaut Lake (16316). Phone 814/382-3999.* Tours and tastings. (Daily) **FREE**

Pymatuning Spillway. *2660 Williamsfield Rd, Jamestown. NW via Hwy 6 on N end of reservoir. Phone 724/932-3141.* Part of Pymatuning State Park. When fish are fed bread, they flock so thickly that ducks walk on them. **FREE**

Pymatuning State Park. *2660 Williamsfield Rd, Jamestown (16134). SW via Hwy 322, 1 mile W of Jamestown. Phone 724/932-3141.* Approximately 21,100 acres with 17-mile lake. Swimming beach, fishing, boating (rentals, mooring, launching, marina); hunting, hiking, cross-country skiing, snowmobiling, sledding, ice skating, picnicking, playground, tent and trailer areas along shore, cabins. Waterfowl museum and refuge; fish hatchery.

Wildlife Learning Center. *12590 Hartstown Rd, Linesville (16424). 9 miles W on Hwy 285, then N on Hartstown-Linesville Rd. Phone 814/683-5545.* Part of Pennsylvania Game Commission; birds and animals indigenous to Pymatuning Reservoir area; bald eagle's nest visible from museum. Educational and interpretive programs. (Apr-mid Oct, Wed-Sun) **FREE**

Connellsville (D-2)

See also New Stanton, Uniontown

Population 9,146
Elevation 885 ft
Area Code 724
Zip 15425
Information Greater Connellsville Chamber of Commerce, 923 W Crawford Ave; phone 724/628-5500

Located in an area visited by George Washington and where he owned land, the region has many references to him in place names. The restored Crawford

Cabin near the river was the home of Colonel William Crawford, surveyor of these properties and Washington's surveying pupil.

Northwest of town in Perryopolis are many historic restorations. The town square is named for Washington, who some believe planned the design of the town.

What to See and Do

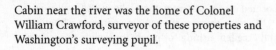

★ Fallingwater (Kaufmann Conservation on Bear Run). *Hwy 381 S, Mill Run. 8 miles E on Hwy 711, then 8 miles S on Hwy 381, near Mill Run. Phone 724/329-8501.* One of the most famous structures of the 20th century, Fallingwater, designed by Frank Lloyd Wright in 1936, is cantilevered on three levels over a waterfall; interior features Wright-designed furniture, textiles, and lighting, as well as sculpture by modern masters; extensive grounds are heavily wooded and planted with rhododendron, which blooms in early July. Visitor center with self-guided orientation program; concession; gift shop. Guided tours (Mid-Mar-Nov, Tues-Sun; winter, Sat-Sun). No children under six; child-care center. No pets. Reservations required.

Linden Hall. *4 miles S on Hwy 201, then 1 mile N on Hwy 819, left on River Rd in Dawson. Phone 724/529-7543.* (1913) Conference and convention center in mountaintop mansion, situated in picturesque Laurel Highlands. Swimming, fishing; golf, tennis, walking trail. Guided tours of mansion (Mar-Dec, Mon-Fri; weekends by appointment). **$$$**

Specialty Lodging

The following lodging establishment is approved by Mobil Travel Guide, but due to its unique and individualized nature has not been given a traditional Mobil Star rating. Included in this listing you may find bed-and-breakfasts, limited-service inns, guest ranches, and other unique hotel properties.

NEWMYER HOUSE. *507 S Pittsburgh St, Connellsville (15425). Phone 724/626-0141.* Restored Queen Anne-style mansion built in 1892; antiques. 4 rooms, 3 story. Children over 12 years only. Complimentary full breakfast. Check-in 3 pm, check-out 11 am. **$**

Conshohocken

Restaurant

★★ COYOTE CROSSING. *800 Spring Mill Ave, Conshohocken (19428). Phone 610/825-3000; fax 610/828-4015. www.coyotecrossing.com.* Mexican, Southwestern menu. Lunch, dinner. Closed Jan 1, July 4, Dec 25. Bar. Outdoor seating. **$$**

Cornwall

See also Ephrata, Hershey, Lancaster, Lebaron, Manheim, Massena

Settled 1732
Population 3,486
Elevation 680 ft
Area Code 717
Zip 17016
Information Pennsylvania Rainbow Region Vacation Bureau, 625 Quentin Rd, PO Box 329, Lebanon 17042; phone 717/272-8555

The Cornwall Ore Banks were a major source of magnetic iron ore for nearly 250 years.

What to See and Do

Cornwall Iron Furnace. *Rexmont Rd and Boyd St, Cornwall. Phone 717/272-9711.* In operation 1742-1883. Open pit mine; 19th-century Miners Village still occupied. Furnace building houses "great wheel" and 19th-century steam engine. Visitor center, exhibits, book store. (Tues-Sun; closed Jan 1, Thanksgiving, Dec 25) **$$**

Historic Schaefferstown. *Hwy 419 N, Schaefferstown. 6 miles SE of Lebanon at junction Hwy 419, 501, 897. Phone 717/949-2244.* An 18th-century farm established by Swiss-German settlers. Village square with authentic log and stone and half-timber buildings; site of first waterworks in US (1758), still in operation. Schaeffer Farm Museum has Swiss Bank House and Barn (1737); early farm tools; colonial farm garden. The museum north of the square has antiques and artifacts of settlers. (See SPECIAL EVENT) House and museum (open during festivals; also June-Sept, by appointment). **$$**

Special Event

Historic Schaefferstown Events. Events during the year include Cherry Fair, fourth Sat in June; Folk Festival, mid-July; Harvest Fair & Horse Plowing Contest, second weekend in Sept.

Danville (B-5)

See also Bloomsburg, Lewisburg

Population 4,897
Elevation 490 ft
Area Code 570
Zip 17821
Information Danville Area Chamber of Commerce, 206 Walnut St; phone 570/275-5200
Web site www.danvillepa.org

What to See and Do

Joseph Priestley House. *472 Priestley Ave, Northumberland (17857). SW via Hwy 11. Phone 570/473-9474.* (1798) American house of the 18th-century Englishman and Unitarian theologian who, in 1774, isolated the element oxygen. (Tues-Sat; closed holidays) **$$**

PP & L Montour Preserve. *700 Preserve Rd, Danville (17821). From I-80 exit 33, then Hwy 54 W to Washingtonville, and NE on local roads. Phone 570/437-3131.* Fishing, boating (no gasoline motors) on 165-acre Lake Chillisquaque. Hiking and nature trails, picnicking. Birds of prey exhibit in visitor center; scheduled programs (Daily, fee for some). **FREE**

Limited-Service Hotel

★ **QUALITY INN & SUITES.** *15 Valley West Rd, Danville (17821). Phone 570/275-5100; fax 570/275-1886. www.choicehotels.com.* 77 rooms, 2 story. Check-out noon. Outdoor pool. **$**

Full-Service Inn

★★★ **PINE BARN INN.** *1 Pine Barn Pl, Danville (17821). Phone 570/275-2071; toll-free 800/627-2276; fax 570/275-3248. www.pinebarninn.com.* This quiet inn is only a 20-minute drive from downtown and the lake. Each room features a full bath, some with Jacuzzi tubs. 65 rooms, 2 story. Check-out 1 pm. Restaurant, bar. **$**

Restaurant

★★ **PINE BARN INN.** *1 Pine Barn Pl, Danville (17821). Phone 570/275-2071; fax 570/275-3248. www.pinebarninn.com.* Seafood, steak menu. Breakfast, lunch, dinner, Sun brunch. Closed holidays. Bar. Children's menu. Converted 19th-century barn. Outdoor seating. **$$**

Delaware Water Gap (B-6)

See also Milford, Pocono Mountains, Stroudsburg

It is difficult to believe that the quiet Delaware River could carve a path through the Kittatinny Mountains, which are nearly 1/4 of a mile high at this point. Conflicting geological theories account for this natural phenomenon, which is part of a national recreation area. The prevailing theory is that the mountains were formed after the advent of the river, rising up from the earth so slowly that the course of the Delaware was never altered.

Despite the speculation about the origin of the gap, there is no doubt about the area's recreational value. A relatively unspoiled area along the river boundary between Pennsylvania and New Jersey, stretching approximately 35 miles from Matamoras to an area just south of I-80, the site of the Delaware Water Gap is managed by the National Park Service.

Trails and overlooks (year-round) offer scenic views. Also here are canoeing and boating, hunting and fishing; camping is nearby at the Dingmans Campground within the recreation area. Swimming and picnicking at Smithfield and Milford beaches. Dingmans Falls and Silver Thread Falls, two of the highest waterfalls in the Poconos, are near here (see MILFORD). Several 19th-century buildings are in the area, including Millbrook Village (several buildings open May-Oct) and Peters Valley (see BRANCHVILLE, NJ). The visitor center is located off I-80 in New Jersey, at Kittatinny Point (Apr-Nov, daily; rest of year, Sat and Sun only; closed Jan 1, Dec 25), phone 908/496-4458 or 717/588-2451. Park headquarters are in Bushkill, PA.

Denver/ Adamstown

See also Ephrata, Lancaster, Reading

Population 3,332
Elevation Denver 380 ft; Adamstown 500 ft
Area Code 717
Zip Denver 17517; Adamstown 19501
Information Pennsylvania Dutch Convention and Visitors Bureau, 501 Greenfield Rd, Lancaster 17601; phone 717/299-8901 or toll-free 800/PADUTCH
Web site www.800padutch.com

Located near a Pennsylvania Turnpike exit, Denver and Adamstown are in the center of an active antique marketing area, which preserves its Pennsylvania German heritage.

What to See and Do

Stoudt's Black Angus. *Rte 272, Adamstown. PA Tpke exit 21 to just beyond Adamstown. Phone 717/484-4385.* More than 350 dealers display quality antiques for sale. (Sun)

Special Event

Bavarian Summer Fest. *SW via Hwy 272 at Black Angus Bier Garten. Phone 717/484-4385 (weekends).* Oompah bands, schuhplattler dance groups; Oktoberfest atmosphere. Includes special events, German folklore, German food, displays, shops. Fri-Sun, early Aug-Labor Day; Sun only Oct.

Limited-Service Hotels

★ ★ **BLACK HORSE LODGE & SUITES.** *PO Box 343, Denver/Adamstown (17517). Phone 717/336-7563; toll-free 800/610-3805; fax 717/336-1110. www.blackhorselodge.com.* Located on 10 acres of land, this lodge comprises three buildings, all found next to the outdoor pool. The property offers large suites with the living and bedroom areas separated by French doors, a king size bed and marble bathroom. 74 rooms, 2 story. Pets accepted. Complimentary full breakfast. Check-out noon. Restaurant, bar. Pool. **$**

★ ★ **HOLIDAY INN.** *1 Denver Rd, Denver (17517). Phone 717/336-7541; toll-free 800/437-5711; fax 717/336-0515. www.holiday-inn.com.* 110 rooms, 2 story. Check-out noon. Restaurant, bar. Outdoor pool. **$**

Specialty Lodging

The following lodging establishment is approved by Mobil Travel Guide, but due to its unique and individualized nature has not been given a traditional Mobil Star rating. Included in this listing you may find bed-and-breakfasts, limited-service inns, guest ranches, and other unique hotel properties.

INNS OF ADAMSTOWN. *62 W Main St, Adamstown (19501). Phone 717/484-0800; toll-free 800/594-4808; fax 717/484-1384. www.adamstown.com.* Two inns; built in 1925; Victorian décor; antiques, family heirlooms. 4 rooms (Adamstown Inn), 5 rooms (Amethyst Inn), 2 story. Children over 12 years only. Complimentary continental breakfast. Check-in 3-6 pm, check-out 10 am. **$**

Restaurant

★ ★ **BLACK HORSE.** *2180 N Reading Rd, Denver (17517). Phone 717/336-6555; fax 717/336-1110. www.blackhorselodge.com.* This restaurant is located in the heart of Pennsylvania Dutch country. The adjacent tavern features over 100 microbrews and imported beers, 350 different liquers, and 30 types of premium cigars. Seafood, steak menu. Dinner. Closed Dec 25. Bar. Children's menu. **$$$**

Donegal

See also Connellsville, Champion, Greensburg, Ligonier, Somerset

Population 165
Elevation 1,814 ft
Area Code 724
Zip 15628

What to See and Do

Seven Springs Mountain Resort Ski Area. *12 miles SE of PA Tpke exit 9 on Champion-Trent Rd. Phone toll-free 800/452-2223. www.7springs.com.* Three quad, five triple chairlifts; two rope tows, six-passenger high-speed chair; patrol, school, rentals; snowmaking; cafeteria, restaurant, bar; lodge. Longest run 1 1/4 miles; vertical drop 750 feet. Night skiing. (Dec-Mar, daily) Alpine slide (May-Sept, daily). Hotel and conference center; summer activities include 18-hole golf, tennis, rope course, horseback riding, and swimming. **$$$$**

Special Event

Seven Springs Wine and Food Festival. *777 Waterwheel Dr, Champion (15622). Phone 814/352-7777; toll-free 800/452-2223. www.7springs.com.* In the middle of Pennsylvania is the Seven Springs Resort and its annual wine tasting festival. Sample some of the best local producers have to offer and drink from the complimentary wine glass given to you with the price of admission. With easy access from the Pennsylvania turnpike, you can head to Champion to try your hand (that is, your feet!) at stomping grapes or simply enjoy the cuisine of the Keystone State. Third weekend in Aug.

Limited-Service Hotel

★ DAYS INN. *Hwy 31, Donegal (15628). Phone 724/593-7536; fax 724/593-6165. www.daysinn.com.* 50 rooms. Complimentary continental breakfast. Check-out 11 am. Outdoor pool. **$**

Full-Service Resort

★ ★ SEVEN SPRINGS MOUNTAIN RESORT. *Rd 1, County Line Rd, Champion (15622). Phone 814/352-7777; toll-free 800/452-2223; fax 814/352-7911. www.7springs.com.* With plenty of accommodations and more activities then one could imagine, this is a great stop for vacationers. During the winter months this is an active ski resort, while summer time brings golfer, hikers, and mountain bikers. 405 rooms, 10 story. Check-in 5 pm, check-out noon. Restaurant, bar. Children's activity center. Fitness room. Indoor pool, outdoor pool, children's pool. Golf. Tennis. Airport transportation available. **$$**

Restaurants

★ ★ ★ HELEN'S. *777 Waterwheel Dr, Champion (15622). Phone 814/352-7777. www.7springs.com.* The formal service, complete with tableside carving and preparations, is a surprise considering the rural setting. Though the menu changes with the seasons, it leans towards classics. American menu. Lunch, dinner. Bar. Reservations recommended. **$$$**

★ ★ ★ NINO BARSOTTI'S. *Hwy 31, Mt Pleasant (15666). Phone 724/547-2900.* American, Italian menu. Lunch, dinner, Sun brunch. Closed Mon; holidays. Bar. Children's menu. Valet parking. **$$**

Downingtown (D-5)

See also King of Prussia, West Chester

Settled 1702
Population 7,589
Elevation 244 ft
Area Code 484 and 610
Zip 19335
Information Chester County Conference and Visitors Bureau, 400 Exton Sq Pkwy, Exton, 19341; phone 610/280-6145 or toll-free 800/228-9933
Web site www.brandywinevalley.com

Settled by emigrants from Birmingham, England, Downingtown honors Thomas Downing, who erected a log cabin here in 1702. The borough was first called Milltown, after the mill built here by Roger Hunt in 1765. The town, with its many historically interesting homes, retains much of its colonial charm. Jacob Eichholtz, a leading early American portrait artist, was born here.

What to See and Do

Hibernia County Park. *1 Park Ave, Coatesville (19320). From Hwy 30 Bypass take Hwy 82 approximately 2 miles N to Cedar Knoll Rd, then left 1 1/4 miles to park entrance on left. Phone 610/384-0290.* Once the center of an iron works community, it is now the largest of the county parks, encompassing 800 acres of woodlands and meadows. The west branch of the Brandywine Creek, Birch Run, and a pond are stocked with trout; hiking trails, picnicking, tent and trailer camping (dump station). Park features Hibernia Mansion; portions of house date from 1798, period furnishings. Tours of mansion (Memorial Day-Labor Day, Sun; fee). **FREE**

Historic Yellow Springs. *1685 Art School Rd, Chester Springs (19425). 10 miles NE via Hwy 113, NW on Yellow Springs Rd. Phone 610/827-7414.* From its beginnings as a fashionable spa, this historic village has been everything from a Revolutionary War hospital to an art school. Countryside covers 145 acres with buildings, medicinal herb garden, and mineral springs. Events and educational programs throughout the year (some fees). Self-guided tour. Office (Mon-Fri).

Special Events

Hibernia Mansion Christmas Tours. *Hibernia County Park, 1 Park Ave, Coatesville (19320).* First week in Dec.

Old Fiddlers' Picnic. *Hibernia County Park, 1 Park Ave, Coatesville (19320).* Second Sat in Aug.

Limited-Service Hotel

★ ★ INN AT CHESTER SPRINGS. *815 N Pottstown Pike, Exton (19341). Phone 610/363-1100; fax 610/524-2329.* 225 rooms, 4 story. Check-out 11 am. Restaurant, bar. Indoor pool, outdoor pool. Airport transportation available. **$**

Full-Service Hotel

★ ★ ★ SHERATON GREAT VALLEY HOTEL. *707 Lancaster Pike, Downingtown (19355). Phone 610/524-5500; fax 610/524-1808. www.sheraton.com.* 198 rooms, 5 story. Check-in 3 pm, check-out noon. Restaurant, bar. Fitness room. Pool, whirlpool. Business center. **$$**

Restaurant

★ ★ DULING-KURTZ HOUSE. *146 S Whitford Rd, Exton (19341). Phone 610/524-1830; fax 610/524-6258. www.duling-kurtz.com.* This cozy, historic country inn features fireplaces in each of its dining rooms. French menu. Lunch, dinner. Bar. Valet parking Fri, Sat. Seven dining rooms. **$$$**

Doylestown (Bucks County) (C-6)

See also Bucks County, Philadelphia, Quakertown (Bucks County)

Settled 1735
Population 8,227
Elevation 340 ft
Area Code 215
Zip 18901
Information Bucks County Conference and Visitors Bureau, 152 Swamp Rd; phone 215/345-4552 or toll-free 800/836-2825
Web site www.buckscountycvb.org

Doylestown is the county seat of historic and colorful Bucks County.

What to See and Do

Covered bridges. Descriptive list, map of 11 bridges in Bucks County may be obtained at Bucks County Tourist Commission.

James A. Michener Art Museum. *138 S Pine St, Doylestown. Phone 215/340-9800. www.michenerartmuseum.org.* This museum, a former prison modeled after the Eastern State Penitentiary in Philadelphia, is as large as a football field and was named for Doylestown's most famous son, the Pulitzer-Prize winning writer James Michener. He supported the arts and dreamed of a regional art museum dedicated to preserving, interpreting, and exhibiting the art and cultural heritage of the Bucks County region. The museum is home to more than 2,500 paintings, sculptures, drawings, and photographs; stained glass collections; an outdoor gallery paying homage to the local landscape; a café; a museum shop; and a research and reference library. (Tues-Sun; closed holidays) **$$**

Mercer Mile. Three reinforced-concrete structures built between 1910-1916 within a 1-mile radius by Dr. Henry Chapman Mercer, archaeologist, historian, world traveler, and tile maker. They include

Fonthill Museum. *525 E Court St, Doylestown. Phone 215/348-9461.* Concrete castle of Henry Chapman Mercer (1856-1930) displays his collection of tiles and prints from around the world. Guided tours (times vary) **$$$**

Mercer Museum. *84 S Pine St, Doylestown. Phone 215/345-0210. www.mercermuseum.org.* In this towering castle built in 1969, visitors will find implements, folk art, and furnishings of early America before mechanization. See a Conestoga wagon, a whaling boat, carriages, and an antique fire engine. Fifty thousand pieces of more than 60 early American crafts and varying trade tools on display. (Daily; closed Jan 1, Thanksgiving, Dec 25) **$$$**

The Moravian Pottery and Tile Works. *130 Swamp Rd, Doylestown. Between Court and North sts. Phone 215/345-6722.* This historic landmark is a working history museum in which visitors can witness tiles produced in their original handmade manner. Henry Chapman Mercer, a historian, archaeologist, collector, ceramist, and major proponent of the Arts & Crafts movement in America, left behind three historic buildings in his hometown of Doylestown: his home, Fonthill; the Mercer Museum (see also MERCER MUSEUM); and the Moravian Pottery and Tile Works. Visitors will see original installations and selected aspects of current tile production, and may purchase tiles made on site in the tile shop. (Daily; closed holidays) **$**

★ **Pearl S. Buck House.** *520 Dublin Rd, Perkasie. 8 miles NW via Hwy 611, 313. Phone 215/249-0100.* (1835) House of Pulitzer and Nobel Prize winning author Pearl S. Buck. Original furnishings include desk at which The Good Earth was written; memorabilia, Chinese artifacts. Picnicking on grounds. Gift shop. One-hour guided tours (Mar-Dec, Tues-Sun; closed holidays). **$$$**

Limited-Service Hotel

★ **COMFORT INN.** *678 Bethlehem Pike, Montgomeryville (18936). Phone 215/361-3600; fax 215/361-7949. www.choicehotels.com.* 84 rooms, 3 story. Complimentary continental breakfast. Check-out 11 am. Internet access in some rooms. **$**

Du Bois (B-2)

See also Clearfield (Clearfield County)

Settled 1865
Population 8,123
Elevation 1,420 ft
Area Code 814
Zip 15801
Information Du Bois Area Chamber of Commerce, 31 N Brady St; phone 814/371-5010

At the entrance to the lowest pass of the Allegheny Range, Du Bois is a transportation center—once the apex of huge lumbering operations. Destroyed by fire in 1888, the town was rebuilt on the ashes of the old community and today ranks as one of the 12 major trading centers in the state.

Limited-Service Hotels

★ **HAMPTON INN.** *RR 8, Box 3A, Du Bois (15801). Phone 814/375-1000; fax 814/375-4668. www.hamptoninn.com.* 96 rooms, 3 story. Complimentary continental breakfast. Check-out noon. Indoor pool, whirlpool. **$**

★ ★ **HOLIDAY INN.** *Hwy 219 and I-80, Du Bois (15801). Phone 814/371-5100; toll-free 800/959-3412; fax 814/375-0230. www.holiday-inn.com.* 160 rooms, 2 story. Pets accepted, some restrictions. Check-out noon. Restaurant, bar. Pool, children's pool. Airport transportation available. **$**

Full-Service Inn

★ ★ ★ **TOWNE HOUSE INN.** *138 Center St, Saint Mary's (15857). Phone 814/781-1556; toll-free 800/851-1180; fax 814/834-4449. www.townehouseinn.com.* 57 rooms, 3 story. Complimentary continental breakfast. Check-out 11 am. Restaurant. Fitness room. Stained glass, antiques in 7 historic (1890s) townhouses. **$**

East Petersburg

Restaurant

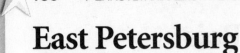

★★★ **HAYDN ZUG'S.** *1987 State St, East Petersburg (17520). Phone 717/569-5746; fax 717/569-8450.* Owner and Chef Terry Lee hails from Petersburg. With its award winning wine list and exceptional cuisine, it makes a day journey worthwhile. Winner of the *Wine Spectator* Award of Excellence. American menu. Lunch, dinner. Closed Sun, Mon; holidays. Bar. Casual attire. Reservations recommended. **$$**

East Stroudsburg (B-6)

Restaurant

★ **DANSBURY DEPOT.** *50 Crystal St, East Stroudsburg (18360). Phone 570/476-0500; fax 571/476-0723.* Continental menu. Lunch, dinner. Closed Thanksgiving, Dec 25. Bar. Children's menu. Converted railroad station depot and freight house, built in 1864. Display of railroad memorabilia. Small trains move around the room, overhead on the walls. **$**

Easton (C-6)

See also Allentown, Bethlehem

Founded 1752
Population 26,263
Elevation 300 ft
Area Code 484 and 610
Zip 18042
Information Two Rivers Area Chamber of Commerce, 1 S 3rd St, PO Box 637, 18044-0637; phone 610/253-4211
Web site www.eastonareachamber.org

Named by Thomas Penn, one of the proprietors, for the English birthplace of his bride, Easton today is the gateway to the great industrial Lehigh Valley. Lafayette College, with its beautiful campus, and the historic Great Square are of interest. Easton, the seat of Northampton County, is part of a larger metropolitan area, the Lehigh Valley, which also includes Allentown and Bethlehem.

What to See and Do

Canal Museum. *30 Centre Sq, Easton (18042). Hwy 611, 1 mile S of Hwy 22, Two Rivers Landing. Phone 610/250-6700.* Exhibits include photographs, models, documents, and artifacts from the era of mule-drawn canal boats in the 1800s; electronic map and audiovisual programs. Changing exhibits. (Memorial Day-Labor Day, daily; rest of year, Tues-Sun; closed Jan 1, Thanksgiving, Dec 25) **$$$**

The Crayola Factory. *30 Centre Sq, Easton (18042). Phone 610/515-8000.* See how crayons and markers are created. Visit Crayola Hall of Fame; enjoy dozens of interactive exhibits featuring the wonders of light and color. Same location and schedule as Canal Museum.

The Great Square. Center of business district. Now called Center Square. Dominated by Soldiers' and Sailors' Monument. Bronze marker shows replica of Old Courthouse, which stood until 1862 on land rented from the Penns for one red rose a year. From Old Courthouse steps, the Declaration of Independence was read on July 8, 1776, when the Easton Flag, the first Stars and Stripes of the united colonies, was unfurled here.

Hugh Moore Park. *S 25th St, Easton (18042). 2 miles S of Hwy 22. Phone 610/250-6700.* Restored Lehigh Canal, locks, and locktender's house; mule-drawn canal boat rides (early May-Labor Day, daily; early-late Sept, weekends) Also hiking, picnicking; boat rentals in park. Park (daily). **FREE**

Lafayette College. *Hwy 22 and Hwy 78, Easton (18042). N side of town. Phone 610/250-5000.* (1826) (2,000 students) Bronze statue of Lafayette by Daniel Chester French in front of college chapel; American historical portrait collection in Kirby Hall of Civil Rights. Tour of campus.

Northampton County Historical Society. *101-107 S 4th St, Easton (18042). Diagonally opposite Parsons-Taylor House. Phone 610/253-1222.* Changing exhibits; library; museum. (By appointment) **$**

Restaurant

★ ★ PEARLY BAKER'S ALE HOUSE. *11 Center Sq, Easton (18042). Phone 610/253-9949; fax 610/253-6133.* International menu. Lunch, dinner. Closed Mon; holidays. Bar. Children's menu. Reservations recommended. Outdoor seating. Austrian chandelier in main dining room. **$$**

Ebensburg (C-2)

See also Altoona, Johnstown

Population 3,091
Elevation 2,140 ft
Area Code 814
Zip 15931
Information Johnstown/Cambria County Convention & Visitors Bureau, 416 Main St, Suite 200, Johnstown 15901-1608; phone 814/536-7993 or toll-free 800/237-8590
Web site www.visitjohnstownpa.com

What to See and Do

Allegheny Portage Railroad National Historic Site. *110 Federal Park Rd, Gallitzin (16641). 12 miles E on Hwy 22. Phone 814/886-6150.* Remains of railroad built 1831-1834 to link east and west divisions of the Pennsylvania Mainline Canal. Cars were pulled up ten inclined planes by ropes powered by steam engines. Horses or locomotives pulled the cars over the level stretches of the 36-mile route across the Alleghenies from Hollidaysburg to Johnstown. The Skew Arch Bridge, an engine house exhibit, and the Lemon House, a historic tavern, help tell the story of the Allegheny Portage Railroad. A visitor center (daily; closed Dec 25) has exhibits and a 20-minute film. There are ranger-led programs (summer, daily) and costumed demonstrations (summer); picnic area (daily), hiking and cross-country trails. **$$**

Portage Station Museum. *400 Lee St, Portage (15946). Phone 814/736-8918.* This historic station was once a stop on the Pennsylvania Railroad. The first floor, with its original lighting fixtures, oak wainscoting, and woodwork, contains the Master's Office and waiting room. Exhibits on the second floor include artifacts from the newly renovated Mainline Mining Museum. (Wed, Sat and Sun afternoons). **FREE**

Edinboro (A-1)

See also Conneaut Lake, Erie, Meadville

Population 6,950
Elevation 1,210 ft
Area Code 814
Zip 16412

This is a resort town on Edinboro Lake and the home of Edinboro State College.

What to See and Do

Mountain View Ski Area. *14510 Mount Pleasant Rd, Cambridge Springs (16403). 4 miles E on Hwy 6 N, then 3 miles S on Hwy 86. Phone 814/734-1641. www.skimtview.org.* Two T-bars, Pomalift; patrol, school, rentals; snowmaking; cafeteria. Longest run 2,500 feet; vertical drop 320 feet. (Dec-Mar, daily) Half-day and evening rates. **$$$$**

Limited-Service Hotel

★ ★ EDINBORO INN RESORT AND CONFERENCE CENTER. *401 W Plum St, Edinboro (16412). Phone 814/734-5650; fax 814/734-7532.* 105 rooms, 2 story. Pets accepted; fee. Check-out noon. Restaurant, bar. Indoor pool. **$**

Full-Service Inn

★ ★ ★ RIVERSIDE INN. *1 Fountain Ave, Cambridge Springs (16403). Phone 814/398-4645; toll-free 800/964-5173; fax 814/398-8161. www.theriversideinn.com.* Opened in 1885, this inn continues to provide excellent service to its visitors. The inn is found nestled in a quiet and peaceful area overlooking French Creek. Guests will enjoy golf, swimming, tennis, and other activities. 74 rooms, 3 story. Closed Jan-mid-Apr. Complimentary full breakfast. Check-in 3 pm, check-out 11 am. Restaurant, bar. Pool. **$**

Emmaus (C-6)

Restaurant

★★ THE FARMHOUSE. *1449 Chestnut St, Emmaus (18049). Phone 610/967-6225; fax 610/965-6225.* This charming restaurant is situated in an 1830s farmhouse in a small city near Allentown. The owner offers several "rotating" draft beers and has a reputation for cooking with beer and pairing beer with food. American menu. Dinner. Closed Sun, Mon. Bar. Outdoor seating. **$$$**

Ephrata (D-5)

See also Bird-in-Hand, Cornwall, Denver/Adamstown, Lancaster, Lebanon, Reading

Settled 1732
Population 13,213
Elevation 380 ft
Area Code 717
Zip 17522
Information Chamber of Commerce, 77 Park Ave, Suite 1; phone 717/738-9010
Web site www.ephrata-area.org

What to See and Do

Ephrata Cloister. *632 W Main St, Ephrata. Phone 717/733-6600. www.phmc.state.pa.us.* Buildings stand as a monument to an unusual religious experiment. In 1732 Conrad Beissel, a German Seventh-Day Baptist, began to lead a hermit's life here; within a few years he established a religious community of recluses, with a Brotherhood, a Sisterhood, and a group of married "householders." The members of the solitary order dressed in concealing white habits; the buildings (1735-1749) were without adornment, the halls were narrow, the doorways were low, and board benches served as beds and wooden blocks as pillows. Their religious zeal and charity, however, proved to be their undoing. After the Battle of Brandywine, the cloistered community nursed the Revolutionary sick and wounded, but contracted typhus, which decimated their numbers. Celibacy also contributed to the decline of the community, but the Society was not formally dissolved until 1934. An orientation exhibit and video prepare each visitor for their relaxing journey back through time. Surviving and restored buildings include the Sisters' House, Chapel, Almonry, and eight others. Craft demonstrations (summer). (Mon-Sat; closed holidays) **$$$**

Museum and Library of the Historical Society of Cocalico Valley. *249 W Main St, Ephrata. Phone 717/733-1616.* Italianate Victorian mansion contains period displays; historical exhibits; genealogical and historical research library (fee) on Cocalico Valley area and residents. (Mon, Wed, Thurs, Sat) **FREE**

Special Event

Street Fair. One of largest in the state. Last full week in Sept.

Specialty Lodgings

The following lodging establishments are approved by Mobil Travel Guide, but due to their unique and individualized nature have not been given a traditional Mobil Star rating. Included in this listing you may find bed-and-breakfasts, limited-service inns, guest ranches, and other unique hotel properties.

THE INNS AT DONECKERS. *318-324 N State St, Ephrata (17522). Phone 717/738-9502; toll-free 800/377-2206; fax 717/738-9554. www.doneckers.com.* 35 rooms, 3 story. Complimentary continental breakfast. Check-in 3 pm, check-out 11 am. Restored clockmaker's house (1777). Hand-cut stenciling. **$**

SMITHTON BED & BREAKFAST COUNTRY INN. *900 W Main St, Ephrata (17522). Phone 717/733-6094. www.historicsmithtoninn.com.* 17 rooms, 3 story. Complimentary full breakfast. Check-in 3:30 pm, check-out noon. Historic stone inn (1763). **$**

Restaurant

★★★ THE RESTAURANT AT DONECKERS. *333 N State St, Ephrata (17522). Phone 717/738-9501; fax 717/738-9512. www.doneckers.com.* Guests can opt for formal atmosphere amidst antiques and artwork in the main dining room, or a more casual setting in the bistro. Check for special events, such as theme dinners, wine tastings, and the like. American, French menu. Lunch, dinner. Closed Wed, Sun; holidays. Bar. Children's menu. **$$$**

Erie (A-1)

See also Edinboro, North East

Settled 1753
Population 103,717
Elevation 744 ft
Area Code 814
Information Erie Area Convention and Visitors Bureau, 208 E Bayfront Pkwy, Suite 103, 16507; phone 814/454-7191 or toll-free 800/524-3743
Web site www.eriechamber.com

Erie, Pennsylvania's premier beach resort, is on beautiful Presque Isle Bay, one of the world's best-protected harbors. The fourth-largest city in Pennsylvania, Erie is the state's only port on the Great Lakes and boasts a wealth of natural beauty and fascinating historical tales. Visitors enjoy Presque Isle State Park with its 7 miles of sandy beaches and hiking and biking trails. Downtown offers big-city cultural and entertainment options like Broadway shows, classical ballet, philharmonic performances, and comedy clubs.

The lake and city take their name from the Eriez tribe, who were killed by the Seneca about 1654. On the south shore of Presque Isle Bay, Commodore Oliver Hazard Perry built his fleet, floated the ships across the sandbars, and fought the British in the Battle of Lake Erie (1813). Fort Presque Isle, built by the French in 1753 and destroyed by them in 1759, was rebuilt by the English, burned by Native Americans, and rebuilt again in 1794 by Americans.

What to See and Do

Bicentennial Tower. *7 Dobbins Landing, Erie (16507). Erie's Bayfront, at the foot of State St. Phone 814/455-6055.* Commemorating Erie's 200th birthday, this 187-foot tower features two observation decks with an aerial view of the city, bay, and Lake Erie. Concessions in tower lobby. (Apr-Sept, daily; rest of year, call for schedule; closed holidays) Free admission Tues. **$**

Erie Art Museum. *411 State St, Erie. Phone 814/459-5477. www.erieartmuseum.org.* Temporary art exhibits in a variety of media; regional artwork and lectures in the restored Greek Revival Old Customs House (1839). Art classes, concerts, lectures, and workshops are also offered. (Tues-Sat, also Sun afternoons; closed holidays) Free admission Wed. **$**

Erie Zoo. *423 W 38th St, Erie. 3 miles N of I-90 State St exit 7. Phone 814/868-3651. www.eriezoo.org.* Zoo houses more than 300 animals, including gorillas, polar bears, and giraffes; children's zoo (May-Sept); one-mile tour of grounds on Safariland Express Train (fee). Indoor ice rink (Sept-Mar) **$$**

Firefighters Historical Museum. *428 Chestnut St, Erie. Phone 814/456-5969.* More than 1,300 items of firefighting memorabilia are displayed in the old #4 Firehouse. Exhibits include fire apparatus dating from 1823, alarm systems, uniforms, badges, ribbons, helmets, nozzles, fire marks and fire extinguishers; fire safety films are shown in the Hay Loft Theater. (May-Oct, Sat-Sun) **$$**

Gridley's Grave. *Lakeside Cemetery, 1718 E Lake Rd, Erie. Phone 814/459-8200.* Final resting place of Captain Charles Vernon Gridley, to whom, at the Battle of Manila Bay in 1898, Admiral Dewey said, "You may fire when ready, Gridley." Gridley died in Japan; his body was returned here for burial. Four old Spanish cannons from Manila Harbor, built in 1777, guard the grave. Offers view of peninsula, Lake Erie and entrance to Erie Harbor from cliff by Gridley Circle.

Land Lighthouse. *2 Lighthouse St, Erie (16507). Foot of Lighthouse St. Phone 814/452-3937.* (1867) The first lighthouse on the Great Lakes was constructed on this site in 1813.

Misery Bay. *NE corner of Presque Isle Bay.* State monument to Perry; named after Perry defeated British and the fleet suffered cold and privations of a bitter winter.

Presque Isle State Park. *1 Peninsula Dr, Erie. N off Hwy 832. Phone 814/833-7424. www.presqueisle.org.* Peninsula stretches 7 miles into Lake Erie and curves back toward city. Approximately 3,200 acres of recreation and conservation areas. Swimming, fishing, boating (rentals, mooring, launching, marina); hiking, birding, trails, cross-country skiing, ice skating, ice fishing, ice boating, picnicking, concessions. Visitor center, environmental education, and interpretive programs.

Waldameer Park & Water World. *220 Peninsula Dr, Erie. At entrance to Presque Isle State Park. Phone 814/838-3591.* Rides, midway, kiddieland, water park, picnic area, food, dance pavilion. (Memorial Day-Labor Day, Tues-Sun; open Mon holidays) **$$$$**

Watson-Curtze Mansion. *356 W 6th St, Erie. Phone 814/871-5790.* Housed in 1890s Victorian mansion. Museum features regional history and decorative arts exhibits; restored period rooms; changing exhibits (Tues-Sat afternoons; closed holidays). Also planetarium with shows (Sat afternoons). **$$**

Wayne Memorial Blockhouse. *560 E 3rd St, Erie. On grounds of State Soldiers' and Sailors' Home. Phone 814/871-4531.* Replica of blockhouse in which General Anthony Wayne died Dec 15, 1796, after becoming ill on a voyage from Detroit. He was buried at the foot of the flagpole; later, his son had the body disinterred and the remains moved to Radnor. (Memorial Day-Labor Day, daily) **FREE**

Limited-Service Hotels

★ **GLASS HOUSE INN.** *3202 W 26th St, Erie (16506). Phone 814/833-7751; toll-free 800/956-7222; fax 814/833-4222. www.glasshouseinn.com.* 30 rooms. Complimentary continental breakfast. Check-out 11 am. Outdoor pool. **$**

★ **HAMPTON INN.** *3041 W 12th St, Erie (16505). Phone 814/835-4200; toll-free 800/426-7866; fax 814/835-5212. www.hamptoninn.com.* 100 rooms, 3 story. Complimentary continental breakfast. Check-out noon. Pool. **$**

★ ★ **RAMADA INN DOWNTOWN.** *18 W 18th St, Erie (16501). Phone 814/456-2961; toll-free 800/832-9101; fax 814/456-7067. www.ramada.com.* 133 rooms, 4 story. Complimentary full breakfast. Check-out noon. Restaurant, bar. Fitness room. Pool. Airport transportation available. Business center. **$**

★ **QUALITY INN.** *8040 Perry Hwy, Erie (16509). Phone 814/864-4911; fax 814/864-3743. www.choicehotels.com.* 107 rooms, 2 story. Pets accepted, some restrictions; fee. Check-out 11 am. Restaurant, bar. Pool. Airport transportation available. Business center. **$**

Restaurant

★ ★ **PUFFERBELLY.** *414 French St, Erie (16507). Phone 814/454-1557; fax 814/455-6138.* Restored firehouse (1907). Outdoor seating. Dinner, Sun brunch. Closed holidays. Bar. **$$**

Erwinna

See also New Hope

Full-Service Inn

★ ★ ★ **EVERMAY ON THE DELAWARE.** *889 River Rd, Erwinna (18920). Phone 610/294-9100; toll-free 877/864-2365; fax 610/294-8249. www.evermay.com.* Built in the 1700s, this inn is situated on 25 acres of pastures, woodlands and gardens, and close to antique shops, galleries, historic sites, parks, and much more. 18 rooms, 4 story. Children over 13 years only. Complimentary continental breakfast. Check-in 2 pm, check-out noon. Restaurant. **$$**

Restaurants

★ ★ ★ **EVERMAY.** *889 River Rd, Erwinna (18920). Phone 610/294-9100; toll-free 877/864-2365; fax 610/294-8249. www.evermay.com.* A sumptuous meal is available at this formal carriage house in a beautiful country setting. Stay at the inn after dining to experience the full romance of the place. American menu. Dinner. Closed Mon-Thurs. Bar. Casual attire. **$$$**

★ ★ ★ **GOLDEN PHEASANT INN.** *763 River Rd (PA 32), Erwinna (18920). Phone 610/294-9595; fax 610/294-9882. www.goldenpheasant.com.* This provincial and romantic weekend hideaway sits nestled between the Delaware River and the Pennsylvania Canal. Located an hour and a half from New York City, and 20 minutes outside of Philadelphia. French menu. Dinner, Sun brunch. Closed Mon. Bar. **$$**

Fort Washington

Population 3,680
Elevation 250 ft
Area Code 215
Zip 19034
Information Valley Forge Convention & Visitors Bureau, 600 W Germantown Pike, Suite 130, Plymouth Meeting 19462; phone 610/834-1550
Web site www.valleyforge.org

What to See and Do

Fort Washington State Park. *500 Bethlehem Pike, Fort Washington. Phone 215/646-2942.* Commemorates the site of Washington's northern defense line against the British in 1777. Fishing; hiking, ball fields, picnicking.

The Highlands. *7001 Sheaff Ln, Fort Washington. Phone 215/641-2687.* (1796) Late-Georgian mansion on 43 acres built by Anthony Morris, active in both state and federal government. Formal gardens and crenellated walls built circa 1845. Tours. (Mon-Fri) **$$**

Hope Lodge. *553 Bethlehem Pike, Fort Washington. 1 mile S. Phone 215/646-1595.* (Circa 1745) Colonial Georgian mansion; headquarters for Surgeon General John Cochran after Battle of Germantown. Historic furnishings, paintings, ceramics. (Tues-Sun; closed holidays) **$$**

Restaurant

★★ PALACE OF ASIA. *285 Commerce Dr, Fort Washington (19034). Phone 215/646-2133; fax 215/646-2953. www.palaceofasia.citysearch.com.* Indian menu. Lunch, dinner, brunch. Closed Dec 24. Bar. Reservations recommended. **$$**

Franklin (Venango County) (B-1)

See also Meadville, Oil City, Titusville

Settled 1787
Population 7,212
Elevation 1,020 ft
Area Code 814
Zip 16323
Information Franklin Area Chamber of Commerce, 1259 Liberty St; phone 814/432-5823
Web site www.franklin-pa.org

A series of French and British forts was erected in this area. The last one, Fort Franklin, was razed by local settlers who used the stone and timber in their own buildings. Old Garrison took its place in 1796 and later served as the Venango County Jail. In 1859, James Evans, a blacksmith, made tools to drill an oil well that brought an oil boom to the area. For years, oil was dominant in the area's industries.

What to See and Do

DeBence Antique Music World. *1261 Liberty St, Franklin. Phone 814/432-5668.* Features nickelodeons, band organs, calliopes, German organs, a variety of music boxes, many other items. Unique "see and hear" museum. Guided tours. (Mid-Mar-Dec, Tues-Sun; closed holidays) **$$$**

Hoge-Osmer House. *South Park and Elk sts, Erie. Phone 814/437-2275.* (Circa 1865) Museum owned by Venango County Historical Society; houses displays of materials and artifacts relating to Venango County history; period furnishings, research library. House open (May-Dec, Tues-Thurs and Sat; rest of year, Sat; closed holidays). Inquire for genealogy library hours. **FREE**

Pioneer Cemetery. *Otter and 15th sts, Franklin.* (1795-1879) Self-guided walking tour booklets can be purchased at the Chamber of Commerce.

Venango County Court House. *1168 Liberty St, Franklin. Phone 814/432-9500.* (1868). Unique styling; contains display of Native American artifacts. (Mon-Fri; closed holidays)

Special Events

Applefest. *1259 Liberty St, Franklin. Phone 814/432-5823. Downtown.* Apple pie-baking contest; arts and crafts; entertainment; classic car show. Kids Korner. Five-km race; horse-drawn buggy rides. First full weekend in Oct.

Franklin Silver Cornet Band Concerts. *City Park, Franklin.* Thurs, mid-June-Aug.

Rocky Grove Fair. July.

Specialty Lodging

The following lodging establishment is approved by Mobil Travel Guide, but due to its unique and individualized nature has not been given a traditional Mobil Star rating. Included in this listing you may find bed-and-breakfasts, limited-service inns, guest ranches, and other unique hotel properties.

LAMBERTON HOUSE BED AND BREAKFAST. *1331 Otter St, Franklin (16323). Phone 814/432-7908.* 5 rooms, 2 story. Complimentary full breakfast. Check-in 3 pm, check-out 11 am. Historic building (1874). **$**

Galeton (A-3)

See also Wellsboro

Population 1,325
Elevation 1,325 ft
Area Code 814
Zip 16922
Information Potter County Recreation, PO Box 245, Coudersport 16915; phone 814/435-2290 or toll-free 888-POTTER2

What to See and Do

Ole Bull State Park. *Oleona. 18 miles SW on Hwy 144. Phone 814/435-5000.* At upper reaches of the Kettle Creek. Site of unsuccessful effort by the famous Norwegian violinist, Ole Bornemann Bull, to establish a colony called "New Norway." Approximately 125 acres. Swimming beach, fishing; hunting, hiking, cross-country skiing, snowmobiling, tent and trailer sites (electric hookups). Interpretive program.

Pennsylvania Lumber Museum. *5660 Hwy 6 W, Galeton. 10 miles W on Hwy 6. Phone 814/435-2652.* Exhibits on lumbering and its techniques, forest industries, and products; reconstructed lumber camp and sawmill; restored locomotive and log-loader; nature trails, picnicking. Slide show in visitor center. (Apr-Nov, daily; closed holidays) (See SPECIAL EVENTS) **$$**

Ski Denton/Denton Hill. *5661 Hwy 6, Coudersport (16915). 10 miles W on Hwy 6. Phone 814/435-2115. www.skidenton.com.* Double, triple chairlifts; two Pomalifts; patrol, school, rentals, snowmaking; cafeteria, restaurant, lodge, cabins. Longest run 1 mile; vertical drop 650 feet. Snowboarding. (Dec-Mar, daily) 100 miles of cross-country trails; night skiing; camping. (See SPECIAL EVENTS) **$$$$**

Special Events

Bark Peeler's Convention. *5660 Hwy 6 W, Galeton. Phone 814/435-2652. On grounds of Pennsylvania Lumber Museum.* Re-creation of old-time festival held by lumber camp workers celebrating the end of the work year. Features many demonstrations, including cross-cut sawing, hewing, bark peeling; entertainment; period music; exhibits. July 4-5.

Bowhunter's Festival. *Denton Hill, Galeton.* Weekend late Aug.

Germania Old Home Day. *Germania. 7 miles SE via Hwy 144. Phone 814/435-8881.* Food, dancing, events, games, entertainment. Early Sept.

Woodsmen's Carnival. *Cherry Springs State Park, Cherry Springs. 12 miles SW on West Branch Rd. Phone 814/435-5010.* Horse-pulling and woodcutting competitions; food; displays. First full weekend in Aug.

Gettysburg (D-4)

See also Hanover, York

Founded 1798
Population 7,490
Elevation 560 ft
Area Code 717
Zip 17325
Information Convention & Visitors Bureau, 35 Carlisle St; phone 717/334-6274
Web site www.gettysburg.com

Because of the historical nature of this area and the many attractions in this town, visitors may want to stop in at the Gettysburg Convention & Visitors Bureau for complete information about bus tours, guide service (including a tape-recorded and self-guided tour) and help in planning their visit here.

What to See and Do

A. Lincoln's Place. *571 Steinwehr Ave, Gettysburg (17325). Phone 717/334-6049.* Live portrayal of the 16th president; 45 minutes. (Mid-June-Labor Day, Mon-Fri) **$$$**

Boyds Bear Country. *75 Cunningham Rd, Gettysburg (17325). 5 miles S of Gettysburg on Hwy 15 S. Phone 717/630-2600; toll-free 866/367-8338. www.boydsbearcountry.com.* "The World's Most Humungous Teddy Bear Store" features four floors of bears, bears, and more bears (plus rabbits, moose, and other furry friends) in a giant barn. At the Boyds Teddy Bear Nursery, kids can adopt their very own baby bear; personalize your bear at the Make-N-Take-Craft Center. Live entertainment every weekend adds to the merriment. Restaurant; museum. (Daily 10 am-6 pm; closed holidays)

Eisenhower National Historic Site. *Rural Rte 9.* (see GETTYSBURG NATIONAL MILITARY PARK)

General Lee's Headquarters. *401 Buford Ave, Gettysburg (17325). Phone 717/334-3141.* Robert E. Lee planned Confederate strategy for the Gettysburg battle in this house; contains collection of historical items from the battle. (Mid-Mar-mid-Nov, daily) **$$**

Gettysburg Battle Theatre. *571 Steinwehr Ave, Gettysburg (17325). Phone 717/334-6100.* Battlefield diorama with 25,000 figures; 30-minute film and electronic maps program showing battle strategy. (Mar-Nov, daily) **$$$**

Gettysburg College. *300 N Washington St, Gettysburg (17325). 3 blocks NW of Lincoln Sq off US 15 Business. Phone 717/337-6000. www.gettysburg.edu.* (1832) (2,000 students) Liberal arts; oldest Lutheran-affiliated college in the US. Pennsylvania Hall was used as Civil War hospital; Eisenhower House and statue on grounds. Tour of campus.

Gettysburg Scenic Rail Tours. *Washington St, Gettysburg (17325). Phone 717/334-6932.* A 22-mile round trip to Aspers on a steam train. Also charter trips and special runs. (June, Thurs-Sun; July-Aug, Tues-Sun; Sept Sat-Sun afternoons) **$$$**

Ghosts of Gettysburg Candlelight Walking Tours. *271 Baltimore St, Gettysburg (17325). Phone 717/337-0445.* Armed with tales from Mark Nesbitt's *Ghosts of Gettysburg* books, knowledgeable guides lead 1 1/4-hour tours through sections of town that were bloody battlefields 130 years ago. (June-Oct, daily evenings; Apr, May, Nov, weekend evenings) **$$$**

Hall of Presidents and First Ladies. *789 Baltimore St, Gettysburg (17325). Adjacent to National Cemetery. Phone 717/334-5717.* Costumed life-size wax figures of all the presidents; reproductions of their wives' inaugural gowns; "The Eisenhowers at Gettysburg" exhibit. (Mid-Mar-Nov, daily) **$$$**

Land of Little Horses. *125 Glenwood Dr, Gettysburg (17325). 5 miles W off Hwy 30, on Knoxlyn Rd to Glenwood Dr; follow signs. Phone 717/334-7259.* A variety of performing horses—all in miniature. Continuous entertainment; indoor arena; exotic animal races. Saddle and wagon rides. Picnic area, snack bar, gift shop. (May-late Aug, daily; Apr, Sept, Oct, weekends) **$$$**

Lincoln Room Museum. *12 Lincoln Sq, Gettysburg (17325). Phone 717/334-8188.* Preserved bedroom in Wills House; collection of Lincoln items; huge plaque inscribed with Gettysburg Address, audiovisual display. (Apr-Nov, daily) **$$**

The Lincoln Train Museum. *425 Steinwehr Ave, Gettysburg (17325). 1/2 mile S via US 15 on Steinwehr Ave. Phone 717/334-5678.* Museum features more than 1,000 model trains and railroad memorabilia; Lincoln Train Ride—simulated trip of 15 minutes. (Mar-Nov, daily) **$$$**

Lutheran Theological Seminary. *61 Seminary Ridge, Gettysburg (17325). Confederate Ave, 1 mile W of Lincoln Sq on Hwy 30. Phone 717/334-6286. www.ltsg.edu.* (1826) (250 students) Oldest Lutheran seminary in US; cupola on campus used as Confederate lookout during battle. Old Dorm, now home of Adams County Historical Society, served as hospital for both Union and Confederate soldiers.

National Civil War Wax Museum. *297 Steinwehr Ave, Gettysburg (17325). Phone 717/334-6245.* Highlights

Gettysburg: A Town Gripped by War

A three-day Civil War battle in July 1863 unfolded about a mile outside Gettysburg, which was a small rural community at the time. The town suffered from the battle, and the impact can be seen in a one-hour, 1-mile walking tour that visits several of the well-preserved buildings that witnessed the conflict. Begin at Lincoln Square, the commercial heart of Gettysburg. Abraham Lincoln stayed at the David Wills House, now a small museum at No. 12, the night before he gave the "Gettysburg Address" dedicating the nearby National Cemetery. Just outside the door is a life-size statue of Lincoln in somber attire appearing to help a visiting tourist casually dressed in a colorful sweater and cords. Among the townsfolk, it is called the "Perry Como statue" because that's who the tourist looks like. Head south on Baltimore Street to Nos. 242-246, the Jennie Wade Birthplace. Wade, the only civilian to be killed in the battle, is believed to have been shot by a Confederate sharpshooter while baking bread and biscuits for Union troops in her sister's nearby house. That house, on Baltimore Street, is a museum, the Jennie Wade House. Between the two homes, stop at the Schriver house at 309 Baltimore. Built for George Schriver and his family, its garret was occupied by Confederate sharpshooters who poked still-visible holes in the wall for their rifles. Now a museum, the Schriver House details life in the town during and immediately after the battle. Across the street at No. 304, formerly the Methodist parsonage, note the shell near the second-story window in front. The parson's daughter, Laura, was said to have narrowly escaped injury when a shell crashed through the brick wall into her room. Later, the shell was placed in the hole to mark the spot. Return to Lincoln Square via Washington Street. At the corner of West Middle Street, pause in front of the Michael Jacobs House at No. 101. A meteorologist, Jacobs recorded the weather throughout his life, leaving important details to posterity of weather and cloud conditions during the battle.

Civil War era and Battle of Gettysburg. (Mar-Dec: daily; rest of year: Sat and Sun; closed Jan 1, Thanksgiving, Dec 25) **$$**

Schriver House. *309 Baltimore St, Gettysburg (17325). Phone 717/337-2800.* Built prior to the Civil War, this two-story brick house was used by Confederate sharpshooters, who knocked still-visible holes in the garret walls through which to aim their weapons. Private owners have restored and furnished the house as a period museum; the 30-minute guided tour details the Schriver family's experience during the battle, as well as the experience of other townspeople. (Apr-Nov: daily; Dec-Mar: weekends) **$$$**

Ski Liberty. *78 Country Club Trail, Carroll Valley (17320). 9 miles W on Hwy 116. Phone 717/642-8282. www.skiliberty.com.* Two quad, three double chairlifts; J-bar, handle tow; patrol, school, rentals; snowmaking; cafeteria, restaurant, bar; nursery, lodge. Longest run approximately 1 mile; vertical drop 600 feet. (Dec-Mar, daily) **$$$$**

Soldiers' National Museum. *777 Baltimore St, Gettysburg (17325). Phone 717/334-4890.* Dioramas of major battles, with sound; Civil War collection. (Mar-Nov, daily; schedule may vary) **$$$**

Special Events

Apple Blossom Festival. *South Mountain Fairgrounds, 35 Carlisle St, Gettysburg (17325). 10 miles NW of Gettysburg on Rte 234.* Early May.

Apple Harvest Festival. *South Mountain Fairgrounds, 218 Mercer St, Gettysburg (17325). 10 miles NW of Gettysburg on Rte 234.* Demonstrations; arts and crafts; guided tours of orchard, mountain areas. First and second weekends in Oct.

Civil War Heritage Days. Lectures by historians; Civil War collectors' show; entertainment; Civil War book show; firefighters' festival; fireworks. Late June-early July.

Limited-Service Hotels

★ **BEST INN.** *301 Steinwehr Ave, Gettysburg (17325). Phone 717/334-1188; toll-free 800/237-8466; fax 717/334-1188. www.gettysburgbestinn.com.* 77 rooms, 2 story. Pets accepted. Complimentary continental breakfast. Check-in 3 pm, check-out noon. Outdoor pool. **$**

★★ **BEST WESTERN GETTYSBURG HOTEL.** *1 Lincoln Sq, Gettysburg (17325). Phone 717/337-2000; toll-free 866/378-1797; fax 717/337-2075. www.bestwestern.com.* 96 rooms, 6 story. Check-in 3 pm, check-out 11 am. Two restaurants, bar. Outdoor pool. **$**

★ **HOLIDAY INN EXPRESS.** *869 York Rd, Gettysburg (17325). Phone 717/337-1400; toll-free 800/465-4329; fax 717/337-0159. www.hiexpress.com.* 51 rooms, 2 story. Complimentary continental breakfast. Check-in 3 pm, check-out 11 am. Indoor pool, whirlpool. **$**

★ **QUALITY INN.** *401 Buford Ave, Gettysburg (17325). Phone 717/334-3141; fax 717/334-1813. www.choicehotels.com.* 45 rooms. Complimentary continental breakfast. Check-in 2:30 pm, check-out noon. Bar. Fitness room. Outdoor pool. **$**

Full-Service Inn

★★★ **THE HERR TAVERN AND PUBLICK HOUSE.** *900 Chambersburg Rd, Gettysburg (17325). Phone 717/334-4332; toll-free 800/362-9849; fax 717/334-3332. www.herrtavern.com.* 16 rooms, 3 story. Children over 12 years only. Complimentary continental breakfast. Check-in 4 pm, check-out 11 am. Restaurant, bar. Built in 1815, served as Confederate hospital. **$$**

Specialty Lodgings

The following lodging establishments are approved by Mobil Travel Guide, but due to their unique and individualized nature have not been given a traditional Mobil Star rating. Included in this listing you may find bed-and-breakfasts, limited-service inns, guest ranches, and other unique hotel properties.

BALADERRY INN. *40 Hospital Rd, Gettysburg (17325). Phone 717/337-1342; toll-free 800/220-0025. www.baladerryinn.com.* Built in 1812; used as a field hospital during the Civil War battle of Gettysburg. Restored; furnished with antiques and reproductions. 9 rooms, 2 story. Children over 12 years only. Complimentary full breakfast. Check-in 3 pm, check-out 11 am. Tennis. **$**

BATTLEFIELD BED AND BREAKFAST INN. *2264 Emmitsburg Rd, Gettysburg (17325). Phone 717/334-8804; toll-free 888/766-3897. www.gettysburgbattlefield.com.* Built in 1809, this Civil War inn is found on the Gettysburg battlefield. Guests can enjoy a carriage ride and a historic demonstration with real muskets, cannons, and cavalry. 8 rooms, 2 story. Complimentary full breakfast. Check-in 2:30-8 pm, check-out 11:30 am. **$$**

BRAFFERTON INN. *44 York St, Gettysburg (17325). Phone 717/337-3423; toll-free 866/337-3427. www.brafferton.com.* First house built in town (1786); antiques. 14 rooms, 2 story. Closed Dec 25. Children over 8 years only. Complimentary full breakfast. Check-in 2-6 pm, check-out 11 am. **$**

THE GASLIGHT INN. *33 E Middle St, Gettysburg (17325). Phone 717/337-9100; toll-free 800/914-5698; fax 717/337-1100. www.thegaslightinn.com.* This bed-and-breakfast is located in the center of historic Gettysburg, near shopping, restaurants, and local attractions. 9 rooms, 3 story. Closed Dec 25, Children over 11 years only. Complimentary full breakfast. Check-in 3-6 pm, check-out 11 am. **$$**

JAMES GETTYS HOTEL. *27 Chambersburg St, Gettysburg (17325). Phone 717/337-1334; toll-free 800/900-5275; fax 717/334-2103. www.jamesgettyshotel.com.* Built in 1804. 11 rooms, 4 story, all suites. Complimentary continental breakfast. Check-in 3-8 pm, check-out 11 am. **$$**

Restaurants

★★ **DOBBIN HOUSE.** *89 Steinwehr Ave, Gettysburg (17325). Phone 717/334-2100; fax 717/334-6905. www.dobbinhouse.com.* Built for Reverend

Alexander Dobbin in 1776, this colonial restaurant is listed on the National Register of Historic Places. Meals are served against a backdrop of traditional 18th-century décor, including stone walls, fireplaces, and carved woodwork. American, seafood menu. Lunch, dinner. Closed Jan 1, Thanksgiving, Dec 25. Bar. Children's menu. **$$**

★★ FARNSWORTH HOUSE INN. *401 Baltimore St, Gettysburg (17325). Phone 717/334-8838; fax 717/334-5862. www.farnsworthhousedining.com.* Built in 1810; tour available. Outdoor seating. American menu. Dinner. Closed Jan 1, Thanksgiving, Dec 25. Children's menu. **$$**

★ GINGERBREAD MAN. *217 Steinwehr Ave, Gettysburg (17325). Phone 717/334-1100. www.thegingerbreadman.net.* American menu. Lunch, dinner. Closed holidays. Bar. Children's menu. **$$**

★★ THE HERR TAVERN & PUBLICK HOUSE. *900 Chambersburg Rd, Gettysburg (17325). Phone 717/334-4332; fax 717/334-3332. www.herrtavern.com.* Restored antebellum tavern with period art and antiques. American menu. Lunch, dinner. Closed Jan 1, Dec 24-25. Bar. Children's menu. **$$**

Gettysburg National Military Park (D-4)

See also Gettysburg, Hanover

Visitor Center is located between Taneytown Rd (State Rte 134) and Steinwehr Ave (Business Rte 15).

Web site www.nps.gov/gett/

The hallowed battlefield of Gettysburg, scene of one of the most decisive battles of the Civil War and immortalized by Lincoln's Gettysburg Address, is preserved by the National Park Service. The town itself is still a college community, as it was more than a hundred years ago on July 1-3, 1863, when General Robert E. Lee led his Confederate Army in its greatest invasion of the North. The defending Northerners under Union General George Meade repulsed the Southern assault after three days of fierce fighting, which left 51,000 men dead, wounded, or missing.

The Gettysburg National Military Park has more than 35 miles of roads through 5,900 acres of the battlefield area. There are more than 1,300 monuments, markers, and tablets of granite and bronze; 400 cannons are also located on the field.

Visitors may wish to tour the battlefield with a Battlefield Guide, licensed by the National Park Service (two-hour tour; fee). The guides escort visitors to all points of interest and sketch the movement of troops and details of the battle. Or visitors may wish to first orient themselves at the Electric Map at the Visitor Center; then using the park folder, the battlefield can be toured without a guide. Audio cassettes are also available for self-guided tours.

The late President Dwight D. Eisenhower's retirement farm, a National Historic Site, adjoins the battlefield. It is open to the public on a limited-tour basis. All visitors must obtain tour tickets at the tour information center, located at the lobby of the Visitor Center-Electric Map building. Transportation to the farm is by shuttle (fee). For further information contact Gettysburg National Military Park, 97 Taneytown Rd, Gettysburg 17325; 717/334-1124.

What to See and Do

The Angle. Spot where Pickett's Charge was repulsed on July 3, referred to as "high water mark" of the Confederacy.

Culp's Hill. Site of longest sustained fighting during battle.

Cyclorama Center. *97 Taneytown Rd, Gettysburg (17325).* Adjacent to visitor center. Instructive film and exhibits: 356-foot Cyclorama painting of Pickett's Charge. (Daily) **$$**

Devil's Den. Stronghold of Confederate sharpshooters following its capture during action on the second day.

East Cemetery Hill. Rallying point for Union forces on first day of battle. Scene of fierce fighting on evening of second day.

Eisenhower National Historic Site. *97 Taneytown Rd (Visitor Center), Gettysburg Natl Military Park. Phone 717/338-9114 (advance tickets).* Farm and home of the 34th President of the United States and his wife, Mamie. Tour of grounds and home (1 1/2-2 hours). Self-guided tours explore the farm and skeet range. Reception Center houses exhibits and bookstore; 11-minute video is shown. Access to site is by shuttle only, from the National Park Service Visitor Center. (Daily; closed Jan 1, Thanksgiving, Dec 25) **$$$**

The Eternal Light Peace Memorial. On Oak Ridge. Erected in 1938 and dedicated by President Roosevelt to "peace eternal in a nation united."

The Gettysburg National Cemetery. Site of Lincoln's Gettysburg Address.

Little Round Top. Key Union position during second and third days of battle.

Memorials to State Units. Includes Pennsylvania State Monument, with names of more than 34,500 Pennsylvanian soldiers who participated in the battle.

Seminary Ridge. Main Confederate battle line.

★ Visitor Center-Electric Map-Gettysburg Museum of the Civil War. *35 Carlisle St, Gettysburg (17325). On Hwy 134. Electric map.* Visits to the park should begin here. Park information, including a self-guided auto tour, and guides may be obtained at the center. Story of battle told on 750-square-foot electric map surrounded by 525 seats (every 45 minutes; fee). Gettysburg Museum of the Civil War has an extensive collection of Civil War relics (free). (Daily; closed Jan 1, Thanksgiving, Dec 25) **$$**

The Wheatfield and Peach Orchard. Scene of heavy Union and Confederate losses on the second day of fighting.

Whitworth Guns on Oak Hill. Only breech-loading cannon used here.

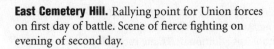

Greensburg (C-2)

See also Connellsville, Donegal, Ligonier, New Stanton

Founded 1785
Population 15,889
Elevation 1,099 ft
Area Code 724
Zip 15601
Information Laurel Highlands Visitors Bureau, 120 E Main St, Ligonier 15658; phone 724/238-5661
Web site www.laurelhighlands.org

Greensburg was named for Revolutionary General Nathanael Greene.

What to See and Do

Bushy Run Battlefield. *Bushy Run Rd, Jeannette. NW on Hwy 993. Phone 724/527-5584.* Here, Colonel Henry Bouquet defeated united Native American forces during Pontiac's War on Aug 5 and 6, 1763. The battle lifted the siege of Fort Pitt and was the turning point of the war. Picnicking, park (free), hiking trails. Visitor center exhibits depict battle (Wed-Sun; closed holidays). **$$**

Historic Hanna's Town. *951 Old Salem Rd, Greensburg (15601). 3 miles NE via Hwy 119. Phone 724/836-1800.* Costumed tour guide tells story of Hanna's Town, site of first court west of Alleghenies. Includes reconstructed courthouse, tavern, jail, and stockaded fort; picnic area. (June-Aug, Tues-Sun; May, Sept and Oct, weekends only) **$$**

Lincoln Highway Heritage Corridor. *114 S Market St, Greensburg. Phone 724/238-9030.* A 140-mile stretch of Hwy 30 extending from Greensburg to Chambersburg. Pass through and explore countless historical and recreational areas. Driving guide available (fee) **$**

Westmoreland County Courthouse. *Main and Pittsburgh sts, Greensburg. Phone 724/830-3000.* Building in style of Italian Renaissance; restored in 1982. (Mon-Fri; closed holidays)

Westmoreland Museum of American Art. *221 N Main St, Greensburg. Phone 724/837-1500.* 18th-, 19th-, and early 20th-century American paintings, sculpture, furniture and decorative arts. 19th- and early 20th-century southwestern Pennsylvania paintings. Extensive toy collection. Lectures, guided tours. (Wed-Sun; closed holidays) **DONATION**

Limited-Service Hotel

★ ★ FOUR POINTS BY SHERATON. *100 Sheraton Dr (Rte 30E), Greensburg (15601). Phone 724/836-6060; fax 724/834-5640. www.sheraton.com.* 146 rooms, 2 story. Check-out noon. Restaurant, bar. Fitness room. Indoor pool. Golf, pro shop, putting green. **$**

Restaurant

★ ★ CARBONE'S. *Hwy 119, Crabtree (15624). Phone 724/834-3430; fax 724/836-2501. www.carbonepasta.com.* American, Italian menu. Dinner. Closed Sun; holidays. Children's menu. **$$**

Hamburg (C-5)

See also Kutztown, Reading, Shartlesville

Founded 1779
Population 4,114
Elevation 373 ft
Area Code 484 and 610
Zip 19526
Information Reading/Berks County Visitors Bureau, 352 Penn St, Reading 19602; phone 610/375-4085 or toll-free 800/443-6610
Web site www.readingberkspa.com

Situated on the banks of the Schuylkill River, Hamburg is a center for one of the finest farming sections in Pennsylvania. The town's industries include the manufacture of brooms, iron and steel castings, knitwear, and soft-drink products.

What to See and Do

Blue Rocks. *341 Sousley Rd, Lenhartsville (19534). 5 miles E on I-78 to Lenhartsville, then 2 miles N on Hwy 143. Phone 610/756-6366.* Covers 125 acres; pool, fishing (stocked pond); picnicking, two pavilions; hiking, Appalachian Trail; camping, trailer facilities (fee; hookups additional). Game room. **$**

Hawk Mountain Sanctuary. *1700 Hawk Mountain Rd, Kempton (19529). 11 miles N via Hwys 61 and 895; follow signs. Phone 610/756-6961.* Hawk and eagle flights visible with binoculars from lookouts mid-Aug-mid-Dec; museum, bookstore. (Daily; closed Jan 1, Thanksgiving, Dec 25) **$$$**

Wanamaker, Kempton & Southern, Inc. *5 miles E on I-78 to Lenhartsville exit, then 5 miles N on Hwy 143 to Kempton. Phone 610/756-6469.* A 6-mile, 40-minute round trip on steam or deisel train along the Ontelaunee Creek at the foot of Hawk Mountain. Model railroad (Sun), antique shop. Snack bar, picnic area. Steam train (July-Aug and Oct, Sat and Sun afternoons; May and June, Sun afternoons). Diesel train (June and Sept, first and third Sat afternoons only). Also special events throughout the year. **$$**

Hanover (D-4)

See also Gettysburg, Gettysburg National Military Park, York

Founded 1763
Population 14,535
Elevation 609 ft
Area Code 717
Zip 17331
Information Hanover Area Chamber of Commerce, 146 Carlisle St; phone 717/637-6130
Web site www.hanoverchamber.com

Known in early days as "McAllisterstown" (for founder Colonel Richard McAllister) and "Rogue's Harbor" (for lack of law enforcement), Hanover is in the rich Conewago Valley. Here, on June 30, 1863, Confederate General J. E. B. Stuart's cavalry tangled with Union forces under Generals Kilpatrick and Custer. The battle prevented Stuart from reaching Gettysburg in time to function as "the eyes of Lee's army."

Among the products of the town's diversified industry are books, wirecloth, yarns, furniture, industrial machinery, textiles, and foods, including the famous pretzel maker, Snyder's of Hanover.

What to See and Do

Codorus State Park. *1066 Blooming Grove Rd, Hanover (17331). 3 miles E on Hwy 216. Phone 717/637-2816.* Approximately 3,300 acres. Swimming pool, fishing in 1,275-acre Lake Marburg, boating (rentals, mooring, launching, marina); hunting, hiking, bridle trails, cross-country skiing, snowmobiling, sledding, ice skating, ice boating, ice fishing, picnicking, mountain biking, snack bar, tent and trailer sites.

Conewago Chapel. *30 Basilica Dr, Hanover (17331). 2 miles W on Hwy 116, then 2 miles N. Phone 717/637-2721.* (1741) Oldest stone Catholic church in the US. Designated Sacred Heart Basilica in 1962. Cemetery dates from 1752. (Daily) **FREE**

Neas House Museum. *113 W Chestnut St, Hanover (17331). Phone 717/632-3207.* Neas House (circa 1783), restored Georgian mansion, serves as local history museum. (May-Nov, Tues-Fri) Special events (spring, summer, late Dec). **FREE**

Utz Quality Foods, Inc. *900 High St, Hanover (17331). Phone 717/637-6644.* Producers of potato chips and snack foods. Glass-enclosed tour gallery overlooks production area; push-to-talk audio program and closed-circuit TV monitors. (Mon-Thurs; closed holidays) **FREE**

Specialty Lodging

The following lodging establishment is approved by Mobil Travel Guide, but due to its unique and individualized nature has not been given a traditional Mobil Star rating. Included in this listing you may find bed-and-breakfasts, limited-service inns, guest ranches, and other unique hotel properties.

THE BEECHMONT BED AND BREAKFAST INN. *315 Broadway, Hanover (17331). Phone 717/632-3013; toll-free 800/553-7009; fax 717/632-2769. www.thebeechmont.com.* Built in 1834, this bed-and-breakfast is located just 14 miles outside of Gettysburg. It offers four large guest rooms and three suites, each furnished with fine antiques. Breakfast can be enjoyed in the dining room, on the porch or in the rooms. 7 rooms, 2 story. Children over 12 years only. Complimentary full breakfast. Check-in 3 pm, check-out 11 am. **$**

Harmony

See also Beaver Falls, Butler, Pittsburgh

Founded 1804
Population 937
Elevation 925 ft
Area Code 724
Zip 16037
Information Butler County Chamber of Commerce, 112 Woody Dr, PO Box 1082, Butler, 16003; phone 724/283-2222
Web site www.butlercountychamber.com

First settlement of George Rapp's Harmony Society, Harmony served the colony only until 1814. More than 100 of the original group are buried in Harmonists Cemetery, southeast of town. Several of the Rappite Society's sturdy brick houses still stand in the village.

What to See and Do

Harmony Museum. *218 Mercer St, Harmony (16037). Phone 724/452-7341.* (1809) Exhibits depict early life under Harmonists and Mennonites; regional history. The Harmony Society was one of America's most successful experiments in communal living. Harmony was the society's first home (1804). Tour. (Tues-Sun afternoons) **$$**

Special Events

Christmas Open House. *218 Mercer St, Harmony (16037).* Candlelight tour of Harmony Museum, Wagner House and Ziegler log house. Entertainment, refreshments. Contact museum for schedule. Early Dec.

Dankfest. *218 Mercer, Harmony (16037). Phone 722/452-7341.* Pioneer craft festival held on grounds of Harmony Museum (see). Crafts, entertainment, tours, refreshments. Contact museum for schedule. Late Aug.

Harrisburg (C-4)

See also Carlisle, Hershey, York

Settled 1718
Population 48,950
Elevation 360 ft
Area Code 717
Information Capital Regional Chamber of Commerce, 3211 N Front St, 17110-1342, phone 717/232-4099; or the Harrisburg-Hershey-Carlisle Tourism & Convention Bureau, 25 N Front St, 17101, phone 717/231-7788
Web site www.harrisburgregionalchamber.org

This midstate metropolis is graced by what many consider the finest capitol building in the nation. Its riverside park (known as City Island), Italian Lake, unique museum, and beautiful Forum are the showplaces; commerce, industry, and politics keep the city going.

The site was viewed in 1615 by Etienne Brulé on a trip down the Susquehanna, but more than a century passed before John Harris, the first settler, opened his trading post here. His son established the town in 1785. It became the seat of state government in 1812; the cornerstone of the first capitol building was laid in 1819.

What to See and Do

Capitol Hill buildings. *N 3rd and Walnut sts, Harrisburg. Phone 717/787-6810.* Clustered in a 45-acre complex, the major buildings are

The Capitol. *Third and State sts, Harrisburg.* (Dedicated 1906) Italian Renaissance building covers 2 acres, has 651 rooms; 26,000-ton, 272-foot dome, imitating that of St. Peter's in Rome, dominates city skyline. Includes murals by Abbey and Okley. Tours (daily; closed holidays). **FREE**

Finance Building. Ceiling murals by Maragliotti, Eugene Savage; mural in south vestibule illustrates The Collection of Taxes. (Mon-Fri)

Forum Building. Includes auditorium below constellation-bedecked ceiling; walls review man's progress through time. Main lobby boasts a Maragliotti ceiling. General and law libraries.

North Office Building. Map inscribed on main lobby floor shows state highways, seals of Pennsylvania cities.

South Office Building. Colorful murals by Edward Trumbull depict Penn's Treaty with the Indians and The Industries of Pittsburgh.

The State Museum of Pennsylvania. *3rd and North sts, Harrisburg. N of Capitol Building. Phone 717/787-4978.* A six-story circular building housing four stories of galleries, authentic early country store, Native American life exhibit, technological and industrial exhibits, collection of antique autos and period carriages; planetarium; natural history and geology exhibits and one of the world's largest framed paintings, Rothermel's *The Battle of Gettysburg.* Planetarium has public shows (Sat and Sun; fee). (Tues-Sun; closed holidays) **FREE**

Dauphin County Courthouse. *Front and Market sts, Harrisburg. Phone 717/255-2741.* Seven imposing courtrooms; outline map on floor of main foyer pictures borough and township boundaries. (Mon-Fri; closed holidays)

Fort Hunter Park. *6 miles N on N Front St.* Historic 37-acre property; site of British-built fort erected in 1754 to combat mounting threats prior to the French and Indian War. In 1787, the land was purchased and became a farm that eventually grew into a self-sufficient village. The Pennsylvania Canal runs through the park; on the grounds are historic buttonwood trees dating from William Penn's time; a 19th-century boxwood garden; herb gardens; paths along the banks of the Susquehanna River; picnic area. Also here are an ice house, springhouse (circa 1800), Centennial barn (1876), and corncrib (1880). Also on the grounds, but not open to the public because of restoration, are the old tavern (1800), and stone stable. Outstanding feature of park is

Fort Hunter Mansion. *5300 N Front St, Harrisburg. Phone 717/599-5751.* Federal-style stone mansion, built in three sections. Front stone portions were built in 1786 and 1814; rear wooden portion built in 1870. Spacious mansion displays period furnishings, clothing, toys, and other artifacts. Guided tours. (May-Dec, Tues-Sun) **$$**

Indian Echo Caverns. *368 Middletown Rd, Hummelstown. 10 miles E on Hwys 322, 422. Phone 717/566-8131.* Stalagmite and stalactite formations. Picnicking, playground. (Daily, schedule varies; closed Jan 1, Thanksgiving, Dec 25) **$$$**

Italian Lake. *N 3rd and Division sts, Harrisburg.* Bordered with flowers, shrubs, and shade trees in summer.

John Harris Mansion. *219 S Front St, Harrisburg. Phone 717/233-3462.* Home of city's founder, now Historical Society of Dauphin County headquarters. Stone house has 19th-century furnishings, library (Mon-Thurs; fee), collection of county artifacts. Tours (Mon-Thurs and by appointment). **$$$**

Penn National Race Course. *I-81, exit 28, Grantville. Phone 717/469-2211.* Live year-round Thoroughbred racing (Wed, Fri-Sun). Nationwide simulcasts (daily). Terrace dining room; gift shop. **$$**

Reservoir Park. *Walnut and N 19th sts, Harrisburg.* View of east end of city, five nearby counties.

Riverfront Park. Four miles along Susquehanna River, with park promenade flanking Front St, concrete walk along river.

Rockville Bridge. *4 miles N on Hwy 22.* (1902) A 3,810-foot stone-arch bridge; 48 spans carry four tracks of Penn Central Railroad main line.

Special Events

Eastern Sports & Outdoor Show. *State Farm Show Complex, 2301 N Cameron, Harrisburg (17110). Phone 717/787-5373.* Early-mid-Feb.

Kipona. Boating and water-related activites. Labor Day weekend.

Pennsylvania National Horse Show. *1509 Cedar Cliff Dr, Harrisburg. Phone 717/975-3677.* Ten days in mid-Oct.

Pennsylvania State Farm Show. *State Farm Show Complex, 2301 N Cameron St, Harrisburg. Phone 717/787-5373.* State fair. Early-mid-Jan.

Limited-Service Hotels

★ ★ BEST WESTERN HARRISBURG/ HERSHEY HOTEL & SUITES. *300 N Mountain Rd, Harrisburg (17112). Phone 717/652-7180; fax 717/ 541-8991. www.bestwestern.com.* 49 rooms, 2 story. Pets accepted, some restrictions; fee. Check-out 11 am. Restaurant, bar. **$**

★ DAYS INN. *3919 N Front St, Harrisburg (17110). Phone 717/233-3100; fax 717/233-6415. www.daysinn .com.* 116 rooms, 3 story. Complimentary continental breakfast. Check-in 3 pm, check-out noon. Fitness room. Outdoor pool. **$**

★ ★ FOUR POINTS BY SHERATON. *800 E Park Dr, Harrisburg (17111). Phone 717/561-2800; toll-free 800/644-3144; fax 717/561-8398. www.fourpoints .com.* 174 rooms, 3 story. Check-in 3 pm, check-out noon. Restaurant, bar. Fitness room. Indoor pool, whirlpool. Airport transportation available. **$**

★ HAMPTON INN. *4230 Union Deposit Rd, Harrisburg (17111). Phone 717/545-9595; fax 717/ 545-6907. www.hamptoninn.com.* 145 rooms, 5 story. Complimentary continental breakfast. Check-in 3 pm, check-out noon. Fitness room. Outdoor pool, whirlpool. Airport transportation available. **$**

★ ★ HOLIDAY INN. *148 Sheraton Dr, New Cumberland (17070). Phone 717/774-2721; fax 717/ 774-2485. www.holilday-inn.com.* 196 rooms, 2 story. Pets accepted; fee. Check-out 11 am. Restaurant, bar. Fitness room. Indoor pool, whirlpool. Airport transportation available. Business center. **$**

★ ★ RADISSON PENN HARRIS HOTEL & CONVENTION CENTER. *1150 Camp Hill Byp, Camp Hill (17011). Phone 717/763-7117; fax 717/ 763-4518. www.radisson.com.* 250 rooms, 3 story. Pets accepted, some restrictions; fee. Check-out 11 am. Restaurant, bar. Fitness room. Pool. Airport transportation available. Business center. **$**

Full-Service Hotels

★ ★ ★ CROWNE PLAZA. *23 S 2nd St, Harrisburg (17101). Phone 717/234-5021; toll-free 800/2CROWNE; fax 717/234-6797. www.crowneplaza.com.* 261 rooms, 10 story. Pets accepted, some restrictions; fee. Check-in 3 pm, check-out noon. Restaurant, bar. Fitness room. Indoor pool. Airport transportation available. **$**

★ ★ ★ HILTON HARRISBURG AND TOWERS. *1 N 2nd St, Harrisburg (17101). Phone 717/233-6000; fax 717/233-6830. www.hilton.com.* 356 rooms, 15 story. Check-in 4 pm, check-out noon. High-speed Internet access. Restaurant, bar. Fitness room. Indoor pool. Airport transportation available. **$**

★ ★ ★ WYNDHAM HARRISBURG HERSHEY. *4650 Lindle Rd, Harrisburg (17111). Phone 717/564-5511; fax 717/564-6173. www.wyndham.com.* 348 rooms, 10 story. Pets accepted, fee. Check-in 4 pm, check-out 11 am. High-speed Internet access. Restaurant, bar. Fitness room. Indoor pool, outdoor pool, whirlpool. Airport transportation available. **$**

Hawley (B-6)

See also Carbondale, Milford, Scranton

Settled 1827
Population 1,303
Elevation 920 ft
Area Code 570
Zip 18428
Information Pocono Mountains Vacation Bureau, 1004 Main St, Stroudsburg 18360; phone 570/424-6050; for brochures phone toll-free 800/POCONOS
Web site www.poconos.org

A major attraction in this Pocono resort area is man-made Lake Wallenpaupack, offering summer recreation on the lake, as well as winter recreation nearby.

What to See and Do

Claws 'N Paws Wild Animal Park. *Lakeville. 12 miles W via Hwy 590, near Lake Wallenpaupack. Phone 570/698-6154.* A zoo in the woods with more than 100 species of exotic animals. Petting zoo with tame deer, lambs, and goats. Farmyard area. Parrot, reptile shows; zookeeper talks (schedule varies). Picnicking, snack bar. (May-Oct, daily) **$$$**

Gravity Coach. *W of town on Hwy 6.* Car used on Pennsylvania Gravity Railroad (22 inclined planes between Hawley and Scranton, 1850-1885).

Lake Wallenpaupack. *Hwy 6. Phone 570/226-2141.* One of the largest man-made lakes in the state (5,600 acres), formed by the damming of Wallenpaupack Creek. Swimming beach (Memorial Day-Labor Day; fee), fishing, boating, water sports; ice fishing, camping. The information center is 1/2 mile NW on Hwy 6 at Hwy 507 (daily; closed Easter, Thanksgiving, Dec 25).

PPL. *Approximately 1 1/2 miles E on Hwy 6. Phone 570/226-3702.* Hydroelectric facilities, dam; recreation area. Superintendent's office has information on campgrounds, hiking trails, picnic groves (Mon-Fri); observation point. (Daily) **FREE**

Promised Land State Park. *Greentown. 12 miles S on Hwy 390. Phone 570/676-3428.* Approximately 2,950 acres. Swimming beach, fishing, boating (rentals, mooring, launch); hiking, cross-country skiing, snowmobiling, ice skating, ice fishing, picnicking, snack bar, tent and trailer sites, cabins. Nature center, interpretive program. **$$$$**

Tanglwood. *Hwy 390 Paper Birch, Tafton. 4 miles S via Hwy 390, off I-84. Phone 570/226-7669. www.tanglwood.com.* Two double chairlifts, two rope tows, beginner lift; patrol, school, rentals, snowmaking; cafeteria, bar; nursery. Longest run 1 mile; vertical drop 415 feet. Night skiing. (Early Dec-late Mar, daily) Half-day rates. **$$$$**

Limited-Service Hotel

★ GRESHAM'S LAKE VIEW MOTEL. *Hwy 6, Hawley (18428). Phone 570/226-4621; fax 570/226-4621.* 21 rooms, 2 story. Check-out 11 am. **$**

Full-Service Resort

★ ★ ★ CAESARS COVE HAVEN. *RR 590, Lakeville (18438). Phone 570/226-4506; toll-free 800/233-4141; fax 570/226-4697.* 282 rooms, 3 story. No children allowed. Check-out 11 am. Bar. Fitness room. Indoor pool, outdoor pool, whirlpool. Tennis. **$$**

Full-Service Inn

★ ★ ★ SETTLERS INN AT BINGHAM PARK. *4 Main Ave, Hawley (18428). Phone 570/226-2993; toll-free 800/833-8527; fax 570/226-1874. www.thesettlersinn.com.* 23 rooms, 2 story. Complimentary full breakfast. Check-in 2 pm, check-out noon. Restaurant. Airport transportation available. Tudor Revival manor (1927); stone fireplace, sitting rooms with many antiques. Bingham Park is opposite. **$**

Specialty Lodging

The following lodging establishment is approved by Mobil Travel Guide, but due to its unique and individualized nature has not been given a traditional Mobil Star rating. Included in this listing you may find bed-and-breakfasts, limited-service inns, guest ranches, and other unique hotel properties.

ROEBLING INN ON THE DELAWARE. *155 Scenic Dr, Lackawaxen (18435). Phone 570/685-7900; fax 570/685-1718. www.roeblinginn.com.* This classic Greek Revival mansion is located at the junction of the Delaware and the Lackawaxen rivers. Many local restaurants are nearby. 6 rooms, 2 story. Complimentary full breakfast. Check-in 2:30 pm, check-out 11:30 am. **$**

Restaurant

★★ THE SETTLERS INN. *4 Main Ave, Hawley (18428). Phone 570/226-2993; fax 570/226-1874. www.thesettlersinn.com.* Seafood menu. Lunch, dinner, Sun brunch. Closed Dec 23-25. Bar. Children's menu. Dining room of Tudor-style hotel constructed in 1920s. **$$**

Hazleton (B-5)

See also Ashland, Bloomsburg, Jim Thorpe, Wilkes Barre

Settled 1809
Population 23,329
Elevation 1,660 ft
Area Code 570
Zip 18201
Information Greater Hazleton Chamber of Commerce, 1 S Church St, Suite 200; phone 570/455-1508
Web site www.hazletonchamber.org

On top of Spring Mountain, Hazleton calls itself the highest city in Pennsylvania. Rich agricultural land surrounds Hazleton, and its early and rapid economic growth was spurred by the rich anthracite coal reserves found in the area. Although coal dominated the town's economy during the 19th century, today there are many diversified industries located here, producing building materials, textiles, office furniture, business forms, foods and food containers, boxes, heavy fabricated steel, plastics, electronic parts, and other products.

What to See and Do

Eckley Miners' Village. *10 miles NE off Hwy 940, near Freeland. Phone 570/636-2070.* (Pennsylvania Anthracite Museum Complex) Mining coal patch town (1850s) portrays life in the anthracite region until about 1940. Walking tour (Memorial Day-Labor Day; fee). (Daily; closed holidays) **$$**

National Shrine of the Sacred Heart. *1 Church Pl, Harleigh (18225). 1 1/2 miles NE on Hwys 309, 940, in Harleigh section of Hazleton. Phone 570/455-1162.* Large outdoor shrine includes stations of the cross and crucifixion scene; picnic area. (Mar-Oct, daily) **FREE**

Limited-Service Hotels

★ BEST WESTERN GENETTI LODGE. *PA 309, RR1, Hazleton (18201). Phone 570/454-2494; fax 570/455-7793. www.bestwestern.com.* 89 rooms, 3 story. Complimentary continental breakfast. Check-out 11 am. Pool. **$**

★★ RAMADA. *Rte 309 N, Hazleton (18201). Phone 570/455-2061; fax 570/455-9387.* 107 rooms, 2 story. Pets accepted; fee. Check-out noon. Restaurant, bar. Pool. **$**

Restaurant

★ TOM'S KITCHEN. *26 Woods Path Ln, Sugarloaf (18249). Phone 570/788-3808.* Breakfast, lunch, dinner. Closed holidays. Children's menu. **$**

Hershey (C-4)

See also Cornwall, Harrisburg, Lebanon

Founded 1903
Population 12,771
Elevation 420 ft
Area Code 717
Zip 17033
Information Hersheypark, 100 W Hersheypark Dr; phone toll-free 800/HERSHEY (information) or 800/533-3131 (reservations)
Web site www.800hershey.com

One of America's most fascinating success stories, this planned community takes its name from founder M. S. Hershey, who established his world-famous chocolate factory here in 1903, then built a town around it. The streets have names like Chocolate and Cocoa, and streetlights are shaped like chocolate kisses. But there's more than chocolate here. Today, Hershey is known as one of the most diverse entertainment and resort areas in the eastern United States. Hershey is also known as the "golf capital of Pennsylvania," and has a number of well-known golf courses.

What to See and Do

Founders Hall. *801 Spartan Ln, Hershey (17033). Phone 717/520-2000.* Campus center of Milton Hershey School, noted for its striking rotunda. (Daily; closed holidays)

Hershey's Chocolate World. *800 Hershey Park Dr, Hershey (17033). Entrance adjacent to Hersheypark. Phone 717/534-4900.* Tour via automated conveyance; simulates steps of chocolate production from cacao bean plantations through chocolate-making in Hershey. Also tropical gardens, shopping village. (Daily; closed Dec 25) **FREE**

Hershey Gardens. *170 Hotel Rd, Hershey (17033). Phone 717/534-3492.* From mid-June to first frost, 8,000 rose plants bloom on 23 acres. Tulip garden (mid-Apr-mid-May); chrysanthemums and annuals; butterfly house featuring 400-500 butterflies; six theme gardens. (Mid-Apr-Oct, daily) **$$$**

Hershey Museum. *170 W Hershey Park Dr, Hershey (17033). Near entrance to Hersheypark. Phone 717/534-3439.* Pennsylvania German, Native American, Eskimo collections; displays of Stiegel glass; "Apostolic Clock" depicting life of Christ; Milton Hershey history. (Daily; closed Jan 1, Thanksgiving, Dec 25) **$$** Adjacent is

> **Hersheypark Arena.** *100 Hershey Park Dr, Hershey (17033). Phone 717/534-3911.* Capacity 10,000; professional hockey, basketball, ice skating, variety shows, concerts.

Hersheypark. *100 W Hershey Park Dr, Hershey (17033). Phone toll-free 800/437-7439.* 110-acre theme park includes Rhine Land, Tudor Square, Dutch crafts barn; more than 60 rides include six roller coasters; live family shows. (Mid-May-Labor Day, daily; May and Sept, selected weekends) **$$$$** Also here is

> **ZooAmerica.** *Phone 717/534-3860.* An 11-acre environmental zoo depicting five climatic regions of North America; home to more than 200 animals. (Daily; closed holidays) Combination admission with Hersheypark available. **$$$**

Hersheypark Stadium/Star Pavilion. *100 W Hershey Park Dr, Hershey (17033). Phone 717/534-3911.* Stadium seats 25,000, Star Pavilion seats 7,200; sports and entertainment events.

Seltzer's Lebanon Bologna Company. *230 N College St, Palmyra. 3 blocks N of Hwy 422. Phone 717/838-6336.* Outdoor wooden smokehouses since 1902. (Mon-Sat; closed holidays) **FREE**

Special Events

Antique Automobile Club. National fall rally. Second weekend in Oct.

Chocolate Lovers' Weekend. *Hotel Hershey, 100 Hotel Rd, Hershey (17033).* Feb.

Christmas Candylane. *Hersheypark, 100 W Hershey Park Dr, Hershey (17033).* Hersheypark is transformed into "Christmas Candylane" to mark the beginning of the Christmas season. Mid-Nov-Dec.

Hersheypark Balloonfest. *Hersheypark, 100 W Hershey Park Dr, Hershey (17033). Phone 717/534-3900.* Oct.

Limited-Service Hotels

★ DAYS INN. *350 W Chocolate Ave, Hershey (17033). Phone 717/534-2162; toll-free 800/329-7466; fax 717/533-6409. www.daysinn.com/hershey06452.* 100 rooms, 4 story. Pets accepted; fee. Complimentary continental breakfast. Check-in 4 pm, check-out 11 am. Fitness room. Indoor pool, whirlpool. Airport transportation available. **$$**

★ ★ HOLIDAY INN. *604 Station Rd, Grantville (17028). Phone 717/469-0661; toll-free 800/465-4329; fax 717/469-7755. www.stayholiday.com.* 200 rooms, 4 story. Pets accepted. Check-in 4 pm, check-out

11 am. Two restaurants, bar. Fitness room. Indoor pool, outdoor pool, whirlpool. Airport transportation available. **$$**

★**SPINNERS INN.** *845 E Chocolate Ave, Hershey (17033). Phone 717/533-9157; toll-free 800/800-5845; fax 717/534-1189. www.spinnersinn.com.* 52 rooms, 2 story. Complimentary continental breakfast. Check-in 3 pm, check-out 11 am. Fitness room. Outdoor pool. **$**

Full-Service Hotel

★★★ **HERSHEY LODGE AND CONVENTION CENTER.** *W Chocolate Ave and University Dr, Hershey (17033). Phone 717/533-3311; toll-free 800/437-7439; fax 717/533-9642. www.hersheypa.com.* 665 rooms, 2 story. Check-in 4 pm, check-out 11 am. Five restaurants, two bars. Children's activity center. Fitness room. Indoor pool, outdoor pool, children's pool, whirlpool. Tennis. Airport transportation available. **$$**

Full-Service Resort

★★★★ **THE HOTEL HERSHEY.** *One Hotel Rd, Hershey (17033). Phone 717/533-2171; toll-free 800/533-3131; fax 717/534-3125. www.hersheypa.com.* Indulge in the delicious world of the Hotel Hershey. This Mediterranean masterpiece of old-world elegance was the realization of a dream for chocolate empire founder Milton Hershey. Perched atop a hill overlooking the town, the Hotel Hershey is a palatial retreat of 300 acres of formal gardens, fountains, and reflecting pools. The hotel impresses visitors of all ages with its signature touches such as evening turndown with chocolate kisses. Its rooms and suites are traditional and refined. Recreational opportunities abound, from 72 holes of golf, 6 miles of nature trails, basketball, volleyball, and tennis courts to the pools and fitness center. Gourmets delight in the Fountain Café, while others enjoy snacks and light meals at the coffeehouse or fireside lounge. The Spa at Hotel Hershey is a wonderfully sinful place, where whipped cocoa baths and chocolate fondue wraps tempt guests. 234 rooms, 5 story. Check-in 4 pm, check-out noon. High-speed Internet access. Two restaurants, bar. Children's activity center. Fitness room, spa. Indoor pool, outdoor pool, children's pool, whirlpool. Golf. Tennis. Business center. Airport transportation available. **$$$**

Spa

★★★ **THE SPA AT THE HOTEL HERSHEY.** *100 W Hersheypark Dr, Hershey (17033). Phone 717/533-2171; toll-free 800/437-7439. www.spaathotelhershey.com.* The Spa at the Hotel Hershey is a sinful place of chocolate indulgence. Styled like a gracious manor home, this alluring space is particularly inviting and welcoming. The terrace off the relaxation room enjoys sweeping views of the manicured grounds and is a perfect spot for reflection and inspiration. The facility includes an inhalation room, a quiet room for meditation, soaking tubs, steam rooms, saunas, and signature showers for hydrotherapy treatments. A nail and hair salon primps and pampers, while personal training sessions keep you in tiptop shape. Chocolate reigns at this spa, where most of the innovative treatments incorporate this delicious ingredient. Calorie-watchers need not fear, though, as these chocolate concoctions won't add to your waistline. From the chocolate bean polish and whipped cocoa bath to the chocolate fondue wrap and the chocolate scrub, this spa experience is pure heaven for chocoholics.

Restaurants

★★★ **CIRCULAR DINING ROOM.** *One Hotel Rd, Hershey (17033). Phone 717/534-8800; toll-free 800/437-7439. www.hersheypa.com.* American menu. Breakfast, lunch, dinner, Sun brunch. Children's menu. Jacket required (dinner, Sun brunch). **$$$**

★★ **DIMITRI'S.** *1311 E Chocolate Ave, Hershey (17033). Phone 717/533-3403; fax 717/533-1405.* Greek menu. Lunch, dinner. Closed Sun. Bar. Children's menu. **$$$**

★★ **UNION CANAL HOUSE.** *107 S Hanover St, Hershey (17033). Phone 717/566-0054; fax 717/566-5867. www.unioncanalhouse.com.* American menu. Dinner. Closed Sun; holidays. Bar. Children's menu. **$$$**

Honesdale (B-6)

See also Hawley, Scranton

Founded 1826
Population 4,874
Elevation 980 ft
Area Code 570
Zip 18431
Information Wayne County Chamber of Commerce, 303 Commercial St; phone 570/253-1960 or toll-free 800/433-9008
Web site www.waynecountycc.com

Named in honor of Philip Hone, a mayor of New York City and first president of the Delaware & Hudson Canal Company, Honesdale was for many years the world's largest coal storage center, shipping millions of tons of anthracite. A gravity railroad brought coal here in winter; in spring it was reshipped by canal boats to tidewater. The Stourbridge Lion, first steam locomotive to operate in the United States (1829), was used by the Delaware & Hudson Canal Company, but when the rail bed proved too weak, mule power replaced the steam engine. Today, Honesdale manufactures textile products, business forms, and furniture, and is surrounded by dairy farms in the beautiful rolling countryside.

What to See and Do

Replica of the Stourbridge Lion. *Main St.* (Original is in Smithsonian Institution) First steam locomotive to operate in the US (1829).

Stourbridge Rail Excursions. Scenic rail excursions from Honesdale to Lackawaxen, centering on the change of seasons, with entertainment and activities. Contact the Chamber of Commerce for schedule, fees.

Triple W Riding Stable. *Hwy 6 through Hawley, left at post office, 3 1/2 miles to "Triple W" sign, turn right. Phone 570/226-2620.* A 181-acre horse ranch in the NE range of Pocono Mountains. Variety of trail rides for beginners or advanced riders; 1/2- and full-day trips; overnight camping trips. Hay and sleigh rides (seasonal; by appointment). (Daily) **$$$$**

Wayne County Historical Society Museum. *810 Main St, Honesdale (18431). Phone 570/253-3240.* Delaware and Hudson-Canal exhibit, Native American exhibit. (Jan-Feb, Sat; Mar-Dec, Wed-Sat; closed Jan 1, Thanksgiving, Dec 25) **$**

Special Event

Wayne County Fair. *545 W Butler St, Mercer.* Exhibits, livestock, horse racing. First full week in Aug.

Hopewell Furnace National Historic Site (D-5)

See also Pottstown, Reading

(15 miles SE of Reading via Hwys 422, 82 to Birdsboro, then SE on Birdsboro-Warwick Rd/Hwy 345; 10 miles NE of Tpke Morgantown Interchange)

Hopewell, an early industrial community, was built around a charcoal-burning cold-blast furnace, which made pig iron and many other iron products from 1771-1883. Nearby mines and forests supplied ore and charcoal for the furnace. The National Park Service has restored the buildings, and interpretive programs emphasize the community's role in the history of American industry. Hopewell is surrounded by the approximately 7,330-acre French Creek State Park (see POTTSTOWN).

The Visitor Center has a museum and audiovisual program on ironmaking and community life. Self-guided tour includes: charcoal house, where fuel for furnace was stored; anthracite furnace ruin; waterwheel and blast machinery; casting house, where 16 molders produced up to 5,000 stoves annually; cold-blast charcoal-burning furnace; blacksmith shop; tenant houses; barn for horses and mules transporting charcoal, ore, iron products to market; office store, which was source of staples, clothing, and house furnishings; springhouse, which supplied "refrigeration"; ironmaster's house, home of proprietor or manager. Stove molding and casting demonstrations (late June-Labor Day; fee). Captioned slide program for the hearing impaired; Braille map and large-print pamphlets for the visually impaired; wheelchair access. (Daily; closed winter holidays) **$$**

Hopwood

Restaurants

★★★ CHEZ GERARD AUTHENTIC FRENCH RESTAURANT. *1187 National Pike, Hwy 40 E, Hopwood (15445). Phone 724/437-9001; fax 724/437-4907. www.chezgerard.net.* The all-French staff prides themselves on providing the most authentic French experience next to visiting the countyside itself. The restaurant resides in the historic Hopwood House which dates back to 1790. The interior combines provincial elegance with farmhouse charm. It is located in Fayette County, a region rich in French and American history. French menu. Lunch, dinner, Sun brunch. Closed Tues. Bar. Children's menu. Outdoor seating. **$$$**

★★ SUN PORCH. *Hwy 40 E, Hopwood (15445). Phone 724/439-5734.* American menu. Lunch, dinner. Closed Mon; Dec 24-25. Children's menu. **$$**

Huntingdon (C-3)

See also Altoona, Orbisonia

Founded 1767
Population 6,918
Elevation 643 ft
Area Code 814
Zip 16652
Information Raystown County Visitors Bureau, 241 Mifflin St; phone 814/643-3577 or toll-free 888/RAYSTOWN
Web site www.raystown.org

Founded on the site of an Oneida village in the Juniata Valley, Huntingdon was first called Standing Stone—for a 14-foot etched stone pillar venerated by Native Americans.

What to See and Do

Indian Caverns. *Hwy 45, Spruce Creek (16683). 13 miles NW via Hwys 22, 45. Phone 814/632-7578. www.indiancaverns.com.* Indian Caverns was first excavated by Harold and Leonore Wertz just before the beginning of the Great Depression. When their expedition uncovered arrowheads and human remains, it became clear the site belonged to the Mohawk and Algonquin peoples. Today, the site is preserved and includes areas used for rituals of fire and sacrifice, carvings hundreds of years old, and even a former hideout for notorious criminal David Lewis. Still on some of the walls are examples of American Indian picture writing. (Apr-Oct, daily 10 am-4 pm; until 6 pm late May-Labor Day) **$$**

Lincoln Caverns. *3 miles W on Hwy 22. Phone 814/643-0268.* The one-hour tour of two caves includes Frozen Niagara, Diamond Cascade; visitor center and gift shop. (Apr-Nov, daily; Mar and Dec, weekends only) **$$$**

Raystown Lake. *7 Points Rd, Hesston (16647). 7 miles S on Hwy 26, follow signs to Hesston. Phone 814/658-3405.* Large man-made lake, with 110 miles of shoreline. Swimming, fishing, boating; hunting, hiking, picnicking, camping. Restaurant. Observation area. Fee for some activities.

Swigart Auto Museum. *Hwy 22 E, Mill Creek. 4 miles E on Hwy 22. Phone 814/643-0885. www.swigartmuseum.com.* Changing exhibits of American steam, gas, electric autos. Large collection of nameplates, license plates, and auto memorabilia; picnic area. (Memorial Day-Oct, daily) **$$**

Special Event

Hartslog Day. *Alexandria. 7 miles NW via Hwy 22.* Heritage festival includes crafts, food, music, games. Second Sat in Oct.

Limited-Service Hotel

★★ DAYS INN. *Hwy 22 and 4th St, Huntingdon (16652). Phone 814/643-3934; fax 814/643-3005. www.daysinn.com.* 76 rooms, 3 story. Check-out 11 am. Restaurant, bar. **$**

Indiana (C-2)

See also Johnstown

Founded 1805
Population 14,895
Elevation 1,310 ft
Area Code 724
Zip 15701
Information Indiana County Tourist Bureau, 2334 Oakland Ave, Suite 7; phone 724/463-7505
Web site www.indiana-co-pa-tourism.org

Named after the Native American population in the area, this borough was established on 250 acres donated for a county seat by George Clymer of Philadelphia, a signer of the Declaration of Independence. Indiana University of Pennsylvania (1875) is located here. This is also the birthplace of actor Jimmy Stewart.

What to See and Do

County parks. **Blue Spruce.** *Phone 724/463-8636 (park commission).* Covers 420 acres. Fishing for bass, perch, catfish, and crappie; boating (rowboat, canoe rentals); winter sports area, picnicking, grills, playground. (Daily) 6 miles N off Hwy 110. **Pine Ridge.** Covers 630 acres. Trout fishing; hiking, picnicking. Nature study. (Daily) SW via Hwy 22 near Blairsville. **Hemlock Lake.** Covers 200 acres. Fishing; small game hunting, hiking, ice skating. Nature study, photography. W on Hwy 286 near Rossiter. (Daily)

Jimmy Stewart Museum. *Indiana Public Library Building, third floor, 9th and Philadelphia sts, Indiana. Phone 724/349-6112; toll-free 800/835-4669.* Highlights the namesake's accomplishments on film, radio, and TV. His roles as a military hero, civic leader, family man, and world citizen are woven into displays, film presentations and gallery talks. Fifty-seat vintage theater. (Daily) **$$**

Yellow Creek State Park. *170 Hwy 259, Penn Run (15765). 12 miles E via Hwy 422. Phone 724/357-7913.* Approximately 3,000 acres. Swimming beach, fishing, boating; hunting, hiking, cross-country skiing, snowmobiling, sledding, ice skating, ice fishing, ice boating, picnicking, playground.

Limited-Service Hotels

★★ BEST WESTERN UNIVERSITY INN. *1545 Wayne Ave, Indiana (15701). Phone 724/349-9620; toll-free 888/299-9620; fax 724/349-2620. www.bestwestern.com.* 107 rooms, 2 story. Check-out noon. Restaurant. Pool. **$**

★★ HOLIDAY INN. *1395 Wayne Ave, Indiana (15701). Phone 724/463-3561; toll-free 800/477-3561; fax 724/463-8006. www.holiday-inn.com.* 159 rooms, 2 story. Pets accepted. Check-out noon. Restaurant, bar. Indoor pool, whirlpool. **$**

Jenkintown

See also Fort Washington, Philadelphia, Willow Grove

Population 4,478
Elevation 250 ft
Area Code 215
Zip 19046
Information Valley Forge Convention & Visitors Bureau, 600 W Germantown Pike, Suite 130, Plymouth Meeting 19462; phone 610/834-1550
Web site www.valleyforge.org

What to See and Do

Abington Art Center. *515 Meetinghouse Rd, Jenkintown. Located in historic Alverthorpe Manor. Phone 215/887-4882.* Contemporary art, sculpture garden (daily, dawn to dusk), gallery and gallery shop. (Tues-Sat) **FREE**

Beth Sholom Synagogue. *8231 Old York Rd, Elkin Park (19027). Old York and Foxcroft rds, 1 mile S. Phone 215/887-1342.* The only synagogue designed by Frank Lloyd Wright. (By appointment) **$$**

Jim Thorpe (C-5)

See also Hazleton

Settled 1815
Population 4,804
Elevation 600 ft
Area Code 570
Zip 18229
Information Carbon County Tourist Promotion Agency Information Center, PO Box 90; phone 570/325-3673 or toll-free 888/JIM-THORPE

The twin towns, Mauch Chunk (Bear Mountain) and East Mauch Chunk, built on the sides of a narrow gorge of the Lehigh River, merged in 1954 and adopted the name of Jim Thorpe, the great Native American athlete. This, together with a "nickel-a-week" plan whereby each man, woman, and child paid five cents to promote the community and attract industry, gave the area (formerly dependent on coal mining) a new lease on economic life. Little has changed in appearance after more than a century; a walking tour will reveal 19th-century architecture.

What to See and Do

Asa Packer Mansion. *Packer Hill. Phone 570/325-3229.* Former showplace home of founder of Lehigh Valley Railroad and Lehigh University, one of state's wealthiest men. Packer's house, treasures, and money were left to the borough. (June-Nov, daily; Apr-May, weekends; first two weeks in Dec) **$$** Adjacent is

Jim Thorpe Memorial. *1 mile E on Hwy 903.* A 20-ton granite mausoleum built in memory of the 1912 Olympic champion.

Old Jail Museum. *128 W Broadway, Jim Thorpe (18229). Phone 570/325-5259.* Built in 1871, the Old Jail, which was an active prison until Jan 1995, contains 28 original cells, warden's living quarters, and 16 dungeon cells. Famous for hangings of Molly Maguires; one Molly, to claim his innocence, placed his hand on his cell wall and said his hand print would remain forever as a sign of his innocence. The hand print is still on the wall of Cell 17. (Late May-early Nov) **$$**

Stone Row. *Race St. Downtown.* Sixteen town houses built by Asa Packer for the engineers on his railroad; reminiscent of Philadelphia's Elfreth's Alley. Some are stores open to the public. Also here is

St. Mark's Church. *Phone 570/325-2241.* Has Tiffany windows and copy of reredos from Windsor Castle. (June-Oct, Wed-Sat afternoons)

Whitewater rafting. On upper and lower gorges of Lehigh River.

Jim Thorpe River Adventures, Inc. *1 Adventure Ln, Jim Thorpe. Phone 570/325-2570.* (Mar-Nov, daily) **$$$$**

Pocono Whitewater Adventures. *RR 903, Jim Thorpe. 8 miles NE of Jim Thorpe Bridge on Hwy 903. Phone 570/325-3655.* Also bike tours. (Mar-Nov, daily) **$$$$**

Special Events

Fall Foliage Festival. Arts and crafts, food, entertainment. Scenic three-hour train rides. Second weekend in Oct.

Laurel Blossom Festival. Arts and crafts, entertainment, food, steam train rides. Second weekend in June.

Specialty Lodging

The following lodging establishment is approved by Mobil Travel Guide, but due to its unique and individualized nature has not been given a traditional Mobil Star rating. Included in this listing you may find bed-and-breakfasts, limited-service inns, guest ranches, and other unique hotel properties.

HARRY PACKER MANSION. *Packer Hill, Jim Thorpe (18229). Phone 570/325-8566. www.murdermansion.com.* This mansion served as a model for the haunted mansion in Disney World. If you are not interested in a Murder Mystery event at the property, there are numerous activities in the area including hiking, biking, and exploring the historical past of the community. 13 rooms, 3 story. Children over 12 years only. Complimentary full breakfast. Check-in 4 pm, check-out 11 am. **$**

Johnstown (C-2)

See also Ebensburg, Indiana, Ligonier

Settled 1800
Population 23,906
Elevation 1,180 ft
Area Code 814
Information Greater Johnstown/Cambria County Convention & Visitors Bureau, 416 Main St, 15901; phone 814/536-7993 or toll-free 800/237-8590
Web site www.visitjohnstownpa.com

On May 31, 1889, a break in the South Fork Dam that impounded an old reservoir 10 miles to the east poured a wall of water onto the city in the disastrous "Johnstown Flood." The death toll rose to 2,209 and property damage totaled $17 million. The city has been flooded 22 times since 1850, most recently in 1977.

Founded by a Swiss Mennonite, Joseph Johns, the city today is the center of Cambria County's iron and steel industry, producing iron and steel bars, railroad cars, parts, and railroad supplies.

What to See and Do

Conemaugh Gap. *Located at the W end of the city.* Gorge, 7 miles long and 1,700 feet deep, cuts between Laurel Hill Ridge and Chestnut Ridge.

Grandview Cemetery. *801 Mill Creek Rd, Westmont (15905). 1 mile W on Hwy 271. Phone 814/535-2652.* The 777 unidentified victims of the 1889 flood are buried under blank headstones in the "Unknown Plot."

Inclined Plane Railway. *Vine St and Roosevelt Blvd, Johnstown. Phone 814/536-1816.* Joins Johnstown and Westmont. Ride is on steep (72% grade) passenger incline with 500-foot ascent. Counterbalanced cable cars take 50 passengers and two automobiles each. (Daily; closed Jan 1, Dec 25) **$$**

Johnstown Flood Museum. *304 Washington St, Johnstown. Phone 814/539-1889.* Museum depicts history of Johnstown, with permanent exhibits on 1889 Johnstown Flood; Academy Award-winning film, photographs, artifacts, memorabilia. (Daily; closed holidays) **$$**

Johnstown Flood National Memorial. *Lake Rd. Jct Hwys 219, 869. Phone 814/495-4643.* Commemorates 1889 Johnstown Flood; preserved remnants of the South Fork Dam. Visitor center with exhibits, 30-minute movie (daily; closed Dec 25). **$**

Limited-Service Hotels

★ COMFORT INN. *455 Theatre Dr, Johnstown (15904). Phone 814/266-3678; fax 814/266-9783. www.choicehotels.com.* 117 rooms, 5 story. Pets accepted, some restrictions; fee. Complimentary continental breakfast. Check-out noon. Fitness room. Indoor pool, whirlpool. Airport transportation available. Business center. **$**

★ ★ HOLIDAY INN. *250 Market St, Johnstown (15901). Phone 814/535-7777; toll-free 800/443-5663; fax 814/539-1393. www.holiday-inn.com.* 164 rooms, 6 story. Pets accepted, some restrictions. Check-out noon. Restaurant, bar. Fitness room. Indoor pool, whirlpool. Airport transportation available. Business center. **$**

★ SLEEP INN. *453 Theatre Dr, Johnstown (15904). Phone 814/262-9292; fax 814/262-0486. www.sleepinn.com.* 62 rooms, 3 story. Pets accepted; fee. Complimentary continental breakfast. Check-out noon. Airport transportation available. **$**

Restaurant

★ ★ SURF N' TURF. *100 Valley Pike, Johnstown (15905). Phone 814/536-9250; fax 814/539-4641.* Seafood, steak menu. Dinner. Closed Dec 25. Bar. Children's menu. **$$**

Kane (A-2)

See also Bradford, Clarion, Warren

Settled 1864
Population 4,126
Elevation 2,000 ft
Area Code 814
Zip 16735
Information Seneca Highlands Tourist Association, junction Hwys 770 W and 219, PO Box H, Custer City 16725; phone 814/368-9370

Situated on a lofty plateau, Kane offers hunting, fishing, and abundant winter sports. Summers are cool and winters are bracing. Allegheny National Forest is to the north, west, and south; there are scenic drives through 4,000 acres of virgin timber. General Thomas L. Kane of "Mormon War" fame settled here and laid out the community, which prospered as a lumber and railroad town. General Ulysses Grant was once arrested here for fishing without a license.

What to See and Do

Bendigo State Park. *Glen Hazel Rd, Johnsonburg. 9 miles SE on Hwy 321, then 7 miles S on Hwy 219, then 3 miles NE on unnumbered road. Phone 814/965-2646.* Approximately 100 acres. Swimming pool, fishing; sledding.

Kinzua Bridge State Park. *Glen Hazel Rd, Mount Jewett. 12 miles E via Hwy 6. Phone 814/965-2646.* An approximately 300-acre park surrounds Kinzua Bridge. When built in 1882, it was the highest railroad bridge in the world, taking its 2,053-foot span 301 feet above the Kinzua Creek. Overlooks, picnicking. (Daily) **FREE**

Thomas L. Kane Memorial Chapel. *30 Chestnut St, Kane. Phone 814/837-9729.* (1878) Built as a chapel for the new town under the direction of General Kane, a Civil War hero and humanitarian who championed the persecuted Mormons. Visitor center includes film of General Kane's life; small museum. (Tues-Sat) **FREE**

Twin Lakes. *8 miles S of E Kane on Hwy 321, then 2 miles N on Forest Rd 191, in Allegheny National Forest. Phone 814/723-5150.* Swimming (fee), fishing; hiking, picnicking, camping (fee).

Kennett Square (D-5)

See also Chester, West Chester; also see Wilmington, DE

Settled 1705
Population 5,273
Elevation 370 ft
Area Code 484 and 610
Zip 19348
Information Chester County Conference and Visitors Bureau, 400 Exton Sq Pkwy, Exton, 19341; phone 610/280-6145 or toll-free 800/228-9933; or the Southeastern Chester County Chamber of Commerce, 206 E State St, PO Box 395, phone 610/444-0774
Web site www.brandywinevalley.com

What to See and Do

Barns-Brinton House. *630 Baltimore Pike, Chadds Ford (19317). 5 1/2 miles NE on Hwy 1. Phone 610/388-7376.* (1714) Authentically restored 18th-century tavern, now a house museum furnished in the period. Guides in colonial costume offer interpretive tours; domestic art demonstrations. (May-Sept, Sat-Sun; also by appointment) **$$**

Brandywine Battlefield. *Baltimore Pike, Chadds Ford. 2 miles W of junction Hwys 1 and 202, near Chadds Ford. Phone 610/459-3342.* Includes Lafayette's quarters and Washington's headquarters. Here, and around Chadds Ford, the Battle of the Brandywine (1777) took place—a decisive battle for Washington. Visitor center with exhibits; tours of historic buildings; museum shop. Picnicking. (Tues-Sun; closed holidays) **$$**

Brandywine River Museum. *Hwy 1, Chadds Ford. 7 miles NE on Hwy 1. Phone 610/388-2700.* Converted 19th-century gristmill houses largest collection of paintings by Andrew Wyeth and other Wyeth family members; also collections of American illustration, still life, and landscape painting. Nature trail, wildflower gardens; restaurant, museum shop, guided tours. (Daily; closed Dec 25) **$$$**

Chaddsford Winery. *632 Baltimore Pike, Chadds Ford (19317). 5 miles NE on Hwy 1. Phone 610/388-6221.* Tours of boutique winery, housed in renovated old barn; view of production process; tasting room. Tours; tastings. (Schedule varies) **$$**

John Chads House. *1736 Creek Rd, Chadds Ford (19317). 7 miles NE via Hwy 1, then 1/4 mile N on Hwy 100. Phone 610/388-7376.* Stone building (circa 1725) is fine example of early 18th-century Pennsylvania architecture; authentically restored and furnished as a house museum. Narrated tours by guides in colonial costume; baking demonstrations in beehive oven. (May-Sept, Sat-Sun; also by appointment) **$**

★ **Longwood Gardens.** *3 miles NE on Hwy 1. Phone 610/388-1000. www.longwoodgardens.org.* Longwood Gardens is a stately horticultural display garden created by Pierre S. du Pont, offering more than 1,000 acres of indoor and outdoor gardens, woodlands, and meadows. Lovers of living things are treated to greenhouses heated year-round, more than 10,000 different types of plants, spectacular fountains, flower shows, and gardening demonstrations. Children's programs are available as well. The Orangery and Exhibition Hall are centerpieces, with a sunken marble floor flooded with reflective water. (Daily) **$$$**

Limited-Service Hotel

★ BRANDYWINE RIVER HOTEL. *Hwys 1 and 100, Chadds Ford (19317). Phone 610/388-1200; toll-free 800/274-9644; fax 610/388-1200.* 40 rooms, 2 story. Pets accepted, some restrictions; fee. Complimentary continental breakfast. Check-in 2 pm, check-out 11 am. Fitness room. Airport transportation available. **$**

★ ★ MENDENHALL HOTEL. *323 Kennett Pike, Mendenhall (19357). Phone 610/388-2100; fax 610/388-1184. www.mendenhallinn.com.* 70 rooms, 3 story. Complimentary continental breakfast. Check-out noon. Restaurant, bar. Fitness room. Airport transportation available. Business center. **$**

Specialty Lodgings

The following lodging establishments are approved by Mobil Travel Guide, but due to their unique and individualized nature have not been given a traditional Mobil Star rating. Included in this listing you may find bed-and-breakfasts, limited-service inns, guest ranches, and other unique hotel properties.

FAIRVILLE INN. *506 Kennett Pike, Chadds Ford (19317). Phone 610/388-5900; toll-free 877/285-7772; fax 610/388-5902. www.innbook.com.* 15 rooms, 2 story. No children allowed. Complimentary continental breakfast. Check-in 3 pm, check-out 11 am. Built in 1826; antiques, period décor. View of surrounding countryside. **$$**

SCARLETT HOUSE BED AND BREAKFAST. *503 W State St, Kennett Square (19348). Phone 610/444-9592; toll-free 800/820-9592; fax 610/925-0373. www.bedandbreakfast.com.* 4 rooms, 2 story. Complimentary full breakfast. Check-in 4-6 pm, check-out 11 am. American Foursquare house built in 1910; Victorian décor. **$**

Restaurants

★ ★ KENNETT SQUARE INN. *201 E State St, Kennett Square (19348). Phone 610/444-5687; fax 610/444-4904. www.kennettinn.com.* Lunch, dinner. Closed Jan 1, Dec 25. Bar. Restored country inn (1835). **$$$**

★ ★ MENDENHALL INN. *PA 52, Mendenhall (19357). Phone 610/388-1181; fax 610/388-1184. www.mendenhallinn.com.* American menu. Lunch, dinner, Sun brunch. Closed Dec 25. Bar. Children's menu. Reservations recommended. Valet parking. **$$$**

★ ★ TERRACE. *Longwood Gardens, Kennett Square (19348). Phone 610/388-6771; fax 610/388-7064. www.longwoodgardens.org.* Located in Longwood Gardens, this restaurant offers a unique blend of regional favorites and American comfort foods. Lunch, dinner. Closed Jan-Mar. Bar. Children's menu. Outdoor seating. Admission to Longwood Gardens required. **$$**

King of Prussia (C-6)

See also Chester, Downingtown, Norristown, Philadelphia, West Chester

Settled early 1700s
Population 18,511
Elevation 200 ft
Area Code 484 and 610
Zip 19406
Information Valley Forge Convention & Visitors Bureau, 600 W Germantown Pike, Suite 130, Plymouth Meeting 19462; phone 610/834-1550
Web site www.valleyforge.org

Originally named Reeseville for the Welsh family that owned the land, the town changed its name to that of the local inn, which is still standing. The area around the town is full of historic interest.

What to See and Do

Harriton House. *500 Harriton Rd, Bryn Mawr (19010). 6 miles SE via Old Gulph Rd to Harriton Rd. Phone 610/525-0201.* (1704) Early American domestic architecture of the Philadelphia area. Originally 700-acre estate, now 16 1/2 acres. House of Charles Thomson, Secretary of the Continental Congresses; restored to early 18th-century period. Nature park. (Wed-Sat; Sun by appointment; closed holidays) **$**

King of Prussia Mall. *160 North Golph Rd, King of Prussia (19406). On Hwy 202 at Mall Blvd, where the expressway meets the turnpike. Phone 610/265-5727 (Plaza). www.kingofprussiamall.com.* The king of malls on the eastern seaboard is located just 18 miles west of central Philadelphia. Bloomingdale's, Neiman Marcus, Nordstrom, Macy's, Lord & Taylor, JCPenney, Sears, and Strawbridge's anchor this mall, and its 365 specialty shops and 40 restaurants will keep you from staying in one place too long. (Daily)

Mill Grove. *Pawlings and Audubon rds, Audubon (19407). 5 miles NW via Hwy 422 and Audubon Rd, N of Valley Forge National Historic Park, on Pawlings Rd. Phone 610/666-5593.* (1762) Includes 175-acre wildlife sanctuary, developed around the first American home of ornithologist John James Audubon, now a museum. Prints, including complete elephant folio. Hiking trails. (Tues-Sat, also Sun afternoons; closed Jan 1, Thanksgiving, Dec 25) **FREE**

Swiss Pines. *Malvern. 6 miles SW via Hwy 202, Great Valley exit, on Charlestown Rd. Phone 610/933-6916.* Japanese gardens featuring azalea and rhododendron collection; ponds, waterfalls, winding pathway; herb and groundcover garden. Children under 12 years not permitted. (Mid-Apr-Nov, Mon-Fri, also Sat mornings; closed holidays and inclement weather) **FREE**

Limited-Service Hotels

★ BEST WESTERN THE INN AT KING OF PRUSSIA. *127 S Gulph Rd; Hwy 202 N, King of Prussia (19406). Phone 610/265-4500; fax 610/354-8905. www.bestwestern.com.* 168 rooms, 2 story. Complimentary continental breakfast. Check-out noon. Pool. Airport transportation available. **$**

★ ★ COURTYARD BY MARRIOTT. *1100 Drummers Ln, Wayne (19087). Phone 610/687-6700; toll-free 800/320-5748; fax 610/687-1149. www.courtyard.com.* 150 rooms, 2 story. Check-out 1 pm. Restaurant, bar. Fitness room. Indoor pool, whirlpool. Business center. **$**

★ ★ HOLIDAY INN. *260 Mall Blvd, King of Prussia (19406). Phone 610/265-7500; fax 610/265-4076. www.holiday-inn.com.* 225 rooms, 5 story. Check-out 11 am. Restaurant, bar. Business center. **$**

★ MCINTOSH INN OF KING OF PRUSSIA. *260 N Gulph Rd, King of Prussia (19406). Phone 610/768-9500; toll-free 800/444-2775; fax 610/768-0225. www.mcintoshinn.com.* 210 rooms, 7 story. Complimentary continental breakfast. Check-out 11 am. **$**

★ SPRINGHILL SUITES. *430 Plymouth Rd, Plymouth Meeting (19462). Phone 610/940-0400; toll-free 888/236-2427; fax 610/940-0700; www.springhillsuites.com.* Guests will enjoy a comfortable stay in rooms featuring separate areas for sleeping, eating, working, and relaxing. 201 rooms, 8 story, all suites. Complimentary continental breakfast. Check-in 3 pm, check-out noon. Fitness room. Indoor pool, whirlpool. **$**

Full-Service Hotels

★ ★ ★ HILTON VALLEY FORGE. *251 W Dekalb Pike, King of Prussia (19406). Phone 610/337-1200; toll-free 800/879-8372; fax 610/337-2224. www.hilton.com.* 340 rooms, 9 story. Check-out noon. Restaurant, bar. Fitness room. Indoor pool, outdoor pool, whirlpool. Airport transportation available. Business center. **$**

★ ★ ★ WAYNE HOTEL. *139 E Lancaster Ave, Wayne (19087). Phone 610/687-5000; toll-free 800/962-5850; fax 610/687-8387. www.waynehotel.com.* Located 18 miles west of Philadelphia, this restored property reflects the elegance of a time past with its wraparound porch, antique reproduction furnishings, and carpeted, subdued lobby. Individually decorated guest rooms feature voice mail, data ports, and direct dial telephones. 38 rooms, 6 story. Complimentary continental breakfast. Check-out noon. Restaurant, bar. Pool. Airport transportation available. Restored Victorian building (1906) with ornate furnishings, antiques. **$**

★ ★ ★ WYNDHAM VALLEY FORGE HOTEL. *888 Chesterbrook Blvd, Wayne (19087). Phone 610/647-6700; fax 610/889-9420. www.wyndham.com.* 229 rooms, 5 story. Check-out noon. Restaurant, bar. Fitness room. Indoor pool, whirlpool. Airport transportation available. **$$**

Restaurants

★ ★ CREED'S. *499 N Gulph Rd, King of Prussia (19406). Phone 610/265-2550; fax 610/265-2733. www.creedskop.com.* Seafood, steak menu. Lunch, dinner. Closed Sun; holidays; also first week in July. Bar. **$$**

★ ★ LOTUS INN. *402 W Swedesford Rd, Berwyn (19312). Phone 610/725-8888; fax 610/725-8285.* Chinese, Japanese menu. Lunch, dinner. Closed Thanksgiving. Bar. Children's menu. Reservations recommended. **$$**

★★ **WILD ONION.** *900 Conestoga Rd, Rosemont (19010). Phone 610/527-4826; fax 610/527-5051. www.thewildonion.com.* Seafood menu. Lunch, dinner. Bar. Children's menu. **$$**

Kulpsville

See also Norristown, Philadelphia

Population 1,200
Elevation 290 ft
Area Code 215
Zip 19443
Information Valley Forge Country Convention & Visitors Bureau, 600 W Germantown Pike, Suite 130, Plymouth Meeting 19462; phone 610/834-1550
Web site www.valleyforge.org

What to See and Do

Morgan Log House. *850 Weikel Rd, Kulpsville. E on Hwy 63, then N on Troxel Rd, E on Snyder Rd and N on Weikel Rd. Phone 215/368-2480.* (1695) Built by the grandfather of General Daniel Morgan and Daniel Boone, this is the oldest and finest surviving medieval-style log house in the country. Partially restored; authentic early 18th-century furnishings. It exhibits fine, early antiques, including 18th-century Pennsylvania furniture. Guided tours (Apr-Dec, weekends; other times by appointment). **$$**

Restaurant

★★ **MAINLAND INN.** *17 Main St, Kulpsville (19451). Phone 215/256-8500; fax 215/256-9308.* Seafood menu. Lunch, dinner, Sun brunch. Closed holidays. Bar. **$$$**

Kutztown (C-5)

See also Allentown, Hamburg, Pennsylvania Dutch Area, Reading

Founded 1771
Population 5,067
Elevation 417 ft
Area Code 484 and 610
Zip 19530

Home of a popular folk festival, Kutztown is named for its founder, George Kutz. The town's population includes many descendants of the Pennsylvania Germans.

What to See and Do

Crystal Cave Park. *3 Crystal Cave Rd, Kutztown (19530). 3 miles NW off Hwy 222. Phone 610/683-6765.* Discovered in 1871; crystal formations, stalactites, stalagmites, natural bridges—all enhanced by indirect lighting. Also museum (July-Sept); nature trail; miniature golf (July-Sept; fee); theater. Café, rock shop, gift shop. Tours (Mar-Nov, daily). **$$$**

Special Event

Folk Festival. *Festival grounds, Kutztown. Phone 215/679-9610.* Celebration of Pennsylvania Dutch folk culture; quilts, music, dancing, and food of Plain and Fancy Dutch. Craftspeople make baskets, brooms, rugs, toleware and other handcrafts. Late June-early July.

Restaurant

★★ **NEW SMITHVILLE COUNTRY INN.** *10425 Old Rte 22, Kutztown (19530). Phone 610/285-2987; fax 610/285-2032.* Breakfast, lunch, dinner. Closed Memorial Day, Labor Day. Bar. Children's menu. Originally a post office and general store; fireplace, antiques. **$$**

Lakeville

Full-Service Hotel

★★★ **CAESARS POCONO RESORTS.** *Rte 590, Lakeville (18438). Phone 570/226-4506; toll-free 877/822-3333; fax 570/226-4697. www.cpresorts.com.* 276 rooms. Complimentary continental breakfast. Check-in 3 pm, check-out noon. Wireless Internet access. Restaurant, bar. Fitness room. Indoor pool, whirlpool. Airport transportation available. Business center. **$$**

Lancaster (D-5)

See also Bird-in-Hand, Cornwall, Denver/Adamstown, Ephrata, Lebanon, Reading, Wrightsville (York County), York

Settled 1721
Population 56,348
Elevation 380 ft
Area Code 717
Information Pennsylvania Dutch Convention & Visitors Bureau, 501 Greenfield Rd, 17601; phone 717/299-8901 or toll-free 800/723-8824
Web site www.800padutch.com

Lancaster blends the industrial modern, the colonial past, and the Pennsylvania Dutch present. It is the heart of the Pennsylvania Dutch Area (see), one of the East's most colorful tourist attractions. To fully appreciate the area, visitors should leave the main highways and travel on country roads, which Amish buggies share with automobiles. Lancaster was an important provisioning area for the armies of the French and Indian and Revolutionary wars. Its crafters turned out fine guns, which brought the city fame as the "arsenal of the Colonies." When Congress, fleeing Philadelphia, paused here on September 27, 1777, the city was the national capital for one day. It was the state capital from 1799 to 1812.

What to See and Do

Abe's Buggy Rides. *2596 Old Philadelphia Pike, Bird-in-Hand. 6 miles E on Hwy 340. Phone 717/392-1794.* A tour through Amish country in an Amish family carriage. (Mon-Sat) **$$$**

Amish Country Tours. *3121 Old Philadelphia Pike (Hwy 340), Bird-In-Hand (17505). Phone 717/768-3600.* Tours of Amish farmlands and Philadelphia. **$$$$**

Amish Farm and House. *2395 Lincoln Hwy E, Lancaster (17602). 4 1/2 miles E via Hwy 30. Phone 717/394-6185.* Typical Amish farm in operation. Lecture on the Amish and tour through early 19th-century stone buildings furnished and decorated as old-order Amish household; waterwheels, windmill, hand-dug well, carriages, spring wagon, sleighs. (Daily; closed Dec 25) **$$$**

Brunswick Tours. *2102 Lincoln Hwy E, Lancaster. Phone 717/397-7541.* Private guide and auto tape tours. **$$$$**

★ **Bube's Brewery.** *102 N Market St, Mount Joy. Phone 717/653-2056.* Historic brewery built before the Civil War is the only brewery left in the country that has remained intact since the mid-1800s; now operates as a restaurant. Guided tours take visitors 43 feet below the street into the brewery's aging vaults and passages, built from a cave and later part of the Underground Railroad; narrator tells history of brewery and explains methods of producing beer in a Victorian-age brewery. Tours (Memorial Day-Labor Day, daily). Restaurant open all year (free tour included with reservations for Catacombs restaurant). **FREE**

Candy Americana Museum. *48 N Broad St, Lititz. 5 miles N via Hwy 501 at Wilbur Chocolate Company. Phone 717/626-3249.* Antique candy production equipment, confectionery molds, unusual candy containers; outlet store. (Mon-Sat; call for hours) **FREE**

Choo-Choo Barn, Traintown, USA. *Hwy 741 E, Strasburg. E via Hwy 30, then SE on Hwy 741. Phone 717/687-7911.* A 1,700-square-foot layout of Lancaster County in miniature, featuring 20 operating trains and more than 150 animated and automated figures and vehicles. Gift shop. Picnicking. (Apr-Dec, daily; closed holidays) **$$**

Dutch Wonderland. *2249 Lincoln Hwy E, Lancaster (17602). 4 miles E via Hwy 30. Phone 717/291-1888.* Family fun park with rides, botanical gardens, diving shows, shops. Monorail (fee). (Memorial Day-Labor Day: daily; Mid-May-Memorial Day and after Labor Day-Oct: Sat and Sun) **$$$$** Adjacent is

> **National Wax Museum of Lancaster County.** *2251 Lincoln Hwy E, Lancaster. Phone 717/393-3679.* Figures re-create Lancaster County's history from the 1700s to present. (Daily; closed Dec 25) **$$$**

Franklin and Marshall College. *Race and College aves (17602). Phone 717/291-3981.* (1787) (1,810 students) Liberal arts college. Rothman Gallery showcases Pennsylvania-German artifacts: quilts, Fraktur, and stoneware. More than 200 varieties of trees, plants, and shrubs on grounds. Tours of campus. Also here are

Joseph R. Grundy Observatory. *Phone 717/ 291-4136.* Holds 11-inch refractor and 16-inch reflecting telescope demonstrations. **FREE**

North Museum of Natural History and Science. *400 College Ave, Lancaster. Phone 717/291-3941.* General science and natural history; planetarium shows (Sat and Sun); children's Discovery Room; film series; monthly art exhibits. (Tues-Sun) **$$**

Fulton Opera House. *12 N Prince St, Lancaster. Phone 717/394-7133.* (1852) One of the oldest American theaters; many legendary people have performed here. It is believed that more than one ghost haunts the theater's Victorian interior. Professional regional theater; home of community theater, opera and symphony organizations. **$$$$**

Hans Herr House. *1849 Hans Herr Dr, Lancaster. Phone 717/464-4438.* (1719) Example of medieval Germanic architecture; served as an early Mennonite meetinghouse and colonial residence of the Herr family. Mennonite rural life exhibit; blacksmith shop. House tours. (Apr-Nov: Mon-Sat; rest of year: by appointment; closed holidays) **$$**

Heritage Center Museum of Lancaster County. *13 King St, Lancaster (17603). Phone 717/299-6440.* (1795) Houses examples of early Lancaster County arts and crafts. Furniture, tall clocks, quilts, needlework, silver, pewter, Fraktur, rifles. (Mid-Apr-early Jan, Tues-Sat) **FREE**

Historic Lancaster Walking Tour. *100 S Queen St, Lancaster. Phone 717/392-1776.* A 90-minute tour of historic downtown area. Costumed guide narrates 50 points of architectural or historic interest covering 6 square blocks. (Apr-Oct: two tours daily Fri-Sat, one tour daily Mon-Thurs and Sun; rest of year: by appointment) **$$**

Historic Rock Ford. *881 Rockford Rd, Lancaster. 2 miles S on Rock Ford Rd, off S Duke St at Lancaster County Park. Phone 717/392-7223.* (1794) Preserved home of General Edward Hand, Revolutionary War commander, member of Continental Congress. (Apr-Oct, Tues-Fri and Sun) **$$**

James Buchanan's Wheatland. *1120 Marietta Ave, Lancaster. 1 1/2 miles W on Hwy 23. Phone 717/ 392-8721.* (1828) Residence of President James Buchanan from 1848 to 1868; restored Federal mansion with period rooms containing American Empire and Victorian furniture and decorative arts. Guided tours (Apr-Oct: daily; Nov: Fri-Mon). Christmas candlelight tours (early Dec). **$$$**

Landis Valley Museum. *2451 Kissel Hill Rd, Lancaster. 2 1/2 miles N, off Hwy 272. Phone 717/569-0401.* Interprets Pennsylvania German rural life. Largest collection of Pennsylvania German objects in US; craft and living history demonstrations (May-Oct; see SPECIAL EVENTS); farmsteads, tavern, country store among other exhibit buildings. (Mar-Dec, daily; closed holidays) **$$$**

Mennonite Information Center. *2209 Millstream Rd, Lancaster. E on Hwy 30. Phone 717/299-0954.* Tourist information; interpretation of Mennonite and Amish origins, beliefs. Free video. (Mon-Sat; closed Jan 1, Thanksgiving, Dec 25) **FREE** Also here is

Hebrew Tabernacle Reproduction. Tours (Mon-Sat; closed Jan 1, Thanksgiving, Dec 25). **$$**

Mill Bridge Village. *S Ronks and Soudersburg rds, Strasburg. Phone 717/687-8181; toll-free 800/645-2744.* Restored historic colonial mill village with operating water-powered gristmill (1738); covered bridge; country crafts include broommaking, quilting, candlemaking, blacksmithing; quilt log cabin; Amish kitchen exhibit; music boxes and nickelodeons; horse-drawn hay and carriage rides; 1890s playground; picnicking. Amish house and schoolhouse tour available. Oktoberfest (Oct weekends). Camp resort (early Apr-Oct, daily; fee). Village (early Apr-Nov, daily). **$$$**

Muddy Run LLC. *11 miles S on Hwy 272, then 3 1/2 miles SW on Hwy 372. Phone 717/284-4325.* Covers 700 acres with 100-acre lake for boating (rentals; no power boats), fishing; picnicking, playgrounds, snack bar, concession, camping. Park (Apr-early Nov).

National Toy Train Museum. *300 Paradise Ln, Strasburg. E via Hwys 30, 896, 741, to Paradise Ln. Phone 717/687-8976.* Trains from the 1880s to present; live operating layouts; movies; rare, unusual and specialty trains. (May-Oct: daily; Apr and Nov-Dec: Sat-Sun) **$$**

Robert Fulton Birthplace. *14 miles S via Hwy 222. Phone 717/548-2679.* Robert Fulton, a great inventor and accomplished artist, is best known for having built the steamboat *Clermont*, which, in 1807, successfully made a trip up the Hudson River against winds and strong current. This little stone house, where Fulton was born, was nearly destroyed by fire about 1822; now refurbished. (Memorial Day-Labor Day, Sat and Sun) **$**

Strasburg Railroad. *Hwy 741 E, Strasburg. 8 miles SE via Hwys 30, 896, 741. Phone 717/687-7522.* Railroad runs 4 1/2 miles to Paradise. Picnic stop. This 160-year-old line uses late 19th-century coaches, various steam locomotives. (Apr-Oct, daily; winter, weekends) **$$$** Adjacent is

Railroad Museum of Pennsylvania. *300 Gap Rd, Strasburg. Phone 717/687-8628.* More than 50 locomotives, freight and passenger cars dating from 1825; audiovisual exhibits; railroading memorabilia. Picnicking. (Apr-Oct: daily; rest of year: Tues-Sun; closed holidays) **$$$**

Sturgis Pretzel House. *219 E Main St, Lititz. 9 miles N via Hwys 501, 772. Phone 717/626-4354.* First US commercial pretzel bakery (1861), restored as museum. Early equipment (also modern plant); pretzel-making demonstrations, visitors may try twisting pretzels; outlet store. (Mon-Sat; closed Jan 1, Thanksgiving, Dec 25) **$**

Twin Brook Winery. *5697 Strasburg Rd, Gap. 17 miles E via Hwy 30, S on Hwy 41, E on Strasburg Rd. Phone 717/442-4915.* Estate winery housed in a restored 19th-century barn offers wine tasting, tours of wine-making facilities, visits to the vineyard; picnic areas. Outdoor concerts (late June-mid-Sept, Sat evenings; fee); special events throughout the year. (Apr-Dec: Mon-Sat, also Sun afternoons; rest of year: Tues-Sat, also Sun afternoons)

The Watch and Clock Museum. *514 Poplar St, Lancaster. 12 miles W via Hwy 30. Phone 717/684-8261.* National Association of Watch and Clock Collectors living museum of timepieces and related tools and memorabilia. Over 8,000 items representing the 1600s to the present. Extensive research library. Special exhibitions. (May-Sept, Tues-Sat, also Sun afternoons; winter schedule varies; closed holidays) **$$**

Special Events

Harvest Days. *Landis Valley Museum, 2451 Kissel Hill Rd, Lancaster. Phone 717/569-0401.* Demonstrations of more than 80 traditional craft and harvest-time activities. Columbus Day weekend.

Music at Gretna. *1 Alpha Dr, Mount Gretna. 15 miles N via Hwy 72. Phone 717/964-3836.* Chamber music and jazz; well-known artists. Mid-June-early Sept.

Old-Fashioned Sunday. *1120 Marietta Ave, Lancaster. On grounds of Wheatland. Phone 717/392-8721.* Festivities include entertainment, magic show, and 19th-century activities. Mid-May.

Sheep Shearing. *Amish Farm and House, 2395 Lincoln Hwy E, Lancaster. Phone 717/394-6185.* Last Thurs and Fri in Apr, first Fri in Oct.

Victorian Christmas Week. *1120 Marietta Ave, Lancaster. On grounds of Wheatland. Phone 717/392-8721.* Early Dec.

Limited-Service Hotels

★★ BEST WESTERN EDEN RESORT INN & SUITES. *222 Eden Rd, Lancaster (17601). Phone 717/569-6444; fax 717/569-4208. www.edenresort.com.* 276 rooms, 3 story. Pets accepted, some restrictions; fee. Check-out noon. Restaurant, bar. Fitness room. Indoor pool, outdoor pool, whirlpool. Tennis. Airport transportation available. Business center. **$**

★★ DAYS INN. *30 Keller Ave, Lancaster (17601). Phone 717/299-5700; fax 717/295-1907. www.kellerinn.com.* 193 rooms, 3 story. Check-out noon. Restaurant, bar. Indoor pool, outdoor pool, children's pool. Tennis. **$**

★ GARDEN SPOT MOTEL. *2291 Lincoln Hwy E, Lancaster (17602). Phone 717/394-4736; fax 717/299-6339.* 19 rooms. Closed Dec-Mar. Check-out 11:30 am. **$**

★ HERSHEY FARM MOTOR INN. *240 Hartman Bridge Rd, Ronks (17572). Phone 717/687-8635; toll-free 800/827-8635; fax 717/687-8638. www.hersheyfarm.com.* 59 rooms, 2 story. Complimentary full breakfast. Check-out 11 am. Pool. **$**

★★ HILTON GARDEN INN LANCASTER. *101 Granite Run Dr, Lancaster (17601). Phone 717/560-0880; fax 717/560-5400. www.hilton.com.* 156 rooms, 2 story. Restaurant, bar. Fitness room. Indoor pool, whirlpool. Business center. **$**

★★ HOLIDAY INN. *521 Greenfield Rd, Lancaster (17601). Phone 717/299-2551; fax 717/397-0220. www.holiday-inn.com.* 189 rooms, 4 story. Check-out noon. Restaurant, bar. Fitness room. Indoor pool, outdoor pool. Tennis. **$**

★★ PARK INN. *24 S Willowdale Dr, Lancaster (17602). Phone 717/293-9500; toll-free 800/524-3817; fax 717/293-8558. www.rockvaleinn.com.* 113 rooms, 2 story. Check-out 11 am. Restaurant, bar. Pool. **$**

★★ RAMADA INN BRUNSWICK HOTEL. *151 N Queen St, Lancaster (17608). Phone 717/397-4801; toll-free 800/233-0182; fax 717/397-4991. www.ramada.com.* 222 rooms, 7 story. Pets accepted, some restrictions; fee. Check-out noon. Restaurant, bar. Fitness room. Indoor pool. **$**

Full-Service Resort

★★ WILLOW VALLEY RESORT. *2416 Willow St Pike., Lancaster (17602). Phone 717/464-2711; toll-free 800/444-1714; fax 717/464-1722. www.willowvalley.com.* Country view; large landscaped grounds. 342 rooms, 5 story. Check-out noon. Restaurant. Fitness room. Two indoor pools, one outdoor pool, whirlpool. Golf. Tennis. Airport transportation available. **$**

Full-Service Inn

★★★ HISTORIC STRASBURG INN. *1 Historic Dr, Rte 896, Strasburg (17579). Phone 717/687-7691; toll-free 800/872-0201; fax 717/687-6098. www.histoicstrasburginn.com.* 101 rooms, 2 story. Pets accepted, some restrictions; fee. Complimentary full breakfast. Check-out noon. Restaurant, bar. Fitness room. Pool, whirlpool. **$**

Specialty Lodgings

The following lodging establishments are approved by Mobil Travel Guide, but due to their unique and individualized nature have not been given a traditional Mobil Star rating. Included in this listing you may find bed-and-breakfasts, limited-service inns, guest ranches, and other unique hotel properties.

ALDEN HOUSE BED AND BREAKFAST. *62 E Main St, Lititz (17543). Phone 717/627-3363; toll-free 800/584-0753; fax 717/627-5428. www.aldenhouse.com.* Built in 1850. 5 rooms, 3 story. Children over 10 years only. Complimentary full breakfast. Check-in after 3 pm, check-out 11 am. **$**

AUSTRALIAN WALKABOUT INN BED AND BREAKFAST. *837 Village Rd, Lancaster (17537). Phone 717/464-0707; fax 717/464-2501. www.walkaboutinn.com.* Brick house with wrap-around porch built in 1925. 8 rooms, 3 story. Children over 10 years only. Complimentary full breakfast. Check-in 3-8 pm, check-out 10 am. **$$**

COUNTRY LIVING INN. *2406 Old Philadelphia Pike, Lancaster (17602). Phone 717/295-7295; fax 717/295-0994. www.countrylivinginn.com.* 34 rooms, 2 story. Check-out noon. **$**

GENERAL SUTTER INN. *14 E Main St, Lititz (17543). Phone 717/626-2115; fax 717/626-0992. www.generalsutterinn.com.* Built in 1764; antique country and Victorian furniture. 16 rooms, 3 story. Pets accepted; fee. Check-in 3 pm, check-out noon. Restaurant, bar. **$**

KING'S COTTAGE. *1049 E King St, Lancaster (17602). Phone 717/397-1017; toll-free 800/747-8717; fax 717/397-3447. www.kingscottagebb.com.* This bed-and-breakfast is nestled in the center of scenic Lancaster County. It provides a perfect location for travelers looking to explore Pennsylvania Dutch Country. The inn is a Spanish-style mansion providing a comfortable stay for travelers. 8 rooms. Children over 12 years only. Complimentary full breakfast. Check-in 4 pm, check-out 11 am. **$$**

O'FLAHERTY'S DINGELDEIN HOUSE. *1105 E King St, Lancaster (17602). Phone 717/293-1723; toll-free 800/779-7765; fax 717/293-1947. www.dingeldeinhouse.com.* Dutch Colonial mansion built in 1912. 7 rooms, 3 story. Complimentary full breakfast. Check-in 2:30 pm, check-out 11 am. Airport transportation available. **$**

SWISS WOODS BED & BREAKFAST. *500 Blantz Rd, Lititz (17543). Phone 717/627-3358; toll-free 800/594-8018; fax 717/627-3483. www.swisswoods.com.* Each of the seven rooms at this bed-and-breakfast offers goose down comforters on the beds, natural wood work, and handcrafted furnishings. Its location puts it near hiking and biking trails, farmers markets, and the lake. 7 rooms, 2 story. Children over 12 years only. Complimentary full breakfast. Check-in 3-7 pm, check-out 11 am. **$**

Restaurants

★ ★ D & S BRASSERIE. *1679 Lincoln Hwy E, Lancaster (17602). Phone 717/299-1694; fax 717/299-4687. www.dandsbrasserie.com.* American menu. Lunch, dinner. Closed Thanksgiving, Dec 25. Bar. House built in 1925; original woodwork, fireplaces. Outdoor seating. **$$$**

★ ★ LOG CABIN. *11 Lehoy Forest Dr, Leola (17540). Phone 717/626-1181; fax 717/626-0969. www.logcabinrestaurant.com.* American menu. Dinner. Closed holidays. Bar. Children's menu. Entry through covered. **$$$**

★ ★ OLDE GREENFIELD INN. *595 Greenfield Rd, Lancaster (17601). Phone 717/393-0668; fax 717/393-0908. www.theoldegreenfieldinn.com.* American menu. Dinner. Closed holidays. Bar. Children's menu. In restored stone farmhouse; dining available on balcony and in wine cellar. Casual attire. Outdoor seating. **$$$**

Lebanon (C-5)

See also Cornwall, Ephrata, Hershey, Lancaster, Pennsylvania Dutch Area

Founded 1756
Population 24,461
Elevation 460 ft
Area Code 717
Zip 17042
Information Pennsylvania Rainbow Region Vacation Bureau, 625 Quentin Rd, PO Box 329; phone 717/272-8555

This industrial city, steeped in German traditions, is the marketplace for colorful Lebanon County. Many Hessians were confined here after the Battle of Trenton. Today, Lebanon bologna factories and food processing are important to the city's economy. Master planning for redevelopment of city and county combines with the traditional atmosphere to make this a charming community.

What to See and Do

Coleman Memorial Park. *Hwy 72 and N 12th St, Lebanon (17046). 2 miles N on Hwy 72, W Maple St. Phone 717/228-4470.* This 100-acre former estate has swimming pool (Memorial Day-Labor Day, daily; fee); tennis courts, athletic fields, picnic facilities. Fee for some activities. Park (daily). **FREE**

The Daniel Weaver Company. *15th Ave and Weavertown Rd, Lebanon. Phone 717/274-6100; toll-free 800/932-8377.* Manufacturers, since 1885, of Weaver's Famous Lebanon Bologna and other wood-smoked gourmet meats; smoked in 100-year-old outdoor smokehouses. Samples. Tours. (Mon-Sat) **FREE**

Fort Zeller. *Newmanstown. 11 miles E on Hwy 422, then S on Hwy 419. Phone 610/589-4301.* One of state's oldest existing forts; originally built of logs, rebuilt of stone in 1745; has 12-foot-wide Queen Anne fireplace in kitchen. (By appointment) **DONATION**

Middlecreek Wildlife Management Area. *Kleinfeltersville. 11 miles SE on Hwy 897 to Kleinfeltersville, then 1 mile S. Phone 717/733-1512. www.pgc.state.pa.us.* A 6,254-acre tract provides refuge for waterfowl, forest, and farmland wildlife. Permit and open hunting areas, inquire at visitor center for regulations. Fishing, boating (Feb-Nov); hiking, picnicking. Visitor center (Mar-Nov, Tues-Sun). **FREE**

Stoevers Dam Recreational Area. *943 Miller St, Lebanon (17046). 2 miles N on Hwy 343. Phone 717/228-4470.* A 153-acre park with 52-acre lake for fishing, boating (electric motors only), canoeing; 1 1/2-mile trail for jogging, hiking, and bicycling; primitive camping (permit only; fee). Nature trails; nature barn (Apr-Oct, Tues-Sun; winter, by appointment). Community park (daily). **FREE**

Stoy Museum of the Lebanon County Historical Society. *924 Cumberland St, Lebanon. Phone 717/272-1473.* Local historical museum containing 30 permanent room and shop displays on three floors of house built in 1773 and used as first county courthouse; research library. Tours. (Mon-Fri, Sun; closed Mon and Sun of holiday weekends) **$$**

Limited-Service Hotels

★ ★ LANTERN LODGE MOTOR INN. *411 N College St, Myerstown (17067). Phone 717/866-6536; toll-free 800/262-5564; fax 717/866-8857. www.thelanternlodge.com.* 83 rooms, 2 story. Check-in 2 pm, check-out 11 am. Restaurant. **$**

★ ★ QUALITY INN. *625 Quentin Rd, Lebanon (17042). Phone 717/273-6771; toll-free 800/626-8242; fax 717/273-4882. www.choicehotels.com.* 130 rooms, 5 story. Check-out noon. Restaurant, bar. Pool. **$**

Specialty Lodging

The following lodging establishment is approved by Mobil Travel Guide, but due to its unique and individualized nature has not been given a traditional Mobil Star rating. Included in this listing you may find bed-and-breakfasts, limited-service inns, guest ranches, and other unique hotel properties.

SWATARA CREEK INN. *10463 Jonestown Rd, Annville (17003). Phone 717/865-3259. www.swataracreekinn.com.* 10 rooms, 3 story. Complimentary full breakfast. Check-in 3 pm, check-out 11 am. Victorian mansion built in 1860; country setting. **$**

Lewisburg (B-4)

See also Danville, Williamsport

Settled 1785
Population 5,620
Elevation 460 ft
Area Code 570
Zip 17837
Information Susquehanna Valley Visitors Bureau, Rural Rte 3, 219-D Hafer Rd; phone 570/524-7234 or toll-free 800/525-7320
Web site www.svvb.com

Home of Bucknell University (1846), this college community also has light industry. The Native American village of Old Muncy Town was located nearby before the region was opened by Ludwig (Lewis) Doerr.

What to See and Do

Fort Augusta. *1150 N Front St, Sunbury. 9 miles SE on Hwy 147. Phone 570/286-4083.* (1757) Museum collection of Northumberland County Historical Society. (Mon, Wed, Fri, afternoons) **FREE**

Packwood House Museum. *15 N Water St, Lewisburg. Phone 570/524-0323.* A three-story, 27-room log and frame building begun in the late 18th century. Former hostelry houses a wide-ranging collection of Americana, period furnishings, textiles, and decorative arts. Changing exhibits; museum shop. Tours. (Tues-Sun; closed holidays) **$$**

Slifer House Museum. *80 Magnolia Dr, Lewisburg (17837). 1 mile N, on grounds of Riverwoods. Phone 570/524-2245.* Elaborate three-story, 20-room Victorian mansion. First and second floors have been restored, complete with Victorian parlor, dining room, library, and five bedrooms. Gift shop. (Apr-late Dec, Tues-Sun; rest of year, Tues-Fri afternoons, also by appointment; closed holidays) **$$**

Limited-Service Hotel

★ BEST WESTERN COUNTRY CUPBOARD INN. *Rte 15 N, Lewisburg (17837). Phone 570/524-5500; fax 570/524-4291. www.bestwestern.com.* 106 rooms, 3 story. Complimentary continental breakfast. Check-out 11 am. Fitness room. Pool. **$**

Restaurant

★ COUNTRY CUPBOARD. *101 Hafer Rd, Lewisburg (17837). Phone 570/523-3211; fax 570/524-9299.* Breakfast, lunch, dinner. Closed Dec 25. Children's menu. Country dining. **$$**

Lewistown (C-4)

Settled 1754
Population 9,341
Elevation 520 ft
Area Code 717
Information Juniata Valley Area Chamber of Commerce, 3 W Monument Sq, 17044; phone 717/248-6713

Surrounded by rich farmland and beautiful forested mountain ranges, Lewistown lies in the scenic Juniata River Valley in the heart of central Pennsylvania. Lewistown retains the charm of its rustic surroundings, which yearly attract thousands of sportsmen and outdoor enthusiasts to the area's fine hunting, fishing, and camping facilities. A large Amish population that thrives on the farmland of the Kishacoquillas Valley has contributed greatly to the area's culture and heritage.

What to See and Do

Brookmere Farm Vineyards. *5369 Hwy 655, Belleville (17004). Approximately 5 miles N via Hwy 322, then SW on Hwy 655, near Belleville. Phone 717/935-5380. www.brookmere.com.* In 19th-century stone and wood barn. Winery tour, wine tasting; picnicking. (Mon-Sat, also Sun afternoons; closed holidays) **FREE**

Greenwood Furnace State Park. *Hwy 305 and Broadmountain Rd, Huntingdon. 5 miles N on Hwy 322, then 9 miles W on Hwy 655, then NW on Hwy 305. Phone 814/667-1800.* Remains of Greenwood Works, last iron furnace to operate in area (circa 1833-1904); restored stack. Approximately 400 acres. Swimming beach, fishing; hiking, snowmobiling, ice skating, ice fishing, picnicking, playground, snack bar, store, tent and trailer sites. Visitor center, interpretive program.

Reeds Gap State Park. *8 miles N off Hwy 322 and unnumbered road. Phone 717/667-3622.* Approximately 200 acres. Swimming pool, fishing; hiking, picnicking, snack bar. Tent sites only.

Limited-Service Hotel

★★ CLARION HOTEL. *13015 Furguson Valley Rd, Burnham (17009). Phone 717/248-4961; toll-free 800/252-7466; fax 717/242-3013. www.choicehotels.com.* 119 rooms, 2 story. Check-out noon. Restaurant, bar. Pool. **$**

Ligonier (C-2)

See also Donegal, Greensburg, Johnstown

Founded 1816
Population 1,695
Elevation 1,200 ft
Area Code 724
Zip 15658
Information Ligonier Valley Chamber of Commerce, Town Hall, 120 E Main St; phone 724/238-4200
Web site www.ligonier.com

Fort Ligonier, built in 1758 by the British, was the scene of one of the key battles of the French and Indian War. It also served as a supply base during Pontiac's War in 1763.

What to See and Do

Compass Inn Museum. *Hwy 30 E, Laughlintown. 3 miles E on Hwy 30. Phone 724/238-4983.* A 1799 stagecoach stop; original log and stone inn authentically restored and furnished; log barn houses.

Conestoga wagon and stagecoach; cookhouse with beehive oven and fireplace; blacksmith shop contains working forge. (May-Oct, Tues-Sun) **$$**

Fort Ligonier. *Hwys 30 and 711, Ligonier (15658). S Market St, on Hwys 30, 711. Phone 724/238-9701.* Reconstructed 18th-century British fort; includes buildings with period furnishings. Museum houses outstanding French and Indian War collection, 18th-century artifacts; introductory film. (May-Oct, daily) (See SPECIAL EVENTS) **$$**

Idlewild Park. *Hwy 30 E, Ligonier. Phone 724/238-3666.* Amusement rides; entertainment; picnicking; children's play area; water park. (Memorial Day-late Aug, Tues-Sun) **$$$$** Adjacent is

> **Story Book Forest.** *Phone 724/238-3666.* Admission included with Idlewild Park. Children's park with animals, people, and buildings portraying nursery rhymes. (Memorial Day-late Aug, Tues-Sun)

St. Vincent Archabbey and College. *Latrobe. 8 miles W on Hwy 30. Phone 724/537-4560.* (1846) (1,200 students) Includes Benedictine monastery, seminary, and coeducational liberal arts college. St. Vincent Theatre has performances in theater-in-the-round. Free self-guided tape tours.

Special Events

Fort Ligonier Days. *120 E Main St, Ligonier (15658). Phone 724/238-4200.* Living history program of the French and Indian War. Parade, 150 juried crafters, food, and special events. Usually second weekend in Oct.

Ligonier Highland Games and Gathering of the Clans of Scotland. *Idlewild Park, Ligonier (15102). Phone 724/238-3666.* Sports; massed pipe bands, Highland dancing competitions, Scottish fiddling; sheep dog, wool spinning, and weaving demonstrations; genealogy booth, Scottish fair. First Sat after Labor Day.

Ligonier Ice Fest. *Phone 724/238-4200.* Professional ice sculptures on the Diamond and in front of businesses; collegiate ice-carving competition. Super Bowl weekend, Jan.

Mountain Playhouse. *Hwy 985 N, Jennerstown. Phone 814/629-9201. www.mountainplayhouse.com.* A professional summer theater company that performs world premiere and classic favorite comedies, musicals, and dramas in a restored gristmill (1805). Matinees and evening performances. June-mid-Oct. **$$$$**

Limited-Service Hotel

★ ★ RAMADA. *216 W Loyalhanna St, Ligonier (15658). Phone 724/238-9545; fax 724/238-9803. www.ramada.com.* 66 rooms, 3 story. Check-out noon. Restaurant, bar. Pool. **$**

Limerick (C-6)

See also Norristown, Pottstown, Reading

Population 800
Elevation 302 ft
Area Code 484 and 610
Zip 19468
Information Valley Forge Convention & Visitors Bureau, 600 W Germantown Pike, Suite 130, Plymouth Meeting 19462; phone 610/834-1550
Web site www.valleyforge.org

What to See and Do

Spring Mountain Ski Area. *6 miles N, off Hwy 29. Phone 610/287-7900. www.springmountain-fun.com.* Triple, three double chairlifts; two rope tows; patrol, school, rentals; snowmaking; cafeteria, lodge. Longest run 1/2 mile; vertical drop 420 feet. Also camping available (fee; hookups). (Mid-Dec-mid-Mar, daily) **$$$$**

Lock Haven (B-4)

See also Williamsport

Founded 1833
Population 9,149
Elevation 564 ft
Area Code 570
Zip 17745
Information Clinton County Tourist Promotion Agency, Court House Annex, 151 Susquehanna Ave; phone 570/893-4037

Founded on the site of pre-Revolutionary Fort Reed, the community takes its name from two sources. The lock of the Pennsylvania Canal once crossed the West Branch of the Susquehanna River here, and the town was once a "haven" for the rafts and lumberjacks of nearby logging camps. Near the geographic center of the state, the town today is a center of commerce and small industry.

What to See and Do

Bald Eagle. *Hwys 150 and 26, Howard (16841). 13 miles SW off Hwy 150. Phone 814/625-2775.* A 1,730-acre lake on approximately 5,900 acres. Swimming beach, fishing, boating (rentals, mooring, launching, marina); hunting, hiking, sledding, ice skating, ice boating, picnicking, playground, snack bar, store, tent and trailer sites.

Bucktail Natural Area. Scenic area extends from mountain rim to mountain rim for 75 miles from Lock Haven north to Renovo and west to Emporium. Connecting the three towns and weaving through the park is Hwy 120, an outstanding drive through mountain scenery. Historic site west of Renovo commemorates Bucktail Trail, which served pioneers and Civil War volunteers. Fishing.

Bull Run School House. *Phone 570/893-4037.* (1899) Only remaining one-room schoolhouse in county; fully restored with all of its original equipment, including double desks, schoolmaster's and recitation desks, Waterbury clock, bell. (Hours vary) **FREE**

The Heisey Museum. *362 E Water St, Lock Haven. Phone 570/748-7254.* Victorian house museum; early 1800s kitchen; ice house containing logging, farming, and canal artifacts. (Tues-Fri; also by appointment) **DONATION**

Hyner View. *22 miles NW on Hwy 120.* At 2,000 feet, "Laurel Drive to the top of the world" provides panoramic view of valley, river, highway and forest. Site of state and national hang gliding competitions.

Kettle Creek. *Hwy 62, Renovo (17764). 35 miles NW on Hwy 120 to Westport, then 7 miles N on Hwy 4001. Phone 570/923-6004.* Approximately 1,600 acres. Winds through beautiful valley developed as tourist area. Swimming beach, fishing, boating (mooring, launching); hunting, hiking, bridle trail, snowmobiling, sledding, ice skating, picnicking, playground, tent and trailer sites (electric hookups).

Special Event

Flaming Foliage Festival. *Renovo (17764). 29 miles NW on Hwy 120, near the traffic light. Phone 570/923-2411.* Includes parade, craft show, and contest for festival queen. Second weekend in Oct.

Specialty Lodging

The following lodging establishment is approved by Mobil Travel Guide, but due to its unique and individualized nature has not been given a traditional Mobil Star rating. Included in this listing you may find bed-and-breakfasts, limited-service inns, guest ranches, and other unique hotel properties.

VICTORIAN INN BED AND BREAKFAST. *402 E Water St, Lock Haven (17745). Phone 570/748-8688; toll-free 888/653-8688; fax 570/748-2444.* 12 rooms, 2 story. Pets accepted, some restrictions. No children allowed. Complimentary full breakfast. Check-in 2 pm, check-out 1 pm. Built in 1859; garden atrium. **$**

Lumberville

See also New Hope

Specialty Lodging

The following lodging establishment is approved by Mobil Travel Guide, but due to its unique and individualized nature has not been given a traditional Mobil Star rating. Included in this listing you may find bed-and-breakfasts, limited-service inns, guest ranches, and other unique hotel properties.

1740 HOUSE. *3690 River Rd Rte 32, Lumberville (18933). Phone 215/297-5661; fax 215/297-5243. www.1740house.com.* 25 rooms, 2 story. Complimentary full breakfast. Check-in 2 pm, check-out noon. Pool. **$$**

Restaurant

★★ CUTTALOSSA INN. *3478 River Rd (PA 32), Lumberville (18933). Phone 215/297-5082. www.cuttalossainn.com.* American menu. Lunch, dinner. Closed Sun; Jan 1, Dec 24-25; also three weeks in Jan. Bar. Outdoor seating. **$$$**

Manheim

See also Cornwall, Lancaster, Lebanon

Founded 1762
Population 4,784
Elevation 400 ft
Area Code 717
Zip 17545
Information Manheim Area Chamber of Commerce, 210 S Charlotte St; phone 717/665-6330
Web site www.manheimchamber.com

Baron Henry William Stiegel founded Manheim and started manufacturing the flint glassware that bore his name. In 1770 he owned the town; by 1774 he was in debtor's prison, the victim of his own generosity and his poor choice of business associates. After his imprisonment, he made a meager living teaching here.

What to See and Do

Mount Hope Estate & Winery. *1/2 mile S of exit 20 at junction Hwy 72 and PA Tpke. Phone 717/665-7021.* Restored sandstone mansion was originally built in the Federal style (circa 1800), then increased its size to 32 rooms with an extension built in 1895, which changed the house's style to Victorian. Turrets, winding walnut staircase, hand-painted 18-foot ceilings, Egyptian marble fireplaces, grand ballroom, crystal chandeliers; greenhouse, solarium, gardens. Wine tasting in billiards room. (Daily; closed Jan 1, Thanksgiving, Dec 25) (See SPECIAL EVENTS) **FREE**

Zion Lutheran Church. *2 S Hazel St, Manheim. 1 block E of Hwy 72. Phone 717/665-5880.* (1891) Victorian-Gothic structure built on site of original church; Stiegel donated the ground (1772) in exchange for one red rose from the congregation every year. (Mon-Fri)

Special Events

Pennsylvania Renaissance Faire. *83 Mansion House Rd, Manheim. Mt. Hope Estate and Winery.* A 16th-century village is created in the acres of gardens surrounding the mansion. Eleven stages includes a jousting arena with capacity of 6,000. Highlights includes medieval jousting tournament, trial and dunking, human chess match, knighthood ceremonies. Weekends, Aug-mid-Oct.

Rose Festival. Celebration during which Stiegel descendant accepts annual rent of one red rose for church grounds. Second Sun in June.

Mansfield (A-4)

See also Wellsboro

Population 3,411
Elevation 1,120 ft
Area Code 570
Zip 16933
Information Wellsboro Area Chamber of Commerce, 114 Main St, PO Box 733, Wellsboro 16901; phone 570/724-1926
Web site www.wellsboropa.com

What to See and Do

Cowanesque Lake. *15 miles N on Hwy 15 to Lawrenceville, then 3 1/2 miles W on Bliss Rd. Phone 570/835-5281.* Same facilities as Tioga-Hammond Lakes (see). (May-Sept)

Hills Creek State Park. *Hills Creek Lake, Wellsboro. 6 miles W, then N on unnumbered road. Phone 570/724-4246.* Approximately 400 acres. Swimming beach; fishing for muskellunge, largemouth bass, walleye in Hills Creek Lake; boating (rentals, mooring, launching); hiking, sledding, ice skating, ice fishing, picnicking, playground, snack bar, tent and trailer sites, cabins. Interpretive program.

Tioga-Hammond Lakes. *Tioga. 10 miles N on Hwy 15, then 7 miles SW on Hwy 287. Phone 570/835-5281.* Twin lakes and dams for flood control and recreation. Swimming, fishing, boating; hunting, trails, picnicking, camping (fee; some sites free). (Late Apr-Dec)

Limited-Service Hotel

★ **COMFORT INN.** *300 Gateway Dr, Mansfield (16933). Phone 570/662-3000; toll-free 800/822-5470; fax 570/662-2551. www.choicehotels.com.* 100 rooms, 2 story. Pets accepted, some restrictions; fee. Complimentary continental breakfast. Check-out noon. Fitness room. **$**

Meadville (A-1)

See also Conneaut Lake, Edinboro, Franklin (Venango County)

Settled 1788
Population 13,685
Elevation 1,100 ft
Area Code 814
Zip 16335
Information Crawford County Convention & Visitors Bureau, 211 Chestnut St; phone 814/333-1258 or toll-free 800/332-2338
Web site www.visitcrawford.org

David Mead—Revolutionary War ensign, tavern-keeper, and major general in the War of 1812—and his brothers established Mead's Settlement in 1788. Colonel Lewis Walker started manufacture of hookless slide fasteners here; since 1923 these fasteners (now known as "zippers") have been the leading local industry. The city is also a major producer of yarn and thread and is home to many tool-and-die manufacturers.

What to See and Do

Allegheny College. *485 Chestnut St, Meadville. Phone 814/332-3100.* (1815) (1,850 students) Bentley Hall (1820) is a fine example of Federalist architecture. Also on campus are Bowman, Penelec, and Megahan Art Galleries. Library has colonial, Ida Tarbell, and Lincoln collections. Tours of campus.

Baldwin-Reynolds House Museum. *639 Terrace St, Meadville. Phone 814/724-6080.* (1841-1843) Restored mansion of Henry Baldwin, congressman and US Supreme Court justice. First and second floors refurbished in period; basement exhibits 19th-century kitchen and Land Office. Also on grounds is 1890 doctor's office. Elaborate landscaping on 3-acre grounds feature pond and icehouse. Tours (late May-Labor Day, Wed-Sun). **$$**

Colonel Crawford Park. *6 miles NE via Hwys 86, 198. Phone 814/724-6879 (summer).* Within park is Woodcock Creek Lake. Swimming (fee), fishing, boating; hunting, nature trail, picnicking, camping (fee). Park (Memorial Day-Labor Day, daily). **FREE**

Erie National Wildlife Refuge. *11296 Wood Duck Ln, Guys Mills (16327). 10 miles E on Hwy 27. Phone 814/789-3585.* Over 250 species of birds, as well as woodchuck, white-tailed deer, fox, beaver, and muskrat are found on this 8,777-acre refuge. Fishing and hunting permitted, regulations at refuge office; nature and ski trails, overlook, photo blind. (Daily). **FREE**

Special Event

Crawford County Fair. *Phone 814/337-2154.* Third week in Aug.

Limited-Service Hotel

★ DAYS INN. *18360 Conneaut Lake Rd, Meadville (16335). Phone 814/337-4264; toll-free 800/275-9093; fax 814/337-7304. www.daysinn.com.* 163 rooms, 2 story. Pets accepted, some restrictions; fee. Check-out 11 am. Restaurant, bar. Indoor pool, whirlpool. **$**

Media (D-6)

See also Chester, Kennett Square, King of Prussia, Philadelphia, West Chester

Population 5,533
Area Code 484 & 610
Information Delaware County Convention & Visitors Bureau, 200 E State St, Suite 100, 19063; phone 610/565-3679 or toll-free 800/343-3983

What to See and Do

Franklin Mint Museum. *Hwy 1, Franklin (19091). 4 miles SW. Phone 610/459-6168.* Houses original works by Andrew Wyeth and Norman Rockwell; collectibles on display include books, dolls, jewelry, furniture; artworks in porcelain, bronze, pewter, crystal, and precious metals; one of the world's largest private mints. (Daily; closed holidays) **FREE**

Newlin Mill Park. *219 S Cheyney Rd, Glen Mills (19342). 7 miles SW via Hwy 1. Phone 610/459-2359.* Park with operating stone gristmill (1704), furnished miller's house (1739), springhouse, blacksmith shop; milling exhibit. Tours, picnicking, fishing, nature trails. (Daily) **$**

Ridley Creek State Park. *S on Hwy 1, then N on Hwy 352. Phone 610/892-3900.* Approximately 2,600 acres of woodlands and meadows. Fishing; hiking, bicycling, sledding, picnicking, playground. Within park is

Colonial Pennsylvania Plantation. *Phone 610/566-1725.* A 200-year-old farm is a living history museum that re-creates the life of a typical farm family of the late 1700s. Period tools and methods are used to perform seasonal and daily chores. Tours (Tues-Fri, by appointment). Visitors may participate in some activities. (Mid-Apr-Nov, Sat and Sun) **$$**

Tyler Arboretum. *515 Painter Rd, Media (19063). Phone 610/566-5431.* Approximately 650 acres of ornamental and native plants. Outdoor "living museum" with a 20-mile system of trails; special fragrant garden and bird garden; notable trees planted in the 1800s; bookstore. Guided walks and educational programs each week. **$$**

Restaurant

★ ★ D'IGNAZIO'S TOWNE HOUSE. *117 Veterans Sq, Media (19063). Phone 610/566-6141; fax 610/566-3840. www.townehouse.com.* Italian, seafood menu. Dinner. Closed Dec 25. Bar. Children's menu. Singing maitre'd. **$$**

Mercer (B-1)

See also Franklin (Venango County)

Settled 1795
Population 2,391
Elevation 1,270 ft
Area Code 724
Zip 16137
Information Mercer Area Chamber of Commerce, PO Box 473; phone 724/662-4185

What to See and Do

Magoffin House Museum. *119 S Pitt St, Mercer. Phone 724/662-3490.* (1821) Houses collection of Native American artifacts, pioneer tools, furniture, children's toys, clothing; military items. Some original furnishings; memorabilia. Special collection of artifacts from John Goodsell's trip to the North Pole with Peary in 1908-1909, as well as early maps, historic records; restored print shop. Office of Mercer County Historical Society is located in the Anderson House, just off Court House Square. (Tues-Sat; closed holidays) **FREE**

Wendell August Forge, Inc. *620 Madison Ave, Grove City. 10 miles SE on Hwy 58. Phone 724/458-8360.* Creators of hand-hammered aluminum, bronze, copper, pewter, sterling silver, and glass and crystal items hand-cut on stone wheel lathe; also limited-edition collectors' items. Gift shop. Self-guided tours (15-30 minutes). (Daily; closed holidays) **FREE**

Special Event

Penn's Woods West-Folk & Arts Festival. *545 W Butler St, Mercer. Phone 412/662-1490. Mercer Area High School, W Butler St.* Fine arts and country crafts. 130 artisans, live entertainment and demonstrations, children's activities, home-cooked food. Mid Feb.

Limited-Service Hotel

★ ★ HOWARD JOHNSON. *835 Perry Hwy, Mercer (16137). Phone 724/748-3030; toll-free 800/542-7674; fax 724/748-3484. www.hojo.com.* 102 rooms, 2 story. Pets accepted. Check-out noon. Restaurant, bar. Fitness room. Pool. Amish craft shop in lobby. **$**

Mercersburg

Restaurant

★ ★ ★ MERCERSBURG INN. *405 S Main St, Mercersburg (17236). Phone 717/328-5231; fax 717/328-3403. www.mercersburginn.com.* Built in 1909, this Georgian-style mansion resides in a charming, 230-year-old village. French menu. Dinner. Closed Sun-Wed; also Dec 24-25. Bar. Reservations recommended. **$$$**

Merion

What to See and Do

The Barnes Foundation. *300 N Latch's Ln, Merion. Phone 610/667-0290. www.barnesfoundation.org.* Paintings by Renoir, Cézanne, Picasso, and Matisse hang among Native American pottery, Pennsylvania German decorative furniture, and sculpture and art from Mexico, China, Africa, early Greece, and Rome in this gallery, arboretum, and library learning hub.

Garden enthusiasts can admire an exceptional collection of flowers and woodland species, and students of art history can lose themselves in the historical archives, which include more than 5,000 volumes on art history and horticulture. (Wed-Sun) **$$**

Middletown (D-4)

Restaurant

★★★ ALFRED'S VICTORIAN RESTAURANT. *38 N Union St, Middletown (17057). Phone 717/944-5373; fax 717/944-6385.* Housed in a picturesque, 1888-Victorian brownstone, this 30-year-old restaurant offers five intimate dining rooms each with authentically restored design elements and period decor. The continental menu shows northern Italian influence and offers 30 different entrées including lobster tail and filet mignon. Italian menu. Lunch, dinner. Closed holidays. Bar. Victorian mansion; antique chandeliers, furnishings; floor-to-ceiling windows; fireplaces. Outdoor seating. **$$$**

Milford (B-6)

See also Bushkill, Delaware Water Gap, Hawley

Settled 1733
Population 1,104
Elevation 503 ft
Area Code 570
Zip 18337
Information Pocono Mountains Vacation Bureau, 1004 Main St, Stroudsburg 18360; phone 570/424-6050; for free brochures phone toll-free 800/POCONOS
Web site www.poconos.org

The borough of Milford was settled by Thomas Quick, a Hollander. Noted forester and conservationist Governor Gifford Pinchot lived here. His house, Grey Towers, is near the town.

What to See and Do

Canoeing, rafting, kayaking, and tubing. *Kittatinny Canoes. S to Dingmans Ferry via Hwy 209, then 1/2 mile E via Hwy 739 S, at Dingmans Ferry toll bridge. Phone 570/828-2338; toll-free 800/356-2852.* Trips travel down the Delaware River. Camping. (Mid-Apr-Oct, daily)

Dingmans Falls and Silver Thread Falls. *8 miles S and W on Hwy 209 near Dingmans Ferry. Phone 570/588-2451.* Part of Delaware Water Gap National Recreation Area (see). Two of the highest waterfalls in the Pocono Mountains; many rhododendrons bloom in July. **FREE**

Grey Towers. *151 Grey Tower Dr, Milford (18337). Phone 570/296-6401.* (1886) A 100-acre estate originally built as summer house for philanthropist James W. Pinchot; became residence of his son, Gifford Pinchot, "father of American conservation," governor of Pennsylvania and first chief of USDA Forest Service. Now site of Pinchot Institute for Conservation Studies. Tours. (Memorial Day weekend-Labor Day weekend, daily; after Labor Day-Veterans Day, afternoons Mon and Fri-Sun; rest of year, by appointment; occasionally closed for conferences.) **DONATION**

Limited-Service Hotels

★★ BEST WESTERN INN AT HUNT'S LANDING. *120 Hwy 6, Matamoras (18336). Phone 570/491-2400; toll-free 800/308-2378; fax 570/491-2422. www.bestwestern.com.* 108 rooms, 4 story. Pets accepted, some restrictions. Check-out 11 am. Restaurant, bar. Indoor pool. **$**

★ MYER MOTEL. *600 Hwys 6 and 209, Milford (18337). Phone 570/296-7223; toll-free 800/764-6937. www.myermotel.com.* 20 rooms. Check-out 11 am. **$**

Full-Service Inn

★★★ CLIFF PARK INN. *155 Cliff Park Rd, Milford (18337). Phone 570/296-6491; toll-free 800/225-6535; fax 570/296-3982. www.cliffparkinn.com.* This is an inn and golf course located on 500 acres overlooking the Delaware River. Nearby activities include cross-country skiing, hiking trails, swimming, and more. 18 rooms, 3 story. Restaurant. Golf. Classic country inn; originally a farmhouse built 1820. **$**

Specialty Lodging

The following lodging establishment is approved by Mobil Travel Guide, but due to its unique and individualized nature has not been given a traditional Mobil Star rating. Included in this listing you may find bed-and-breakfasts, limited-service inns, guest ranches, and other unique hotel properties.

PINE HILL FARM BED AND BREAKFAST. *181 Pine Hill Farm Rd, Milford (18337). Phone 570/296-5261. www.pinehillfarm.com.* 6 rooms, 2 story. Children over 12 years old only. Complimentary full breakfast. Check-in 3 pm, check-out 11 am. Located atop hill overlooking the Delaware River. Includes 268 acres of fields and forests, with 5 miles of 1800s logging trails for walking, birdwatching. **$**

Mount Airy

What to See and Do

Lee's Hoagie House. *19th St and Cheltenham Ave, Mount Airy. Phone 215/549-7600. www.leeshoagiehouse.com.* You might call them subs, grinders, or torpedoes, but in Philadelphia they are hoagies, and Lee's Hoagie House is an institution where this local favorite is concerned. Lee's was putting every fresh ingredient you could think of on oversized Italian rolls well before Jared was born. There are more than 20 stores throughout Philadelphia and the surrounding areas.

Mount Joy (D-5)

Restaurants

★★ CATACOMBS AT BUBE'S BREWERY. *102 N Market St, Mount Joy (17552). Phone 717/653-2056; fax 717/653-9337. www.bubesbrewery.com.* In old Victorian hotel and brewery (1876); dining areas are located in original bottling plant, original dining rooms of the hotel portion (Victorian décor) and below ground, in the cellars (medieval atmosphere, costumes, entertainment). American menu. Lunch, dinner. Closed holidays. Bar. Outdoor seating. Guided tours. **$$$**

★★ GROFF'S FARM RESTAURANT. *650 Pinkerton Rd, Mount Joy (17552). Phone 717/653-2048; fax 717/653-1115. www.groffsfarmrestaurant.com.* Pennsylvania Dutch specialties are served family style at this immensely popular restaurant. Many of the dishes are prepared from recipes that have been passed down through generations to owner Betty Groff. Dinner. Closed Dec 24-26; also weekdays Jan-mid-Feb. Children's menu. Reservations recommended. **$$**

Mount Pocono (B-6)

See also Pocono Mountains

Population 2,742
Elevation 1,840 ft
Area Code 570
Zip 18344
Information Pocono Mountains Vacation Bureau, Inc, 1004 Main St, Stroudsburg 18360; phone 570/424-6050; for brochures phone toll-free 800/POCONOS
Web site www.poconos.org

One of the many thriving resort communities in the heart of the Pocono Mountains, Mount Pocono offers recreation year-round in nearby parks, lakes, and ski areas.

What to See and Do

Gouldsboro State Park. *Hwy 423, Tobyhanna. 10 miles N on Hwy 611 and I-380, then NE on Hwy 507. Phone 570/894-8336.* Approximately 2,800 acres; 250-acre lake. Swimming beach, fishing, boating (rentals, mooring, launching); hunting, hiking, ice skating, ice fishing.

Memorytown, USA. *Grange Rd, Mount Pocono. 2 miles E via Hwy 940. Phone 570/839-1680.* Old-time village includes hex shop, country store, store with artifacts; ice-cream parlor; paddle-boats; entertainment; lodging, restaurant, and tavern. Summer festivals. Fee for some activities. (Daily) **FREE**

Mount Airy Lodge Ski Area. *42 Wood Land, Mount Pocono (18344). Just E of town via Hwy 940 to Hwy 611. Phone toll-free 800/441-4410. www.mountairylodge.com.* Two double chairlifts; patrol, school, rentals, snowmaking; cafeteria, restaurant, bar, nursery, lodge. Longest run 1,800 feet; vertical drop 250 feet. Also country trails. (Mid-Dec-late Mar) **$$$$**

Pocono Knob. *1 1/2 miles E on Knob Rd.* Excellent view of surrounding countryside.

Tobyhanna State Park. *Hwy 423, Tobyhanna. 5 miles N on Hwy 611, then NE on Hwy 423. Phone 570/894-8336.* Approximately 5,440 acres with 170-acre lake. Swimming beach; fishing, hunting; boating (rentals, mooring, launching). Hiking, biking; cross-country skiing. Snowmobiling, ice skating, ice fishing. Tent and trailer sites.

Full-Service Resorts

★ ★ ★ CAESARS PARADISE STREAM. *Hwy 940, Mount Pocono (18344). Phone 570/226-2101; toll-free 800/233-4141; fax 570/226-2109. www.caesarsparadisestream.com.* 164 rooms. No children allowed. Check-in 3 pm, check-out 11 am. Restaurant, bar. Fitness room. Indoor pool, outdoor pool, whirlpool. Tennis. **$$$**

★ ★ ★ POCONO MANOR INN AND GOLF CLUB. *Hwy 314, Pocono Manor (18349). Phone 570/839-7111; toll-free 800/233-8150; fax 570/839-0708. www.poconomanor.com.* 255 rooms. Check-in 4 pm, check-out 11 am. Restaurant, bar. Children's activity center. Fitness room. Indoor pool, outdoor pool. Golf. Tennis. On 3,100-acre mountain estate. **$$**

Full-Service Inns

★ ★ ★ FRENCH MANOR. *Huckleberry Rd, South Sterling (18460). Phone 570/676-3244; toll-free 800/523-8200; fax 570/676-9786. www.thefrenchmanor.com.* 9 rooms, 3 story. No children allowed. Check-in 2 pm, check-out 11 am. Restaurant. Airport transportation available. French chateau-style; Spanish slate roof; patio; 38-foot-high dining room with beamed ceilings; Great Hall has two floor-to-ceiling fireplaces. **$$**

★ ★ ★ STERLING INN. *PA 191, South Sterling (18460). Phone 570/676-3311; toll-free 800/523-8200; fax 570/676-9786. www.sterlinginn.com.* 54 rooms, 3 story. Check-in 4 pm, check-out 11 am. Restaurant. Indoor pool, whirlpool. Golf. Tennis. Airport transportation available. Built in the 1850s; country and Victorian suites. **$**

Restaurant

★ TOKYO TEAHOUSE. *RR 940, Mount Pocono (18346). Phone 570/839-8880; fax 570/839-1888.* Japanese menu. Lunch, dinner. Closed Tues in July, Aug. **$$$**

New Castle (B-1)

See also Beaver Falls, Harmony

Settled 1798
Population 26,309
Elevation 860 ft
Area Code 724
Information Lawrence County Tourist Promotion Agency, Celli Central Station, 229 S Jefferson, 16101; phone 724/654-8408
Web site www.lawrencecounty.com/tourism

At the junction of the Shenango, Mahoning, and Beaver rivers, this was long an important Native American trading center; the Delawares used it as their capital. Today the fireworks and plastics industries have become an integral part of the community.

What to See and Do

Greer House. *408 N Jefferson, New Castle. Phone 724/658-4022.* Turn-of-the-century restored mansion houses the Lawrence County Historical Society. Museum has extensive Shenango and Castleton china collections, Sports Hall of Fame, fireworks room. Archives; workshops and speakers. (Tues-Sat; also by appointment) **DONATION**

Hoyt Institute of Fine Arts. *124 E Leasure Ave, New Castle. Phone 724/652-2882.* Cultural arts center housed in two early 20th-century mansions on 4 acres of landscaped grounds; permanent art collection, changing exhibits, period rooms, performing arts programs, classes. Tours. (Tues-Sat; closed holidays) **DONATION**

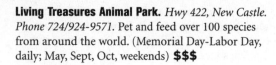

Living Treasures Animal Park. *Hwy 422, New Castle. Phone 724/924-9571.* Pet and feed over 100 species from around the world. (Memorial Day-Labor Day, daily; May, Sept, Oct, weekends) **$$$**

McConnell's Mill State Park. *12 miles E via Hwy 422. Phone 724/368-8091.* Approximately 2,500 acres. Century-old mill surrounded by beautiful landscape and scenery. Fishing, hunting; whitewater boating. Hiking. Picnicking, store. Historical center, interpretive program.

Scottish Rite Cathedral. *614 Center Ave, New Castle. Phone 724/654-6683.* On hillside; six 32-foot columns dominate city's skyline. Large auditorium; cathedral; ballroom. Local Masonic headquarters. Tours (by appointment). **$**

Limited-Service Hotel

★ COMFORT INN. *1740 New Butler Rd, New Castle (16101). Phone 724/658-7700; fax 724/658-7727. www.choicehotels.com.* 79 rooms, 2 story. Pets accepted, some restrictions; fee. Complimentary continental breakfast. Check-out noon. Fitness room. **$**

New Hope (C-6)

See also Doylestown (Bucks County), Erwinna, Lumberville

Founded 1681
Population 2,252
Elevation 76 ft
Area Code 215 and 267
Zip 18938
Information Information Center, 1 W Mechanic St, PO Box 633, phone 215/862-5880 or Bucks County Conference and Visitors Bureau, Inc, 152 Swamp Rd, Doylestown 18901, phone 215/345-4552 or toll-free 800/836-2825
Web site www.buckscountycvb.org

The river village of New Hope was originally the largest part of a 1,000-acre land grant from William Penn to Thomas Woolrich of Shalford, England. In the 20th century the area gained fame as the home of artists and literary and theatrical personalities.

What to See and Do

Bucks County River Country. *2 Walters Ln, Point Pleasant (18950). Phone 215/297-5000. www.rivercountry.net.* On the Delaware River; two- to four-hour canoeing, rafting, tubing and kayaking trips; one-day outings to full vacation trips. (May-Oct) **$$$$**

Coryell's Ferry. *22 S Main St, New Hope. Phone 215/862-2050.* Passenger and charter rides aboard the *Major William C. Barnett*, a 65-foot Mississippi-style sternwheel riverboat, on the Delaware River. (Memorial Day-Labor Day, daily; call for extended season) **$$$**

Ghost Tours. *Main and Ferry sts, New Hope. Phone 215/957-9988.* Follow a lantern-led walk to learn about the area's ghosts. (Oct, Fri and Sat evenings; June-Sept, Sat evening only) **$$$**

New Hope & Ivyland Railroad. *32 W Bridge St, New Hope (18938). W Bridge St, adjacent to Delaware Canal. Phone 215/862-2332. www.newhoperail.com.* A 9-mile, 50-minute narrated train ride through Bucks County. Reading Railroad passenger coaches from the 1920s depart from restored 1890 New Hope Station. Gift shop. (Early Apr-Nov, daily; Dec, special Santa Train Fri-Sun; rest of year, weekends) **$$$**

Parry Barn. *S Main St, New Hope (19040). Opposite mansion.* (1784). Owned by New Hope Historical Society; operated as commercial art gallery. **FREE**

Parry Mansion Museum. *S Main and Ferry sts, New Hope. Phone 215/862-5652.* (1784). Restored stone house built by Benjamin Parry, prosperous merchant and mill owner. Eleven rooms on view, restored and furnished to depict period styles from late 18th to early 20th centuries. (May-Dec, Fri-Sun; also by appointment) **$$**

Peddler's Village. *Hwys 202 and 263, Lahaska (18931). 5 miles S on Hwy 202. Phone 215/794-4000. www.peddlersvillage.com.* This 18th-century-style country village with 42 acres of landscaped gardens and winding brick paths makes a great day trip from Philadelphia. Browse through a selection of more than 70 specialty shops for handicrafts, toys, accessories, leather goods, collectibles, and gourmet foods. Take the kids for a ride on an antique carousel, or take advantage of the many free family events and seasonal festivals. (Daily; closed Jan 1, Thanksgiving, Dec 25) Also in village is

Carousel World. *Peddlers Vlg Shop # 165, Lahaska. Phone 215/794-8960.* Learn about history of the carousel in turn-of-the-century park. Antique carousel rides. Gift shop. (Daily) **$**

Washington Crossing Historic Park. *7 miles S on Hwy 32.* (see).

Special Events

New Hope Arts and Crafts Festival. *1 W Mechanic St, New Hope (18938). Phone 215/862-5880.* Contemporary and traditional crafts. Painting, photography, sculpture. Oct.

Scarecrow Festival. *Peddler's Village, between Hwys 202 and 263 LaHaska PA, New Hope (18931). Phone 215/794-4000.* Scarecrow making, pumpkin painting. Jack-o-lantern and gourd art contest. Square dancing, entertainment. Sept.

Teddy Bear's Picnic. *Peddler's Village, between Hwys 202 and 263 LaHaska PA, New Hope (18931). Phone 215/794-4000.* Teddy bear vendors, parades, competitions. "Bear clinic" for hurt bears. Appraisals. Music. July.

Full-Service Inns

★ ★ ★ CENTRE BRIDGE INN. *2998 N River Rd, New Hope (18938). Phone 215/862-2048; fax 215/862-3244. www.centrebridgeinn.com.* 9 rooms, 2 story. Complimentary continental breakfast. Check-in 3 pm, check-out noon. Restaurant, bar. **$**

★ ★ ★ GOLDEN PHEASANT INN. *763 River Rd, Erwinna (18920). Phone 610/294-9595; fax 610/294-9882. www.goldenpheasant.com.* 6 rooms, 2 story. Pets accepted, some restrictions; fee. Complimentary continental breakfast. Check-in 3 pm, check-out noon. Restaurant. **$**

★ ★ ★ GOLDEN PLOUGH INN. *SR 202, Lahaska (18931). Phone 215/794-4004; fax 215/794-4008. www.peddlersvillage.com.* 72 rooms, 3 story. Complimentary continental breakfast. Check-in 3 pm, check-out 11 am. Restaurant. **$**

★ ★ ★ HOTEL DU VILLAGE. *2535 N River Rd, New Hope (18938). Phone 215/862-9911; fax 215/862-9788. www.hotelduvillage.com.* 20 rooms, 2 story. Complimentary continental breakfast. Check-in after 2 pm, check-out 11 am. Restaurant, bar. Pool. Tennis. Small Tudor-style country inn on spacious grounds; former estate. **$**

Specialty Lodgings

The following lodging establishments are approved by Mobil Travel Guide, but due to their unique and individualized nature have not been given a traditional Mobil Star rating. Included in this listing you may find bed-and-breakfasts, limited-service inns, guest ranches, and other unique hotel properties.

1870 WEDGWOOD INN OF NEW HOPE. *111 W Bridge St, New Hope (18938). Phone 215/862-3936; fax 215/862-3937. www.1870wedgwoodinn.com.* 12 rooms, 2 story. Pets accepted, some restrictions; fee. Complimentary full breakfast. Check-in 3 pm, check-out 11 am. Built in 1870; antiques, large Wedgwood collection. Carriage rides. **$**

AARON BURR HOUSE. *80 W Bridge St, New Hope (18938). Phone 215/862-2343; fax 215/862-3937. www.new-hope-inn.com.* 5 rooms, 2 story. Pets accepted, some restrictions; fee. Complimentary full breakfast. Check-in 2 pm, check-out 11 am. Built in 1873. **$**

BARLEY SHEAF FARM BED & BREAKFAST. *PO Box 10, Holicong (18928). Phone 215/794-5104; fax 215/794-5332. www.barleysheaf.com.* 15 rooms, 3 story. Complimentary full breakfast. Check-in 2 pm, check-out 11 am. Pool. Thirty-acre farmhouse; built in 1740. **$$**

FOX AND HOUND BED AND BREAKFAST OF NEW HOPE. *246 W Bridge St, New Hope (18938). Phone 215/862-5082; toll-free 800/862-5082; fax 215/862-5082. www.foxhoundinn.com.* 8 rooms,

3 story. Children over 12 years only. Complimentary continental breakfast; full breakfast on weekends. Check-in 2 pm, check-out 11 am. Stone manor house built in 1850. **$**

HOLLILEIF BED & BREAKFAST. *677 Durham Rd (SR 413), Newtown (18940). Phone 215/598-3100.* 5 rooms, 3 story. Complimentary full breakfast. Check-in 3 pm, check-out 11:30 am. 18th-century house; antiques, fireplace. **$**

INN TO THE WOODS. *150 Glenwood Dr, Washington Crossing (18977). Phone 215/493-1974; toll-free 800/574-1974; fax 215/493-7592. www.inn-bucks.com.* 6 rooms, 3 story. Children over 12 years only. Complimentary full breakfast. Check-in 3 pm, check-out 11 am. **$$**

MANSION INN. *9 S Main St, New Hope (18938). Phone 215/862-1231; fax 215/862-0277. www.themansioninn.com.* 15 rooms, 3 story. Children over 16 years only. Complimentary full breakfast. Check-in 2 pm, check-out 11 am. Pool. Built (1865); Victorian décor. **$$**

PINEAPPLE HILL BED AND BREAKFAST. *1324 River Rd, New Hope (18938). Phone 215/862-1790; toll-free 888/866-8404. www.pineapplehill.com.* 8 rooms, 3 story. Complimentary full breakfast. Check-in 3 pm, check-out 11 am. Pool. Built in 1790. On river. **$**

TATTERSALL INN. *16 Cafferty N River Rd, Point Pleasant (18950). Phone 215/297-8233; toll-free 800/297-4988; fax 215/297-5093. www.tattersallinn.com.* 6 rooms, 2 story. Complimentary full breakfast. Check-in 3 pm, check-out 11 am. **$**

Restaurants

★★ CENTRE BRIDGE INN. *2998 N River Rd, New Hope (18938). Phone 215/862-2048; fax 215/862-3244. www.centrebridgeinn.com.* American menu with French influences. Lunch, dinner, Sun brunch. Closed Mon; Dec 25. Bar. Valet parking Sat. Outdoor seating. **$$$**

★★★ THE CHAMPAGNE ROOM. *9 S Main St, New Hope (18938). Phone 215/862-6260; fax 215/862-0277. www.themansioninn.com.* International menu. Lunch, dinner. Closed Mon-Wed. Bar. Casual attire. Outdoor seating. **$$**

★★ COCK N' BULL. *Hwys 202 and 263, Lahaska (18931). Phone 215/794-4000; fax 215/794-4001. www.peddlersvillage.com.* Steak menu. Dinner. Closed Jan 1, Dec 25. Bar. Casual attire. Reservations recommended. **$$**

★★ INN AT PHILLIPS MILL. *2590 N River Rd, New Hope (18938). Phone 215/862-9919; fax 215/862-0530.* French country menu. Dinner. Closed Jan 1, Dec 25. Casual attire. Reservations recommended. Outdoor seating. **$$**

★★★ ODETTE'S. *S River Rd, New Hope (18938). Phone 215/862-2432; fax 215/862-2142. www.odettes.com.* American menu. Lunch, dinner, Sun brunch. Bar. Children's menu. Built in 1794 as bargeman's inn; overlooks Delaware River; memorabilia of Odette Myrtil Logan of South Pacific fame. Reservations recommended. Valet parking. **$$**

★ SPOTTED HOG. *Hwys 202 and 263, New Hope (18931). Phone 215/794-4000; fax 215/794-4008. www.peddlersvillage.com.* Breakfast, lunch, dinner. Closed Thanksgiving, Dec 25. Bar. Children's menu. **$$**

New Stanton

See also Connellsville, Greensburg

Population 1,906
Elevation 980 ft
Area Code 724
Zip 15672
Information Laurel Highlands Visitors Bureau, Town Hall, 120 E Main St, Ligonier 15658; phone 724/238-5661
Web site www.laurelhighlands.org

What to See and Do

L. E. Smith Glass Co. *1900 Liberty St, New Stanton (15672). Phone 724/547-3544 (for tour schedule).* Reproductions of several styles of antique handcrafted glass. Tours. Children under six years not admitted on tour. (Mon-Fri; closed first two weeks in July) **FREE**

Limited-Service Hotel

★★ **DAYS INN.** *127 W Byers Ave, New Stanton (15672). Phone 724/925-3591; toll-free 800/329-7466; fax 724/925-9859. www.daysinn.com.* 135 rooms, 3 story. Check-out 11 am. Restaurant, bar. Fitness room. Pool. **$**

New Wilmington

Restaurant

★★ **THE TAVERN.** *108 N Market St, New Wilmington (16142). Phone 724/946-2020.* Country décor; built in 1840. Lunch, dinner. Closed Tues; July 4, Thanksgiving, Dec 24-25. **$$**

Norristown (D-6)

See also King of Prussia, Kulpsville, Limerick, Philadelphia

Founded 1704
Population 31,282
Elevation 130 ft
Area Code 484 & 610
Information Valley Forge Convention and Visitors Bureau, 600 W Germantown Pike, Suite 130, Plymouth Meeting 19462; phone 610/834-1550
Web site www.valleyforge.org

William Penn, Jr., owner of the 7,600-acre tract around Norristown, sold it to Isaac Norris and William Trent for 50 cents an acre in 1704. It became a crossroads for colonial merchants and soldiers; Washington's army camped nearby. Dutch, German, Swedish, Welsh, and English immigrants left their mark on the city. Today Norristown, still a transportation hub, houses many industries and serves as a county government center.

What to See and Do

Elmwood Park Zoo. *1661 Harding Blvd, Norristown. Phone 610/277-3825.* Features extensive North American waterfowl area; cougars, bobcats, bison, elk; outdoor aviary; birds of prey; children's zoo barn; museum with exhibit on animal senses. (Daily; closed Jan 1, Thanksgiving, Dec 25) **$$**

Peter Wentz Farmstead. *Schultz Rd, Worcester. 10 miles NW via Hwy 202, W via Hwy 73 on Schultz Rd. Phone 610/584-5104.* Restored and furnished mid-18th-century country mansion, twice used by Washington during the Pennsylvania campaign. More than 70 acres with demonstration field and crops of the period. Slide presentation; reconstructed 1744 barn with farm animals. (Tues-Sun; closed holidays) **FREE**

Full-Service Hotel

★★★ **SHERATON BUCKS COUNTY HOTEL.** *400 Oxford Valley Rd, Norristown (19047). Phone 215/547-4100; fax 215/269-3400. www.sheraton.com.* 187 rooms, 15 story. Check-in 3 pm, check-out noon. Restaurant, bar. Fitness room. Indoor pool, whirlpool. Business center. **$$**

Full-Service Inn

★★★ **WILLIAM PENN INN.** *US 202 & Sumneytown Pike, Gwynedd (19436). Phone 215/699-9272; fax 215/699-4808. www.williampenninn.com.* 4 rooms, 2 story. Complimentary continental breakfast. Check-in 1 pm, check-out 11 am. Restaurant. **$**

Restaurants

★★ **GYPSY ROSE.** *505 Bridge Rd (Hwy 113), Collegeville (19426). Phone 610/489-1600. www.gogypsyrose.com.* This site was once an 18th-century farmhouse that has evolved into a wonderful inn. The restaurant enjoys a view of breathtaking landscaped grounds which may be viewed on a brick terrace that is open seasonally (Apr-Oct). Dinner, Sun brunch. Closed holidays. Bar. Children's menu. Outdoor seating. **$$**

★★★ **THE JEFFERSON HOUSE.** *2519 DeKalb Pike, Norristown (19401). Phone 610/275-3407; fax 610/275-1275. www.thejeffersonhouserestaurant.com.* American menu. Lunch, dinner, Sun brunch. Closed holidays. Bar. Children's menu. Manor house set on extensive, landscaped grounds; former Buckland estate. **$$$**

★★ **WILLIAM PENN INN.** *US 202 and Sumneytown Pike, Gwynedd (19436). Phone 215/699-9272; fax 215/699-4808. www.williampenninn.com.* American menu. Lunch, dinner, Sun brunch. Closed Dec 25. Bar. Originally built as a tavern (1714); antiques. **$$$**

North East (A-1)

See also Erie

Settled 1794
Population 4,601
Elevation 801 ft
Area Code 814
Zip 16428
Information Chamber of Commerce, 21 S Lake St; phone 814/725-4262

When Pennsylvania bought from the federal government the tract containing North East in 1778, the state gained 46 miles of Lake Erie frontage, a fine harbor, and some of the best Concord grape country in the nation.

What to See and Do

Heritage Wine Cellars. *12162 E Main Rd, North East. Phone 814/725-8015.* Guided tours; wine tastings. (Daily; closed holidays) **FREE**

Mazza Vineyards. *11815 E Lake Rd, North East. Phone 814/725-8695.* Guided tours; wine tastings. (Daily; closed holidays) **FREE**

Penn-Shore Vineyards and Winery. *10225 E Lake Rd, North East. Phone 814/725-8688.* Guided tours; wine tastings. (Daily; closed holidays) **FREE**

Special Events

Cherry Festival. Concessions, rides, games, parade. Mid-July.

Wine Country Harvest Festival. *21 S Lake St, North East. Gravel Pit Park and Gibson Park. Phone 814/725-4262.* Arts and crafts, bands, buses to wineries, food. Last full weekend in Sept.

Oil City (B-1)

See also Franklin (Venango County), Titusville

Population 11,504
Elevation 1,000 ft
Area Code 814
Zip 16301

Spreading on both sides of Oil Creek and the Allegheny River, Oil City was born of the oil boom. Oil refining and the manufacture of oil machinery are its major occupations today. Nearby are natural gas fields. Seven miles northwest stood the famous oil-boom town of Pithole. In 1865, it expanded from a single farmhouse to a population of more than 10,000 in five months as its first oil well brought in 250 barrels a day.

Limited-Service Hotel

★★ **HOLIDAY INN.** *1 Seneca St, Oil City (16301). Phone 814/677-1221; fax 814/677-0492. www.holiday-inn.com.* 106 rooms, 5 story. Pets accepted; fee. Check-out noon. Restaurant, bar. Pool. **$**

Orbisonia (C-3)

See also Chambersburg, Huntingdon

Population 425
Elevation 640 ft
Area Code 814
Zip 17243

What to See and Do

East Broad Top Railroad. *On Hwy 522. Phone 814/447-3011.* The oldest surviving narrow-gauge railroad east of the Rockies. Train ride (70 minutes); fascinating old equipment, buildings. Picnic area. (June-Oct, weekends only) **$$$** Opposite is

Rockhill Trolley Museum. *Meadow St, Rockhill Furnace. 1/2 mile W off Hwy 522, on Hwy 994, in Rockhill Furnace. Phone 814/447-9576.* Old-time trolleys; car barn and restoration shop tours. A 2-mile ride on Shade Gap Electric Railway. Gift shop. (Memorial Day-Oct, weekends) **$$**

Pennsylvania Dutch Area

See also Allentown, Bird-in-Hand, Ephrata, Kutztown, Lancaster, Lebanon, Manheim, Reading

Web site www.800padutch.com

From the Rhineland and Palatinate of Germany came great migrations of settlers to Pennsylvania in the 18th century, first near Philadelphia and then moving west. Because they retained their customs and speech and developed beautiful and bountiful farms, the Pennsylvania Dutch (corruption of the German Deutsch) country is one of the state's greatest tourist attractions. There are all degrees of conservatism among these descendants of German immigrants, ranging from the Amish to the Brethren, but all share tremendous vigor, family devotion, love of the Bible, and belief in thrift and hard work.

Many of the "plain people"—the Amish, Old Order Mennonites, and Bretren (Dunkards)—live today much as they did a century ago. Married men wear beards, black coats, and low-crowned black hats; women wear bonnets and long, simple dresses. They drive horses and buggies instead of cars, work long hours in the fields, shun the use of modern farm machinery, and turn to the Bible for guidance. Despire their refusal to use machinery they are master farmers. (They were among the first to rotate crops and practice modern fertilization methods.) Their harvests are consistently among the best in the country.

Many of the Amish regard photographs as "graven images"; visitors should not take pictures of individuals without their permission.

Philadelphia (D-6)

See also Burlington, Camden, Bristol, Chester, Doylestown (Bucks County), Jenkintown, King of Prussia, Kulpsville, Media, Norristown; also see Wilmington, DE

Founded 1682
Population 1,517,550
Elevation 45 ft
Area Code 215 and 267
Information Convention & Visitors Bureau, 1515 Market St, 19102; phone 215/636-3300
Web site www.pcvb.org
Suburbs Bristol, Chester, Fort Washington, Jenkintown, Kennett Square, King of Prussia, Media, Norristown, West Chester, Willow Grove; also Wilmington, DE and Camden, NJ.

The nation's first capital has experienced a rebirth in the past few decades. Philadelphia has successfully blended its historic past with an electricity of modern times, all the while keeping an eye on the future. In the mid-18th century, it was the second-largest city in the English-speaking world. Today, Philadelphia is the second-largest city on the East Coast and the fifth largest in the country. Here, in William Penn's City of Brotherly Love, the Declaration of Independence was written and adopted, the Constitution was molded and signed, the Liberty Bell was rung, Betsy Ross was said to have sewn her flag, and Washington served most of his years as president.

This is the city of "firsts," including the first American hospital, medical college, women's medical college, bank, paper mill, steamboat, zoo, sugar refinery, daily newspaper, US mint, and public school for black children (1750).

The first Quakers, who came here in 1681, lived in caves dug into the banks of the Delaware River. During the first year, 80 houses were raised; by the following year, William Penn's "greene countrie towne" was a city of 600 buildings. The Quakers prospered in trade and commerce, and Philadelphia became the leading port in the colonies. Its leading citizen for many years was Benjamin Franklin—statesman, scientist, diplomat, writer, inventor, and publisher.

The fires of colonial indignation burned hot and early in Philadelphia. Soon after the Boston Tea Party, a protest rally of 8,000 Philadelphians frightened off a British tea ship. In May 1774, when Paul Revere rode from Boston to Philadelphia to report Boston's harbor had been closed, all of Philadelphia went into mourning. The first and second Continental Congresses convened here, and Philadelphia became the headquarters of the Revolution. After the Declaration of Independence was composed and accepted by Congress the city gave its men, factories, and shipyards to the cause. But British General Howe and 18,000 soldiers poured in on September 26, 1777, to spend a comfortable and social winter here while Washington's troops endured the bitter winter at Valley Forge. When the British evacuated the city, Congress returned. Philadelphia continued as the seat of government until 1800, except for a short period when New York City held the honor. The Constitution of the United States was written here, and President George Washington graced the city's halls and streets.

Since those historic days, Philadelphia has figured importantly in the politics, economy, and culture of the country. Here, national conventions have nominated presidents. During four wars the city has served as an arsenal and a shipyard. More than 1,400 churches and synagogues grace the city. There are over 25 colleges, universities, and professional schools in Philadelphia as well. Fine restaurants are in abundance, along with exciting nightlife to top off an evening. Entertainment is offered by the world-renowned Philadelphia Orchestra, theaters, college and professional sports, outstanding parks, recreation centers, and playgrounds. Shoppers may browse major department stores, hundreds of specialty shops, and antique shopping areas.

For 10 blocks between the Delaware River and 9th Street lies a history-rich part of Philadelphia. Here are the shrines of American liberty: Independence Hall, the Liberty Bell Pavilion, and many other historical sites in and around Independence National Historical Park.

Additional Visitor Information

There is also a visitor center at 3rd & Chestnut sts, operated by the National Park Service. (Daily) Phone 215/597-8975 or 215/597-8974 for information on park attractions.

Philadelphia Fun Facts

- Betsy Ross made the first American flag in Philadelphia.
- Benjamin Franklin founded the Philadelphia Zoo. This was the first zoo in the United States.

The Visitors Center of the Philadelphia Convention and Visitors Bureau, 16th St and John F. Kennedy Blvd, 19102, has tourist information and maps (daily; closed Thanksgiving, Dec 25). Phone 215/636-1666 or 800/537-7676.

Public Transportation

Subway and elevated trains, commuter trains, buses, trolleys (SEPTA), phone 215/580-7800

Airport **Philadelphia International Airport.** Weather phone 215/936-1212.

Information Phone 215/937-6800 or toll-free 800/PHL-GATE

Lost and Found Phone 215/937-6888

Airlines Air Jamaica, Air Canada, Air France, AirTran, America West, American Eagle, American Airlines, ATA - American Trans Air, British Airways, Continental, Continental Express, Delta Air Lines, Delta Connection, Lufthansa, Midwest Express, United Express, US Airways, US Airways (Int'l), US Airways Express, USA 3000, Northwest Airlines, United Airlines

What to See and Do

9th Street Italian Market. *9th St between Wharton and Fitzwater, Philadelphia (19147). Located in the heart of historic Philadelphia. Phone 215/923-5637. www.phillyitalianmarket.com.* Stroll through this outdoor market and you'll get more than a just a whiff of Italy. Sip on Italian gourmet coffee, inhale imported cheeses, or treat yourself to a cannoli. With more than 100 merchants selling their wares, this is the largest working outdoor market in the US, calling this neighborhood home for more than a century. But there's local flavor here as well. Pinch a Jersey tomato, stop for a famous soft pretzel, or take home fresh-baked Amish bread.

And if you want to sit for a while, there are plenty of choices for every budget, from fine Italian dining to lunch counters to an outdoor snack tent. **FREE**

Academy of Music. *Broad and Locust sts, Philadelphia (19102). Phone 215/893-1999. www.academyofmusic.org.* (1857). City's opera house, concert hall; home of Philadelphia Orchestra, Philly Pops, Opera Company of Philadelphia and Pennsylvania Ballet.

Academy of Natural Sciences Museum. *1900 Ben Franklin Pkwy, Philadelphia (19103). Phone 215/299-1000. www.acnatsci.org.* (1812). Dinosaurs, Egyptian mummies, animal displays in natural habitats, live animal programs, hands-on children's museum. (Daily; closed Jan 1, Thanksgiving, Dec 25) **$$**

African-American Museum Philadelphia. *701 Arch St, Philadelphia (19106). Phone 215/574-0380.* Built to house and interpret African-American culture. Changing exhibits; public events include lectures, workshops, films, and concerts. (Tues-Sun; closed Jan 1, Thanksgiving, Dec 25) **$$$**

American Swedish Historical Museum. *1900 Pattison Ave (19145). Phone 215/389-1776. www.americanswedish.org.* From tapestries to technology, the museum celebrates Swedish influence on American life. Special exhibits on the New Sweden Colony. Research library, collections. (Tues-Fri 10 am-4 pm, Sat-Sun from noon; closed holidays) **$$**

Antique Row. *9th and Pine sts, Philadelphia (19103). From 9th to 17th Sts along Pine St, Philadelphia.* Dozens of antique, craft and curio shops.

Arch Street Meetinghouse. *320 Arch St, Philadelphia (19106). Phone 215/627-2667. www.archstreetfriends.org.* (1804). Perhaps the largest Friends meetinghouse in the world. Exhibits, slide show, tours. (Daily except Sun; closed Jan 1, Thanksgiving, Dec 25) **DONATION**

The Atwater Kent Museum of Philadelphia. *15 S 7th St, Philadelphia (19106). Phone 215/685-4830. www.philadelphiahistory.org.* Hundreds of fascinating artifacts, toys and miniatures, maps, prints, paintings, and photographs reflect the city's social and cultural history. (Daily 10 am-5 pm; closed holidays) **$**

Balch Institute for Ethnic Studies. *18 S 7th St, Philadelphia (19106). Phone 215/925-8090. www.hsp.org.* A multicultural library, archive, museum, and education center that promotes intergroup understanding using education; 300 years of US immigration are documented here. Features "Peopling of Pennsylvania," as well as changing exhibits. (Mon-Tues, Thurs-Fri 1-5:30 pm, Wed to 8:30 pm; closed holidays) **$$**

Betsy Ross House. *239 Arch St, Philadelphia (19106). Phone 215/686-1252. www.betsyrosshouse.org.* Where the famous seamstress is said to have made the first American flag. Upholsterer's shop, memorabilia. Flag Day ceremonies, June 14. (Apr-Oct, daily 10 am-5 pm; Tues-Sun rest of year; closed Jan 1, Thanksgiving, Dec 25) **DONATION**

Blue Cross River Rink. *Fetival Pier at Penn's Landing, Columbus Blvd and Spring Garden St, Philadelphia (19123). Phone 215/925-7465. www.riverrink.com.* Few outdoor ice skating rinks are as well located as this one along the Delaware River. Visitors have a great vantage point from which to view the Benjamin Franklin Bridge and the Philadelphia skyline. This Olympic-size rink, at 200 feet x 85 feet, can accommodate 500 skaters. After a hearty skate, warm yourself in the heated pavilion, which features a video game area and concessions. (Mon-Thurs 6-9 pm, Fri-Sat 12:30 pm-1 am, Sun 12:30-9 pm, Nov-mid Mar) **$$**

The Bourse. *5th St, Philadelphia (19106). 5th St, across from Liberty Bell Pavilion.* (1893-1895) Restored Victorian building houses shops and restaurants.

Burial Ground of Congregation Mikveh Israel. *Spruce and 8th sts, Philadelphia (19106).* (1738). Graves of Haym Salomon, Revolutionary War financier, and Rebecca Gratz, probable model for "Rebecca" of Sir Walter Scott's *Ivanhoe.*

Centipede Tours. *1315 Walnut St, Philadelphia (19107). Phone 215/735-3123. www.centipede.com.* Candlelight strolls (1 1/2 hours) through historic Philadelphia and Society Hill areas led by guides in 18th-century dress; begins and ends at City Tavern. (Mid-May-mid-Oct, Fri-Sat) Reservations preferred. **$$**

Christ Church. *2nd and Market sts, Philadelphia (19106). 2nd St between Market and Arch sts. Phone 215/922-1695. www.christchurchphila.org.* (Episcopal). Patriots, Loyalists, and heroes have worshiped here since 1695. Sit in pews once occupied by Washington,

Franklin, and Betsy Ross. (Mar-Dec, daily; rest of year, Wed-Sun; closed Jan 1, Thanksgiving, Dec 25) **FREE**

Christ Church Burial Ground. *5th and Arch sts, Philadelphia (19106). Phone 215/922-1695.* Resting place of Benjamin Franklin, his wife, Deborah, and six other signers of the Declaration of Independence. (Call for hours)

City Hall. *Broad and Market sts, Philadelphia (19107). Phone 215/686-2840.* A granite statue of William Penn stands 510 feet high above the heart of the city on top of this municipal building, which is larger than the Capitol. It is known as Penn Square, and was designated by Penn as the location for a building of "publick concerns." It also functions as Philadelphia's City Hall. It is one of the finest examples of French Second-Empire architectural style and a sculptural achievement. Constructing this building with the tallest statue (37,000 feet) in the world on its top took 30 years. Penn's famous hat is more than 7 feet in diameter, and the brim creates a 2-foot-wide track. There are more than 250 sculptures around this marble, granite, and limestone structure, 20 elevators, and a four-faced, 50-ton clock. (Mon-Fri; closed holidays)

Civil War Library and Museum. *1805 Pine St, Philadelphia (19103). Phone 215/735-8196.* Four-story brick 19th-century townhouse filled with 18,000 books and periodicals dealing with events leading up to the American Civil War, the war itself, and early Reconstruction. Unique collection of arms, uniforms, flags of the period, memorabilia, and artifacts begun in 1888 by former officers of the Union Army. Exhibits on Lincoln, Grant, and Meade; also the Navy Room and the Armory. (Thurs-Fri; closed holidays) **$$**

Cliveden. *6401 Germantown Ave, Philadelphia (19144). Between Johnson and Cliveden sts. Phone 215/848-1777. www.cliveden.org.* (1767) A 2 1/2-story stone Georgian house of individual design built as a summer home by Benjamin Chew, Chief Justice of colonial Pennsylvania. On Oct 4, 1777, British soldiers used the house as a fortress to repulse Washington's attempt to recapture Philadelphia. Used as the Chew family residence for 200 years; many original furnishings. A National Trust for Historic Preservation property. (Apr-Dec, Thurs-Sun afternoons; closed Easter, Thanksgiving, Dec 25) **$$$**

Deshler-Morris House. *5442 Germantown Ave, Philadelphia (19144). Phone 215/596-1748. www.nps.gov/demo/.* (1772-1773) Residence of President Washington in the summers of 1793, 1794; period furnishings, garden. (Wed-Sun afternoons, or by appointment; closed holidays) **$**

Edgar Allan Poe National Historic Site. *532 N 7th St, Philadelphia (19123). At Spring Garden St. Phone 215/597-8780. www.nps.gov/edal/.* Where Poe lived before his move to New York in 1844. The site is the nation's memorial to the literary genius of Edgar Allan Poe. Exhibits, slide show, tours, and special programs. (Wed-Sun 9 am-5 pm; closed Jan 1, Dec 25) **FREE**

Electric Factory. *421 N 7th St, Philadelphia (19123). Phone 215/569-9400. www.electricfactory.com.* This all-ages live music venue offers accessibility to lesser-known bands, although Tori Amos, Garbage, Brian Setzer, and other well-known artists have played here. Because it can accommodate 3,000 people, it can feel crowded; there is no seating on the main level. But early arrivers can position themselves at bar tables in the upstairs balcony overlooking the stage. (Daily)

Elfreth's Alley. *126 Elfreth's Alley, Philadelphia (19106). Located on 2nd Street, between Race and Arch. Phone 215/574-0560. www.elfrethsalley.org.* Philadelphians still live in these Georgian- and Federal-style homes along cobblestoned Elfreth's Alley, the nation's oldest continued-use residential street. A few homes have been converted into museums, offering guided tours, a quaint gift shop, and handcrafted memorabilia. Culture and architecture appreciators will pick up all sorts of historical facts through photos and the collections. (Mar-Oct: Mon-Sat 10 am-5 pm, Sun from noon; Nov-Feb: Thurs-Sat 10 am-5 pm, Sun from noon) **$**

★ **Fairmount Park.** *4231 N Concourse Dr, Philadelphia (19131). Begins at Philadelphia Museum of Art, extends NW on both sides of Wissahickon Creek and Schuylkill River. Phone 215/685-0000. www.phila.gov/fairpark.* At 8,900 acres, Fairmount Park is the largest city park in America. The park can please the very active and the moderately active, as well as the artistically and historically inclined. It is home to 100 miles of beautifully landscaped paths for walking and horseback riding. Cyclists love to bike along the Pennypack and Wissahickon trails. Walkers stroll or power-hike in Valley Green alongside the ducks. In-line skaters and rowing and sculling enthusiasts at Boathouse Row enjoy the sights along the Schuykill River on Kelly Drive. Within the park are the Philadelphia Zoo (see), the Shofuso Japanese House, the Philadelphia Museum of Art (see), the outdoor festival center Robin Hood Dell, and the Philadelphia Orchestra's summer amphitheater (Mann Music Center—see also PHILADELPHIA ORCHESTRA), as well as 127 tennis courts and numerous picnic spots. The park contains America's largest collection of authentic colonial homes, features majestic outdoor sculptures, and includes Memorial Hall, the only building remaining from the 1876 Centennial Exhibition. (Daily) In park are

Boathouse Row Rowing Regattas. *Boathouse Row, Kelly Dr, Philadelphia. On the E bank of the river. Phone 215/978-6919 (for rowing, regatta schedules). www.boathouserow.org.* The Schuylkill River along Kelly Drive beckons competitive rowers. Powerboats are not allowed on this scenic 28-mile river. With Fairmount Park surrounding the 14 historic boathouses where the boats are kept and the Art Museum as a backdrop, it is among the most picturesque rowing courses in the world. Several well-attended events take place here from spring into fall, including the Stotesbury Cup Regatta, the Dad Vail Regatta, the Head of the Schuylkill Regatta, Independence Day Regatta, and the Schuylkill Navy Regatta. **FREE**

Colonial Mansions. *Phone 215/684-7922.* Handsome 18th-century dwellings in varying architectural styles, authentically preserved and furnished, include Mount Pleasant (1761) (Tues-Sun); Cedar Grove (1756) (Tues-Sun); Strawberry Mansion (1797) (Tues-Sun); Sweetbriar (1797) (Mon, Wed-Sun); Lemon Hill (1799) (Wed-Sun); Woodford (1756) (Tues-Sun); Laurel Hill (1760) (Wed-Sun). Further details and guided tours from Park Houses office at Philadelphia Museum of Art. **$**

Japanese Exhibition House. *Fairmount Park Horticulture Center, Horticultural Dr, Philadelphia. Phone 215/878-5097.* Re-creates a bit of Japan, complete with garden, pond, bridge. (May-Labor Day, Tues-Sun; Labor Day-Oct, Sat and Sun) **$**

Philadelphia Museum of Art. *26th St and Ben Franklin Pkwy, Philadelphia. Take I-676 W to the Ben Franklin Pkwy exit (22nd St, museum area), on the right side. At the end of the exit ramp, turn right onto 22nd St and move into the far left lane. Turn left onto the outside lanes of the parkway toward the museum, follow the Art Museum signs, and turn left at the stoplight. Follow this to the west entrance of the museum, where limited parking is available. Phone 215/763-8100. www.philamuseum.org.* Modeled after a Greco-Roman temple, this massive museum amplifies the beauty of more than 300,000 works of art, and offers spectacular natural views. From the top of the steps outside (made famous by Sylvester Stallone in the movie *Rocky*), visitors discover a breathtaking view of the Ben Franklin Parkway toward City Hall. Inside, the collections span 2,000 years and many more miles. There's a lavish collection of period rooms, a Japanese teahouse, a Chinese palace hall, and a celebrated selection of Oriental carpets. Art lovers will also find East Asian art costumes, Indian and Himalayan pieces, European decorative arts, Medieval sculptures, Renaissance paintings, Impressionist and Post-Impressionist paintings, and modern and contemporary works in many media. (Tues, Thurs, Sat-Sun 10 am-5 pm, Wed and Fri to 8:45 pm; closed holidays) **$$**

Philadelphia Orchestra. *260 S Broad St, #1600, Philadelphia. Phone 215/893-1999. www.philorch.org.* The internationally renowned Philadelphia Orchestra has distinguished itself as a leading American orchestra through a century of acclaimed performances, historic international tours, and best-selling recordings. Performances are held at The Kimmel Center for the Performing Arts at Broad and Spruce Streets; the Mann Center for the Performing Arts, 52nd Street and Parkside Avenue; Saratoga Performing Arts Center in upstate New York; and annually at New York's Carnegie Hall.

Philadelphia Zoo. *3400 W Girard Ave, Philadelphia (19104). Located at the corner of 34th St and Girard Ave in Fairmount Park. Phone 215/243-1100. www.phillyzoo.org.* The Philadelphia Zoo may have been America's first zoo—it was home to the nation's first white lions and witnessed its first successful chimpanzee birth—but you'll see no signs of old age here. Over the last century, the zoo has transformed itself into much more. The zoo is a preservation spot for rare and endangered animals, as well as a garden and wildlife destination point. Lovers of living things will appreciate the opportunity to see 1,600 live animals, from red pandas to Rodrigues fruit bats, in realistic re-creations of their natural habitats. Inclined to reach out and touch? Take a pony, camel, or elephant ride; feed nectar to a parrot in a walk-through aviary; or engage with a playful wallaby. Prefer less hands-on contact? Pedal a boat around Bird Lake. If you are happier at arm's length, pretend that you're a giraffe and explore a four-story tropical tree or take a soaring balloon 400 feet up on the country's first passenger-carrying Zooballoon. (Feb-Nov: daily 9:30 am-5 pm, Dec-Jan: daily 9:30 am-4 pm; closed Jan 1, Jun 12, Thanksgiving, Dec 24-25, Dec 31) **$$$$**

Robin Hood Dell East. *Ridge Ave, Philadelphia. Near 33rd St. Phone 215/685-9560. www.delleast.org.* (See SPECIAL EVENTS)

Fireman's Hall Museum. *147 N 2nd St, Philadelphia (19106). Phone 215/923-1438.* Collection of antique firefighting equipment; displays and exhibits of fire department history since its beginning in 1736; library. (Tues-Sat 9 am-4:30 pm; closed holidays) **DONATION**

First Presbyterian Church. *201 S 21st St, Philadelphia (19103). Phone 215/567-0532. www.fpcphila.org.* This more than 300-year-old church was designed in the Victorian Gothic style, combining French and English medieval Gothic cathedral motifs with massive details, flamboyant decoration, and mixed materials, including granite, sand-toned brick, six types of marble, terra-cotta, and stone. No plaster was used anywhere within the original building, a matter of some architectural significance toward the end of the 19th century. **FREE**

The Five Spot. *5 S Bank St, Philadelphia (19106). Phone 215/574-0070. www.thefivespot.com.* Originally opened as a swing club during the late-1990s "swing trend," The Five Spot is now a live music and dance club that features everything from rock music and live DJs to salsa and swing. The club hosts a live cabaret act called the Peek-a-boo Revue the first Saturday of every month, as well as Latin salsa on Thursdays, open-mike nights on Tuesdays (where many musicians claim to have gotten their start), and weekly swing lessons. (Daily) **$**

Fort Mifflin. *Fort Mifflin Rd and Enterprise Ave, Philadelphia (19153). From I-95 S take exit 13 to Island Ave, left at stop sign, follow signs. From I-95 N take exit 10, pass the airport, turn right at Island Ave and follow the road around; turn right onto Fort Mifflin Rd. Phone 215/685-4192. www.libertynet.org/ftmifflin.* Fort Mifflin is a complex of 11 restored buildings that bring the area's only existing fort to life. It was a Revolutionary War fort strategically located in the Delaware River at the mouth of the Schuylkill. Here, you can climb into a bombproof enclosure used to shelter troops; witness the uniform and weapons demonstrations that take place throughout the year; explore the 4-foot-thick walls of the Arsenal, soldiers' barracks, officers' quarters, and blacksmith's shop; or simply enjoy the spectacular view of Philadelphia and the Delaware from the Northeast Bastion. Self-guided and one-hour guided tours are available. (Apr-Nov, Wed-Sun) **$$**

Franklin Institute Science Museum. *222 N 20th St, Philadelphia (19103). Phone 215/448-1200. sln.fi.edu.* This 300,000-square-foot science museum complex and memorial hall brings biology, earth science, physics, mechanics, aviation, astronomy, communications, and technology to life with a variety of highly interactive exhibits honoring Philadelphia's mechanical inventor Ben Franklin. (A 30-foot marble statue of Franklin sits in a Roman Pantheon-inspired chamber known as the Benjamin Franklin National Memorial.) The kids can play tic-tac-toe with a strategically adept computer, climb into the cockpit of an Air Force jet trainer, experiment with the laws governing flight, or test water quality in the Mandell Center, located in a 38,000-square-foot garden. Stargazers can witness the birth of the universe, see galaxies form, or discover wondrous nebulae under the Fels Planetarium dome. Budding physicists and bike fanatics will appreciate the 28-foot-high bicycle perched on a 1-inch cable demonstrating gyroscopic stability in the Sky Bike exhibit. And every member of the family can lose themselves in the 56-speaker sounds and larger-than-life-size images at the Tuttleman IMAX Theater. (Daily 9:30 am-5 pm; closed holidays) **$$$$**

Franklin Mills Mall. *1455 Franklin Mills Cir, Philadelphia (19154). I-95 and Woodhaven Rd, 15 minutes N of Center City Philadelphia; daily shuttle bus available. Phone 215/632-1500. www.franklin-mills-mall.com.* Bargain hunters will feel like they've hit the jackpot in the more than 200 discount stores in this mega-shopping complex, just 15 miles outside Center City Philadelphia, which touts itself as "Pennsylvania's most visited attraction." Shoppers will find outlets of such well-known retailers as Kenneth Cole, Tommy Hilfiger, Casual Corner, The Gap, Old Navy, Nine West, Neiman Marcus, Saks Fifth Avenue, and Marshalls. There is no sales tax on apparel in Pennsylvania, which makes slashed prices even more appealing. Two food courts, seven restaurants, and a 14-screen movie theater will engage any non-shoppers in the group. If you don't want to fight for a parking spot, take advantage of the daily shuttle services from area hotels, airport, and train stations. (Mon-Sat 10 am-9:30 pm, Sun 11 am-7 pm) **FREE**

The Gallery. *9th and Market sts, Philadelphia (19107). Phone 215/925-7162.* Concentration of 250 shops and restaurants in a four-level mall with glass elevators, trees, fountains, and benches.

Gloria Dei Church National Historic Site. *Columbus Blvd and Christian St, Philadelphia (19147). 8 blocks S of Chestnut. Phone 215/389-1513. www.nps.gov/glde.* (1700) The state's oldest church. Memorial to John Hansen, president of the Continental Congress under the Articles of Confederation. (Daily)

Haverford College. *370 Lancaster Ave, Haverford (19041). 10 miles W on Rte 30. Phone 610/896-1000. www.haverford.edu.* (1833) (1,138 students) Founded by members of the Society of Friends. The 204-acre campus includes Founders Hall; James P. Magill Library; Arboretum; Morris Cricket Library and Collection (by appointment only; phone 610/896-1162). Tours of arboretum and campus.

Historic Bartram's Garden. *54th St and Lindbergh Blvd, Philadelphia (19143). Phone 215/729-5281. www.bartramsgarden.org.* Pre-Revolutionary home of John Bartram, the royal botanist to the colonies under George III, naturalist, and plant explorer. The 18th-century stone farmhouse ($), barn, stable, and cider mill overlook the Schuylkill River. Museum shop. (Daily 10 am-5 pm; closed holidays) **FREE**

Historical Society of Pennsylvania. *1300 Locust St, Philadelphia (19107). Phone 215/732-6200. www.hsp.org.* Museum exhibit features first draft of Constitution, 500 artifacts and manuscripts, plus video tours of turn-of-the-century urban and suburban neighborhoods. Research library and archives house historical and genealogical collections. (Mon, Tues, Thurs-Fri 1-5:30 pm, Wed to 8:30 pm; closed holidays) **$$**

★ **Independence National Historical Park.** *3rd and Chestnut sts, Philadelphia (19106). Phone 215/597-8974.* The park has been called "America's most historic square mile." The Independence Visitor Center at 6th & Market sts has a tour map, information on all park activities and attractions, and a 30-minute film entitled *Independence.* Unless otherwise indicated, all historic sites and museums in the park are open daily and are free. In the park are

Bishop White House. *309 Walnut St, Philadelphia (19106).* (1786-1787) House of Bishop William White, first Episcopal Bishop of Pennsylvania. Restored and furnished. Free tickets at park's Visitor Center. Admission by tour only.

Carpenters' Hall. *320 Chestnut St, Philadelphia (19106).* (1770) Constructed as guild hall; meeting site of First Continental Congress (1774). Historical museum since 1857; still operated by Carpenters Co. Contains original chairs; exhibits of early tools. (Tues-Sun 10 am-4 pm)

Congress Hall. *6th and Chestnut sts, Philadelphia (19106). Phone 215/597-8974.* Congress met here during the last decade of the 18th century. House of Representatives and Senate chambers are restored.

Declaration House. *701 Market St, Philadelphia (19106). Phone 215/597-8974.* Reconstructed house on the site of the writing of the Declaration of Independence by Thomas Jefferson; two rooms Jefferson rented have been reproduced. Short orientation and movie about Jefferson, his philosophy on the common man, and the history of the house.

The First Bank of the United States. *3rd and Walnut sts, Philadelphia. Between Walnut and Chestnut sts.* (1797-1811). Organized by Alexander Hamilton; country's oldest bank building; exterior restored. Closed to the public.

Franklin Court. *316-322 Market St, Philadelphia. Between Market and Chestnut Sts, in block bounded by 3rd and 4th Sts. Phone 215/597-8974.* The site of Benjamin Franklin's house has been developed as a tribute to him; area includes working printing office and bindery, underground museum with multimedia exhibits, an archaeological exhibit, and the B. Franklin Free Post Office.

Independence Hall. *5th and Chestnut sts, Philadelphia. Phone 215/597-8974. www.nps.gov/inde/.* Built in the mid-1700s, Independence Hall is the site of the first public reading of the Declaration of Independence. It also played host to large political rallies during the country's founding years. It is considered a fine example of Georgian architecture. Visitors often find the Hall a good first stop for their tour of Independence National Historic Park, which includes the Liberty Bell (see), Congress Hall (see), Old City Hall (see), and

Carpenter's Hall (see). The building is open for tours only. Admission by tour only.

Independence Square. *Philadelphia. Bounded by Chestnut, Walnut, 5th and 6th sts.* Known as State House Yard in colonial times. Contains Independence Hall, Congress Hall, Old City Hall, and Philosophical Hall.

★ **The Liberty Bell.** *Liberty Bell Center, 6th St between Market and Chestnut sts, Philadelphia. Phone 215/597-8974. www.nps.gov/inde/liberty-bell.* "Proclaim liberty throughout all the land unto all the inhabitants thereof," reads the inscription on this irreparably damaged, 2,000-pound historic bell housed in the Liberty Bell Center. An international icon and one of the most venerated stops in Independence Park, the bell is a representation of the fragile but enduring nature of the republic it reflects. This mostly copper symbol of religious freedom, justice, and independence is believed to hang from its original yoke. (Daily) **FREE**

Library Hall. *105 S 5th St, Philadelphia (19106). Phone 215/440-3400.* Reconstruction of Library Company of Philadelphia (1789-1790) building is occupied by library of American Philosophical Society. Open to scholars. (Mon-Fri)

The Merchant's Exchange. *3rd and Walnut sts, Philadelphia (19106).* Designed by William Strickland, this building is one of the East's finest examples of Greek Revival architecture. Exterior restored; now houses regional offices of the National Park Service. Closed to the public.

Museum Shop (Pemberton House). *Chestnut St, Philadelphia. Between 3rd and 4th sts.* Reconstruction of Quaker merchant's house; now shop with items relating to historic sites.

New Hall Military Museum. *4th and Chestnut sts, Philadelphia. In Carpenters' Court. Phone 215/597-8974.* This reconstruction houses the US Marine Corps Memorial Museum, featuring exhibits on the early history of the Marines, and the Army-Navy Museum. (Daily 2-5 pm)

Old City Hall. *5th and Chestnut sts, Philadelphia (19106).* (1789) Built as City Hall, but was also home of first US Supreme Court, 1791-1800. Exterior restored. Interior depicts the judicial phase of the building.

Philosophical Hall. *104 S 5th St, Philadelphia (19106). 5th St side of Square. www.amphilsoc.org.* (1785-1789) Home of the American Philosophical Society, oldest learned society in America (1743), founded by Benjamin Franklin. Not open to the public.

Thaddeus Kosciuszko National Memorial. *301 Pine St, Philadelphia (19106). Phone 215/597-8974 (voice). www.nps.gov/thko/.* House of Polish patriot during his second visit to US (1797-1798). He was one of the 18th century's greatest champions of American and Polish freedom and one of the first volunteers to come to the aid of the American Revolutionary Army. Exterior and second-floor bedroom have been restored. (Wed-Sun)

Todd House. *4th and Walnut sts, Philadelphia.* (1775) House of Dolley Payne Todd, who later married James Madison and became First Lady; 18th-century furnishings depict middle-class Quaker family life. Free tickets at park's Visitor Center. Admission by tour only.

Independence Seaport Museum. *211 S Columbus Blvd, Philadelphia (19106). Take I-95 to exit 20. At the traffic light turn left onto Columbus Blvd (aka Delaware Ave.). Pass the Hyatt Regency Philadelphia at Penn's Landing on the right; the next building is the Museum. Turn right into the museum just before the bridge. The circular driveway leads to the entrance to the Penn's Landing parking lot. Phone 215/925-5439. www.phillyseaport.org.* Maritime enthusiasts of all ages will appreciate the creative interactive exhibits about the science, history, and art of boat building along the region's waterways at the Independence Seaport Museum. Oral histories of the men and women who have lived and worked here take visitors through immigration, commerce, defense, industry, and the recreational aspects of boats. You can watch how builders assemble a boat, walk (or crawl) through a full-size replica of a Delaware River Shad Skiff, or pull shapes through a 10-foot tank of water to examine drag-affecting speed. Or you can chart a course for Penn's Landing or learn about navigation as you travel beneath a three-story replica of the Ben Franklin Bridge and make your way along a model of the Delaware River. (Daily 10 am-5 pm; closed Jan 1, Thanksgiving, Dec 25) **$$**

Jeweler's Row. *7th and Sansom sts, Philadelphia (19106).* Largest jewelry district in the country other than New York City. More than 300 shops, including wholesalers and diamond cutters.

John Heinz National Wildlife Refuge at Tinicum. *86th and Lindbergh Blvd, Philadelphia (19153). S via I-95, W Hwy 291 exit, right on Bartram Ave, left on 84th St, left on Lindbergh Blvd. Phone 215/365-3118. www.fws.gov.* Largest remaining freshwater tidal wetland in the state, protecting more than 1,000 acres of wildlife habitat. Area was first diked by Swedish farmers in 1643; Dutch farmers and the colonial government added dikes during the Revolutionary War. More than 280 species of birds and 13 resident mammal species. Hiking, bicycling, nature observation, canoeing on Darby Creek, fishing. (Daily 8 am-sunset) **FREE**

Laff House Comedy Club. *221 South St, Philadelphia (19147). Phone 215/440-4242. www.laffhouse.com.* This humor hub located on the city's artsy and alternative South Street hosts comedy events all week. There are Open Mic nights ($), Comedy Spotlights ($$), and comedy competitions. Laff Club attracts up-and-comers as well as established comics such as Dave Attell of Comedy Central's *Insomniac.*

Library. *1901 Vine St, Philadelphia (19103). Logan Sq. Phone 215/686-5322. www.library.phila.gov.* Large central library with over 9 million indexed items in all fields. Rare books, maps, theater scripts, and orchestral scores; automobile reference collections; changing exhibits. (Memorial Day-Labor Day, Tues-Sun; rest of year, daily; closed holidays) **FREE**

Manayunk. *Take 76 from the Center City to Manayunk exit 338. At the bottom of the ramp, turn left and cross the Green Ln bridge to the traffic light, which is Main St, and turn right into Manayunk. Phone 215/482-9565. www.manayunk.com.* This historic district, just 7 miles from Center City, makes a great destination point or place to hang out. Appreciators of old things will marvel over the rail lines, canal locks, and old textile mills dotting this quaint town. Joggers, walkers, hikers, and off-road cyclists will enjoy traveling the towpath that edges the town while their shop-a-holic counterparts check out the more than 70 boutiques and galleries. The word *Manayunk* is derived from the Lenape Indian word *manaiung,* which means "where we go to drink," after the canal that flows into town, and this town offers a selection of charming watering holes. Serious shoppers will find collectibles, furnishings, crafts, clothing, and accessories that you can't find just anywhere.

Masonic Temple. *1 N Broad St, Philadelphia (19107). Phone 215/988-1900. www.pagrandlodge.org/home.html.* Philadelphia's Masonic Temple was designed for the Fraternal Order of Freemasons, of which Benjamin Franklin and George Washington were members. The interior houses seven different halls, including the Gothic Hall, Oriental Hall, and the better-known Egyptian Hall. It showcases treasures of freemasonry, including a book written by Franklin and a Masonic apron of Washington's. A tour helps illuminate the mysteries of this unusual religious order. (Mon-Sat) **FREE**

Morris Arboretum of the University of Pennsylvania. *100 Northwestern Ave, Philadelphia (19128). Approximately 12 miles NW in Chestnut Hill; entrance on Northwestern Ave, between Stenton and Germantown Ave. Phone 215/247-5777. www.upenn.edu/arboretum/.* (1887). Public garden with more than 14,000 accessioned plants on 166 acres; special garden areas such as Swan Pond, Rose Garden, and Japanese gardens. Tours (Sat and Sun afternoon; one each day) (Daily; closed holidays) **$$**

Mummer's Museum. *1100 S 2nd St, Philadelphia (19147). Phone 215/336-3050. riverfrontmummers.com.* Participatory exhibits and displays highlighting the history and tradition of the Mummer's Parade (see SPECIAL EVENTS). Costumes and videotapes of past parades. Free outdoor string band concerts (May-Sept, Tues evenings, weather permitting); 20 string bands, different every week. (Tues-Sun; closed Mon, holidays, and Sun in July-Aug) **$**

Mutter Museum. *19 S 22nd St, Philadelphia (19103). Phone 215/563-3737. www.collphyphil.org/muttpg1.shtml.* This collection of one-of-a-kind, hair-raising medical curiosities includes President Cleveland's jawbone; the thorax of John Wilkes Booth; a plaster cast of Siamese twins; human bones shattered by bullets; a liver in a jar; and a drawer full of buttons, coins, and teeth removed from human stomachs without surgery. Located at the esteemed College of Physicians of Philadelphia, the gallery holds an internationally revered collection of creepy anatomical and pathological specimens, medical instruments, and illustrations. (Mon-Sun 10 am-5 pm; closed Jan 1, Thanksgiving, Dec 25) **$$**

National Museum of American Jewish History. *Independence Mall East, 55 N 5th St (19106). Phone 215/923-3811. www.nmajh.org.* The museum presents experiences and educational programs that preserve, explore, and celebrate the history of Jews in America.

Philadelphia Soft Pretzel

The famous Philadelphia soft pretzel is not your average hard, crunchy, plastic-wrapped snack. You know you're getting the real deal when you are handed this hand-rolled, freshly baked, coarsely salted, buttery, golden-brown comfort food in a paper bag. A Philadelphia pretzel's texture is as vital as its taste: that means not too dry (read: stale) and certainly not too moist. Aficionados claim that Amish girls in hairnets sell the best ones at Fishers in Reading Terminal Market. But serious pretzel hunters can also find these chewy twists of dough, considered to be the country's oldest snack food, in food carts at city intersections, family-owned restaurants, and the airport. Try one with a dollop or two of yellow—not Dijon—mustard.

(Mon-Thurs 10 am-5 pm, Fri to 3 pm, Sun noon-5 pm; closed Jan 1, Thanksgiving, also Jewish holidays) **FREE**

Old Pine Street Presbyterian Church. *412 Pine St, Philadelphia (19106). At 4th St. Phone 215/925-8051.* (1768) Colonial church and graveyard, renovated in 1850s in Greek Revival style. (Daily)

Old St. George's United Methodist Church. *235 N 4th St, Philadelphia (19106). Phone 215/925-7788.* (1769) Oldest Methodist Church in continuous service in the US. Colonial architecture; collection of Methodist memorabilia; has only Bishop Asbury bible and John Wesley chalice cup in America. (Daily)

Old St. Mary's Church. *252 S 4th St, Philadelphia (19106). Between Locust and Spruce sts. Phone 215/923-7930.* (1763) Commodore John Barry, "father of the US Navy," is interred in graveyard behind the city's first Catholic cathedral. (Daily)

Penn's Landing. *Columbus Blvd and Spruce St, Philadelphia (19106).* Here are

Gazela of Philadelphia. *Phone 215/218-0110. www.gazela.com.* (1883) Portuguese square-rigger, tall ship. (Sat-Sun 10 am-5 pm when not sailing)

USS _Olympia_. *Phone 215/925-5439.* Commodore Dewey's flagship during Spanish-American War; restored. Naval museum has weapons, uniforms, ship models, and naval relics of all periods. Also here is World War II submarine, USS *Becuna.* (Daily; closed holidays) **$$$**

Pennsylvania Academy of Fine Arts. *118 N Broad St, Philadelphia. Phone 215/972-7600. www.pafa.org.* This is the nation's oldest art museum and school of fine arts. Within the Gothic Victorian structure are paintings, works on paper, and sculptures by American artists ranging from colonial masters to contemporary artists. Many of the nation's finest artists, including Charles Willson Peale, Mary Cassatt, William Merritt Chase, and Maxfield Parrish, were founders, teachers, or students here. (Tues-Sat) **$$$**

Pennsylvania Ballet. *1101 S Broad St, Philadelphia (19147). Phone 215/336-2000. www.paballet.org.* This company with a George Balanchine influence includes a varied repertoire of ballets ranging from classics like *The Nutcracker* to original works. Performances are held at the Academy of Music and the Merriam Theatre.

Pennsylvania Hospital. *8th and Spruce sts, Philadelphia (19107).* (1751) First in country, founded by Benjamin Franklin.

Pentimenti Gallery. *133 N 3rd St, Philadelphia (19106). Phone 215/625-9990. www.pentimenti.com.* Exhibiting works of art in all modes ranging from figurative to abstract by local, regional, and international artists. (Wed-Sat) **FREE**

Philadelphia 76ers (NBA). *First Union Center, 3601 S Broad St, Philadelphia (19148). At Pattison Ave. Phone 215/339-7676. www.nba.com/sixers/.*

Philadelphia Carriage Company. *500 N 13th St, Philadelphia (19123). Phone 215/922-6840.* Guided tours via horse-drawn carriage covering Society Hill and other historic areas; begin and end on 5th St at Chestnut. (Daily, weather permitting; closed Dec 25) **$$$$**

Philadelphia Eagles (NFL). *Lincoln Financial Field, 11th St and Pattison Ave, Philadelphia (19148). Phone 215/463-2500. www.philadelphiaeagles.com.*

Philadelphia Flyers (NHL). *First Union Center, 3601 S Broad St, Philadelphia (19148). Phone 215/336-2000.*

Philadelphia Phillies (MLB). *Citizens Bank Park, Pattison Ave, Philadelphia (19148). Pattison Ave between 11th and Darien sts. Phone 215/463-5000. www.philadelphiaphillies.com.*

Please Touch Museum for Children. *210 N 21st St, Philadelphia (19103). 21st St and Race. Phone 215/963-0667. www.pleasetouchmuseum.org.* A group of artists, educators, and parents conceived of this award-winning, interactive exploratory learning center for children ages 1 to 7 in 1976. The safe, hands-on learning laboratory has since become a model for children's museums nationwide. Story lovers will enjoy having tea with the Mad Hatter or hanging out with Max in the forest "where the wild things are." Children who don't want to sit still can board the life-size bus or shop at the miniature supermarket. The ones who like to get their hands dirty can engage in science experiments. Creature lovers can interact with fuzzy human-made barnyard animals. And the entertainment-minded can see themselves on television or audition for a news anchor position. (Daily) **$$$**

Reading Terminal Market. *12th and Arch sts, Philadelphia (19107). Phone 215/922-2317. www.readingterminalmarket.org.* The nation's oldest continuously operating farmers' market is alive and well—and thriving—in downtown Philadelphia. An indoor banquet for the senses, the market offers an exhilarating array of baked goods, meats, poultry, seafood, produce, flowers, and Asian, Middle Eastern, and Pennsylvania Dutch foods. Locals recommend the family-run stands, three of which are descendants of the original market. (Mon-Sat 8 am-6 pm)

Rita's Water Ice. *235 South St, Philadelphia (19147). Phone 215/629-3910. www.ritasice.com/contact.html.* The best water ice is not a solid and not quite a liquid, and visitors to Philadelphia will find it at Rita's. With locations throughout the city and surrounding area, Rita's is the city's favorite for frozen water ice, offering a changing selection of smooth, savory water ice, as well as ice cream and gelati. (Daily)

Rittenhouse Square. *1800 Walnut St, Philadelphia (19103). Bordered by 18th, 19th, and Walnut sts. www.rittenhouserow.org.* In the blocks that surround this genteel urban square in Philadelphia's most fashionable section of town are exclusive shops, restaurants, and cafés. Discover what's new at chic boutiques—Francis Jerome, Sophy Curson, Nicole Miller, or Ralph Lauren—or experience department store shopping of old at the historic Wanamaker's building, which is now a Lord & Taylor.

Rodin Museum. *22nd St and Franklin Pkwy, Philadelphia (19101). Phone 215/763-8100. www.rodinmuseum.org.* This museum, built in the Beaux Arts style, houses more than 200 sculptures created by Auguste Rodin (1840-1917) and is considered the largest collection of his works outside his native France. *The Thinker,* Rodin's most famous piece, greets visitors outside at the gateway to the museum. Tours available. (Tues-Sun 10 am-5 pm; closed holidays) **$$**

Schuylkill Center for Environmental Education. *8480 Hagy's Mill Rd, Philadelphia (19128). 9 miles NW. Phone 215/482-7300.* A 500-acre natural area with more than 7 miles of trails; discovery room; gift shop/bookstore. (Daily; closed holidays) **$$**

Sesame Place. *100 Sesame Rd, Philadelphia (19047). 20 miles NE via I-95 to Levittown exit (25 E). Follow signs for the Oxford Valley Mall on the Rte 1 Bypass.* *(See BRISTOL)*

Shops at the Bellevue. *200 S Broad St, Philadelphia (19102). Broad St at Walnut. Phone 215/875-8350.* Beaux Arts architecture of the former Bellevue Stratford Hotel has been preserved and transformed; it now contains offices, a hotel, and a four-level shopping area centered around an atrium court. (Mon-Sat)

Society Hill Area. *7th and Lombard sts, Philadelphia (19106). Area between the Delaware River and Washington Sq (5th St), bounded by Walnut St to the N and Lombard St to the S. www.ushistory.org/tour/tour_sochill.htm.* Secret parks, cobblestone walkways, and diminutive alleys among beautifully restored brick colonial town-homes make this historic area a treasure for visitors. A popular daily 30-minute walking tour will inspire history fans as well architecture lovers. Highlights along the way include a courtyard designed by famed architect I. M. Pei; gardens planted by the Daughters of the American Revolution; a sculpture of Robert Morris, one of the signers of the Declaration of Independence; Greek Revival-style architecture now home to the National Portrait Gallery; and the burial ground of Revolutionary War soldiers. Admire the gardens, immerse yourself in the history of Independence National Historical Park, or stroll through the exquisitely landscaped Washington Square Park. In the summer months, the area hosts outdoor arts festivals in Headhouse Square. It's also home to some of Philadelphia's finest restaurants. In this area are

Athenaeum of Philadelphia. *219 S 6th St, Philadelphia. Phone 215/925-2688. www.philaathenaeum.org.* Landmark example of Italian Renaissance architecture (1845-1847); restored building has American neoclassical-style decorative arts, paintings, sculpture; research library; furniture and art from the collection of Joseph Bonaparte, King of Spain and older brother of Napoleon; changing exhibits of architectural drawings, photos, and rare books. Tours by appointment. (Mon-Fri; closed holidays) **FREE**

Physick House. *321 S 4th St, Philadelphia. Phone 215/925-7866.* (1786) House of Dr. Philip Sung Physick, "father of American surgery," from 1815-1837. Restored Federal-style house with period furnishings; garden. (Thurs-Sun afternoons) **$$**

Powel House. *244 S 3rd St, Philadelphia. Phone 215/627-0364.* (1765) Georgian townhouse of Samuel Powel, last colonial mayor of Philadelphia and first mayor under the new republic. Period furnishings, silver and porcelain; garden. Tours (Thurs-Sun afternoons; closed holidays). **$$**

South Street District. *From the Schuylkill Expy, take the South St exit east. From the Center City area, it's 5 blocks south of Market St. Phone 215/413-3713. www.south-street.com.* On South Street, the young and hip will enjoy the search for thrift store finds, the aroma of incense, the light refracting from crystals, and a fashion show of the pierced and tattooed sort. The rest can rifle through dusty rare books, cruise the art galleries, or try on every manner of hat. These blocks at the southern boundary of the city—as well as the numbered streets just off of it—are chock full of offbeat shops, cafés, street musicians, and water ice stands, all within walking distance of Penn's Landing and Society Hill. For a Philadelphia signature treat, visitors of all tastes should not miss the legendary Jim's Steaks for cheesesteaks.

St. Peter's Church. *3rd and Pine sts, Philadelphia (19106). Phone 215/925-5968. www.stpetersphila.org.* (1761 Episcopal) Georgian colonial architecture; numerous famous people buried in churchyard.

Stenton House. *4601 N 18th St, Philadelphia (19140). 18th St between Courtland St and Windrim Ave. Phone 215/329-7312. www.stenton.org.* (1723-1730) Mansion built by James Logan, secretary to William Penn. Excellent example of Pennsylvania colonial architecture, furnished with 18th- and 19th-century antiques. General Washington spent Aug 23, 1777, here and General Sir William Howe headquartered here for the Battle of Germantown. Colonial barn, gardens, kitchen. (Apr-Dec, Tues-Sat afternoons; rest of year, by appointment; closed holidays) **$$**

Temple University. *Cecil B Moore Ave and Broad St, Philadelphia (19122). Phone 215/204-7000. www.temple.edu.* (1884) (33,000 students) Undergraduate, professional, and research school. Walking tours of campus.

The Trocadero Theatre. *1003 Arch St, Philadelphia (19107). Phone 215/922-5483. www.thetroc.com.* This former 1870s opera house hosted vaudeville, burlesque, and Chinese movies before it became the beautiful, contemporary live music venue that it is today. The theater, which includes upstairs and downstairs seating, now hosts many well-known rock and pop artists, as well as the annual eight-hour Philadelphia Pop Festival held in June, which highlights local bands. Recently, it has gone back to one of its previous incarnations—a movie house. On "Movie Mondays," the theater holds free screenings (on its original screen) of such classic movies as *Apocalypse Now* and *Escape from New York*.

University of Pennsylvania. *Chestnut to Pine Sts and 32nd to 40th sts. Phone 215/898-5000. www.upenn.edu.* (1740) (23,000 students) On campus are the restored Fisher Fine Arts Library (phone 215/898-8325), Annenberg Center for performing arts (phone 215/898-6791); University Museum of Archaeology and Anthropology and the Institute of Contemporary Art, located at 36th and Sansom sts (Wed-Sun; phone 215/898-7108; fee). Also here is

University of Pennsylvania Museum of Archaeology and Anthropology. *33rd and Spruce sts, Philadelphia. Phone 215/898-4000. www.upenn.edu/museum/.* World-famous archaeological and ethnographic collections developed from the museum's own expeditions, gifts, and purchases; features Chinese, Near Eastern, Greek, ancient Egyptian, African, Pacific, and North, Middle, and South American materials; library. Restaurant, shops. (Tues-Sun; closed holidays, also Sun in summer) **$$**

US Mint. *5th and Arch sts, Philadelphia (19106). On Independence Mall. Phone 215/408-0114. www.usmint .gov.* Produces coins of all denominations. Gallery affords visitors an elevated view of the coinage operations. Medal making may also be observed. Audiovisual, self-guided tours. Rittenhouse Room on the mezzanine contains historic coins, medals, and other exhibits. (July-Aug, daily; rest of year, Mon-Fri; closed Jan 1, Thanksgiving, Dec 25) **FREE**

Wagner Free Institute of Science. *1700 W Montgomery Ave, Philadelphia (19121). At 17th St. Phone 215/763-6529.* Victorian science museum with more than 50,000 specimens illustrating the various branches of the natural sciences. Dinosaur bones, fossils, reptiles, and rare species are all mounted in the Victorian style. Reference library and research archives. (Tues-Fri) **FREE**

Walnut Street Theatre. *825 Walnut St, Philadelphia (19107). At 9th St. Phone 215/574-3550. www. wstonline.org.* (1809) America's oldest theater. The Walnut Mainstage offers musicals, classical, and contemporary plays. Two studio theaters provide a forum for new and avant-garde works.

Washington Square. *Walnut and 6th sts, Philadelphia (19107).* Site where hundreds of Revolutionary War soldiers and victims of the yellow fever epidemic are buried. Life-size statue of Washington has tomb of Revolutionary War's Unknown Soldier at its feet. Across the street is

Philadelphia Savings Fund Society Building. (1816) Site of oldest savings bank in the US. Not open to the public.

Wok N' Walk Tours of Philadelphia Chinatown. *1002 Arch St, Philadelphia (19107). Located at the corner of 10th and Arch sts in Center City. Phone 215/928-9333. www.josephkpoon.com/home.* Considered one of the best culinary tours in the country, Joseph Poon's Wok N' Walk Tour is rich with Chinese history and culture as well as calories. This two-and-a-half-hour tour begins at Poon's Asian restaurant. (Be sure to try Chef Poon's trademark potato carvings.) Walkers are treated to a tai chi demonstration, Poon's state-of-the-art kitchen, and a vegetable carving lesson. Along the tour, you visit a Chinese herbal medicine expert, a fortune cookie factory, and a Chinese noodle shop; see exotic fish and places of worship; and, best of all, snack on free samples from a Chinese bakery in one of the city's more vibrant ethnic communities. (Daily) **$$$$**

Special Events

American Music Theater Festival. *123 S Broad St, Philadelphia (19109). Phone 215/893-1570.* Repertory includes new opera, musical comedy, cabaret-style shows, revues, and experimental works. Mainstage productions Mar-June.

Army-Navy Football Game. *John F. Kennedy Memorial Stadium or Veterans Stadium.* First Sat in Dec.

The Book and the Cook. *1528 Walnut St, Philadelphia (19102). Phone 215/686-3662.* Sample fine cuisine as world-famous cookbook authors team up with the city's most respected chefs to create culinary delights. Wine tastings, market tours, film festival. Mar.

CoreStates US Pro Cycling Championship. *Broad and Walnut sts, Philadelphia (19102).* At 156 miles, it's the longest (and richest) single-day cycling event in the country. Mid-June.

Delaware Valley First Fridays. *In the Old City, 2nd and 3rd sts, from Market to Race. www.dvfirstfridays .com.* First Fridays is a citywide cultural event that takes place at rotating venues with alternating formats on the first Friday of every month, with socializing and networking as goals. Galleries, shops, theaters, restaurants, and sidewalks in the Old City area along Second and Third streets from Market to Race have hosted record label release parties, live concerts, comedy shows, children's festivals, fashion shows, and vendor expositions. Proceeds go to African-American charitable organizations. First Fri of every month.

Devon Horse Show. *Approximately 20 miles NW via Hwy 30, at Horse Show Grounds, in Devon. Phone 610/964-0550. www.thedevonhorseshow.org.* One of America's leading equestrian events. More than 1,200 horses compete; country fair; antique carriage drive. Nine days beginning Memorial Day weekend.

Elfreth's Alley Fete Days. *126 Elfreth's Alley, Philadelphia (19106). Phone 215/574-0560. www.elfrethsalley.org.* Homes open to the public, costumed guides, demonstrations of colonial crafts; food, entertainment. Second weekend in June.

Fairmount Park Historical Christmas Tours. *2600 Ben Franklin Pkwy, Philadelphia (19130). Phone 215/684-7922.* Period decorations in 18th-century mansions. Early Dec.

Head House Open Air Craft Market. *Pine and 2nd sts, Philadelphia (19147). In Society Hill area in Head House Sq.* Crafts demonstrations, children's workshops. Sat and Sun, June-Aug.

Horse racing. *Philadelphia Park, 3001 Street Rd, Bensalem (19020). Phone 215/639-9000. www.philadelphiapark.com.* Flat racing at Philadelphia Park.

Mann Center for the Performing Arts. *Fairmount Park, 123 S Broad St, #1930, Philadelphia (19131). 52nd St and Parkside Ave. Phone 215/546-7900. www.manncenter.org.* Orchestra performs late June-July, Mon, Wed, and Thurs. Also popular music attractions. June-Sept.

Mummer's Parade. *1100 S 2nd St, Philadelphia (19147). Phone 215/336-3050. www.mummers.com.* The Mummer's Parade is Philadelphia's version of New Orleans' Mardi Gras or Spain's Carnival. It is an annual tradition to dress in outlandish costumes and noisily parade down the streets of Philadelphia on New Year's Day (the word *mummer* comes from an old French word that means to wear a mask). Jan 1.

The Opera Company of Philadelphia. *Academy of Music, 510 Walnut St, Philadelphia (19106). Phone 215/928-2100. www.operaphilly.com/.* Oct-Apr.

PECO Energy Jazz Festival. *2301 Market St, Philadelphia (19101). Phone toll-free 800/537-7676.* Jazz concerts around the city. Four days mid-Feb.

Penn Relays. *Franklin Field, 235 S 33rd St, Philadelphia (19104). 33rd and South sts. Phone 215/898-6151. www.thepennrelays.com.* These races originally served as a way to dedicate Franklin Field to the University of Pennsylvania. That was in 1895. Today, the Penn Relays hold the record for being the longest uninterrupted amateur track meet in the country. Thousands of men and women, ranging in age from 8 to 80, have competed. More than 400 races take place, one every five minutes, to keep spectators glued. Last weekend in Apr. **$$$**

Philadelphia Flower Show. *Pennsylvania Convention Center, 12th and Arch sts, Philadelphia (19107). Phone 215/988-8899. www.theflowershow.com.* The country's first formal flower show took place here in 1829 in the city's Masonic Hall on Chestnut Street. More than 150 years later, exotic and rare flowers are still on display in this town, but in a new location: the Pennsylvania Convention Center. Flower lovers will be dazzled by more than 275,000 flowers from Africa, Germany, Japan, England, France, Holland, Italy, and Belgium. Early Mar. **$$$$**

Philadelphia Open House. *325 Walnut St, Philadelphia (19106). Phone 215/928-1188.* House and garden tours in different neighborhoods; distinguished selection of over 150 private homes, gardens, historic sites. Many tours include lunches, candlelight dinners, or high teas. Late Apr-mid-May.

Philadelphia Theatre Company. *Plays and Players Theatre, 1714 Delancey St, Philadelphia (19103). Phone 215/568-1920.* Four contemporary American plays per season. Oct-June.

Robin Hood Dell East. *Fairmount Park, 33rd and Ridge sts, Philadelphia (19101). Phone 215/685-9560. www.delleast.org.* Top stars in popular music stage outdoor concerts. July-Aug.

Thanksgiving Day Parade. *Franklin Pkwy, Philadelphia (19103). Phone 215/878-9700.* Giant floats; celebrities.

Limited-Service Hotels

★ BEST WESTERN INDEPENDENCE PARK HOTEL. *235 Chestnut St, Philadelphia (19106). Phone 215/922-4443; fax 215/922-4487. www.bestwestern.com.* Located in historic Old City Philadelphia, this hotel—on the National Register of Historic Places—blends in well with its surroundings. The city's most historic square mile, Society Hill, Penn's Landing, and Independence National Historic Park are all nearby. Start the day with a complimentary European-style breakfast, including make-your-own Belgian waffles, served in a glass-enclosed courtyard. Afternoon tea and cookies are served in the Grand Parlor. The traditionally decorated guest rooms boast high ceilings and modern baths. 36 rooms. Pets accepted, some restrictions; fee. Complimentary continental breakfast. Check-in 3 pm, check-out noon. **$**

★★ **COURTYARD BY MARRIOTT.** *21 N Juniper St, Philadelphia (19107). Phone 215/496-3200; toll-free 800/321-2211; fax 215/496-3696. www.courtyard.com.* 498 rooms, 15 story. Check-in 3 pm, check-out noon. High-speed Internet access. Restaurant, bar. Fitness room. Indoor pool, whirlpool. Business center. **$**

★★ **DOUBLETREE HOTEL.** *237 S Broad St, Philadelphia (19107). Phone 215/893-1600; fax 215/893-1663. www.doubletree.com.* 434 rooms, 26 story. Check-out noon. Restaurant, bar. Fitness room. Indoor pool, whirlpool. Airport transportation available. **$**

★★ **DOUBLETREE HOTEL.** *640 W Germantown Pike, Plymouth Meeting (19462). Phone 610/834-8300; toll-free 800/222-TREE; fax 610/834-1751. www.doubletree.com.* 252 rooms, 7 story, all suites. Check-in 3 pm, check-out noon. Restaurant, bar. Fitness room. Indoor pool, children's pool, whirlpool. Airport transportation available. **$$**

★★ **EMBASSY SUITES CITY CENTER.** *1776 Benjamin Franklin Pkwy, Philadelphia (19103). Phone 215/561-1776; fax 215/561-5930. www.embassysuites.com.* Enjoy panoramic views of the city from the balconies of this all-suite hotel, located just off of historic Logan Square. Within the approximately 750-square-foot suites, guests enjoy a separate living room with a queen-size sleeper sofa and dining area, plus a bedroom. Suites are equipped with conveniences such as microwave ovens, refrigerators, and coffeemakers. In-suite dataports, high-speed Internet connections, and voice mail cater to business travelers' needs. 288 rooms, all suites. Check-in 4 pm, check-out noon. High-speed Internet access. Restaurant, bar. Airport transportation available. Business center. **$**

★★ **HILTON GARDEN INN.** *1100 Arch St, Philadelphia (19107). Phone 215/923-0100; toll-free 800/774-1500; fax 215/925-0800. www.hiltongardeninn.com.* This hotel's location—adjacent to the Pennsylvania Convention Center and attached to the Gallery Mall, with more than 150 shops and restaurants—makes it convenient for both business and leisure travelers. Guest rooms and suites are equipped with modern conveniences and technology. Hotel services and amenities include a complimentary 24-hour business center and Pavilion Pantry featuring beverages and snacks. A restaurant and lounge on the top floor overlook the city. 279 rooms. Check-in 4 pm, check-out 11 am. High-speed Internet access. Restaurant, bar. Fitness room. Indoor pool, whirlpool. Business center. **$**

★★ **THE RADISSON PLAZA WARWICK HOTEL.** *1701 Locust St, Philadelphia (19103). Phone 215/735-6000; fax 215/789-6105. www.radisson.com.* 545 rooms, 21 story. Check-out noon. Restaurant, bar. Fitness room. **$$**

Full-Service Hotels

★★★★ **FOUR SEASONS HOTEL PHILADELPHIA.** *1 Logan Sq, Philadelphia (19103). Phone 215/963-1500; fax 215/963-9506. www.fourseasons.com/philadelphia.* Philadelphia's rich heritage comes alive at the Four Seasons Hotel. Located on historic Logan Square, the hotel puts the city's museums, shops, and businesses within easy reach. The eight-story Four Seasons is a Philadelphia institution in itself, from its dramatic Swann Fountain to its highly rated Fountain Restaurant (see), considered one of the better dining establishments in town. The rooms and suites are a celebration of federalist décor, and some accommodations incorporate little luxuries like deep soaking tubs and high-speed Internet access. City views of the Academy of Natural Science, Logan Square, and the tree-lined Ben Franklin Parkway provide a sense of place for some guests, while other rooms offer tranquil views over the inner courtyard and gardens. The Four Seasons spa focuses on nourishing treatments, while the indoor pool resembles a tropical oasis with breezy palm trees and large skylights. 364 rooms, 8 story. Pets accepted, some restrictions. Check-in 3 pm, check-out noon. High-speed Internet access. Restaurant, bar. Fitness room, spa. Indoor pool, whirlpool. Business center. **$$$**

★ ★ ★ **THE HILTON INN AT PENN.** *3600 Sansom St, Philadelphia (19104). Phone 215/222-0200; toll-free 800/774-1500; fax 215/222-4600. www.hilton .com.* Experience a distinctly collegiate environment at this hotel, located in the middle of Penn's campus, not far from Philadadelphia's central business district. Travelers find the Inn at Penn easily accessible from I-76, Amtrak's 30th Street Station, and the Philadelphia International Airport. The Penn Restaurant and Wine Bar features regional Italian cuisine with fresh pasta made daily. 238 rooms. Check-in 3 pm, check-out noon. High-speed Internet access. Two restaurants, two bars. Whirlpool. Business center. **$$**

★ ★ ★ **HYATT REGENCY PHILADELPHIA AT PENN'S LANDING.** *201 S Columbus Blvd, Philadelphia (19106). Phone 215/928-1234; fax 215/ 521-6600. www.hyatt.com.* 363 rooms, 22 story. Check-in 3 pm, check-out noon. High-speed Internet access. Restaurant, bar. Fitness room. Indoor pool, whirlpool. Business center. **$**

★ ★ ★ **LATHAM HOTEL.** *135 S 17th St, Philadelphia (19103). Phone 215/563-7474; toll-free 877/528-4261; fax 215/568-0110. www.lathamhotel .com.* This charming hotel is a favorite of guests looking for an intimate setting in downtown Philly. Conveniently located, it is just blocks away from Independence Hall and the Pennsylvania Convention Center. 139 rooms, 14 story. Check-out noon. Restaurant, bar. Fitness room. Business center. **$**

★ ★ ★ **LOEWS PHILADELPHIA HOTEL.** *1200 Market St, Philadelphia (19107). Phone 215/627-1200; fax 215/564-1985. www.loewshotels.com.* 583 rooms, 32 story. Check-in 3 pm, check-out noon. High-speed Internet access. Restaurant, bar. Fitness room. Indoor pool, whirlpool. Business center. **$$**

★ ★ ★ **MARRIOTT PHILADELPHIA AIRPORT.** *One Arrivals Rd, Philadelphia (19153). Phone 215/492-9000; fax 215/492-6799. www.marriott.com.* 419 rooms, 15 story. Check-in 4 pm, check-out noon. High-speed Internet access. Restaurant, bar. Fitness room. Indoor pool, whirlpool. Business center. **$$**

★ ★ ★ **MARRIOTT PHILADELPHIA DOWNTOWN.** *1201 Market St, Philadelphia (19107). Phone 215/625-2900; fax 215/625-6000. www.marriott .com.* 1,408 rooms, 20 story. Check-out noon. Restaurant, bar. Fitness room. Indoor pool, children's pool, whirlpool. Business center. **$$$**

★ ★ ★ **MARRIOTT PHILADELPHIA WEST.** *111 Crawford Ave, West Conshohocken (19428). Phone 610/941-5600; toll-free 800/237-3639; fax 610/941-4425. www.marriott.com.* This hotel is located just miles from the Valley Forge National Park, Philadelphia Zoo, Museum of Art, and the Franklin Institute, as well as many other local points of interest. 286 rooms, 17 story. Check-in 3 pm, check-out noon. High-speed Internet access. Restaurant, bar. Fitness room. Indoor pool, whirlpool. Airport transportation available. **$$**

★ ★ ★ **OMNI HOTEL AT INDEPENDENCE PARK.** *401 Chestnut St, Philadelphia (19106). Phone 215/925-0000; fax 215/931-4260. www.omnihotels.com.* 150 rooms, 14 story. Check-in 4 pm, check-out 11 am. Restaurant, bar. Fitness room. Indoor pool, whirlpool. Business center. **$$**

★ ★ ★ **PARK HYATT PHILADELPHIA.** *Broad and Walnut sts, Philadelphia (19102). Phone 215/ 893-1234; toll-free 800/228-9000; fax 215/732-8518. www.parkphiladelphia.hyatt.com.* 172 rooms, 5 story. Check-in 3 pm, check-out noon. Restaurant, bar. Fitness room, spa. Whirlpool. Business center. **$$$**

★ ★ ★ **PENN'S VIEW HOTEL.** *Front and Market sts, Philadelphia (19106). Phone 215/922-7600; toll-free 800/331-7634; fax 215/922-7642. www.pennsviewhotel .com.* 54 rooms, 5 story. Complimentary continental breakfast. Check-in 3 pm, check-out noon. Restaurant. Airport transportation available. **$$**

★ ★ ★ **RADNOR HOTEL.** *591 E Lancaster Ave, Saint Davids (19087). Phone 610/688-5800; toll-free 800/ 537-3000; fax 610/341-3299. www.radnorhotel.com.* 171 rooms, 4 story. Check-out noon. Restaurant, bar. Fitness room. Pool, children's pool. Airport transportation available. Business center. **$$**

★★★ THE RITTENHOUSE HOTEL. *210 W Rittenhouse Sq, Philadelphia (19103). Phone 215/546-9000; toll-free 800/635-1042; fax 215/732-3364. www.rittenhousehotel.com.* The Rittenhouse Hotel is a jewel in the heart of Philadelphia. This intimate hotel occupies a particularly enviable address across from the leafy Rittenhouse Square and among the prestigious town houses of this exclusive area. The accommodations are among the most spacious in the city and are decorated with a sophisticated flair. Guests at The Rittenhouse are treated to the highest levels of personalized service. Fitness and business centers cater to travelers visiting for work or pleasure, while the Adolf Biecker Spa and Salon pampers and primps its clients in a peaceful setting. From the mood-lifting décor of the gracious Cassatt Lounge and the striking contemporary style of Lacroix (see) to the rowing memorabilia of Boathouse Row Bar and the traditional steakhouse feel of Smith & Wollensky, the Rittenhouse Hotel also provides memorable dining experiences to match every taste. 98 rooms, 9 story. Pets accepted, some restrictions. Check-in 3 pm, check-out 1 pm. High-speed Internet access. Restaurant, bar. Fitness room, spa. Indoor pool. Business center. **$$**

★★★ THE RITZ-CARLTON, PHILADELPHIA. *Ten Avenue of the Arts, Philadelphia (19102). Phone 215/523-8000; toll-free 888/505-3914; fax 215/568-0942. www.ritzcarlton.com.* The Ritz-Carlton breathes new life into a magnificent historic building in the center of Philadelphia's downtown business district. This one-time home to Girard and Mellon Banks was designed in the 1900s by the architectural firm of McKim, Mead, and White, and was inspired by Rome's Pantheon. Marrying historic significance with trademark Ritz-Carlton style, this Philadelphia showpiece boasts handsome and striking décor. Impressive marble columns dominate the lobby, where guests can pause for reflection over light meals in the Rotunda. The rooms and suites are the last word in luxury, while Club Level accommodations transport guests to heaven with a private lounge filled with five food and beverage selections daily. Dedicated to exceeding visitors' expectations, The Ritz-Carlton even offers a pillow menu, a bath butler, and other unique services. Dining options are plentiful, and the Sunday jazz brunch is a local favorite. 330 rooms, 31 story. Pets accepted, some restrictions; fee. Check-in 3 pm, check-out noon. High-speed Internet access. Restaurant, bar. Fitness room. Business center. **$$**

★★★ SHERATON RITTENHOUSE SQUARE, AN ENVIRONMENTAL HOTEL. *227 S 18th St, Philadelphia (19103). Phone 215/546-9400; fax 215/893-0955. www.sheratonrittenhouse.com.* 193 rooms, 16 story. Complimentary continental breakfast. Check-in 3 pm, check-out noon. Restaurant, bar. Children's activity center. Fitness room. Airport transportation available. Business center. **$$$**

★★★ SHERATON SOCIETY HILL. *One Dock St, Philadelphia (19106). Phone 215/238-6000; toll-free 888/345-7333; fax 215/238-6652. www.sheraton.com.* Situated in downtown Philadelphia, this hotel is conveniently located near Independence Hall, Society Hill, the Liberty Bell, the Philadelphia Zoo, and the Pennsylvania Convention Center. 378 rooms, 4 story. Check-out noon. Restaurant, bar. Fitness room. Indoor pool, children's pool, whirlpool. **$**

★★★ SHERATON UNIVERSITY CITY. *36th and Chestnut sts, Philadelphia (19104). Phone 215/387-8000; fax 215/387-7920. www.sheraton.com.* 374 rooms, 15 story. Check-in 3 pm, check-out noon. Restaurant, bar. Fitness room. Outdoor pool, whirlpool. Business center. **$**

★★★ SOFITEL. *120 S 17th St, Philadelphia (19103). Phone 215/569-8300; toll-free 800/SOFITEL; fax 215/569-1492. www.sofitel.com.* Modern French style permeates the Sofitel Philadelphia. This elegant hotel sits on the former site of the Philadelphia Stock Exchange, and its downtown location makes it ideal for business travelers. The rooms and suites are exceedingly stylish, with soft colors offset by bold fabrics. Warm and inviting, the accommodations welcome with a variety of thoughtful touches, such as fresh flowers and plush towels. This hotel is the essence of relaxed elegance, and its fashionable design extends to the restaurant and bar. Comfortable chic defines the lobby bar, La Bourse, while the bistro fare and unique setting of Chez Colette recall the romance of 1920s Paris. 306 rooms, 14 story. Pets accepted, some restrictions; fee. Check-in 3 pm, check-out noon. High-speed Internet access. Restaurant, bar. Fitness room. Pool, whirlpool. Business center. **$$**

Specialty Lodgings

The following lodging establishments are approved by Mobil Travel Guide, but due to their unique and individualized nature have not been given a traditional Mobil Star rating. Included in this listing you may find bed-and-breakfasts, limited-service inns, guest ranches, and other unique hotel properties.

ALEXANDER INN. *Spruce and 12th sts, Philadelphia (19107). Phone 215/923-3535; toll-free 877/253-9466; fax 215/923-1004. www.alexanderinn.com.* This restored, historic structure houses a relatively new hotel, designed with modern Deco décor reminiscent of the lavish cruise ships of the 1930s. The public spaces and the 48 guest rooms are adorned with beautiful artwork. All accommodations have private baths. Work off the baked goods from the daily breakfast buffet in the 24-hour fitness center, or walk the nearby Antique Row. The Betsy Ross House, Penn's Landing, and the Historic District of Independence Hall are all nearby. 48 rooms. Complimentary continental breakfast. Check-in 3 pm, check-out noon. Fitness room. **$**

GASKILL HOUSE B&B. *312 Gaskill St, Philadelphia (19147). Phone 215/413-0669. www.gaskillhouse.com.* Check into this bed-and-breakfast—a private residence since 1828, listed with the National Registry of Historic Homes—and enter a tranquil oasis in the heart of Philadelphia's Society Hill historic district. The fully restored double townhouse blends period furnishings with modern comforts and amenities, including private bath and either a whirlpool or fireplace in each of the three guest rooms. After a day spent exploring nearby attractions, relax in the library or private sun garden. Guests are served a complimentary full American breakfast each morning. 3 rooms. Complimentary full breakfast. Check-in 3-6 pm, check-out 11 am. **$$**

RITTENHOUSE SQUARE B&B. *1715 Rittenhouse Sq, Philadelphia (19103). Phone 215/546-6500; toll-free 877/791-6500; fax 215/546-8787. www.rittenhousebb.com.* This renovated 1900s carriage house affords guests a choice of ten deluxe rooms in an ideal setting just off of Rittenhouse Square—one of the city's most fashionable locations. Rooms feature marble bathrooms, telephone and cable TV, and workstations with Internet access. Guests are made comfortable with 24-hour concierge service, nightly turndown service, a nightly complimentary wine and snack reception, and continental breakfast served in the café. 10 rooms. Complimentary continental breakfast. Check-in 3 pm, check-out noon. **$$**

THOMAS BOND HOUSE. *129 S 2nd St, Philadelphia (19106). Phone 215/923-8523; toll-free 800/845-2663; fax 215/923-8504.* 12 rooms, 2 story. Complimentary continental breakfast. Check-in 3-9 pm, check-out noon. Airport transportation available. Restored guest house (1769) built by Dr. Thomas Bond, founder of the country's first public hospital. **$**

Restaurants

★★ **ADEN RESTAURANT.** *614 N 2nd St, Philadelphia (19123). Phone 215/627-9844; fax 215/925-9771. www.adenrestaurant.com.* Mediterranean menu. Lunch, dinner. Casual attire. Outdoor seating. **$$**

★★ **ADRIATICA.** *217 Chestnut St, Philadelphia (19106). Phone 215/592-8001; fax 215/592-8002. www.adriaticarestaurant.com.* Mediterranean, seafood menu. Dinner, late-night. Bar. Casual attire. Outdoor seating. **$$**

★★★ **AZALEA.** *401 Chestnut St, Philadelphia (19106). Phone 215/925-0000; fax 215/925-1263. www.omnihotelindependencepark.com.* Just a block from historic Independence Hall and the Liberty Bell, this restaurant at the Omni Hotel at Independence Park (see) is a restful spot to enjoy a meal. The décor is stylishly eclectic, and executive chef Peter Paul Meyer's menus are rooted in classic French technique, and feature contemporary touches and international accents. Dishes range from comfortingly rich (house-made herb spaetzle baked with Gruyere and Emmantal cheeses and assorted summer vegetables) to heart-healthy (mustard-glazed salmon over golden whipped potatoes with a sauce ver jus and baby bok choy). American menu. Dinner. Bar. Casual attire. Valet parking. **$$$**

★★ **BISTRO ROMANO.** *120 Lombard St, Philadelphia (19147). Phone 215/925-8880; fax 215/925-9888. www.bistroromano.com.* Italian menu. Dinner. Closed Jan 1, Thanksgiving, Dec 25. Bar. Children's menu. **$$**

★★ **BOOKBINDER'S.** *215 S 15th St, Philadelphia (19102). Phone 215/545-1137; fax 215/732-2560.* Seafood menu. Lunch, dinner. Closed Thanksgiving, Dec 25. Bar. Children's menu. Casual attire. **$$$**

★★★★ **BRASSERIE PERRIER.** *1619 Walnut St, Philadelphia (19103). Phone 215/568-3000; fax 215/568-7855. www.brasserieperrier.com.* Brasserie Perrier, the less formal, younger sibling of Le Bec-Fin (see), is a terrific spot for first-rate modern French fare with Italian and Asian influences. While the menu is more reasonably priced than the one at its more refined relative, the quality here remains just as high. In traditional French brasserie style, you'll find plats du jour, steak frites, and frisée aux lardons among other perfectly prepared standards. The kitchen also departs from the traditional brasserie-style menu, offering a fantastic selection of sweet and savory fondues (a ton of fun to share as an appetizer or for dessert), as well as creative takes on pasta and entrées painted with eclectic flavors from around the globe. The impressive wine list is mostly French, although some American bottles are also featured. The modern Art Deco dining room is warmed by plush banquettes, vintage silver leaf ceilings, light cherry wood, and golden lighting, making it a wonderful choice for many occasions, from an after-work drink to a lunch meeting. French menu. Lunch, dinner. Closed holidays. Bar. Reservations recommended. Valet parking. Outdoor seating. **$$$**

★★ **BRIDGET FOY'S SOUTH STREET GRILL.** *2nd and South sts, Philadelphia (19147). Phone 215/922-1813; fax 215/922-6551. www.bridgetfoys.com.* Lunch, dinner. Closed Thanksgiving, Dec 25. Bar. Outdoor seating. **$$**

★★★ **BUDDAKAN.** *325 Chestnut St, Philadelphia (19106). Phone 215/574-9440; fax 215/574-8994. www.buddakan.com.* Slick, sexy, and spectacular, Buddakan is one of Philadelphia's hottest spots for dining, drinking, and lounging. Whether you're seated in the shadow of the restaurant's 10-foot gilded Buddha at the elevated communal table or at one of the other more intimate tables for two in chairs backed with black-and-white photo portraits, you will never guess that this den of fabulousness was once a post office. If your mail carrier were feasting on Buddakan's brand of splashy Asian fusion fare, like lobster fried rice with Thai basil and saffron and crisp thin pizza topped with seared tuna and wasabi, you can be sure that the mail would never arrive on time. Entrées are meant for sharing and arrive steamy and fragrant, arranged with a minimalist, Zenlike artistry. The wine and sake list is impressive, as is the lengthy selection of house cocktails. A nice way to kick off the evening is with the signature Buddalini, a sexy sipper made from Champagne, Cointreau, and fresh mango juice. Pan-Asian menu. Lunch, dinner. Closed holidays. Two bars. **$$$**

★★ **CAFE SPICE.** *35 S 2nd St, Philadelphia (19106). Phone 215/627-6273; fax 215/627-6280. www.cafespice.com.* Indian menu. Lunch, dinner, late-night. Bar. Outdoor seating. **$$**

★★★ **CHEZ COLETTE.** *120 S 17th St, Philadelphia (19103). Phone 215/569-8300.* French menu. Breakfast, lunch, dinner. Bar. **$$$**

★★★ **CIRCA.** *1518 Walnut St, Philadelphia (19102). Phone 215/545-6800; fax 215/545-7683. www.circarestaurant.com.* Still echoing its past function as a bank, the building that houses Circa offers guests the chance to dine in a vault, or under the soaring cathedral ceiling of the original bank proper. Austere setting aside, executive chef Tom Harkin's Mediterranean menu is all warmth and sunshine. Wood-grilled prawns come with sweet corn mashed potatoes and sun-dried tomato reduction. There's a superb Moroccan lamb sirloin with grilled fennel, tomato, and chicken puree, and the pan-roasted organic chicken is stuffed with sweet sausage and served with a confit of leg meat and mustard spaetzle. Desserts also glow. Lunch, dinner. Closed Jan 1, Dec 25. Bar. Valet parking. **$$$**

★★ **CITY TAVERN.** *138 S 2nd St, Philadelphia (19106). Phone 215/413-1443; fax 215/413-3043. www.citytavern.com.* 18th-century American menu. Lunch, dinner. Closed Mon in Jan. Bar. Children's menu. Historical colonial tavern (1773). Outdoor seating. **$$$**

★★ **CUVEE NOTRE DAME.** *1701 Green St, Philadelphia (19130). Phone 215/765-2777.* Belgian menu. Lunch, dinner, Sun brunch. Closed Thanksgiving, Dec 25. Bar. Children's menu. Outdoor seating. **$$**

★★ DARK HORSE. *Head House Sq, Philadelphia (19147). Phone 215/928-9307; fax 215/928-0232. www.dickensinn.com.* American menu. Lunch, dinner, Sun brunch. Closed Mon; Jan 1, Dec 25. Bar. Children's menu. In historic Harper House (1788); Victorian décor; artwork imported from England. **$$**

★★★ DEUX CHEMINEES. *1221 Locust St, Philadelphia (19107). Phone 215/790-0200; fax 215/790-0202. www.deuxchem.com.* Featuring classic and regional French cuisine in five beautifully appointed dining rooms, Deux Cheminees ("two fireplaces") is a testament to the fact that some traditions endure for good reason. Located in two 19th-century town houses, the formal restaurant offers fixed-price five-course menus and special value three-course dinners for early diners. This is the place for foie gras, pates and terrines, sweetbreads and escargot. And the house specialty—rack of lamb for two—is roasted to order and served with truffle-filled sauce Perigord. French menu. Dinner. Closed Sun, Mon; holidays. Reservations recommended. **$$$$**

★ DIMITRI'S. *795 S 3rd St, Philadelphia (19147). Phone 215/625-0556.* Mediterranean menu. Dinner. Closed Easter, Thanksgiving, Dec 24-25. **$$**

★★ DINARDO'S. *312 Race St, Philadelphia (19106). Phone 215/925-5115; fax 215/592-1112. www.dinardos.com.* Seafood menu. Lunch, dinner. Closed Easter, Thanksgiving, Dec 25. Bar. Children's menu. Historic building (1740). **$$**

★ FAMOUS 4TH STREET DELI. *700 S 4th St, Philadelphia (19147). Phone 215/922-3274; toll-free 888/922-3535. www.famouscookies.com.* Family owned since 1923, this Jewish delicatessen is worth a stop for a corned beef, roast beef, roast turkey brisket, or smoked fish sandwich. But it's the freshly baked award-winning cookies that put the Famous in "Famous 4th Street Deli." These large, chunky cookies come in chocolate chip, chocolate walnut, peanut butter, and oatmeal raisin. Deli menu. Breakfast, lunch. Closed Rosh Hashanah, Yom Kippur. **$**

★★ FELICIA'S. *1148 S 11th St, Philadelphia (19147). Phone 215/755-9656; fax 215/755-6056.* Italian menu. Lunch, dinner. Closed Mon; holidays. Bar. Valet parking. **$$**

★★ FEZ. *620 S 2nd St, Philadelphia (19147). Phone 215/925-5367; fax 215/925-8844. www.fezrestaurant.com.* Moroccan menu. Dinner. Casual attire. Reservations recommended. **$$**

★★★ FOUNTAIN RESTAURANT. *1 Logan Sq, Philadelphia (19103). Phone 215/963-1500; fax 215/963-9506. www.fourseasons.com/philadelphia.* The wine list at The Fountain, the stunning flagship restaurant of the Four Seasons Hotel Philadelphia (see), weighs as much as a light barbell. If you need to work your biceps, it makes for a good substitute. The extensive list—covering all of France as well as Germany, Italy, the United States, Australia, New Zealand, and South America—is just one of the highlights of dining here. The kitchen often serves ingredients from local producers and includes the farms' names on the menu, so you'll know which farmer planted your baby greens and where your beets were picked. This thoughtfulness adds to the experience by giving you a real sense of connection to the food and the care that is taken to find the best ingredients. As you'll see here, the best ingredients really do make a difference. Vegetarian items are available on request, and the kitchen offers several selections that are marked "nutritionally balanced, healthier fare." If you choose one of these "lighter" options, you can definitely opt for the heavenly chocolate soufflé for dessert. Since it is a house specialty, you really should make a point of having it regardless of what you decide to eat for dinner. *Secret Inspector's Notes: The dining room at The Fountain is just lovely, ideal for a special occasion or business dinner. Consult the fantastic sommelier for wine assistance, but in case it's an off-evening, be prepared for absent-minded staff and food that on occasion lacks interesting flavor and textural excitement.* French menu. Breakfast, lunch, dinner, Sun brunch. Bar. Children's menu. Jacket required. Valet parking. **$$$$**

★ GENO'S STEAKS. *1219 S 9th St, Philadelphia (19147). Phone 215/389-0659; fax 215/389-4166. www.genossteaks.com.* American menu. Breakfast, lunch, dinner, late-night. Closed Thanksgiving, Dec 25, Dec 31. Casual attire. Outdoor seating. **$**

★★ THE ITALIAN BISTRO OF CENTER CITY. *211 S Broad St, Philadelphia (19107). Phone 215/731-0700; fax 215/731-0702. www.italianbistro.com.* Italian menu. Lunch, dinner. Closed Thanksgiving, Dec 25. Bar. Children's menu. **$$**

★★★ JAKE'S RESTAURANT. *4365 Main St, Manayunk (19127). Phone 215/483-0444; fax 215/487-7122. www.jakesrestaurant.com.* Located in Manayunk, Philadelphia's funky, high-energy, artsy neighborhood, Jake's Restaurant is a lively, sexy spot to meet friends for drinks and stay for dinner. Be warned, though; this is a place you may not want to leave. Chef/owner Bruce Cooper's chic regulars make a habit of staying all night, savoring his unique brand of stylish, regional American food. While at the bar, go for one of Jake's wild house cocktails or take a chance on a unique microbrew. After drinks, settle into the lively, butter-yellow dining room and get ready for a fabulous meal. While fine dining can be pretentious or stuffy, at Jake's it is neither. The kitchen is in sync with its customers' desire for both fun and flavor in their food. For instance, on a recent visit, the prix fixe menu was titled "Jake's Clam Bake," which featured a popular four-course clam bake-style shellfish menu paired with wine. Unfortunately, sunshine and the seashore are not included, but with the steady buzz from the bright energy in the room, you won't need them. American menu. Lunch, dinner, Sun brunch. Bar. Reservations recommended. Outdoor seating. **$$$**

★★ JOSEPH POON. *1002 Arch St, Philadelphia (19107). Phone 215/928-9333; fax 215/928-9368. www.josephpoon.com.* Pan-Asian menu. Lunch, dinner. Closed Mon; Thanksgiving, Dec 25; also Chinese New Year. Bar. **$$**

★★ KNAVE OF HEARTS. *230 South St, Philadelphia (19147). Phone 215/922-3956.* Lunch, dinner, Sun brunch. Closed Dec 25. Bar. **$$**

★★★★ LACROIX AT THE RITTENHOUSE. *210 West Rittenhouse Sq, Philadelphia (19103). Phone 215/790-2533. www.rittenhousehotel.com.* Set in the stately Rittenhouse Hotel, Lacroix is a restaurant of understated elegance featuring the haute culinary creations of chef Jean-Marie Lacroix. The kitchen plays up fresh local ingredients with a delicate French hand, while guests dine in posh, sophisticated luxury and enjoy transporting views of the charming Rittenhouse Square. For an intimate dinner party, consider the private dining room that can seat up to 18 guests. French menu. Breakfast, lunch, dinner. Bar. Children's menu. Jacket required. **$$$**

★★★ LE BAR LYONNAIS. *1523 Walnut St, Philadelphia (19102). Phone 215/567-1000; fax 215/568-1151. www.lebecfin.com.* Since Georges Perrier added Le Bar Lyonnais to his internationally renowned Le Bec-Fin restaurant in 1990, the bar has achieved status as one of Philadelphia's best French bistros, winning kudos for its comfortable setting and accessible menu. Open from lunch to late-night, the bistro features dishes such as a cassolette of snails in champagne and hazelnut butter sauce, grilled Dover sole with herb gnocchi in beurre blanc, and veal tenderloin with calves liver and onions. Best bar munchies? The crisp frites with dipping sauces. French bistro menu. Lunch, dinner. Closed Sun; holidays. Bar. Valet parking. **$$$**

★★★★★ LE BEC-FIN. *1523 Walnut St, Philadelphia (19102). Phone 215/567-1000; fax 215/568-1151. www.lebecfin.com.* Still sparkling from its recent renovation, Georges Perrier's Le Bec-Fin, which opened in 1970, remains a shining star for elegant haute cuisine of the French variety. Perrier unveiled his better-than-ever culinary temple after closing the restaurant for one month. During that time, he had architects, draftsmen, designers, and painters working around the clock to transform the Louis XVI-style room into a "turn-of-the-century Parisian dining salon." Indeed, the room is a bastion of civility with fresh flowers, tawny-toned carpeting, amber lighting, and finely dressed tabletops. In addition to the stunning physical changes to the space, the menu has been treated to a warm wave of fresh air. Perrier's talented team brings out the brilliance in classic dishes while offering several new creations that are destined to be classics. Perrier's signature crab cake with haricot verts has remained on the menu through the renovation. It joins an exciting menu divided between Les Entrees (appetizers); an impressive and unusual selection of Les Poissons (fish), depending on availability; and an equally terrific assortment of Les Viandes (meats), also listed according to season and availability. Le Cave, as the restaurant's wine cellar is known, has also seen improvement. The list has been expanded from 200 to 700 bottles and includes many sought-after vintages and rare selections from private collections. Reborn, Le Bec-Fin is better than ever. *Secret Inspector's Notes: The service here is as warm and attentive as you could imagine. Each guest's wants and needs are consistently attended to, and the staff manages to keep the interaction fun and light while achieving the utmost professionalism.* French menu. Lunch, dinner. Closed Sun; holidays. Bar. Jacket required. Valet parking. **$$$$**

★ ★ ★ LE CASTAGNE RISTORANTE. *1920 Chestnut St, Philadelphia (19103). Phone 215/751-9913; fax 215/751-9919. www.lecastagne.com.* Italian menu. Lunch, dinner. Closed Sun. Bar. Outdoor seating. **$$$**

★ MANAYUNK BREWING AND RESTAURANT. *4120 Main St, Manayunk (19127). Phone 215/482-8220; fax 215/482-3555. www.manayunkbrewery.com.* Lunch, dinner. Children's menu. On the river. **$$**

★ MANAYUNK DINER. *3720-3740 Main St, Philadelphia (19127). Phone 215/483-4200; fax 215/483-0840.* American menu with Greek influences. Breakfast, lunch, dinner, late-night. Bar. Children's menu. Casual attire. Outdoor seating. **$$**

★ ★ ★ MONTE CARLO LIVING ROOM. *150 South St, Philadelphia (19147). Phone 215/925-2220; fax 215/925-9956.* Rounding the corner on this, their showcase restaurant's 20th year, Giorgio Giuliani and Umberto Degli Estosti recently completed an extensive remodel. The resulting ambience in the 45-seat dining room and club upstairs is elegant, warm, and welcoming. The chef's weekly-changing menus represent fine contemporary Mediterranean cuisine at its best. A starter duet of foie gras and sweetbreads is coupled with Firelli pears and aged balsamic vinegar, and in the entrée section, the roasted lamb is fragrant with sage and paired with cranberry beans and Barolo sauce. Cheese course selections are well thought out, and the desserts are creative. Italian menu. Dinner. Closed holidays. Bar. Jacket required. **$$$$**

★ ★ ★ MOONSTRUCK. *7955 Oxford Ave, Philadelphia (19111). Phone 215/725-6000; fax 215/722-7177. www.moonstruckrestaurant.com.* Formerly known as Ristorante DiLullo, this elegantly casual northern Italian gem has been doing business for more than 20 years. Menus let customers choose among a wide range of antipasti, primi piatti (pasta appetizers), secondi piatti (second courses), and piatti tradizionale (traditional classics). The latter menu section features one special dish per night, ranging from Friday's caciucco—a bouillabaisse of seafood and fish—to Tuesday's osso buco, braised veal shank with pesto risotto. Italian menu. Dinner. Closed Jan 1, July 4, Dec 25. **$$**

★ ★ ★ MORIMOTO. *723 Chestnut St, Philadelphia (19106). Phone 215/413-9070; fax 215/413-9075. www.morimotorestaurant.com.* Japanese fusion cuisine from "Iron Chef" Masaharu Morimoto of New York's Nobu fame (he was executive chef at Nobu Matsuhisa's restaurant for six years) pulsates with life and creativity. His Philadelphia outpost—stunningly shaped by local restaurant impresario Stephen Starr—is Morimoto's first restaurant in the US. Ceilings undulate, booths change color, and the sushi bar at the back never stops bustling. The best way to challenge your taste buds is to select one of Morimoto's omakase (multicourse tasting) menus. Japanese menu. Lunch, dinner. Closed Jan 1, Thanksgiving, Dec 25. Bar. Reservations recommended. **$$$**

★ NAIS CUISINE. *13-17 W Benedict Ave, Havertown (19083). Phone 610/789-5983.* French, Thai menu. Dinner. Reservations recommended. **$$**

★ ★ ★ OVERTURES. *609 E Passyunk Ave, Philadelphia (19147). Phone 215/627-3455.* Chef/proprietor Peter LamLein has been creating his finely tuned menus of French/Mediterranean fare for Philadelphians for more than a decade. The setting is elegantly Empire, with murals on the garden room walls and additional paintings by pastry chef Ron Weisberg throughout. There's a nice selection of à la carte dishes, including an appetizer of fresh anchovies in lemon oil with garlic and roasted peppers, and an entrée of veal sweetbreads in hazelnut crumbs with orange Cognac sauce. But the best values are LamLein's fixed-price menus—$50 for four courses and $20.04 (the price matches the year) for three courses—three nights a week. Bring your own alcoholic beverages, as there is no bar. Fresh juices and mixers are stocked, however, and the waitstaff will uncork and pour your wines. Mediterranean menu. Dinner. Closed Mon; holidays. Reservations recommended. **$$$**

★★ PALOMA. *6516 Castor Ave, Philadelphia (19149). Phone 215/533-0356. www.palomarestaurant.com.* French, Mexican menu. Dinner. Closed Mon; Dec 25. Bar. Children's menu. **$$$**

★★★ PASION! *211 S 15th St, Philadelphia (19102). Phone 215/875-9895; fax 215/875-9935. www.pasionrestaurant.com.* Award-winning chef Guillermo Pernot's passion is Nuevo Latino cuisine—a melding of ancient cooking influences plumbed from Mexico, Central America, and South America with fun, contemporary stylings. Known for his meal-starting seviches (five different versions are featured daily), Pernot is equally creative with main courses, such as a plantain and wasabi pea-crusted salmon with creamy fufu and recao beurre blanc sauce. The upscale Latin-themed dining room, run by Pernot's business partner Michael Dombkoski, was recently doubled in size and features newly updated fabrics and furniture. Nuevo Latino menu. Dinner. Closed holidays. Bar. **$$$**

★★ PHILADELPHIA FISH. *207 Chestnut St, Philadelphia (19106). Phone 215/625-8605; fax 215/625-9529. www.philadelphiafish.com.* Seafood menu. Dinner. Closed Thanksgiving, Dec 25. Bar. Children's menu. Casual attire. Outdoor seating. **$$**

★★ THE PLOUGH & THE STARS. *123 Chestnut St, Philadelphia (19106). Phone 215/733-0300; fax 215/829-1097. www.ploughstars.com.* This upscale Irish pub is situated in a spectacular location in a beautiful historically preserved building with 245-foot ceilings, molded Corinthian columns, and dramatic 16-foot windows. Plan to stop here for Irish tea and scones after a day of touring Philadelphia's historic places, as it's just a few blocks from art galleries and several movie theaters as well as the Liberty Bell, Independence Hall, and Penn's Landing. Pints of Guinness and shepherd's pie are the specialties of the house, made more festive around the roaring fireplace or, in good weather, outdoors. Contemporary Irish menu. Dinner. Bar. Children's menu. Outdoor seating. **$$**

★★ RANGOON BURMESE RESTAURANT. *112 N 9th St, Philadelphia (19107). Phone 215/829-8939; fax 215/629-2370.* Burmese menu. Lunch, dinner. Closed Thanksgiving. Bar. **$$**

★ THE RESTAURANT SCHOOL. *4207 Walnut St, Philadelphia (19104). Phone 215/222-4200.* This restaurant offers a unique dining experience in a "restaurant school" that consists of two buildings: a restored 1856 mansion is linked by a large atrium dining area to a new building housing the kitchen and classrooms. Eclectic/International, seasonal menu. Dinner. Closed Sun, Mon; also during student breaks. Bar. **$**

★★★ RISTORANTE PANORAMA. *Front and Market sts, Philadelphia (19106). Phone 215/922-7800; toll-free 800/331-7634; fax 215/922-7642. www.pennsviewhotel.com.* Located right at the bridge to Penn's Landing in a building that's on the National Register of Historic Places, Panorama is part of the Penn's View Hotel (see). The cuisine is gutsy old-world Italian, featuring dishes such as paillard of beef rolled in garlic, cheese, egg, and herbs, slow-cooked in tomato sauce, and served with house-made gnocchi. But it's wine that this place is known for. Daily wine lists offer from 22 to 26 different flights (five wines per flight), plus dozens more by-the-glass options. The quality—made possible by the restaurant's cruvinet preservation and dispensing system—is exceptional, earning Panorama numerous "Best Wines by the Glass" awards from national food magazines. Northern Italian menu. Dinner. Closed most holidays. Bar. Casual attire. **$$$**

★★★ RUTH'S CHRIS STEAK HOUSE. *260 Broad St, Philadelphia (19102). Phone 215/790-1515; toll-free 800/544-0808; fax 215/790-9480. www.ruthschris.com.* Steak menu. Dinner. Closed holidays. Bar. **$$$**

★★★ THE SALOON. *750 S 7th St, Philadelphia (19147). Phone 215/627-1811; fax 215/627-6765.* Richard Santore has been operating this venerable establishment in Philadelphia's Bellavista neighborhood, bordering Center City and South Philly, for more than 30 years. The food is classic Italian fare, served for lunch and dinner, in a dining room featuring lots of framed mirrors and old glass. Appetizers include poached pear and gorgonzola salad with roasted walnuts, baby greens, and red onion with pear vinaigrette. Fettuccini Lobster Amatriciana is a toss of house-made fettuccini with lobster, bacon, onion, fresh tomato, and pecorino cheese in tomato sauce. Daily dinner specials range from beef carpaccio drizzled with truffle essence and served with fava beans to a double veal chop marinated in white wine, pan seared and served with Yukon gold potatoes. Italian menu. Lunch, dinner. Closed Sun; holidays. Bar. **$$**

★ ★ ★ **SALT.** *253 S 20th St, Philadelphia (19103). Phone 215/545-1990.* American menu. Dinner. Bar. Outdoor seating. **$$$**

★ ★ **SERRANO.** *20 S 2nd St, Philadelphia (19106). Phone 215/928-0770; fax 215/928-0805. www.tinangel .com.* International menu. Dinner. Closed holidays. Bar. **$$**

★ ★ **SONOMA.** *4411 Main St, Philadelphia (19127). Phone 215/483-9400; fax 215/487-7894. www.sonomarestaurant.com.* California menu. Lunch, dinner. Closed Thanksgiving. Bar. Children's menu. Casual attire. Valet parking. Outdoor seating. **$$$**

★ **SOUTH STREET DINER.** *140 South St, Philadelphia (19147). Phone 215/627-5258; fax 215/ 629-3954.* Greek menu. Breakfast, lunch, dinner, late-night. Closed Dec 25. Bar. Children's menu. Outdoor seating. **$$**

★ ★ **STEPHEN'S.** *1415 City Line Ave, Wynnewood (19096). Phone 610/896-0275.* Italian menu. Lunch, dinner. Closed Jan 1, Dec 25. Bar. Reservations recommended. Valet parking. **$$**

★ ★ ★ **SUSANNA FOO.** *1512 Walnut St, Philadelphia (19102). Phone 215/545-2666; fax 215/ 546-9106. www.susannafoo.com.* Thanks to the plethora of greasy Chinese takeout joints, Chinese food has been much maligned over the years. But at Susanna Foo, a Zenlike dining oasis, the delicious, traditional cuisine of China sheds its unfortunate reputation and gains the respect it deserves. For the past 20 years, chef/owner Susanna Foo has been dressing up the dishes of her native land with sophisticated French flair and modern, global accents. Foo's dim sum can be a meal on their own, and that's a wonderful way to approach dinner here, as long as you order the stellar signature Hundred Corner crabcakes. The entrées are equally mouthwatering, especially the famous tea-smoked Peking duck breast. You may never be able to order takeout again. Chinese, French menu. Lunch, dinner. Closed holidays. Bar. Valet parking. **$$$**

★ ★ ★ **SWANN CAFE.** *1 Logan Sq, Philadelphia (19103). Phone 215/963-1500; toll-free 866/516-1100; fax 215/963-9562. www.fourseasons.com/philadelphia.* Named for the spectacular Logan Square fountain situated right in front of the Four Seasons Hotel (see) that houses this café, Swann is the more accessible of the hotel's exceptional restaurants. (The other, Fountain Restaurant (see), is one of Philadelphia's premier special-occasion restaurants.) Menus are overseen by executive chef Martin Hamann and range from light and lovely dishes such as an appetizer ragout of forest mushrooms and asparagus tips to a zesty sandwich of pulled osso bucco with aged provolone and spicy pepper and onion relish on a Stirato roll. American menu. Lunch, dinner. Bar. Children's menu. Casual attire. Valet parking. **$$**

★ ★ ★ **TANGERINE.** *232 Market St, Philadelphia (19106). Phone 215/627-5116; fax 215/627-5117. www.tangerinerestaurant.com.* Moroccan menu. Specializes in spiced rouget, harissa gnocchi, tagines (traditional Morrocan stews), lamb and honey, mustard-crusted tuna with curreied lentils, crispy cabash duck, shrimp and scallops. Dinner. Bar. **$$**

★ ★ **THOMAS' RESTAURANT AND BAR.** *4201 Main St, Philadelphia (19127). Phone 215/483-9075; fax 215/483-2109.* American, Asian, French menu. Dinner, brunch. Closed Jan 1, Thanksgiving, Dec 25. Bar. Outdoor seating. **$$**

★ ★ **UMBRIA.** *7131 Germantown Ave, Philadelphia (19119). Phone 215/242-6470.* Eclectic menu. Dinner. Closed Sun-Tues; holidays. **$$**

★ ★ ★ **VETRI.** *1312 Spruce St, Philadelphia (19107). Phone 215/732-3478; fax 215/732-3487. www.vetriristorante.com.* Chef Mark Vetri learned to prepare rustic Italian cuisine (rabbit loin and sweetbreads wrapped in pancetta with morels; baby goat poached in milk and then oven roast to crispness) from Italy's best chefs and then brought his skills home to Philly. Ensconced in the tiny, 35-seat space once occupied by other pinnacle establishments (Le Bec-Fin, Chanterelle), Vetri is intent on creating likewise legendary meals. Sweet quirkiness is his trademark (Vetri shaves prosciutto on a 1936 Berkel meat slicer right in the dining room). The wine list has been nationally lauded, and the service is seamless. On Saturdays, indulge in Vetri's five- or seven-course fixed-price menus (not available during the summer). Italian menu. Dinner. Closed Sun; holidays. Casual attire. **$$$**

★★ **WHITE DOG CAFE.** *3420 Sansom St, Philadelphia (19104). Phone 215/386-9224; fax 215/386-1185. www.whitedog.com.* Lunch, dinner, brunch. Closed Thanksgiving, Dec 25. Bar. Children's menu. Former house (circa 1870) of author Madame Blavatsky, founder of the Theosophical Society. Outdoor seating. **$$**

★★ **ZOCALO.** *3600 Lancaster Ave, Philadelphia (19104). Phone 215/895-0139.* Contemporary Mexican menu. Lunch, dinner. Closed holidays. Bar. Outdoor seating. **$$**

Pittsburgh (C-1)

See also Ambridge, Beaver Falls, Butler, Connellsville, Harmony, New Stanton, Washington, Weirton

Settled 1758
Population 334,563
Elevation 760 ft
Area Code 412
Information Greater Pittsburgh Convention & Visitors Bureau, 425 6th Ave 30th Floor 15219; phone toll-free 800/366-0093
Web site www.visitpittsburgh.com

Pittsburgh has had a remarkable renaissance to become one of the most spectacular civic redevelopments in America, with modern buildings, clean parks, and community pride. In fact, it has been named "all-American city" by the National Civic League. The new Pittsburgh is a result of a rare combination of capital-labor cooperation, public and private support, enlightened political leadership, and imaginative, venturesome community planning. Its $1-billion international airport was designed to be the most user-friendly in the country.

After massive war production, Pittsburgh labored to eliminate the 1930s image of an unsophisticated mill town. During the 1950s and 1960s Renaissance I began, a $500-million program to clean the city's air and develop new structures such as Gateway Center, the Civic Arena, and Point State Park. The late 1970s and early 1980s ushered in Renaissance II, a $3-billion expansion program reflecting the movement away from industry and toward high technology.

Today Pittsburgh has completed this dramatic shift from industry to a diversified base including high technology, health care, finance, and education, and continues its transition to a services-oriented city.

Pittsburgh's cultural personality is expressed by the Pittsburgh Symphony Orchestra, Pittsburgh Opera, Pittsburgh Ballet, Phipps Conservatory, and the Carnegie Museums of Pittsburgh, which include the Museum of Natural History and the Museum of Art. The city has 25 parks, 45 "parklets," 60 recreation centers, and 27 swimming pools.

Born of frontier warfare in the shadow of Fort Pitt, the city is named after the elder William Pitt, the great British statesman. Its strategic military position was an important commercial asset and Pittsburgh soon became a busy river port and transit point for the western flow of pioneers.

Industry grew out of the West's need for manufactured goods; foundries and rolling mills were soon producing nails, axes, frying pans, and shovels. The Civil War added tremendous impetus to industry, and by the end of the war, Pittsburgh was producing half the steel and one-third of the glass made in the country. Such captains of industry and finance as Thomas Mellon, Andrew Carnegie, and Henry Clay Frick built their industrial empires in Pittsburgh. The American Federation of Labor was born here (1881); the city has been the scene of historic clashes between labor and management.

World War I brought a fresh boom to the city, as well as changes in its industrial character. It was a vast arsenal for the Allies during World War II.

Additional Visitor Information

For additional accommodations, see PITTSBURGH INTERNATIONAL AIRPORT AREA, which follows PITTSBURGH.

For additional information about Pittsburgh, contact the Greater Pittsburgh Convention and Visitors Bureau, 425 6th Ave, 30th Floor, 15219 (Mon-Fri); 412/281-7711 or 800/366-0093. A Visitor Information Center is along Liberty Ave, adjacent to 4 Gateway Center (Mar-Dec, daily; rest of year, Mon-Sat). Other centers can be found in the Carnegie Library's Mount Washington branch and on the University

Oakland, the City Beautiful

Once known as the "Forge of the Universe," industrial Pittsburgh was a smoky, pulsating mill town that fed the fortunes of such corporate giants as Carnegie, Westinghouse, and Mellon. Since then, the city has cleansed its air and its reputation to rank as one of America's most delightful big cities. Before this renaissance, Pittsburgh's 19th-century elite created a second city just 3 miles east of downtown called Oakland. A sparkling cultural and educational center, it was an antidote to the blue-collar grime from which many of them profited. Under the patronage of Andrew Carnegie and others, Oakland became, as historians have described it, "The City Beautiful," a lavish fantasy of parks and monumental structures housing museums and universities. This one-hour, 1-mile tour is an introduction to this rich heritage bequeathed to the public. To explore it fully might take days. Begin on the steps of The Carnegie at 4400 Forbes Avenue. An immense gray building, it is shared by the Museum of Art and the Museum of Natural History. Born to a poor family in Scotland in 1835, founder Carnegie came to the United States with his parents at age 12. Starting his career as telegraph messenger, he went on to make a fortune in steel. A generous man, he gave The Carnegie to the city. For the Museum of Art, he sought contemporary artwork, thus creating what is considered the first museum of modern art in America. It boasts a fine collection of impressionists. Acquiring Jurassic Age fossils, Carnegie put the Museum of Natural History in the paleontology business. The Hall of Dinosaurs is particularly impressive. Across Forbes Avenue is the Foster Memorial, where composer Stephen Collins Foster is cited for the "beautiful ideals" given voice in his enduring music. Soaring above the memorial is the University of Pittsburgh's 42-story Tower of Learning, one of the largest academic buildings in the world. It was built in the early 1930s as a symbol of power and achievement. A ten-minute walk away in adjacent Schenley Park is Phipps Conservatory on Schenley Drive (west from the Carnegie), an elegant Beaux-Art greenhouse that is believed to be the largest in the country. When it opened in 1893, it was one of the nation's first large-scale enclosed botanical gardens. Conclude your tour by strolling among its many exhibits, from tropical flowers to a major assortment of bonsai.

of Pittsburgh's campus, Log Cabin, Forbes Ave. For a schedule of events in Pittsburgh, 24-hour visitor information, phone 800/366-0093.

Public Transportation

Subway and surface trains, buses (Port Authority of Allegheny County), phone 412/442-2000

What to See and Do

Alcoa Building. *425 6th Ave, Pittsburgh.* Pioneer in aluminum for skyscraper construction, exterior work was done from inside; no scaffolding was required. Draped in aluminum waffle, 30 stories high; considered to be one of the country's most daring experiments in skyscraper design.

Allegheny County Courthouse. *Grant St and 5th Ave, Pittsburgh.* One of the country's outstanding Romanesque buildings, the 2-square-city-block structure was designed by Henry Hobson Richardson in 1884. (Mon-Fri; closed holidays) **FREE**

Andy Warhol Museum. *117 Sandusky St, Pittsburgh. Phone 412/237-8300.* The most comprehensive single-artist museum in the world. More than 500 works. (Tues-Sun) **$$$**

Benedum Center for the Performing Arts. *719 Liberty Ave. Phone 412/456-6666.* Expansion and restoration of the Stanley Theater, a movie palace built in 1928. Gilded plasterwork, 500,000-piece crystal chandelier and a nine-story addition to backstage area make this an exceptional auditorium with one of the largest stages in the country. The center is home to Pittsburgh Ballet Theatre, the Pittsburgh Dance Council, the Pittsburgh Opera, and Civic Light Opera. Free guided tours (by appointment).

Boyce Park Ski Area. *18 miles E on I-376 to Plum exit (16B); follow signs to park. Phone 724/733-4656.* Beginner-intermediate slopes; two double chairlifts; two surface lifts; patrol, school, rentals, snowmaking; cafeteria. Longest run, 1/4 mile; vertical drop, 160 feet. Night skiing. (Dec-Mar, daily) **$$$$**

Carnegie Mellon University. *5000 Forbes Ave, Pittsburgh (15213). Adjacent to Schenley Park. Phone 412/268-2000. www.cmu.edu.* (1900) 7,900 students. Founded by Andrew Carnegie. Composed of seven colleges. Tours of campus.

★ **The Carnegie Museums of Pittsburgh.** *4400 Forbes Ave, Pittsburgh. Phone 412/622-3360.* Public complex built by industrialist Andrew Carnegie. (Daily except Mon; closed holidays) **$$** Includes

Carnegie Museum of Art. Possibly America's first modern art museum, as Carnegie urged the gallery to exhibit works dated after 1896. Collection of Impressionist and Post-Impressionist paintings; Hall of Sculpture; Hall of Architecture; films, videos.

Carnegie Museum of Natural History. Houses one of the most complete collections of dinosaur fossils. Exhibits include Dinosaur Hall, Polar World, Hillman Hall of Minerals and Gems, the Walton Hall of Ancient Egypt; changing exhibits.

Library of Pittsburgh. Central branch contains more than 4 1/2 million books. Houses first department of science and technology established in a US public library.

Music Hall. Home to Mendelssohn Choir, Pittsburgh Chamber Music Society and River City Brass Band. Elaborate gilt and marble foyer; walls of French eschallion, 24 pillars made of green stone and a gold baroque ceiling.

The Carnegie Science Center. *One Allegheny Ave. On Ohio River. Phone 412/237-3400.* Learning and entertainment complex has over 40,000 square feet of exhibit galleries that demonstrate how human activities are affected by science and technology. USS *Requin,* moored in front of the center, is a World War II diesel-electric submarine; tours (40 minutes) demonstrate the electronic, visual, and voice communication devices on board. Henry Buhl Jr. Planetarium and Observatory is a technologically sophisticated interactive planetarium with control panels at every seat. Also here are the 350-seat OMNIMAX Theater and the Health Sciences Amphitheater. Restaurant, gift shop. (Daily; closed Dec 25) **$$$$**

County parks. *South Park. 12 miles S on Hwy 88. North Park, 14 miles N on Hwy 19. Boyce Park, 14 miles E on I-376, Hwy 22. Settler's Cabin Park, 9 miles W on I-279, Hwy 22. Phone 412/350-2455 (county park information and permits).* Swimming; fishing; boating. Bicycling (rentals), ball fields; golf, tennis. Cross-country skiing, ice skating (winter, daily). Picnicking. Parks open daily. Fees for activities. Attractions for each park vary.

★ **Fallingwater.** *Hwy 381, Mill Run. 27 miles S on Hwy 51, 10 miles E on Hwy 201 to Connellsville, 8 miles E on Hwy 711, then 8 miles S on Hwy 381, near Mill Run.* (See CONNELLSVILLE)

★ **The Frick Art and Historical Center.** *7227 Reynolds St, Pittsburgh. Phone 412/371-0600.* Museum complex built on grounds of estate once belonging to industrialist Henry Clay Frick; gardens, carriage house museum, greenhouse, cafe and restored children's playhouse that now serves as a visitor's center. (Tues-Sun; closed holidays) **FREE** Also on grounds are

Clayton, the Henry Clay Frick Home. A restored four-story Victorian mansion with 23 rooms; only remaining house of area in East End once known as "Millionaire's Row." Some original décor and personal mementos of the Fricks. Tours; reservation recommended. **$$$**

The Frick Art Museum. *Phone 412/371-0600.* Collection of Helen Clay Frick, daughter of Henry Clay Frick, includes Italian Renaissance, Flemish, and French 18th-century paintings and decorative arts. Italian and French furniture, Renaissance bronzes, tapestries, Chinese porcelains. Also changing exhibits; concerts, lectures. **FREE**

Frick Park. *Beechwood Blvd and English Ln, Pittsburgh. Phone 412/422-6536.* Covers 476 acres, largely in natural state; nature trails wind through ravines and over hills; also nature center (2005 Beechwood Blvd), tennis courts, picnic areas, playgrounds. Park (Daily). **FREE**

Gateway Center. *420 Fort Duquesne Blvd, Pittsburgh (15222). Covers 23 acres adjacent to Point State Park. Phone 412/392-6000.* Complex includes four skyscrapers of Trizec Properties, Inc. Gateway Center Plaza, a 2-acre open-air garden over underground parking garage, has lovely walks, three fountains, more than 90 types of trees and 100 varieties of shrubs and seasonal flowers. (Mon-Fri; closed holidays)

Guided Bus and Walking Tours. *1 Station Sq, Suite 450, Pittsburgh (15219). Phone 412/471-5808. www.phlf.org.* Offered through the Pittsburgh History and Landmarks Foundation. **$$**

Hartwood. *215 Saxonburg Blvd, Pittsburgh. 12 miles N via Hwy 8. Phone 412/767-9200.* (1929). A 629-acre re-creation of English country estate; Tudor mansion with many antiques; formal gardens, stables. Tours (Tues-Sun; closed holidays). Also music and theater events during summer. **$$**

★ **Inclines.** (Hill-climbing trolleys). Travel to the top of Mount Washington for an excellent view of Golden Triangle, where the Allegheny and Monongahela rivers join to form the Ohio River.

Duquesne Incline. *1220 Grandview Ave, Pittsburgh. Lower station, W Carson St, opposite the fountain, SW of Fort Pitt Bridge; upper station, in restaurant area. Phone 412/381-1665.* Built 1877; restored and run by community effort; observation deck. (Daily) Free parking at lower station. **$**

Monongahela Incline. *Station on W Carson St near Station Sq and Smithfield St Bridge. Phone 412/442-2000.* Panoramic views from observation deck. (Daily) **$**

James L. Kelso Bible Lands Museum. *616 N Highland, Pittsburgh. On grounds of Pittsburgh Theological Seminary. Phone 412/362-5610.* Artifacts and displays from the ancient Near East, especially Palestine. (Call for hours) **FREE**

Kennywood Park. *4800 Kennywood Blvd, West Mifflin. 8 miles SE on Hwy 837. Phone 412/461-0500. www.kennywood.com.* Combines modern rides with rides from traditional streetcar parks, popular at the turn of the 20th century. Lost Kennywood, with lagoon, Victorian-era buildings, shopping. Gardens, picnic groves. (Mid-May-Labor Day, daily) **$$$$**

Mellon Arena. *66 Mario Lemieux Pl, Pittsburgh. www.mellonarena.com.* This $22-million all-weather amphitheater accommodates 17,500 people. Retractable roof can fold up within 2 1/2 minutes.

Museum of Photographic History. *531 E Ohio, Pittsburgh. Phone 412/231-7881.* Photo gallery and museum. Selections from 100,000 antique photographic images. (Mon-Sat; closed holidays) **$$**

National Aviary. *Allegheny Commons West, approximately 1 mile W of downtown. Phone 412/323-7235.* The Aviary is home to one of the world's premier bird collections and is the only indoor bird facility independent of a larger zoo in North America. A veritable jungle of colorful, amusing and exotic birds. (Daily; closed Dec 25) **$$**

Pittsburgh Children's Museum. *10 Childrens' Way. Phone 412/322-5058.* Hands-on exhibits. Hands-on silkscreen studio; storytelling; regularly scheduled puppet shows; live performances; two-story climber. (Memorial Day-Labor Day, daily; rest of year, Tues-Sat, also Sun afternoons) **$$**

Pittsburgh Penguins (NHL). *66 Mario Lemieux Pl. Phone 412/323-1919.* Teams play at Mellon Arena.

Pittsburgh Pirates (MLB). *115 Federal St. Phone 412/323-5000.* Teams play at PNC Park.

Pittsburgh Steelers (NFL). *600 Stadium Circle. Phone 412/432-7800.* Teams play at Heinz Field.

The Pittsburgh Zoo. *1 Wild Pl, Pittsburgh (15260). NE on Highland Ave in Highland Park area. Phone 412/665-3639.* Over 70 acres containing over 6,000 animals, children's farm (late May-Oct), discovery pavilion, reptile house, tropical and Asian forests, African savanna and aqua zoo. Merry-go-round and train rides (fee). Highland Park covers 75 acres and has tennis courts, picnic grounds, shelters (some require permit), twin reservoirs, swimming pool (fee). (Daily; closed Dec 25) **$$$**

Point State Park. *Fort Duquesne and Fort Pitt blvds. Phone 412/471-0235.* "Point" where the Allegheny and Monongahela rivers meet to form the Ohio; 36 acres. A 150-foot fountain symbolizes the joining of the rivers. There are military drills with fifes and drums, muskets and cannon (May-Labor Day; some Sun afternoons). In the park are

Block House of Fort Pitt. *Fort Duquesne and Fort Pitt blvds, Pittsburgh.* Last remaining building of original fort (1767). (Wed-Sun) **FREE**

Fort Pitt Museum. *101 Commonwealth Pl, Pittsburgh. Phone 412/281-9284.* Built on part of original fort. Exhibits on early Pittsburgh and Fort Pitt; military struggles between France and Britain for western Pennsylvania and the Old Northwest Territory. (Wed-Sun; closed holidays) **$$**

PPG Place. *Market Sq.* Designed by Philip Johnson, this is Pittsburgh's most popular Renaissance II building. PPG Place consists of six separate buildings designed in a postmodern, Gothic skyscraper style. Shopping and a food court can be found in Two PPG Place.

Riverview Park. *2 miles N on US 19.* Covers 251 acres. Swimming pool (mid-June-Labor Day, daily, fee); tennis courts (Apr-Nov, daily); picnic shelter (May-Sept, permit required). Also playgrounds, parklet; nature, jogging trail. Fee for some activities. **FREE** In the park is

Allegheny Observatory. *159 Riverview Ave, Pittsburgh. Phone 412/321-2400.* Slides, tour of building. Maintained by University of Pittsburgh. Children under 12 years only with adult. Reservation required. (Apr-Oct, Thurs-Fri; closed holidays) **FREE**

Rodef Shalom Biblical Botanical Garden. *4905 5th Ave. Phone 412/621-6566. www.rodefshalom.org/garden.* The natural world of ancient Israel is re-created here in settings that specialize in plants of the Bible. A waterfall, desert, and stream all help simulate the areas of the Jordan, Lake Kineret, and the Dead Sea. Tours (by appointment). Special programs and exhibits. (June-mid-Sept, Mon-Thurs, Sat-Sun; Sat hours limited) **FREE**

Sandcastle Water Park. *1000 Sandcastle Dr (15120). Approximately 5 miles SE of downtown via I-376 and PA 837. Phone 412/462-6666. www.sandcastlewaterpark.com.* The city's down-by-the-riverside water park has 15 slides, adult and kiddie pools; boardwalk; food. (First Sat June-Labor Day, daily; closed holidays) **$$$$**

Schenley Park. *5000 Forbes Ave (15217). Adjacent Carnegie-Mellon University. Phone 412/687-1800.* Covers 456 acres; picnic areas; 18-hole golf course, lighted tennis courts; swimming pool; ice skating (winter); softball fields, running track; nature trails; bandstand (summer; free). Fee for some activities. (Daily) **FREE** Also in park is

Phipps Conservatory. *1 Schenley Park, Pittsburgh. Phone 412/622-6914.* Constantly changing array of flowers; tropical gardens; outstanding orchid collection. Children's Discovery Garden with interactive learning opportunities. Seasonal flower shows (see SPECIAL EVENTS). (Tues-Sun) **$$$**

The Senator John Heinz Regional History Center. *1212 Smallman St, Pittsburgh. In Chatauqua Ice Warehouse (1898). Phone 412/454-6000.* Preserves 300 years of region's history with artifacts and extensive collection of archives, photos. Houses the Historical Society of Western Pennsylvania. Library (Tues-Sat). (Daily; closed Jan 1, Thanksgiving, Dec 25) **$$$**

Sightseeing USA/Lenzner Coach USA. *110 Lenzner Ct, Sewickley (15143). Phone 412/741-2720; toll-free 800/342-2349.*

Soldiers and Sailors Memorial Hall and Military History Museum. *4141 5th Ave at Bigelow Blvd. Phone 412/621-4253.* Auditorium has Lincoln's Gettysburg Address inscribed above stage; flags, weapons, uniforms, memorabilia from US wars. (Tues-Fri, also Sat-Sun afternoons; closed holidays) **$$**

Station Square. *450 Landmarks Bldg, 1 Station Sq. Along Monongahela River across from downtown, via Smithfield St Bridge. Phone 412/471-5808. www.stationsquare.com.* This 40-acre area features shopping, dining, and entertainment in and among the historic buildings of the P & LE Railroad. Shopping in warehouses that once held loaded railroad boxcars. (Daily; closed holidays)

Tour-Ed Mine and Museum. *748 Bull Creek Rd, Pittsburgh (15084). 20 miles NW via Hwy 28 (Allegheny Valley Expy) to Tarentum, then 1/4 mile W via Red Belt W. Phone 724/224-4720. www.tour-edmine.com.* Complete underground coal mining operation; sawmill; furnished log house (1789); old company store; historical mine museum; shelters; playground. (May-Labor Day week, daily) **$$$**

Two Mellon Bank Center. *Grant St and 5th Ave, Pittsburgh.* Formerly the Union Trust Building, its Flemish-Gothic style was modeled after a library in Louvain, Belgium. Interior has a glass rotunda.

University of Pittsburgh. *5th Ave and Bigelow Blvd, Pittsburgh. Phone 412/624-4141. www.pitt.edu.* (1787) (33,000 students) Tours of Nationality Rooms in

Cathedral of Learning. Campus of 70 buildings on 125 acres. Buildings include

Cathedral of Learning. *4200 5th Ave, Pittsburgh. Phone 412/624-6000.* (1935). Unique skyscraper of classrooms, stretching its Gothic-Moderne architecture 42 floors high (535 feet); vantage point on 36th floor. Surrounding a three-story Gothic commons room are an Early American Room and 24 Nationality Rooms, each reflecting the distinctive culture of the ethnic group that created and furnished it. Tours (Daily; closed holidays). **$$**

Heinz Chapel. *5th and Bellefield aves, Pittsburgh. E of Cathedral of Learning. Phone 412/624-4157.* Tall stained-glass windows; French Gothic architecture. (Mon-Thurs, Sat-Sun; closed holidays) **FREE**

Henry Clay Frick Fine Arts Building. *Schenley Plaza, 104 Frick Fine Arts, Pittsburgh. Phone 412/648-2400.* Glass-enclosed cloister; changing exhibits; art reference library. (Sept-mid-June, daily; rest of year, Mon-Fri; closed university holidays, also Dec 24-Jan 2) **FREE**

Stephen Foster Memorial. *4301 Forbes Ave, Pittsburgh. Phone 412/624-4100.* Auditorium/ theater. Collection of the Pittsburgh-born composer's music and memorabilia. Said to be one of the most elaborate memorials ever built to a musician. (Mon-Sat, also Sun afternoons; closed holidays)

USX Tower. *Grant St and 7th Ave, Pittsburgh (15219).* Once known as the US Steel Building, it is 64 stories high, and the tallest building in Pittsburgh. Ten exposed triangular columns and an exterior paneling of steel make up its construction.

Special Events

Folk Festival. *105 Mall Blvd, Pittsburgh (15146). Pittsburgh Expo Mart, Monroeville.* Food of many nations; arts and crafts; folk music, dancing. Memorial Day weekend.

Phipps Conservatory Flower Shows. *Schenley Park, 1 Schenley Dr, Pittsburgh. Phone 412/622-6914.* Spring, summer, fall, and holidays.

Pittsburgh/Shop 'N Save Three Rivers Regatta. *Point State Park, Pittsburgh. www.pghregatta.com.* Water, land, and air events; water shows and speedboat races. Last weekend in July and first weekend in Aug.

Pittsburgh Irish Festival. *1 Station Sq, Pittsburgh (15219). I. C. Light Amphitheatre, Station Square. Phone 412/422-1113. www.pghirishfest.org.* Irish foods, dances, and entertainment. Early or mid-Sept.

Pittsburgh Public Theater. *621 Penn Ave, Pittsburgh. Phone 412/316-1600.* City's largest resident professional company. Sept-June.

Pittsburgh Symphony Orchestra. *Heinz Hall for the Performing Arts, 600 Penn Ave, Pittsburgh. Phone 412/392-4900.* Classical, pop, and family concerts. Sept-May.

Three Rivers Arts Festival. *707 Penn Ave, Pittsburgh. Point State Park, Gateway Center, USX Tower, PPG Place. Phone 412/281-8723.* Juried, original works of local and national artists: paintings, photography, sculpture, crafts and videos; artists' market in outdoor plazas. Ongoing performances include music, dance, and performance art. Special art projects; film festival; food; children's activities. Early-mid-June.

Limited-Service Hotels

★ HAWTHORN SUITES. *700 Mansfield Ave, Pittsburgh (15205). Phone 412/279-6300; toll-free 800/331-3131; fax 412/279-4993. www.hawthornsuitespittsburgh.com.* 151 rooms, 2 story. Pets accepted; fee. Complimentary full breakfast. Check-out noon. Pool, whirlpool. Airport transportation available. Chalet-style buildings. **$**

★ ★ HOLIDAY INN. *2750 Mosside Blvd, Monroeville (15146). Phone 412/372-1022; toll-free 800/465-4329; fax 412/373-4065. www.holiday-inn.com.* 188 rooms, 4 story. Pets accepted, some restrictions. Check-out noon. Restaurant, bar. Fitness room. Pool. **$**

★ ★ RAMADA. *1 Bigelow Sq, Pittsburgh (15219). Phone 412/281-5800; toll-free 800/225-5858; fax 412/281-4208. www.ramada.com.* 311 rooms, 20 story. Complimentary continental breakfast. Check-out noon. Restaurant, bar. Fitness room. Indoor pool. **$**

Full-Service Hotels

★★★ HILTON PITTSBURGH. *600 Commonwealth Pl, Pittsburgh (15222). Phone 412/391-4600; fax 412/594-5161. www.hilton.com.* 713 rooms, 24 story. Check-out noon. Restaurant, bar. Fitness room. Airport transportation available. Business center. **$**

★★★ MARRIOTT PITTSBURGH CITY CENTER. *112 Washington Pl, Pittsburgh (15219). Phone 412/471-4000; fax 412/281-4797. www.marriott.com.* 402 rooms, 11 story. Check-in 3 pm, check-out noon. Restaurant, bar. Fitness room. Indoor pool. Business center. **$$**

★★★ OMNI WILLIAM PENN HOTEL. *530 William Penn Pl, Pittsburgh (15219). Phone 412/281-7100; fax 412/553-5252. www.omnihotels.com.* Relive the grandeur of a bygone era at the Omni William Penn. This hotel, built in 1916, fuses historic charm with modern luxury in the heart of downtown Pittsburgh. The sumptuous public spaces invite daydreaming, while the rooms and suites are tastefully and elegantly appointed with a distinguished style. Executives on the go appreciate the hotel's complete business and fitness centers; families adore the Omni Kids Program; and leisure visitors enjoy the spa and salon services and proximity to the city's leading stores. The hotel offers a variety of convenient and tempting dining choices, from Starbucks and Brueggers Bagels for quick bites, snacks and pub food at the Palm Court and Tap Room, and fine dining at the Terrace Room. 596 rooms, 24 story. Check-in 3 pm, check-out noon. Wireless Internet access. Restaurant, bar. Fitness room. Airport transportation available. Business center. **$$**

★★★ RENAISSANCE PITTSBURGH HOTEL. *107 6th St, Pittsburgh (15222). Phone 412/562-1200; fax 412/562-1644. www.renaissancehotels.com.* 300 rooms, 14 story. Check-in 4 pm, check-out 1 pm. Restaurant, bar. Fitness room. Whirlpool. Business center. **$$**

★★★ SHERATON STATION SQUARE HOTEL. *7 Station Square Dr, Pittsburgh (15219). Phone 412/261-2000; toll-free 800/255-7488; fax 412/261-2932. www.sheraton.com.* 292 rooms, 15 story. Check-out noon. Restaurant, bar. Fitness room. Indoor pool, whirlpool. Business center. On riverfront. **$$**

★★★ THE WESTIN CONVENTION CENTER PITTSBURGH. *1000 Penn Ave, Pittsburgh (15222). Phone 412/281-3700; fax 412/227-4500. www.westin.com.* 616 rooms, 26 story. Pets accepted, some restrictions; fee. Check-in 3 pm, check-out noon. Restaurant, bar. Fitness room, spa. Indoor pool, whirlpool. Business center. **$$**

Specialty Lodgings

The following lodging establishments are approved by Mobil Travel Guide, but due to their unique and individualized nature have not been given a traditional Mobil Star rating. Included in this listing you may find bed-and-breakfasts, limited-service inns, guest ranches, and other unique hotel properties.

APPLETREE BED AND BREAKFAST. *703 S Negley Ave, Pittsburgh (15232). Phone 412/661-0631; fax 412/661-7525. www.appletreeb-b.com.* 8 rooms, 3 story. Children over 12 years only. Complimentary full breakfast. Check-in 3-6 pm, check-out 11 am. Historic building (1884). **$$**

INN AT OAKMONT. *300 Rte 909, Oakmont (15139). Phone 412/828-0410; fax 412/828-1358. www.pittsburghbnb.com.* 8 rooms, 2 story. Complimentary full breakfast. Check-in 2 pm, check-out 11 am. Fitness room. **$**

PRIORY INN. *614 Pressley St, Pittsburgh (15212). Phone 412/231-3338; fax 412/231-4838. www.thepriory.com.* 24 rooms, 3 story. Complimentary continental breakfast. Check-in 3 pm, check-out 11 am, weekends noon. European-style inn with fountain and floral arrangements in courtyard. Previously a haven for Benedictine monks (1888). **$**

Restaurants

★★ 1902 LANDMARK TAVERN. *24 Market Sq, Pittsburgh (15222). Phone 412/471-1902.* Italian, American menu. Lunch, dinner. Closed Sun; holidays.

Bar. Restored tavern (1902); ornate tin ceiling, original tiles. **$$**

★ **ABRUZZI'S RESTAURANT.** *52 S Tenth St, Pittsburgh (15203). Phone 412/431-4511.* Italian menu. Dinner. Bar. Casual attire. **$$**

★★★ **CAFE ALLEGRO.** *51 S 12th St, Pittsburgh (15203). Phone 412/481-7788; fax 412/481-4520.* The romantic ambience of the several intimate dining areas draws crowds to this South Side Mediterranean restaurant. Try uncomplicated dishes like fish cooked en papillote and pastas. Italian menu. Dinner. Closed holidays. Bar. Valet parking. **$$**

★★ **CAFE AT THE FRICK.** *7227 Reynolds St, Pittsburgh (15208). Phone 412/371-0600; fax 412/371-6030. www.frickart.org.* Lunch. Closed Mon; holidays. Outdoor seating. **$**

★★★ **CARLTON.** *500 Grant St, Pittsburgh (15219). Phone 412/391-4099; fax 412/391-4240. www.thecarltonrestaurant.com.* American menu. Lunch, dinner. Closed Sun; holidays. Bar. Children's menu. **$$$**

★★ **CASBAH.** *229 S Highland Ave, Pittsburgh (15206). Phone 412/661-5656; fax 412/661-0616. www.bigburrito.com.* Mediterranean menu. Lunch, dinner. Closed holidays. Bar. Casual attire. Outdoor seating. **$$**

★★ **CHEESE CELLAR CAFE & BAR.** *25 Station Sq, Pittsburgh (15219). Phone 412/471-3355; fax 412/281-0549.* French menu. Breakfast, lunch, dinner. Closed Thanksgiving, Dec 25. Bar. Children's menu. Outdoor seating. **$$**

★★ **THE CHURCH BREW WORKS.** *3525 Liberty Ave, Pittsburgh (15201). Phone 412/688-8200; fax 412/688-8201. www.churchbrew.com.* Regional American menu. Dinner. Closed Thanksgiving, Dec 25. Bar. Brew-pub in 1902 church; vaulted ceiling, stained-glass windows. Outdoor seating. **$$**

★★★ **CLIFFSIDE.** *1208 Grandview Ave, Pittsburgh (15211). Phone 412/431-6996.* American menu. Dinner. Closed holidays. Bar. Valet parking. **$$**

★★★ **COMMON PLEA.** *308 Ross St, Pittsburgh (15219). Phone 412/281-5140; fax 412/281-6856. www.commonplea.citysearch.com.* With its dark paneling, glass wall, and subdued lighting, this restaurant caters to the legal crowd. Seafood menu. Lunch, dinner. Closed holidays. Bar. Valet parking (dinner). **$$**

★★ **COZUMEL.** *5507 Walnut St, Pittsburgh (15232). Phone 412/621-5100.* Mexican menu. Lunch, dinner. Bar. Children's menu. Casual attire. **$**

★★ **D'IMPERIO'S.** *3412 William Penn Hwy, Pittsburgh (15235). Phone 412/823-4800; fax 412/823-4804.* Reserve ahead for Friday night alfresco dining in summer. Otherwise, go for traditional Italian favorites accompanied by opera and Italian crooners. American, Italian menu. Lunch, dinner. Closed Sun; holidays. Bar. Children's menu. **$$$**

★ **DAVE AND ANDY'S ICE CREAM PARLOR.** *207 Atwood St, Pittsburgh (15213). Phone 412/681-9906.* Closed holidays. 1930s look; some counters. **$**

★ **DEJAVU LOUNGE.** *2106 Penn Ave, Pittsburgh (15222). Phone 412/434-1144.* American, Pan-Asian menu. Lunch, dinner, late-night. Closed Sun. Bar. Casual attire. Outdoor seating. **$$**

★★ **GEORGETOWN INN.** *1230 Grandview Ave, Pittsburgh (15211). Phone 412/481-4424.* Seafood, steak menu. Lunch, dinner. Closed holidays. Bar. **$$$**

★★★ **GRAND CONCOURSE.** *1 Station Sq, Pittsburgh (15219). Phone 412/261-1717; fax 412/261-6041. www.muer.com.* Continental menu. Lunch, dinner, Sun brunch. Closed Dec 25. Bar. Children's menu. Converted railroad station. Outdoor seating. **$$$**

★★ **INDIA GARDEN.** *328 Atwood St, Pittsburgh (15213). Phone 412/682-3000; fax 412/682-3130. www.indiagarden.net.* Indian menu. Lunch, dinner. **$**

★★ **KAYA.** *2000 Smallman St, Pittsburgh (15222). Phone 412/261-6565; fax 412/261-1526. www.bigburrito.com.* Caribbean menu. Dinner. Closed holidays. Bar. Outdoor seating. **$$$**

★ KENNY B'S EATERY. *123 Sixth St, Pittsburgh (15222). Phone 412/201-1626.* American, Cuban menu. Breakfast, lunch, dinner. Casual attire. **$**

★ ★ LE MONT. *1114 Grandview Ave, Pittsburgh (15211). Phone 412/431-3100; fax 412/431-1204. www.lemontpittsburgh.com.* American menu. Dinner. Closed holidays. Bar. Valet parking. **$$$**

★ ★ ★ LE POMMIER. *2104 E Carson St, Pittsburgh (15203). Phone 412/431-1901. www.lepommier.com.* French menu. Lunch, dinner. Closed Sun; holidays. Bar. Located in oldest storefront in area (1863). Valet parking Fri, Sat. Outdoor seating. **$$**

★ ★ MAX'S ALLEGHENY TAVERN. *537 Suismon St, Pittsburgh (15212). Phone 412/231-1899; fax 412/231-5099. www.maxsalleghenytavern.com.* German menu. Lunch, dinner. Closed holidays. Bar. **$$**

★ ★ MEZZANOTTE CAFE. *4621 Liberty Ave, Pittsburgh (15224). Phone 412/688-8070. www.mezzanottecafe.com.* Modern Italian, Mediterranean menu. Lunch, dinner. Closed Sun; holidays. Bar. Casual attire. **$$**

★ ★ MONTEREY BAY FISH GROTTO. *1411 Grandview Ave, Pittsburgh (15211). Phone 412/481-4414; fax 412/481-4448. www.montereybayfishgrotto.com.* Lunch, dinner. Children's menu. **$$$**

★ ★ OLD EUROPE. *1209 E Carson St, Pittsburgh (15203). Phone 412/488-1700.* Eastern European menu. Dinner. Bar. Casual attire. **$$**

★ ★ PASTA PIATTO. *736 Bellefonte St, Pittsburgh (15232). Phone 412/621-5547; fax 412/621-2164.* Italian menu. Lunch, dinner. Closed holidays. Bar. Children's menu. **$$**

★ PENN BREWERY. *800 Vinial St, Troy Hill, Pittsburgh (15212). Phone 412/237-9402; fax 412/237-9406. www.pennbrew.com.* German menu. Lunch, dinner. Closed Sun; holidays. Bar. Children's menu. Restored 19th-century brewery, German beer hall-style communal dining. Outdoor seating. **$$**

★ ★ PICCOLO MONDO. *661 Andersen Dr, Pittsburgh (15220). Phone 412/922-0920; fax 412/922-0921. www.piccolo-mondo.com.* Northern Italian menu. Lunch, dinner. Closed Sun except Mother's Day; holidays. Bar. Children's menu. Jacket required. **$$**

★ ★ POLI. *2607 Murray Ave, Pittsburgh (15217). Phone 412/521-6400. www.polisince1921.com.* The Poli family has been operating this Italian seafood restaurant for three generations, and pride themselves on serving the freshest fish possible. Seafood, Italian menu. Lunch, dinner. Closed Mon; Thanksgiving, Dec 25. Bar. Children's menu. Casual attire. Valet parking. **$$**

★ PRIMANTI BROTHERS. *46 18th St, Pittsburgh (15222). Phone 412/263-2142. www.primantibros.com.* American, Italian menu. Dinner. Closed holidays. **$**

★ ★ RICO'S. *1 Rico Ln, Pittsburgh (15237). Phone 412/931-1989; fax 412/931-2293. www.ricosrestaurant.com.* Italian, American menu. Lunch, dinner. Closed Sun; holidays. Bar. Jacket required. Valet parking. **$$$**

★ ★ ★ SOBA. *5847 Ellsworth Ave, Pittsburgh (15232). Phone 412/362-5656; fax 412/361-4318. www.bigburrito.com.* Pan-Asian menu. Dinner. Bar. Outdoor seating. **$$$**

★ ★ ★ STEELHEAD GRILL. *112 Washington Pl, Pittsburgh (15219). Phone 412/394-3474; fax 412/394-1017. www.steelheadgrill.com.* Lunch, dinner. Children's menu. **$$$**

★ ★ SUSHI TWO. *2122 E Carson St, Pittsburgh (15203). Phone 412/431-7874; fax 412/431-7864. www.sushi2-too.com.* Japanese menu. Lunch, dinner. Closed Thanksgiving. Bar. **$$$**

★ ★ TAMBELLINI. *860 Saw Mill Run Blvd, Pittsburgh (15226). Phone 412/481-1118; fax 412/481-7565. www.tambellini.com.* Guests should come hungry when visiting Louis Tambellini's place just outside of Pittsburgh. Prime steaks, veal chops, pastas, and seafood dishes await the anxious diner; vegetarian dishes are also available. American menu. Lunch, dinner. Closed Sun; Jan 1, Thanksgiving, Dec 25. Bar. Children's menu. Valet parking (dinner). **$$**

★ ★ TESSARO'S. *4601 Liberty Ave, Pittsburgh (15224). Phone 412/682-6809.* American, Mexican menu. Lunch, dinner. Closed Sun; holidays. Bar.

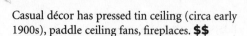

Casual décor has pressed tin ceiling (circa early 1900s), paddle ceiling fans, fireplaces. **$$**

★★ THAI PLACE. *5528 Walnut St, Pittsburgh (15232). Phone 412/687-8586; fax 412/687-7970.* Thai menu. Lunch, dinner. Bar. Casual attire. **$$**

★★★ TIN ANGEL. *1200 Grandview Ave, Pittsburgh (15211). Phone 412/381-1919; fax 412/381-6270. www.tinangel.com.* Located in a prime spot on Grandview Avenue, Tin Angel boasts wonderful views of downtown Pittsburgh in a candlelit setting. Seafood, steak menu. Closed Sun; holidays. Bar. **$$$**

Pittsburgh International Airport Area

See also Pittsburgh

Airport Information

Airport Pittsburgh International Airport.

Information Phone 412/472-3525

Lost and Found Phone 412/472-3500

Airlines Air Canada, Air Tran Airways, America West, American Airlines, American Trans Air, Continental Airlines, Delta Air Lines, Northwest Airlines, United Airlines, US Airways

Limited-Service Hotel

★ HAMPTON INN. *1420 Beers School Rd, Coraopolis (15108). Phone 412/264-0020; fax 412/264-3220. www.hamptoninn.com.* 129 rooms, 5 story. Pets accepted, some restrictions. Complimentary continental breakfast. Check-out noon. Airport transportation available. **$**

Full-Service Hotel

★★★ HYATT REGENCY PITTSBURGH INTERNATIONAL AIRPORT. *1111 Airport Blvd, Pittsburgh (15231). Phone 724/899-1234. www.hyatt.com.* 336 rooms, 11 story. Check-in 3 pm, check-out noon. Restaurant, bar. Fitness room. Indoor pool. Business center. **$**

Restaurant

★★★ HYEHOLDE. *190 Hyeholde Dr, Moontownship (15108). Phone 412/264-3116; fax 412/264-5723. www.hyeholde.com.* Don a jacket and tie for this long-standing outpost of English-country elegance 20 minutes from downtown Pittsburgh. The game and seafood menu and manor-like setting of rich tapestries, exposed wood beams, and candlelight are a popular choice for special events. Continental menu. Lunch, dinner. Closed Sun; holidays. Valet parking. Outdoor seating. Herb garden. **$$$**

Pocono Mountains (B-6)

See also Bushkill, Canadensis, Hawley, Milford, Mount Pocono, Shawnee on Delaware

Information Pocono Mountains Vacation Bureau, 1004 Main St, Stroudsburg 18360; phone 717/424-6050; for free brochures phone toll-free 800/POCONOS (Northeast Pennsylvania resort area)
Web site www.poconos.org

The Pocono Mountains area in northeast Pennsylvania extends north from Wind Gap and Delaware Water Gap into Pike, Carbon, Monroe, and Wayne counties. Within its 2,400 square miles almost every form of recreation can be found.

This scenic country with 500 lakes, including Lake Wallenpaupack (see HAWLEY), has hundreds of accommodations and is a well-established resort area. Visitors, many of whom return year after year, take advantage of the large plush resorts, smaller family-run resorts, housekeeping cottage resorts, camping resorts, country inns, and bed-and-breakfasts. There is primitive, forested country for those who wish to rough it. For the hunter, there are deer, bear, wildcat, and fox. For the freshwater angler, there are black bass, trout, pickerel, and walleye.

Summer offers boating, swimming, hiking, horseback riding, mountain biking, golf, theaters, and a host of other diversions. In the autumn, there is a magnificent display of foliage, as well as heritage festivals and country fairs. The first snowfall brings skiing, snowboarding, snow tubing, ice skating, sleigh rides, tobogganing, and snowmobiling.

The name "Pocono" was probably taken from the Native American pocohanne, meaning a stream between the mountains. Settled in the mid-1700s, the Poconos yielded iron and, later, coal. The lakes and forest still retain their charm. The land "between the mountains" is as inviting as it always has been.

Port Allegany (A-3)

See also Bradford

Settled 1816
Population 2,355
Elevation 1,481 ft
Area Code 814
Zip 16743
Information Chamber of Commerce, 22 Church St; phone 814/642-2181

Native Americans called this spot "canoe place" because here on the portage route between the Allegheny and Susquehanna headwaters they paused to build canoes. Early settlers followed their route. Soon after the town was established, lumbering operations reached their peak; later industrial expansion included coal mining and tanning. In the late 1890s, the borough became the center of a boom resulting from the discovery of natural gas and glass sand.

What to See and Do

Eldred World War II Museum. *201 Main St, Eldred (16731). 15 miles N on Hwy 155, 5 miles N on Hwy 446. Phone 814/225-2220.* Exhibits include battle maps, posters, dioramas with narrative, periscope, video history. Centerpiece is "Remembering the Women Behind the Front Lines" exhibit. Library. (Tues, Thurs, Sat-Sun) **FREE**

Sizerville State Park. *Sizerville State Park, Emporium. 19 miles S on Hwy 155. Phone 814/486-5605.* Approximately 385 acres. Swimming pool; fishing, hunting; cross-country skiing, snowmobiling. Picnicking, playground, snack bar. Tent and trailer sites.

Pottstown (C-5)

See also Hopewell Furnace National Historic Site, Limerick, Norristown, Reading

Settled 1701
Population 21,859
Elevation 160 ft
Area Code 610
Zip 19464
Information TriCounty Area Chamber of Commerce, 135 High St; phone 610/326-2900
Web site www.tricopa.com

An iron forge operating in 1714 at Manatawny Creek, about 3 miles north of Pottstown, was the first industrial establishment in the state. The borough was established by John Potts, an ironmaster, on land William Penn had earlier deeded to his son, John. Today, the community is the commercial and cultural hub for an area with a population of 130,000. Nearly 200 modern industries are located here.

What to See and Do

Boyertown Museum of Historic Vehicles. *85 S Walnut St, Boyertown (19512). 7 miles N via Hwys 100, 73. Phone 610/367-2090.* Collection of over 100 antique autos, trucks, sleighs, buggies, and bicycles. Also includes the Hill, which was among the first gasoline-powered cars. (Tues-Sun) **$$**

French Creek State Park. *843 Park Rd, Elverson (19520). 9 miles W on Hwy 724, then 4 miles S on Hwy 345. Phone 610/582-9680.* Approximately 7,330 acres, two lakes. Boating (rentals, mooring, launching), fishing. Swimming pool. Hiking trails. Playground, disc golf. Ice fishing. Picnicking. Tent and trailer sites, cabins.

Merritt's Museum of Childhood. *907 Ben Franklin Hwy W, Douglassville. 1 mile W on Hwy 422. Phone 610/385-3408.* Antique toys, costumed figures, furnishings; gift shop in lobby. (Mon, Wed-Sun; closed holidays) **$$** Admission includes

Mary Merritt Doll Museum. *843 Ben Franklin Hwy W, Pottstown. Phone 610/385-3809.* Antique dolls and toys dating from 1725 to 1900. (Mon, Wed-Sun; closed holidays)

Pottsgrove Manor. *W King St and Hwy 100. Phone 610/326-4014.* (1752) Newly restored house of John Potts, 18th-century ironmaster and founder of Pottstown; outstanding example of early Georgian architecture and furniture. Includes recently discovered slave quarters and Potts's office. Slide orientation. Museum shop. (Tues-Sun; closed holidays) **FREE**

Ringing Rocks Park. *1500 Ringing Rocks Park, Pottstown (19464). 3 miles N off Hwy 663. Phone 610/323-6560.* Roller skating (Fri-Sun; fee); nature trails, picnicking, interesting rock formations. (Daily) **FREE**

Special Event

Duryea Day Antique & Classic Auto Show. *Boyertown Community Park, 28 Warwick St, Pottstown.* Antique autos, trucks and other vehicles; displays, arts and crafts, flea market with automotive memorabilia, activities, Pennsylvania Dutch food. Labor Day weekend.

Limited-Service Hotels

★ **COMFORT INN.** *Hwy 100 and Shoemaker Rd, Pottstown (19464). Phone 610/326-5000; toll-free 800/879-2477; fax 610/970-7230. www.pottstownpacomfortinn.com.* 121 rooms, 4 story. Pets accepted, some restrictions; fee. Complimentary continental breakfast. Check-out noon. Pool. **$**

★ **HOLIDAY INN EXPRESS.** *1600 Industrial Hwy, Pottstown (19464). Phone 610/327-3300; toll-free 800/386-0031; fax 610/327-9447. www.hiexpottstownpa.com.* 120 rooms, 4 story. Complimentary continental breakfast. Check-out noon. Pool. **$**

Specialty Lodging

The following lodging establishment is approved by Mobil Travel Guide, but due to its unique and individualized nature has not been given a traditional Mobil Star rating. Included in this listing you may find bed-and-breakfasts, limited-service inns, guest ranches, and other unique hotel properties.

TWIN TURRETS INN. *11 E Philadelphia Ave, Boyertown (19512). Phone 610/367-4513; toll-free 877/877-7897; fax 610/369-7898. www.twinturrets.com.* 10 rooms, 3 story. Children over 12 years preferred. Complimentary full breakfast. Check-in 1 pm, check-out 11 am. Business center. Original Boyer mansion built in 1850; antiques and original art. **$**

Restaurants

★★★ **COVENTRY FORGE INN.** *3360 Coventryville Rd, Pottstown (19465). Phone 610/469-6222; fax 610/469-1909.* The regions first French restaurant is still its best. Housed in one of the oldest homes in the country, this dining establishment is a bit tricky to find, but worth the drive. French menu. Dinner. Closed Sun except Mother's Day, Mon; Jan 1, Dec 25. Bar. Built in 1717; antiques. **$$$**

★★ **GRACIE'S 21ST CENTURY CAFE.** *Mana Tawny Rd, Pine Forge (19548). Phone 610/323-4004. www.gracies21stcentury.com.* Contemporary American menu. Dinner. Closed July 4, Thanksgiving, Dec 25. Bar. Reservations recommended. Valet parking. Outdoor seating. Ultramodern facility. **$$$**

Quakertown (Bucks County) (C-6)

See also Allentown, Bethlehem, Doylestown (Bucks County), Pottstown

Founded 1715
Population 8,931
Elevation 500 ft
Area Code 215
Zip 18951
Information Upper Bucks County Chamber of Commerce, 2170 Portzer Rd; phone 215/536-3211 or Bucks County Conference and Visitors Bureau, 152 Swamp Rd, Doylestown 18901, phone 215/345-4552 or toll-free 800/836-2825
Web site www.ubcc.org

Once a station on the Underground Railroad, Quakertown today still retains some of its colonial appearance. In 1798, angered by what they considered an unfair federal tax and incited by one John Fries, Quakertown housewives started greeting tax assessors with pans of hot water. The "hot water" rebellion cooled down when federal troops arrived, but the town switched political parties (from Federalist to Jeffersonian) almost en masse.

What to See and Do

Mennonite Heritage Center. *565 Yoder Rd, Harleysville. 4 miles S of Hwy 309 on Hwy 113. Phone 215/256-3020.* An interpretive video and exhibits including quilts, Pennsylvania German Fraktur, furniture, books, deeds, and clothing show the history of local Mennonites through three centuries. (Tues-Sun) **DONATION**

Restaurants

★ LA PIAZZA CAFE. *1408 W Broad St, Quakertown (18951). Phone 215/536-2452; fax 215/536-7538.* Italian menu. Lunch, dinner. Closed holidays. Children's menu. Reservations recommended. **$$**

★ ★ MEYERS RESTAURANT. *Hwy 309, Quakertown (18951). Phone 215/536-4422. www.meyersrestaurant.com.* American menu. Breakfast, lunch, dinner. Closed 3 days late Dec. Bar. Children's menu. Casual attire. **$$**

Reading (C-5)

See also Denver/Adamstown, Ephrata, Hamburg, Hopewell Furnace National Historic Site, Kutztown, Lancaster, Limerick, Pottstown

Founded 1748
Population 81,207
Elevation 260 ft
Area Code 484 & 610
Information Reading & Berks County Visitors Bureau, 352 Penn St 19602; phone 610/375-4085 or toll-free 800/443-6610
Web site www.readingberkspa.com

A city of railroads and industry famous for its superb pretzels, Reading (RED-ing) was the second community in the United States to vote a Socialist government into office; however, the city has not had such a government for many years. Love of music and the thrift and vigor of the "Dutch" are reflected in the character of this unofficial capital of Pennsylvania Dutch land.

William Penn purchased the land now occupied by Reading from the Lenni-Lenape Native Americans and settled his two sons, Thomas and Richard, on it. They named it Reading (fern meadow) for their home in England. During the Revolution, the citizens of Reading mustered troops for the Continental army, forged cannon, and provided a depot for military supplies and a prison for Hessians and British. The hundreds of skilled German craftspeople, plus canal and railroad transportation, ignited Reading's industrial development. Today, some of the world's leading industries continue to headquarter here.

What to See and Do

Berks County Heritage Center. *2201 Tulpehocken Rd, Reading (19610). 4 miles N via Hwy 183, then W onto Red Bridge Rd. Phone 610/374-8839.* Historical interpretive complex. Here are the Gruber Wagon Works (1882), where finely crafted wagons were produced for farm and industry; Wertz's Red Bridge (1867), the longest single-span covered bridge in the state; Deppen Cemetery, with graves of Irish workers who died of "swamp fever" while building the Union Canal; C. Howard Hiester Canal Center, with its collection of canal artifacts. Tours of wagon works and canal center; orientation slide program. (May-Oct, Tues-Sun) **$$**

Conrad Weiser Homestead. *14 miles W via Hwy 422. Phone 610/589-2934.* (1729) Restored and furnished house of colonial "ambassador" to the Iroquois nation; springhouse; gravesite; visitor center; picnicking in 26-acre park. (Wed-Sun) **$$**

Daniel Boone Homestead. *400 Daniel Boone Rd, Reading (19508). 7 miles E on Hwy 422 to Baumstown, then N on Boone Rd. Phone 610/582-4900.* Birthplace of Daniel Boone in 1734. Approximately 570 acres; includes Boone House, barn, blacksmith shop, and sawmill. Picnicking. Nature trails. Youth camping. Visitor's center. (Tues-Sun; closed holidays) **$$**

Historical Society of Berks County. *940 Centre Ave, Reading. Phone 610/375-4375.* Local history exhibits; decorative arts, antiques, transportation displays. (Tues-Sat; closed holidays) **$$**

Koziar's Christmas Village. *782 Christmas Village Rd, Bernville. 12 miles N via Hwy 183. Phone 610/488-1110.* Valley set aglow with over 500,000 Christmas lights; Wishing Well Lane; two barns filled with handmade items, decorations; theme exhibits, Santa's Post Office. (Thanksgiving-Dec) **$$$**

Mid-Atlantic Air Museum. *Reading Regional Airport, Hwy 183 and Van Reed Rd, Reading. Phone 610/372-7333.* Aviation museum dedicated to the preservation of vintage aircraft; planes are restored to flying condition by volunteers. Collection of 40 airplanes and helicopters; 20 on public display, including Martin 4-0-4 airliners, B-25 bomber, and others. (Daily; closed Jan 1, Thanksgiving, Dec 25) **$$**

Outlet Shopping. *801 N 9th St, Reading (19604). Phone 610/375-4085; toll-free 800/443-6610.* More than 300 factory outlet stores can be found at five different shopping complexes. Contact Visitors Bureau.

Reading Public Museum and Art Gallery. *500 Museum Rd, Reading. Phone 610/371-5850.* In 25-acre Museum Park with stream. Exhibits of art and science. (Tues-Sun; closed holidays) **$$** Adjacent is

Planetarium. *Phone 610/371-5854.* Changing exhibits. Starand laser light shows. **$$**

Limited-Service Hotels

★★ BEST WESTERN DUTCH COLONY INN & SUITES. *4635 Perkiomen Ave, Reading (19606). Phone 610/779-2345; toll-free 800/828-2830; fax 610/779-8348. www.bestwestern.com.* 71 rooms, 2 story. Pets accepted; fee. Check-out noon. Restaurant, bar. Pool. **$**

★ COMFORT INN. *2200 Stacy Dr, Reading (19605). Phone 610/371-0500; fax 610/478-9421. www.choicehotels.com.* 60 rooms, 2 story. Complimentary continental breakfast. Check-out 11 am. Fitness room. Airport transportation available. **$**

★★ INN AT READING. *1040 N Park Rd, Wyomissing (19610). Phone 610/372-7811; toll-free 800/383-9713; fax 610/372-4545. www.innatreading.com.* 250 rooms, 2 story. Check-out 11 am. Restaurant, bar. Fitness room. Pool. Airport transportation available. Business center. **$**

★★ READING HOTEL. *1741 W Papermill Rd, Wyomissing (19610). Phone 610/376-3811; fax 610/375-7562.* 254 rooms, 5 story. Pets accepted; fee. Check-out noon. Restaurant, bar. Fitness room. Indoor pool, whirlpool. Airport transportation available. **$**

Restaurants

★★ ALPENHOF BAVARIAN. *903 Morgantown Rd, Reading (19607). Phone 610/373-1624; fax 610/373-8040. www.alphenhofonline.com.* American, German menu. Lunch, dinner. Closed Jan 1, Dec 25. Bar. Outdoor seating. **$$**

★★ ANTIQUE AIRPLANE. *4635 Perkiomen Ave, Reading (19606). Phone 610/779-2345; fax 610/779-8348.* Breakfast, lunch, dinner. Closed Jan 1, Dec 25. Bar. Children's menu. Casual elegance; aviation theme. **$$**

★★★ GREEN HILLS INN. *2444 Morgantown Rd, Reading (19607). Phone 610/777-9611.* French, American menu. Dinner. Closed Sun. **$$$**

Scranton (B-5)

See also Carbondale, Hawley, Honesdale, Pocono Mountains, Wilkes Barre

Settled 1771
Population 76,415
Elevation 754 ft
Area Code 570
Information Northeast Pennsylvania Convention and Visitors Bureau Montage Mountain Rd; phone 570/963-6363 or toll-free 800/22-WELCOME
Web site www.visitnepa.org

The first settlers here found a Monsey Native American village on the site. In 1840, George and Seldon Scranton built five iron furnaces using the revolutionary method of firing with anthracite coal instead of charcoal. Manufacture of iron and steel remained an important industry until 1901, when the mills moved to Lake Erie to ease transportation problems.

After World War II, Scranton thoroughly revamped its economy when faced with depletion of the anthracite coal mines, which for more than a century had fired its forges. Scranton's redevelopment drew nationwide attention and served as a model for problem cities elsewhere. Today, Scranton is the home of electronic and printing industries and is host to several major trucking firm terminals.

What to See and Do

Catlin House. *232 Monroe Ave, Scranton. Phone 570/344-3841.* (1912) Headquarters of Lackawanna Historical Society; period furnishings (colonial-1900s), historic exhibits, antiques; research library (fee). Tours available (fee). (Tues-Fri, also Sat afternoons; closed holidays) **FREE**

Lackawanna County Stadium. *235 Montage Mountain Rd, Scranton. Exit 51 off I-81. Phone 570/969-2255.* Open-air stadium/civic arena seats 11,000. Home of AAA baseball, high school and college football and marching band competitions. (Apr-Nov)

Montage Ski Area. *1000 Montage Mountain Rd, Scranton. S on I-81, exit 51, follow signs. Phone 570/969-7669. www.skimontage.com.* Quad, double, three triple chairlifts; school, rentals; snowmaking; bar, restaurant; lodge. Vertical drop 1,000 feet. Night skiing. More than 130 acres of trails set in 400 acres of mountainside. (Early Dec-late Mar, daily) Summer activities include water slides, batting cages, amphitheater (June-Labor Day). **$$$$**

Nay Aug Park. *Arthur Ave and Mulberry St, Scranton. Phone 570/348-4186.* More than 35 acres with memorials to pioneer days. Picnicking; swimming pool (fee); walking trail; refreshment stands; and the "Pioneer," a gravity railroad car dating back to 1850; weekend concerts (summer). (Daily) In park is

Anthracite Heritage Museum. *Keyser Ave and Bald Mountain Rd, Scranton. Phone 570/963-4804.* History and culture of anthracite region. Other affiliated parts of the complex are the Iron Furnaces; Museum of Anthracite Mining (see ASHLAND), with emphasis on the technology of the industry, and the 19th-century miners' village of Eckley, near Hazleton (see). (Daily; closed holidays) **$$**

Everhart Museum. *1901 Mulberry St, Scranton. Phone 570/346-7186. www.everhart-museum.org.* Permanent collections includes 19th- and 20th-century American art; Dorflinger glass; Native American, Asian, and primitive art; natural history displays, including Dinosaur Hall. Gift shop. (Tues-Sun; closed holidays) **$$**

Lackawanna Coal Mine Tour. *McDade Park, Scranton. Phone 570/963-MINE; toll-free 800/238-7245.* Underground coal mine 300 feet below ground shows world of anthracite miners. Conditions are authentic (damp, dark, slippery, and cold); dress appropriately. Above-ground facilities include a "shifting shanty" exhibit room with photo-mural graphic displays, mine artifacts, and video presentations; gift shop; restaurant. (Apr-Nov, daily; closed Thanksgiving) **$$$**

Scranton Iron Furnaces. *159 Cedar Ave, Scranton. Phone 570/963-3208.* Partially restored site of four anthracite-fired iron furnaces built 1848-1857 and used until 1902. Visitor center, outdoor exhibits. Self-guided tours (daily). Guided tours (late May-early Sept, Mon-Thurs). **FREE**

Steamtown National Historic Site. *150 S Washington Ave, Scranton. Phone toll-free 888/693-9391. www.nps.gov/stea.* Site with large collection of steam locomotives and other memorabilia located in an authentic freight yard. Steam train ride through yard (Memorial Day-Dec; daily). 25-mile train excursion (July 4-mid-Oct, Sat and Sun). **$$$**

Limited-Service Hotels

★ ★ CLARION HOTEL. *300 Meadow Ave, Scranton (18505). Phone 570/344-9811; toll-free 800/347-1551; fax 570/344-7799. www.choicehotels.com.* 125 rooms, 6 story. Check-out noon. Restaurant, bar. Pool. Airport transportation available. **$**

★ HAMPTON INN. *22 Montage Mountain Rd, Scranton (18507). Phone 570/342-7002; fax 570/342-7012. www.hamptoninn.com.* 129 rooms, 4 story. Complimentary continental breakfast. Check-out noon. Fitness room. Indoor pool, whirlpool. Airport transportation available. **$**

★ ★ INN AT NICHOLS VILLAGE. *1101 Northern Blvd, Clarks Summit (18411). Phone 570/587-1135; toll-free 800/642-2215; fax 570/586-7140. www.*

nicholsvillage.com. This inn is made of four separate buildings surrounded by a courtyard garden. Both an indoor pool and a sauna are available for guests to enjoy along with two family restaurants and one fine dining room. 135 rooms, 4 story. Check-out noon. Restaurant, bar. Fitness room. Indoor pool. Airport transportation available. 12 acres include over 1,000 rhododendrons; forestland. **$**

★★ **RADISSON LACKAWANNA STATION HOTEL SCRANTON.** *700 Lackawanna Ave, Scranton (18503). Phone 570/342-8300; fax 570/342-0380. www.radisson.com.* 145 rooms, 6 story. Check-out noon. Restaurant, bar. Fitness room. Whirlpool. Airport transportation available. Located in the historic Lackawanna train station building. **$**

★★ **SHADOWBROOK INN AND RESORT.** *615 Rte 6 E, Tunkhannock (18657). Phone 570/836-2151; toll-free 800/955-0295; fax 570/836-5655. www.shadowbrookresort.com.* 73 rooms, 3 story. Complimentary continental breakfast. Check-in 2 pm, check-out noon. Restaurant, bar. Fitness room. Pool. Golf, pro. **$**

Restaurant

★ **COOPER'S SEAFOOD HOUSE.** *701 N Washington Ave, Scranton (18509). Phone 570/346-6883; fax 570/346-8049. www.coopers-seafood.com.* Lunch, dinner. Closed holidays. Bar. Children's menu. **$$**

Sellersville

Restaurant

★★ **WASHINGTON HOUSE.** *136 N Main St, Sellersville (18960). Phone 215/257-3000; fax 215/257-3166. www.washington-house.com.* This beautifully restored Victorian restaurant was originally a farmhouse built in the 18th century. American menu. Lunch, dinner, late-night. Closed Jan 1, July 4, Dec 25. Bar. Children's menu. Casual attire. **$$**

Shamokin Dam (C-4)

Settled 1790
Population 1,502
Elevation 500 ft
Area Code 570
Zip 17876

Full-Service Inns

★★★ **INN AT NEW BERLIN.** *321 Market St, New Berlin (17855). Phone 570/966-0321; toll-free 800/797-2350; fax 570/966-9557. www.newberlin-inn.com.* 9 rooms, 2 story. Complimentary full breakfast. Check-in 3 pm, check-out noon. Restaurant. **$**

Sharon (B-1)

See also Mercer

Settled 1802
Population 16,328
Elevation 998 ft
Area Code 724
Zip 16146
Information Mercer County Convention & Visitors Bureau, 50 N Water Ave, 16146; phone 724/748-5315 or toll-free 800/637-2370
Web site www.mercercountypa.org

In the heart of the rich Shenango Valley, Sharon is a busy industrial city that started with a lonely mill on the banks of the Shenango River. Steel, fabrication of steel products, and manufacture of electric transformers are a major part of the economic base. The Shenango Dam and its reservoir are northeast of town, near Sharpsville, and offer many recreational activities.

What to See and Do

Shenango Lake. *2442 Celly Rd, Hermitage (16148). 6 miles N of I-80, Hwy 18. Phone 724/646-1115 (camping).* Swimming, waterskiing; fishing, hunting; boating (ramps). Picnicking. More than 300 tent and trailer sites (mid-May-Labor Day; rest of Sept, reduced number of sites; electric hookups additional).

Special Event

The Small Ships Review. *101 Chestnut Ave, Sharon. Downtown. Phone 724/981-3123.* Parade of ships, entertainment, fireworks, food. July.

Full-Service Inn

★ ★ ★ TARA COUNTRY INN. *2844 Lake Rd, Clark (16113). Phone 724/962-2992; toll-free 800/782-2803; fax 724/962-3250. www.tara-inn.com.* 27 rooms, 2 story. No children allowed. Check-in 3 pm, check-out noon. Restaurants. Indoor pool, outdoor pool. Business center. **$$$**

Restaurant

★ QUAKER STEAK & LUBE. *101 Chestnut St, Sharon (16146). Phone 724/981-9464; fax 724/981-1504. www.quakersteakandlube.com.* Steak menu. Lunch, dinner. Bar. Children's menu. Former gas station; vintage automobiles, license plates, memorabilia. Casual attire. Outdoor seating. **$$**

Shartlesville

See also Hamburg, Reading

Population 300
Elevation 560 ft
Area Code 610
Zip 19554

What to See and Do

Roadside America. *109 Roadside Dr, Shartlesville. Just off Hwy 22, exit I-78. Phone 610/488-6241.* This miniature "village" consists of O-gauge trains, villages and scenes, with 66 miniature displays re-creating 200 years of life in rural America. Started in 1903, displays now cover 6,000 square feet. (Daily; closed Dec 25) **$$**

Restaurants

★ BLUE MOUNTAIN FAMILY RESTAURANT. *I-78, Shartlesville (19554). Phone 610/488-0353; fax 610/488-0500.* American menu. Breakfast, lunch, dinner. Closed Jan 1, Dec 25. Bar. Children's menu. **$$**

★ HAAG'S HOTEL. *Main and Third sts, Shartlesville (19554). Phone 717/362-3476.* American menu. Breakfast, lunch, dinner. Closed Dec 25. Bar. In former hotel (1914); Early American décor. **$$**

Shawnee on Delaware

See also Bushkill, Stroudsburg

Population 400
Elevation 320 ft
Area Code 717
Zip 18356
Information Pocono Mountains Vacation Bureau Inc, 1004 Main St, Stroudsburg 18360; phone 717/424-6050; for free brochures, phone toll-free 800/POCONOS
Web site www.poconos.org

What to See and Do

Shawnee Mountain Ski Area. *Hollow Rd, Shawnee on Delaware. 6 miles N on I-80, exit 52, follow signs. Phone 570/421-7231. www.shawneemt.com.* Quad, triple, seven double chairlifts; patrol, school, rentals; snowmaking; cafeteria, bar; nursery. 23 slopes and trails; longest run 1 mile; vertical drop 700 feet. (late Nov-Mar, daily) Night skiing. Half-day rates. **$$$$**

Shawnee Place Play & Water Park. *Hollow Rd, Shawnee on Delaware. I-80, exit 52, Rte 209 N and follow signs. Phone 570/421-7231.* Kids can jump in a pool of plastic balls, swing on a cable glide, climb on cargo nets, glide down water slides, and splash in a wading pool. Magic shows, picnics, video games, snack bar. (Mid-June-early Sept, daily; late May-mid-June, weekends only). **$$$**

Limited-Service Hotel

★ ★ SHAWNEE INN AND GOLF RESORT. *1 River Rd, Shawnee on Delaware (18356). Phone 570/424-4000; toll-free 800/742-9633; fax 570/424-9168. www.shawneeinn.com.* 103 rooms, 3 story. Check-in 4 pm, check-out noon. Restaurant, bar. Children's activity center. Indoor pool, three outdoor pools, children's pool. Golf. Tennis. **$$**

Somerset (D-2)

See also Donegal, Johnstown, Ligonier

Settled 1773
Population 6,762
Elevation 2,190 ft
Area Code 814
Zip 15501
Information Somerset County Chamber of Commerce, 601 N Center Ave; phone 814/445-6431
Web site www.shol.com/smrst/somrst.htm

Somerset, a county seat, is also the marketing place for farms, lumber mills, and coal mines in the area. James Whitcomb Riley described the countryside in his poem *'Mongst the Hills of Somerset.* The county offers fishing, swimming, boating, hiking, biking, camping, skiing, and ice skating.

What to See and Do

Hidden Valley Ski Area. *1 Craighead Dr, Hidden Valley. 12 miles W of PA Tpke Somerset exit 10; 8 miles E of PA Tpke Donegal exit 9, on Hwy 31. Phone 814/443-8000; toll-free 800/443-7544 (snow conditions). www.hiddenvalleyresort.com.* Six chairlifts, beginner's lift; patrol, school, rentals; snowmaking; cafeteria, restaurant, bars; nursery. Longest run 5,280 feet; vertical drop 610 feet; 28 slopes (Dec-Mar, daily). 30 miles of cross-country trails (rentals). Night skiing. Shuttle service. Conference center, lodging. Year-round facilities, activities. **$$$$**

Kooser State Park. *9 miles NW on Hwy 31. Phone 814/445-8673.* Approximately 220 acres, this park contains a 4-acre lake with fishing and a swimming beach (Memorial Day-Labor Day). The park also offers cross-country skiing and sledding in winter and picnicking and camping in summer (tent and trailer sites, cabins).

Laurel Hill State Park. *1454 Laurel Hill Park Rd, Somerset (15501). 8 miles W on Hwy 31, then SW on unnumbered road. Phone 814/445-7725.* Approximately 3,900 acres. Swimming beach, snack bar; boating (mooring, launching). Hiking, hunting; snowmobiling, ice fishing. Picnicking. Tent and trailer sites.

Mount Davis. *26 miles S on Hwy 219 to Salisbury, then W on unnumbered road. Phone 724/238-9533.* Highest point in state (3,213 feet).

Somerset Historical Center. *10649 Somerset Pike, Somerset (15501). 5 miles N on Hwy 985. Phone 814/445-6077.* Museum exhibits on rural life; outdoor display includes log house, log barn, covered bridge, sugarhouse. Bus tour (fee). (Tues-Sat; closed holidays) **$$**

Special Events

Farmers' and Threshermen's Jubilee. *New Centerville. 9 miles SW via Hwy 281. Phone 814/926-3142.* Equipment demonstrations; tractor-pulling, horseshoe-pitching, tobacco-spitting contests; antique car show and flea market; food. Early Sept.

Maple Festival. *Festival Park, 120 Meyers Ave, Somerset. Phone 814/634-0213.* Apr.

Mountain Craft Days. *Somerset Historical Center, 10649 Somerset Pike, Somerset. Phone 814/445-6077.* More than 150 traditional craft demonstrations; antique exhibits; entertainment. Early Sept.

Somerfest. *Laurel Arts/Phillip Dressler Center for the Arts, 214 Harrison Ave, Somerset. Phone 814/443-2433.* German festival: dancing, competitions, entertainment, food, tours. Mid-July.

Springs Folk Festival. *Between Salisbury, PA (Hwy 219) and Grantsville, MD (Hwy 40, I-68 exit 19). Phone 814/662-4158.* Crafts demonstrations include bread baking, wheat weaving, basket and broom making, candle dipping, quilt stitching; entertainment featuring banjo and fiddle music; pioneer exhibits on forest trail; maple sugaring, apple butter boiling, log hewing; museum adjacent with antique tools, furnishings, historical artifacts. Early Oct.

Limited-Service Hotel

★ RAMADA. *215 Ramada Rd, Somerset (15501). Phone 814/443-4646; fax 814/445-7539. www.ramada.com.* 152 rooms, 2 story. Pets accepted. Check-out noon. Restaurant, bar. Indoor pool, whirlpool. **$**

Full-Service Resort

★★ HIDDEN VALLEY RESORT CONFERENCE CENTER. *1 Craighead Dr, Hidden Valley (15502). Phone 814/443-6454; toll-free 800/458-0175; fax 814/443-1907. www.hiddenvalleyresort.com.* 206 rooms, 3 story. Check-in 4 pm, check-out noon. Restaurant, bar. Children's activity center. Fitness room. Indoor pool, three outdoor pools, whirlpool. Golf. Tennis. Airport transportation available. Located in scenic Laurel Highlands mountain area. **$$**

Full-Service Inn

★★★ INN AT GEORGIAN PLACE. *800 Georgian Place Dr, Somerset (15501). Phone 814/443-1043; fax 814/443-6220. www.theinnatgeorgianplace.com.* 11 rooms, 3 story. Pets accepted, some restrictions. Children over 5 years only. Complimentary full breakfast. Check-in 3 pm, check-out noon. Restaurant. Georgian mansion built in 1915; chandeliers, marble foyer. **$**

Specialty Lodging

The following lodging establishment is approved by Mobil Travel Guide, but due to its unique and individualized nature has not been given a traditional Mobil Star rating. Included in this listing you may find bed-and-breakfasts, limited-service inns, guest ranches, and other unique hotel properties.

BAYBERRY INN BED AND BREAKFAST. *611 N Center Ave, Somerset (15501). Phone 814/445-8471.* 11 rooms, 2 story. Children over 12 years only. Complimentary continental breakfast. Check-in 3 pm, check-out 11 am. Brick house built 1902. **$**

Restaurants

★ COUNTRY COTTAGE. *2817 New Centerville Rd, Somerset (15557). Phone 814/926-4078.* Breakfast, lunch, dinner. Closed holidays. Children's menu. **$**

★★ OAKHURST TEA ROOM. *2409 Glades Pike, Somerset (15501). Phone 814/443-2897; fax 814/445-3781. www.oakhursttearoom.com.* American menu. Lunch, dinner, brunch. Closed Mon; Dec 25. Bar. Children's menu. Outdoor seating. **$$**

★★ PINE GRILL. *800 N Center Ave, Somerset (15501). Phone 814/445-2102; fax 814/443-6043.* Breakfast, lunch, dinner. Closed Dec 25. Bar. Children's menu. Opened 1941. **$**

State College (C-3)

See also Bellefonte

Settled 1859
Population 38,420
Elevation 1,154 ft
Area Code 814
Information Centre County Convention & Visitors Bureau, 800 E Park Ave, 16803; phone 814/231-1400 or toll-free 800/358-5466
Web site www.visitpennstate.org

The home of Pennsylvania State University and principally concerned with services to this institution, this borough is near the geographic center of the state. In the beautiful Nittany Valley, State College is surrounded by farmland famous for its production of oats and swine. Iron ore was discovered just east of town in 1790, and many iron furnaces later sprang up.

What to See and Do

Columbus Chapel–Boal Mansion Museum. *Business Rte 322, Boalsburg. 4 miles E on Hwy 322. Phone 814/466-6210.* The mansion has been the Boal family home since 1789 and includes original furnishings, china, tools, and weapons. Colonel Theodore Davis Boal, who outfitted his own troop for World War I, lived here. The 16th-century chapel belonged to the family of Christopher Columbus in Spain and was brought here in 1909 by Boal relatives. It contains religious items and Renaissance and baroque art, as well as an admiral's desk and explorer's cross that belonged to Columbus himself. Summer concerts on grounds. (May-early-Oct, Tues-Sun) **$$$**

Mount Nittany Vineyard & Winery. *7 miles E on Hwy 322, E on Hwy 45, N on Linden Hall Rd. Phone 814/466-6373.* Stone-faced, chalet-style building nestled on southern slopes of Mount Nittany. Tasting room offers variety of wines and view of large pond, vineyard, and mountains. Group tastings (by appointment). (Fri-Sun; closed holidays, also Jan) **FREE**

Penn's Cave. *222 Penns Cave Rd, Centre Hall (16828). NE on Hwy 26, SE on Hwy 144, then 5 miles E of Centre Hall on Hwy 192. Phone 814/364-1664.* A one-hour, 1-mile boat trip through cavern; stalactites, stalagmites; plus ride-through wildlife park. Picnic area; visitor center; gift shop; snack bar. (Mid-Feb-Nov, daily) **$$$$**

Pennsylvania Military Museum. *Boalsburg. 4 miles E on Hwy 322, in Boalsburg. Phone 814/466-6263.* On grounds of 28th Division Shrine; dioramas; battle exhibits and equipment from the Revolutionary War to the present. Audiovisual program; military bookstore. (Tues-Sun; closed holidays) **$$**

Pennsylvania State University. *College and Atherton sts, State College (16802). On Hwy 322 in University Park. Phone 814/865-4700.* (1855) (41,000 students) Approximately 760 major buildings on a 15,984-acre campus; it is the land grant institution of Pennsylvania. On campus are

Ag Hill, The College of Agriculture. Showplace for state's dairy industry including the dairy center, off Park Rd near stadium, with five herds of cows, automatic milking equipment (daily). The creamery, Curtain Rd, has retail salesroom for cheeses, milk, cream, ice cream (daily; closed holidays). Also test flower gardens off Park Rd near East Halls (July-Sept). **FREE**

Earth and Mineral Sciences Museum. *Pollock Rd, State College. Steidle Building. Phone 814/865-6427.* Exhibitions of ores, gems, and fossils; automated displays; art gallery. (Mon-Fri; closed holidays) **FREE**

Old Main. *E of Mall near Pollock Rd. Phone 814/865-2501.* (1929) Present building, on site of original Old Main (1863), uses many of the original stones; topped by lofty bell tower. Here are Henry Varnum Poor's land grant frescoes. (Mon-Fri; closed holidays) **FREE**

Whipple Dam State Park. *10 miles S on Hwy 26, then 1 mile E on unnumbered road. Phone 814/667-3808.* Approximately 250 acres. Swimming beach; fishing, hunting; boating (launching, mooring). Hiking. Snowmobiling, ice skating, ice fishing. Picnicking, snack bar.

Special Events

Central Pennsylvania Festival of the Arts. *403 S Allen St # 201, State College. Phone 814/237-3682.* Open-air display of visual and performing arts; indoor exhibits; demonstrations of arts and crafts; food booths. Mid-July.

Centre County Grange Fair. *237 Hoffer St, State College (16828). Hwy 144 S, at Grange Park in Centre Hall. Phone 814/364-9674.* Exhibits, livestock show, rides, concessions, entertainment. Last week in Aug.

Memorial Day Celebration. *1402 S Atherton St, State College. In Boalsburg. Phone 814/231-1400.* Celebrate the holiday in the birthplace of Memorial Day.

Limited-Service Hotels

★★ AUTOPORT MOTEL & RESTAURANT. *1405 S Atherton St, State College (16801). Phone 814/237-7666; toll-free 800/932-7678; fax 814/237-7456. www.autoport.statecollege.com.* 86 rooms, 3 story. Check-out 11 am. Restaurant, bar. Pool. **$**

★★ DAYS INN. *240 S Pugh St, State College (16801). Phone 814/238-8454; toll-free 800/258-3297; fax 814/237-1607. www.daysinn.com.* 184 rooms, 6 story. Pets accepted, some restrictions; fee. Complimentary continental breakfast. Check-out noon. Restaurant, bar. Fitness room. Indoor pool. Airport transportation available. Business center. **$**

★ HAMPTON INN. *1101 E College Ave, State College (16801). Phone 814/231-1590; fax 814/238-7320. www.hamptoninn.com.* 121 rooms, 3 story. Complimentary continental breakfast. Pool. Airport transportation available. **$**

Full-Service Hotels

★★★ ATHERTON HOTEL. *125 S Atherton St (US 322 Business), State College (16801). Phone 814/231-2100; toll-free 800/832-0132; fax 814/237-1130. www.atherton.statecollege.com.* This inn is located 1/2 mile from Penn State. The Anthropology Museum, Historic Boalsburg Village, and Palmer Museum of Art are also nearby. 150 rooms, 7 story. Check-out noon. Restaurant, bar. Airport transportation available. **$**

★★★ NITTANY LION INN. *200 W Park Ave, State College (16803). Phone 814/865-8500; toll-free 800/233-7505; fax 814/865-8501. www.pshs.psu.edu.* 237 rooms, 3 story. Check-in 3 pm, check-out noon. Restaurant, bar. Fitness room. Airport transportation available. Located on the main campus of Penn State. **$**

Full-Service Resort

★★★ TOFTREES RESORT AND FOUR STAR GOLF CLUB. *1 Country Club Ln, State College (16803). Phone 814/234-8000; toll-free 800/458-3602; fax 814/238-4404. www.toftrees.com.* 113 rooms, 3 story. Check-in 3 pm, check-out noon. Restaurant, bar. Fitness room. Pool. Golf. Tennis. Airport transportation available. Mediterranean décor. **$**

Full-Service Inn

★★★ CARNEGIE HOUSE. *100 Cricklewood Dr, State College (16803). Phone 814/234-2424; toll-free 800/229-5033; fax 814/231-1299. www.cmagic.com/ch.* 22 rooms, 3 story. Complimentary continental breakfast. Check-in 3 pm, check-out 11 am. Restaurant. Airport transportation available. Décor and ambiance is reminiscent of Scotland. **$**

Restaurants

★★ TAVERN. *220 E College Ave, State College (16801). Phone 814/238-6116. www.thetavern.com.* Dinner. Closed holidays. Bar. Children's menu. **$$**

★★★ VICTORIAN MANOR. *901 Pike St, Lemont (16851). Phone 814/238-5534; fax 814/237-7890.* Each individually decorated dining room in this Victorian house offers a charming setting for a lovely meal. French, American menu. Dinner. Closed Mon; holidays. Historic building (1891). Victorian décor. **$$**

Stroudsburg (B-6)

See also Easton, Pocono Mountains, Shawnee on Delaware

Settled 1769
Population 5,756
Elevation 430 ft
Area Code 570
Zip 18360
Information Pocono Mountains Vacation Bureau, Inc, 1004 Main St; phone 570/424-6050; for free brochures, phone toll-free 800/POCONOS
Web site www.poconos.org

This is a center for the Pocono Mountains resort area and the surrounding rural community. It is the Monroe County seat.

What to See and Do

Alpine Mountain Ski Area. *Hwy 447, Analomink. 6 miles N via Hwy 191, 447 N, just outside Analomink. Phone 570/595-2150; toll-free 800/233-8240. www.alpinemountain.com.* Two quad, one double chairlift; patrol, school, rentals; snowmaking; lodge, restaurant, bar; child-care center. Vertical drop 500 feet. 21 trails and slopes. Night skiing. (Dec-Mar, daily) **$$$$**

Canoeing. *Phone 570/421-0180.* Canoe trips on the Delaware River; equipment provided; also transportation to and from the river. (May-Oct) Contact Chamberlain Canoes, PO Box 155, Minisink Hills 18341. **$$$$**

Quiet Valley Living Historical Farm. *1000 Turkey Hill Rd, Stroudsburg (18360). 3 1/2 miles SW on Hwy 209 Business, then 1 1/2 miles S (follow signs). Phone 570/992-6161.* A log house (1765) with kitchen and parlor added 1892; 12 other original or reconstructed buildings. Demonstrations of seasonal farm activities. Farm animals, garden, gift shop. Guided tours with costumed guides, 1 1/2-2 hours. (Late June-Labor Day, Tues-Sun) **$$$**

Stroud Mansion. *900 Main St, Stroudsburg (18360). Phone 570/421-7703.* (18th century). Built by founder of city; houses Historical Society of Monroe County. Historical artifacts, genealogical records. Tours. (Tues-Fri, also Sun afternoons; closed holidays) **$**

Limited-Service Hotels

★★ BEST WESTERN POCONO INN. *700 Main St, Stroudsburg (18360). Phone 570/421-2200; toll-free 888/508-2378; fax 570/421-5561. www.bestwestern.com.* 90 rooms, 4 story. Check-out 11 am. Restaurant, bar. Indoor pool, whirlpool. **$**

★★ SHANNON INN. *US Rte 209 and State Rte 447, Stroudsburg (18301). Phone 570/424-1951; toll-free 800/424-8052; fax 570/424-7782.* 120 rooms, 2 story. Complimentary continental breakfast. Check-out 11 am. Restaurant, bar. Indoor pool. **$**

Full-Service Resort

★ ★ **CAESARS POCONO PALACE.** *Rte 209, Marshalls Creek (18335). Phone 570/226-2101; toll-free 800/233-4141; fax 570/226-2109. www.caesarspoconos resorts.com.* 189 rooms. No children allowed. Check-in 3 pm, check-out 11 am. Restaurant, bar. Fitness room. Indoor pool, outdoor pool, whirlpool. Golf. **$$**

Restaurants

★ **ARLINGTON DINER.** *834 N 9th St, Stroudsburg (18360). Phone 570/421-2329.* Dinner. Closed Jan 1, Thanksgiving, Dec 25. Children's menu. **$$**

★ **BROWNIE'S IN THE BURG.** *700 Main St, Stroudsburg (18360). Phone 570/421-2200.* Seafood, steak menu. Lunch, dinner. Bar. **$$**

★ **LEE'S.** *PA 611, Bartonsville (18321). Phone 570/ 421-1212. www.leesrestaurant.com.* Chinese, Japanese menu. Lunch, dinner. Closed Thanksgiving. Bar. Reservations recommended. **$$**

★ **SARAH STREET GRILL.** *550 Quaker Alley, Stroudsburg (18360). Phone 570/424-9120; fax 570/ 424-9535. www.sarahstreetgrill.com.* American menu. Lunch, dinner. Bar. Children's menu. Casual attire. Outdoor seating. **$$**

★ ★ **STONEBAR INN.** *PA 209, Stroudsburg (18360). Phone 570/992-6634; fax 570/992-6884.* Dinner. Closed holidays. Bar. Children's menu. Reservations recommended. Outdoor seating. Fireside dining. **$$**

Tannersville

See also Pocono Mountains, Stroudsburg

Population 1,200
Elevation 890 ft
Area Code 570
Zip 18372
Information Pocono Mountains Vacation Bureau Inc, 1004 Main St, Stroudsburg 18360; phone 570/424-6050; for free brochures, phone toll-free 800/POCONOS.
Web site www.poconos.org

What to See and Do

Camelback Ski Area. *Camelback Rd. 3 1/2 miles W off I-80, exit 45, in Big Pocono State Park. Phone 570/ 629-1661; toll-free 800/233-8100 (mid-atlantic states, ski report). www.skicamelback.com.* Two quad, three triple, seven double chairlifts, surface lift; patrol, school, rentals; snowmaking; cafeteria, restaurant, bar; nursery. Longest run 1 mile; vertical drop 800 feet. Night skiing. (Late Nov-late Mar, daily) 33 trails. Alpine slide, water slides, swimming pool, bumper boats, entertainment (mid-June-Labor Day, daily; mid-May-mid-June and Labor Day-Oct, weekends only). Single and combination tickets. **$$$$**

Full-Service Resort

★ ★ **CAESARS POCONO RESORTS.** *Rte 611, Brookdale Rd, Scotrun (28374). Phone 570/839-8844; toll-free 800/233-4141; fax 570/839-2414. www. caesarspoconoresorts.com.* 127 rooms, 2 story. Check-in 3 pm, check-out 11 am. Restaurant, bar. Children's activity center. Fitness room. Indoor pool, outdoor pool, children's pool, whirlpool. Tennis. **$$**

Titusville (A-1)

See also Franklin (Venango County), Meadville, Oil City

Settled 1796
Population 6,146
Elevation 1,199 ft
Area Code 814
Zip 16354
Information Titusville Area Chamber of Commerce, 202 W Central Ave; phone 814/827-2941

Titusville spreads from the banks of Oil Creek, so called because of the oil that appeared on its surface. Edwin L. Drake drilled the first successful oil well in the world on Aug 27, 1859. Overnight, Titusville became the center of the worldwide oil industry.

What to See and Do

Drake Well Museum. *East Bloss and Allen St Ext. 1 mile SE of Hwy 8. Phone 814/827-2797.* Site of world's first oil well; operating replica of Drake derrick and engine house; picnic area. Museum contains dioramas, working models, life-size exhibits depicting history of oil. (May-Oct: daily; Nov-Apr: Tues-Sat, also Sun afternoons) **$$**

Limited-Service Resort

★★ **CROSS CREEK RESORT.** *Rte 8 S, Titusville (16354). Phone 814/827-9611; toll-free 800/461-3173; fax 814/827-2062. www.crosscreekresort.com.* 94 rooms, 2 story. Check-out 2 pm. Restaurant, bar. Pool. Golf. Tennis. **$**

Towanda (A-5)

See also Mansfield, Scranton

Settled 1794
Population 1,131
Elevation 737 ft
Area Code 570
Zip 18848
Information Endless Mountains Visitors Bureau, 712 Rte 6E, Tunkhannock 18657-9232; phone 570/836-5431 or toll-free 800/769-8999
Web site www.endlessmountains.org

On the north branch of the Susquehanna River, Towanda takes its name from a Native American word meaning "where we bury the dead."

In 1793, the Asylum Company purchased 1,600 acres of these wild valleys as a refuge for Marie Antoinette of France, should she escape to America. "La Grande Maison," a queenly house, was built. French noblemen settled here and a thriving community (called Azilum) was planned. The colony was unsuccessful and most of its founders returned to France. Many of their descendants, however, still live in Bradford County.

What to See and Do

David Wilmot's Burial Place. *Riverside Cemetery, William and Chestnut sts, Towanda.* Congressman (1845-1851), senator (1861-1863), leader of the Free Soil Party, Wilmot introduced the Wilmot Proviso in Congress, which would have required the US to outlaw slavery in any lands purchased from Mexico. This was an important factor in the dissension between North and South that led to the Civil War.

French Azilum. *8 miles SE via Hwys 6, 187. Phone 570/265-3376.* Site of colony for refugees from the French Revolution (1793-1803). Three cabins with crafts, tool exhibits; log cabin museum (1793); Laporte House (1836), built by son of one of colony's founders, reflects elegant French influence. Special events. Guided tours. (June-Aug, Wed-Sun; May, Sept-Oct, Sat, Sun) **$$**

Tioga Point Museum. *724 S Main St, Athens. 17 miles N off Hwy 220, on Hwy 199, Spalding Memorial Building. Phone 570/888-7225.* Mementos of French Azilum; Civil War, Stephen Foster and Native American exhibits; historical displays of early canals and steam railroad. (Tues, Thurs and Sat; closed holidays) **DONATION**

Valley Railroad Museum. *S Lehigh Ave, Sayre. 15 miles N off Hwy 220. Phone 570/888-1881.* Century-old Lehigh Valley passenger station houses museum with displays of railroad memorabilia and railroad exhibit of Lehigh Valley in miniature; gift shop. (Tues-Sun; closed holidays) **$$**

Limited-Service Hotel

★★ **BEST WESTERN GRAND VICTORIAN INN.** *255 Spring St, Sayre (18840). Phone 570/888-7711; toll-free 800/627-7972; fax 570/888-0541. www.bestwestern.com.* 100 rooms, 4 story. Check-out 11 am. Restaurant, bar. Fitness room. Indoor pool, whirlpool. Tennis. **$**

Tunkhannock

Restaurant

★ **FIREPLACE.** *1111 PA 6W, Tunkhannock (18657). Phone 570/836-9662; fax 570/836-5795.* Lunch, dinner. Closed Dec 25. Bar. Children's menu. **$$**

Uniontown (D-1)

See also Connellsville

Settled 1768
Population 12,422
Elevation 999 ft
Area Code 724
Zip 15401
Information Laurel Highlands Visitors Bureau, 120 E Main St, Ligonier 15658; phone 724/238-5661
Web site www.laurelhighlands.org

Coal and its byproducts made Uniontown prosperous, but with the decline in coal mining the city has developed a more diversified economic base. First known as Union, this city has been the Fayette County seat since 1784. General Lafayette and his son, George Washington de Lafayette, came on a visit after the Revolutionary War and were welcomed by Albert Gallatin, one-time senator and secretary of the Treasury. Uniontown was a hotbed of the Whiskey Rebellion, and federal troops were sent here in 1794.

What to See and Do

Braddock's Grave. *200 Caverns Park Rd, Farmington (15437).* Granite monument marks burial place of British General Edward Braddock, who was wounded in battle with French and Native American forces on July 9, 1755, and died four days later.

Fort Necessity National Battlefield. *1 Washington Pkwy, Farmington (15437). 11 miles SE on Hwy 40. Phone 724/329-5512.* (1754) The site of Washington's first major battle and the opening battle of the French and Indian War (1754). This land was known as the Great Meadows. A portion was later purchased by Washington, who owned it until his death. A replica of the original fort was built on the site following an archaeological survey in 1953. Picnic area (mid-spring-late fall). **$$** Nearby and included in the admission fee is

Visitor Center. Exhibits on battle at Great Meadows; audiovisual program. (Daily; closed Dec 25)

Friendship Hill National Historic Site. *15 miles S on Hwy 119 to Hwy 166. Phone 724/329-5512.* Preserves the restored home of Albert Gallatin, a Swiss immigrant who served his adopted country, in public and private life, for nearly seven decades. Gallatin made significant contributions to our young Republic in the fields of finance, politics, diplomacy, and scholarship. He is best known as the Treasury Secretary under Jefferson and Madison. Exhibits, audiovisual program, and audio tour provide information on Albert Gallatin. (Daily; closed Dec 25) **FREE**

Jumonville Glen. *200 Caverns Park Rd, Uniontown (15437). 7 miles from Fort Necessity, 2 1/2 miles N of Hwy 40 on Summit Rd.* Site of skirmish between British and French forces that led to the battle at Fort Necessity. (Mid-Apr-mid-Oct)

Laurel Caverns. *200 Caverns Park Rd, Farmington. 5 miles SE on Hwy 40, then 5 miles S on marked road. Phone 724/438-3003.* Colored lighting; unusual formations. Indoor miniature golf. Repelling (fee). Guided tours. Exploring trips. (May-Oct, daily) **$$$$**

Ohiopyle State Park. *Dinner Bell Rd, Ohiopyle. 10 miles SE on Hwy 40, then 6 miles NE off Hwy 381. Phone 724/329-8591.* Approximately 18,700 acres of overlooks, waterfalls. Fishing, hunting; whitewater boating. Hiking, bicycling. Cross-country skiing, snowmobiling, sledding. Picnicking, playground, snack bar. Tent and trailer sites. Nature center, interpretive program.

River tours. Whitewater rafting on the Youghiogheny River; some of the wildest and most scenic in the eastern US. Cost includes equipment and professional guides. Age limits are imposed because of level of difficulty.

Laurel Highlands River Tours. *Sherman St, Ohiopyle. Phone 724/329-8531; toll-free 800/472-3846.* For info contact PO Box 107, Dept PM, Ohiopyle 15470. **$$$$**

Mountain Streams & Trails Outfitters. *Phone 724/329-8810; toll-free 800/723-8669.* Also on the Youghiogheny, Big Sandy, Cheat and Tygart's Valley rivers. Also rentals of whitewater rafts, canoes, trail bikes. **$$$$**

White Water Adventurers. *Phone toll-free 800/992-7238.* Contact Director, PO Box 31, Ohiopyle 15470. **$$$$**

Wilderness Voyageurs. *Phone toll-free 800/272-4141.* Trips on the lower and middle Youghiogheny. Also bicycle, canoe rentals; kayak and canoe lessons. PO Box 97, Ohiopyle (15470). **$$$$**

Limited-Service Hotel

★★ HOLIDAY INN. *700 W Main St, Uniontown (15401). Phone 724/437-2816; toll-free 800/465-4329; fax 724/437-3505. www.holiday-inn.com.* 179 rooms, 2 story. Pets accepted, some restrictions. Check-out 11 am. Restaurant, bar. Indoor pool, whirlpool. Tennis. **$**

Full-Service Resorts

★★★★ NEMACOLIN WOODLANDS RESORT & SPA. *1001 Lafayette Dr, Farmington (15437). Phone 724/329-8555; toll-free 800/422-2736;*

fax 724/329-6153. www.nemacolin.com. Leave quotidian distractions behind and escape to Nemacolin Woodlands Resort & Spa. Tucked away in Pennsylvania's scenic Laurel Highlands, this comprehensive resort is the sort of place you go to rediscover your inner child. Young and old alike delight in the multitude of recreational opportunities available here, from the Hummer driving club, equestrian center, and shooting academy to the adventure and activities centers, culinary classes, and art museums. Two golf courses and a renowned golf academy delight players, while special activities entertain children and teenagers. There is something to suit every taste at Nemacolin, even down to the lodging. Grand European style defines the guest accommodations at Chateau LaFayette, while the Lodge maintains a rustic charm. Families enjoy the spacious accommodations in the townhouses, while the luxury homes add a touch of class to group travel. Echoing the resort's commitment to satisfying all styles, dining also runs the gamut from fine gourmet meals to casual fare. 220 rooms, 5 story. Check-in 3 pm, check-out noon. Restaurant, bar. Children's activity center. Fitness room. Two indoor pools, two outdoor pools, whirlpools. Golf. Tennis. Situated on 1,250 acres with seven lakes; landing strip. **$$$**

★ ★ ★ **SUMMIT INN RESORT.** *101 Skyline Dr, Farmington (15437). Phone 724/438-8594; fax 724/438-3917. www.summitinnresort.com.* 100 rooms, 3 story. Closed early Nov-mid-Apr. Check-in 4 pm, check-out noon. Restaurant, bar. Fitness room. Indoor pool, outdoor pool, whirlpool. Golf. Tennis. Built in 1907. Atop Mount Summit. **$**

Specialty Lodging

The following lodging establishment is approved by Mobil Travel Guide, but due to its unique and individualized nature has not been given a traditional Mobil Star rating. Included in this listing you may find bed-and-breakfasts, limited-service inns, guest ranches, and other unique hotel properties.

INNE AT WATSON'S CHOICE. *234 Balsinger Rd, Uniontown (15401). Phone 724/437-4999; toll-free 888/820-5380. www.watsonschoice.com.* Built in 1820; German architecture. 7 rooms, 2 story. No children allowed. Complimentary full breakfast. Check-in after 3 pm, check-out 11 am. **$**

Spa

★ ★ ★ ★ **WOODLANDS SPA AT NEMACOLIN.** *1001 LaFayette Dr, Farmington (15437). Phone 724/329-8555; toll-free 800/422-2736. www.nemacolin.com.* The Far East meets the mountains at the Woodlands Spa, where Asian design principles are married with indigenous materials. Feng shui, the ancient Chinese philosophy of balancing the forces of nature, heavily influences the spa's décor. Achieving inner tranquility is a focal point at the spa, and the treatments embrace this guiding principle. An extensive massage menu includes favorites such as Swedish, sports, aromatherapy, shiatsu, and deep tissue as well as Eastern methods such as reflexology and reiki. The Ayurvedic rebalancer and the hot stone shirodhara are massage experiences that use ancient Indian wisdom to balance your mind, body, and spirit and help you achieve complete relaxation. In addition to Asian principles of well-being, the Woodlands Spa honors European traditions. Kila bodywork, a spa signature, combines Russian, Swedish, and Eastern massage techniques. Mineral- and herb-enriched baths and body kurs that incorporate a variety of natural ingredients are popular treatments here, where hydrotherapy plays a defining role. The water path ritual begins with a walk through hot and cold water, particularly efficacious for increasing circulation and energy. The walk is followed by an invigorating Swiss shower and ends with a soothing soak in a tub filled with mineral salts from the Sarvar Springs in Hungary. The body scrub odysseys exceed the ordinary and celebrate the diverse cultures of the world. From Japanese citrus and Balinese hibiscus to German chamomile and Greek mint, each scrub embodies a different international personality. Fitness and nutrition also play significant roles at the Woodlands Spa, where consultations with nutritionists and conditioning experts help you gain insight into your body and its needs. Innovative and informative programs target women's nutritional needs, eating for better energy, and increasing metabolism for weight control. A delicious spa restaurant makes healthy eating easier.

Restaurant

★ ★ ★ **COAL BARON.** *7606 National Pike, Uniontown (15401). Phone 724/439-0111. www.coalbaron.com.* This 20-year-old restaurant is located 2 miles outside of town and offers a broad, continental menu. A painting of a coal tipple adorns the dining room wall, in honor of the establishment's name. American menu. Lunch, dinner. Closed Mon; Dec 24, 25. Bar. Children's menu. Jacket required. Valet parking. **$$**

Valley Forge National Historical Park (D-6)

See also King of Prussia, Philadelphia

Information Superintendent, PO Box 953, Valley Forge 19482; phone 610/783-1077
Web site www.nps.gov/vafo

Two thousand soldiers died here from hunger, disease, and cold, but General George Washington and his beleaguered army ultimately triumphed over the British in 1778. Today, Valley Forge has come to symbolize American perseverance and sacrifice on a lush, 3,600-acre hilly expanse with rich historical significance and beautiful scenery. Visitors can tour the park by car or bus and see Washington's restored stone headquarters, log soldier huts, bronze statues and monuments, and weapons and equipment used during the American Revolution. You can even learn how Washington's soldiers were taught to load and fire their muskets. The visitors' center features exhibits, artifacts, a gift shop, and an 18-minute film. Actively inclined history buffs will enjoy choosing from a 16-mile walking trail, 10-mile horse trails, a bike path, or a 10-mile self-guided tour. Picnic areas are available as well. (Daily 9 am-5 pm; closed Dec 25)

What to See and Do

Auto Tape Tour. *Phone 610/783-5788.* Self-guided tour dramatizes Washington's winter encampment. (2-hour tape rental, May-Oct, daily) Bookstore. **$$$**

Bus Tour. *Phone 610/783-5788.* Narrated tour (approximately 90 minutes) includes stops at historic sites. (June-Labor Day: tour departures every 1/2-hour; Labor Day-Oct: weekends only) Tours leave from Visitor Center. **$$$**

National Memorial Arch. Built in 1917 to commemorate Washington's army. Inscribed in the arch is a quote from General Washington: "Naked and starving as they are, we cannot enough admire the incomparable patience and fidelity of the soldiery."

Soldier Life Program. Interpreters present programs detailing camp life of the Continental Army soldier (offered at various times during the year).

Visitor Center. *Hwy 23 and N Golf Rd, Valley Forge Natl Historical Park (19482). Just inside park. Phone 610/783-1077.* Information, exhibits, audiovisual program, tour maps. Bus tours depart from here. (Daily)

Washington Headquarters. Park staff will provide information about the house where Washington lived for six months and which served as military headquarters for the Continental Army during that time. (Daily) Fee charged Apr-Nov. **$**

Washington Memorial Chapel. *Hwy 23, Valley Forge. Phone 610/783-0120.* Private property within park boundaries. Stained-glass windows depict the story of the New World, its discovery and development; hand-carved oak choir stalls, Pews of the Patriots, and Roof of the Republic bearing the State Seal of all the states. Also part of the chapel is the 58 cast-bell Washington Memorial National Carillon, with bells honoring states and territories. **FREE**

Restaurants

★ ★ ★ KENNEDY-SUPPLEE MANSION. *1100 W Valley Forge Rd, Valley Forge (19406). Phone 610/337-3777; fax 610/337-3567. www.kennedysupplee .com.* American menu. Lunch, dinner. Closed Sun; some holidays. Bar. Jacket required (dinner). Valet parking. Eight dining rooms in mansion (1850s). **$$$**

★ ★ KIMBERTON INN. *Kimberton Rd, Kimberton (19442). Phone 610/933-8148; fax 610/935-3430. www.kimbertoninn.com.* American menu. Dinner, Sun brunch. Closed Mon. Bar. Tavern (1796) on 4 1/2 acres of gardens. **$$$**

★ ★ SEVEN STARS INN. *263 Hoffecker Rd, Phoenixville (19460). Phone 610/495-5205; fax 610/495-5340. www.sevenstarsinn.com.* Seafood menu. Dinner. Closed Mon; holidays. Bar. Children's menu. **$$$**

Warren (A-2)

See also Bradford, Kane

Founded 1795
Population 10,259
Elevation 1,200 ft
Area Code 814
Zip 16365
Information Warren County Chamber of Commerce, 308 Market St, PO Box 942; phone 814/723-3050; or Travel Northern Alleghenies, 315 Second St, at the point, PO Box 804, phone 814/726-1222
Web site www.warrenpachamber.com

At the junction of the Allegheny and Conewango rivers, Warren is the headquarters and gateway of the famous Allegheny National Forest. Named for General Joseph Warren, American patriot killed in the Battle of Bunker Hill, the town was once the point where great flotillas of logs were formed for the journey to Pittsburgh or Cincinnati.

What to See and Do

Allegheny National Forest. *222 Liberty St, Warren (16365). Phone 814/723-5150.* More than 510,000 acres S and E on Hwys 6, 62, located in Warren, Forest, McKean, and Elk counties. Black bear, whitetail deer, wild turkey, a diversity of small birds and mammals; streams and reservoirs with trout, walleye, muskellunge, northern pike, and bass; rugged hills, quiet valleys, open meadows, dense forest. These lures, plus swimming, boating, hiking, camping, and picnicking facilities, draw more than 2 million visitors a year. Hundreds of campsites; fees are charged at some recreation sites. In forest are

Buckaloons Recreation Area. *Klondike, Bradford. 6 miles W on Hwy 6. Phone 814/362-4613.* Site of former Native American village on the banks of the Allegheny River. Boat launching. Picnicking. Camping (fee). Seneca Interpretive Trail.

Kinzua Dam and Allegheny Reservoir. *1205 Kinzua Rd, Warren. Phone 814/726-0661.* Dam (179 feet high, 1,897 feet long) with 27-mile-long lake. Swimming; fishing; boating (ramps, rentals; fees). Picnicking, overlooks. Camping (fee). Kinzua Dam Visitor Center has displays. Kinzua Point Information Center, 4 miles NE of dam, phone 814/726-1291. Some fees. 3 miles SE on Hwy 6, then 6 miles E on Hwy 59. (It is possible that the Hwy 59 bridge, 1 1/2 miles E of Kinzua Dam, will be closed; phone ahead for information.)

Chapman State Park. *RR 1, Clarendon. 7 miles SE on Hwy 6, then W at light. Phone 814/723-0250.* Approximately 800 acres. Lake and creek stocked with trout and bass. Swimming beach; fishing, hunting; boating (rentals, mooring, launching). Hiking. Cross-country skiing, snowmobiling, sledding, ice skating, ice fishing. Picnicking, snack bar. Tent and trailer sites available (some with electric; fee). Interpretive program.

Washington (D-1)

See also Pittsburgh

Founded 1781
Population 15,268
Elevation 1,120 ft
Area Code 724
Zip 15301
Information Washington County Tourism Promotion Agency, Franklin Mall, 1500 W Chestnut St; phone 724/228-5520 or toll-free 800/531-4114
Web site www.washpatourism.org

Originally a Native American village known as Catfish Camp, the village of Bassettown became Washington during the Revolution. During the Whiskey Rebellion the town was a center of protest against the new federal government's tax; arrival of federal troops quieted the rebellious farmers. Washington and Jefferson College (1781) is located here.

What to See and Do

David Bradford House. *175 S Main St, Washington. Phone 724/222-3604.* (1788) Restored frontier home of a leader of the Whiskey Rebellion. (May-mid-Dec, Wed-Sat, limited hours, also Sun afternoons)

LeMoyne House. *49 E Maiden St, Washington. Phone 724/225-6740.* (1812) Abolitionist's home, built by the LeMoyne family, was a stop on the underground railroad; period furnishings, paintings, library; gardens; museum shop. Administered by Washington County Historical Society. (Jan-Feb: Tues-Fri; Mar-Dec: Tues-Sat) **$$**

Magna Entertainment Corporation. *Race Track Rd, Meadow Lands. 4 miles N on Rte 19. Phone 724/225-9300.* Harness racing. Parimutuel betting. (Tues, Thurs-Sat evenings) Simulcasts (daily).

Meadowcroft Museum of Rural Life. *401 Meadowcroft Rd, Avella (15312). 19 miles NW via Hwys 18, 50. Phone 724/587-3412.* A 200-acre outdoor museum complex that preserves the history of life on the land in western Pennsylvania. General store, restored log houses, one-room schoolhouse, blacksmith shop, and archaeology exhibit. (May-Oct, Wed-Sun) **$$**

Pennsylvania Trolley Museum. *1 Museum Rd, Washington (15301). I-79 N, exit 41 (Meadowlands), follow signs. Phone 724/228-9256.* Museum displays include more than 35 trolley cars dating from 1894. Scenic trolley ride; car barn and trolley-restoration shop; visitor center and gift shop with exhibit, video presentation and picnic area. (June-Aug: daily; Apr-May and Sept-Dec: weekends) **$$$**

Limited-Service Hotels

★★ HOLIDAY INN. *340 Racetrack Rd, Washington (15301). Phone 724/222-6200; toll-free 800/465-4329; fax 724/228-1977. www.holiday-inn.com.* 138 rooms, 7 story. Pets accepted, some restrictions. Check-out noon. Restaurant, bar. Fitness room. Pool, whirlpool. Airport transportation available. Meadows Racetrack is adjacent. **$**

Washington Crossing Historic Park (Bucks County) (C-6)

See also Doylestown (Bucks County), New Hope, Philadelphia

Information Superintendent, PO Box 103, Washington Crossing, 18977; phone 215/493-4076

Two sections: Bowman's Hill, 2 miles S of New Hope on Hwy 32, and Washington Crossing, 7 miles S of New Hope on Hwy 32.

In a blinding snowstorm on Christmas night 1776, George Washington and 2,400 soldiers crossed the Delaware River from the Pennsylvania shore and marched to Trenton, surprising the celebrating Hessian mercenaries and capturing the city. Washington's feat was a turning point of the Revolutionary War. Park (Tues-Sun; closed holidays).

What to See and Do

Area of Embarkation. Marked by tall granite shaft supporting Washington's statue.

Bowman's Hill Wildflower Preserve. *Located in SE Hwy in Bucks County, about 40 miles NE of Philadelphia. Phone 215/862-2924.* If you'd like to explore outside the city, Bowman's Hill Wildflower Preserve is a great place to start. Pennsylvania's native plants come into focus at this 100-acre preserve located 40 miles northeast of Philadelphia. Hike or walk along a beautiful woodland, meadow, creek, or arboretum. Botanic enthusiasts will discover 1,000 species of trees, shrubs, ferns, vines, and herbaceous wildflowers. If you're an animal lover, don't forget to bring binoculars to watch for frogs. Photographers can catch a magnified moment in the display gardens. There are many contemplative places for meditation and study, scenic picnic spots, and several historic sites within hiking distance. Then head 5 miles south to Washington Crossing Historic Park (215/493-4076), where George Washington crossed the Delaware River in 1776. Bowman's Hill Tower, a lookout commemorating the American Revolution, offers a view of the Delaware River and rolling countryside 1 mile on foot or by car (215/862-3155). Nearby is New Hope, a perfect place for antiquing, art gallery hopping, shopping, or taking a mule barge ride on the Delaware Canal. (Daily; Closed Jan 1, Thanksgiving, Dec 25) **$$**

Concentration Valley. Where Washington assembled troops for raid on Trenton.

McConkey Ferry Inn. (1752) Restored as historic house. Sold in 1777 to Benjamin Taylor, whose descendents established the 19th-century village of Taylorsville.

Memorial Building. *1112 River Rd, Washington Crossing. Phone 215/493-4076.* Near Point of Embarkation. Houses copy of Emanuel Leutze's painting, Washington Crossing the Delaware. Movie shown five times a day.

Memorial Flagstaff. *Bowman's Hill.* Marks graves of unknown Continentals who died during encampment.

Special Event

The Crossing. *1112 River Rd, Washington Crossing Historic Park. Phone 215/493-4076.* Reenactment of Washington's crossing of the Delaware River, Christmas night in 1776. Dec.

Wayne

Restaurants

★★★ 110 RESTAURANT AND BAR. *110 N Wayne Ave, Wayne (19087). Phone 610/687-8333; fax 610/293-0770.* Located in a former 19th-century bank building, this American grill has become a popular spot with the Main Line crowd. American menu. Dinner, Sun brunch. Closed holidays. Bar. **$$$**

★★★ TAQUET. *139 E Lancaster Ave, Wayne (19087). Phone 610/687-5005; fax 610/687-5292. www.taquet.com.* This elegant Main Line restaurant prides itself on serving local products that are prepared with a French sensibility. There is a lovely porch for outdoor dining in summer months and the wine list is among the best in the area. French menu. Lunch, dinner. Closed Sun; Jan 1, Dec 25. Bar. Victorian décor. Outdoor seating. **$$**

★★ TOWN AND COUNTRY GRILLE. *888 Chesterbrook Blvd, Wayne (19087). Phone 610/647-6700; fax 610/964-9086. www.wyndhamvalleyforge.com.* This casual eatery is located in the Wyndham Valley Forge Hotel. Consider it if you're visiting Chesterbrook Corporate Center, where the hotel resides, or nearby Valley Forge National Park and King of Prussia Mall. Breakfast, lunch, dinner, Sun brunch. Bar. Children's menu. Country furnishings. **$$**

★★ VILLA STRAFFORD. *115 Strafford Ave, Wayne (19087). Phone 610/964-1116; fax 610/964-9086. www.villastrafford.com.* This recently restored mansion may be seen as a perfect location for a wedding. The continental cuisine is served with formal elegance. A wonderful weekend getaway for live jazz buffs. American menu. Dinner. Closed Sun; Jan 1. Bar. Mansion built in 1909. **$$$**

Wellsboro (A-4)

See also Galeton, Mansfield

Settled 1799
Population 3,328
Elevation 1,311 ft
Area Code 570
Zip 16901
Information Wellsboro Area Chamber of Commerce, 114 Main St, PO Box 733; phone 570/724-1926
Web site www.wellsboropa.com

Wellsboro is the gateway to Pennsylvania's "canyon country." Settled largely by New Englanders, it is sustained by an assortment of industries. The area yields coal, natural gas, hardwoods, maple syrup, and farm products.

What to See and Do

Auto tours. There are more than a million acres of forests, mountains, and streams to be explored. The Wellsboro Area Chamber of Commerce has published a map of three tours.

Red Arrow Tour. Follows Hwy 660 SW 10 miles from Wellsboro to Leonard Harrison State Park. Lookout Point, near the parking area, has large picnic area nearby. Path winds 1 mile from park to bottom of gorge, through shady glens, past waterfalls.

White Arrow Tour. Leads from the Switchbacks (1 1/2 miles W of Bradley Wales Park), 3 miles S to Leetonia, once a prosperous lumber village, now occupied by State Forest Rangers; then W & N to Cushman View, Wilson Point Rd, Lee Fire Tower, Cedar Run Mountain Rd and Hwy 6; approximately 75 miles.

Yellow Arrow Tour. Leads from Leonard Harrison State Park, back on Hwy 660, NW on Hwy 362, then 1/4 mile W on Hwy 6 to Colton Point Rd for views of the canyon and Four Mile Run Country. At Colton Point State Park (observation points, picnic shelters, fireplaces) the arrows follow Pine Creek S on old lumbering railroad tracks, converted into roadways called the "Switchbacks," to Bradley Wales Park overlooking Tiadaghton, the next lookout point on Pine Creek. From here continue S on W Rim Rd to Blackwell. From Blackwell, NE on Hwy 414 to Morris, then N on Hwy 287 to Wellsboro—a circle of 65 miles.

Robinson House Museum. *120 Main St, Wellsboro. Phone 570/724-6116.* (Circa 1820) Houses turn-of-the-century artifacts; genealogical library. (Mon-Fri afternoons) **FREE**

Ski Sawmill Family Resort. *Oregon Hill Rd, 16 miles S via Hwy 287. Phone 570/353-7521; toll-free 800/ 532-7669. www.skisawmill.com.* Chairlift, three T-bars; patrol, school, rentals; snowmaking; cafeteria, restaurant, bar. Longest run 3,250 feet; vertical drop 515 feet. (Dec-Mar, daily) Year-round activities. **$$$$**

Special Event

Pennsylvania State Laurel Festival. *114 Main St, Wellsboro.* Week-long event includes parade of floats, marching musical and precision units, antique cars, laurel queen contestants; crowning of the queen; arts and crafts; children's pet and hobby parade, exhibits and displays. Mid-June.

Limited-Service Hotels

★ CANYON MOTEL. *18 East Ave, Wellsboro (16901). Phone 570/724-1681; toll-free 800/255-2718; fax 570/724-1681. www.canyonmotel.com.* 31 rooms. Pets accepted, some restrictions; fee. Complimentary continental breakfast. Check-in 2 pm, check-out 11 am. Fitness room. Indoor pool, whirlpool. **$**

★★ PENN WELLS HOTEL & LODGE. *62 Main St, Wellsboro (16901). Phone 570/724-2111; toll-free 800/545-2446; fax 570/724-3703. www.pennwells.com.* 73 rooms. Check-out noon. Restaurant, bar. Fitness room. Indoor pool, whirlpool. Built in 1869; high ceilings, oak and cherry woodwork, antiques, early Americana. **$**

★ SHERWOOD MOTEL. *2 Main St, Wellsboro (16901). Phone 570/724-3424; toll-free 800/626-5802; fax 570/724-5658. www.sherwoodmotel.org.* 42 rooms, 2 story. Check-out 11 am. Pool. **$**

Specialty Lodging

The following lodging establishment is approved by Mobil Travel Guide, but due to its unique and individualized nature has not been given a traditional Mobil Star rating. Included in this listing you may find bed-and-breakfasts, limited-service inns, guest ranches, and other unique hotel properties.

KALTENBACH'S BED AND BREAKFAST. *Stony Fork Rd, Wellsboro (16901). Phone 570/724-4954; toll-free 800/772-4954. www.kaltenbachsinn.com.* 10 rooms. Complimentary full breakfast. Check-in noon, check-out 11 am. **$**

West Chester (D-6)

See also Chester, Downingtown, Kennett Square, King of Prussia, Media, Philadelphia

Founded 1788
Population 17,861
Elevation 459 ft
Area Code 484 & 610
Information Chester County Tourist Bureau, 601 Westtown Rd, Suite 170, 19382; phone 610/344-6365 or toll-free 800/228-9933
Web site www.brandywinevalley.com

In the heart of three Pennsylvania Revolutionary War historic sites—Brandywine, Paoli, and Valley Forge—West Chester today is a university and residential community with fine examples of Greek Revival and Victorian architecture.

What to See and Do

Brinton 1704 House. *Dilworthtown. 5 miles S just off Hwy 202, Oakland Rd. Phone 302/478-2853.* Stone house built by Quaker farmer William Brinton, authentically restored and furnished. (May-Oct, Sat, Sun; also by appointment) **$**

Limited-Service Hotels

★★ BEST WESTERN CONCORDVILLE HOTEL & CONFERENCE CENTER. *Hwys 322 and 1, Concordville (19331). Phone 610/358-9400; toll-free 800/522-0070; fax 610/358-9381. www.concordville.com.* 116 rooms, 5 story. Complimentary continental breakfast. Check-out noon. Restaurant, bar. Fitness room. Indoor pool, whirlpool. **$**

★★ HOLIDAY INN. *943 S High St, West Chester (19382). Phone 610/692-1900; fax 610/436-0159. www.holiday-inn.com.* 143 rooms, 3 story. Check-out noon.

Restaurant, bar. Fitness room. Pool. Airport transportation available. **$**

Full-Service Inn

★★★ **DULING-KURTZ HOUSE & COUNTRY INN.** *146 S Whitford Rd, Exton (19341). Phone 610/524-1830; fax 610/524-6258. www.duling-kurtz.com.* This small inn is located within walking distance to shopping, the train station, and more. 20 rooms, 3 story. Complimentary continental breakfast. Check-in 3 pm, check-out 11 am. Restaurant. Built in 1783; period furniture, sitting room. **$**

Restaurants

★★ **GILMORE'S.** *133 E Gay St, West Chester (19380). Phone 610/431-2800; fax 610/431-9464. www.gilmoresrestaurant.com.* French menu. Dinner. Closed Sun, Mon; holidays; also one week in winter and one week in summer. **$$$**

★★ **YE OLDE CONCORDVILLE INN.** *US 1 and US 322, Concordville (19331). Phone 610/459-2230; fax 610/459-1446. www.concordville.com.* American menu. Lunch, dinner. Closed Dec 25. Bar. Children's menu. Outdoor seating. **$$**

West Middlesex

Population 929
Elevation 840 ft
Area Code 724
Zip 16159

Limited-Service Hotels

★★ **HOLIDAY INN.** *3200 S Hermitage Rd, Hermitage (16159). Phone 724/981-1530; toll-free 800/465-4329; fax 724/981-1518. www.holiday-inn.com.* 180 rooms, 3 story. Pets accepted, some restrictions. Check-out 11 am. Restaurant, bar. Pool. **$**

★★ **RADISSON HOTEL SHARON.** *I-80 and Rte 18, West Middlesex (16159). Phone 724/528-2501; toll-free 800/358-7260; fax 724/528-2306. www.radisson.com.* 153 rooms, 3 story. Pets accepted, some restrictions. Check-out 11 am. Restaurant, bar. Fitness room. Indoor pool, whirlpool. **$**

White Haven

See also Hazleton, Jim Thorpe, Pocono Mountains, Wilkes Barre

Population 1,182
Elevation 1,221 ft
Area Code 570
Zip 18661
Information Pocono Mountains Vacation Bureau, 1004 Main St, Stroudsburg 18360, phone 570/424-6050; for free brochures, phone toll-free 800/POCONOS
Web site www.poconos.org

What to See and Do

Big Boulder. *Hwy 940 and Moseywood Rd, Lake Harmony. 1 mile E off Hwy 903. Phone 570/722-0100.* Five double, two triple chairlifts; patrol, school, rentals; snowmaking; cafeteria, bar; nursery, lodge. Night skiing. Longest run approximately 3/4 mile; vertical drop 475 feet. (Dec-Mar, daily) **$$$$**

Hickory Run State Park. *Hickory Run. 6 miles S on Hwy 534 off I-80, exit 41. Phone 570/443-0400.* Approximately 15,500 acres of scenic area. Swimming beach; fishing, hunting; hiking; cross-country skiing, snowmobiling, sledding, ice skating, ice fishing. Picnicking, playground, snack bar, store. Tent and trailer sites.

Jack Frost. *Rte 940, Blakeslee. 6 miles E on Hwy 940. Phone 570/443-8425.* Two triple, five double chairlifts; patrol, school, rentals; snowmaking; cafeteria, restaurant, bar; nursery. Longest run approximately 1/2 mile; vertical drop 600 feet. (Dec-Mar, daily) Half-day rate. **$$$$**

Limited-Service Hotels

★ **COMFORT INN.** *Rte 940, White Haven (18661). Phone 570/443-8461; fax 570/443-7988. www.choicehotels.com.* 123 rooms, 6 story. Check-out noon. Bar. Pool. **$**

★★ **RAMADA.** *Rte 940, Lake Harmony (18624). Phone 570/443-8471; toll-free 800/251-2610; fax*

570/443-0326. www.poconoramada.com. 138 rooms, 4 story. Pets accepted, some restrictions; fee. Check-out noon. Restaurant, bar. Indoor pool. Airport transportation available. **$**

Full-Service Resort

★ ★ MOUNTAIN LAUREL RESORT AND SPA. *I-80 at PA Tpke NE exit, White Haven (18661). Phone 570/443-8411; fax 570/443-5518. www.mountainlaurelresort.com.* 250 rooms, 3 story. Check-in 4 pm, check-out noon. Restaurant, bar. Children's activity center. Fitness room. Indoor pool, outdoor pool, whirlpool. Golf. Tennis. Airport transportation available. Business center. **$$**

Restaurant

★ ★ ★ POWERHOUSE. *I-80, exit 273, White Haven (18661). Phone 570/443-4480; fax 570/443-7784. www.powerhouseeatery.com.* Exposed pipes and valves let diners remember the history of Powerhouse's building while they dine on basic Italian specialties. American, Italian menu. Closed Dec 24, 25. Bar. Located in old power plant. **$$**

Wilkes Barre (B-5)

See also Hazleton, Pocono Mountains, Scranton, White Haven

Founded 1769
Population 43,123
Elevation 550 ft
Area Code 570
Information Northeast Pennsylvania Convention & Visitors Bureau, 99 Glenmaura National Blvd, Scranton, 18507; phone toll-free 800/22WELCOME
Web site www.visitnepa.org

Named in honor of two members of the British Parliament who championed individual rights and supported the colonies, Wilkes-Barre (WILKS-berry) and the Wyoming Valley were settled by pioneers from Connecticut. Pennsylvania and Connecticut waged the Pennamite-Yankee War, the first phase ending in 1771 with Connecticut in control of the valley. It was later resumed until Connecticut relinquished its claims in 1800. Wilkes-Barre was burned by the Native Americans and Tories during the Revolution and again by Connecticut settlers protesting the Decree of Trenton (1782), in which Congress favored Pennsylvania's claim to the territory. Discovery of anthracite coal in the valley sparked the town's growth after Judge Jesse Fell demonstrated that anthracite could be burned in a grate without forced draft.

Limited-Service Hotels

★ ★ BEST WESTERN EAST MOUNTAIN INN & SUITES. *2400 E End Blvd, Wilkes Barre (18702). Phone 570/822-1011; fax 570/822-6072. www.bestwestern.com.* 156 rooms, 7 story. Check-out noon. Restaurant, bar. Fitness room. Indoor pool, whirlpool. Airport transportation available. **$**

★ HAMPTON INN. *1063 Hwy 315, Wilkes Barre (18702). Phone 570/825-3838; fax 570/825-8775. www.hamptoninn.com.* 123 rooms, 5 story. Complimentary continental breakfast. Check-out noon. **$**

★ ★ HOLIDAY INN. *880 Kidder St, Wilkes Barre (18702). Phone 570/824-8901; toll-free 888/466-9272; fax 570/824-9310. www.holiday-inn.com.* 120 rooms, 2 story. Pets accepted, some restrictions. Check-out noon. Restaurant, bar. Pool, children's pool. **$**

Full-Service Resort

★ ★ ★ WOODLANDS INN & RESORT. *1073 Hwy 315, Wilkes Barre (18702). Phone 570/824-9831; toll-free 800/762-2222; fax 570/824-8865. www.thewoodlandsresort.com.* The Woodlands Inn & Resort offers urban warriors a chance to bask in the simple joys of nature. This wooded resort on 40 acres in the foothills of the Poconos is a perfect place to spend a family vacation, a romantic getaway, or even a corporate retreat. Golf and skiing are just a short distance away, while the property is a veritable playground with walking trails, tennis courts, and shimmering pools. Evenings are spent living it up at the resort's five nightclubs, bars, and lounges, where live jazz and dancing are among the pastimes. Thymes restaurant features delicious all-day European-influenced dining with scenic views of the Laurel Run Stream. 179 rooms, 9 story. Check-out noon. Restaurant, bar. Fitness room. Indoor pool, outdoor pool, whirlpool. Tennis. Airport transportation available. **$**

Specialty Lodging

The following lodging establishment is approved by Mobil Travel Guide, but due to its unique and individualized nature has not been given a traditional Mobil Star rating. Included in this listing you may find bed-and-breakfasts, limited-service inns, guest ranches, and other unique hotel properties.

PONDA - ROWLAND BED AND BREAKFAST. *RR 1, Box 349, Dallas (84532). Phone 570/639-3245; toll-free 888/855-9966; fax 570/639-5531. www. pondarowland.com.* 5 rooms, 2 story. Complimentary full breakfast. Check-in 1 pm, check-out noon. On 130-acre farm. **$**

Restaurant

★ ★ SABER ROOM. *94 Butler St, Wilkes Barre (18702). Phone 570/829-5743; fax 570/829-5311. www. saberroom.com.* Courteous service is found at this fine-dining establishment. American menu. Lunch, dinner. Closed Sun; Easter, July 4. Bar. Reservations recommended. **$$**

Williamsport (B-4)

See also Lewisburg, Lock Haven

Settled 1795
Population 30,706
Elevation 528 ft
Area Code 570
Zip 17701
Information Lycoming County Tourist Promotion Agency, 454 Pine St; phone toll-free 800/358-9900

Now famous as the birthplace of Little League baseball, Williamsport once was known as the "lumber capital of the world." In 1870, a log boom extended 7 miles up the Susquehanna River; 300 million feet of sawed lumber were produced each year. When the timber was exhausted the city developed diversified industry and remained prosperous. The historic district of Williamsport, known as "millionaire's row," includes homes of former lumber barons.

What to See and Do

Hiawatha. *I-180, Reach Rd exit, in Susquehanna State Park. Phone toll-free 800/248-9287.* Sightseeing trips down Susquehanna River aboard replica of an old-fashioned paddlewheel riverboat. Public cruises (May-Oct, Tues-Sun).

Little League Baseball International Headquarters. *1 mile S on Hwy 15. Phone 570/326-1921.* Summer baseball camp and Little League World Series Stadium are here. (Mon-Fri; closed holidays) **FREE** Adjacent is

Little League Baseball Museum. *Hwy 15, Williamsport. 1 mile S on Hwy 15. Phone 570/ 326-3607.* (Memorial Day-Labor Day, daily; rest of year, Mon, Thurs-Sun; closed Jan 1, Thanksgiving, Dec 25) **$$**

Little Pine State Park. *15 miles SW via Hwy 220, then 13 miles N via Hwy 44 and Legislative Rte 4001. Phone 570/753-6000.* Approximately 2,000 acres. Swimming beach; fishing, hunting; boating (ramps, mooring); cross-country skiing, snowmobiling, sledding, ice skating, ice fishing. Picnicking, playground, store. Tent and trailer sites (electric hook-ups). Interpretive program.

Thomas T. Thaber Museum of the Lycoming County Historical Society. *858 W 4th St, Williamsport. Phone 570/326-3326.* Exhibits on regional history from 10,000 BC to present. Exhibits include Native American, frontier era; canals, steam fire engine and hose cart; military history; general store, blacksmith shop, woodworker's shop, gristmill, crafts and industry; Victorian parlor and furnished period rooms; wildlife, sports and Little League; lumber business. (May-Oct, daily; rest of year, Tues-Sun; closed holidays) **$$** Within museum is

Shempp Toy Train Collection. Extensive toy train collection. More than 350 train sets on display, including the entire Lionel collection. Two detailed running displays allow visitors to start trains, blow whistles. Twelve unique trains include an American Flyer #3117 and Lionel "Super #381."

Special Events

Little League World Series. Teams from all over the world compete. Third week in Aug.

Lycoming County Fair. *Williamsport. 20 miles SE via Hwy 220, at Hughesville Fairgrounds.* More than 50 acres of amusements, commercial displays, livestock judging, demolition derbies, grandstand entertainment, food. Mid-July.

Victorian Sunday. House tours, flower show, entertainment. Second Sun in June.

Limited-Service Hotels

★ ★ **HOLIDAY INN.** *1840 E 3rd St, Williamsport (17701). Phone 570/326-1981; toll-free 800/369-4572; fax 570/323-9590. www.holiday-inn.com.* 170 rooms, 2 story. Pets accepted. Check-out 11 am. Restaurant, bar. Pool. **$**

★ ★ **RADISSON HOTEL WILLIAMSPORT.** *100 Pine St, Williamsport (17701). Phone 570/327-8231; fax 570/322-2957. www.radisson.com.* This hotel is conveniently located near the Williamsport Regional Airport. 148 rooms, 5 story. Pets accepted, some restrictions. Check-out noon. Restaurant, bar. Indoor pool. Airport transportation available. **$**

Full-Service Hotel

★ ★ **GENETTI HOTEL & SUITES.** *200 W 4th St, Williamsport (17701). Phone 570/326-6600; toll-free 800/321-1388; fax 570/326-5006. www.genetti.com.* 206 rooms, 10 story. Pets accepted. Check-out 11 am. Restaurant, bar. Fitness room. Pool. Airport transportation available. **$**

Willow Grove

See also Jenkintown, Philadelphia

Population 35
Elevation 310 ft
Area Code 215 & 267
Zip 19090

What to See and Do

Bryn Athyn Cathedral. *1000 Cathedral Rd, Bryn Athyn. 3 miles N of PA Tpke, exit 27 on Hwy 611 N, then 4 miles E on County Line Rd to Hwy 232. Phone 215/947-0266.* Outstanding example of Gothic architecture. Free guided tours (Apr-Nov, Tues-Sun). On grounds adjacent is

Glencairn Museum. *1001 Cathedral Rd, Willow Grove. At Hwy 232. Phone 215/938-2600.* Romanesque building features medieval sculpture and one of the largest privately owned collections of stained glass in the world; also Egyptian, Greek, Roman, ancient Near East, and Native American collections. (Mon-Fri by appointment) **$$**

Graeme Park. *859 County Line Rd, Horsham (19044). 5 miles N on Hwy 611. Phone 215/343-0965.* (1722) A fine example of Georgian architecture; stone house built by Sir William Keith, colonial governor of colony 1717-1726. Tours. (Wed-Sun; closed holidays) **$$**

Limited-Service Hotels

★ ★ **COURTYARD BY MARRIOTT.** *2350 Easton Rd, Willow Grove (19090). Phone 215/830-0550; fax 215/830-0572. www.courtyard.com.* 149 rooms, 3 story. Check-out noon. Restaurant, bar. Fitness room. Indoor pool, whirlpool. Airport transportation available. **$$**

★ **HAMPTON INN.** *1500 Easton Rd, Willow Grove (19090). Phone 215/659-3535; fax 215/659-4040. www.hamptoninn.com.* 150 rooms, 5 story. Complimentary continental breakfast. Check-out noon. Fitness room. Airport transportation available. **$**

Full-Service Inn

★ ★ ★ **JOSEPH AMBLER INN.** *1005 Horsham Rd, North Wales (19454). Phone 215/362-7500; fax 215/361-5924. www.josephamblerinn.com.* 37 rooms, 3 story. Complimentary full breakfast. Check-in 3 pm, check-out 11 am. Restaurant. Business center. Four buildings built 1734-1820; antiques. **$**

Restaurant

★ ★ **CASABLANCA.** *1111 Easton Rd, Warrington (18976). Phone 215/343-7715; fax 215/328-0774. www.casablancarestaurants.com.* Moroccan menu. Dinner. Children's menu. Reservations recommended. **$$**

★ ★ ★ **JOSEPH AMBLER INN.** *1005 Horsham Rd, Montgomeryville (19454). Phone 215/362-7500; fax 215/361-5924. www.josephamblerinn.com.* Complex combinations of local fare and European cuisine make up the innovative menu at this rustic country inn. Dinner. Bar. In 1820s stone barn. Outdoor seating. **$$$**

Wrightsville

See also Bird-in-Hand, Lancaster, Pennsylvania Dutch Area, Wrightsville

Population 2,223
Elevation 306 ft
Area Code 717
Zip 17368
Information York County Visitors Information Center, 1618 Toronita St, York 17402; phone 717/848-4000 or toll-free 800/673-2429
Web site www.yorkpa.org

What to See and Do

Donegal Mills Plantation & Inn. *Mt Joy. 5 miles N via Hwys 30, 441, 772, in Mt Joy (Lancaster Co). Phone 717/653-2168.* (1800). Historic village and resort dating from 1736. Mansion, bake house, gardens; restaurant and lodging (year-round). Plantation tours (Mar-Dec, Sat and Sun afternoons). **$$**

York (D-4)

See also Gettysburg, Hanover, Harrisburg, Lancaster, Pennsylvania Dutch Area, Wrightsville

Founded 1741
Population 40,862
Elevation 400 ft
Area Code 717
Information Convention and Visitors Bureau, 1 Market Way East, PO Box 1229, 17405, phone toll-free 800/673-2429; or the Visitors Information Center, 1618 Toronita St, 17402, phone 717/843-6660
Web site www.yorkpa.org

York claims to be the first capital of the United States. The Continental Congress met here in 1777 and adopted the Articles of Confederation, using the phrase "United States of America" for the first time. The first Pennsylvania town founded west of the Susquehanna River, York was and is still based on an agricultural and industrial economy. The city is dotted with 17 historical markers and 35 brass or bronze tablets marking historical events or places. There are more than 10 recreation areas in the county.

What to See and Do

Bob Hoffman Weightlifting Hall of Fame. *3300 Board Rd, York (17402). 4 miles N via I-83, exit 11; at York Barbell Co corporate headquarters. Phone 717/767-6481.* Weightlifting section honors Olympic weightlifters, powerlifters, bodybuilders, and strongmen; displays include samples of Iron Game artifacts, memorabilia, and photos. (Mon-Sat; closed holidays) **FREE**

Central Market House. *34 W Philadelphia St, York. Phone 717/848-2243.* Opened in March 1888. Over 70 vendors offer fresh produce, homemade baked goods, regional handcrafts, and specialty items. (Tues, Thurs, Sat; closed holidays) **FREE**

Fire Museum of York County. *757 W Market St, York. Phone 717/843-0464.* Turn-of-the-century firehouse preserves two centuries of firefighting history; from leather bucket brigades to hand-drawn hose carts and pumps, horse-drawn equipment, and finally to motorized equipment; artifacts and memorabilia; fire chief's office and firefighter's sleeping quarters are re-created, complete with brass slide pole. (Apr-Oct, Sat and second Sun every month; also by appointment; closed holidays) **$**

Friends Meeting House. *135 W Philadelphia St, York. Phone 717/843-2285.* (1766) Original virgin pine paneling; restored. Regular meetings are still held here. (By appointment) **FREE**

Gifford Pinchot State Park. *2200 Rosstown Rd, Lewisberry (17339). 14 miles NW on Hwy 74 to Rossville, then NE on Hwy 177. Phone 717/432-5011.* Approximately 2,300 acres; 340-acre lake. Fishing, hunting; boating (rentals, mooring, launching). Hiking. Cross-country skiing, ice skating, ice fishing, ice boating. Picnicking, store. Tent and trailer sites, cabins. Nature center, interpretive center.

Harley-Davidson, Inc. *1425 Eden Rd, York. 2 miles E on Hwy 30. Phone 717/848-1177.* Guided tour through motorcycle assembly plant and the Rodney Gott Antique Motorcycle Museum. Children under 12 and cameras not permitted on plant tour. Plant and museum combination tour (Mon-Fri); museum tour (Sat). **FREE**

Historical Society of York County. *250 E Market St, York. Phone 717/848-1587.* Includes library with genealogical records (Tues-Sat; fee for nonmembers).

Museum features exhibits on the history of York County. Combination ticket for all historic sites maintained by the society. (Daily; closed holidays) **$** Sites include

Bonham House. *152 E Market St, York. Phone 717/848-1587.* (Circa 1875). Historic house reflects life in late 19th century. (By appointment; closed holidays) **$**

General Gates' House. *157 W Market St, York. Enter on N Pershing Ave.* (1751) It was here that Lafayette gave a toast to Washington, marking the end of a movement to replace him. Also here are Golden Plough Tavern (1741), one of the earliest buildings in York, which reflects the Germanic background of many of the settlers in its furnishings and half-timber architecture, and the Bobb Log House (1811), furnished with painted and grained furniture. (Tues-Sat; closed holidays) **$$**

Ski Roundtop. *925 Roundtop Rd, Lewisberry (17339). 12 miles NW on Hwy 74, then 1/2 mile N on Hwy 177 to Mt Airy Rd, then to Roundtop Rd, follow signs. Phone 717/432-9631; toll-free 800/767-4766 (snow report). www.skiroundtop.com.* Two quad, triple, two double chairlifts; two J-bars, one magic carpet, two tubing lifts; patrol, school, rentals; snowmaking; cafeteria; nursery. Longest run 4,100 feet; vertical drop 600 feet. (Mid-Nov-mid-Mar, daily) **$$$$**

Warrington Friends Meeting House. *14 miles NW on Hwy 74.* (1769; expanded in 1782) Fine example of early Quaker meetinghouse.

York County Colonial Court House. *W Market and Pershing aves. Phone 717/848-1587.* Replica of 1754 original. Exhibits include multimedia presentation of Continental Congress's adoption of the Articles of Confederation, audiovisual story of 1777-1778 historic events; original printer's copy of Articles of Confederation, historic documents, and artifacts. Tours. (Daily) **$**

Special Event

River Walk Art Festival. *1 Market Way W, York.* Along Codorus Creek at York County Colonial Court House. Late Aug.

Limited-Service Hotels

★BEST WESTERN WESTGATE INN. *1415 Kenneth Rd, York (17404). Phone 717/767-6931; fax 717/767-6938. www.bestwestern.com.* 105 rooms, 3 story. Complimentary continental breakfast. Check-out noon. **$**

★ HAMPTON INN. *1550 Mt Zion Rd, York (17402). Phone 717/840-1500; fax 717/840-1567. www.hamptoninn.com.* 144 rooms, 5 story. Complimentary continental breakfast. Check-out 11 am. Fitness room. Pool. **$**

★★HOLIDAY INN. *2000 Loucks Rd, York (17404). Phone 717/846-9500; toll-free 800/465-4329; fax 717/767-1973. www.holiday-inn.com.* 181 rooms, 2 story. Pets accepted. Check-out 11 am. Restaurant, bar. Fitness room. Indoor pool, outdoor pool, whirlpool. **$**

Full-Service Hotel

★ ★ YORKTOWNE HOTEL. *48 E Market St, York (17405). Phone 717/848-1111; toll-free 800/233-9324; fax 717/854-7678. www.yorktowne.com.* Open since 1925, this hotel has hosted such guests as Eleanor Roosevelt, Mickey Mantle, Lucille Ball, and Richard Nixon. 122 rooms, 8 story. Check-out noon. Restaurant, bar. Fitness room. Airport transportation available. **$**

Restaurants

★ ★ ★ ACCOMAC INN. *6330 S River Dr, York (17368). Phone 717/252-1521; fax 717/252-5711. www.accomac.com.* This elegant country restaurant comes complete with white tablecloths and tableside preparation. French menu. Dinner, Sun brunch. Closed Dec 25. Bar. **$$$**

★ ★ SAN CARLO'S. *333 Arsenal Rd US 30, York (17402). Phone 717/854-2028; fax 717/846-2983. www.sancarlosrestaurant.com.* American menu. Dinner. Bar. Children's menu. Renovated 175-year-old barn; original fieldstone walls. **$$**

Virginia

Settled by Elizabethans and named for their Virgin Queen, the first of the Southern states still retains a degree of the graceful courtliness that reached its peak just before the Civil War. Evidence of strong ties with the past are apparent in the Old Dominion. More than 1,600 historical markers dot its 55,000 miles of paved roads. More than 100 historic buildings are open all year; hundreds more welcome visitors during the statewide Historic Garden Week (usually the last week in April).

Population: 6,377,000
Area: 40,767 square miles
Elevation: 0-5,729 feet
Peak: Mount Rogers (between Smyth, Grayson Counties)
Entered Union: Tenth of original 13 states (June 25, 1788)
Capital: Richmond
Motto: Thus Always To Tyrants
Nickname: Old Dominion
Flower: American Dogwood
Bird: Cardinal
Fair: Late September-early October in Richmond
Time Zone: Eastern
Web site: www.virginia.org

Permanent English settlement of America began in Jamestown in 1607 and started a long line of Virginia "firsts": the first legislative assembly in the Western Hemisphere (1619); the first armed rebellion against royal government (Bacon's Rebellion, 1676); the first stirring debates, in Williamsburg and Richmond, which left pre-Revolutionary America echoing Patrick Henry's inflammatory "Give me liberty, or give me death!" Records show that America's first Thanksgiving was held December 4, 1619, on the site of what is now Berkeley Plantation.

To Virginia the nation owes its most cherished documents—Thomas Jefferson's Declaration of Independence, George Mason's Bill of Rights, James Madison's Constitution. From here came George Washington to lead the Revolution and to become the first of eight US presidents to hail from Virginia.

Ironically, the state so passionately involved in creating a new nation was very nearly the means of its destruction. Virginia was the spiritual and physical capital of the Confederacy; the Army of Northern Virginia was the Confederacy's most powerful weapon, General Robert E. Lee its greatest commander. More than half the fighting of the Civil War took place in Virginia; and here, in the courthouse of the quaint little village of Appomattox, the war finally came to an end.

When chartered in 1609, the Virginia territory included about one-tenth of what is now the United States; the present state ranks 36th in size, but the remaining area is remarkably diverse. Tidewater Virginia—the coastal plain—is low, almost flat, arable land cut by rivers and bays into a magnificent system of natural harbors. It was vital to commerce and agriculture in the early days. Today it is still important commercially (the Hampton Roads port is one of the world's great naval and shipbuilding bases) and is a perennial lure to vacationers as well.

Inland lies the gentle rolling Piedmont, covering about half the state. Here is Virginia's leading tobacco area; it also produces apples, corn, wheat, hay, and dairy products. The world's largest single-unit textile plant is in Danville; the Piedmont also manufactures shoes, furniture, paper products, clay, glass, chemicals, and transportation equipment.

West of the Piedmont rise the Blue Ridge Mountains; high, rugged upland plateaus occur to the south. Further west is the Valley of Virginia, a series of fertile valleys. Best known is the Shenandoah, which contains some of the

Calendar Highlights

April

Garden Week *(Charlottesville).* Some fine private homes and gardens in the area are open. For more information, contact the Garden Club of Virginia/Richmond headquarters, phone 804/644-7776.

Garden Week in Historic Lexington *(Lexington). Phone 540/463-3777.* Tour of homes and gardens in the Lexington and Rockbridge County areas.

International Azalea Festival *(Norfolk). Downtown and Norfolk Botanical Garden. Phone 757/664-6620.* To honor NATO. Parade, coronation ceremony, air show (held at Norfolk Naval Air Station), events, concerts, fair, ball, entertainment.

May

Jamestown Weekend *(Jamestown, Colonial National Historical Park). Phone 757/229-1733.* Original Jamestown site. Commemorates arrival of first settlers in 1607; special tours and activities.

June

Natural Chimneys Jousting Tournament *(Harrisonburg). Natural Chimneys Regional Park. Phone 540/350-2510.* America's oldest continuous sporting event, held annually since 1821. "Knights" armed with lances charge down an 80-yard track and attempt to spear three small rings suspended from posts.

Red Cross Waterfront Festival *(Alexandria). Phone 703/549-8300.* Commemorates Alexandria's maritime heritage. Features "tall ships," blessing of the fleet, river cruises, races, arts and crafts, exhibits, food, variety of music; fireworks.

July

Pony Penning *(Chincoteague).* The "wild" ponies are rounded up on Assateague Island, then swim the inlet to Chincoteague, where foals are sold at auction before the ponies swim back to Assateague. Carnival amusements. For more information, contact the Chincoteague Chamber of Commerce, phone 757/336-6161.

September

Publick Times *(Williamsburg). Colonial Williamsburg. Phone 757/220-7645 or toll-free 800/246-2099.* Re-creation of colonial market days; contests, crafts, auctions, military encampment.

Virginia State Fair *(Richmond). Phone 804/228-3200.* Animal and 4-H contests, music, horse show, carnival.

October

Blue Ridge Folklife Festival *(Martinsville). Blue Ridge Farm Museum. Phone 540/365-4415.* Gospel, blues, and string band music; traditional regional crafts; regional foods; quilt show, antique autos, steam and gas-powered farm equipment. Sports events include horse-pulling and log-skidding contests, coon dog swimming and treeing contests.

December

Christmas Candlelight Tour *(Fredericksburg).* Historic homes open to the public; carriage rides; Christmas decorations and refreshments of the colonial period. Contact the Visitor Center, phone 540/373-1776 or toll-free 800 678-4748.

richest—and once bloodiest—land in the nation. Civil War fighting swept the valley for four years; Winchester changed hands 72 times.

To the southwest are the Appalachian Plateaus, a rugged, forested region of coal mines. Here the splendid outdoor drama, *Trail of the Lonesome Pine,* romanticized by the novelist John Fox, is performed.

For the vacationer today, the state offers colonial and Civil War history at every turn, seashore and mountain recreation year-round, such natural oddities as caverns in the west and the Dismal Swamp in the southeast, and the Skyline Drive (see SHENANDOAH NATIONAL PARK), one of the loveliest scenic drives in the East.

When to Go/Climate

Virginia summers can be hot and humid, marked by brief, powerful thunderstorms; winter snows are common in the mountains. Moderate temperatures, light rainfall, verdant flowering gardens, and brilliant foliage make spring and fall the best seasons to visit.

AVERAGE HIGH/LOW TEMPERATURES (° F)

Richmond

Jan 46/26	**May** 78/54	**Sept** 81/59
Feb 49/28	**June** 85/63	**Oct** 71/47
Mar 60/36	**July** 88/68	**Nov** 61/38
Apr 70/45	**Aug** 87/66	**Dec** 50/30

Roanoke

Jan 44/25	**May** 76/53	**Sept** 79/57
Feb 47/27	**June** 83/60	**Oct** 68/45
Mar 58/36	**July** 86/65	**Nov** 58/37
Apr 67/44	**Aug** 85/64	**Dec** 48/29

Parks and Recreation

Water-related activities, hiking, various other sports, picnicking and visitor centers, as well as camping, are available in many state parks. State park facilities and services are operated on a seasonal basis. Parking for noncampers, $1.50-$2.50/car/day, Memorial Day-Labor Day. Admission to State Historical Parks $1.25; children $1. Swimming, boat rentals, cafes, and concessions, Memorial Day-Labor Day; fees for activities. Pets are allowed in camping and cabins, but must be kept inside at night. At all other times pets must be on a leash not longer than 6 feet. Facilities for the disabled at many parks.

Tent and trailer campgrounds are available in 19 state parks generally from March-November; maximum stay is 2 weeks. $11/site/night, $19.25 at Seashore (up to 6 persons, 1 vehicle); electricity and water $15/site/night where available. Reservations may be made 180 days-1 week in advance (see below for addresses). Seven parks offer housekeeping cabins (May-Sept). Douthat (see CLIFTON FORGE) has a guest lodge for 15. Reservations for campsites are accepted beginning in late March. Campsite and cabin reservations may be made by phoning 800/933-PARK or 804/225-3867. Booklets with details on each park may be obtained from the Virginia Department of Conservation & Recreation, 203 Governor St, Suite 213, Richmond 23219. A campground directory is available from Virginia Tourism Corporation, 901 E Byrd St, Richmond 23219. Phone 804/786-4484.

FISHING AND HUNTING

Saltwater fishing on ocean, bay, river, or creek is a major sport. Virginia is blessed with many miles of shoreline: 120 miles on the Atlantic Ocean, 300 miles on Chesapeake Bay, and 1,300 miles of tidal shores. There is no closed season for saltwater fishing except for striped bass. There are some species size and bag limits. No license is required to fish in ocean waters or seaside of the eastern shore, but a license is required to fish in the Chesapeake and tidal tributaries. Information concerning size limits and bag limits on saltwater game fish may be obtained from the Virginia Marine Resources Commission, PO Box 756, Newport News 23607; phone 800/937-9247. The Commonwealth of Virginia sponsors an annual Saltwater Fishing Awards Program (see VIRGINIA BEACH), open to the public. Contact Virginia Saltwater Fishing Tournament, 968 S Oriole Dr, Suite 102, Virginia Beach 23451. Phone 757/491-5160.

Freshwater fishing is excellent in many of the state's large reservoirs and rivers for such species as large-mouth and smallmouth bass, landlocked striped bass, muskie, and a wide variety of panfish. Lake Anna, Smith Mountain Lake, Lake Gaston, James River, Lake Moomaw, and Buggs Island Lake are nationally known for excellent bass and landlocked striped bass fishing. Nonresident license: $30;

$30 additional for license for trout in designated stocked waters. Five-day license to fish statewide, $6; other special fees. Fishing in a national forest requires an additional fishing/hunting stamp, $3.

Hunting for upland game and migratory waterfowl in season. Nonresident license: $60; 3-day license: $30; bear, deer, turkey, $60 additional; nonresident muzzleloader license, $25; nonresident special archery license to hunt during special archery season, $25. Hunting in a national forest requires an additional fishing/hunting stamp, $3. There is a 50¢ issuance fee for all licenses. For fishing and hunting regulations and information write Department of Game and Inland Fisheries, 4010 W Broad St, Richmond 23230, or phone 804/367-1000.

Driving Information

Safety belts are mandatory for all persons in front seat of vehicle. Children under 4 years must be in approved safety seats anywhere in vehicle. For further information, phone 804/367-0538.

INTERSTATE HIGHWAY SYSTEM

The following alphabetical listing of Virginia towns in this book shows that these cities are within 10 miles of the indicated Interstate highways. Check a highway map for the nearest exit.

Highway Number	Cities/Towns within 10 Miles
Interstate 64	Ashland, Charlottesville, Chesapeake, Clifton Forge, Covington, Hampton, Jamestown, Lexington, Newport News, Norfolk, Portsmouth, Richmond, Staunton, Virginia Beach, Waynesboro, Williamsburg, Yorktown.
Interstate 66	Alexandria, Arlington County, Fairfax, Falls Church, Front Royal, Manassas, McLean.
Interstate 77	Wytheville.
Interstate 81	Abingdon, Blacksburg, Bristol, Front Royal, Harrisonburg, Lexington, Marion, Natural Bridge, New Market, Radford, Roanoke, Salem, Staunton, Strasburg, Winchester, Woodstock, Wytheville.
Interstate 85	Petersburg, South Hill.
Interstate 95	Alexandria, Arlington County, Ashland, Emporia, Fairfax, Falls Church, Fredericksburg, Hopewell, McLean, Petersburg, Richmond, Springfield, Triangle.

Additional Visitor Information

Recreational and tourist information, including travel guides, brochures, and maps, is available from the Virginia Tourism Corporation, 901 E Byrd St, Richmond 23219; phone 800/932-5827. Virginia Department of Transportation, 1401 E Broad St, Richmond 23219, phone 804/786-2838, offers an official state map.

There are ten welcome information centers in Virginia at the following locations: the northern end of the state, on I-81 in Clear Brook, and on I-66 in Manassas; at the northeastern side, on I-95 in Fredericksburg; around the bay area on the eastern side, on Hwy 13 in New Church; around the southerly border, on I-95 in Skippers, and on I-85 in Bracey; in the southwest part of the state, on I-81 in Bristol, and I-77 in Lambsburg; and on the western side, on I-64 in Covington, and on I-77 in Rocky Gap.

GEORGE WASHINGTON'S PLANTATIONS

Ask any historically knowledgeable American to name George Washington's home, and the answer you would expect is Mount Vernon, just south of Alexandria, Virginia. But this is only partly correct. In his youth, Washington lived on two other plantations–both of which, like Mount Vernon, honor the country's first president. Each unique home tells a different aspect of his life. All three can be visited in a one-day, 170-mile round-trip. Make sure to get an early start, and begin in Alexandria, a Potomac River port long before the Capitol at Washington, DC was conceived. Paralleling the Potomac, the scenic Mount Vernon Parkway winds south for about 10 miles to Mount Vernon, a sprawling estate Washington inherited at the age of 20 from a half-brother. Here, you can tour his stately white mansion, enjoy the Potomac views as he surely did, walk among the 18th-century farm fields and gardens, and pay homage at his and Martha's tombs. At Mount Vernon, you'll learn about Washington the farmer, the soldier, and the statesman, an imposing man of laudable qualities. Plan to spend much of the morning at the estate. About noon, head south to Washington's two childhood homes to get to know the youth who became the "father of his country." Your first stop is Popes Creek Plantation, which is officially called George Washington Birthplace National Monument. From Mount Vernon, take State Route 235 West to Hwy 1 South and follow the signs to I-95 South to Fredericksburg–about 40 miles. In Fredericksburg, take State Route 3 east for about 36 miles. Make a left turn onto State Route 204, which ends at the plantation in about 2 miles. This is where Washington was born on February 22, 1732. Unlike Mount Vernon, nothing remains of the original house except a few foundation bricks and grand Potomac River views. And yet the 550-acre park–re-created in part as a colonial farm with fields, pastures, and livestock–does a fine job of exploring Washington's origins. His great-grandfather John, an English seaman, settled in the area in 1657, prospered, and was eventually buried in the park. You can tour Memorial House, a Colonial-style farmhouse similar to one that might have stood on the property in 1732. Nearby are other reconstructed period farm buildings and a large herb garden. Walking trails trace the river's shoreline past a grove of towering cedars, and a shaded picnic area is provided. Packing a picnic is a good idea since the park has no food service. Plan on staying about 90 minutes here, giving yourself time to return to Fredericksburg and Ferry Farm, where Washington's family moved when he was six. At the city outskirts, bear right onto Business Route 3. A sign to Ferry Farm will indicate a U-Turn at a stoplight. It is at Ferry Farm that Washington might have chopped down a cherry tree–wild cherries still grow on the property–and where he might have tossed a coin across the Rappahannock River. Archaeological digs, sometimes open to visitors, are underway, and a small museum describes the life Washington as a lad on these hilly, wooded acres. Return to Alexandria via Route 3 and I-95 North. Conclude your day there with dinner in early American style at Gadsby's Tavern, built in 1792. **(Approximately 170 miles)**

NORTHERN VIRGINIA WINE COUNTRY

Fifteen years ago, a tour of Virginia's Wine Country would have struck wine connoisseurs as preposterous. But that was then. The state now counts more than 60 wineries, many of them producing award-winning vintages. Even California, home to some of America's most notable wines, is taking notice because several of Virginia's winemakers are producing new and different wines from grapes not yet grown on the West Coast. In recent years, wine-tasting has become an inviting pastime for weekenders. Fortunately, many of the wineries are clustered conveniently to make a visit to three or four in half a day quite practical, though many visitors combine a sampling tour with a stay in a country inn that serves Virginia wines. Part of the fun of visiting Virginia's wineries is that they tend to be located in out-of-the way corners of the country-side. To get to them, you have to negotiate winding back roads over which you might not otherwise travel.

This one-day, 150-mile tour from Fairfax County (a Washington, DC suburb) traverses the scenic foothills of the Blue Ridge Mountains. Here and there it edges Shenandoah National Park, where a detour of a few miles will take you to one of the lofty overlooks along Skyline Drive, the famed ridge-top parkway. Begin in the tour on I-66 West just north of Fairfax City. Near Manassas, stop at the Visitor Information Center to pick up the latest edition of *Virginia Wineries Festival and Tour Guide.* It lists the operating hours of the tasting rooms, many of which are open daily, some only on weekends. If Civil War history interests you, stop briefly at Manassas National Battlefield Park, which commemorates the first major clash between the North and South. At Gainesville, head south on Hwy 29 past Culpeper to the village of Leon; the Prince Michel Vineyards will be on the right. A visit begins with a self-guided tour of the wine-making facility. This French-owned facility produces a very nice Chardonnay. Its gourmet restaurant, serving lunch and dinner, overlooks acres of vineyards draped across rolling hills. From St. Michel, continue south on Hwy 29 to Madison, and turn right onto State Route 231 North. For about 20 miles, this stretch of the road is a Virginia Scenic Byway. On your left, the high, forested ridge rising overhead is Shenandoah National Park. On both sides of the road, stately plantation homes carry descriptive names. Just south of Sperryville, pick up Hwy 522 North. In Sperryville, browse the sprawling Sperryville Antiques Market and stop for a bite–or at least a peek–at The Appetite Repair Shop, a café in used-auto motif. A "Sub in a Hub" is a sandwich served in a hub cap. Continue north on Hwy 522 toward Front royal, turning right at Route 635. For about a mile, the road glides beneath towering tree; Oasis Winery is on the right. Oasis is best known for its sparkling wines. After you visit to Oasis, return to Hwy 522 and continue north to Front Royal. Head east (right) on Route 55 to Linden. Turn right onto Route 638 and proceed 2 miles to Linden. Perched atop a small hill, its outdoor deck offers gorgeous Blue Ridge views. Linden is one of Virginia's finest wineries, and one of the prettiest. Linden's Seyval, a dry white wine, is popular with wine fanciers looking for something new. Return to Route 55 and turn west (left) 1 mile to the entrance to I-66. Take I-66 east back to Fairfax City. **(Approximately 150 miles)**

Abingdon (F-2)

See also Bristol, Marion

Settled circa 1770
Population 7,780
Elevation 2,069 ft
Area Code 540
Zip 24210
Information Abingdon Convention & Visitors Bureau, 335 Cummings St; phone toll-free 800/435-3344
Web site www.abingdon.com

Daniel Boone passed through this area in 1760 and dubbed it "Wolf Hill" after a pack of wolves from a nearby cave disturbed his dogs. Wolf Hill had long been a crossing for buffalo and Native Americans; Boone later used it for his own family's westward migration. Later, Black's Fort was built here and the community adopted that name. Now known as Abingdon, this summer resort in the Virginia Highlands just north of Tennessee is the Washington County seat, Virginia's largest burley tobacco market, and a livestock auction center.

What to See and Do

Grayson Highlands State Park. *35 miles SE on Hwy 58. Phone 276/579-7092.* Within this 4,935-acre park are rugged peaks, some more than 5,000 feet; alpine scenery. Hiking, horse trails, picnicking, camping, visitor center, interpretive programs, pioneer life displays (June-Aug). Adjacent to Mount Rogers National Recreation Area (see MARION). (Daily)

White's Mill. *12291 White's Mill Rd, Abingdon (24210). Phone 276/676-0285.* Old gristmill and general store, still in operation. (Wed-Sat) **$**

Special Events

Barter Theatre. *133 W Main St, Abingdon (24210). Hwy 11 off I-81, in former Town Hall. Phone 540/628-3991.* America's oldest, longest-running professional repertory theater. Founded during the Depression on the theory that residents would barter their abundant crops for first-rate professional entertainment. Designated State Theatre of Virginia in 1946. Barter Players perform Mar-Dec. Children's theater June-Aug.

Virginia Highlands Festival. *208 W Main St, Abingdon (24210).* Exhibits, demonstrations of rustic handicrafts; plays, musical entertainment; historical reenactments; historic house tours, antique market. Early-mid-Aug.

Limited-Service Hotels

★ COMFORT INN. *170 Old Jonesboro Rd, Abingdon (24210). Phone 276/676-2222; fax 276/676-2222. www.choicehotels.com.* 80 rooms, 2 story. Complimentary continental breakfast. Check-out noon. Outdoor pool. **$**

★ DAYS INN. *887 Empire Dr SW, Abingdon (24210). Phone 276/628-7131; fax 276/628-7158. www.daysinn.com.* 105 rooms, 2 story. Check-out 11 am. Restaurant. **$**

Full-Service Inn

★ ★ ★ THE MARTHA WASHINGTON INN. *150 W Main St, Abingdon (24210). Phone 276/628-3161; toll-free 888/888-5252; fax 276/628-8885. www.camberleyhotels.com.* Experience Southern hospitality at its finest in this historic inn, built as a private residence for a Virginia general in 1832. The original architecture has been painstakingly maintained and period decor of glistening wood floors, crystal chandeliers, and plaster detailing finishes the authentic look. Dining is an updated element and meals served in The Dining Room are innovative and well-prepared. 62 rooms. Check-in 3 pm, check-out 11 am. Three restaurants, bar. **$$$**

Alexandria (C-8)

See also Arlington County (Ronald Reagan Washington-National Airport Area), Fairfax, Falls Church, Mount Vernon; also see District of Columbia

Settled 1670
Population 128,283
Elevation 52 ft
Area Code 703
Information Convention/Visitors Association, 421 King St, 22314-3209; phone 703/838-4200
Web site www.funside.com

A group of English and Scottish merchants established a tobacco warehouse at the junction of Hunting Creek and the "Potowmack" River in the 1740s. The little settlement prospered and 17 years later surveyor John West, Jr., and his young assistant, George Washington, arrived and "laid off in streets and 84 half-acre lots" the town of Alexandria. Among the first buyers on the July morning in 1749 when the lots were offered for public sale were Lawrence Washington and his brother Augustus, William Ramsay, the Honorable William Fairfax, and John Carlyle. Erecting handsome town houses, these gentlemen soon brought a lively and cosmopolitan air to Alexandria with parties, balls, and horse racing. It was also the hometown of George Mason and Robert E. Lee and home to George Washington.

In 1789, Virginia ceded Alexandria to the District of Columbia, but in 1846, the still Southern-oriented citizens asked to return to the Old Dominion, which Congress allowed.

During the Civil War, Alexandria was cut off from the Confederacy when Union troops occupied the town to protect Potomac River navigation. Safe behind Union lines, the city escaped the dreadful destruction experienced by many other Southern towns. After the war, even with seven railroads centering here for transfer of freight, Alexandria declined as a center of commerce and was in trade doldrums until about 1914, when the Alexandria shipyards were reopened and the Naval Torpedo Station was built. Today, it has developed into a trade, commerce, transportation, and science center. More than 250 national associations are based here.

What to See and Do

Alexandria Black History Resource Center. *638 N Alfred St, Alexandria (22314). Phone 703/838-4356.* Photographs, letters, documents, and artifacts relate the history of African Americans in Alexandria. (Tues-Sat; closed holidays) **DONATION**

The Athenaeum. *201 Prince St, Alexandria (22314). Phone 703/548-0035.* Greek Revival structure (1851) built as a bank now houses the Fine Arts Association. Art shows, dance performances. (Wed-Fri and Sat-Sun afternoons; closed holidays)

Atlantic Kayak. *1201 N Royal St, Alexandria (22314). Phone 703/838-9072; toll-free 800/297-0066. www.atlantickayak.com.* See the capital's sights from a new perspective: as a kayaker on the Potomac. Atlantic Kayak runs short trips that include a brief lesson; all equipment is included, and no experience is required. Sunset and moonlight tours are an especially beautiful way to view DC's monuments. Another outing takes you to the Dyke Marsh Wildlife Area, where you'll see ospreys, great blue herons, and other birds. There's even a tour with fireworks viewing on July 4. (Apr-Oct, daily)

Doorways to Old Virginia. *221 King St, Alexandria (22314). Departs from Ramsay House. Phone 703/548-0100. www.chesapeakejubilee.org.* Offers guided walking tours of the historic district. (Mar-Oct, Fri-Sun, evenings) **$$$**

Fort Ward Museum and Historic Site. *4301 W Braddock Rd, Alexandria (22304). Phone 703/838-4848.* Restored Union Fort from the Civil War; museum contains a Civil War collection. Museum (Tues-Sun; closed Jan 1, Thanksgiving, Dec 25). Park, picnicking (daily to sunset). **FREE**

George Washington Masonic National Memorial. *101 Callahan Dr, Alexandria (22301). W end of King St. Phone 703/683-2007. www.gwmemorial.org.* American Freemasons' memorial to their most prominent member, this 333-foot-high structure houses a large collection of objects that belonged to George Washington, which were collected by his family or the masonic lodge where he served as the first Master. Guided tours explore a replica of Alexandria-Washington Lodge's first hall, a library, museum, and an observation deck on the top floor. (Daily 9 am-4 pm; closed Jan 1, Thanksgiving, Dec 25) **FREE**

Gunston Hall. *10709 Gunston Rd, Mason Neck (22079). 18 miles S on Hwy 1, then 4 miles E on Hwy 242. Phone 703/550-9220. www.gunstonhall.org.* (1755-1759) The 550-acre estate of George Mason, framer of the Constitution and father of the Bill of Rights. Restored 18th-century mansion with period furnishings; reconstructed outbuildings; display of historic livestock on a working farm; museum; boxwood gardens on grounds; nature trail; picnic area; gift shop. (Daily 9:30 am-5 pm; closed Jan 1, Thanksgiving, Dec 25) **$$**

King Street. *In Old Town.* Street is lined with trendy restaurants, shops, and fine antique stores.

Oxon Hill Farm. *6411 Oxon Hill Rd, Oxon Hill (20745). Entrance from Oxon Hill Rd, 300 yds W of jct Hwy 210 and I-95. Phone 301/839-1177.* Living history farm (circa 1898-1914) located on a working farm with livestock; participatory activities. Represents life from early 1800s to present. (Daily; closed Jan 1, Thanksgiving, Dec 25) **FREE**

Pohick Bay Regional Park. *6501 Pohick Bay Dr, Lorton (22079). Phone 703/339-6104. www.nvrpa.org/pohickbay.html. Near Gunston Hall.* Activities in this 1,000-acre park include swimming (Memorial Day-Labor Day), boating (ramp, rentals, fee); 18-hole golf, miniature and Frisbee golf, camping (7-day limit; electric hookups available; fee), picnicking. Park (all year). Fee charged for activities.

Pohick Episcopal Church. *9301 Richmond Hwy, Lorton (22079). 16 miles S on Hwy 1. Phone 703/550-9449.* (1774) The colonial parish church of Mount Vernon and Gunston Hall. Built under the supervision of George Mason and George Washington; original walls; interior fully restored. (Daily) **FREE**

Sightseeing boat tours. *Phone 703/684-0580.* Tours of the Alexandria waterfront. Contact the Potomac Riverboat Company. **$$$**

Torpedo Factory Arts Center. *105 N Union St, Alexandria (22314). Phone 703/838-4565. www.torpedofactory.org.* Renovated munitions plant houses an artists' center with more than 160 professional artists of various media. Studios, cooperative galleries, school. Also the home of Alexandria Archaeology offices, lab, and museum; phone 703/838-4399. (Daily 10 am-5 pm; closed holidays) **FREE**

★ **Walking tour of historic sites.** *221 King St, Alexandria (22314). Tours depart from the Ramsay House, King at Fairfax St. Phone 703/838-4200.* Start at the Visitor Center in Ramsay House (circa 1725), which is the oldest house in Alexandria and has been used as a tavern, grocery store, and cigar factory. Here, you can obtain special events information and a free visitors' guide, as well as purchase block tickets good for reduced admission to three of the city's historic properties. Guided walking tours depart from here (spring-fall, weather permitting). The bureau also issues free parking permits, tour and highway maps, and hotel, dining, and shopping information. (Daily; closed Jan 1, Thanksgiving, Dec 25) One block N on Fairfax St is

Carlyle House. *121 N Fairfax St, Alexandria (22314). Phone 703/549-2997.* (1753) This stately stone mansion built in Palladian style was the site of a 1755 meeting between General Edward Braddock and five British colonial governors to plan the early campaigns of the French and Indian War. (Tues-Sun; closed holidays) **$$**

Stabler-Leadbeater Apothecary Museum. *105 S Fairfax St, Alexandria (22314). Phone 703/836-3713.* (1792) Largest collection of apothecary glass in its original setting in the country; more than 1,000 apothecary bottles. Original building is now a museum of early pharmacy; collection of old prescriptions, patent medicines, scales, and other 18th-century pharmacy items. George Washington, Robert E. Lee, and John Calhoun were regular customers. (Daily; closed Jan 1, Thanksgiving, Dec 25)

Old Presbyterian Meeting House. *321 S Fairfax St, Alexandria (22314). Phone 703/549-6670. www.opmh.org.* (1774) Tomb of the unknown soldier of the Revolution is in the churchyard. (Mon-Fri) **FREE**

Lafayette House. *301 S St. Asaph St, Alexandria (22314).* Fine example of Federal architecture. House was loaned to Lafayette for his last visit to America (1825). (Private)

The Lyceum. *201 S Washington St, Alexandria (22314). Phone 703/838-4994.* Museum, exhibitions; Virginia travel information (limited). (Daily; closed Jan 1, Thanksgiving, Dec 25) **FREE**

Christ Church. *118 N Washington St, Alexandria (22314). Phone 703/549-1450. www.historicchristchurch.org.* (1773) Washington and Robert E. Lee were pewholders. Fine Palladian window; interior balcony; wrought-brass and crystal chandelier brought from England. Structure is extensively restored but has changed little since it was built. Exhibit, gift shop at Columbus Street entrance. (Mon-Sat, also Sun afternoons; closed holidays; also for weddings, funerals)

Home of General Henry "Light Horse Harry" Lee. *611 Cameron St, Alexandria (22314).* (Private)

Lee-Fendall House. *614 Oronoco St, Alexandria (22314). Phone 703/548-1789. www.leefendallhouse.org.* (1785) Built by Phillip Richard Fendall and lived in by the Lee family for 118 years. Both George Washington and Revolutionary War hero "Light Horse Harry" Lee were frequent visitors to the house. Remodeled in 1850, the house is furnished with Lee family belongings. (Tues-Sat 10 am-4 pm, Sun 1-4 pm, weekend hours may vary; closed holidays) **$**

Boyhood Home of Robert E. Lee. *607 Oronoco St, Alexandria (22314). Phone 703/548-8454.* Federalist architecture. Famous guests include Washington and Lafayette.

Gadsby's Tavern Museum. *134 N Royal St, Alexandria (22314). Phone 703/838-4242.* (1770, 1792) Famous hostelry frequented by Washington and other patriots. Combines two 18th-century buildings; interesting architecture. (Tues-Sun; closed holidays) **$$**

Special Events

George Washington Birthday Celebrations. Events include a race and a Revolutionary War reenactment; climaxed by a birthday parade on the federal holiday. Feb.

House tours. *221 King St, Alexandria (22314). Tours depart from the Ramsay House. Phone 703/838-4200.* Fine colonial and Federalist houses are open to the public: Historic Garden Week (Apr); Hospital Auxiliary Tour of Historic Houses (Sept); Scottish Christmas Walk (Dec). Tickets, additional information at Alexandria Convention/Visitors Association.

Red Cross Waterfront Festival. *123 N Alfred St, Alexandria (22314). Phone 703/549-8300.* Commemorates Alexandria's maritime heritage. Features "tall ships," blessing of the fleet, river cruises, races, arts and crafts, exhibits, food, a variety of music, and fireworks. June.

Scottish Christmas Walk. *Ramsay House, 221 King St, Alexandria (22314). Phone toll-free 800/388-9119.* Parade, house tour, concerts, greens and heather sales, and a dinner/dance to emphasize city's Scottish origins. First Sat in Dec.

Virginia Scottish Games. *Ramsay House, 221 King St, Alexandria (22314). Phone 703/838-4200.* Athletic competition, Highland dance and music, antique cars, displays, and food. Fourth weekend in July.

Limited-Service Hotels

★ BEST WESTERN OLD COLONY INN. *1101 N Washington St, Alexandria (22314). Phone 703/739-2222; toll-free 800/780-7234; fax 703/549-2568. www.bestwestern.com.* 49 rooms, 2 story. Complimentary full breakfast. Check-out noon. High-speed Internet access. Airport transportation available. **$**

★ HAMPTON INN. *4800 Leesburg Pike, Alexandria (22302). Phone 703/671-4800; fax 703/671-2442. www.hamptoninn.com.* 130 rooms, 4 story. Complimentary continental breakfast. Check-out noon. Fitness room. Outdoor pool. **$**

★★ HOLIDAY INN. *480 King St, Alexandria (22314). Phone 703/549-6080; toll-free 800/368-5047; fax 703/684-6508. www.holiday-inn.com.* 227 rooms, 6 story. Pets accepted, some restrictions. Complimentary continental breakfast. Check-in 3 pm, check-out noon. Restaurant, bar. Fitness room. Indoor pool. Airport transportation available. Business center. **$$**

★★ RADISSON HOTEL OLD TOWN ALEXANDRIA. *901 N Fairfax St, Alexandria (22314). Phone 703/683-6000; fax 703/683-7597. www.radisson.com.* 258 rooms, 12 story. Check-out noon. Restaurant, bar. Outdoor pool. Airport transportation available. Business center. **$**

Full-Service Hotels

★★★ HILTON ALEXANDRIA MARK CENTER. *5000 Seminary Rd, Alexandria (22311). Phone 703/845-1010; fax 703/845-7662. www.hilton.com.* 495 rooms, 30 story. Check-out noon. Restaurant, bar. Fitness room. Indoor pool, outdoor pool, whirlpool. Tennis. Airport transportation available. Business center. Located on 50 wooded acres with nature preserve. **$**

★★★ RELAIS & CHATEAUX MORRISON HOUSE. *116 S Alfred St, Alexandria (22314). Phone 703/838-8000; toll-free 800/367-0800; fax 703/684-6283. www.morrissonhouse.com.* The quaint, brick-lined streets of charming Old Town Alexandria are a perfect match for the historical flavor of the Morrison House. Just down the river from the Capitol, this Federal-style mansion presents visitors with a peaceful alternative to the bustling city. Decorative fireplaces, four-poster mahogany beds, and silk sofas define the guest rooms, all furnished in early American décor. The amenities are decidedly 21st century, however, with oversized marble bathrooms and luxurious Frette linens. The Grille attracts a smart casual set with its clubby ambience and live piano music, but it is the exceptional Elysium (see) that is not to be missed. Menus are banished here, the dishes determined by the chef's conversations with each patron. Diners sip Champagne and fine wines as he concocts creative, personalized meals. Rather like having a private chef for the evening, this is truly a singular experience. 45 rooms, 5 story. Check-in 3 pm, check-out noon. Restaurant, bar. **$$**

★★★ SHERATON SUITES ALEXANDRIA. *801 N St. Asaph St, Alexandria (22314). Phone 703/836-4700; toll-free 800/325-3535; fax 703/548-4514. www.sheraton.com.* Located just 2 miles from National Airport and the Pentagon, this hotel offers amenities for both business and leisure travelers. 247 rooms, 10 story, all suites. Check-out 1 pm. Restaurant, bar. Fitness room. Indoor pool, whirlpool. Airport transportation available. **$$**

Restaurants

★ THE ALAMO. *100 King St, Alexandria (22314). Phone 703/739-0555; fax 703/549-8441.* Nouvelle Southwestern menu. Lunch, dinner. Closed Thanksgiving, Dec 25. Bar. In 1871 Corn Exchange Building. **$$**

★★ BILBO BAGGINS. *208 Queen St, Alexandria (22314). Phone 703/683-0300; fax 703/683-1857. www.bilbobaggins.net.* American menu. Lunch, dinner, Sun brunch. Closed July 4, Thanksgiving, Dec 25. Bar. Children's menu. Upstairs in an 1898 structure; stained glass, skylights. **$$**

★★ BISTROT LA FAYETTE. *1118 King St, Alexandria (22314). Phone 703/548-2525; fax 703/548-0220.* French menu. Lunch, dinner. Closed Sun. Bar. Casual attire. **$$$**

★★ BLUE POINT GRILL. *600 Franklin St, Alexandria (22314). Phone 703/739-0404; fax 703/684-1853. www.suttongourmet.com.* Seafood menu. Lunch, dinner, Sun brunch. Closed Dec 25. Outdoor seating. **$$**

★★ CALVERT GRILLE. *3106 Mount Vernon Ave, Alexandria (22305). Phone 703/836-8425; fax 703/836-0539.* Breakfast, lunch, dinner, brunch. Bar. Children's menu. **$$**

★★ CHART HOUSE. *1 Cameron St, Alexandria (22314). Phone 703/684-5080; fax 703/684-7364. www.chart-house.com.* Seafood menu. Lunch, dinner, Sun brunch. Bar. Children's menu. Outdoor seating. **$$$**

★★★ CHEZ ANDRE. *10 E Glebe Rd, Alexandria (22305). Phone 703/836-1404; fax 703/836-2530.* Choose from three different dining rooms at this restaurant that has been family owned for nearly 40 years. French menu. Lunch, dinner. Closed Sun; holidays. Bar. Reservations recommended. **$$**

★ COPELAND'S OF NEW ORLEANS. *4300 King St, Alexandria (22302). Phone 703/671-7997; fax 703/578-1082.* Cajun/Creole menu. Lunch, dinner, Sun brunch. Closed Thanksgiving, Dec 25. Bar. Children's menu. Outdoor seating. **$**

★★ ECCO CAFE. *220 N Lee St, Alexandria (22314). Phone 703/684-0321; fax 703/684-1785. www.eccocafe.com.* American, Italian menu. Lunch, dinner, Sun brunch. Closed Thanksgiving, Dec 25. Bar. In a restored 1890s warehouse building; eclectic décor. **$$**

★★★ ELYSIUM. *116 S Alfred St, Alexandria (22314). Phone 703/838-8000; toll-free 800/367-0800; fax 703/684-6283. www.morrisonhouse.com.* Have you ever dreamed of having a chef of your very own—someone who would come to your table and say something like, "Good evening. So nice to see you. What would you like me to make for you this evening?" Open your eyes. This is not a dream. You are at Elysium, a magical restaurant in the Morrison House hotel (see) in historic Alexandria, where you create your very own "Flight of Food" based on what the chef has purchased from local markets and farmers that very day. Instead of a dinner menu, you'll be presented with a wine list (a nice big one with lots of terrific international choices) and then a personal visit from the chef to discuss what you're in the mood to eat. He'll give you the list of ingredients, and you work together to develop the menu. It's very interactive and very exciting. This is living. After dinner, a butler will escort you to the parlor for an after-dinner drink or a wonderful, aromatic pot of special-blend loose tea made for the Morrison House. Eclectic menu. Breakfast, dinner. Closed Jan 1. Bar. Children's menu. Casual attire. **$$$**

★ **FACCIA LUNA.** *823 S Washington St, Alexandria (22314). Phone 703/838-5998. www.faccialuna.com.* American, Italian menu. Lunch, dinner. Closed holidays. Bar. Children's menu. Outdoor seating. **$$**

★ ★ **FISH MARKET.** *105 King St, Alexandria (22314). Phone 703/836-5676; fax 703/836-4659. www.fishmarketoldtown.com.* Seafood menu. Lunch, dinner. Closed Thanksgiving, Dec 25. Bar. Children's menu. Casual attire. In a restored 18th-century warehouse built of bricks carried to the New World as the ballast in a ship's hold; nautical décor. **$$**

★ ★ **GADSBY'S TAVERN.** *138 N Royal St, Alexandria (22314). Phone 703/548-1288; fax 703/548-5324.* American menu. Lunch, dinner, Sun brunch. Closed Jan 1, Dec 25, children's menu. Outdoor seating. Built in 1792; Georgian architecture; colonial décor and costumes. Strolling minstrels. Gadsby's Tavern Museum adjacent. **$$**

★ ★ **GERANIO.** *722 King St, Alexandria (22314). Phone 703/548-0088; fax 703/548-0091. www.geranio.net.* A roaring fireplace and stylish décor create a comfortable blend of old and new at this innovative restaurant. Regional favorites make up the diverse and gratifying menu. Italian menu. Lunch, dinner. Closed Jan 1, Thanksgiving, Dec 25. Casual attire. **$$**

★ **HARD TIMES CAFE.** *1404 King St, Alexandria (22314). Phone 703/683-5340; fax 703/683-8801. www.hardtimes.com.* Lunch, dinner. Closed holidays. Housed in a former church; rustic décor; collection of state flags. **$**

★ ★ **IL PORTO.** *121 King St, Alexandria (22314). Phone 703/836-8833; fax 703/836-8835. www.ilportoristorante.com.* A very skilled kitchen staff turns out classic dishes at this cozy restaurant, a local favorite for years. Set in a renovated warehouse, the atmosphere is just as rustic as the food. Italian menu. Lunch, dinner. Closed Thanksgiving. Bar. Children's menu. Casual attire. Reservations recommended. **$$**

★ ★ ★ **LA BERGERIE.** *218 N Lee St, Alexandria (22314). Phone 703/683-1007; fax 703/519-6114. www.labergerie.com.* A historic brick warehouse is the setting for this local favorite. Pleasant, tuxedoed waiters serve classic, often-forgotten dishes from the Basque region. French menu. Lunch, dinner. Closed Sun except Mother's Day; also holidays. Reservations recommended. **$$**

★ ★ **LANDINI BROTHERS.** *115 King St, Alexandria (22314). Phone 703/836-8404; fax 703/549-2211. www.landinibrothers.com.* Italian menu. Lunch, dinner. Closed holidays. Bar. Reservations recommended. 1790s building. **$$**

★ ★ **LE GAULOIS.** *1106 King St, Alexandria (22314). Phone 703/739-9494; fax 703/739-9496.* French menu. Lunch, dinner. Closed holidays. Casual attire. Reservations recommended. Outdoor seating. **$$**

★ ★ **LE REFUGE.** *127 N Washington St, Alexandria (22314). Phone 703/548-4661.* French menu. Lunch, dinner. Closed Sun; holidays. Bar. Reservations recommended. **$$$**

★ **MANGO MIKE'S.** *4580 Duke St, Alexandria (22304). Phone 703/823-1166; fax 703/370-4424. www.mangomikes.com.* Caribbean menu. Lunch, dinner, Sun brunch. Closed Thanksgiving, Dec 25. Bar. Children's menu. Outdoor seating. **$**

★ ★ **MONROE'S.** *1603 Commonwealth Ave, Alexandria (22301). Phone 703/548-5792; fax 703/548-5914.* Italian menu. Dinner, Sun brunch. Closed holidays. Bar. Children's menu. Reservations recommended. Outdoor seating. Contemporary trattoria with large murals. **$$**

★ ★ **R. T.'S.** *3804 Mt. Vernon Ave, Alexandria (22305). Phone 703/684-6010; fax 703/548-0417.* Cajun/Creole menu. Lunch, dinner. Closed holidays. Bar. Children's menu. **$$**

★ ★ **SANTA FE EAST.** *110 S Pitt St, Alexandria (22314). Phone 703/548-6900; fax 703/519-0798.* Southwestern menu. Lunch, dinner, Sun brunch. Closed July 4, Thanksgiving, Dec 25. Bar. Outdoor seating. In historic (1790) building. Fountain in courtyard. **$$**

★ ★ **SCOTLAND YARD.** *728 King St, Alexandria (22314). Phone 703/683-1742; fax 703/683-6989. www.scotlandyardrestaurant.com.* Scottish menu. Dinner. Closed Mon; Thanksgiving. Reservations recommended. **$$$**

★★ TEMPO. *4231 Duke St, Alexandria (22304). Phone 703/370-7900; fax 703/370-7902. www.tempo-restaurant.com.* Italian, French menu. Lunch, dinner, Sun brunch. Closed holidays. Bar. Reservations recommended. Outdoor seating. **$$**

★★ THAI HUT. *408 S Van Dorn St, Alexandria (22304). Phone 703/823-5357; fax 703/823-2931.* Thai menu. Lunch, dinner. Closed Thanksgiving, Dec 25. **$**

★★ UNION STREET PUBLIC HOUSE. *121 S Union St, Alexandria (22314). Phone 703/548-1785; fax 703/548-0705. www.usphalexandria.com.* American menu. Lunch, dinner, Sun brunch. Closed Thanksgiving, Dec 25. Bar. Children's menu. In a sea captain's house and warehouse (circa 1870). **$$**

★★ VILLA D'ESTE. *600 Montgomery St, Alexandria (22314). Phone 703/549-9477; fax 703/549-8809. www.villadesterestaurant.com.* Italian menu. Lunch, dinner. Closed holidays. Bar. Reservations recommended. **$$$**

★★ WHARF. *119 King St, Alexandria (22314). Phone 703/836-2834; fax 703/836-3028.* Seafood menu. Lunch, dinner. Closed Jan 1, Thanksgiving, Dec 25. Bar. Children's menu. Late 18th-century building. **$$**

Appomattox Court House National Historical Park (E-6)

See also Lynchburg

(3 miles NE of Appomattox on Hwy 24)

The series of clashes between General Ulysses S. Grant and General Robert E. Lee that started with the Battle of the Wilderness (May 5, 1864) finally ended here on Palm Sunday, April 9, 1865, in the little village of Appomattox.

A week earlier, Lee had evacuated besieged Petersburg and headed west in a desperate attempt to join forces with General Johnston in North Carolina. Ragged and exhausted, decimated by desertions, without supplies, and beset by Union forces at every turn, the once-great Army of Northern Virginia launched its last attack at dawn on April 9. By 10 am, it was clear that further bloodshed was futile; after some difficulty in getting a message to Grant, the two antagonists met in the parlor of the McLean House. By 3 pm, the generous surrender terms had been drafted and signed. The war was over. Three days later, 28,231 Confederate soldiers received their parole here.

The 1,743-acre park includes the village of Appomattox, restored and reconstructed to appear much as it did in 1865. Uniformed park rangers or interpreters in period dress answer questions about the residents and events. (Daily; closed holidays Nov-Feb) Golden Eagle Passport accepted (see MAKING THE MOST OF YOUR TRIP). Audiovisual programs, Braille guide folders, audio guide, and large-print folder available for the hearing and visually impaired. For further information contact the Superintendent, PO Box 218, Appomattox 24522; 804/352-8987.

What to See and Do

★ Appomattox Courthouse Building. Reconstructed building houses visitor center, museum; audiovisual slide program (every half hour, second floor). Self-guided tour of village begins here and includes

Clover Hill Tavern and outbuildings. (1819) Oldest structure in village; bookstore, rest rooms.

Confederate Cemetery.

County jail. (1870) Furnished.

McLean House and outbuildings. Reconstruction of house where Generals Lee and Grant met on April 9, 1865.

Meek's Store and Meek's Storehouse. With period furnishings.

Stacking of Arms. On the fourth anniversary of the firing on Fort Sumter, which triggered the outbreak of war, Confederate soldiers laid down their weapons here.

Woodson Law Office. With period furnishings.

Holliday Lake State Park. *9 miles NE of Appomattox on Hwy 24, then 6 miles SE via Hwys 626, 692. Phone 434/248-6308.* Approximately 250 acres in Buckingham-Appomattox State Forest. Swimming beach, bathhouse, fishing, boating (launch, rentals) on 150-acre lake; hiking trails, picnicking, concession, tent and trailer sites. Visitor center, interpretive programs. Park (daily); most activities, including camping (Memorial Day-Labor Day).

Arlington County (Ronald Reagan Washington-National Airport Area)

See also Alexandria, Fairfax, Fall Church, McLean; also see District of Columbia

Web site www.co.arlington.va.us

Airport Information

Subway trains and buses (Metro Transit System), phone 202/962-1234. Information 202/637-7000

Airport Ronald Regan Washington-National Airport.

Information Phone 703/417-8000

Lost and Found Phone 703/417-8560

Web site www.mwaa.com/national/index.htm

Airlines Air Canada, Alaska Airlines, America West, American Airlines, American Eagle, American Trans Air (ATA), Continental Airlines, Continental Express, Delta Air Lines, Delta Connection, Delta Shuttle, Frontier Airlines, Midwest Express Airlines, Northwest Airlines, United Airlines, US Airways, US Airways Shuttle, US Airways Express

> **Arlington County Fun Fact**
>
> The Pentagon building in Arlington is the largest office building in the world.

What to See and Do

Arlington Farmers' Market. *N Courthouse Rd and N 14th St, Arlington. Adjacent to Arlington County Courthouse. Phone 703/228-6423. www.arlingtonfarmersmarket.com.* Irresistibly fresh berries, peaches, and heirloom tomatoes are just some of the pleasures available at this lively market, which has been featuring the produce of farmers within 125 miles of Arlington since 1979. Don't miss the grass-fed meats, specialty goat cheeses, and unusual varieties of familiar fruits and vegetables (one longtime vendor grows 35 different types of apples). Expect a great selection in any season at this year-round market: more than 30 producers are on hand on a typical Saturday. (Sat)

★ **Arlington National Cemetery.** *W end of Memorial Bridge. Phone 703/979-0690. www.arlingtoncemetery.org.* The solemn grounds of Arlington National Cemetery are a profoundly stirring sight. Gentle hills are studded as far as the eye can see with white stones marking the graves of more than 260,000 Americans who served in the nation's military, from the American Revolution to more recent conflicts. Many visitors stop at the Tomb of the Unknowns, which contains the unidentified remains of servicemen killed in the world wars and the Korean conflict and provides quiet tribute to anonymous sacrifice. Most also pay their respects at the eternal flame marking the granite-paved gravesite of President John F. Kennedy and his wife, Jacqueline, and that of Robert F. Kennedy nearby. These graves are situated on a grassy slope below Arlington House, the elegantly columned mansion that was Civil War general Robert E. Lee's home for 30 years and is now maintained as a public memorial to him. **FREE** Also located here are

Arlington House, the Robert E. Lee Memorial. *Phone 703/557-0613. www.nps.gov/arho/.* National memorial to Robert E. Lee. Built between 1802 and 1818 by George Washington Parke Custis, Martha Washington's grandson and foster son of George Washington. In 1831 his daughter, Mary Anna Randolph Custis, married Lieutenant Robert E. Lee; six of the seven Lee children were born here. As executor of the Custis estate, Lee took extended leave from the US Army and devoted his time to managing and improving the estate. It was the Lee homestead for 30 years before the Civil War. On April 20, 1861, following the secession of Virginia, Lee made his decision to stay with Virginia. Within a month, the house was vacated. Some of the family possessions were moved for safekeeping, but most were stolen or destroyed when Union troops occupied the house during the Civil War. In 1864, when Mrs. Lee could not appear personally to pay property tax, the estate was confiscated by the federal government; a 200-acre section was set aside for a national cemetery. (There is some evidence that indicates this was done to ensure the Lee family could never again live on the estate.) G. W. Custis Lee, the general's son, later regained title to the property through a Supreme Court decision and sold it to the US government in 1883 for $150,000. Restoration of the house to its 1861 appearance was begun in 1925. The Classic Revival house is furnished with authentic pieces of the period, including some Lee family originals. From the grand portico with its six massive, faux-marble Doric columns there is a panoramic view of Washington, DC. (Daily; closed Jan 1, Dec 25)

Memorial Amphitheatre. This impressive white marble edifice is used for ceremonies such as Memorial Day, Easter sunrise, and Veterans Day services.

Tomb of the Unknowns. On November 11, 1921, the remains of an unknown American soldier of World War I were entombed here. A memorial was erected in 1932 with the inscription "Here rests in honored glory an American soldier known but to God." On Memorial Day 1958, an unknown warrior who died in World War II and another who died in the Korean War were laid beside him. On Memorial Day 1984, an unknown soldier from the Vietnam War was interred here. Sentries stand guard 24 hours a day; changing of the guard is every hour on the hour Oct-Mar, every 30 minutes Apr-Sept.

Crystal City Shops. *Crystal Dr, Arlington (22202). Between 15th and 23rd sts. Phone 703/922-4636. www.thecrystalcityshops.com.* Crystal City, a mixed-use residential and commercial development, has an underground shopping complex and a lot of street-level activity. It's currently being upgraded to provide more of a "Main Street" feel, with outdoor cafés and other seating as well as improved landscaping and opportunities for window-shopping. You'll find jewelry and gift shops, men's and women's apparel, books, and home furnishings, as well as a Japanese steakhouse, two American steakhouses, and a Legal Sea Foods. (Daily)

Fashion Centre at Pentagon City. *1100 S Hayes St, Arlington (22202). Off I-395 at jct S Hayes St and Army-Navy Dr, S of the Pentagon. Phone 703/415-2400.* The presence of the Ritz-Carlton Hotel dictates a glamorous tone at this huge, glittering mall, anchored by Macy's and Nordstrom and home to more than 150 other tantalizing shops and restaurants. Of-the-moment women's fashions and accessories are everywhere—don't miss bebe, Betsey Johnson, and MAC Cosmetics. For home furnishings, check out Crate & Barrel and Williams-Sonoma; Bang & Olufsen is here, too, if your needs are aural. Recover from strenuous browsing at the skylit food court. (Daily; closed Thanksgiving, Dec 25)

Iwo Jima Statue. *On Arlington Blvd, near Arlington National Cemetery.* Marine Corps War Memorial depicts raising of the flag on Mount Suribachi, Iwo Jima, February 23, 1945; this is the largest sculpture ever cast in bronze. Sunset Parade concert with performances by US Marine Drum and Bugle Corps, US Marine Corps Color Guard, and the Silent Drill Team (late May-late Aug, Tues evenings).

★ **The Newseum.** *1101 Wilson Blvd, Arlington (22209). Phone 703/284-3700; toll-free 888/639-7386.* This 72,000-square-foot interactive museum of news takes visitors behind the scenes to see and experience how and why news is made. Be a reporter or newscaster; relive great news stories through multimedia exhibits; see today's news as it happens on a block-long video wall. (Wed-Sun; closed holidays) **FREE** Located on the grounds is

Freedom Park. Nearly 1,000 feet in length, the park occupies a never-used bridge. The park also features a memorial to the journalists killed in the line of duty and various icons of freedom.

The Pentagon. *Jefferson Davis Hwy, Washington Blvd, and I-395, Arlington. Phone 703/695-1776. www.defenselink.mil/pubs/pentagon/.* With some 6 million square feet of floor area, this is one of the largest office buildings in the world. It houses the offices of the Department of Defense. **FREE**

Sur La Table. *1101 S Joyce St, Suite B-20, Arlington (22202). Phone 703/414-3580. www.surlatable.com.* In the 1970s, Seattle spawned this clearinghouse for hard-to-find kitchen gear, and it soon became known as a source for cookware, small appliances, cutlery, kitchen tools, linens, tableware, gadgets, and specialty foods. Sur La Table has since expanded to include cooking classes ($$$$), chef demonstrations, and cookbook author signings, as well as a catalog and online presence. Cooking connoisseurs discover such finds as cool oven mitts, zest graters, copper whisks, onion soup bowls, and inspired TV dinner trays. (Daily)

Special Events

Arlington County Fair. *3308 S Stafford St, Arlington (22206). Phone 703/920-4556.* Countywide fair; arts, crafts, international foods, children's activities. Aug.

Army 10-miler. *The Pentagon, Arlington. Phone 202/685-3361. www.armytenmiler.com.* America's largest 10-mile road race, attracting thousands of military and civilian runners. Early Oct.

Marine Corps Marathon. *Rte 110 and Marshall Dr, Arlington (22201). Phone toll-free 800/786-8762. www.marinemarathon.com.* Cheer on your favorite runner at the Marine Corps Marathon—with 16,000 contestants participating, there will be awesome physiques to admire everywhere you look. The 26-mile, 385-yard route starts and ends near the Iwo Jima Memorial and winds through Arlington, Georgetown, and DC, passing the Capitol, the Pentagon, and other inspiring sights along the way. The Marine Corps Marathon 5K race, organized in conjunction with the Special Olympics competition, starts at the Memorial at 9:10 am. Late Oct. **FREE**

Memorial Day Service Ceremony. *Arlington National Cemetery.* Wreaths placed at the Tomb of the Unknown Soldier. The National Symphony Orchestra gives a free concert later in the evening on the lawn of the Capitol. Memorial Day.

Limited-Service Hotels

★ ★ COURTYARD BY MARRIOTT. *2899 Jefferson Davis Hwy, Arlington (22202). Phone 703/549-3434; fax 703/549-7440. www.courtyard.com.* 272 rooms, 14 story. Check-out 1 pm. Restaurant, bar. Fitness room. Indoor pool, whirlpool. Airport transportation available. **$$**

★ ★ EMBASSY SUITES. *1300 Jefferson Davis Hwy, Arlington (22202). Phone 703/979-9799; fax 703/920-5947. www.embassysuitesdcmetro.com.* Convenient to downtown Washington and close to the airport, this property is in the center of Crystal City. 267 rooms, 11 story, all suites. Complimentary full breakfast. Check-in 3 pm, check-out noon. Restaurant, bar. Fitness room. Indoor pool, whirlpool. Airport transportation available. **$$**

★ HAMPTON INN. *2000 Jefferson Davis Hwy, Arlington (22202). Phone 703/418-5901; toll-free 800/329-7466; fax 703/521-5901. www.hamptoninn.com.* 247 rooms, 8 story. Check-out 11 am. High-speed Internet access. Restaurant, bar. Fitness room. Indoor pool. Airport transportation available. **$**

★ ★ QUALITY INN. *1200 N Courthouse Rd, Arlington (22201). Phone 703/524-4000; toll-free 888/987-2555; fax 703/522-6814. www.choicehotels.com.* 392 rooms, 10 story. Pets accepted, some restrictions; fee. Check-out noon. Restaurant, bar. Fitness room. Outdoor pool. **$**

Full-Service Hotels

★ ★ ★ CROWNE PLAZA. *1489 Jefferson Davis Hwy, Arlington (22202). Phone 703/416-1600; fax 703/416-1615. www.crowneplaza.com/was-natlapt.* 308 rooms, 11 story. Check-in 3 pm, check-out noon. Two restaurants, bar. Fitness room. Outdoor pool. Airport transportation available. Business center. **$$**

★ ★ ★ HILTON ARLINGTON AND TOWERS. *950 N Stafford St, Arlington (22203). Phone 703/528-6000; fax 703/812-5127. www.hilton.com.* This hotel is part of the Balliston Metro Center and is close to shopping and the National Science Foundation. 209 rooms, 7 story. Check-out 1 pm. Restaurant, bar. Indoor pool, whirlpool. **$$**

★ ★ ★ HYATT ARLINGTON. *1325 Wilson Blvd, Arlington (22209). Phone 703/525-1234; fax 703/875-3393. www.arlingtonhyatt.com.* This hotel is located across the bridge from Washington and close to Arlington National Cemetery. 304 rooms, 16 story. Check-in 3 pm, check-out noon. Restaurant, bar. Fitness room. Business center. **$$**

★ ★ ★ MARRIOTT CRYSTAL CITY AT REAGAN NATIONAL AIRPORT. *1999 Jefferson Davis Hwy, Arlington (22202). Phone 703/413-5500; toll-free 800/331-3131; fax 703/413-0192. www.marriott.com.* 343 rooms, 12 story. Check-in 4 pm, check-out 1 pm. Restaurant, bar. Fitness room. Indoor pool, whirlpool. Airport transportation available. Business center. Near Metrorail. **$$**

★★★★ THE RITZ-CARLTON, PENTAGON CITY. *1250 S Hayes St, Arlington (22202). Phone 703/415-5000; fax 703/415-5061. www.ritzcarlton.com.* Five minutes from Washington National Airport, The Ritz-Carlton, Pentagon City provides its guests with an effortless way to visit the capital region. Although businesses, monuments, and other attractions are only minutes away, visitors leave the hectic pace behind when staying here. Tailored elegance is the hallmark of this hotel, and the guest rooms are no exception. Feather beds and Egyptian cotton linens make demanding travelers loyal fans; updated technology is a boon for business travelers; and club-level accommodations take pampering to another level. Massages and personal fitness assessments are available at the fitness center, and the indoor access to the area's popular Fashion Centre puts smiles on the faces of devoted shoppers. Afternoon tea takes on a whimsical edge with the Winnie-the-Pooh children's tea service in the Lobby Lounge, and The Grill (see) never ceases to delight diners with its all-day dining. 366 rooms, 18 story. Check-in 3 pm, check-out noon. Restaurant, bar. Children's activity center. Fitness room. Indoor pool, whirlpool. Business center. **$$$**

★★★ SHERATON CRYSTAL CITY HOTEL. *1800 Jefferson Davis Hwy, Arlington (22202). Phone 703/486-1111; toll-free 800/862-7666; fax 703/769-3970. www.sheraton.com.* 210 rooms, 15 story. Check-in 3 pm, check-out 1 pm. Restaurant, bar. Fitness room. Outdoor pool. Airport transportation available. Business center. **$$**

Restaurants

★★ ALPINE. *4770 Lee Hwy, Arlington (22207). Phone 703/528-7600; fax 703/528-7625.* Italian menu. Lunch, dinner. Closed Mon; holidays. Bar. **$$**

★★ BISTRO BISTRO. *4021 S 28th St, Arlington (22206). Phone 703/379-0300; fax 703/931-1036. www.bistro-bistro.com.* Mediterranean menu. Lunch, dinner, Sun brunch. Closed Thanksgiving, Dec 24-25. Bar. Outdoor seating. **$$**

★ CAFE DALAT. *3143 Wilson Blvd, Arlington (22201). Phone 703/276-0935.* Vietnamese menu. Lunch, dinner. Closed July 4, Thanksgiving, Dec 25; also Chinese New Year. **$$**

★★ CARLYLE GRAND CAFE. *4000 S 28th St, Arlington (22206). Phone 703/931-0777; fax 703/931-9420. www.greatamericanrestaurants.com/carlyle/cm.htm.* American menu. Lunch, dinner, Sun brunch. Closed Thanksgiving, Dec 25. Bar. Outdoor seating. **$$**

★ COWBOY CAFE. *4792 Lee Hwy, Arlington (22207). Phone 703/243-8010.* American menu. Breakfast, lunch, dinner. Bar. **$**

★ FACCIA LUNA. *2909 Wilson Blvd, Arlington (22201). Phone 703/276-3099. www.faccialuna.com.* Italian menu. Lunch, dinner. Closed Thanksgiving, Dec 24-25. Bar. Children's menu. Outdoor seating. Upscale trattoria. **$$**

★★★ THE GRILL. *1250 S Hayes St, Arlington (22202). Phone 703/412-2760; fax 703/415-5061. www.ritzcarlton.com.* The Grill at the Ritz-Carlton offers upscale American classics in a warm, clubby dining room decked out in mahogany wood. It features a crackling fireplace and fresh flowers. The Grill's formal yet inviting atmosphere makes it ideal for all sorts of gatherings, whether business, pleasure, or both. The seasonal menu features lots of pin-up worthy dishes. Lobster, filet mignon, foie gras, caviar, and oysters are in attendance in abundance, giving those in need of culinary luxury an easy and delicious fix. Weekends are busy for The Grill, as it houses one of the best brunches in the area. American menu. Breakfast, lunch, dinner, brunch. Children's menu. Casual attire. Valet parking. **$$$**

★★ J. W.'S STEAKHOUSE. *1401 Lee Hwy, Arlington (22209). Phone 703/524-6400; fax 703/524-8964. www.marriott.com.* Seafood, steak menu. Dinner, Sun brunch. Closed Jan 1. Bar. **$$$**

★★ LA COTE D'OR CAFE. *6876 Lee Hwy, Arlington (22213). Phone 703/538-3033; fax 703/573-0409.* French menu. Lunch, dinner, Sun brunch. Closed Jan 1, Dec 25. Bar. Outdoor seating. **$$**

★★ **LITTLE VIET GARDEN.** *3012 Wilson Blvd, Arlington (22201). Phone 703/522-9686.* Vietnamese menu. Lunch, dinner. Closed Thanksgiving, Dec 25. Bar. Outdoor seating. **$**

★ **MATUBA.** *2915 Columbia Pike, Arlington (22204). Phone 703/521-2811.* Japanese menu. Lunch, dinner. **$$**

★★ **QUEEN BEE.** *3181 Wilson Blvd, Arlington (22201). Phone 703/527-3444; fax 703/525-2750.* Vietnamese menu. Lunch, dinner. **$**

★★ **R. T.'S SEAFOOD KITCHEN.** *2300 Clarendon Blvd, Arlington (22201). Phone 703/841-0100; fax 703/841-0597.* Cajun menu. Lunch, dinner. Closed holidays. Bar. Children's menu. Outdoor seating. **$$**

★ **RED HOT AND BLUE.** *1600 Wilson Blvd, Arlington (22209). Phone 703/276-8833. www.redhotandblue.com.* Barbecue menu. Lunch, dinner. Closed Thanksgiving, Dec 25. Bar. Memphis blues memorabilia. **$$**

★ **SILVER DINER.** *3200 Wilson Blvd, Arlington (22201). Phone 703/812-8667; fax 703/812-8669.* American menu. Breakfast, lunch, dinner, brunch. Closed Dec 25. Children's menu. **$$**

★★ **TIVOLI.** *1700 N Moore St, Arlington (22209). Phone 703/524-8900; fax 703/524-4971. www.tivolirestaurant.net.* Italian menu. Lunch, dinner. Closed Sun; holidays. Bar. Reservations recommended. **$$**

★ **VILLAGE BISTRO.** *1723 Wilson Blvd, Arlington (22209). Phone 703/522-0284; fax 703/522-7797.* American menu. Lunch, dinner. Closed Thanksgiving, Dec 25. Bar. Outdoor seating. Monet prints on walls. **$$**

★★ **WOO LAE OAK.** *1500 S Joyce St, Arlington (22202). Phone 703/521-3706; fax 703/521-0014. www.woolaeoak.com.* Korean menu. Lunch, dinner. Closed Jan 1. **$$**

Ashland (D-8)

See also Richmond

Founded 1858
Population 6,619
Elevation 221 ft
Area Code 804
Zip 23005
Information Ashland/Hanover Visitor Information Center, 112 N Railroad Ave; phone 804/752-6766 or toll-free 800/897-1479
Web site www.vatc.org

Ashland was founded when the president of the Richmond, Fredericksburg, and Potomac Railroad bought land here. He dug a well, struck mineral water, and started a health resort—Slash Cottage (wilderness acres were called "slashes"). A thriving village grew up and took the name of Henry Clay's Kentucky estate. In 1866, the railroad company gave land to the Methodist Church and induced the church to move Randolph-Macon College here. A section of early 1900s houses along the railroad tracks has been set aside as a historic district.

What to See and Do

Paramount's Kings Dominion. *16000 Theme Pkwy, Doswell (23047). 1 mile E on Hwy 54, then 7 miles N on I-95. Phone 804/876-5561; toll-free 800/553-7277. www.kingsdominion.com.* A 400-acre family theme park consisting of six theme areas, including Water Werks; Action Epic Theatre; the Anaconda, a looping roller coaster that passes through an underwater tunnel; also Shockwave stand-up roller coaster; The Outer Limits roller coaster; 33-story likeness of the Eiffel Tower with panoramic view; whitewater raft ride; live entertainment; shops. (Late May-Aug: daily; late Mar-late May and Sept-Oct: weekends) **$$$$**

Patrick Henry Home. *16120 Chiswell Ln, Beaverdam (23015). 11 miles NW via Hwys 54, 671, County 685 (Scotchtown Rd), left onto Chiswell Ln, in Beaverdam. Phone 804/227-3500.* The 1719 Scotchtown was American Revolution-era hero Patrick Henry's home from 1771 to 1778. It was also the girlhood home of

Dolly Madison. Fine colonial architecture. (Apr-Oct, Tues-Sat 10 am-4:30 pm, Sun 1:30-4:30 pm; closed Easter, Mother's Day, July 4) **$$**

Randolph-Macon College. *204 Henry St, Ashland (23005). 1 mile W of I-95. Phone 804/752-7305.* (1830) (1,100 students) Coeducational, liberal arts, Methodist-affiliated college. Historic buildings include Washington-Franklin Hall, Old Chapel, and Pace Hall. **FREE**

Limited-Service Hotels

★ BEST WESTERN HANOVER HOUSE. *10296 Sliding Hill Rd, Ashland (23005). Phone 804/550-2805; fax 804/550-2104. www.bestwestern.com.* 93 rooms, 2 story. Check-out noon. Restaurant. Fitness room. Outdoor pool. **$**

★★ QUALITY INN. *810 England St, Ashland (23005). Phone 804/798-4231; fax 804/798-9074. www.choicehotels.com.* 56 rooms, 2 story. Check-out 11 am. Restaurant, bar. Fitness room. Outdoor pool, children's pool. **$**

Full-Service Inn

★★★ HENRY CLAY INN. *114 N Railroad Ave, Ashland (23005). Phone 804/798-3100; toll-free 800/343-4565; fax 804/752-7555. www.henryclayinn.com.* This inn, an authentic reproduction of a Georgian Revival inn, is near the historic areas of Williamsburg, Charlottesville, and Fredericksburg. 11 rooms, 3 story. Complimentary continental breakfast. Check-in 2 pm, check-out 11 am. Restaurant. Authentic reproduction of Georgian Revival inn. **$**

Restaurant

★★ IRONHORSE. *100 S Railroad Ave, Ashland (23005). Phone 804/752-6410; fax 804/752-6441.* American menu. Lunch, dinner. Closed Sun; holidays; also week after Jan 1 and week after July 4. Bar. **$$$**

Basye (C-6)

See also Luray, New Market, Woodstock

Population 200
Elevation 1,354 ft
Area Code 540
Zip 22810
Information Bryce Resort, PO Box 3; phone 540/856-2121
Web site www.bryceresort.com

What to See and Do

Bryce Resort. *1982 Fairway Dr, Bayse (22810). Phone toll-free 800/821-1444. www.bryceresort.com.* Bryce Resort sits in the Shenandoah Valley, and Stony Creek winds through the course, coming into play on seven different holes. This par-71 course is just a shade under 6,300 yards from the championship tees, and the challenging distance is never more evident than on the 575-yard opening hole. The course is played moderately, with about 30,000 rounds going off each year, but it's kept in great condition, and the teaching pros on staff are always willing to help even the most inexperienced golfer. **$$$$**

Bryce Resort Ski Area. *1982 Fairway Dr, Basye (22810).*

Winter. Day and night skiing. Two double chairlifts, three surface lifts; patrol, school, rentals; snowmaking; ski shop; restaurant, cafeteria, bar. Longest run 2,750 feet; vertical drop 500 feet. (Mid-Dec-mid-Mar, daily)

Summer. Fishing, swimming, boating; horseback riding, tennis, hiking, grass skiing. Fee for activities.

Limited-Service Hotel

★★ BEST WESTERN SHENANDOAH VALLEY. *250 Conickville Blvd, Mount Jackson (22842). Phone 540/477-2911; fax 540/477-2392. www.bestwestern.com.* 98 rooms, 2 story. Pets accepted, some restrictions; fee. Check-out 11 am. Restaurant, bar. Outdoor pool, children's pool. Tennis. **$**

Specialty Lodging

The following lodging establishment is approved by Mobil Travel Guide, but due to its unique and individualized nature has not been given a traditional Mobil Star rating. Included in this listing you may find bed-and-breakfasts, limited-service inns, guest ranches, and other unique hotel properties.

WIDOW KIP'S COUNTRY INN. *355 Orchard Dr, Mount Jackson (22842). Phone 540/477-2400; toll-free 800/478-8714. www.widowkips.com.* This restored 1830 Victorian home is set on 7 acres of rural countryside with a view of the Shenandoah River and the valley. 5 rooms. Pets accepted; fee. Complimentary full breakfast. Check-in 3 pm, check-out 11 am. Outdoor pool. **$**

Big Stone Gap (F-2)

See also Breaks Interstate Park, Wise

Founded 1888
Population 4,856
Elevation 1,488 ft
Area Code 540
Zip 24219
Information Lonesome Pine Tourist Information Center, 619 Gilley Ave, PO Box 236; phone 540/523-2060

This rugged mountain country gave John Fox, Jr., his inspiration for *Trail of the Lonesome Pine* and *Little Shepherd of Kingdom Come.* The town lies at the junction of three forks of the Powell River, which cuts a pass through Stone Mountain.

What to See and Do

John Fox, Jr., House & Museum. *117 Shawnee Ave, Big Stone Gap (24219). Phone 276/523-2747.* Occupied from 1888 by the author of *Trail of the Lonesome Pine* and *Little Shepherd of Kingdom Come,* best-selling novels of the early 1900s. Memorabilia and original furnishings. Guided tours (June-Sept: Tues-Sun; Oct: weekends).

June Tolliver House. *Jerome St and Clinton Ave, junction Hwys 23, 58A. Phone 276/523-1235.* Heroine in *Trail of the Lonesome Pine* lived here; period furnishings; now an arts and crafts center; restored 1890 house. (June-late Dec, Tues-Sun) **FREE**

Natural Tunnel State Park. *Hwy 871, Duffield. 18 miles SE, off Hwy 23. Phone 276/940-2674. www.dcr.state.va.us.* Consists of 648 acres. Giant hole chiseled through Purchase Ridge by Stock Creek; pinnacles or "chimneys." Railroad and stream are accommodated in this vast tunnel—100 feet or more in diameter, 850 feet long. Tunnel, visitor center with exhibits. Swimming, pool, fishing; hiking, picnicking, concession, camping, tent and trailer sites (Memorial Day-Labor Day). Interpretive programs. Chairlift. Park (daily); tunnel and most activities (Memorial Day-Labor Day; daily).

Southwest Virginia Museum. *10 W 1st St, Big Stone Gap (24219). W 1st St and Wood Ave. Phone 540/523-1322.* Four-story mansion contains exhibits dealing with life in southwestern Virginia during original coal boom of the 1890s; also Native Americans of the area and early pioneers. (Memorial Day-Labor Day: daily; Mar-late May and early Sept-Dec: Tues-Sun; closed Thanksgiving, Dec 25) **$$**

Special Event

Trail of the Lonesome Pine. *June Tolliver Playhouse, adjacent to June Tolliver House.* Outdoor musical drama. For reserved seats phone 540/523-1235. Thurs-Sat, late June-Labor Day.

Blacksburg (E-4)

See also Radford, Roanoke, Salem

Founded 1798
Population 39,573
Elevation 2,080 ft
Area Code 540
Zip 24060
Information Blacksburg Regional Chamber of Commerce, 1995 S Main St, Suite 901; phone 540/522-4503 or toll-free 800/288-4061
Web site www.blacksburg-chamber.com

The Washington and Jefferson national forests, which lie to the northwest, provide a colorful backdrop of azaleas, flowering dogwood, and redbud in spring and brilliant hardwoods in fall. Virginia Polytechnic Institute and State University is a source of employment for the town. The forests' Blacksburg Ranger District office is located here.

What to See and Do

Mountain Lake. *20 miles NW on Hwys 460, 700.* A resort lake, particularly inviting in late June and early July, when azaleas and rhododendron are in bloom.

Smithfield Plantation. *460 Bypass and Hwy 314, Blacksburg. 1/4 mile W off Hwy 460 bypass, at VA Tech exit. Phone 540/231-3947.* (1773) Restored pre-Revolutionary house; original woodwork. Home of Colonel William Preston and three governors. Architectural link between Tidewater and Piedmont plantations of Virginia and those of the Mississippi Valley. Grounds restored by Garden Club of Virginia. (Apr-Nov, Thurs-Sun 1-5 pm) **$**

Limited-Service Hotels

★ ★ BEST WESTERN RED LION INN. *900 Plantation Rd, Blacksburg (24060). Phone 540/552-7770; fax 540/552-6346. www.bestwestern.com.* 104 rooms, 2 story. Check-out noon. Restaurant, bar. Outdoor pool. Tennis. **$**

★ COMFORT INN. *3705 S Main St, Blacksburg (24060). Phone 540/951-1500; toll-free 800/228-5150; fax 540/951-1530. www.choicehotels.com.* 80 rooms, 4 story. Pets accepted. Complimentary continental breakfast. Check-out 11 am. High-speed Internet access. Fitness room. Outdoor pool. **$**

★ ★ FOUR POINTS BY SHERATON. *900 Price's Fork Rd, Blacksburg (24060). Phone 540/552-7001; fax 540/552-0827. www.sheraton.com.* 148 rooms, 2 story. Check-out noon. Restaurant, bar. Indoor pool, outdoor pool, children's pool. Tennis. **$**

★ ★ RAMADA. *3503 Holiday Ln, Blacksburg (24060). Phone 540/951-1330; toll-free 800/684-9628; fax 540/951-4847. www.ramada.com.* 98 rooms, 2 story. Pets accepted, some restrictions; fee. Check-out noon. Restaurant, bar. Outdoor pool, children's pool. **$**

Specialty Lodging

The following lodging establishment is approved by Mobil Travel Guide, but due to its unique and individualized nature has not been given a traditional Mobil Star rating. Included in this listing you may find bed-and-breakfasts, limited-service inns, guest ranches, and other unique hotel properties.

OAKS VICTORIAN INN. *311 E Main St, Christiansburg (24073). Phone 540/381-1500; toll-free 800/336-6257; fax 540/381-3036.* This Queen Anne Victorian (1889) is home to seven historic oak trees, one of which is the largest white oak in the area. Built in 1889, the inn provides guests with many amenities including down comforters and claw foot bathtubs to name a few. 7 rooms, 3 story. Children over 14 years only. Complimentary full breakfast. Check-in 4 pm, check-out noon. Whirlpool. Airport transportation available. **$**

Blue Ridge Parkway (D-6)

See also Roanoke, Waynesboro

Elevation 649-6,050 ft; average 3,000 ft

Winding 469 mountainous miles between the Shenandoah and Great Smoky Mountains national parks (about 217 miles are in Virginia), the Blue Ridge Parkway represents a different concept in highway travel. It is not an express highway (speed limit 45 miles per hour) but a road intended for leisurely travel. All towns are bypassed. Travelers in a hurry would be wise to take state and US routes, where speed limits are higher.

The parkway follows the Blue Ridge Mountains for about 355 miles, then winds through the Craggies, Pisgahs, and Balsams to the Great Smokies. Overlooks, picnic and camp sites, visitor centers, nature trails, fishing streams and lakes, and points of interest are numerous and well-marked.

Accommodations are plentiful in cities and towns along the way. Food availability is limited on the parkway.

The parkway is open all year, but the best time to drive it is between April and November. Some sections are closed by ice and snow for periods in winter and early spring. Fog may be present during wet weather. The higher sections west of Asheville to Great Smoky Mountains National Park and north of Asheville to Mount Mitchell may be closed January through March due to hazardous driving conditions.

For maps, pamphlets and detailed information contact Superintendent, 199 Hemphill Road, Asheville, NC 28803; phone 828/298-0398.

What to See and Do

Camping. Tent and trailer sites at Otter Creek, Peaks of Otter, Roanoke Mountain, Rocky Knob, Doughton Park, Julian Price Memorial Park, Linville Falls, Crabtree Meadows, and Mount Pisgah. (May-Oct) 14-day limit, June-Labor Day. No electricity; pets on leash only; water shut off with first freeze, usually late Oct. Fee/site/night. Primitive winter camping at Linville Falls when roads are passable.

Fishing. Rainbow, brook, brown trout and smallmouth bass in streams and lakes. State licenses required.

Folk Art Center. *Mile 382.* Craft Guild Headquarters, sales, parkway travel information, park ranger. (Daily)

Horseback riding. *Mile 292.7.* 20 miles of trails in Moses H. Cone Memorial Park. Horses for hire at Blowing Rock, NC.

Interpretive programs. *Mile 60.8, 86, 169, 241.1, 297.1, 316.3, 340, and 408.6.* Outdoor talks (mid-June-Labor Day) at Otter Creek (mile 60.8), Peaks of Otter (mile 86), Rocky Knob (mile 169), Doughton Park (mile 241.1), Price Park (mile 297.1), Linville Falls (mile 316.3), Crabtree Meadows (mile 340), and Mount Pisgah (mile 408.6). Obtain schedules at Parkway Visitor Centers.

Northwest Trading Post. *Mile 258.6.* Country store sells native handicrafts.

Parkway Craft Center. *Mile 294, Blowing Rock, NC.*

Self-guided trails. Moderate grades. Walks take from five minutes to one hour. Trails on the parkway include

Cascades Trail. *Mile 272.* Leads to waterfall.

Cone Park Trail. *Mile 294.* Manor house wild garden.

Craggy Gardens Trail. *Mile 364.6.* Traverses high mountain.

Elk Run Trail. *Mile 86.* Forest, plant, animal community.

Flat Rock Trail. *Mile 308.2.* Magnificent valley and mountain views.

Greenstone Trail. *Mile 8.8.* Of geologic interest.

Linville Falls Trail. *Mile 316.4.* Views of falls, Linville River Gorge.

Mabry Mill Trail. *Mile 176.* Old-time mountain industry.

Mountain Farm Trail. *Mile 5.8.* Typical mountain farm, reconstructed.

Richland Balsam Trail. *Mile 431.* Spruce-fir forests. Highest spot on parkway.

Rocky Knob Trail. *Mile 168.* Leads to overlook of Rock Castle Gorge.

Trail of the Trees. *Mile 63.6.* Leads to overlook of James River.

★ **Visitor Centers.** Exhibits, travel information, interpretive publications. (Daily during peak travel season) Centers include

Craggy Gardens Visitor Center. *Mile 364.6.* 5,892-foot elevation. Natural history exhibits, naturalist. (Mid-June-Labor Day, daily; May-mid-June, early Sept-Oct, weekends)

Humpback Rocks Visitor Center. *Mile 5.8.* Pioneer mountain farm, park ranger.

James River Wayside. *Mile 63.6.* Story of James River and Kanawha Canal, park ranger.

Linn Cove Information Center. *Mile 304.*

Mabry Mill. *Mile 176.* Old-time mountain industry, including tannery exhibits, picturesque mill, blacksmith shop.

Museum of North Carolina Minerals. *Mile 331.* (Daily, winter hours vary; closed holidays)

Peaks of Otter Visitor Center. *Mile 86.* Wildlife exhibits, park ranger.

Rocky Knob Information Station. *Mile 169.* Information, exhibits, park ranger.

Waterrock Knob Information Center. *Mile 451.* Panoramic views, visitor information, exhibits, publications.

Limited-Service Hotel

★ ★ PEAKS OF OTTER LODGE. *Blue Ridge Pkwy, Bedford (24523). Phone 540/586-1081; toll-free 800/542-5927; fax 540/586-4420. www.peaksofotter.com.* Nestled between two mountains that make up the Peaks of Otter, this lodge overlooks Abbott Lake. Each room has a view of the lake and the Sharp Top Mountains. 63 rooms, 2 story. Check-out noon. Restaurant, bar. **$**

Full-Service Resort

★ ★ DOE RUN LODGE RESORT AND CONFERENCE CENTER. *Blue Ridge Pkwy, Fancy Gap (24343). Phone 276/398-2212; toll-free 800/325-6189; fax 276/398-2833. www.doerunlodge.com.* Located along Blue Ridge Parkway, this nature-lover's retreat with its fresh, clean mountain air is truly delightful. 47 rooms, 2 story. Pets accepted, some restrictions; fee. Check-out noon. Restaurant, bar. Outdoor pool. Tennis. **$**

Specialty Lodging

The following lodging establishment is approved by Mobil Travel Guide, but due to its unique and individualized nature has not been given a traditional Mobil Star rating. Included in this listing you may find bed-and-breakfasts, limited-service inns, guest ranches, and other unique hotel properties.

THE OSCEOLA MILL COUNTRY INN. *Hwy 56, Steele's Tavern (24476). Phone 540/377-6455; fax 540/377-5148. www.osceolamill.com.* 12 rooms, 2 story. Complimentary full breakfast. Check-in 2 pm, check-out 11 am. Outdoor pool. In renovated 1849 mill, mill store, and restored 1873 miller's house. **$**

Restaurant

★ ★ PEAKS OF OTTER. *Mile Post 86, Blue Ridge Pkwy (24523). Phone 540/586-9263; fax 540/586-4420. www.peaksofotter.com.* Breakfast, lunch, dinner, Sun brunch. Bar. Children's menu. **$$**

Booker T. Washington National Monument (E-5)

See also Roanoke

(Approximately 18 miles S on Hwy 116 from Roanoke to Burnt Chimney, then continue 6 miles E on Hwy 122)

The 1861 property inventory of the Burroughs plantation listed, along with household goods and farm implements, the entry "1 Negro boy (Booker)—$400." Freed in 1865, the boy and his family moved to Malden, West Virginia. There, while working at a salt furnace and in coal mines, the youngster learned the alphabet from Webster's Blueback Spelling Book. Later, by working at the salt furnace before school, then going to work at the mine after school, he got the rudiments of an education. When he realized that everyone else at the school roll call had two names, he chose Washington for his own.

At age 16 he started the 500-mile trip from Malden to Hampton Institute, where he earned his way. He taught at Malden for two years, attended Wayland Seminary, and returned to Hampton Institute to teach. In July 1881 he started Tuskegee Institute in Alabama with 30 pupils, two run-down buildings, and $2,000 for salaries. When Washington died in 1915 the Institute had 107 buildings, more than 2,000 acres, and was assessed at more than $500,000.

The 224-acre monument includes most of the original plantation. A 1/4-mile self-guided plantation trail passes reconstructed farm buildings, a slave cabin, crops, and animals of the period; there is also a 1 1/2 mile self-guided Jack-O-Lantern Branch nature trail. Picnic facilities. Visitor Center has an audiovisual program, exhibits depicting his life (Daily; closed January 1, Thanksgiving, December 25). Phone 540/721-2094.

Breaks Interstate Park (E-2)

See also Big Stone Gap, Wise

(7 miles SE of Elkhorn City, KY and 8 miles N of Haysi, VA on Hwy 80)

Web site www.breakspark.com

Where the Russell Fork of the Big Sandy River plunges through the mountains is called the "Grand Canyon of the South," the major focus of this 4,600-acre park on the Kentucky-Virginia border. From the entrance, a paved road winds through an evergreen forest and then skirts the canyon rim. Overlooks provide a spectacular view of the "Towers," a huge pyramid of rocks. Within the park are extraordinary rock formations, caves, springs, a profusion of rhododendron and, of course, the 5-mile-long, 1,600-foot-deep gorge.

The visitor center houses historical and natural exhibits, including a coal exhibit (Apr-Oct, daily). Laurel Lake is stocked with bass and bluegill. Swimming pool, pedal boats; hiking, bridle, and mountain bike trails, picnicking, playground, camping (Apr-Oct, fee); motor lodge, cottages (year-round), restaurant, gift shop. Park (daily); facilities (Apr-late Dec, daily). Contact Breaks Interstate Park, PO Box 100, Breaks, VA 24607. Phone 276/865-4413 or toll-free 800/982-5122.

Limited-Service Hotel

★★ **BREAKS INTERSTATE.** *Hwy 1, Breaks (24607). Phone 540/865-4414; toll-free 800/982-5122; fax 540/865-5561. www.breakspark.com.* 34 rooms, 2 story. Closed late Dec-Mar. Check-out 11 am. Restaurant. Outdoor pool, children's pool. Woodland setting; overlooks Breaks Canyon. **$**

Bristol (F-2)

See also Abingdon

Founded 1771
Population 17,367
Elevation 1,680 ft
Area Code 540 (VA); 423 (TN)
Zip 24201 (VA); 37620 (TN)
Information Chamber of Commerce, 20 Volunteer Pkwy, TN, or PO Box 519, VA 24203; phone 423/989-4850
Web site www.bristolchamber.org

Essentially a city in two states, Bristol is actually two cities—Bristol, Tennessee and Bristol, Virginia—sharing the same main street and the same personality. Each has its own government and city services. Together they constitute a major shopping center. Named for the English industrial center, Bristol is an important factory town in its own right. These cities carry on the pioneer tradition of an ironworks established here about 1784 which made the first nails for use on the frontier.

What to See and Do

Bristol Caverns. *5 miles SE on Hwy 435, off I-81. Phone 423/878-2011.* Unusual rock formations seen from lighted, paved walkways winding through caverns and along an underground river. Guided tours every 20 minutes. Picnic area. (Daily; closed Easter, Dec 25) **$$$**

Rocky Mount Historic Site. *200 Hyder Hill Rd, Bristol (24201). 11 miles SW on US 11 E. Phone 423/538-7396.* Features the 2 1/2-story log house (1770) that served from 1790 to 1792 as capital under William Blount, governor of the Territory of the United States South of the River Ohio. Restored to its original simplicity; 18th-century furniture. On grounds are restored log kitchen, slave cabin, barn, blacksmith shop, and smokehouse. (Daily; closed Thanksgiving, Dec 21-Jan 5; also weekends in Jan, Feb) **$$**

Special Event

Bristol Motor Speedway. *2801 Hwy 11 E, Bristol (24201). 5 miles S on Hwy 11 E. Phone 423/764-1161.* Apr, June, and Aug.

Limited-Service Hotels

★ COMFORT INN. *2368 Lee Hwy, Bristol (24201). Phone 276/466-3881; fax 276/466-6544. www.choicehotels.com.* 60 rooms, 2 story. Complimentary continental breakfast. Check-out 11 am. Outdoor pool. **$**

★ LA QUINTA INN. *1014 Old Airport Rd, Bristol (24201). Phone 276/669-9353; fax 276/669-6974. www.laquintainn.com.* 123 rooms, 4 story. Pets accepted. Complimentary continental breakfast. Check-out noon. Outdoor pool. **$**

★ ★ RAMADA. *2221 Euclid Ave, Bristol (24201). Phone 276/669-7171; fax 276/669-7171. www.ramada.com.* 123 rooms, 2 story. Check-out noon. Restaurant, bar. Outdoor pool. **$**

Brookneal (E-6)

See also Lynchburg, South Boston

Settled circa 1790
Population 1,259
Elevation 560 ft
Area Code 804
Zip 24528

What to See and Do

Patrick Henry National Memorial (Red Hill). *1250 Red Hill Rd, Brookneal (24528). 3 miles E on Hwy 40, 2 miles S on Hwy 600 and 619. Phone 434/376-2044.* Last home and burial place of Patrick Henry. Restoration of family cottage, cook's cabin, smokehouse, stable, kitchen. Patrick Henry's law office. Museum and gift shop on grounds. Interpretive video. (Daily; closed Jan 1, Thanksgiving, Dec 25) **$$$**

Cape Charles (E-9)

See also Hampton, Newport News, Norfolk, Portsmouth, Virginia Beach

Population 1,134
Elevation 10 ft
Area Code 757
Zip 23310
Information Chesapeake Bay Bridge & Tunnel District, Public Relations Department, PO Box 111; phone 757/331-2960, ext 20
Web site www.cbbt.com

The Chesapeake Bay Bridge-Tunnel (17.6 miles long) leads from Cape Charles (12 miles south of the town) to Virginia Beach/Norfolk. There is a scenic stop, gift shop, restaurant, and fishing pier (bait available). Note: Noncommercial vehicles entering with compressed gas containers are limited to (a) two nonpermanently-mounted containers with a maximum individual capacity of 105 pounds water or 45 pounds LP gas each, or one container with a maximum capacity of 60 pounds LP gas; or (b) not more than two permanently-mounted containers with a total capacity of 200 gallons water when LP gas is used as a motor fuel. One-way passenger car toll.

Specialty Lodging

The following lodging establishment is approved by Mobil Travel Guide, but due to its unique and individualized nature has not been given a traditional Mobil Star rating. Included in this listing you may find bed-and-breakfasts, limited-service inns, guest ranches, and other unique hotel properties.

WILSON-LEE HOUSE BED AND BREAKFAST. *403 Tazewell Ave, Cape Charles (23310). Phone 757/331-1954; fax 757/331-8133. www.wilsonleehouse.com.* 6 rooms. Children over 12 years only. Complimentary full breakfast. Check-in 4-6 pm, check-out 11 am. Built in 1906. **$**

Restaurant

★ LITTLE ITALY. *10277 Rogers Dr, Nassawadox (23413). Phone 757/442-7831; fax 757/442-3634. www.francolittleitaly.com.* Italian menu. Lunch, dinner. Closed Sun; holidays. Bar. Children's menu. Former country grocery store. **$$**

Cape Henry Memorial (F-9)

See also Norfolk, Virginia Beach

(10 miles E of Norfolk on Hwy 60)

The first English settlers of Jamestown landed here on April 26, 1607. They claimed the land for England, stayed four days, named their landing spot for Henry (then Prince of Wales and oldest son of King James I), and put up a cross.

A cross put up by the Daughters of the American Colonists in 1935 marks the approximate site of the first landing. An interpretive display describes the Battle of the Capes, a sea battle fought between England and France in 1781 and a prelude to the Battle of Yorktown. Nearby is Cape Henry Lighthouse, first lighthouse in the United States authorized and built by the federal government (1791). The memorial is in Fort Story Military Reservation.

Centreville (C-8)

Limited-Service Hotel

★ **SPRINGHILL SUITES.** *5920 Trinity Pkwy, Centreville (20120). Phone 703/815-7800; toll-free 888/287-9400; fax 703/815-4100. www.springhillsuites.com.* Guests looking for spacious and functional accommodations will enjoy suites that feature a separate area for eating, sleeping, working, and relaxing. 136 rooms, 4 story, all suites. Complimentary continental breakfast. Check-in 3 pm, check-out noon. Fitness room. Indoor pool, whirlpool. **$**

Restaurants

★ ★ **SWEETWATER TAVERN.** *14250 Sweetwater Ln, Centreville (22020). Phone 703/449-1100; fax 703/449-1108.* Lunch, dinner. Closed Thanksgiving, Dec 25. Bar. Children's menu. **$$**

★ **WINFIELD'S.** *5127 Westfield Blvd, Centreville (20120). Phone 703/803-1040; fax 703/803-6310.* Seafood, steak menu. Lunch, dinner. Closed holidays. Bar. Children's menu. Reservations recommended. Outdoor seating. **$$**

Charlottesville (D-6)

See also Waynesboro

Founded 1762
Population 45,049
Elevation 480 ft
Area Code 434
Information Charlottesville/Albemarle Convention & Visitors Bureau, 600 College Dr, Charlottesville 22902; phone 804/977-1783 or toll-free 877/386-1102
Web site www.charlottesvilletourism.org

Popularly known as the #1 small city in the South, Charlottesville is famous as the home of Thomas Jefferson, the third president of the United States, and the University of Virginia, which Jefferson founded and designed. Fewer people know that Jefferson and two of his friends—James Madison, America's fourth president, and James Monroe, the nation's fifth, who lived very nearby—actually governed the country for 25 consecutive years. An even better kept secret is that Charlottesville offers much more than history. The downtown pedestrian mall streetscape at the center of the historic district is alive with more than 120 shops and 30 restaurants, outdoor cafés, theaters, bookstores, and a skating rink. Charlottesville is also able to brag about its beautiful parks, top-notch museums, and award-winning wineries and an outstanding lineup of entertainment.

As you follow the silhouettes of the three presidents on your way to the area's historic attractions, including Monticello, Michie Tavern, Ash Lawn-Highland (Monroe's home), and Montpelier, you can enjoy the Art in Place program of constructed sculptures that pop up along the roadways. If the outdoors is your pleasure, you can meander through the area's rolling hills on a myriad of scenic byways, hiking trails, and river paths; play golf on a mountaintop; or enjoy the Blue Ridge Parkway, considered by some to be America's most beautiful drive.

What to See and Do

Albemarle County Courthouse. *Court Sq.* North wing was used in 1820s as a "common temple" shared by Episcopalian, Methodist, Presbyterian, and Baptist sects, one Sunday a month to each but with all who wished attending each Sunday. Jefferson, Monroe, and Madison worshiped here.

★ **Ash-Lawn Highland.** *1000 James Monroe Pkwy, Charlottesville. 4 1/4 miles SE on County 795. Phone 434/293-9539.* (1799) Built on a site personally selected by Thomas Jefferson, this 535-acre estate was the home of President James Monroe (1799-1823). The estate is now owned by Monroe's alma mater, the College of William and Mary. This early 19th-century working plantation offers guided tours of the house with Monroe possessions, spinning and weaving demonstrations, old boxwood gardens, peacocks, picnic spots. Special events include Summer Music Festival (June-Aug) of arts, evening concerts, children's shows (Sat), Plantation Days Weekend, spring and Christmas programs. (Daily; closed Jan 1, Thanksgiving, Dec 25) **$$$**

George Rogers Clark Memorial. *W Main and Jefferson Park Ave, Charlottesville (22906). W Main St, E of university.* Brother of William Clark and soldier on the frontier, this intrepid explorer who opened up the Northwest Territory was an Albemarle County native son.

Historic Michie Tavern. *683 Thomas Jefferson Pkwy, Charlottesville (22902). 1 mile S on Hwy 20. Phone 434/977-1234.* (Circa 1784) Located near Jefferson's Monticello. Visitors dine on hearty Midday Fare in the Tavern's Ordinary where servers in period attire greet them. Afterwards, a tour of the original tavern features living history where guests participate in 18th-century activities, including a lively Virginia dance. (Daily; closed Jan 1, Dec 25) **$$$**

Lewis and Clark Monument. *Midway Park, Ridge and Main sts, Charlottesville.* Memorial to Jefferson's secretary, Meriwether Lewis, who explored the Louisiana Territory with his friend William Clark.

★ **Monticello.** *2 miles SE on Hwy 53. Phone 434/984-9822. www.monticello.org.* Located on a mountaintop, Monticello is one of the most beautiful estates in Virginia and is considered a classic of American architecture. The house was designed by Thomas Jefferson and built over the course of 40 years, symbolizing the pleasure he found in "putting up and pulling down." Jefferson moved into the first completed outbuilding of his new home in 1771, although construction continued until 1809. Most of the interior furnishings are original. Tours of the restored orchard, vineyard, 1,000-foot-long vegetable garden, and Mulberry Row, once the site of plantation workshops. Jefferson died at Monticello on July 4, 1826, and was buried in the family cemetery. The Thomas Jefferson Memorial Foundation maintains the house and gardens. (Mar-Oct: daily 8 am-5 pm; Nov-Feb: daily 9 am-4:30 pm; closed Dec 25) **$$$** Approximately 2 miles W of here is

Monticello Visitors Center. *Hwy 20 S and I-64, Charlottesville. Phone 434/984-9822.* Personal and family memorabilia; architectural models and drawings; *Thomas Jefferson: The Pursuit of Liberty,* a 35-minute film, shown twice daily. (Daily; closed Dec 25) **FREE**

Robert E. Lee Monument. *1st and Jefferson sts, Charlottesville.*

Stonewall Jackson on Little Sorrel. *Adjacent to courthouse.* By Charles Keck.

University of Virginia. *914 Emmet St N, Charlottesville (22903). W end of Main St. Phone 434/924-1019.* (1819) (18,100 students) Founded by Thomas Jefferson and built according to his plans. Handsome red brick buildings with white trim, striking vistas, smooth lawns, and ancient trees form the grounds of Jefferson's "academical village." The serpentine walls, one brick thick, which Jefferson designed for strength and beauty, are famous. Room 13, West Range, occupied by Edgar Allan Poe as a student, is displayed for the public. Walking tours start at the Rotunda (daily; closed three weeks mid-Dec-early Jan). **FREE**

Walking tour. *Phone 434/977-1783.* The Charlottesville/Albemarle Information Center, located on Hwy 20 S in the Monticello Visitors Center Building, has information for a walking tour of historic Charlottesville.

Wintergreen Resort. *Hwy 664, Wintergreen. W on Hwy 250 to Hwy 151, then S to Hwy 664, turn right, follow signs (approximately 4 1/2 miles). Phone 434/325-2200. www.wintergreenresort.com.* Quad, three triple, double chairlifts; patrol, school, rentals, snow making; lodge (see RESORTS); nursery. Twenty runs; longest run 1 1/2 miles; vertical drop 1,003 feet. (Dec-

Mar, daily) Night skiing. Summer activities include fishing, boating; golf, tennis, horseback riding. **$$$$**

Special Events

Dogwood Festival. Parade, lacrosse and golf tournaments, carnival. Nine days mid-Apr.

Founder's Day. (Jefferson's Birthday) Commemorative ceremonies. Apr 13.

Garden Week. Some fine private homes and gardens in the area are open. Mid-Apr.

Limited-Service Hotels

★ BEST WESTERN CAVALIER INN. *105 Emmet St N, Charlottesville (22903). Phone 434/296-8111; fax 434/296-3523. www.bestwestern.com.* 120 rooms, 5 story. Complimentary continental breakfast. Check-in 3 pm, check-out noon. Outdoor pool. Airport transportation available. Business center. **$**

★ ★ DAYS INN. *1600 Emmet St N, Charlottesville (22901). Phone 434/293-9111; toll-free 800/493-9111; fax 434/977-2780. www.daysinn.com.* 129 rooms, 3 story. Pets accepted; fee. Check-in 2 pm, check-out noon. Restaurant, bar. Fitness room. Outdoor pool, children's pool. Airport transportation available. **$**

★ ★ DOUBLETREE HOTEL. *990 Hilton Heights Rd, Charlottesville (22901). Phone 434/973-2121; toll-free 800/494-7596; fax 434/978-7735. www.charlottesville.doubletree.com.* Close to the historic sites, this hotel services both the leisure and business traveler. The Blue Ridge Parkway, with its many activities, is nearby. 247 rooms, 9 story. Check-in 3 pm, check-out noon. Restaurant, bar. Fitness room. Indoor pool, outdoor pool, whirlpool. Tennis. Airport transportation available. **$**

★ ENGLISH INN OF CHARLOTTESVILLE. *2000 Morton Dr, Charlottesville (22903). Phone 434/971-9900; toll-free 800/786-5400; fax 434/977-8008. www.wytestone.com/eic.* 88 rooms, 3 story. Complimentary full breakfast. Check-in 2 pm, check-out noon. Indoor pool. Airport transportation available. **$**

★ HAMPTON INN. *2035 India Rd, Charlottesville (22901). Phone 804/978-7888; fax 804/973-0436. www.hamptoninn.com.* 123 rooms, 5 story. Complimentary continental breakfast. Check-in 2 pm, check-out noon. Outdoor pool. Airport transportation available. **$**

Full-Service Hotel

★ ★ ★ OMNI CHARLOTTESVILLE HOTEL. *235 W Main St, Charlottesville (22902). Phone 434/971-5500; fax 434/979-4456. www.omnihotels.com.* Located on a downtown mall, this hotel is within walking distance to the government buildings. 211 rooms, 6 story. Pets accepted, some restrictions; fee. Check-in 3 pm, check-out noon. Restaurant, bar. Fitness room. Indoor, outdoor pools; whirlpool. **$**

Full-Service Resorts

★ ★ ★ BOAR'S HEAD INN. *W Rte 250, Charlottesville (22903). Phone 434/296-2181; toll-free 800/476-1988; fax 434/972-6019. www.boarsheadinn.com.* Located in the Blue Ridge Mountains, this resort welcomes guests to visit the past as well as enjoy the present. Guests can visit past presidential homes, stroll through local wineries, or enjoy a panoramic view by hot-air balloon. 171 rooms, 4 story. Check-in 4 pm, check-out noon. Restaurants, bar. Children's activity center. Fitness room. Three pools. Golf. Tennis. Airport transportation available. Business center. **$$**

★ ★ ★ WINTERGREEN RESORT. *Rte 664, Wintergreen (22958). Phone 434/325-2200; toll-free 800/266-2444; fax 434/325-8004. www.wintergreenresort.com.* 315 rooms, 3 story. Check-in 4 pm, check-out 11 am. Restaurant, bar. Children's activity center. Fitness room. Indoor pool, five outdoor pools, children's pool, whirlpool. Golf, 36 holes. Tennis. Airport transportation available. Business center. **$**

Full-Service Inns

★ ★ ★ PROSPECT HILL PLANTATION INN. *2887 Poindexter Rd, Louisa (23093). Phone 540/967-0844; toll-free 800/277-0844; fax 540/967-0102. www.prospecthill.com.* This romantic 1732 manor house is set on 50 acres of lawn. 13 rooms, 2 story. Closed Dec 24 evening, Dec 25. Complimentary full breakfast. Check-in 3 pm, check-out 11 am. Restaurant. Outdoor pool. **$$$**

★ ★ ★ **SILVER THATCH INN.** *3001 Hollymead Dr, Charlottesville (22911). Phone 434/978-4686; fax 434/973-6156. www.silverthatch.com.* Built in 1780, this clapboard home is full of history and is one of the oldest buildings in the area. 7 rooms, 2 story. Children over 12 years only. Complimentary full breakfast. Check-in 3 pm, check-out 11 am. Restaurant. Outdoor pool. **$**

Specialty Lodgings

The following lodging establishments are approved by Mobil Travel Guide, but due to their unique and individualized nature have not been given a traditional Mobil Star rating. Included in this listing you may find bed-and-breakfasts, limited-service inns, guest ranches, and other unique hotel properties.

200 SOUTH STREET INN. *200 W South St, Charlottesville (22902). Phone 434/979-0200; fax 434/979-4403. www.southstreetinn.com.* 24 rooms, 4 story. Complimentary continental breakfast. Check-in 2 pm, check-out 11 am. Built 1856; antiques. **$**

INN AT MONTICELLO. *Rte 20 S; 1188 Scottsville Rd, Charlottesville (22902). Phone 434/979-3593; fax 434/296-1344. www.innatmonticello.com.* Guests can choose to relax by a fireplace in winter or sit on the porch in summer at this country manor house built in the mid-1800s. Guest rooms are decorated with period antiques and reproductions. 5 rooms, 2 story. Children over 12 years only. Complimentary full breakfast. Check-in 4 pm, check-out 11 am. **$$**

Restaurants

★ ★ **ABERDEEN BARN.** *2018 Holiday Dr, Charlottesville (22901). Phone 434/296-4630; fax 434/979-6397. www.aberdeenbarn.com.* Seafood, steak menu. Dinner. Closed Thanksgiving, Dec 25. Bar. Children's menu. **$$$**

★ ★ **C & O.** *515 E Water St, Charlottesville (22902). Phone 434/971-7044; fax 434/963-4789. www.candorestaurant.com.* Eclectic/International, French menu. Dinner. Closed holidays. Bar. **$$**

★ ★ **CARMELLO'S.** *400 Emmet St, Charlottesville (22903). Phone 434/977-5200.* Italian menu. Dinner. Closed Jan 1, Dec 25. Bar. **$$**

★ ★ **HARDWARE STORE.** *316 E Main St, Charlottesville (22902). Phone 434/977-1518; toll-free 800/426-6001; fax 434/979-7555.* Eclectic menu. Lunch, dinner. Closed Sun; holidays. Outdoor seating. In 1890s hardware store; vintage signs displayed. **$$**

★ ★ **IVY INN.** *2244 Old Ivy Inn, Charlottesville (22903). Phone 434/977-1222; fax 434/977-1377. www.ivyinnrestaurant.com.* Dinner. Closed Sun. Victorian-style house (1804); fireplaces. Reservations recommended. Outdoor seating. **$$$**

★ ★ **L'AVVENTURA.** *220 W Market St, Charlottesville (22902). Phone 804/977-1912; fax 804/977-8458. www.vinegarhilltheatre.com.* Country Italian menu. Dinner. Closed Sun-Tues; Thanksgiving, Dec 25. Bar. Outdoor seating. **$$**

★ ★ **MAHARAJA.** *139 Zan Rd, Charlottesville (22901). Phone 434/973-0440.* Indian, seafood, vegetarian menu. Lunch, dinner. Closed Jan 1, Thanksgiving, Dec 25. Bar. Casual attire. Outdoor seating. **$$**

★ ★ ★ **OLD MILL ROOM.** *US 250 W, Charlottesville (22905). Phone 804/972-2230; fax 804/972-6024. www.boarsheadinn.com.* This dining room is located in the Boar's Head Inn at the University of Virginia. Entrées are served with vegetables from their own garden. American menu. Breakfast, lunch, dinner. Bar. Valet parking. Outdoor seating. Children's menu. 19th-century décor with mahogany woodwork, fireplaces, framed artwork. **$$$**

★ ★ **ROCOCO'S.** *2001 Commonwealth Dr, Charlottesville (22901). Phone 434/971-7371; fax 434/971-4058. www.rococos.com.* Italian, seafood menu. Lunch, dinner, Sun brunch. Closed Dec 25. Children's menu. **$$**

★ ★ **SCHNITZELHOUSE.** *2208 Fontaine Ave, Charlottesville (22903). Phone 434/293-7185; fax*

434/293-3719. Swiss, German menu. Dinner. Closed Sun-Mon; holidays; also one week in Jan and July. Bar. Children's menu. **$$**

Chesapeake (F-9)

See also Norfolk, Portsmouth, Virginia Beach

Founded 1962
Population 199,184
Elevation 12 ft
Area Code 757
Information Chesapeake Conventions & Tourism Bureau; phone 757/382-2540 or toll-free 888/889-5551
Web site www.visitchesapeake.org

For those who enjoy the beach yet seek a vacation off the beaten path, Chesapeake is an excellent choice. You'll be minutes away from 18th-century America, the oceanfront boardwalk of Virginia Beach, theme parks, and more, while remaining very near world-class natural environments. The active Atlantic Intra-coastal Waterway, home to a myriad of birds and wildlife, is complemented by the 49,000-acre Great Dismal Swamp National Wildlife Refuge managed by the Nature Conservancy. Bring your binoculars, your camera, and your lifelong checklist of birds, because if you can't add a few species in our environs, you probably aren't paying attention!

Farther up the coast, the Back Bay National Wildlife Refuge encompasses a series of barrier islands that feature large sand dunes, maritime forests, freshwater marshes, and ponds populated with large flocks of wintering waterfowl. Whether you meander through the bay on the unique trolley designed not to disturb the wildlife, kayak on the waterway itself, or stroll on the more than 19 miles of hiking trails at First Landing State Park, you'll enjoy the remote nature of it all. If you enjoy sneaking up on wildlife in its natural habitat, you've come to the right place!

Chesapeake Fun Fact

Opened in 1964, the Chesapeake Bay Bridge-Tunnel is 18 miles long and has two bridges and two mile-long tunnels. It extends over the mouth of the Chesapeake Bay and connects the cities of Cape Charles and Norfolk.

What to See and Do

Northwest River Park. *1733 Indian Creek Rd, Chesapeake (23322). Off Battlefield Blvd (Hwy 168). Phone 757/421-3145.* Approximately 8 miles of hiking/nature trails wind through this 763-acre city park. Fishing, boating, canoeing (ramp, rentals); picnicking (shelters), playground, nine-hole miniature golf, camping, tent and trailer sites (Apr-Dec, daily; fee; hookups, dump station). Shuttle tram. (Daily; closed Jan 1, Dec 25) Fragrance trail for the visually impaired. **FREE**

Special Event

Chesapeake Jubilee. *City Park, 1500 Mount Pleasant Rd, Chesapeake (23322).* National and regional entertainment, carnival, food booths, fireworks. Third weekend in May.

Limited-Service Hotels

★ COMFORT INN. *1550 Crossways Blvd, Chesapeake (23320). Phone 757/420-1600; toll-free 800/428-0562; fax 757/420-0099. www.choicehotels.com.* 123 rooms, 3 story, all suites. Complimentary continental breakfast. Check-in 3 pm, check-out 11 am. Fitness room. Outdoor pool, whirlpool. **$**

★ HAMPTON INN. *701 A Woodlake Dr, Chesapeake (23320). Phone 757/420-1550; fax 757/424-7414. www.hamptoninn.com.* 120 rooms, 4 story. Complimentary continental breakfast. Check-out noon. Outdoor pool. **$**

★★ HOLIDAY INN. *725 Woodlake Dr, Chesapeake (23320). Phone 757/523-1500; fax 757/523-0683. www.holiday-inn.com.* 258 rooms, 7 story. Check-in 2 pm, check-out noon. Restaurant, bar. Fitness room. Indoor pool, whirlpool. Airport transportation available. **$**

Restaurants

★★ KYOTO. *1412 Greenbriar Pkwy, Chesapeake (23320). Phone 757/420-0950; fax 757/420-0692.* Japanese menu. Lunch, dinner. Closed July 4, Thanksgiving, Dec 25. Bar. Children's menu. **$$**

★★ **LOCKS POINTE.** *136 N Battlefield Blvd, Chesapeake (23320). Phone 757/547-9618; fax 757/548-3229.* American, seafood menu. Lunch, dinner, Sun brunch. Closed Mon; Dec 24-25. Bar. Children's menu. Outdoor seating. On Intracoastal Waterway; dockage. **$$**

Chincoteague (D-10)

Founded 1662
Population 4,317
Elevation 4 ft
Area Code 757
Zip 23336
Information Chamber of Commerce, 6733 Maddox Blvd, PO Box 258; phone 757/336-6161
Web site www.chincoteaguechamber.com

Chincoteague oysters, wild ponies, and good fishing are the stock in trade of this small island, connected with Chincoteague National Wildlife Refuge by a bridge and to the mainland by 10 miles of highway (Hwy 175, from Hwy 13), causeways, and bridges.

The oysters, many of them grown on the hard sand bottoms off Chincoteague from seed or small oysters brought from natural beds elsewhere, are among the best in the East. Clams and crabs are also plentiful. Commercial fishing has always been the main occupation of the islanders, but now, catering to those who fish for fun is also important economically.

Chincoteague's wild ponies are actually small horses but when full-grown are somewhat larger and more graceful than Shetlands. They are thought to be descended from horses that swam ashore from a wrecked Spanish galleon, their limited growth caused by generations of marsh grass diet.

What to See and Do

★ **Assateague Island.** *8586 Beach Rd, Chincoteague (23336). Phone 410/641-1441. www.nps.gov/asis. Accessible by bridge from town. Includes Chincoteague National Wildlife Refuge and the Virginia unit of Assateague Island National Seashore.* A 37-mile barrier island, Assateague's stretches of ocean and sand dunes, forest, and marshes create a natural environment unusual on the East Coast. Sika deer, a variety of wildlife, and countless birds, including the peregrine falcon (autumn), can be found here, but wild ponies occasionally roaming the marshes offer the most exotic sight for visitors. Nature and auto trails; interpretive programs. Swimming (bathhouse), lifeguards in summer, surf fishing; camping, hike-in and canoe-in camp sites and day-use facilities. Picnicking permitted in designated areas; cars are limited to designated roads. No pets allowed. Obtain information at Toms Cove Visitor Center (spring-fall, daily) and at Chincoteague Refuge Visitor Center (daily). Access for the disabled to all facilities. For more information, contact the Chief of Interpretation, Assateague Island National Seashore, 7206 National Seashore Ln, Berlin, MD 21811. (See OCEAN CITY, MD.) Also contact the Refuge Manager, Chincoteague National Wildlife Refuge, PO Box 62, 23336; phone 757/336-6122. **$$**

Captain Barry's Back Bay Cruises & Expeditions. *Phone 757/336-6508 (information).* Includes Bird Watch Cruise, Back Bay Expedition, Champagne Sunset Cruise, Moonlight Excursions, and Fun Cruise. Trips vary from one to four hours. Reservations recommended. **$$$$**

NASA Visitor Center. *Wallops Island. 5 miles S on Hwy 175. Phone 757/824-1344.* Showcases world of past, present, and future flight. Features moon rock brought from *Apollo 17* mission; scale models of space probes, satellites, and aircraft; displays of current and future NASA projects; full-scale aircraft and rockets; films on space and aeronautics. Model rocket demonstrations (Mar-Nov: first Sat; June-Aug: also third Sat, weather permitting). Picnic facilities. Gift shop. (July 4-Labor Day: daily; Sept-Nov and Mar-June: Mon and Thurs-Sun; closed holidays) **FREE**

Oyster and Maritime Museum of Chincoteague. *7125 Maddox Blvd, Chincoteague (23336). Phone 757/336-6117.* Museum contains diorama, aquarium, shellfish industry interpretation. Also has the Wyle Maddox Library. (May-Aug: daily; Sept-Oct: Sat and Sun) **$$**

Refuge Waterfowl Museum. *7059 Maddox Blvd, Chincoteague (23336). Phone 757/336-5800.* Rotating displays of antique decoys and hunting tools. Decoy making and waterfowl art. Call ahead for hours. (Daily; closed Dec 25) **$$**

Special Events

Chincoteague Power Boat Regatta. *Phone 757/336-6161.* Late June.

Easter Decoy & Art Festival. *Phone 757/336-6161.* Easter weekend.

Oyster Festival. *6733 Maddox Blvd, Chincoteague (23336).* Columbus Day weekend.

Pony Penning. *Phone 757/336-6161.* The "wild" ponies are rounded up on Assateague Island, then swim the inlet to Chincoteague, where foals are sold at auction before the ponies swim back to Assateague. Carnival amusements. Last Wed and Thurs in July.

Waterfowl Week. *8231 Beach Rd, Chincoteague (23336).* National Wildlife Refuge open to vehicles during peak migratory waterfowl populations. Late Nov.

Limited-Service Hotels

★ COMFORT SUITES. *4195 Main St, Chincoteague (23336). Phone 757/336-3700; toll-free 800/517-4000; fax 757/336-5452. www.choicehotels.com.* 87 rooms, all suites. Check-in 3 pm, check-out 11 am. Fitness room. Indoor pool, whirlpool. **$**

★ DRIFTWOOD LODGE. *7105 Maddox Blvd, Chincoteague (23336). Phone 757/336-6557; toll-free 800/553-6117; fax 757/336-6558. www.driftwoodmotorlodge.com.* 53 rooms, 3 story. Check-out 11 am. Outdoor pool. At entrance to Assateague National Seashore. **$**

★ ★ ISLAND MOTOR INN. *4391 Main St, Chincoteague (23336). Phone 757/336-3141; toll-free 800/832-2925; fax 757/336-1483.* This waterfront location is within walking distance of shops, restaurants, and art galleries. All rooms have a private balcony and the boats on Chincoteague Bay can be watched from an observation deck. 60 rooms, 3 story. Check-out 11 am. Restaurant. Fitness room. Indoor pool, outdoor pool, whirlpool. **$**

★ REFUGE MOTOR INN. *7058 Maddox Blvd, Chincoteague (23336). Phone 757/336-5511; toll-free 800/544-8469; fax 757/336-6134. www.refugeinn.com.* 70 rooms, 2 story. Check-out 11 am. Fitness room. Indoor, outdoor pool, whirlpool. Near wildlife refuge and national seashore. Chincoteague ponies on grounds. **$**

Specialty Lodgings

The following lodging establishments are approved by Mobil Travel Guide, but due to their unique and individualized nature have not been given a traditional Mobil Star rating. Included in this listing you may find bed-and-breakfasts, limited-service inns, guest ranches, and other unique hotel properties.

CEDAR GABLES SEASIDE INN. *6095 Hopkins Ln, Chincoteague (23336). Phone 757/336-6860; fax 757/336-1291. www.cedargable.com.* This is a waterfront bed-and-breakfast inn overlooking Oyster Bay and the Chincoteague Wildlife Refuge. All rooms open to waterfront decks and offer breathtaking views of Assateague Island. The rooms have cable TV, fireplaces, Jacuzzis. Nearby, guests can enjoy the beach, wildlife refuge, fishing, biking, and hiking. 4 rooms, 3 story. Closed 1 week in late Dec. Children over 14 years only. Complimentary full breakfast. Check-in 3 pm, check-out 11 am. Outdoor pool, whirlpool. **$$**

CHANNEL BASS INN. *6228 Church St, Chincoteague (23336). Phone 757/336-6148; toll-free 800/249-0818; fax 757/336-6599. www.channelbass-inn.com.* Originally built in 1892 as a private home, it was converted to a small hotel in the 1920s. Today, it offers uniquely appointed guest rooms, some with views of the Chincoteague Bay. A traditional English afternoon tea and full breakfast are included. The inn's proximity to the nearby Assateague Island makes it a perfect getaway for birdwatchers and nature lovers. 6 rooms, 3 story. Closed Jan-mid-Mar, Nov. Children over 8 years only. Complimentary full breakfast. Check-in 2 pm, check-out 11 am. **$$**

THE GARDEN AND THE SEA INN. *4188 Nelson Rd, New Church (23415). Phone 757/824-0672; toll-free 800/824-0672. www.gardenandseainn.com.* This lovely Victorian inn offers romantically decorated rooms. The complimentary breakfast can be enjoyed in either the dining room overlooking the gardens or in the garden by the lily pond. 8 rooms. Closed Dec-Apr. Pets accepted. Complimentary continental breakfast. Check-in 3 pm, check-out 11 am. Restaurant. Outdoor pool. **$$**

MISS MOLLY'S INN. *4141 Main St, Chincoteague (23336). Phone 757/336-6686; toll-free 800/221-5620; fax 757/336-0600. www.missmollys-inn.com.* 7 rooms, 3 story. Complimentary full breakfast. Check-in 2 pm, check-out 11 am. In historic building (1886); library, sitting room; antiques. Marguerite Henry stayed here while writing *Misty of Chincoteague.* **$**

WATSON HOUSE. *4240 Main St, Chincoteague (23336). Phone 757/336-1564; toll-free 800/336-6787; fax 757/336-5776. www.watsonhouse.com.* 6 rooms, 2 story. Closed Dec-Apr. Children over 10 years only. Complimentary full breakfast. Check-in 2 pm, check-out 11 am. Victorian residence (1874). **$**

Restaurants

★ DON'S SEAFOOD. *4113 Main St, Chincoteague Island (23336). Phone 757/336-5715. www.donsseafood.com.* Lunch, dinner. Closed mid-Jan-late Mar. Bar. Children's menu. View of channel. **$$**

★★ THE GARDEN AND THE SEA INN. *4188 Nelson Rd, New Church (23415). Phone 757/824-0672. www.gardenandseainn.com.* This casual respite in a Victorian inn specializes in fresh dishes: just-caught seafood and produce from local farms. Entrees of elegant fare are accompanied by rich, flavorful sauce. French, seafood menu. Dinner. Closed Mon-Wed; also Dec-Mar. **$$**

★ STEAMERS SEAFOOD. *6251 Maddoc Blvd, Chincoteague (23336). Phone 757/336-5478.* Seafood menu. Dinner. Closed Nov-Apr. Children's menu. **$$**

Clarksville (F-6)

See also South Boston, South Hill

Population 1,329
Elevation 359 ft
Area Code 804
Zip 23927
Information Clarksville Lake Country Chamber of Commerce, 105 2nd St, PO Box 1017; phone 804/374-2436
Web site www.kerrlake.com/chamber

What to See and Do

Occoneechee State Park. *1 1/2 miles E on Hwy 58. Phone 434/374-2210.* Approximately 2,700 acres under development; long shoreline on John H. Kerr Reservoir (Buggs Island Lake). Fishing, boat launching; hiking, picnic shelters, tent and trailer sites (hookups, season varies). Amphitheater; interpretive programs. (Daily)

Prestwould. *429 Prestwould Dr, Clarksville (23927). 2 miles N on US 15. Phone 434/374-8672.* (1795) Manor house built by Sir Peyton Skipwith; rare French scenic wallpaper; original and period furnishings; restored gardens. (Mid-Apr-Oct: daily; rest of year: by appointment) **$$$**

Special Events

Native American Heritage Festival and Powwow. *Occoneechee State Park, 105 2nd St, Clarksville (23927). Phone 804/374-2436.* Native American music, dances, crafts. Second weekend in May.

Virginia Lake Festival. *Occoneechee State Park, 1105 2nd St, Clarksville (23927). Phone 804/374-2436.* Juried arts and crafts show, beach music, dancers, gymnasts. Fun Run, antique car show, sailboat race, hot-air balloons. Food vendors. Third weekend in July.

Limited-Service Hotel

★ BEST WESTERN ON THE LAKE. *103 2nd St, Clarksville (23927). Phone 434/374-5023; fax 434/374-0900.* 50 rooms, 2 story. Complimentary continental breakfast. Check-out 11 am. Outdoor pool. **$**

Clifton

Restaurants

★★ HEART-IN-HAND. *7145 Main St, Clifton (20124). Phone 703/830-4111; fax 703/803-9028. www.heartinhandrestaurant.com.* Lunch, dinner, Sun brunch. Closed holidays. Converted general store (circa 1870). Outdoor seating. **$$**

★★★ **HERMITAGE INN.** *7134 Main St, Clifton (20124). Phone 703/266-1623; fax 703/968-0259. www.hermitageinnrestaurant.com.* A historic clapboard inn is the setting for an intimate dining experience. Mediterranean menu. Lunch, dinner. Closed Mon-Tues; Jan 1, July 4. **$$$**

Clifton Forge (D-5)

See also Covington, Lexington, Warm Springs

Settled 1878
Population 4,289
Elevation 1,079 ft
Area Code 540
Zip 24422
Information Alleghany Highlands Chamber of Commerce, 501 E Ridgeway St; phone 540/862-4969
Web site members.aol.com/ahchamber

The town, named after a tilt-hammer forge that operated profitably for almost a hundred years, is at the southern tip of the Shenandoah Valley just west of the Blue Ridge Parkway.

What to See and Do

C & O Historical Society Archives. *312 E Ridgeway St, Clifton Forge (24422). Opposite terminal building. Phone 540/862-2210.* Includes C & O Railroad artifacts, old blueprints for cars and engines, books, models, collection of photos. (Mon-Sat; closed holidays) **FREE**

Douthat State Park. *8 miles N on Hwy 629. Phone 540/862-7200.* Nearly 4,500 acres, high in the Allegheny Mountains, with 50-acre lake. Swimming beach, bathhouse, trout fishing (fee/day), boating (Memorial Day-Labor Day; rentals, some electric and water hook-ups, launching, electric motors only); hiking, self-guided trails, picnicking, restaurant, concession, camping (fee), tent and trailer sites (Mar-Sept; no hookups), cabins (all year). Visitor center, interpretive programs. (Daily) **FREE**

Iron Gate Gorge. *2 miles S on Hwy 220.* Perpendicular walls of rock rise from banks of Jackson River. James River Division of C & O Railroad and US 220 pass through gorge. Restored chimney of old forge is here.

Colonial National Historical Park (E-9)

Made up of four independent areas—Cape Henry Memorial, the Colonial Parkway, Jamestown (see all three), and Yorktown Battlefield (see YORKTOWN)—this is where America as we know it began. Jamestown, Yorktown, and Williamsburg (not a National Park Service area) are connected by the Colonial Parkway. Abundant in natural as well as historical wealth, the park boundaries enclose more than 9,000 acres of forest woodlands, marshes, shorelines, fields, and a large variety of wildlife.

Colonial Parkway (E-9)

See also Colonial National Historical Park, Jamestown (Colonial National Historical Park), Williamsburg, Yorktown

The Colonial Parkway is a 23-mile link between the three towns that formed the "cradle of the nation"—Jamestown, Williamsburg, and Yorktown. It starts at the Visitor Center at Jamestown, passes through Williamsburg (the Colonial Williamsburg Information Center is near the north underpass entrance), and ends at the Visitor Center in Yorktown.

At turnouts and overlooks along the route, information signs note such historic spots as Glebeland, Kingsmill, Indian Field Creek, Powhatan's Village, Fusilier's Redoubt, and others. A free picnic area is provided during the summer at Ringfield Plantation, midway between Williamsburg and Yorktown. The parkway is free to private vehicles, and the speed limit is 45 miles per hour. There are no service stations along the way.

Covington (D-5)

See also Clifton Forge, Hot Springs, White Sulphur Springs

Founded 1833
Population 6,303
Elevation 1,245 ft
Area Code 540
Zip 24426
Information Alleghany Highlands Chamber of Commerce, 501 E Ridgeway St, Clifton Forge 24422; phone 540/862-4969
Web site members.aol.com/ahchamber

Named for its oldest resident, Covington developed from a small village on the Jackson River. It is located in the western part of Virginia known as the Allegheny Highlands. The James River Ranger District office of the Washington and Jefferson national forests is located here.

What to See and Do

Humpback Bridge. *3 miles W just off Hwy 60/I-64.* Erected in 1857, this 100-foot-long structure was made of hand-hewn oak held together with locust-wood pins. In use until 1929, it is now maintained as part of a 5-acre state highway wayside and is the only surviving curved-span covered bridge in the US.

Lake Moomaw. *13 miles N via Hwys 220, 687, follow signs to Gathright Dam. Phone 540/962-2214.* This 12-mile-long lake has a rugged shoreline of more than 43 miles set off by towering mountains. It is surrounded by the Gathright Wildlife Management Area and portions of the Washington and Jefferson national forests. Boating, swimming, fishing, water-skiing; picnicking, camping (fee). Visitor center. (Apr-Oct, daily)

Limited-Service Hotel

★★ BEST WESTERN MOUNTAIN VIEW. *820 E Madison St, Covington (24426). Phone 540/962-4951; fax 540/965-5714. www.bestwestern.com.* 79 rooms, 2 story. Pets accepted; fee. Check-out 11 am. Restaurant. Outdoor pool, children's pool. **$**

Specialty Lodging

The following lodging establishment is approved by Mobil Travel Guide, but due to its unique and individualized nature has not been given a traditional Mobil Star rating. Included in this listing you may find bed-and-breakfasts, limited-service inns, guest ranches, and other unique hotel properties.

MILTON HALL BED AND BREAKFAST INN. *207 Thorny Ln, Covington (24426). Phone 540/965-0196; fax 540/962-8232.* Built in 1874, this Gothic English manor is now an elegant bed-and-breakfast. The property and its formal English gardens sit on 44 acres of mostly wooded land, adjoining the George Washington National Forest. At the forest, guests can enjoy hiking, horseback riding, fishing, and hunting. 6 rooms, 2 story. Pets accepted, some restrictions. Complimentary full breakfast. Check-in 3 pm, check-out noon. **$$**

Culpeper (D-7)

See also Orange, Warrenton

Founded 1748
Population 9,664
Elevation 430 ft
Area Code 540
Zip 22701
Information Chamber of Commerce, 133 W Davis St; phone 540/825-8628

Volunteers from Culpeper, Fauquier, and Orange counties marched to Williamsburg in 1777 in answer to Governor Patrick Henry's call to arms. Their flag bore a coiled rattlesnake with the legends "Don't Tread on Me" and "Liberty or Death."

In the winter of 1862-1863, churches, homes, and vacant buildings in Culpeper were turned into hospitals for the wounded from the battles of Cedar Mountain, Kelly's Ford, and Brandy Station. Later, the Union Army had headquarters here.

Today, Culpeper is a light industry and trading center for a five-county area, with a healthy agriculture industry.

What to See and Do

Dominion Wine Cellars. *1 Winery Ave, Culpeper. 2 miles S on Hwy 3. Phone 540/825-8772.* Tours and tasting. (Daily; closed holidays) **FREE**

Limited-Service Hotels

★ COMFORT INN. *890 Willis Ln, Culpeper (22701). Phone 540/825-4900; fax 540/825-4904. www.choicehotels.com.* 49 rooms, 2 story. Pets accepted; fee. Complimentary continental breakfast. Check-out 11 am. Outdoor pool. **$**

★ ★ HOLIDAY INN. *791 James Madison Rd S, Culpeper (22701). Phone 540/825-1253; fax 540/825-7134. www.holiday-inn.com.* 159 rooms, 2 story. Check-out noon. Restaurant, bar. Outdoor pool, children's pool. **$**

Specialty Lodgings

The following lodging establishments are approved by Mobil Travel Guide, but due to their unique and individualized nature have not been given a traditional Mobil Star rating. Included in this listing you may find bed-and-breakfasts, limited-service inns, guest ranches, and other unique hotel properties.

FOUNTAIN HALL BED AND BREAKFAST. *609 S East St, Culpeper (22701). Phone 540/825-8200; toll-free 800/298-4748; fax 540/825-7716. www.fountainhall.com.* This charming bed and breakfast is located on the foothills of the Blue Ridge Mountains in historic downtown Culpeper. The Colonial Revival house (1859) was converted and now offers uniquely decorated rooms. Guests can relax in one of the spacious parlors or go off to discover some of the many neighboring historic sites, bike trails, or scenic countryside. 6 rooms, 2 story. Complimentary continental breakfast. Check-in 2 pm, check-out 11 am. **$**

GRAVES' MOUNTAIN LODGE. *Hwy 670, Syria (22743). Phone 540/923-4231; fax 540/923-4312. www.gravesmountain.com.* 40 rooms. Closed Dec-mid-Mar. Pets accepted, some restrictions; fee. Check-in 3 pm, check-out 11 am. Restaurant. Outdoor pool, children's pool. Tennis. **$**

Restaurant

★ ★ ★ PRINCE MICHEL. *154 Winery Ln, Leon (22725). Phone 540/547-9720. www.princemichel.com.* Meals are served on gold-rimmed china in a refined setting to create a romantic dining experience. French menu. Lunch, dinner. Closed Mon-Wed; holidays; also Dec 25-mid-Jan, mid-June-mid-July. Outdoor seating. **$$$**

Danville (F-5)

See also Martinsville, South Boston

Founded 1792
Population 48,411
Elevation 500 ft
Area Code 804
Information Danville Area Chamber of Commerce, 635 Main St, PO Box 1538, 24543; phone 804/793-5422
Web site www.danvillechamber.com

This textile and tobacco center blends the leisurely pace of the Old South with the modern tempo of industry. It is one of the nation's largest brightleaf tobacco auction markets. Dan River, Inc. houses the largest single-unit textile mill in the world; other major industries are also located here. Nancy Langhorne, Viscountess Astor, the first woman to sit in the British House of Commons, was born in Danville in 1879.

What to See and Do

Chatham. *38 Main St, Chatham (24531). 17 miles N via Hwy 29. Phone 434/432-1650.* Founded in 1777, this county seat of Pittsylvania County has many historically interesting houses, schools, and public buildings: Hargrave Military Academy (1909) with the Owen R. Cheatham Chapel and Yesteryear Hall (museum); Chatham Hall (1894) with Renaissance Chapel, stained-glass windows of women, and St. Francis mural in Commons Building; Old Clerk's Office (1813) restored as museum; Courthouse (1853) in Greek Revival style with delicate plaster ceiling frescoes and portraits; Emmanuel Episcopal Church (1844) with Gothic interior and signed Tiffany windows; and Sims-Mitchell House (1860s). Also of interest are the Educational and Cultural Center with planetarium and museum; antique shops, restaurants, trolley diners, and many private houses, several of which offer overnight accommodations. Self-guided walking tour information for town and county may be obtained at the Chamber of Commerce.

Danville Museum of Fine Arts and History. *975 Main St, Danville (24541). Phone 434/793-5644.* Home of Major W. T. Sutherlin; built in 1857. President Jefferson Davis and his cabinet fled to Danville after receiving news of General Lee's retreat from Richmond. It was during this time that the Sutherlin mansion served as the last capital of the Confederacy. Victorian restoration in historical section of house (parlor, library, and Davis bedroom). Rotating art exhibits by national and regional artists. (Tues-Fri, also Sat and Sun afternoons; closed holidays, also Dec 24-Jan 2) **FREE**

Danville Science Center. *677 Craghead St, Danville (24541). Phone 434/791-5160.* Hands-on museum for the entire family. Located in a restored Victorian train station. (Daily; closed Thanksgiving, Dec 25) **$$**

Tobacco auctions. *635 Main St, Danville (24541). Phone 434/793-5422.* Several huge warehouses ring with the chants of tobacco auctioneers. (Aug-early-Nov, Mon-Thurs; closed Labor Day, Columbus Day, Veterans Day) **FREE**

"Wreck of the Old 97" Marker. *Riverside Dr (Hwy 58), Danville. Between N Main and Locust Ln overpass.* Site of celebrated train wreck (September 27, 1903), made famous by a folk song.

Special Events

Danville Harvest Jubilee. *125 S Floyd St, Danville (24541). Phone 804/799-5200.* Celebration of tobacco harvest season. Mid-Sept.

Festival in the Park. *125 S Floyd St, Danville (24541). Phone 804/799-5200.* Arts, crafts, entertainment. Third weekend in May.

Limited-Service Hotels

★ HOLIDAY INN EXPRESS. *2121 Riverside Dr, Danville (24540). Phone 434/793-4000; fax 434/799-5516. www.holiday-inn.com.* 98 rooms, 3 story. Complimentary continental breakfast. Check-out noon. Outdoor pool. Deck overlooking river. **$**

★★ STRATFORD INN. *2500 Riverside Dr, Danville (24540). Phone 434/793-2500; fax 434/793-6960.* 151 rooms, 2 story. Pets accepted; fee. Complimentary full breakfast. Check-out noon. Restaurant, bar. Fitness room. Pool, children's pool, whirlpool. **$**

Dulles International Airport Area

See also Fairfax

Airport Information

Airport Dulles International Airport.

Information Phone 703/572-2700

Lost and Found Phone 703/572-8479

Web site www.metwashairports.com/dulles

Airlines Aeroflot, Air Canada, Air France, Air Tran Airways, Alaska Airlines, ANA (All Nippon Airways), American Airlines, America West, ACA (Atlantic Coast Airlines), Austrian Airlines, BMI British Midland, British Airways, BWIA International Airways, Continental Airlines, Continental Express, Delta Air Lines, Delta Connection, Delta Express, Grupo TACA, Ethiopian Airlines, jetBlue, KLM Royal Dutch, Korean Air, Lufthansa, Northwest Airlines, Saudi Arabian Airlines, SAS (Scandinavian Airlines), Song, SWISS, United Airlines, United Express, US Airways, Virgin Atlantic Airways

What to See and Do

Reston Town Center. *1921 Freedom Dr, Reston (20190). Adjacent Dulles Toll Rd (Hwy 267) at Reston Pkwy. Phone 703/709-8500. www.restontowncenter.com.* A 20-acre urban development incorporating elements of a traditional town square. Includes more than 50 retail shops and restaurants, movie theater complex, office space, and hotel. (See SPECIAL EVENTS)

Special Events

Fountain Square Holiday Celebration. *Reston Town Center, 11921 Freedom Dr 980, Reston (20190).* Choral groups, puppeteers, magicians, ice shows, dancers, parade. Thanksgiving-Dec 24.

Fountain Square Ice Rink. *Reston Town Center, 11921 Freedom Dr, Reston (20190).* Outdoor public ice rink. Mid-Nov-mid-Mar.

Northern Virginia Fine Arts Festival. *Reston Town Center, 11921 Freedom Dr, Reston (20190).* Art sale, children's activity area, barbecue. Mid-May.

Oktoberfest. *Reston Town Center, 11921 Freedom Dr, Reston (20190).* Biergarten with authentic German music, food. Mid-Sept.

Summer concerts. *Reston Town Center, 11921 Freedom Dr, Reston (20190).* Sat evenings June-Aug; also Thurs evenings in July.

Taste of the Town. *Fairfax.* Selected restaurants offer sample-size specialties. Last weekend in June.

Limited-Service Hotels

★ COMFORT INN. *200 Elden St, Herndon (20170). Phone 703/437-7555; fax 703/437-7572. www.choicehotels.com.* 103 rooms, 3 story. Complimentary continental breakfast. Check-out 11 am. Fitness room. Airport transportation available. **$**

★ ★ DAYS INN. *2200 Centreville Rd, Herndon (20170). Phone 703/471-6700; fax 703/742-8965. www.daysinn.com.* 205 rooms, 4 story. Complimentary continental breakfast. Check-out noon. Restaurant, bar. Fitness room. Outdoor pool, whirlpool. Airport transportation available. **$**

★ ★ HOLIDAY INN. *1000 Sully Rd, Sterling (20166). Phone 703/471-7411; fax 703/709-0785. www.holiday-inn.com.* 296 rooms, 2 story. Pets accepted, some restrictions. Check-out noon. Restaurant, bar. Fitness room. Indoor pool, whirlpool. Airport transportation available. Business center. **$$**

Full-Service Hotels

★ ★ ★ HYATT REGENCY RESTON. *1800 President's St, Reston (22190). Phone 703/709-1234; fax 703/709-2291. www.hyatt.com.* Located in the heart of Fairfax County's technology hub, this property offers resortlike ambiance in a suburban setting. 514 rooms, 12 story. Check-out noon. Restaurant, bar. Fitness room. Indoor pool, whirlpool. Airport transportation available. Business center. **$$**

★ ★ ★ MARRIOTT SUITES DULLES WORLDGATE. *13101 Worldgate Dr, Herndon (20170). Phone 703/709-0400; fax 703/709-0426. www.marriott.com.* 253 rooms, 11 story. Check-out noon. Restaurant, bar. Fitness room. Indoor pool, outdoor pool, whirlpool. Airport transportation available. **$$**

★ ★ ★ SHERATON RESTON HOTEL. *11810 Sunrise Valley, Reston (20191). Phone 703/620-9000; fax 703/860-1594. www.sheraton.com.* 301 rooms, 5 story. Check-in 3 pm, check-out noon. High-speed Internet access. Restaurant, bar. Fitness room. Outdoor pool, whirlpool. Business center. **$$**

Full-Service Resort

★ ★ ★ MARRIOTT WESTFIELDS RESORT AND CONFERENCE CENTER. *14750 Conference Center Dr, Chantilly (20151). Phone 703/818-0300; fax 703/818-3655. www.marriott.com.* Whether you are away on business or vacation, this hotel will accommodate all of your needs. The rooms are beautifully decorated and welcoming. 340 rooms, 4 story. Pets accepted, some restrictions; fee. Check-in 3 pm, check-out 1 pm. High-speed Internet access. Restaurant, bar. Fitness room. Indoor pool, outdoor pool, whirlpool. Golf. Tennis. Airport transportation available. Business center. **$$**

Restaurants

★ ★ CLYDE'S. *11905 Market St, Reston (20190). Phone 703/787-6601; fax 703/787-0390. www.clydes.com.* American, seafood menu. Lunch, dinner, Sun brunch. Closed Dec 25. Bar. Outdoor seating. **$$**

★ ★ FORTUNE. *1428 N Point Village Ctr, Reston (20194). Phone 703/318-8898; fax 703/318-8990.* Chinese menu. Lunch, dinner. Reservations recommended. **$$**

★ ★ **IL CIGNO.** *1617 Washington Plz N, Reston (20190). Phone 703/471-0121; fax 703/471-4259. www.ilcigno.com.* Italian menu. Lunch, dinner. Closed holidays. Bar. Reservations recommended. Outdoor seating. **$$**

★ ★ ★ **MARKET STREET BAR AND GRILL.** *1800 Presidents St, Reston (20190). Phone 703/709-6262; fax 703/709-6244. www.msbg.net.* American, Asian menu. Breakfast, lunch, dinner, Sun brunch. Bar. Reservations recommended. Valet parking. Outdoor seating. **$$**

★ ★ ★ **PALM COURT.** *14750 Conference Ctr Dr, Chantilly (20151). Phone 703/818-3522; fax 703/818-0363.* Housed in the Marriott Westfields Resort (see), this restaurant's menu is a throwback to the days of tableside dining. The buffet-style Sunday brunch is an extravaganza with tuxedo-clad waiters, mimosas, and an unending array of sweets. American menu. Breakfast, lunch, dinner, Sun brunch. Bar. Children's menu. Reservations recommended. Valet parking. **$$$**

★ ★ ★ **RUSSIA HOUSE.** *790 Station St, Herndon (20170). Phone 703/787-8880; fax 703/319-1765. www.russiahouserestaurant.com.* The decor is contemporary with Russian artwork displayed. Russian menu. Lunch, dinner. Closed holidays. Bar. **$$$**

★ ★ **SIAM ASIAN BISTRO.** *328 Elden St, Herndon (20170). Phone 703/742-8881; fax 703/437-5967.* Asian, Thai menu. Lunch, dinner. Closed Dec 25. Bar. Reservations recommended. Outdoor seating. **$$**

★ **TORTILLA FACTORY.** *648 Elden St, Herndon (20172). Phone 703/471-1156; fax 703/318-0390.* Mexican menu. Lunch, dinner. Closed holidays. Children's menu. Own tortillas. **$$**

Eastville

Restaurant

★ ★ ★ **EASTVILLE MANOR.** *6058 Willow Oak Rd, Eastville (23347). Phone 757/678-7378; fax 757/678-9005. www.eastvillemanor.com.* Chef/owner William Scalley and his wife Melody preside over this 1886 Victorian country inn and restaurant located in a tiny rural town. Polished wood floors, chandeliers, and antiques dominate the interior, while landscaped grounds create a tranquil setting outside. Community produce and fish and herbs from the backyard garden make their way onto the creative, internationally inspired menu. American menu. Dinner. Closed Sun-Mon; also Tues Sept-May. Children's menu. **$$**

Emporia (F-8)

Population 5,665
Elevation 110 ft
Area Code 804
Zip 23847

Limited-Service Hotels

★ **BEST WESTERN EMPORIA.** *1100 W Atlantic St, Emporia (23847). Phone 434/634-3200; toll-free 800/528-1234; fax 434/634-5459. www.bestwestern.com.* 99 rooms, 2 story. Pets accepted; fee. Complimentary continental breakfast. Check-out 11 am. Fitness room. Outdoor pool. **$**

★ **HAMPTON INN.** *1207 W Atlantic St, Emporia (23847). Phone 804/634-9200; toll-free 800/426-7866; fax 804/348-0071. www.hamptoninn.com.* 115 rooms, 2 story. Pets accepted. Complimentary continental breakfast. Check-out 11 am. Outdoor pool. **$**

Fairfax (C-8)

See also Alexandria, Arlington County (Ronald Reagan Washtington-National Airport Area), Dulles International Airport Area, Falls Church, McLean; also see District of Columbia

Founded 1874
Population 21,498
Elevation 447 ft
Area Code 703
Information Fairfax County Convention & Visitors Bureau, 8300 Boone Blvd, Suite 450, Tyson's Corner-Vienna 22182; phone 703/790-3329, 703/550-2450 (visitor center), or toll-free 800/7-FAIRFAX
Web site www.visitfairfax.org

Upon arriving in Fairfax, nestled in northern Virginia in the shadow of Washington, DC, you'll believe that you've landed in another century. In this quaint historic town, you can still envision the approaching troops as they raided the Fairfax County Courthouse on June 1, 1861. This battle cost John Quincy Marr his life, and he became the first Confederate casualty of the war. Today, Fairfax and the surrounding county have become a government center, home to many major corporations and a thriving technology industry.

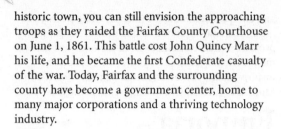

What to See and Do

County parks. *12055 Government Center Pkwy, Fairfax (22035). Phone 703/324-8700.* For additional information contact Fairfax County Park Authority, 12055 Government Center Pkwy, Suite 927, 22035.

Burke Lake. *7315 Ox Rd, Fairfax Station (22039). 6 miles S on Hwy 123. Phone 703/323-6601.* Consists of 888 acres. Fishing, boating (ramp, rentals); picnicking, playground, concession, miniature train, carousel (summer, daily; early May and late Sept, weekends), 18-hole and par-three golf, camping (May-Sept; seven-day limit). Beaver Cove Nature Trail; fitness trail. Fee for activities. (Daily) **$$**

Lake Fairfax. *1400 Lake Fairfax Dr, Reston (20190). On Hwy 606 near Leesburg Pike. Phone 703/471-5415.* Pool, boat rentals, fishing, excursion boat; picnicking, carousel, miniature train (late May-Labor Day, daily), camping (Mar-Dec; seven-day limit; electric additional fee). Fee for activities. (Daily)

George Mason University. *4400 University Dr, Fairfax (22030). Phone 703/993-1000. www.gmu.edu.* (1957) (24,000 students) This state-supported university started as a branch of the University of Virginia. Performing Arts Center features concerts, theater, dance; Fenwick Library maintains largest collection anywhere of material pertaining to Federal Theatre Project of the 1930s. Research Center for Federal Theatre Project contains 7,000 scripts, including unpublished works by Arthur Miller, sets and costume designs, and oral history collection of interviews with former Federal Theatre personnel. (Mon-Fri; closed holidays)

Regional parks. *5400 Ox Rd, Fairfax Station (22039). Phone 703/352-5900.* Contact Northern Virginia Regional Park Authority at above address.

Algonkian. *47001 Fairway Dr, Fairfax. 6 miles NE on Hwy 123 to Hwy 7, then 9 miles NW to Cascades Pkwy N, then 3 miles N near Sterling. Phone 703/450-4655.* An 800-acre park on the Potomac River; swimming (Memorial Day-Labor Day, fee), fishing, boating (ramp); golf, miniature golf, picnicking, vacation cottages, meeting and reception areas. **FREE**

Bull Run. *7700 Bull Run Dr, Fairfax. From Beltway I-66 W, exit at Centreville, W on Hwy 29 3 miles to park sign. Phone 703/631-0550.* Consists of 1,500 acres. Themed swimming pool (Memorial Day-Labor Day, daily; fee); camping (one to four persons, fee; electricity available; reservations accepted, phone 703/631-0550), concession, picnicking, playground, miniature golf, Frisbee golf, public shooting center, nature trail. (Mid-Mar-Dec) **$$$**

Meadowlark Botanical Gardens. *9750 Meadowlark Gardens Ct, Vienna (22182). On Beulah Rd between Rtes 7 and 123. Phone 703/255-3631. www.washacadsci.org/meadowlark-gardens/.* Lilac, wildflower, herb, hosta, native plants, and landscaped gardens on 95 acres. Includes three ponds; water garden; gazebos; trails. Visitor center. (Daily) Children under 7 free. **$$**

Sully. *3601 Sully Rd, Fairfax (20151). 10 miles W on Hwy 50, then N on Hwy 28 (Sully Rd), near Chantilly. Phone 703/437-1794.* (1794) Restored house of Richard Bland Lee, brother of General "Light Horse Harry" Lee; some original furnishings; kitchen-washhouse, log house store, smokehouse on grounds. Guided tours. (Mon, Wed-Sun; closed Jan 1, Thanksgiving, Dec 25) **$$**

Special Events

Antique Car Show. *3601 Sully Rd, Fairfax (20151).* Four hundred antique cars, flea market, and music. June.

Barns of Wolf Trap. *1624 Trap Rd, Vienna (22182). 3/4 mile S of Wolf Trap Farm Park. Phone 703/938-2404.* A 350-seat theater with chamber music, recitals, mime, jazz, folk, theater, and children's programs. For schedule contact the Barns. Late Sept-early May.

Quilt Show. *3601 Sully Rd, Fairfax (22181).* Quilts for sale, quilting demonstrations, and antique quilts on display. Sept.

Wolf Trap Farm Park for the Performing Arts. *1624 Trap Rd, Vienna (22182). 8 miles NE on Hwy 123,* *then W on Hwy 7 to Towlston Rd (Trap Rd), then follow signs. Phone 703/255-1900.* Varied programs include ballet, musicals, opera, classical, jazz, and folk music. Filene Center open theater seats 3,800 under cover and 3,000 on lawn. Picnicking on grounds, all year. Also free interpretive children's programs, July-Aug. For schedules and prices contact Wolf Trap Foundation at above address. Late May-Sept.

Limited-Service Hotel

★ **COMFORT INN.** *11180 Main St, Fairfax (22030). Phone 703/591-5900; toll-free 800/223-1223; fax 703/591-3507. www.choicehotels.com.* 205 rooms, 6 story. Complimentary continental breakfast. Check-out 11 am. Restaurant, bar. Fitness room. Indoor pool, outdoor pool. Airport transportation available. **$**

Full-Service Hotel

★ ★ ★ **HYATT FAIR LAKES.** *12777 Fair Lakes Cir, Fairfax (22033). Phone 703/818-1234; fax 703/653-6190. www.hyatt.com.* 316 rooms, 14 story. Check-in 3 pm, check-out noon. Restaurant, bar. Fitness room. Indoor pool, whirlpool. Airport transportation available. Business center. **$$**

Full-Service Inn

★ ★ ★ **THE BAILIWICK INN.** *4023 Chain Bridge Rd, Fairfax (22030). Phone 703/691-2266; toll-free 800/366-7666; fax 703/934-2112. www.bailiwickinn.com.* A restored Federal-style inn (1800), this majestic bed-and-breakfast offers individually decorated guest rooms, all graciously appointed with antiques. Each room is named after a famous Virginian and includes a small library of books dedicated to the namesake. The first Civil War skirmish occured here in June of 1861. 14 rooms, 4 story. Complimentary full breakfast. Check-in 2 pm, check-out 11 am. Restaurant. **$$**

Restaurants

★ ★ **ARTIE'S.** *3260 Old Lee Hwy, Fairfax (22030). Phone 703/273-7600; fax 703/273-9433. www.greatamericanrestaurants.com.* American menu. Lunch, dinner, late-night, Sun brunch. Closed Thanksgiving, Dec 25. Bar. Children's menu. Casual attire. **$$**

★ ★ ★ **BAILIWICK INN.** *4023 Chain Bridge Rd, Fairfax (22030). Phone 703/691-2266; fax 703/934-2112. www.bailiwickinn.com.* This Federal-style inn and restaurant, on the National Register of Historic Places, offers French-American cuisine in a quaint, romantic space. Visit for one of the seasonal wine dinners or for traditional English high tea in one of the intimate parlors. American, Mediterranean, seafood menu. Lunch, dinner. Closed Mon, Tues. Reservations recommended. Outdoor seating. **$$$**

★ **BLUE OCEAN.** *9440 Main St, Fairfax (22031). Phone 703/425-7555; fax 703/425-8274. www.blueocean-sushi.com.* Japanese menu. Lunch, dinner. Closed holidays. **$$**

★ ★ **BOMBAY BISTRO.** *3570 Chain Bridge Rd, Fairfax (22030). Phone 703/359-5810; fax 703/359-5811. www.bombaybistro.com.* Indian menu. Lunch, dinner, brunch. Closed Thanksgiving. Bar. Outdoor seating. **$$**

★ ★ **CONNAUGHT PLACE.** *10425 North St, Fairfax (22030). Phone 703/352-5959; fax 703/591-2568.* Indian menu. Lunch, dinner, brunch. Closed Thanksgiving, Dec 25. Bar. Sitar Fri, Sat. **$$$**

★ **P. J. SKIDOO'S.** *9908 Lee Hwy, Fairfax (22030). Phone 703/591-4515; fax 703/591-5407. www.pjskidoos.com.* American menu. Lunch, dinner, Sun brunch. Closed Thanksgiving, Dec 25. Bar. Children's menu. Outdoor seating. **$$**

Falls Church (C-8)

See also Alexandria, Arlington County (Ronald Reagan Washington-National Airport Area), Fairfax, McLean; also see District of Columbia

Population 10,377
Elevation 340 ft
Area Code 703
Information Greater Falls Church Chamber of Commerce, 417 W Broad St, PO Box 491, 22040-0491; phone 703/532-1050
Web site www.fallschurchchamber.org

Falls Church is a pleasant, cosmopolitan suburb of Washington, DC, just over the Arlington County line, graced with many interesting old houses. This was a crossover point between the North and the South through which pioneers, armies, adventurers, and merchants passed.

What to See and Do

The Falls Church. *115 E Fairfax St, Falls Church (22046). At Washington St, on Hwy 29. Phone 703/532-7600.* (1769) Episcopal. This building replaced the original wooden church built in 1732. Served as a recruiting station during the Revolutionary War; abandoned until 1830; used during the Civil War as a hospital and later as a stable for cavalry horses. Restored according to original plans with gallery additions in 1959. (Mon-Fri, Sun; closed holidays) Worship services Wed noon and Sun at 8 am and noon. **FREE**

Fountain of Faith. *7400 Lee Hwy, Falls Church (22042). In National Memorial Park. Phone 703/560-4400.* Memorial dedicated to the four chaplains—two Protestant, one Jewish, one Catholic—who were aboard the USS *Dorchester* when it was torpedoed off Greenland in 1943. They gave their life jackets to four soldiers on deck who had none.

Full-Service Hotel

★★★ MARRIOTT FAIRVIEW PARK. *3111 Fairview Park Dr, Falls Church (22042). Phone 703/849-9400; fax 703/849-8692. www.marriott.com.* Sitting on a park-like setting, this property offers jogging paths through woods and around a lake. 394 rooms, 15 story. Check-out noon. Restaurant, bar. Fitness room. Indoor, outdoor pool; whirlpool. Business center. **$$**

Restaurants

★★ BANGKOK STEAKHOUSE. *926 W Broad St #A, Falls Church (22046). Phone 703/534-0095; fax 703/534-3096. www.bangkokbluesrestaurant.com.* Thai, Laotian menu. Lunch, dinner. **$$**

★★★ DUANGRAT'S. *5878 Leesburg Pike, Falls Church (22041). Phone 703/820-5775; fax 703/820-6206. www.duangrats.com.* Thai menu. Lunch, dinner. Bar. **$$**

★★★ HAANDI. *1222 W Broad St (Hwy 7), Falls Church (22046). Phone 703/533-3501; fax 703/533-3502. www.haandi.com.* The accolades are plentiful for this fine dining restaurant that is renowned as one of the best in the region. The depth of flavor and unique spices found in each dish are unmatched. Indian menu. Lunch, dinner. Closed Dec 25. **$$**

★★ PEKING GOURMET INN. *6029 Leesburg Pike (Hwy 7), Falls Church (22041). Phone 703/671-8088; fax 703/671-5912. www.pekinggourmet.com.* Chinese menu. Lunch, dinner. Closed Thanksgiving. Reservations recommended. Favorite of Washington politicians. **$$**

★★ PILIN THAI. *116 W Broad St (Hwy 7), Falls Church (22046). Phone 703/241-5850; fax 703/241-7556.* Thai menu. Lunch, dinner. Closed holidays. Bar. Reservations recommended. **$$**

★★ SECRET GARDEN BEEWON. *6678 Arlington Blvd, Falls Church (22042). Phone 703/533-1004; fax 703/533-1056.* Korean, Japanese menu. Lunch, dinner. Closed Jan 1. Bar. Reservations recommended. **$$**

★ SIR WALTER RALEIGH INN. *8120 Gatehouse Rd, Falls Church (22042). Phone 703/560-6768; fax 703/560-7134.* Seafood, steak menu. Lunch, dinner. Closed Dec 25. Bar. Children's menu. **$**

Farmville (E-7)

See also Keysville

Population 6,845
Elevation 304 ft
Area Code 804
Zip 23901

Longwood College's Jeffersonian buildings provide architectural interest in downtown Farmville.

What to See and Do

Sailor's Creek Battlefield Historic State Park. *State Rtes 307 N and 17, Fredericksburg (23966). 9 miles E on Hwy 460, then 7 miles NE on Hwy 307 and 2 miles N on Hwy 617. Phone 804/392-3435.* The site of last major battle of the Civil War on Apr 6, 1865, preceding Lee's surrender at Appomattox by three days. Auto tour. **FREE**

Limited-Service Hotel

★ **COMFORT INN.** *Hwy 15 and US 460 Bypass, Farmville (23901). Phone 434/392-8163; toll-free 800/228-5150; fax 434/392-3691. www.choicehotels.com.* 51 rooms, 2 story. Check-out noon. Outdoor pool. **$**

Fredericksburg (D-8)

See also Triangle

Settled 1727
Population 19,279
Elevation 61 ft
Area Code 540
Information Visitor Center, 706 Caroline St, 22401; phone 540/373-1776 or toll-free 800/678-4748.
Web site www.fredericksburgvirginia.net

One of the seeds of the American Revolution was planted here when a resolution declaring independence from Great Britain was passed on April 29, 1775. Here is where George Washington went to school, where his sister Betty lived, and his mother, Mary Ball Washington, lived and died. James Monroe practiced law in town. Guns for the Revolution were manufactured here, and four of the most savage battles of the Civil War were fought nearby.

Captain John Smith visited the area in 1608 and gave glowing reports of its possibilities for settlement. In 1727, the General Assembly directed that 50 acres of "lease-land" be laid out and the town called Fredericksburg, after the Prince of Wales.

Ships from abroad sailed up the Rappahannock River to the harbor—ampler then than now—to exchange their goods for those brought from "upcountry" by the great road wagons and river carriers. The town prospered.

The Civil War left Fredericksburg ravaged. Situated midway between Richmond and Washington, it was recurringly an objective of both sides; the city changed hands seven times and the casualties were high. Even so, many buildings put up before 1775 still stand. Proudly aware of their town's place in the country's history, the townspeople keep Fredericksburg inviting with fresh paint, beautiful lawns, and well-kept gardens.

What to See and Do

Belmont (The Gari Melchers Estate and Memorial Gallery). *224 Washington St, Fredericksburg (22405). Phone 540/654-1843.* Residence from 1916 to 1932 of American-born artist Gari Melchers (1860-1932), best known for his portraits of the famous and wealthy, including Theodore Roosevelt, William Vanderbilt, and Andrew Mellon, and as an important impressionist artist of the period. The artist's studio comprises the nation's largest collection of his works, housing more than 1,800 paintings and drawings. The site is a registered National and State Historic Landmark and includes a 27-acre estate, frame house built in the late 18th century and enlarged over the years, and a stone studio built by Melchers. Owned by the state of Virginia, Belmont is administered by Mary Washington College. (Daily; closed holidays) **$$$**

Confederate Cemetery. *Washington Ave between Amelia and William sts.* There are 2,640 Confederate Civil War soldiers buried here, some in graves marked "Unknown."

Fredericksburg Area Museum (Town Hall). *907 Princess Anne St, Fredericksburg (22401). Phone 540/371-3037.* (1814) Museum and cultural center interpret the history of Fredericksburg area from its first settlers to the 20th century. Changing exhibits. Children's events. (Daily; closed Jan 1, Thanksgiving, Dec 25) **$$**

Fredericksburg Masonic Lodge #4, AF and AM. *Princess Anne and Hanover sts, Fredericksburg (22401). Phone 540/373-5885.* Washington was initiated into this Lodge November 4, 1752; the building, dating from 1812, contains relics of his initiation and membership; authentic Gilbert Stuart portrait; 300-year-old Bible on which Washington took his Masonic oath. (Mon-Sat, also Sun afternoons; closed Jan 1, Thanksgiving, Dec 25) **$**

George Washington's Ferry Farm. *268 Kings Hwy, Fredericksburg (22405). 1 mile E on Hwy 3. Phone 540/370-0732.* The site of George Washington's boyhood home. Once a tobacco plantation, it now serves

Fredericksburg's Presidential Legacy

Midway between Washington and Richmond, the old colonial river port of Fredericksburg earned the dubious nickname of "battlefield city" in the Civil War, as the site of four major battles between 1862 and 1864. As a result, many visitors overlook its colonial antecedents and its unique status as the hometown of both George Washington and James Monroe, who were born now far away. This one-hour, 1-mile stroll down its quiet tree-shaded streets is an introduction to this presidential legacy. Begin by visiting the Fredericksburg Visitor Center at 706 Caroline Street. Walk north along Caroline Street, the Historic District's attractive main street, which is lined with interesting shops and cafés. At George Street, turn left one block to Charles Street, and then go right to 908 Charles, the James Monroe Museum. As a young man, Monroe practiced law in an office on this site. The museum displays rich pieces of furniture he took with him to the White House as the country's fifth president. Continue north on Charles Street to Lewis Street and turn left onto Washington Avenue. Turn right a half block to Kenmore Plantation, the lovely mansion and garden at 2101 Washington. Built in 1752, it was the home of Betty Lewis, who was George Washington's sister, and her husband Fielding Lewis, a financier and gun manufacturer who aided the Revolutionary cause. The house is particularly noted for its richly decorated, hand-molded ceilings. From Kenmore, retrace your steps on Lewis Street for three blocks to Charles Street. At 1200 Charles Street stands the Mary Washington House, which George Washington bought for his mother in 1772 so she could be more easily looked after by daughter Betty. Though busy George, who lived 40 miles north at Mount Vernon, was a dutiful son, his mother often accused him of neglect, a story told at the museum. Continue east on Lewis to Caroline Street, and turn north (left) to the Rising Sun Tavern at 1306, the tour's conclusion. Built in 1760 as a private home by Charles Washington, George's younger brother, it has been restored to the 18th-century tavern it became in 1792.

as an archaeological dig and a nature preserve. Guided tours. (Daily) **$**

Hugh Mercer Apothecary Shop. *1020 Caroline St, Fredericksburg (22401). Phone 540/373-3362.* This 18th-century medical office and pharmacy offers exhibits on the medicine and methods of treatment used by Dr. Hugh Mercer before he left to join the Revolutionary War as brigadier general. Authentic herbs and period medical instruments. (Daily; closed holidays) **$$**

James Monroe Museum. *908 Charles St, Fredericksburg (22401). Phone 540/654-1043.* As a young lawyer, James Monroe lived and worked in Fredericksburg from 1786 to 1789, and even served on Fredericksburg's City Council. This museum houses one of the nation's largest collections of Monroe memorabilia, articles, and original documents. Included are the desk bought in France in 1794 during his years as ambassador and used in the White House for signing of the Monroe Doctrine, formal attire worn at Court of Napoleon, and more than 40 books from Monroe's library; also garden. The site is a National Historic Landmark owned by the Commonwealth of Virginia and administered by Mary Washington College. (Daily; closed holidays) **$$**

Kenmore. *1201 Washington Ave, Fredericksburg (22401). Phone 540/373-3381.* (1752) Considered one of finest restorations in Virginia; former home of Colonel Fielding Lewis, commissioner of Fredericksburg gunnery, who married George Washington's only sister, Betty. On an original grant of 863 acres, Lewis built a magnificent home; three rooms have full decorative molded plaster ceilings. Diorama of 18th-century Fredericksburg. (Daily; closed Jan, Feb, holidays) **$$$**

Mary Washington House. *1200 Charles St, Fredericksburg (22401). Phone 540/373-1569.* Bought by George for his mother in 1772; she lived here until her death in 1789. Here she was visited by General Lafayette. Some original furnishings. Boxwood garden. (Daily; closed holidays) **$$**

Mary Washington Monument. *Washington Ave and Pitt St, Fredericksburg (22401).* Where Mrs. Washington often went to rest and pray and where she is buried.

Masonic Cemetery. *George and Charles sts, Fredericksburg (22401).* One of nation's oldest Masonic burial grounds.

Old Slave Block. *William and Charles sts, Fredericksburg (22401).* Circular block of sandstone about 3 feet high from which ladies mounted their horses and slaves were auctioned in antebellum days.

Presbyterian Church. *Princess Anne and George sts, Fredericksburg (22401). SW corner. Phone 540/373-7057.* (1833) Cannonballs in the front pillar and other damages inflicted in 1862 bombardment. Pews were torn loose and made into coffins for soldiers. Clara Barton, founder of the American Red Cross, is said to have nursed wounded here. A plaque to her memory is in the churchyard. Open on request (Mon-Fri, Sun).

Rising Sun Tavern. *1306 Caroline St, Fredericksburg (22401). Phone 540/371-1494.* (Circa 1760) Washington's youngest brother Charles built this tavern, which became a social and political center and stagecoach stop. Restored and authentically refurnished as an 18th-century tavern; costumed tavern staff, English and American pewter collection. (Daily; closed holidays) **$$**

St. George's Episcopal Church and Churchyard. *Princess Anne and George sts, Fredericksburg (22401). NE corner. Phone 540/373-4133.* Patrick Henry, uncle of the orator, was the third rector. Headstones in the churchyard bear the names of illustrious Virginians. (Daily)

St. James House. *1300 Charles St, Fredericksburg (22401). Phone 540/373-1569.* Frame house built in 1760s, antique furnishings, porcelain and silver collections; landscaped gardens. (Open Historic Garden Week in Apr and first week in Oct; other times by appointment) **$**

The University of Mary Washington. *1301 College Rd, Fredericksburg (22401). Phone 540/654-1000; toll-free 800/468-5614.* (1908) (3,700 students) Coeducational liberal arts and sciences institution that offers historic preservation, computer science, and business administration. College also includes 275 acres of open and wooded campus; red brick, white-pillared buildings. President of the college occupies Brompton (private), house built in 1830 on land sold to Fielding Lewis in 1760 and expanded by a later owner, Colonel John Lawrence Marye. Campus tours.

Visitor Center. *706 Caroline St, Fredericksburg (22401).* Orientation film; information; obtain walking tour brochure and combination tickets here.

Special Events

Christmas Candlelight Tour. *604 William St # A, Fredericksburg (22401).* Historic homes open to the public; carriage rides; Christmas decorations and refreshments of the Colonial period. First weekend in Dec.

Historic Garden Week. *Fredericksburg.* Private homes open. Usually third week in Apr.

Market Square Fair. *Fredericksburg.* Entertainment, crafts demonstrations, food. Mid-May.

Quilt Show. *Fredericksburg.* Exhibits at various locations. Demonstrations and sale of old and new quilts. Sept.

Limited-Service Hotels

★ BEST WESTERN CENTRAL PLAZA. *3000 Plank Rd, Fredericksburg (22401). Phone 540/786-7404; toll-free 800/528-1234; fax 540/785-7415. www.bestwestern.com.* 76 rooms, 3 story. Pets accepted, some restrictions. Complimentary continental breakfast. Check-out noon. **$**

★ COMFORT INN. *5422 Jefferson Davis Hwy, Fredericksburg (22407). Phone 540/898-5550; toll-free 800/221-2222; fax 540/891-2861. www.choicehotels.com.* 125 rooms, 5 story. Complimentary continental breakfast. Check-out noon. Fitness room. Indoor pool, whirlpool. **$**

★ ★ RAMADA INN. *5324 Jefferson Davis Hwy, Fredericksburg (22408). Phone 540/898-1102; toll-free 800/272-6232; fax 540/898-2017. www.ramada.com.* 195 rooms, 2 story. Pets accepted, some restrictions. Check-out noon. Restaurant, bar. Fitness room. Indoor pool, whirlpool. **$**

Full-Service Hotel

★★ HOLIDAY INN. *2801 Plank Rd, Fredericksburg (22404). Phone 540/786-8321; toll-free 800/682-1049; fax 540/786-0397. www.holiday-inn.com.* 195 rooms, 3 story. Pets accepted, some restrictions; fee. Check-out noon. Restaurant, bar. Fitness room. Outdoor pool, children's pool. Tennis. Airport transportation available. **$**

Specialty Lodgings

The following lodging establishments are approved by Mobil Travel Guide, but due to their unique and individualized nature have not been given a traditional Mobil Star rating. Included in this listing you may find bed-and-breakfasts, limited-service inns, guest ranches, and other unique hotel properties.

FREDERICKSBURG COLONIAL INN. *1707 Princess Anne St, Fredericksburg (22401). Phone 540/371-5666.* 39 rooms, 2 story. Complimentary continental breakfast. Check-in 2 pm, check-out 11 am. Built 1928; antiques. **$**

KENMORE INN. *1200 Princess Anne St, Fredericksburg (22401). Phone 540/371-7622; fax 540/371-5480. www.kenmoreinn.com.* 9 rooms, 2 story. Complimentary continental breakfast. Check-in 2 pm, check-out 11 am. Restaurant, bar. Structure built in the late 1700s; in historic district. **$$**

RICHARD JOHNSTON INN. *711 Caroline St, Fredericksburg (22401). Phone 540/899-7606.* 9 rooms, 3 story. Complimentary continental breakfast. Check-in 2-6 pm, check-out 11 am. Built in 1787. In historic district. **$**

Restaurants

★★ LA PETITE AUBERGE. *311 William St, Fredericksburg (22401). Phone 540/371-2727.* American, French menu. Lunch, dinner. Closed Sun; holidays. Bar. Outdoor seating. **$$$**

★★★ RENATO. *422 William St, Fredericksburg (22401). Phone 540/371-8228; fax 540/371-2311. www.renatos1.com.* In the center of old town, this cozy dining room offers an extensive menu. All breads, pasta, and pastries are made fresh daily on the premises. Italian menu. Lunch, dinner. Closed holidays. Bar. **$$**

Fredericksburg and Spotsylvania National Military Park (D-7)

See also Fredericksburg

What to See and Do

Chancellorsville Visitor Center. *120 Chatham Ln, Fredericksburg (22405). 7 miles W of I-95 on Hwy 3. Phone 540/786-2880.* Slide program, museum with exhibits; dioramas. (Daily; closed Jan 1, Dec 25) **$$**

Chatham Manor. *120 Chatham Ln, Fredericksburg (22405). Phone 540/371-0802.* Georgian brick manor house, owned by a wealthy planter, was converted to Union headquarters during two of the battles of Fredericksburg. The house was eventually used as a hospital where Clara Barton and Walt Whitman nursed the wounded. (Daily; closed Jan 1, Dec 25) **$$**

Fredericksburg Visitor Center. *Lafayette Blvd (Hwy 1) and Sunken Rd, Fredericksburg (22401). Phone 540/373-6122.* Information and directions for various parts of park. Tours should start here. (Daily; closed Jan 1, Dec 25) **$$** Center includes

> **Fredericksburg National Cemetery.** *Lafayette Blvd and Sunken Rd, Fredericksburg (22401).* More than 15,000 Federal interments; almost 13,000 unknown.
>
> **Museum.** *1900 E Kanawha, Fredericksburg (22401).* Slide program, diorama, exhibits. (Same days as Visitor Center) **$$**

Old Salem Church. *Fredericksburg. 1 mile W of I-95 on Hwy 3.* (1844) Building used as a field hospital and refugee center. Scene of battle on May 3-4, 1863.

Stonewall Jackson Shrine. *120 Chatham Ln, Fredericksburg (22405). 12 miles S on I-95 to Thornburg exit, then 5 miles E on Hwy 606 to Guinea. Phone 804/633-6076.* Plantation office where on May 10, 1863, Confederate General Jackson, ill with pneumonia and with his shattered left arm amputated, murmured, "Let us cross over the river, and rest under the shade of the trees," and died. (Mid-June-Labor Day: daily; Apr-mid-June, after Labor Day-Oct: Mon, Tues, Fri-Sun; rest of year: Mon, Sat-Sun) **$$**

Front Royal (C-7)

See also Winchester, Woodstock

Founded 1788
Population 13,589
Elevation 567 ft
Area Code 540
Zip 22630
Information Chamber of Commerce of Front Royal-Warren County, 414 E Main St; phone 540/635-3185 or toll-free 800/338-2576
Web site www.frontroyal.com

Once known as "Hell Town" for all the wild and reckless spirits it attracted, Front Royal was a frontier stop on the way to eastern markets. The present name is supposed to have originated in the command, "Front the royal oak," given by an English officer to his untrained mountain militia recruits.

Belle Boyd, the Confederate spy, worked here extracting military secrets from Union officers. It is said that she invited General Nathaniel Banks, whose regiment was occupying the town, and his officers to a ball once. Later she raced on horseback to tell General Jackson what she had learned. The next morning (May 23, 1862), the Confederates attacked and captured nearly all of the Union troops, providing Jackson one of his early victories in the famous Valley Campaign.

Front Royal was a quiet little village until the entrance to Shenandoah National Park (see) and the beginning of Skyline Drive opened in 1935, just 1 mile to the south. With millions of motorists passing through every year, the town has grown rapidly. The production of automotive finishes, limestone, and cement contributes to the town's economy, but the tourism industry remains one of its largest.

What to See and Do

Belle Boyd Cottage. *101 Chester St, Front Royal (22630). Behind Ivy Lodge. Phone 540/636-1446.* Relocated to its present site, the two-story cottage has been restored to reflect life in Front Royal between 1840 and 1860. For a two-year period during the Civil War, Belle Boyd stayed in this cottage while visiting relatives and used the opportunity to spy on Union troops occupying the town. This modest dwelling was also used to house wounded soldiers of both armies. (Mid-Apr-Oct, Mon-Fri, weekends by appointment; closed holidays) **$**

Jackson's Chase Golf Course. *65 Jackson's Chase Dr, Front Royal (22630). Phone 540/635-7814. www.jacksonschase.com.* Jackson's Chase is built on a tract of land that was used by Conferderate General "Stonewall" Jackson to chase Nathaniel Banks' Union forces through the Shenandoah Valley and into the eventual first Battle of Winchester. The course itself incorporates the area's rolling terrain into plateau fairways and holes lined with water. Holes three through eight surround a small area being developed for homes with 1-acre lots, for those who wish to live in full view of history and good golf. **$$$$**

Shenandoah Valley Golf Club. *134 Golf Club Circle, Front Royal (22630). Phone 540/636-4653. www.svgcgolf.com.* Nestled into the Blue Ridge Mountains, Shenandoah Valley offers 27 holes and has hosted such prestigious tournaments as the PGA Tour's Kemper Open. If you want to play, make sure to reserve a tee time at least a week in advance. Once you do, you'll be happy with a course that is very affordable and playable for most any golfer. **$$$$**

Skyline Caverns. *10344 Stonewall Jackson Hwy, Front Royal (22630). 1 mile S on Hwy 340. Phone 540/635-4545; toll-free 800/296-4545.* Extensive, rare, intricate flowerlike formations of calcite (anthodites); sound and light presentation; 37-foot waterfall; clear stream stocked with trout (observation only). Electrically lighted; 54°F year-round. Miniature train provides trip through surrounding wooded area (Mar-mid-Nov, daily, weather permitting). Snack bar; gift shop. Cavern tours start every few minutes. (Daily) **$$$**

Sky Meadows State Park. *11012 Edmonds Ln, Delaplane (20144). 20 miles E on Hwy 66, 7 miles N on Hwy 17. Phone 540/592-3556.* A 1,862-acre park. Fishing pond; hiking and bridle trails, picnicking, primitive walk-in camping. Visitor center; programs. (Daily) **$$**

Warren Rifles Confederate Museum. *95 Chester St, Front Royal (22630). Phone 540/636-6982.* Historic relics and memorabilia of War between the States. (Mid-Apr-Oct: daily; rest of year: by appointment) **$$**

Special Events

Festival of Leaves. Arts and crafts, demonstrations; historic exhibits; parade. Second weekend in Oct.

Virginia Mushroom and Wine Festival. Mushrooms, wine, and cheese. Entertainment. Third Sat in May.

Warren County Fair. Entertainment, livestock exhibits and sale, contests. First week in Aug.

Warren County Garden Tour. Garden Club sponsors tours of historic houses and gardens. Last week in Apr.

Limited-Service Hotel

★★ **QUALITY INN.** *10 S Commerce Ave, Front Royal (22630). Phone 540/635-3161; toll-free 888/821-4488; fax 540/635-6624. www.choicehotels.com.* 107 rooms, 3 story. Check-out 11 am. Restaurant. Outdoor pool. **$**

Specialty Lodging

The following lodging establishment is approved by Mobil Travel Guide, but due to its unique and individualized nature has not been given a traditional Mobil Star rating. Included in this listing you may find bed-and-breakfasts, limited-service inns, guest ranches, and other unique hotel properties.

CHESTER HOUSE. *43 Chester St, Front Royal (22630). Phone 540/635-3937; toll-free 800/621-0441; fax 540/636-8695. www.chesterhouse.com.* This Georgian-style property, built in 1905, is located 1 mile from Skyline Drive, where there are scenic drives and hiking trails. 5 rooms, 2 story. Children over 12 years only. Complimentary full breakfast. Check-in 3 pm, check-out 11 am. **$$**

Galax (F-4)

See also Wytheville

Settled 1904
Population 6,837
Elevation 2,382 ft
Area Code 540
Zip 24333
Information Galax-Carroll-Grayson Chamber of Commerce, 405 N Main St; phone 540/236-2184

Galax is named for the pretty evergreen with heart-shaped leaves that florists use in various arrangements. It grows in the mountainous regions around Galax and is gathered for sale all over the United States. Nearby are three mountain passes: Fancy Gap, Low Gap, and Piper's Gap.

What to See and Do

Jeff Matthews Memorial Museum. *606 W Stuart Dr, Galax (24333). Phone 276/236-7874.* Two authentically restored log cabins (1834 and 1860s). Relocated to present site and furnished with items used in the period in which the cabins were inhabited. Also houses collection of photos of Civil War veterans, artifacts and memorabilia of the area; covered wagon; farm implements. Restored log cabin used as a blacksmith's shop. (Wed-Sun) **FREE**

Recreation. Swimming, boating, fishing on New River; hunting and hiking. Canoeing and other activities can be found at

Cliffview Trading Post. *442 Cliffview Rd, Galax. Phone 276/238-1530.* Bike rentals (Tues-Sat; closed Thanksgiving, Dec 25) and horse rentals (Apr-Nov, Tues-Sat); trail rides in New River Trail State Park.

Special Event

Old Fiddler's Convention. *Felts Park, Galax.* Folk songs, bands, and dancing. Second week in Aug.

George Washington Birthplace National Monument (D-8)

See also Fredericksburg, Montrose

(38 miles E of Fredericksburg on Hwy 3, then 2 miles E on Hwy 204)

George Washington, first child of Augustine and Mary Ball Washington, was born February 11, 1732 (celebrated February 22 according to the new-style calendar) at his father's estate on Popes Creek on the south shore of the Potomac. The family moved in 1735 to Little Hunting Creek Plantation (later called Mount Vernon), then in 1738 to Ferry Farm near Fredericksburg.

The 538-acre monument includes much of the old plantation land. (Daily; closed Jan 1, Dec 25)

What to See and Do

Family burial ground. *1732 Popes Creek Rd, George Washington Birthplace National Monument. 1 mile NW on Bridges Creek. Phone 804/224-1732.* Site of 1664 home of Colonel John Washington, first Washington in Virginia and great-grandfather of the first president. Washington's ancestors are buried here.

Memorial House. *1732 Popes Creek Rd, George Washington Birthplace National Monument. Phone 804/224-1732.* Original house burned (1779) and was never rebuilt. The Memorial House is not a replica of the original; it represents a composite of typical 18th-century Virginia plantation house. Bricks were handmade from nearby clay. Furnishings are typical of the times.

Colonial Farm. "Living" farm designed to show 18th-century Virginia plantation life; livestock, colonial garden, several farm buildings, furnished colonial kitchen, household slave quarters, and spinning and weaving room.

Picnic area. *1732 Popes Creek Rd, George Washington Birthplace National Monument. Phone 804/224-1732.* 1/4 mile N of house.

Visitor Center. *1732 Popes Creek Rd, George Washington Birthplace National Monument. Phone 804/224-1732.* Orientation film; museum exhibits. **$**

Glen Allen

Limited-Service Hotel

★ SPRINGHILL SUITES. *9701 Brook Rd, Glen Allen (23059). Phone 804/266-9403; fax 804/266-6703. www.springhillsuites.com.* Located near many restaurants and shops, this property features studio suites and is easily accessible from both I-295 and I-95. 136 rooms, 4 story, all suites. Complimentary continental breakfast. Check-in 3 pm, check-out noon. Fitness room. Indoor pool, whirlpool. **$**

Gloucester (E-9)

See also Newport News, Williamsburg, Yorktown

Founded 1769
Population 900
Elevation 70 ft
Area Code 804
Zip 23061
Information Chamber of Commerce, PO Box 296; phone 804/693-2425.

In the spring, acres of daffodil blooms make this area a treat for the traveler. This elm-shaded village is the commercial center of Gloucester (GLOSS-ter) County. There are many old landmarks and estates nearby, including the birthplace of Walter Reed, at the junction of Hwys 614 and 616.

What to See and Do

County Courthouse. *6489 Main St, Gloucester (23061). On Hwy 17 Business. Phone 804/693-4042.* (18th century) Part of Gloucester Court House Circle Historic District. Portraits of native sons in the courtroom; plaques memorializing Nathaniel Bacon, leader in the rebellion of 1676, first organized resistance to British authority, and Major Walter Reed, surgeon and conqueror of yellow fever. (Mon-Fri; closed holidays) **FREE** Nearby are Debtors Prison, the pre-Revolutionary Botetourt Building, and the

Roswell Historic Ruins. *6549 Main St, Gloucester (23061). Phone 804/693-2585.* Three-story Georgian mansion's brickwork was put in place over 250 years ago. Majestic ruins hint at projecting pavilions, arched windows, and stone-capped chimney stacks. Tours by appointment. (Apr-Oct: Sun; winter: by appointment) **FREE**

Virginia Institute of Marine Science, College of William and Mary. *1208 Greate Rd, Gloucester Point (23062). Phone 804/684-7000.* Small marine aquarium and museum display local fish, and invertebrates; marine science exhibits, bookstore. (Mon-Fri; closed holidays) **FREE**

Great Dismal Swamp National Wildlife Refuge (F-9)

See also Chesapeake, Portsmouth

Harriet Beecher Stowe found Virginia's Dismal Swamp a perfect setting for her antislavery novel, *Dred* (1856); modern hunters, fishermen, and naturalists find the area fits their ambition just as well. From its northern edge just southwest of Norfolk, the swamp stretches almost due south like a great ribbon, 25 miles long and 11 miles wide. Centuries of decaying organic matter have created layers of peat so deep that fires would sometimes smolder under the surface for weeks.

Creation of the refuge began in 1973 when the Union Camp Corporation donated 49,100 acres of land to the Nature Conservancy, which in turn conveyed it to the Department of Interior. The refuge was officially established through the Dismal Swamp Act of 1974 and is managed for the primary purpose of protecting and preserving a unique ecosystem. The refuge now consists of over 107,000 acres of forested wetlands that have been greatly altered by drainage and logging operations.

Near the center is Lake Drummond, 3,100 acres of juniper water, which is water that combines the juices of gum, cypress, and maple with a strong infusion of juniper or white cedar. The chemical mix added by the tree resins results in a water that remains sweet, or fresh, indefinitely. In the days of long sailing voyages, when ordinary water became foul after a few weeks, this "dark water" was highly valued.

The Great Dismal Swamp has also been commercially exploited for its timber, particularly cypress and cedar. A company organized by George Washington and several other businessmen bought a large piece of the swamp and used slave labor to dig the Dismal Swamp Canal, which both facilitated drainage of timber land and provided a transportation route in and out of the swamp.

Animal and bird life continues to abound in this eerie setting. There are white-tailed deer and rarely observed black bear, foxes, bobcats—and a large number of snakes, including copperheads, cottonmouths, and rattlesnakes. Birding is popular in the swamp from April-June; the peak of spring migration is mid-April-mid-May.

Hampton (E-9)

See also Cape Charles, Newport News, Norfolk, Portsmouth, Virginia Beach

Settled 1610
Population 146,437
Elevation 12 ft
Area Code 757
Information Hampton Visitor Center, 710 Settlers Landing Rd, 23669; phone 757/727-1102 or toll-free 800/800-2202
Web site www.hampton.va.us

Hampton is the oldest continuously English-speaking community in the United States (Jamestown, settled in 1607, is a national historical park, but not a town). The settlement began at a place then called Kecoughtan, with the building of Fort Algernourne as protection against the Spanish. In the late 1600s and early 1700s the area was harassed by pirates. Finally in 1718, the notorious brigand Blackbeard was killed by Lieutenant Robert Maynard and organized piracy came to an end here.

Hampton was shelled in the Revolutionary War, sacked by the British in the War of 1812, and burned in 1861 by retreating Confederates to prevent its occupation by Union forces. Only the gutted walls of St. John's Church survived the fire. The town was rebuilt after the Civil War by its citizens and soldiers. Computer technology, manufacturing, aerospace research, and commercial fishing are now big business here.

Langley Air Force Base, headquarters for the Air Combat Command, Fort Monroe, headquarters for the US Army's Training and Doctrine Command, and the NASA Langley Research Center are located here.

What to See and Do

Air Power Park and Aviation History Center. *413 W Mercury Blvd, Hampton (23666). Hwy 258. Phone 757/727-1163.* Over 50 indoor and outdoor exhibits feature real fighter aircraft, missiles, and rockets; local aviation history and model aircraft exhibits. Picnicking, playground. (Daily; closed Jan 1, Thanksgiving, Dec 25) **FREE**

Bluebird Gap Farm. *60 Pine Chapel Rd, Hampton (23666). Phone 757/727-6739.* This 60-acre farm includes barnyard zoo; indigenous wildlife such as deer and wolves; antique and modern farm equipment and farmhouse artifacts. Picnicking, playground. (Wed-Sun; closed holidays) **FREE**

Buckroe Beach. *22 Lincoln St, Hampton (23669). 4 miles E on Hwy 351, foot of E Pembroke Ave on Chesapeake Bay. Phone 757/727-6347.* Swimming; public park, concerts. Lifeguards (Memorial Day-Labor Day). **FREE**

Fort Monroe. *3 miles SE via Mercury Blvd, Ingalls Rd.* First fort here was a stockade called Fort Algernourne (1609); the second, Fort George, though built of brick, was destroyed by a hurricane in 1749; present fort was completed about 1834. **FREE** Here are

Casemate Museum. *20 Bernard Rd, Hampton (23651). Phone 757/788-3391.* Provides insight on heritage of the fort, Old Point Comfort, and the Army Coast Artillery Corps. Museum offers access to a series of casemates and a walking tour of the fort. Jefferson Davis casemate contains cell in which the Confederacy's president was confined on false charges of plotting against the life of Abraham Lincoln. Museum features Civil War exhibits, military uniforms, and assorted artwork, including three original Remington drawings, along with audiovisual programs. Scale models of coast artillery guns and dioramas represent the role of the coast artillery from 1901 to 1946. (Daily; closed Jan 1, Thanksgiving, Dec 25) **FREE**

Chapel of the Centurion. (1858) One of the oldest churches on the Virginia peninsula. Woodrow Wilson worshiped here occasionally.

Hampton Carousel. *602 Settlers Landing Rd, Hampton (23669). Downtown, on waterfront. Phone 757/727-6381.* (1920) Completely restored in 1991, antique carousel is housed in its own pavilion and features 48 hand-carved horses. (Apr-Sept: Mon-Sat, also Sun afternoons; Oct-Nov: daily, weather permitting; Dec 1-15: weekends) **$**

Hampton University. *Cemetery Rd and Frissell Ave, Hampton (23669). E end of Queen St, 1/4 mile off I-64 exit 267. Phone 757/727-5253. www.hampton.edu.* (1868) (6,100 students) Founded by Union Brigadier General Samuel Chapman Armstrong, chief of the Freedman's Bureau, to prepare the youth of the South, regardless of color, for the work of organizing and instructing schools in the Southern states; many blacks and Native Americans came to be educated. Now Virginia's only coeducational, nondenominational, four-year private college. The Hampton choir is famous. It "sang up" a building, Virginia-Cleveland Hall, in 1870 on a trip through New England and Canada, raising close to $100,000 at concerts. On campus are

Emancipation Oak. The Emancipation Proclamation was read here.

Museum. *Huntington Building, Cemetery Rd and Frissell Ave, Hampton.* Collection of ethnic art; Native American and African artifacts; contemporary African-American works; paintings by renowned artists. (Daily; closed school holidays) **FREE**

***Miss Hampton II* Harbor Cruises.** *764 Settlers Landing Rd, Hampton (23669). Phone 757/722-9102.* Narrated three-hour cruise includes a stop at Fort Wool, a Civil War island fortress. (Apr-Oct) **$$$$**

Settlers Landing Monument. *1/2 mile S, on grounds of the Veterans Affairs Medical Center between Hampton River and Mill Creek, off I-64 exit 268.* Marks approximate site of first settlers' landing near Strawberry Banks in 1607. Painting by Sidney King depicts visit to Kecoughtan by colonists en route to Jamestown. (Daily) **FREE**

St. John's Church and Parish Museum. *W Queens Way and Franklin St, Hampton. Phone 757/722-2567.* (1728) Fourth site of worship of Episcopal parish established in 1610. Bible dating from 1599; communion silver from 1618; Colonial Vestry Book; taped historical message. (Daily)

Virginia Air and Space Center and Hampton Roads History Center. *600 Settlers Landing Rd, Hampton (23669). Downtown, off I-64 exit 267. Phone 757/727-0900; toll-free 800/296-0800. www.vasc.org.* Exhibits show the historical link between Hampton Roads' seafaring past and spacefaring future. Exhibits include 19 full-sized air- and spacecraft, the *Apollo 12* Command Module, a moon rock, and rare NASA artifacts. Films shown in 283-seat IMAX theater (daily). Gift shop. (Daily; closed Thanksgiving, Dec 25) **$$$**

Special Events

Hampton Bay Days. *Phone 757/727-6122.* Arts and crafts, rides, science exhibits; entertainment. Mid-Sept.

Hampton Cup Regatta. *Phone toll-free 800/800-2202.* Inboard hydroplane races. Mid-Aug.

Hampton Jazz Festival. *Hampton Coliseum, 1000 Coliseum Dr, Hampton. Phone 757/838-4203.* Three days late June.

Limited-Service Hotels

★ HAMPTON INN. *1813 W Mercury Blvd, Hampton (23666). Phone 757/838-8484; fax 757/826-0725. www.hamptoninn.com.* 131 rooms, 6 story. Complimentary continental breakfast. Check-in 3 pm, check-out noon. Fitness room. **$**

★ ★ HOLIDAY INN. *1815 W Mercury Blvd, Hampton (23666). Phone 757/838-0200; fax 757/838-4964. www.holiday-inn.com.* 390 rooms, 4 story. Check-out 11 am. Restaurant, bar. Fitness room. Indoor pool, outdoor pool, whirlpool. Airport transportation available. Business center. **$**

★ ★ RADISSON HOTEL HAMPTON. *700 Settlers Landing, Hampton (23669). Phone 757/727-9700; fax 757/722-4557. www.radisson.com.* Located on the waterfront in downtown Hampton, this hotel is conveniently located between Williamsburg and Virginia Beach and is close to business and leisure districts and military bases. 177 rooms, 9 story. Check-in 3 pm, check-out noon. Restaurant, bar. Fitness room. Outdoor pool, whirlpool. Airport transportation available. On Hampton River. **$**

Restaurant

★ SAMMY AND NICK'S. *2718 W Mercury Blvd, Hampton (23666). Phone 757/838-9100; fax 757/838-9612.* Steak menu. Lunch, dinner. Closed Thanksgiving, Dec 25. Bar. Children's menu. Casual attire. **$$**

Harrisonburg (D-6)

See also Franklin, Luray New Market, Staunton

Founded 1780
Population 40,468
Elevation 1,352 ft
Area Code 540
Information Harrisonburg-Rockingham Convention and Visitors Bureau,10 E Gay St, 22802; phone 540/434-2319
Web site www.hrcvb.org

Originally named Rocktown due to the limestone outcroppings prevalent in the area, Harrisonburg became the county seat of Rockingham County when Thomas Harrison won a race against Mr. Keezle of Keezletown, 3 miles east. They had raced on horseback to Richmond to file their respective towns for the new county seat. Harrisonburg is noted for good hunting and fishing, recreational opportunities, beautiful scenery, and turkeys. The annual production of more than 5 million turkeys, most of them processed and frozen, has made Rockingham County widely known. This is a college town with three 4-year universities. Much of the Washington and Jefferson national forests are here.

What to See and Do

Caverns. There are several caverns within 24 miles of Harrisonburg. They include

Grand Caverns Regional Park. *Dogwood Ave, Grottoes. 12 miles S on I-81, then 6 miles E on Hwy 256. Phone 540/249-5705; toll-free 888/430-2283. home.rica.net/uvrpa.* Known for its immense underground chambers and spectacular formations. Visited by Union and Confederate troops during the Civil War. Unique shield formations. Electrically lighted; 54°F. Park facilities include a swimming pool ($), tennis courts, miniature golf, picnic pavilions, and hiking and bicycle trails. Guided tours. (Apr-Oct: daily; Nov-Mar: weekends) **$$$$**

Shenandoah Caverns. *24 miles N on Hwy 11.* (See NEW MARKET)

Eastern Mennonite University. *1200 Park Rd, Harrisonburg (22802). 2 miles NW on Hwy 42. Phone 540/432-4000.* (1917) (1,350 students) Many Mennonites live in this area. On campus is an art gallery, planetarium (shows by appointment, free), natural history museum, and the Menno Simons Historical Library, containing many 16th-century Mennonite volumes (school year, Mon-Sat). Campus tours.

George Washington and Jefferson National Forests. *5162 Valleypointe Pkwy, Roanoke (24019). 10 miles W on Hwy 33. Phone 540/265-5100. www.southernregion.fs.fed.us/gwj.* Consist of approximately nearly 2 million acres. Swimming; fishing for trout, bluegill, and bass; hunting for deer, bear, wild turkey, and small game; riding trails, camping, picnicking. Scenic drives past Crabtree Falls, hardwood forests, and unusual geologic features. Overlooks of the Shenandoah Valley. Part of the Appalachian Trail crosses through the forest. Fees are charged at some recreation sites. Trails for the visually impaired. **FREE**

Recreation areas. *Coeburn Rd, Wise. Phone 540/328-2931.* In the George Washington and Jefferson National Forests. **High Knob,** 4 miles S on I-23 to Norton, then 3 miles S via Hwy 619, 1 1/2 miles E on FS Rd 238. Camping, swimming, picnicking. **Bark Camp,** 7 miles W of Big Stone Gap on I-58 A, then 1 mile N on Hwy 622, then 3 miles W on Hwy 621. Camping (fee). Swimming. **North Fork of Pound Lake,** I-23 to Pound, then W on Hwy 671. Camping (fee), picnicking, swimming, boat ramp, hiking. The Clinch Ranger District office is in Wise.

James Madison University. *800 S Main St, Harrisonburg (22807). Phone 540/568-3621.* (1908) (15,000 students) Interesting old bluestone buildings. Campus tours through Visitor Center phone 540/568-5681. On campus is

Miller Hall Planetarium and Sawhill Art Gallery. *Phone 540/568-3621 (for schedules).* **FREE**

Lake Shenandoah. *3 miles E.*

Lincoln Homestead. *9 miles N on Hwy 42.* Brick house, the rear wing of which was built by Abraham Lincoln's grandfather, and where his father was born. Main portion of the house was built about 1800 by Captain Jacob Lincoln. (Private)

Natural Chimneys Regional Park. *Mount Solon. 15 miles SW off Hwy 42. Phone 540/350-2510.* Seven colorful and massive rock towers rise 120 feet above the plain. Pool; picnic facilities, camping (fee; limited Nov-Feb), bicycle and nature trails, playground. Park (daily). **$$**

Shenandoah River. Good bass fishing.

Shenandoah Valley Folk Art and Heritage Center. *115 Bowman Rd, Harrisonburg. Phone 540/879-2681. www.heritagecenter.com.* Featured is the Stonewall Jackson Electric Map that depicts his Valley Campaign of 1862. The 12-foot vertical relief map fills an entire wall and lets visitors see and hear the campaign, battle by battle. Also displays of Shenandoah Valley history, artifacts. (Mon-Sat; closed holidays) **$$**

Silver Lake. *Dayton. 5 miles SW on Hwy 42.*

Virginia Quilt Museum. *301 S Main St, Harrisonburg (22801). Phone 540/433-3818.* Resource center for the study of quilts and quilting. (Mon, Thurs-Sat, also Sun afternoons; closed holidays) **$$**

Special Events

Natural Chimneys Jousting Tournament. *Natural Chimneys Regional Park, 94 Natural Chimneys Ln, Harrisonburg.* America's oldest continuous sporting event, held annually since 1821. "Knights" armed with lances charge down an 80-yard track and attempt to spear three small rings suspended from posts. Each knight is allowed three rides at the rings, thus a perfect score is nine rings. Ties are run off using successively smaller rings. Third Sat in June and Aug.

Rockingham County Fair. *4808 S Valley Pike, Harrisonburg (22801).* Mid-Aug.

Limited-Service Hotels

★ COMFORT INN. *1440 E Market St, Harrisonburg (22801). Phone 540/433-6066; fax 540/433-0793. www.choicehotels.com.* 60 rooms, 2 story. Pets accepted, some restrictions. Complimentary continental breakfast. Check-out noon. Outdoor pool. **$**

★★ **FOUR POINTS BY SHERATON.** *1400 E Market St, Harrisonburg (22801). Phone 540/433-2521; toll-free 800/708-7037; fax 540/434-0253. www.fourpoints.com.* 140 rooms, 5 story. Pets accepted; fee. Check-out noon. Restaurant, bar. Fitness room. Indoor pool, children's pool, whirlpool. **$**

★ **HAMPTON INN.** *85 University Blvd, Harrisonburg (22801). Phone 540/432-1111; fax 540/432-0748. www.hamptoninn.com.* 164 rooms, 4 story. Complimentary continental breakfast. Check-out noon. Outdoor pool. **$**

★★ **VILLAGE INN.** *4979 S Valley Pike, Harrisonburg (22801). Phone 540/434-7355; toll-free 800/736-7355. www.shenandoah.org/villageinn.* 36 rooms. Pets accepted; fee. Check-out noon. Restaurant. Outdoor pool. **$**

Hopewell (E-8)

See also Petersburg, Petersburg National Battlefield, Richmond, Surry, Williamsburg

Founded 1613
Population 22,354
Elevation 50 ft
Area Code 804
Zip 23860
Information Hopewell Area-Prince George Chamber of Commerce, 210 N 2nd Ave; phone 804/458-5536

The second permanent English settlement in America has been an important inland port since early times, having a fine channel 28 feet deep and 300 feet wide. It was the birthplace of statesman John Randolph of Roanoke. Edmund Ruffin, an early agricultural chemist who fired the first shot at Fort Sumter, was born near here.

"Cittie Point," at the junction of the James and Appomattox rivers, finally became one of Virginia's big cities during World War I when an E. I. du Pont de Nemours Company dynamite plant on Hopewell Farm supplied guncotton to the Allies.

What to See and Do

City Point Unit of Petersburg National Battlefield. *Cedar Ln and Pecan Ave, Hopewell (23860). Phone 804/458-9504.* Grant's headquarters during the siege of Petersburg and largest Civil War supply depot. Includes Appomattox Manor, home to one family for 340 years; Grant's headquarters were on the front lawn. Many other buildings. (Daily; closed holidays) **$**

Flowerdew Hundred. *1617 Flowerdew Hundred Rd, Hopewell (23860). 10 miles SE on Hwy 10. Phone 804/541-8897.* Outdoor museum on the site of an early English settlement on the south bank of the James River. Originally inhabited by Native Americans, settled by Governor George Yeardley in 1618. Thousands of artifacts dating from the prehistoric period through the present have been excavated and are on exhibit in the museum. A replicated 19th-century detached kitchen and working 17th-century-style windmill are open to visitors. Exhibits, interpretive tours. Picnicking. (Apr-Nov: Sat and Sun or by appointment; rest of year: by appointment) **$$**

Merchants Hope Church. *11500 Merchants Hope Rd, Hopewell (23860). 6 miles E on Hwy 10, then 1/2 mile S on Hwy 641. Phone 804/458-6197.* (1657) Given the name of a plantation that was named for a barque plying between Virginia and England. The exterior has been called the most beautiful colonial brickwork in America. Oldest operating Protestant church in the country. (Open by request) **DONATION**

Special Events

Hooray for Hopewell Festival. *Downtown.* Arts and crafts, food, entertainment, children's rides. Third weekend in Sept.

Prince George County Heritage Fair. *Flowerdew Hundred.* Arts and crafts; educational exhibits and demonstrations; music, food, children's rides, hayrides. Last weekend in Apr.

Limited-Service Hotel

★ **HOLIDAY INN EXPRESS.** *4911 Oaklawn Blvd, Hopewell (23860). Phone 804/458-1500; fax 804/458-9151. www.holiday-inn.com.* 115 rooms, 2 story. Complimentary continental breakfast. Check-out 11 am. Fitness room. Outdoor pool, whirlpool. **$**

Hot Springs (E-5)

See also Clifton Forge, Covington, Warm Springs

Population 300
Elevation 2,238 ft
Area Code 540
Zip 24445

A Ranger District office of the Washington and Jefferson national forests is located here.

What to See and Do

The Homestead. *Hwy 220, Hot Springs (24445). Phone toll-free 800/838-1766. www.thehomestead.com.* Double chairlift, T-bar, J-bar, baby rope tow; patrol, school, rentals; snowmaking; cafeteria, bar. Ice curling, ice skating rink (Thanksgiving-Mar). **$$$$**

Full-Service Resort

★★★ **THE HOMESTEAD.** *Hwy 220, Hot Springs (24445). Phone 540/839-1766; toll-free 800/838-1766; fax 540/839-7556. www.thehomestead.com.* Founded ten years before the American Revolution, The Homestead is one of America's finest resorts. For more than two centuries, presidents and other notables have flocked to this idyllic mountain resort on 15,000 acres in the scenic Allegheny Mountains. Mindful of its historical obligations, the resort carefully adds creature comforts to the traditional accommodations. From the fresh mountain air and natural hot springs to the legendary championship golf, this Georgian-style resort is the embodiment of a restorative retreat. A leading golf academy sharpens skills, while three courses challenge players. History abounds at the resort; for example, America's oldest continuously played tee is located here at the Old Course. Guests take to the waters as they have done for 200 years, while the spa incorporates advanced therapies for relaxation and rejuvenation. Eight restaurants tempt guests with a variety of options, from continental cuisine in formal settings to fun flavors in relaxed environments. 513 rooms, 12 story. Check-in 4 pm, check-out noon. Restaurant, bar. Children's activity center. Fitness room, spa. Indoor pool, outdoor pool. Golf. Tennis. Airport transportation available. Business center. **$$**

Specialty Lodging

The following lodging establishment is approved by Mobil Travel Guide, but due to its unique and individualized nature has not been given a traditional Mobil Star rating. Included in this listing you may find bed-and-breakfasts, limited-service inns, guest ranches, and other unique hotel properties.

VINE COTTAGE INN. *Hwy 220, Hot Springs (24445). Phone 540/839-2422; toll-free 800/410-9755. www.vinecottageinn.com.* 15 rooms, 3 story. Closed two weeks in Mar. Pets accepted; fee. Complimentary full breakfast. Check-in 3 pm, check-out noon. Built in 1894; family-oriented Victorian inn. **$**

Restaurants

★ **COUNTRY CAFE.** *Hwy 220 S, Hot Springs (24445). Phone 540/839-2111.* American menu. Breakfast, lunch, dinner. Closed Mon; holidays, children's menu. **$$**

★★ **SAM SNEAD'S TAVERN.** *Main St, Hot Springs (24445). Phone 540/839-7666. www.thehomestead.com.* American, seafood menu. Dinner. Reservations recommended. **$$$**

Irvington

See also Lancaster

Population 673
Elevation 31 ft
Area Code 804
Zip 22480

What to See and Do

Historic Christ Church. *420 Christ Church Rd, Irvington. 2 1/2 miles W, off Hwy 200. Phone 804/438-6855.* (1735) Built by Robert Carter, ancestor of eight governors of Virginia, two presidents, three signers of the Declaration of Independence, a chief justice, and many others who served the country with distinction. Restored; original structure and furnishings, triple-decker pulpit. Built on site of earlier wooden church (1669); family tombs. Tours. (Apr-Nov, daily) **FREE** On the grounds is

Carter Reception Center. Narrated video presentation; museum with artifacts from Corotoman, home of Robert Carter, and from the church construction; photographs of the restoration. Guides. (Apr-Nov, daily) **FREE**

Full-Service Resort

★★★ **TIDES INN.** *480 King Carter Dr, Irvington (22480). Phone 804/438-5000; toll-free 800/843-3746; fax 804/438-5222. www.tidesinn.com.* The Tides Inn is a superior vacation destination. This comprehensive resort enjoys a splendid setting in Virginia's "Northern Neck," where rich history and beautiful scenery enchant visitors. Bordered by the Chesapeake Bay, Potomac River, Rappahannock River, and with views of gentle Carters Creek, water figures largely in the experience here. A 64-slip marina is a boater's paradise. Golf, tennis, croquet, biking, blissing out in the spa, and exploring the nearby historic sites are just some of the ways guests fill their days while staying here. Dining runs the gamut from the elegant setting at The Dining Room and dinner river cruises on the *Miss Ann* to the casual atmospheres of Commodore's, Cap'n B's, and the Chesapeake Club. 106 rooms. Closed Jan-mid-Mar. Pets accepted, some restrictions; fee. Check-in 4 pm, check-out noon. Restaurant, bar. Children's activity center. Fitness room, spa. Beach. Saltwater pool, indoor pool. Golf, 27 holes. Tennis. **$$**

Jamestown (Colonial National Historical Park) (E-9)

See also Colonial Parkway, Newport News, Surry, Williamsburg, Yorktown

On May 13, 1607, in this unpromising setting, the first permanent English settlement in the New World was founded. From the beginning, characteristics of the early United States were established—self-government, industry, commerce, and the plantation system. The 104 men and boys who landed here that day and the people who followed them forecast the varied origins of the American populace. There were English, Germans, Africans, French, Italians, Poles, and Irish.

The *Susan Constant* (120 tons), the *Godspeed* (40 tons), and the *Discovery* (20 tons) brought the settlers here after a landing at Cape Henry. Thus, 20 years after the tragic failure to establish a colony at Roanoke Island and 13 years before the Pilgrims landed at Plymouth, Massachusetts, the English succeeded in settling in America.

The landing was not auspicious. Captain John Smith, ablest man in the group, was in chains; most of the others possessed a singular ineptitude for existing in a strange, hostile wilderness. Smith's ability and driving personality soon made him the acknowledged leader. For about a year he kept the bickering at a minimum, and the establishment of a colony was well under way.

The London Company, under whose patronage the colonists had set forth, continued to send "gentlemen" and adventurers to reinforce the colony. The second such shipment (September 1608) elicited the famous "Smith's rude answer" to company demands for gold and assorted riches. He wrote in part, "I entreat you rather send but thirty carpenters, husbandmen, gardeners, fishermen, blacksmiths, masons, and diggers up of trees, roots … than a thousand of such as we have: for except we be able both to lodge them and feed them, the most will consume with want of necessaries before they can be made good for anything."

Good for anything or not, this little band made glass in 1608, introduced the first commercial tobacco cultivation in 1612, and produced the country's first representative legislative body in 1619. In the earliest years, clapboards (some of which were shipped back to England) were made here, and later bricks, fishing nets, pottery, a variety of tools, and other items needed in the colony.

The first Africans were brought to the colony in 1619 on a Dutch privateer. They were probably indentured servants, pledged to work until their passage had been paid off. This was a common arrangement at the time.

There was not an easy day for any of the colonists for years. Crops failed and rats ate the corn. Until John Rolfe married Pocahontas, daughter of Chief Powhatan, in 1614, the Native Americans were suspicious and unfriendly. Disease plagued the settlers. The winter of 1609-1610 was called the "starving time." The 350-person colony was reduced to about 60 emaciated, defeated survivors who decided to give up and return to England. The June 1610 arrival of

Lord de la Warre with reinforcements and supplies dissuaded them. Then the colony began to build and hope returned.

When Jamestown became a Royal Colony in 1624, feeling against personal (and often high-handed) government began to mount. By 1676 there was open revolt, led by Nathaniel Bacon, the younger. Bacon's forces finally burned the town, calling it a "stronghold of oppression." It was partially rebuilt but decline was inevitable, in part due to the damp, unhealthy climate of the area. The statehouse burned in 1698 and in 1699 the government moved to Middle Plantation and renamed it Williamsburg. By Revolutionary War days Jamestown was no longer an active community. About the same time, the James River washed away the sandy isthmus and the site became an island.

Nothing of the 17th-century settlement remains above ground except the Old Church Tower. Since 1934, however, archaeological exploration by the National Park Service has made the outline of the town clear. Cooperative efforts by the Park Service and the Association for the Preservation of Virginia Antiquities (which owns 22.5 acres of the island, including the Old Church Tower) have exposed foundations and restored streets, property ditches, hedgerows, fences, and the James Fort site from 1607. Markers, recorded messages, paintings, and monuments are everywhere. Entrance station (daily; closed Dec 25). Contact the Superintendent, PO Box 210, Yorktown 23690; phone 757/898-3400. Jamestown Island entrance fee $5/adult (over age 16); Golden Access, Age, and Eagle passports accepted (see MAKING THE MOST OF YOUR TRIP).

What to See and Do

Confederate Fort. *Near Old Church Tower.* (1861) One of two Civil War fortifications on the island.

Dale House. *1367 Colonial Pkwy, Jamestown (23081).* Archaeological laboratory. A viewing area is open to the public.

First landing site. *Colonial Historic Pkwy and Jamestown Rd, Jamestown (23185).* Fixed by tradition as point in river, about 200 yards from present seawall, upriver from Old Church Tower.

Glasshouse. *Colonial National Historic Pkwy and Jamestown Rd, Jamestown (23185).* Colonists produced glass here in 1608. Demonstration exhibits, glassblowing (daily; closed Dec 25).

James Fort site. *Colonial Historic Pkwy and Jamestown Rd, Jamestown (23185).* Excavation of first fort (1607) can be viewed between seawall and Old Church Tower.

Jamestown Settlement. *Rte 31 S Jamestown Rd, Williamsburg. Adjacent to historic Jamestown. Phone 757/253-4838; toll-free 888/593-4682. www.historyisfun .org.* Living history museum re-creates the first permanent English settlement in the New World. Recalls early-17th-century Jamestown with full-scale reproductions of ships which arrived in 1607 and the triangular James Fort. The Powhatan Indian Village depicts Native American culture encountered by English colonists. Museum complex features an orientation film, changing gallery, and three exhibit galleries focusing on the history of Jamestown and the Powhatan. Food service available. Combination ticket with Yorktown Victory Center (see YORKTOWN) available. (Daily; closed Jan 1, Dec 25) **$$$$**

Memorial Church. *Colonial National Historic Pkwy and Jamestown Rd, Jamestown (23185).* Built in 1907 by the National Society of the Colonial Dames of America over foundations of original church. Within are two foundations alleged to be of earlier churches, one from 1617 that housed the first assembly.

New Towne. *1367 Colonial Pkwy, Jamestown (23081).* Area where Jamestown expanded around 1620 may be toured along "Back Streete" and other original streets. Section includes reconstructed foundations indicating sites of Country House, Governor's House, homes of Richard Kemp, builder of one of the first brick houses in America, Henry Hartwell, a founder of College of William and Mary, and Dr. John Pott and William Pierce, who led the "thrusting out" of Governor John Harvey in 1635.

Old Church Tower. Only standing ruin of the 17th-century town. Believed to be part of the first brick church (1639). Has 3-foot-thick walls of handmade brick.

Tercentenary Monument. *Located near Jamestown Visitor Center.* Erected by US (1907) to commemorate 300th Jamestown anniversary. Other monuments include Captain John Smith statue (by William

Couper), Pocahontas Monument (by William Ordway Partridge), House of Burgesses Monument (listing members of first representative legislative body in America).

Trails. Three- and five-mile auto drives provide access to entire area. Visitor center has 45-minute auto drive and town site tape tours available.

Visitor Center. *Colonial National Historic Pkwy and Jamestown Rd, Jamestown (23185).* Guide leaflets, introductory film, and exhibits. Post office. (Daily; closed Dec 25)

Special Events

First Assembly Day. *Jamestown, the original town site.* Commemorates first legislative assembly in 1619. Late July.

Jamestown Weekend. *Jamestown, the original town site.* Commemorates arrival of first settlers in 1607; special tours and activities. Mid-May.

Keswick (D-6)

See also Charlottesville

Full-Service Resort

★★★ KESWICK HALL AT MONTICELLO. *701 Club Dr, Keswick (22947). Phone 434/979-3440; toll-free 800/274-5391; fax 434/977-4171. www.keswick.com.* Keswick Hall inspires its guests with its stately Italianate architecture and serenely beautiful setting. The 600-acre estate, set at the foot of the Blue Ridge Mountains, introduces visitors to a rarefied world of luxury and comfort. Individually designed, the guest rooms reflect a modern interpretation of early American style through the use of overstuffed furniture, club chairs, Aubusson carpets, and canopied four-poster beds. Views over the magnificent formal gardens are particularly coveted. Guests choose from three fantastic restaurants or enjoy the privacy of room service. The rolling hills of the Shenandoah Valley invite exploration and the historic halls of Monticello are only minutes away, but this resort also entices its guests with a variety of recreational opportunities. The members-only Keswick Hall, adjacent to the hotel, presents an exclusive opportunity for guests to enjoy its indoor/outdoor pool, tennis courts, fitness facility, spa services, and 18-hole Arnold Palmer golf course. 48 rooms, 3 story. Pets accepted. Check-in 3 pm, check-out noon. Restaurant. Children's activity center. Fitness room, spa. Indoor pool, outdoor pool, whirlpool. Golf. Tennis. Airport transportation available. **$$$**

Restaurant

★★★ MAIN DINING ROOM. *701 Club Dr, Keswick (22947). Phone 434/979-3440; fax 434/923-4378. www.keswick.com.* "A feast for the eyes" best describes the chef's classicly inspired culinary creations. And most appropriate given the lush atmosphere of this formal dining room with its trompe l'oeil wall murals and expansive garden views. American menu. Breakfast, dinner. Bar. Children's menu. Casual attire. Reservations recommended. Valet parking. Outdoor seating. **$$$**

Keysville (E-6)

See also Farmville

Population 817
Elevation 642 ft
Area Code 804
Zip 23947

What to See and Do

Twin Lakes State Park. *Farmville. 15 miles NE on Hwy 360, then 1 1/2 miles NW off Hwy 613. Phone 434/392-3435.* More than 250 acres of state forest; two lakes. Swimming, bathhouse, fishing, boating (rentals, launching, electric motors only); hiking, bicycle, and self-guided trails; picnicking, playground, concession, camping, hook-ups, tent and trailer sites, cabins (Mar-Dec); pavilion.

Lancaster

See also Irvington

Population 150
Elevation 89 ft
Area Code 804
Zip 22503

The family of Mary Ball Washington, mother of George Washington, were early settlers of this area. Washington's maternal ancestors are buried in the churchyard of St. Mary's Whitechapel Church 5 miles west of Lancaster.

What to See and Do

Lancaster County Courthouse Historic District. Sycamore trees surround this area around the antebellum courthouse (1860). Marble obelisk is one of the first monuments erected to Confederate soldiers (1872).

Mary Ball Washington Museum and Library Complex. *8346 Mary Ball Rd, Lancaster (22503). Phone 804/462-7280.* Contains the Old Clerk's Office (1797), the Old Jail (1819), Lancaster House (1800), the headquarters and main museum building. Also Virginia genealogical research center. (Wed-Sat, Tues by appointment) **$**

St. Mary's Whitechapel Church. *5 miles W on Hwy 622.* (1740-1741) Church where Mary Ball and her family worshiped; many of the tombstones bear the Ball name.

Specialty Lodging

The following lodging establishment is approved by Mobil Travel Guide, but due to its unique and individualized nature has not been given a traditional Mobil Star rating. Included in this listing you may find bed-and-breakfasts, limited-service inns, guest ranches, and other unique hotel properties.

INN AT LEVELFIELD. *10155 Mary Ball Rd, Lancaster (22503). Phone 804/435-6887; fax 804/435-7440. www.innatlevelefields.com.* This 1857 antebellum landmark homestead is situated on 54 acres, with 12 acres of lawn and 42 acres of timberland. The building features a double-tiered portico and four massive chimneys, as well as a 1,000-foot driveway. 6 rooms, 2 story. Complimentary full breakfast. Check-in 3 pm, check-out 11 am. Outdoor pool. **$**

Leesburg (C-7)

See also Arlington County (Ronald Reagan Washtington-National Airport Area), McLean; also see District of Columbia

Founded 1758
Population 28,311
Elevation 352 ft
Area Code 703
Information Loudoun Tourism Council, 108-D South St SE, 20175; phone 703/771-2170 or toll-free 800/752-6118
Web site www.visitloudoun.org

Originally named Georgetown for King George II of England, this town was later renamed Leesburg, probably after Francis Lightfoot Lee, a signer of the Declaration of Independence and a local landowner. Leesburg is located in a scenic area of rolling hills, picturesque rural towns, and Thoroughbred horse farms, where point-to-point racing and steeplechases are popular.

What to See and Do

Ball's Bluff Battlefield. *N via Hwy 15.* One of the smallest national cemeteries in the US marks site of the third armed engagement of the Civil War. On October 21, 1861, four Union regiments suffered catastrophic losses while surrounded by Confederate forces; the Union commander, a US senator and presidential confidant, was killed here along with half his troops, who were either killed, wounded, captured, or drowned while attempting to recross the Potomac River. Oliver Wendell Holmes, Jr., later to become a US Supreme Court justice, was wounded here.

Loudoun Museum. *16 Loudoun St SW, Leesburg (20175). Phone 703/777-7427.* Century-old restored building contains exhibits and memorabilia of the area; audiovisual presentation "A Special Look at Loudoun." Brochures, information about Loudoun County; walking tours; self-guided tour booklets (fee). (Daily; closed Thanksgiving, Dec 25; also Jan) **$**

Morven Park. *Old Waterford Rd. 1 mile N of Leesburg. Phone 703/777-2414.* Originally the residence of Thomas Swann, early Maryland governor, the estate was enlarged upon by Westmoreland Davis, governor of Virginia from 1918 to 1922. The 1,200-acre park includes a 28-room mansion, boxwood gardens, Winmill Carriage Museum with more than 70 horse-drawn vehicles, Museum of Hounds and Hunting with video presentation and artifacts depicting the history of fox hunting, and Morven Park International Equestrian Center (see SPECIAL EVENTS). (Apr-Nov, Fri-Mon afternoons) **$$$**

Oatlands. *20850 Oatlands Plantation Ln, Leesburg (20175). 6 miles S on Hwy 15. Phone 703/777-3174.* (1803) A 261-acre estate; Classical Revival mansion, built by George Carter, was the center of a 5,000-acre plantation; house was partially remodeled in 1827, which was when the front portico was added. Most of the building materials, including bricks and wood, came from or were made on the estate. Interior furnished with American, English, and French antiques; reflects period between 1897 and 1965 when the house was owned by Mr. and Mrs. William Corcoran Eustis, prominent Washingtonians. Formal garden has some of the finest boxwood in US. Farm fields provide equestrian area for races and horse shows. (Early Apr-Dec, daily; closed Thanksgiving, Dec 24-25)

Vineyard and Winery Tours. *Phone toll-free 800/752-6118.* For a list of area winery tours contact the Loudoun Tourism Council, 108-D South St SE.

Waterford. *3 miles NW on Hwy 7, 1/4 mile on Hwy 9, then 2 miles N on Hwy 662. Phone 703/771-2170.* Eighteenth-century Quaker village, designated a National Historic Landmark, has been restored as a residential community. An annual homes tour (first full weekend in Oct) has craft demonstrations, exhibits, traditional music. Waterford Foundation has brochures outlining self-guided walking tours. **$**

Special Events

August Court Days. *108 South St SE, Leesburg (20175). Phone 703/771-2170 or 800/752-6118.* Reenactment of the opening of the 18th-century judicial court. Festivities resemble a country fair with craft demonstrations, games, entertainers on the street. Third weekend in Aug.

Christmas at Oatlands. *20850 Oatlands Plantation Ln, Leesburg (20175).* Candlelight tours, 1800s decorations, refreshments. Mid-Nov-Dec, Sat evenings.

Homes and Gardens Tour. Sponsored by Garden Club of Virginia. Late Apr.

Loudoun Hunt Pony Club Horse Trials. *Morven Park International Equestrian Institute, 4173 Tutt Ln, Leesburg. Phone 703/777-2890.* Competition in combined training: dressage, cross-country, and stadium jumping. Late Mar.

Sheep Dog Trials. *Oatlands, 20850 Oatlands Plantation Ln, Leesburg (20175).* May.

Wine Festival. *Morven Park, 17263 Southern Planter Ln, Leesburg (20176). Phone 202/537-0961.* Many wineries participate; includes seminar for home/commercial wine growers; grape-stomping, waiters' race, jousting tournament, music, wine tastings, awards presentations. Mid-July.

Limited-Service Hotels

★ DAYS INN. *721 E Market St, Leesburg (20176). Phone 703/777-6622; toll-free 800/329-7466; fax 703/777-4119. www.daysinn.com.* 81 rooms, 2 story. Pets accepted; fee. Complimentary continental breakfast. Check-out noon. **$**

★ ★ HOLIDAY INN. *1500 E Market St, Leesburg (20176). Phone 703/771-9200; toll-free 888/850-8545; fax 703/771-1575. www.holiday-inn.com.* 126 rooms, 2 story. Pets accepted, some restrictions. Check-out noon. Restaurant, bar. Fitness room. Outdoor pool. Airport transportation available. Colonial mansion (1773). **$**

Full-Service Resort

★ ★ ★ LANSDOWNE RESORT. *44050 Woodridge Pkwy, Leesburg (20176). Phone 703/729-8400; toll-free 800/541-4801; fax 703/729-4096. www.lansdowneresort.com.* Comprising a nine-story tower and two five-story wings, this hotel offers guests woodland views from the guest rooms. 305 rooms, 9 story. Check-out noon. Restaurant, bar. Children's activity center. Fitness room. Indoor pool, outdoor pool, whirlpool. Golf. Tennis. Airport transportation available. Business center. **$$**

Full-Service Inn

★★★ LEESBURG COLONIAL INN. *19 S King St, Leesburg (20175). Phone 703/777-5000; toll-free 800/392-1332; fax 703/777-7000. www.leesburgcolonialinn.com.* 10 rooms, 2 story. Complimentary full breakfast. Check-in 2 pm, check-out noon. Restaurant. Airport transportation available. Historic building (1759) built of same stone as Capitol in DC. **$**

Specialty Lodgings

The following lodging establishments are approved by Mobil Travel Guide, but due to their unique and individualized nature have not been given a traditional Mobil Star rating. Included in this listing you may find bed-and-breakfasts, limited-service inns, guest ranches, and other unique hotel properties.

LITTLE RIVER INN. *39307 John Mosby Hwy, Aldie (20105). Phone 703/327-6742; fax 703/327-6645. www.aldie.com.* 9 rooms, 2 story. Complimentary full breakfast. Check-in 3 pm, check-out noon. Built in 1810. In foothills of Bull Run Mountains. **$**

NORRIS HOUSE INN. *108 Loudoun St SW, Leesburg (20175). Phone 703/777-1806; toll-free 800/644-1806; fax 703/771-8051. www.norrishouse.com.* Located in the historic district of Leesburg, this rambling colonial house dates from 1760. Filled with antiques and plenty of charm, both the common rooms and guest rooms are comfortable and relaxing. The Stone House Tea Room serves an elegant afternoon tea. 6 rooms, 3 story. Complimentary full breakfast. Check-in 4-8 pm, check-out noon. Airport transportation available. **$**

Restaurants

★★ GREEN TREE. *15 S King St, Leesburg (20175). Phone 703/777-7246; fax 703/777-7000.* American menu. Lunch, dinner, Sun brunch. Authentic 18th-century recipes. Windows open to street. **$$**

★★ LAUREL BRIGADE INN. *20 W Market St, Leesburg (20176). Phone 703/777-1010; fax 703/777-9001.* American menu. Lunch, dinner. Closed Mon. Children's menu. Oldest section dates from 1759; colonial décor, stone walls, fireplace. Outdoor seating. **$$$**

★★ LEESBURG COLONIAL INN. *19 S King St, Leesburg (20175). Phone 703/777-5000; fax 703/777-9001. www.leesburgcolonialinn.com.* American menu. Lunch, dinner. Bar. Children's menu. Outdoor seating. **$$**

Lexington (D-5)

See also Clifton Forge, Natural Bridge

Founded 1777
Population 6,867
Elevation 1,060 ft
Area Code 540
Zip 24450
Information Visitors Bureau, 106 E Washington St; phone 540/463-3777
Web site www.lexingtonvirginia.com

Lexington was home to two of the greatest Confederate heroes: Robert E. Lee and Thomas J. "Stonewall" Jackson. Both are buried here. Sam Houston, Cyrus McCormick, and James Gibbs (inventor of the sewing machine) were born nearby.

Set in rolling country between the Blue Ridge and Allegheny mountains, this town is the seat of Rockbridge County. Lexington is known for attractive homes, trim farms, fine old mansions, and two of the leading educational institutions in the Commonwealth: Washington and Lee University and Virginia Military Institute.

What to See and Do

Goshen Pass. *19 miles NW on Hwy 39.* Scenic mountain gorge formed by Maury River. Memorial to Matthew Fontaine Maury is here.

Lexington Carriage Company. *106 E Washington St, Lexington (24450). Phone 540/463-5647.* Approximately 45-minute narrated horse-drawn carriage tours of historic Lexington. Groups of ten or more by appointment only. (Apr-Oct, daily, weather permitting) Tours depart across street from Visitor Center. **$$$$**

Stonewall Jackson House. *8 E Washington St, Lexington (24450). Phone 540/463-2552. www.stonewalljackson.org.* Only home owned by Confederate General Stonewall Jackson, restored to its appearance of 1859-1861. Many of the furnishings were once owned by Jackson. Interpretive slide presentation and guided tours (1/2 hour). Restored gardens; shop. (Daily; closed holidays) **$$**

Stonewall Jackson Memorial Cemetery. *White and Main sts, Lexington. E side of S Main St.* General Jackson and more than 100 other Confederate soldiers are buried here.

Virginia Horse Center. *487 Maury River Rd, Lexington (24450). Hwy 11 N to Hwy 39 W. Phone 540/463-2194.* Sprawling across nearly 400 acres, the Center provides a versatile site for numerous horse-related functions year-round: shows, clinics, auctions, festivals. Fees vary.

Virginia Military Institute. *On Hwy 11. Phone 540/464-7207. www.vmi.edu.* (1839) (1,300 cadets) State military, engineering, sciences, and arts college. Coeducational since 1997. Stonewall Jackson taught here, as did Matthew Fontaine Maury, famed naval explorer and inventor. George Catlett Marshall, a general of the army and author of the Marshall Plan, was a graduate. Mementos of these men on display in VMI museum (daily; closed Jan 1, Thanksgiving, Dec 24-31). Dress parade (most Fri afternoons, weather permitting). **FREE** Located on the south end of the parade ground is

> **George C. Marshall Museum.** *VMI Parade Ground, Lexington. Faces parade ground. Phone 540/463-7103.* (1964) Displays on life and career of the illustrious military figure and statesman (1880-1959); World War I electric map and recorded narration of World War II; Marshall Plan; gold medallion awarded with his Nobel Prize for Peace (1953). (Daily; closed Jan 1, Thanksgiving, Dec 25) **$$**

Washington and Lee University. *W Washington St, Lexington. Phone 540/463-8400.* (1749) (2,137 students) Liberal arts university situated on an attractive campus with white colonnaded buildings; also includes Washington and Lee Law School. Founded as Augusta Academy in 1749; became Liberty Hall in 1776; name changed to Washington Academy in 1798 after receiving 200 shares of James River Canal Company stock from George Washington, and then to Washington College. General Robert E. Lee served as president from 1865-1870; soon after Lee's death in 1870 it became Washington and Lee University. On campus is

> **Lee Chapel.** Robert E. Lee is entombed here. Also houses Lee family crypt and museum, marble "recumbent statue" of Lee, portions of art collection of Washington and Lee families. Lee's office remains as he left it. (Daily; closed holidays) **FREE**

Special Events

Garden Week in Historic Lexington. *106 E Washington St, Lexington (24450). Phone 540/463-3777.* Tour of homes and gardens in the Lexington, Rockbridge County area. Late Apr.

Holiday in Lexington. *Phone 540/463-3777.* Parade, plays, children's events. Early Dec.

Lime Kiln Arts Theater. *14 S Randolph St, Lexington (24450). Phone 540/463-3074.* Professional theatrical productions and concerts in outdoor theater. Memorial Day-Labor Day.

Limited-Service Hotels

★★ BEST WESTERN INN AT HUNT RIDGE. *Willow Springs Rd, Lexington (24450). Phone 540/464-1500; toll-free 800/464-1501; fax 540/463-5345. www.bestwestern.com.* 100 rooms, 3 story. Pets accepted; fee. Check-out 11 am. Restaurant, bar. Indoor pool, outdoor pool. **$**

★ COMFORT INN. *US 11 and I-64, Lexington (24450). Phone 540/463-7311; toll-free 800/628-1956; fax 540/463-4590. www.choicehotels.com.* 80 rooms, 4 story. Pets accepted, some restrictions; fee. Complimentary continental breakfast. Check-out 11 am. Indoor pool. **$**

★ HOLIDAY INN EXPRESS. *US 11 and I-64, Lexington (24450). Phone 540/463-7351; fax 540/463-5464. www.holiday-inn.com.* 72 rooms, 2 story. Pets accepted; fee. Complimentary continental breakfast. Check-out 11 am. View of mountains. **$**

Full-Service Inn

★ ★ ★ **INN AT UNION RUN.** *325 Union Run, Lexington (24450). Phone 540/463-9715; toll-free 800/528-6466; fax 540/463-3526. www.unionrun.com.* This Federal-style farmhouse was built in 1883, in the heart of the Shenandoah Valley, just 3 miles from historic Lexington, Virginia. In addition to the guest rooms in the main building and carriage house (built in 1992), the inn features a fine dining room. 8 rooms, 2 story. Children over 10 years only. Complimentary full breakfast. Check-in 3 pm, check-out 11 am. Restaurant. **$**

Specialty Lodgings

The following lodging establishments are approved by Mobil Travel Guide, but due to their unique and individualized nature have not been given a traditional Mobil Star rating. Included in this listing you may find bed-and-breakfasts, limited-service inns, guest ranches, and other unique hotel properties.

ALEXANDER WITHROW INN. *3 W Washington St, Lexington (24450). Phone 540/463-2044; fax 540/463-7262. www.lexingtonhistoricinns.com.* 16 rooms, 4 story. Complimentary continental breakfast. Check-in 2 pm, check-out noon. Built in 1809. **$**

HUMMINGBIRD INN. *30 Wood Ln, Goshen (24439). Phone 540/997-9065; toll-free 800/397-3214; fax 540/997-0289. www.hummingbirdinn.com.* Located on the edge of Shenandoah Valley, near Goshen Pass, this historic bed-and-breakfast is made for relaxing. Sit on the wraparound veranda, sleep late in one of the individually decorated rooms, or unwind with a day of trout fishing nearby. 5 rooms, 2 story. Pets accepted, some restrictions; fee. Children over 12 years only. Complimentary full breakfast. Check-in 3 pm, check-out 11 am. **$**

MAPLE HALL COUNTRY INN. *3111 N Lee Hwy, Lexington (24450). Phone 540/463-6693; fax 540/463-2114. www.lexingtonhistoricinns.com.* Plantation house built in 1850; period furnishings. 21 rooms, 3 story. Complimentary continental breakfast. Check-in 2 pm, check-out noon. Restaurant. Outdoor pool. Tennis. **$**

STEELES TAVERN MANOR. *Hwy 11, Steeles Tavern (24476). Phone 540/377-6444; toll-free 800/743-8666; fax 540/377-5937. www.steelestavern.com.* Built in 1916, this Georgian manor home offers guests a relaxing vacation spot with afternoon tea and sherry, nearby trout fishing, and beautiful green landscaping. Guest rooms feature refrigerators with complimentary soda, double Jacuzzis, and snack baskets. 5 rooms, 2 story. Children over 13 years only. Complimentary full breakfast. Check-in 3 pm, check-out 11 am. **$$**

Restaurants

★ **REDWOOD.** *898 N Lee Hwy, Lexington (24450). Phone 540/463-2168.* Seafood, steak menu. Breakfast, lunch, dinner. Closed Dec 25. Children's menu. Family restaurant with home-style cooking; casual atmosphere. **$**

★ ★ ★ **WILLSON-WALKER HOUSE.** *30 N Main St, Lexington (24450). Phone 540/463-3020; fax 540/464-1635. www.willsonwalker.com.* The service is as gracious as one might expect at this historic antebellum mansion. Dress is casual but the food is not. The contemporary southern-style menu includes many elegant variations of American fare. Lunch, dinner, brunch. Closed Sun, Mon; Jan 1, Thanksgiving, Dec 24-25; also Sat lunch Dec-Mar. Children's menu. Outdoor seating. **$$**

Luray (C-6)

See also Basye, Front Royal, Harrisonburg, New Market

Founded 1812
Population 4,871
Elevation 789 ft
Area Code 540
Zip 22835
Information Page County Chamber of Commerce, 46 E Main St; phone 540/743-3915
Web site www.luraypage.com

The name of this town is of French origin; its fame comes from the caverns discovered here in 1878. Situated at the junction of Hwys 211 and 340, Luray is 9 miles away from, and within sight of, Shenandoah National Park (see) and Skyline Drive. Headquarters of the park are here. There are three developed recreation areas north and west of town in Washington and Jefferson national forests.

What to See and Do

Luray Caverns. *970 Hwy 211/340 W. W edge of town on Hwy 211. Phone 540/743-6551.* One of the largest caverns in the east. Huge underground rooms (one is 300 feet wide, 500 feet long, with a 140-foot ceiling) connected by natural corridors and paved walkways are encrusted with colorful rock formations, some delicate as lace, others massive. In one chamber is the world's only "stalacpipe" organ, which produces music of symphonic quality from stone formations. Indirect lighting permits taking of color photos within caverns. Temperature is 54°F. One-hour guided tours start about every 20 minutes. (Daily) **$$$$** Fee includes

> **Car and Carriage Museum.** Exhibits include 140 restored antique cars, carriages, and coaches featuring history of transportation from 1625.

Luray Singing Tower. *970 Hwy 211/340 W. Phone 540/743-6551.* Houses 47-bell carillon; largest bell weighs 7,640 lbs. Features 45-minute recitals by celebrated carillonneur. (June-Aug: Tues, Thurs, and Sun evenings; Mar-May and Sept-Oct: weekend afternoons) In park adjacent to caverns. **FREE**

Luray Zoo. *1087 Hwy 211 W. 1/2 mile W on Hwy 211. Phone 540/743-4113.* Features large reptile collection, exotic animals, and tropical birds; petting zoo; live animal shows; life-sized dinosaur reproductions. Gift shop. (Mid-Apr-Oct, daily) **$$$**

Massanutten One-room School. *In Lawn Park. Contact Chamber of Commerce.* Restored and furnished as it was in the 1800s. Period displays and pictures. (By appointment) **FREE**

Special Events

Mayfest Street Festival. *46 E Main St, Luray (22835).* Entertainment, crafts. Third Sat in May.

Page County Heritage Festival. Arts and crafts exhibits. Self-guided tour of churches and old homes. Columbus Day weekend.

Limited-Service Hotels

★★ BEST WESTERN INTOWN OF LURAY. *410 W Main St, Luray (22835). Phone 540/743-6511; toll-free 800/526-0942; fax 540/743-2917. www.bestwestern.com.* 40 rooms, 2 story. Pets accepted; fee. Check-out noon. Restaurant. Outdoor pool. **$**

★★ BIG MEADOWS LODGE. *Skyline Dr, Luray (22835). Phone 540/999-2221; toll-free 800/999-4714; fax 540/999-2011. www.visitshenandaoh.com.* 92 rooms. Closed Dec-mid-May. Check-out noon. Restaurant, bar. Panoramic view of Shenandoah Valley. **$**

★ DAYS INN. *138 Whispering Hill Rd, Luray (22835). Phone 540/743-4521; fax 540/743-6863. www.daysinn.com.* 101 rooms, 2 story. Check-out noon. Restaurant, bar. Outdoor pool. **$**

★ LURAY CAVERNS MOTEL. *Box 748, Luray (22835). Phone 540/743-4531; fax 540/743-7088. www.luraycaverns.com.* 64 rooms. Outdoor pools. Views of Blue Ridge Mountains. **$**

★★ SKYLAND LODGE. *Skyline Dr, Luray (22835). Phone 540/999-2211; toll-free 800/999-4714; fax 540/999-2231.* 177 rooms. Closed Dec-Mar. Check-out noon. Restaurant, bar. **$**

Full-Service Inn

★★★ JORDAN HOLLOW FARM INN. *326 Hawksbill Park Rd, Stanley (22851). Phone 540/778-2285; toll-free 888/418-7000; fax 540/778-1759. www.jordanhollow.com.* Find serene relaxation at this restored colonial horse farm. Some guest rooms feature beautiful vistas of the Blue Ridge Mountains. The Shenandoah Valley location offers many outdoor recreations, not the least of which is simply taking in the scenery. 20 rooms, 2 story. Complimentary full breakfast. Check-in 3 pm, check-out noon. Restaurant, bar. **$**

Specialty Lodgings

The following lodging establishments are approved by Mobil Travel Guide, but due to their unique and individualized nature have not been given a traditional Mobil Star rating. Included in this listing you may find bed-and-breakfasts, limited-service inns, guest ranches, and other unique hotel properties.

CABINS AT BROOKSIDE. *2978 Hwy 211 E, Luray (22835). Phone 540/743-5698; toll-free 800/299-2655; fax 540/743-1326. www.brooksidecabins.com.* The privacy and seclusion of your own log cabin is the draw to this vacation development located 4 1/2 miles from the entrance to Skyline Drive. The cabins have a plush country décor, front porches, and are set into the woods. A cozy restaurant on the property serves homestyle food. 9 rooms. Check-out noon. **$**

MAYNEVIEW BED AND BREAKFAST. *439 Mechanic St, Luray (22835). Phone 540/743-7921; fax 540/743-1191. www.mayneview.com.* This lovely inn is nestled in the heart of the Shenandoah Valley and has a wonderful wraparound porch. Visitors can take day trips to the famous Luray Caverns, the New Market Battlefield, and several antique shops. 5 rooms, 3 story. Complimentary full breakfast. Check-in 3 pm, check-out noon. Whirlpool. Victorian building (1865). **$$**

WOODRUFF HOUSE BED AND BREAKFAST. *330 Mechanic St, Luray (22835). Phone 540/743-1494; fax 540/743-1722.* Three 1800s Victorian houses make up this bed-and-breakfast located near many local attractions including the Shenandoah National Park, Luray Caverns, and the George Washington National Forest. 5 rooms, 3 story. Children over 10 years only. Check-in 3 pm, check-out noon. **$$$**

Restaurants

★ BROOKSIDE. *2978 Hwy 211 E, Luray (22835). Phone 540/743-5698; fax 540/743-1326. www.brooksidecabins.com.* Seafood, steak menu. Breakfast, lunch, dinner. Closed mid-Dec-mid-Jan. Children's menu. **$**

★ ★ PARKHURST. *2547 Hwy 211 W, Luray (22835). Phone 540/743-6009; fax 540/743-7009.* Seafood, steak menu. Lunch, dinner. Closed holidays. Bar. **$$**

Lynchburg (E-6)

See also Appomattox Court House National Historical Park, Brookneal

Settled 1757
Population 65,269
Elevation 795 ft
Area Code 804
Information Visitors Information Center, 12th and Church sts, 24504; phone 804/847-1811 or toll-free 800/732-5821

Lynchburg is perched on hills overlooking the James River, which was for many years its means of growth. Today, the city is home to more than 3,000 businesses and diversified industries. Educational institutions located here include Lynchburg College, Randolph-Macon Women's College, and Liberty University.

One of the first buildings in the town was a ferry house built by John Lynch. The same enterprising young man later built a tobacco warehouse, probably the first one in the country. During the Civil War, Lynchburg was important as a supply base and hospital town. In June 1864, General Jubal A. Early successfully defended the town from an attack by Union forces. More than 2,200 Confederates are buried in the Confederate Cemetery, located in the Old City Cemetery.

What to See and Do

Anne Spencer House. *1313 Pierce St, Lynchburg (24501). Phone 434/845-1313.* House of noted poet, only black woman and only Virginian to be included in the *Norton Anthology of Modern American and British Poetry.* On grounds is Spencer's writing cottage "Edan Kraal." Many dignitaries have visited here. Museum with artifacts, memorabilia, period antique furnishings; formal garden. (House by appointment; gardens daily) **$$**

Blackwater Creek Natural Area. *In center of city.* Ruskin Freer Nature Preserve (115 acres) includes trails with plants; athletic area; bikeway winds past wildflower area and historical sites, ending downtown; Creekside Trunk Trail, natural grass trail with typical Piedmont species of plants, moist ravines, north-facing rocky bluffs. (Daily) **FREE**

Fort Early. *Memorial and Fort aves, Lynchburg.* Defense earthwork for Lynchburg's closest battle during the Civil War. Confederates under General Jubal A. Early turned back forces under General David Hunter in 1864. (Daily) **FREE**

Jefferson's Poplar Forest. *Poplar Forest Dr and Fox Hall Rd, Forest. SW of Lynchburg on Hwy 221, then left on Hwy 811 and left again on Hwy 661 in Bedford County. Phone 434/525-1806.* Designed and built by Thomas Jefferson as a personal retreat; begun in 1806. Restoration in progress; house unfurnished. (Apr-Nov, daily; closed Thanksgiving) **$$$**

Old Court House Museum. *901 Court St, Lynchburg (24504). Phone 434/847-1459.* (1855) Restored to original Greek Revival appearance. Three galleries have exhibits on early history of the area, highlighting Quaker settlement and role of tobacco; restored mid-19th-century courtroom. (Daily; closed holidays) **$**

Pest House Medical Museum. *Old City Cemetery, 4th and Taylor sts, Lynchburg. Phone 434/847-1465.* The 1840s white frame medical office of Quaker physician Dr. John Jay Terrell has been joined with Pest House quarantine hospital to typify the standard of medicine during the late 1800s. Original medical instruments include operating table, hypodermic needle, clinical thermometer, and chloroform mask. Period furnishings on one side duplicate Dr. Terrell's office during the Civil War; other side represents quarantine hospital for Confederate soldiers in which Dr. Terrell volunteered to assume responsibility. Window displays with audio description. Tours (by appointment). (Daily) **FREE**

Point of Honor. *112 Cabell St, Lynchburg (24504). Phone 804/847-1459.* (1815) Restored mansion on Daniel's Hill above the James River, built by Dr. George Cabell, Sr., physician to Patrick Henry. Federalist style with octagon bay facade and finely crafted interior woodwork; period furnishings; gardens and grounds being restored. (Daily; closed holidays) **$$**

Randolph-Macon Women's College. *2500 Rivermont Ave, Lynchburg (24503). Phone 434/947-8000.* (1891) 748 women. A 100-acre campus on historic Rivermont Ave near James River. First college for women in the South granted a Phi Beta Kappa chapter. Campus is interesting mixture of architecture including Vincent Kling design for Houston Chapel. Tours (by appointment). On campus is

Maier Museum of Art. *Phone 804/947-8136.* Collection is representative of 19th- and 20th-century American painting. Artists include Thomas Hart Benton, Edward Hicks, Winslow Homer, James McNeil Whistler, Mary Cassatt, and Georgia O'Keeffe. Changing exhibits. (Academic year, Tues-Sun afternoons) **FREE**

Riverside Park. *Rivermont Ave.* (Daily) **FREE** In park is

Packet Boat *Marshall.* Mounted on a stone base, the boat carried the remains of Stonewall Jackson home to Lexington; for many years packets were the principal mode of transportation along the James River and Kanawha Canal.

South River Meeting House. *5810 Fort Ave, Lynchburg (24502). Phone 804/239-2548.* Completed in 1798, the stone building remained the site of Quaker worship and activity until the 1840s. John Lynch, founder of Lynchburg, and other early leaders of community are buried in adjacent historic cemetery. (Daily; closed holidays) **FREE**

Limited-Service Hotels

★ ★ DAYS INN. *3320 Candlers Mountain Rd, Lynchburg (24502). Phone 434/847-8655; toll-free 800/787-3297; fax 434/846-3297. www.daysinn.com.* 131 rooms, 5 story. Check-out noon. Restaurant. Outdoor pool. Airport transportation available. **$**

★ ★ HOLIDAY INN. *601 Main St, Lynchburg (24505). Phone 434/528-2500; fax 434/528-0062. www.holiday-inn.com.* 243 rooms, 8 story. Pets accepted; fee. Check-out noon. Restaurant, bar. Fitness room. Outdoor pool. Airport transportation available. **$**

★ HOLIDAY INN EXPRESS. *5600 Seminole Ave, Lynchburg (24501). Phone 434/237-7771; fax 434/239-0659. www.holiday-inn.com.* 104 rooms, 3 story. Complimentary continental breakfast. Check-out noon. Outdoor pool. **$**

★ ★ HOWARD JOHNSON. *PO Box 735, Madison Heights (24572). Phone 804/845-7041; fax 804/845-4718. www.hojo.com.* 70 rooms, 2 story. Check-out noon. Restaurant. Outdoor pool, children's pool. Airport transportation available. **$**

Full-Service Hotel

★ ★ ★ RADISSON HOTEL LYNCHBURG. *2900 Candlers Mountain Rd, Lynchburg (24502). Phone 434/237-6333; toll-free 800/221-4982; fax 434/237-4277. www.hilton.com.* Located at the foot of the Blue Ridge Mountains, this hotel sits on a unique

10-acre landscaped and wooded spread. The Natural Bridge, one of the seven natural wonders of the world, is easily accessible. 168 rooms, 5 story. Check-out 11 am. Restaurant, bar. Fitness room. Indoor pool, whirlpool. Airport transportation available. Business center. **$**

Specialty Lodging

The following lodging establishment is approved by Mobil Travel Guide, but due to its unique and individualized nature has not been given a traditional Mobil Star rating. Included in this listing you may find bed-and-breakfasts, limited-service inns, guest ranches, and other unique hotel properties.

1880'S MADISON HOUSE. *413 Madison St, Lynchburg (24504). Phone 434/528-1503. www. madisonhousebb.com.* This 1880s restored Victorian bed-and-breakfast is located in the Garland Hill historic district. An ornate, cast iron front porch welcomes guests, and the house features antiques and a library full of books including many on the Civil War. Guests can relax in the garden with a good book and refreshments. 4 rooms, 2 story. Complimentary full breakfast. Check-in 3-6 pm, check-out 11 am. Airport transportation available. **$**

Restaurants

★ ★ CROWN STERLING. *6120 Fort Ave, Lynchburg (24502). Phone 434/239-7744.* American menu. Dinner. Closed Sun; holidays. **$$**

★ ★ ★ SACHIKO'S PORTERHOUSE. *126 Old Graves Mill Rd, Lynchburg (24502). Phone 804/237-5655; fax 804/237-2934.* This restaurant has been in business for 25 years. American menu. Dinner. Closed Sun; holidays. Bar. **$$$**

★ T. C. TROTTER'S. *2496 Rivermont Ave, Lynchburg (24503). Phone 434/846-3545.* American menu. Lunch, dinner. Closed Mon; Thanksgiving, Dec 25. Bar. Children's menu. Outdoor seating. **$$**

Madison (D-7)

See also Charlottesville

Restaurant

★ ★ BERTINE'S NORTH CARIBBEAN. *206 S Main St, Madison (22727). Phone 540/948-3463.* Caribbean menu. Dinner. Closed Tues-Thurs; also Easter, Dec 25. Outdoor seating. **$$**

Manassas (C-8)

See also Arlington County (Ronald Reagan Washington-National Airport Area), Fairfax, Falls Church, Triangle; also see District of Columbia

Population 35,135
Elevation 321 ft
Area Code 703
Information Prince William County/Manassas Conference & Visitors Bureau, 14420 Bristow Rd, 20112; phone 703/792-4254 or toll-free 800/432-1792
Web site www.visitpwc.com

Though the Native Americans who had lived in this area for thousands of years were driven out under a treaty in 1722, settlement remained concentrated along the Potomac River until the coming of the railroad in 1858. The Manassas rail junction was vital to the South, and many troops were stationed along this line of communication. Control of this junction led to two major battles nearby (see MANASSAS (BULL RUN) NATIONAL BATTLEFIELD PARK).

What to See and Do

Kastle Greens Golf Club. *11446 Rogues Rd, Midland (22728). Phone toll-free 877/283-4653. www. kastlegreens.com.* Built in 1998, Kastle Greens is within an hour's drive of both Washington, DC and Richmond. Walking the more than 6,700 yards from the blue tees may make this course seem like it's for big hitters, but make no mistake that this is also a target golf course, with several doglegs and possible blind shots if your tee shot does not land where it should. A challenge, to be sure. **$$$$**

The Manassas Museum. *9101 Prince William St, Manassas (20110). Phone 703/368-1873.* Museum features collections dealing with Northern Virginia Piedmont history from prehistoric to modern times, with special emphasis on Civil War. (Tues-Sun; closed holidays) **$$**

Special Event

Prince William County Fair. *9101 Prince William St, Manassas (20110). Phone 703/368-0173.* Carnival, entertainment, tractor pull, exhibits, contests. Mid-Aug.

Limited-Service Hotel

★★ HOLIDAY INN. *10800 Vandor Ln, Manassas (20109). Phone 703/335-0000; fax 703/361-8440. www.holiday-inn.com.* 158 rooms, 5 story. Pets accepted, some restrictions; fee. Complimentary continental breakfast. Check-in 3 pm, check-out noon. Restaurant, bar. Fitness room. Indoor pool, outdoor pool. Near Manassas (Bull Run) Battlefield. **$**

Restaurants

★★★ CARMELLO'S AND LITTLE PORTUGAL. *9108 Center St, Manassas (20110). Phone 703/368-5522; fax 703/369-9874. www.carmellos.com.* Italian and Portuguese cuisine are beautifully combined to create generous contemporary dishes. The restaurant's intimate atmosphere makes it a popular spot for special occasions. Italian, Portuguese menu. Lunch, dinner. Closed holidays. Bar. **$$**

★★ JAKE'S. *9412 Main St, Manassas (20110). Phone 703/330-1534; fax 703/335-6934. www.jakesofmanassas.com.* American menu. Lunch, dinner. Bar. Outdoor seating. **$$**

★★★ PANINO. *9116 Mathis Ave, Manassas (20110). Phone 703/335-2566; fax 703/257-6394.* Although off the beaten track, this chef-owned and operated restaurant has, for the past ten years, offered perhaps the best best regional Italian cuisine outside the Beltway. Only the freshest of ingredients are used. Italian menu. Lunch, dinner. Closed Sun; holidays. Reservations recommended. **$$**

Manassas (Bull Run) National Battlefield Park (C-7)

See also Falls Church, Manassas

(SW of Washington, DC)

Web site www.nps.gov/mana/

This 5,000-acre park was the scene of two major Civil War battles. More than 26,000 men were killed or wounded here in struggles for control of a strategically important railroad junction. The first major land battle of the war was fought here on July 21, 1861 between poorly trained volunteer troops from both North and South. The battle finally evolved into a struggle for Henry Hill, where "Stonewall" Jackson earned his nickname. With the outcome in doubt, Confederate reinforcements arrived by railroad from the Shenandoah Valley and turned the battle into a rout.

Thirteen months later (August 28-30, 1862), in the second battle of Manassas, General Robert E. Lee outmaneuvered and defeated Union General John Pope and cleared the way for a Confederate invasion of Maryland. (Daily; closed Dec 25)

What to See and Do

Chinn House Ruins. The house served as a field hospital in both engagements and marked the left of the Confederate line at First Manassas; also the scene of Longstreet's counterattack at Second Manassas.

Dogan House. An original structure at Groveton, a village around which the battle of Second Manassas was fought.

Stone Bridge. Where Union artillery opened the Battle of First Manassas; it afforded an avenue of escape for the Union troops after both First and Second Manassas.

Stone House. *Phone 703/361-1339.* Originally a tavern (circa 1848), used as field hospital in both battles. (Summer, daily)

Unfinished Railroad. Fully graded railroad bed, never completed, behind which Stonewall Jackson's men were positioned during the second battle.

Visitor Center. *6511 Sudley Rd, Manassas (20109). On Henry Hill, just N of I-66 off Hwy 234. Phone 703/361-1339. www.nps.gov/mana/.* Hill affords view of much of the first battlefield. Information; self-guided tours start here (walking tour of First Manassas, directions for driving tour of Second Manassas). Markers throughout park explain various aspects of battles. Ranger-conducted tours (summer). In the same building is

Battlefield Museum. Exhibits reflect incidents of battles; audiovisual presentations offer orientation. (Daily; closed Dec 25)

Marion (F-3)

See also Abingdon, Wytheville

Founded 1835
Population 6,349
Elevation 2,178 ft
Area Code 540
Zip 24354
Information Smyth County Chamber of Commerce, 124 W Main St, 24354; phone 540/783-3161
Web site www.marionva.org

This popular vacation spot is surrounded by the George Washington and Jefferson national forests, abounding in game and birds, near a state park, and high enough to promise an invigorating climate. The seat of Smyth County, it was named for General Francis Marion, known during the American Revolution as the "Swamp Fox."

What to See and Do

George Washington and Jefferson National Forests. (See HARRISONBURG) SE of town via Hwy 16 is the

Mount Rogers National Recreation Area. *3714 Hwy 16, Marion (24354). Phone 276/783-5196.* A 140,000-acre area that includes Mount Rogers, the state's highest point (5,729 feet), mile-high open meadows known as "balds," and a great variety of animals and plants. Swimming, fishing; hunting, camping (fee at some areas), four visitor centers, approximately 400 miles of hiking, bicycle, and bridle trails. Mount Rogers Scenic Byway (auto); Virginia Creeper Trail (hikers, bicycles, horses) follows an abandoned railroad grade through spectacular river gorges. Adjacent to New River Trails State Park (see ABINGDON). Visitor Center (Daily all year) (Mid-May-Mid-Sept: daily; rest of year: Mon-Fri) Some fees.

Hungry Mother State Park. *2854 Park Blvd, Marion (24354). 3 miles N on Hwy 16. Phone 276/781-7400.* More than 2,180 acres amid the mountains with a 108-acre lake; panoramic views. Swimming beach, bathhouse, fishing, boating (rentals, launching, electric motors only); hiking, self-guided trails, picnicking, restaurant, concession, tent and trailer sites (electrical hookups, late Mar-Dec), cabins (year round). Hilltop visitor center, interpretive programs. **$**

Special Events

Chilhowie Apple Festival. Mid-Sept.

Hungry Mother Arts and Crafts Festival. *Hungry Mother State Park, 2854 Park Blvd, Marion (24354).* Mid-July.

Whitetop Ramp Festival. Mid-May.

Limited-Service Hotel

★★ BEST WESTERN MARION. *1424 N Main St, Marion (24354). Phone 276/783-6031; toll-free 800/528-1234; fax 276/782-9990. www.bestwestern.com.* 79 rooms, 2 story. Complimentary continental breakfast. Check-out noon. Restaurant, bar. Outdoor pool. **$**

Martinsville (F-5)

See also Danville

Founded 1793
Population 15,416
Elevation 1,020 ft
Area Code 540
Information Martinsville-Henry County Chamber of Commerce, 115 Broad St, PO Box 709, 24114; phone 540/632-6401
Web site www.mhcchamber.com

Martinsville was named for Joseph Martin, a pioneer who settled here in 1773. Henry County takes its name from Patrick Henry, who lived here. When Henry County Court first opened in October 1776, 640 residents pledged an oath of allegiance to the United States; 40 refused to renounce allegiance to England. Located near the beautiful Blue Ridge Mountains, this community is home to Bassett Furniture and E. I. du Pont de Nemours.

What to See and Do

Blue Ridge Farm Museum. *Hwy 40, Ferrum. Phone 540/365-4415.* Presents the heritage of mountain region through reconstructed farmsteads and "folklife galleries." Authentic buildings from 1800 German heritage farm, include log house, kitchen, blacksmith shop, and barn. Costumed interpreters demonstrate farm and household chores. Special events (fees). (Mid-May-mid-Aug: weekends; rest of year: by appointment) **$$**

Fairy Stone State Park. *Hwy 346, Stuart. 21 miles NW via Hwys 220, 57, 346. Phone 276/930-2424.* Consists of 4,570 acres, with a 168-acre lake adjoining Philpott Reservoir. Nestled in the foothills of the Blue Ridge Mountains, this park is named for the "fairy stones" (staurolites) found near the southern tip of its boundary. Swimming beach, bathhouse, fishing, boating (launch, rentals, electric motors only); hiking and bicycle trails, picnic shelters, concession, cafe, tent and trailer sites (dump station, electrical hookups), cabins (Mar-Dec). Visitor center, evening programs. (Daily)

Philpott Lake. *1058 Philpott Lake Rd, Martinsville (24055). Just NE of Fairy Stone State Park. Phone 276/629-2703.* State's fourth-largest lake, formed by Philpott Dam, a US Army Corps of Engineers project. Swimming, skin diving, waterskiing, boating, fishing; hunting, hiking, picnicking; four camping areas (Apr-Oct), one area free, some fees.

Virginia Museum of Natural History. *1001 Douglas Ave, Martinsville (24112). Phone 276/666-8600.* State museum focuses on preservation, study, and interpretation of Virginia's natural heritage. Features visual and hands-on exhibits; includes a computer-animated triceratops dinosaur and a life-size ground sloth model. Special events during the year include Earth Day (Apr) and Virginia Indian Festival (Sept). (Mon-Sat; closed holidays) **FREE**

Special Events

Blue Ridge Folklife Festival. *Blue Ridge Farm Museum, Martinsville. Phone 540/365-4415.* Gospel, blues, and string band music; traditional regional crafts; regional foods; quilt show, antique autos, steam and gas-powered farm equipment. Sports events include horse-pulling and log-skidding contests, coon dog swimming and treeing contests. Late Oct.

Stock car races. *Martinsville Speedway. 3 miles S. Phone 540/956-3151.* Miller Genuine Draft 300, mid-Mar. Hanes 500, late Apr. Goody's 500, late Sept. Taco Bell 300, mid-Oct.

Limited-Service Hotel

★ ★ BEST WESTERN MARTINSVILLE INN. *1755 Virginia Ave, Martinsville (24112). Phone 276/632-5611; toll-free 800/528-1234; fax 276/632-1168. www.bestwestern.com.* 97 rooms, 2 story. Pets accepted, some restrictions. Check-out noon. Restaurant, bar. Fitness room. Outdoor pool, children's pool. **$**

McLean (C-8)

See also Arlington County (Ronald Reagan Washington-National Airport Area), Fairfax, Falls Church, Leesburg; Tysons Corner; also see District of Columbia, Rockville, MD

Population 38,929
Elevation 300 ft
Area Code 703
Information Fairfax County Convention & Visitors Bureau, 8300 Boone Blvd, Suite 450, Tyson's Corner 22182; phone 703/790-3329 or toll-free 800/7-FAIRFAX
Web site www.visitfairfax.org

What to See and Do

Claude Moore Colonial Farm. *6310 Georgetown Pike, McLean (22101). 2 miles E on Hwy 193 (Georgetown Pike). Phone 703/442-7557. At Turkey Run.* Demonstration of 1770s low-income working farm; costumed interpreters work with crops and animals using 18th-century techniques. (Apr-mid-Dec, Wed-Sun weather permitting; closed Thanksgiving) **$**

Colvin Run Mill Historic Site. *10017 Colvin Run Rd, Great Falls (22066). 3 miles W via Hwy 123, then 5 miles NW via Hwy 7, on Colvin Run Rd. Phone 703/759-2771.* Tours of historical gristmill. General store, miller's house exhibit, barn and grounds (free). (Mar-Dec: Mon and Wed-Sun; rest of year: weekends; closed Jan 1, Thanksgiving, Dec 25) **$$**

Great Falls Park. *George Washington Memorial Pkwy, McLean (22101). Phone 703/285-2965. www.nps.gov/gwmp/grfa.* Spectacular natural beauty is only 15 miles from the nation's capital at Great Falls Park, where the usually peaceful Potomac River narrows into a series of dramatically cascading rapids and 20-foot waterfalls before heading through Mather Gorge. Enjoy the view from a scenic overlook, and then explore some of the park's 15 miles of trails, which take you past the remains of the Patowmack Canal, part of an 18th-century engineering project backed by George Washington, among others. (Daily 7 am-dark; closed Dec 25) **$**

Tysons Corner Center. *1961 Chain Bridge Rd, McLean (22102). Phone 703/893-9400; toll-free 888/289-7667. www.shoptysons.com.* More than 250 stores, including Norstrom, Bloomingdale's, and L.L.Bean. (Mon-Sat 10 am-9:30 pm, Sun 11 am-6 pm; closed Thanksgiving, Dec 25)

Limited-Service Hotel

★★ **HOLIDAY INN.** *1960 Chain Bridge Rd, McLean (22102). Phone 703/893-2100; fax 703/356-8218. www.holiday-inn.com.* 316 rooms, 9 story. Check-out 1 pm. Restaurant, bar. Fitness room. Indoor pool, whirlpool. Airport transportation available. Business center. **$$**

Restaurants

★★ **CAFE OGGI.** *6671 Old Dominion Dr, McLean (22101). Phone 434/442-7360.* Italian menu. Lunch, dinner. Closed holidays. Reservations recommended. **$$**

★★ **CAFE TAJ.** *1379 Beverly Rd, McLean (22101). Phone 703/827-0444; fax 703/827-2707.* Indian menu. Lunch, dinner. Closed July 4. Bar. Outdoor seating. **$$**

★★ **DA DOMENICO.** *1992 Chain Bridge Rd, McLean (22102). Phone 703/790-9000.* Italian menu. Lunch, dinner. Closed Sun; holidays. Bar. Reservations recommended. **$$**

★★★ **DANTE.** *1148 Walker Rd, Great Falls (22066). Phone 703/759-3131; fax 703/759-0457. www.danterestaurant.com.* A historic Victorian home is the setting for this restaurant. Italian menu. Lunch, dinner. Closed holidays. Bar. Children's menu. Converted country house. Reservations recommended. Outdoor seating. **$$$**

★★ **J GILBERT'S STEAKHOUSE.** *6930 Old Dominion Dr, McLean (22101). Phone 703/893-1034; fax 703/893-1036.* Seafood, steak menu. Lunch, dinner, Sun brunch. Closed Dec 25. Bar. Children's menu. Outdoor seating. **$$**

★★ **J. R.'S GOODTIMES.** *8130 Watson St, McLean (22102). Phone 703/821-0546; fax 703/356-9426. www.jrsbeef.com.* Seafood menu. Lunch, dinner. Closed holidays. Bar. Reservations recommended. **$$**

★★ **KAZAN.** *6813 Redmond Dr, McLean (22101). Phone 703/734-1960; fax 703/734-9636.* Turkish menu. Lunch, dinner. Closed Sun. Children's menu. **$$**

★★★ **L'AUBERGE CHEZ FRANCOIS.** *332 Springvale Rd, Great Falls (22066). Phone 703/759-3800. www.laubergechezfrancois.com.* Rich, hearty dishes at this Alsatian-themed restaurant are served by dirndl-clad waitresses and waiters in red vests. French menu. Dinner. Closed Mon; Jan 1, July 4, Dec 25. Jacket required. Reservations recommended. Outdoor seating. **$$$**

★★★ **LE RELAIS.** *1025-I Seneca Rd, Great Falls (22066). Phone 703/444-4060. www.lerelaisonline.com.* French menu. Lunch, dinner. Closed Mon. Bar. Outdoor seating. **$$$**

★★ **PULCINELLA.** *6852 Old Dominion Dr, McLean (22101). Phone 703/893-7777; fax 703/893-0208. www.pulcinella.com.* Italian menu. Lunch, dinner. Closed Thanksgiving, Dec 25. Bar. **$$**

★★★ **SERBIAN CROWN.** *1141 Walker Rd, Great Falls (22066). Phone 703/759-4150; fax 703/759-1010. www.serbiancrown.com.* Russian and French cuisine are fearlessly combined to create an elegant menu. Russian menu. Lunch, dinner. Bar. Reservations recommended. Outdoor seating. **$$$**

★★ **TACHIBANA.** *6715 Lowell Ave, McLean (22101). Phone 703/847-1771. www.j-netusa.com/com/tachibana/.* Japanese menu. Lunch, dinner. Closed holidays. Circular dining room. **$$$**

Monterey (D-5)

See also Staunton, Warm Springs

Population 158
Elevation 2,881 ft
Area Code 540
Zip 24465
Information Highland County Chamber of Commerce, PO Box 223; phone 540/468-2550

Special Event

Highland County Maple Festival. *Phone 540/468-2550.* Tours of sugar camps producing maple syrup and maple sugar products. Juried craft show; food, entertainment. Mid-Mar.

Full-Service Inn

★★★ **HIGHLAND INN.** *PO Box 40, Monterey (24465). Phone 540/468-2143; toll-free 888/466-4682; fax 540/468-3143. www.highland-inn.com.* 18 rooms, 3 story. Check-in 2 pm, check-out 11 am. Restaurant, bar. Victorian building furnished with period antiques. Built in 1904. **$**

Montross (D-8)

See also George Washington Birthplace National Monument

Population 315
Elevation 149 ft
Area Code 804
Zip 22520

What to See and Do

Stratford Hall Plantation. *Hwys 3 E and 214 (22558). 6 miles N on Hwy 3 to Lerty, then E on Hwy 214. Phone 804/493-8038.* Boyhood home of Richard Henry Lee and Francis Lightfoot Lee and birthplace of General Robert E. Lee. Center of restored, working plantation is monumental Georgian house built circa 1735, famous for its uniquely grouped chimney stacks. Interiors span approximately a 100-year period and feature a Federal-era parlor and neoclassical paneling in the Great Hall. Flanking dependencies include kitchen, plantation office, and gardener's house. Boxwood garden; 18th- and 19th-century carriages; working mill; visitor center with museum, video presentations. Plantation luncheon (daily). (Daily; closed Jan 1, Thanksgiving, Dec 25) **$$$**

Westmoreland State Park. *Hwy 347. 5 miles NW on Hwy 3, then N on Hwy 347. Phone 804/493-8821.* Approximately 1,300 acres on Potomac River. Sand beach, swimming pool, bathhouse, fishing, boating (ramp, rentals); hiking trails, picnicking, playground, concession, camping, tent and trailer sites (Mar-Nov; dump station, electrical hookups), cabins (Mar-Dec). Visitor center, evening programs.

Mount Vernon

See also Alexandria, Fairfax, Springfield; also see District of Columbia

What to See and Do

Gristmill. *3 miles W on Hwy 235. Phone 703/780-3383.* This mill was reconstructed in 1930 on the original foundation of a mill George Washington operated on the Dogue Run. Visitor center, programs. (Memorial Day-Labor Day, daily) **$**

Potomac Spirit. *Pier 4, 6th and Water sts, Washington (20024). Pier 4. Phone 202/923-4354; toll-free 866/211-3811. www.spiritcitycruises.com.* Offers round-trip, Potomac River cruises from Washington, DC to Mount Vernon. The five-hour excursion is sufficient for a complete tour of the house, gardens, and tomb (late Mar-early June: one trip daily; early June-late Aug: two trips daily). **$$$$**

Woodlawn Plantation. *9000 Richmond Hwy, Alexandria (22309). 3 miles W of George Washington Pkwy on Hwy 1. Phone 703/780-4000. www.woodlawn1805.org.* (1800-1805) In 1799, George Washington gave 2,000 acres of land as a wedding present to Eleanor Parke Custis, his foster daughter, who married his nephew, Major Lawrence Lewis. Dr. William Thornton, first architect of the US Capitol, then designed this mansion. The Lewises entertained such notables as Andrew Jackson, Henry Clay, and the Marquis de Lafayette. The house was restored in the early 1900s and later became the residence of a US senator; 19th-century period rooms; many original furnishings. Formal gardens. (Mar-Dec, daily; closed Jan-Feb, Thanksgiving, Dec 25) A National Trust for Historic Preservation property. **$$** Also here is

Frank Lloyd Wright's Pope-Leighey House. (1940) Erected in Falls Church in 1940, the house was disassembled (due to the construction of a new highway) and rebuilt at the present site in 1964. Built of cypress, brick, and glass, the house is an example of Wright's "Usonian" structures, which he proposed as a prototype of affordable housing for Depression-era middle-income families; original Wright-designed furniture. (Mar-Dec, daily; closed Jan-Feb, Thanksgiving, Dec 25) A National Trust for Historic Preservation property. Combination ticket ($$$) for both houses available. **$$**

Restaurant

★★ MOUNT VERNON INN. *On the grounds of Mount Vernon, Mount Vernon (22121). Phone 703/780-0011; fax 703/780-1704.* Lunch, dinner. Bar. Children's menu. Waiters in colonial costume. Hand-painted murals of colonial scenes. **$$**

Natural Bridge (D-5)

See also Lexington

Founded 1774
Population 200
Elevation 1,078 ft
Area Code 540
Zip 24578
Information Natural Bridge of Virginia, Hwys 11 and 130, PO Box 57; phone 540/291-2121 or toll-free 800/533-1410
Web site www.naturalbridgeva.com

Native Americans worshiped at the stone bridge nature formed across a deep gorge; town and county were both named after it. The limestone arch, 215 feet high, 90 feet long, and 150 feet wide in some places, attracted the interest of Thomas Jefferson, who purchased the bridge and 157 surrounding acres from King George III for 20 shillings, about $2.49, in 1774. Fully appreciative of this natural wonder, Jefferson built a cabin for visitors and installed caretakers. His guest book reads like a colonial "Who's Who." Surveyed by George Washington and painted by many famous artists, the bridge easily accommodates Hwy 11. The Glenwood Ranger District of the Washington and Jefferson National Forests has its office in Natural Bridge.

What to See and Do

Cave Mountain Lake Recreation Area. *7 miles S via Hwy 130, right on Hwy 759, then right on Forest Service Rd 781 in George Washington and Jefferson national forests. Phone 540/291-2189.* Swimming; picnicking, camping (fee). (May-Oct) **$$**

Natural Bridge. *Hwys 11 and 130. I-81, exit 175 or 180. Phone 540/291-2121; toll-free 800/533-1410.* Self-guided tours (one hour). (Daily) **$$$** Ticket includes entrance to

Caverns of Natural Bridge. *Hwy 11 and I-81, Natural Bridge.* More than 300 feet below ground on three levels; streams, hanging gardens of formations, flowstone cascade, totem pole, colossal dome, and more. One-mile guided tour (one hour). (Mar-Nov, daily) **$$$**

Drama of Creation. Musical presentation, viewed from beneath Natural Bridge, includes light show cast under and across arch. (Nightly)

Natural Bridge Wax Museum. *70 Wert Faulkner Hwy, Natural Bridge. Hwys 11 and 130.* Wax figures depicting local history; self-guided factory tours. (Daily) **$$$**

Natural Bridge Zoo. *Hwy 11. I-81 between exits 175 and 180. Phone 540/291-2420.* State's largest and most complete zoo with over 400 reptiles, birds, and mammals. Petting area; safari shop; picnic grounds. (Mar-Nov, daily) **$$$**

Limited-Service Hotels

★★ NATURAL BRIDGE INN & CONFERENCE CENTER. *Hwy 11, Natural Bridge (24578). Phone 540/291-2121; toll-free 800/*

533-1410; fax 540/291-1551. www.naturalbridgeva .com. 180 rooms. Check-out noon. Restaurant, bar. Indoor pool. Tennis. **$**

★★ WATTSTULL COURT. *130 Arcadia Rd, Buchanan (24066). Phone 540/254-1551.* 26 rooms. Pets accepted, some restrictions; fee. Check-out 11 am. Restaurant. Pool, children's pool. Panoramic view of Shenandoah Valley. **$**

New Market (C-6)

See also Basye, Harrisonburg, Luray

Settled 1761
Population 1,637
Elevation 1,060 ft
Area Code 540
Zip 22844
Information Shenandoah Valley Travel Association, PO Box 1040; phone 540/740-3132
Web site www.svta.org

New Market, situated in the Shenandoah Valley, gained its niche in Virginia history on May 15, 1864 when, in desperation, Confederate General Breckinridge ordered the cadets from Lexington's Virginia Military Institute to join the battle against the forces of General Franz Sigel. The oldest was just 20, but they entered the fray fearlessly, taking prisoners and capturing a battery. Their heroism inspired the Confederate defeat of Sigel's seasoned troops.

What to See and Do

Bedrooms of America. *9386 Congress St, New Market (22844). I-81 exit 264. Phone 540/740-3512.* Authentic furnishings from William and Mary through Art Deco periods. Antique dolls. Gift shop. (Daily; closed Dec 25) **$**

Endless Caverns. *1800 Endless Caverns Rd, New Market. Via I-81, exit 257 or 264, then approximately 3 miles on Hwy 11 to entrance. Phone 540/896-2283.* Lighted display of unusual rock formations; stalagmites and stalactites, columns, shields, flowstone and limestone pendants, presented in natural color. Temperature 55°F summer and winter. Camping. Guided tours (75 minutes). (Daily; closed Dec 25) **$$$**

New Market Battlefield State Historical Park. *8895 Collins Dr, New Market. 1 mile N of I-81 exit 264. Phone 540/740-3101. www.vmi.edu/museum/nm.* Site of Civil War Battle of New Market (May 15, 1864), in which 257 VMI cadets played a decisive role. Original Bushong farmhouse and outbuildings restored, period furnishings. Hall of Valor; exhibits; films. Scenic overlooks, walking tour. (Daily; closed Jan 1, Thanksgiving, Dec 24-25) Also here is

New Market Battlefield Military Museum. *9500 George R. Collins Dr, New Market. 1/4 mile N of I-81 exit 264. Phone 540/740-8065.* Located on actual site of Battle of New Market, the museum houses a private collection of more than 2,000 military artifacts and genuine, personal artifacts of the American soldier from 1776 to the present. Includes uniforms, weapons, battlefield diaries, medals, mementos; film (30 minutes). Bookshop has more than 500 titles, some antique. Union and Confederate troop position markers are on museum grounds. (Mid-Mar-Nov, daily) **$$$**

Shenandoah Caverns. *261 Caverns Rd, New Market (22847). 4 miles N, off I-81 exit 269. Phone 540/477-3115.* Elevator lowers visitors 60 feet to large subterranean rooms, fascinating rock formations; snack bar, picnic areas. Interior a constant 54° F. (Daily; closed Dec 25) **$$$$**

Limited-Service Hotel

★ BUDGET INN. *2192 Old Valley Pike, New Market (22844). Phone 540/740-3105; toll-free 800/296-6835; fax 540/740-3108. www.budgetinn.com.* 14 rooms. Pets accepted, some restrictions; fee. Check-out 11 am. **$**

★★ SHENVALEE GOLF RESORT. *9660 Fairway Dr, New Market (22844). Phone 540/740-3181; fax 540/740-8931. www.shenvalee.com.* 42 rooms, 2 story. Check-out 1 pm. Restaurant, bar. Outdoor pool, children's pool. Tennis. On 200 acres. **$**

Newport News (E-9)

See also Cape Charles, Gloucester, Hampton, Jamestown (Colonial National Historical Park), Portsmouth, Virginia Beach, Yorktown

Settled 1619
Population 180,150
Elevation 25 ft
Area Code 757
Information Visitor Center, 13560 Jefferson Ave, 23603; phone 757/886-7777 or toll-free 888/4-WE-R-FUN
Web site www.newport-news.org

One of the three cities (also see NORFOLK and PORTSMOUTH) that make up the Port of Hampton Roads, Newport News has the world's largest shipbuilding company, Newport News Shipbuilding. Fourteen miles long and 40 feet deep, Hampton Roads is one of the world's finest natural harbors, formed by the James, York, Elizabeth, and Nansemond rivers as they pass into Chesapeake Bay. The largest ships are accommodated at Newport News docks; huge tonnages of coal, ore, tobacco, and grain are shipped from the port annually. During the two World Wars it was a vitally important point of embarkation and supply. The area still has many important defense establishments.

Newport News is located on the historic Virginia Peninsula between Williamsburg and Virginia Beach. The peninsula contains Hampton, Yorktown, Jamestown, and Williamsburg. Some of the earliest landings in this country were here. The name of the town is said to derive from the good "news" of the arrival of Captain Christopher Newport, who brought supplies and additional colonists to the settlement at Jamestown.

What to See and Do

Fort Eustis. *213 Calhoun St, Newport News (23604). NW end of city on Mulberry Island, I-64 exit 250A. Phone 757/878-4920.* Headquarters of US Army Transportation Center. Self-guided auto tour available; brochures at Public Affairs Office (Building 213). **FREE** On grounds is

US Army Transportation Museum. *1387 Jackson Ave, Newport News (23604). Phone 757/878-1115.* Depicts development of Army transportation from 1776 to the present; "flying saucer," amphibious vehicles, trucks, helicopters. Gift shop. (Tues-Sun; closed holidays) **FREE**

Historic Hilton Village. *Warwick Blvd and Main St, Newport News. I-64 exit 263 A.* Listed on the National Register of Historic Places, this village was built between 1918-1920 to provide wartime housing for workers at Newport News Shipbuilding. Architecturally significant neighborhood features 500 English cottage-style homes and antique and specialty shops. **FREE**

Mariners' Museum. *100 Museum Dr, Newport News (23606). Warwick and J. Clyde Morris blvds. From Williamsburg, take I-64 E to exit 258A. Travel 2 1/2 miles S on J. Clyde Morris Blvd; the Museum entrance is straight ahead. Phone 757/596-2222. www.mariner.org.* Exhibits and displays represent international nautical history; ship models, figureheads, scrimshaw, paintings, decorative arts, and small craft. Age of Exploration Gallery chronicles advancements in shipbuilding, ocean navigation, and cartography that led to early transoceanic exploration. The Chesapeake Bay Gallery exhibits Native American artifacts, workboats, racing shells, multimedia exhibits, a working steam engine, and hundreds of artifacts and photos that tell the story of this body of water. The Crabtree Collection of Miniature Ships showcases 16 detailed miniatures that illustrate the evolution of the sailing ship. Small craft gallery showcases vessels from five continents. A short film, *Sea Power Beyond the Horizon,* shows the historic and modern importance of the sea. Historical interpreters; research library; museum shop. A 550-acre park on the James River features 5-mile Noland Trail with 14 pedestrian bridges; picnic area. Guided tours. (Daily; closed Thanksgiving, Dec 25) **$$$**

Newport News Park. *13560 Jefferson Ave, Newport News (23603). Jct Hwys 105, 143, I-64 exit 250B. Phone 757/886-7912.* Facilities of this 8,065-acre park include freshwater fishing, canoes, paddleboats, boat rentals; history and nature trails, bicycle paths (rentals), archery, arboretum, discovery center, picnicking, Civil War earthworks, 188 campsites. (All year) Some fees. **$$$$**

Peninsula Fine Arts Center. *101 Museum Dr, Newport News (23606). I-64 exit 258A. Phone 757/596-8175. www.pfac-va.org.* Changing bimonthly exhibits ranging from national traveling exhibitions to regional artists; classes, workshops, and special events. Children's hands-on activity area; museum shop. (Daily; closed holidays) **$$**

Virginia Living Museum. *524 J. Clyde Morris Blvd, Newport News (23601). From Williamsburg take I-64 E to exit 258A and go S on J. Clyde Morris Blvd. Approximately 2 miles. Phone 757/595-1900. www.virginialivingmuseum.org.* Exhibits on natural science; wildlife, all native to Virginia, living in natural habitats; indoor and outdoor aviaries; aquariums; wildflower gardens; planetarium with daily shows; observatory; children's hands-on Discovery Center. (Daily; closed holidays) **$$**

Virginia War Museum. *9285 Warwick Blvd, Newport News (23607). In Huntington Park, on Hwy 60, I-64 exit 263A. Phone 757/247-8523. www.warmuseum.org.* More than 60,000 artifacts, including weapons, uniforms, vehicles, posters, insignias, and accoutrements relating to every major US military involvement from the Revolutionary War to the Vietnam War. Military history library and film collection. Civil War tours and educational programs available. (Mon-Sat, also Sun afternoons; closed Jan 1, Thanksgiving, Dec 25). **$$**

Limited-Service Hotels

★ COMFORT INN. *12330 Jefferson Ave, Newport News (23602). Phone 757/249-0200; toll-free 800/368-2477; fax 757/249-4736. www.choicehotels.com.* 124 rooms, 3 story. Pets accepted; fee. Complimentary continental breakfast. Check-in 2 pm, check-out noon. Outdoor pool. Airport transportation available. **$**

★ HAMPTON INN. *12251 Jefferson Ave, Newport News (23602). Phone 757/249-0001; fax 757/249-3911. www.hamptoninn.com.* 120 rooms, 4 story. Complimentary continental breakfast. Check-out noon. Outdoor pool. Airport transportation available. Business center. **$**

Full-Service Hotel

★★★ OMNI NEWPORT NEWS HOTEL. *1000 Omni Blvd, Newport News (23606). Phone 757/873-6664; fax 757/873-1732. www.omnihotels.com.* An upscale suburban hotel located in the Newport News central business district. 187 rooms, 9 story. Check-in 3 pm, check-out 11 am. Restaurant, bar. Fitness room. Indoor pool, whirlpool. Business center. **$**

Restaurants

★★ AL FRESCO. *11710 Jefferson Ave, Newport News (23606). Phone 757/873-0644; fax 757/873-2355.* French, Vietnamese menu. Lunch, dinner. Closed Sun; holidays. Bar. **$$**

★★ DAS WALDCAFE. *12529 Warwick Blvd, Newport News (23606). Phone 757/930-1781.* German menu. Dinner. Closed Mon; holidays. Bar. **$$**

★★ HERMAN'S HARBOR HOUSE. *663 Deep Creek Rd, Newport News (23606). Phone 757/930-1000; fax 757/930-3831.* Seafood menu. Lunch, dinner. Closed Dec 25. Bar. Casual attire. **$$**

★★ PORT ARTHUR. *11137 Warwick Blvd, Newport News (23601). Phone 757/599-6474; fax 757/595-7599.* Chinese menu. Lunch, dinner. Closed Thanksgiving, Dec 25. Bar. Children's menu. Casual attire. **$$$**

Norfolk (F-9)

See also Cape Charles, Chesapeake, Hampton, Newport News

Founded 1682
Population 243,403
Elevation 12 ft
Area Code 757
Information Norfolk Convention and Visitors Bureau, 232 E Main St, 23510; phone 757/664-6620 or toll-free 800/368-3097
Web site www.norfolkcvb.com
Suburbs Chesapeake, Hampton, Newport News, Portsmouth, Virginia Beach. (See individual alphabetical listings.)

This city is part of the Port of Hampton Roads. It is a bustling trade center and has many historic, cultural, and resort areas nearby to attract the tourist. Harbor tours depart from Norfolk's downtown waterfront.

In 1682, the General Assembly bought from Nicholas Wise, a pioneer settler, 50 acres on the Elizabeth River for "ten thousand pounds of tobacco and caske." By 1736, the town that developed was the largest in Virginia. On January 1, 1776, Norfolk was shelled by the British and later burned by the colonists to prevent a British takeover. The battle between the Merrimac and the Monitor in Hampton Roads in March 1862 was followed by the fall of the city to Union forces in May of that year. In 1883, the first shipment of coal to the port by the Norfolk and Western Railway (now Norfolk Southern) began a new era of prosperity for the city.

Norfolk and Portsmouth are connected by bridge tunnels and a pedestrian ferry. Norfolk houses the largest naval facility in the world. It is also headquarters for the United States Navy's Atlantic Fleet and NATO's Allied Command Atlantic. Norfolk has shipbuilding and ship repair companies, consumer and industrial equipment manufacturers, and food-processing plants. The city ships coal, tobacco, grain, seafood, and vegetables. It is also the region's cultural center, home to the Virginia Opera, Virginia Symphony, Virginia Waterfront International Arts Festival, and Virginia Stage Company.

Old Dominion University (1930), Virginia Wesleyan College (1967), Norfolk State University (1935), and Eastern Virginia Medical School (1973) are located here. This area is also the headquarters for year-round resort activities. Within a 50-mile radius are ocean, bay, river, and marsh fishing and hunting; nearby there are 25 miles of good beaches. The 17.6-mile-long Chesapeake Bay Bridge-Tunnel between Norfolk and the Delmarva Peninsula opened in 1964; toll for passenger cars is $10, including passengers.

Public Transportation

Buses (Tidewater Regional Transit), phone 757/640-6300.

Airport Norfolk International Airport. Weather 757/666-1212.

Information Phone 757/857-3351

Lost and Found Phone 757/857-3344

What to See and Do

American Rover. *Waterside Marina, Waterside Dr exit off I-264. Phone 757/627-SAIL.* This 135-foot, three-masted topsail passenger schooner cruises the "smooth waters" of Hampton Roads historical harbor; spacious sun decks; below-deck lounges; concessions. Tour passes historic forts, merchant and US Navy ships. Some tours pass the naval base (inquire for tour schedule). (Apr-mid-Oct, two- and three-hour tours daily)

***Carrie B* Harbor Tours.** *Departs from the Waterside. Phone 757/393-4735.* Replica of 19th-century riverboat takes narrated 90-minute tour of naval shipyard and inner harbor (Apr-Oct, daily); narrated 2 1/2-hour tour of naval base (Apr-Oct, daily); 2 1/2-hour sunset cruise to Hampton Roads and naval base (June-Labor Day, daily).

Chrysler Museum of Art. *245 W Olney Rd, Norfolk (23510). At Mowbray Arch. Phone 757/664-6200.* Art treasures representing nearly every important culture, civilization, and historical period of the past 4,000 years. Photography gallery; fine collection of Tiffany decorative arts and glass, includes the 8,000-piece Chrysler Institute of Glass. (Wed-Sun; closed holidays) **$$$**

General Douglas MacArthur Memorial. *City Hall Ave and Bank St, Norfolk (23510). Phone 757/441-2965.* Restored former city hall (1847) where MacArthur is buried. Nine galleries contain memorabilia of his life and military career. There are three other buildings on MacArthur Square: a theater where a film biography is shown, a gift shop, and the library/archives. (Mon-Sat 10 am-5 pm, Sun from 11 am; closed Jan 1, Thanksgiving, Dec 25) **DONATION**

Hermitage Foundation Museum. *7637 N Shore Rd, Norfolk (23505). Phone 757/423-2052.* Guided tours of fine arts museum in Tudor-style mansion. Collections of tapestries, Chinese bronzes and jade, ancient glass. (Daily; closed Jan 1, Thanksgiving, Dec 25) **$$**

Hunter House Victorian Museum. *240 W Freemason St, Norfolk (23510). Phone 757/623-9814.* Built in 1894 and rich in architectural details, the house contains the Hunter family's collection of Victorian furnishings and decorative pieces, including a Renaissance Revival bedchamber suite, a nursery with children's playthings, an inglenook, and stained-glass windows; lavish period reproduction floor and wall coverings, lighting fixtures, and drapery. Also exhibited is a collection of early-20th-century medical memorabilia. Tours begin every 30 minutes. (Apr-Dec, Wed-Sat, also Sun afternoons; closed Jan 1, Thanksgiving, Dec 25). **$$**

Moses Myers House. *331 Bank St, Norfolk (23510). Phone 757/333-6283.* (1792) Excellent example of Georgian architecture; many pieces of original furniture, silver and china. (Apr-Dec: Tues-Sun; rest of year: Tues-Sat; closed holidays) **$$**

Nauticus—The National Maritime Center. *1 Waterside Dr, Norfolk (23510). Phone 757/664-1000; toll-free 800/664-1080. www.nauticus.org.* Interprets aspects from marine biology and ecology to exploration, trade, and shipbuilding. Interactive computer exhibits allow visitors to navigate a simulated ocean voyage, design a model ship, pilot a virtual reality submarine, and view actual researchers at work in two working marine laboratories. Active US Navy ships and scientific research vessels periodically moor at Nauticus and open to visitors. Also 350-seat, 70mm wide-screen theater; shark petting tank. (Memorial Day-Labor Day: daily; rest of year: Tues-Sun; closed Jan 1, Thanksgiving, Dec 24 and 25). **$$$** Also here is

> **Hampton Roads Naval Museum.** *Phone 757/444-8971.* Interprets the extensive naval history of the Hampton Roads area; including detailed ship models, period photographs, archaeological artifacts, and a superior collection of naval prints and artwork. (Daily; closed Jan 1, Thanksgiving, Dec 25) **FREE**

Norfolk Botanical Garden. *6700 Azalea Garden Rd, Norfolk (23518). Adjacent Norfolk International Airport. Phone 757/441-5830. www.norfolkbotonicalgarden.org.* Azaleas, camellias, rhododendrons, roses (May-Oct), dogwoods, and hollies on 155 acres. Japanese, Colonial, perennial, and rose gardens; flowering arboretum; Hill of Nations; fragrance garden for the visually impaired; picnicking, restaurant, and gift shop; tropical pavilion. Flowering displays best from early Apr-Oct. Gardens (daily; closed special events). Information center (daily; closed Jan 1, Dec 25). Narrated boat ride (30 minutes) and tram tours (mid-Mar-Labor Day: daily; through Oct: weekends, trams only). **$$$**

Norfolk Naval Base and Norfolk Naval Air Station. *Hampton Blvd and I-564, Norfolk. Phone 757/444-7955.* The largest naval installation in the world. Ship visitors should check in at the Naval Base Pass Office on Hampton Blvd, opposite Gate 5. Naval base tours are also offered. Tour buses from Tour and Information Office, 9079 Hampton Blvd (Apr-Oct, daily). **$$**

Spirit of Norfolk. *Departs from the Waterside. Phone 757/625-1748.* Harbor cruise aboard 600-passenger cruise ship. Captain's narration highlights the harbor's famous landmarks, including Waterside Festival Marketplace, Portsmouth Naval Hospital, Old Fort Norfolk, Blackbeard's hiding place, Norfolk Naval Base, and downtown area's dynamic skyline. Luncheon cruise (Tues-Sun); evening dinner cruise (Tues-Sun); moonlight party cruise (Fri-Sat, in season).

St. Paul's Episcopal Church. *201 St. Paul's Blvd, Norfolk (23510). At City Hall Ave. Phone 757/627-4353.* (1739) Only building to survive burning of Norfolk in 1776. (Tues-Fri, also by appointment) **DONATION**

Virginia Zoological Park. *3500 Granby St, Norfolk (23504). Phone 757/441-5227. www.virginiazoo.org.* A combination zoo, park, and conservatory. Playground, tennis courts, basketball courts; picnic area, concession. (Daily 10 am-5 pm; closed Jan 1, Dec 25). **$$**

Waterside Festival Marketplace. *333 Waterside Dr, Norfolk (23510). www.watersidemarketplace.com.* A waterfront pavilion creating a lively marketplace with more than 90 shops, restaurants. (Mon-Sat 10 am-9 pm, Sun noon-6 pm; closed Thanksgiving, Dec 25) Bordering the Waterside are the city's marina and dock areas, where harbor tour vessels take on passengers. A brick promenade skirting the marina connects the Waterside to

> **Town Point Park.** *120 W Main St, Norfolk (23510). Phone 757/441-2345.* Home to Norfolk Festevents, the park hosts more than 100 free outdoor concerts, parties, dances, movies, and festivals each year.

Willoughby-Baylor House. *601 E Freemason St, Norfolk (23510). Phone 757/664-6200.* (1794) Restored town house with period furnishings; herb and flower garden adjacent. (By appointment; inquire at Moses Myers House) **$$**

Special Events

Harborfest. *Town Point Park, 120 W Main St, Norfolk (23510). Downtown waterfront on Wayside Dr. Phone 757/441-2149.* Sailboat and speedboat races, tall ships, ship tours, waterskiing, military demonstrations, entertainment, children's activities, fireworks, seafood. First full weekend in June.

International Azalea Festival. *Downtown and Norfolk Botanical Garden.* To honor NATO. Parade, coronation ceremony, air show (held at Norfolk Naval Air Station), events, concerts, fair, ball, entertainment. Late Apr.

Virginia Children's Festival. *Town Point Park, 120 W Main St, Norfolk (23510). Phone 757/441-2149.* More than 200 educational, creative, and interactive activities; entertainment. Early Oct.

Virginia Opera. *160 E Virginia Beach Blvd, Norfolk (23510). Phone 757/623-1223. Harrison Opera House and other select locations.* Statewide opera company; traditional and contemporary works. Features young American artists. Oct-Apr.

Virginia Symphony. *Phone 757/892-6366. Chrysler Hall and other select locations.* Five performance series. Sept-May.

Virginia Waterfront International Arts Festival. *Phone 757/664-6492.* Eighteen days of classical and contemporary music, dance, visual arts and theater performances. Late Apr-mid-May.

Limited-Service Hotels

★★ BEST WESTERN CENTER INN. *235 N Military Hwy, Norfolk (23502). Phone 757/461-6600; toll-free 800/237-5517; fax 757/466-9093. www.bestwestern.com.* 154 rooms, 2 story. Check-in 3 pm, check-out noon. Restaurant, bar. Fitness room. Indoor pool, outdoor pool, whirlpool. Airport transportation available. Near airport. **$**

★ BEST WESTERN HOLIDAY SANDS INN & SUITES. *1330 E Oceanview Ave, Norfolk (23503). Phone 757/583-2621; toll-free 800/525-5156; fax 757/587-7540.* 95 rooms, 5 story. Complimentary continental breakfast. Check-out 11 am. Fitness room. Outdoor pool. Airport transportation available. **$**

★★ CLARION HOTEL. *345 Granby St, Norfolk (23510). Phone 757/622-6682; toll-free 888/402-6682; fax 757/623-5949. www.choicehotels.com.* 125 rooms, 8 story. Pets accepted, some restrictions; fee. Check-in 3 pm, check-out noon. Restaurant, bar. Fitness room. **$**

★ COMFORT INN. *8051 Hampton Blvd, Norfolk (23505). Phone 757/451-0000; fax 757/451-8394. www.choicehotels.com.* 120 rooms, 2 story. Complimentary continental breakfast. Check-in 3 pm, check-out 11 am. Indoor pool, whirlpool. **$**

★★ DOUBLETREE HOTEL. *880 N Military Hwy, Norfolk (23502). Phone 757/461-9192; toll-free 800/933-9600; fax 757/461-8290. www.doubletreehotel.com.* This hotel is conveniently located in Norfolk's Military Circle Mall, close to the Virginia Beach oceanfront, military installations, and historic downtown Norfolk. 208 rooms, 14 story. Check-in 3 pm, check-out noon. High-speed Internet access. Restaurant, bar. Fitness room. Outdoor pool. Airport transportation available. Business center. **$**

★ HAMPTON INN. *1450 N Military Hwy, Norfolk (23502). Phone 757/466-7474; fax 757/466-0117. www.hamptoninn.com.* 130 rooms, 2 story. Check-out noon. Outdoor pool. Airport transportation available. **$**

Full-Service Hotels

★★★ HILTON NORFOLK AIRPORT. *1500 N Military Hwy, Norfolk (23502). Phone 804/466-8000; toll-free 800/422-7474; fax 804/466-7806. www.norfolkhilton.com.* Conveniently located 2 miles from Norfolk International Airport, this hotel is ideal for those visiting the business district or military installations. 254 rooms, 6 story. Check-in 3 pm, check-out 1 pm. Restaurant, bar. Fitness room. Outdoor pool, whirlpool. Tennis. Airport transportation available. **$**

★★★ MARRIOTT NORFOLK WATERSIDE. *235 E Main St, Norfolk (23510). Phone 804/627-4200; fax 804/628-6466. www.marriott.com.* 405 rooms, 24 story. Check-in 4 pm, check-out 11 pm. Restaurant, bar. Fitness room. Indoor pool, whirlpool. Business center. **$$**

★★★ SHERATON NORFOLK WATERSIDE HOTEL. *777 Waterside Dr, Norfolk (23510). Phone 757/622-6664; fax 757/625-8271. www.sheraton.com.* Adjacent to Waterside Marketplace on the Elizabeth

River, this landmark hotel affords great views of the harbor and downtown skyline. 445 rooms, 10 story. Check-in 3 pm, check-out noon. High-speed Internet access. Restaurant, bar. Outdoor pool. Business center. **$**

Specialty Lodging

The following lodging establishment is approved by Mobil Travel Guide, but due to its unique and individualized nature has not been given a traditional Mobil Star rating. Included in this listing you may find bed-and-breakfasts, limited-service inns, guest ranches, and other unique hotel properties.

PAGE HOUSE. *323 Fairfax Ave, Norfolk (23507). Phone 757/625-5033; toll-free 800/599-7659; fax 757/623-9451. www.pagehouseinn.com.* This Georgian Revival mansion (1898), originally a family home and completely renovated in 1990, is located in the fashionable Ghent historic district. 7 rooms, 3 story. Children under 12 years only by reservations. Check-in 2-9 pm, check-out 11 am. Fitness room. **$$**

Restaurants

★★ BAKER'S CRUST. *330 W 21st St, Norfolk (23517). Phone 757/625-3600; fax 757/625-1855. www.bakerscrust.com.* Steak menu. Lunch, dinner. Bar. Children's menu. Casual attire. Outdoor seating. **$$**

★ THE BANQUE. *1849 E Little Creek Rd, Norfolk (23518). Phone 757/480-3600; fax 757/583-9622.* Dinner. Closed Mon; Thanksgiving, Dec 24-25. Bar. Western décor. **$$**

★★ FREEMASON ABBEY. *209 W Freemason St, Norfolk (23510). Phone 757/622-3966; fax 757/490-7678.* American, seafood menu. Lunch, dinner, Sun brunch. Bar. Children's menu. Casual attire. Renovated church (1873); many antiques. **$$**

★★★ LA GALLERIA. *120 College Pl, Norfolk (23510). Phone 757/623-3939; fax 757/623-9108.* Fine cuisine is the mainstay of this refreshingly cosmopolitan restaurant. All of the delectable desserts are made in-house. Italian menu. Lunch, dinner. Closed Sun; Thanksgiving, Dec 25. Bar. Children's menu. Valet parking. Outdoor seating. **$$**

★★ MONASTERY. *443 Granby St, Norfolk (23510). Phone 757/625-8193; fax 757/437-0513.* Czech, Eastern European menu. Lunch, dinner. Closed Mon; Easter, Thanksgiving, Dec 25; also July-Aug. Bar. Reservations recommended. **$$**

★★★ SHIP'S CABIN. *4110 E Ocean View Ave, Norfolk (23518). Phone 757/362-4659; fax 757/362-0627. www.shipscabin.com.* Only the freshest seafood is served, thanks to the proprietor's years in the boating business. A popular option is the "mix and match" menu: choose a tailored combination of fish, preparation method, and sauce to accompany. The atmosphere is casual, in keeping with its beach setting. Dinner. Bar. Outdoor seating. **$$**

★ UNCLE LOUIE'S. *132 E Little Creek Rd, Norfolk (23505). Phone 757/480-1225; fax 757/480-3540. www.unclelouies.com.* Breakfast, lunch, dinner. Closed Thanksgiving, Dec 25. Bar. Children's menu. **$**

Orange (D-7)

See also Charlottesville, Culpeper

Founded 1749
Population 4,123
Elevation 521 ft
Area Code 540
Zip 22960

This is the seat of Orange County, named for William, Prince of Orange, in 1734. Located in the Piedmont (foothills) of the Blue Ridge Mountains, Orange was settled by Germans under the leadership of Alexander Spotswood between 1714 and 1719.

This is riding and hunting country, drawing its livelihood from farming, livestock, and light industry. There are many antebellum houses in the county.

What to See and Do

James Madison Museum. *129 Caroline St, Orange (22960). Phone 540/672-1776.* Exhibits commemorating Madison's life and his contributions to American history; also Orange County history and Hall of Agriculture that includes an 18th-century homestead. (Mar-Nov: daily; rest of year: Mon-Fri) **$$**

Montpelier. *11407 Constitution Hwy, Montpelier Station (22957). 4 miles SW, on Hwy 20, in Montpelier Station. Phone 540/672-0006. www.montpelier.org.* The former residence of James Madison, fourth president of the United States. Madison was the third generation of his family to live on this extensive plantation. He inherited Montpelier and enlarged it twice. After his presidency, he and Dolley Madison retired to the estate, which Mrs. Madison sold after the president's death to pay off her son's gambling debts. In 1901, the estate was bought by William du Pont, who enlarged the house, added many outbuildings, including a private railroad station, built greenhouses, and planted gardens. Today, under the stewardship of the National Trust for Historic Preservation, a long-term research and preservation project has begun. Self-guided tours of the arboretum, nature trails, and formal garden. (Apr-Oct: daily 9:30 am-5:30 pm; Nov-Mar: daily 9:30 am-4:30 pm; closed Jan 1, Thanksgiving, Dec 25; also first Sat in Nov) **$$$**

Specialty Lodgings

The following lodging establishments are approved by Mobil Travel Guide, but due to their unique and individualized nature have not been given a traditional Mobil Star rating. Included in this listing you may find bed-and-breakfasts, limited-service inns, guest ranches, and other unique hotel properties.

HIDDEN INN. *249 Caroline St, Orange (22960). Phone 540/672-3625; toll-free 800/841-1253; fax 540/672-5029. www.hiddeninn.com.* This inn is located close to Monticello, Montpelier, and Skyline drive and offers activities that include biking, hiking, antique shopping, boating, and fishing. Four buildings make up the inn with the main house being over 100 years old. It was built by descendents of Thomas Jefferson. Verandahs wrap around the building and look out over the wooded gardens. 10 rooms, 2 story. Complimentary full breakfast. Check-in 3 pm, check-out noon. Late 19th-century residence; on 7-1/2 wooded acres. **$**

HOLLADAY HOUSE. *155 W Main St, Orange (22960). Phone 540/672-4893; toll-free 800/358-4422; fax 540/672-3028. www.holladayhousebandb.com.* 6 rooms, 3 story. Complimentary full breakfast. Check-in 3 pm, check-out 11 am. Restaurant. Whirlpool. Federal-style residence (circa 1830). **$**

Pearisburg (E-4)

See also Blacksburg, Radford

Population 2,729
Elevation 1,804 ft
Area Code 540
Zip 24134

What to See and Do

Walnut Flats. *110 Southpark Dr, Pearisburg. 11 miles S on Hwy 100, then 10 1/2 miles W on Hwy 42 to County 606, N 1 mile to County 201, 2 1/2 miles. Phone 540/552-4641.* Fishing in Dismal Creek; hunting (in season), hiking, primitive camping. Dismal Falls and Flat Top Mountain are here. **FREE** Approximately 1/2 mile from Walnut Flags on County 201 is

> **White Pine Horse Camp.** Primitive camping, horse trails. **FREE**

White Rocks Recreation Area. *Hwys 635 and 613. In George Washington and Jefferson national forests. Phone 540/552-4641.* Fishing in Big Stony Creek; hunting (in season), hiking, camping (fee). (Apr-Nov)

Petersburg (E-8)

See also Hopewell, Petersburg National Battlefield, Richmond

Settled 1645
Population 33,740
Elevation 87 ft
Area Code 804
Information Petersburg Visitors Center, 425 Cockade Alley, 23803; phone 804/733-2402 or toll-free 800/368-3595

This city, Lee's last stand before Appomattox (1864-1865), was settled in 1645 when the General Assembly authorized construction of Fort Henry at the falls of the Appomattox River. In 1784, three separate towns united to become the single city of Petersburg.

British troops under Generals Benedict Arnold and William Phillips occupied the town in 1781; on May 24 that same year Cornwallis started the journey to his surrender at Yorktown. Between the Revolutionary War and Civil War, the town was a popular stopping place with a social life that, for a time, eclipsed that of Richmond.

Physically untouched during the early years of the Civil War (though the town sent 17 companies to the front), Petersburg, in 1864, was the scene of Lee's final struggle against Grant. In April 1865, when Lee's supply routes were finally cut and he was forced to evacuate the city, the Confederacy collapsed. A week later Lee surrendered at Appomattox.

The shattered city made a new start after the war, showing amazing recuperative powers; in 1870, Petersburg had 20 more industries than there had been in 1850. Today, besides being a storehouse of colonial and Civil War history, Petersburg is a thriving industrial city.

What to See and Do

Appomattox River Park. *Western part of town, on River Rd. Phone 804/733-2394.* A 137-acre park with canal for canoeing or fishing; access to rapids; picnic area. (Mid-Apr-Oct, daily)

Blandford Church and Cemetery. *321 S Crater Rd, Petersburg (23803).* Church (1735) and cemetery (1702); since 1901 a memorial to the Confederacy, has 15 Tiffany stained-glass windows. (Daily; closed holidays) **$$**

Centre Hill Mansion. (1823) Federalist mansion visited by Presidents Tyler, Lincoln, and Taft. Chandeliers, finely detailed carvings; antiques, 1886 Knabe Art grand piano with hollywood inlaid on rosewood. (Daily; closed holidays) **$$**

Farmers Bank. *19 Bollingbrook St, Petersburg (23803).* (1817) Banking memorabilia including original plates and press for printing Confederate currency. Tours depart from Visitor Center, Old Market Square. (Apr-Oct, daily) **$$**

Fort Lee. *3 miles NE on Hwy 36.* Army training center in World War I and World War II. Here is

> **US Army Quartermaster Museum.** *Blvg 5218, Ave A, Petersburg. Phone 804/734-4203.* Uniforms, flags, weapons, equestrian equipment from 200 years of military service. Civil War and Memorial rooms. (Tues-Sun; closed Jan 1, Thanksgiving, Dec 25) **FREE**

Lee's Retreat. *Phone toll-free 800/673-8732.* A 98-mile driving tour follows route of General Robert E. Lee's retreat from Petersburg to Appomattox. Roadside pull-overs, signs, and audio interpretation at important Civil War sites. For brochures, maps, and audio tapes, contact the Petersburg Visitors Center. **FREE**

Lee Memorial Park. *S part of town, off Johnson Rd. Phone 804/733-2394.* Facilities of this 864-acre park include lake (launch fee), fishing (fee; license required); game fields and courts (fee), picnic area. (Daily; lake facilities closed mid-Oct-mid-Apr) Also here is

> **USSSA Softball Hall of Fame Museum.** *3935 S Crater Rd, Petersburg. 1 mile off I-95. Phone 804/732-4099.* Honors outstanding persons in amateur softball. Numerous displays, exhibits, photographs; 7-minute film. (Daily; closed holidays) **$**

Pamplin Park Civil War Site. *6125 Boydton Plank Rd, Petersburg (23803). Phone 804/861-2408.* Site of General Ulysses S. Grant's decisive victory over Confederate forces in 1865. This 422-acre park includes battle trails, reconstructed soldier huts, plantation home. Interpretive Center, and museum. Guided tours available. (Daily; closed Jan 1, Thanksgiving, Dec 25) Also here is

> **National Museum of the Civil War Soldier.** Exhibit on the Civil War's common soldier, one of the country's largest Civil War bookshops. Gift shop; restaurant.

Poplar Grove (Petersburg) National Cemetery. *S off I-85.* On self-guided tour of Petersburg National Battlefield (see). Of 6,315 graves, 4,110 are unidentified.

Siege Museum. *15 W Bank St, Petersburg (23803). Phone 804/733-2402.* Greek Revival building houses exhibits describing the ten-month Civil War siege of Petersburg. Film *The Echoes Still Remain,* with Joseph Cotten, is shown every hour on the hour. (Daily; closed holidays) **$$**

St. Paul's Episcopal Church. *110 N Union, Petersburg (23803). Between W Washington and Tabb sts. Phone 804/733-3415.* (1856) Lee worshiped here during the siege of Petersburg (1864-1865). Open on request (Mon-Thurs).

Trapezium House. *Market and High sts, Petersburg (23803).* (1817) Built by eccentric Irish bachelor Charles O'Hara in the form of a trapezium, with no right angles and no parallel sides. O'Hara is said to have believed the superstitions of his West Indian servant, who thought that ghosts and evil spirits inhabited right angles. Tours depart from Siege Museum, 15 W Bank St. (Apr-Oct, daily) **$$**

Limited-Service Hotels

★ ★ **BEST WESTERN STEVEN KENT.** *12205 S Crater Rd, Petersburg (23805). Phone 804/733-0600; fax 804/862-4549. www.bestwestern.com.* 138 rooms, 2 story. Pets accepted, some restrictions; fee. Check-out 11 am. Restaurant, bar. Outdoor pool, children's pool. Tennis. **$**

★ **DAYS INN.** *12208 S Crater Rd, Petersburg (23805). Phone 804/733-4400; toll-free 877/512-4400; fax 804/861-9559. www.daysinn.com.* 155 rooms, 2 story. Pets accepted, some restrictions; fee. Check-out 11 am. Fitness room. Outdoor pool, children's pool. **$**

Restaurant

★ **ALEXANDER'S.** *101 W Bank St, Petersburg (23803). Phone 804/733-7134.* American, Greek, Italian menu. Breakfast, lunch, dinner. Closed Sun; Jan 1, Thanksgiving, Dec 25; also week of July 4. Children's menu. In old town storefront. **$**

Petersburg National Battlefield (E-8)

See also Hopewell, Petersburg, Richmond

(Hwy 36 and I-95)

Web site www.nps.gov/pete

The campaign that spelled doom for the Confederacy occurred in a huge 40-mile semicircle around Richmond and Petersburg at the price of 70,000 Union and Confederate casualties.

After his unsuccessful attempt to take Richmond by frontal assault (at Cold Harbor, June 3, 1864), General Grant withdrew and attacked Petersburg. After four days of fighting and failing to capture the city, Grant decided to lay siege. Petersburg was the rail center that funneled supplies to Lee and Richmond.

The siege lasted ten months, from June 15, 1864, to April 2, 1865, with the two armies in almost constant contact. When Petersburg finally fell, Lee's surrender was only a week away.

The park, more than 2,700 acres, preserves Union and Confederate fortifications, trenches, and gun pits. Another unit of the battlefield, Five Forks Unit, is located 23 miles to the west. Park (daily). Living history programs daily during summer. Access for the disabled includes several paved trails and ramps to the Visitor Center. For further information contact the Superintendent, 1539 Hickory Hill Rd, Petersburg 23803-4721; phone 804/732-3531. Golden Eagle, Golden Age, and Golden Access Passports honored (see MAKING THE MOST OF YOUR TRIP).

What to See and Do

Battery 5. Strongest original Confederate position, captured on opening day of battle. From here "the Dictator," a Union mortar, shelled Petersburg, 2 1/2 miles away. A similar mortar is nearby.

Battery 8. Confederate artillery position captured and used by Union as Fort Friend.

Battery 9. Confederate position on original line. Site of reconstructed Union camp and living history programs.

City Point Unit. (See HOPEWELL)

Colquitt's Salient. Section of Confederate defense line.

The Crater. Hole remaining after Union troops tunneled beneath Confederate artillery position and exploded four tons of powder (July 30, 1864). The resulting breach in Confederate lines failed as a major breakthrough. Several special monuments in vicinity.

First Maine Monument. Memorial to Maine dead in greatest regimental loss in a single action of the war.

Five Forks Unit. *1539 Hickory Hill Rd, Petersburg (23803). Approximately 6 miles SW via Hwy 613 (White Oak Rd), to junction Dinwiddie Courthouse Rd (Hwy 627) and Wheeler Pond Rd (Hwy 645). Phone 804/265-8244.* (1,115 acres) This road junction, beyond Lee's extreme right flank, led to the only remaining Confederate supply line, the South Side Railroad. The Battle of Five Forks (April 1, 1865) saw Union forces under General Philip H. Sheridan smash Confederates commanded by General George Pickett and gain access to the tracks beyond. On April 2, Grant ordered an all-out assault, crumbling Lee's right flank. Only a heroic stand by Confederate forces at Fort Gregg held off the Union advance while Lee evacuated Petersburg on the night of April 2. Visitor contact station (summer). **FREE**

Fort Haskell. One of the points where Union troops stopped a desperate attempt by Lee to break the siege.

Fort Stedman. Lee's "last grand offensive" concentrated here (March 25, 1865). The battle lasted four hours; the Confederates failed to hold their breakthrough.

Gracie's Dam. Site of one of several Confederate dams intended to flood area between lines.

Harrison's Creek. First Grant (June 1864), then Lee (March 1865) had advances checked here.

Spring Garden. Heaviest Union artillery concentration during Battle of Crater was along this ridge.

Visitor Center. *Off Hwy 36.* Information, exhibits; maps for self-guided tours. (Daily; closed Jan 1, Dec 25) Self-guided tour starts near center building.

Portsmouth (F-9)

See also Cape Charles, Chesapeake, Hampton, Newport News, Norfolk, Virginia Beach

Founded 1752
Population 100,565
Elevation 15 ft
Area Code 757
Information Portsmouth Convention and Visitors Bureau, 505 Crawford St, Suite 2, 23704; phone 757/393-5327 or toll-free 800/767-8782
Web site www.portsmouth.va.us

Connected to Norfolk by two bridge tunnels and a pedestrian ferry that cross the Elizabeth River, Portsmouth is part of the great Hampton Roads port, unrivaled for commercial shipping and shipbuilding activity. It is also the headquarters of the United States Coast Guard Atlantic Fleet.

In Gosport, long a part of Portsmouth, Andrew Sprowle, a Scot, built a marine yard in 1767 which became in turn a British naval repair station and, after the Revolutionary War, a federal navy yard. Now called the Norfolk Naval Shipyard, it is the largest naval shipyard in the world. The *Chesapeake,* sister of the *Constitution* and one of the US Navy's first warships, was built here. So was the *Merrimac,* which was seized by the Confederates, changed into an ironclad in 1861, and rechristened the CSS *Virginia.* The oldest drydock (1831) here is still in use.

What to See and Do

***Carrie B* Harbor Tours.** *Departs from Portside, 6 Crawford Pkwy, Portsmouth. Phone 757/393-4735.* Replica of 19th-century riverboat makes narrated tour (90-minutes) of naval shipyard and inner harbor (Apr-Oct, daily); narrated tour (2 1/2 hours) of naval base and Hampton Roads (Apr-May and Sept-Oct, daily); sunset cruise (2 1/2 hours) to Hampton Roads and naval base (June-Labor Day, daily). (Also see NORFOLK).

Hill House. *221 North St, Portsmouth (23704). Phone 757/393-0241.* Headquarters of the Portsmouth Historical Association. Built in early 1820s, this four-story English basement-style (with a raised basement) house contains original furnishings collected by generations of the Hill family. In near-original condition, the house has undergone only limited renovation through the years. Garden restored. (Apr-Dec, Wed, Sat-Sun) **$**

Historic houses. *6 Crawford Pkwy, Portsmouth (23704). Phone 757/393-5111.* Portsmouth has over 300 years of history represented by more than 20 examples of colonial, Federal, and antebellum houses. Among them is the Nivison-Ball House (circa 1730-1750), 417 Middle Street, where Andrew Jackson and General Lafayette were entertained. These houses are private and may be viewed only from the exterior. Obtain Olde Towne Portsmouth walking tour brochures with map and descriptions of churches, homes, and old buildings from the Visitor Center at High Street Landing.

Monumental United Methodist Church. *450 Dinwiddie St, Portsmouth (23704). 1 block N of High St. Phone 757/397-1297.* (1772) Methodist. Oldest Methodist congregation in the South; history room. Guided tour (Mon-Fri, by appointment; closed holidays).

The Portsmouth Museums. *221 High St, Portsmouth (23704). Phone 757/393-8983.* Located in a four-block radius, the museum complex has facilities housing artistic, educational, and historic exhibits. (Memorial Day-Labor Day, daily; closed Jan 1, Thanksgiving, Dec 25) The complex includes

Children's Museum of Virginia. More than 60 interactive activities in 12 areas; planetarium. (Mid-June-Labor Day, Mon-Sat, also Sun afternoons) **$$**

Court House Galleries. *420 High St, Portsmouth (23704).* Changing exhibits. **$**

Lightship Museum. *London Slip and Water St, Portsmouth (23704).* Built in 1915, commissioned in 1916 as Lightship 101, it served 48 years in Virginia, Delaware, and Massachusetts. Retired in 1964 and renamed Portsmouth. **$**

Naval Shipyard Museum. *2 High St, Portsmouth (23704). On Elizabeth River.* Thousands of items of naval equipment, plus flags, uniforms, prints, maps, and models, including models of the CSS *Virginia;* the US Ship-of-the-line *Delaware,* built in Portsmouth; and the first ship drydocked in the US. **$**

Trinity Church. *500 Court St, Portsmouth (23704). Phone 757/393-0431.* Episcopal. Oldest church building (1762) and parish in Portsmouth. Legend says the church bell cracked while ringing out news of Cornwallis' surrender; it was later recast. Confederate Memorial window. Commodore James Barron, many colonial patriots are buried here. Open on request (Mon-Fri); office behind church in parish hall.

Limited-Service Hotel

★★ HOLIDAY INN. *8 Crawford Pkwy, Portsmouth (23704). Phone 757/393-2573; toll-free 800/456-2811; fax 757/399-1248. www.holiday-inn.com.* 222 rooms, 4 story. Pets accepted. Check-in 4 pm, check-out 11 am. Restaurant, bar. Fitness room. Outdoor pool. **$**

Full-Service Hotel

★★★ RENAISSANCE PORTSMOUTH HOTEL. *425 Water St, Portsmouth (23704). Phone 757/673-3000; fax 757/673-3030. www.renaissancehotels.com.* 254 rooms, 16 story. Check-in 3 pm, check-out noon. Restaurant, bar. Fitness room. Indoor pool, whirlpool. Business center. **$**

Restaurants

★★ CAFE EUROPA. *319 High St, Portsmouth (23704). Phone 757/399-6652.* Mediterranean menu. Lunch, dinner. Closed Sun, Mon; holidays. Bar. Casual attire. **$$**

★ THE CIRCLE. *3010 High St, Portsmouth (23707). Phone 757/397-8196; fax 757/399-3074.* Seafood, steak menu. Breakfast, lunch, dinner. Closed Dec 25. Bar. Children's menu. Casual attire. Rotunda dining room with extensive buffet. **$$**

Radford (E-4)

See also Blacksburg, Pearisburg, Salem

Settled 1756
Population 15,859
Elevation 1,820 ft
Area Code 540
Zip 24141
Information Chamber of Commerce, 1126 Norwood St; phone 540/639-2202
Web site www.radfordchamber.com

What to See and Do

Claytor Lake State Park. *4400 State Park Rd, Radford (24084). On Hwy 660, 6 miles SW, just S of I-81 exit 101. Phone 540/674-5492.* Consists of 472 acres in wooded hills adjacent to 5,000-acre lake. Swimming, sand beach, bathhouse, fishing, boating (ramp, rentals, marina); hiking and bridle trails, picnicking, concession, tent and trailer sites (electrical hookups, Apr-Sept), cabins (Mar-early Dec). Visitor center, interpretive programs. Park office and visitor center in Howe House (1876-1879), built on land once settled by Dunkers (Dunkards), a religious sect that fled persecution in Germany in the 1720s.

Radford University. *801 Norwood St, Radford (24142). On US 11, I-81 exit 109. Phone 540/831-5324. www.radford.edu.* (1910) (9,142 students) Flossie Martin Gallery in Powell Hall houses visual arts with an emphasis on regional and contemporary; changing exhibits. Corinna de la Burde Sculpture Court, adjacent to the gallery, is an open-air museum displaying large-scale sculpture; changing exhibits, and permanent installations. Archives in the McConnell Library contain pamphlets, campus information, local history, oral history of Appalachia, and rare books. Greenhouse (daily). Dedmon Center, a recreation-convocation complex, features air-supported roof, arena seating 5,600; swimming pool; indoor tennis and handball courts. (Daily)

Limited-Service Hotels

★ BEST WESTERN RADFORD INN. *1501 Tyler Ave, Radford (24141). Phone 540/639-3000; toll-free 800/628-1955; fax 540/633-0251. www.bestwestern.com.* 72 rooms, 2 story. Pets accepted, some restrictions; fee. Check-out noon. Fitness room. Indoor pool, children's pool, whirlpool. **$**

★ COMFORT INN. *4424 Cleburne Blvd, Dublin (24084). Phone 540/674-1100; toll-free 800/638-7949; fax 540/674-2644. www.choicehotels.com.* 98 rooms, 2 story. Complimentary continental breakfast. Check-out noon. Outdoor pool. **$**

Reston (C-8)

(See Dulles International Airport Area)

Richmond (E-8)

See also Ashland, Hopewell, Petersburg, Petersburg National Battlefield, Richmond National Battlefield Park, Tappahannock

Settled 1607
Population 197,790
Elevation 150 ft
Area Code 804
Information Convention and Visitors Bureau, 550 E Marshall St, 23219; phone 804/782-2777 or toll-free 800/370-9004
Web site www.richmondva.org

Located at the falls of the James River, Richmond had to wait 170 years before becoming the state capital. Four hundred years later, with a history as old as Jamestown itself, the city blends its heritage with vibrant contemporary commerce and trade. Its location equidistant from the plantations of Tidewater Virginia and the Piedmont of central Virginia gives the city a unique mix of heritage, culture, and geography. It continues to be a city of contrasts and multiple perspectives that hosts the treasures of colonial times along with state-of-the-art contemporary offerings.

Richmond has served as the capital of Virginia and of the Confederate States of America. The heritage of these two dramatically different situations can be found in places like St. John's Church, site of Patrick Henry's famous speech ("Give me liberty or give me death"), and The Museum and White House of the Confederacy, the residence of Confederate President Jefferson Davis.

A gateway to the Virginia Piedmont and Tidewater, Richmond also serves as a gateway to Southside, the central, south-central part of Virginia that is less traveled and less explored. Travelers will find the rural communities, the pace, and the byways of Southside a welcome contrast to today's hectic times.

The Virginia Historical Society's Story of Virginia does a phenomenal job of laying out the complex history of the Richmond region. Beginning with "Becoming a Homeplace," illustrating its founding by John Smith, Richmond's story continues with "Becoming Virginians," followed by "Becoming Southerners," "Becoming Confederates," and "Becoming New Southerners," "Becoming Americans Again" and lastly "Becoming Equal." Supported with 10,000 artifacts, the story ultimately covers the gamut of American culture.

With all this heritage in one place, Richmond has something for everyone. Toss in a strong arts community, good restaurants, and Southern gentility, and you have a great place to visit and explore.

There have been few dull moments in Richmond's history. Native Americans and settlers fought over the ground on which it now stands. In 1775, Patrick Henry made his "liberty or death" speech in St. John's Church, and in 1780, the city was named capital of the state. At that time, Virginia extended all the way to the Mississippi. British soldiers plundered it brutally in the Revolutionary War. As the capital of the Confederacy from 1861 to 1865, it was constantly in danger. Finally, in 1865, the city was evacuated and retreating Confederate soldiers burned the government warehouse; a portion of the rest of the city also went up in flames.

However, Richmond did survive. As Virginia's capital, it proudly exemplifies the modern South. It is a city that is industrially aggressive yet culturally aware, respectful of its own historical background yet receptive to new trends in architecture and modes of living. Richmond esteems both the oldest monuments and the newest skyscrapers.

Tobacco and tobacco products, paper and paper products, aluminum, chemicals, textiles, printing and publishing, and machinery contribute to the city's economy. Richmond is also an educational center; Virginia Commonwealth University, Virginia Union University, and the University of Richmond are based here.

What to See and Do

17th Street Farmers' Market. *17th and Main sts, Richmond (23219). Phone 804/646-0477. www.17thstreetfarmersmarket.com.* Farmers market built on the site of a Native American trading village. Seasonal produce, flowers, and holiday greens. (Daily)

6th Street Marketplace. *6th St, Richmond (23219). Between Coliseum and Grace St, downtown.* Restored area of shops, restaurants, and entertainment.

Agecroft Hall. *4305 Sulgrave Rd, Richmond (23221). Cary St exit off I-195, turn onto N Thompson Ave, then right on Cary to Malvern, then left on Cantebury to Sulgrave Rd. Phone 804/353-4241. www.agecrofthall.com.* Half-timbered Tudor manor built in the late 15th century near Manchester, England. Disassembled, brought here, and rebuilt during the late 1920s in a spacious setting of formal gardens and grassy terraces overlooking the James River. English furnishings from 16th and 17th centuries. Audiovisual presentation explains the history of the house. (Tues-Sun; closed holidays) **$$**

★ **Capitol Square.** *9th and Grace sts, Richmond (23219). Bounded by Broad, Governor, Bank, and 9th sts, downtown. Phone 804/784-5736.* On Capitol Square are

Equestrian Statue of Washington. By Thomas Crawford; cast in Munich over an 18-year period. Base features allegorical representations of six famous Revolutionary War figures from Virginia.

Governor's Mansion. *E of State Capitol. Phone 804/371-2642.* (1813) This two-story Federal-style house was built after the capital was moved from Williamsburg. Oldest governor's mansion in the US still in use as a governor's residence. Tours (by appointment). **FREE**

State Capitol. *Capitol Sq. Phone 804/698-1788.* (1785-1788) Modeled after La Maison Carrée, an ancient Roman temple at Nímes, France, the Capitol was designed by Thomas Jefferson. In this building, where America's oldest continuous English-speaking legislative bodies still meet, is the famous Houdon statue of Washington. The rotunda features the first interior dome in the US; here Aaron Burr was tried for treason, Virginia ratified the Articles of Secession, and Robert E. Lee accepted command of the forces of Virginia; the Confederate Congress also met in the building. (Mon-Sat, also Sun afternoons; closed Jan 1, Thanksgiving, Dec 25)

Virginia State Library and Archives. *800 E Broad St, Richmond (23219). Phone 804/692-3500. www.lva.lib.va.us.* Outstanding collection of books, maps, and manuscripts. (Mon-Sat; closed holidays) **FREE**

Carytown. *Between Boulevard St and I-95.* Eight blocks of shops, restaurants, and theaters adjacent to the historic Fan neighborhood.

Church Hill Historic Area. *Bounded by Broad, 29th, Main, and 21st sts, E of Capitol Sq.* Neighborhood of 19th-century houses, more than 70 of which predate Civil War. Some Church Hill houses are open during Historic Garden Week (see SPECIAL EVENTS). In center of Church Hill is

Edgar Allan Poe Museum. *1914-1916 E Main St, Richmond (23223). Phone 804/648-5523. www.poemuseum.org.* Old Stone House portion is thought to be oldest structure in Richmond (1737). Three additional buildings house Poe mementos; James Carling illustrations of "The Raven"; scale model of the Richmond of Poe's time. Guided tours. (Tues-Sun; closed holidays). **$$**

Richmond's Historical Legacy

Richmond was the Civil War "Capital of the Confederacy," and this aspect of its past can easily be recalled on a two-hour, 2-mile walking tour of the city center. The city also enjoys other, less-troubling claims to historical fame, which will be pointed out along the way. Begin this walk at the Virginia State Capitol, designed in 1785 by Thomas Jefferson, himself a state governor, in the style of a classical temple. Surrounded by Capitol Square's expanse of well-tended lawn, it displays such majesty that it still commands the eye despite the modern-day structures that surround it. Step inside the Rotunda to see the famous life-size statue of George Washington, the only one executed of him from life. From Capitol Square, walk north (right) on 9th Street across Broad Street to the neighborhood once known as Court End, which now bustles with students and faculty of the Medical College of Virginia. At 818 East Marshall Street (intersecting 9th) stands the most important residence of Court End, the home of John Marshall, the distinguished chief justice of the US Supreme Court from 1801 to 1835. Built in 1790, the two-story brick house where he lived for 45 years is a museum dedicated to his memory. Though it's a seven-block detour, head west on Marshall Street to 2nd Street and turn north (right) two blocks to 110 East Leigh Street, the Maggie Walker National Historic Site. A museum, the modest two-story brick home on a quiet residential street, honors a black woman of impressive ability. Despite physical handicaps, Walker became America's first female bank president, establishing the Penny Savings Bank in 1903 as a way of helping local blacks during the Jim Crow period. Double back via Marshall Street past the John Marshall House to the Valentine Museum at 1015 East Clay Street. A small, innovative museum with a contemporary outlook, it focuses on the people and history of Richmond. Conclude the tour a block down the street at 12th and East Clay at the adjacent Museum of the Confederacy and the White House of the Confederacy. Not surprisingly, the museum emphasizes Southern leaders, featuring mementos of General Robert E. Lee. The White House, a neoclassical mansion built in 1818, recounts the home life during the Civil War of Confederate President Jefferson Davis and his wife, Varina.

St. John's Episcopal Church. *25th and Broad sts, Richmond (23223). Phone 804/648-5015.* (1741) Where Patrick Henry delivered his stirring "liberty or death" speech. Reenactment of the Second Virginia Convention (late May-early Sept, Sun). Guided tours. (Daily; closed holidays)

City Hall Observation Deck. *900 E Broad St, Richmond (23219). Phone 804/646-7000.* Eighteenth-floor observation deck offers a panoramic view of the city, including the Capitol grounds, James River, and Revolutionary and Civil War-era buildings contrasted with modern skyscrapers. (Mon-Fri) **FREE**

★ **The Fan and Monument Avenue.** *Bounded by Franklin St and Monument Ave, Boulevard, Main, and Belvidere sts. Phone 804/643-3589.* Named for the layout of streets that fan out from Monroe Park toward the western part of town. Historical neighborhood has restored antebellum and turn-of-the-century houses, museums, shops, restaurants, and famed Monument Avenue. The fashionable boulevard, between Lombard and Belmont streets, is dotted with imposing statues of Generals Lee, Stuart, and Jackson; of Jefferson Davis; and of Commodore Matthew Fontaine Maury, inventor of the electric torpedo. Within this area are

Children's Museum of Richmond. *2626 W Broad St, Richmond (23220). Phone 804/474-2667; toll-free 877/295-2667. www.c-mor.org.* Exhibits on arts, nature, and the world around us designed for children 2-12 years old; many hands-on exhibits. (July-Aug: daily; rest of year: Tues-Sun; closed holidays) **$$**

Science Museum of Virginia. *2500 W Broad St, Richmond (23220). N of Monument Ave. Phone 804/864-1400. www.smv.org.* Hands-on museum. Major exhibits include aerospace, computers, electricity, visual perception, physical phenomena and astronomy, and Foucault pendulum. The Ethyl Universe Planetarium Space Theater features Omnimax films and planetarium shows (inquire for schedule). (Tues-Sun; closed Thanksgiving, Dec 25) **$$$**

Virginia Historical Society. *428 N Boulevard, Richmond (23220). Phone 804/358-4901. www.vahistorical.org.* Comprehensive collection of Virginia history housed in the Museum of Virginia History with permanent and changing exhibits, and the Library of Virginia History with historical and genealogical research facilities. (Mon-Sat, museum also Sun afternoons; closed holidays) **$$**

Virginia Museum of Fine Arts. *2800 Grove Ave, Richmond (23220). At Boulevard St. Phone 804/340-1400. www.vmfa.state.va.us.* America's first state-supported museum of art. Collections of paintings, prints, and sculpture from major world cultures; Russian Imperial Easter eggs and jewels by Faberge; decorative arts of the Art Nouveau and Art Deco movements; sculpture garden; changing exhibits. Cafeteria. (Tues-Sun; closed holidays) **FREE**

Federal Reserve Money Museum. *701 E Byrd St, Richmond (23219). Downtown, on first floor of bank. Phone 804/697-8000. www.rich.frb.org/econed/museum/.* Exhibits of currency, include rare bills; gold and silver bars; money-related artifacts. (Mon-Fri 9:30 am-3:30 pm; closed holidays) **FREE**

Historic Richmond Tours. *707 E Franklin St, Richmond (23219). Phone 804/649-0711.* Offers guided van tours with pickup at Visitor Center and major hotels (daily); reservations required. Also guided walking tours (Apr-Oct, daily; fee). **$$$$**

Hollywood Cemetery. *412 S Cherry St, Richmond (23220). At Albemarle St. Phone 804/648-8501. www.hollywoodcemetery.org.* (1847) James Monroe, John Tyler, Jefferson Davis, other notables, and 18,000 Confederate soldiers are buried here; audiovisual program (Mon-Fri). (Daily 8 am-5 pm; walking tours Apr-Oct, Mon-Sat at 10 am) **FREE**

Jackson Ward. *Broad and Belvidere sts, Richmond (23218). Bounded by I-95, 7th, Broad, and Belvidere sts.* Historic downtown neighborhood that was home to many famous black Richmonders, including Bill "Bojangles" Robinson. The area has numerous 19th-century, Greek Revival, and Victorian buildings with ornamental ironwork that rivals the wrought iron of New Orleans. Within the ward are

Bill "Bojangles" Robinson Statue. *Leigh and Adams sts, Richmond.* Memorial to the famous dancer who was born at 915 N 3rd St.

Black History Museum and Cultural Center. *Clay St, Richmond. Phone 804/780-9093. www.blackhistorymuseum.org.* Limited editions, prints, art, photographs; African memorabilia; Sam Gilliam collection. (Tues-Sun 10 am-5 pm) **$$**

Maggie Walker National Historic Site. *110 1/2 E Leigh St, Richmond (23219). Phone 804/771-2017. www.nps.gov/malw.* Commemorates the life and career of Maggie L. Walker, daughter of former slaves, who overcame great hardships to become successful in banking and insurance; early advocate for women's rights and racial equality. Two-story, red brick house was home to her family from 1904 to 1934. (Mon-Sat; closed Jan 1, Thanksgiving, Dec 25) **FREE**

John Marshall House. *818 E Marshall St, Richmond (23219). Phone 804/648-7998.* (1790) Restored house of famous Supreme Court justice features original woodwork and paneling, family furnishings, and mementos. (Tues-Sun; closed holidays) Combination ticket available for Marshall House, Valentine Museum, Museum of the Confederacy, and White House of the Confederacy. **$**

Kanawha Canal Locks. *12th and Byrd sts, Richmond (23219). Downtown. Phone 804/780-0107 (walking tour).* Impressive stone locks were part of the nation's first canal system, planned by George Washington. Narrated audiovisual presentation explains the workings of the locks and canal. Picnic grounds. (Mon-Sat) **FREE**

Meadow Farm Museum. General Sheppard Crump Memorial Park, *8600 Dixon Powers Dr, Richmond (23273). Phone 804/501-5520. www.co.henrico.va.us/rec/mfarm.htm.* Living history farm museum depicting rural life in the 1860s. Orientation center, farmhouse, barn, outbuildings, crop demonstration fields, and 1860s doctor's office. Also a 150-acre park with picnic shelters, playground. (Mar-Dec, Tues-Sun) **$**

Monumental Church. *1224 E Broad St, Richmond (23219). N of Capitol Sq.* (1812) Located on the Medical College of Virginia campus of Virginia Commonwealth University. Octagonal domed building designed by Robert Mills, architect of the Washington Monument. Commemorative structure was built on the site where many prominent persons, including the governor, perished in a theater fire in

1811. Interior closed. Behind the church is the distinctive Egyptian Building (1845).

Museum of the Confederacy. *1201 E Clay St, Richmond (23219). Phone 804/649-1861. www.moc.org.* Contains the nation's largest collection of Confederate military and civilian artifacts, including uniforms; equipment; flags; personal belongings of Jefferson Davis, Robert E. Lee, and J. E. B. Stuart; documents; manuscripts; and artwork. (Mon-Sat 10 am-5 pm, Sun noon-5 pm; closed Jan 1, Thanksgiving, Dec 25) **$$**

Paddlewheeler *Annabel Lee.* *Departs from Intermediate Terminal. Broad St E to 21st St, turn right on 21st St to Dock St, turn left on Dock, follow until you reach the terminal. Phone 804/377-2020; toll-free 800/752-7093. www.spiritcitycruises.com/Richmond/onboard/.* Triple-decked, 350-passenger, 19th-century-style riverboat cruises the James River. Narrated tour; entertainment. Lunch, brunch, dinner, and plantation cruises. (Apr-Dec, at least one cruise Tues-Sun)

Parks. *Phone 804/780-5733.* For general information, contact the Department of Parks and Recreation.

Bryan. *Bellevue Ave and Hermitage Rd, Richmond (23227).* A 279-acre park, 20 acres of which are an azalea garden with more than 55,000 plants (best viewed late Apr-mid-May). Picnic facilities, tennis courts. **FREE**

James River. *W 22nd St and Riverside Dr, Richmond (23225).* Five sections. Fishing, pedestrian bridges with overlook of James River, whitewater canoe and inner-tube accesses; bird watching, wildlife sanctuary, self-guided tours, bicycle and hiking trails, visitor center with display, information station, interpretive programs. **FREE**

Lewis Ginter Botanical Garden. *1800 Lakeside Ave, Lakeside (23228). Phone 804/262-9887. www.lewisginter.org.* Victorian-era estate features the Grace Arents Garden and the Henry M. Flagler Perennial Garden; seasonal floral displays; emphasis on daffodils, daylilies, azaleas, and rhododendrons. (Daily) **$$**

Maymont. *1700 Hampton St, Richmond (23220). At Pennsylvania Ave. Phone 804/358-7166.* Dooley mansion, late Victorian in style, houses an art collection and decorative arts exhibits (Tues-Sun; fee). Also here are formal Japanese and Italian gardens, an arboretum, a nature center with wildlife habitat for native species, an aviary, a children's farm, and a working carriage collection. (Daily) **FREE**

Pocahontas State Park. *10301 State Park Rd, Chesterfield (23838). S on Hwy 10, then W on Hwy 655. Phone 804/796-4255. www.dcr.state.va.us/parks/pocahont.htm.* More than 7,000 acres; Swift Creek Lake. Swimming, pool, bathhouse, fishing, boating (launch, rentals, electric motors only); hiking trails, bicycle path (rentals), picnicking, concession, tent and trailer sites (seasonal), group cabins. Nature center; evening interpretive programs (summer). (Daily)

William Byrd. *Boulevard St and Idlewood Ave, Richmond (23220).* Includes 287 acres of groves, artificial lakes, picnic areas. Tennis courts, softball fields, and a fitness course. Amphitheater (June-Aug). Virginia's World War I memorial, a 240-foot, pink brick carillon tower.

Plantation tours. *401 E Marshall St, Richmond (23220). Phone 804/783-7450.* The Richmond-Petersburg-Williamsburg area has many fine old mansions and estates. Some are open most of the year; others only during Historic Garden Week (see SPECIAL EVENTS). The Metro Richmond Visitors Center has maps, information folders, and suggestions.

Shockoe Slip. *11 S 12th St, Richmond (23219). E Cary St between 12th and 14th sts, downtown.* Restored area of historic buildings and gaslit cobblestone streets; shopping, restaurants, and galleries.

St. Paul's Church. *815 E Grace St, Richmond (23219). W of Capitol Sq. Phone 804/643-3589. www.stpauls-episcopal.org.* (Episcopal) Established in 1843, the church survived the Civil War intact. It was here that Jefferson Davis received news of Robert E. Lee's retreat from Petersburg to Appomattox. Beginning in 1890, the church added many fine stained-glass windows, including eight from the Tiffany studios. Sanctuary ceiling features decorative plasterwork interweaving Greek, Hebrew, and Christian motifs around a central panel. A Tiffany mosaic of da Vinci's *Last Supper* surmounts the altar. (Daily; closed holidays)

Valentine Museum. *1015 E Clay St, Richmond (23219). N of Capitol Sq. Phone 804/649-0711. www.valentinemuseum.com.* Traces the history of Richmond. Exhibits focus on city life, decorative arts, costumes and textiles, and industrial and social history; tour of restored 1812 Wickham House. Lunch is served in a walled garden (Apr-Oct). (Daily; closed holidays). **$$**

Virginia Aviation Museum. *5701 Huntsman Rd, Richmond (23250). At Richmond International Airport. Phone 804/236-3622. www.vam.smv.org.* Exhibits and artifacts on the history of aviation, with an emphasis on Virginia pioneers. (Daily; closed Thanksgiving, Dec 25) **$$**

Virginia House. *4301 Sulgrave Rd, Windsor Farms (23221). 1/2 mile off Hwy 147 (Cary St). Phone 804/353-4251. www.vahistorical.org.* A Tudor building constructed of materials from Warwick Priory (built in England in 1125 and rebuilt in 1565 as a residence); moved here in 1925. The west wing is modeled after Sulgrave Manor, at one time the home of Lawrence Washington. Furniture, tapestries, and paintings from the 15th to 20th centuries. Formal gardens. Tours by appointment only except during Historic Garden Week (see SPECIAL EVENTS). (Fri-Sat 10 am-4 pm, Sun 12:30-5 pm, otherwise by appointment; closed holidays) **$$**

Virginia War Memorial. *621 S Belvidere St, Richmond (23220). Downtown at N end of Robert E. Lee Bridge. Phone 804/786-2060. www.vawarmemorial.org.* Honors Virginians who died in World War II and the Korean and Vietnam wars. Mementos of battles; eternal flame; more than 12,000 names engraved on glass and marble walls. (Daily) **FREE**

White House of the Confederacy. *12th and E Clay sts, Richmond (23219). N of Capitol Sq. Phone 804/649-1861. www.moc.org/exwhite.htm.* Classical Revival house (1818) used by Jefferson Davis as his official residence during the period when Richmond was the capital of the Confederacy. Abraham Lincoln met with troops here during the Union occupation of the city. Restored to pre-wartime appearance; original furnishings. (Daily; closed Jan 1, Thanksgiving, Dec 25) **$$**

Wilton House Museum. *215 S Wilton Rd, Richmond (23226). Off Cary St, 8 miles W. Phone 804/282-5936. www.wiltonhousemuseum.org.* (1753) Georgian mansion built by William Randolph III. Fully paneled, authentic 18th-century furnishings. Headquarters of the National Society of Colonial Dames in Virginia. (Tues-Sun; closed holidays) Open during Historic Garden Week (see SPECIAL EVENTS). **$**

Special Events

Historic Garden Week in Virginia. *12 E Franklin St, Richmond (23219). Phone 804/644-7776. www.vagardenweek.org.* Many private houses and gardens of historic or artistic interest are opened for this event, which includes more than 200 houses and gardens throughout the state. Tours. Mid-late Apr.

June Jubilee. *Downtown.* Performing and visual arts festival with ethnic foods, folk dances, music, and crafts. First weekend in June.

Richmond Newspapers Marathon. Last Sun in Oct.

Virginia State Fair. *600 E Laburnum Ave, Richmond (23222). Phone 804/228-3200. www.statefair.com.* Animal and 4-H contests, music, horse show, and carnival. Late Sept-early Oct.

Limited-Service Hotels

★★ COURTYARD BY MARRIOTT. *6400 W Broad St, Richmond (23230). Phone 804/282-1881; toll-free 800/321-2211; fax 804/288-2934. www.courtyard.com.* 145 rooms, 3 story. Check-out noon. High-speed Internet access. Restaurant, bar. Fitness room. Outdoor pool, whirlpool. **$**

★★ DOUBLETREE HOTEL. *5501 Eubank Rd, Sandston (23150). Phone 804/226-6400; fax 804/226-1269. www.doubletree.com.* This hotel is just 40 minutes from Colonial Williamsburg and directly across from the Richmond International Airport. Area attractions include Kings Dominion, Busch Gardens, Richmond Coliseum, Aviation Museum, and the Museum of the Confederacy. 160 rooms, 5 story. Check-out noon. Restaurant, bar. Fitness room. Outdoor pool, whirlpool. Airport transportation available. **$**

★★ EMBASSY SUITES. *2925 Emerywood Pkwy, Richmond (23294). Phone 804/672-8585; toll-free 800/362-2779; fax 804/672-3749. www.embassysuites.com.* 224 rooms, 8 story, all suites. Complimentary full breakfast. Check-out noon. Restaurant, bar. Fitness room. Indoor pool, whirlpool. Business center. **$**

★ **LA QUINTA INN.** *6910 Midlothian Tpke, Richmond (23225). Phone 804/745-7100; toll-free 800/531-5900; fax 804/276-6660. www.laquinta.com.* 130 rooms, 3 story. Pets accepted. Complimentary continental breakfast. Check-out noon. Outdoor pool. **$**

★ **QUALITY INN.** *8008 W Broad St, Richmond (23294). Phone 804/346-0000; fax 804/346-4547. www.choicehotels.com.* 191 rooms, 6 story. Pets accepted; fee. Complimentary continental breakfast. Check-out 11 am. Fitness room. Outdoor pool. **$**

★ ★ **SHERATON RICHMOND WEST HOTEL.** *6624 W Broad St, Richmond (23230). Phone 804/285-2000; toll-free 800/228-9000; fax 804/288-3961. www.sheraton.com.* 372 rooms, 8 story. Check-in 3 pm, check-out noon. Restaurant, bar. Fitness room. Indoor pool, outdoor pool. Tennis. Airport transportation available. Business center. **$$**

Full-Service Hotels

★ ★ ★ **THE BERKELEY HOTEL.** *1200 E Cary St, Richmond (23219). Phone 804/780-1300; toll-free 888/780-4422; fax 804/648-4728. www.berkeleyhotel.com.* This hotel opened in 1988 but appears to be a property of days gone by. It is located at the crossroads of the business district and Historic Shockoe Slip. Dark wood paneling adorns the lobby and dining room. Dramatic windows to the ceiling give it a European appearance, and diners at the hotel's restaurant get a view of the Slip's cobblestone and lamplights. 56 rooms, 6 story. Check-out noon. Restaurant, bar. **$**

★ ★ ★ **CROWNE PLAZA.** *555 E Canal St, Richmond (23219). Phone 804/788-0900; fax 804/788-7087. www.richmondcrowneplaza.com.* Just 9 miles from Richmond International Airport, this hotel is situated in the heart of the historic district and minutes from area attractions such as Shockoe Slip, Sixth Street Market Place, museums, theaters, and fine dining. 299 rooms, 16 story. Check-out noon. Restaurant, bar. Fitness room. Indoor pool, whirlpool. Business center. **$$**

★ ★ ★ ★ ★ **THE JEFFERSON HOTEL.** *101 W Franklin St, Richmond (23220). Phone 804/788-8000; toll-free 800/424-8014; fax 804/225-0334. www.jefferson-hotel.com.* The Jefferson Hotel is an institution in the heart of Richmond. Imaginations run wild at this historic landmark, dating to 1895. It's easy to conjure a beautifully dressed debutante gliding down the hotel's sweeping staircase, or influential politicians having a heated debate under the impressive marble-style columns. The guest rooms are furnished in a traditional style defined by antique reproductions and fine art, while modern amenities and inimitable Southern hospitality ensure the comfort of all guests. Pedigreed residents take afternoon tea here. TJ's provides a casual setting for fine dining with local dishes like oyster chowder and peanut soup. The hotel's star restaurant is Lemaire (see), with its sparkling ambience and refined menu. 264 rooms, 9 story. Pets accepted; fee. Check-in 3 pm, check-out noon. Restaurant, bar. Children's activity center. Fitness room. Indoor pool. Business center. **$$$**

★ ★ ★ **MARRIOTT RICHMOND.** *500 E Broad St, Richmond (23219). Phone 804/643-3400; fax 804/788-1230. www.marriott.com.* 410 rooms, 17 story. Check-in 3 pm, check-out noon. Restaurant, bar. Fitness room. Indoor pool, whirlpool. Business center. **$**

★ ★ ★ **OMNI RICHMOND HOTEL.** *100 S 12th St, Richmond (23219). Phone 804/344-7000; fax 804/648-6704. www.omnihotels.com.* This contemporary hotel is located in the center of the financial and historic districts and features views of the scenic James River. 369 rooms, 19 story. Check-out noon. Restaurant, bar. Indoor pool. Business center. **$**

Specialty Lodgings

The following lodging establishments are approved by Mobil Travel Guide, but due to their unique and individualized nature have not been given a traditional Mobil Star rating. Included in this listing you may find bed-and-breakfasts, limited-service inns, guest ranches, and other unique hotel properties.

EMMANUEL HUTZLER HOUSE. *2036 Monument Ave, Richmond (23220). Phone 804/353-6900. www.bensonhouse.com.* 4 rooms, 3 story. Children over 12 years only. Complimentary full breakfast. Check-in 4 pm, check-out noon. Built in 1914; antiques. **$**

LINDEN ROW INN. *100 E Franklin St, Richmond (23219). Phone 804/783-7000; toll-free 800/348-7424; fax 804/648-7504. www.lindenrowinn.com.* 68 rooms, 4 story. Complimentary continental breakfast. Check-in 3 pm, check-out 11 am. Restaurant (public by reservation). In a block of Greek Revival row houses (1847), around a courtyard thought to be the playground of Edgar Allan Poe; antique and period furnishings and décor. **$**

Restaurants

★ ★ ACACIA. *3325 W Cary St, Richmond (23221). Phone 804/354-6060; fax 804/354-6062. www.acaciarestaurant.com.* American menu. Lunch, dinner. Closed Sun. In an old renovated church. **$$**

★ ★ AMICI. *3343 W Cary St, Richmond (23221). Phone 804/353-4700; fax 804/278-6291. www.amiciristorante.net.* Italian menu. Lunch, dinner. Closed holidays. Bar. Outdoor seating. **$$**

★ BYRAM'S LOBSTER HOUSE. *3215 W Broad St, Richmond (23230). Phone 804/355-9193. www.byrams.com.* Seafood menu. Lunch, dinner. Closed Jan 1, Dec 25. Bar. **$$**

★ ★ CABO'S CORNER BISTRO. *2053 W Broad St, Richmond (23220). Phone 804/355-1144.* Seafood menu. Dinner. Closed Sun-Mon. Bar. Casual attire. **$$**

★ ★ CAFE MANDOLIN. *1309 W Main St, Richmond (23220). Phone 804/355-8558.* International menu. Lunch, dinner. Closed Sun-Mon. Bar. Casual attire. Outdoor seating. **$$**

★ CAFFE DI PAGLIACCI. *214 N Lombardy St, Richmond (23220). Phone 804/353-3040; fax 804/358-2509. www.caffedipagliacci.com.* Italian menu. Dinner, Sun brunch. Closed Mon; holidays. Bar. Casual attire. **$$**

★ ★ ★ THE DINING ROOM AT THE BERKELEY HOTEL. *1200 E Cary St, Richmond (23219). Phone 804/225-5105; fax 804/343-1885. www.berkleyhotel.com.* Located in a European-style hotel, this handsomely decorated dining room serves elegant, impeccably prepared meals in an atmosphere that is sophisticated and tranquil. Many fine Virginia products are served, and classical preparations prevail. Breakfast, lunch, dinner. Children's menu. **$$$**

★ ★ HALF WAY HOUSE. *10301 Jefferson Davis Hwy, Richmond (23237). Phone 804/275-1760.* American menu. Lunch, dinner. Bar. Antique-furnished manor house (1760) was a stop on the Petersburg stagecoach line until the late 19th century; hosted Washington, Lafayette, Patrick Henry, and Jefferson, among others. Used as a Union headquarters during the 1864 siege of Richmond. **$$$**

★ ★ HELEN'S. *2527 W Main St, Richmond (23220). Phone 804/358-4370; fax 804/358-4553.* American menu. Dinner. Closed Mon; holidays. **$$**

★ ★ ★ KABUTO JAPANESE HOUSE OF STEAK. *8052 W Broad St, Richmond (23294). Phone 804/747-9573.* Japanese menu. Lunch, dinner. Closed Thanksgiving, Dec 25. Bar. Children's menu. **$$**

★ ★ LA PETIT FRANCE. *2108 Maywill St, Richmond (23230). Phone 804/353-8729; fax 804/353-4692. www.lapetitefrance.net.* French menu. Lunch, dinner. Closed Sun-Mon; holidays; also the last two weeks in Aug. Children's menu. Jacket required (dinner). **$$$**

★ ★ ★ LEMAIRE. *101 W Franklin, Richmond (23220). Phone 804/788-8000; fax 804/344-5162. www.jefferson-hotel.com.* Old-world fine dining comes to life at Lemaire, located in the historic Jefferson Hotel (see). The restaurant is named for Etienne Lemaire, who served as maitre d' to President Jefferson and was widely credited for introducing the fine art of cooking with wines to America. His love of food and wine is continued at Lemaire, where contemporary Southern cooking goes upscale with French accents, homegrown herbs, featherweight sauces, and seasonal ingredients. Professional and friendly service and quiet, intimate surroundings make dining at Lemaire a delight. American menu. Breakfast, lunch, dinner. Closed Memorial Day. Bar. Children's menu. Jacket required. Valet parking. **$$$**

★ MILLIE'S. *2603 E Main St, Richmond (23223). Phone 804/643-5512; fax 804/648-4321. www.milliesdiner.com.* Thai menu. Lunch, dinner, Sun brunch. Closed Mon. In front of old tobacco warehouses; huge collection of old 45 singles with mini-jukeboxes in booths. **$$**

★★★ THE OLD ORIGINAL BOOKBINDER'S. *2306 E Cary St, Richmond (23223). Phone 804/643-6900; fax 804/643-6690. www.oldoriginalbookbinders.com.* Seafood, steak menu. Dinner. Closed holidays. Bar. Children's menu. Valet parking. **$$$**

★ O'TOOLES. *4800 Forest Hill Ave, Richmond (23225). Phone 804/233-1781; fax 804/232-1737.* Seafood, steak menu. Lunch, dinner. Closed Dec 24-25. Bar. Children's menu. **$$**

★★ PEKING PAVILION. *1302 E Cary St, Richmond (23219). Phone 804/649-8888; fax 804/649-8147.* Chinese menu. Lunch, dinner, Sun brunch. Closed Thanksgiving. Bar. **$$**

★★★ RUTH'S CHRIS STEAK HOUSE. *11500 Huguenot Rd, Richmond (23113). Phone 804/378-0600; fax 804/378-0776. www.sizzlingsteak.com.* Located in the historic Bellgrade Plantation House, this restaurant offers fine dining with elegant Southern hospitality. Dine on the patio or in a private room with period furnishings. Dinner. Closed holidays. Bar. Outdoor seating. Organist Tues-Sun. **$$**

★★ SAM MILLER'S WAREHOUSE. *1210 E Cary St, Richmond (23219). Phone 804/644-5465; fax 804/644-5470. www.sammillers.com.* Seafood menu. Lunch, dinner. Closed Labor Day, Dec 25. Children's menu. Casual attire. In a historic district; display of antique mirrors. Lobster tank. **$$$**

★★ SKILLIGALEE. *5416 Glenside Dr, Richmond (23228). Phone 804/672-6200; fax 804/755-1312. www.skilligalee.com.* Seafood menu. Lunch, dinner. Closed Thanksgiving, Dec 25. Bar. Children's menu. **$$$**

★ STRAWBERRY STREET CAFE. *421 Strawberry St, Richmond (23220). Phone 804/353-6860; fax 804/358-3569. www.strawberrystreetcafe.com.* Lunch, dinner. Children's menu. Stained glass throughout the restaurant. **$$**

★ TANGLEWOOD ORDINARY. *2210 River Rd W, Maidens (23102). Phone 804/556-3284. www.ordinary.com.* Traditional Southern menu. Dinner. Closed Mon-Tues; holidays. Collection of *The Saturday Evening Post* dating from 1913. **$$**

★★ TOBACCO COMPANY. *1201 E Cary St, Richmond (23219). Phone 804/782-9555; fax 804/788-8913. www.thetobaccocompany.com.* American menu. Lunch, dinner, Sun brunch. Closed Jan 1, Dec 25. Bar. In a former tobacco warehouse (circa 1880); built around a skylit atrium with an antique cage elevator; many unusual antiques. **$$$**

★ TRAK'S. *9115 Quioccasin Rd, Richmond (23229). Phone 804/740-1700; fax 804/740-1700.* Mediterranean menu. Lunch, dinner. Closed Sun; holidays. Children's menu. **$$**

★★ YEN CHING. *6601 Midlothian Tpke, Richmond (23225). Phone 804/276-7430. www.yenchingdining.com.* Chinese menu. Lunch, dinner. Closed Thanksgiving. Bar. **$$**

Richmond National Battlefield Park (E-8)

See also Ashland, Richmond

(Headquarters located in Chimborazo Park)

Web site www.nps.gov/rich

A total of seven Union drives on Richmond, the symbol of secession, were made during the Civil War. Richmond National Battlefield Park, 770 acres in ten different units, preserves sites of the two efforts that came close to success—McClellan's Peninsula Campaign of 1862 and Grant's attack in 1864.

What to See and Do

Main Visitor Center. *3215 E Broad St, Richmond. In Chimborazo City Park on Hwy 60 E. Phone 804/226-1981.* Information, exhibits, film, slide program. (Daily; closed Jan 1, Thanksgiving, Dec 25) **FREE**

Self-guided tour. Auto drive (60 miles) with markers, maps, recorded messages providing background, detailed information for specific places. Visitors may select own route, including all or part of the drive.

Other Visitor Centers. *Richmond.* Cold Harbor, 16 miles NE on Hwy 156 (daily, unstaffed) and Fort Harrison, 10 miles SE on Hwy 5 and Battlefield Park Rd (June-Aug, daily). **FREE**

Roanoke (E-5)

See also Blacksburg, Blue Ridge Parkway, Harrisonburg, Salem

Settled 1740
Population 94,911
Elevation 948 ft
Area Code 540
Information Roanoke Valley Convention & Visitors Bureau, 114 Market St, 24011; phone 540/342-6025 or toll-free 800/635-5535
Web site www.visitroanokeva.com

Nestled in the heart of the Blue Ridge Mountains, Roanoke has location, location, location. The view from the top of Mill Mountain standing under the famous Roanoke Star (the world's largest man-made star) reveals the spectacular beauty and vastness of the Roanoke Valley, which seems to go on forever in every direction.

Tucked in the center, the city itself evolved from a thriving industrial railroading nexus in the late 1800s to a state-of-the-art destination where electrons are now the currency of choice. Over the years, Roanoke has become a sophisticated place, with a thriving arts community, a wealth of museums, and varied entertainment and theater offerings, which now share the stage with several world-class educational institutions. The hustle and bustle of the Norfolk and Southern Railroad has given way to health care, education, travel, conventions, industry, and trade. From the history of the Center in the Square and Virginia's Explore Park to the high-tech Hotel Roanoke Conference Center, you can enjoy it all!

What to See and Do

Center in the Square. *1 Market Sq, Roanoke (24011). Downtown. Phone 540/342-5700.* Restored 20th-century furniture warehouse housing five independent cultural organizations: three museums, including Art Museum of Western Virginia, and two professional theater companies (see SPECIAL EVENTS). (Tues-Sun; closed holidays) Also here are

History Museum of Western Virginia. Permanent exhibits deal with Roanoke history from days of Native Americans to present. Archives, library (by appointment). (Tues-Sun; closed holidays) **$**

Science Museum of Western Virginia & Hopkins Planetarium. *Phone 540/342-5710.* Museum contains hands-on exhibits in the natural and physical sciences: animals of land and ocean, computers, TV weather station. Workshops, programs, and classes for children and adults; special exhibits. Hopkins Planetarium shows films. (Tues-Sun; closed holidays) **$$$**

George Washington and Jefferson National Forests. (See HARRISONBURG)

Mill Mountain Zoological Park. *Hwy 220/I-581 and Blue Ridge Pkwy, Roanoke (24014). Phone 540/343-3241. www.mmzoo.org.* Zoo sits atop Mill Mountain; offers picnic areas with magnificent views of city and valley. (Daily; closed Dec 25) **$$$**

Virginia's Explore Park. *3900 Rutrough Rd SE, Roanoke (24014). Blue Ridge Pkwy, mile 115. Phone toll-free 800/842-9163. www.explorepark.org.* This 1,300-acre living history museum and nature center features re-created frontier settlement that depicts life in western Virginia in 1671, 1740, and 1850. Six miles of hiking trails. Picnic areas. (May-Oct, Wed-Sun) **$$$**

Virginia Museum of Transportation. *303 Norfolk Ave, Roanoke (24016). Downtown. Phone 540/342-5670. www.vmt.org.* Vehicles from the past and present. Large steam, diesel, and electric locomotive collection. Aviation exhibits; model of miniature traveling circus. Hands-on exhibits. (Mar-Dec: daily; rest of year: Wed-Sun; closed holidays) **$$$**

Special Events

Festival in the Park. *119 Park Ave, Roanoke (23510). Phone 757/625-1445.* Art exhibits, crafts, sports, food, parade, entertainment. Two weekends beginning the Fri before Memorial Day.

Mill Mountain Theatre. *1 Market Sq SE, Roanoke (24011). Center in the Square. For reservations phone 540/342-5740.* Musicals, comedies, dramas. Nightly Tues-Sun; Sat-Sun matinees. Regular season, Oct-Aug.

Virginia State Championship Chili Cookoff. *City Market, Roanoke. Phone 540/342-4716.* Teams compete to represent Virginia in World Cook-off. Samples, entertainment. Contact Roanoke Special Events Committee, 210 Reserve Ave SW, 24016. First Sat in May.

Limited-Service Hotels

★★ CLARION HOTEL. *2727 Ferndale Dr NW, Roanoke (24017). Phone 540/362-4500; fax 540/362-4506. www.choicehotels.com.* 154 rooms, 5 story. Pets accepted, some restrictions; fee. Check-out noon. Restaurant, bar. Fitness room. Indoor pool, outdoor pool, whirlpool. Tennis. Airport transportation available. **$**

★★ DOUBLETREE HOTEL. *110 Shenandoah Ave, Roanoke (24016). Phone 540/985-5900; fax 540/853-8264.* This vintage 1882 hotel has been lovingly restored to its rich, 19th-century elegance and is listed in the National Register of Historic Places. It is just a short walk across the Market Square Bridge to downtown Roanoke. 332 rooms, 7 story. Check-out noon. High-speed Internet access. Restaurant, bar. Pool, whirlpool. Airport transportation available. Business center. **$**

★ HAMPTON INN. *3816 Franklin Rd SW, Roanoke (24014). Phone 540/989-4000; fax 540/989-0250. www.hamptoninn.com.* 59 rooms, 2 story. Complimentary continental breakfast. Check-out 11 am. **$**

★★ HOLIDAY INN. *4468 Starkey Rd, Roanoke (24014). Phone 540/774-4400; toll-free 888/228-5040; fax 540/774-1195. www.holiday-inn.com.* 196 rooms, 5 story. Pets accepted; fee. Check-out noon. Restaurant, bar. Outdoor pool. Airport transportation available. **$**

★★ RAMADA INN. *1927 Franklin Rd SW, Roanoke (24014). Phone 540/343-0121; fax 599/343-0121. www.ramada.com.* 127 rooms, 4 story. Pets accepted; fee. Complimentary full breakfast. Check-out noon. Restaurant, bar. Outdoor pool. Near river. **$**

Full-Service Hotel

★★★ PATRICK HENRY HOTEL. *617 S Jefferson St, Roanoke (24011). Phone 540/345-8811; toll-free 800/303-0988; fax 540/345-1648. www.patrickhenryroanoke.com.* 117 rooms, 10 story. Complimentary continental breakfast. Check-out noon. Restaurant, bar. Airport transportation available. **$**

Specialty Lodging

The following lodging establishment is approved by Mobil Travel Guide, but due to its unique and individualized nature has not been given a traditional Mobil Star rating. Included in this listing you may find bed-and-breakfasts, limited-service inns, guest ranches, and other unique hotel properties.

CLAIBORNE HOUSE. *185 Claiborne Ave, Rocky Mount (24151). Phone 540/483-4616. www.claibornehouse.net.* 5 rooms, 2 story. Complimentary full breakfast. Check-in 3 pm, check-out 11 am. Built in 1895; Victorian-style décor. **$**

Restaurants

★★ BILLY'S RITZ. *102 Salem Ave SE, Roanoke (24011). Phone 540/342-3937.* Steak menu. Dinner. Closed holidays; Jan 1-16. Bar. Outdoor seating. **$$**

★★ KABUKI JAPANESE STEAK HOUSE. *3503 Franklin Rd SW, Roanoke (24014). Phone 540/981-0222; fax 540/342-0406.* Japanese menu. Dinner. Closed holidays; also Jan 2, Super Bowl Sun. Bar. Children's menu. Reservations recommended. **$$**

★★★ LIBRARY. *3117 Franklin Rd, Roanoke (24014). Phone 540/985-0811; fax 540/345-6588.* French, American menu. Dinner. Closed Sun; holidays. Bar. Jacket required. **$$$**

Salem (E-5)

See also Blacksburg, Radford, Roanoke

Founded 1802
Population 24,747
Elevation 1,060 ft
Area Code 540
Zip 24153
Information Salem/Roanoke County Chamber of Commerce, 9 N College Ave, PO Box 832; phone 540/387-0267

Salem, part of the industrial complex of the Roanoke Valley, shares with Roanoke the beautiful setting between the Blue Ridge and Allegheny mountains. Historic markers throughout Salem indicate the city's colonial heritage.

What to See and Do

Dixie Caverns. *5753 W Main St, Salem (24153). Off I-81 at exit 132. Phone 540/380-2085.* Stalactites in lofty chambers; modern lighting system makes 45-minute tour comfortable as well as interesting. Pottery shop and mineral shop (all year). Camping facilities (fee). (Daily; closed Dec 25) **$$$**

Roanoke College. *221 College Ln, Salem (24153). Off I-81. Phone 540/375-2282.* (1842) (1,750 students) One of the few Southern colleges to remain open during the Civil War. Many historic buildings, some antebellum. Olin Hall, fine arts building, has theater, art gallery, and sculptures. Excellent exhibit of paintings, photographs, and other items concerning Mary, Queen of Scots (by appointment only; phone 540/375-2487). Tours.

Limited-Service Hotels

★ HOLIDAY INN EXPRESS. *1535 E Main St, Salem (24153). Phone 540/986-1000; toll-free 800/465-4329; fax 540/986-0355. www.holiday-inn.com.* 70 rooms, 3 story. Complimentary continental breakfast. Check-out 11 am. **$**

★ ★ RAMADA INN. *1671 Skyview Rd, Salem (24153). Phone 540/389-7061; fax 540/389-7060. www.ramada.com.* 102 rooms, 3 story. Complimentary continental breakfast. Check-out noon. Restaurant. Outdoor pool, children's pool. **$**

Restaurant

★ SHANGHAI. *1416 Colorado St, Salem (24153). Phone 540/389-4151; fax 540/389-7049.* Chinese menu. Lunch, dinner, Sun brunch. Closed Thanksgiving, Dec 25. Bar. Children's menu. **$**

Shenandoah National Park (C-7)

See also Front Royal, Harrisonburg, Luray, New Market

About 450 million years ago, the Blue Ridge was at the bottom of a sea. Today, it averages 2,000 feet above sea level; some 300 square miles of the loveliest Blue Ridge area are included in Shenandoah National Park.

The park is 80 miles long and 2-13 miles wide. Running its full length is the 105-mile Skyline Drive. Main entrances are the North Entrance (Front Royal), from I-66, Hwys 340, 522, and 55; Thornton Gap Entrance (31.5 miles south), from Hwy 211; Swift Run Gap Entrance (65.7 miles south), from Hwy 33; and the South Entrance (Rockfish Gap), from I-64, Hwy 250, and the Blue Ridge Parkway (see). The drive, twisting and turning along the crest of the Blue Ridge, is one of the finest scenic trips in the East. Approximately 70 overlooks give views of the Blue Ridge, the Piedmont, and, to the west, the Shenandoah Valley and the Alleghenies.

The drive offers much, but the park offers more. Exploration on foot or horseback attracts thousands of visitors who return again and again. Most of the area is wooded, predominantly in white, red, and chestnut oak, with hickory, birch, maple, hemlock, tulip poplar, and nearly 100 other species scattered here and there. At the head of Whiteoak Canyon are hemlocks that are more than 300 years old. The park bursts with color and contrast in the fall, which makes this season particularly popular with visitors. The park is a sanctuary for deer, bears, foxes, and bobcats, along with more than 200 varieties of birds.

Accommodations are available in the park, with lodges, motel-type units, and cabins at Big Meadows and Skyland and housekeeping cabins at Lewis Mountain. For reservations and rates (which vary), contact ARA-MARK Virginia Sky-Line Company, Inc, PO Box 727, Luray 22835-9051; phone toll-free 800/999-4714. Nearby communities provide a variety of accommodations. In the park, there are restaurants at Panorama, Skyland, and Big Meadows; light lunches and groceries are available at Elkwallow, Big Meadows, Lewis Mountain, and Loft Mountain waysides.

The park is open all year; lodge and cabin accommodations, usually Mar-Dec; phone ahead for the schedule. Skyline Drive is occasionally closed for short periods during Nov-Mar. As in all national parks, pets must be on a leash. The speed limit is 35 miles per hour. $10 per car per week, annual permit $20; Golden Age, Golden Access, and Golden Eagle Passports are accepted (see MAKING THE MOST OF YOUR TRIP).

Park Headquarters is 5 miles east of Luray on Hwy 211. Detailed information and pamphlets may be obtained by contacting the Superintendent, Shenandoah National Park, 3655 Hwy 211 E, Luray 22835; phone 540/999-3500.

What to See and Do

Camping. *Phone toll-free 800/365-CAMP.* First-come, first-served tent and trailer sites (no hookups) at Mathews Arm, Lewis Mountain, and Loft Mountain. Big Meadows requires reservations. Fourteen-day limit. Campers must register and check out (spring-fall). Write to the Park Superintendent, 3655 Hwy 211 E, Luray 22835, for information. **$$$$**

Fishing. Trout. Regulations and directions at entrance stations, Dickey Ridge, Panorama, Big Meadows, and Loft Mountain. State or five-day nonresident license necessary.

Hiking. The 500 miles of trails include 101 miles of the Appalachian Trail. Along the trail, which winds 2,100 miles from Maine to Georgia, are numerous side trails to mountaintops, waterfalls, and secluded valleys. The trail crosses Skyline Drive at several points and can be entered at many overlooks. Overnight backcountry use requires a permit. No open fires are allowed. Regulations and permits may be obtained at any park entrance station, visitor center, or at Park Headquarters. The backcountry may be closed during periods of high fire danger. Visitor centers and lodges post schedules of evening programs and ranger-led hikes. Self-guided walks ranging from 1/2 to two hours are at Dickey Ridge (mile 4.6), Skyland (mile 1.7), Big Meadows (mile 51.1), Lewis Mountain (mile 57.5), and Loft Mountain (mile 79.5).

Interpretive program. Guided walks, illustrated campfire talks. (Usually mid-June-mid-Oct; rest of year, on a limited basis) Obtain a schedule at Park Headquarters, entrance stations, visitor centers, or concessions.

Picnicking. Near Dickey Ridge Visitor Center, Elkwallow, Pinnacles, Big Meadows, Lewis Mountain, South River, and Loft Mountain.

★ Points of special interest on Skyline Drive. Mileposts are numbered north to south, starting at Front Royal. Periods of operation are estimated—phone ahead.

Big Meadows. *Mile 51.1, Shenandoah.* (3,500 feet) Accommodations, restaurant; store, gas; tent and trailer sites; picnic grounds; nature trail. (Usually Apr-Nov)

Byrd Visitor Center. *Mile 51, Shenandoah.* Exhibits, information, book sales, orientation programs, maps. (Usually Apr-Nov, daily)

Dickey Ridge Visitor Center. *Mile 4.6, Shenandoah.* Exhibits, programs, information, book sales; picnic grounds. (Usually Apr-Nov, daily)

Elkwallow. *Mile 24.1, Shenandoah.* (2,445 feet) Picnic grounds; food, store. (May-Oct, daily)

Lewis Mountain. *Mile 57.5, Shenandoah.* (3,390 feet) One- and two-bedroom cabins with heat; tent and trailer sites; picnic grounds, store. (Usually May-Oct)

Loft Mountain. *Mile 79.5, Shenandoah.* (3,380 feet) Picnicking, camping (May-Oct); wayside facility; gas, store (May-Oct).

Loft Mountain Information Center. *Mile 79.5, Shenandoah.* Exhibits, information; programs, nature trail. (Usually May-Nov)

Mary's Rock Tunnel. *Mile 32.4, Shenandoah.* (2,545 feet) Drive goes through 600 feet of rock (clearance 13 feet).

Panorama. *Mile 31.5, at junction Hwy 211, Shenandoah.* (2,300 feet) Dining room, gift shop. Trail to Mary's Rock. Closed in winter.

Pinnacles. *Mile 36.7, Shenandoah.* (3,500 feet) Picnic grounds.

Skyland. *Mile 41.7, Shenandoah.* (3,680 feet) Accommodations, restaurant, gift shop; guided trail rides; Stony Man Nature Trail.

South River. *Mile 62.8, Shenandoah.* (2,940 feet) Picnic grounds, 2 1/2-mile round-trip trail to falls.

Riding. Many miles of horseback trails. Trail rides (ponies for children) for rent at Skyland.

South Boston (F-6)

See also Brookneal, Clarksville, Danville

Population 8,491
Elevation 407 ft
Area Code 804
Zip 24592

What to See and Do

Staunton River State Park. *1170 Staunton Trl, Scottsburg (24589). 8 miles NE on Hwy 304, then 11 miles SE on Hwy 344, in Scottsburg. Phone 804/572-4623.* Approximately 1,600 acres of woods, meadows, and lengthy shoreline on John H. Kerr Reservoir (Buggs Island Lake) and the Dan and Staunton rivers. Swimming pool, wading pool, bathhouse, fishing, boating (ramp); hiking and nature trails, tennis courts, picnic facilities, shelters, children's playground, concession, tent and trailer sites, seven cabins (Mar-Dec). **$**

South Hill (F-7)

See also Clarksville

Population 4,403
Elevation 440 ft
Area Code 804
Zip 23970

Limited-Service Hotel

★ HOLIDAY INN EXPRESS. *101 Thompson St, South Hill (23950). Phone 434/955-2777; fax 434/955-2700. www.holiday-inn.com.* 55 rooms, 2 story. Complimentary continental breakfast. Check-out 11 am. Fitness room. Outdoor pool. **$**

Springfield (B-6)

See also Alexandria, Arlington County (Ronald Reagan Washington-National Airport Area), Fairfax, Mount Vernon; also see District of Columbia

Population 30,417
Elevation 300 ft
Area Code 703

Limited-Service Hotels

★ BEST WESTERN POTOMAC MILLS. *14619 Potomac Mills Rd, Woodbridge (22192). Phone 703/494-4433; toll-free 800/543-2392; fax 703/385-2627. www.bestwestern.com.* 176 rooms, 9 story. Complimentary continental breakfast. Check-out noon. Fitness room. Outdoor pool. **$**

★ HAMPTON INN. *6550 Loisdale Ct, Springfield (22150). Phone 703/924-9444; toll-free 800/426-7866; fax 703/971-6944. www.hamptoninn.com.* 153 rooms, 7 story. Pets accepted. Complimentary continental breakfast. Check-out noon. Outdoor pool. **$**

Full-Service Hotel

★★★ HILTON SPRINGFIELD. *6550 Loisdale Rd, Springfield (22150). Phone 703/971-8900; fax 703/971-8527. www.hilton.com.* This property is located just 15 minutes from Washington DC. 244 rooms, 12 story. Restaurant, bar. Indoor pool. Check-out 1 pm. Fitness room. **$**

Restaurant

★★ MIKE'S AMERICAN GRILL. *6210 Backlick Rd, Springfield (22150). Phone 703/644-7100; fax 703/866-3769.* Steak menu. Lunch, dinner. Closed Thanksgiving, Dec 25. Bar. **$$**

Staunton (D-6)

See also Harrisonburg, Monterey, Waynesboro

Settled 1736
Population 23,853
Elevation 1,385 ft
Area Code 540
Zip 24401
Information Travel Information Center, 1250 Richmond Rd; phone 540/332-3972 or toll-free 800/332-5219

To historians, Staunton (STAN-ton) is known as the birthplace of Woodrow Wilson, and to students of government, as the place where the city manager plan was first conceived and adopted. Set in fertile Shenandoah Valley fields and orchards between the Blue Ridge and Allegheny mountain ranges, the area around Staunton produces poultry, livestock, and wool. Manufacturing firms in the city make air conditioners, razors, candy, and clothing.

A Ranger District office of the George Washington and Jefferson national forests is located here.

What to See and Do

Augusta Stone Church. *28 Old Stone Church Ln, Fort Defiance (24437). 7 miles N on Hwy 11. Phone 540/248-2634.* (1747) Oldest Presbyterian church in continuous use in state. Once used as fort during Native American raids. Museum of early church artifacts (by appointment).

Frontier Culture Museum. *1290 Richmond Rd, Staunton (24401). I-81 exit 222, Hwy 250 W. Phone 540/332-7850.* Living history museum consists of working farms brought together from England, Germany, Northern Ireland, and an American farm. The European farms represent what America's early settlers left; the American farm, from the Valley of Virginia, reflects the blend of the various European influences. Visitors are able to see and take part in life as it was lived on these 17th-, 18th-, and 19th-century farmsteads. Costumed interpreters demonstrate daily life at all four sites. Visitor center. (Daily; closed first week in Jan, Thanksgiving, Dec 25) **$$$**

Gypsy Hill Park. *Chruchville and Thornrose aves, Staunton (24401). Phone 540/332-3945.* Lake stocked with fish, swimming (late May-Labor Day, fee); lighted softball field with concession stand, outdoor basketball courts, tennis, 18-hole golf, picnicking, miniature train ride, playgrounds, fairgrounds. (Daily)

McCormick Memorial Wayside. *McCormick Farm Cir, Steeles Tavern. 16 miles SW via Hwy 11, I-81; 1 mile E of I-81 on Hwy 606 near Steeles Tavern. Phone 540/377-2255.* Cyrus McCormick's first reaper is displayed here. Picnic grounds. (Daily) **FREE**

Trinity Episcopal Church. *120 W Beverley St, Staunton (24401). Phone 540/886-9132.* (1855) Founded as Augusta Parish Church (1746), original building on this site served as Revolutionary capital of state for 16 days in 1781. Open on request (Mon-Fri).

Woodrow Wilson Birthplace and Presidential Museum. *24 N Coalter St, Staunton (24401). Near I-81, I-64, and Hwy 11. Phone 540/885-0897.* Restored Greek Revival manse with period furnishings and Wilson family mementos from 1850s; museum building on grounds houses seven-gallery presidential exhibit, "The Life and Times of Woodrow Wilson," and his 1919 Pierce-Arrow limousine. Victorian gardens. (Daily; closed Jan 1, Thanksgiving, Dec 25) **$$$**

Special Event

Jazz in the Park. *Gypsy Hill Park, 1000 Montgomery Ave, Staunton (24401).* Thurs nights. July-Aug.

Limited-Service Hotels

★ BEST WESTERN STAUNTON INN. *260 Rowe Rd, Staunton (24401). Phone 540/885-1112; toll-free 800/752-9471; fax 540/885-0166. www.bestwestern.com.* 80 rooms, 4 story. Complimentary continental breakfast. Check-out 11 am. Indoor pool. **$**

★ COMFORT INN. *1302 Richmond Ave, Staunton (24401). Phone 540/886-5000; fax 540/886-6643. www.choicehotels.com.* 98 rooms, 5 story. Pets accepted, some restrictions; fee. Complimentary continental breakfast. Check-out 11 am. Outdoor pool. **$**

★★ HOLIDAY INN. *I-81; Hwy 275, Staunton (24401). Phone 540/248-6020; fax 540/248-2902. www.holiday-inn.com.* 116 rooms, 4 story. Check-out noon. Restaurant, bar. Fitness room. Indoor pool, outdoor pool. Golf. Tennis. Airport transportation available. **$**

Full-Service Inn

★★★ BELLE GRAE INN. *515 W Frederick St, Staunton (24401). Phone 540/886-5151; fax 540/886-6641. www.bellegrae.com.* 14 rooms, 2 story. Children over 12 years only. Complimentary full breakfast. Check-in 3 pm, check-out 11 am. Restaurant. Airport transportation available. 1870s restored Victorian mansion. **$**

Specialty Lodgings

The following lodging establishments are approved by Mobil Travel Guide, but due to their unique and individualized nature have not been given a traditional Mobil Star rating. Included in this listing you may find bed-and-breakfasts, limited-service inns, guest ranches, and other unique hotel properties.

FREDERICK HOUSE. *28 N New St, Staunton (24401). Phone 540/885-4220; toll-free 800/334-5575; fax 540/885-5180. www.frederickhouse.com.* 23 rooms, 2 story. Complimentary full breakfast. Check-in 3 pm, check-out 11 am. Encompasses 6 adjacent townhouses built 1810-1919. **$$**

THORNROSE HOUSE. *531 Thornrose Ave, Staunton (24401). Phone 540/885-7026; toll-free 800/861-4338; fax 540/885-6458. www.thornrosehouse.com.* 5 rooms, 2 story. Complimentary full breakfast. Check-in 3 pm, check-out 11 am. Georgian Revival house (1912); wraparound veranda. Opposite park. **$**

Restaurants

★ THE PULLMAN RESTAURANT. *36 Middlebrook Ave, Staunton (24401). Phone 540/885-6612; fax 540/885-6774. www.thepullman.com.* Seafood menu. Lunch, dinner, Sun brunch. Closed holidays. Children's menu. **$**

★ ROWE'S. *74 Rowe Rd, Staunton (24401). Phone 540/886-1833; fax 540/886-0910. www.mrsrowes.com.* Breakfast, lunch, dinner. Closed holidays. Children's menu. **$**

Strasburg (C-7)

See also Front Royal, Winchester, Woodstock

Founded 1761
Population 4,017
Elevation 578 ft
Area Code 540
Zip 22657
Information Chamber of Commerce, PO Box 42; phone 540/465-3187

Lying at the base of Massanutten Mountain and on the north fork of the Shenandoah River, Strasburg was founded in 1761 by German settlers. Prospering in the early 19th century as a center of trade and flour milling, the village later became identified with the manufacture of high quality pottery, earning the nickname "Pottown" after the Civil War. The town's location on the Manassas Gap Railroad and the Shenandoah Valley Turnpike gave Strasburg a pivotal role in Stonewall Jackson's Campaign of 1862. The first western Virginia town to be served by two railroads, Strasburg became prominent after 1890 as a railroad town, manufacturing center, and home of printing and publishing businesses.

Today Strasburg, located near the entrance to the Skyline Drive, offers historical and cultural museums. It attracts visitors with its antebellum and Victorian architecture and its burgeoning art community. The town calls itself the "antique capital of Virginia" because of its many antique shops.

What to See and Do

Belle Grove. *336 Belle Grove Rd, Strasburg (22645). 4 miles N on Hwy 11. Phone 540/869-2028.* (1794) The design of this limestone mansion reflects the influence of Thomas Jefferson. Used as Union headquarters during the Battle of Cedar Creek, October 19, 1864. Unusual interior woodwork; herb garden in rear. Guided tours. (Apr-Oct, daily) A National Trust for Historic Preservation property. (See SPECIAL EVENTS) **$$$**

Hupp's Hill Battlefield Park and Study Center. *33229 Old Valley Pike, Strasburg (22657). I-81 to exit 298, S 1/2 mile on Hwy 11. Phone 540/465-5884.* Former campsite for six different Civil War generals' troops, now a museum and hands-on interpretive center. Artifacts, documents, exhibits. Guided battlefield tours (by appointment; fee). (Daily; closed holidays) **$$**

Strasburg Museum. *440 E King St, Strasburg (22657). Phone 540/465-3175.* Blacksmith, cooper, and potter shop collections; displays from colonial homes; relics from Civil War and railroad eras; Native American artifacts. Housed in Southern Railway Depot. (May-Oct, daily) **$**

Special Events

Battle of Cedar Creek Reenactment. *Belle Grove, 8437 Valley Pike, Middletown (22645). Phone 830/278-2016.* Mid-Oct.

Mayfest. Celebration of town's German heritage with parade, entertainment and arts, crafts, antiques, and foods fairs. Third weekend in May.

Wayside Theatre. *7853 Main St, Middletown (22645). On Hwy 11, I-81 exit 302. Phone 540/869-1776.* Professional performances. Wed-Sun. Reservations required. Late May-mid-Oct and Dec.

Full-Service Inns

★ ★ ★ HOTEL STRASBURG. *213 S Holliday St, Strasburg (22657). Phone 540/465-9191; toll-free 800/348-8327; fax 540/465-4788. www.hotelstrasburg.com.* Queen Anne, Renaissance Revival, and Eastlake-style antiques make up many of the furnishings of this Victorian-style hotel. Guests are welcome to explore each room to view the antiques, and most are available for purchase. 29 rooms, 3 story. Complimentary continental breakfast (Mon-Fri). Check-in 2 pm, check-out 11 am. Restaurant, bar. Victorian building. **$$**

★ ★ ★ WAYSIDE INN - MIDDLETOWNE. *7783 Main St, Middletown (22645). Phone 540/869-1797; fax 540/869-6038. www.waysideofva.com.* Operating since 1797, this inn is located in the Shenandoah Valley at the foot of the Massanutten Mountains. Canopied beds, English, French, and Oriental antiques, brocades, chintzes, and silks decorate the property. Fresh cuisine is prepared and served in seven different dining rooms. 22 rooms, 3 story. Check-in 2 pm, check-out 11 am. Restaurant, bar. **$**

Restaurants

★ ★ ★ HOTEL STRASBURG. *213 S Holliday St, Strasburg (22657). Phone 540/465-9191; fax 540/465-4788. www.hotelstrasburg.com.* The inn's ornate Victorian lobby gives way to an invitingly cozy country restaurant, where locals and travelers alike dine on fine wines and elegant cuisine. American menu. Lunch, dinner, Sun brunch. Bar. Children's menu. Reservations recommended. **$$**

★ ★ WILKINSON'S TAVERN. *7783 E Main St (Hwy 11), Middletown (22645). Phone 540/869-1797; fax 540/869-6038.* Breakfast, lunch, dinner, Sun brunch. Bar. Children's menu. In restored colonial-era inn; many antiques. **$$**

Surry (E-8)

See also Colonial Parkway, Hopewell, Jamestown (Colonial National Historical Park), Newport News, Williamsburg

Population 262
Elevation 122 ft
Area Code 757
Zip 23883

What to See and Do

Chippokes Plantation State Park. *695 Chippokes Park Rd, Surry (23883). 6 miles E via Hwy 10, 634. Across James River from Jamestown. Phone 757/294-3625 (park).* Plantation continuously operated since 1619. Approximately 1,600 acres. Swimming pool, fishing; hiking and bicycle paths, interpretive tour road, picnicking, concession. Visitor center, programs. Tours of mansion, carriage house, kitchen, and formal gardens (Memorial Day-Labor Day: Wed-Sun; Apr-Oct: weekends). (See SPECIAL EVENT) Farm and Forestry Museum (Memorial Day-Labor Day: Wed-Sun; Apr-Oct: weekends). **$**

Special Event

Pork, Peanut, and Pine Festival. *Chippokes Plantation, Surry.* Pork products, peanuts, crafts, pine decorations. Third weekend in July.

Tangier Island (D-9)

Settled 1666
Population 604
Elevation 3 ft
Area Code 757
Zip 23440

Bought from Native Americans for two overcoats, Tangier was first settled by a mainland family named West. In 1686, John Crockett moved here with his four sons and four daughters. They were later joined by a few other families. Descendants of these families now populate the island. Life is simple and lacks most urban complexities. Most of the men are anglers, oystering and clamming in one season, crabbing in another.

This tranquil little island (approximately 4 miles long) is 12 miles out in Chesapeake Bay. The island offers good duck hunting, fishing, swimming, and relaxation. There is an airfield here, and there are excursion boats from Reedville and Onancock, Virginia, and Crisfield, Maryland. Accommodations include a boarding house, Chesapeake House, with seven rooms, family-style meals. Contact PO Box 194; phone 757/891-2331 for reservations.

Tappahannock (D-8)

See also Lancaster, Montross, Richmond

Founded 1680
Population 2,068
Elevation 22 ft
Area Code 804
Zip 22560
Information Chamber of Commerce, PO Box 481; phone 804/443-5241

Bartholemew Hoskins patented the first land here in 1645. Following his lead, others came and a small village soon sprang up, known at that time as Hobbes His Hole. Formally chartered in 1682 as New Plymouth, the town was to experience yet another name change. Built around the Rappahannock River, which means "running water," the town port became known as Tappahannock or "on the running water." Four hundred men gathered here in 1765 to protest the Stamp Act.

Today the area around Prince and Duke streets and Water Lane of Tappahannock has been declared a historic district. Highlights include the beautifully renovated Ritchie House, the Anderton House, once used for the prizing of tobacco into hogsheads, and Scot's Arms Tavern.

Limited-Service Hotel

★ **DAYS INN.** *Rte 17 Tappahannock Blvd, Tappahannock (22560). Phone 804/443-9200; fax 804/443-2663. www.daysinn.com.* 60 rooms, 2 story. Complimentary continental breakfast. Check-out 11 am. **$**

Restaurant

★★ **LOWERY'S SEAFOOD RESTAURANT.** *Rte 17 and 360, Tappahannock (22560). Phone 804/443-4314; fax 804/443-4474. www.lowerysrestaurant.com.* Seafood menu. Lunch, dinner. Closed Dec 25. **$$**

Toano (E-8)

What to See and Do

The Tradition Golf Club at Stonehouse. *9700 Mill Pond Run, Toano (23168). Phone 757/566-1138. www.traditionalclubs.com/stone.* This picturesque par-71 course, laid out over 6,962 yards, has steep hills, deep ravines, broad fairways, and huge greens. Call for tee times. (Daily) **$$$$**

Triangle (C-8)

See also Alexandria, Fredericksburg, Manassas; also see District of Columbia

Population 5,500
Elevation 150 ft
Area Code 703
Zip 22172
Information Prince William County/Manassas Conference & Visitors Bureau, 8609 Sudley Rd, Suite 105, Manassas 20110; phone 703/396-7130
Web site www.visitpwc.com

Quantico Marine Corps Base is 3 miles east of town.

What to See and Do

Marine Corps Air-Ground Museum. *715 Broadway St, Quantico (22134). 2 miles E, in OCS area on Quantico Marine Corps Base. Phone 703/640-7965.* Chronological presentation of the Marine Corps Air-Ground Team's role in American history; artifacts on exhibit include aircraft, engines, armor, tracked and wheeled vehicles, artillery, small arms, uniforms, dioramas, and photographs in pre-World War II aviation hangars. (Apr-late Nov, Tues-Sun) **FREE**

Prince William Forest Park. *18100 Park Headquarters Rd, Triangle (22172). From I-95, 1/4 mile W on Hwy 619. Phone 703/221-7181. www.nps.gov/prwi.* Consists of 18,000 acres. Hiking, bicycling, picnicking, camping (14-day limit; no hookups; fee; group cabins by reservations only), trailer campground off Hwy 234 (fee; hookups, showers, laundry). Naturalist programs. (Daily) **$$**

Tysons Corner (C-8)

See also Arlington County (Ronald Reagan Washington-National Airport Area), Fairfax, Falls Church, McLean, Vienna; also see District of Columbia

Population 18,540
Area Code 703
Information Fairfax County Convention & Visitors Bureau, 8300 Boone Blvd, Suite 450, Tysons Corner 22182; phone 703/790-3329 or toll-free 800/7-FAIRFAX
Web site www.visitfairfax.org

This Virginia suburban area of Washington, DC, is the location of one of the largest shopping centers in the nation.

Limited-Service Hotel

★ **COMFORT INN.** *1587 Spring Hill Rd, Vienna (22182). Phone 703/448-8020; toll-free 800/828-3297; fax 703/448-0343. www.comfortinntysons.com.* 250 rooms, 3 story. Pets accepted, some restrictions; fee. Complimentary continental breakfast. Check-out noon. Outdoor pool. Airport transportation available. **$**

Full-Service Hotels

★★★ **HILTON MCLEAN TYSONS CORNER.** *7920 Jones Branch Dr, McLean (22102). Phone 703/847-5000; toll-free 800/932-3322; fax 703/761-5100. www.mclean.hilton.com.* Located close to the famous shopping area of Tyson Corners, this hotel has a glass-domed and vaulted atrium lobby and piano music for the enjoyment of guests. 458 rooms, 9 story. Check-out noon. Restaurant, bar. Indoor pool. Business center. **$$**

★★★ **MARRIOTT TYSONS CORNER.** *8028 Leesburg Pike, Vienna (22182). Phone 703/734-3200; fax 703/734-5763. www.marriott.com.* This property is located in the heart of Tysons Corner, next to a major shopping mall. 390 rooms, 15 story. Check-out noon. Restaurant, bar. Fitness room. Indoor pool, whirlpool. Business center. **$$**

★★★★ **THE RITZ-CARLTON, TYSONS CORNER.** *1700 Tyson's Blvd, McLean (22102). Phone 703/506-4300; fax 703/506-2694. www.ritzcarlton.com.* The Ritz-Carlton, Tysons Corner is northern Virginia's premier hotel. Only 12 miles from Washington, DC, this hotel offers an escape from the daily grind. The guest rooms are tastefully appointed with a stylishly refined aesthetic, and windows look out over the city or the Blue Ridge Mountains. Culinary works of art are created each day at Maestro (see). Its sensational contemporary Italian cuisine is complemented by the casually elegant décor; the open kitchen design allows guests to watch as the chef prepares their flavorful meals. Visitors to the Ritz-Carlton Day Spa check their worries at the door, and proper primping and pampering are the order of the day. Rose body wraps and hot stone therapy are just two of the wonderful signature treatments to be experienced here. Others opt for retail therapy and hit the more than 230 stores at the adjacent Tysons Galleria and Tysons Mall. 398 rooms, 24 story. Check-in 3 pm, check-out noon. Restaurant, bar. Fitness room, spa. Indoor pool, whirlpool. Business center. **$$**

Restaurants

★★ **AARATHI.** *409 Maple Ave E, Vienna (22180). Phone 703/938-0100; fax 703/319-0111.* Indian menu. Lunch, dinner. Closed July 4, Dec 25. Reservations recommended. **$$**

★★ **BISTRO 123.** *246 E Maple Ave, Vienna (22180). Phone 703/938-4379; fax 703/255-9042. www.bistro123vienna.com.* French menu. Lunch, dinner. Closed Sun. Bar. Outdoor seating. **$$**

★★ **BONAROTI.** *428 Maple Ave E, Vienna (22180). Phone 703/281-7550; fax 703/281-7587.* Italian menu. Lunch, dinner. Closed Sun; holidays. Bar. Children's menu. **$$**

★★ **CLYDE'S.** *8332 Leesburg Pike, Vienna (22182). Phone 703/734-1901; fax 703/790-1422. www.clydes.com.* Seafood menu. Lunch, dinner, Sun brunch. Bar. Children's menu. **$$**

★★ **HUNAN LION.** *2070 Chain Bridge Rd, Vienna (22182). Phone 703/734-9828; fax 703/893-2972. www.hunanlion.com.* Chinese menu. Lunch, dinner. Closed Thanksgiving. Bar. **$**

★★★ **LA PROVENCE.** *144 W Maple Ave, Vienna (22180). Phone 703/242-3777; fax 703/242-3983.* French Provençal menu. Lunch, dinner. Closed Sun; holidays. Bar. Reservations recommended. **$$**

★★★ **LE CANARD.** *132 Branch Rd, Vienna (22180). Phone 703/281-0070; fax 703/255-3465. www.lecanardrestaurant.com.* The formal interior of dark red fabrics and mahogany wood sets the tone for an elegantly traditional dining experience. Rich, sumptuous dishes are followed by unique flaming specialty coffees. French menu. Lunch, dinner. Bar. Reservations recommended. **$$**

★★★★ **MAESTRO.** *1700 Tysons Blvd, Tysons Corner (22102). Phone 703/506-4300; fax 703/917-5499. www.maestrorestaurant.com.* Tucked inside the supremely elegant Ritz-Carlton, Tysons Corner, Maestro is a culinary work of art. Power brokers and sophisticates flock to this regal dining room complete with rich, dark woods and priceless artwork. This refined restaurant's menu reads like a love letter to the cuisine of Italy, celebrating the intoxicating flavors and cooking styles of the country. Two distinct menus, along with an exceptional tasting menu, encourage diners to mix and match. Those who prefer the classics will want to sample La Tradizione, where favorite Italian dishes are enhanced with the chef's signature modern pizzazz. Diners who want to embark on a palate-pleasing journey should look to L'Evoluzione for inspiration, which showcases the chef's talent and revolutionary approach to Italian cooking. Presentation is everything at Maestro, and the service here is peerless. The extensive wine list is easily navigable with the assistance of the award-winning sommelier. The exceedingly lavish decor goes hand-in-hand with the grandiose cuisine and service. Several of the fusion-inspired items are prepared tableside with the finest ingredients. The beautifully sculpted desserts are a must. Italian menu. Dinner, Sun brunch. Children's menu. Valet parking. **$$$**

★★ **MARCO POLO.** *245 Maple Ave W, Vienna (22180). Phone 703/281-3922; fax 703/281-3926. www.marcopolorestaurant.com.* Italian, seafood menu. Lunch, dinner. Closed Sun except Mother's Day. **$$**

★★★ **MORTON'S OF CHICAGO.** *8075 Leesburg Pike, Vienna (22182). Phone 703/883-0800; fax 703/883-0673. www.mortons.com.* Consistent with expectations, this outlet serves the same famed entrées as its sister restaurants. The tableside menu presentation reveals generous portions and high-quality ingredients. A warm, club-like atmosphere is the backdrop for a succulent meal. Steak menu. Lunch, dinner. Closed holidays. Bar. Jacket required. Reservations recommended. Valet parking. **$$$**

★★★ **NIZAM'S.** *523 Maple Ave W, Vienna (22180). Phone 703/938-8948; fax 703/938-0453. www.nizamsrestaurant.com.* Doner kebob, otherwise known as gyros, is the legendary mainstay of this refined Turkish restaurant. Thin, tender slices of marinated, spit-roasted lamb nestle inside soft pita bread in a dish that rivals anything Istanbul could turn out. Service is polished and attentive. Lunch, dinner. Closed Mon; also Jan 1, Thanksgiving, Dec 25. Bar. Reservations recommended. **$$**

★★ **PANJSHIR II.** *224 W Maple Ave, Vienna (22180). Phone 703/281-4183; fax 703/281-4183.* Vegetarian menu. Lunch, dinner. Closed Mon; Jan 1, also July 4, Thanksgiving. Bar. **$$**

★★ **TARA THAI.** *226 Maple Ave W, Vienna (22180). Phone 703/255-2467; fax 703/255-2867. www.tarathai.com.* Thai menu. Lunch, dinner. Closed Dec 25. Bar. Reservations recommended. **$$**

★★ **THAT'S AMORE.** *150 Branch Rd SE, Vienna (22180). Phone 703/281-7777; fax 703/281-4132. www.thatsamore.com.* Italian menu. Lunch, dinner. Closed Labor Day, Thanksgiving, Dec 25. Bar. **$$$**

Virginia Beach (F-9)

See also Cape Charles, Chesapeake, Hampton, Newport News, Norfolk, Portsmouth

Population 425,257
Elevation 12 ft
Area Code 757
Information Visitor Information Center, 2100 Parks Ave, 23451; phone 757/437-4882 or toll-free 800/446-8038
Web site www.vbfun.com

As an Atlantic Coast vacation resort, Virginia Beach consistently ranks at the top. Strolling down the newly expanded boardwalk, you can relive the pleasures of your youth and enjoy the buzz of exciting entertainment, good food, and people-watching at its finest.

The area's historical sites tie Virginia Beach to the first permanent English settlement of over 400 years ago. In fact, First Landing State Park is where John Smith alighted before he went on to Jamestown. They've got museums too, including the Virginia Marine Science Museum, voted on of the top ten marine science aquariums/museums in the US.

If you think Virginia Beach is only beach, you're missing the boat. More than 106 square miles of wetlands and water, a 3,000-acre state park, and two wildlife refuges await. Amazingly, being this close to Virginia's largest city, the natural ecological areas surrounding Virginia Beach are among the most pristine and undiscovered ecological areas along the mid-Atlantic. Even on a rainy day (and there aren't many), the wildlife, including native birds, whales, and dolphins, are close enough for you to get a good look at them up close and personal.

What to See and Do

Adam Thoroughgood House. *1636 Parish Rd, Virginia Beach (23455). Phone 757/431-4000.* (Circa 1680) One of the oldest remaining brick houses in US; restored, furnished; restored gardens. (Apr-Dec: Tues-Sun; rest of year: Tues-Sat; closed holidays) **$$**

Association for Research and Enlightenment. *67th St and Atlantic Ave, Virginia Beach. Phone 757/428-3588. www.are-cayce.com.* Headquarters for study and research of work of psychic Edgar Cayce. Visitor Center has bookstore, library, displays, ESP-testing machine, movie, and daily lecture. (Daily; closed Thanksgiving, Dec 25) **FREE**

Contemporary Art Center of Virginia. *2200 Parks Ave, Virginia Beach (23451). Phone 757/425-0000. www.cacv.org.* This 32,000-square-foot facility is devoted to the presentation of 20th-century art through exhibitions, education, performing arts, and special events. (Mon-Sat, Sun afternoons; closed holidays) **$$**

First Landing/Seashore State Park. *2500 Shore, Virginia Beach (23451). 5 miles N on Hwy 60 at Cape Henry. Phone 757/412-2300.* More than 2,700 acres with lagoons, cypress trees, and sand dunes. Swimming at own risk, fishing, boating (ramp); hiking, bicycle, and self-guided nature trails; picnicking, tent and trailer sites (Mar-Nov; fee), 20 cabins (open all year round). Visitor center, interpretive programs. Access for disabled to nature trail. (Daily) **$$**

Fishing. *Linkhorn Bay and Rudee Inlet.* In the Lynnhaven and Rudee Inlets for channel bass, speckled trout, spots, croakers, flounder, and whiting in season; in the Back Bay area, 18 miles S on Hwy 615, for largemouth black bass, pickerel, and perch. Pier fishing and surf casting from piers jutting into the Atlantic and piers in the Chesapeake Bay. Reef, deep-sea, and Gulf Stream fishing from charter boats, for sea bass, weakfish, flounder, cobia, bonito, tuna, marlin, false albacore, blue, and dolphin. Lake and stream fishing at Lake Smith, Lake Christine, and the inland waterways of the Chesapeake and Albemarle Canal. Crabbing for blue crabs in Lynnhaven waters, Linkhorn Bay, and Rudee Inlet. (No license or closed season for saltwater fishing.)

Francis Land House Historic Site and Gardens. *3131 Virginia Beach Blvd, Virginia Beach (23452). On the S side of the boulevard, between Rosemont Rd and Lynnhoven Pwky. Phone 757/431-4000.* Late 18th-century plantation home features period rooms, special exhibits, gardens, and museum gift shop. (Tues-Sat, also Sun afternoons; closed holidays) **$$**

Lynnhaven House. *4405 Wishart Rd, Virginia Beach (23455). Phone 757/460-1688.* (Circa 1725). This stately story-and-a-half masonry structure is a well-preserved example of 18th-century architecture and decorative arts. (May and Oct: weekends only; June-Sept: Tues-Sun) **$$**

Motor World. *700 S Birdneck Rd, Virginia Beach (23451). Phone 757/422-6419.* Park includes go-carts, arcade. Also a 36-hole miniature Shipwreck Golf Course, batting cages, and large Children's Zone. (May-early Sept, daily)

Norwegian Lady Statue. *25th St and Boardwalk, Virginia Beach.* A gift to Virginia Beach from the people of Moss, Norway. The statue commemorates the tragic wreck of the Norwegian bark Dictator off the shores of Virginia Beach in 1891.

Ocean Breeze Water Park. *849 General Booth Blvd, Virginia Beach (23451). Phone 757/422-4444 (recording); toll-free 800/678-9453.* "Get wet, get wild" at this Caribbean paradise with slides, wave pool, rapids, and children's water amusements (mid-May-early Sept, daily). **$$$$**

Old Cape Henry Lighthouse and Memorial Park. *On Fort Story, an active army base. 6 miles N on Hwy 60.* First US-government-built lighthouse (circa 1791).

Old Coast Guard Station. *24th St and Atlantic Ave, Virginia Beach. Phone 757/422-1587. www.oldcoastguardstation.com.* Former Coast Guard Station (1903); visual exhibits of numerous shipwecks along the Virginia coastline tell of past bravery and disaster. "The War Years" exhibit relates United States Coast Guard efforts during World War I and World War II. Photographs, ship models, artifacts. Gift shop. (Memorial Day-Sept: daily; rest of year: Tues-Sun; closed holidays) **$$**

Virginia Marine Science Museum. *717 General Booth Blvd, Virginia Beach (23451). 2 miles S of resort area. Phone 757/425-3474. www.vmsm.com.* Live animals, interactive exhibits, six-story screen, 300-seat IMAX 3-D theater. Exhibits include ocean aquarium with sharks, large fish; sea turtle aquarium; seal and other habitats; aviary; salt marsh preserve; touch tank; river room; garden. (Daily; closed Thanksgiving, Dec 25) **$$$**

Special Events

Boardwalk Art Show. Works by more than 350 artists from US and abroad. Mid-June.

East Coast Surfing Championship. *8437 Valley Pike, Middletown (22645). Phone 830/278-2016.* Fourth weekend in Aug.

Neptune Festival. *265 Kings Grand Rd, Virginia Beach (23452).* Last two weeks in Sept.

Pungo Strawberry Festival. *916 Princess Anne Rd, Virginia Beach (23457).* Sat and Sun of Memorial Day weekend.

Virginia Saltwater Fishing Tournament. *968 S Oriole Dr, Virginia Beach (23451). Phone 757/491-5160.* The Commonwealth of Virginia sponsors this annual program. No entry fee or registration requirements; open to everyone who fishes in tournament waters and complies with tournament rules. For information contact Virginia Saltwater Fishing Tournament at above address. Mar-Dec.

Winter whale-watching boat trips. *Phone 757/437-4882.* Mon, Wed, Fri-Sun. Jan-Mar.

Limited-Service Hotels

★ ★ CLARION HOTEL. *4453 Bonney Rd, Virginia Beach (23462). Phone 757/473-1700; toll-free 800/847-5202; fax 757/456-5778. www.choicehotels.com.* 149 rooms, 8 story. Check-in 3 pm, check-out 11 am. Restaurant, bar. Fitness room. Indoor pool, whirlpool. Business center. **$**

★ COMFORT INN. *2800 Pacific Ave, Virginia Beach (23451). Phone 757/428-2203; toll-free 800/441-0684; fax 757/422-6043. www.choicehotels.com.* 137 rooms, 7 story. Complimentary full breakfast. Check-in 3 pm, check-out 11 am. Fitness room. Beach. Indoor pool, outdoor pool, whirlpool. **$**

★ ★ DOUBLETREE HOTEL. *1900 Pavilion Dr, Virginia Beach (23451). Phone 757/422-8900; fax 757/428-6948. www.doubletree.com.* Adjacent to the Virginia Beach Pavilion Convention Center and only 6 blocks from the beach, this hotel offers amenities for both leisure and business travelers. 292 rooms, 12 story. Check-out 11 am. Restaurant, bar. Fitness room. Indoor pool. Tennis. Business center. **$$**

★ ★ HOLIDAY INN. *2607 Atlantic Ave, Virginia Beach (23451). Phone 757/491-6900; toll-free 800/810-2400; fax 757/491-2125. www.holiday-inn.com.* 143 rooms, 10 story. Check-in 4 pm, check-out 11 am.

Restaurant, bar. Fitness room. Beach. Indoor pool, whirlpool. **$**

★★ **RAMADA.** *5700 Atlantic Ave, Virginia Beach (23451). Phone 757/428-7025; toll-free 800/265-3032; fax 757/428-2921. www.ramada.com.* Located on the ocean in what locals refer to as the North End, this hotel provides guests with spectacular views. Explore the beach or rent a bike, boat, or jet ski. 216 rooms, 17 story. Check-out 11 am. Restaurant, bar. Children's activity center. Fitness room. Beach. Indoor pool, outdoor pool, whirlpool. Business center. **$$**

Full-Service Hotel

★★★ **FOUNDERS INN.** *5641 Indian River Rd, Virginia Beach (23464). Phone 757/424-5511; toll-free 800/926-4466; fax 757/366-0613. www.foundersinn.com.* Sitting on 26 manicured acres, this Georgian-style inn has a Southern-colonial décor and a unique combination of intimate charm and extensive meeting space. 249 rooms. Check-out noon. Restaurant. Children's activity center. Fitness room. Indoor pool, outdoor pool. Tennis. Airport transportation available. Business center. **$**

Full-Service Resort

★★ **OCEAN SANDS RESORT.** *2207 Atlantic Ave, Virginia Beach (23451). Phone 757/428-5141; toll-free 800/874-8661; fax 757/422-8436. www.oceansandsresort.com.* This oceanfront property offers brightly colored rooms and a variety of leisure recreations. 105 rooms, 14 story. Check-in 4 pm, check-out 10 am. Restaurant. Fitness room, spa. Indoor pool, whirlpool. Airport transportation available. Beach. **$**

Restaurants

★★ **ALDO'S.** *1860 Laskin Rd, Virginia Beach (23454). Phone 757/491-1111; fax 757/491-0597. www.gohamptonroad.com.* Italian menu. Lunch, dinner. Closed Thanksgiving, Dec 25. Bar. Outdoor seating. **$$**

★★ **BLUE PETE'S SEAFOOD AND STEAK.** *1400 N Muddy Creek Rd, Virginia Beach (23456). Phone 757/426-2005; fax 757/721-3792.* Seafood menu. Dinner. Closed Mon. Bar. Children's menu. Outdoor seating. **$$$**

★★ **COASTAL GRILL.** *1427 N Great Neck Rd, Virginia Beach (23454). Phone 757/496-3348. www.coastalgrill.com.* Seafood menu. Dinner. Closed holidays. Bar. Children's menu. **$$**

★ **CUISINE AND COMPANY.** *3004 Pacific Ave, Virginia Beach (23451). Phone 757/428-6700; fax 757/428-0138. www.cuisineandcompany.com.* California menu. Breakfast, lunch, dinner. Closed Jan 1, Thanksgiving, Dec 25. **$**

★★ **DUCK-IN RESTAURANT AND GAZEBO.** *3324 Shore Dr, Virginia Beach (23451). Phone 757/481-0201; fax 757/481-9780. www.duck-in.com.* Where can you find the best place in Virginia Beach to eat and drink simply and cheaply and then kick back? Try this eatery. For beachcombers looking for a watering hole on the shore, this is the top pick. Try the fired popcorn shrimp and other seafood entrées, made simple and fresh. Seafood menu. Lunch, dinner. Children's menu. **$$**

★★ **IL GIARDINO.** *910 Atlantic Ave, Virginia Beach (23451). Phone 757/422-6464; fax 757/422-1175. www.ilgiardino.com.* Italian menu. Dinner. Closed Thanksgiving, Dec 25. Bar. Children's menu. Valet parking. Outdoor seating. **$$**

★★ **INLET.** *3319 Shore Dr, Virginia Beach (23451). Phone 757/481-7300; fax 757/481-0625. www.theinletrestaurant.com.* Seafood menu. Lunch, dinner, Sun brunch. Bar. Children's menu. Valet parking. Outdoor seating. Lobster tank. On Lynnhaven Inlet; 2-story saltwater aquarium in dining area. **$$**

★★ **THE LIGHTHOUSE.** *1st St and Atlantic Ave, Virginia Beach (23451). Phone 757/428-7974; fax 757/422-9914. www.thelighthouseva.com.* Seafood menu. Lunch, dinner, brunch. Bar. Children's menu. **$$**

★★ **LUCKY STAR.** *1608 Pleasure House Rd, Virginia Beach (23455). Phone 757/363-8410; fax 757/460-4714.* Eclectic, seafood menu. Dinner. Closed Sun; holidays. Bar. Reservations recommended. **$$**

★★ **LYNNHAVEN FISH HOUSE.** *2350 Starfish Rd, Virginia Beach (23451). Phone 757/481-0003; fax 757/481-3474. www.lynnhavenfishhouse.net.* Seafood menu. Lunch, dinner. Closed Thanksgiving, Dec 25. Bar. Children's menu. Valet parking. Lobster tank. On Lynnhaven fishing pier. **$$**

★ **PUNGO GRILL.** *1785 Princess Anne Rd, Virginia Beach (23456). Phone 757/426-6655.* Regional American menu. Lunch, dinner. Closed Mon; Thanksgiving, Dec 24-25; also Jan-Feb. Bar. Children's menu. Outdoor seating. Dining room on enclosed porch of 1919 Aladdin house. **$$**

★★ **RUDEE'S.** *227 Mediterranean Ave, Virginia Beach (23451). Phone 757/425-1777; fax 757/425-5107. www.rudees.com.* Seafood, steak menu. Lunch, dinner, Sun brunch. Closed Thanksgiving, Dec 25. Bar. Children's menu. Valet parking. Outdoor seating. On inlet; transient slips available for boats. **$$$**

Warm Springs (D-5)

See also Clifton Forge, Covington, Hot Springs, Monterey

Population 425
Elevation 2,260 ft
Area Code 540
Zip 24484

Nestled at the foot of Little Mountain (3,100 feet), the spring wildflowers and groves of fall foliage make Warm Springs a very scenic spot for sightseeing, hiking, or water activities. Visitors also enjoy walking tours to view the many historic buildings.

Full-Service Inn

★★★ **INN AT GRISTMILL SQUARE.** *PO Box 359, Warm Springs (24484). Phone 540/839-2231; fax 540/839-5770. www.gristmillsquare.com.* This inn is comprised of five restored 19th-century buildings including a gristmill and blacksmith shop. 15 rooms. Complimentary continental breakfast. Check-in 2 pm, check-out noon. Restaurant, bar. Outdoor pool. Tennis. Airport transportation available. Consists of five restored 19th-century buildings. **$**

Restaurant

★★★ **WATERWHEEL.** *Rte 619, Warm Springs (24484). Phone 540/839-2231; fax 540/839-5770. www.gristmillsquare.com.* A restored gristmill circa 1900 is the rustic setting for a unique dining experience. Guests venture to the wine cellar to make their selection directly from the bins. American menu. Dinner, Sun brunch. Bar. **$$$**

Warrenton (C-7)

See also Culpeper, Fairfax, Front Royal, Manassas

Population 6,670
Elevation 560 ft
Area Code 540
Zip 20186
Information Warrenton-Fauquier County Visitor Center, 183 A Keith St; phone 540/347-4414 or toll-free 800/820-1021
Web site www.fauquierchamber.org

The seat of Fauquier County, Warrenton was named for General Joseph Warren, who fought at Bunker Hill in the Revolutionary War. The town is situated in the valley of the Piedmont near the foothills of the Blue Ridge Mountains and is known for its cattle and Thoroughbred horse farms. Many old buildings and houses provide for an interesting walking tour of the town.

Special Event

Flying Circus. *Morrisville Rd and Brookes Store Dr, Warrenton. Phone 540/439-8661.* Flying shows of the barnstorming era, from comedy acts to precision and stunt flying. Rides, picnic area. 7 miles S on Hwy 15/29, then 7 miles SE on Hwy 17 near Bealeton. Sun. May-Oct.

Limited-Service Hotel

★ **COMFORT INN.** *7379 Comfort Inn Dr, Warrenton (20187). Phone 540/349-8900; fax 540/347-5759. www.choicehotels.com.* 97 rooms. Pets accepted, some restrictions; fee. Complimentary continental breakfast. Check-out 11 am. Fitness room. Outdoor pool. **$**

Restaurant

★ ★ **NAPOLEON'S.** *67 Waterloo St, Warrenton (20186). Phone 540/347-1200. www.napoleonsrestaurant .com.* French menu. Lunch, dinner. Closed Dec 25. Bar. Outdoor seating. Attractive flower gardens. Historic 1838 mansion owned by Confederate General Eppa Hunton. **$$**

Washington (C-8)

See also Warrenton

Founded 1796
Population 183
Elevation 690 ft
Area Code 540
Zip 22747

The oldest of more than 25 American towns to be named after the first president, this town was surveyed in 1749 by none other than George Washington himself. The streets remain laid out exactly as surveyed and still bear the names of families who owned the land on which the town was founded. It is rumored that Gay Street was named by the 17-year-old Washington after the lovely Gay Fairfax.

The town, seat of Rappahannock County, is situated in the foothills of the Blue Ridge Mountains, which dominate the western horizon.

Full-Service Inn

★ ★ ★ ★ ★ **THE INN AT LITTLE WASHINGTON.** *309 Main St, Washington (22747). Phone 540/675-3800; fax 540/675-3100.* Savvy epicureans book a room—and a table—at The Inn at Little Washington. Just far enough away from the nation's capital and tucked away in a sweet village in the foothills of the Blue Ridge Mountains, The Inn offers visitors a taste of the good life. Urban warriors are swayed by the Victorian charms of the public and private rooms, and the pastoral setting in Virginia's hunt country soothes even the most frayed nerves. Sophisticated without being pretentious, this romantic country house's amiable staff welcomes visitors with the comforts of home, including a delightful afternoon tea with scones and tartlets. Tempting as it may be to indulge, guests save their appetites for the evening's superlative cuisine. Many make special trips just for the talented chef's award-winning and artfully prepared meals, although lucky guests recount their memorable feasts while ensconcing themselves in one of the inn's lovely rooms. 14 rooms, 2 story. Closed Tues in Jan-Mar and July; also Dec 24-25. Complimentary continental breakfast. Check-in 3 pm, check-out noon. Restaurant, bar. Airport transportation available. **$$$$**

Specialty Lodgings

The following lodging establishments are approved by Mobil Travel Guide, but due to their unique and individualized nature have not been given a traditional Mobil Star rating. Included in this listing you may find bed-and-breakfasts, limited-service inns, guest ranches, and other unique hotel properties.

BLEU ROCK INN. *12567 Lee Hwy, Washington (22747). Phone 540/987-3190; fax 540/987-3193. www. bleurockinn.com.* 5 rooms, 2 story. Closed Mon, Tues; Jan 1, Dec 24-25. Complimentary full breakfast. Check-in 3 pm, check-out 11 am. Restaurant. Restored farmhouse (1899) on lake; rustic setting; vineyard. **$**

MIDDLETON INN. *176 Main St, Washington (22747). Phone 540/675-2020; toll-free 800/816-8157; fax 540/675-1050. www.middleton-inn.com.* This historic country estate was built in 1850 by Middleton Miller, who designed and manufactured the Confederate uniform of the Civil War. The inn faces the Blue Ridge Mountains, and the original slaves' quarters have been converted into a two-story guest cottage. 4 rooms, 2 story. Children over 12 years only. Complimentary full breakfast. Check-in 3 pm, check-out 11 am. **$$**

SYCAMORE HILL HOUSE AND GARDENS. *110 Menefee Mountain Ln, Washington (22747). Phone 540/675-3046. www.sycamorehillhouseandgardens .com.* 3 rooms, 2 story. Children over 12 years only. Complimentary full breakfast. Check-in 2 pm, check-out 11 am. On top of a hill, with a view of the mountains. **$**

Restaurants

★ ★ ★ **BLEU ROCK INN.** *12567 Lee Hwy, Washington (22747). Phone 540/987-3190. www. bleurockinn.com.* This country-inn farmhouse is located on 80 acres of rolling hillside overlooking the Blue Ridge Mountains and adjoining vineyards. It is a great place to stop between Harrisonburg and Washington, DC. American, French menu. Dinner, brunch. Closed Mon, Tues; Dec 25. Outdoor seating. **$$$**

★ ★ **FOUR AND TWENTY BLACKBIRDS.** *650 Zachary Taylor Hwy, Flint Hill (22627). Phone 540/675-1111.* American menu. Dinner, Sun brunch. Closed Mon, Tues; July 4, Dec 25; also the first two weeks of Jan and Aug. Originally built in 1910 as carpenter's shop. **$$**

★ ★ ★ ★ ★ **THE INN AT LITTLE WASHINGTON.** *309 Main St, Washington (22747). Phone 540/675-3800; fax 540/675-3100.* Opulent, luxurious, romantic, mind-altering, and magnificent: these are just a handful of adjectives that come to mind after experiencing dinner at The Inn at Little Washington. Set in the foothills of the Blue Ridge Mountains, the Inn's dining room is heavy with charm, appointed with rich draperies, tasseled lampshades, and vases overflowing with elaborate flower arrangements. As for the food, it's spectacular. Chef Patrick O'Connell has amassed almost every culinary award in existence. (He must have a separate house for all his plaques and trophies.) For the wonderful opportunity to be a guinea pig in his gifted presence, you will fork over a tidy sum, but your financial indulgence will be well rewarded. Plates are breathtaking, assembled from pristine seasonal ingredients that sparkle and balanced flavors that dazzle. Seasonal dishes that should be considered required eating include the crab cake "sandwich" with fried green tomatoes and tomato vinaigrette; the sesame-crusted Chilean seabass with baby shrimp, artichokes, and grape tomatoes; the rabbit braised in apple cider with wild mushrooms and garlic mashed potatoes; and, for dessert, the pistachio and white chocolate ice cream terrine with blackberry sauce. An amazing wine list will give you the right buzz to match your meal. To make matters even better, coddling is a specialty of the house, so be prepared to have your every whim catered to with grace and warmth. American menu. Breakfast, dinner. Closed Tues (except in May and Oct), Dec 24-25. Bar. Casual attire. Valet parking. Outdoor seating. **$$$$**

Waynesboro (D-6)

See also Charlottesville, Shenandoah National Park, Blue Ridge Parkway, Staunton

Settled circa 1739
Population 19,520
Elevation 1,300 ft
Zip 22980
Information Waynesboro Augusta County Chamber of Commerce, 301 W Main St; phone 540/949-8203

Waynesboro is at the southern end of the Skyline Drive and the northern end of the Blue Ridge Parkway.

What to See and Do

P. Buckley Moss Museum. *150 P. Buckley Moss Dr, Waynesboro. Phone 540/949-6473.* Museum's exhibits and programs examine the symbolism and aesthetic ideas of one of America's most notable living artists. (Mon-Sat 10 am-6 pm, Sun 12:30-5:30 pm; closed Jan 1, Thanksgiving, Dec 25) **FREE**

Shenandoah National Park. *1 mile E to Skyline Dr.* (see).

Shenandoah Valley Art Center. *600 W Main St, Waynesboro (22980). Phone 540/949-7662.* Art galleries, studios. Working artists; performing arts. (Tues-Sun) **DONATION**

Sherando Lake Recreation Area. *16 miles SW on Blue Ridge Pkwy, in George Washington and Jefferson national forests. Phone 540/942-5965 (summer).* Facilities include 21-acre lake with sand beach and bathhouses, swimming, fishing; picnicking, camping (Apr-Oct, fee). Amphitheater, campfire programs. (Apr-Nov, daily) **$$**

Special Event

Fall Foliage Festival. First and second weekends in Oct.

Limited-Service Hotels

★ **QUALITY INN.** *640 W Broad St, Waynesboro (22980). Phone 540/942-1171; fax 540/942-4785. www.choicehotels.com.* 75 rooms. Pets accepted, some restrictions. Check-out noon. Outdoor pool, children's pool. **$**

★ DAYS INN. *2060 Rosser Ave, Waynesboro (22980). Phone 540/943-1101; toll-free 800/943-1102; fax 540/949-7586. www.daysinn.com.* 98 rooms, 2 story. Pets accepted; fee. Check-out 11 am. Outdoor pool. **$**

Specialty Lodging

The following lodging establishment is approved by Mobil Travel Guide, but due to its unique and individualized nature has not been given a traditional Mobil Star rating. Included in this listing you may find bed-and-breakfasts, limited-service inns, guest ranches, and other unique hotel properties.

IRIS INN. *191 Chinquapin Dr, Waynesboro (22980). Phone 540/943-1991; fax 540/942-2093. www.irisinn.com.* This inn overlooks the Shenandoah Valley and is near the Blue Ridge Mountains. The Great Room, with its 28-foot stone fireplace and a large mural of the wildlife in the mountains, is a central focus. A full and hearty breakfast is included as well as a "bottomless" cookie jar. 9 rooms, 2 story. Complimentary full breakfast. Check-in 3 pm, check-out 11 am. Wooded setting overlooking Shenandoah Valley. **$**

Williamsburg (E-8)

See also Colonial Parkway, Gloucester, Hopewell, Jamestown (Colonial National Historical Park), Newport News, Surry, Yorktown

Settled 1633
Population 11,998
Elevation 86 ft
Area Code 757
Information Chamber of Commerce, 201 Penniman Rd, PO Box 3620, 23187; phone 757/229-6511
Web site www.williamsburgcc.com

After the Native American massacre of 1622, this Virginia colony built a palisade across the peninsula between the James and York rivers. The settlement that grew up around the palisade was called Middle Plantation and is now the site of Colonial Williamsburg.

Middle Plantation figured prominently in Bacon's Rebellion against Governor Berkeley. In 1693, it was chosen as the site of the College of William and Mary, and in 1699, the seat of Virginia government was moved here. The capitol was built to replace the Jamestown statehouse, which had burned the year before. Renamed in honor of William III of England, the new capital gradually became a town of about 200 houses and 1,500 residents. For 81 years, Williamsburg was the political, social, and cultural capital of Virginia.

The colony's first successful printing press was established here by William Parks, and in 1736 he published Virginia's first newspaper. The capitol was the scene of such stirring colonial events as Patrick Henry's Stamp Act speech (1765).

The First Continental Congress was called from here by the dissolved House of Burgesses in 1774. Two years later, the Second Continental Congress was boldly led by delegates from Virginia to declare independence; George Mason's Declaration of Rights, which became the basis for the first ten amendments to the Constitution, was adopted here.

Williamsburg's exciting days came to an end in 1780 when the capital was moved to Richmond for greater safety and convenience during the Revolutionary War. For a century and a half it continued as a quiet little college town, its tranquility interrupted briefly by the Civil War. In 1917, when a munitions factory was built near the town and cheap housing for the factory's 15,000 workers was hastily erected, Williamsburg seemed destined to live out its days in ugliness.

In 1926, however, John D. Rockefeller, Jr. and Dr. W. A. R. Goodwin, rector of Bruton Parish Church, who saw the town as a potential treasurehouse of colonial history, shared the broad vision that inspired the restoration of Williamsburg. For more than 30 years, Rockefeller devoted personal attention to the project and contributed funds to accomplish this nonprofit undertaking.

Today, after many years of archaeological and historical research, the project is near completion. The Historic Area, approximately a mile long and a half-mile wide, encompasses most of the 18th-century capital. Eighty-eight of the original buildings have been restored; 50 major buildings, houses, and shops and many smaller outbuildings have been reconstructed on their original sites; 45 of the more historically significant buildings contain more than 200 exhibition rooms, furnished either with original pieces or reproductions and open to the public on regular seasonal schedules.

Visitors stroll Duke of Gloucester Street and mingle with people in 18th-century attire. Craftsmen at about 20 different shops ply such trades as wigmaking and blacksmithing, using materials, tools, and techniques of pre-Revolutionary times.

Williamsburg is beautiful year-round. November through March is an excellent time to visit, when it is less crowded and the pace is more leisurely; some holiday weekends may be busy. The Historic Area is closed to private motor vehicles 8 am-10 pm.

What to See and Do

Abby Aldrich Rockefeller Folk Art Center. *307 S England St, Williamsburg (23187).* An outstanding collection of American folk art. Items in this collection were created by artists not trained in studio techniques, but who faithfully recorded aspects of everyday life in paintings, sculpture, needlework, ceramics, toys, and other media. (Daily, hours vary by season)

America's Railroads on Parade. *1915 Pocahontas Trl, Williamsburg (23185). In the Village Shops at Kingsmill. Phone 757/220-8725.* More than 4,000 square feet of model train layouts, hands-on exhibits, and a gift shop. (Daily; closed Jan 1, Thanksgiving, Dec 25) **$$**

Brush-Everard House. Home of an early mayor, with programs on slave life.

Bruton Parish Church. *331 Duke of Gloucester St, Williamsburg. Just W of Palace Green. Phone 757/229-2891. www.brutonparish.org.* One of America's oldest Episcopal churches, in continuous use since 1715. Organ recitals (Mar-Dec, Tues and Sat). (Daily; no tours during services)

Busch Gardens Williamsburg. *1 Busch Gardens Blvd, Williamsburg (23187). 3 miles E on US 60. Phone 757/253-3000; toll-free 800/343-7946. www.buschgardens.com.* This European-style theme park on 360 acres features re-created 17th-century German, English, French, Italian, Scottish, and Canadian villages. Attractions include more than 30 thrill rides, including the Drachen Fire roller coaster, one of the nation's largest; the 3-D movie Haunts of the Olde Country, with in-theater special effects; live shows, an antique carousel, celebrity concerts, miniature of Le Mans racetrack, and rides for small children. Theme restaurants; shops. Transportation around the grounds by sky ride or steam train. A computer-operated monorail links the park with the Anheuser-Busch Hospitality Center, where visitors can take a brewery tour. (Mid-Apr-Aug: daily; late Mar-mid-Apr and Sept-Oct: weekends) **$$$$**

Carriage and wagon rides. Take a ride through the Historic Area in a carriage or wagon driven by a costumed coachman. General admission ticket holders can make reservations on the day of the ride at the Lumber House ticket office. (Daily, weather permitting) **$$$**

Children's tours. Special programs, tours, and experiences exclusively for children and families are offered in the summer.

College of William and Mary. *Richmond Rd, Williamsburg. W end of Duke of Gloucester St. Phone 757/221-4000. www.wm.edu.* (1693) With a student body of 7,000, William and Mary is America's second-oldest college (only Harvard is older). It initiated an honor system, an elective system of studies, and schools of law and modern languages; it was the second to have a school of medicine (all in 1779). The prestigious Phi Beta Kappa Society was founded here as well (1776). On campus are

> **Muscarelle Museum of Art.** *Jamestown Rd, Williamsburg. Phone 757/221-2700. www.wm.edu/muscarelle.* Traveling displays and exhibitions from an extensive collection. (Wed, Sat-Sun noon-4 pm; Thurs-Fri 10 am-4:45 pm; closed holidays) **FREE**
>
> **Wren Building.** *I-64, Williamsburg.* Oldest (1695-1699, restored 1928) academic building in America; designed by the great English architect Sir Christopher Wren. Tours (daily). **FREE**

The Colonial Golf Course. *8285 Diascund Rd, Lanexa (23187). 10 miles W of Williamsburg. Phone 757/566-1600; toll-free 800/566-6660. www.golfcolonial.com.* This course, designed by Lester George and Robert Wrenn, was Williamsburg's first daily-fee facility and offers the only year-round golf academy in the state.

The 18 holes have a par of 72, with yardage ranging from 4,568 to 6,885. (Daily) **$$$$**

Colonial Williamsburg Visitor Center. *102 Information Center Dr, Williamsburg (23185). Colonial Pkwy and Hwy 132. Phone 757/220-7645; toll-free 800/246-2099. www.colonialwilliamsburg.com.* An admission ticket is necessary to enjoy the full scope of Colonial Williamsburg. Three types of general admission tickets are available: The Basic Ticket provides admission on the Colonial Williamsburg transportation system and entrance to the exhibits in the Historic Area for one day. (This ticket does not provide admission to the Governor's Palace, the DeWitt Wallace Decorative Arts Gallery, Carter's Grove, or the Abby Aldrich Rockefeller Folk Art Center.) The Patriot's Pass (valid for one year) provides admission on the transporation system and entrance to all historic buildings, colonial houses, craft shops, Governor's Palace, Carter's Grove, DeWitt Wallace Decorative Arts Gallery, Abby Aldrich Rockefeller Folk Art Center, and historical film. Ticket prices vary. Ticket sales, sightseeing information; orientation film; lodging and dining assistance; bookstore; transportation. Center (daily).

The Candle Factory. *7521 Richmond Rd, Williamsburg (23188). Phone 757/564-3354. www.candlefactory.com.* Open since 1964, the family-owned and -operated Candle Factory produces more than 6 million soaps and candles each year. You can watch while soaps and candles are being made. (Daily 9 am-5:30 pm; closed Jan 1, Thanksgiving, Dec 25)

The Capitol. *Duke of Gloucester St, Williamsburg (23187). E end of Duke of Gloucester St.* The House of Burgesses met here (1704-1779); it was also the scene of Patrick Henry's speech against the Stamp Act.

The Magazine. *Duke of Gloucester St, 1 block E of Palace Green.* Arsenal and military storehouse of Virginia Colony; authentic arms exhibited.

The Music Theatre of Williamsburg. *7575 Richmond Rd, Williamsburg. Phone 757/564-0200; toll-free 888/687-4220. www.musictheatre.com.* This 752-seat theater, which opened in 1998, features ever-changing shows that appeal to and are appropriate for all ages. Call for the performance schedule. **$$$$**

Courthouse. *Duke of Gloucester St, E of Palace Green.* County and city business was conducted here from 1770 until 1932. The interior has been carefully restored to its original appearance. Visitors often participate in scheduled reenactments of court sessions.

DeWitt Wallace Decorative Arts Gallery. *Henry and Francis sts, Williamsburg. Phone 757/220-7724; toll-free 800/447-8679.* Modern museum adjoining Public Hospital, features exhibits, lectures, films, and related programs centering on British and American decorative arts of the 17th to early 19th centuries. (Fri-Wed) **$$$$**

Disabled Visitor Information. *Phone toll-free 800/246-2099.* Efforts are made to accommodate the disabled while still retaining the authenticity of colonial life. Many buildings have wheelchair access once inside, but it should be noted that most buildings are reached by steps. The Visitor Center has a list detailing accessibility of each building; wheelchair ramps may be made available at some buildings. In addition, there are wheelchair rentals and parking. A hands-on tour of several historic trades may be arranged for the visually impaired and sign language tours are available with advance notice.

Evening entertainment. Colonial Williamsburg presents "rollicking 18th-century plays" throughout the year; wide variety of cultural events, concerts, and historical reenactments (fees vary). Chowning's Tavern offers colonial "gambols" (games), music, entertainment and light food and drink (evenings).

Ford's Colony Williamsburg. *240 Ford's Colony Dr, Williamsburg (23188). Phone toll-free 800/334-6033. www.fordscolony.com.* This Dan Maples-designed course features 54 holes, comprising the par-72 Marsh Hawk Course, the par-71 Blackheath Course, and the par-72 Blue Heron Course, and was chosen as one of America's best golf courses by *Golf Week Magazine.* The course touts itself as a "player's course" that appeals to golfers of all levels. **$$$$**

Go-Karts Plus. *6910 Richmond Rd, Hwy 60 W, Williamsburg (23187). Phone 757/564-7600. www.gokartsplus.com.* This 8-acre park has four go-kart tracks that appeal to various ages and driving skills, as well as bumper cars and boats, a miniature golf course, and an arcade. Admission is free; tickets must be purchased for activities. (Memorial Day weekend through Labor Day: daily 11 am-11 pm; shorter hours in spring and fall; closed Nov-late Mar)

Governor's Palace and Gardens. *N end of Palace Green.* Residence of Royal Governor, one of the most elegant mansions in colonial America; set in 10-acre restored gardens. **$$$$**

Haunted Dinner Theater. *5363 Richmond Rd, Williamsburg. Phone 757/258-2500; toll-free 888/426-3746. www.haunteddinnertheater.com.* Help unravel a murder mystery—tame enough for little ones—while feasting on a 71-item, all-you-can-eat dinner buffet at Capt. George's World Famous Restaurant. Performances are held Wed-Sun evenings at 7 pm. **$$$$**

Historic trades. Craftsmen in 18th-century costume pursue old trades of apothecary, printer, bookbinder, silversmith, wigmaker, shoemaker, blacksmith, harnessmaker, cabinetmaker, miller, milliner, gunsmith, wheelwright, basketmaker, cook, cooper, and carpenter.

James Geddy House. Once home of a prominent silversmith with working brass, bronze, silver, and pewter foundry.

James River State Park. *Phone 434/933-4355; toll-free 800/933-7275. www.dcr.state.va.us/parks/jamesriv.htm.* This 1,500-acre park has three fishing ponds and 3 miles of river frontage. The park offers pond and river fishing. An excellent spot is Pony Pasture, located on the south bank 2 miles downstream from the Huguenot Bridge on Riverside Dr. The area is also considered one of Richmond's best locations for bird-watching and inner-tubing. **$$**

Lanthorn Tour. *Phone toll-free 800/246-2099.* A costumed interpreter conducts evening walking tour of selected shops that are illuminated by candlelight. (Mar-Dec, daily) **$$$**

Peyton Randolph House. (1716) Home of president of First Continental Congress. Rochambeau's headquarters prior to Yorktown campaign.

Play Booth Theater. Scenes from 18th-century plays in open-air theater. Open to all Colonial Williamsburg ticket holders. (Spring-fall, daily)

Public Gaol. Where debtors, criminals, and pirates (including Blackbeard's crew) were imprisoned.

Public Hospital. Reconstruction of first public institution in the English colonies devoted exclusively to treatment of mental illness.

Raleigh Tavern. Frequent meeting place for Jefferson, Henry, and other Revolutionary patriots; a social center of the Virginia Colony.

Ride with Me to Williamsburg. *Phone 301/299-7817; toll-free 800/840-7433.* Informative and entertaining 90-minute audiocassette describes events from Williamsburg's colorful colonial, revolutionary, and Civil War past. The town's famous restoration is summarized by one of the architects who worked on the project. Contact RWM Associates, PO Box 1324, Bethesda, MD 20817.

Shirley Pewter Shop. *417 Duke of Gloucester St, Williamsburg (23185). Phone 757/229-5356; toll-free 800/550-5356. www.shirleypewter.com.* This shop features Williamsburg's own brand of pewter, "Shirley Pewter." Items available include dinnerware, oil lamps, and tableware. Many items can be engraved. (Daily)

Shopping. Superior wares typical of the 18th century are offered in nine restored or reconstructed stores and shops; items include silver, jewelery, herbs, candles, hats, and books. Two craft houses sell approved reproductions of the antiques on display in the houses and museums.

Skate Park. *5301 Longhill Rd, Williamsburg (23187). Phone 757/259-3200. www.james-city.va.us/recreation/skatepark.html.* A great, safe place for inline skating, skateboarding, and biking. The park is open to ages 9 and up, and all skaters and bikers must wear protective gear. (Nov-Mar: closed Mon-Tues, Thurs; rest of year: daily) **$$**

Special focus and orientation tours. Orientation tours (30 minutes) for first-time visitors; special tours (90 minutes), called history walks, include African-American life, gardens, religion, and women of Williamsburg. Reservations are available at any ticket sales location.

Water Country USA. *176 Water Country Pkwy, Williamsburg (23187). Phone 757/253-3350; toll-free 800/343-7946. www.watercountryusa.com.* This park, the mid-Atlantic's largest water park, features water slides, thrill rides, and live entertainment. A retro surf theme sets a festive mood. If you're interested in visiting Busch Gardens as well, which is just 3 miles from Water Country USA, you can save money by purchasing a Bounce Pass, which gains you admission to both parks. (May, early-mid-Sept: weekends from 10 am; Jun-Aug: daily from 10 am) **$$$$**

Wetherburn's Tavern. One of the most popular inns of the period.

Williamsburg National Golf Course. *3700 Centerville, Williamsburg (23188). Phone 757/258-9738; toll-free 800/859-9182. www.wngc.com.* This 18-hole, par-72 public course is the only Jack Nicklaus-designed course in Virginia. Call for tee times. **$$$$**

Williamsburg Winery. *5800 Wessex Hundred, Williamsburg (23185). Phone 757/229-0999. www.williamsburgwinery.com.* Founded in 1985, the winery carries on a Virginia tradition that began with the Jamestown settlers in 1607. Located 2 miles from the Histoic Area, it has 50 acres of vineyards. Visitors can take 30-45 minute guided walking tours, and tastings are available after the tour. (Daily) **$$$$**

Wythe House. Home of George Wythe, America's first law professor, teacher of Jefferson, Clay, and Marshall. This was Washington's headquarters before siege of Yorktown, Rochambeau's after.

York River State Park. *5526 Riverview Rd, Williamsburg (23188). 8 miles NW via I-64, exit 231B, then 1 mile N on Hwy 607 to Hwy 606 E. Phone 757/566-3036.* A 2,500-acre park along the York River and its related marshes. Includes the Taskinas Creek National Estuarine Research Reserve. Fishing, boating (launch), canoe trips; hiking and bridle trails, picnicking, interpretive center, programs, nature walks. (Daily)

Special Events

18th-Century Comedy. *5363 Richmond Rd (Williamsburg Lodge Auditorium), Williamsburg. Phone 800/HISTORY.* Sat nights, Mar-Dec.

Antiques Forum. *102 Information Center Dr, Colonial Williamsburg (23185). Phone toll-free 800/447-8679.* Mid-Feb.

Colonial Weekends. *Phone toll-free 800/246-2099.* Package weekends on 18th-century theme, features introductory lecture, guided tours, banquet at Colonial Williamsburg. Jan-early Mar.

Fife and Drum Corps. *Carter's Grove and S England St, Colonial Williamsburg. Phone 757/220-7453.* Performances in the Historic Area. Sat, Apr-Oct.

Garden Symposium. *102 Information Center Dr, Colonial Williamsburg (23185). Phone toll-free 800/447-8679.* Lectures and clinics. Last week in Apr.

Learning Weekend. *8437 Valley Pike, Middletown (22645). Colonial Williamsburg. Phone 830/278-2016.* Family-oriented weekend of discovery on a single topic. Mar.

Living History Programs. *1340 S Pleasant Valley Rd, Colonial Williamsburg. (22601).* Includes An Assembly, Cross or Crown, and Cry Witch! Varying schedule weekly. Spring, summer, and fall.

Military Drill. *Duke of Gloucester and Colonial sts (Market Sq Green), Williamsburg. Phone 757/229-6511.* Costumed weekly drill by Williamsburg Independent Company. Mid-Mar-Oct.

Prelude to Independence. *102 Information Center Dr, Colonial Williamsburg. (23185). Phone toll-free 800/447-8679.* Mid-May.

Publick Times. *102 Information Center Dr, Colonial Williamsburg. (23185). Phone toll-free 800/447-8679.* Re-creation of colonial market days; contests, crafts, auctions, military encampment. Labor Day weekend.

Traditional Christmas Activities. *102 Information Center Dr, Colonial Williamsburg (23185). Phone toll-free 800/447-8679.* Featuring grand illumination of city; fireworks. Dec.

Washington's Birthday Celebration. *8437 Valley Pike, Middletown (22645). Phone 830/278-2016.* President's Day weekend.

Limited-Service Hotels

★ HAMPTON INN. *201 Bypass Rd, Williamsburg (23185). Phone 757/220-0880; fax 757/229-7175. www.hamptoninn.com.* 121 rooms, 4 story. Complimentary continental breakfast. Check-in 3 pm, check-out 11 am. Indoor pool, whirlpool. **$**

★★ RADISSON FORT MAGRUDER HOTEL & CONFERENCE CENTER. *6945 Pocahontas Trail, Williamsburg (23185). Phone 757/220-2250; toll-free 800/582-1010; fax 757/221-6982.* 303 rooms, 4 story. Check-out 11 am. Restaurant, bar. Fitness room. Indoor pool, outdoor pool, children's pool, whirlpool. Tennis. Business center. **$**

★★ WILLIAMSBURG LODGE. *310 S England St, Williamsburg (23185). Phone 757/220-7976; toll-free 800/447-8679; fax 757/220-7799. www.history.org.* A lobby with native Virginia cypress paneling and flagstone floors greets guests to this year-round inn. Folk art decorates the guest rooms and public areas and most overlook the gardens and lawns. 264 rooms, 3 story. Complimentary continental breakfast. Check-in 4 pm, check-out 11 am. Restaurant, bar. Children's activity center. Fitness room, spa. Indoor pool, outdoor pool, children's pool, whirlpool. Golf. Tennis. **$$**

Full-Service Hotels

★★★ MARRIOTT WILLIAMSBURG. *50 Kingsmill Rd, Williamsburg (23185). Phone 757/220-2500; toll-free 800/288-2662; fax 757/221-0653. www.marriott.com.* This hotel is close to Busch Gardens as well as Colonial Williamsburg, Jamestown and Yorktown sites, and shopping and outlet centers. 295 rooms, 6 story. Check-in 4 pm, check-out noon. Restaurant, bar. Children's activity center. Fitness room. Indoor, outdoor pools; whirlpool. Tennis. Business center. **$**

★★★ MARRIOTT'S MANOR CLUB AT FORD'S COLONY. *101 St. Andrews Dr, Williamsburg (23188). Phone 804/258-1120; fax 804/258-5705. www.marriott.com.* Just minutes away from historic Williamsburg, this 2,500-acre Colonial-style property, offers the ultimate in vacation luxuries. 135 rooms, 3 story. Check-out 10 am. Restaurant. Fitness room. Indoor pool, outdoor pool, whirlpools. Golf. Tennis. **$$$**

★★★★ THE WILLIAMSBURG INN. *136 E Francis St, Williamsburg (23187). Phone 757/229-1000; fax 757/220-7096.* Pedigreed patriots make the Williamsburg Inn their home away from home while exploring the rich history of colonial America. The inn rolls out the red carpet for its guests, offering fine accommodations, gourmet dining, and unsurpassed levels of service. Furnished in English Regency style, the guest rooms have just the right amount of sophistication to appeal to adults while keeping children comfortable and satisfied. Blessed with a central location in the heart of this re-created 18th-century village, the inn is within a leisurely stroll of the blacksmith's shop, the candlemaker, and the cobbler. After reliving history, guests reap the rewards of the inn's plentiful activities and play a round of golf, dive into the spring-fed pool, rally on the clay tennis courts, head to the fitness center to keep in shape, or spoil themselves at the spa or gourmet restaurant. 110 rooms, 2 story. Complimentary full breakfast. Check-in 4 pm, check-out 11 am. Restaurant, bar. Children's activity center. Indoor pool, outdoor pool, children's pool, whirlpool. Golf. Tennis. Airport transportation available. Business center. **$$$**

★★★ WOODLANDS HOTEL AND SUITES. *105 Visitor Center Dr, Williamsburg (23185). Phone 757/220-7960; toll-free 800/447-8679; fax 757/565-8942. www.colonialwilliamsburg.org.* Woodland tones are found in the rooms in these guest quarters located on the grounds of the visitor center and surrounded by pine trees. 300 rooms. Complimentary continental breakfast. Check-in 4 pm, check-out 11 am. Restaurant. Children's activity center. Outdoor pool, children's pool. **$**

Full-Service Resort

★★★ KINGSMILL RESORT. *1010 Kingsmill Rd, Williamsburg (23185). Phone 757/253-1703; toll-free 800/832-5665; fax 757/253-3993. www.kingsmill.com.* Colonial Williamsburg may only be 3 miles down the road, but the Kingsmill Resort is decidedly 21st century. This playground for adults attracts golfers, tennis players, and those seeking rest and relaxation to its 2,900 manicured acres along the James River. Three 18-hole golf courses and a nine-hole par-three course challenge and charm players, while the Golf Academy provides clinics and individual instruction. Tennis players take their pick from fast-drying clay, Deco-Turf, and hydro courts at the state-of-the-art facility, while other racquet sports and a fitness center are discovered at the Sports Club. The spa rejuvenates and restores with its wide variety of treatments. After a day filled with activities, hearty appetites are always satisfied at the resort's six restaurants and lounges. 412 rooms, 2 story. Complimentary continental breakfast. Check-in 4-6 pm, check-out 11 am. Restaurant, bar. Children's activity center. Fitness room, spa. Beach. Indoor pool, outdoor pool, children's pool, whirlpool. Golf. Tennis. Business center. **$$$**

Specialty Lodgings

The following lodging establishments are approved by Mobil Travel Guide, but due to their unique and individualized nature have not been given a traditional Mobil Star rating. Included in this listing you may find bed-and-breakfasts, limited-service inns, guest ranches, and other unique hotel properties.

COLONIAL CAPITAL BED AND BREAKFAST. *501 Richmond Rd, Williamsburg (23185). Phone 757/229-0233; toll-free 800/776-0570; fax 757/253-7667. www.ccbb.com.* 5 rooms, 3 story. Children over 8 years only. Complimentary full breakfast. Check-in 2 pm, check-out 11 am. Built in 1926; antiques. **$**

COLONIAL GARDENS INN. *1109 Jamestown Rd, Williamsburg (23185). Phone 757/220-8087; toll-free 800/886-9715; fax 757/253-1495. www.colonial-gardens.com.* 4 rooms, 2 story. Complimentary full breakfast. Check-in 2-6 pm, check-out 11 am. Built in 1960; Southern design. **$$**

COLONIAL HOUSES-HISTORIC LODGING. *302-B Francis St, Williamsburg (23185). Phone 757/565-8440; toll-free 800/447-8679; fax 757/565-8444.* These 18th-century historic buildings are very secluded, located on the 173 acres of Colonial Williamsburg. Guests can choose from a small house or a larger one with with up to 16 rooms, each furnished with period reproductions. All are within walking distance of shops, museums, and horse-drawn carriages. 77 rooms, 2 story. Complimentary continental breakfast. Check-in 4 pm, check-out 11 am. Business center. **$$**

EDGEWOOD BED AND BREAKFAST. *4800 John Tyler Memorial Hwy, Charles City (23030). Phone 804/829-2962; fax 804/829-2962.* This Gothic home built in 1870 houses a collection of country primitives. It is famous for its ghost which has been experienced by generations of occupants. The property includes a gristmill that ground corn for both the Union and Confederate armies. 8 rooms, 3 story. Children over 12 years only. Complimentary full breakfast. Check-in 3 pm, check-out 11:30 am. Pool. **$**

LIBERTY ROSE BED AND BREAKFAST. *1022 Jamestown Rd, Williamsburg (23185). Phone 757/253-1260; toll-free 800/545-1825. www.libertyrose.com.* This restored house is decorated in a Victorian-style with European antiques and is located just 1 mile from Colonial Williamsburg's historic village. 4 rooms, 2 story. Children over 12 years only. Complimentary full breakfast. Check-in 3 pm, check-out 11 am. **$$**

NORTH BEND PLANTATION BED AND BREAKFAST. *12200 Weyanoke Rd, Charles City (23030). Phone 804/829-5176. www.northbendplantation.com.* 4 rooms, 2 story. Complimentary full breakfast. Check-in 3 pm, check-out 11 am. Pool. **$**

PINEY GROVE. *16920 Southall Plantation Ln, Charles City (23030). Phone 804/829-2480; fax 804/829-6888. www.pineygrove.com.* 4 rooms, 2 story. Complimentary full breakfast. Check-in 4 pm, check-out noon. Pool. Two historic farmhouses (circa 1800). **$**

WILLIAMSBURG SAMPLER BED AND BREAKFAST. *922 Jamestown Rd, Williamsburg (23185). Phone 757/253-0398; toll-free 800/722-1169; fax 757/253-2669. www.williamsburgsampler.com.* This 18th-century, plantation-style colonial home is located in the City of Williamsburg's Architectural Corridor Protection District. 4 rooms, 3 story. Complimentary full breakfast. Check-in 1 pm, check-out 11 am. **$**

Restaurants

★ ★ ABERDEEN BARN. *1601 Richmond Rd, Williamsburg (23185). Phone 757/229-6661; fax 757/227-4440. www.aberdeen-barn.com.* Dinner. Closed Thanksgiving, Dec 25; also first two weeks in Jan. Bar. Children's menu. **$$$**

★★ BERRET'S SEAFOOD RESTAURANT AND TAPHOUSE GRILL. *199 S Boundary St, Williamsburg (23185). Phone 757/253-1847; fax 757/220-0415. www.berrets.com.* American, seafood menu. Lunch, dinner. Closed Jan 1, Dec 25; also Mon in Jan and Feb. Bar. Children's menu. Casual attire. Outdoor seating. **$$**

★★ COACH HOUSE TAVERN. *12604 Harrison Landing Rd, Charles City (23030). Phone 804/829-6003; fax 804/829-6907.* Seafood menu. Lunch, dinner, Sun brunch. Closed Dec 25. Bar. Children's menu. Reservations recommended. **$$$**

★★★ THE DINING ROOM AT FORD'S COLONY. *240 Ford's Colony Dr, Williamsburg (23188). Phone 757/258-4107; fax 757/258-4168. www.fordscolony.com.* Rich, imaginative American and European dishes are served by an impeccable waitstaff in a quiet, elegant dining room. American, seafood menu. Dinner, Sun brunch. Closed Sun, Mon; also early Jan. Bar. Children's menu. Jacket required. **$$$**

★★ GIUSEPPE'S. *5601 Richmond Rd, Williamsburg (23188). Phone 757/565-1977; fax 757/564-0853. www.giuseppes.com.* Italian menu. Lunch, dinner. Closed Sun; holidays. Bar. Children's menu. Outdoor seating. **$$**

★★ INDIAN FIELDS TAVERN. *9220 John Tyler Memorial Hwy, Charles City (23030). Phone 804/829-5004; fax 804/829-5411. www.indianfields.com.* Lunch, dinner, Sun brunch. Closed Dec 24-25; also Mon in Jan. Bar. Children's menu. Turn-of-the-century farmhouse on working farm. Screened porch dining area. **$$$**

★★ JEFFERSON INN. *1453 Richmond Rd, Williamsburg (23185). Phone 757/229-2296; fax 757/258-2533.* Seafood menu. Dinner. Closed Thanksgiving, Dec 24-25. Bar. Children's menu. Casual attire. **$$**

★★ KING'S ARMS TAVERN. *416 E Duke of Glouchester St, Williamsburg (23185). Phone 757/229-2141; fax 757/565-8806. www.colonialwilliamsburg.com.* American menu. Lunch, dinner. Bar. Children's menu. Restored 18th-century tavern; colonial décor. Reservations recommended. Outdoor seating. Own apple cider. Colonial balladeers. **$$$**

★★★ KITCHEN AT POWHATAN. *3601 Ironbound Rd, Williamsburg (23188). Phone 757/220-0741; fax 757/253-0987. www.kitchenatpowhatan.com.* An 18th-century plantation kitchen is the setting for this cozy, intimate restaurant. The simple menu features contemporary American dishes inspired by fresh local ingredients. Dinner. Closed Mon. Bar. **$$$**

★★ LE YACA. *1915 Pocahontas Trail #C10, Williamsburg (23185). Phone 757/220-3616; fax 757/259-0138.* Southern French menu. Lunch, dinner. Closed Sun. Bar. **$$$**

★ OLD CHICKAHOMINY HOUSE. *1211 Jamestown Rd, Williamsburg (23185). Phone 757/229-4689; fax 757/253-2276. www.visitwilliamsburg.com.* Southern menu. Breakfast, lunch. Closed Thanksgiving, Dec 25. Casual attire. 18th-century stagecoach stop atmosphere. **$**

★★ PEKING. *122 Waller Mill Rd, Williamsburg (23185). Phone 757/229-2288. www.peking-va.com.* Chinese menu. Lunch, dinner, brunch. Closed Thanksgiving. Bar. Reservations recommended. **$$**

★ PIERCE'S PITT BAR-B-QUE. *447 Rochambeau Dr, Williamsburg (23188). Phone 757/565-2955.* Barbecue menu. Breakfast, lunch, dinner. Closed Thanksgiving, Dec 25. **$**

★★ PRIME RIB HOUSE. *1433 Richmond Rd, Williamsburg (23185). Phone 757/229-6823. www.primeribhouse.com.* Southwestern menu. Dinner. Bar. Children's menu. **$$**

★★★ REGENCY DINING ROOM. *136 E Francis St, Williamsburg (23185). Phone 757/229-2141; fax 757/220-7096. www.colonialwilliamsburg.com.* Set in the charming Williamsburg Inn (see), the Regency Dining Room offers diners a graceful place to relax and enjoy a leisurely dinner of well executed and beautifully presented contemporary regional Southern fare. The menu runs the gamut from modern dishes like tomato-rosemary ravioli with smoked duck and oxtail rillettes to tried-and-true classics like Chateaubriand and the signature Williamsburg Inn crab cake. Diners with two left feet may want to brush up on their waltzing before dinner, as live music and dancing are served up on Friday and Saturday nights. American menu. Breakfast, lunch, dinner. Bar. Children's menu. Jacket required. Outdoor seating. **$$$**

★★ SEASONS CAFE. *110 S Henry, Williamsburg (23185). Phone 757/259-0018; fax 757/259-0513. www.seasonsofwilliamsburg.com.* International menu. Lunch, dinner, brunch. Closed Dec 25. Bar. Children's menu. Casual attire. **$$**

★★★ THE TRELLIS. *403 Duke of Gloucester St, Williamsburg (23185). Phone 757/229-8610; fax 757/221-0450. www.thetrellis.com.* American menu. Lunch, dinner, brunch. Bar. Casual attire. Outdoor seating. **$$$**

★★ WHALING COMPANY. *494 McLaw Cir, Williamsburg (23185). Phone 757/229-0275. www.whalingcompany.com.* Steak menu. Dinner. Bar. Children's menu. **$$**

★★ YORKSHIRE STEAK AND SEAFOOD HOUSE. *700 York St, Williamsburg (23185). Phone 757/229-9790; fax 757/229-7685. www.yorkshire-wmbg.com.* Dinner. Closed Dec 25. Bar. Children's menu. In colonial-style building. **$$**

Winchester (C-7)

See also Charles Town, Front Royal, Strasburg

Settled 1732
Population 23,585
Elevation 720 ft
Area Code 540
Information Winchester-Frederick County Visitor Center, 1360 S Pleasant Valley Rd, 22601; phone 540/662-4135 or toll-free 800/662-1360

This is the oldest colonial city west of the Blue Ridge, a Civil War prize that changed hands 72 times (once, 13 times in a day). Sometimes called the "apple capital of the world," it is located at the northern approach to the Shenandoah Valley.

George Washington, a red-haired 16-year-old, blithely headed for Winchester and his first surveying job in 1748, and began a decade of apprenticeship for the awesome military and political responsibilities he would later assume as a national leader. During the French and Indian Wars, Colonel Washington made the city his defense headquarters while he built Fort Loudoun in Winchester. Washington was elected to his first political office as a representative from Frederick County to the House of Burgesses.

At the intersection of travel routes, both east-west and north-south, Winchester grew and prospered. By the time of the Civil War it was a major transportation and supply center, strategically located to control both Union approaches to Washington and Confederate supply lines through the Shenandoah Valley. More than 100 minor engagements and six battles took place in the vicinity. General Stonewall Jackson had his headquarters here during the winter of 1861-1862. From his headquarters in Winchester, Union General Philip Sheridan started his famous ride to rally his troops at Cedar Creek, 11 miles away, and turn a Confederate victory into a Union rout.

Approximately 3.5 million bushels of apples are harvested annually in Frederick County and are one of Winchester's economic mainstays today. The world's largest apple cold storage plant and one of the world's largest apple processing plants are here.

What to See and Do

Abram's Delight and Log Cabin. *1340 S Pleasant Valley Ave, Winchester. Phone 540/662-6519.* (1754) Oldest house in city, restored, furnished in 18th-century style; boxwood garden; log cabin, basement kitchen. (Apr-Oct: daily; rest of year: by appointment, weather permitting) Inquire about combination ticket. **$$**

First Presbyterian Church of Winchester. *116 S Loudoun St, Winchester. Phone 540/662-3824.* (1788) Building has been used as a church, a stable by Union troops in Civil War, a public school, and an armory; restored in 1941. (Daily)

Handley Library and Archives. *100 W Piccadilly St, Winchester. Phone 540/662-9041.* Completed in 1913, public library was designed in Beaux Arts style. Rotunda is crowned on the outside with a copper-covered dome and on the inside by a dome of stained glass. Interesting interior features include wrought-iron staircases and glass floors. Historical archives are housed on lower level (nonresident fee). (Mon-Sat; closed holidays)

Stonewall Jackson's Headquarters. *415 N Braddock St, Winchester. Phone 540/667-3242.* Jackson's headquarters November 1861-March 1862; now a museum housing Jackson memorabilia and other Confederate items of the war years. (Apr-Oct: daily; rest of year: by appointment, weather permitting) Inquire about combination ticket. **$$**

Washington's Office-Museum. *Cork and Braddock sts, Winchester (22601). Phone 540/662-4412.* Building used by George Washington in 1755-1756 during construction of Fort Loudoun. Housed in this museum are French and Indian, Revolutionary, and Civil War relics. (Apr-Oct: daily; rest of year: by appointment, weather permitting) **$**

Special Events

Apple Harvest Arts & Crafts. *Jim Barnett Park.* Pie contests, apple-butter making, music, arts and crafts. Third weekend in Sept.

Historic Garden Tour. *1340 S Pleasant Valley Rd, Winchester. Phone 540/662-6550.* Open house and gardens in historic Winchester. Mid-Apr.

Shenandoah Apple Blossom Festival. *135 N Cameron St, Winchester. Phone 540/662-3863.* Apple Blossom Queen, parades, arts and crafts, band contests, music, food, and attractions. Late-Apr-early May.

Limited-Service Hotels

★ ★ BEST WESTERN LEE-JACKSON MOTOR INN. *711 Millwood Ave, Winchester (22601). Phone 540/662-4154; fax 540/662-2618. www.bestwestern.com.* 140 rooms, 2 story. Pets accepted; fee. Check-out noon. Restaurant, bar. Outdoor pool. Airport transportation available. **$**

★ COMFORT INN. *167 Town Run Ln, Stephens City (22655). Phone 540/869-6500; fax 540/869-2558. www.choicehotels.com.* 58 rooms, 2 story. Complimentary continental breakfast. Check-out noon. Outdoor pool. **$**

★ HAMPTON INN. *1655 Apple Blossom Dr, Winchester (22601). Phone 540/667-8011; fax 540/667-8033. www.hamptoninn.com.* 103 rooms, 4 story. Complimentary continental breakfast. Check-out noon. Outdoor pool. **$**

★ ★ HOLIDAY INN. *1017 Millwood Pike, Winchester (22602). Phone 540/667-3300; fax 540/722-2730. www.holiday-inn.com.* 175 rooms, 2 story. Check-out noon. Restaurant, bar. Outdoor pool. Tennis. **$**

Full-Service Inns

★ ★ ★ ASHBY INN. *692 Federal St, Paris (20130). Phone 540/592-3900; fax 540/592-3781. www.ashbyinn.com.* This restored 1829 inn is charming and elegant. Guests should certainly make a point to dine in the restaurant, which features seasonal fare. 9 rooms, 3 story. Children over 10 years only. Complimentary full breakfast. Check-in 3 pm, check-out noon. Restaurant. **$**

★ ★ ★ L'AUBERGE PROVENÇAL FRENCH COUNTRY INN. *Rte 340 S, Boyce (22663). Phone 540/837-1375; toll-free 800/638-1702; fax 540/837-2004. www.laubergeprovencale.com.* This French-style inn, decorated with Victorian and European antiques, is located in the heart of Virginia hunt country. 14 rooms, 2 story. Children over 10 years only. Complimentary full breakfast. Check-in 3 pm, check-out 11 am. Restaurant. Whirlpool. Airport transportation available. **$$**

Specialty Lodging

The following lodging establishment is approved by Mobil Travel Guide, but due to its unique and individualized nature has not been given a traditional Mobil Star rating. Included in this listing you may find bed-and-breakfasts, limited-service inns, guest ranches, and other unique hotel properties.

THE INN AT VAUCLUSE SPRING. *231 Vaucluse Spring Ln, Stephens City (22655). Phone 540/869-0200; toll-free 800/869-0525; fax 540/869-9546.* Located on 100 acres of land, this inn is spread over four buildings: the Manor House, Chumley Homeplace, Gallery, and Millhouse Studio. Visitors will enjoy the nearby wineries and scenic location. 10 rooms,

2 story. Children over 10 years only. Complimentary full breakfast. Check-in 3-5 pm, check-out 11 am. Outdoor pool. Business center. **$$**

Restaurants

★★★ **ASHBY INN.** *692 Federal St, Paris (20130). Phone 540/592-3900; fax 540/592-3781. www.ashbyinn.com.* Seasonal provisions inspire the simple, hearty menu that rivals those of trendy city restaurants. Look for garden fresh tomatoes in the summer and wild game in the fall. Relax in a very warm, very country atmosphere. Dinner, Sun brunch. Closed Mon, Tues; Jan 1, July 4, Dec 25. Reservations recommended. Outdoor seating. **$$**

★★★ **L'AUBERGE PROVENÇAL.** *Rte 340 S, Boyce (22620). Phone 540/837-1375. www.laubergeprovencale.com.* This country inn has earned a reputation for fine cuisine served with detailed, personal attention. Innkeeper/chef Alain Borel, from Avignon, and his wife Celeste provide an authentic, garden-inspired menu. French Provençal menu. Dinner. Closed Mon-Tues; July 4, Dec 25. Bar. Outdoor seating. **$$$**

Woodstock (C-6)

See also Basye, Front Royal, Luray, New Market, Strasburg

Founded 1761
Population 3,952
Elevation 780 ft
Area Code 540
Zip 22664
Information Chamber of Commerce, 143 N Main St, PO Box 605; phone 540/459-2542
Web site www.woodstockva.com/chamber

A German immigrant, Jacob Mller, received a land grant from Lord Fairfax and came here in 1752 with his wife and six children. A few years later he set aside 1,200 acres for a town, first called Müllerstadt, later Woodstock. In a small log church here, John Peter Gabriel Mühlenberg, in January 1776, preached his famous sermon based on Ecclesiastes 3:1-8: "There is a time to every purpose. . a time to war and a time to peace," at the end of which he flung back his vestments to reveal the uniform of a Continental colonel and began to enroll his parishioners in the army that was to overthrow British rule.

The *Shenandoah Valley-Herald,* a weekly newspaper established in 1817, is still published here.

What to See and Do

Shenandoah County Court House. *Main St, Woodstock.* (1792) Oldest courthouse still in use west of the Blue Ridge Mountains; interior restored to original design. (Mon-Fri)

Shenandoah Vineyards. *3659 S Ox Rd, Woodstock (22824). From I-81 exit 279 at Edinburg, W on Hwy 675, make first right on Hwy 686, go 1 1/2 miles to winery. Phone 540/984-8699.* Valley's first winery. Premium wines; hand-picked and processed in the European style. Picnic area. Tours, free tastings available. (Daily; closed Jan 1, Thanksgiving, Dec 25) **FREE**

Woodstock Tower. *4 miles E on Mill Rd, crest of Massanutten Mountain.* Panoramic view of seven horseshoe bends of the Shenandoah River.

Special Events

Shenandoah County Fair. *300 Fairgrounds Rd, Woodstock (22664). Phone 540/459-3867.* One of the oldest county fairs in the state. Harness racing last four days. Late Aug-early Sept.

Shenandoah Valley Music Festival. *102 N Main St, Woodstock (22664). Phone 540/459-3396.* Symphony pops, classical, folk, jazz, country, and big band concerts. Pavilion and lawn seating. Outdoor pavilion on grounds of historic Orkney Springs Hotel in Orkney Springs. Contact Festival, PO Box 12; phone 540/459-3396. Four weekends, mid-July-Labor Day weekend.

Limited-Service Hotel

★ **RAMADA.** *1130 Motel Dr, Woodstock (22664). Phone 540/459-5000; fax 540/459-8219. www.ramada.com.* 124 rooms, 3 story. Check-out noon. Restaurant, bar. Outdoor pool. **$**

Specialty Lodging

The following lodging establishment is approved by Mobil Travel Guide, but due to its unique and individualized nature has not been given a traditional Mobil Star rating. Included in this listing you may find bed-and-breakfasts, limited-service inns, guest ranches, and other unique hotel properties.

INN AT NARROW PASSAGE. *Rte 11; 30 Chapman Landing Rd, Woodstock (22664). Phone 540/459-8000; toll-free 800/459-8002; fax 540/459-8001. www.innatnarrowpassage.com.* This restored colonial wagon stop along the Old Valley Pike is located on the Shenandoah River. The guest rooms are decorated with Early American reproductions and antiques are available. Views of both the river and the Massanutten Mountains are enjoyed. 12 rooms, 2 story. Complimentary full breakfast. Check-in 2 pm, check-out 11 am. **$**

Restaurant

★★ SPRING HOUSE TAVERN. *325 S Main St (US 11), Woodstock (22664). Phone 540/459-4755.* Lunch, dinner. Bar. Children's menu. Five dining rooms include a log lounge. **$$**

Wytheville (F-3)

See also Galax, Marion

Founded 1792
Population 7,804
Elevation 2,284 ft
Area Code 540
Zip 24382
Information Wytheville-Wythe-Bland Chamber of Commerce, 150 E Monroe St, PO Box 563; phone 540/223-3365
Web site chamber.wytheville.com

With lead mines and the only salt mine in the South nearby, Wytheville was a Union target during the Civil War. One story states a detachment of Union cavalry attempted to take the town in July 1863, only to be thwarted by Molly Tynes, who rode 40 miles over the mountains from Rocky Dell to tell the countryside that the Yankees were coming. The alerted home guard turned them away. A transportation center today, Wytheville is a vacationland nestled between the Blue Ridge and Allegheny mountains. Rural Retreat Lake is nearby. Wythe Ranger District office for the George Washington and Jefferson national forests (see HARRISONBURG) is located here.

What to See and Do

Big Walker Lookout. *12 miles N on Hwy 52; on Big Walker Mountain Scenic Byway. Phone 276/228-4401.* A 120-foot observation tower at 3,405-foot elevation; swinging bridge. Gift shop; snack bar. (Apr-late May: Thurs-Sun; Memorial Day-Oct: Tues-Sun) **$$**

Shot Tower Historical Park. *176 Orphanage Dr, Wytheville (24360). At Jackson's Ferry, 6 miles E on I-81, then 7 miles S on Hwy 52; or I-77 S, Poplar Camp exit. Phone 540/699-6778 (New River Trail State Park).* (1807) On bluff overlooking New River. One of three shot towers still standing in US; fortresslike stone shaft has 2 1/2 foot thick walls rising 75 feet above ground and boring 75 feet below to a water tank. Molten lead was poured through sheet iron colanders from the tower top; during the 150-foot descent it became globular before hitting the water. Pellets were then sorted by rolling them down an incline; well-formed shot rolled into a receptacle; faulty ones zig-zagged off and were remelted. Visitor center, programs; hiking trails, picnicking. (Memorial Day-Labor Day, daily) **$**

Wytheville State Fish Hatchery. *1260 Red Hollow Rd, Wytheville (05301). 12 miles SE on Hwy 52 to Hwy 629. Phone 276/637-3212.* Approximately 150,000 pounds of rainbow trout produced annually. Five-tank aquarium; displays. Self-guided tours. (Daily) **FREE**

Special Event

Chautauqua Festival. Held over a nine-day period. Includes parade, educational events, performing arts, art shows, children's activities, music, food, entertainment. Third week in June.

Limited-Service Hotels

★ BEST WESTERN WYTHEVILLE INN. *355 Nye Rd, Wytheville (24382). Phone 276/228-7300; fax 276/228-4223. www.bestwestern.com.* 100 rooms, 2 story. Pets accepted, some restrictions; fee. Complimentary continental breakfast. Check-out noon. Outdoor pool. **$**

★ DAYS INN. *150 Malin Dr, Wytheville (24382). Phone 276/228-5500; fax 276/228-6301. www.daysinn.com.* 118 rooms, 3 story. Check-out noon. View of mountains. **$**

★ ★ HOLIDAY INN. *1800 E Main St, Wytheville (24382). Phone 276/228-5483; toll-free 800/465-4329; fax 276/228-5417. www.holiday-inn.com.* 199 rooms, 4 story. Pets accepted, some restrictions; fee. Check-out 11 am. Restaurant, bar. Outdoor pool, children's pool. **$**

Restaurant

★ LOG HOUSE. *520 E Main St, Wytheville (24382). Phone 540/228-4139.* American menu. Lunch, dinner. Closed Sun; Dec 25. Children's menu. Colonial motif; built 1776. Outdoor seating. **$$**

Yorktown (E-9)

See also Colonial Parkway, Gloucester, Jamestown (Colonial National Historical Park), Newport News, Williamsburg

Founded 1691
Population 203
Elevation 54 ft
Information Colonial National Historical Park, PO Box 210, 23690; phone 757/898-3400
Web site www.nps.gov/colo

Free land offered in 1630 to those adventurous enough "to seate and inhabit" the 50-foot bluffs on the south side of the York River "formerly known by ye Indyan name of Chiskiacke" brought about the beginning of settlement. When the Assembly authorized a port, started in 1691, the town slowly expanded and in the following years became a busy shipping center, with prosperity reaching a peak about 1750. From then on the port declined along with the Tidewater Virginia tobacco trade.

Yorktown's moment in history came in 1781. British commander Cornwallis, after raiding up and down Virginia with minimal resistance from the Marquis de Lafayette, was sent here to establish a naval base in which supplies and reinforcements could be shipped to him. The Comte de Grasse's French fleet effectively blockaded the British, however, by controlling the mouth of the Chesapeake Bay. At the Battle of the Capes on September 5, 1781, a British fleet sent to investigate the French presence was defeated by the French. Cornwallis found himself bottled up in Yorktown by combined American and French forces under Washington, which arrived on September 28.

Shelling began October 9. The siege of Yorktown ended on October 17 with Cornwallis requesting terms of capitulation. On October 19, Cornwallis' troops marched out with flags and arms cased, their bands playing. Then they laid down their arms, bringing the last major battle of the Revolutionary War to a close.

Yorktown Battlefield, part of Colonial National Historical Park, surrounds the village. Though Yorktown itself is still an active community, many surviving and reconstructed colonial structures supply an 18th-century atmosphere.

What to See and Do

Grace Episcopal Church. *111 Church St, Yorktown. Phone 757/898-3261.* (1697) Walls of local marl (a mixture of clay, sand, and limestone); damaged in 1781, gutted by fire in 1814. A 1649 communion service is still in use. (Daily)

★ Yorktown Battlefield in Colonial National Historic Park. *From Williamsburg, take the Colonial Parkway 13 miles E to Yorktown. Phone 757/898-2410. www.nps.gov.* Surrounds and includes part of town. Remains of 1781 British fortifications, modified and strengthened by Confederate forces in Civil War. Reconstructed American and French lines lie beyond. Roads lead to headquarters, encampment areas of Americans, French. Admission fee includes access to Visitor Center, battlefield tour, Moore House, and Nelson House. Golden Access, Age, and Eagle passports honored (see MAKING THE MOST OF YOUR TRIP). (Daily; closed Dec 25) **$** Stop first at

Moore House. *Located along battlefield tour road. Phone 757/898-3400.* In this 18th-century house the "Articles of Capitulation" were drafted. These were signed by General Washington in the captured British Redoubt #10 on October 19. (Mid-June-mid-Aug: daily; spring and fall: weekends)

Nelson House. *Nelson and Main sts, Yorktown.* Original restored mansion built by "Scotch Tom" Nelson in the early 1700s. Home of his grandson, Thomas Nelson, Jr., a signer of the Declaration of Independence. Impressive example of Georgian architecture. (Apr-Oct, daily)

Self-guided battlefield tour. Markers, displays aid in visualizing siege. Highlights include headquarters sites of Lafayette, von Steuben, Rochambeau, Washington; American Battery #2; Grand French Battery; a key point is Surrender Field where British forces laid down their arms.

Visitor Center. *Colonial Pkwy and Yorktown Visitor Center, Yorktown. E side of town, at end of Colonial Pkwy. Phone 757/898-3400.* Information; special exhibits, General Washington's field tents. (Daily; closed Dec 25)

Yorktown National Civil War Cemetery. 2,183 interments (1,436 unknown).

Yorktown Victory Monument. *E end of Main St.* Elaborately ornamented 95-foot granite column memorializes American-French alliance in Revolutionary War.

Yorktown Victory Center. *31 Rte S Jamestown Rd, Williamsburg. 1/2 mile W on Hwy 238. Phone 757/253-4838; toll-free 888/593-4682.* Museum of the Revolutionary War chronicles the struggle for independence from the beginnings of colonial unrest to the formation of the new nation. Exhibit galleries, living history Continental Army encampment, and late-18th-century farm. (Daily; closed Jan 1, Dec 25) Combination ticket with Jamestown Settlement (see JAMESTOWN COLONIAL NATIONAL HISTORICAL PARK) available. **$$$$**

Special Event

Yorktown Day. Observance of America's Revolutionary War victory at Yorktown in 1781. Oct 19.

Limited-Service Hotel

★★ DUKE OF YORK MOTOR HOTEL. *508 Water St, Yorktown (23690). Phone 757/898-3232; fax 757/898-5922.* 57 rooms, 3 story. Check-in 2 pm, check-out noon. Restaurant. Beach. Outdoor pool. **$**

Restaurant

★★ RIVER'S INN RESTAURANT & CRAB DECK. *8109 Yacht Haven Dr, Gloucester Point (23062). Phone 804/642-9942; toll-free 888/780-2722; fax 804/642-9945. www.riversinnrestaurant.com.* Seafood menu. Lunch, dinner. Closed Dec 25; also Mon-Tues from Oct-Mar. Bar. Children's menu. Casual attire. Outdoor seating. **$$**

District of Columbia

Designed by Major Pierre Charles L'Enfant in about 1791, Washington was the first American city planned for a specific purpose. It is a beautiful city, with wide, tree-lined streets laid out according to a design that is breathtaking in its scope and imagination. For its purpose, the broad plan still works well even though L'Enfant could not have foreseen the automobile or the fact that the United States would come to have a population of more than 250 million people. Nevertheless, L'Enfant's concept was ambitious, allowing for vast growth. Washington, named for the first US president, has been the nation's capital since 1800. The city's business is centered around government and tourism; there is little heavy industry.

Population: 572,059
Area: 63 square miles
Elevation: 1-410 feet
Peak: Tenleytown
Entered Union: Founded in 1790
Flower: American Beauty Rose
Bird: Wood Thrush
Time Zone: Eastern
Web site: www.washington.org
Fun Facts:

- The Bureau of Engraving and Printing (BEP), located in Washington, DC, is responsible for designing and printing paper currency for the United States.
- During World War II, to protect the city from possible enemy invasion, anti-aircraft guns were placed on top of several government office buildings. One of those guns accidentally went off and the projectile hit the roof of the Lincoln Monument.

The District of Columbia and Washington are one and the same. Originally, the District was a 10-mile-square crossing the Potomac River into Virginia, but the Virginia portion (31 square miles) was returned to the state in 1846. Residences of DC workers spill into Virginia and Maryland; so do government offices. In 1800, there were 130 federal employees; at the end of the Civil War, there were 7,000; now there are well over half a million. Although the city was a prime Confederate target in the Civil War, it was barely damaged. The assassination of Abraham Lincoln, however, struck a blow to the nation and drove home to Americans the fact that Washington was not merely a center of government. What happens here affects everyone.

This is a cosmopolitan city. Perhaps no city on earth has a populace with so many different origins. Representatives from all nations and men and women from every state work here—and vote in their home states by absentee ballot. It is a dignified, distinguished capital. Many who visit the city go first to the House of Representatives or Senate office buildings and chat with their representatives, who receive constituent visitors when they can. At these offices, visitors obtain tickets to the Senate and House galleries. From the top of the Washington Monument, there is a magnificent view of the capital. The Lincoln and Jefferson memorials cannot fail to capture the imagination.

When to Go/Climate

DC winters are relatively mild, while summers are hot and humid. The city is alive with color in spring and fall—cherry blossoms bloom in April and May, and vibrant fall foliage begins around September.

AVERAGE HIGH/LOW TEMPERATURES (° F)

Washington National Airport

Jan 47/27	**May** 76/57	**Sept** 80/63
Feb 46/29	**June** 85/67	**Oct** 69/50
Mar 57/38	**July** 89/71	**Nov** 58/41
Apr 67/46	**Aug** 87/70	**Dec** 47/32

Additional Visitor Information

The Washington, DC Convention and Visitors Association, 1212 New York Ave NW, Suite 600, Washington, DC 20005, has brochures and schedules of events; phone 202/789-7000 (Mon-Fri, 9 am-5 pm).

By writing to your representative or senator ahead of time, you can obtain free passes to the House and Senate visitors' galleries to watch congressional sessions in progress. Without this ticket, the chambers can be viewed only when Congress is not in session.

Write to your senator at the United States Senate, Washington, DC 20510. Address your representative at the United States House of Representatives, Washington, DC 20515. In the letter, include the dates you will be in Washington, first- and second-choice dates for the tours, and the number of people in your party. Also include your home phone number, should your representative's or senator's aide need to contact you. You can also get tickets, if available, directly from the office of your senator or representative after you arrive in Washington.

The National Park Service maintains information kiosks at several key points in the city as well as a White House Visitor Center at 1450 Pennsylvania Ave NW, which distributes free tickets to tour the White House.

For additional attractions and accommodations, see ARLINGTON COUNTY (RONALD REAGAN WASHINGTON-NATIONAL AIRPORT AREA) and DULLES INTERNATIONAL AIRPORT AREA in Virginia. Also see BALTIMORE/WASHINGTON INTERNATIONAL AIRPORT AREA in Maryland.

The following suburbs and towns in the Washington, DC, area are included in this book. For information on any one of them, see the individual alphabetical listing. In Virginia: Alexandria, Arlington County (Ronald Reagan Washington-National Airport Area), Fairfax, Falls Church, McLean, Springfield, Tyson's Corner. In Maryland: Bethesda, Bowie, College Park, Laurel, Rockville, Silver Springs.

Washington

Founded 1790
Population 572,059
Elevation 1-410 feet
Area Code 202
Web site www.washington.org

You won't see any skyscrapers in Washington, DC—by law, no building may be taller than the 12-story-high Washington Monument—but you will find world-renowned museums, first-rate restaurants and shopping, captivating monuments and memorials, quaint neighborhoods, grassy parks and tree-lined streets, a modern and efficient mass-transit system, a thriving arts scene, and a zoological park housing not one, but two giant pandas. So if you want skyscrapers, head elsewhere. For everything else, pay a visit to Washington.

Washington is best known as the capital of the United States, but the city did not even exist at the time the nation gained its independence in 1789. For a year, the nation's new government met in New York City, before relocating to Philadelphia. Dissension soon grew between the northern and southern states over the location of the permanent capital. Ultimately, it was agreed that the capital would be situated in the southern region, but only after the northern states were relieved of debts incurred during the Revolutionary War. In 1790, President George Washington selected a site for the nation's capital at the junction of the Potomac and Anacostia rivers, 14 miles north of his home in Mount Vernon. Andrew Ellicott conducted a survey of the area, which consisted mainly of swampland and dense forest. Ellicott was aided by Benjamin Banneker, a free black from Maryland. Using celestial calculations, Banneker, a self-taught astronomer and mathematician, laid out 40 boundary stones at 1-mile intervals to mark the city's borders.

President Washington chose Pierre-Charles L'Enfant to plan the new capital. L'Enfant, a French-born architect and urban designer who served in the American Revolutionary Army, created a bold and original plan, one that is widely considered the nation's greatest achievement in municipal planning. L'Enfant's plan called for a grid pattern of streets, with these streets intersected by wide, diagonal avenues. The diagonal avenues would meet at circles, and these circles would anchor the residential neighborhoods. An example can be seen today at Logan Circle, where four different thoroughfares converge, including Rhode Island and Vermont avenues. The large open circle sits at the core of a beautiful neighborhood, with many of the residences built soon after the Civil War in the Late Victorian and Richardsonian Romanesque styles.

L'Enfant envisioned the "Congress House" (now the Capitol) situated atop Jenkins Hill, which offered sweeping views of the Potomac River. To the west of Jenkins Hill, L'Enfant planned a 400-foot-wide avenue (now the National Mall) bordered by embassies and cultural institutions. Not everyone was pleased with his plan. Though he had the support of President Washington, L'Enfant faced opposition from some of the district commissioners who had been appointed to oversee the capital city's development. Secretary of State Thomas Jefferson, a noted architect in his own right, disapproved of the plan, but L'Enfant refused to compromise or modify his vision for the capital. In 1792, following a series of incidents between L'Enfant and those who challenged his plan, Washington dismissed the genius planner whom he had appointed only a year earlier. In L'Enfant's place, Washington appointed Andrew Ellicott to prepare a map of the city. With the help of his assistant, Benjamin Banneker, Ellicott produced a map of the city that adhered closely to L'Enfant's plan.

L'Enfant sought $95,500 for his services in planning the capital city, though he was ultimately paid less than $4,000. L'Enfant lived with friends during his later years. He died in 1825, financially destitute and never having received acclaim for his work in planning Washington. He was buried in Maryland, then disinterred and reburied at Arlington National Cemetery in 1909. A marble monument marks the site of his grave.

L'Enfant's visionary plan fostered the growth of the city's eclectic mix of neighborhoods, each containing its own distinct qualities: the surprising charm of Capitol Hill, with its 19th-century row houses and brick-lined streets; the massive stone monuments, museums, and government buildings in and around the National Mall; the quaint shops and restaurants of Georgetown; the cosmopolitan style and atmosphere of Dupont Circle; the bustling nightlife of Adams

Morgan; and the leaf-shaded residential streets of Woodley Park. The layout of the city, with its broad avenues converging on circles and squares designated for public use, made the growth of these neighborhoods possible. As a result, the city as a whole has a small-town feel even though its population exceeds 570,000.

Most first-time visitors to Washington are surprised by the city's considerable natural beauty. L'Enfant's plan, which identified parks and open spaces as essential elements in urban design, helped to shape a city that is not merely functional but also quite lush and green, possessing the "sorts of places," as L'Enfant wrote, that "may be attractive to the learned and afford diversion to the idle." Were he alive today, L'Enfant would be pleased to see congressional staffers playing softball on the National Mall, walkers strolling alongside the Potomac River, and hikers venturing off for a trek on the trails within Rock Creek Park. Pulitzer Prize-winning historian David McCullough has expressed his appreciation of the capital's natural beauty. "In many ways it is our most civilized city," McCullough wrote of Washington. "It accommodates its river, accommodates trees and grass, makes room for nature as other cities don't."

The C&O Canal Towpath is a popular destination for bikers and hikers. The towpath begins in Georgetown and parallels the Potomac River, meandering 184 miles west to Cumberland, Maryland. Just outside of Washington, the towpath cuts through Great Falls Park. The park's ferocious rapids and giant boulders may cause visitors to forget that they're only a few miles from the city. The George Washington Parkway leads from the park back to the capital. McCullough penned of this route, "There is no more beautiful entrance to any of our cities than the George Washington Parkway, which sweeps down the Virginia side of the Potomac. The views of the river gorge are hardly changed from Jefferson's time."

Beyond the gorge, the capital unfolds in a rich blend of people, neighborhoods, parks, embassies, offices, memorials, monuments, and museums. Rising above it all, the white marble of the Washington Monument stretches for the sky, a constant reminder of the capital's namesake and the remarkable history and growth of not just this great city but also the nation it serves and represents.

Public Transportation

The Metrorail system is the least expensive means of getting around the capital. Metro (as it is called) provides a coordinated transportation system between buses and rail. The rapid rail system links major commercial districts and neighborhoods from the Capitol to the Pentagon and from the National Zoo to the National Airport and beyond. Trains operate every 6-12 minutes on the average: Monday-Friday, 5:30 am-midnight; Saturday and Sunday from 8 am. Phone 202/637-7000.

What to See and Do

2:K:9. *2009 8th St NW, Washington (20001). Phone 202/667-7750.* Flash helps you get in the door here (no jeans or athletic wear, please); pulsating hip-hop, house, and techno beats will keep you dancing until all hours. Dazzling lighting effects and a powerful sound system make the enormous dance floor rock. Exhausted? Take a breather at the swank 42-foot bar or just hang back and watch the dancers in cages—always inspiring. The place draws a glam, multiethnic crowd of under-30s. **$$$**

African American Civil War Memorial. *1200 U St NW, Washington (20001). 10th and U sts NW. Phone 202/667-2667.* Sculpture pays tribute to the more than 200,000 African American soldiers who fought in the Civil War.

American Red Cross. *1730 E St NW, Washington (20006). Phone 202/737-8300. www.redcross.org.* National headquarters includes three buildings bounded by 17th, 18th, D, and E sts NW. The 17th St building includes marble busts Faith, Hope, and Charity by sculptor Hiram Powers and three original Tiffany stained-glass windows. (Daily 8:30 am-4 pm, closed most federal holidays) **FREE**

Arena Stage. *1101 6th St, Washington (20024). At Maine Ave SW. Phone 202/488-3300. www.arena-stage.org.*

Art Museum of the Americas, OAS. *201 18th St NW, Washington (20006). Phone 202/458-6016. www.museum.oas.org.* Dedicated to Latin American and Caribbean contemporary art; paintings, graphics, sculpture. (Tues-Sun 10 am-5 pm; closed holidays) **FREE**

B'nai B'rith Klutznick Museum. *1640 Rhode Island Ave NW, Washington (20036). B'nai B'rith International Center. Phone 202/857-6583.* Permanent exhibition of Jewish ceremonial and folk art. Changing exhibits. (Mon-Fri, Sun; closed holidays, Jewish holidays) **FREE**

Basilica of the National Shrine of the Immaculate Conception. *400 Michigan Ave NE, Washington (20017). Phone 202/526-8300.* Largest Roman Catholic church in the US and one of the largest in the world. Byzantine and Romanesque architecture; extensive and elaborate collection of mosaics and artwork. (Daily) Carillon concerts (Sun afternoons); organ recitals (June-Aug, Sun evenings). Guided tours (daily). **FREE**

Black History Recreation Trail. *1100 Ohio Dr SW, Washington (20001). Phone 202/619-7222.* Trail through Washington neighborhoods highlights important sites in African American history.

Blair-Lee House. *1651 Pennsylvania Ave NW, Washington (20503).* (1824) Guest house for heads of government and state who are visiting the US as guests of the president. Not open to the public.

Blues Alley. *1073 Wisconsin Ave NW, Washington (20007). Phone 202/337-4141. www.bluesalley.com.* For nearly 40 years, serious jazz lovers have flocked to this intimate club to hear such noted artists as Dizzy Gillespie, Sarah Vaughan, and Maynard Ferguson, along with a host of outstanding but lesser-known musicians. Nightly shows run the gamut from vocal and instrumental sounds to solo performers to larger ensembles. Housed in an 18th-century brick carriage house in Georgetown, the club has a sophisticated ambience and a Creole-themed dinner menu to match. **$$**

Bureau of Engraving and Printing. *14th and C sts SW, Washington (20228). S of the Mall; enter on 14th St. Phone 202/874-3019. www.bep.treas.gov.* Watch millions of dollars being made—printed, that is—on the tour of this site, which takes visitors through many of the steps involved in producing currency. You'll see large, blank sheets of paper transformed, as if by magic, into wallet-size bills and learn about the latest high-tech steps the Bureau has taken to thwart counterfeiting. You can buy uncut sheets of bills in different denominations, as well as shredded cash, at the BEP store. Guided tours 9 am-2 pm. (Closed weekends, federal holidays, and Dec 24-Jan 3) **FREE**

Capital Children's Museum. *800 3rd St NE, Washington (20002). Phone 202/675-4120. www.ccm.org.* Make delicious tortillas and hot chocolate in "Mexico," slide down a fire pole in "Cityscapes," or design a cartoon character in "Chuck Jones: An Animated Life"—learning and playing feel pretty much the same at this lively, hands-on museum. Young problem-solvers will enjoy the challenge of the 20 puzzling tasks of "Brain Teasers," while their younger siblings can take on "Teasers for Tots." The charming old building that houses the museum is a former convent. (Daily 10 am-5 pm; closed Mon during the school year except holidays) **$$**

The Capitol. *Capitol Hill, Washington (20002). Between Constitution and Independence aves, at Pennsylvania Ave, E end of the National Mall. Phone 202/225-6827. www.aoc.gov.* With its graceful dome making it one of the most famous American landmarks, the Capitol has been the seat of the legislative branch of the US government for more than 200 years. Visitors can take guided tours of several sections, including the beautifully restored Old Supreme Court Chamber and Old Senate Chamber. The breathtaking Rotunda, a ceremonial space beneath the soaring dome, is a gallery for paintings and sculptures of historic significance. Below it is the Crypt, built for the remains of George Washington (who asked to be buried at Mount Vernon instead), now used for exhibits. Don't miss the National Statuary Hall, where statues of prominent citizens have been donated by all 50 states, and the ornate Brumidi Corridors, named for the Italian artist who designed their murals and many other decorative elements in the Capitol. A state-of-the-art visitor center, currently under construction, is scheduled to open in 2005. (Mon-Sat; closed Jan 1, Thanksgiving, Dec 25) Tickets for tours are available at the Capitol Guide Service kiosk near the intersection of First St SW and Independence Ave. **FREE**

Congress. *Capitol Hill, Washington (20002).* Tickets to the House and Senate visitors' galleries can be obtained from the office of your representative or senator. Foreign visitors can obtain passes to the Senate Gallery from the appointment desk, first floor, Senate Wing; and to the House of Representatives Gallery from the check stand, third floor, House wing (identification required).

Old Senate Chamber. *First and Constitution aves NE, Washington (20002). N of rotunda. Phone 202/225-6827.* Original Senate chamber has been restored to its 1850s appearance.

West Front. *Capitol Hill, Washington (20002). Phone 202/225-6827.* Along the Capitol's west front are terraces, gardens, and lawns designed by Frederick Law Olmstead, who also planned New York City's Central Park. Halfway down the hill are the Peace Monument (on the north) and the Garfield Monument (on the south). At the foot of Capitol Hill is Union Square with a reflecting pool and Grant Monument.

Capitol City Brewing Company. *2 Massachusetts Ave NE, Washington (20002). Phone 202/842-2337. www.capcitybrew.com.* Shiny copper vats and a large oval copper bar are the centerpieces of this huge—and hugely popular—brew pub situated in the beautifully restored 1911 Postal Square Building. Hill staffers and tourists crowd in for made-on-the-premises ales, lagers, and pilsners that go down well with warm pretzels and mustard or with whole meals. This is one of four Capitol City pubs in the area, and the only one swathed in neoclassical marble. (Mon-Sat 11-1:30 am, Sun to midnight)

Catholic University of America. *620 Michigan Ave NE, Washington (20064). Phone 202/319-5000.* (1887) (5,510 students) Open to all faiths. Performances at Hartke Theatre (year-round).

Chesapeake & Ohio Canal Boat Rides. *1057 Thomas Jefferson St NW, Washington (20007). Thomas Jefferson St NW, between 30th and 31st sts. Phone 202/653-5190.* Narrated one-hour round-trip canal tours by park rangers in period clothing aboard mule-drawn boats. The ticket office is adjacent. (Apr-Nov, Wed-Sun) **$$**

Chesapeake & Ohio Canal Towpath. *1057 Thomas Jefferson St NW, Washington (Georgetown Visitor Center) (20007). Phone 202/653-5190. www.nps.gov/choh/co_visit.htm.* Biking (or simply strolling) along the fascinating Chesapeake & Ohio Canal towpath is a great way to immerse yourself in both history and nature. The canal, which runs 184.5 miles between Georgetown and Cumberland, Maryland, was completed in 1850. The mostly level path takes you past locks, lockhouses, aqueducts, and other intriguing original structures from the route's commercial heyday. Expect spectacular scenery and all manner of wildlife along the way, including deer, fox, and woodpeckers. Fee ($) per cyclist at Great Falls. Georgetown Visitor Center (Sat-Sun).

Chinatown. *G and H sts, between 6th and 8th sts NW.* Recognizable by the Chinatown Friendship Archway at 7th and H sts. The archway is decorated in Chinese architectural styles of Qing and Ming dynasties and is topped with nearly 300 painted dragons.

Clara Barton National Historic Site. *5801 Oxford Rd, Glen Echo (20812). 8 miles NW. Phone 301/492-6245. www.nps.gov/clba.* Thirty-six-room house (1891) of unusual architecture was both the national headquarters of the Red Cross and the home of Clara Barton for the last 15 years of her life. Contents include many items belonging to the founder of the American Red Cross. Period costumes worn during some special programs. Guided tours only. (Daily 10 am-5 pm; closed Jan 1, Thanksgiving, Dec 25) **FREE**

Constitution Gardens. *Constitution Ave and 18th St, Washington (20011). Phone 202/426-6841.* This 50-acre park, with a man-made lake, is also the site of the Signers of the Declaration of Independence Memorial. **FREE**

Corcoran Gallery of Art. *500 17th St NW, Washington (20006). 17th St between New York Ave and E St NW. Phone 202/639-1700. www.corcoran.org.* The city's oldest art museum—and its largest non-federal one—is also one of its liveliest. Known for its strong collection of 19th-century American art (don't miss John Singer Sargent's luminous *Oyster Gatherers of Cancale*) and its support for local artists, the museum also shows important European pieces and eye-opening contemporary works, including photography, performance art, and new media. A glamorous, Frank Gehry-designed addition to the landmark beaux arts building is in the works. (Wed, Fri-Mon 10 am-5 pm, Thurs to 9 pm; closed Jan 1, Thanksgiving, Dec 25) Free admission Mon, Thurs after 5 pm. **$**

DAR Headquarters. *1776 D St NW, Washington (20006). Phone 202/628-1776. www.dar.org.* Includes Memorial Continental Hall (1904) and Constitution Hall (1920); DAR Museum Gallery, located in the administration building, has 33 state period rooms; outstanding genealogical research library (fee for nonmembers). Guided tours (Mon-Sat). **FREE**

DC United (MLS). *RFK Memorial Stadium, 2400 E Capitol St, Washington (20003). Phone 202/547-9077. www.dcunited.com.* Professional soccer team.

Department of Commerce Building. *1401 Constitution Ave NW, Washington (20230). Pennsylvania Ave, between 14th and 15th sts NW. Phone 202/482-4883. www.commerce.gov.* (1932)

Department of Energy. *1000 Independence Ave SW, Washington (20585). Phone 202/586-5575. www.energy.gov.* Includes the Interstate Commerce Commission (1934), Constitution Ave between 12th and 13th sts NW; Customs Department, Constitution Ave between 13th and 14th sts NW; and the District Building, Pennsylvania Ave between 13th and 14th sts NW, Washington's ornate 1908 city hall.

Department of Justice Building. *950 Pennsylvania Ave, Washington (20530).* (1934) *Pennsylvania Ave between 9th and 10th sts NW.* (Not open to the public) Across Pennsylvania Ave is

FBI Headquarters. *J. Edgar Hoover Bldg, 935 Pennsylvania Ave NW, Washington (20535). Between 9th and 10th sts NW; tour entrance on 9th St NW. Phone 202/324-3000. www.fbi.gov.* Tours of historical exhibits, includes FBI laboratory; very large firearm collection; demonstration of firearms. (Mon-Fri; closed holidays) **FREE**

Department of State Building. *2201 C St NW, Washington (20520). 21st, 22nd, C and D St NW. Phone 202/647-3241.* The State Department's diplomatic reception rooms, furnished with 18th-century American furniture and decorative art, are used by the Secretary of State and cabinet members for formal entertaining. Tours (Mon-Fri; closed federal holidays and special events; three to four weeks advance reservations; children over 12 years only preferred). **FREE**

Department of the Interior. *1849 C St NW, Washington (20240). Between 18th and 19th sts NW. Phone 202/208-3100. www.doi.gov.* (1938) Within is a museum including exhibits and dioramas depicting the history and activities of the department and its various bureaus. A photo ID is required for admission. (Mon-Fri; closed holidays) Reference library is open to the public. **FREE**

Department of the Treasury. *1500 Pennsylvania Ave NW, Washington (20501). E of the White House. Phone 202/622-0896. www.treasury.gov.* According to legend, this Greek Revival building, one of the oldest (1836-1869) in the city, was built in the middle of Pennsylvania Ave because Andrew Jackson, tired of endless wrangling over the location, walked out of the White House, planted his cane in the mud, and said, "Here." The building has been extensively restored. **FREE**

Dumbarton Oaks. *1703 32nd St NW, Washington (20007). Garden entrance at 31st and R sts. Phone 202/339-6401. www.doaks.org.* (1800) Famous gardens spanning 16 acres are both formal and Romantic in design. Mansion has antiques and European art, including El Greco's *The Visitation*, galleries of Byzantine art, and a library of rare books on gardening and horticulture. Museum of pre-Columbian artifacts housed in structure by Philip Johnson. Gardens (daily afternoons; closed holidays); house and museum (Tues-Sun afternoons; closed holidays). **$$**

Dupont-Kalorama Museum Walk. *www.dkmuseums.com.* A joining of forces of seven museums to create an awareness of the area. Information and brochures are available at any of the museums in the group. Participating museums are

Anderson House Museum. *2118 Massachusetts Ave NW, Washington (20008). Phone 202/785-2040.* Museum of the Revolutionary War and national headquarters of the Society of the Cincinnati has portraits by early American artists; 18th-century paintings; 17th-century tapestries; decorative arts of Europe and Asia; and displays of books, medals, swords, silver, glass, and china. (Tues-Sat afternoons; closed holidays) **FREE**

Fondo del Sol. *2112 R St NW, Washington (20008). Phone 202/483-2777.* Dedicated to presenting, promoting, and preserving cultures of the Americas, the museum presents exhibitions of contemporary artists and crafters, holds special events, and hosts traveling exhibits for museums and other institutions. (Tues-Sat 12:30-5:30 pm; closed holidays) **$$**

Meridian International Center. *1624 Crescent Pl NW, Washington (20009). Phone 202/939-5568. www.meridian.org.* Housed in two historic mansions designed by John Russell Pope, the center hosts international exhibits, concerts, lectures, and symposia promoting international understanding. Period furnishings, Mortlake tapestry; gardens with linden grove. (Wed-Sun 2-5 pm; closed holidays) **FREE**

Phillips Collection. *1600 21st St NW, Washington (20009). Phone 202/387-2151. www.phillipscollection.org.* First museum of modern art in the nation. Founded in 1918, the museum continues to emphasize the work of emerging as well as established international artists. Permanent collection of 19th- and 20th-century Impressionist, Post-Impressionist, and modern painting and sculpture. (Tues-Wed, Fri-Sat 10 am-5 pm, Thurs to 8:30 pm, Sun noon-7 pm; closed holidays) Introductory tours (Wed and Sat). Concerts (Sept-May, Sun). Weekday admission by donation. **$$**

Textile Museum. *2320 S St NW, Washington (20008). Phone 202/667-0441. www.textilemuseum.org.* Founded in 1925 with the collection of George Hewitt Myers, the museum features changing exhibits of non-Western textiles, Oriental rugs, and other handmade textile art. Guided tours (Sept-May, Wed, Sat, Sun; by appointment). (Mon-Sat 10 am-5 pm, Sun from 1 pm) **DONATION**

Woodrow Wilson House. *2340 S St NW, Washington (20008). Phone 202/387-4062. www.woodrowwilsonhouse.org.* (1915) Red brick Georgian Revival town house to which President Wilson retired after leaving office; family furnishings and gifts-of-state. A National Trust for Historic Preservation property. (Tues-Sun 10 am-4 pm; closed Jan 1, Thanksgiving, Dec 25) **$**

Eastern Market. *225 7th St SE, Washington (20003). Phone 202/546-2698.* Meat, fish, and produce are sold. Also crafts and farmers market on weekends. (Tues-Sun)

Eighteenth Street Lounge. *1212 18th St NW, Washington (20036). Phone 202/466-3922. www.eslmusic.com.* Lovers of modern dance music and techno all over the world know about ESL, the music label; DC residents and visitors flock to the lounge itself, a cooler-than-cool, atmospheric three-story space where the music, often spun by the DJ duo Thievery Corporation (one member is an owner), never stops. Relax by a fireplace or hang out on the patio, depending on the weather. A strict door policy weeds out wearers of athletic garb and the attitudinally impaired. (Tues-Sat) **$$$$**

Emancipation Statue. *Lincoln Park, 11th and E Capitol St NE, Washington (20003).* Bronze work of Thomas Ball paid for by voluntary subscriptions from emancipated slaves, depicting Lincoln presenting the Emancipation Proclamation to a black man, was dedicated on April 14, 1876, the 11th anniversary of Lincoln's assassination, with Fredrick Douglass in attendance. Also here is

Mary McLeod Bethune Memorial. *E Capitol St SE, Washington.* Honors the noted educator and advisor to President Lincoln and founder of the National Council of Negro Women.

Embassy Row. *Massachusetts Ave and 23rd St NW, Washington (20036).* This neighborhood, within the city's northwest quadrant, is centered around Sheridan Circle. Dozens of foreign legations can be found in the area and north along Massachusetts Ave.

Explorers Hall. *1145 17th St NW, Washington (20036). 17th and M sts NW. Phone 202/857-7588 (recording).* National Geographic Society headquarters. Several traveling exhibits, call for information. (Daily; closed Dec 25) **FREE**

Federal Reserve Building. *C and 21st sts NW, Washington (20002). Phone 202/452-3149.* (1937) Primarily an office building but noteworthy for its architecture; rotating art exhibits; film (20 minutes). **FREE**

Federal Trade Commission Building. *6th St and Pennsylvania Ave NW, Washington (20001). Phone 202/326-2222. www.ftc.gov.* (1938) (Mon-Fri; closed holidays) **FREE**

Federal Triangle. *Pennsylvania Ave and 13th St NW, Washington (20004).* The Triangle consists of a group of government buildings, nine of which were built for $78 million in the 1930s in modern classic design. The "crown jewel" of the triangle is the Ronald Reagan International Trade Center, located on Pennsylvania Ave at 13th St NW.

★ **Ford's Theatre.** *511 10th St NW, Washington (20004). Phone 202/426-6924 (visitor information). www.fordstheatre.org.* Seeing a play in this historic old theater, famous as the site of Abraham Lincoln's assassination, is deeply moving. A museum in the basement exhibits the clothes the president was wearing that night, as well as John Wilkes Booth's derringer; upstairs, the presidential box has been restored to its 1865 condition. Ford's became a working theater again in 1968; recent productions have included the play *Inherit the Wind* and a one-man show about George Gershwin. Self-guided tours (daily 9 am-5 pm; closed Dec 25). In basement is

Lincoln Museum. *Phone 202/347-4833.* Exhibits and displays focus on Lincoln's life and assassination. (Daily; closed during matinees; also Dec 25) **FREE** Nearby is

Petersen House. *516 10th St NW, Washington (20004).* The house where President Lincoln was taken after the shooting at Ford's Theatre; he died here the following morning. The house has been restored to its appearance at that time. (Daily 9 am-5 pm; closed Dec 25) **FREE**

Fort Dupont Park. *Randle Cir and Minnesota Ave SE, Washington (20019). Phone 202/426-7723. www.nps.gov/fodu/.* Picnicking, hiking, and bicycling in hilly terrain; cultural arts performances in summer (see SPECIAL EVENTS). Also films, slides, and activities involving natural science; environmental education programs; nature discovery room; Junior Ranger program; programs for senior citizens and disabled persons; and garden workshops and programmed activities by reservation. **FREE** Nearby is

Fort Dupont Sports Complex. *3779 Ely Pl SE, Washington (20019). E on Pennsylvania Ave SE; N on Minnesota Ave; E on Ely Pl. Phone 202/584-5007 (ice rink).* Skating, ice hockey (fee); tennis courts, basketball courts, ball fields (daily; free), jogging.

Fort Stevens Park. *13th and Quackenbos St NW, Washington (20019). Piney Branch Rd and Quackenbos St NW. Phone 202/895-6000.* General Jubal Early and his Confederate troops tried to invade Washington at this point on July 11-12, 1864. President Lincoln risked his life at the fort during the fighting. (Daily) **FREE**

Fort Washington National Park. *13551 Fort Washington Rd, Fort Washington, MD (20744). 4 miles S on Hwy 210, 3 1/2 miles. Phone 301/763-4600. www.nps.gov/fowa.* Earliest defense of the city (1809), the original fort was destroyed in 1814; reconstructed by 1824. View of the Potomac River; picnicking; history exhibits. (Apr-late Sept: daily 9 am-5 pm; Oct-late Mar: daily 9 am-4:30 pm) **$$**

Franciscan Monastery. *1400 Quincy St NE, Washington (20017). Phone 202/526-6800.* Within the church and grounds is the "Holy Land of America"; replicas of sacred Holy Land shrines including the Manger at Bethlehem, the Garden of Gethsemane, and the Holy Sepulchre. Also the Grotto at Lourdes and Roman catacombs. Guided tours by the friars (daily). **DONATION**

★ **Franklin Delano Roosevelt Memorial.** *West Basin Dr, Washington (20003). West Potomac Park near the Lincoln Memorial. Phone 202/426-6841. www.nps.gov/fdrm.* This newer memorial, dedicated in 1997, features a series of sculptures depicting the 32nd US President Franklin Roosevelt and his wife, Eleanor. Four outdoor rooms represent each of FDR's four presidential terms, which began in the Great Depression and ended at the close of World War II. Visitors can feel his presence in broadcasts of his "fireside chats" throughout the exhibits. (Daily 24 hours; interpretive ranger staff on site 8 am-11:45 pm; closed Dec 25) **FREE**

Frederick Douglass National Historic Site. *1411 W St SE, Washington (20020). Phone 202/426-5961; toll-free 800/967-2283 (tour reservations). www.nps.gov/frdo/freddoug.html.* This 21-room house on 9 acres is where Douglass, a former slave who became minister to Haiti and a leading black spokesman, lived from 1877 until his death in 1895; visitor center with film, memorabilia. (Daily; closed Jan 1, Thanksgiving, Dec 25) **FREE**

Fresh Farm Market. *20th St NW, Washington (20036). Between Massachusetts Ave and Q St NW. Phone 202/331-7300. www.freshfarmmarket.org.* Looking for the slenderest stalks of asparagus? Herbs that really taste like herbs? How about a bright bouquet of tulips? You'll find those delights and many others, including in-season fruits, mushrooms, artisanal cheeses, and organic offerings, at this weekly market, which brings together more than 25 local farmers with customers who prefer to skip the middleman. Vendors here sell only goods grown or produced on their land; every dollar spent goes directly to them. (Daily, Sun 9 am-1 pm)

General Services Administration Building. *18th and F sts NW, Washington (20405).* (1917) Was originally the Department of Interior.

Georgetown Flea Market. *Wisconsin Ave NW, Washington (20007). Just N of S St. Phone 202/296-4989. www.georgetownfleamarket.com.* This friendly neighborhood flea market has been giving local collectors of antique furniture, jewelry, books, rugs, toys, linens, and other vintage treasures a reason to get out of the house on Sundays since 1973. It's also known as a place to spot celebrities (actress Diane Keaton has been a frequent patron). About 70 dealers set up booths year-round; come early for the biggest selection or late for the best bargains, but feel free to dicker anytime. (Sun)

Georgetown University. *Main entrance at 37th and O sts NW, Washington. Phone 202/687-0100.* (1789) (12,000 students) Oldest Catholic college in the US, a Jesuit school. Campus tours (Mon-Sat, by reservation).

George Washington University. *2033 K St NW, Washington (20006). 19th to 24th sts NW, F St to Pennsylvania Ave. Phone 202/994-1000. www.gwu.edu.* (1821) (20,000 students) Theater; art exhibits in Dimock Gallery (Mon-Fri; closed holidays) and University Library.

Glow. *714 6th St NW, Washington (20001). Phone 202/271-1171. www.clubglow.com.* Mix eye-popping special effects—heavy, high-tech lighting with a state-of-the-art sound system, add some of the city's hippest DJs and hundreds of gotta-dance clubgoers, and you've got—on Saturday nights, anyway—the party to end all parties. A once-a-week club within a club, Glow fills gigantic Club Insomnia with the hottest trance, techno, British, and Latin sounds, working the young, sexily dressed crowd (no boots or athletic wear) into a froth of sensory overload. (Sat) **$$$$**

Government Printing Office. *710 N Capitol St NW, Washington (20403). On N Capitol St, between G and H sts. Phone 202/512-0132.* Four buildings with 35 acres of floor space where most of the material issued by US government, including production and distribution of the Congressional Record, Federal Register, and US passports, is printed. (No public tours; for information on the agency, call 202/512-1991.) Office includes the Main Government Bookstore, Nearly 20,000 publications available (Mon-Fri; closed holidays).

Gray Line bus tours. *50 Massachusetts Ave NE, Washington (20002). Phone 301/386-8300; toll-free 800/862-1400.* Tours of city and area attractions depart from Union Station. Contact 5500 Tuxedo Rd, Tuxedo, MD 20781.

Great Falls of the Potomac. (See CHESAPEAKE AND OHIO CANAL NATIONAL HISTORICAL PARK in Maryland)

Harness racing. Rosecroft Raceway. *6336 Rosecroft Dr, Fort Washington (20744). 8 miles SE. Phone 301/567-4000.* (Daily, races Thurs-Sat) **$$**

House Office Buildings. *Independence and New Jersey aves, Washington (20500). Along Independence Ave, S side of Capitol grounds. Phone 202/224-3121.* Pedestrian tunnel connects two of the oldest House office buildings with the Capitol.

Howard University. *2400 6th St NW, Washington (20059). Main campus: 2400 6th St NW between W and Harvard sts NW (20059). West campus: 2900 Van Ness St NW (20008). Three other campuses in the area. Phone 202/806-6100.* (1867) (12,000 students) Main campus has a Gallery of Fine Art with a permanent Alain Locke African Collection; changing exhibits (Sept-July, Mon-Fri).

HR-57. *1610 14th St NW, Washington (20009). Phone 202/667-3700. www.hr57.org.* This ultra-friendly, bare-bones spot is the performance arm of the Center for the Preservation of Jazz and Blues, a not-for-profit cultural center that named its club after a 1987 House Resolution designating jazz as "a rare and valuable national American treasure." Musical integrity—and the ability to appreciate a great jam—are everything here; expect to hear well-known and lesser-known artists at the top of their game, and a crowd that eats it up. (Wed-Sat) **$$**

The Improv. *1140 Connecticut Ave NW, Washington (20036). Phone 202/296-7008. www.dcimprov.com.* The crowd is youngish and the comedy free-flowing here, where almost anything is good for a laugh, especially the local industry: politics. Onstage talent includes established stars as well as hilariously original newcomers you may have caught on *Comedy Central* or elsewhere on TV. Open mic nights enable wannabe comics to step into the limelight and compete for prizes. Appetizers, sandwiches, beer, and wine are available. (Daily) **$$$$**

International Spy Museum. *800 F St NW, Washington (20004). Phone 202/393-7798; toll-free 866/779-6873. www.spymuseum.org.* Learn more about people who keep secrets for a living at this private museum that opened in 2002. It sheds light on the world of international espionage with artifacts that run the gamut from invisible ink and high-tech eavesdropping devices to a through-the-wall camera and a KGB lipstick pistol. Find out how codes were made and broken throughout history, how successful disguises are created, and what real-life James Bonds think of the high-stakes "game" of spying. (Daily from 10 am; closed Jan 1, Thanksgiving, Dec 25). **$$$$**

Islamic Center. *2551 Massachusetts Ave NW, Washington (20008). Phone 202/332-8343.* Leading mosque in the US has landscaped courtyard, intricate interior mosaics. (Daily; no tours during Fri prayer service)

Iwo Jima Statue. *Meade St, Washington (22211). Across Theodore Roosevelt Bridge on Arlington Blvd.* (See ARLINGTON COUNTY in Virginia)

John F. Kennedy Center for the Performing Arts. *2700 F St NW, Washington (20566). Phone 202/467-4600; toll-free 800/444-1324. www.kennedy-center.org.* The glittering home of the National Symphony Orchestra and Washington Opera hosts an impressive array of internationally known artists in dance, theater, and music. It opened in 1971 as a memorial to John F. Kennedy; a large bronze bust of the former president graces the Grand Foyer. The sleekly designed complex houses a number of dazzling performance spaces and reception areas, as well as paintings, sculptures, and other artwork presented by foreign governments. (Daily) **FREE**

Judiciary Square. *D, E, and F sts, between 4th and 5th sts NW.* Two square blocks of judiciary buildings, including five federal and district courts, the US District Court (1820), and the US Court of Appeals (1910). At D St halfway between 4th and 5th sts is the first completed statue of Abraham Lincoln (1868).

Kenilworth Aquatic Gardens. *Anacostia Ave and Douglas St NE, Washington (20019). Phone 202/426-6905. www.nps.gov/nace/keag.* Water lilies, lotuses, and other water plants bloom from mid-May until the frost. Gardens (daily). Guided walks (Memorial Day-Labor Day, Sat-Sun, and holidays, also by appointment; closed Jan 1, Thanksgiving, Dec 25). **FREE**

Korean War Memorial. *French Dr SW and Independence Ave, Washington (20242). Adjacent to the Lincoln Memorial. Phone 202/426-6841. www.nps.gov/kwvm.* This massive sculpture honors the Americans who served in the Korean conflict, showing 19 soldiers dressed and armed for battle heading toward the American flag, their symbolic goal. The adjacent wall features etched photographs that pay tribute to military support personnel. (Daily 8 am-11:45 pm; closed Dec 25) **FREE**

Labor Department. *Francis H. Perkins Building, 200 Constitution Ave NW, Washington (20210). Phone 202/219-6992 (library); toll-free 866/487-2365. www.dol.gov.* Lobby contains the Labor Hall of Fame, an exhibit depicting labor in the US; the library on the second floor is open to the public. (Mon-Fri; closed holidays) **FREE**

Lafayette Square. *Pennsylvania Ave NW, Washington (20004). Phone 202/673-7647.* Statue of Andrew Jackson on horseback in the center was the first equestrian figure in Washington (1853). One of the park benches was known as Bernard Baruch's office in 1930s and is dedicated to him. On the square is

Decatur House Museum. *748 Jackson Pl NW, Washington (20006). Phone 202/842-0920. www.decaturhouse.org.* (1818) Federal townhouse built for naval hero Commodore Stephen Decatur by Benjamin H. Latrobe, second architect of the Capitol. After Decatur's death in 1820, the house was occupied by a succession of American and foreign statespeople and was a center of political and social life in the city. The ground floor family rooms reflect Decatur's Federal-period lifestyle. Operated by the National Trust for Historic Preservation. (Tues-Fri 10 am-3 pm, Sat-Sun noon-4 pm; closed Jan 1, Thanksgiving, Dec 25) **FREE**

Library of Congress. *10 1st St SE, Washington (20540). Phone 202/707-6400 (reading room schedule, calendar of events). www.loc.gov.* (1800) Treasures include a Gutenberg Bible, the first great book printed with movable metal type; the Giant Bible of Mainz, a 500-year-old illuminated manuscript. Collection includes books, manuscripts, newspapers, maps, recordings, prints, photographs, posters, and more than 30 million books and pamphlets in 60 languages. In the elaborate Jefferson Building is the Great Hall, decorated with murals, mosaics, and marble carvings; exhibition halls. In the Madison Building, a 22-minute audiovisual presentation, America's Library, provides a good introduction to the library and its facilities.

(Mon-Sat 10 am-5:30 pm; closed federal holidays) **FREE** Library complex includes

Folger Shakespeare Library. *201 E Capitol St SE, Washington (20003). Phone 202/544-4600. www.folger.edu.* (1932) Houses the finest collection of Shakespeare materials in the world, including the 1623 First Folio edition and large holdings of rare books and manuscripts of the English and continental Renaissance. The Great Hall offers year-round exhibits from the Folger's extensive collection. The Elizabethan Theatre, which was designed to resemble an innyard theater of Shakespeare's day, is the site of the Folger Shakespeare Library's series of museum and performing arts programs, which include literary readings, drama, lectures, and education and family programs. Self-guided tours. Guided tours (11 am). (Mon-Sat 10 am-4 pm; closed federal holidays) **FREE**

★ **Lincoln Memorial.** *23rd St NW, Washington (20242). At Daniel French and Henry Beacon Dr. Phone 202/426-6841. www.nps.gov/linc.* Dedicated in 1922, Daniel Chester French's Abraham Lincoln looks across a reflecting pool to the Washington Monument and the Capitol. Lincoln's Gettysburg Address and Second Inaugural Address are inscribed on the walls of the templelike structure, which is particularly impressive at night. The 36 columns represent the 36 states in the Union in existence at the time of Lincoln's death. (Daily 8 am-midnight; closed Dec 25) **FREE**

Lulu's Club Mardi Gras. *1217 22nd St NW, Washington (20013). Phone 202/861-5858. www.lulusclub.com.* This freewheeling spot is all about raucous music, dancing, and checking out members of the opposite sex. Beer is the beverage of choice; food is served until 10 pm. Salsa lessons draw regular crowds, but Lulu's is also known for special events such as "Shred Your Ex, Meet Your Next," where patrons are invited—in a spirit of communal catharsis—to run photos of formerly significant others through a shredder. (Mon-Thurs 4 pm-2 am, Fri-Sat to 3 am) **$$**

Martin Luther King, Jr. Memorial Library. *901 G St NW, Washington (20001). www.dclibrary.org/mlk.* (1972) Main branch of the DC public library was designed by architect Mies van der Rohe. Martin Luther King mural. Books, periodicals, photographs, films, videocassettes, recordings, microfilms, Washingtoniana, and the *Washington Star* collection. Library for the visually impaired; librarian for the hearing impaired; black studies division; AP wire service machine; community information service. Underground parking. (Mon-Sat, also Sun afternoons; closed holidays) **FREE**

MCI Center. *601 F St NW, Washington (20004). Phone 202/628-3200. www.mcicenter.com.* This 20,000-seat, state-of-the-art arena, home to the NBA's Washington Wizards, the WNBA's Washington Mystics, the NHL's Washington Capitals, and the Georgetown Hoyas, is also a popular venue for concerts and other events, from Liza Minnelli to the Harlem Globetrotters. Even when nothing is scheduled, you can check out Nick and Stef's Steakhouse (open for dinner every day, lunch Mon-Fri), the F Street Sports Bar, or Modell's Sporting Goods for team-themed athletic wear. (Mon-Sat; closed holidays; days and fees for events vary) Located here is

MCI National Sports Gallery. *Phone 202/661-5133.* This 25,000-square-foot museum commemorates and showcases the best of American sports history. Includes sports memorabilia collections; participatory and technology-driven exhibits with basketball, football, hockey, and baseball themes. Rotating exhibits feature special-interest sports. Home of the American Sportscasters Association Hall of Fame and Museum, honoring the memorable voices that brought great sports moments. **$$$**

National Academy of Sciences. *2100 C St NW, Washington (20418). Between 21st and 22nd sts NW. Phone 202/334-2000. www.nationalacademies.org.* (1924) Established in 1863 to stimulate research and communication among scientists and to advise the federal government in science and technology. A famous 21-foot bronze statue of Albert Einstein by Robert Berks is on the front lawn. Art exhibits, concerts. (Schedule varies) **FREE**

National Aquarium. *Dept of Commerce Bldg, 14th St and Constitution Ave NW, Washington (20230). Phone 202/482-2825. www.nationalaquarium.com.* The nation's oldest public aquarium was established in 1873. It now exhibits more than 1,700 specimens representing approximately 260 species, both fresh-water and saltwater. Touch tank; theater. Shark feedings (Mon, Wed, Sat); piranha feedings (Tues, Thurs, Sun). (Daily 9 am-5 pm; closed Dec 25) **$**

National Archives. *700 Pennsylvania Ave NW, Washington (20408). Between 7th and 9th sts NW; exhibition entrance is on Constitution Ave. Phone 202/501-5205. www.archives.org.* (1934) Original copies of the Declaration of Independence, the Bill of Rights, and the Constitution; a 1297 version of the Magna Carta and other historic documents, maps, and photographs. Guided tours by appointment only. Archives are also available to the public for genealogical and historical research (Mon-Sat; closed federal holidays). (Daily 10 am-5:30 pm; closed Dec 25) **FREE**

National Building Museum. *401 F St NW, Washington (20001). Housed in the Old Pension Building. Phone 202/272-2448. www.nbm.org.* Deals with architecture, design, engineering, and construction. Permanent exhibits include drawings, blueprints, models, photographs, artifacts, and the architectural evolution of Washington's buildings and monuments. The museum's enormous Great Hall is supported by eight of the world's largest Corinthian columns. Group and open tours daily. (Mon-Sat 10 am-5 pm, Sun 11 am-5 pm; closed Jan 1, Thanksgiving, Dec 25) **FREE**

National Colonial Farm. *3400 Bryan Point Rd, Accokeek (20607). I-95 exit 3 A, then 10 miles S on Hwy 210, right on Bryan Point Rd, 3 miles. Phone 301/283-2113.* Approximately 150 acres in Piscataway National Park. A "living history" farm of mid-18th century; crops, herb garden, livestock, methods of the period are used; replicated farm buildings. (Tues-Sun 10 am-5 pm; closed Jan 1, Thanksgiving, Dec 25) **$**

National Gallery of Art. *600 Constitution Ave NW, Washington (20002). Between 3rd and 7th sts. Phone 202/737-4215. www.nga.gov.* The West Building (1941), designed by John Russell Pope, contains Western European and American art spanning periods between the 13th and 20th centuries: highlights include the only Leonardo da Vinci painting on display outside of Europe, *Ginevra de' Benci;* a comprehensive collection of Italian paintings and sculpture; major French Impressionists; numerous Rembrandts and examples of the Dutch school; masterpieces from the Mellon, Widener, Kress, Dale, and Rosenwald collections; special exhibitions. The East Building (1978), designed by architect I. M. Pei, houses the gallery's growing collection of 20th-century art, including Picasso's *Family of Saltimbanques* and Jackson Pollock's *Lavender Mist.* (Daily; closed Jan 1, Dec 25) **FREE**

National Museum of Health and Medicine. *Walter Reed Army Medical Center, Building #54, 6900 Georgia Ave and Elder St, Washington (20307). Walter Reed Army Medical Center, Building #54. Phone 202/782-2200.* One of the most important medical collections in America. Interprets the link between history and technology; AIDS education exhibit; an interactive exhibit on human anatomy and lifestyle choices; and a collection of microscopes, medical teaching aids, tools, and instruments (1862-1965) and famous historical icons exhibits. (Daily 10 am-5:30 pm; closed Dec 25) **FREE**

National Museum of Women in the Arts. *1250 New York Ave NW, Washington (20005). Phone 202/783-5000; toll-free 800/222-7270. www.nmwa.org.* Focus on women's contributions to the arts. More than 1,200 works by women artists from the Renaissance to the present. Paintings, drawings, sculpture, pottery, prints. Library, research center by appointment. Performances. Guided tours (by appointment). (Mon-Sat 10 am-5 pm, Sun noon-5 pm; closed Jan 1, Thanksgiving, Dec 25) **$**

National Portrait Gallery. *8th and F sts NW, Washington (20560). Phone 202/275-1738. www.npg.si.edu.* Portraits and statues of people who have made significant contributions to the history, development, and culture of the US. (Daily 10 am-5:30 pm; closed Dec 25)

National Presbyterian Church and Center. *4101 Nebraska Ave NW, Washington (20016). Phone 202/537-0800. www.natpresch.org.* Chapel of the President contains memorabilia of past US presidents; faceted glass windows depict the history of man and church. Self-guided tours (daily; no tours holidays). Guided tours (Sun following service).

National Theatre. *1321 Pennsylvania Ave NW, Washington (20004). Phone 202/628-6161 (information); toll-free 800/447-7400 (tickets). www.nationaltheatre.org.* Sarah Bernhardt, Laurence Olivier, and the Barrymores are just some of the theatrical luminaries who have performed at this historic playhouse, which is said to be haunted by the ghost of a murdered actor. These days, you'll see touring productions of such shows as *The Tale of the Allergist's Wife* and *42nd Street.* On Mondays, there are films in summer and performances drawing on local talent the rest of the year. Saturday mornings feature children's shows. Tours (Mon-Fri) by reservation, phone 202/783-6854. Fees vary by performance.

Navy Yard. *901 M St SE, Washington (20374). Between 1st and 11th sts SE. Phone 202/433-4882.* Along the Anacostia River at a location chosen by George Washington, the yard was founded in 1799 and was nearly destroyed during the War of 1812. Outside the yard at 636 G St SE is the John Philip Sousa house, where the "March King" wrote many of his famous compositions; the house is private. One block east is

Marine Barracks. *8th St and I St SE, Washington (20390). Entrance to Navy Yard is at end of 9th St at M St SE. Inside is G St between 8th and 9th sts SE. Phone 202/433-6060.* The parade ground, more than two centuries old, is surrounded by handsome and historic structures, including the Commandant's House facing G St, which is said to be the oldest continuously occupied public building in the city. The spectacular parade is open to the public Tuesday and Friday evenings in summer (see SPECIAL EVENTS).

Marine Corps Museum. *Building 58, 901 M St SE, Washington (20374). Building 58, Washington Navy Yard. Phone 202/433-3840.* Weapons, uniforms, maps, flags, and other artifacts describe the history of the US Marine Corps. Housed in a restored 19th-century structure; also used as marine barracks from 1941 to 1975. (Mon, Wed-Sat 10 am-4 pm, Sun noon-5 pm; Fri to 8 pm from May-late Aug; closed Jan 1, Dec 25) **FREE**

Navy Museum. *805 Kidder Breese SE, Washington (20374). Building 76, Washington Navy Yard. Phone 202/433-6897.* History of the US Navy from the Revolutionary War to the space age. Dioramas depict achievements of early naval heroes; displays development of naval weapons; fully rigged foremast fighting top and gun deck from frigate Constitution on display; World War II guns that can be trained and elevated; submarine room has operating periscopes. Approximately 5,000 objects on display including paintings, ship models, flags, uniforms, naval decorations, and the bathyscaphe Trieste. Two-acre outdoor park displays 19th- and 20th-century guns, cannon, other naval artifacts; US Navy destroyer *Barry* located on the waterfront. (Apr-early Sept: Mon-Fri 9 am-5 pm; early Sept-late Mar: Mon-Fri 9 am-4 pm, Sat-Sun 10 am-5 pm; closed Jan 1, Dec 24-25. Tours Mon-Fri) **FREE**

New York Avenue Presbyterian Church. *1313 New York Ave NW, Washington (20005). Phone 202/393-3700. www.nyapc.org.* The church where Lincoln worshipped. It was rebuilt 1950-1951, with Lincoln's pew. Dr. Peter Marshall was pastor from 1937 to 1949. Mementos on display include the first draft of the Emancipation Proclamation. (Daily, services Sun morning; closed holidays)

The Octagon Museum. *1799 New York Ave NW, Washington (20006). At 18th and E sts NW. Phone 202/638-3221. www.archfoundation.org/octagon/.* (1799-1801) Federal townhouse built for Colonel John Tayloe III, based on designs by Dr. William Thornton. It served as temporary quarters for President and Mrs. James Madison after the White House burned in the War of 1812; it also was the site of the ratification of the Treaty of Ghent. Restored with period furnishings (1800-1828). Changing exhibits on architecture and allied arts. (Tues-Sun 10 am-4 pm; closed Jan 1, Thanksgiving, Dec 25) **$**

Old Executive Office Building. *17th St and Pennsylvania Ave NW, Washington (20501). Phone 202/395-5895.* (1875) Second Empire/Victorian architecture. Built as War Office; was also home to State Department; now offices for president's staff. Guided tours by appointment (Sat morning only). **FREE**

Old Stone House. *3051 M St NW, Washington (20007). Phone 202/426-6851 (also TTY service). www.nps.gov/rocr/oldstonehouse/.* (1765) Believed to be the oldest pre-Revolutionary building in Washington. Constructed on parcel No. 3 of the original tract of land that was then Georgetown, the house was used as both a residence and a place of business; five rooms are furnished with household items that reflect a middle-class residence of the late 18th century. The grounds are lush with fruit trees and seasonal blooms. (Sat-Sun noon-5 pm; closed holidays) **FREE**

Organization of American States (OAS). *17th St NW and Constitution Ave, Washington (20006). Phone 202/458-3000. www.oas.org.* Headquarters of OAS, set up to maintain international peace and security and to promote integral development in the Americas. Tropical patio, Hall of Heroes and Flags, Hall of the Americas, Aztec Garden, Council Chamber. (Mon-Fri; closed holidays) **FREE**

P. B. Dye Golf Club. *9526 Dr. Perry Rd, Ijamsville, MD (21754). Phone 301/607-GOLF (4653). www.pbdyegolf.com.* Designed by and named for renowned course mapper Pete Dye, this layout features five tees and Dye's signature railroad ties all over the course. While most of the greens are very large, the holes that lead up to them can be incredibly difficult. There are plenty of doglegs (some of them turn severely), and irregularly shaped bunkers guard many of the greens. Many approach shots, especially on the par-threes, require tee shots through openings guarded by tall trees, so an errant first shot can ruin an entire hole. A very challenging course from start to finish. **$$$$**

Pavilion at the Old Post Office. *1100 Pennsylvania Ave NW, Washington (20004). Phone 202/289-4224. www.oldpostofficedc.com.* (1899) Romanesque structure, which for years was headquarters of the US Postal Service, has been remodeled into a marketplace with 100 shops and restaurants and daily entertainment. In the 315-foot tower are replicas of the bells of Westminster Abbey, a Bicentennial gift from Great Britain; the tower, which is the second-highest point in DC, offers spectacular views from an open-air observation deck (free). Above the Pavilion shops are headquarters for the National Endowment for the Arts. (Daily 10 am-5 pm; closed Jan 1, Thanksgiving, Dec 25) **FREE**

Polly Esther's. *605 12th St NW, Washington (20005). Phone 202/737-1970. www.pollyesthers.com.* Sometimes familiarity breeds fun! If your idea of the good old days is the 1970s, '80s, or '90s, you'll love it here, where dancing to a retro beat is all the rage and the Hustle is more than a memory. Period kitsch adds to the ambience; the moderately priced drink list includes potions made with Tang. Part of a New York-based chain, this Polly Esther's is especially popular for bachelorette parties. (Thurs 5 pm-2 am, Fri 5 pm-3 am, Sat 8 pm-3 am) **$$**

Potomac Park (East and West). *1100 Ohio St SW, Washington (22213). NW and SE of the Jefferson Memorial. Phone 202/619-7222 (park information). www.nps.gov/nacc/.* A more beautiful urban playground would be hard to find. Features 720 riverfront acres divided by Washington's famous Tidal Basin into East and West Potomac Parks. East Potomac Park has three golf courses, a large swimming pool, picnic grounds, tennis courts, and biking and hiking paths. Pedal boats can be rented at the Tidal Basin. At West Potomac Park, you'll find the Vietnam, Korean, Lincoln, Jefferson, and FDR memorials; Constitution Gardens; a small island where ducks live; and the Reflecting Pool. Beyond these family-friendly activities, you'll find one of the most glorious—albeit one of the briefest—sights of the city: the famous two-week burst of pink and white cherry blossoms from more than 3,000 trees, a 1912 gift of friendship from Japan, in late Mar/early Apr. The Cherry Blossom Festival (see SPECIAL EVENTS) begins each year with the lighting of the 300-year-old Japanese Stone Lantern, presented by the governor of Tokyo back in 1954.

★ **President Kennedy's Gravesite.** *South Gate, Arlington National Cemetery.* (See ARLINGTON COUNTY in Virginia)

Rock Creek Park. *3545 Williamsburg Ln NW, Washington (20008). From downtown DC, take the Rock Creek and Potomac Pkwy N to Beach Dr. Exit onto Beach Dr N, take it to Broad Branch Rd, make a left and then a right onto Glover Rd, and follow the signs to the Nature Center. Phone 202/895-6070 or 202/426-6829. www.nps.gov/rocr.* Leave urban commotion behind by going for a brisk hike in Rock Creek Park. Just 5 miles from the White House are dozens of miles of clearly marked, well-maintained, easy and moderately hard hiking trails through the park's 1,754 acres of meadows and woodlands. There's also a gentle walk along Beach Drive that takes you through dramatic Rock Creek Gorge; on weekends and holidays, cars are prohibited, making it even more peaceful. (Daily dawn-dusk) **FREE** Also here are

Art Barn. *2401 Tilden St NW, Washington (20008). At Beach Dr NW. Phone 202/244-2482.* Historic carriage house (1831). Art exhibitions. (Thurs-Sun afternoons) **FREE**

Carter Barron Amphitheatre. *4850 Colorado Ave NW, Washington (20011). 16th St and Colorado Ave NW. Phone 202/426-0486. www.nps.gov/rocr/cbarron/cbarron.htm.* This 4,200-seat outdoor theater in a wooded area is the setting for summer performances of symphonic, folk, pop, and jazz music and Shakespearean theater.

Nature Center. *5200 Glover Rd NW, Washington (20015). Phone 202/865-6070.* Planetarium, films, exhibits, nature demonstrations. (Wed-Sun 9 am-5 pm; closed holidays) **FREE**

Senate Office Buildings. *114 Constitution Ave NE, Washington (20002). Constitution Ave on both sides of 1st St NE.* Linked by private subway to the Capitol.

Sewall-Belmont House. *144 Constitution Ave NE, Washington (20002). Phone 202/546-1210. www.sewallbelmont.org.* (1680, 1800) The Sewall-Belmont House is a monument to Alice Paul, the author of the Equal Rights Amendment. From this house, she spearheaded the fight for the passage of the amendment. Now a national landmark, the house contains portraits and sculptures of women from the beginning of the suffrage movement; extensive collection of artifacts of the suffrage and equal rights movements; historic headquarters of the National Woman's Party. (Tues-Fri 11 am-3 pm, Sat noon-4 pm; closed Jan 1, Thanksgiving, Dec 25) **FREE**

Shakespeare Theatre at the Lansburgh. *450 7th St NW, Washington (20004). Phone 202/547-1122. www.shakespearedc.org.*

Shops at Georgetown Park. *3222 M St NW, Washington (20007). Phone 202/298-5577. www.shopsatgeorgetownpark.com.* This stylish urban mall has four levels of upscale shops and restaurants to explore, and is especially strong in apparel. Look for Ann Taylor, Abercrombie & Fitch, J. Crew, Talbots, and other nationally popular brands. If your energy flags, you'll find fresh-baked pretzels and cookies to munch on, as well as Godiva chocolates. An accommodating Concierge Center on Level One offers gift wrapping, stroller and wheelchair loan, postal services, parking validation, photocopying, faxing, and other amenities. (Mon-Sat 10 am-9 pm, Sun noon-6 pm)

Shops at National Place. *1331 Pennsylvania Ave NW, Washington (20004). Enter at 13th and F sts. Phone 202/662-1200.* Trilevel marketplace—at, above, and below street grade—featuring more than 100 specialty shops and restaurants. (Mon-Sat 10 am-7 pm, Sun noon-5 pm)

★ **Smithsonian Institution.** *1000 Jefferson Dr SW, Washington (20560). Phone 202/357-2700 (general information and schedule). www.si.edu.* The majority of Smithsonian museums are located on the National Mall. Smithsonian headquarters are in the Smithsonian Institution Building, the "Castle" (1855), located at 1000 Jefferson Dr SW, on the Mall. The headquarters contain administrative offices, Smithson's crypt, and the Smithsonian Information Center, which has information on all Smithsonian museums. Many visitors begin their day here. (All buildings open daily 10 am-5:30 pm; closed Dec 25; Anacostia Museum and National Zoo hours vary) **FREE** Smithsonian museums on the Mall include

Anacostia Museum. *1901 Fort Pl SE, Washington (20020). Phone 202/357-2700. www.si.edu.* An exhibition and research center for black heritage in the historic Anacostia section of southeast Washington. Changing exhibits. (Daily 10 am-5 pm; closed Dec 25) **FREE**

Arthur M. Sackler Gallery. *1200 Jefferson Dr SW, Washington (20560). Phone 202/357-2700.* Changing exhibitions of Asian art, both Near- and Far-Eastern, from major national and international collections. Permanent collection includes Chinese and South and Southeast Asian art objects presented by Arthur Sackler. Between the Freer Gallery and the Arts and Industries Building is the Enid A. Haupt Garden, 4 acres that compose the "roof" of the Sackler Gallery, the International Gallery, an underground Smithsonian research and education complex, and 1050 Independence Ave SW. **FREE**

Arts and Industries Building. *900 Jefferson Dr SW, Washington (20560). Phone 202/357-2700. www.si.edu/ai/.* The south hall contains the Experimental Gallery, an exhibit space dedicated to innovative and creative exhibits from museums in the Smithsonian and from around the world. Discovery Theater (fee) hosts performances for children. **FREE**

Freer Gallery. *1200 Jefferson Dr SW, Washington (20560). Phone 202/357-2700. www.asia.si.edu.* Asian art with objects dating from Neolithic period to the early 20th century. Also works by late 19th- and early 20th-century American artists, including a major collection of James McNeill Whistler's work, highlighted by the famous Peacock Room. Next to the Freer is the Smithsonian Institution Building, or "the Castle." **FREE**

Hirshhorn Museum and Sculpture Garden. *Independence Ave and 7th St SW, Washington (20560). Phone 202/357-2700. www.hirshhorn.si.edu.* The cool modernity of the paintings and sculptures here—and of the curvy building itself—are a delicious respite for history-sated visitors. Inside is some of the most interesting art produced in the last 100 years: everything from

Constantin Brancusi's egglike "Sleeping Muse I" to Nam June Paik's "Video Flag" made with 70 video monitors. Outdoors, the greenery of the plaza (7:30 am-5:30 pm) and sculpture garden (7:30 am-dusk) make this an inviting spot for a National Mall rendezvous. **DONATION**

National Air and Space Museum. *600 Independence Ave SW, Washington (20560). Between 7th and 4th sts SW. Phone 202/357-1387. www.nasm.si.edu.* This popular museum thrills those who have lived through the age of space exploration, as well as those whose memories go back further. View the Wright brothers' 1903 *Kitty Hawk Flyer,* Charles Lindbergh's *Spirit of St. Louis,* and the command module *Columbia,* which carried the first men to walk on the moon. World War II buffs will want to see not only American fighter planes but also the British Supermarine *Spitfire,* the Japanese *Mitsubishi Zero,* and the German *Messerschmitt.* In the Apollo to the Moon exhibit, you'll see lunar rocks, spacesuits, and John Glenn's squeeze-tube beef stew, among other artifacts. An IMAX theater enables you to view on a huge, five-story-high screen Earth as seen from the space shuttle. And don't miss the high-tech shows at the Albert Einstein Planetarium, which combine ideas about the size and origins of the universe with eye-popping images taken from the Hubble Space Telescope and Mars Global Surveyor. **FREE**

National Museum of African Art. *950 Independence Ave SW, Washington. Phone 202/633-4600. www.nmafa.si.edu.* With everything from masks to musical instruments, sacred objects to simple wooden headrests, the diverse cultures of Africa past and present are on view at this small but fascinating museum. Permanent exhibits display ceramics, textiles, household tools, and the visual arts of the sub-Sahara. Traveling shows cover even more ground; recent ones have featured colonial-era photography and Ethiopian religious icons. A full schedule of films, musical presentations, lectures, and children's events keeps things lively. (Daily 10 am-5:30 pm; closed Dec 25) **FREE**

National Museum of American History. *14th St and Constitution Ave NW, Washington (20560). Phone 202/357-2700. www.americanhistory.si.edu.* More than 17 million artifacts cover aspects of American cultural heritage large and small, public and private. Want to see Julia Child's gleaming black six-burner stove? Check out the cheerfully comfortable kitchen from the famous chef's longtime home in Cambridge, Massachusetts, reassembled here in 2001. Or watch textile conservators take painstaking steps to restore the fragile Star-Spangled Banner, the actual flag that inspired Francis Scott Key in 1814 to write the poem that became America's national anthem. The museum's endlessly fascinating collections include everything from the lap desk at which Thomas Jefferson drafted the Declaration of Independence to Henry Ford's 1913 Model-T, from first ladies' inaugural gowns to Dorothy's ruby slippers from *The Wizard of Oz.* Children will especially enjoy the Hands On History Room, where they can harness a life-size model of a mule or tap out a telegraph message in Morse code. **FREE**

National Museum of Natural History. *Constitution Ave and 10th St NW, Washington (20560). Phone 202/633-1000. www.mnh.si.edu.* Before you enter this museum, stop on the Ninth Street side of the building to see the mesmerizing Butterfly Garden. You'll see the different relationships between plants and butterflies in four separate habitats: wetland, meadow, wood's edge, and urban garden. But the fascination only begins here. The National Museum of Natural History holds more than 124 million artifacts and specimens dating back to the Ice Age. For a fun first stop, try the first-floor Discovery Room. Here the whole family can learn about different cultures and other aspects of natural history through a wealth of interactive activities. Other museum exhibits include an insect zoo with thousands of live specimens, a section on gems (including the 45.52-carat, billion-year-old Hope Diamond), dinosaur skeletons, a live coral reef, and botanical, zoological, and geological materials. This is where Western civilization can be traced, literally, to its roots. **FREE**

National Zoo. *3001 Connecticut Ave NW, Washington (20008). Main entrance at 3000 block of Connecticut Ave NW; other entrances at Beach Dr (Rock Creek Pkwy) and the junction of Adams Mill Rd and Harvard St. Phone 202/673-4800. natzoo.si.edu.* A branch of the Smithsonian Institution, the National Zoo features 5,000 animals of 500 species. Come when the zoo first opens or after 2 pm if you want to see giant pandas Tian Tian and Mei Xiang without waiting in long lines. The pair, on ten-year loan from China, are this lovely and interesting zoological park's most famous residents, but the other animals, from butterflies to American bison, have charms of their own and shouldn't be missed. The zoo is set amid the urban greenery of Rock Creek Park. (Daily from 10 am; closed Dec 25) **FREE**

Renwick Gallery at the American Art Museum. *Pennsylvania Ave at 17th St NW, Washington (20006). Phone 202/275-1500. www.americanart.si.edu.* The Patent Office Building, home of the American Art Museum, is closed for renovations until 2006, but the museum's Renwick Gallery, housed in an elegant Second Empire-style building, remains open, and its exhibitions of American crafts and decorative arts are knockouts. The permanent collection features superb, one-of-a-kind pieces in clay, fiber, glass, metal, and wood. Make sure to see the sculptural furniture by Sam Maloof and the playful "Game Fish" by Larry Fuente. (Daily 10 am-5:30 pm; closed Dec 25) **FREE**

St. John's Church Georgetown Parish. *3240 O St NW, Washington (20007). Phone 202/338-1796.* Oldest Episcopal congregation in Georgetown, established 1796; original design of church by William Thornton, architect of the Capitol. Many presidents since Madison have worshiped here. Francis Scott Key was a founding member. Tours (by appointment).

Supreme Court of the United States. *1st St NE and Maryland Ave, Washington (20024). E of the Capitol. Phone 202/479-3211.* Designed by Cass Gilbert in Neoclassical style. Court is in session Oct-Apr (Mon-Wed, at two-week intervals from the first Mon in Oct) and on the first workday of each week in May and June; court sessions are open to the public (10 am and 1 pm), on a first-come, first-served basis; lectures are offered in the courtroom (Mon-Fri except when court is in session; 20-minute lectures hourly on half hour); on the ground floor are exhibits and a film (23 minutes), cafeteria, snack bar, and gift shop (Mon-Fri; closed holidays). **FREE**

Theodore Roosevelt Memorial. *18050 W Basin Dr SW, Arlington (20024). N end of Theodore Roosevelt Island, accessible only by footbridge from George Washington Memorial Pkwy, northbound lane.* The island is an 88-acre wilderness preserve; the 17-foot statue of Roosevelt was designed by Paul Manship. (Daily; closed Dec 25) **FREE**

★ **Thomas Jefferson Memorial.** *East Basin Dr SW, Washington (20003). S edge of Tidal Basin. Phone 202/426-6841. www.nps.gov/thje.* This memorial, dedicated in 1943, honors the third President of the United States and the author of both the Declaration of Independence and the Bill of Rights. The white marble dome surrounded by columns, representing the classic style that Jefferson introduced to the US, is a memorable Washington landmark and is quite beautiful especially when lit up at night. In the basement, you'll find a museum and the plaster statue from which the 19-foot bronze one in the center of the monument was created. (Daily 8 am-midnight; closed Dec 25) **FREE**

Tourmobile Sightseeing. *1000 Ohio Dr SW, Washington (20024). Phone 202/554-5100. www.tourmobile.com.* Narrated shuttle tours to 18 historic sites on the National Mall and in Arlington National Cemetery. Unlimited reboarding throughout day (daily; no tours Dec 25). Additional tours separately or in combinations: Arlington National Cemetery; Mount Vernon (seasonal) and Frederick Douglass Home (seasonal). **$$$$**

Tudor Place. *1644 31st St NW, Washington (20007). Phone 202/965-0400. www.tudorplace.org.* (1805) This 12-room Federal-style mansion was designed by Dr. William Thornton, architect of the Capitol, for Martha Custis Peter, granddaughter of Martha Washington. The Peter family lived in the house for 180 years. All furnishings and *objets d'art* are original. More than 5 acres of gardens (Mon-Sat). Guided tours (Tues-Sat, by reservation; closed holidays). **$$**

Union Station. *50 Massachusetts Ave NE, Washington (20002). On Massachusetts Ave NE between 1st and 2nd sts. Phone 703/371-9441. www.unionstationdc.com.* This is shopping in some of the most elegant surroundings imaginable—architect Daniel Burnham's extraordinary 1907 Union Station, restored to its former glory and reopened in 1988. The white granite Beaux Arts masterpiece is still a functioning train station and is now home to more than 130 upscale restaurants and shops, many of them catering to the special needs of travelers. But many locals patronize the shops too (including President Bill Clinton, who regularly bought holiday presents here). Also located within the station are the Amtrak depot and Gray Line and Tourmobile Sightseeing operators (see both). (Daily) **FREE**

US Botanic Garden. *100 Maryland Ave SW, Washington (20002). At base of Capitol Hill. Phone 202/225-8333. www.usbg.gov.* The Botanic Garden, one of the oldest in the country, was established by Congress in 1820 for public education and exhibition. It features plants collected by the famous Wilkes Expedition of the South Seas. Conservatory has tropical, subtropical, and desert plants; seasonal displays. Exterior gardens are planted for seasonal blooming; also here is Bartholdi Fountain, designed by the sculptor of the Statue of Liberty. (Daily 10 am-5 pm) **FREE**

★ **US Holocaust Memorial Museum.** *100 Raoul Wallenberg Plz SW, Washington (20024). Entrances at Raoul Wallenberg Plz (15th St SW) and at 14th St SW. Phone 202/488-0400. www.ushmm.org.* Opened in 1993, this privately funded museum is noteworthy for its effective presentation of information, images, and artifacts in an architectural setting that enhances visitors' understanding of the Holocaust. Temporary exhibits cover everything from the diary of Anne Frank to the role of Oskar Schindler in saving the lives of hundreds of Jews. At the heart of the museum is its self-guided Permanent Exhibition, which includes powerful photos; film footage; eyewitness testimonies; clothing, suitcases, children's drawings, and other victims' belongings; and reconstructions of concentration camp buildings. Especially stirring is the Hall of Faces, a narrow, three-story-high space crammed with framed photographs of the Jewish residents of a single Lithuanian town, more than 3,000 of whom were murdered in September 1941. Visitors are welcome to reflect privately on their experience in the quiet, skylighted Hall of Remembrance and to light memorial candles in the niches of its walls. (Daily 10 am-5:30 pm; closed Yom Kippur, Dec 25). Timed daily-use passes are necessary for visiting the museum's permanent exhibition and can be obtained each day at the museum starting at 10 am or in advance by calling toll-free 800/400-9373. **FREE**

US National Arboretum. *3501 New York Ave NE, Washington (20002). Phone 202/245-2726. www.usna.usda.gov.* Floral displays in spring, summer, fall, and winter on 446 acres; Japanese garden, National Bonsai and Penjing Museum (daily); National Herb Garden, major collections of azaleas (15,000), wildflowers, ferns, magnolias, crabapples, cherries, and dogwoods; aquatic plantings; dwarf conifers (the world's largest evergreen collection). (Daily; closed Dec 25) Under 16 years admitted only with adult. **FREE**

US Navy Memorial. *701 Pennsylvania Ave NW, Washington (20001). Pennsylvania Ave, at 7th and 9th sts NW. Phone 202/737-2300. www.lonesailor.org.* Dedicated to those who have served in the Navy in war and in peacetime. A 100-foot-diameter granite world map dominates the Plaza, where the *Lone Sailor,* a 7-foot bronze sculpture, stands and the US Navy Band stages performances (Memorial Day-Labor Day, Tues evenings). Visitor Center features electronic kiosks with interactive video displays on naval history; also Navy Memorial Log Room and US Presidents Room. (Tues-Sat) **FREE** Also here is

> ***At Sea.*** *Arleigh and Roberta Burke Theater. Phone toll-free 800/777-2238.* Underwritten by ExxonMobil, this award-winning high-resolution 70mm film conveys the experience of being at sea aboard a US Navy aircraft carrier. The 241-seat theater employs a two-story, 52-foot-wide screen and six-track digital audio to surround the audience with the sights and sounds of carrier operations. Showings (Mon-Sat, four times daily; Sun, two times).

★ **Vietnam Veterans Memorial.** *900 Ohio Dr SW, Washington (20242). Constitution Ave between Henry Bacon Dr and 21st St NW. Phone 202/426-6841. www.nps.gov/vive.* Designed by Maya Ying Lin and funded by private citizens' contributions, this memorial's polished black granite walls are inscribed with the names of the 58,175 US servicemen who died in or remain missing from the Vietnam War (a large directory helps visitors locate specific names). Deliberately apolitical, the memorial aims to foster reconciliation and healing given the divisiveness the war caused in American society. Also on site are the Three Servicemen Statue and Flagpole and the Vietnam Women's Memorial. (Daily; closed Dec 25) **FREE**

Voice of America. *330 Independence Ave SW, Washington (20237). Between 3rd and 4th sts SW; enter on C St. Phone 202/619-3919.* Live radio broadcasts to foreign countries; 45-minute guided tours (Mon-Fri, reservations required; closed holidays). **FREE**

Warner Theatre. *13th and E sts NW, Washington (20004). Phone 202/783-4000. www.warnertheatre.com.* This theater, with over 1,800 seats, has been restored to its 1924 glory, with a sparkling chandelier, stained-glass lamps, and Portuguese draperies. The Warner is host to many performances today, including comedies, musicals, an annual *Nutcracker* performance, and, from time to time, movie premiers.

Washington Capitals (NHL). *MCI Center, 601 F St NW, Washington (20004). Phone 202/661-5050. www.*

washingtoncapitals.com. The Capitals advanced to the NHL finals once in the 1990's, but success has been sporadic, at best. The team plays its home games in the MCI Center, one of the newer facilities in the league, which the team shares with the Washington Wizards (see) of the NBA. Going to games provides a good chance to see Washington movers and shakers like politicians and celebrities—and it could be argued that more people go for this reason than for the hockey.

Washington Convention Center. *801 Mount Vernon Pl, Washington (20001). Phone 202/249-3000; toll-free 800/368-9000. www.dcconvention.com.* Washington's biggest building is also one of its newest. Opened in 2003, the Washington Convention Center occupies six city blocks, housing 700,000 square feet of exhibit space and 125,000 square feet of meeting space. The roof of the structure alone covers 17 acres. Monolithic in size but not in design, the building's aesthetically tasteful exterior features a nice balance of glass, limestone, and granite. The Washington Convention Center is located immediately north of Mount Vernon Square, offering convenient access to some of the city's finest hotels and restaurants. Many other attractions can be found nearby, including Chinatown, the National Portrait Gallery, Ford's Theatre, and the MCI Center—home to the NBA's Wizards, the WNBA's Mystics, and the NHL's Capitals.

Washington Dolls' House & Toy Museum. *5236 44th St NW, Washington (20015). Phone 202/244-0024. www.dollshousemuseum.com.* Splendid collection of antique doll houses, dolls, toys, and games; museum shop. (Tues-Sat 10 am-5 pm, Sun from noon; closed Jan 1, Thanksgiving, Dec 25) **$$**

Washington Harbour. *3000 K St NW, Washington (20007).* Dining and shopping complex that features lavish fountains, life-size statuary, and a boardwalk with a view of the Potomac River.

★ **Washington Monument.** *15th St SW, Washington (20242). Mall at 15th St SW. Parking lot on N side, off Constitution Ave. Phone 202/426-6841. www.nps.gov/wamo.* This obelisk, the tallest masonry structure in the world at 555 feet, was dedicated in 1885 to the memory of the first US president, George Washington. Before its dedication, it had been under construction for almost 40 years, a lack of funds and the Civil War both getting in the way of its completion. You can see where construction resumed after a 28-year delay about a quarter of the way up the monument, where two different shades of marble meet. Views of the majestic structure can be enjoyed anytime, but to enter, you must have a ticket. You can try your luck at getting one of the free tickets distributed at the kiosk at 15th and Madison starting at 8 am for same-day tours, or you can reserve tickets ahead of time by calling 800/967-2283. There is an elevator to the observation room at the 500-foot level. To take the 898 steps up or down, arrangements must be made in advance. (Daily 9 am-4:45 pm; closed Dec 25) **FREE**

Washington Mystics (WNBA). *MCI Center, 601 F St NW, Washington (20004). Phone 202/661-5050. www.wnba.com/mystics/.* Professional women's basketball team.

★ **Washington National Cathedral.** *3000 Wisconsin Ave NW, Washington (20016). Massachusetts and Wisconsin aves NW. Phone 202/537-6207 (tours). www.cathedral.org/cathedral.* This inspiring edifice, 83 years in the making, was completed in 1990, its $65 million cost covered by private donations. It was built largely of Indiana limestone using traditional methods, with flying buttresses rather than steel providing support. Graced with intricate carvings inside and out, it has a 30-story central tower and 215 stained-glass windows, including one that contains a piece of lunar rock presented by the astronauts of *Apollo XI.* Bring binoculars if you want to see, close up, the more than 100 gargoyles, which depict not just dragons but also a child with his hand in a cookie jar and *Star Wars* villain Darth Vader. Worshippers of all faiths are welcome at services held daily. There are also frequent musical events, including recitals given on the magnificent pipe organ most Sundays at 5 pm. Famous Americans interred at the cathedral include Woodrow Wilson and Helen Keller. (Mon-Sat 10 am-4:30 pm, Sun from 12:30 pm) **DONATION**

Washington Redskins (NFL). *FedEx Field, 1 Redskins Rd, Landover (20785). Phone 301/276-6050. www.redskins.com.* The Redskins have made some significant changes lately, including moving out of historic RFK Stadium and into state-of-the-art FedEx Field before the start of the 2002 season. Historians will remember the contributions made to the team by Hall of Fame players like Joe Theisman, Art Monk, and John Riggins.

Washington Walks. *Phone 202/484-1565. www.washingtonwalks.com.* Guided tours sponsored by

Washington Walks are a great way to see the city up close. The group (along with Children's Concierge) runs two tours that kids will especially like: for Goodnight Mr. Lincoln, children can show up in pajamas at the Lincoln Memorial for stories, games, and music about Honest Abe. The White House Un-Tour offers role-playing (you might be asked to impersonate the president who loved bowling) and fun facts about the executive mansion. (Apr-Oct: days vary; rest of year: by appointment) **$$**

Washington Wizards (NBA). *MCI Center, 601 F St NW, Washington (20004). Phone 202/661-5050. www.nba.com/wizards.* The Wizards got a publicity boost in the early 2000's, as Michael Jordan came out of retirement for a second time to play for the team. Still, the team never made the playoffs under Jordan, and he retired again after the 2003 season finale. The team plays its home games in the MCI Center, and tickets are easy to come by on most nights, depending on who the Wizards' competition is.

★ **The White House.** *1600 Pennsylvania Ave NW, Washington (20502). Phone 202/456-7041 (recording). www.whitehouse.gov.* Constructed in 1800 under the supervision of George Washington, the house has been lived in by every US president since John Adams. It was burned by the British during the War of 1812 and reconstructed under the guidance of James Monroe (1817-1825). The West Wing, which includes the Oval Office, was built during Theodore Roosevelt's administration (1901-1909); before its construction, executive offices shared the second floor with the president's private quarters. The interior of the White House was gutted and rebuilt, using modern construction techniques, during the Truman administration; President Truman and family resided at Blair House for four years during the reconstruction. The Library and the Vermeil Room (on the Ground Floor); the East, Green, Blue, and Red Rooms; and the State Dining Room (on the State Floor) are accessible to groups of ten for tours. In this era of heightened security, you'll find Secret Service agents in every room, doubling as tour guides. Obtain tickets through your congressperson or senator. (Tues-Sat 7:30-11:30 am; closed Jan 1, Dec 25, and presidential functions) **FREE**

World War II Memorial. *National Mall and Memorial Parks, 900 Ohio Dr SW (20024). Phone 202/426-6841. www.nps.gov/nwwm.* The World War II Memorial honors America's "Greatest Generation," the men and women who emerged from the Depression to rise up against forces of tyranny, ultimately triumphing in a hard-fought war that took the lives of 50 million people worldwide. Situated on the National Mall between the Lincoln Memorial and the Washington Monument, this memorial opened to visitors in the spring of 2004. Twin Atlantic and Pacific pavilions are divided by an oval-shaped pool, symbolizing a war fought across two oceans. Fifty-six wreath-adorned stone pillars—each representing a US state or territory—form semicircles on the memorial's north and south sides. The wide entrance on the memorial's east side features bas-relief sculptures depicting scenes of America at war. To the west, the Reflecting Pool cascades over twin waterfalls that bookend the Freedom Wall, which glitters with 4,000 gold stars (one-tenth the number of Americans who lost their lives in the war). National park rangers staff an information station south of the memorial, answering questions and providing brochures.

Yellow House. *1430 33rd St NW, Washington (20007).* (1733) One of Georgetown's oldest homes (a private residence), typical of the area's mansions.

Special Events

Cherry Blossom Festival. *Tidal Basin and Ohio Dr NW, Washington (20003). Tidal Basin, West Potomac Park, East Potomac Park, Washington Monument grounds. Phone 202/547-1500. www.nationalcherryblossomfestival.org.* Nothing says spring more spectacularly than the sight of thousands of cherry trees in full bloom around the Jefferson Memorial. About 150 trees remain from the original 1912 gift of 3,000 from the city of Tokyo, but thousands of others have been planted in parks along the Tidal Basin, and for two weeks each year their lush pink and white blooms transform the cityscape. The festival celebrates this annual event with activities that appeal to visitors of all ages. Don't miss the Smithsonian's Kite Festival on the National Mall, the rousing parade, or Sakura Matsuri, a day-long Japanese street festival. Visitors can enjoy drummers, traditional dancers, and musical performances; demonstrations of flower arranging, calligraphy, and martial arts; a Taste of Japan food fair (who says that sushi isn't street food?); and the bustling Ginza Arcade, with shops selling everything from origami paper to antique kimonos. Late Mar-early Apr.

Concerts. *Independence and 15th St NW, Washington (20008). Phone 202/619-7222.* **Sylvan Theater,** Washington Monument grounds, June-Aug, days vary, phone 202/619-7222. **US Capitol,** west terrace, June-late Aug, Mon-Wed, Fri, Sun, phone 202/619-7222. **National Gallery of Art,** west garden court, Oct-June, Sun evenings; first-come basis, phone 202/842-6941. **Phillips Collection,** at Dupont-Kalorama Museum, Sept-May, Sun, phone 202/387-2151.

Easter Egg Roll. *White House Lawn, 1600 Pennsylvania Ave NW, Washington (20502). Phone 202/456-2200.* First introduced to Washington by Dolley Madison. Mon after Easter.

Evening Parade. *8th and I sts SE, Washington (20390). US Marine Barracks, I St between 8th and 9th sts SE. Phone 202/433-6060.* Spectacular parade with Marine Band, US Marine Drum and Bugle Corps, Color Guard, Silent Drill Team, and marching companies. Submitting a written request for reservations at least three weeks in advance is recommended. Tues and Fri evenings, early May-late Aug.

Festival of American Folklife. *National Mall, Constitution Ave, Washington (20004). Phone 202/357-2700.* Festival of folklife traditions from America and abroad. Sponsored by the Smithsonian Institution and National Park Service. Late June-early July.

Fort Dupont Summer Theatre. *Fort Dupont Park, Minnesota Ave and Randle Cir, Washington (20019). Phone 202/426-7723.* Musicals, concerts, plays, and dancing. Fri evenings, late June-late Aug.

Georgetown Garden Tour. *3224 N St NW, Washington (20007). Phone 202/333-6896.* Fourteen or more different gardens open to the public. Proceeds go to Georgetown Children's House; includes "Evermay" garden, which features grand expanses, fountains, and sculptures. Self-guided tours. Second Sat in May.

Georgetown House Tour. *3240 O St NW, Washington (20007). Phone 202/338-1796. www.georgetownhousetour.com.* Held since 1927, participants view 12 well-known and less well-known houses in Georgetown. St. John's Episcopal Church members serve as hosts and guides, and serve tea in the Parish Hall in the afternoon. Late Apr. **$$$$**

Goodwill Industries Embassy Tour. *220 S Dakota Ave NE, Washington (20018). Phone 202/636-4225.* The only time six to eight embassies are open to the public. This is a walking tour with shuttle bus transportation between embassies. Visitors can view artifacts and design peculiar to each government's legation, and complimentary refreshments and an illustrated tour booklet are given to each guest. Tickets are limited. No children under age 10 permitted. Second Sat in May.

July 4th Fireworks on the Mall. *National Mall, Washington (20001). Phone 202/426-6841. www.nps.gov/nama/events/july4/july4.htm.* You have to like a city that holds its fireworks show on the Fourth of July and not on the 3rd or whenever it's convenient. This display is extra-spectacular because the bombs burst in air over the monuments on the National Mall—a truly stirring sight. One of the best viewing spots is the Capitol, where the National Symphony Orchestra gives a rousing concert before the fireworks begin. Arrive early (the crowds get quite large) and picnic while you wait. July 4. **FREE**

Musical programs. *Carter Barron Amphitheater, Rock Creek Park, 5000 Glover Rd NW, Washington (20015). Phone 202/619-7222.* Mid-June-Aug.

Pageant of Peace. *Ellipse, south of White House, 15th and E sts NW, Washington (20319). Phone 202/619-7222.* Seasonal music, caroling; giant Christmas tree near the White House is lit by the president. Dec.

Taste of DC. *Pennsylvania Ave NW, Washington (20004). Between 7th and 14th sts. Phone 202/789-7002. www.washington.org/taste/.* Enjoy sample-size portions of scrumptious fare from local restaurants at the biggest, liveliest food and music festival on the East Coast. In an area as culturally diverse as DC, the vendors represent many of the world's great cuisines, including Indian, Jamaican, Italian, and Thai. Enjoy music and other live entertainment as you munch on your jerk chicken and vegetable samosas, and make sure to save room for key lime pie or an old-fashioned funnel cake. Columbus Day weekend. **FREE**

Washington National Cathedral Open House. *3000 Wisconsin Ave NW, Washington (20016). Phone 202/537-6200.* Special tours, entertainment, food; demonstrations of cathedral arts. It's the only day of the year when the central tower is open to the public. Sat nearest Sept 29. **FREE** (Small fee for some activities)

Limited-Service Hotels

★ ★ GEORGETOWN INN. *1310 Wisconsin Ave NW, Washington (20007). Phone 202/333-8900; toll-free 800/368-5922; fax 202/333-8308. www.georgetowninn.com.* This hotel, located in the heart of historic Georgetown, puts travelers close to the eclectic and charming shops and restaurants for which this neighborhood is known. Guests luxuriate in the inn's marble bathrooms, fluffy terry-cloth robes, and complimentary turn-down service. The inn's restaurant, the Daily Grill, serves classic American fare. 98 rooms, 6 story. Check-in 3 pm, check-out noon. Restaurant, bar. Fitness room. **$$**

★ ★ THE HAMILTON CROWNE PLAZA. *14th and K sts NW, Washington (20005). Phone 202/682-0111; fax 202/682-9525. www.hamiltoncrowneplazawashingtondc.com.* This 1920s hotel is large, but it has the feel of a smaller, intimate inn. The rooms are elegantly decorated in a blue and gold palette, but still maintain your comfort. They feature plush duvet beds with feather comforters. Several of the rooms offer beautiful views of the DC skyline, as well as Franklin Square. Because it's located in the heart of DC, you will be within easy walking distance of major attractions, such as the White House, Smithsonian museums, and the monuments. 318 rooms, 14 story. Pets accepted. Check-in 3 pm, check-out noon. High-speed Internet access. Restaurant, bar. Fitness room. Business center. **$$**

★ ★ HOLIDAY INN GEORGETOWN. *2101 Wisconsin Ave NW, Washington (20007). Phone 202/338-4600; toll-free 800/465-4328; fax 202/333-6113. www.higeorgetown.com.* Bass Hotels and Resorts awarded this hotel its "Quality of Excellence Award." Families seeking a fun location and a reasonable price will enjoy the hotel's convenience to downtown DC, as well as a variety of shopping, sightseeing, and dining venues. It also offers a free shuttle to travelers visiting nearby Georgetown University. 296 rooms, 7 story. Check-in 3 pm, check-out noon. Restaurant, bar. Fitness room. Outdoor pool. **$**

★ ★ HOLIDAY INN ON THE HILL. *415 New Jersey Ave NW, Washington (20001). Phone 202/638-1616; toll-free 800/638-1116; fax 202/638-0707. www.holidayinnonthehill.com.* The sleek, contemporary, styling of this Holiday Inn is not what you would expect of a chain hotel. Decorated in eye-catching cobalt blue and black, the rooms feature leather-based platform beds with high wood-and-fabric headboards, while the lobby sports a unique "bubble" wall. Its location in Capitol Hill—and its amenities—make it a great port for families and business travelers alike. Each room has high-speed Internet access, and Wi-Fi is also available in the lobby, restaurant, and meeting rooms. An in-house business center provides 24-hour access to computers, copiers, or fax services. 343 rooms, 10 story. Check-in 3 pm, check-out noon. High-speed Internet access. Restaurant, bar. Fitness room. Outdoor pool. Business center. **$**

★ ★ HOTEL WASHINGTON. *Pennsylvania Ave and 15th St NW, Washington (20004). Phone 202/638-5900; toll-free 800/424-9540; fax 202/638-1595. www.hotelwashington.com.* Opened in 1917, this is the oldest and continuously operated hotel in DC, located one block from the White House. The hotel's architectural details are sumptuous, and include pegged teak flooring and the lobby's beautiful crystal chandeliers. Its rooftop Sky Terrace Restaurant boasts one of the most magnificent views of the city. The hotel's rich history has allowed it to serve an impressive clientele that includes past presidents, movie stars, and even the White House's National Turkey every Thanksgiving! 344 rooms, 11 story. Pets accepted. Check-in 3 pm, check-out 1 pm. Restaurant, bar. Fitness room. Business center. **$$**

★ JURYS NORMANDY INN. *2118 Wyoming Ave NW, Washington (20008). Phone 202/483-1350; toll-free 800/423-6953; fax 202/387-8241. www.jurysdoyle.com.* 75 rooms, 6 story. Check-out noon. **$**

★ ★ ONE WASHINGTON CIRCLE HOTEL. *1 Washington Cir NW, Washington (20037). Phone 202/872-1680; toll-free 800/424-9671; fax 202/223-3961. www.onewashcirclehotel.com.* A multimillion-dollar renovation and close proximity to DC's downtown are only a few reasons that this hotel is perfect for business or leisure. Nearly all the rooms in this suite hotel have full kitchens and spacious balconies that offer sweeping city views. Guests can dine out at nearby restaurants or try the hotel's well-reviewed Circle Bistro. 151 rooms, 9 story. Check-in 3 pm, check-out noon. Restaurant, bar. Fitness room. Outdoor pool. **$$**

★★ RIVER INN. *924 25th St NW, Washington (20037). Phone 202/337-7600; toll-free 800/424-2741; fax 202/337-6520. www.theriverinn.com.* This all-suite hotel recently underwent a complete renovation. The rooms are equipped with full kitchens with marble floors and high-speed Internet access. Close to George Washington University and Foggy Bottom, the hotel offers turn down service, the morning paper, and even grocery shopping, if needed. Dish, the in-house restaurant, boasts home-style biscuits and 1950s root beer floats. 126 rooms, all suites. Pets accepted; fee. Check-out noon. Restaurant, bar. Fitness room. **$$**

★★ TOPAZ HOTEL. *1733 North St NW, Washington (20036). Phone 202/393-3000; toll-free 800/424-2950; fax 202/296-5945. www.topazhotel.com.* 99 rooms, 10 story. Complimentary continental breakfast. Pets accepted. Check-out noon. Restaurant, bar. On the site of the "Little White House" where Theodore Roosevelt lived during his vice-presidency and the first weeks of his presidency. **$$**

★ WINDSOR PARK HOTEL. *2116 Kalorama Rd NW, Washington (20008). Phone 202/483-7700; toll-free 800/247-3064; fax 202/332-4547. www.windsorparkhotel.com.* 43 rooms, 5 story. Complimentary continental breakfast. Check-out noon. **$**

Full-Service Hotels

★★★ THE FAIRMONT WASHINGTON, DC. *2401 M St NW, Washington (20037). Phone 202/429-2400; toll-free 800/257-7544; fax 202/457-5010. www.fairmont.com.* The Fairmont is a refined choice in Washington, DC. This elegant hotel is amenity-rich, with one of the city's largest fitness centers and a complete business center. Located in the West End, this hotel is an ideal base for corporate travelers or vacationers wanting to take in the many cultural treasures of the nation's capital. The well-appointed rooms and suites are comfortable and spacious, and guests on the Gold Floor level are treated to additional perks, such as private check-in and dedicated concierge service. Hotel guests and local denizens celebrate the weekend at the Colonnade's special brunch, while the Bistro is an informal spot for contemporary American fare. 415 rooms, 10 story, all suites. Pets accepted, some restrictions; fee. Check-in 3 pm, check-out noon. High-speed Internet access. Restaurant, bar. Fitness room, spa. Indoor pool, whirlpool. Airport transportation available. Business center. **$$**

★★★★ FOUR SEASONS HOTEL WASHINGTON, DC. *2800 Pennsylvania Ave NW, Washington (20007). Phone 202/342-0444; fax 202/944-2076. www.fourseasons.com.* This Four Seasons Hotel is nestled within Washington's lovely and historic Georgetown neighborhood. Just outside the hotel's doors are enticing shops, energetic nightlife, and delectable dining. The warm and inviting atmosphere of the Four Seasons is instantly recognizable in the gracious lobby, where bountiful floral displays and Oriental rugs set a refined, residential tone. The guest accommodations are some of the most spacious in the city and are magnificently appointed with polished formal furnishings, beautiful fabrics, and exquisite attention to detail. The views of Rock Creek Park (see) and the C & O Canal further enhance the relaxing mood. Popular fitness classes are offered in the extremely well-equipped fitness center, complete with a lap pool, while the seven spa treatment rooms provide a restful alternative for personal well-being. Consistently delicious meals are available at Seasons (see), or you can retreat to the cozy Garden Lounge for afternoon tea or cocktails. Not only is the food memorable, but the politically charged crowd is unparalleled! *Secret Inspector's Notes: No time to finish your e-mails before lunch? No problem! When dining at Seasons for lunch, guests are greeted not only with gracious charm but also with the offer of wireless connectivity from an available laptop.* 257 rooms, 6 story. Pets accepted, some restrictions. Check-in 3 pm, check-out noon. High-speed Internet access. Restaurant, bar. Fitness room, spa. Indoor pool, whirlpool. Business center. **$$$$**

★★★ GRAND HYATT WASHINGTON. *1000 H St NW, Washington (20001). Phone 202/582-1234; fax 202/628-1641. www.grandwashington.hyatt.com.* A convenient downtown location, situated close to the MCI Center, the US Capitol, and other federal agencies, makes this hotel a popular choice for travelers. 888 rooms, 12 story. Check-in 3 pm, check-out noon. Restaurant, bar. Fitness room. Indoor pool, whirlpool. Business center. **$$$**

★★★★ THE HAY-ADAMS. *16th and H sts NW, Washington (20006). Phone 202/638-6600; toll-free 800/424-5054; fax 202/293-2716. www.hayadams.com.* The Hay-Adams seems to radiate the power of the nation's capital. Set on Lafayette Square across from the White House, the hotel has been welcoming notables since the 1920s. Reading like a "Who's Who" of American history, the Hay-Adams' guest list is truly fascinating. If only these walls could talk! Originally designed as the private residences of two influential men, the hotel retains the majestic style of its former incarnation. The guest rooms are a happy marriage of historic preservation and 21st-century conveniences; intricately carved plaster ceilings and ornamental fireplaces reside alongside high-speed Internet access and multiline telephones. Windows frame views of the White House, St. John's Church, and Lafayette Square, further convincing visitors that they are in the center of Washington's universe. All-day dining is available at Lafayette, while the Off the Record bar is a popular watering hole for politicians and hotel guests. 145 rooms, 8 story. Pets accepted, some restrictions. Check-in 3 pm, check-out noon. Restaurant, bar. **$$$$**

★★★ HILTON WASHINGTON EMBASSY ROW. *2015 Massachusetts Ave NW, Washington (20036). Phone 202/265-1600; fax 202/328-7526. www.hilton.com.* This elegant hotel is in the heart of DC's international business community. It is located a half a block from the Metro, so you will find it easy to arrange business or sightseeing. In the evening, you can relax with drinks and hors d'oeuvres in the lobby lounge or take in the fabulous view of DC from the seasonal rooftop pool. The International Marketplace restaurant features—as its name suggests—cuisine from around the world. 193 rooms, 9 story. Check-in 3 pm, check-out noon. Restaurant, bar. Children's activity center. Fitness room. Outdoor pool. Business center. **$$**

★★★ HOTEL GEORGE. *15 E St NW, Washington (20001). Phone 202/347-4200; toll-free 800/576-8331; fax 202/347-4213. www.hotelgeorge.com.* The Hotel George shakes things up in the nation's capital. In a city well known for its power brokers and style makers, travelers book this boutique hotel for its dynamic interiors and central Capitol Hill location. The dramatic rooms and suites are the very definition of modern living, with bold artwork, monochromatic tones, clean lines, and high-tech amenities. The hotel's hip quotient is furthered by its restaurant, Bistro Bis (see), which is often considered one of the top tables in town. Its industrial chic design is the perfect complement to the hotel's sleek personality, and its French bistro fare is a favorite of politicos and celebrities. 139 rooms, 8 story. Pets accepted. Check-in 3 pm, check-out noon. High-speed Internet access. Restaurant, bar. Fitness room. **$$$**

★★★ J. W. MARRIOTT HOTEL ON PENNSYLVANIA AVENUE. *1331 Pennsylvania Ave NW, Washington (20004). Phone 202/393-2000; fax 202/626-6991. www.marriotthotels.com/wasjw.* Located in the heart of Washington, this elegant hotel offers guests superb service and a relaxing stay. Centrally located to theaters, shops, and some wonderful sightseeing, this hotel has something for everyone. 772 rooms, 12 story. Check-out noon. High-speed Internet access. Restaurant. Fitness room. Indoor pool, whirlpool. Business center. **$$**

★★★ THE JEFFERSON. *1200 16th St NW, Washington (20036). Phone 202/347-2200; fax 202/331-7982. www.thejeffersondc.com.* Just four blocks from the White House, this Beaux Arts hotel dating to 1923 is a masterpiece of quiet luxury. The antique-filled public rooms recall the elegance of the past, and the museum-quality collection of artwork and original documents signed by Thomas Jefferson is astounding. The guest rooms are a stylish blend of old and new. The seamless, attentive service is outstanding and satisfies every need. A fitness center is available, as are privileges at the University Club, with its Olympic-size pool. The restaurant feels like old Washington with its faux tortoiseshell walls and leather chairs, yet its New American cuisine is all the rage. 100 rooms, 8 story. Pets accepted, some restrictions. Check-in 3 pm, check-out 1 pm. Restaurant, bar. Fitness room. **$$**

★ ★ ★ **LATHAM HOTEL.** *3000 M St NW, Washington (20007). Phone 202/726-5000; toll-free 800/368-5922; fax 202/337-4250. www.thelatham.com.* The quaintness of Georgetown sits just steps away from this European-style boutique hotel, given its prime location on the city's main street. Simply walk outside its front doors and you'll find good shopping and tasty food. For the latter, however, you may not even want to leave The Latham. Michele Richard, a high-profile local chef with an international reputation, owns and operates the onsite Michele Richard Citronelle (see) restaurant, where diners savor award-winning French and American cuisine. The well-appointed guest rooms come with marble showers, high-speed Internet access, and more. In summer, cool off in the rooftop swimming pool. 143 rooms, 10 story. Check-in 3 pm, check-out 11 am. High-speed Internet access. Restaurant. Outdoor pool. **$$**

★ ★ ★ **LOEWS L'ENFANT PLAZA HOTEL.** *480 L'Enfant Plz SW, Washington (20024). Phone 202/484-1000; toll-free 800/636-5065; fax 202/646-4456. www.loewshotels.com.* Because DC isn't just for politicians, this hotel lays out the welcome mat for pets and families. In addition to special packages for kids, the hotel also offers them for four-legged guests, and provides a special area in which to walk them. But the hotel caters to adult tastes, too. Its rooms, which offer diverse views of the city, are enhanced by thoughtful amenities, such as mini-TV/radios and scales in each bathroom. And convenience has not been sacrificed. A shopping complex and Metro station are located in the lower level of the building, and the hotel is only steps away from the Air and Space and Holocaust museums. 370 rooms. Pets accepted. Check-in 3 pm, check-out noon. Restaurant, bar. Children's activity center. Fitness room. Indoor pool, outdoor pool. Business center. **$$**

★ ★ ★ **THE MADISON.** *15th and M sts NW, Washington (20005). Phone 202/862-1600; toll-free 800/424-8577; fax 202/785-1255. www.themadisondc.com.* The beautiful Georgian architecture and clock tower cupola are not the only things that distinguish this hotel. The owners and staff are dedicated to providing the highest level of hospitality. Its traditional and elegant atmosphere is enhanced by numerous, contemporary amenities, such as a fitness center, high-speed Internet access, and an indoor pool. The hotel offers a complimentary continental breakfast in the lobby, but be sure to check out Rod's Steak and Seafood Grille, which has won *New Jersey* magazine's "Best Steak" award. 353 rooms. Check-in 3 pm, check-out noon. High-speed Internet access. Restaurant, bar. Fitness room. Airport transportation available. Business center. **$$$**

MANDARIN ORIENTAL, WASHINGTON, DC (Too new to be rated). *1330 Maryland, Washington (20024). Phone 202/554-8588; fax 202/554-8999. www.mandarin-oriental.com.* For a bit of Asian flair in the nation's capital, discerning travelers book the Mandarin Oriental. This fashionable hotel caters to contemporary business and leisure travelers with its wide array of services, including a comprehensive business center, full-service Asian-influenced spa, and fine dining. Overlooking the Tidal Basin with views of the Jefferson Memorial, this hotel enjoys a scenic and central location. The rooms and suites respect the hotel chain's Asian heritage while incorporating a bit of classic Washington style. Imported linens, state-of-the-art technology, and aromatherapy bath products are among the many in-room creature comforts offered at this hotel. Contemporary Asian cuisine pleases palates in the two restaurants, while the lounge offers a casual alternative with light fare and cocktails. 400 rooms. Check-in 3 pm, check-out noon. High-speed Internet access. Two restaurants, two bars. Fitness room. Airport transportation available. Business center. **$$$**

★ ★ ★ **MARRIOTT WARDMAN PARK HOTEL.** *2660 Woodley Rd NW, Washington (20008). Phone 202/328-2000; toll-free 888/733-3222; fax 202/234-0015. www.marriotthotels.com/wasdt.* This hotel gracefully combines historic charm, beauty, and convenience. Its Wardman Tower, built in 1928, is listed on the National Historic Register. The award-winning gardens have been featured on the *NBC Nightly News* and boast nearly 100,000 seasonal flowers. With an in-house gourmet market, full-service Starbucks, jewelry store, and other numerous amenities, you can easily make this your home away from home. In addition, the hotel's excellent location within the Woodley Park neighborhood puts you just minutes away from major attractions, such as the National Zoo, and only steps away from a number of unique restaurants. 1,334 rooms, 10 story. Pets accepted, some restrictions. Check-in 4 pm, check-out noon. High-speed Internet access. Restaurant, bar. Fitness room, spa. Two outdoor pools. Business center. **$$**

★ ★ ★ OMNI SHOREHAM HOTEL. *2500 Calvert St NW, Washington (20008). Phone 202/234-0700; fax 202/756-5145. www.omnihotels.com.* A resort atmosphere in a city hotel is what you will find at the Omni Shoreham. Luxuriate in the full-service spa, where you can relax with a facial, massage, or manicure. The fitness center is outfitted with state-of-the-art equipment, and the heated pool and hot tub are available for a quick swim or soak. If you prefer the outdoors, hike, bike, jog, or even horseback ride through the scenic trails of nearby Rock Creek Park. But the amenities of DC are still at your fingertips; the hotel's Woodley Park location puts you close to attractions and restaurants, and the eclectic Adams-Morgan neighborhood is only minutes away. 836 rooms, 8 story. Pets accepted, some restrictions; fee. Check-in 3 pm, check-out noon. Restaurant, bar. Fitness room, spa. Indoor pool, outdoor pool, children's pool, whirlpool. Business center. **$$$**

★ ★ ★ PARK HYATT WASHINGTON. *24th and M sts NW, Washington (20037). Phone 202/789-1234; fax 202/457-8823. www.hyatt.com.* The awe-inspiring monuments and world-class museums of Washington, DC are within easy reach of the Park Hyatt. Located in the city's West End, the hotel is several blocks from Georgetown and downtown. The Park Hyatt maintains a handsome style throughout the hotel, from the gleaming lobby with its palette of gold and cream to the guest rooms and suites, which include the latest technology while maintaining a cozy ambience. Rivaling a small museum, the hotel boasts an impressive art collection: Picasso, Leger, Matisse, and Miró adorn the walls of the public and private spaces. Melrose (see) is recognized for its distinguished cuisine, served in the formal dining room or outside on the terrace during warmer months. The health club is comprehensive, including the latest exercise equipment, indoor pool, whirlpool, and sauna. 223 rooms, 10 story. Pets accepted. Check-in 3 pm, check-out noon. Restaurant, bar. Fitness room, spa. Indoor pool, whirlpool. **$$$**

★ ★ ★ RENAISSANCE MAYFLOWER HOTEL. *1127 Connecticut Ave NW, Washington (20036). Phone 202/347-3000; fax 202/776-9182. www.renaissancehotels.com.* If you like to get comfortable in stately old hotels, you'll want to book a room at this high-rise property in the heart of the city's business district. Built in 1925 for Calvin Coolidge's inauguration, this hotel played host to the likes of Franklin Delano Roosevelt and J. Edgar Hoover. You'll find popular shops and restaurants just outside its front doors; the White House is only four blocks away. Be ready for the eye-pleasing view when you check in: all the gilded trim, crystal chandeliers, and Oriental rugs in the block-long lobby will awe you. The guest rooms themselves are quite homey, so you'll likely feel right at home in yours. For business travelers, each room has a desk with work lamp, a two-line phone with a dataport, and a speakerphone. For groups, the Mayflower offers state-of-the-art meeting facilities. 660 rooms, 10 story. Pets accepted, some restrictions; fee. Check-in 3 pm, check-out noon. Restaurant, bar. Fitness room. Business center. **$**

★ ★ ★ ★ THE RITZ-CARLTON, GEORGETOWN. *3100 South St NW, Washington (20007). Phone 202/912-4100; fax 202/912-4199. www.ritzcarlton.com.* Embassy delegations often stay at this elegant, intimate hotel that blends contemporary décor with a historical setting. It's located on the banks of the Potomac River in Washington Harbour, an entertainment/residential/office complex located on land that was once the site of the original village of George Towne. Many of its executive suites and deluxe rooms offer gorgeous river views, and each comes with all the extra creature comforts you'd expect from a Ritz-Carlton, including feather duvets, goose-down pillows, and oversized marble baths. But don't spend all your time in your cushy room. Sip one of the fire-red martinis served in the Degrees Bar and Lounge, and then dine in Fahrenheit, which dishes out American/Italian cuisine. Soothe yourself with a facial or a full-body massage at the Boutique Spa, or tone those muscles at the fully equipped fitness center. 86 rooms. Pets accepted, some restrictions. Check-in 3 pm, check-out noon. Restaurant, bar. Fitness room, spa. **$$$$**

★★★★ THE RITZ-CARLTON, WASHINGTON DC. *1150 22nd St NW, Washington (20037). Phone 202/835-0500; fax 202/835-1588. www.ritzcarlton.com.* A convenient West End location, stylish accommodations, and superior service make The Ritz-Carlton, Washington, DC a favorite of sophisticated travelers. The supremely knowledgeable staff truly pampers its guests. The Ritz-Carlton's attention to detail is marvelous, and it continues to exceed expectations with innovative amenities. On-call technology butlers assist with computer woes, while the Luggage-less Travel program is offered to frequent guests, inviting them to leave behind items for their next visit. Traditional European décor defines the rooms and suites, and Club Level accommodations are treated to five food and beverage presentations daily. Perhaps most impressive is the Sports Club/LA access granted to all guests of The Ritz-Carlton. Adjacent to the hotel, this massive 100,000-square-foot complex is a veritable nirvana for fitness buffs with cutting-edge fitness programming, multiple athletic courts, and a pool. The complex also includes Splash, one of Washington's leading day spas. 300 rooms, 15 story. Pets accepted, some restrictions. Check-in 3 pm, check-out noon. Restaurant, bar. Fitness room, spa. Indoor pool, whirlpool. Business center. **$$$**

★★★ SOFITEL. *806 15th NW, Washington (20005). Phone 202/730-8800; fax 202/730-8500. www.sofitel.com.* 237 rooms. Pets accepted. Check-in 3 pm, check-out noon. Restaurant, bar. Fitness room. **$$$**

★★★★ THE ST. REGIS, WASHINGTON, DC. *923 16th and K sts NW, Washington (20006). Phone 202/638-2626; toll-free 800/562-5661; fax 202/638-4231. www.starwood.com/stregis/.* The St. Regis is a treasure in the nation's capital. Since 1926, the St. Regis has been a preferred residence of discerning travelers visiting Washington. Just a stone's throw from the White House, the hotel enjoys a prime city location with nearly all of Washington's attractions nearby. Stepping into this esteemed hotel offers an enchanting glimpse of a grander time. Its gilded lobby of coffered ceilings and sparkling chandeliers is a work of art. Reflecting its Italian Renaissance roots, the rooms and suites recall the splendor of European palaces with silk-covered walls and antique furnishings. English-style butlers attend to the individual needs of each guest. Formal afternoon tea is served to the gentle strains of a harp, and dining at the Library Restaurant completes this sublimely elegant experience. 193 rooms, 8 story. Pets accepted, some restrictions; fee. Check-in 3 pm, check-out 1 pm. Restaurant, bar. Fitness room. **$$$**

★★★ THE WATERGATE HOTEL. *2650 Virginia Ave NW, Washington (20037). Phone 202/965-2300; fax 202/965-1173. www.watergatehotel.com.* The circular architecture of this hotel is as distinct as its infamous history. Its unique curved shaped allows for large-sized rooms with all the expected amenities. Situated on the banks of the Potomac, the hotel has several rooms with balconies that give you a fabulous view of the river. Catch a show next door at the famous Kennedy Center. Take a short stroll to the upscale boutiques and fine dining of Georgetown. Or hop on the nearby Foggy Bottom Metro and explore other DC attractions. 250 rooms, 13 story. Pets accepted, some restrictions; fee. Check-in 3 pm, check-out noon. High-speed Internet access. Restaurant, bar. Fitness room, spa. Indoor pool, whirlpool. Business center. **$$**

★★★ THE WESTIN EMBASSY ROW. *2100 Massachusetts Ave NW, Washington (20008). Phone 202/293-2100; toll-free 800/434-9990; fax 202/293-0641. www.westin.com/.* Since 1927, this Embassy Row property has welcomed guests with turn-of-the-century style. All rooms and suites are decorated with Federal and Empire furnishings, including rich fabrics and antique reproductions, and boast beautiful views of Washington National Cathedral and historic Georgetown. Join the distinguished political and social crowd at the Jockey Club for innovative American cuisine. 206 rooms, 8 story. Pets accepted. Check-in 3 pm, check-out noon. High-speed Internet access. Restaurant, bar. Fitness room. Business center. **$$$**

★★★ THE WESTIN GRAND. *2350 M St NW, Washington (20037). Phone 202/429-0100; toll-free 888/627-8406; fax 202/429-9759. www.westin.com.* Not as glitzy as many of the other top DC hotels, the Westin offers attentive service and a more private, low-key environment. The rooms are comfortable and stylish, with ultra-comfortable beds and sizable bathrooms. 263 rooms, 4 story. Pets accepted, some restrictions. Check-in 3 pm, check-out noon. High-speed Internet access. Restaurant, bar. Fitness room. Outdoor pool. Business center. **$$**

★ ★ ★ **WILLARD INTERCONTINENTAL WASHINGTON.** *1401 Pennsylvania Ave NW, Washington (20004). Phone 202/628-9100; fax 202/637-7326. www.washington.interconti.com.* The Willard InterContinental is steeped in history. Only two blocks from the White House, this legendary beaux arts hotel has been at the center of Washington's political scene since 1850. The Willard's lobby has always served as a drawing room to the world; it is here that Lincoln held fireside staff meetings, Grant escaped the rigors of the White House to enjoy brandy and cigars, and the term "lobbyist" was coined. Henry Clay shared the secret of the mint julep in the Round Robin Bar, while the Willard Room's continental cuisine (see) makes history today. This landmark's guest rooms and suites are a traditional blend of Edwardian and Victorian styles furnished in deep jewel tones. The Jenny Lind suite is perfect for honeymooners with its mansard roof and canopy bed, while the Oval suite, inspired by the office of the same name, makes guests feel like masters of the universe. 341 rooms, 12 story. Pets accepted. Check-in 3 pm, check-out noon. High-speed Internet access. Restaurant, bar. Fitness room. Business center. **$$$$**

★ ★ ★ **WYNDHAM CITY CENTER HOTEL.** *1143 New Hampshire Ave NW, Washington (20037). Phone 202/775-0800; toll-free 800/526-7495; fax 202/331-9491. www.wyndham.com/citycenter.* This hotel puts guests close to two of DC's trendiest neighborhoods—Georgetown and Dupont Circle. Along with the convenient location, the hotel offers comfortable rooms that feature Herman Miller Aeron desk chairs and cordless phones. Shula's Steak House, named for Don Shula and the 1972 Miami Dolphins, provides fine dining. 352 rooms, 9 story. Check-in 3 pm, check-out noon. Restaurant, bar. Fitness room. Business center. **$$**

Restaurants

★ ★ ★ **1789.** *1226 36th St NW, Washington (20007). Phone 202/965-1788; fax 202/337-1541. www.1789restaurant.com.* This quietly elegant establishment, located in a restored mansion just on the edge of Georgetown University's campus, is a top destination for students with visiting relatives. American menu. Dinner. Closed Dec 25. Bar. Jacket required. **$$$**

★ ★ ★ **701 RESTAURANT.** *701 Pennsylvania Ave NW, Washington (20004). Phone 202/393-0701; fax 202/393-0242.* Overlooking the Navy Memorial fountains, this restaurant features a varied menu as well as a caviar bar. The roomy tables, comfortable chairs, and live piano music provide a nice atmosphere. American menu. Lunch, dinner. Closed holidays. Bar. Outdoor seating. **$$$**

★ ★ **ADITI.** *3299 M St NW, Washington (20007). Phone 202/625-6825.* Indian menu. Lunch, dinner. Closed Thanksgiving. Bar. **$**

★ **AFTERWORDS.** *1517 Connecticut Ave NW, Washington (20036). Phone 202/387-1462; fax 202/232-6777.* American menu. Breakfast, lunch, dinner, brunch. Closed Thanksgiving, Dec 25. Bar. Outdoor seating. In two-story greenhouse and terrace behind Kramer Books bookshop. **$**

★ ★ **ANNA MARIA'S.** *1737 Connecticut Ave NW, Washington (20009). Phone 202/667-1444; fax 202/667-2699.* Italian menu. Lunch, dinner, late-night. Closed holidays. Bar. Casual attire. **$$**

★ **AUSTIN GRILL.** *2404 Wisconsin Ave NW, Washington (20007). Phone 202/337-8080. www.austingrill.com.* Tex-Mex menu. Lunch, dinner, Sun brunch. Closed Thanksgiving, Dec 25. Bar. **$$**

★ ★ **BACCHUS.** *1827 Jefferson Pl NW, Washington (20036). Phone 202/785-0734; fax 202/785-1811. www.bacchusdc.net.* Middle Eastern menu. Lunch, dinner. Closed Sun; holidays. Casual attire. **$$**

★★ **BEDUCI.** *2100 P St NW, Washington (20037). Phone 202/223-3824; fax 202/296-1143. www.beduci .com.* Mediterranean menu. Lunch, dinner. Closed holidays. Bar. Casual attire. Outdoor seating. Three dining areas. **$$$**

★ **BILLY MARTIN'S TAVERN.** *1264 Wisconsin Ave NW, Washington (20007). Phone 202/333-7370; fax 202/333-6089. www.billymartinstavern.com.* American menu. Breakfast, lunch, dinner, late-night, brunch. Closed Dec 25. Bar. Casual attire. Established 1933. **$$**

★★★ **BISTRO BIS.** *15 E St NW, Washington (20001). Phone 202/661-2700; fax 202/661-2747. www. bistrobis.com.* The long zinc bar is the only concession to the bistro theme at this sleek downtown spot. The food is classic French bistro, with well-executed items. As unstuffy as DC gets; a fun night out. French bistro menu. Lunch, dinner, brunch. Closed Dec 25. Children's menu. **$$**

★★ **BISTRO FRANCAIS.** *3128 M St NW, Washington (20007). Phone 202/338-3830; fax 202/338-1421.* Country French menu. Lunch, brunch. Closed Dec 24-25. **$$**

★★ **BISTROT LEPIC & WINE BAR.** *1736 Wisconsin Ave NW, Washington (20007). Phone 202/333-0111; fax 202/333-2209. www.bistrotlepic.com.* French menu. Lunch, dinner. Closed Mon; holidays. Bar. Casual attire. Reservations recommended. Storefront restaurant. **$$**

★★★ **BOMBAY CLUB.** *815 Connecticut Ave NW, Washington (20006). Phone 202/659-3727; fax 202/659-5012.* This restaurant maintains its position as one of the most respected Indian restaurants in the area. The menu is divided into sections including house, vegetarian, Goan, Moghlai, and Northwest Frontier specialties. Indian menu. Lunch, dinner, Sun brunch. Closed Jan 1, Dec 25. Bar. Outdoor seating. **$$**

★★ **BOMBAY PALACE.** *2020 K St NW, Washington (20006). Phone 202/331-4200; fax 202/ 331-1505. www.bombay-palace.com.* Indian menu. Lunch, dinner. Bar. Indian décor and original art; 350-gallon fish tank. **$$**

★ **THE BREAD LINE.** *1751 Pennsylvania Ave NW, Washington (20006). Phone 202/822-8900; fax 202/822-8256.* Breakfast, lunch. Closed Sat-Sun. Outdoor seating. The menu is inspired by international street foods. **$**

★ **BURMA.** *740 6th St NW, Washington (20001). Phone 202/638-1280.* Burmese menu. Lunch, dinner. Closed holidays. **$**

★★ **BUSARA.** *2340 Wisconsin Ave NW, Washington (20007). Phone 202/337-2340; fax 202/333-1364. www.busara.us.* Thai menu. Lunch, dinner. Closed Thanksgiving. Bar. Casual attire. Outdoor seating. **$$**

★ **C. F. FOLKS.** *1225 19th St NW, Washington (20036). Phone 202/293-0162; fax 202/457-9078. www. cffolks.com.* Lunch. Closed Sat-Sun; holidays. Outdoor seating. No credit cards accepted. **$**

★★★ **CAFE 15.** *806 15th St NW, Washington (20005). Phone 202/737-8800; fax 202/730-8500.* Located in the sophisticated Sofitel (see), Cafe 15 does a strong job of competing in the culinary politics of high-end DC dining. You'll find an airy, bright dining room with a gracious staff and an ambitious team of chefs turning out contemporary French-Alsatian fare of the lofty, super-foodie variety. The wine list is deep and rare and well suited to heavy-hitter expense accounts. French menu. Breakfast, lunch, dinner. Bar. Casual attire. Outdoor seating. **$$$**

★★ **CAFE ATLANTICO.** *405 8th St NW, Washington (20004). Phone 202/393-0812; fax 202/393-0555. www.cafeatlanticodc.com.* Latin American menu. Lunch, dinner. Closed Thanksgiving, Dec 24-25. Bar. Casual attire. Reservations recommended. Valet parking. Outdoor seating. **$$$**

★★ **CAFE MILANO.** *3251 Prospect St NW, Washington (20007). Phone 202/333-6183; fax 202/333-6594. www.cafemilano.net.* Italian menu. Lunch, dinner, late-night. Closed Dec 25. Bar. Casual attire. Reservations recommended. Outdoor seating. **$$$**

★ **CAFE MOZART.** *1331 H St NW, Washington (20005). Phone 202/347-5732; fax 202/347-4958. www.cafemozartgermandeli.com.* Austrian, German menu. Breakfast, lunch, dinner. Closed Jan 1, Thanksgiving, Dec 25. Bar. Children's menu. German deli on premises. **$$**

★ ★ ★ THE CAPITAL GRILLE. *601 Pennsylvania Ave NW, Washington (20004). Phone 202/737-6200; fax 202/637-8821. www.thecapitalgrille.com.* Steak menu. Lunch, dinner. Closed Thanksgiving, Dec 25. Bar. Valet parking (dinner). **$$$**

★ ★ CASHION'S EAT PLACE. *1819 Columbia Rd NW, Washington (20009). Phone 202/797-1818; fax 202/797-0048. www.cashionseatplace.com.* Eclectic menu. Dinner, Sun brunch. Closed Mon; hours vary. Bar. Casual attire. Reservations recommended. Valet parking. Outdoor seating. **$$$**

★ ★ ★ CHRISTOPHER MARKS. *1301 Pennsylvania Ave NW, Washington (20004). Phone 202/628-5938; fax 202/737-0072.* You'll feel like a power player upon stepping into this clubby restaurant. The menu is a bit predictable, but all of the choices are well executed and served by a professional staff. Seafood menu. Lunch, dinner. Closed Sun. Children's menu. **$$$**

★ ★ CLYDE'S OF GEORGETOWN. *3236 M St NW, Washington (20007). Phone 202/333-9180.* One of the oldest saloons in Washington, this is the original Clyde's (now one of a dozen establishments owned by the Clyde's Group). Its cozily crowded main bar draws a loyal following with its nice selection of draft beers. The brass-and-wood dining room features ambitious menu choices well beyond the burgers and chili for which the place is famous. American, seafood menu. Lunch, dinner, Sun brunch. Closed Dec 25. Bar. Children's menu. Atrium dining. **$$**

★ ★ ★ DC COAST. *1401 K St NW, Washington (20005). Phone 202/216-5988; fax 202/371-2221. www.dccoast.com.* Seafood menu. Lunch, dinner. Closed Sun; holidays. Bar. Casual attire. **$$$**

★ ★ DISTRICT CHOPHOUSE & BREWERY. *509 7th St NW, Washington (20004). Phone 202/347-3434; fax 202/347-3388. www.districtchophouse.com.* American menu. Lunch, dinner, late-night. Closed Thanksgiving, Dec 25. Bar. Children's menu. Casual attire. **$$$**

★ FRAN O'BRIEN'S STADIUM STEAK HOUSE. *1001 16th St NW, Washington (20036). Phone 202/783-2598; fax 202/783-3444. www.fobss.com.* Seafood, steak menu. Lunch, dinner. Closed holidays. Bar. Children's menu. **$$**

★ ★ GABRIEL. *2121 P St NW, Washington (20037). Phone 202/956-6690; fax 202/956-6641. www.washingtonpost.com/yp/gabriel.* American menu. Breakfast, dinner, Sun brunch. Closed Mon; Dec 25. Bar. **$$**

★ ★ ★ GALILEO. *1110 21st St NW, Washington (20036). Phone 202/293-7191; fax 202/331-9364. www.robertodonna.com.* This is the flagship enterprise of Roberto Donna, the celebrity chef whose reputation in the area is legendary (he is also behind Il Radicchio, I Matti, and many others). In keeping with the cutting-edge trends, there's even a much-sought-after kitchen table. Italian menu. Lunch, dinner. Closed Memorial Day, July 4, Dec 25-Jan 1. Bar. Children's menu. Casual attire. Reservations recommended. Outdoor seating. **$$$**

★ GARRETT'S. *3003 M St NW, Washington (20007). Phone 202/333-1033; fax 202/333-8055. www.garrettsdc.com.* American menu. Lunch, dinner. Bar. 1794 landmark building; originally the house of Maryland governor T. S. Lee. **$$**

★ ★ ★ GEORGIA BROWN'S. *950 15th St NW, Washington (20005). Phone 202/393-4498; fax 202/393-7134. www.gbrowns.com.* At this McPherson Square spot, one of Washington's favorite restaurants for several years running, diners have trouble choosing from among the many creative, modern dishes. The dining room is the definition of "casual elegance." Southern menu. Lunch, dinner, Sun brunch. Closed holidays. Bar. Casual attire. Reservations recommended. **$$**

★ ★ ★ ★ GERARD'S PLACE. *915 15th St NW, Washington (20005). Phone 202/737-4445; fax 202/737-5555.* Gerard's Place is an intimate little hideaway for people who love the art of dining. Elegant and civilized, it is perfect for romance, special occasions, or dinner with close friends. The menu is a product of meticulous attention to detail. Fresh ingredients are at work here, as are classic French technique and a healthy dose of creativity. Aromatic herbs like sage, mint, basil, lavender, sorrel, and lemon thyme often play supporting roles. Meals are served on mismatched china plates—a nice touch that adds a sweet sense of home to this prized establishment. The kitchen offers a five-course tasting menu as well as a tempting à la carte menu. The wine list is lengthy and features mostly French bottles, with a more modest American selection. Desserts are all made to order and must be selected at the beginning of the meal, or at least 25 minutes before you'd like to dig in. These desserts are worth the wait, so don't miss out. French menu. Lunch, dinner. Closed Sun; holidays. Casual attire. Outdoor seating. **$$$**

★ ★ ★ THE GRILL AT RITZ-CARLTON, WASHINGTON, DC. *1150 22nd St NW, Washington (20037). Phone 202/835-0500; fax 202/974-5505. www.ritzcarlton.com.* Eclectic/International menu. Breakfast, lunch, dinner. Bar. Children's menu. Casual attire. **$$$**

★ GRILL FROM IPANEMA. *1858 Columbia Rd NW, Washington (20009). Phone 202/986-0757; fax 202/265-4229. www.thegrillfromipanema.com.* Brazilian menu. Dinner, brunch. Closed holidays. Bar. **$$**

★ GUAPO'S. *4515 Wisconsin Ave NW, Washington (20016). Phone 202/686-3588; fax 202/686-5490. www.guaposrestaurant.com.* Latin American, Mexican menu. Lunch, dinner. Bar. Outdoor seating. **$$**

★ GUARDS. *2915 M St NW, Washington (20007). Phone 202/965-2350; fax 202/342-6112.* American, seafood menu. Lunch, dinner, Sun brunch. Bar. **$$**

★ HAAD THAI. *1100 New York Ave NW, Washington (20005). Phone 202/682-1111; fax 202/682-0824. www.haadthai.com.* Thai menu. Lunch, dinner. Closed holidays. Bar. **$**

★ ★ HOGATE'S. *800 Water St SW, Washington (20024). Phone 202/484-6300; fax 202/484-3840.* American menu. Lunch, dinner, Sun brunch. Closed Dec 25. Bar. Children's menu. Outdoor seating. **$$$**

★ HUNAN CHINATOWN. *624 H St NW, Washington (20001). Phone 202/783-5858; fax 202/393-1375. www.marriottworldcenter.com.* Chinese menu. Lunch, dinner. Closed Thanksgiving. Casual attire. **$$**

★ J. PAUL'S. *3218 M St NW, Washington (20007). Phone 202/333-3450; fax 202/342-6721. www.j-pauls.com.* American menu. Lunch, dinner, Sun brunch. Bar. Children's menu. **$$**

★ ★ JALEO. *480 7th St NW, Washington (20004). Phone 202/628-7948; fax 202/628-7952. www.jaleo.com.* Spanish menu. Lunch, dinner, late-night. Closed Thanksgiving, Dec 24-25. Bar. Casual attire. Valet parking. Outdoor seating. Murals of flamenco dancers. **$$**

★ ★ ★ THE JEFFERSON. *1200 16th St NW, Washington (20036). Phone 202/833-6206; fax 202/331-7982. www.thejeffersondc.com.* Here, diners seeking an intimate, secluded restaurant find professional and discreet service, perfect for those seeking anonymity in this high-profile town. The chef demonstrates a high degree of culinary talent and sensibility with the freshest seasonal ingredients. American menu. Breakfast, lunch, dinner, Sun brunch. Bar. Children's menu. Casual attire. Valet parking. **$$$**

★ ★ ★ JEFFREY'S AT THE WATERGATE. *2650 Virginia Ave NW, Washington (20037). Phone 202/298-4455; fax 202/298-4483.* Contemporary American menu. Breakfast, lunch, dinner, Sun brunch. Bar. Children's menu. Casual attire. Valet parking. **$$$**

★ ★ ★ KINKEAD'S. *2000 Pennsylvania Ave NW, Washington (20006). Phone 202/296-7700; fax 202/296-7688. www.kinkead.com.* Senators, journalists, models, financiers, and media moguls rub elbows at chef/owner Bob Kinkead's stunning spot for jazzy, distinctive, and fun-to-eat global fare. The deep cherry wood-paneled dining room has an intimate, clubby feel to it, with warm, low lighting, vintage wrought-iron staircases, tufted chocolate leather seating, and elegant table settings. As for what to eat, diners here have a tough choice to make. The palatial raw bar is a great place to start. But then again, the menu, which changes daily and draws influences from Spain, France, Italy, Morocco, and Asia, offers a terrific selection of appetizers, soups, salads, chops, and seafood, not to mention incredibly creative side dishes. It is not possible to order a disappointment. To complement the menu, you'll find one of the most user-friendly wine lists in the capital. The list is color coded from light to dark according to nose, weight, body, and flavor. Kinkead's hosts live jazz in the evenings and is a perfect choice for a lively meal with family, friends, or colleagues. Seafood menu. Lunch, dinner. Closed holidays. Bar. Casual attire. Outdoor seating. **$$$**

★ **KRUPIN'S.** *4620 Wisconsin Ave NW, Washington (20016). Phone 202/686-1988; fax 202/686-3566.* Deli menu. Breakfast, lunch, dinner. Closed Thanksgiving, Dec 25. Children's menu. Casual attire. **$$**

★ ★ **LA CHAUMIERE.** *2813 M St NW, Washington (20007). Phone 202/338-1784; fax 202/965-4597.* Country French menu. Lunch, dinner. Closed Sun; holidays. **$$**

★ ★ **LA COLLINE.** *400 N Capitol St NW, Washington (20001). Phone 202/737-0400; fax 202/737-3026.* French menu. Breakfast, lunch, dinner. Closed Sun; holidays. Bar. Outdoor seating. Across from Union Station. **$$**

★ ★ **LAURIOL PLAZA.** *1835 18th St NW, Washington (20009). Phone 202/387-0035; fax 202/387-8311. www.lauriolplazarestaurant.com.* Latin American menu. Lunch, dinner, brunch. Closed Thanksgiving, Dec 25. Bar. Casual attire. Outdoor seating. **$$**

★ ★ **LAVANDOU.** *3321 Connecticut Ave NW, Washington (20008). Phone 202/966-3002; fax 202/966-0982. www.lavandourestaurant.net.* French menu. Lunch, dinner. Closed holidays; Aug. Bar. Casual attire. **$$**

★ **LES HALLES.** *1201 Pennsylvania Ave NW, Washington (20004). Phone 202/347-6848; fax 202/347-6911. www.leshalles.net.* American, French menu. Lunch, dinner, brunch. Bar. Children's menu. Outdoor seating. Three-level dining area. **$$$**

★ ★ **LUIGINO.** *1100 New York Ave NW, Washington (20005). Phone 202/371-0595; fax 202/371-6482. www.luigino.com.* Italian menu. Lunch, dinner. Closed Jan 1, Labor Day, Dec 24-25. Bar. Casual attire. Reservations recommended. Outdoor seating. **$$**

★ **MARKET INN.** *200 E St SW, Washington (20024). Phone 202/554-2100; fax 202/863-1052. www.marketinndc.com.* American menu. Lunch, dinner, Sun brunch. Closed Thanksgiving, Dec 25. Bar. Children's menu. Outdoor seating. English pub ambience. **$$**

★ ★ ★ **MELROSE.** *24th at M St NW, Washington (20037). Phone 202/955-3898; fax 202/408-6118.* Finding a hotel restaurant that feels like a dining experience and not just an obligatory feeding ground for the hotel's guests can be a tough task. The Melrose Restaurant, located in the Park Hyatt (see), is far from a standard hotel feeder. It is fairly formal in its décor, with cushioned neutral-toned seating, cream-colored walls, high ceilings, lots of windows, and lots of sunlight. The room is lovely, but in a battle between décor and food, the food wins hands down. The kitchen sees food as an inspiration for energy and creativity, and this contemporary menu is filled with dishes that are alive with flavor and ingenuity. It is clear that the chefs behind closed doors are not afraid to play with products from around the world. The menu shows a special fondness for Asian ingredients, but nods are also made to Spanish, Italian, and regional American styles of cooking. Eclectic/International menu. Breakfast, lunch, dinner, Sun brunch. Bar. Children's menu. Casual attire. Valet parking. Outdoor seating. **$$$**

★ ★ ★ **MENDOCINO GRILL AND WINE BAR.** *2917 M St NW, Washington (20007). Phone 202/333-2912; fax 202/625-7888.* The excellent, all-American wine list is the most impressive feature of this wine bar-cum-restaurant. The food is designed to complement the wine, and the menu is comprised of creative choices that all sound tempting. The décor is upscale 1960s modern (think *Brady Bunch* wine bar), but it somehow manages to work. American menu. Lunch, dinner. **$$$**

★ ★ ★ ★ **MICHEL RICHARD CITRONELLE.** *3000 M St NW, Washington (20007). Phone 202/625-2150; fax 202/339-6326. www.citronelledc.com.* Citronelle's chef/owner Michel Richard is one talented guy. Not only has he created a restaurant that has stood the test of time (he's had it for more than ten years), but he has also managed to keep the menu vibrant, exciting, and just on the safe side of daring. Like his food, the restaurant is stylish and elegant. Filled with fresh flowers and lit with a creamy, golden glow, the room has a chic vibe and an open kitchen for a bird's-eye view of the chefs, dressed in white and hard at work. This is a terrific spot for most any occasion so long as fine dining is the order of business. Ingredients are the stars here; the chef manages to wow diners by highlighting the simple flavors of each dish's main component. Global accents—herbs, spices, fruits, nuts, and vegetables—come into play to draw out flavors, to spotlight sweetness or acidity, and to maintain balance on the palate. Richard is a poetic culinarian. Nabbing a seat at one of his coveted tables is like winning the lottery. French menu. Breakfast, lunch, dinner. Closed holidays. Bar. Children's menu. Jacket required. Outdoor seating. **$$$**

★★ **MONOCLE.** *107 D St NE, Washington (20002). Phone 202/546-4488; fax 202/546-7235.* American menu. Lunch, dinner. Closed Sat-Sun; holidays. Bar. Children's menu. Valet parking. Located in 1865 Jenkens Hill building. Close to the Capitol; frequented by members of Congress and other politicians. **$$**

★★ **MORRISON-CLARK.** *1015 L St NW, Washington (20001). Phone 202/289-8580; fax 202/289-8576. www.morrisonclark.com.* American, Caribbean menu. Lunch, dinner, Sun brunch. Closed holidays. Bar. Outdoor seating. **$$$**

★ **MR. SMITH'S.** *3104 M St NW, Washington (20007). Phone 202/333-3104. www.mrsmiths.com.* American menu. Lunch, dinner, brunch. Bar. Outdoor seating. **$$**

★ **MR. YUNG'S.** *740 6th St NW, Washington (20001). Phone 202/628-1098; fax 202/628-1128.* Chinese menu. Lunch, dinner. Outdoor seating. **$$**

★ **MURPHY'S OF DC.** *2609 24th St NW, Washington (20008). Phone 202/462-7171; fax 202/462-7901. www.murphysofdc.com.* American, Irish menu. Lunch, dinner. Children's menu. Outdoor seating. **$$**

★ **NATHAN'S.** *3150 M St NW, Washington (20007). Phone 202/338-2000; fax 202/333-2509.* American menu. Dinner, brunch. Closed Dec 25. Bar. Casual attire. **$$**

★★ **NEW HEIGHTS.** *2317 Calvert St NW, Washington (20008). Phone 202/234-4110; fax 202/234-0789. www.newheightsrestaurant.com.* American menu. Dinner, brunch. Closed holidays. Bar. Casual attire. Outdoor seating. **$$$**

★★★ **OBELISK.** *2029 P St NW, Washington (20036). Phone 202/872-1180.* Italian menu. Dinner. Closed Sun-Mon; holidays. Intimate dining room on the second floor of a townhouse. **$$$**

★★ **OCCIDENTAL GRILL.** *1475 Pennsylvania Ave NW, Washington (20004). Phone 202/783-1475; fax 202/783-1478. www.occidentaldc.com.* American menu. Lunch, dinner. Closed Thanksgiving, Dec 25. Bar. **$$$**

★★ **OLD EBBITT GRILL.** *675 15th St NW, Washington (20005). Phone 202/347-4800; fax 202/347-6136. www.ebbitt.com.* Proximity to the White House, monuments, and museums makes this famous watering hole a draw for the power-hungry as well as the merely hungry. Known for big breakfasts in the early hours and oysters and burgers later, Old Ebbitt also serves seasonal specialties such as corn on the cob and berry cobbler. Its beaux arts façade and glamorous marble, brass, and mahogany interior allow tourists to feel like high-placed political insiders. American menu. Breakfast, lunch, dinner, late-night, Sun brunch. Closed Dec 25. Bar. Children's menu. Casual attire. **$$**

★★ **OLD EUROPE.** *2434 Wisconsin Ave NW, Washington (20007). Phone 202/333-7600; fax 202/625-0553. www.old-europe.com.* German menu. Lunch, dinner. Closed July 4, Dec 24. Bar. Children's menu. Casual attire. **$$**

★★ **OVAL ROOM.** *800 Connecticut Ave NW, Washington (20006). Phone 202/463-8700; fax 202/785-9863. www.ovalroom.com.* American menu. Lunch, dinner. Closed Sun; July 4, Dec 25. Bar. Outdoor seating. **$$$**

★★ **THE PALM.** *1225 19th St NW, Washington (20036). Phone 202/293-9091; fax 202/775-1468. www.thepalm.com.* Steak menu. Lunch, dinner. Closed holidays. Bar. Casual attire. Valet parking. **$$$**

★★ **PAOLO'S.** *1303 Wisconsin Ave NW, Washington (20007). Phone 202/333-7353; fax 202/342-2846. www.capitalrestaurants.com.* Italian menu. Lunch, dinner, late-night, brunch. Closed Dec 25. Bar. Children's menu. Casual attire. Outdoor seating. Wood-burning pizza oven. **$$**

★★ **PESCE.** *2016 P St NW, Washington (20036). Phone 202/466-3474; fax 202/466-8302. www.pescebistro.com.* Seafood menu. Lunch, dinner. Closed holidays. Casual attire. Valet parking. **$$**

★ **PIZZERIA PARADISO.** *2029 P St NW, Washington (20036). Phone 202/223-1245; fax 202/223-5699.* Pizza, sandwich menu. Lunch, dinner. Closed holidays. Casual attire. **$$**

★★★ **PRIME RIB.** *2020 K St NW, Washington (20006). Phone 202/466-8811; fax 202/466-2010. www.theprimerib.com.* This K Street spot remains one of the best steakhouses inside the Beltway. Seafood, steak menu. Lunch, dinner. Closed Sun; holidays. Bar. Jacket required. **$$$**

★ **RAKU.** *1900 Q St NW, Washington (20009). Phone 202/265-7258; fax 202/265-5488. www.raku/dc.com.* Pan-Asian menu. Lunch, dinner. Closed Thanksgiving, Dec 25. Bar. Outdoor seating. **$$**

★★★ **RED SAGE.** *605 14th St NW, Washington (20005). Phone 202/638-4444; fax 202/628-8430. www.redsage.com.* The flavors of colors of the vibrant Southwest come to the Northeast at Red Sage, one of DC's trendiest and liveliest venues. Political movers and shakers, media magnates, and the like crowd into Red Sage nightly to relax and wind down with chilly, potent margaritas, and fiery new-wave fare that incorporates the robust chile-centric ingredients of the American Southwest. This is a perfect spot for dinner with friends who crave heat, and the scene, with dinner. American menu. Lunch, dinner. Closed holidays. Bar. Children's menu. Casual attire. Outdoor seating. **$$$**

★★★ **RESTAURANT NORA.** *2132 Florida Ave NW, Washington (20008). Phone 202/462-5143; fax 202/234-6232. www.noras.com.* Organic seasonal ingredients, many purchased from local family farms, are the stars of this intimate, former 19th-century grocery store turned organic American eatery. Chef/owner Nora Pouillon is a pioneer in the organic movement; Restaurant Nora was the first certified organic restaurant in the country (95 percent of the products used are organic). And it's not only the purity of the edible ingredients that is attended to—all the water used at Nora is filtered three times on premises, including the water that washes your dishes and is used for cooking. While Nora's focuses on healthful cooking, this is not flavorless spa cuisine. Pouillon coaxes intense flavors from nature's superstar ingredients, creating stylish, delicious meals that integrate accents from places far and near—from the American South to Spain, and from Latin America to Asia and India. (If you're looking for a soy burger on spelt bread, this is not the place.) The mouthwatering and imaginative menu changes daily and includes a selection of starters, main-course salads, and entrées, as well as two tasting menus. The rustic dining room is decorated with dried flowers and museum-quality antique Mennonite and Amish quilts. Soothing amber lighting warms the room, and Nora's wonderful food warms the tummy. Continental menu. Dinner. Closed Sun; holidays; also late Aug-early Sept. Bar. **$$$**

★★★ **SAM AND HARRY'S.** *1200 19th St NW, Washington (20036). Phone 202/296-4333; fax 202/785-1070. www.samandharrys.com.* Steak menu. Lunch, dinner. Closed Sun; holidays. Bar. Casual attire. Reservations recommended. Valet parking. **$$$**

★★ **SEA CATCH.** *1054 31st St NW, Washington (20007). Phone 202/337-8855; fax 202/337-7159. www.seacatchrestaurant.com.* Seafood menu. Lunch, dinner. Closed Sun. Bar. Valet parking. Outdoor seating on a deck overlooking the historic Chesapeake and Ohio Canal. **$$$**

★★★ **SEASONS.** *2800 Pennsylvania Ave NW, Washington (20007). Phone 202/342-0444; fax 202/944-2076. www.fourseasons.com.* Enclosed in glass and tastefully decorated with deep armchairs, dark wood, fresh flowers, and a good dose of style, Seasons is the elegant flagship restaurant of the Four Seasons Hotel (see). The sophisticated American menu offers simple, elegant fare that makes this an ideal locale for a business meal. The kitchen is not trying to win awards for wild, far-out food. The dishes here will all be familiar, but even the most familiar foods can surprise you when they're prepared with the best ingredients, passion, and skill. To complement the classic menu, you can choose from old-world or North American wines, or an extensive selection of wines by the glass. For an afternoon delight, stop by the Garden Terrace for tea service with all the trimmings—scones with clotted cream, cucumber and watercress sandwiches with the crusts cut off, petit fours, chocolate-dipped strawberries, and assorted butter cookies. American menu. Breakfast, lunch, dinner, Sun brunch. Bar. Children's menu. Casual attire. Valet parking. Outdoor seating. **$$$**

★★ **SEQUOIA.** *3000 K St NW, Washington (20007). Phone 202/944-4200; fax 202/944-4210. www.arkrestaurants.com.* American menu. Lunch, dinner, Sun brunch. Bar. Casual attire. Outdoor seating. **$$**

★ **SUSHI-KO.** *2309 Wisconsin Ave NW, Washington (20007). Phone 202/333-4187; fax 202/333-7594. www.sushiko.us.* Japanese menu. Lunch, dinner. Closed July 4, Thanksgiving, Dec 25. Casual attire. **$$$**

★ ★ ★ **TABERNA DEL ALABARDERO.** *1776 I St NW, Washington (20006). Phone 202/429-2200; fax 202/775-3713. www.alabardero.com.* The joyousness of this restaurant (a favorite of DC celebrities for birthdays) is only matched by the highly skilled staff. Spanish, Mediterranean menu. Lunch, dinner. Closed Sun; holidays. Bar. Casual attire. Outdoor seating. **$$$**

★ ★ ★ **TEATRO GOLDONI.** *1909 K St NW, Washington (20006). Phone 202/955-9494; fax 202/955-9594. www.teatrogoldoni.com.* This restaurant serves innovative, complex Venetian dishes. Italian menu. Lunch, dinner. Closed Sun; holidays. Bar. Casual attire. Valet parking. **$$$**

★ **THAI KINGDOM.** *2021 K St NW, Washington (20006). Phone 202/835-1700; fax 202/466-4147.* Thai menu. Lunch, dinner. Closed holidays. Bar. **$$**

★ **THE TOMBS.** *1226 36th St NW, Washington (20007). Phone 202/337-6668; fax 202/337-1541. www.clydes.com.* Did someone say "Rah"? Since 1962, this classic sports-themed bar and grill has been dear to the hearts of Georgetown University students, faculty, and alums—raucously dear to them when GU teams have a home game or are playing on TV. Vintage sporting prints and rowing paraphernalia contribute to the ambience. You'll find burgers, pizza, and other bar standards on the menu, as well as desserts (and a good wine list) from the restaurant upstairs, 1789 (see). American menu. Lunch, dinner, Sun brunch. Closed Thanksgiving, Dec 24-25. Bar. **$$**

★ **TONY AND JOE'S SEAFOOD PLACE.** *3000 K St NW, Washington (20007). Phone 202/944-4545; fax 202/944-4587. www.tonyandjoes.com.* Seafood menu. Lunch, dinner, late-night, Sun brunch. Closed Dec 25. Bar. Casual attire. Outdoor seating. **$$$**

★ ★ **TWO QUAIL.** *320 Massachusetts Ave NE, Washington (20002). Phone 202/543-8030; toll-free 800/543-8030; fax 202/543-8035. www.twoquail.com.* Eclectic/International menu. Lunch, dinner. Closed holidays. Casual attire. Reservations recommended. Outdoor seating. **$$**

★ ★ ★ **VIDALIA.** *1990 M St NW, Washington (20036). Phone 202/659-1990; fax 202/223-8572. www.vidaliadc.com.* Chef/owner Jeffrey Buben, taking his lead from the South as well as from the Chesapeake Bay area, transforms regional cuisine into a delectable art. Southern/Soul menu. Lunch, dinner. Closed holidays; Sun in July, Aug. Bar. Children's menu. Casual attire. **$$$**

★ ★ ★ **WILLARD ROOM.** *1401 Pennsylvania Ave NW, Washington (20004). Phone 202/637-7440; fax 202/637-7326. www.washington.interconti.com.* Located in the Willard InterContinental Washington hotel (see), The Willard Room may look familiar to you if you've seen the Steven Spielberg film *Minority Report*—a scene was filmed in the restaurant. But you needn't be Tom Cruise on a mission to enjoy a meal at this sophisticated Victorian-style dining room. An eclectic American menu that changes with the seasons is offered at lunch and dinner. Spa selections are popular choices for those on a waistline-preservation plan; these dishes are marked with an asterisk to indicate that they are lower in fat, cholesterol, and sodium. Those who have no interest in anything labeled "Spa," unless it means a massage, will be fine with the menu's other choices—innovative takes on fish, shellfish, game, lamb, beef, and poultry prepared with a French flair. In addition to dessert, the restaurant offers an after-dinner cheese course for those who are extremely anti-spa. The Willard Room also houses a wonderful selection of wines from France and Italy, as well as new-world bottles from Australia and North America. Another perk is the classic cocktail list that adds to the old-world charm of dining here. *Secret Inspector's Notes: This restaurant has been (and continues to be) a hotbed of politicos. You'll feel as if coalitions are being formed around you as you glance from table to table.* American menu. Breakfast, lunch, dinner. Closed Sun. Bar. Jacket required. Reservations recommended. Valet parking. **$$$$**

★ **ZED'S ETHIOPIAN CUISINE.** *1201 28th St NW, Washington (20007). Phone 202/333-4710; fax 202/333-1085. www.zeds.net.* Ethiopian menu. Lunch, dinner. Closed Thanksgiving, Dec 25. Silverware provided at customer's request; communal dining from trays. **$$**

West Virginia

The wild, rugged topography that made settlement of this area difficult in the early days has today made West Virginia a paradise for outdoor enthusiasts. The state's ski industry has taken advantage of the highest total altitude of any state east of the Mississippi River by opening several Alpine and Nordic ski areas. Outfitters offer excellent whitewater rafting on the state's many turbulent rivers. Rock climbing, caving, and hiking are popular in the Monongahela National Forest, and West Virginia also boasts an impressive state park system, as well as extensive hunting and fishing areas.

Population: 1,808,344
Area: 24,078 square miles
Elevation: 240-4,863 feet
Peak: Spruce Knob (Pendleton County)
Entered Union: June 20, 1863 (35th state)
Capital: Charleston
Motto: Mountaineers Are Always Free
Nickname: Mountain State
Flower: Rhododendron
Bird: Cardinal
Tree: Sugar Maple
Fair: August in Lewisburg
Time Zone: Eastern
Web site: www.state.wv.us
Fun Facts:

- Nearly 75 percent of West Virginia is covered by forests.
- West Virginia was the first state to have sales tax. It became effective July 1, 1921.

The nickname "Mountain State" gives only a hint of West Virginia's scenic beauty, which is unsurpassed in the East. West Virginia is also a land of proud traditions, with many festivals held throughout the year as tributes to the state's rich heritage. These events include celebrations honoring the state's sternwheel riverboat legacy, its spectacular autumn foliage, and even its strawberries, apples, and black walnuts.

The occupation of West Virginia began with the Mound Builders, a prehistoric Ohio Valley culture that left behind at least 300 conical earth mounds that challenge the imagination. Many have been worn away by erosion, but excavations in some have revealed elaborately adorned human skeletons and artifacts of amazing beauty and utility.

Pioneers who ventured into western Virginia in the 18th century found fine vistas and forests, curative springs, and beautiful rivers. George Washington and his family frequented the soothing mineral waters of Berkeley Springs (see), and White Sulphur Springs (see) later became a popular resort among the colonists. But much of this area was still considered "the wild West" in those days, and life here was not easy.

The Commonwealth of Virginia largely ignored its western citizens—only one governor was elected from the western counties before 1860. When the counties formed their own state during the Civil War, it was the result of many years of strained relations with the parent state. The move had been debated over the years and the war finally provided the opportunity the counties needed to break away from Virginia. Although many sentiments in the new state remained pro-South, West Virginia's interests were best served by staying with the Union.

The first land battle of the Civil War took place in the western counties (see PHILIPPI) soon after Fort Sumter was fired upon in April 1861. Through the rest of 1861 and into 1862, Union forces under Generals George McClellan and William S. Rosecrans chased the Confederates back toward rebel Virginia. Succeeding battles were fought farther and farther south until major Confederate

Calendar Highlights

May

Vandalia Gathering *(Charleston). Phone 304/344-5075.* A festival of traditional arts; craft demonstrations, clogging, gospel music, fiddling, banjo picking, special exhibits.

Webster Springs Woodchopping Festival *(Webster Springs).* Southeastern World Woodchopping Championships; state championship turkey calling contest, draft horse pull, horse show, fireman's rodeo; arts and crafts, music, parades, concessions.

June

Mountain Heritage Arts and Crafts Festival *(Harpers Ferry). Phone 304/725-2055 or toll-free 800/624-0577.* More than 190 craftspeople and artisans demonstrate quilting, wool spinning, pottery throwing, vegetable dyeing, and other crafts; concerts. Also in Sept.

July

Jamboree in the Hills *(Wheeling). Phone toll-free 800/828-3097.* A four-day country music festival featuring more than 30 hours of music; top country stars. Camping is available.

August

State Fair *(Lewisburg). Fairgrounds. Phone 304/645-1090.* Exhibitors from a number of other states; horse shows, harness racing.

September

Sternwheel Regatta Festival *(Charleston). Phone 304/348-6419.* Sternwheel and towboat races, parades, contests, hot air balloon race, fireworks; nationally known entertainers nightly; arts and crafts.

Stonewall Jackson Heritage Arts and Crafts Jubilee *(Weston). Jackson's Mill State 4-H Conference Center. Phone 304/269-1863.* Mountain crafts, music, dance, and food.

October

Bridge Day *(Fayetteville). New River Gorge Bridge. Contact Fayetteville Chamber of Commerce, phone 304/465-5617.* Bridge is opened to pedestrians; parachutists test their skills by jumping off the bridge and floating to the bottom of the gorge.

Mountain State Forest Festival *(Elkins). Some events on campus of Davis & Elkins College. Phone 304/636-1824.* Queen Silvia is crowned; carnival, parades, entertainment, tilting at rings on horseback, sawing and woodchopping contests, marksmanship tests, State Championship Fiddle and Banjo Contest, juried craft fair and art exhibit.

resistance became impossible. For the rest of the war, Confederate Army activity in the state was limited to destructive lightning raids designed to wreck railroad lines and damage Union supply sources.

The war left West Virginia a new state, but like other war-ravaged areas, it had suffered heavy losses of life and property. The recovery took many years. West Virginians eventually rebuilt their state; new industry was developed, railroads were built, and resources like coal, oil, and natural gas brought relative prosperity.

West Virginia continues to be an important source of bituminous coal and a major producer of building stone, timber, glass, and chemicals. The state is also the home of such technological wonders as the National Radio Astronomy Observatory (see MARLINTON), where scientists study the universe via radio telescopes, and the New River Gorge Bridge (see GAULEY BRIDGE), the world's longest steel span bridge.

When to Go/Climate

West Virginia summers are hot and humid, although temperatures in elevated areas rarely top 90° F. Snowfall can range from 10-15 feet in some areas.

AVERAGE HIGH/LOW TEMPERATURES (° F)

Charleston

Jan 41/23	**May** 76/52	**Sept** 79/57
Feb 45/26	**June** 83/60	**Oct** 68/44
Mar 57/35	**July** 86/64	**Nov** 57/36
Apr 67/43	**Aug** 84/63	**Dec** 46/28

Elkins

Jan 38/16	**May** 71/44	**Sept** 74/50
Feb 41/18	**June** 78/52	**Oct** 64/37
Mar 52/27	**July** 80/57	**Nov** 53/30
Apr 62/35	**Aug** 79/56	**Dec** 43/21

Parks and Recreation

Water-related activities, hiking, riding, various other sports, picnicking and visitor centers, as well as camping, are available in many state parks. There is a small fee for swimming and game court use. Campgrounds with picnic facilities are available in 22 state parks and forests; all have drinking water and sanitary facilities; some have showers, coin laundries, utility hookups; 2-week limit; $6-$14/night for 6 persons or less, $1 each additional person. Camping season runs from mid-April-October in all parks except Canaan Valley and Pipestem resorts, which are open year-round. Campground reservations may be made at Babcock, Beech Fork, Blackwater Falls, Bluestone, Canaan Valley Resort, Cedar Creek, Chief Logan, Holly River, North Bend, Pipestem Resort, Stonewall Jackson Lake, Tomlinson Run, Twin Falls Resort, Tygart Lake, and Watoga state parks and at Greenbrier and Kanawha state forests. There is a $5 handling fee; reservations must be made 7-14 days in advance. Camping at all other state parks is on a first-come, first-served basis. Pets on leash only. Many cabins and lodges are available for seasonal or year-round use; seven-day minimum from the second Monday in June-Labor Day. Most parks are open daily, 8 am-sunset. For information and reservations contact individual parks or phone 800/225-5982 (except AK and HI).

FISHING AND HUNTING

In addition to a million acres of prime federal hunting and fishing land, West Virginia has 48 wildlife management areas. Nonresident statewide fishing license $30; three-day license $5. Nonresident (except KY, OH, PA) hunting, basic license $100; archery deer, muzzleloader deer, and turkey stamps $30; six-day, small-game license $20. Nonresident migratory waterfowl stamp $5. A conservation stamp is required in addition to all regular hunting and fishing licenses (nonresident $5). For further information, contact the Division of Natural Resources, Wildlife Resources Section, State Capitol Complex, Building 3, Charleston 25305. Phone 304/558-2771.

Driving Information

Children under 9 must be in an approved passenger restraint anywhere in vehicle; ages 3-8 may use a regulation safety belt; children under 3 years must use an approved safety seat. For more information, phone 304/746-2121.

INTERSTATE HIGHWAY SYSTEM

The following alphabetical listing of West Virginia towns in this book shows that these cities are within 10 miles of the indicated interstate highways. Check a highway map for the nearest exit.

Highway Number	Cities/Towns within 10 Miles
Interstate 64	Beckley, Charleston, Huntington, Lewisburg, Nitro, White Sulphur Springs.
Interstate 70	Wheeling.
Interstate 77	Charleston, Parkersburg, Princeton, Ripley.
Interstate 79	Charleston, Clarksburg, Fairmont, Morgantown, Sutton.
Interstate 81	Martinsburg.

Additional Visitor Information

Travel materials, including information on accommodations, skiing, caving, rock climbing, whitewater rafting, and other activities, are available from the West Virginia Division of Tourism, State Capitol Complex, 2101 Washington St E, Charleston 25305. Phone 800/225-5982. The Information & Education Section, Department of

Natural Resources, State Capitol, Charleston 25305, publishes a monthly magazine, *Wonderful West Virginia.*

Information on hiking along the completed portion of the Allegheny Trail, including a hiking guide (fee), is available from the West Virginia Scenic Trails Association, 633 West Virginia Ave, Morgantown 26505. The trail runs north-south from the Pennsylvania state line near Coopers Rock State Forest to Peters Mountain, SE of Lindside, at the Virginia state line.

There are several welcome centers in West Virginia; visitors who stop by will find information and brochures most helpful in planning stops at points of interest. Locations are as follows: on I-64, westbound near White Sulphur Springs and eastbound near Huntington; on I-81, southbound by the West Virginia/Maryland border and northbound near the West Virginia/Virginia border; on I-79, southbound north of Morgantown; on I-77, southbound near Mineral Wells; on I-70, westbound near the West Virginia/Pennsylvania border. The West Virginia Information Center is located at Harpers Ferry. All centers are open daily (closed Jan 1, Thanksgiving, Dec 25). Personnel at any of these locations will also assist visitors in making lodging reservations. In addition, information may be obtained at the Capitol Guides Desk in the rotunda of the State Capitol at Charleston (Memorial Day-Labor Day, Mon-Sat, also Sun afternoons).

CANYON COUNTRY-AROUND NEW RIVER GORGE

The New River, a twisted strand of tumbling water, has cut a deep and narrow gorge for more than 50 miles through the rugged mountains of southeastern West Virginia. Rafting enthusiasts consider the New to be one of the best whitewater rivers in the nation. It's also very pretty to look at while standing on a cliff's edge high above. This two-day, 300-mile scenic drive out of Charleston, which circles the gorge, provides plenty of scenic viewing opportunities. At the same time, the tour offers a look at the state's coal-mining heritage. At the turn of the century King Coal rules the gorge, and at one time two dozen coal-mining towns prospered on the banks of the New. Now, much of the gorge is protected as the New River Gorge National River. From Charleston, head east on Highway 60, following the old Midland Trail up the Kanawha River. In the first few miles, the highway winds past industrial plants, which are interesting to see in their ugly strangeness. The mountain scenery begins in about 30 miles at Gauley Bridge, where the New flows into the Kanawha. Here, as the New begins to display whitewater turbulence, the road climbs steeply and you spot the first of many waterfalls spilling from overhead. One of finest gorge views is just ahead at Hawk's Nest State Park, which has a 31-room lodge at cliff's edge. A steep hiking trail down to the river provides a chance to stretch your legs. About 25 minutes on, detour south on Highway 19 to the Canyon rim Visitor Center, which provides information about the park and the region. You also get a good look at the New River Gorge Bridge, one of the highest bridges in the country. Linking the north and south rims of the gorge, it has become famous for its once-a-year parachute jumps in October. Dozens of parachutists leap from its concrete safety barriers and float 876 feet to the river sandbar below. A stairway takes you partway down the cliff for more river and bridge views. Continue east on Highway 60 to Route 41, where you again detour south (right) to Babcock State Park to see its old stone gristmill and to try its hiking trails. Back on Highway 60, head east to Route 20 south to Hinton, a picturesque riverfront town. A river-level road leads to view of Sandstone Falls on the New. You can stay in Hinton or continue south on Route 20 to Pipestem Resort State Park, a 4,000-acre preserve with a 113-room lodge and an 18-hole golf course. From Pipestem, double back on Route 20 to Route 3 west to Highway 19 north to Beckley. Here you can ride a coal car deep into the Beckley Exhibition Coal Mine. From Beckley, take Route 61 north to Glen Jean and then head east on Route 25 to Thurmond, a former riverside mining boom town. The still-active train tracks run down the main street next to the sidewalk. An Amtrak station doubles as a railroad museum. Return to Route 61 north to I-64/I-77 and back to Charleston. **(Approximately 300 miles)**

Spruce Knob/Monongahela High Country

In the big cities of the Mid-Atlantic, it is sometimes hard to believe that there is a vast and rugged mountain wilderness just to the west. You can find plenty of this unspoiled nature in West Virginia, where soaring mountain ridges stretch into the distance and countless splashing streams beckon. This one-day, 150-mile loop out of the pretty college town of Elkins takes you through some of the Mid-Atlantic's most scenic mountain terrain. The route crisscrosses 100,000-acre Spruce Knob-Seneca Rocks National Recreation Area in the Monongahela National Forest. From Elkins, take Hwy 250 south through the national forest to Thornwood. Mile after mile, the road climbs and dips alongside splashing streams. At Thornwood, head north on Route 28 toward Riverton. Two miles south of Riverton, turn west (left) onto Forest Service Road 112 and follow the signs to Spruce Knob, about 15 miles. At an altitude of 4,861 feet, Spruce Knob is the state's loftiest mountain peak—although peak isn't really an apt description. The summit is a broad, oddly flat plateau scattered with piles of age-smoothed rocks. A thin forest of red spruce, stunted by the strong and nearly constant westerly winds, struggles for a foothold. This is one of the most remote and rugged areas of the Mid-Atlantic that can be reached in a passenger sedan. A rock-lined trail leads to the Observation Tower, a three-story stone structure that boosts sightseers above the trees for a majestic 360-degree panorama. Return to Route 28 and continue north to Seneca Rocks, a slender 900-foot-high forested ridge favored by rock climbers. You can watch them from the Discovery Center or take the easier 1 1/2-mile trail to the summit. Pause for snacks or lunch at Harper's Old Country Store. To continue, head west on Route 55 to Harmon and pick up Route 32 north to Davis. The road passes alongside 6,000-acre Canaan Valley Resort State Park, where you can stop to hike, bicycle, or go for a swim in the outdoor pool. A year-round resort, the park operates a downhill skiing complex. In summer, the chairlift will carry you to the top for grand views. About 15 miles long and 3 miles wide, the valley is situated at an altitude of 3,200 feet, which all but guarantees moderate summer temperatures. Just to the north, the town of Davis has become a major center for mountain biking, mostly on abandoned US Forest Service roads. Outfitters offer rentals and maps. On the edge of Davis, turn left into Blackwater Falls State Park, a rumpled expanse of woodland ridges and valleys cut by the impressively deep canyon of the Blackwater River. Motorists approach the park's 55-room lodge on a long, winding road that carries them deeper and deeper into the forest. Suddenly a clearing appears, revealing the lodge clinging to the precipitous edge of the canyon. The river races far below, the thunder of crashing whitewater clearly audible. Visitors can view the 65-foot plunge of Blackwater Falls from the canyon rim just upriver from the lodge or descend 214 steps to its base. In summer, the beach at little Pendleton Lake makes a refreshing rest stop. Continue north 2 miles to Thomas, an old mining town built in a double tier on a mountainside, and then return to Elkins on Hwy 219 south. **(Approximately 150 miles)**

Aurora (B-5)

See also Davis, Grafton

Settled 1787
Population 150
Elevation 2,641 ft
Area Code 304
Zip 26705

Located at the summit of Cheat Mountain, Aurora offers visitors clean air and high altitude.

What to See and Do

Cathedral State Park. *1 mile E on Hwy 50. Phone 304/735-3771. www.cathedralstatepark.com.* Hiking trails through 132 acres of deep, virgin hemlock forest; cross-country skiing, picnicking.

Beckley (D-3)

See also Gauley Bridge, Hinton

Founded 1838
Population 17,254
Elevation 2,416 ft
Area Code 304
Information Southern West Virginia Convention & Visitors Bureau, PO Box 1799, 25802; phone 304/252-2244 or toll-free 800/VISIT-WV
Web site www.visitwv.org

The "smokeless coal capital of the world" is a center for more than 200 small mining and farming towns. Beckley is situated on a high plateau surrounded by fertile valleys. During the Civil War the village was held at various times by both armies; Union troops shelled it in 1863. Coal was found here in 1774 but was not mined until 1890. Smokeless coal became the standard bunker fuel during World War I, and the demand continued for years thereafter. Beckley now serves as a commercial, medical, and tourist center.

What to See and Do

Babcock State Park. *13 miles NE via Hwy 19 to Hwy 41, near Landisburg. Phone 304/438-3003; toll-free 800/225-5982.* More than 4,100 acres of rugged mountain scenery with trout stream and waterfalls, views of New River Canyon, rhododendrons (May-July); restored operating gristmill. Swimming pool, lake and stream fishing, boating (rowboat, paddleboat rentals); hiking trails, horseback riding, game courts (equipment rentals), cross-country skiing, camping (electrical hookups), 26 cabins (rentals, spring and fall). Nature and recreation programs (summer). (Mid-Apr-Oct)

Beckley Exhibition Coal Mine. *513 Ewart Ave, Beckley (25801). 1 1/2 miles SE off I-77, exit 44 on Ewart Ave in New River Park. Phone 304/256-1747.* Riding tours in coal cars through 1,500 feet of underground passageways, constant 56°F temperature; museum, coal company house, superintendent of coal mines' house, church, campground. (Apr-Oct, daily) **$$$$**

Grandview Unit of New River Gorge National River. *4700 Grandview Rd, Beckley (25813). 5 miles SE on Hwy 19, then 5 miles NE via Airport, Glen Hedrick and Grandview rds. Phone 304/763-3715.* Nearly 900 wooded acres at the northern end of the New River Gorge National River area (see HINTON); offers spectacular overlooks of New River Gorge and Horseshoe Bend; rhododendron gardens. Hiking trails, game courts (some fees), cross-country skiing, picnicking, playgrounds, and concession. Outdoor dramas (June-Labor Day, Tues-Sun).

Lake Stephens. *350 Lake Stephens Rd, Beckley (25801). W of town. Phone 304/934-5323.* A 303-acre lake with swimming, fishing, and boating, plus trailer camping (with hookups).

Plum Orchard Lake Wildlife Management Area. *11 miles N on I-77 to Pax exit, then E on Rural Rte 23. Phone 304/469-9905.* More than 3,200 acres with rabbit, grouse, squirrel hunting. Also a 202-acre lake with more than 6 miles of shoreline; boating; fishing for bass, channel catfish, crappie, and bluegill; picnicking, playground, camping.

Twin Falls Resort State Park. *Hwy 97, Mullens. 25 miles SW via Hwy 16 and Hwy 54, then W on Hwy 97, near Maben. Phone 304/294-4000.* Approximately 4,000 acres with restored pioneer house and farm. Swimming pool; hiking trails, 18-hole golf course, clubhouse, tennis, game courts, picnicking, playground, restaurant, lodge, camping, 14 cabins (equipment rentals). Recreation center, programs. (Daily)

Whitewater rafting. *New River Park. Phone 304/252-2244; toll-free 800/847-4898.* Many outfitters offer guided trips on the New and Gauley rivers. For a list of outfitters, contact the Southern West Virginia Convention & Visitors Bureau, PO Box 1799, 25802.

WinterPlace Ski Resort. *100 Old Flat Top Mountian Rd, Flat Top. 17 miles S via I-77, exit 28 (Ghent/Flat Top), follow signs. Phone 304/787-3221; toll-free 800/607-7669. www.winterplace.com.* On southern West Virginia's highest peak. Two quad, three triple, two double chairlifts; two surface lifts; ski school, rentals; snowmaking; snow-tubing; cafeteria, lounge; restaurants; entertainment; children's program; sporting goods shops. Night skiing. Twenty-seven runs; longest run 1 1/4 miles; vertical drop 603 feet. Snowboard park. (Dec-late Mar, daily) **$$$$**

Youth Museum of Southern West Virginia. *106 Adair St, Beckley (25801). Ewart Ave, in New River Park. Phone 304/252-3730.* Hands-on exhibits, planetarium, log house. (May-Labor Day: daily; rest of year: Tues-Sat) **$$**

Special Events

Appalachian Festival. *245 N Kanewha St, Beckley (25801). Phone 304/252-7328.* Exhibitions and demonstrations of native crafts; entertainment, food. Aug.

Theatre West Virginia. *4700 Grandview Rd, Beaver (25813). Cliffside Amphitheatre at Grandview Park, W on I-64, exit 129B. Phone 304/256-6800; toll-free 800/666-9142.* Outdoor musical dramas. Mid-June-mid-Aug.

Limited-Service Hotel

★ HAMPTON INN. *110 Harper Park Dr, Beckley (25801). Phone 304/252-2121; fax 304/255-6238. www.hamptoninn.com.* 108 rooms, 5 story. Complimentary continental breakfast. Check-in 2 pm, check-out noon. Fitness room. Outdoor pool. **$**

Berkeley Springs (B-7)

See also Martinsburg

Founded 1776
Population 735
Elevation 612 ft
Area Code 304
Zip 25411
Information Berkeley Springs-Morgan County Chamber of Commerce, 127 Fairfax St; phone 304/258-3738 or toll-free 800/447-8797
Web site www.berkeleysprings.com

Popularized by George Washington, who surveyed the area for Lord Fairfax in 1748, Berkeley Springs is the oldest spa in the nation. Fairfax later granted the land around the springs to Virginia. The town is officially named Bath, for the famous watering place in England, but the post office is Berkeley Springs. The waters, which are piped throughout the town, are fresh and slightly sweet, without the medicinal flavor of most mineral springs. Washington and his family returned again and again. The popularity of the resort reached its peak after the Revolutionary War, becoming something of a summer capital for Washingtonians in the 1830s. But like all resort towns, Berkeley Springs declined as newer, more fashionable spas came into vogue. The Civil War completely destroyed the town's economy. Today, the town is again visited for its healthful waters, spas, and charming downtown.

What to See and Do

Berkeley Springs State Park. *121 S Washington St (25411). Center of town. Phone 304/258-2711.* Famous resort with health baths of all types (fees); five warm springs. Main bathhouse (daily; closed holidays). Roman bathhouse with second-floor museum (Memorial Day-mid-Oct, daily). Swimming pool (Memorial Day-Labor Day, daily; fee).

Cacapon Resort State Park. *10 miles S off Hwy 522. Phone 304/258-1022.* More than 6,100 acres with swimming, sand beach, fishing, boating (rowboat and paddleboat rentals); hiking and bridle trails, horseback riding, 18-hole golf course, tennis, game

George Washington's Spa and Berkeley Springs

Tucked in a narrow, rock-shadowed valley along the Cacapon River, the little mountain community of Berkeley Springs has transformed itself into "Spa Town USA." A total of five separate spas employ more than 40 massage therapists—three times the number of practicing lawyers, town official claim. The clustering of so many spas in the town is relatively new, but Berkeley Springs has a long heritage as a spa destination. Well before white settlers arrived, Native Americans sought out the warm, 74.3-degree mineral springs. Still bubbling forth from the base of Warm Springs Ridge at 2,000 gallons per minute, the water was believed to have curative powers. George Washington, who first visited the springs in 1748 as a 16-year-old surveyor, returned nearly a dozen times in later years seeking health benefits. In 1776, he and prominent friends and family established the Town of Bath, intent on making it a popular spa, and the first bath houses were built. Because of this, Berkeley Springs claims to be "the country's first spa." You can explore the town's spa heritage in a 30-minute, half-mile stroll in Berkeley Springs State Park, which doubles as the community's town square. One of America's most curious public parklands, the 7-acre Berkeley Springs State Park operates year-round as a very affordable government-run spa. Begin a loop around the park at the large public swimming pool, fed by spring waters. Heading clockwise, take a peek inside the Main Bath House, where you can enjoy a private hot-tub soak and Swedish-style massage. Continue on to a stone-lined natural pool of flowing spring water, dubbed "George Washington's Bath Tub" in his honor. Move on to the Gentlemen's Spring House, where you are welcome to draw jugs of the famed drinking water for free. Conclude this plunge into historic bathing with a look into the Roman Bath House, where you can indulge in a private hot-tub soak without an accompanying message.

courts, cross-country skiing, picnicking, playground, concession, restaurant, lodge. No camping; 30 cabins. Nature, recreation programs. Nature center.

Sleepy Creek Wildlife Management Area. *1910 Sleepy Creek Rd, Berkley Springs (25427). 15 miles SE, E of Hwy 522. Phone 304/754-3855.* Approximately 23,000 acres of rugged forest offer wild turkey, deer, grouse, and squirrel hunting; boating and bass fishing on 205-acre lake; primitive camping (fee). Also 70 miles of hiking trails crossing two mountains, several valleys.

View from Prospect Peak. *On Hwy 9, near town.* Potomac River winds through what the National Geographic Society has called one of the nation's outstanding vistas.

Special Event

Apple Butter Festival. *304 Fairfax St, Berkeley Springs (25411). Phone toll-free 800/447-8797.* Crafts demonstrations, music, contests. Columbus Day weekend.

Limited-Service Hotels

★ ★ CACAPON RESORT STATE PARK. *818 Cacapon Dr, Berkeley Springs (25411). Phone 304/258-1022; fax 304/258-5323. www.cacaponresort.com.* 52 rooms, 3 story. Check-in 3 pm, check-out noon. Restaurant. Children's activity center. Golf, 18 holes. Tennis. **$**

★ SUPER 8. *118 Limestone Rd, Hancock (21750). Phone 301/678-6101; fax 301/678-5376. www.super8.com.* 50 rooms, 2 story. Complimentary continental breakfast. Check-in 3 pm, check-out noon. **$**

Full-Service Resort

★ ★ COOLFONT RESORT. *3621 Cold Run Valley Rd, Berkeley Springs (25411). Phone 304/258-4500; toll-free 800/888-8768; fax 304/258-5499. www.coolfont.com.* 19 rooms, 3 story. Check-in 4 pm, check-out 11 am. Complimentary full breakfast. Restaurant, bar. Children's activity center. Fitness room, spa. Indoor pool, whirlpool. Tennis. **$$**

Full-Service Inn

★★ THE INN & SPA AT BERKELEY SPRINGS. *207 S Washington St, Berkeley Springs (25411). Phone 304/258-2210; toll-free 800/822-6630; fax 304/258-3986. www.theinnandspa.com.* This colonial-style inn enjoys the healthful waters of the area and provides access for guests to mineral baths and spa. 68 rooms, 3 story. Complimentary continental breakfast. Check-in 3 pm, check-out 11 am. Restaurant, bar. Spa. Airport transportation available. **$**

Specialty Lodging

The following lodging establishment is approved by Mobil Travel Guide, but due to its unique and individualized nature has not been given a traditional Mobil Star rating. Included in this listing you may find bed-and-breakfasts, limited-service inns, guest ranches, and other unique hotel properties.

HIGHLAWN INN. *171 Market St, Berkeley Springs (25411). Phone 304/258-5700; toll-free 888/290-4163. www.highlawninn.com.* This Victorian-style manor, built in the late 1890s, has authentic furnishings and ornate fireplaces. The mineral bath waters of the area are an added feature. 12 rooms, 3 story. Children over 14 years only. Complimentary full breakfast. Check-in 2 pm, check-out noon. **$**

Bethany

See also Weirton, Wheeling

Population 985
Elevation 932 ft
Area Code 304
Zip 26032

What to See and Do

Bethany College. *1 Main St, Bethany (26032).* (1840) (800 students) Founded by Alexander Campbell, the leading influence in the 19th-century religious movement that gave rise to the Disciples of Christ, Churches of Christ, and Christian churches. Historic buildings on the 300-acre campus include Old Main, styled after the University of Glasgow in Scotland; Pendleton Heights, a 19th-century house used as the college president's residence; Old Bethany Meeting House (1852); Delta Tau Delta Founder's House (1854); and

Campbell Mansion. *Phone 304/829-7285.* A 24-room house where Campbell lived; antique furnishings. On property is hexagonal brick study, one-room schoolhouse, and smokehouse. The Campbell family cemetery, "God's Acre," is across from the mansion. (Apr-Oct: Tues-Sun; rest of year: by appointment) **$$**

Bluefield (E-3)

See also Princeton

Founded 1889
Population 11,451
Elevation 2,611 ft
Area Code 304
Zip 24701
Information Convention & Visitors Bureau, 500 Bland St, PO Box 4099; phone 304/325-8438 or toll-free 800/221-3206
Web site www.bluestonecvb.com

Named for the bluish chicory covering the nearby hills, Bluefield owes its existence to the Pocahontas Coal Field. The town came to life in the 1880s when the railroad came through to transport coal. This commercial and industrial center of southern West Virginia is known as nature's "air-conditioned city" because of its altitude—one-half mile above sea level. Bluefield has a sister city by the same name in Virginia, directly across the state line.

What to See and Do

Eastern Regional Coal Archives. *Craft Memorial Library, 600 Commerce St, Bluefield (24701). Phone 304/325-3943.* Center highlights the history of West Virginia coal fields; exhibits, photographs, mining implements; films, research material. (Mon-Fri afternoons; closed holidays) **FREE**

Panther State Forest. *50 miles NW off Hwy 52 near Panther. Phone 304/938-2252.* More than 7,800 acres of rugged hills. Swimming pool (Memorial Day-Labor Day), fishing; hunting, hiking trails, picnicking, playground, concession, camping.

Pinnacle Rock State Park. *PO Box 1, Bluefield (24715). 7 miles NW on Hwy 52. Phone 304/248-8565.* Approximately 250-acre park contains a 15-acre lake and interesting sandstone formations, which resemble a giant cockscomb. Hiking, picnicking.

Limited-Service Hotels

★ **EAST RIVER MOUNTAIN INN.** *3175 E Cumberland Rd, Bluefield (24701). Phone 304/325-5421; toll-free 888/613-9080; fax 304/325-6045.* 98 rooms, 2 story. Pets accepted, some restrictions; fee. Complimentary continental breakfast. Check-in 2 pm, check-out noon. Bar. Fitness room. Indoor pool, children's pool, whirlpool. **$**

★ ★ **HOLIDAY INN.** *3350 Big Laurel Hwy, Bluefield (24701). Phone 304/325-6170; toll-free 800/465-4329; fax 304/323-2451. www.holiday-inn.com.* 120 rooms, 2 story. Pets accepted, some restrictions. Check-in 2 pm, check-out noon. Restaurant, bar. Fitness room. Outdoor pool. **$**

Restaurant

★ **MAYFLOWER I.** *105 Hockman Pike, Bluefield (24605). Phone 540/322-4578.* American menu. Dinner. Closed Mon; holidays. Children's menu. Casual attire. **$$**

Buckhannon (C-4)

See also Elkins, Philippi, Weston

Settled 1770
Population 5,725
Elevation 1,433 ft
Area Code 304
Zip 26201
Information Buckhannon-Upshur Chamber of Commerce, 16 S Kanawha St, PO Box 442; 304/472-1722

What to See and Do

Audra State Park. *8 miles N on Hwy 119, then 6 miles E on Hwy 11. Phone 304/457-1162.* Approximately 360 acres offer swimming in a natural mountain stream surrounded by tall timber; bathhouse. Hiking trails, picnicking, playground, concession, tent and trailer camping.

Holly River State Park. *Webster Springs. 32 miles S of Buckhannon on Hwy 20. Phone 304/493-6353.* More than 8,100 acres and the second largest state park in the state. Camping, cabins, picnicking, hiking.

West Virginia State Wildlife Center. *Hwy 20 S, French Creek. 12 miles S on Hwy 4, 20. Phone 304/924-6211.* Fenced-in habitats of approximately 50 species of birds and animals native to West Virginia, including deer, elk, buffalo, timber wolf, mountain lion, and black bear. Loop walkway (1 1/4 miles). Trout pond; picnicking, concession. (May-Oct: daily; Apr and Nov: weekends and holidays only; Dec-Mar: days vary) **$**

West Virginia Wesleyan College. *59 College Ave, Buckhannon (26201). College Ave and Meade St. Phone 304/473-8000.* (1890) 1,600 students. An 80-acre campus featuring Georgian architecture. Wesley Chapel, the largest place of worship in the state, contains a Casavant organ with 1,474 pipes.

Special Event

West Virginia Strawberry Festival. *Phone 304/472-9036.* Parades, dances, exhibits, air show, arts and crafts, other activities. Usually the week before Memorial Day.

Limited-Service Hotels

★ **BICENTENNIAL MOTEL.** *90 E Main St, Buckhannon (26201). Phone 304/472-5000; toll-free 800/762-5137; fax 304/472-9159.* 45 rooms, 2 story. Pets accepted, some restrictions. Check-in 2 pm, check-out 11 am. Bar. Outdoor pool. **$**

★ **HAMPTON INN.** *1 Commerce Blvd, Buckhannon (26201). Phone 304/473-0900; fax 304/473-0900. www.hamptoninn.com.* 62 rooms. Complimentary continental breakfast. Check-in 2 pm, check-out noon. Fitness room. Indoor Pool. **$**

Charles Town (B-7)

See also Harpers Ferry, Martinsburg, Shepherstown; also see Winchester, VA

Founded 1786
Population 2,907
Elevation 530 ft
Area Code 304
Zip 25414
Information Jefferson County Chamber of Commerce, 201 Frontage Rd, PO Box 426; phone 304/725-2055
Web site www.jeffersoncounty.com/chamber

Charles Town is serene, aristocratic, and full of tradition, with orderly, tree-shaded streets and 18th-century houses. It was named for George Washington's youngest brother, Charles, who laid out the town and named most of the streets after members of his family. Charles Washington's family lived here for many years. Charles Town is also famed as the place where John Brown was jailed, tried, and hanged in 1859 after his antislavery raid on Harpers Ferry.

What to See and Do

Charles Town Races and Gaming. *Flowing Springs Rd, Rte 340 N, Charles Town. 1 mile E on Hwy 340. Phone 304/725-7001; toll-free 800/795-7001.* Thoroughbred racing; clubhouse, video machines, dining room. (Daily; closed holidays) **FREE**

Jefferson County Courthouse. *100 E Washington, Charles Town (25414). N George and E Washington sts. Phone 304/728-3240.* (1836) This red brick, Georgian colonial structure was the scene of John Brown's trial, one of three treason trials held in the US before World War II. The courthouse was shelled during the Civil War but was later rebuilt; the original courtroom survived both the shelling and fires and is open to the public. In 1922, leaders of the miners' armed march on Logan City were tried here; one, Walter Allen, was convicted and sentenced to ten years. (Mon-Fri; closed holidays) **FREE**

Jefferson County Museum. *200 E Washington, Charles Town (25414). N Samuel and E Washington sts. Phone 304/725-8628.* Houses John Brown memorabilia, old guns, Civil War artifacts. (Apr-Nov, Mon-Sat) **DONATION**

Site of John Brown Gallows. *S Samuel and Hunter sts, Charles Town.* Marked by a pyramid of three stones supposedly taken from Brown's cell in Charles Town jail. At the execution, 1,500 troops were massed around the scaffold. Some were commanded by Major Thomas "Stonewall" Jackson; among them was John Wilkes Booth, Virginia militiaman.

Tours of Charles Town. *Phone 304/728-7713.* Historical walking tours; candlelit tours of Jefferson County Courthouse (evenings); carriage rides. All tours by appointment. **FREE**

Zion Episcopal Church. *300 E Congress St, Charles Town (25414). E Congress between S Mildred and S Church sts. Phone 304/725-5312.* (1852) Buried in the cemetery around the church are about 75 members of the Washington family, as well as many Revolutionary War and Confederate soldiers. (Interior, by appointment)

Special Events

Founders Day-Washington Heritage. *Phone toll-free 800/733-5469.* Exhibits, performances, tours. First weekend in May.

Jefferson County Fair. *Fairgrounds, 3 miles W of Charles Town on Leetown Pike. Phone 304/728-7415. www.jeffersoncountyfair.org.* Livestock show, entertainment, amusement rides, exhibits. Late Aug.

Limited-Service Hotel

★★ TURF MOTEL. *608 E Washington St, Charles Town (25414). Phone 304/725-2081; toll-free 800/422-8873; fax 304/728-7605. www.turfmotel.com.* 45 rooms, 2 story. Pets accepted, some restrictions; fee. Check-in 2 pm, check-out 11:30 am. Restaurant. Outdoor pool. **$**

Charleston (D-3)

See also Nitro

Settled 1794
Population 53,421
Elevation 601 ft
Area Code 304
Information Convention & Visitors Bureau, Charleston Civic Center, 200 Civic Center Dr, 25301; phone 304/344-5075 or toll-free 800/733-5469
Web site www.charlestonwv.com

Charleston, the state capital, is the trading hub for the Great Kanawha Valley, where deposits of coal, oil, natural gas, and brine have greatly contributed to this region's national importance as a production center for chemicals and glass. Two institutions of higher learning, West Virginia State College and the University of Charleston, are located in the metropolitan area. Charleston is also the northern terminus of the spectacular West Virginia Turnpike.

Daniel Boone lived around Charleston until 1795. During his residence he was appointed a lieutenant colonel in the county militia in 1789 and was elected to the Virginia assembly the same year. The area became important as a center of salt production in 1824, when steam engines were used to operate brine pumps. After Charleston became the capital of West Virginia in 1885, following a dispute with Wheeling, the town came into its own. During World War I, an increased demand for plate and bottle glass, as well as for high explosives, made Charleston and the nearby town of Nitro (see) boom.

What to See and Do

Coonskin Park. *2000 Coonskin Dr, Charleston (25311). 3/4 mile N off Hwy 114. Phone 304/341-8000.* Recreation area includes swimming, fishing for bass and catfish, pedal boating; hiking trails, 18-hole golf, miniature golf, tennis. Picnicking, playground, concession. (Daily; closed Dec 25; some activities seasonal) Fees for activities.

Cultural Center. *1900 E Kanawha Blvd, Charleston (25305). Next to the state capitol, on Greenbrier St. Phone 304/558-0220.* The Center houses the Division of Culture and History and Library Commission; archives library (Mon-Sat); state museum; special events, changing exhibits. (Daily; closed holidays) **FREE** Also here is

Mountain Stage. *Phone 304/342-5757.* Live public radio show heard on stations nationwide; features jazz, folk, blues, and rock. Visitors may watch show; afternoon performances (Sun). **$$$**

Elk River Scenic Drive. Beautiful drive along the Elk River from Charleston northeast to Sutton (approximately 60 miles). Begins just north of town; take Hwy 119 NE to Clendenin, then Hwy 4 NE to Hwy 19 in Sutton.

Kanawha State Forest. *Loudendale Rd. 7 miles S off Hwy 119. Phone 304/558-3500.* Approximately 9,300 acres with a swimming pool, bathhouse (Memorial Day-Labor Day); hunting, hiking, interpretive trail for the disabled, horseback riding, cross-country skiing, picnicking, playground, concession, and camping.

State Capitol. *1900 E Kanawha Blvd, Charleston (25305). On river at E Kanawha Blvd between Greenbrier St and California Ave. Phone 304/558-4839; toll-free 800/225-5982.* (1932) One of America's most beautiful state capitols, the building was designed by Cass Gilbert in Italian Renaissance style. Within the gold-leaf dome, which rises 300 feet above the street, hangs a 10,080-piece, hand-cut imported chandelier weighing more than two tons. Guided tours available. (Mon-Fri, Sat afternoons) **FREE** Across the grounds is the

Governor's Mansion. *1716 Kanawha Blvd E, Charleston (25305). Phone 304/558-3809.* (1925) Beautiful Georgian structure of red Harvard brick with white Corinthian columns. Tours (Thurs and Fri; also by appointment). **FREE**

Sunrise Museum. *746 Myrtle Rd, Charleston (25314). Across South Side Bridge. Phone 304/344-8035.* On 16 acres of wooded grounds with gardens and trails, this art and science museum is housed in two historic mansions built by William MacCorkle, ninth governor of West Virginia. Guided tours by appointment. (Wed-Sun; closed holidays) **$$** Located here are

Art Museum. American paintings, graphics, and sculpture from the 19th and 20th centuries; rotating exhibits; films and lectures. **$$**

Science Museum. Exhibits in natural sciences and technology; planetarium, programs, lectures. Interactive exhibits, demonstrations. **$$**

West Virginia State College. *Rte 25 Barron Dr, Institute. 8 miles W via I-64 exit 50. Phone 304/766-3000.* (1891) (4,635 students) On campus are Davis Fine Arts Building with periodic exhibits (Mon-Sat; closed holidays); Asian art collection in library (daily; closed holidays); and East Hall (1895), formerly president's residence. Tours.

Whitewater rafting. *90 Mac Corkle Ave SW, Charleston (25303). Phone toll-free 800/225-5982.* Many outfitters offer guided rafting, canoeing, and fishing trips on the New and Gauley rivers. For a list of outfitters contact the West Virginia Division of Tourism, Research, and Development, 90 Mac Corkle Ave SW, South Charleston, WV 25303.

Special Events

Sternwheel Regatta Festival. *Phone 304/348-6419.* Sternwheeler and towboat races, parades, contests, hot-air balloon race, fireworks; nationally known entertainers nightly; arts and crafts. Late Aug-early Sept.

Vandalia Gathering. *1900 Kanawha Blvd E, Charleston (25305). Phone 304/558-0220.* A festival of traditional arts; craft demonstrations, clogging, gospel music, fiddling, banjo picking, special exhibits. Memorial Day weekend.

Limited-Service Hotels

★ COUNTRY INN & SUITES BY CARLSON. *105 Alex Ln, Charleston (25304). Phone 304/925-4300; fax 304/925-1500.* 64 rooms. Pets accepted. Check-in 3 pm, check-out noon. Fitness room. Indoor pool, whirlpool. **$**

★ HAMPTON INN. *1 Preferred Pl, Charleston (25309). Phone 304/746-4646; fax 304/746-4665. www.hamptoninn.com.* 104 rooms, 5 story. Complimentary continental breakfast. Check-in 2 pm, check-out noon. Fitness room. Indoor pool, whirlpool. Airport transportation available. Business center. **$**

★ HAMPTON INN. *1 Virginia St W, Charleston (25302). Phone 304/343-9300, fax 304/342-9393. www.hamptoninn.com.* 110 rooms, 5 story. Complimentary continental breakfast. Check-in 2pm, check-out noon. Fitness room. Indoor pool, whirlpool. Airport transportation available. Business center. **$**

★ HAWTHORN INN & SUITES. *107 Alex Ln, Charleston (25304). Phone 304/925-1171; fax 304/925-2252.* 67 rooms. Pets accepted. Complimentary continental breakfast. Check-in 3 pm, check-out noon. Fitness room. Indoor pool, whirlpool. **$**

★ ★ HOLIDAY INN. *600 Kanawha Blvd E, Charleston (25301). Phone 304/344-4092; fax 304/345-4847. www.holiday-inn.com.* 256 rooms, 11 story. Check-in 3 pm, check-out noon. High-speed Internet access. Two restaurants, two bars. Fitness room. Outdoor pool. Airport transportation available. Business center. **$**

★ HOLIDAY INN EXPRESS. *100 Çivic Center Dr, Charleston (25301). Phone 304/345-0600; fax 304/343-1322. www.charleston-holidayinn.com.* 196 rooms, 6 story. Pets accepted, some restrictions; fee. Complimentary continental breakfast. Check-in 3 pm, check-out noon. High-speed Internet access. Fitness room. Airport transportation available. **$**

★ SUPER 8 MOTEL. *1010 Washington St E, Charleston (25301). Phone 304/345-9779; fax 304/345-6120. www.super8.com.* 160 rooms. Complimentary continental breakfast. Check-in 3 pm, check-out noon. Outdoor pool. **$**

Full-Service Hotel

★ ★ ★ MARRIOTT CHARLESTON TOWN CENTER. *200 Lee St E, Charleston (25301). Phone 304/345-6500; fax 304/353-3722. www.marriott.com.* This hotel, which is conveniently located in the heart of downtown Charleston, offers many services and amenities. There are many recreational activities, restaurants, and shops in the immediate area. 347 rooms, 15 story. Pets accepted. Check-in 4 pm, check-out noon. High-speed Internet accesss. Two restaurants, bar. Fitness room. Indoor pool, whirlpool. Airport transportation available. Business center. **$**

Restaurants

★ ★ BLOSSOM DELI. *904 Quarrier St, Charleston (25301). Phone 304/345-2233; fax 304/345-4412.* Don't be fooled by the name. Although it operates as a New York-style deli during the day, at night it is transformed into a romantic French-style bistro. And if longevity is a criteria for success, they first opened their doors in 1930 as a deli/soda fountain and, according to locals, it just keeps getting better. American menu. Breakfast, lunch, dinner. Closed Sun; holidays. **$$**

★ ★ CHEF DAN'S. *222 Leon Sullivan Blvd, Charleston (25301). Phone 304/344-2433; fax 304/344-2446.* American, Italian menu. Lunch, dinner. Closed Sun; holidays. Bar. Children's menu. **$$**

★ ★ JOE FAZIO'S SPAGHETTI HOUSE. *1008 Bullitt St, Charleston (25301). Phone 304/344-3071.* Just five minutes from downtown, this restaurant has the feeling of Little Italy at its finest. Choose from one of four dining rooms where big portions of food are served in a casual, no-frills atmosphere. Italian menu. Dinner. Closed Mon; Jan 1, Easter, Dec 24-25. Children's menu. **$$**

★ ★ ★ **LAURY'S.** *350 MacCorkle Ave SE, Charleston (25314). Phone 304/343-0055.* Located downtown near the Kanawha River in the old C&O Railroad Depot, this continental restaurant has welcomed diners since 1979. The dining room is an elegant, charming space. American menu. Lunch, dinner. Closed Sun; holidays. Bar. **$$**

Chesapeake and Ohio Canal National Historical Park (C-8)

(See Maryland)

Clarksburg (B-4)

See also Fairmont, Grafton, Weston

Settled 1773
Population 16,743
Elevation 1,007 ft
Area Code 304
Zip 26301
Information Greater Bridgeport Conference & Visitors Center, 164 W Main St, Bridgeport 26330; phone 304/842-7272 or toll-free 800/368-4324
Web site www.bridgeport-clarksburg.com

In the heart of the West Virginia hills, Clarksburg is the trading center for an area of grading lands, coal mines, and oil and gas fields. The Criminal Justice Information Services Division of the FBI is located here. During the Civil War it was an important supply base for Union troops. The famous Civil War General "Stonewall" Jackson was born in Clarksburg in 1824. His statue stands before the courthouse.

What to See and Do

North Bend Rail Trail. *121 N Court St, Harrisville (26362). I-79, exit 119 to Hwy 50. Phone 304/643-2500; toll-free 800/899-6278.* Seventy-one miles of scenic countryside trails featuring 13 tunnels, numerous bridges, and several historic sites. Bike, hike, or horseback ride trail from nearby Wilsonburg to North Bend State Park (see PARKERSBURG). **FREE**

Salem International University. *223 W Main St, Salem (26426). 12 miles W. Phone 304/782-5011. www.salemiu.edu.* (1888) (750 students) On campus is the Jennings Randolph Center (by appointment; fee), which houses papers and memorabilia of the former senator. Also here is

> **Fort New Salem.** *Phone 304/782-5245.* A collection of 20 log houses from throughout the state were relocated to the campus; pioneer history is re-created through crafts and folklore. Special events throughout the year (fee); summer concerts (July, Sat evenings). (Memorial Day weekend-Oct: Wed-Sun; Apr-mid-May: Mon-Fri) **$$**

Stealey-Goff-Vance House. *123 W Main St, Clarksburg (26301). Phone 304/842-3073.* (1807) House restored by Harrison County Historical Society as a museum with period rooms, antique furniture, tools, and Native American artifacts. (May-Sept, Fri, limited hours) **$**

Watters Smith Memorial State Park. *Rural Rte 1, Duck Creek Rd, Lost Creek. 8 miles S on Hwy 19, then SE on unnumbered road. Phone 304/745-3081.* More than 500 acres on Duck Creek with visitor center/museum and 19th-century pioneer homestead. Swimming pool (seasonal); hiking, game courts, picnicking, playground, concession. Recreation building.

Special Event

West Virginia Italian Heritage Festival. *309 Clark St, Clarksburg (26301). Phone 304/622-7314.* Italian arts, music, contests, entertainment. Labor Day weekend.

Limited-Service Hotels

★ ★ **HOLIDAY INN.** *100 Lodgeville Rd, Bridgeport (26330). Phone 304/842-5411; fax 304/842-7258. www.holiday-inn.com.* 158 rooms, 2 story. Pets accepted. Check-in 3 pm, check-out noon. Restaurant, bar. Outdoor pool. Airport transportation available. **$**

★ **SUTTON INN.** *250 Emily Dr, Clarksburg (26301). Phone 304/623-2600; toll-free 866/726-2322; fax 304/622-5240.* 112 rooms, 2 story. Complimentary continental breakfast. Check-in 3 pm, check-out noon. **$**

Restaurants

★★★ **JIM REID'S.** *1422 Buckhannon Pike, Nutter Fort (26301). Phone 304/623-4909; fax 304/623-5043.* A cheerful, dedicated Margaret Reid still presides over her late husband's namesake establishment that has welcomed diners for over 32 years. The expanded, small-town dining room now boasts more space and a charming fireplace. Seafood, steak menu. Lunch, dinner. Closed Mon; holidays. Bar. Children's menu. **$$$**

★★ **MINARD'S SPAGHETTI INN.** *813 E Pike St, Clarksburg (26301). Phone 304/623-1711.* Italian menu. Lunch, dinner. Closed holidays. Bar. Children's menu. Casual attire. **$$**

Davis (C-5)

See also Aurora, Elkins

Founded 1883
Population 624
Elevation 3,099 ft
Area Code 304
Zip 26260
Information West Virginia Mountain Highlands, PO Box 1456, Elkins 26241; phone 304/636-8400

Davis, the highest town in the state, was founded by Henry Gassaway Davis, US senator from 1871 to 1883. Senator Davis established the first night train in America (1848). He and his son-in-law, Senator Stephen B. Elkins, became wealthy from coal, lumber, and railroading.

What to See and Do

Blackwater Falls State Park. *County Rte 29, Davis. 2 miles W off Hwy 32. Phone 304/259-5216. www.blackwaterfalls.com.* This 1,688-acre park includes a deep river gorge with 66-foot falls of dark, amber-colored water. Swimming in lake (fee), bath houses (Memorial Day-Labor Day), fishing, boating (rowboat, paddleboat rentals); nature trails, horseback riding; cross-country ski trails, center (rentals, school); sledding, picnicking, playground, concession, lodge, cabins, tent and trailer campground. Nature, recreation programs and tours. Paved falls viewing area for the disabled.

Canaan Valley Resort State Park. *Hwy 32, Davis (26260). Phone 304/866-4121; toll-free 800/622-4121. www.canaanresort.com.* Quad, two triple chairlifts, Pomalift; patrol, school, SKIwee program, rentals; snowmaking; restaurant, cafeteria; lodging, nursery; night skiing (Fri-Sun). Twenty-two trails, 34 slopes; vertical drop 850 feet. (Dec-Mar, daily) 18 miles of cross-country trails. Chairlift rides (early May-Oct, daily). Special programs for the disabled. **$$$$**

Timberline Four Seasons Resort. *Hwy 32, Davis (26260). 8 miles S off Hwy 32. Phone 304/866-4801; toll-free 800/766-9464. www.timberlineresort.com.* Triple, two double chairlifts; patrol, school, SKIwee program, rentals; snowmaking; restaurant, bar; nursery; lodging, night skiing and special events. Thirty-five slopes and trails; longest run 2 miles, vertical drop 1,000 feet. (Dec-Apr, daily) cross-country skiing. Chairlift rides (July-Oct, Sat-Sun, also Mon holidays). **$$$$**

White Grass Touring Center. *Freeland Rd, Davis (26260). 9 miles S on Hwy 32 to Freeland Rd; 1/2 mile N of Canaan Valley Resort State Park. Phone 304/866-4114. www.whitegrass.com.* Thirty-six miles of cross-country trails, some machine-groomed; patrol, school, rentals; snowfarming; restaurant; telemark slopes, guided tours. (Late Nov-Mar, daily) **$$$**

Whitewater rafting. *200 Sycamore St, Davis (26260). Phone toll-free 800/225-5982.* Many outfitters offer guided trips on the Cheat River. For a list of outfitters contact the West Virginia Division of Tourism, Research, and Development, 90 Mac Corkle Ave SW, South Charleston, WV 25303

Special Event

Tucker County Alpine Winter Festival. *William Ave and Fourth St, Davis (26260). Phone 304/866-4121.* Governor's Cup ski races. First weekend in Mar.

Limited-Service Hotel

★★ **ALPINE LODGE.** *Williams Ave, Davis (26260). Phone 304/259-5245; fax 304/259-5168.* 46 rooms, 2 story. Check-out 11 am. Restaurant. Indoor pool. **$**

Full-Service Resorts

★ ★ **BLACKWATER LODGE.** *County Rte 29, Davis (26260). Phone 304/259-5216; toll-free 800/ 225-5982; fax 304/259-5881.* 80 rooms, 2 story. Lodge: Check-in 3 pm, check-out noon. Cabins: Check-in 4 pm, check-out 10 am. Restaurant. Children's activity center. Fitness room. Indoor pool, whirlpool. Tennis. All state park facilities available. **$**

★ ★ **CANAAN VALLEY RESORT AND CONFERENCE CENTER.** *Hwy 32, Davis (26260). Phone 304/866-4121; toll-free 800/622-4121; fax 304/866-2172. www.canaanresort.com.* Whether you visit in the winter or summer, this resort holds wonderful surprises for the young at heart. 256 rooms, 2 story. Check-in 4 pm, check-out 11 am. Restaurant. Children's activity center. Fitness room. Indoor pool, outdoor pool, whirlpool. Golf. Tennis. Naturalist program. **$**

Elkins (C-5)

See also Buckhannon, Davis, Philippi

Founded 1890
Population 7,032
Elevation 1,830 ft
Area Code 304
Zip 26241
Information West Virginia Mountain Highlands, PO Box 1456; phone 304/636-8400

Elkins was named for US Senator Stephen B. Elkins, an aggressive politician and powerful industrial magnate who was Secretary of War under Benjamin Harrison (1888-1892). This town is in a coal and timber region and is also a railroad terminus and trade center. Some of the finest scenery in the state can be seen in and around Elkins.

Seneca Rocks

Serious rock climbers rate West Virginia's massive Seneca Rocks as one of the top East Coast destinations for their sport. More than 375 major mapped climbing routes ascend the sheer, slender rocks that thrust 900 feet above the tumbling North Fork River. On any nice day you're apt to see a half-dozen or more climbers laboriously pulling themselves, hand over hand, slowly up the wall. It might take them hours to get to the top; you can enjoy the same view from the summit as they get, but without the effort. A 1-mile foot trail—rated only moderately difficult—zig zags to the top. Heavily traveled and well-marked, it is a non-climber's introduction to West Virginia's panoramic vistas. A notable West Virginia landmark, the dramatic rock formation is worth a visit simply as a scenic attraction. From the edge of the river, which tumbles in a fury of white water, a thickly forested ridge forms an imposing pedestal for the rocks. From this base, the twin towers seem to leap into the sky. They form a rough, craggy wall with a knife's-edge point barely 15 feet wide. Begin your ascent near the foot of the rocks at Seneca Rocks Discovery Center, a beautiful structure of stone and glass. Inside, exhibits detail the natural history of the rocks; outside, the deck is positioned for great views of the climbers. The hiker's trail to the top begins just across the river from the Discovery Center. It climbs steadily through shady woods. Sturdy benches are placed along the way if you need to rest. At several especially steep points, stone steps seem to stretch endlessly above, but that's only your imagination. From the summit overlooks, the view of the river-traced valley below is a generous reward for your pains. Give yourself an hour to reach the top, 30 minutes to enjoy your lofty perch, and another 30 minutes for the much easier descent. Afterward, cross the road (State Route 55) for refreshments in the village of Seneca Rocks at Harper's Old Country Store, which looks much as it must have on its opening day in 1902.

What to See and Do

Bowden National Fish Hatchery. *10 miles E on Old US 33. Phone 304/637-0238.* Produces brook, brown, and rainbow trout for stocking in state and national forest streams; also striped bass for Chesapeake Bay restoration project. Hatchery (daily). Visitor center (Memorial Day-mid-Oct, daily). **FREE**

The Old Mill. *WV 32, Harman. 25 miles E via US 33 to WV 32 N. Phone 304/227-4466.* (1877) A gristmill powered by water turbines rather than a waterwheel. It was also used for planing wood and for producing white flour. Today it still uses water power to grind corn, wheat, rye, and buckwheat. Observation hive has live bees. West Virginia crafts shop includes rug weaving. (Memorial Day-Labor Day, Mon-Sat) **DONATION**

Special Events

Augusta Festival. *100 Campus Dr, Elkins (26241). Phone 304/637-1209. On campus of Davis & Elkins College.* Celebration of traditional folk life and arts, featuring local and national performers, dances, juried craft fair, storytelling sessions, children's activities, and homemade foods. Mid-Aug.

Mountain State Forest Festival. *101 Lough St, Elkins (26241). Phone 304/636-1824. Some events on campus of Davis & Elkins College.* Queen Silvia is crowned; carnival, parades, entertainment, tilting at rings on horseback, sawing and woodchopping contests, marksmanship tests, State Championship Fiddle and Banjo Contest; juried craft fair and art exhibit. Late Sept-early Oct.

Limited-Service Hotels

★★ ELKINS MOTOR LODGE. *Harrison Ave, Elkins (26241). Phone 304/636-1400; toll-free 877/636-1863; fax 304/636-6318.* 55 rooms, 2 story. Pets accepted; fee. Check-out noon. Restaurant. Airport transportation available. **$**

★ SUPER 8. *350 Beverly Pike; Rte 219 S, Elkins (26241). Phone 304/636-6500; fax 304/636-6500. www.super8.com.* 44 rooms, 2 story. Pets accepted. Complimentary continental breakfast. Check-out 11 am. **$**

Specialty Lodging

The following lodging establishment is approved by Mobil Travel Guide but, due to its unique and individualized nature has not been given a traditional Mobil Star rating. Included in this listing you may find bed-and-breakfasts, limited-service inns, guest ranches, and other unique hotel properties.

THE WARFIELD HOUSE. *318 Buffalo St, Elkins (26241). Phone 304/636-4555; toll-free 888/636-4555. www.warfieldhousebandb.com.* The nearby attractions include Blackwater Falls State Park, Spruce Knob-Seneca Rocks Recreation Area, and the Cass Scenic Railroad. 5 rooms, 2 story. Children over 12 years only. Complimentary continental breakfast. Check-in 6 pm, check-out 11 am. **$**

Restaurant

★★ CHEAT RIVER INN. *Hwy 33 E, Elkins (26241). Phone 304/636-6265; fax 304/636-4495. www.cheatriverlodge.com.* Dinner. Closed Mon; holidays. Bar. Children's menu. Outdoor seating. Mounted fish on display. **$$**

Fairmont (B-5)

See also Clarksburg, Morgantown

Settled 1793
Population 19,097
Elevation 883 ft
Zip 26554
Information Convention & Visitors Bureau of Marion County, 110 Adams St, PO Box 58, 26555-0058; phone 304/368-1123 or toll-free 800/834-7365
Web site www.marioncvb.com

Fairmont was a Union supply depot plundered by Confederate cavalry in April 1863. General William Ezra Jones's division swept through town, took 260 prisoners, destroyed the $500,000 bridge across the Monongahela River, and raided the governor's residence. After the war, resources in the region were developed and coal became the mainstay. Today Fairmont manufactures aluminum, mine machinery, and other products.

What to See and Do

Fairmont State College. *1201 Locust Ave, Fairmont (26554). Phone 304/367-4000.* (1867) (7,000 students) On campus is a one-room schoolhouse with original desks, books, and other artifacts related to the early era of education (Apr-Oct, schedule varies).

Marion County Museum. *211 Adams St, Fairmont (26554). Adjacent to courthouse. Phone 304/367-5398.* Displays of B & O china, five furnished rooms covering 1776-1920s; doll, train, and toy collection. (Mon-Fri 10 am-2 pm; also Sat from Memorial Day-Labor Day; closed holidays) **FREE**

Prickett's Fort State Park. *I-79, exit 139, then 2 miles W. Phone 304/363-3030 (museum); toll-free 800/225-5982.* Approximately 200 acres with reconstructed 18th-century log fort, colonial trade and lifestyle demonstrations by costumed interpreters, outdoor historical drama (July, Wed-Sat). Boating (ramps); picnicking. Visitor center. Fort and museum (mid-Apr-Oct, daily). Museum (fee).

Special Event

Three Rivers Festival. *Palatine Park, Fairmont. Phone 304/363-2625.* Entertainment, parade, Civil War reenactment, carnival, games. Third weekend in May.

Limited-Service Hotels

★ COMFORT INN. *1185 Airport Rd, Fairmont (26554). Phone 304/367-1370; toll-free 800/228-5150; fax 304/367-1806. www.choicehotels.com.* 82 rooms, 2 story. Complimentary continental breakfast. Check-in 2 pm, check-out noon. Wireless Internet access. Fitness room. Outdoor pool. **$**

★★ HOLIDAY INN. *930 E Grafton, Fairmont (26554). Phone 304/366-5500; fax 304/363-3975. www.holiday-inn.com.* 106 rooms, 2 story. Pets accepted, some restrictions. Check-in 3 pm, check-out noon. Restaurant, bar. Outdoor pool. **$**

Restaurant

★★ MURIALE'S. *1742 Fairmont Ave, South Fairmont (26554). Phone 304/363-3190; fax 304/363-0828.* Italian menu. Lunch, dinner. Closed Dec 25. Bar. Children's menu. Casual attire. Outdoor seating. **$$**

Franklin (C-5)

See also Petersburg; also see Harrisonburg, VA

Settled 1794
Population 797
Elevation 1,731 ft
Area Code 304
Zip 26807
Information West Virginia Mountain Highlands, PO Box 1456, Elkins 26241; phone 304/636-8400

What to See and Do

Seneca Caverns. *Approximately 15 miles NW on Hwy 33 to Riverton, then 3 miles E. Phone 304/567-2691; toll-free 800/239-7647.* Caves contain magnificent stalagmites and stalactites; were used as a refuge by the Seneca people. (Daily) **$$$**

Special Event

Treasure Mountain Festival. *Phone 304/249-5422.* Square dancing, clogging; parade, gospel and mountain music, drama; rifle demonstration, cross-cut sawing contest; children's contests, games; trail rides craft exhibits, country food. Third weekend in Sept.

Gauley Bridge (D-4)

See also Beckley, Charleston, Summersville

Population 738
Elevation 680 ft
Area Code 304
Zip 25085
Information Upper Kanawha Valley Chamber of Commerce, PO Box 831, Montgomery 25136; phone 304/442-5756

This town at the junction of the New and Gauley rivers was the key to the Kanawha Valley during the Civil War. In November 1861 Union General W. S. Rosecrans defeated Confederate General John B. Floyd, a victory that assured Union control of western Virginia. Stone piers of the old bridge, which was destroyed by retreating Confederates in 1861, can be seen near the present bridge.

What to See and Do

Contentment Museum Complex. *7 miles E on Hwy 60, 1 mile E of Hawk's Nest State Park. Phone 304/658-5695.* (Circa 1830) Former residence of Confederate Colonel George W. Imboden contains original woodwork, period furniture, toy collection. Adjacent Fayette County Historical Society Museum features displays of Native American relics, local artifacts, Civil War items; restored one-room schoolhouse. (June-Aug: Mon-Sat; rest of year: by appointment) **$$**

Hawk's Nest State Park. *6 miles E on Hwy 60. Phone 304/658-5212.* Approximately 280 acres on Gauley Mountain, with fine views of New River Gorge from rocks 585 feet above the river. A 600-foot aerial tramway carries passengers to canyon floor. Swimming pool, fishing; hiking trails, tennis, picnic area, playground, concession, restaurant, lodge. Log museum with early West Virginia artifacts (May-Nov, daily; free).

New River Gorge Bridge. *Hwy 19, Lansing. 13 miles SE on Hwy 60, then 6 miles SW on Hwy 19, near Fayetteville. Phone 304/574-2115.* A masterpiece of engineering, this four-lane, single arch steel-span bridge rises 876 feet above the New River Gorge National River (see HINTON), making it the second-highest bridge in the US, and at 3,030 feet, the longest bridge of its type in the world. Just north of the bridge on Hwy 19 is the Canyon Rim Visitors Center (daily; closed Dec 25), providing two overlooks of the bridge and river, a 70-foot descending boardwalk, slide presentation, exhibits, and ranger-guided walks (May-Oct).

Whitewater rafting. *Phone toll-free 800/225-5982.* Many outfitters offer guided trips on the New and Gauley rivers. For a list of outfitters, contact the West Virginia Division of Tourism, Research, and Development, 90 Mac Corkle Ave SW, South Charleston 25303 or the Fayette County Chamber of Commerce, 310 Oyler Ave, Oak Hill 25901.

Special Event

Bridge Day. *New River Gorge Bridge. Phone 304/442-5756.* Bridge is opened to pedestrians; parachutists test their skills by jumping off the bridge and floating to the bottom of the gorge. Third Sat in Oct.

Limited-Service Hotel

★★ HAWKS NEST STATE PARK LODGE. *Rte 60, Ansted (25812). Phone 304/658-5212; toll-free 800/225-5982; fax 304/658-4549. www.hawksnestsp.com.* 31 rooms, 4 story. Check-in 3 pm, check-out noon. Restaurant. Children's activity center. Outdoor pool. Golf, 9 holes. Tennis. **$**

Grafton (B-5)

See also Aurora, Clarksburg, Fairmont, Morgantown, Philippi

Founded 1856
Population 5,489
Elevation 1,004 ft
Area Code 304
Zip 26354
Information Grafton-Taylor County Convention and Visitors Bureau, 214 W Main St, Room 205; phone 304/265-3938

Mother's Day started in Grafton in 1908 when Anna Jarvis observed the anniversary of her mother's death during a religious service. The idea caught on nationally, and in 1914 President Woodrow Wilson issued a proclamation urging nationwide observance. The International Shrine to Motherhood in the original Mother's Day church is located at 11 East Main Street.

During the Civil War Grafton was an important railroad center; 4,000 Union troops camped here before the Battle of Philippi in 1861. General McClellan also had his headquarters in the town. The first land soldier killed in the war, T. Bailey Brown, fell at Grafton. He is buried in the Grafton National Cemetery.

What to See and Do

Tygart Lake State Park. *2 miles S off Hwys 119, 250. Phone 304/265-3383.* This scenic 2,100-acre park contains one of the largest concrete dams east of the Mississippi (1,900 feet by 209 feet). Swimming, waterskiing, fishing, boating (ramp, rentals, marina); hiking, game courts, picnic area, playground, concession, lodge, tent and trailer camping, ten cabins. Nature and recreation programs, dam tours (summer; phone 304/265-1760).

Special Event

Taylor County Fair. *Fairgrounds, Hwy 50, Grafton. Phone 304/265-4155.* Horse racing, livestock shows, auctions, carnival, crafts. Last week of July.

Limited-Service Hotels

★ CRISLIP MOTOR LODGE. *300 Moritz Ave, Grafton (26354). Phone 304/265-2100; fax 304/265-2017.* 40 rooms, 2 story. Pets accepted. Check-in 4 pm, check-out 11 am. Outdoor pool. **$**

★ ★ TYGART LAKE STATE PARK LODGE. *Hwy 1, Grafton (26354). Phone 304/265-6144; toll-free 800/225-5982; fax 304/265-6147. www.tygartlake.com.* 20 rooms, 1 story. Closed Jan-Apr. Check-in 4 pm, check-out noon. Restaurant, bar. Children's activity center. **$**

Harpers Ferry (B-7)

See also Charles Town, Martinsburg, Shepherdstown

Settled 1732
Population 307
Elevation 247 ft
Area Code 304
Zip 25425
Information Jefferson County Chamber of Commerce, 201 Frontage Rd, PO Box 426, Charles Town 25414; phone 304/725-2055
Web site www.jeffersoncounty.com/chamber

Scene of abolitionist John Brown's raid in 1859, Harpers Ferry is at the junction of the Shenandoah and Potomac rivers, where West Virginia, Virginia, and Maryland meet. A US armory and rifle factory made this an important town in early Virginia; John Brown had this in mind when he began his insurrection. He and 16 other men seized the armory and arsenal the night of October 16 and took refuge in the engine house of the armory when attacked by local militia. On the morning of the 18th, the engine house was stormed, and Brown was captured by 90 marines from Washington under Brevet Colonel Robert E. Lee and Lt. J. E. B. Stuart. Ten of Brown's men were killed, including two of his sons. He was hanged in nearby Charles Town (see) for treason, murder, and inciting slaves to rebellion.

When war broke out, Harpers Ferry was a strategic objective for the Confederacy, which considered it the key to Washington. "Stonewall" Jackson captured 12,693 Union prisoners here before the Battle of Antietam in 1862. The town changed hands many times in the war, during which many buildings were damaged. In 1944, Congress authorized a national monument here, setting aside 1,500 acres for that purpose. In 1963, the same area was designated a National Historical Park, now occupying more than 2,200 acres.

What to See and Do

Harpers Ferry National Historical Park. *Shenandoah and High sts, Harpers Ferry (25425). Phone 304/535-6298. www.nps.gov/hafe.* Here the old town has been restored to its 19th-century appearance; exhibits and interpretive presentations explore the park's relation to the water-power industry, the Civil War, John Brown, and Storer College, a school established for freed slaves after the war. A Visitor Center is located just off Hwy 340. Visitors should park there; a bus will take them to Lower Town. Contact the Visitor Center, PO Box 65. **$$** (Daily 8 am-6 pm; to 5 pm in winter; closed Jan 1, Thanksgiving, Dec 25) Located in the park are

Camp Hill. Four restored, private houses built 1832-1850.

Harper House. Three-story stone house built between 1775 and 1782 by the founder of the town; both George Washington and Thomas Jefferson were entertained as overnight guests. Restored and furnished with period pieces.

Information Center. *S side of Shenandoah St. Phone 304/535-6029.* Restored Federalist house built in 1859 by US government as residence for the master armorer of the US Armory. During the Civil War, it was used as headquarters by various commanding officers. Also on this street is the site of the US Armory that John Brown attempted to seize; it was destroyed during the Civil War.

Jefferson's Rock. From here Thomas Jefferson, in 1783, pronounced the view "one of the most stupendous scenes in nature."

John Brown's Fort. *On Arsenal Sq.* Where John Brown made his last stand; rebuilt and moved near original site.

John Brown Museum. *Arsenal Sq and High St.* Contains an exhibit and film on John Brown and a ten-minute slide presentation on the history of the park. Exiting the museum to the right is High St, which has two Civil War museums and two black history museums.

Lockwood House. (1848) Greek Revival house used as headquarters, barracks, and stable during Civil War; later used as a classroom building by Storer College (1867), which was founded to educate freed men after the war.

Other buildings. Open to the public during the summer are the dry goods store, provost, office, and blacksmith shop.

The Point. Three states, West Virginia, Virginia, and Maryland, and two rivers, the Shenandoah and Potomac, meet at the Blue Ridge Mountains.

Ruins of St. John's Episcopal Church. Used as a guardhouse and hospital during the Civil War.

John Brown Wax Museum. *168 High St, Harpers Ferry (25425). Phone 304/535-6342.* Sound and animation depict Brown's exploits, including the raid on Harpers Ferry. **$$**

Whitewater rafting. *Phone toll-free 800/225-5982.* Many outfitters offer guided trips on the Shenandoah and Potomac rivers. For a list of outfitters, contact the West Virginia Division of Tourism, Research, and Development, 90 Mac Corkle Ave SW, South Charleston 25303.

Special Events

Election Day 1860. *Along Shenandoah and High sts. Phone 304/535-6298.* More than 100 people in 19th-century attire reenact the 1860 presidential election. Second Sat in Oct.

Mountain Heritage Arts and Crafts Festival. *102 Frontage Rd, Harpers Ferry (25414). Phone 304/725-2055.* More than 190 craftspeople and artisans demonstrate quilting, wool spinning, pottery throwing, vegetable dyeing, and other crafts; concerts. Second full weekend in June and last full weekend in Sept.

Old Tyme Christmas. *Phone 304/925-8019.* Caroling, musical programs, children's programs, taffy pull, candlelight walk. First two weekends of Dec.

Limited-Service Hotel

★ COMFORT INN. *Rte 340 and Union St, Harpers Ferry (25425). Phone 304/535-6391; toll-free 800/535-9909; fax 304/535-6395. www.choicehotels.com.* 50 rooms, 2 story. Complimentary continental breakfast. Check-in 3 pm, check-out 11 am. **$**

Hillsboro (D-4)

See also Marlinton

Settled 1765
Population 243
Elevation 2,303 ft
Area Code 304
Zip 24946
Information West Virginia Mountain Highlands, PO Box 1456, Elkins 26241; phone 304/636-8400

Civil War troops marched through Hillsboro and Confederates camped in town before the decisive Battle of Droop Mountain. Novelist Pearl S. Buck was born in her grandparents' house while her parents, missionaries on leave from China, were visiting.

What to See and Do

Beartown State Park. *1 1/2 miles S off Hwy 219, near Droop Mountain. Phone 304/653-4254. www.beartownstatepark.com.* Approximately 110 acres of dense forest with unique rock formations created by erosion; a boardwalk with interpretive signs winds through the park. Standard hours.

Droop Mountain Battlefield State Park. *5 miles S on Hwy 219. Phone 304/653-4254. www.droopmountainbattlefield.com.* Encompasses approximately 285 acres on site where on Nov 6, 1863, Union forces under General William W. Averell defeated Confederates under General John Echols, destroying the last major rebel resistance in the state. Park features graves, breastworks, and monuments. Hiking, picnic areas, playground. Museum. Battle reenactments (second week of Oct, every even year).

★ Pearl S. Buck Birthplace Museum. *1/2 mile N on Hwy 219. (Stulting House) Phone 304/653-4430.* Birthplace of the Pulitzer and Nobel Prize-winning novelist, restored to its 1892 appearance; original and period furniture; memorabilia. Sydenstricker House, home of Buck's father and his ancestors, was moved 40 miles from its original site and restored here. Guided tours. (May-Nov, Mon-Sat; closed Jan 1, Thanksgiving, Dec 25) **$$**

Watoga State Park. *Hwy 39 and Beaver's Creek Rd, Hillsboro (24954). 1 mile N on Hwy 219, then SE. Phone 304/799-4087.* More than 10,100 acres make this West Virginia's largest state park. Watoga, derived from the Cherokee term watauga, means "river of islands." It aptly describes the Greenbrier River, which forms several miles of the park's boundary. Swimming pool, bathhouses, fishing, boating on 11-acre Watoga Lake (rentals); hiking and bridle trails, horseback riding, tennis, game courts, cross-country skiing, picnicking, playground, concession, restaurant (seasonal), tent and trailer camping, 33 cabins. Brooks Memorial Arboretum; nature, recreation programs (summer). Adjacent to the park is

Calvin Price State Forest. *Hwy 39 and Beaver's Creek Rd, Hillsboro (24954). Phone 304/799-4087.* This vast, undeveloped forest has more than 9,400 acres for fishing; deer and small-game hunting, hiking, and primitive camping (fee).

Hinton (E-4)

See also Beckley

Founded 1873
Population 2,880
Elevation 1,382 ft
Area Code 304
Zip 25951
Information Summers County Chamber of Commerce, 200 Ballangee St; phone 304/466-5332

Hinton, a railroad town on the banks of the New River, is the seat of Summers County, where the Bluestone and Greenbrier rivers join the scenic and protected New River.

What to See and Do

Bluestone State Park. *5 miles S on Hwy 20. Phone 304/466-2805.* More than 2,100 acres on Bluestone Lake, which was created by the Bluestone Dam. Swimming pool (Memorial Day-Labor Day), wading pool, bathhouses, waterskiing, fishing, boating (ramps, marina nearby; canoe, rowboat, and motorboat rentals); hiking trails, game courts, picnicking, playground, tent and trailer camping (dump station), 25 cabins. Nature, recreation programs (summer). Gift shop. Standard hours, fees.

New River Gorge National River. *104 Main St, Glen Jean (25846). Phone 304/465-0508.* One of the oldest rivers on the continent, the New River rushes northward through a deep canyon with spectacular scenery. The 52-mile section from Hinton to Fayetteville is popular among outdoor enthusiasts, especially whitewater rafters and hikers. The Hinton Visitor Center is located along the river at Hwy 3 Bypass (Memorial Day-Labor Day, daily); phone 304/466-0417. A year-round visitor center is located on Hwy 19 near the New River Gorge Bridge (see GAULEY BRIDGE). For further information and a list of whitewater outfitters, contact Superintendent, PO Box 246, Glen Jean 25846.

Pipestem Resort State Park. *12 miles SW on Hwy 20. Phone 304/466-1800.* More than 4,000 acres with 3,600-foot aerial tramway to Bluestone River complex. Swimming, bathhouses, fishing, canoeing, paddleboating; hiking trails, horseback riding, 9- and 18-hole golf courses, miniature golf, tennis, archery, lighted game courts, cross-country skiing, sledding, playground, two lodges, four restaurants, tent and trailer camping (dump station), 25 cabins. Visitor center; nature, recreation programs. Aerial tramway, arboretum, observation tower. Amphitheater; dances.

Full-Service Resort

★ ★ MOUNTAIN CREEK LODGE. *Pipestem State Park, Pipestem (25979). Phone 304/466-1800; toll-free 800/922-5582; fax 304/466-5679.* 174 rooms, 7 story. Check-in 4 pm, check-out noon. Restaurant, bar. Fitness room. Indoor pool, outdoor pool, children's pool. Tennis. Mountain Creek Lodge (open May-Oct) is located at foot of Bluestone Canyon; accessible only by aerial tram. The resort is state-owned and operated; all state park facilities are available to guests. **$**

Restaurants

★ ★ BLUESTONE DINING ROOM. *Pipestem Resort, Pipestem (25979). Phone 304/466-1800.* American menu. Breakfast, lunch, dinner. Children's menu. Casual attire. **$$**

★ KIRK'S. *RR 3, Hinton (25951). Phone 304/466-4600.* American menu; hamburgers, hot dogs. Breakfast, lunch, dinner. Closed Thanksgiving, Dec 25. Casual attire. Outdoor seating. **$**

★ ★ MOUNTAIN CREEK. *Pipestem Resort, Pipestem (25979). Phone 304/466-1800.* French, American menu. Dinner. Closed Nov-Apr. Bar. Children's menu. Casual attire. Park in Pipestem Resort State Park. Dining room at 1,000-foot-deep gorge; accessible by tram only. **$$$**

★ ★ OAK SUPPER CLUB. *Just N of Pipestem State Park entrance, Pipestem (25979). Phone 304/466-4800; fax 304/466-4800.* American menu. Dinner. Closed Sun, Mon; Thanksgiving, Dec 25; also Jan-mid-Feb. Bar. Children's menu. Casual attire. **$$**

Huntington (D-2)

Founded 1871
Population 51,475
Elevation 564 ft
Area Code 304
Information Cabell-Huntington Convention & Visitors Bureau, PO Box 347, 25708; phone 304/525-7333 or toll-free 800/635-6329
Web site www.wvvisit.org

The millionaire president of the Chesapeake & Ohio Railroad, Collis P. Huntington, founded this city and named it for himself. Originally a rail and river terminus, commerce and industry have made it the second-largest city in the state. Thoroughly planned and meticulously laid out, Huntington is protected from the Ohio River by an 11-mile floodwall equipped with 17 pumping stations and 45 gates. Glass, railroad products, and metals are important city industries.

What to See and Do

Beech Fork State Park. *5601 Longbranch Rd, Huntington (25504). Approximately 15 miles SE via Hwy 10, then 7 miles W on Hughes Branch Rd, near Bowen. Phone 304/528-5794.* Nearly 4,000 acres on 720-acre Beech Fork Lake. Fishing, boating (ramp, marina); hiking trails, physical fitness trail, tennis, game courts, picnicking, camping. Store. Visitor center; nature, recreation programs (summer). Meeting rooms.

Blenko Glass Company. *Fairground Rd, Milton. 16 miles E via Hwy 60; I-64, exit 28. Phone 304/743-9081.* Famous glass factory; makers of Country Music Award, presidential gifts, and original supplier to Colonial Williamsburg. Visitor center (daily; closed holidays) has stained glass from nine leading studios; observation gallery for viewing hand-blown glass-making and blown stained glass. (Mon-Fri; closed holidays; also first two weeks of July, Dec 25-Jan 1) Museum of Historical Glass; Garden of Glass beside a 3-acre lake. **FREE**

Camden Park. *Hwy 60 E, Huntington. Phone 304/429-4231.* Amusement park with 27 rides, games, concession; boat and train rides, log flume, miniature golf, roller rink, picnicking. (Mid-Apr-Memorial Day: Sat-Sun; Memorial Day-Labor Day: Tues-Sun) Rides individually priced; also unlimited ride plan. **$$$**

East Lynn Wildlife Management Area. *McClintic Rd, Point Pleasant. 15 miles SE via Hwy 152 and Hwy 37, near East Lynn. Phone 304/675-0871.* Almost 23,000 acres used primarily by sportsmen; trails, primitive camping (fee).

Heritage Village. *210 11th St, Huntington (25701). 11th St and Veterans Memorial Blvd. Phone 304/696-5954.* Restored Victorian B & O Railroad yard surrounding brick courtyard. Restaurant in original passenger station (1887), restored Pullman car, shops in renovated freight and box cars, warehouses. (Mon-Sat) **FREE**

Huntington Museum of Art. *2033 McCoy Rd, Huntington (25701). I-64, exit 8. Phone 304/529-2701.* Museum with American and European paintings, prints, and sculpture; Herman P. Dean Firearms Collection; Georgian silver; Asian prayer rugs; pre-Columbian art; Appalachian folk art; Ohio Valley historical and contemporary glass. Complex includes exhibition galleries, library, studio workshops, amphitheater, auditorium, sculpture garden, observatory, art gallery for young people, nature trails. (Tues-Sat, also Sun afternoons; closed holidays) **FREE**

Limited-Service Hotels

★ DAYS INN. *5196 Hwy Rte 60 E, Huntington (25705). Phone 304/733-4477; toll-free 800/694-8999; fax 304/733-4493. www.daysinn.com.* 153 rooms, 2 story. Complimentary continental breakfast. Check-in 3 pm, check-out noon. Outdoor pool. **$**

★ ★ RADISSON HOTEL HUNTINGTON. *1001 3rd Ave, Huntington (25701). Phone 304/525-1001; toll-free 800/333-3333; fax 304/691-5417. www.radisson.com.* This high-rise hotel is located downtown, just one block from Riverfront Park. 202 rooms, 11 story. Check-in 3 pm, check-out noon. High-speed Internet access. Complimentary continental breakfast. Two restaurants, bar. Fitness room. Outdoor pool. Airport transportation available. Business center. **$**

Restaurants

★★ **HERITAGE STATION.** *11th St and Veterans Memorial Blvd, Huntington (25701). Phone 304/523-6373; fax 304/523-6399.* American menu. Lunch, dinner. Closed Sun; Thanksgiving, Dec 25. Bar. Children's menu. Casual attire. Outdoor seating. Former railroad station built in 1887; memorabilia, antiques. **$$$**

★★ **REBELS & REDCOATS TAVERN.** *412 W 7th Ave, Huntington (25701). Phone 304/523-8829; fax 304/697-8676.* This family-owned restaurant offers a varied menu and has been in business for 35 years. The casual, colonial dining room has a pleasant red and green décor with rustic finishes and a fireplace. American menu. Lunch, dinner. Closed Sun, Mon; holidays; also the week of July 4. Bar. Children's menu. Casual attire. **$$$**

Lewisburg (D-4)

See also White Sulphur Springs

Founded 1782
Population 3,624
Elevation 2,099 ft
Area Code 304
Zip 24901
Information Greenbrier County Convention & Visitors Center, 105 Church St; phone 304/645-1000 or toll-free 800/833-2068
Web site www.greenbrierwv.com

At the junction of two important Native American trails, the Seneca (now Hwy 219) and the Kanawha (now Hwy 60), Lewisburg was the site of colonial forts as well as a Civil War battle. The town's 236-acre historic district has more than 60 buildings from the 18th and 19th centuries in a variety of architectural styles.

What to See and Do

Lost World Caverns. *Fairview Rd, Lewisburg. 1 mile N on Fairview Rd. Phone 304/645-6677.* Scenic trail over subterranean rock mountain; prehistoric ocean floor; stalagmites, stalactites; flow stone, ribbons, hex stones. Self-guided tours (daily; closed holidays). **$$$**

North House Museum. *301 W Washington St, Lewisburg (24901). Phone 304/645-3398.* Colonial and 19th-century objects and artifacts. (Mon-Sat) **$$**

Old Stone Presbyterian Church. *200 Church St, Lewisburg (24901). Phone 304/645-2676.* Original log church (1783) was replaced by present native limestone structure (1796). (Daily) **FREE**

Organ Cave. *417 Masters Rd, Ronceverte (24970). Phone 304/645-7600.* One of the longest caves in the US. Forty-five miles of mapped passageways. (Daily)

Special Event

State Fair. *Fairgrounds, Hwy 219 S, Lewisburg (24902). 2 miles S on Hwy 219. Phone 304/645-1090.* Exhibitors from a number of other states; horse shows, harness racing. Mid-Aug.

Limited-Service Hotel

★★ **BRIER INN & CONFERENCE CENTER.** *540 N Jefferson St, Lewisburg (24901). Phone 304/645-7722; fax 304/645-7865. www.brierinn.com.* 162 rooms, 2 story. Pets accepted, some restrictions; fee. Check-in 3 pm, check-out 11 am. Restaurant, bar. Fitness room. Outdoor pool. **$**

Full-Service Inn

★★★ **GENERAL LEWIS INN.** *301 E Washington St, Lewisburg (24901). Phone 304/645-2600; toll-free 800/628-4454; fax 304/645-2601. www.generallewisinn.com.* Operating as a guest house since 1928, this bed-and-breakfast was built in the early 1800s. It is surrounded by flower gardens and lawns with a lily pond. Every room is furnished with antiques and crafts made by early settlers. 25 rooms, 2 story. Check-in 3 pm, check-out 11 am. Restaurant, bar. **$**

Marlinton (D-5)

See also Hillsboro

Settled 1749
Population 1,204
Elevation 2,130 ft
Area Code 304
Zip 24954
Information West Virginia Mountain Highlands, PO Box 145, Elkins 26241; phone 304/636-8400

Marlinton is the seat of Pocahontas County, an area known for its wide variety of outdoor recreational opportunities. A Ranger District office of the Monongahela National Forest (see ELKINS) is located in the town.

What to See and Do

Cass Scenic Railroad State Park. *Hwy 66, Cass (24927). 5 miles E on Hwy 39, then 19 miles N on Hwy 28 to Hwy 66. Phone 304/456-4300; toll-free 800/225-5982. www.cassrailroad.com.* Steam train makes an 8-mile round-trip (90 minutes) up the mountain to Whittaker (daily) and a 22-mile round-trip (4 1/2 hours) to the top of Bald Knob (Tues-Sun); picnic stopover. Dinner trains (some Sat starting in June; call for reservations). On the 1,089-acre property are two museums, a country store, and 14 renovated logging camp houses now serving as tourist cottages. Picnicking, camping. Three train departures daily. **$$$$**

Cranberry Mountain Visitor Center-Monongahela National Forest. *Hwy 150 and Hwy 39/55, Marlinton (26261). Approximately 7 miles NW of Mill Point via Hwy 219 and Hwy 39. Phone 304/653-4826.* Exhibits, videos, and publications on conservation and forest management. (Apr-Nov, daily) **FREE** 2 miles west is

> **Cranberry Glades.** *Hwy 150 and Hwy 39-55, Marlinton. Phone 304/653-4826.* A USDA Forest Service botanical area. Approximately 750 acres featuring open bog fringed by forest and alder thicket. Boardwalk with interpretive signs. Guided tours leave from visitor center (June-Labor Day, wkends). Glades (year-round, weather permitting). **FREE**

Elk River Touring Center. *Hwy 219, Slatyfork. 16 miles N on US 219, follow signs, near Slatyfork. Phone 304/572-3771. www.ertc.com.* Features 34 miles of cross-country trails in the Monongahela National Forest (see); rentals; restaurant; lodging. Night skiing. Also guided mountain bike tours, cave tours in season. **$$$$**

Greenbrier River Trail. *Hwy 39 and Beaver's Creek Rd, Marlinton (24954). Phone 304/799-4087.* Part of the state park system, this 76-mile trail runs along the Greenbrier River from the town of Cass, on the north, through Marlinton to North Caldwell, on the south; passes through small towns, over 35 bridges, and through two tunnels. Originally the trail was part of the Chesapeake & Ohio Railroad. Activities include backpacking, bicycling, and cross-country skiing; trail also provides access for fishing and canoeing. No developed sites.

National Radio Astronomy Observatory. *Hwys 28 and 92, Green Bank (24944). 5 miles SE on Hwy 39, then 21 miles N on Hwy 28, 92 in Green Bank. Phone 304/456-2209.* Study of the universe by radio telescopes. Slide show, exhibits, and one-hour bus tour of site. (Mid-June-Labor Day weekend: daily; Memorial Day weekend-mid-June and after Labor Day-Oct: Sat-Sun) **FREE**

Pocahontas County Historical Museum. *810 2nd Ave, Marlinton (24954). On US 219 S, at WV 39. Phone 304/799-4973.* Displays on history of the county from its beginnings to present. Extensive photo collection. (Early June-Labor Day, daily) **$**

Seneca State Forest. *5 miles E via Hwy 39, then 10 miles NE on Hwy 28. Phone 304/799-6213.* Approximately 12,000 acres with fishing and boating on a 4-acre lake; hunting, hiking trails, picnicking, playground. Camping, eight rustic cabins.

Snowshoe Mountain Resort. *1 Snowshoe Dr, Snowshoe. 26 miles N on Hwy 219, near Slatyfork. Phone 304/572-4636 (ski report).* Four quad, seven triple chairlifts; two handle tows; patrol, school, rentals; snowmaking; restaurants, lodging, nursery, health club, four pools. Fifty-six slopes and trails; longest run 6,200 feet; vertical drop 1,500 feet. Night skiing. (Mid-Nov-mid-Apr, daily) Summer activities include horseback riding, fishing, and hiking. **$$$$**

Special Event

Pioneer Days. *900 9th St, Marlinton (24954). Phone 304/799-4315.* Craft exhibits and demonstrations; horse-pulling contests, frog and turtle races; bluegrass and mountain music shows; 4x4 truck pulling; parade; antique car show. Early-mid-July.

Martinsburg (B-7)

See also Berkeley Springs, Charles Town, Hagerstown, Harpers Ferry, Shepherdstown; also see Hagerstown, MD

Settled 1732
Population 14,972
Elevation 457 ft
Area Code 304
Zip 25401
Information Martinsburg-Berkeley County Chamber of Commerce, 198 Viking Way; phone 304/267-4841 or toll-free 800/332-9007
Web site www.berkeleycounty.org

Martinsburg is located in the center of an apple- and peach-producing region in the state's eastern panhandle. Because of its strategic location at the entrance to the Shenandoah Valley, the town was the site of several battles during the Civil War. The famous Confederate spy Belle Boyd was a resident. Officially chartered in 1778, Martinsburg is recognized for the preservation of its many 18th- and 19th-century houses and mercantile and industrial buildings.

What to See and Do

General Adam Stephen House. *309 E John St, Martinsburg (25401). Phone 304/267-4434.* (1789) Restored residence of Revolutionary War soldier and surgeon Adam Stephen, founder of Martinsburg. Period furnishings; restored smokehouse and log building. (May-Oct, Sat-Sun, limited hours; also by appointment) **FREE** Adjacent is

> **Triple-Brick Building.** Completed in three sections just after the Civil War, the structure was used to house railroad employees. A museum of local history is located on the top two floors. (May-Oct, Sat-Sun, limited hours; also by appointment) **FREE**

Special Event

Mountain State Apple Harvest Festival. *Phone 304/263-2500.* Parade, celebrity breakfast, contests, entertainment, Apple Queen coronation, square dancing, grand ball, arts and crafts show. Third weekend in Oct.

Limited-Service Hotels

★ COMFORT INN. *1872 Edwin Miller Blvd, Martinsburg (25401). Phone 304/263-6200; fax 304/267-0995. www.choicehotels.com.* 109 rooms, 5 story. Complimentary continental breakfast. Check-in 3 pm, check-out noon. Fitness room. Outdoor pool. Airport transportation available. **$**

★★ HOLIDAY INN. *301 Foxcroft Ave, Martinsburg (25401). Phone 304/267-5500; fax 304/264-9157. www.holiday-inn.com.* 120 rooms, 5 story. Pets accepted, some restrictions. Check-in 3 pm, check-out noon. Restaurant, bar. Fitness room. Indoor pool, outdoor pool, whirlpool. Tennis. **$**

★ SUPER 8. *2048 Edwin Miller Blvd, Martinsburg (25401). Phone 304/263-0801; toll-free 800/800-8000; fax 304/263-0801. www.super8.com.* 43 rooms, 3 story. Pets accepted, some restrictions. Complimentary continental breakfast. Check-in 1 pm, check-out 11 am. **$**

★★ WOODS RESORT & CONFERENCE CENTER. *Mountain Lake Rd, Hedgesville (25427). Phone 304/754-7977; toll-free 800/248-2222; fax 304/754-8146. www.thewoodsresort.com.* This resort is adjoined to the 23,000-acre Sleepy Creek Wilderness. 58 rooms, 2 story. Complimentary full breakfast. Check-in 4 pm, check-out noon. Restaurant, bar. Children's activity center. Fitness room. Indoor pool, three outdoor pools, children's pools, whirlpool. Golf, 36 holes. Tennis. **$**

Monongahela National Forest (C-5)

(Entrance is E of Elkins on Hwy 33)

This 901,000-acre forest, in the heart of the Alleghenies, has some of the loftiest mountains in the East. Spruce Knob (4,862 ft) is the highest point in the state. Headwaters of the Ohio and Potomac rivers are here. The forest is a meeting ground of northern and southern plant life, with stands of red spruce and northern hardwoods joining with oak, hickory, and other southern hardwoods. There are also many interesting secondary and tertiary plants and wildflowers. Several recreation areas, including five wilderness areas, Spruce Knob/Seneca Rocks National Recreation Area near Petersburg (see), and Blue Bend and Lake Sherwood recreation areas near White Sulphur Springs (see), are all located within the forest. Swimming, fishing, boating; hunting, hiking, rock climbing, caving, picnicking, camping (fee). Fees charged at the more developed recreation sites. Part of the Greenbrier River Trail (see MARLINTON) runs through the southern section of the forest. Forest headquarters in Elkins (see); Cranberry Mountain Visitor Center near Marlinton (see); and Seneca Rocks Visitor Center in Seneca Rocks (see PETERSBURG).

Moorefield (C-6)

See also Petersburg

Settled 1777
Population 2,375
Elevation 821 ft
Area Code 304
Zip 26836
Information West Virginia Mountain Highlands, PO Box 1456, Elkins 26241; phone 304/636-8400

What to See and Do

Lost River State Park. *18 miles E on Hwy 55 to Baker, then 13 miles S on Hwy 259, near Mathias. Phone 304/897-5372; toll-free 800/225-5982.* More than 3,700 acres where Lee's White Sulphur Springs was once a famous resort; an original cabin still stands; museum. Swimming pool, wading pool (Memorial Day-Labor Day); hiking trails, horseback riding, tennis, game courts, picnicking, playground, restaurant, 24 cabins. Recreation building; nature programs (summer); scenic overlooks.

Special Event

Hardy County Heritage Weekend. *Main St and Winchester, Moorefield (26836). Phone 304/538-6560.* Tours of antebellum houses; medieval jousting, crafts, traditional events. Last full weekend in Sept.

Morgantown (B-5)

See also Fairmont, Grafton

Settled 1776
Population 26,809
Elevation 892 ft
Area Code 304
Zip 26505
Information Greater Morgantown Convention & Visitors Bureau, 709 Beechurst Ave; phone 304/292-5081 or toll-free 800/458-7373
Web site www.mgtn.com

Morgantown is both an educational and industrial center. West Virginia University was founded here in 1867, the Morgantown Female Collegiate Institute in 1839. Known internationally for its glass, Morgantown is home to a number of glass plants which produce wares ranging from lamp parts to decorative paper weights and crystal tableware. The town is also home to a number of research laboratories maintained by the federal government.

What to See and Do

Coopers Rock State Forest. *10 miles E on I-68. Phone 304/594-1561.* More than 12,700 acres. Trout fishing; hunting, hiking trails to historical sites; Henry Clay iron furnace (1834-1836). Cross-country ski trails, picnicking, playground, concession, tent and trailer camping. Adjacent is

Chestnut Ridge Regional Park. *Sand Springs Rd, Bruceton Mills. Phone 304/594-1773.* Swimming beach, fishing; tent and trailer camping (hookups, dump station), rustic cabins, lodge (fees), hiking, picnicking, cross-country ski trails (Dec-Feb). Nature center. Park (daily).

West Virginia University. *Visitors Resource Center, One Waterfront Pl, Morgantown (26501). www.wvu.edu.* (1867) (22,712 students) University has 15 colleges. Tours (Mon-Sat; for reservations phone 304/293-3489). The Visitors Center in the Communications Building on Patterson Drive has touch-screen monitors and video presentations about the university and upcoming special events (phone 304/293-6692 for 24-hour event information). Of special interest on the downtown campus are Stewart Hall and the university's original buildings, located on Woodburn Circle. In the Evansdale area of Morgantown are the Creative Arts Center, the 75-acre Core Arboretum, and the 63,500-seat Coliseum. Also in the Evansdale area are

Cook-Hayman Pharmacy Museum. *1 Medical Dr, Morgantown. Health Sciences Center North, room 1136. Phone 304/293-5101.* Re-creates pharmacy of yesteryear with old patent medicines. (Mon-Fri; weekends by request; closed holidays) **DONATION**

Personal Rapid Transit System (PRT). *88 Beechhurst Ave, Morgantown (26505). Phone 304/293-5011.* A pioneering transit system, the PRT is the world's first totally automated system. Operating without conductors or ticket takers, computer-directed cars travel between university campuses and downtown Morgantown. (Mon-Sat; may not operate holidays and university breaks) **$**

Whitewater rafting. *Phone toll-free 800/458-7373.* Many outfitters offer guided trips on the Cheat and Tygart rivers. For a list of outfitters contact the Greater Morgantown Convention and Visitors Bureau, 709 Beechurst Ave.

Special Events

Mason-Dixon Festival. *Morgantown Riverfront Park, Morgantown. Phone 304/599-1104.* River parade, boat races, arts and crafts, concessions. Mid-Sept.

Mountaineer Balloon Festival. *Morgantown Municipal Airport, 100 Hart Field Rd, Morgantown (26505). Phone 304/296-8356.* Hot air balloon races, carnival, music, food. Mid-Oct.

Limited-Service Hotels

★ ★ CLARION HOTEL. *127 High St, Morgantown (26505). Phone 304/292-8200; fax 888/241-7944. www.clarionhotelmorgan.com.* Historic brick hotel (1925). 76 rooms, 5 story. Complimentary continental breakfast. Check-in 3 pm, check-out 11 am. Restaurant, bar. Fitness room. Business center. **$**

★ COMFORT INN. *225 Comfort Inn Dr, Morgantown (26508). Phone 304/296-9364; fax 304/296-0469. www.choicehotels.com.* 80 rooms, 2 story. Pets accepted, some restrictions; fee. Complimentary continental breakfast. Check-in 3 pm, check-out noon. Fitness room. Outdoor pool, whirlpool. **$**

★ HAMPTON INN. *1053 Van Voorhis Rd, Morgantown (26505). Phone 304/599-1200; fax 304/598-7331. www.hamptoninn.com.* 107 rooms, 5 story. Complimentary continental breakfast. Check-in 2 pm, check-out noon. Business center. **$**

★ ★ HOLIDAY INN. *1400 Saratoga Ave, Morgantown (26505). Phone 304/599-1680; fax 304/598-0989. www.holiday-inn.com.* 147 rooms, 4 story. Pets accepted; fee. Check-in 3 pm, check-out noon. Restaurant, bar. Outdoor pool. **$**

Full-Service Resort

★ ★ ★ LAKEVIEW SCANTICON GOLF RESORT, SPA & CONFERENCE CENTER. *1 Lakeview Dr, Morgantown (26508). Phone 304/594-1111; toll-free 800/624-8300; fax 304/594-9405. www.lakeviewresort.com.* Even the most stressed-out guest will find true relaxation at this resort. 187 rooms, 3 story. Check-in 4 pm, check-out noon. High-speed Internet access. Pets accepted, some restrictions. Two restaurants, two bars. Children's activity center. Fitness room, spa. Indoor pool, whirlpool. Golf. Tennis. Airport transportation available. Business center. **$**

Restaurants

★ ★ BACK BAY. *1869 Mileground, Morgantown (26505). Phone 304/296-3027; fax 304/296-2624. www.backbaywv.com.* Seafood menu. Lunch, dinner. Closed holidays. Bar. Children's menu. Casual attire. Outdoor seating. **$$**

★ **PUGLIONI'S.** *1137 Van Voorhis Rd, Morgantown (26505). Phone 304/599-7521.* Italian menu. Lunch, dinner. Closed holidays. Bar. Children's menu. Casual attire. **$$**

Nitro (D-3)

See also Charleston

Founded 1918
Population 6,824
Elevation 604 ft
Area Code 304
Zip 25143
Information Putnam County Chamber of Commerce, 5664 Hwy 34, PO Box 553, Teays 25569; phone 304/757-6510
Web site www.putnamcounty.org

Nitro experienced explosive growth around a huge smokeless powder plant during World War I, when the town's population reached 35,000 overnight and some 3,400 buildings were erected. When the war ended the demand for smokeless powder fizzled and the town dried up; factory buildings were scrapped and whole houses were shipped down the river. Now a western suburb of Charleston, Nitro produces chemicals.

What to See and Do

Tri-State Greyhound Park. *1 Greyhound Dr, Cross Lanes (25313). E via I-64 exit 47A to Goff Mountain Rd, then to Greyhound Dr. Phone 304/776-1000.* Indoor grandstand, clubhouse, concessions. (Mon-Sat evenings; matinees Sat-Sun, and holidays) Must be 18 to wager.

Waves of Fun. *2 Valley Park Rd, Hurricane (25526). W via I-64 exit 39, then 3 miles S on Hwy 34, at Valley Park. Phone 304/562-0518.* Water park featuring three water slides, wave pool, swimming areas, bathhouse, tube rentals (fee), lockers, concessions; miniature golf. (Memorial Day-June: weekends; early June-Labor Day: daily) **$$$**

Limited-Service Hotels

★ **COMFORT INN.** *102 Racer Dr, Cross Lanes (25313). Phone 304/776-8070; toll-free 800/798-7886; fax 304/776-6460. www.choicehotels.com.* 112 rooms, 2 story. Complimentary continental breakfast. Check-in 3 pm, check-out noon. Bar. Fitness room. Outdoor pool, whirlpool. Airport transportation available. Business center. **$**

★★ **WELLINGTON'S.** *1 Dairy Rd, Poca (25159). Phone 304/755-8219; fax 304/755-3229. www.wellingtons.webatonce.com.* Located at the Scarlet Oaks Country Club, this restaurant provides a fine-dining atmosphere. Guests will enjoy the three intimate dining rooms filled with the sounds of live piano on Fridays and Saturdays. American, French menu. Lunch, dinner. Closed Sun; holidays. Children's menu. Casual attire. **$$$**

Parkersburg (B-3)

Settled 1785
Population 33,099
Elevation 616 ft
Area Code 304
Zip 26101
Information Parkersburg/Wood Co Convention & Visitor's Bureau, 350 7th St; phone 304/428-1130 or toll-free 800/752-4982
Web site www.parkersburgcvb.org

In 1770, George Washington came to this area to inspect lands awarded to him by Virginia for his military services. After the Revolutionary War, Blennerhassett Island, in the Ohio River west of Parkersburg, was the scene of the alleged Burr-Blennerhassett plot. Harman Blennerhassett, a wealthy Irishman, built a lavish mansion on this island. After killing Alexander Hamilton in a duel, Aaron Burr came to the island, allegedly with the idea of seizing the Southwest and setting up an empire; Blennerhassett may have agreed to join him. On December 10, 1806, the plot was uncovered. Both men were acquitted of treason but ruined financially in the process. The Blennerhassett mansion burned in 1811 but was later rebuilt.

Today Parkersburg is the center for many industries, including glass, chemicals, petrochemicals, and ferrous and other metals. Fishing is popular in the area, especially below the Belleville and Willow Island locks and dams on the Ohio River.

What to See and Do

Actors Guild Playhouse. *724 Market St, Parkersburg (26101). 8th and Market sts. Phone 304/485-1300.* Musical, comedic, and dramatic performances. (Fri-Sun) **$$$**

Blennerhassett Island Historical State Park. *137 Juliana St, Parkersburg (26101). 2 miles S in the Ohio River. Phone 304/420-4800.* A 500-acre island accessible only by sternwheeler. There are self-guided walking tours of the island, horse-drawn wagon rides, and tours of the Blennerhassett mansion. Bicycle rentals, picnicking, concessions. Tickets are available for the boat ride at the Blennerhassett Museum. (May-Labor Day: Tues-Sun; Sept-Oct: Thurs-Sun) **$$**

Blennerhassett Museum. *2nd and Juliana sts, Parkersburg (26101). Phone 304/420-4840.* Features archaeological and other exhibits relating to history of Blennerhassett Island and Parkersburg area; includes artifacts dating back 12,000 years. Theater with video presentation. (May-Oct: Tues-Sun; rest of year: Sat-Sun; closed Jan 1, Thanksgiving, Dec 25) **$**

City Park. *Park Ave and 23rd St, Parkersburg (26101). Phone 304/424-8572.* A 55-acre wooded area with the Cooper Log Cabin Museum, which dates from 1804. Swimming pool, fishing, paddle boats; miniature golf, tennis, shelters and picnic facilities.

Middleton Doll Company. *1301 Washington Blvd, Parkersburg (26101). 2 miles W via Hwy 50. Phone 740/423-1481.* Tour of vinyl and porcelain doll factory (20 minutes). Factory store (Mon-Sat; closed holidays). **FREE**

Mountwood Park. *Volcano Rd, Waverly. 12 miles E via Hwy 50 to Volcano Rd. Phone 304/679-3611.* Wooded area with fishing, boating (no gasoline motors); hiking, mountain biking, nature trails; picnic area. **FREE**

North Bend State Park. *22 miles E on Hwy 50, then 7 miles SE on Hwy 31, near Cairo. Phone 304/643-2931; toll-free 800/225-5982.* Approximately 1,400 acres in the wide valley of the North Fork of the Hughes River; scenic overlooks of famous horseshoe bend. Swimming pool, bathhouse, fishing; miniature golf, tennis, game courts; hiking, bicycle, and bridle trail; 71-mile North Bend Rail Trail (see Clarksburg). Picnicking, playground, concession, restaurant, lodge, tent and trailer camping (dump station), eight cabins. Nature, recreation programs. Nature trail for disabled.

Parkersburg Art Center. *725 Market St, Parkersburg (26101). Phone 304/485-3859.* Changing exhibits. (Tues-Sun; closed holidays) **$**

Rubles Sternwheelers Riverboat Cruises. *Point Park, 2nd and Ann sts, Parkersburg (26101). Depart from Point Park. Phone 740/423-7268.* To Blennerhassett Island. (May-early Sept: Tues-Sun; early Sept-Oct: Thurs-Sun) **$$$**

Special Events

Parkersburg Homecoming. *Point Park, 2nd and Avery sts, Parkersburg (26101). Just off Hwy 68 at foot of 2nd St. Phone 304/422-3588.* Riverfront celebration features entertainment, parade, sternwheeler races, waterskiing show, miniature car races, fireworks. Third weekend in Aug.

West Virginia Honey Festival. *4-H Grounds, Parkersburg. Phone 304/428-1130.* Honey-related exhibits, baking, food, arts and crafts. Mid-Sept.

Limited-Service Hotels

★★ HOLIDAY INN. *Hwy 50 and I-77, Parkersburg (26104). Phone 304/485-6200; fax 304/485-6761. www.holiday-inn.com.* 149 rooms, 2 story. Check-in 3 pm, check-out noon. Restaurant, bar. Fitness room. Indoor pool, children's pool, whirlpool. **$**

★★ NORTH BEND STATE PARK LODGE. *RR 1 Box 221, Cairo (26337). Phone 304/643-2931; toll-free 800/225-5982; fax 304/643-2970. www.northbendsp.com.* 29 rooms, 2 story. Check-in 4 pm, check-out noon (lodge), 10 am (cabins). Restaurant. Children's activity center. Outdoor pool, indoor pool, children's pool. Tennis. On river. View of mountains. State owned, operated. **$**

Full-Service Hotel

★★ BLENNERHASSETT HOTEL. *320 Market St, Parkersburg (26101). Phone 304/422-3131; toll-free 800/262-2536; fax 304/485-0267. www.theblennerhassett.com.* This landmark hotel was built before the turn of the century in the "gaslight era" and was fully restored in 1986. The Victorian style of the hotel is evident in the rich crown mouldings, authentic English doors, brass and leaded-glass chandeliers, and antiques. 94 rooms, 5 story. Check-in 3 pm, check-out noon. Restaurant, bar. Airport transportation available. **$**

Specialty Lodging

The following lodging establishment is approved by Mobil Travel Guide but, due to its unique and individualized nature has not been given a traditional Mobil Star rating. Included in this listing you may find bed-and-breakfasts, limited-service inns, guest ranches, and other unique hotel properties.

WILLIAMS' HOUSE BED-AND-BREAKFAST. *5406 Grand Central Ave, Vienna (26105). Phone 304/295-7212; fax 304/295-5550.* At this romantic getaway near the Ohio state line, hosts Barbara and Bob Williams run a bed-and-breakfast out of their country home. Barbara even makes a full breakfast that usually includes hot biscuits, grits, and the like. 5 rooms, 3 story. Complimentary full breakfast. Check-in 2 pm, check-out noon. Fitness room. Outdoor pool. Airport transportation available. Built in 1920. **$**

Restaurant

★ MOUNTAINEER FAMILY RESTAURANT. *4006 E 7th St, Parkersburg (26101). Phone 304/422-0101.* American menu. Breakfast, lunch, dinner, late-night. Closed Dec 25. Children's menu. Casual attire. **$**

Petersburg (C-6)

See also Franklin, Moorefield

Settled 1745
Population 2,423
Elevation 937 ft
Area Code 304
Zip 26847
Information West Virginia Mountain Highlands, 1200 Harrison Ave, Lower Level, Suite A, Elkins 26241; phone 304/636-8400

A Ranger District office of the Monongahela National Forest (see) is located in Petersburg.

What to See and Do

Monongahela National Forest. *USDA Forest Service, H659, PO Box 240. Phone 304/257-4488.* Recreation area is popular for canoeing, hiking, and other outdoor sports. Camping (fee). **FREE**

Smoke Hole Caverns. *Hwy 28 S, Seneca Rocks (26884). 8 miles S on WV 28 and 55. Phone 304/257-4442; toll-free 800/828-8478. www.smokehole.com.* These caverns were used centuries ago by the Seneca both for shelter and the smoking of meat. During the Civil War, they were used by troops on both sides for storing ammunition. Later, they hid "moonshiners," illegal distillers of corn whiskey. It is claimed that the caverns contain the longest ribbon stalactite and the second highest cave room in the world. Guided tours. Large gift shop with wildlife exhibits; concessions. Tours. (Daily 9 am-5 pm; closed Thanksgiving, Dec 25) **$$**

Limited-Service Hotels

★★ HERMITAGE MOTOR INN. *203 Virginia Ave, Petersburg (26847). Phone 304/257-1711; toll-free 800/437-6482; fax 304/257-4330.* 38 rooms, 2 story. Complimentary continental breakfast. Check-out noon. Restaurant. Outdoor pool. Craft shop, bookstore in 1840s inn. **$**

★ SMOKE HOLE HOTEL & LOG CABINS. *Hwy 28 S, Seneca Rocks (26884). Phone 304/257-4442; toll-free 800/828-8478; fax 304/257-2745. www.smokehole.com.* 10 rooms, 1 story. Check-out 11 am. Outdoor pool. Adjacent to Smoke Hole Caverns. **$**

Philippi (C-5)

See also Buckhannon, Clarksburg, Elkins, Grafton

Settled 1780
Population 2,870
Elevation 1,307 ft
Area Code 304
Zip 26416
Information Barbour County Chamber of Commerce, PO Box 5000; phone 304/457-1958

The first land battle of the Civil War, a running rout of the Confederates known locally as the Philippi Races, was fought here on June 3, 1861. A historical marker on the campus of Alderson-Broaddus College marks the site. The Union attacked to protect the Baltimore & Ohio Railroad, whose main line between Washington and the West ran near the town.

What to See and Do

Barbour County Historical Society Museum. *146 N Main St, Philippi (26416). Phone 304/457-4846.* This B & O Railroad station (1911), used until 1956, is now restored as a museum; also local arts and crafts. (May-Oct: daily; rest of year: by appointment)

Covered bridge. *200 N Main St, Philippi (26416). Phone 304/645-7195.* Spanning the Tygart River since 1852; restored in recent years; believed to be the only two-lane bridge of its type still in daily use on a federal highway (Hwy 250).

Special Events

Barbour County Fair. *Hwy 250 between Phillipi and Belington, Philippi (26416). Fairgrounds, 5 miles SE on Hwy 250. Phone 304/823-1328 or 304/457-3254.* Horse and antique car shows, quilt and livestock exhibits, carnival rides, nightly entertainment, parade, and more. Week before Labor Day.

Blue & Gray Reunion. *Phone 304/457-4265.* Commemorates the first land battle of the Civil War; reenactment, parade, crafts. First weekend in June.

Limited-Service Hotel

★ **SUPER 8.** *US 250 S Rte 4 Box 155, Philippi (26416). Phone 304/457-5888; fax 304/457-5888. www.super8.com.* 39 rooms, 2 story. Pets accepted. Check-in 2 pm, check-out 11 am. **$**

Point Pleasant (C-2)

See also Ripley

Settled 1774
Population 4,637
Elevation 569 ft
Area Code 304
Zip 25550
Information Mason County Area Chamber of Commerce, 305 Main St; phone 304/675-1050

On October 10, 1774, British-incited Shawnees under Chief Cornstalk fought a battle here against 1,100 frontiersmen. The colonists won and broke the Native American power in the Ohio Valley. Historians later argued that this, rather than the battle at Lexington, Massachusetts, was the first battle of the Revolutionary War. In 1908, the US Senate rewrote history by recognizing this claim.

What to See and Do

Krodel Park and Lake. *Hwys 2 and 62, Point Pleasant (25550). 1 mile SE via WV 62/2. Phone 304/675-1068 (seasonal).* A 44-acre park with a replica of Fort Randolph (circa 1775). Fishing (license required), paddle boats (fee); miniature golf (fee), playground, camping (Apr-Nov; fee). **FREE**

McClintic Wildlife Management Area. *McClintic Rd, Point Pleasant. 7 miles NE off Hwy 62. Phone 304/675-0871.* Approximately 2,800 acres with primitive camping (fee). Also fishing and hunting (licenses required).

Tu-Endie-Wei State Park. *1 Main St, Point Pleasant (25550). In Tu-Endie-Wei Park (Wyandotte Indian for "where two rivers meet"). Phone 304/675-0869. www.wvparks.com/pointpleasant.* An 84-foot granite shaft was erected here in 1909, after the US Senate agreed to a claim made by historians that the first battle of the Revolutionary War was fought here. The park also contains a marker where Joseph Celeron de Bienville buried a leaden plate in 1749, claiming the land for France, and the graves of Chief Cornstalk and "Mad Anne" Bailey, a noted pioneer scout. **FREE** Also here is

> **Mansion House.** (1796) Oldest log building in Kanawha Valley, restored as a museum. (May-Oct, daily) **FREE**

West Virginia State Farm Museum. *Hwy 1, Point Pleasant (25550). 4 miles N via Hwy 62, adjacent to county fairgrounds. Phone 304/675-5737.* Contains more than 30 farm buildings depicting early rural life, including a log church, one-room schoolhouse, kitchen, scale house, and four-unit building. Barn contains mount of one of the largest horses in the world; also animals. (Apr-Nov, Tues-Sun) **FREE**

Special Event

Mason County Fair. *County Fairgrounds, Point Pleasant. Phone 304/675-5463.* Livestock show, arts and crafts, contests, Nashville entertainers. Mid-Aug.

Limited-Service Hotel

★ **LOWE HOTEL.** *401 Main St, Point Pleasant (25550). Phone 304/675-2260.* 42 rooms, 4 story. Check-out noon. **$**

Princeton (E-3)

See also Bluefield

Settled 1826
Population 6,347
Elevation 2,446 ft
Area Code 304
Zip 24740
Information Princeton-Mercer County Chamber of Commerce, 910 Oakvale Rd; phone 304/487-1502
Web site www.pmcc.com

Princeton is the southern terminus of the spectacular 88-mile West Virginia Turnpike and a trade center for an agricultural, industrial, and coal mining area.

What to See and Do

Camp Creek State Park. *Hwy 19, Camp Creek. 13 miles N on I-77, exit 20, then 2 miles NW, at Camp Creek. Phone 304/425-9481.* Approximately 500 acres. Fishing; hiking trails, game courts, biking, horseback riding, picnicking, playgrounds, camping.

Ripley (C-3)

See also Point Pleasant

Settled 1768
Population 3,263
Elevation 616 ft
Area Code 304
Zip 25271

What to See and Do

Washington's Lands Museum and Park. *6 miles N via I-77 exit 146 to Ravenswood, then 2 1/2 miles S on Hwy 68. Phone 304/372-5343.* Housed in converted river lock building and restored Sayre Log House; exhibits trace the pioneer and river history of the area. Park, on the Ohio River, has picnicking and boat launching facilities. Museum (Memorial Day-Labor Day, Sat-Sun afternoons). **DONATION**

Special Events

Mountain State Art & Craft Fair. *Cedar Lakes Conference Center, Ripley. Phone 304/372-7860.* Features traditional crafts, art, folk music, and foods. Early July.

West Virginia Black Walnut Festival. *273 E Main St, Spencer (25276). 25 miles E on Hwy 33/119 in Spencer. Phone 304/927-1780.* Parade, carnival, band festival, car show, contests, livestock show, arts and crafts. Mid-Oct.

Limited-Service Hotels

★★ **BEST WESTERN MCCOYS INN & CONFERENCE CENTER.** *701 Main St, Ripley (25271). Phone 304/372-9122; toll-free 800/288-9122; fax 304/372-4400. www.bestwestern.com.* 123 rooms, 2 story. Pets accepted. Check-in 3 pm, check-out 11 am. Restaurant, bar. Fitness room. Outdoor pool. **$**

★ **HOLIDAY INN EXPRESS.** *1 Hospitality Dr, Ripley (25271). Phone 304/372-5000; toll-free 800/465-4329; fax 304/372-5600. www.holiday-inn.com.* 65 rooms, 2 story. Pets accepted. Complimentary continental breakfast. Check-in 3 pm, check-out 11 am. Fitness room. **$**

Roanoke

Full-Service Resort

★★★ **STONEWALL RESORT.** *940 Resort Dr, Roanoke (26447). Phone 304/269-7400; toll-free 888/278-8150; fax 304/269-4358.* 198 rooms, 3 story. Check-in 4 pm, check-out 11 am. Restaurant, bar. Children's activity center. Fitness room, spa. Indoor pool, outdoor pool, whirlpool. Golf. **$**

Shepherdstown (B-7)

See also Charles Town, Harpers Ferry, Martinsburg; also see Frederick, Hagerstown, MD

Settled circa 1730
Population 803
Elevation 406 ft
Area Code 304
Zip 25443
Information Jefferson County Chamber of Commerce, 201 Frontage Rd, PO Box 426, Charles Town 25414; phone 304/725-2055
Web site www.jeffersoncounty.com/chamber

In 1787, Shepherdstown was the site of the first successful public launching of a steamboat. However, James Rumsey, inventor of the craft, died before he could exploit his success. Rival claims by John Fitch, and Robert Fulton's commercial success with the *Clermont* 20 years later, have clouded Rumsey's achievement.

The state's first newspaper was published here in 1790, and Shepherdstown almost became the national capital. (George Washington considered it as a possible site, according to letters in the Library of Congress.) Shepherdstown is also the location of one of the early gristmills, which is believed to have been constructed around 1739 and finally ceased production in 1939. This is the oldest continuously settled town in the state.

What to See and Do

Historic Shepherdstown Museum. *129 E German St, Shepherdstown. In the old Entler Hotel (1786), German and Princess sts. Phone 304/876-0910.* Artifacts dating to the 1700s, including many items concerning the founding of the town. Guided tours (by appointment). (Apr-Oct, daily) **FREE** Also available here are

Guided walking tours. Historic sites in Shepherdstown. **$$**

Full-Service Inn

★★★ BAVARIAN INN & LODGE. *Hwy 34, Shepherdstown (25443). Phone 304/876-2551; fax 304/876-9355. www.bavarianinnwv.com.* This inn is decorated with Federal period reproductions and provides European-style hospitality. Four-poster mahogany beds, brass chandeliers, and bathrooms with imported marble grace each room. 72 rooms, 4 story. Check-in 3 pm, check-out noon. High-speed Internet access. Restaurant, bar. Fitness room. Outdoor pool. Tennis. **$$**

Specialty Lodging

The following lodging establishment is approved by Mobil Travel Guide but, due to its unique and individualized nature has not been given a traditional Mobil Star rating. Included in this listing you may find bed-and-breakfasts, limited-service inns, guest ranches, and other unique hotel properties.

THOMAS SHEPHERD INN. *PO Box 1162, Shepherdstown (25443). Phone 304/876-3715; toll-free 888/889-8952; fax 304/876-3313. www.thomasshepherdinn.com.* This cozy inn was built in 1868 in the Federal style of architecture. The guest rooms have been lovingly restored, feature the original floors, Oriental rugs, wardrobes, and a variety of corner cupboards. 6 rooms, 2 story. Children over 8 years only. Complimentary full breakfast. Check-in 3 pm, check-out 11 am. **$**

Restaurants

★★★ BAVARIAN INN AND LODGE. *Hwy 34, Shepherdstown (25443). Phone 304/876-2551. www.bavarianinnwv.com.* Few places serve traditional German fare that's so authentic. Stone fireplaces and dark woods create a rustic yet elegant ambience. German menu. Breakfast, lunch, dinner. Bar. Children's menu. **$$$**

★ OLD PHARMACY CAFE & SODA FOUNTAIN. *138 E German St, Shepherdstown (25443). Phone 304/876-2085; fax 304/876-4376.* American menu. Lunch, dinner. Closed Jan 1, Thanksgiving, Dec 25. Bar. Children's menu. In former pharmacy (1911); many original pieces including a marble soda fountain. **$$**

★★★ YELLOW BRICK BANK & LITTLE INN. *201 German at Princess St, Shepherdstown (25443). Phone 304/876-2208; fax 304/876-2208.* Housed in a 19th-century bank building in a rural town near the upper Potomac, this surprisingly inventive restaurant serves creative cuisine in an airy, high-ceilinged dining room. Lunch, dinner, Sun brunch. Closed Thanksgiving, Dec 25. Bar. Overnight stays available. **$$**

Summersville (D-4)

See also Gauley Bridge

Founded 1824
Population 3,294
Elevation 1,894 ft
Area Code 304
Zip 26651
Information Chamber of Commerce, 411 Old Main Dr, PO Box 567; phone 304/872-1588

Twenty-year-old Nancy Hart led a surprise Confederate attack on Summersville in July 1861, captured a Union force, and burned the town. She was captured, but her jail guard succumbed to her charms. The guard was then disarmed and killed by the young woman. She escaped to Lee's lines. After the war she returned to Summersville.

What to See and Do

Carnifex Ferry Battlefield State Park. *12 miles W on Hwy 39, then SE on Hwy 129, near Kesslers Cross Lanes. Phone 304/872-0825.* Here on Sept 10, 1861, 7,000 Union troops under General William S. Rosecrans fought and defeated a lesser number of Confederates under General John B. Floyd. The 156-acre park includes Patteson House Museum (Memorial Day-weekend after Labor Day, Sat, Sun, holidays), which displays Civil War relics. Hiking trails, picnicking, game courts, playgrounds, concession. Civil War reenactment (weekend after Labor Day). Park (May-early Sept, daily). **FREE**

Gauley River National Recreation Area. *104 Main St, Glen Jean (25846). Phone 304/465-0508.* Designated a federally protected area in Oct 1988, the 25-mile stretch of the Gauley from the Summersville Dam west to just above the town of Swiss is famous for whitewater rafting. There are no developed sites. Large tracts of land along the river are privately owned. For further information and a list of whitewater outfitters, contact Superintendent, New River Gorge National River, PO Box 246, Glen Jean 25846.

Summersville Lake. *5 miles S on Hwy 19. Phone 304/872-3459.* A 2,700-acre lake. Swimming, waterskiing, fishing, boating; hiking, picnicking. Battle Run Campground is 3 miles W on Hwy 129 (fee). (May-Oct, daily) Fee for some activities.

Special Events

Nicholas County Fair. *616 Church St, Summersville (26651). 3 miles N at Nicholas County Memorial Park. Phone 304/872-1454.* Midway; flower show; agricultural and crafts exhibits. July.

Nicholas County Potato Festival. *411 Old Main Dr, Summersville (26651). Citywide. Phone 304/872-3722.* Includes parades, entertainment, volleyball tournament, arts and crafts show, bed races. First full week in Sept.

Limited-Service Hotels

★ ★ BEST WESTERN SUMMERSVILLE LAKE MOTOR LODGE. *1203 S Broad St, Summersville (26651). Phone 304/872-6900; toll-free 800/214-9551; fax 304/872-6908. www.bestwestern.com.* 57 rooms, 3 story. Pets accepted; fee. Complimentary continental breakfast. Check-in 1 pm, check-out 11 am. Restaurant, bar. **$**

★ COMFORT INN. *903 Industrial Dr N, Summersville (26651). Phone 304/872-6500; toll-free 800/872-1752; fax 304/872-3090. www.choicehotels.com.* 99 rooms, 2 story. Pets accepted, some restrictions; fee. Complimentary continental breakfast. Check-in 3 pm, check-out 11 am. Fitness room. Outdoor pool. **$**

Sutton (C-4)

Settled 1826
Population 1,011
Elevation 840 ft
Area Code 304
Zip 26601

What to See and Do

Sutton Lake. *S Stonewall St, Sutton. Phone 304/765-2816. Dam is 1 mile E.* Swimming in designated areas, boat launch (fee); camping (May-Dec; some electric hookups; fees) at Gerald R. Freeman Campground, 16 miles E on Hwy 15; and at Mill Creek-Bakers Run Area, 16 miles SE on Hwy 17.

Limited-Service Hotel

★ ★ **DAYS INN.** *2000 Sutton Ln, Sutton (26601). Phone 304/765-5055; toll-free 866/700-7284; fax 304/765-2067. www.flatwoodsusa.com.* 201 rooms, 5 story. Check-in 3 pm, check-out noon. Restaurant, bar. Fitness room. Indoor pool, whirlpool. **$**

Webster Springs (D-4)

Settled 1860
Population 990
Elevation 1,509 ft
Area Code 304
Zip 26288
Information Mayor's Office, 146 McGraw Ave; phone 304/847-5411.

Once a resort famed for its medicinal "lick," or spring, the town is now a trading center and meeting place for sportsmen.

What to See and Do

Holly River State Park. *20 miles N on Hwy 20 to Hacker Valley, then 1 mile E. Phone 304/493-6353.* More than 8,000 acres of heavy forest with excellent trout fishing in Laurel Fork. Swimming pool, bathhouse; hiking trails to waterfalls and Potato Knob, tennis, game courts, picnicking, playground, restaurant (seasonal), camping (dump station), nine cabins. Nature, recreation programs (summer).

Kumbrabow State Forest. *25 miles NE on Hwy 15, then 5 miles N, near Monterville. Phone 304/335-2219. www.kumbrabow.com.* More than 9,400 acres of wild, rugged country with trout fishing; deer, turkey, and grouse hunting; hiking trails, cross-country skiing, picnicking, playground, tent and trailer camping, five rustic cabins.

Special Events

Webster County Fair. *11 miles S on Hwy 20 to 4-H Camp Caesar. Phone 304/226-3888.* Rides, agricultural exhibits, entertainers, horse show. Labor Day week.

Webster Springs Woodchopping Festival. *Phone 304/847-7666.* Southeastern World Woodchopping Championships; state championship turkey calling contest, draft horse pull, horse show, fireman's rodeo; arts and crafts, music, parades, concessions. Memorial Day weekend.

Weirton (A-4)

See also Bethany, Wheeling

Founded 1910
Population 20,411
Elevation 760 ft
Area Code 304
Zip 26062
Information Chamber of Commerce, 3200 Maine St; phone 304/748-7212

Weirton has been a steel producing town since its founding in 1910 by Ernest T. Weir, who also founded the Weirton Steel Company. In 1984, Weirton Steel became the largest employee-owned steel company in the world. Modern plants produce tin plate and hot-rolled, cold-rolled, and galvanized steels for containers, automobiles, appliances, and other products.

What to See and Do

Mountaineer Racetrack & Resort. *Hwy 2, Chester. 12 miles N on Hwy 2. Phone 304/387-2400.* Thoroughbred racing on 1-mile track; three restaurants. (Mon, Thurs-Sun)

Tomlinson Run State Park. *15 miles N off Hwy 8. Phone 304/564-3651.* Approximately 1,400 acres. Swimming pool, bathhouse, fishing, boating on 27-acre lake (rowboat and paddleboat rentals); hiking trails, miniature golf, tennis, picnicking, playground, tent and trailer camping (dump station). Nature, recreation programs (summer).

Weirton Steel Corp and Half Moon Industrial Park. *400 Three Springs Dr (26062). Phone 304/748-7212.* Tours of Alpo and others. Contact Chamber of Commerce for details.

Weston (C-4)

See also Buckhannon, Clarksburg

Settled 1784
Population 4,317
Elevation 1,009 ft
Area Code 304
Zip 26452
Information Lewis County Convention & Visitors Bureau, 345 Center St, PO Box 379; phone 304/269-7328.

Surveyed originally by "Stonewall" Jackson's grandfather, Weston today is a center for coal, oil, and gas production, as well as the manufacture of glass products. The Weston State Hospital, completed in 1880 and said to be the largest hand-cut stone building in the nation, is located in town.

What to See and Do

Cedar Creek State Park. *31 miles SW off Hwy 33/119, near Glenville. Phone 304/462-8517.* More than 2,400 acres. Swimming pool, bathhouse, fishing, boating (rentals); hiking trails, miniature golf, tennis, game courts, picnicking, playground, concession, tent and trailer camping (dump station). Park office in restored log cabin.

Jackson's Mill State 4-H Conference Center. *Jackson's Mill Rd, Weston. 4 miles N off Hwy 19. Phone 304/269-5100.* First camp of its kind in US; 43 buildings, gardens, swimming pool, amphitheater, interfaith chapel. Picnicking. Also here is

> **Jackson's Mill Historic Area.** Includes Blaker's Mill, an operating water-powered gristmill; blacksmith shop; McWharten cabin (circa 1700s); Mary Conrad's cabin (circa 1800s); and Jackson's Mill Museum, where "Stonewall" Jackson lived and worked as a boy. Museum represents grist and saw milling agriculture and home arts of the area as practiced 100 years ago. (Memorial Day-Labor Day: Tues-Sun; May and after Labor Day-mid-Oct: weekends only) **$$**

Stonewall Jackson Lake and Dam. *Rte 33 W, Weston. Just S off I-79 exit 96, follow signs to dam. Phone 304/269-4588.* Approximately 2,500-acre lake with over 82 miles of shoreline created by impounding the waters of the West Fork River. Swimming, scuba diving, waterskiing, fishing, boating (ramps, rentals, marinas); picnicking, camping. Visitor center.

Stonewall Jackson Lake State Park. *Rte 33 W. 11 miles S on US 19. Phone 304/269-0523.* Approximately 3,000 acres. Fishing, boating (launch, marina); nature and fitness trails, picnicking, playground, camping (hookups). Visitor center. Standard hours, fees.

Special Events

Horse show. *Trefz Farm, Rte 88 and National Rd, Weston (26003). 3 miles E on Hwy 33. Phone 304/269-3257.* Saddle, walking, harness, pony, western, and Arabian riding. Usually July.

Stonewall Jackson Heritage Arts & Crafts Jubilee. *Jackson's Mill State 4-H Conference Center, Weston. Phone 304/269-1863.* Mountain crafts, music, dance, and food. Labor Day weekend.

Limited-Service Hotel

★ COMFORT INN. *Exit 99 off I-79, Weston (26452). Phone 304/269-7000; toll-free 800/228-5150; fax 304/269-7249. www.choicehotels.com.* 70 rooms, 2 story. Pets accepted, some restrictions; fee. Complimentary continental breakfast. Check-in 3 pm, check-out noon. Outdoor pool. **$**

Wheeling (A-4)

See also Bethany, Weirton

Settled 1769
Population 31,419
Elevation 678 ft
Area Code 304
Zip 26003
Information Convention & Visitors Bureau, 1401 Main St; phone 304/233-7709 or toll-free 800/828-3079
Web site www.wheelingcvb.com

Wheeling stands on the site of Fort Henry, built in 1774 by Colonel Ebenezer Zane and his two brothers, who named the fort for Virginia's Governor Patrick Henry. In 1782, the fort was the scene of the final battle of the Revolutionary War, a battle in which the valiant young pioneer Betty Zane was a heroine. The fort had withstood several Native American and British sieges during the war. However, during the last siege (after the war was officially ended), the defenders of the fort ran out of powder. Betty Zane, sister of the colonel, volunteered to run through the gunfire to the outlying Zane cabin for more. With the powder gathered in her apron, she made the 150-yard trek back to the fort and saved the garrison. Zane Grey, a descendant of the Zanes, wrote a novel about Betty and her exploit.

Today Wheeling is home to many industries, including producers of steel, iron, tin, chemical products, pottery, glass, paper, tobacco, plastics, and coal.

What to See and Do

The Artisan Center. *1400 Main St, Wheeling (26003). Heritage Sq. Phone 304/233-4555.* Restored 1860s Victorian warehouse houses River City Ale Works, West Virginia's largest brew pub. "Made in Wheeling" crafts and exhibits; artisan demonstrations. (Daily) **FREE**

Grave Creek Mound State Park. *801 Jefferson Ave, Moundsville (26041). 9 miles S via Hwy 2. Phone 304/843-1410.* Features the nation's largest prehistoric Adena burial mound—79 feet high, 900 feet around, 50 feet across the top. Some excavating was done in 1838; exhibits in Delf Norona Museum & Cultural Center (daily; fee).

Jamboree USA. *Capitol Music Hall, 1015 Main St, Wheeling (26003). Phone 304/234-0050; toll-free 800/624-5456. www.jamboreeusa.com.* Live country music shows presented by WWVA Radio since 1933. (Sat) **$$$$**

Kruger Street Toy & Train Museum. *144 Kruger St, Wheeling (26003). Phone 304/242-8133; toll-free 877/242-8133. www.toyandtrain.com.* Collection of antique toys, games, and playthings in a restored Victorian-era schoolhouse. (Daily 10 am-6 pm; closed holidays) **$$**

Oglebay Resort Park. *3 miles NE of I-70, on Hwy 88. Phone 304/243-4000; toll-free 800/624-6988 (See SPECIAL EVENTS). www.toyandtrain.com.* A 1,650-acre municipal park. Indoor and outdoor swimming pools, fishing, paddle boating on 3-acre Schenk Lake; three 18-hole golf courses, miniature golf, tennis courts, picnicking, restaurant, snack shop, cabins, lodge. Train ride; 65-acre Good Children's Zoo (fee) with animals in natural habitat. Benedum Natural Science Theater; garden center; arboretum with 4 miles of walking paths; greenhouses; observatory. Fee for most activities. Also in the park is

Mansion Museum. *The Burton Center, Wheeling. Phone 304/242-7272.* Period rooms, exhibits trace history from 1835-present. (Daily) **$$**

Site of Fort Henry. *11th and Main sts, Wheeling (26003). Phone 304/233-7709.* Bronze plaque marks the location of the fort that Betty Zane saved.

West Virginia Independence Hall-Custom House. *1528 Market St, Wheeling (26003). Phone 304/238-1300.* (1859) Site of the meeting at which Virginia's secession from the Union was declared unlawful, and the independent state of West Virginia was created. The building, used as a post office, custom office, and federal court until 1912, has been restored. It now houses exhibits and events relating to the state's cultural heritage, including an interpretive film and rooms with period furniture. (Mar-Dec: daily; rest of year: Mon-Sat; closed state holidays) **FREE**

Wheeling Park. *1801 National Rd, Wheeling (26003). 5 miles E on Hwy 40. Phone 304/242-3770.* Approximately 400 acres. Swimming pool, water slide, boating on Good Lake; golf, miniature golf, indoor/outdoor tennis, ice skating (rentals), picnicking, playground, refreshment area with video screen and lighted dance floor. Aviary. Fees for activities. (Daily; some facilities seasonal)

Special Events

City of Lights. *Oglebay Resort Park, Rte 88 North, Wheeling (26003). Phone 304/243-4000.* A 350-acre lighting display featuring lighted buildings, holiday themes with more than 500,000 lights, including 28-foot candy canes and giant swans on Schenk Lake. Winter Fantasy in Good Zoo. Nov-Jan.

Jamboree in the Hills. *1015 Main St, Wheeling (26003). 15 miles W off I-70 exit 208 or 213, in St. Clairsville, OH. Phone toll-free 800/624-5456.* A four-day country music festival featuring more than 30 hours of music; top country stars. Camping available. Third weekend in July.

Oglebayfest. *Oglebay Resort Park, Rte 88 N, Wheeling (26003). Phone 304/243-4000.* Country fair, artists' market, fireworks, parade, ethnic foods, contests, square and round dancing, entertainment. First weekend in Oct.

Limited-Service Hotels

★ ★ BEST WESTERN WHEELING INN. *949 Main St, Wheeling (26003). Phone 304/233-8500; fax 304/233-8500. www.bestwestern.com.* 80 rooms, 4 story. Pets accepted; fee. Complimentary continental breakfast. Check-in 2 pm, check-out 11 am. Restaurant, bar. Fitness room. Whirlpool. **$**

★ HAMPTON INN. *795 National Rd, Wheeling (26003). Phone 304/233-0440; toll-free 800/426-7866; fax 304/233-2198. www.hamptoninn.com.* 104 rooms, 5 story. Complimentary continental breakfast. Check-in 3 pm, check-out noon. Fitness room. **$**

Full-Service Resort

★ ★ OGLEBAY FAMILY RESORT. *Oglebay Park, Wheeling (26003). Phone 304/243-4000; toll-free 800/624-6988; fax 304/243-4070. www.oglebay-resort.com.* This 1,650-acre resort features beautiful gardens and fine accommodations. 212 rooms, 2 story. Pets accepted, some restrictions. Check-in 3 pm, check-out 11 am. Bar. Children's activity center. Fitness room, spa. Indoor pool, outdoor pool, children's pool, whirlpool. Golf. Tennis. Airport transportation available. Business center. Mansion museum, garden center. Stables. Children's zoo. Rustic setting in Oglebay Park. **$$**

Restaurant

★ ★ ★ ERNIE'S ESQUIRE. *1015 E Bethlehem Blvd, Wheeling (26003). Phone 304/242-2800; fax 304/242-2809.* A local landmark for nearly 50 years, this fine dining restaurant serves a wide variety of options to suit any palate. Lunch, dinner, late-night, Sun brunch. Closed Dec 25. Bar. Children's menu. Casual attire. Valet parking. **$$$**

White Sulphur Springs (D-4)

See also Lewisburg; also see Covington, VA

Settled 1750
Population 2,315
Elevation 1,923 ft
Area Code 304
Zip 24986
Information Chamber of Commerce, PO Box 11, 24986; phone 304/536-2500
Web site www.wsswv.com

In the 18th century, White Sulphur Springs became a fashionable destination for rich and famous colonists, who came for the "curative" powers of the mineral waters. It has, for the most part, remained a popular resort ever since. A number of US presidents summered in the town in the days before air conditioning made Washington habitable in hot weather. The John Tylers spent their honeymoon at the famous "Old White" Hotel. In 1913 the Old White Hotel gave way to the present Greenbrier Hotel, where President Wilson honeymooned with the second Mrs. Wilson. During World War II the hotel served as an internment camp for German and Japanese diplomats and, later, as a hospital.

The first golf course in America was laid out near the town in 1884, but the first game was delayed when golf clubs, imported from Scotland, were held for three weeks by customs men who were suspicious of a game played with "such elongated blackjacks or implements of murder."

What to See and Do

Fishing, swimming, boating, camping, hiking. *Phone 304/536-2144.* In **Monongahela National Forest** (see): **Blue Bend Recreation Area,** 6 miles N on WV 92, then 4 miles W on WV 16/21; **Lake Sherwood Recreation Area,** 23 miles N via WV 92, then 11 miles NE on WV 14.

Greenbrier State Forest. *Harts Run Rd, Caldwell. 3 miles W on Hwy 60, then 1 1/2 miles S on Harts*

Run Rd. Phone 304/536-1944. More than 5,100 acres. Swimming pool (Memorial Day-Labor Day), bass fishing in Greenbrier River; hunting, hiking trails, picnicking, playground, tent and trailer camping, 12 cabins. Nature, recreation programs (summer).

Memorial Park. *Greenbrier Ave, White Sulphur Springs.* Swimming pool (Memorial Day-Labor Day; fee); tennis courts, ball fields, track, horseshoe pits, playground. (Daily)

National Fish Hatchery. *400 E Main St, White Sulphur Springs (24986). On US 60. Phone 304/536-1361.* Rainbow trout in raceways and ponds. Visitor center has display pool, aquariums, and exhibits. (Memorial Day-Labor Day, daily) **FREE**

Special Events

Dandelion Festival. *Phone 304/536-2323.* Entertainment, exhibits; arts and crafts. Memorial Day weekend.

Full-Service Resort

★★★★ THE GREENBRIER. *300 W Main St (Hwy 60), White Sulphur Springs (24986). Phone 304/536-1110; toll-free 800/624-6070; fax 304/536-7874. www.greenbrier.com.* Resting on a 2,500-acre estate in the picturesque Allegheny Mountains of West Virginia, The Greenbrier is one of America's oldest and finest resorts. Fiercely proud of its 200-year history, this all-encompassing resort continues to appeal to active-minded visitors seeking a respite from the everyday. This resort is the embodiment of a sportsman's paradise, with more than 50 activities on its sprawling grounds. In addition to three championship golf courses, the highly acclaimed Sam Snead Golf Academy, tennis courts, and fitness and spa facilities, guests are invited to partake in unique adventures like falconry, trap and skeet shooting at the Gun Club, and the Land Rover Driving School. The fascinating tour of the federal government's Cold War bunker constructed under the resort is particularly notable. Comprised of rooms, suites, estate houses, and guest houses, the accommodations reflect the resort's aristocratic tradition, while seven restaurants satisfy all appetites. 803 rooms, 6 story. Check-in 4 pm, check-out noon. High-speed Internet access. Four restaurants, four bars. Children's activity center. Fitness room, spa. Indoor pool, outdoor pool, children's pool, whirlpool. Golf. Tennis. Hunt club and game preserve. Airport transportation available. Business center. **$$$**

Restaurants

★★★ THE GREENBRIER MAIN DINING ROOM. *300 W Main St (Hwy 60), White Sulphur Springs (24986). Phone 304/536-1110; fax 304/536-7854. www.greenbrier.com.* Capitol Hill elite and local celebrities alike get a dose of gracious Southern hospitality at this legendary resort. French, American menu. Breakfast, dinner. Children's menu. Jacket required. Reservations recommended. Valet parking. **$$$**

★★★★ THE TAVERN ROOM. *300 W Main St, White Sulphur Springs (24986). Phone 304/536-1110; toll-free 800/624-6070; fax 304/536-7854. www.greenbrier.com.* Located in the majestic Greenbrier Resort at White Sulphur Springs, The Tavern Room is a cozy, intimate restaurant with exposed brick walls, high wine cellar-styled archways, dark wood accents, glowing hurricane lamps, and deep garnet-colored walls that lend richness and rusticity to the warm dining room. Magnificent floral arrangements and pretty tabletops dressed up with petite vases of fresh flowers add a burst of natural color to the space. The contemporary French menu is elegant and refined but approachable and simple, offering a variety of classically prepared fish, beef, lamb, and poultry (most purchased from regional farmers), as well as traditional French indulgences like caviar and foie gras. Attentive service and soothing live piano music add to the luxury and serenity of dining at The Tavern Room. American menu. Dinner. Closed Wed, Sun; early May-Oct. Bar. Jacket required. Reservations recommended. Valet parking. **$$$$**

Williamson (E-2)

Founded 1892
Population 3,414
Elevation 665 ft
Area Code 304
Zip 25661
Information Tug Valley Chamber of Commerce, 45 E 2nd Ave, PO Box 376; phone 304/235-5240
Web site www.tugvalleychamberofcommerce.com

The center of the "billion-dollar coal field," Williamson is truly a coal town; the walls of the local Chamber of Commerce building, at the west corner of Courthouse Square, are made of coal. The surrounding Tug River Valley was the scene of the bitter Hatfield-McCoy mountaineer family feud.

What to See and Do

Cabwaylingo State Forest. *38 miles N off Hwy 52, Hwy 152 near Wilsondale. Phone 304/385-4255.* Approximately 8,100 acres. Swimming pool (Memorial Day-Labor Day), fishing; hunting, hiking trails, game courts, picnicking, playground, concession, tent and trailer camping (dump station), 13 cabins.

Matewan. *12 miles SW via Hwy 49. Phone 304/426-4239.* This tiny hamlet was the site of the famous feud between the West Virginia Hatfields and the Kentucky McCoys. On Election Day, Aug 7, 1882, three McCoy sons stabbed and shot Ellison Hatfield. Devil Anse Hatfield avenged his brother by executing the three McCoys. Soon Kentucky bounty hunters made raids into West Virginia to capture the Hatfieds, who retaliated in 1888 by attacking a McCoy homestead. By 1890 the killings had ended but the feud continued to be sensationalized. In 1920, Matewan was the scene of a shootout between union organizers and coal company operators that left ten dead, including the mayor.

Special Event

King Coal Festival. *28 Oak St, Williamson (25661). Phone 304/235-5560.* Entertainment, exhibits; theatrical presentation; country music, square dancing. Mid-Sept.

Index

E

O

P

Notes

Notes

Notes

Notes

Notes

Notes

Notes

Notes

Notes

Notes

Notes

Notes

Notes

Notes